The Autocourse History of the Grand Prix Car 1966-91

To everyone in Formula 1 who aimed high . . .

'There's always room at the top, and it's damned crowded down below.
Why shouldn't one get there? It only needs a little more push and a little
more attention to detail than the average fellow is prepared to give.'
Sir Henry O'Neil de Hane Segrave

The Autocourse
History of
the Grand Prix Car
1966-91

by Doug Nye

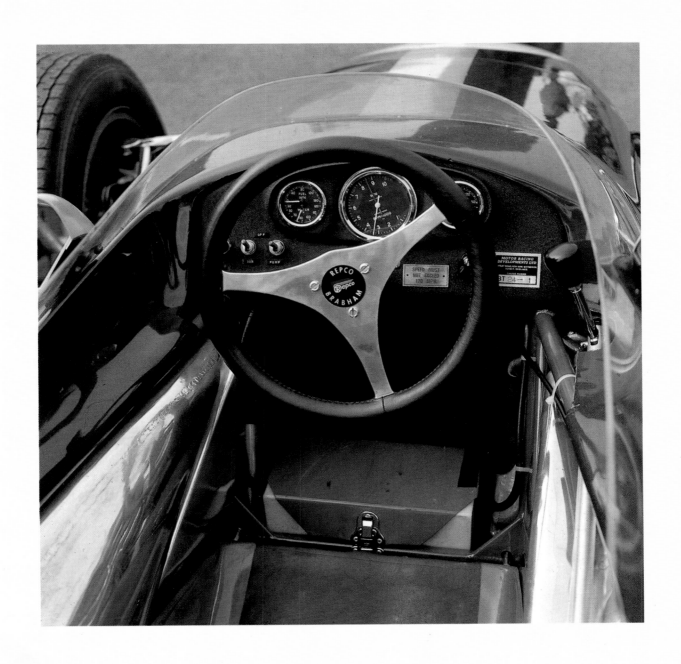

Hazleton Publishing, Richmond, Surrey

COSWORTH®
RACING

The success of Cosworth engines in international motor racing is legendary. Today, with new challenges, continuous research, development and production technology form the centre of our race ethic. Our commitment to excellence ensures that Cosworth will continue to achieve the competitive edge vital for tomorrows success.

Cosworth Engineering
St James Mill Road
Northampton NN5 5JJ, UK.
Telephone: (0) 604 752444

▼ A division of Vickers PLC

Contents

PUBLISHER
Richard Poulter

EXECUTIVE PUBLISHER
Elizabeth Le Breton

PRODUCTION MANAGER
George Greenfield

ART EDITOR
Steve Small

HOUSE EDITOR
Peter Lovering

This second edition published in
1992 by
Hazleton Publishing
3 Richmond Hill, Richmond,
Surrey TW10 6RE.

Printed in Spain by
Graficas Estella SA, Estella.

ISBN: 0-905138-94-5

DISTRIBUTORS
UNITED KINGDOM
George Philip Ltd
59 Grosvenor Street
London W1X 9DA

NORTH AMERICA
Motorbooks International
PO Box 2, 729 Prospect Ave.
Osceola, Wisconsin 54020 USA

Title page photograph:
'SPEED MUST NOT EXCEED 170 MPH' reads the dash-panel sticker while the chassis-plate announces this cockpit as belonging to Repco Brabham 'BT24-1'. These were the last multi-tubular spaceframe-chassised cars to win the Formula 1 Constructors' World Championship title (in 1967). Note grey-enamelled chassis tube, wrapped-over glass-fibre body mouldings, polished welded-aluminium strap-in fuel tanks and clip-cover battery box beneath the driver's thighs . . . all typical Sixties practice.

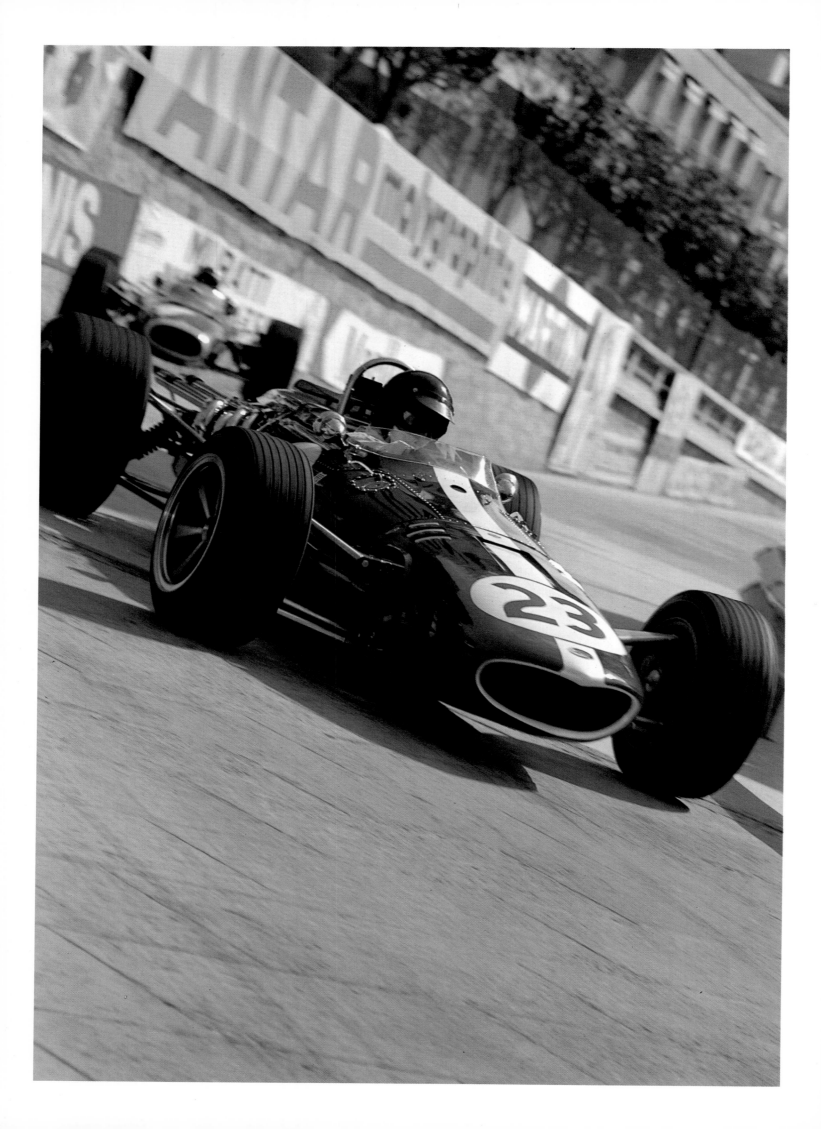

Introduction

From 1966 to 1976 we could quite properly describe the contemporary Formula 1 as the '3-litre Formula'. Renault changed all that in 1977 when they pioneered exploitation of the hitherto-ignored clause which permitted use of supercharged engines of up to 1500 cc.

Renault chose to employ exhaust-driven turbocharging for their forced-induction 1500. By 1981, the normally aspirated 3-litre brigade headed by Cosworth-Ford was fighting a valiant rearguard action against the proliferation of major-manufacturer turbocharged cars then under development. By the end of 1982 the Constructors' Championship had for the first time fallen to turbocharged 1500 cc cars. No longer was this the '3-litre Formula'.

Naturally aspirated 3-litre F1 cars fought their last battles through 1983 and into 1984 had no chance of winning, vanishing altogether during 1985.

Following a controversial ruling which banned the Cosworth engine's last redoubt, the Tyrrell team, from racing, the Austrian GP at the Österreichring on 19 August 1984 was run without a single 3-litre engine competing. In the next race, at Monza, for the first time in 17 years there was not even a single 3-litre 'Cossy' in the paddock.

They would return to sing their swansong in the Tyrrell cars of early 1985 but when a Tyrrell-DFY ran in that season's German GP on 4 August, it was the end. Formula 1 was now purely 1500 cc turbocharged, and for 1986 the 3-litre naturally aspirated option was finally deleted. So the father gave way to the son, and by evolution the '3-litre Formula' had run its course, with a 20-season period surveyed in the first edition of this book.

Now we have updated the story to the end of 1991, to cover the final seasons of 1.5-litre turbocharged racing into 1988, and the birth of the new 3.5-litre naturally aspirated class which was phased in to take over completely in 1989.

So here we have a full quarter-century of premier-Formula motor racing to encapsulate within these covers. The broad subject of 'The Grand Prix Car' has been covered in the past by other learned analyses which effectively traced its development up to 1953. I make no excuses for paying tribute to the late Laurence Pomeroy's magnificent if flawed two-volume work published nearly 40 years ago.

As will be apparent to those who are, I am neither an engineer nor a student of engineering. However, like many fellow enthusiasts, I am fascinated by the backroom effort behind the superstars' exploits on circuit and by the design, manufacture and development of the vehicles they drive.

In the following pages I set out to record the detailed history of each of our 26 Formula 1 Constructors' Championship-winning cars from 1966 to 1991, highlighting details of their design, construction, modification and operation, while a detailed Appendix gives a reference run-down on the 427 mainstream Formula 1 races run during this period.

By definition, most racing cars are unsuccessful – there just is not enough winning to go around. Their place is in the Team Directory section which covers every car to compete in international major-league Formula 1 during the period. Engines are covered in a similar manner.

A brief Overview provides a summary of technical progress and innovation while some topics of special interest are highlighted in boxed paragraphs placed within the text.

We have tried to avoid any easy options in compiling this survey and I hope it gives the reader as much interest as it has caused me and my publisher agonies in production.

I hope that when reading this book, you can marvel – as I always do – at the devotion and dedication of those involved in what is effectively a technological war fought at a frightening pace under incredible and unrelenting pressures. This is what enables Formula 1 racing to attract and employ such fine people – people who do not pack up and go home until the work is done, people to whom winning is reward for total effort. People I admire.

What follows is dedicated to all of them. The achievements are theirs, while the inevitable errors in a work of this magnitude are mine, and for those I apologize in advance.

Doug Nye,
Farnham, Surrey.
September 1992

Spirit of '3-litre' Formula 1: Dan Gurney's gorgeous AAR Eagle-Weslake V12 rounding Monte Carlo's harbour-front Tabac corner during the 1967 Monaco Grand Prix meeting, Jackie Stewart's 2.1-litre BRM P261 in pursuit.

GOODYEAR FOR WINNING TECHNOLOGY FOR ROAD AND TRACK

THE technology of the Grand Prix car advanced at a spectacular rate throughout the 26 seasons between 1966 and 1991. Engine power, braking performance and aerodynamic efficiency were all dramatically increased and, with the competition growing ever more intense, lap times were steadily reduced.

Only relentless research and development enabled the racing tyre to keep pace with this spiralling progress.

Goodyear, the only tyre manufacturer involved in Formula 1 in each of those 26 seasons, has been at the forefront of this development, constant testing enabling the tyres to develop in step with the demands made on them.

Of the 375 World Championship Grands Prix held in this period, 263 were won by cars running on Goodyear tyres, conclusive proof of the company's commitment to excellence.

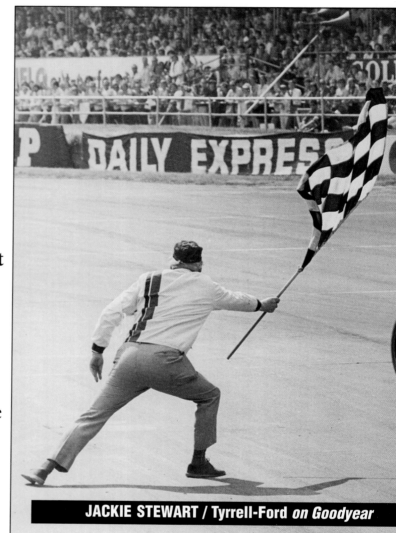

JACKIE STEWART / Tyrrell-Ford *on Goodyear*

That commitment has inevitably been reflected in the Eagle high-performance road tyres produced by Goodyear which have benefited from the lessons learned in the highly demanding environment of Grand Prix racing.

There can be no doubt that in this instance racing has truly improved the breed.

RICHIE GINTHER / Honda *on Goodyear*

AYRTON SENNA / McLaren-Honda *on Goodyear*

NIGEL MANSELL / Williams-Renault *on Goodyear*

Acknowledgements

As you can imagine, the body of work presented within these pages would not have been possible without help. Any journalist is only as good as his sources and I only hope my work has been worthy of mine.

I must pay special tribute to the assistance provided by Patrick Head of Williams Grand Prix Engineering, John Barnard of McLaren International, Ferrari and Benetton, Gordon Murray of Motor Racing Developments and Dr Harvey Postlethwaite of Ferrari for their special and decidedly expert assistance, opinion and advice.

Permission to use original factory drawings was granted by Mr Ferrari via Dr Franco Gozzi, by Peter Warr of Team Lotus, by Ken Tyrrell, and by Patrick Head of Williams Grand Prix Engineering.

Most immediate and wide-ranging help in a variety of trials, tribulations and confusions came from my friends Geoff Goddard – who took many of the photographs which follow – Denis Jenkinson of *Motor Sport*, Maurice Hamilton of *The Observer*, Alan Henry of *Autocourse* and *The Guardian* and Nigel Roebuck of *Autosport*. Matthew Carter of *Autocar* was also of great help.

Thanks also to . . . Peter Agg (Trojan), *Ing.* Giulio Alfieri (Maserati), James A. Allington, Bert Baldwin (Goodyear), Derek Bell, Herbie Blash (Lotus and Brabham), Dr Helmuth Bott (Porsche), Sir Jack Brabham, BRM, Creighton Brown (McLaren International), Jimmy Buss (Hewland Engineering), Rory Byrne (Toleman), Alan Campbell (Ferodo), Michael Cane, the late Colin Chapman, Alan Charles, Denny Chrobak (Goodyear), Peter Connew, John Cooper, Gordon Coppuck (McLaren, Spirit and Leyton House/March), André de Cortanze (Renault), Michele Cory (BMW), Mike Costin (Cosworth Engineering), Jabby Crombac, Colette Darcy (Renault), Ron Dennis (McLaren International), Gérard Ducarouge (Renault), Bernard Dudot (Renault), Eagle, Andrew Ferguson (Lotus and Vel's Parnelli), Geoff Ferris (Penske), Derek Gardner (Tyrrell), Goodyear, Dan Gurney, Brian Hart, Mr Yoshiyuki Hayashi, without whose enthusiasm I would not have been able to tackle a work of this magnitude, the late Heinz Hofer (Penske), Robin Herd (March, McLaren and Cosworth), John Judd (Repco Brabham and Engine Developments Ltd), Dr Karl Kempf (Goodyear and Tyrrell), Jean-Luc Lagardère (Matra), Lotus, Owen Maddock (Cooper), Uwe Mahle (BMW), Bob Marston (Cooper and Lola), Bob Martin (Firestone), Ted Martin, Tony Matthews, Teddy Mayer (McLaren and Beatrice), Allan McCall (Tecno-Tui), the late Bruce McLaren, Leo Mehl (Goodyear), Hans Mezger (Porsche), Michelin, Vel Miletich (Vel's Parnelli), Andrew Nahum (Science Museum, London), Barry Needham (Alfa Romeo), John Nicholson (Nicholson-McLaren Engines), David North (Brabham), Martin Ogilvie (Lotus), Jack Oliver (Shadow and Arrows), Osella, Tim Parnell (BRM), the late Maurice Phillippe (Lotus, Vel's Parnelli Jones and Tyrrell), Mike Pilbeam (BRM and LEC), Raymond Playfoot (BMW), Duncan Rabagliati (Formula One Register), Alan Rees (March, Shadow and Arrows), Renault, José Rosinski of *Sport Auto*, Tony Rudd (BRM and Lotus), Jean Sage (Renault), Dick Scammell (Lotus and Vel's Parnelli), Betty Sheldon (Formula One Register), Dr K. Paul Sheldon (Formula One Register), Martin Slater (Lyncar), Roger Sloman (Advanced Carbon Composites), Tony Southgate (Arrows and Shadow), Alec Stokes (BRM), John Surtees, Ron Tauranac (Motor Racing Developments, Trojan and Theodore), Len Terry (Lotus, Eagle and BRM), Theodore, John Thorpe (Safir), Sheridan Thynne (Williams Grand Prix Engineering), Mario Tozzi-Condivi (Cooper), Ken Tyrrell, Brenda Vernor (Ferrari), Neil Verweij (Alfa Romeo), Dave Wass (Arrows and Shadow), Tom Wheatcroft, founder of the Donington Collection of Single-Seater Racing Cars, Frank Williams, Aubrey Woods (BRM), Leo Wybrott (McLaren and Lotus) . . . for enabling me finally to commit this work to paper. It covers the 26 busiest seasons in Grand Prix racing history, and I hope records fairly the successes, achievements and failures of all those who pushed a little harder than the average fellow.

Photographs & Illustrations

Photographs and other illustrations have been contributed by the following *(listed by page)*:

COLOUR: Geoffrey Goddard, 3, 6, 26, 27, 31, 129, 130, 131 *top right*, 132, 133 *all*, 134, 135, 136, 137, 138, 139, 140, 141, 142-3, 144, 225, 226, 227, 229, 232 *bottom*, 234 *top row*, 234 *middle row*, 234 *bottom right*; Tony Matthews, 230-1 *centre*; Phipps Photographic, 48, 131 *centre right*, 235 *top*; Renault Sport, 234 *bottom left*; Steve Small, 236 *inset*; Nigel Snowdon, 228, 230 *top*, 231 *bottom right*, 232 *top*, 233, 236-7, 238-9, 240.

BLACK AND WHITE: Alfa Romeo SpA, 186 *bottom*; James Allington/*Autosport*, 61; *Autocar*, 57, 67 *centre*; *Autosport*, 122 *top*, 123 *top*, 146, 159 *bottom*, 220 *top*; Jim Bamber, 99 *top*, 109 *upper middle*; Bill Bennett/*Motoring News*, 257 *bottom*; Gérard Berthoud, 220 *bottom*; BMW Motorsport, 187 *bottom*; Charles Briscoe-Knight/Motofoto, 116 *bottom*, 119 *centre*, 265 *top*; BRM/*Autocar*, 190; Diana Burnett, 112, 149 *top*, 151, 198 *centre*, 218 *bottom*, 253, 267; Camel Team Lotus, 166-7; Pete Coltrin, 263 *top*; Ferrari SpA, 183, 192 *bottom*, 334 *bottom*; Footwork, 209, 273; Ford Motor Company, 59, 196; Geoffrey Goddard, 30, 34, 35, 49 *centre*, 49 *bottom*, 50, 51, 52, 53, 55, 58, 62, 63, 64, 66, 70 *bottom*, 71, 72 *bottom*, 73 *top*, 75, 76, 77, 78, 79, 81, 83, 85, 86 *top left*, 87, 88 *centre*, 89, 90 *top right, bottom left*, 91, 92, 97, 98, 99 *bottom*, 100, 103 *top*, 105, 108, 114 *centre*, 116 *top*, 186 *top*, 191 *top*, 200 *top*, 219 *top*, 223 *centre*, 243 *centre*, 249, 250, 251 *top*, 252, 254, 255 *centre*, 257 *top & centre*, 258, 260, 261, 263 *centre, bottom left & bottom right*; 264, 272, 274 *centre*, 275, 276, 293 *left*, 294, 297, 298 *bottom*, 300, 301 *top*, 316 *top*, 320, 325, 329; Robert Harmeyer Jnr, 218 *top*; Brian Hatton/*Motor*, 65 *bottom*, 73 *bottom*, 255 *bottom*; Michael Hewett, 104; Hewland Engineering, 95 *centre & bottom*; Honda, 199 *bottom*; Jeff Hutchinson, 102 *top*, 220 *centre*; David Hutson, 217 *bottom*, 220 *centre*; International Press Agency, 127, 149 *centre*, 143, 153 *top*, 188, 265 *bottom*, 281 *top*, 306; John Player Team Lotus, 286 *bottom*, 288 *bottom*, 331, 333 *top*; Larrousse-Lola, 284; LAT, 95 *top left*, 109 *top left & right*; Leyton House March, 296; Ligier Gitanes, 282 *bottom*, 283; Tony Matthews, 262 *bottom*; Tony Matthews/LAT, 74, 80, 84, 96, 251 *bottom*, 274 *top*, 295; Matra Sports, 70 *top*, 72 *top*, 73 *centre*, 208, 298 *top right*; *Motor*, 262 *top*; Motor Racing Developments, 244 *top right*; Doug Nye, 299; Theo Page/Ford Motor Co., 54; Phipps Photographic, 68, 93, 94, 101 *bottom*, 109 *lower centre*, 242, 243, 244 *bottom left*, 259 *top*, 279, 307, 308, 314, 316 *centre*; Giorgio Piola, 38, 86 *bottom*, 88 *top*, 103, 106, 109, 110, 118 *bottom*, 121 *top*, 219 *bottom*, 280 *centre*, 287 *top*, 288 *top*, 301 *centre & bottom*, 302; Renault Sport, 210, 309; Rial, 313; Nigel Snowdon, 19, 49 *top*, 60, 82, 101 *centre*; 113, 114 *bottom*, 115, 118 *centre*, 121 *centre*, 122 *bottom*, 123 *centre*, 124, 126 *centre*, 128, 145, 147, 148, 152, 155, 156, 158, 159 *top*, 160-1, 162, 165, 168, 169, 170, 171, 172-3, 174, 175, 176, 177, 178, 184, 192 *centre*, 193, 194, 195, 200 *centre*, 201, 202, 203, 204, 205, 206-7, 212, 215, 216, 217 *top*, 218 *bottom*, 221, 222, 223, 224, 241, 244 *bottom right*, 246, 247, 248, 256, 259 *centre*, 260 *top*, 266, 268, 269, 270, 272, 273, 277, 278, 280 *top*, 282 *centre*, 289, 290, 291, 292, 298 *centre*, 303, 304, 305, 310, 311, 312, 315, 318, 319, 321, 324, 326, 327, 328, 352; Bent Sorensen, 181, 182; STP, 293 *bottom right*; TAG Turbo Engines, 153 *centre*; Leslie Thacker, 286 *top*; Tyrrell Racing Organisation, 323, 332, 335; Williams Grand Prix Engineering, 117, 333 *bottom*, 334 *top*; Peter Wright, 102 *centre & bottom*; Leo Wybrott, 90 *middle right & bottom right*.

SUPERLATIVE PERFORMANCES
1966-91

Every motor race provides three opportunities for a superlative performance – race win, pole position and fastest lap.

In our 26-season period, 375 World Championship-qualifying Grand Prix races were run, supplemented by 52 non-Championship events. Individual race wins and pole positions totalled 427 each, with 433 fastest lap performances, being shared twice in Championship rounds and four times in non-Championship races. The Formula's superlative performances thus total 1287; the following table records victories, pole positions and fastest laps by chassis and by engine, in all races.

ENGINES

Engine	CHAMPIONSHIP			NON-CHAMPIONSHIP			
	Wins	Pole	FL	Wins	Pole	FL	Total
Cosworth-Ford	**159**	**130**	**147**	**29**	**34**	**34**	533
DFV V8	155	130	141	29	34	34	
V6 t/c	—	—	1	—	—	—	
DFR V8	—	—	2	—	—	—	
HB V8	4	—	3	—	—	—	
Ferrari	**64**	**70**	**78**	**9**	**4**	**7**	232
V12 3.0	3	7	4	3	2	4	
flat-12	37	42	44	6	2	2	
V6 t/c	15	18	19	—	—	1	
V12 3.5	9	3	11	—	—	—	
Honda	**65**	**73**	**54**	**—**	**—**	**—**	192
V12 3.0	1	1	2	—	—	—	
V6 t/c	40	35	35	—	—	—	
V10	16	27	13	—	—	—	
V12	8	10	4	—	—	—	
Renault	**31**	**58**	**36**	**—**	**—**	**—**	125
V6 t/c	20	50	22	—	—	—	
V10	11	8	14	—	—	—	
TAG Turbo V6 t/c	**25**	**7**	**18**	**—**	**—**	**—**	50
BMW 4-cyl t/c	**9**	**15**	**14**	**—**	**—**	**—**	38
Repco V8	**8**	**7**	**4**	**4**	**4**	**5**	32
BRM	**6**	**2**	**4**	**3**	**6**	**5**	26
1.9 V8	1	—	—	—	—	—	
2.1 V8	—	—	—	—	—	1	
H16	1	—	—	—	2	—	
V12	4	2	4	3	4	4	
Alfa Romeo	**2**	**5**	**7**	**1**	**1**	**1**	17
flat-12	2	3	6	—	1	—	
V12	—	2	1	1	—	1	
Matra V12	**3**	**4**	**5**	**1**	**1**	**1**	15
Coventry-Climax	**—**	**2**	**1**	**2**	**1**	**1**	7
2.7 4-cyl	—	—	—	1	1	1	
2.0 V8	—	2	1	1	—	—	
Weslake V12	**1**	**—**	**2**	**1**	**1**	**1**	6
Maserati V12	**2**	**1**	**2**	**—**	**—**	**—**	5
Hart 4-cyl t/c	**—**	**1**	**2**	**—**	**—**	**—**	3
Judd CV V8	**—**	**—**	**3**	**—**	**—**	**—**	3
Chevrolet V8 F5000*	**—**	**—**	**—**	**2***	**—**	**1**	3
	375	**375**	**377†**	**52**	**52**	**56†**	**1287**

*Formula F5000 of two minor races; first F1 finishers were BRM V12– and Cosworth V8-powered.
†Two Championship and four non-Championship fastest laps were shared by different engines.

*Two 'Formula 1' races have been won outright by Formula 5000 cars. The Madrid GP at Jarama, 1969, was won by a Lola-Chevrolet T142, pole and fastest lap by a McLaren-Chevrolet M10A. Fastest F1 car in both practice and race as well as 'F1 class' winner was a BRM P261 V12 spl. The 1973 Race of Champions was won by a Chevron-Chevrolet B24, with a McLaren M19-Cosworth the first F1 car home. Chevron also set fastest lap in 1972 Oulton Park Gold Cup.

†These column totals are greater than the total number of races because two GP Championship and four non-Championship fastest laps have each been shared by two manufacturers.

NB: Non-Championship races include '3-litre Formula' dress rehearsal, Rand GP, Kyalami, South Africa, 4-12-1965.

MARQUES

Make	CHAMPIONSHIP			NON-CHAMPIONSHIP			
	Wins	Pole	FL	Wins	Pole	FL	Total
McLaren	**94**	**76**	**65**	**7**	**4**	**8**	254
Cosworth V8	30	17	20	7	3*	7	
TAG V6	25	7	18	—	—	—	
Honda V6	15	15	10	—	—	—	
Honda V10	16	27	13	—	—	—	
Honda V12	8	10	4	—	—	—	
Chevrolet V8*	—	—	—	—	1*	1*	
Ferrari	**64**	**70**	**78**	**9**	**4**	**7**	232
V12 3.0	3	7	4	3	2	4	
flat-12	37	42	44	6	2	2	
V6	15	18	19	—	—	1	
V12 3.5	9	3	11	—	—	—	
Lotus	**55**	**79**	**45**	**6**	**11**	**12**	208
2.1 BRM V8	—	—	—	—	—	1	
2.0 Climax V8	—	2	1	1	—	—	
BRM H16	1	—	—	—	—	—	
Cosworth V8	47	57	36	5	11	11	
Renault V6	5	19	4	—	—	—	
Honda V6	2	1	3	—	—	—	
Judd CV V8	—	—	1	—	—	—	
Williams	**51**	**37**	**54**	**3**	**1**	**2**	148
Cosworth V8	17	10	17	3	1	2	
Honda V6	23	19	22	—	—	—	
Judd CV V8	—	—	1	—	—	—	
Renault V10	11	8	14	—	—	—	
Brabham	**33**	**37**	**37**	**10**	**8**	**9**	134
2.7 Climax 4-cyl	—	—	—	1	1	1	
Repco V8	8	7	4	4	4	5	
Alfa Romeo flat-12	2	3	6	—	1	—	
Cosworth V8	15	14	16	4	2	2	
Alfa V12	—	—	—	1	—	1	
BMW 4-cyl	8	13	11	—	—	—	
Tyrrell	**23**	**14**	**20**	**1**	**4**	**2**	64
Cosworth V8	23	14	19	1	4	2	
Cosworth DFR V8	—	—	1	—	—	—	
Renault V6	**15**	**31**	**17**	**—**	**—**	**—**	63
Matra	**9**	**4**	**12**	**3**	**3**	**3**	34
Cosworth V8	9	2	9	2	2	2	
V12	—	2	3	1	1	1	
Ligier	**8**	**9**	**9**	**—**	**1**	**—**	27
Cosworth V8	5	7	6	—	1	—	
Matra V12	3	2	2	—	—	—	
Renault V6	—	—	1	—	—	—	
BRM	**5**	**2**	**4**	**3**	**6**	**3**	23
1.9 V8	1	—	—	—	—	—	
H16	—	—	—	—	2	—	
V12	4	2	4	3	4	3	
March	**3**	**5**	**7**	**2**	**2**	**1**	20
Cosworth V8	3	5	6	2	2	1	
Judd CV V8	—	—	1	—	—	—	
Benetton	**5**	**2**	**7**	**—**	**—**	**—**	14
BMW 4-cyl	1	2	3	—	—	—	
Cosworth-Ford V6 t/c	—	—	1	—	—	—	
Cosworth DFR V8	—	—	1	—	—	—	
Cosworth-Ford HB V8	4	—	2	—	—	—	
Shadow-Cosworth V8	1	2	2	1	2	2	10
Surtees-Cosworth V8	—	—	3	2	2	2	9
Hesketh-Cosworth V8	1	—	1	1	3	2	8
Eagle-Weslake V12	1	—	2	1	1	1	6
Wolf-Cosworth V8	3	1	2	—	—	—	6
Cooper-Maserati V12	2	1	2	—	—	—	5
Honda V12	1	1	2	—	—	—	4
Alfa Romeo V12	—	2	1	—	—	—	3
Toleman-Hart 4-cyl	—	1	2	—	—	—	3
Arrows-Cosworth V8	—	1	1	—	—	—	2
Ensign-Cosworth V8	—	—	1	—	—	—	1
Fittipaldi-Cosworth V8	—	—	—	—	—	1	1
Jordan-Cosworth-Ford HB V8	—	—	1	—	—	—	1
Kojima-Cosworth V8	—	—	1	—	—	—	1
Parnelli-Cosworth V8	—	—	1	—	—	—	1
Penske-Cosworth V8	1	—	—	—	—	—	1
Theodore-Cosworth V8	—	—	—	1	—	—	1
Chevron-Chevrolet V8*	—	—	—	1*	—	1*	2
Lola-Chevrolet V8*	—	—	—	1*	—	—	1
	375	**375**	**377†**	**52**	**52**	**56†**	**1287**

▶ Today, no-one can claim exclusivity in technological progress; these days, all reputable car manufacturers are well-versed in electronics, engine design and the harmonisation of suspension systems. Much more important is the way in which a manufacturer employs this technology.

▶ One approach, for example, is to equip the dashboard with flashing lights and displays, making it look like the flight deck of an airliner. Another is to provide the driver with unlimited capabilities to vary the suspension settings. Other manufacturers resort to the wind tunnel in their attempts to create an identity and a character for their cars.

▶ At Mercedes-Benz, technology is never used simply for its own sake; progress is associated with terms such as common sense and responsibility. So our engineers not only have the courage and the ability to produce avant-garde products such as the Mercedes-Benz World Championship sports car, they also have sufficient responsibility to delay the introduction of four-valve engines until they are

No unsigh

(Unless you

ly roll bar.

urn it over.)

certain that they will provide the desired additional performance at lower engine speeds.

► Then there is the SL. A car widely recognised as a "technological wonder" and a "super sports car". Yet with all their enthusiasm, our engineers would not release the car until it was not only the most advanced convertible in the world but also probably the safest.

► To this end, they invented a roll-over bar that is only visible when it is required. And when it really is needed, it's there in a flash. It comes up immediately, in less than 0.3 seconds, when the sensors and microprocessors report that the car is in a critical situation.

► In keeping us at the forefront of technology, our engineers are every bit as ingenious as any others. But they are not merely concerned with maintaining our leadership. They are motivated equally by a sense of responsibility. Enjoy your motoring.

Mercedes-Benz

Overview

HIGHLIGHTS OF THE GRAND PRIX FORMULAE 1966-1991

Inevitably, the start of any new racing Formula sees a makeshift year with lashed-up interim cars, teething-troubled new designs and nearly always the best-prepared, most practical and down-to-earth team carrying home the bacon.

This is exactly what happened in 1966 when the '3-litre Formula' began. The modest-engined Repco Brabhams used lightweight and simple multi-tubular spaceframe chassis, BRM and Lotus followed Ferrari's 1965 lead into using the engine as a fully stressed structural member and a number of adventurous new designs made their debut, looking to reach full development and success in 1967.

Most of their optimistic hopes were shattered that year by the emergence of the epochal Cosworth-Ford DFV V8 engine which set near-untouchable new standards of compact practical design allied to standard-setting power and torque.

When it became available to other customer teams in addition to Team Lotus in 1968, Formula 1 was thrown open to anyone and the path was cleared for the mushrooming interest and explosion of commercial sponsorship which entirely changed the superficial face of racing through the Seventies.

The emergence of such engine performance soon overwhelmed chassis and tyre capability into 1969, when some teams laid plans to overcome their traction problems by dividing drive to all four wheels instead of using just the rear pair.

These developments were effectively and neatly rendered unnecessary by the impact of aerodynamic download technology exemplified by the brief era of tall strutted wings and airfoil aids in late 1968/early 1969.

In 1969, the four-wheel drive experiments briefly flowered and died.

Come 1970, and the Lotus 72 and new flat-12 Ferrari 312B emerged. One set new standards in aerodynamic download within wing-restrictive regulations, the other greatly improved mechanical and chassis packaging, clearing airflow beneath the regulation low-level rear wing, as well as sheer horsepower.

The 72 was probably the only net front-end download car that season, all others being in varying degrees of discomfort with net aerodynamic lift around their front wheels.

An increasing rate of aerodynamic testing, pragmatic, intuitive common-sense innovation and logical thought helped shape the Grand Prix car as it went into the mid-Seventies.

Robin Herd's March outfit had been ahead of its time with its low polar moment 721X car of 1972, matched more effectively by Derek Gardner's Tyrrell 005 that same season. Mauro Forghieri's Ferrari 312B3/74 gave notice of what was to come in central mass concentration and the good rear wing performance attainable with only a knee-high flat-12 engine to obstruct flow ahead of it.

Engine and tyre performance held centre-stage through 1975-76 while Gordon Murray's intuitive genius found maturity at Brabham. In 1977, Lotus rang the changes and sparked a real aerodynamic revolution with their Type 78 and its successor the Type 79 of 1978 which established Peter Wright's ground-effects aerodynamics principle.

By harnessing airflow beneath the car in addition to airflow over the top of it, the Lotus R&D group had found a key which unlocked a whole new area of Grand Prix car performance.

All had to follow, but by this time Renault had been seduced into Formula 1 by the promotional hullabaloo now attached to it from big-sponsor exposure. It was now regarded once more as an honourable and potentially profitable arena in which a major production-car manufacturer could appear.

Renault made their first painful steps along the path towards the next revolution to overwhelm Formula 1 – the establishment of turbocharged 1500 cc engines which would have sufficient power to spare to drag huge drag-inducive high-download wings through the air, generating lap times which the naturally aspirated Cosworth brigade were increasingly hard-pressed to match.

The best Cosworth teams such as Williams and Brabham fought back brilliantly with a series of arguably ever-more dubious ploys such as lowering suspensions and post-race fillable 'brake-cooling' water-ballast reservoirs which enabled their bitter rearguard action to be fought successfully against the turbocharged teams until 1982-83.

The sliding skirt ban of 1981 had seen lowering suspension devices introduced to retrieve workable high download ground effects from underwing side pod tunnel sections, and as the law makers floundered about in a morass of their own making so contemporary Formula 1 cars became solid-sprung virtual 550-horsepower go-karts, subjecting their structures and drivers to fearsomely destructive jounce loads.

In 1983 underwing ground-effects sections were suddenly laid to rest once and for all as the governing body applied a new flat-bottom-within-the-wheelbase regulation.

As progressive restrictions were then placed upon available race-distance fuel allowances to come into line with energy-conscious motor industry considerations, the rule makers suffered increasingly cold feet over the 1000-horsepower course that turbocharged Formula 1 was taking.

Costs had rocketed, few teams had competitive engines, there was no really viable customer turbocharged engine available. The future looked bleak, so after a solitary season's pure 1500 cc turbocharged racing – in 1986 – the governing body made its celebrated U-turn, and 3.5-litre naturally aspirated engines were admitted to the premier class.

By 1988 the turbocharged cars were running their final season – one which proved to be a comprehensive walkover for McLaren-Honda – and from 1989 a new era began with such towering industrial names as Honda, Renault, Ford and Fiat-Ferrari slugging it out in the FIA Formula 1 World Championship series. They fielded multi-cylinder atmospherically aspirated racing engines in cars built – with the sole exception of Ferrari (and arguably Lotus) – by dedicated specialist constructors, for whom Formula 1 was the sole means of sustenance.

Grand Prix racing had come a long, long way from the start of the 3-litre Formula in 1966. In the following pages we have tried to tell it like it was, and why it was, in greater depth than ever before. Read on . . .

Formula 1 in the Eighties tried to make its mark on the lucrative US scene using makeshift street circuits as here in Detroit '85. Six different makes and five different engines are represented in this bunch:

Cheever's Alfa Romeo 185T V8 leads Warwick's Renault RE60, de Angelis's Lotus-Renault 97T, Johansson's Ferrari 156/85, Piquet's Brabham-BMW BT54 and Lauda's McLaren-TAG Turbo MP4/2B.

SPORTS PERSONALIT

Y OF THE YEAR

And the winner is...

The new Honda Prelude.

While we're about it, we'd also like to nominate it for best newcomer and best performance.

But does the new Prelude deserve all these plaudits?

We firmly believe it does.

Radically styled to look every inch a sports car, it's also endowed with suitably sporting prowess.

There's a choice of two 16 valve engines; 2.0 litre and 2.3 litre, both fuel-injected and more powerful than ever before. And the 2.3 has electronic four-wheel steering which gives it extraordinarily responsive handling and agility.

But the real beauty of the new Prelude is that it combines all the performance of a sports car with all the reliability of a Honda.

And, unlike many sports cars, it boasts a distinctive and luxurious interior.

With power-steering, ABS and, on the 2.3, a safety SRS airbag, it's no wonder 'World Sports Car' magazine declared: "The Honda Prelude has it all."

But don't take our, or their, word for it.

Visit your Honda dealer and give the new Prelude a personality test of your own.

The new Honda Prelude

SUMMARY

1966
New Formula introduced: widespread use of uprated 1½-litre machinery until new-generation 3-litre engines became available.

1967
Reliable Repco 3-litre V8s in ultra-light Brabham chassis took Championship while pure-bred racing engine from Cosworth-Ford set new performance standards. Gurney-Weslake V12 and BRM H16 reached respective peaks. Growing aerodynamic interest revealed by spoilers added at Spa by Brabham and Lotus, bubble cockpit canopy and gearbox shroud at Monza by Brabham.

1968
Cosworth-Ford DFV V8 engines made available for customer sale: used by McLaren and Matra International in addition to Lotus to dominate results. Small fields, strutted wing aerodynamic aids introduced by Ferrari and Brabham at Spa, developed most rapidly by Lotus thereafter. Engine power outstripped traction, Firestone YB11 tyres performed well, four-wheel drive plans were laid.

1969
500 kg minimum weight to accommodate new onboard extinguisher and roll-over bar requirements. 4WD was tried and discredited. Cosworth cars utterly dominant, led by Stewart in Tyrrell Matras. Barcelona strutted wing collapses caused hasty application of new low-wing restrictions.

1970
Bag tanks, and indirectly therefore monocoque chassis, became mandatory – end of the multitubular spaceframe in Formula 1, 530 kg minimum weight. Lotus 72 dominated, with luck; Ferrari flat-12 made its mark. Lotus introduced engine airbox induction scoops, Matra adopted tall airboxes, starting trend.

1971
Goodyear introduce slick tyres at Kyalami, Firestone slicker ones at Ontario (practice only) and Barcelona. Firestone introduced low-profile tyres and encountered vibration problems. Stewart dominant in new Tyrrell-Cosworth; close racing, Ferrari faltered after dominant early-season. Development of front-wheel fairing bluff noses pioneered in Formula 1 by Matra, proven by Tyrrell. Lotus ran 4WD gas-turbine-powered Formula 1 Type 56B.

1972
16-gauge external fuel tank sheathing required in preparation for deformable structure regulation in 1973, engines with more than 12 cylinders banned. Year of the Lotus 72 and Fittipaldi while Ferrari faltered, Stewart ulcer affected Tyrrell results until end of season.

1973
Deformable structure fuel tank protection devices mandatory from Spanish GP, along with dry-break fuel-line couplings, 250-litre maximum fuel tank capacity, 575 kg minimum weight to compensate. Stewart's Tyrrells versus Lotus twins, Fittipaldi and Peterson; all three shared honours. Far-outrigged rear wings achieved greater download; McLaren introduced Graviner breathable-air driver safety system at Belgian GP.

1974
Rear wing overhang restricted to 1 metre behind rear axle line. Ferrari resurgent with new flat-12

cars; Goodyear resources and success would force Firestone out of racing. Brabham experimented with under-car aerodynamic devices, McLaren and Tyrrell followed suit. Failure of Lotus 72 replacement Type 76 and experimental two-pedal auto-clutch system; Peterson still won three races in obsolete 72. McLaren M23 title. Harvey Postlethwaite tried rubber suspension medium on Hesketh, Gordon Murray adopted successful pullrod rising-rate suspension on Brabham BT44.

1975
Ferrari flat-12s dominant for Lauda and Regazzoni, Cosworth users sought alternative engines, Brabham planned Alfa Romeo flat-12 cars. Final eclipse of classic Lotus 72s. Carbon-composite components, predominantly for wings, made F1 debut on Hesketh and Hill.

1976
New low airbox regulations introduced from Spanish GP, rear wing overhang cut from 1 metre to 80 cm, front overhang maximum 120 cm, 21 in. maximum wheel/tyre width, 13 in. maximum rear rim diameter, front rim diameter free. Maximum overall car width 215 cm. Maximum airbox height 85 cm above lowest sprung part of car. Additional forward roll-over bar mandatory, ban on oil-carrying devices behind rearmost 'casing' prevented siting of outrigged oil coolers under rear wing. 575 kg minimum weight maintained. Season-long Ferrari/McLaren battle. Increasing use of aluminium honeycomb structural panels; McLaren M26 prototype used extensive Kevlar and Nomex lightweight structural honeycomb, team also introduced compressed-air starter system at South African GP. Tyrrell introduced successful six-wheeled Project 34 cars, Brabham experimented with Dunlop carbon brakes.

1977
Airbox height now 95 cm maximum *above ground*; Lotus 78 part-honeycomb design introduced 'wingcar' ground-effects underwing technology; V8 engine unreliability allowed Ferrari first-ever Constructors' Championship hat-trick. Renault first to take advantage of turbocharged 1500 cc engine option.

1978
Single 250-litre fuel cell permitted, old maximum of 80 litres per cell rule waived. Lotus 79 wing-cars destroyed all opposition, new Williams FW06 best of the rest. Gordon Murray adopted small carbon-composite structural panels in Brabham BT48 monocoque. Harvey Postlethwaite used folded aluminium-honeycomb tub in Wolf WR7 series. Maurice Phillippe and Dr Karl Kempf of Tyrrell tested 'computer-controlled' active suspension.

1979
Overall car length fixed at 5 metres, overhang limits unchanged. Ferrari flat-12 resurgent as other teams enjoyed only half-season success – Ligier early on, Williams later dominant. Renault became competitive with turbocharged engine, won first race. Aerodynamic 'porpoising' became evident, notably making Lotus 80 fail.

1980
Height of the ground-effects sliding skirted car era with Williams FW07Bs dominant but Brabham BT49s challenged later. Renault's turbocharged cars consistent and serious challengers. Ferrari announced turbocharged 1500 cc V6 car for '81.

1981
Sliding skirts banned, 6 cm ground clearance regulations enforced but sidestepped by Brabham hydropneumatic lowering suspension ploy, subsequently copied by all teams. Suspension travel minimized to ensure consistent download, compromising chassis (and driver) life. Brabham's Piquet was Drivers' Champion, Williams FW07Cs took team's second consecutive Constructors' Cup victory. John Barnard of McLaren introduced moulded carbon-composite chassis, followed by Lotus whose 'twin-chassis' Type 88 was banned. Ferrari won races in first turbocharged season. Brabham tested BMW turbocharged engine.

1982
Driver survival cell cockpit protection requirements introduced, Ferrari 126C2 turbocharged cars dominated with Renault but accidents marred season. Brabham-BMW turbocharged car won first GP, Gordon Murray introduced pit-stop refuelling and tyre-change race strategy, Renault lost Constructors' Championship to Ferrari, Drivers' title to Rosberg of Williams. Last Cosworth-powered World Champion Driver.

1983
New flat-bottom regulation applied, banning ground-effects underwing sections between wheels. Rear wing width cut from 110 cm to 100 cm, overhang cut from 80 cm to 60 cm, height raised to 100 cm for mirror visibility, minimum weight cut to 540 kg to encourage Cosworth engine users. DFY scored last 3-litre non-turbocharged engine victory. Widespread use of in-race refuelling/tyre-change tactics.

1984
Fuel volume permitted for race cut from 250 litres to 220 litres, original intention expressed to lower it further to 195 litres in 1985. In-race refuelling banned so widespread use of fuel cooling prior to filling car to reduce volume and squeeze more in. Pedal-box lengths respecified. Season notable for McLaren-TAG Turbo *tour de force*, Michelin radial tyres dominant, new Goodyear radials needed to catch up.

1985
Rear wing additional winglets banned, 220-litre fuel restriction enforced for extra year, new nose-box regulations demanded crash testing before acceptance, Lotus introduced turning-vanes to reduce front-wheel drag. Fuel and engine development created massive power increase. Last 3-litre engine raced in German GP, Formula 1 all-turbocharged thereafter. Successful McLaren rearguard action retained Championship titles, BMW most powerful engine, Williams-Honda most effective combination dominating end of season. Toleman introduced effective stepped-monocoque aerodynamic device.

1986
Naturally aspirated engines banned from Formula 1, which became for this unique season a purely 1500 cc turbocharged class. Fuel capacity further reduced to 195 litres. Turbo boost remained unrestricted – engines winding up to 5 bar-plus in qualifying tune. Driver Elio de Angelis asphyxiated in mid-season testing crash at Ricard, slow rescue being blamed for his tragic death after Brabham-BMW BT55 overturned following wing failure. Constructors' Championship effectively three-horse race between Williams-Honda, McLaren-TAG and Lotus-Renault. Williams took nine of the 16 GPs, Senna the

majority of pole positions for Lotus-Renault. Benetton (*née* Toleman) adopted BMW power and on Pirelli tyres notched their maiden GP victory, Gerhard Berger driving non-stop, in Mexico.

1987
Profound FISA U-turn launches new 3.5-litre naturally aspirated F1 class with its own Drivers' and Constructors' Championships run in parallel with the 1.5-litre turbos' traditional series. FISA also applied maximum 4-bar boost-restricting pop-off valves on turbo entries, banned water intercooling, only air/air being permitted; minimum weight for turbocharged cars 540 kg – for new 'atmo' cars (maximum 12 cylinders) 500 kg. Teams given option to swap once only from turbo engines to naturally aspirated, reversion forbidden. Flat-bottomed form maintained, ditto 195 litres fuel capacity for both turbocharged and 'atmo' cars. No contest between allegedly 4-bar turbos and 3.5-litre 'atmos'. Goodyear inherited F1 tyre monopoly upon Pirelli's withdrawal. To minimize costs they offered no qualifying tyres and one control race tyre – save for a compound choice dictated by track conditions in Mexico. Control tyre tailored to turbo car requirements, so unsuited to 'atmos' rendering them even less competitive. Williams-Honda again won nine GPs, Senna two in Active-suspended Lotus 99T. Ferrari resurgent, won last two GPs. In Portugal Alain Prost of McLaren-TAG broke Jackie Stewart's long-standing career record of 27 Championship-qualifying GP wins.

1988
Final year of turbo racing – pop-off boost limit slashed to nominal 2.5 bar, turbo fuel allowance to just 150 litres. Comprehensive frontal and lateral chassis crash testing mandatory, turbo runners permitted to retain existing monocoques to save costs of all-new impact-absorbing footbox structures/pedals behind the front axle line new designs for one season's racing only. For 1989 Formula 1 was to become a pure 3.5-litre 'atmo' class with 195-litre fuel capacity.

McLaren-Honda alone built significant all-new turbo-engined car for '88 – Lotus tried and failed abysmally – so McLaren-Honda dominated accordingly, Ferrari playing second fiddle with updated '87 chassis. The two teams shared all 16 GP wins between them – England 15, Italy 1 . . . 1988 was a joke season – no contest, the most one-sided Formula 1 season in history. McLaren-Honda greatly enjoyed it . . . and take all credit for pulling no punches whatsoever.

1989
New purely 3.5-litre atmospherically aspirated Formula 1. Highly detailed safety regulations include requirements for structural 'survival cell' cockpit design and extensive test procedures to verify its effectiveness. 500 kg minimum weight limit – 150 litres fuel capacity.

The Barnard-masterminded Ferraris driven by Mansell and Berger proved semi-automatic transmission in Formula 1, the Italian team's drivers winning three GPs between them – including the Englishman's famous victory on the new car's debut in Brazil.

McLaren fought back with their Honda V10-engined MP4/5 cars, Senna alone winning six times, Prost four and the Brazilian being rammed by his team-mate in Japan, then recovering to win on the road. He was subsequently disqualified for by-passing a chicane so Prost clinched the Drivers' Championship on his McLaren swansong. McLaren-Honda took the Constructors' Cup, and indulged in a celebrated attempt to have Senna reinstated as Japanese GP winner – and thereby as Champion – to Prost's cost. Boutsen picked up two wins for the new Renault V10-engined Williams, and Nannini's Benetton-Ford was presented with victory in Japan after Senna's disqualification – a maiden win for the Cosworth-Ford HB V8.

1990
The new 3.5-litre 'atmo' Formula really got into its stride this season, with fuel chemistry playing an increasingly significant role, but Senna again scored six victories for McLaren-Honda and Alain Prost five for his new team, Ferrari. The World Championship titles lay between them in the penultimate round in Japan, and Senna promptly took Prost off at the first corner in a celebrated tangle reminiscent of the previous year. This time the incident clinched the Drivers' crown for the Brazilian, and the Constructors' Cup was McLaren-Honda's again.

Williams-Renault also won with Patrese driving at Imola, and Boutsen in Hungary; Ferrari with Mansell driving in Portugal.

1991
As McLaren-Honda adopted new V12 engines, their Formula 1 World Championship domination – seriously challenged by Ferrari in 1990 – was breached by Williams-Renault once their new V10 cars with semi-automatic transmission achieved reliability. While Ferrari fortunes collapsed in a winless season, and Williams-Renault transmission unreliability frustrated returned team leader Mansell and the faithful Patrese, Senna and McLaren-Honda stole away with four consecutive GP victories opening the season. Each was achieved in face of adversity, but Senna and McLaren International were able to hang on to another double World Championship-winning points advantage despite the latest Williams-Renault V10s dominating five consecutive mid-season GPs and winning four of them, three to Mansell, one to Patrese. The Englishman later added further victories at Monza and Barcelona but the chase of Senna was to prove in vain as Honda retrieved competitiveness with revised V12 engine specs enabling Senna to win two more late-season races.

Mansell's fortunes suffered a bungled tyre-change and subsequent disqualification at Estoril. After Mansell spun out of the Japanese GP, Senna backed off just before the finish line to permit team-mate Berger his first McLaren victory.

Piquet for Benetton-Ford inherited a win in Canada after Mansell's engine had died in the last corner while comfortably leading. In retrospect it was one of the hardest-fought and most enjoyable F1 seasons in years . . . But the gulf between the top teams and the cannon fodder was growing ever wider . . . and as the worldwide economic recession deepened, great worries were being expressed for the future of Formula 1.

In years to come images such as this will be regarded fondly as the spirit of an age. The late 1980s/early 1990s were absolutely the era of McLaren-Honda, and of Ayrton Senna – here the MP4/6 V12, at Magny-Cours 1991.

HISTORICAL DEPTH TO SHELL'S 150th GRAND PRIX WIN

When Ayrton Senna took the chequered flag to win the 1991 Belgian Grand Prix at Spa-Francorchamps it represented a milestone in the company's history of motor sport involvement. From a purely statistical viewpoint it was the 150th Grand Prix victory to be won on Shell products since the official World Championship was instigated in 1950. In a wider sense, it represented a symbolic reaffirmation of Shell's commitment to a sport which it has actively supported since the fledgling years of the motor car.

Shell's involvement with the sport has developed steadily over many decades since Count Borghese relied on Shell fuels and lubricants, supplies of which were positioned strategically throughout the route, to win the gruelling 1907 Paris to Peking endurance race. From those early days local Shell companies were quick to capitalise on the publicity available as a by-

product of supporting such racing pioneers.

This *ad hoc* support was offered not only to races, but also to record attempts and other spectacular adventures involving wings and wheels. An example of the wide-ranging nature of Shell's involvement can be judged from the support for Francis Chichester, who later earned a knighthood for his equally heroic yachting exploits, on his daring solo flights from London to Sydney in the early 1930s with a de Havilland Gypsy Moth biplane.

By this stage in motor racing history, the sport had consolidated itself as an internationally organised affair, a far cry from the early days of one-way road races between major cities. Factory teams were already beginning to rule the roost in the classic races and local Shell companies had started to support the most successful.

One of the most historic deals of all was forged by Shell's marketing company in Italy. In 1924 it

concluded an arrangement to support Alfa Romeo, thereby establishing Shell's first link with a works team and a partnership which endured through to the end of the 1951 season when Alfa finally withdrew from the fray with its highly developed 1½-litre supercharged type 159.

This liaison was soon followed by Shell's support for the famous Bentley team at Le Mans, providing it with the fuels and lubricants which carried the British racing green cars to four successive victories at the Sarthe between 1927 and 1930.

After Bentley's withdrawal from racing, Shell-Mex supported many of the private ERAs running in the voiturette class during the mid-1930s and other Shell companies supported Gordini and Auto Union until the outbreak of hostilities in 1939.

In the pre-war years the choice of fuel specification was uninhibited by regulations. The obligatory requirement for 'pump' fuel was several years away – indeed, the 75-octane 'pump'

Left: **Le Mans 1928 and the Bentleys of Birkin and Clement are in the lead at the start.**

Opposite: **Nino Farina at the wheel of the Alfa Romeo 159 in which he won the first official World Championship in 1950.**

For many years Keith Ballisat *(below)* **was very active on the marketing side of the Shell motor sport programme; a capable driver, he is pictured in a Cooper-Climax in 1958.**

fuel of the time was regarded as pretty indifferent stuff for road cars, let alone highly tuned racing engines.

As a result, most racing cars ran on a methanol-based fuel known generically as 80/10/10, which reflected its content of about 80 per cent methanol, ten per cent petrol and ten per cent benzol. This blend could be used in conjunction with a lower compression ratio – and therefore reduced mechanical stress – than pure methanol, which was employed by high-compression engines in shorter-distance sprint events.

As would always be the case, fuel development represented a key element in unlocking increased power outputs and Shell developed complex cocktails of nitro-benzene, methanol, acetone and water specially for the Auto Union team when it was at the height of its battles with Mercedes-Benz in the 1930s.

In the immediate post-war era, Shell's fuel development helped Alfa Romeo increase the power of its 1½-litre engines from just over 250 bhp in 1946 to an amazing 350 bhp six years later, further aided by the introduction of two-stage supercharging.

The problems of heat dissipation within the straight-eight-cylinder engines were considerable and, as a result, the fuel was liberally laced with alcohol as this burns relatively coolly, but even after taking this step (in addition to equipping the engine with sodium-filled valves and revising the water circulation system to direct coolant towards the exhaust ports), the exhaust manifolds were literally glowing.

The Shell-fuelled Alfa Romeos started their domination of the official World Championship when Giuseppe Farina won the 1950 British Grand Prix at Silverstone, the first of three victories he would score that year on his way to becoming the sport's first official World Champion. Team-mate Juan Manuel Fangio would also win three races, but the brilliant Argentinian rising star would have to wait for the following year before winning the first of his record five championships.

In its final incarnation, the remarkable Alfa 159 would develop 404 bhp towards the end of the

1951 season, by which time its fuel consumption was so prodigious that it was not only starting the races with a significant weight handicap, but its consumption necessitated more frequent pit stops. This had been a significant disadvantage for the Alfas and contributed to Louis Chiron's victory in the 1948 French Grand Prix when his plodding 4.5-litre Talbot had benefited from a non-stop run.

However, Alfa had more enduring opposition on the horizon with the development of the Aurelio Lampredi-designed naturally aspirated Ferrari V12s which were developed during the first two years of the new formula. Shell had been associated with Enzo Ferrari since his spell as Alfa Romeo racing manager in the 1930s, so it was logical to expand its involvement to supply fuels and lubricants to the new Ferrari F1 cars which were built under his own name after the war.

Ferrari's F1 programme had started with a 1½-litre supercharged V12 between 1948 and 1950, the engines designed by Gioacchino Colombo, the man who had designed the original Alfa 158 in the immediate pre-war period. However, Ferrari quickly concluded that the 1½-litre supercharged concept was, in the long-term, an unproductive route and assigned Colombo's successor, Lampredi, to construct a non-supercharged V12.

The engine grew from a 3.3-litre version, via a 4.1-litre intermediate size, to the full 4.5 litres which powered the elegant Ferrari 375 during the summer of 1951. Alberto Ascari gave the Alfa Romeos a fright in the Grand Prix de l'ACF at Reims, but then Argentinian José Froilan Gonzalez scored the first victory for the Ferrari/Shell alliance with a memorable win in the British Grand Prix at Silverstone, beating Fangio's Alfa Romeo in a straight fight.

Ascari then followed this up with commanding victories at the Nürburgring and Monza, hammering home the message that the day of the supercharged F1 car was at an end. However, Fangio's victory in the Spanish Grand Prix, the final race of the season, guaranteed that an Alfa driver won that year's World Championship.

In the absence of any financial support from the Italian government, Alfa Romeo announced

that it would be withdrawing from racing at the end of the 1951 season. Ferrari was, of course, fully committed to the sport and Shell would continue supplying fuels and lubricants to Maranello in 1952 and '53 when, due to a shortage of 1½-litre supercharged or 4.5-litre unsupercharged cars, the World Championship was run under 2-litre Formula 2 regulations.

Shell-fuelled Ferraris won every race but one during those two seasons, Ascari taking the championship title on each occasion. In 1952 his team-mate, Piero Taruffi, was the only other driver to win a race, triumphing in the Swiss Grand Prix at Berne, while in '53 Britain's Mike Hawthorn won a sensational battle with Fangio's Maserati at Reims to score a fine victory in the French Grand Prix, while Farina won at the Nürburgring and Fangio triumphed for Maserati at Monza. Between the Belgian Grands Prix of 1952 and '53, Ascari won a total of nine consecutive GPs, a record which remains unmatched to this day.

Shell's continuing association with Ferrari produced two victories in 1954 under the newly introduced 2½-litre regulations. Gonzalez triumphed again at Silverstone with the type 625 – a derivative of the highly successful Formula 2 car which had dominated the previous two seasons – and Mike Hawthorn won the Spanish Grand Prix in the type 553 'Squalo'.

There was only a lucky victory at Monaco to be earned by Shell and Ferrari in 1955, thanks to the efforts of Maurice Trintignant and the old type 625, but better was to come in 1956, when Maranello was bequeathed the superb Lancia D50s, Fangio winning the championship for the fourth time.

There were no Shell/Ferrari victories in 1957, but major changes were afoot to forestall too much experimentation with exotic fuels using nitro-methane, and a new specification was introduced from the start of 1958. The fuel companies in general were anxious to make more advertising capital from their involvement in Grand Prix racing, so the fuel requirements were changed from alcohol-based fuels to so-called 'pump petrol'.

Apart from the obvious difficulty of writing a precise definition of the term 'pump petrol' another immediate snag arose, namely the problem of setting and maintaining minimum acceptable standards for such fuel on a worldwide basis. As a result, it was eventually decided that 130-octane aviation gasoline (AvGas) would be permitted.

For the 1958 season, Ferrari was equipped with its elegant Dino 246 machines driven by Mike Hawthorn and Peter Collins. Mike won the French Grand Prix, Peter the British, and Hawthorn went on to become the first Englishman to win the World Championship after a season-long battle with Stirling Moss in the Vanwall.

The next two seasons of F1 competition were characterised by the rear-engined revolution and Ferrari won only three races with the now outdated Dino through to the end of the 1960 season. Thereafter, Shell expanded its involvement

A BRM V8 racing engine *(left)* undergoing a test by a Shell technician prior to the 1965 Grand Prix season.

Steve McArragher *(bottom)* was involved in the technical development of the fuel supplied to McLaren during their all-conquering turbo years of 1984 and 1985.

in F1 to encompass support for the British BRM team which, after a decade of trying, had finally won its first Grand Prix – the Dutch – in 1959, thanks to the efforts of Swedish driver Jo Bonnier.

The advent of the 1½-litre F1 at the start of 1961 saw the Shell-fuelled Ferrari 156s dominate the first season under the new regulations thanks to having buckled down and developed a suitable power unit immediately the rules were announced rather than attempting to argue the toss with the sport's governing body.

That modest Californian Phil Hill became the first American to win the title at the end of a wearing season which was blighted by the death of his team-mate Wolfgang von Trips – and 13 spectators – in a dreadful accident during the early stages of the Italian Grand Prix.

Meanwhile BRM was preparing the ground for the most serious challenge of its 13-year history, tackling the new formula with a compact 1½-litre V8 engine. BRM was already running on Super Shell and using Shell lubricants by this stage, but now, with the evolution of this new engine, the team developed a close programme of collaboration with Shell and received valuable assistance from its Thornton Research Centre.

Shell's development work on the V8 project was typical of the close relationship which the company has always sustained with the competing teams it has supplied. Even though the prevailing technical regulations called for the use of normal commercial fuel, there was plenty of scope for improving the combustion performance of the early BRM engines.

The Owen Organisation, which owned BRM, became very concerned when the early V8s would only develop between 165 and 190 bhp, far from their intended output of 225 bhp. More confusingly, the BRM engineers could not accurately establish the reason for the variation between a good engine and a bad one.

All the most obvious variables, such as timing and breathing, were apparently eliminated to the point that poor combustion seemed to be the root of the problem. The Owen Organisation technicians had already established that the engine was relatively insensitive to changes in ignition timing, another sure sign of poor combustion.

However, in those days before F1 had the luxury of test teams, the fortnightly schedule of major races hampered any attempts at long-term research. BRM therefore approached Shell, who agreed to collaborate, putting Dr Geoff Harrow of their Thornton Research Centre in charge of the investigation programme based on an engine which had previously produced rather disappointing power outputs.

Considerable work on combustion was in hand at Thornton at the time and certain commonly accepted general principles had been examined in some depth. One of these was that the power output in a normal engine is closely related to the most efficient possible combustion process.

This development work clearly proved worthwhile for, as Ferrari faded from the pace, so the Shell-fuelled BRMs developed into a highly competitive force with Graham Hill winning four races during 1962 to take the World Championship. Hill sustained his competitive momentum into the following year, winning the first of five Monaco victories in 1963 to notch up Shell's 50th win in championship Grands Prix.

In addition, Hill won the US Grand Prix that season, with former motor cycle champion John Surtees putting Ferrari back into the competitive frame with a well-judged win at the Nürburgring. The following year Surtees would add another two wins to his tally on his way to clinching the World Championship, thereby becoming the only man ever to win the title on both two and four wheels.

Ferrari also benefited from Dr Harrow's breathing exercises. Flame propagation and combustion had been so erratic that only by overadvancing the ignition until it pinked would one of the engines deliver anything near full power. That was until Geoff Harrow started to measure flame speeds and combustion rates and experiment with different turbulence schemes.

In addition, Shell scored three other GP victories in 1964, Hill taking two for BRM and Ferrari number two Lorenzo Bandini surviving to win the Austrian Grand Prix on the bumpy Zeltweg aerodrome after most of the regular front-runners were forced into retirement. Shell's three victories in 1965 – the last year of the 1½-litre F1 – came courtesy of BRM's efforts, two from Hill and a splendid win at Monza from new boy Jackie Stewart.

For 1966, the F1 technical regulations, while still calling for 'commercially available' fuel to be used, changed to cater for 3-litre engines. Ferrari produced a very logical development of his V12 sports car engine for Grand Prix purposes, but BRM opted for the complex H16 engine configuration. Basing the design on some tried and tested components, notably the cylinder heads developed in conjunction with Shell Research and Thornton for the successful V8, the team pressed ahead with what turned out to be an overimaginative and excessively complex project.

BRM hedged its bets with a V12 engine which would be available in sports car racing trim, but sustained problems with the H16 over two seasons meant that by 1968 the V12 was being used as the team's front-line F1 weapon. Nevertheless, throughout 1968 work proceeded on a much lighter and more compact version of the H16 which Shell researchers at Thornton concluded had 'excellent breathing; much better than any engine yet tested'. However, by this stage the main role of the revised H16 was as a development medium for the 48-valve cylinder heads which were now under preparation for the V12.

In fact, BRM's Jackie Stewart scored Shell's first victory under the 3-litre regulations at Monaco in 1966. However, the Scot was not driving an H16-powered car, but a '65 chassis equipped with one of the trusty V8 engines enlarged to 2 litres.

He won easily from Bandini's 2.4-litre Ferrari V6 after Surtees's larger Ferrari 3-litre V12 wilted with transmission problems in a race which graphically illustrated the diversity of machinery competing during what was inevitably going to be an interim season from the technical standpoint.

Surtees's Shell-fuelled Ferrari would then win the Belgian Grand Prix at Spa before the British driver's much-publicised split with the team, but the Italian driver Lodovico Scarfiotti raised Shell's tally to three victories that season with a splendid triumph in front of his emotional countrymen at Monza.

In 1967 Shell recorded only a single success when Dan Gurney's Eagle-Weslake V12 won the Belgian Grand Prix at Spa, but 1968 brought with it additional involvements not only with Colin Chapman's Team Lotus, but also with Bruce McLaren's fledgling team. Lotus scored four victories, McLaren three and Ferrari one, making it statistically the most successful season ever in Shell's post-war racing involvement. Two years later, with Lotus notching up six wins, Ferrari four and BRM one, Shell's seasonal record was boosted to a total of 11 victories.

By this stage in its motor racing involvement, Shell had a very focused idea of how to get the best out of its investment. In an internal document entitled *Shell in Motorsport* published in 1969, the company's approach was summed up thus: 'Awareness that leading teams are running on, and winning with, Shell promotes public confidence in Shell products and technical resources, and can be exploited to promote sales. It is Shell's conviction that it is right to be associated with this dynamic and youthful activity which is more and more in the public eye through press and television and in particular attracts the influential enthusiast and the motorists of tomorrow.'

Shell's alliance with Lotus and BRM finished at the end of 1971 while a similar deal with the French Matra team came to an end when they withdrew from F1 at the end of the following year. Although the Ferrari partnership continued to the end of the 1973 season, it would produce only one more victory, Jacky Ickx winning at the Nürburgring in 1972.

A whole dynasty of World Championship McLarens on display in the foyer of the team's factory at Woking.

One of the results of the October 1973 energy crisis was inevitably a sharp fall in the sponsorship of motor sport by the oil companies, a trend reflected by Shell's decision to end its F1 involvement. Although the amount of fuel and lubricant consumed in motor racing was negligible, with advertising and publicity material stressing the conservation message, it was considered to be counter-productive to be publicly associated with motor sport during this troubled period.

For the next decade Shell reduced its front-line F1 involvement, its only success coming in 1977 when the Shell France-fuelled and -lubricated Ligier-Matra won the Swedish Grand Prix in the hands of Jacques Laffite. But in 1984 Shell rekindled its involvement with a major programme of support for the McLaren International team, then using the Porsche-made TAG turbo V6 engine.

Shell lubricants were used by the team from the start of the season, with fuel supply starting only from the French Grand Prix, which Niki Lauda won. Between them, Lauda and his teammate, Alain Prost, won nine races on Shell fuel and lubricants *en route* to a commanding victory in the Constructors' World Championship.

Lauda won the drivers' title in 1984, but Prost would take it from him in 1985 and keep it the following year as the McLaren-TAGs sustained a competitive pace across a three-year period. Demands on fuel and lubricants were progressively intensified during a period when the permitted fuel capacity in F1 was steadily reduced – from 250 litres to 220 litres in 1984, then to 195 litres in 1986, with that limit being retained in conjunction with a 4-bar turbo boost limit the following year.

Balancing the maximum possible power output with optimum economy and a degree of cooling within the combustion chamber itself involved a considerable technical challenge which Shell tackled with wholehearted energy and commitment. Then, in 1988, with the turbo engine regulations in their final year, McLaren switched to Honda V6 power with fuel capacity restricted to 150 litres and a boost maximum of 2.5 bar.

With these turbocharged engines capable of delivering around 700 hp under race conditions and allegedly 1000 hp for a short burst, there was no demand for extra power via the fuel. What was at a premium was fuel economy. More than one race was lost through running out of fuel, or slowing down to avoid running out. When everything that could be done to improve m.p.g. had been done, Shell turned its eyes towards the lubricant.

Since the beginning of racing the demand had always been for a thick, viscous oil which would resist dilution by the excess fuel that goes with rich mixtures. Viscous oils, however, cause drag. Recognising that modern engine management systems and fuel injection systems had practically eliminated dilution of the oil by fuel through precise and timed metering, Shell turned its thoughts to the idea of low-drag, thin oils.

A joint development programme with Honda showed these oils to be the equal of thick oils in terms of protection, while reducing engine drag and friction. This translated into a fractional improvement in fuel economy, or, in racing terms, an extra lap of running at racing speeds, fully justifying the claim of the lubricants engineers that the 'mileage ingredient' is in the oil!

The 1988 season saw the Shell-fuelled and -lubricated Marlboro McLaren-Hondas of Ayrton Senna and Alain Prost win 15 of the season's 16 races between them after exerting a level of technical domination not achieved since the exploits of Alfa Romeo and Ferrari in the early 1950s. Senna clinched his first World Championship.

With the introduction of the 3.5-litre naturally aspirated F1 engine regulations at the start of 1989, Shell's fuel development priorities altered subtly, with engine development concentrating primarily on power output from the new Honda V10 rather than the need to work within very tight consumption limits. The 1989 season saw the Shell-fuelled and -lubricated Honda Marlboro McLaren team win another ten races, with Alain Prost this time taking the Drivers' World Championship.

Honda Marlboro McLaren scored a hat-trick of Constructors' World Championships in 1990 with Ayrton retaking the drivers' title, still using the Honda V10 engine, but the arrival of the latest RA 121E V12 for the start of the 1991 season meant another shift of emphasis in the evolution of Shell's fuel technology. When Senna won the 1991 Belgian Grand Prix at Spa it was Shell's 150th Grand Prix victory, the 151st coming at Suzuka, where Gerhard Berger scored his first win for McLaren and Ayrton clinched his third Drivers' World Championship with second place.

When the Honda V10 appeared, fuel economy, while still of concern, was less critical than it had been with the turbo engine. At the same time the search began for a means of raising power now that the turbo route was banned.

Some of the work done over 20 years before by Geoff Harrow on flame speeds and burning rates provided early clues and by Rio in 1989 a first qualifying fuel was being considered. Fuels with a bias for economy were also developed and made available.

As the V10 'grew' into the V12, a new family of fuels had to be developed to suit this engine's different combustion characteristics, one that was more rewarding in terms of response to fuel property changes. With the heightened competition of the 1991 season, added impetus was given to the quest for power gains via the fuel, with considerable success, and complimentary comments about Shell's contribution to the World Championship triumph were made by Ron Dennis, Yasuoka-San of Honda and reigning title-holder Ayrton Senna.

The 1992 season sees a change to the fuel specification in F1. At long last FISA will bring in an unleaded petrol requirement, strongly advocated by Shell and others for some time. Other restrictions to the specification will to some degree restrict the scope for fuel-derived power gains, but at the same time throw up new challenges.

With increasing attention being drawn to the high-technology image of Grand Prix racing as we enter the last decade of the 20th century, it is understandable that fuel and lubricants should emerge as an area of particular fascination and interest. For Shell, however, this media attention focuses merely on the tip of an iceberg of long-term commitment to technical excellence which has underpinned its involvement in front-line motor sport since the pioneering days of automotive competition.

'There is no doubt in my mind that "racing improves the breed" as they used to say,' says Roger Lindsay, head of fuels development at Shell. 'This is not to say that the technological developments achieved in support of motor racing could not be arrived at by more measured, genteel research programmes. However the "buzz" that is developed by competition and having to do better by the week stretches the imagination and focuses the mind.

'What we've been seeing in F1 fuels/engine behaviour this season is giving us considerable food for thought for the future development of everyday fuel, and our experience with F1 lubricants is already finding its way into the world where Shell shakes hands with 8,000,000 motorists a day.

'And for the people involved at our research centre to meet the World Champion, to see world class in operation in the Honda Marlboro McLaren team and to have the opportunity to get experience of working at otherwise unheard-of levels of performance and precision is perhaps the most valuable contribution of all.'

Chapter 1
The Formula Evolves

Crowded paddocks were a problem for the teams but undoubtedly gave Formula 1 practice periods a charming character which many now miss. Here at Spa-Francorchamps in preparation for the 1968 Belgian GP, Amon's Ferrari 312/68 '007 sports its chassis-mounted strutted wing, prompted by Chaparral out of Michael May via an unofficial Team Lotus Tasman experiment six months previously. Surtees's Honda V12 is beyond Ferrari '0011, Jochen Rindt can be seen pondering his Brabham's four-cam Repco 860 engine and behind him is Bonnier's private yellow McLaren-BRM M5A. Extreme left, just behind their BRM transporter, are Louis (half out of shot) and Jean Stanley, and in orange overalls team Chief Mechanic Cyril Atkins. The more you look, the more you see . . .

What would become known as the '3-litre Formula', despite its inclusion right from the start of a 1500 cc supercharged option, took shape during 1963. The Monaco Grand Prix was held on 26 May that year. During that weekend beside the sea in Monte Carlo, two significant meetings were convened to tap opinion regarding a new Grand Prix Formula, due to take effect 2½ years hence, in 1966.

At that time this meeting could be seen as the contemporary Formula 1's 'mid-life crisis', for it was then 2½ years since its introduction on 1 January 1961. It had replaced the old 1954-1960 Formula, which had limited unsupercharged engines to 2.5 litres and forced supercharged units right down to only 750 cc. Under the new 1961-63 Formula – subsequently extended to the end of 1965 – the supercharged option had remained unchanged but unblown engines were straitjacketed to no more than 1.5 litres and not less than 1.3 litres. What was more, the CSI had then underlined its determination to contain speeds and prevent construction of super-light, potentially fragile racing cars by imposing for the first time a minimum weight limit. This was set at 450 kg (992.07 lb).

Under this Formula only commercially available pump petrol could be used, onboard automatic starters were mandatory for the first time, as were driver-protecting roll-over bars. Oil replenishment during the race was banned, the road wheels had to be exposed, unfaired by streamlined bodywork, and battery cut-out switches became obligatory.

After these regulations had been announced at the end of 1958 by CSI President Augustin Perouse, there was uproar amongst the British Formula 1 establishment. They muttered darkly about supporting a breakaway 3-litre InterContinental Formula which would admit existing 2½-litre machinery and also – they dreamed – attract strong US support. While they fulminated at the CSI, the European interest in GP racing, from Ferrari and now increasingly from Porsche in Germany, quietly got on with the job in hand. The upshot was that they both shone in that first '1½-litre' season of 1961 while the whingeing Brits were too late in building the engines and cars which would largely dominate the class from 1962-65. Nobody of any note adopted the 750 cc supercharged option available under this Formula.

Now, in those Monte Carlo meetings of May 1963, the Grand Prix Drivers' Association first agreed that a replacement 3-litre unblown Formula would offer much more interest for both drivers and spectators, but since only Ferrari amongst contemporary racing manufacturers was at that time building 3-litre engines (for sports and GT competition) the drivers then concluded that the best compromise would in fact be a 2-litre Formula. This would allow, they thought, existing 1½-litre Formula 1 engines to be enlarged, to offer more spectacle and a better driving challenge, while minimizing extra cost.

This was true where BRM's V8s were concerned, but there was insufficient meat on the rival Coventry Climax V8 to allow straightforward enlargement. In any case Climax's new owners, Jaguar, seemed disinclined to sanction a Climax investment in design and manufacture of a larger engine for the new class, if larger it should be. This was mainly because they were increasingly involved up to their necks in other, potentially more lucrative work. Since such leading teams as Lotus, Brabham and Cooper all used Climax engines, their future come 1966, even at this time, looked uncertain.

Immediately after this GPDA meeting, a surprisingly informal get-together was convened by the CSI under its contemporary Swiss President, Maurice Baumgartner. His heart really did seem to be in the right place, as he now canvassed the views of drivers, constructors, race organizers and even the specialist racing press. Yet, perhaps predictably, there was little agreement. Some, notably the British RAC and engine manufacturers, would have preferred to see the existing Formula continue unchanged. It would make life much simpler for them and, in the manufacturers' case, undoubtedly more profitable.

Graham Hill propounded the GPDA's 2-litre preference, adding that the jump from the proposed new 1-litre Formula 2 – which was due to commence in 1964 – to a full 3-litre Formula 1 would be too great for aspiring new drivers. Italians present smiled happily at the thought of a 3-litre Formula giving *La Ferrari* a flying start, while the French simply hoped for a Formula under which somebody, anybody, might be encouraged to construct a French-blue GP car for the first time in almost a decade.

After these naturally inconclusive Monaco meetings, further discussions continued between the CSI and the constructors, with the GPDA offering advice to anyone who would listen. During the United States GP meeting at Watkins Glen that October, another GPDA meeting briefed its delegates to recommend a 3-litre limit with a minimum weight clause of 525 kg (1157.42 lb) at the November CSI meeting in Paris, where minimum cockpit dimensions would also be suggested. That meeting, in the FIA headquarters offices at 8, Place de la Concorde, took place on Thursday and Friday, 21-22 November 1963.

There is a delightful (if probably apocryphal) story about this meeting and how the new Formula was finally decided. The British representatives had long since planned their tactics. It seemed certain the CSI was hell-bent upon ditching the existing unpopular 1½-litre class. They couldn't go to 2½ litres as that had been the preceding Formula. It seemed doubtful that they would allow the quantum performance leap to a full 3 litres. In any case this was virtually the last thing the constructors wanted, as it would render their expensive 1500s obsolete overnight and threatened almost prohibitive cost. They preferred the GPDA's original 2-litre option. It would allow conversion of existing equipment while still adding sufficient speed and power to please both spectators and drivers. But, facing the familiar caprice of the CSI, they decided instead to suggest the 3-litre limit, certain it would be rejected; whereupon, they figured, the most likely compromise would be the 2-litre class which they in fact preferred.

As it happened, when they set out their case for

HOT NOT BOTHERED.

As any motoring journalist will tell you the Renault 5 GT Turbo was a hot act to follow.

But when its natural successor the Clio 16 Valve came along, we confidently offered it up for evaluation. And this for example is what Car Magazine had to say.

"Overall victory then goes to the Clio... it's not just the best hot hatch you can buy, it's also the best driver's car for the money."

The press were well impressed. Hardly surprising, the 137bhp Clio achieves 0 to 60mph in 7.8* seconds and has a top speed of 130mph.

But it's also a bit of a smoothie. Not just in the ride, which is superb, but in terms of equipment too. Metallic paint and ABS brakes** aside, everything else comes as standard.

It has power steering, that rare item which is usually a costly option. An anti-theft device, which can be a costly omission. Then, mounted right by the steering wheel itself are controls for a superb, six speaker Hi-Fi system.

Electric windows and door mirrors are also included, as are remote control central door lock-

**RENAULT
A CERTAIN
FLAIR**

ing and a catalytic converter.

We pay healthy attention to economy too. At a constant 56mph the Clio 16 Valve returns 45.6mpg.† Insurance premiums are also good news. Despite its performance qualities the Clio falls into group 11, whereas the Fiesta XR2i and the Peugeot 1.9 205 GTi would cost dearly in group 14.

It has an eight-year anti-corrosion warranty and the option of Renault Cordiale our budget maintenance scheme where a regular monthly sum covers repairs and servicing for up to three years.

Are you warming to it? Then test drive the Clio 16 Valve.

It's hot but not the slightest bit bothered.

To Renault UK, FREEPOST, PO Box 21, Thame, Oxon OX9 3BR. For more information about the Clio 16 Valve fill in the coupon or call Renault Freephone **0800 525150**. CR HG P 442

Mr/Mrs/Miss (please delete) _____
BLOCK CAPITALS

Address _____

_____

Town and County _____ Postcode _____

Telephone _____ Age (if under 18) _____

Present car make and model _____
(eg Renault 5 GTX)

Registration Letter ____ Month/Year you expect to replace
(eg "F")

RENAULT CLIO 16 VALVE

3 litres the Ferrari representative, Mauro Forghieri, smiled assent, the CSI members nodded sagely, and the proposal went clean through so fast '. . . it hardly touched the sides!'

Certainly that meeting finally agreed the new Formula 1 to take effect from 1 January 1966 and to run initially for three years to the end of 1968. It would restrict unsupercharged engines to 3 litres capacity, and supercharged units to 1500 cc, in essence allowing existing engines to be supercharged. The cars would run on commercially available fuel and the minimum weight would be 500 kg (1102.3 lb) including oil and water but excluding fuel. This compared with the 450 kg (992 lb) minimum for the existing 1500 cc Formula 1 cars.

In addition to the 3-litre unsupercharged/1.5-litre supercharged capacity limits, the CSI also opened the door – as predicted – to both rotary engines and to gas turbines. Rotary engines of the Wankel type would be permitted without capacity restriction but they would have to run on commercial fuel and would be restricted to minimum and maximum weight limits to be fixed at a later date. Gas turbine engines would be permitted without capacity or fuel restrictions, but with weight limitations to be applied after consultation 'with various experts' by 1 March 1964. All regulations for the existing 1500 cc Formula which had not been cancelled by these new proposals would continue to apply, which meant those onboard starters, roll-over hoops, exposed wheels, prohibited addition of oil during races, etc.

In general, these regulations were well received, although some felt that the 2.0 equivalency factor between unsupercharged and supercharged engines (3000 cc divided by 2.0 equalling 1500 cc) was too generous, since past history had demonstrated that supercharged racing engine outputs could match if not actually improve upon normally aspirated engines of three times their capacity. The gas turbine admission was thought to attract potential gas turbine car manufacturers such as Rover in the UK and Chrysler in the USA, while the Wankel clause was hoped to attract Mercedes-Benz who were involved in intensive Wankel engine research and development at that time.

In fact none of these volume car manufacturers would participate in Formula 1. BRM documents typify thinking which was probably shared by their counterparts at Ferrari. On 6 July 1964, BRM Chief Engineer Tony Rudd wrote an internal memo on the new Formula. He considered that since his existing 1.5-litre unblown V8 engines delivered 210 bhp, '. . . we must plan for 425 hp in the first year of the new Formula. Petrol, within the definitions of the formula, will not permit the use of mean cylinder pressures above 250 lbs per sq. in. by the end of the Formula in 1969. Therefore, to obtain 425 bhp from a supercharged 1½-litre, it must turn at 26,000 rpm as it also has to develop enough power to drive the supercharger. Such an engine is not impossible; but it would be fantastically expensive; it would have to exploit the science of metallurgy to the full; it would require heat exchangers etc, and could only be produced reliably by an organisation of the size of Ford, General Motors, Mercedes or Rolls-Royce. The alternative is the unsupercharged 3-litre.' Where Tony's typically logical memo would differ from, for example, Italian thinking in the Ferrari plant at Maranello was in his conclusion regarding his team's 3-litre Formula 1 contender . . .

'We have examined several versions', he wrote, 'and have concluded that a 16-cylinder engine would give us the best chance of success . . . the most desirable layout is an H16, we have prepared a design here at Bourne which is some 18" long, 28" wide and 14" high; this engine would weigh some 375 lbs and fit in the existing monocoque body shape . . . These cars, however, only carry 30 gallons of fuel, whereas a 3-litre engine will require at least 55 gallons, so that the cars will have to be about 1½" wider . . . These engines will cost us nearly twice as much to build; they will have to sell to private owners for between £6,000 and £7,000. The number of

engines sold will obviously be less . . . the oil companies anticipated that the 3-litre engines would cost more like £10,000 each.'

We shall see shortly just how much less expensive an engine could be developed, sufficient to dominate the World Championship results in the first two seasons of the new Formula's life.

Rumours in the winter of 1964/65, with only a year to go before the new regulations took effect, included talk of Brabham almost certainly using a GM-based American V8 engine modified and developed by their financial backers, Repco of Australia. Dan Gurney, the Brabham driver, was at that time receiving a Ford retainer and was organizing a development programme in Los Angeles to build Climax 1½-litre V8 experience into an aluminium American V8. Cooper had contacted BRM for 3-litre engines, since Climax had as yet made no plans to build engines for the new class. Lotus's new engine facility was concentrating upon development of a 4.7-litre Ford Fairlane V8 engine for their Lotus 30 sports-racing car. Lotus chief Colin Chapman appeared disinterested in Climax and was thought to be working with Ford for a 1966 F1 engine. McLaren had backing from Firestone and had already obtained the exclusive European rights to the Traco Oldsmobile V8 aluminium engine, weighing 325 lb and delivering 345 bhp. It would be simple to convert this V8 to 3 litres but Bruce McLaren had already contacted BRM concerning an engine for 1966 when he would be leaving Cooper to build his own 3-litre F1 cars.

Climax were deeply involved in V12 engine development for Jaguar and had abandoned their four-valve per cylinder V8 F1 engine programme in favour of a new 1½-litre flat-16. These complex programmes left them very little spare capacity for a new 1966 3-litre engine. Chief Engineer Walter Hassan was said to want any engine they should build for 1966 to go into a four-wheel drive car, since with the tyre and chassis technology of the time this seemed the only sensible way to put 425 bhp-plus down onto the road. Climax should also either build or approve all the transmission system. This view was not shared by the client teams and appeared to be one of the reasons why Climax did not seem to be working on an engine for 1966, or so the grapevine was telling us . . .

In Germany, the Continental tyre company was

charger; *ergo* it had to be 1500 cc supercharged. This invoked press speculation based on the 1948 Porsche-designed Cisitalia flat-12 1500 which had used twin eccentric-vane superchargers.

Pirelli had shown racing activity and this was linked with a possible comeback by Alfa Romeo. In view of Italy's parlous financial condition, it was thought unlikely that Alfa – which was state-owned – would in fact obtain a racing budget. Several French firms were known to be working on F2 engines, but there was no sign of interest in an F1 project.

As we now know, like all rumour-mongering, some 20 per cent – maybe less – of the above had real substance, 80 per cent was pie in the sky. We shall see how competition within the 3-litre Formula shaped up in its first season and subsequently, but first we should examine how the Formula itself evolved into the longest-running Grand Prix class in history. While still maintaining the basic parameters decided by that long-gone Place de la Concorde meeting of November 1963, so many more clauses and amendments were added subsequently that the overall shape and specification of the Grand Prix car would become increasingly strait-jacketed until our period ends in 1991. This just encouraged the designers' originality to burst out through any unguarded seams to the law makers' perpetual irritation and embarrassment . . . which was, of course, always a healthy sign.

THE FIRST EXTENSION

After its initial three-year run, from 1966 to the end of 1968, the Formula was extended for a further four years, to the end of 1972.

During 1968 there had been a series of motor racing tragedies, which claimed the lives of Jim Clark, Mike Spence, Ludovico Scarfiotti, Lucien Bianchi and Jo Schlesser. Only Schlesser's death came in a Formula 1 car, when his brand new air-cooled Honda V8 crashed and burned during the French GP at Rouen-les-Essarts. Nevertheless, the atmosphere of the time demanded additional safety measures to be taken, and from 1 March 1969 new F1 regulations demanded much-enlarged really practical roll-over bars and the addition of effective onboard fire extinguishing systems.

Two extinguisher circuits had to be provided,

thought to be working on a new racing tyre, suggesting that Mercedes-Benz could be interested in Formula 1, although these tyres might also have been for Porsche.

In Italy, Ferrari were clearly working on their 1966 F1 car and inevitably there were rumours that its 12-cylinder engine had run with a super-

Lotus 49 wing collapses here at Barcelona in 1969 triggered a ban that ended the brief reign of high-strutted 'foils such as this bi-wing arrangement on Piers Courage's Frank Williams-entered Brabham BT26-Cosworth.

It used to be common for visiting GP teams to house their cars in garages near the circuit for overnight preparation. Here at Reims '66, casa Ferrari was wide open for inspection! The car is Bandini's pole-position 312 V12.

which could be fed from a single 5 kg bottle. One had to be a manually operated system which could be triggered by the driver when normally seated, the extinguishant outlets being directed towards the engine induction and injection pump. A secondary system, triggerable by the driver as well as by any helper outside the vehicle, had to discharge into the cockpit. The trigger device had to be indicated by a red-painted circle, with the letter 'E' prominently displayed.

Other changes to Formula 1 included a mandatory electric circuit breaker, which was required on all cars – single-seaters, saloons, sports and GTs – taking part in speed races from 1 January 1969. Its position had to be indicated by a blue triangle with a lightning flash emblem and had to be within easy reach from both inside and outside the car.

Rubber bag safety fuel tanks were described which would become mandatory in F1 and F2 from 1 January 1970, while short-term leak-proof tank fillers and caps which did not protrude beyond the coachwork were required from 1 March 1969. The South African GP at Kyalami opened the new season on that day, so it gave us our first sight of onboard-extinguisher F1 cars with those robust new roll-over bars and dramatic-looking circuit breaker and extinguisher trigger symbols painted on their sides.

To accommodate this extra equipment, the minimum weight limit was raised 10 kg for each system, taking the mark from 500 to 530 kg (1168.44 lb) by the start of 1970.

After the strutted wing proliferation of 1968 had culminated – as will be related – in the Spanish GP Lotus accidents of 1969, an arbitrary wing ban was applied during practice for the next GP on

the calendar, at Monaco, pending formulation of new wing restriction regulations, which took effect from the Dutch GP two weeks later. Now no part of the coachwork, with the exception of the 'safety roll bar', was permitted to exceed in height a horizontal plane 80 cm (31.5 in.) above the lowest point 'of the entirely sprung structure of the car'. Behind the front wheels, coachwork was now restricted to 110 cm (43.3 in.), while maximum width ahead of the front wheels was 150 cm (59.05 in.), although any part ahead of the front wheels exceeding 110 cm in width was prohibited from extending above the height of the front wheel rims.

These more detailed dimensional restrictions upon the size, and indirectly the shape, of eligible F1 cars were the thin end of the wedge. Designers would find themselves progressively hedged about by ever-increasing legislation.

Where structures were concerned, magnesium sheet would now only be permissible if its thickness exceeded 3 mm, thinner stock representing a fire hazard. The onboard battery had to have sufficient capacity to start the engine at least twice, while teams were now permitted to start the engine in the pits or on the dummy starting grid via an external power source. From 1 January 1972 chromium plating of steel suspension members of over 45 tons per square inch tensile strength was forbidden, as it was feared the

process could embrittle the material and then serve to hide incipient crack formation until too late.

DEFORMABLE STRUCTURE REGULATIONS, 1973-75

After the initial extension from 1969 to 1972, a further three-year extension was granted to the end of 1975, but by this time a maximum engine cylinder limit of 12 had been applied. Another BRM H16 would no longer be admissible, neither would such often-rumoured, ultra-expensive but potentially dominant exotica as a W24-cylinder Honda, nor an X36 Yamaha. Interested Formula 1 constructors were by this time not averse to self-protection and preservation of vested interest – Formula 1 had become increasingly a closed shop.

Now minimum weight was up to 550 kg (1212.53 lb). Minimum cockpit opening size was 60 cm (23.62 in.) in length and 45 cm (17.72 in.) in width, maintained for a distance of 30 cm (11.81 in.) from the rearward extremity of the seat backrest towards the front.

Of more obvious significance to the appearance of the Formula 1 car, from 1 January 1972 designers were permitted to increase the overall width of the car to 130 cm (51.18 in.) on condition that the extra 10 cm (3.94 in.) on each side should form a 'deformable structure', containing no fuel, fuel lines, electrical power sources or circuitry.

In effect these new crush pads would serve to protect what were at that time still commonly midship-mounted fuel tanks. However, the rule makers prevented use of this deformable structure innovation as an excuse to add extra aerofoil aids by stipulating that any aerodynamic device situated behind the front wheels must remain

We race.

You get the r

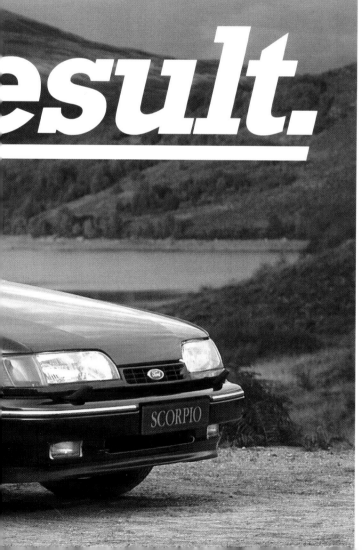

After winning 155 Grand Prix races, the Ford Cosworth V8 engine has become a Formula One legend.

So when Ford decided to build a high performance Scorpio, there was absolutely no doubt where the power would come from.

Drawing on their racing experience, Cosworth further developed and refined the 2.9 litre V6 24-valve engine.

It has the same electronic management module as the Benetton Ford car. The EEC IV, as it is known, is capable of making 250,000 decisions every second.

(Making it the most powerful of its kind in the world.)

The cylinder heads and camshafts are made using a revolutionary casting process in which the molten metal never comes into contact with the atmosphere.

This helps to eliminate impurities and distortion, producing parts that are both exceptionally smooth and accurate.

The fuel injection system also has an F1 background. Sensors inside the engine feed back information on load and speed. The computer then calculates the exact amount of fuel required.

The result is an engine that's smooth, efficient and highly responsive.

And, to meet the world's strictest exhaust emission standards, the Scorpio 24V is only available with a 3-way catalytic converter.

Every time we race, we learn something new that helps to improve our knowledge about engines, tyres and suspension.

And, wherever possible, as you'll see in the Scorpio 24V, we put it on the road.

Everything we do is driven by you.

For a catalogue or the address of your Ford dealer, call the Ford Information Service free on 0800 01 01 12.

within 55 cm (21.65 in.) of the car's centreline. Furthermore, any part of the structure surrounding the fuel tank which was in direct contact with the external airstream now had to include an aluminium sheet skin of at least 1.5 mm (16-gauge) thickness, the alloy specified being aluminium-magnesium with a minimum tensile strength of 14 tons per square inch and a minimum elongation of five per cent.

Red rearward-facing warning lights of at least 15 watts now had to be provided for bad-weather racing, mounted as high as possible on the tail of the car and clearly visible from the rear, ready to be switched on by order of the Clerk of the Course in poor visibility.

From 1 July 1972 a clearly marked external emergency services firing handle had to be fitted, capable of being operated by emergency personnel from a distance if necessary using a hook. This emergency handle had simultaneously to trigger the onboard extinguishing systems, cut out the engine and isolate the battery. From 1 January that year a headrest capable of restraining 17 kg (37.48 lb) under a rearwards acceleration of 5G had to be fitted, so designed as to prevent the driver's head becoming trapped between the roll-over bar and the headrest itself.

By 1973 deformable structure tank protection was to become mandatory, and to accommodate it minimum weight was increased to 575 kg (1267.65 lb). From 1 January that year, overall body dimensions were modified to demand a maximum width in the area between the front and rear wheel trailing and leading edges of not more than 140 cm (55.12 in.). No oil, fuel or electrical lines should be situated beyond 60 cm (23.62 in.).

The shapes of 1970: Ickx's Ferrari 312B (10) lines up outside Rindt's Lotus 72 with Regazzoni's Ferrari (15) and Siffert's March 701 – sans side-wing tanks on row two – Pescarolo's Matra-Simca (14) and Amon's March 701 on row three. Top-ducted radiators appear in all but the hip-radiator Lotus. Two-by-two starting grids robbed Formula 1 of some spectacle as did such sterile circuits as Hockenheim, seen here.

either side of the car's centreline, and they must neither run adjacent to the main fuel cells nor within the crushable structure. Maximum rear wing width remained at 110 cm (43.31 in.).

Self-sealing break-away aircraft-type fuel couplings were now specified to prevent spillage in an accident, and the fuel system itself had to be arranged '. . . so that no part of it is the first object to be struck in an accident'. Total fuel tank capacity was restricted to 250 litres (54.99 Imperial gallons), of which no more than 80 litres (17.59 Imp. gall.) should be contained in any one tank. The deformable structures themselves were required from the first race of the European World Championship series, the Spanish GP.

The entire fuel tank area of the cars in direct contact with the open airstream now had to incorporate a crushable structure, which was specified as featuring sandwich construction based on a fire-resistant core of minimum crushing strength of 25 lb per sq. in. It was permissible to pass water pipes through this core, while the sandwich construction had to include two sheets of 1.5 mm thickness, one being 14 tons tensile aluminium. Minimum sandwich thickness had to be 10 mm (0.3937 in.) but the 'fore and after fuel tank area' should provide for a crushable structure at least 100 mm (3.937 in.) thick at the structure's thickest point, this situation being at the constructors' discretion, over a length of at least 35 cm (13.78 in.) after which it could gradually reduce to 10 mm (0.3937 in.).

During 1973, Formula 1 car rear wings were outrigged ever further behind the rear wheels to seek clean airflow and thus generate ever greater download. For 1974 this move was jumped upon as the regulations were rewritten to insist that '. . . nothing above the rear wheels must protrude more than 1 metre behind the axle of the rear wheels' [sic], 1 metre converting to 39.37 inches.

'THE AIRBOX RULES', 1976-77
By this time the Formula was already nine seasons old, and in its tenth season – 1975 – it was extended for a further two until the end of 1977, regulations being agreed initially for those two with little alteration. However, more significant changes were agreed to at Monza that year, to

take effect from the Spanish GP on 1 May 1976.

From that date total rear overhang, beyond the rear wheels, was reduced from 1 metre to 80 cm (31.49 in.) while front overhang limit was set at 120 cm (47.24 in.). Maximum rear wheel width was fixed Imperially for Goodyear's convenience at 21 in. – the actual term used being 'la roue complète', or 'the complete wheel', defined by the CSI as meaning the wheel and tyre *ensemble*. Rear wheel diameter had to be 13 in. Front wheel diameter was free, but maximum width was again 21 in. Overall width of the car was now restricted to 215 cm (84.65 in.), this dimension being based upon that of the widest contemporary F1 car at the end of 1975, which was the McLaren M23. Ironically, it would be James Hunt's Spanish GP-winning McLaren M23 that May which first fell foul of this very ruling.

In preceding years, engine airboxes had been born and had flourished in variety, size and height. Now they were being restricted, brought within the 80 cm (31.49 in.) envelope measured from the lowest point of the entirely sprung structure of the car so far as the air intake orifice was concerned, while the total height of the airbox was allowed to exceed that dimension by 5 cm (1.97 in.).

To enhance driver protection, a forward roll-over bar was now specified, mounting near the dashboard in such a way that a straight line drawn to its highest point from the top of the main roll-over bar would pass above the driver's helmet when he was sitting normally within the cockpit. It was now rather vaguely specified that 'a substantial structure will extend in front of the pedals', while oil pipes and coolers were to be protected by 10 mm (0.3937 in.) thick crushable structures. This pedal protection was later defined as a structure capable of withstanding a 25G deceleration without causing the pedals to move backwards by more than 150 mm (5.91 in.) with the car carrying driver and a full fluid load. No part of the car containing oil could now be situated aft of the rearmost casing (gearbox or differential), thus banning far-outrigged underwing oil coolers etc, while the maximum height exhaust restriction was now suppressed to give free for all. Despite these changes minimum weight was unaltered at

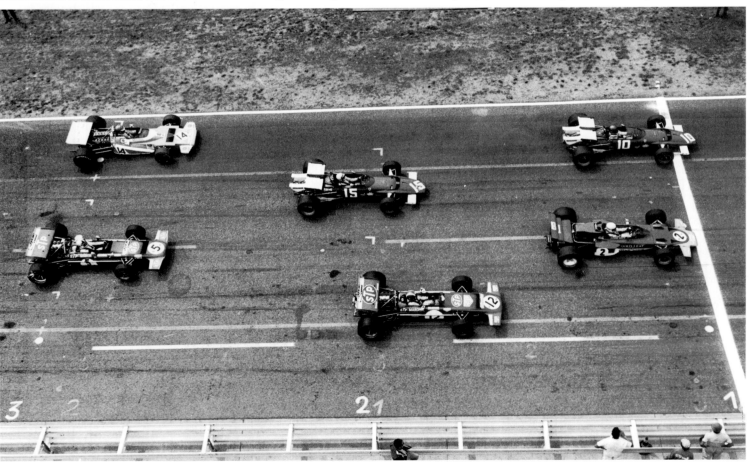

575 kg (1267.65 lb).

In 1977 the coachwork height to the upper extremity of the airbox opening was 90 cm (35.43 in.) measured from the ground. Total airbox height could still exceed that dimension by a further 5 cm (1.97 in.)

FOURTH EXTENSION, 1978-81

Yet again a Formula extension was granted, this time for two more years, to the end of 1979 for most prescriptions, but for four more seasons, to the end of 1981, for engine specifications.

It was decided that from 1 January 1979 the cars' overall length would be limited to 5.0 metres (196.85 in.). Rear overhang limit was set at 80 cm (31.49 in.); front overhang limit was 120 cm (47.24 in.). A waiver was granted to allow total fuel capacity to be concentrated in one single cell in the new breed of narrow monocoque ground-effects cars as introduced by the Lotus 79. This single cell between cockpit and engine was considered to be so deeply protected within side pod structures, monocoque chassis and engine assemblies as to be virtually invulnerable.

By 1979 the approved FIA version of the Formula 1 regulations filled 10 close-print pages of their annual 'Yellow Book' although inevitably by the time this annual had been published each year, numerous detail changes had often been made and the only way to keep abreast of the continuing flow of gobbledy-gook from Paris was to receive and study the CSI's regular technical bulletins.

The 1979 regulations were very comprehensively and carefully framed. Overall width was still restricted to 215 cm (84.65 in.) while coachwork ahead of the front wheels could be extended to a maximum width of 150 cm (59.06 in.), though any part of that coachwork exceeding 110 cm (43.31 in.) in width should not extend above the height of the front wheel rims 'with the driver aboard seated normally and irrespective of the fuel load'.

Regulation wording was even more pernickety now where overhangs were concerned, specifying considerations such as 'Except in the case of front-wheel drive when the measurement will be taken from the centreline of the rearmost substantial load-carrying wheels, no part of the car shall be more than 80 cm behind the centre-line of the rearmost driving wheels. No part of the car shall be more than 120 cm in front of the centre-line of the foremost front wheels . . .' Six-wheelers, and talk of outrigging a pair of dummy wheels abaft the tail for wing extension purposes, had the rule makers on their toes. Interestingly, a regulation now appeared governing refuelling during the race. In the event that any fuel was added after a race start, the container from which it was drawn had to have a leak-proof coupling connecting it to the tank filler on the car, and the air vent on the container itself had to be fitted with a non-return valve.

A group of European Common Market civil servants visited one of the Formula 1 teams, to see what motor racing was all about. During lunch the conversation came round to framing the regulations. One team member declared there were far too many regulations, the Formula would be improved if they were simplified. The bureaucrats vehemently disagreed, one suspects as anyone would whose reason to exist was being challenged. 'No', they insisted, 'One should frame regulations so detailed that they cover every conceivable eventuality'. That was how it would go, though the poachers would consistently try to outwit the gamekeepers . . .

From around 1973 the Formula One Constructors' Association had effectively run Formula 1, with a relatively malleable governing body going along with most of their recommendations. This cosy state of affairs changed with the election of Frenchman Jean-Marie Balestre as CSI President. He was about to crack the whip. This is not the vehicle in which to detail the political differences between FOCA and the CSI – which changed its name to FISA (*Fédération Internationale du Sport Automobile*) in 1979.

Clothes makyth man . . . and smootheth aerodynamic flow. Revson's British GP-winning McLaren M23 sports full bodywork and tall airbox which gave ram induction and faired airflow onto that vital far-outrigged rear wing.

Suffice to record that the two factions fell into increasing dispute as Balestre resolved to retrieve 'the sporting power' for the governing body. FOCA, whose power had developed during the 'kit car' mid-Seventies under the dynamic guidance of Brabham team patron Bernard Ecclestone, vigorously defended its own interests.

The irresistible force and the immoveable object now clashed over a unilateral FISA decision to ban sliding aerodynamic skirts from 1 January 1981. The move was intended to reduce cornering speeds, but British teams with their Cosworth DFV engines perceived hidden motives designed to foster better performances from major industrial company Continental teams like Renault, which after all was now France's great white hope.

When Balestre declared – without FOCA's agreement – that FISA was indeed waiving the normal two-year stability rule to enforce this skirt ban on safety grounds, all hell broke loose. Throughout 1980 a series of disputes simmered bitterly between FOCA and FISA. It extended eventually to FISA seeking to usurp FOCA's established commercial control of Grand Prix racing. Into the winter of 1980/81 there was detailed talk of there being two parallel forms of Formula 1 racing in the coming season, one run by FISA without skirts but supported by the *Grande Costruttori* teams – notably Ferrari, Renault and Alfa Romeo – while the mere British *assemblatori* (known equally derisively as *garagisti*, typified by Williams, Brabham, Lotus or Tyrrell, would run under FOCA's own skirted rules.

FISA promptly threatened dire retribution for circuit promoters who might give FOCA races a home. Something had to give, and in January 1981 representatives from all Formula 1 teams met at Ferrari's plant and concluded the Maranello Agreement for joint presentation as a peace initiative to FISA. Its major proposals formed the basis of peace concluded in Paris that March. It was called the Concorde Agreement; FOCA yielded to the sliding skirts ban, while FISA yielded on Formula 1 finances.

Regulations were drawn up which demanded a consistent 6 cm ground clearance 'at any moment when the car is in motion'. It takes a fleet-footed scrutineer to measure the ground clearance of a racing car at 180 mph, and lowering suspension devices were developed to sidestep the regulation. The poachers had fooled the gamekeepers again.

Later in the year this patently unenforceable regulation was reworded merely to specify that all cars should have a 6 cm ground clearance at the point of measurement in the pit lane. In other words, out on circuit anything goes.

This produced a generation of highly effective ground-effect skirted cars with minimal suspension movement whose jarring high-G ride quality tortured their drivers yet generated terrific cornering forces and high lap speeds.

Apart from the skirt and ground-clearance question, 1981 regulations had included a weight limit of 585 kg (1289.69 lb). In a move which upset many purist engineering enthusiasts the long-lived clauses permitting use of Wankel, diesel, two-stroke and turbine engines were suppressed and these power units specifically prohibited. 'In this time of dispute', declared FISA, 'we want no further source of confusion to unsettle Formula 1'. From 1981 only four-stroke engines with reciprocating pistons were admissible, engines with more than 12 cylinders having long since been outlawed. FISA also announced a ban on cars having more than four wheels and also on four-wheel drive with effect from 1983.

When FOCA accepted the skirt ban, FISA sweetened the pill a little by dropping the minimum weight limit 5 kg to a level the 3-litre cars could comfortably attain and the turbos could not. The non-turbo teams like Williams and Brabham then took this a stage further by adopting what were claimed to be water-cooled braking systems. In these the onboard tank simply formed a legitimate ballast tank fillable prior to post-race scrutineering – as were conventional fluid reservoirs – but in this case to bring an underweight race car up to the legal limit. This ploy would ultimately be stamped out, it would not be permitted to top up fluid reservoirs after the race, and random weighing during qualifying would also restrict the activities of ultra-light qualifying specials as exploited so notably by Brabham.

In addition, tyre company discomfort with the costs of all-out competition brought about a qualifying tyre agreement, in which only two sets of marked and scrutinized qualifying tyres would be made available for each car, and they too would be carefully policed during the qualifying sessions. Sadly, this created great pressures for the drivers to take desperate risks before their precious qualifiers 'went off', and it undoubtedly contributed to Villeneuve's fatal accident. But driver safety had also been considered.

Driver survival-cell regulations were now to apply from 1 January 1982. Two continuous box members, one either side of the driver, were to extend from behind him to a point 30 cm (11.18 in.) in front of the soles of his feet with him seated normally and 'with his feet on the pedals in the inoperative position'.

Structural material cross-section of each box member had to be 10 cm, while the overall cross-section of each box had to be 150 cm² to the soles of the driver's feet, then tapering forward of his

Sticks to corners. Takes some licking. (They ought to commemorate it on a stamp.)

The 205 GTI comes in two denominations – 1.6 and 1.9 litres.

Both, however, will ensure your swift delivery to your destination.

The mid-range acceleration of the Bosch L-Jetronic fuel-injected engine enables you to overtake post-haste.

Its low centre of gravity and low-profile tyres give you first-class handling.

PEUGEOT

205 GTI

And all-round independent suspension prevents you from mysteriously going astray round bends.

The specimen you see opposite is obviously in mint condition.

But even those with much-handled examples in their possession are unwilling to swap them.

The 205 GTI. Wouldn't the sincerest form of flattery be philately?

Giorgio Piola's sketches explain the flat-bottom ruling of November 1982. Top: *Contemporary ground-effect configuration and (centre) flat-bottom requirements showing: 1, protective footbox; 2, sealing side skirts; 3, underwing venturi profiles (dimensions are tail overhang and wing height in cm).* Above: *A uniform flat-plane underside was demanded between trailing edge of 'the complete front wheels' and leading edge of 'the complete rear wheels'. Note venturi diffuser undersurface around gearbox.*

10 metres/second. The protective 'box was to crush in such a progressive manner that there should be no greater mean deceleration than 25G. Such an impact should not cause any deformation of the chassis itself behind the footbox, in a plane behind the pedals in their inoperative position.

Proving tests were mandatory; some teams used a fixed test section and moving 750 kg pendulum (as at Britain's Cranfield Institute), whilst others employed a moving trolley impacting a block (as at MIRA). End-on aluminium honeycomb structures worked well, but many engineers trailed home sadly from early tests with rubbish-bags full of shrapnel – all that remained of their pet footbox theories.

Rear wing regulations were also tightened to ban use of the ahead-of-the-axle-line side winglets adopted for 1984. This cut download available to all teams but by mid-1985 designers had found ways to retrieve lost values, with greater efficiency than hitherto.

THE ONE-YEAR FORMULA – 1986
For this solitary season, FISA finally banned naturally aspirated 3-litre engines from Formula 1, which became a purely 1500 cc turbocharged class.

Fuel capacity was further reduced to 195 litres, but turbocharger boost levels remained unrestricted. Racing was relatively poor despite the cars being quite spectacularly fast and considerable misgivings were expressed about the future of Formula 1 as the expense of turbocharged technology and the paucity of competitive engines available saw the gap widening rapidly between the haves at the front of the starting grids and the have-not teams at the back.

The rule-makers considered that something had to be done, and done quickly, and FISA's response was to make a complete U-turn and a year after having finally removed the naturally aspirated sub-class from Formula 1, it was reintroduced in a new guise for 1987 . . .

As late as the Italian GP meeting in September 1986, FISA was still discussing potential changes to the technical requirements for the '87 season, despite having previously declared rule stability until 1989 when opting for 1500 cc turbo-only racing starting from 1 January 1986!

Amongst the proposals floated for the FISA Executive Committee meeting on 3 October '86 were options for 1000 cc turbo engines, 1500 cc turbo engines with either pop-off valve or air restrictor limitations, 1500 turbos with both forms of restriction, current regulations with just one, Saturday, practice session and starting grid decided on the results of an 80 km preliminary race, or current regulations with 180-litre fuel capacity or a reduction in the fuel octane rating.

Alternative proposals included a ban on turbocharged engines altogether, and their replacement by 3.3-litre atmospherically aspirated cars without any minimum weight limit; a turbo ban and adoption of 3.5-litre 'atmos' instead with 120-litre tanks and in-race refuelling permitted, or finally (paragraph 9) 'Banning of turbocharged engines and adoption of 3500 cc normally aspirated engines with weight to be defined . . .'.

The 3.3-litre option looked attractive, since the Cosworth DFL 540 bhp V8 engine was already widely available, affordable and reliable, but come the 3 October meeting within the conference room of the Automobile Club de France building in the Place de la Concorde, Paris, a compromise sliding-requirements set of regulations was agreed by the FISA Executive which was unanimously ratified next day by the 50-country FISA Plenary Conference.

It was suggested that Honda warned of legal action since rule stability had been guaranteed by FISA 1986-89 and the Japanese company had invested and planned accordingly. FISA President Balestre, however, justified the new requirements by claiming that they '. . . have mainly been inspired by safety reasons, but also by the determination to give a new boost to the World Championship for many years to come. This will reduce costs and ban qualifying engines . . .'.

feet to a 100 cm² section. Furthermore, the internal cross-section of the cockpit, from behind the seat to soles of feet, had nowhere to be less than 700 cm², minimum width 25 cm (9.84 in.) over the whole length of the cockpit, and there were further detail dimensional requirements.

Side panel regulations now demanded 20 cm (7.87 in.) high panels, 60 per cent of wheelbase in length which had to be sited between front and rear wheels at least 55 cm (21.65 in.) from the car's longitudinal axis. They had to be formed from minimum 10 mm thick composite material with a honeycomb core in metal or Nomex with expanded foam compression-resistance, and structural struts to link these panels to the tub, so absorbing lateral impact. The radiators were allowed to perform this role.

As it happened, 1982 was the last season in which underwing-section ground-effects cars were permitted, as on 3 November the FISA technical commission met in Paris and agreed radical rule changes to take effect from the next race, the opening round of the 1983 World Championship.

Any supposedly sacrosanct 'stability' regulation had been handily scrapped in the name of safety. During the season two Formula 1 cars had hurtled into the spectator enclosures at Ricard-Castellet, one in testing, one during the French GP with potentially catastrophic results, fortunately not realized. It was considered that Villeneuve's fatal practice accident at Zolder had been magnified by the bouncing Ferrari's aerodynamic surfaces, while the ground-effect car form in general undoubtedly contributed to his teammate Pironi's career-ending crash in the rain at Hockenheimring.

Under the 3 November 1982 ruling, Formula 1 cars were to be slowed down, especially in cornering, by a ban on aerodynamic skirts and shaped underbodies. Flat bottoms were now mandatory between vertical planes touching the front of the rear tyres and rear edge of the front tyres, wing width was cut from 110 cm (43.31 in.) to 100 cm (39.37 in.) to reduce surface area, and their leverage decreased by reducing overhang beyond the rear axle-line from 80 cm (31.49 in.) to 60 cm (23.62 in.). Wing height was permitted to increase from 90 cm to 100 cm to improve rear mirror visibility. The four-wheel drive ban was confirmed.

As yet another sop to the few surviving non-turbocharged runners, minimum weight was again cut from 580 kg (1278.67 lb) to 540 kg (1190.48 lb).

Then, with the aim of freezing engine power – some hope! – at 500-550 bhp into 1985, FISA decreed that fuel tank volume was to be reduced progressively from the 250 litres allowed in 1983 to 220 litres in 1984 and 195 litres in 1985. Refuelling during the race would itself be banned in 1984 which meant that cars would have to be sufficiently economical to survive race distance on 220 litres only. This would cause many teams problems, not merely on fuel economy, since through the brief refuelling era it had been common to fling extra fuel through the engines purely to cool them and obtain ever-greater power.

The length of Grand Prix races was to be maintained.

Driver safety was also taken into account and was to be improved with augmented survival-cell regulations. Pedal-box length was extended from the mandatory 30 cm (11.81 in.) of 1982 to 50 cm (19.68 in.) in 1983.

For 1985, the footbox regulation required that a vehicle weighing 750 kg (1654 lb) should impact an immoveable object at not less than

TURBOS VERSUS THE 'ATMO' CLASS – 1987-1988

The new 3.5-litre naturally aspirated F1 class was consequently launched in 1987 in conjunction with its own Jim Clark Trophy and Colin Chapman Trophy competitions for a Drivers' and Constructors' Championship run in parallel with the 1.5-litre turbos' traditional and premier series.

FISA declared its intention to develop Formula 1 through a progressive series of annual rule changes until it would emerge as a purely 3.5-litre atmospherically aspirated class in 1989.

Initially to achieve some kind of equality between the 1500 cc turbocharged cars and the new 3.5-litre 'atmos', FISA applied maximum 4-bar boost-restricting pop-off valves to turbo entries, banned multi-stage turbo compressors, water injection and water intercooling – only air/air being permitted – and they also set differential weight minima for the two classes; for turbocharged cars 540 kg (1190.5 lb) – for new 'atmo' cars (maximum 12 cylinders) 500 kg (1102.3 lb). Fuel capacity was unchanged at 195 litres. Oval pistons and engines of more than 12 cylinders were both banned.

For 1988 the cars would be required to have flat bottoms and – as in Indycar racing – the foot pedals would have to be mounted behind the front-wheel centreline. FISA also demanded safety improvements within the cockpit 'survival cell' and specified that comprehensive frontal and lateral crash testing would become mandatory for all chassis, the lateral requirement being a new departure.

Teams were required to declare in advance the type of engine they would be running – turbocharged or atmospheric-induction. They had the option to swap – but once only – from turbo engines to naturally aspirated, reversion being forbidden to prevent a well-funded team from perhaps taking the 'atmo' route on a suitable street circuit, and then reverting to turbo power for the high-speed courses.

Flat-bottomed chassis form was to be maintained, ditto 195-litres fuel capacity for both turbocharged and 'atmo' cars.

In 1988, which was to be the final season in which turbocharged engines were accepted within Formula 1, pop-off valve boost limit was slashed savagely to only 2.5 bar, while fuel cell capacity in turbocharged cars was cut right back to only 150 litres (32.99 gallons).

Comprehensive frontal and lateral chassis crash testing now became mandatory – see shortly – but turbocharged runners were permitted to retain existing monocoques if preferred, which would save them the costs of having to construct all-new impact-absorbing footbox structures/pedals behind the front axle line designs for one season's racing only. Their fuel cell arrangements still had to be adjusted within these monocoques, however, to match the new 150-litre ceiling requirement.

THE 'ATMOSPHERIC' RULES – 1989-1991

In 1989, the new 3.5-litre 'atmo' Formula 1 took full effect, and what had hitherto been the regulations applied to a subsidiary class within the hybrid turbo/'atmo' seasons of 1987-88 took full effect. They were complex, and far reaching, with the accent emphatically upon safety.

The full ramificiations of the regulations which govern the modern Grand Prix car are seldom presented to the enthusiast public in any detail. Well here goes . . .

The FIA's Formula 1 World Championship regulations filled 27 finely spaced pages in a softbound, taped-spine A4 booklet, the technical prescriptions occupying ten of those pages. Their requirements may be summarized as follows.

Coachwork and Dimensions

Overall width not to exceed 215 cm (84.64 in.), coachwork ahead of the front wheels no more than 150 cm (59.05 in.) but no part of it exceeding 110 cm (43.3 in.) span could rise above the height of the front wheel rims with the driver aboard and seated normally, irrespective of fuel load.

Maximum coachwork width behind the rearmost edge of the complete front wheel and ahead of the rear-wheel centreline was 140 cm (55.11 in.) including the mandatory crushable structure.

The 'flat-bottom' requirement read: 'Between the rear edge of the complete front wheels and the front edge of the complete rear wheels all sprung parts of the car visible from directly beneath the car must lie on one plane within a tolerance of plus or minus 5 mm. All these parts must present a uniform, solid, hard, rigid (no degree of freedom in relation to the body/chassis unit), impervious surface, under all circumstances. The periphery of the surface formed by these parts may be curved upwards with a maximum radius of 5 cm. No parts of the bodywork in front of the centreline of the rear wheels and extending above the height of the rear complete wheels may project beyond 50 cm each side of the longitudinal axis of the car.'

Coachwork behind the rear-wheel centreline could be no wider than 100 cm (39.37 in.). No part of the car was permitted to extend beyond 60 cm (23.62 in.) behind the 'centreline of the rearmost driving wheels' (except in the case of front-wheel drive when the measurement would be taken from the centreline of the rearmost substantial load-carrying wheels . . .)

Front-end overhang was limited to a maximum 120 cm (47.24 in.) ahead of the front-wheel centreline.

Except for the safety roll-over structures, no part of the car might exceed 100 cm (39.37 in.) from the ground. No part of the roll-over structure higher than 100 cm from the ground could be shaped to have a significant aerodynamic influence on the car's performance.

Aerodynamic features had to comply with the coachwork regulations, had to be rigidly secured to the entirely sprung part of the car, and had to remain immobile in relation to it. Any devices or construction designed to bridge the gap between the sprung part of the car and the ground was forbidden.

No part having an aerodynamic influence and no part of the coachwork 'may under any circumstances be located below the geometrical plane generated by the plane surface provided for by Article 3.3 . . .' – the flat-bottom rule.

Weight

Minimum weight was 500 kg (1102.3 lb), ballast being acceptable so long as its removal necessitated the use of tools. It had to be possible to fix seals to the ballast 'if deemed necessary by the scrutineers'.

No additions of liquid or any other material whatsoever was permitted to the cars during the race, and the replacement during the race of any part of the car with another part materially heavier was forbidden.

Engine

Four-stroke engines were required with reciprocating pistons – displacing no more than 3500 cc. They had to be unsupercharged, not more than 12 cylinders, the normal section of each cylinder 'must be circular' while Wankel, diesel, two-stroke and turbine engines were all specifically forbidden.

Piping and petrol tanks, cables and electrical equipment

All fuel tanks had to be situated within the main structure of the car, no fuel being carried more than 40 cm (15.74 in.) from the longitudinal axis nor in the longitudinal box members of the chassis.

Rubber bladder fuel bags were mandatory to FIA/FT3 specification, made by any one of 16 FIA-recognized manufacturers based in France, Germany, Italy, Japan, Great Britain and the USA. Each bladder had to carry code markings reflecting its manufacturer's name and the specifications and date of its manufacture. Bladders over five years old were banned.

All fuel fittings had to be metal-bonded into the tank. All connections between tank and chassis had to be frangible – enabling the tank to move relative to the chassis under impact, the connections failing at a load less than 50 per cent of that required to pull the fitting out of the tank.

All cables, lines and electrical equipment had to be fitted in such a manner that any leakage could not result in accumulation of fluid in the cockpit or enable contact between fluid and any electrical line or equipment.

Cables, lines and electrical equipment

Cables and lines passing through the cockpit had to be enclosed within a cover of liquid-tight and fire-resistant material. All external fuel lines outside the cockpit with the exception of those permanently mounted on the engine had to be capable of withstanding 70 kg/cm² (1000 lb psi) pressure and 260°C (500°F) temperature.

Crushable structure

The entire fuel tank area of the car in direct contact with the open airstream had to incorporate a crushable structure which had to be an integral part of the car including the complete area of the body/monocoque construction irrespective of such added items as water radiators, inlet ducts and windscreens etc.

The crushable structure had to be of sandwich construction based on a fire-resistant core of a minimum crushing strength of 25 lb psi (18N/ cm²). It was permissible to pass water pipes through this core but not fuel, oil or electrical lines. The sandwich construction had to include either two 1.5 mm thick sheets – one of which had to be aluminium alloy – having a tensile strength of 14 tons per square inch (225N/mm²) and minimum elongation of 5 per cent; or two 1.5 mm thick sheets having a tensile strength of 14 tons/square inch. Minimum sandwich thickness was 1 cm.

Tank fillers and caps

In-race refuelling was forbidden, while race distance – excluding the warm-up lap – had to be equal to the least number of complete laps which exceeded 305 km, or alternatively a time limit of two hours: 'the leader will be shown the chequered flag when he crosses the start/finish line at the end of the lap in which such period of two hours shall end . . .'.

Oil (sic)

Crushable structures 1 cm thick had to protect all oil storage tanks situated outside the main structure of the car, while no part containing oil could be situated aft of the gearbox or final-drive casing in any rear-drive car, or behind the complete rear wheels in any front-drive car.

All oil lines external to the cockpit with the exception of lines permanently mounted on the engine had to be capable of withstanding 70 kg/cm² (1000 lb psi) and 260°C (500°F).

An oil catch tank of at least 3 litres capacity was necessary when an open-type sump breather was featured. No part containing oil could be more than 70 cm (27.56 in.) from the car's longitudinal centreline. No oil replenishment was permitted in the race.

Starting

Remote starting devices were permissible 'both on the grid and in the pits'.

Transmission to the wheels

Four-wheel drive remained forbidden, while all cars had to have a reverse gear, in working order when the car started the event and which could be operated by the driver when seated normally in the car.

Brakes

Twin-circuit brakes were mandatory, arranged so that in event of a failure the foot pedal would still operate the brakes on at least two wheels.

Front brake cooling ducts could not protrude beyond a plane parallel to the ground 140 mm (5.51 in.) above the wheel centreline; a plane

A degree or two lower and wider than the saloo

PURE, UNDILUTED BMW.

ultivalve engines. M-Technic sports suspension. Z-axle. ABS. The essence of a coupé. The essence of BMW.

THE NEW 3 SERIES COUPÉ.

parallel to the ground 140 mm below the horizontal wheel centreline; and beyond a vertical plane parallel to the inner face of the front rim and displaced from it by 120 mm (4.72 in.) towards the car centreline. When viewed from the side such ducts could not protrude beyond the periphery of the tyre in a forward sense, or the rim in a rearward sense.

Wheels and tyres
Wheels had to be external to the coachwork when the car was viewed in plan 'with the rear aerodynamic device removed . . .'.

The maximum permitted wheel width was 18 in., maximum diameter 26 in., measured horizontally at axle height. The number of wheels was fixed at four.

Cockpit
Cockpit-opening minimum dimensions were set at 60 cm (23.62 in.) long, 45 cm (17.71 in.) wide maintained over 30 cm (11.81 in.) from the rearmost point of the seat backrest to the front. The driver had to achieve access without any door being opened or part of the car removed, and he had to be facing forward when seated at his steering wheel.

It was required that the cockpit be vacatable within five seconds with the steering wheel in place. Two mirrors were mandatory, offering clearly defined rear visibility for the normally seated driver.

Two shoulder straps, one abdominal strap and two straps between the legs were mandatory, these straps having to be securely fitted to the car.

Safety
Specification and application of a 5 kg cockpit extinguisher and a 2.5 kg engine compartment extinguisher were spelled out, together with those for a life support system and electrical master switch. A red rear warning light of at least 25 watts had to be mounted no more than 10 cm (3.93 in.) from the centreline, with a surface of 20-40 cm² (3.1-6.2 sq. in.) capable of being switched on by the normally seated driver. Chromium plating of suspension parts of over 45 tons/sq. in. (725 N/mm²) tensile strength was forbidden. The use of magnesium sheet less than 3 mm thick emained forbidden.

At least two protective roll-over structures were mandatory – one not more than 25 cm (9.84 in.) forward of the steering wheel rim and at least as high as the top of it; the second not less than 50 cm (19.68 in.) behind the first and high enough for a line extended between the peaks of both structures to clear the driver's helmet when he was normally seated, with his helmet on and seat belts fastened.

All such structures when attached to the car had to be capable of withstanding three loads applied simultaneously to their respective top ends – 1.5w laterally ('w' representing the racing weight of the car), 5.5w longitudinally and 7.5w vertically.

Design concept of such safety structures was specifically permitted to be 'free', including the use of forward-facing stays restricting the dimensions of the cockpit access 'provided the driver can exit the cockpit in the time required . . .'.

All cars were furthermore required to have a structure immediately behind the driver's seat which had to be wider than and extending above his shoulders when belted normally into his seat – and capable of withstanding 1.5w lateral load applied to its top.

Survival cell
Survival cell requirements were painstakingly spelled out in eight detailed paragraphs under the regulations' 'Section "f"'.

The cell was to include two continuous box members, one each side of the driver and the chassis had also to incorporate at least one lateral hoop at the main roll-over bar level, one ahead of the pedal-box and a further hoop between these two.

Each box member had to extend from behind the

driver to a point at least 50 cm (19.68 in.) ahead of the soles of his feet – seated normally and with his feet on the pedals in the inoperative position. The foremost 40 cm (15.74 in.) of each box member did not have to be an integral part of the chassis, but had to be 'solidly fixed to it'.

The soles of the driver's feet on the inoperative-position pedals were required to remain behind the vertical plane passing through the centreline of the front wheels. 'Should the car not be fitted with pedals, the driver's feet at the maximum forward extension shall not be situated to the fore of the above referred vertical plane . . .'; a crafty piece of regulatory far-sightedness there!

Throughout its length, the structural material within the cross-section of each box member had to have a minimum area of 10 cm² (1.55 sq. in.), minimum tensile strength of 31 kg/mm² and a minimum panel thickness of 1 mm on unstabilized skins and 5 cm² (0.775 sq. in.) area and 0.5 mm thickness on stabilized skins.

Throughout its length from behind the driver to the soles of his feet, each box had to have a minimum cross-section of 100 cm² (15.5 sq. in.) and a minimal structural material cross-section of 5 cm² (0.775 sq. in.) for unstabilized skins and 2.5 cm² (0.3875 sq. in.) with stabilized skins.

The internal cross-sectional area of the cockpit from the soles of the driver's feet to behind his seat had to be nowhere less than 700 cm² (108.5 sq. in.) and the minimum width 25 cm (9.84 in.) over the whole length of the cockpit.

Minimum height of the box between the front and rear roll-over bar structures had to be no less than 20 cm (7.87 in.)

At least that part of the box members forward of a 'transversal section' 20 cm (7.87 in.) to the rear of the soles of the drivers' feet had to be subjected to an impact test against a solid vertical barrier placed at right angles to the longitudinal axis of the car. If such a part of the box members was tested independently of the rest of the chassis structure it had to be attached to the inertia trolley in such a way that its impact resistance was not increased.

For the purposes of the test the total weight of the trolley and test structure or complete car had to be 780 kg (1719.6 lb) and the impact velocity 10 metres per second (22.369 mph).

The box members' resistance had to be such that during the impact an average deceleration of not more than 25G was recorded, and the final deformation had to be contained within the zone ahead of the soles of the driver's feet.

Additionally, the chassis had to be subjected to a lateral static load test in the cockpit area and in the fuel tank area, in which a pad 10 cm long and 30 cm high (3.93 x 11.81 in.) conforming to the shape of the chassis had to be placed against both sides of its outermost structure with the lowest part of the pad at the lowest part of the chassis. A plane through the vertical centreline of the pads had to pass through the centre of the seat-belt lap-strap fixing. A constant 'transversal load' of 2000 kg (4409.2 lb) then had to be applied to the pads at their centre of area through a pin-jointed junction. After half a minute's application the inner structure of the chassis across the defined plane had to remain unreduced in dimension under the applied load by more than 2 cm (0.78 in.)

The same load conditions were to be applied across the chassis structure in the fuel tank area at a vertical passing through the centre of the fuel tank in side elevation. Under these load conditions there had to be no structural failure of the inner chassis's inner surfaces. Such tests had to be carried out under supervision of a FISA technical delegate in recognized testing laboratories in France, Germany, Italy, the UK or USA as approved by FISA.

A dossier defining the structure, test method and results had to be submitted to FISA before any such relevant model of car would be admitted to an F1 race. Any significant modification introduced into the frontal and/or lateral part of the chassis structure would require it to undergo another test.

All cars had to feature a headrest which would not deflect more than 5 cm (1.96 in.) rearwards when a rearward force of 85 kg (187.4 lb) was applied. The headrest surface had to be not less than 80 cm² (12.4 sq. in.) and it had to be both continuous and without protruding parts. The headrest had to be located in a position such that the headrest was the first point of contact with the driver's helmet in the event of an impact projecting the driver's head rearward when he was normally seated.

Fuel
The only permissible fuel was liberally defined as having a maximum 102RON octane rating, the measurement being made in accordance with International standard ASIM D 2699, the fuel being accepted or rejected according to ASIM D 3244 'with a confidence limit of 95%' – i.e. giving a 5 per cent margin for test variation which would mean a reading of up to 108RON from the standard prescribed test would be deemed acceptable. . . which says much more about the test standard than the fuel itself . . . and which would become a bone of enormous contention come 1992 . . .

A maximum 2 per cent oxygen and 1 per cent nitrogen by weight were permitted, the remainder of the fuel having to consist exclusively of hydrocarbons without any alcohols, nitrocompounds 'or other power-boosting additives'. In events outside Europe each competitor was free to use either a fuel complying with the above prescriptions or the aviation fuel which the organizers were required to supply, and whose technical characteristics would have been supplied to the teams and engine specialists 60 days prior to the race.

The only oxidant permissible to mix with the fuel was air.

Finally, it was confirmed that 'The final text for these regulations is to be the English version which will be used should any dispute arise over their interpretation'.

But at the 1990 Italian GP meeting, FISA's noisy President Balestre declared his intention to propose (if not impose) a number of safety-related regulation changes when the FIA World Congress would be convened the following month. Most radically, he wished to extend the flat-bottom rule from the front edge 'of the complete front wheel' – i.e. wheel and tyre – to the rearmost extremity of the bodywork. His intention was to abolish the downforce-inducing diffuser underfloors beneath the tail of all contemporary F1 cars.

A charitable few construed this as Balestre's way of encouraging alternative proposals for the World Congress. Others viewed his proposals as threatening to write off overnight enormous investment in underfloor technology research and development.

In fact the imminent Congress then confirmed conservative new measures for 1991 as follows: reduction in front wing width – reduction of rear overhang from 60 cm to 50 cm – mandatory roll-over bar apertures to enable crane-strops to be attached easily for removal from the circuit – improved protection for fuel tanks and all fluid lines – conformity of safety harnesses with the specified FIA standard – location, attachment and control system for extinguishers – better definition of the electrical circuit breaker – more explicit positioning regulations for the red tail-guard light.

Against this background, with finely judged detail wording and generally better regard for the spirit of the regulations than for many years past, Formula 1 approached the end of our period. As one top Formula 1 designer put it 'These days you can't argue the meaning of a word – like the celebrated "How rigid is rigid?" dispute of the early '80s when it was claimed that anything flexes if you push it hard enough. If anyone tried a crafty like that these days he'd just be told to go away and think again . . .

'And the general feeling is that this is A Good Thing . . .'

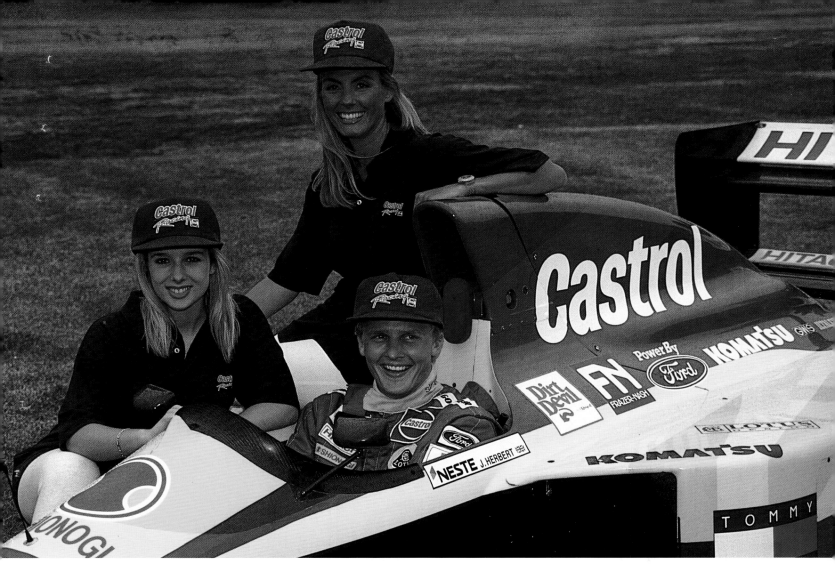

OBVIOUSLY IT'S NOT JUST OUR OIL THAT HELPS HIM GO FASTER.

Castrol are proud to sponsor the Lotus Grand Prix team
and to supply the cars with Castrol Formula RS.

FULL SYNTHETIC ENGINEERING.

IT'S SAID THAT
IS THE TOU
WHO ARE UNIPA

The Unipart F3's young Mansell in 1979.

Unipart was launched in 1969. The range of products available was tiny compared with today, but at that time was the only substantial brand to cover a large number of car models from different manufacturers. Unipart took to developing products in one of the most gruelling testing grounds there is - competitive motor sport.

Unipart F1. Spark plug

By the seventies Unipart were fully committed to ever more demanding competition. Both in the High Street and on the track.

We reasoned that winning in the World's most technologically exacting sport would give us the commercial winning edge that motorsport enforces.

Unipart prepared for Formula 1 the way so many budding drivers do: Formula 3. We learned alongside some of the best in the business.

Nigel Mansell, Britain's new World Champion, honed his talent for winning in our 1979 Formula 3 team of 140 mph March-Triumphs.

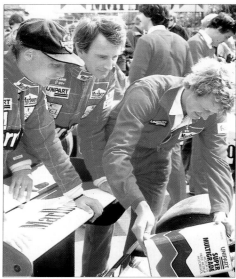

F1, M1, Same One! Unipart Supermultigrade Oil. The right choice for all three!

But we didn't just "Back Britain" at a time when it was deeply unfashionable. Multiple World Champions Niki Lauda and Alain Prost drove Unipart components. So did Le Mans winner Jan Lammers in his time with Ensign. Other international test drivers? Clay Regazzoni, Andrea de Cesaris, John Watson, Michele Alboreto, Jean Alesi,

Julian Bailey, Satoru Nakajima, Olivier Grouillard, Bertrand Gachot, Michael Schumacher, Alessandro Zanardi, Stefano Modena and Mauricio Gugelmin.

1981-84 Developing Excellence with Marlboro McLaren

Unipart product development stretched beyond glamorous drivers. We were in there running our hardware during the most exciting period of the technical change seen in the sport.

The Unipart manufactured Turbo Induction Tube

We count our 1981-84 years with McLaren as particularly rewarding. Ron Dennis and designer John Barnard brought the age of carbon fibre composite construction to Grand Prix in the

FORMULA ONE
GHEST TEST
RT TO DISAGREE?

1981 MP4, overturning years of traditional alloy fabrication and transforming driver safety. Unipart seized its chance. Creating products that met with the tightest specifications in the unforgiving demand for excellence that is Formula One. We met the McLaren standard. Exhausts, multigrade motor oils, hub

1980 the Unipart sponsored Ensign

bearings, spark plugs, engine cooling radiators. Even the high temperature trial of supplying mixture to the fantastically powerful engines of the turbo era, all were Unipart manufacturing tasks. Mo Nunn's brave Ensign equipe wore our colours. The team tested ten of our product lines in our 1980 Formula One debut season.

Filters, Thermostats and clutch bearings, have been tested to the Formula One limit by Tyrrell Grand Prix drivers. In fact we were the sole sponsor for Tyrrell at the beginning of the 1989 season.

Today we continue to work with the "backroom boys" as well as the name drivers. Designer Gary Anderson

The Unipart developed Oil cooler

(remember the F3 Anson? We sponsored that, too), draws on Unipart experience that stretches back to cooling consultancy with current McLaren F1 road car designer, Gordon Murray. Jordan Grand Prix have counted on our support

The 1992 Sasol Jordan Yamaha

The 1992 World Champion Nigel Mansell

since their magnificent 1991 debut year. We bred World Champions on our products. As they progressed, so did we. Today Unipart is Britain's largest independent automotive parts business. You don't get to that position without passing the Formula 1 test. The Toughest Test of all.

So thank you, Nigel. Thanks to all of you, mentioned and unmentioned.

One thing's for sure when we consider if our involvement in Formula One has been both challenging and rewarding. There is only one answer

The Answer is YES.
Now What's the Question?

UNIPART

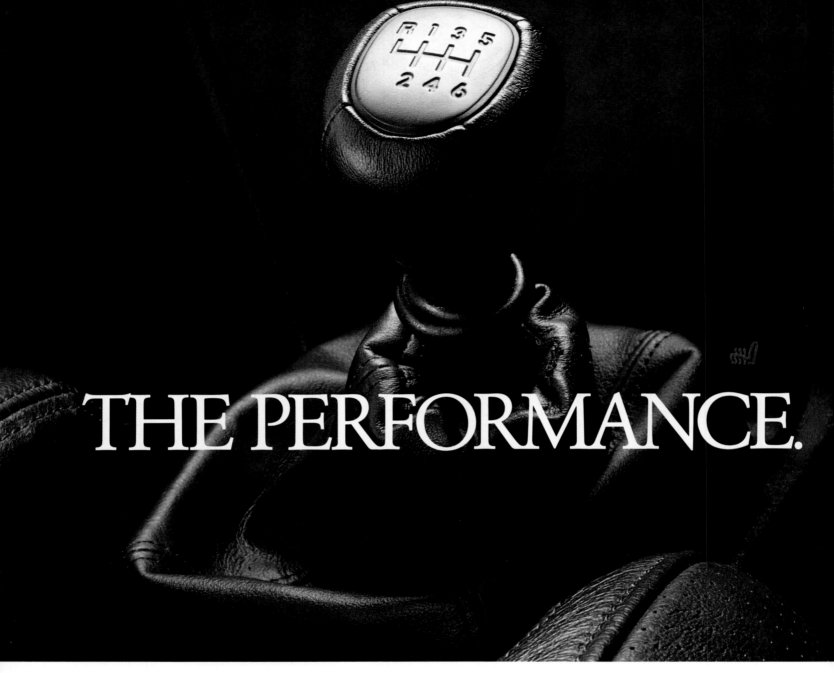

THE PERFORMANCE.

This Calibra has just moved up a gear.

It's the new Turbo 4x4 version with a six speed gearbox unique in its class.

The extra cog is no gimmick. Without it you simply wouldn't appreciate the car's finely-tuned muscle-power.

Balancing the increased performance is a safer, more refined turbo system.

It cuts in swiftly at unusually low engine speeds, giving an immediate response when you want to overtake a slow-moving vehicle.

For the interior, a spot of power-dressing seemed appropriate.

All-black, all-leather heated seats. All matching the door panels, gear knob and steering wheel.

What isn't new about the seats is the now legendary amount of rear legroom.

As any car magazine will tell you, no other car of its type can match the Calibra for accommodation.

(One summed it up rather nicely, claiming it actually defies coupé law.*)

THE BEST SEATS.

Standard features include power steering, trip computer, CAT, deadlocking and alarm.

And a slinky, sophisticated SC804 radio cassette with six speakers. The system has an anti-theft removable display and the latest RDS EON cut-in travel information.

Finally, before launching our flagship, we took another long hard look at the Calibra's unmistakable, sleek styling.

Not that we wanted to change anything, of course. We just like looking at it.

For more details of either the Turbo, or the 8 or 16-valve version, telephone 0800 444200.

THE CALIBRA TURBO 4x4.

 VAUXHALL

Once driven, forever smitten.

Chapter 2

REPCO BRABHAM – THE TWO YEARS B.C.*
1966-67

*Before Cosworth

Simplify and reduce weight. Few 1966 Formula 1 cars were more simple or lighter than Ron Tauranac's Repco V8-engined BT19, seen here driven by Jack Brabham en route to victory in the Dutch GP at Zandvoort. Its simple multi-tubular spaceframe chassis was light and stiff enough to promote good handling on those Goodyear tyres; note 13 in. diameter front wheels, 15 in. rears. The combination won four consecutive mid-season GPs and the World Championship.

The so-called '3-litre Formula' saw two years' racing before the Cosworth-engined cars established their Championship domination. In both these formative years, 1966 and 1967, it was the simple, lightweight spaceframe cars from Brabham which carried off the Championship titles, using Australian-made, initially American production-derived, Repco V8 engines.

Ron Tauranac's Motor Racing Developments (MRD) company, founded in partnership with twice-World Champion driver Jack Brabham, had begun manufacturing production Formula Junior cars in Victoria Road, Surbiton (to the south-west of London), during the winter of 1961/62. In their formative years of Australian racing, both Tauranac and Brabham had been regular customers of Geoffrey Russell's Replacement Parts Pty Ltd company, which had long since adopted the 'Repco' brand name.

They maintained this close triangular relationship throughout Jack Brabham's highly successful years as Cooper number one driver and it continued after Tauranac came to join him in his new British-based engineering ventures in 1960.

Tauranac and Brabham's first MRD prototype Formula Junior car emerged during the summer of 1961, and with a number of customer orders already received they laid down a production batch of a dozen improved versions for 1962. They had found the Victoria Road premises and did a deal with Repco's UK marketing people under which Repco took over warehousing space there and then sub-let production space to MRD.

In August 1962, MRD's first 'Brabham' Formula 1 car, the Climax V8-engined BT3, made its debut with Jack driving in the German GP, and a regular two-car Formula 1 team was then formed for 1963-65 as Jack's own Brabham Racing Organisation company. Tauranac had no formal share in this business, and Formula 1 design and development became something of a chore for him through those final three years of 1½-litre racing.

MRD had to design and build the Formula 1 chassis, which were supplied to BRO at an agreed price. BRO raced them, providing engines, transmissions, drivers and so on. Throughout this period MRD's prime responsibility was always to its paying customers who were buying production Formula 2, Formula Junior, Tasman Formula and even private-owner F1 cars in ever-increasing numbers.

This heavy pressure upon the factory – which was now sited alongside the Wey Navigation Canal at New Haw, within sight of the huge railway embankment which flanks the old Railway Straight at Brooklands Motor Course – meant that F1 work was often delayed. Even so, it occupied much time which could be devoted more profitably to the production cars. Tauranac was as unhappy with this state of affairs as only this fiercely logical, rather short-fused man could be. He declared his unhappiness to Brabham and the production of new Brabham cars for the new Grand Prix Formula was in the balance during the autumn of 1965.

Meanwhile Coventry Climax's much-promised flat-16-cylinder 1500 cc F1 engine had been still-born. MRD had built a specially tailored Brabham chassis ready for it – Cooper and Lotus were in the same boat – and as a new joint agreement was at last worked out between Jack Brabham and his engineering partner, so this idle frame was hurriedly pressed into service to put their green-and-gold colours on the 3-litre Formula grid. Despite the last-minute nature of their project, this Repco Brabham BT19 was actually the first of the new breed of true 3-litre Formula 1 cars to appear. It was also the first to win a race, and the first to win a 3-litre Formula 1 Constructors' World Championship title.

Here I should perhaps explain that from the beginning of Formula Junior production, the MRD-made racing cars had been named 'Repco Brabhams' in mild recognition of the Repco

group's assistance. As Formula Junior was at that time dominated by modified Ford engines, these cars became officially 'Repco Brabham-Fords'. When Climax four-cylinder FPF-engined Tasman cars were first produced by MRD in the winter of 1962/63, they were known as 'Repco Brabham-Climaxes'.

Repco had a major interest in Tasman Formula racing which catered for 2.7-litre, then from 1964 2.5-litre, engined single-seater cars in Australia and New Zealand. The class was dominated by the 2½-litre F1-originated Climax FPF engine, for which Repco made many parts and with Climax's blessing ran a 'down-under' sales and service programme. They eventually fitted Repco Brabham nameplates to these engines and technically speaking the MRD-built cars powered by these units then became pure-bred 'Repco Brabhams'. However, we must not confuse them with the true Repco Brabham V8 Formula 1 engines and cars whose story follows.

THE REPCO V8 ENGINES

What became the World Championship-winning Australian V8 engine was conceived in February 1964, when Repco's Melbourne management had appreciated that supplies of Climax FPF parts would probably dry up within the life of the existing Tasman Formula. Chief Engineer Frank Hallam and Project Engineer Phil Irving – of Vincent motor cycle fame – were authorized to produce a new engine which would fit into existing Repco Brabham Tasman chassis.

Their answer was a V8 using an existing General Motors-made Oldsmobile F85 all-aluminium block. This represented the debris of an enormously costly and unsuccessful attempt by GM to produce a linerless aluminium engine for a 3-litre Buick 'compact'. The linerless idea had failed in production so a few were completed with cast-in ferrous liners, but that proved more fiddly and costly than conventional iron-block construction, and so GM understandably cut their losses and ditched the entire project. Repco picked up some of the pieces – Bruce McLaren's embryo sports-racing car team in England scooping up most of the remainder – and Repco were to turn commercial production failure into a Formula 1 World Champion.

Hallam and Irving had opted for this F85 V8 on the basis that the obvious way to extract more power than an FPF's from the same 2.5-litre capacity was to employ more cylinders, thus increasing both piston area and crankshaft speed. The recently abandoned F85's availability made it possible to sidestep a slow and costly foundry operation by using these proprietary blocks off the shelf.

Irving found that the Olds block could accommodate a range of displacements from 2.5 to 4.4 litres so it could double as both a Tasman Formula or Group 7 sports-racing car power unit. It needed stiffening and overhead camshafts would have to replace the standard centre camshaft within the vee which GM had provided to operate ohv via long pushrods.

In their modifications, the Repco engineers applied two basic parameters: 1) frontal area should be minimized to match existing Repco Brabham body designs; 2) overall width should also fit into the existing chassis frames.

Irving's new cylinder head design produced a simple head common for each cylinder bank. It carried parallel valves angled inwards at 10 degrees from the cylinder axis in simple wedge-shaped combustion chambers. They were actuated from a single chain-driven overhead camshaft.

This modest and very 'un-racy' arrangement was preferred to a twin overhead camshaft system; firstly to keep the engine narrow overall, secondly to reduce the length of unsupported drive chain to each shaft. The uncompromising practicality of the Repco engineers' approach is emphasized by the fact that these new heads were identical in every dimension to minimize expense and to ease the spares requirement for the private owner.

Repco took the bare GM-made aluminium blocks and filled all unwanted holes and spaces original-

ly intended for the now redundant pushrod valvegear. A ladder-formation 3/16 in. thick steel stiffener plate was screwed to the sump flange to stiffen the engine's bottom end.

New main bearing caps were retained by long bolts which penetrated deep into the crankcase casting. The existing 3.5 in. bores were reamed and fitted with 10-thou thick Repco cast-iron liners. Bore and stroke of 85 mm x 55 mm gave the required Tasman Formula displacement of 2.5 litres. Laystall in England machined the crankshafts, which revolved in five Repco plain main bearings. Another short-cut was taken when suitably lightened and balanced Daimler 4-litre V8 production con-rods were found to fit. They were much cheaper than specially made rods – their actual price being £7 each, while a raw unmachined F85 block cost every bit of £11 . . . so who needed 16-cylinder racing engines?

By itself this must have gladdened Jack Brabham's notoriously 'careful' old heart, even though he was only now developing crucial interest in this engine.

Repco's V8 pistons were cast in aluminium-silicon alloy, with shallow valve clearance indents in the crown. Two beautiful magnesium castings completed this conversion; a Y-shaped cam-drive chain cover on the front, and a new 3-inch deep ribbed sump further improving bottom-end rigidity to accommodate the designed power increase.

Adaptors were designed to match either Weber carburettors or Lucas fuel injection, and Repco even made their own specialized oil and water pumps for the new unit. It emerged 25½ in. long overall, excluding the Climax FWB flywheel; 21 in. wide across the heads; 23 in. high, excluding induction equipment on top.

Repco's prototype V8 coughed into life for the first time on the company's Richmond, Victoria, test bed on 21 March 1965, only 51 weeks after Hallam and Irving had first set pen to paper. The run was satisfactory and testing continued while Jack Brabham and Repco made the deal to produce a 3-litre F1 version for the coming year. Phil Irving consequently spent much of that summer in England, working closely with Jack himself on detail 3-litre design.

They chose the standard 3.5 in. (88.9 mm) bore and adopted a stroke of 60.3 mm to displace 2994 cc. Lucas fuel injection was chosen and in early tests this F1 unit delivered 285 bhp at 8000 rpm. Its low stroke:bore ratio of 0.68:1 suggested very high rotational speeds but, despite the short stroke, maximum power was still produced at only 8000 rpm and the engine has been described as being 'neither useful nor safe' beyond 8300 rpm due to ultimate engine breathing and mechanical restrictions.

This is perhaps to forget Irving and Brabham's true objective. Both were intensely practical and *very* experienced. Both recognized what a delusive

Top: *Make-do versus leftover; Brabham's original BT19-Repco leading Clark's 2-litre Lotus-Climax and team-mate Hulme's BT20-Repco during their terrific battle in the 1966 Dutch GP. Note different engine cowl and exhaust layouts in the spaceframe Brabhams.* Centre: *Bottom end of the modified stock GM Repco RB600 aluminium block was stiffened by the steel ladder-plate seen here.* Above: *Two years on, the hybrid-construction BT26-Repco four-cam car of 1968 used riveted-on stress panel triangulation on a simplified tubular base-frame. Workmanship was beautiful, the engine unreliable.*

target ultimate power can be in road racing. Mid-range torque, an engine's ability to provide real 'punch' away from low- and medium-speed corners, is what makes a potential winner on most World Championship circuits – even then when superfast courses like Spa, Reims and Monza were still in unfettered use. Their races could quite logically be surrendered to Ferrari's V12s or perhaps Maserati's similar engine tipped for Cooper, or, if the lessons of history should be overturned, to BRM's fabulous H16. That would still leave Monaco, Zandvoort, Brands Hatch, the Nürburgring, Watkins Glen, Mexico City – all slow or medium-fast circuits, forming two-thirds of the Championship trail.

And never forget that Jack Brabham and his team were professionals, racing for a living. There were potentially good earnings on offer from the non-Championship events at Silverstone (still considered merely 'medium-fast' in those days), Syracuse and Oulton Park where mid-range punch rather than flat-out power should still carry the day. In short, there was *money* to be earned.

This is what concentrates the minds of those racing purely for racing's sake. They are a different breed from those involved in intense technical research or product promotion.

The Repco engine offered a notably broad power spread, with useful torque as low as 3500 rpm, then beginning to fly at 4000 rpm and delivering peak torque – something like 192 psi bmep – at 6500 rpm. And there was still real power available up at 8000 rpm. What's more, the engine weighed only 340 lb. Fuel consumption was also most advantageous, at around 8 mpg which put the finalized cars on the starting grid with only some 35 gallons on board. Thus the light and simple Repco Brabham enjoyed a startline weight advantage over all opposition with greater power, while its relatively humble engine was still man enough to handle any competitive car of comparable weight. It could score on weight over the more powerful Ferrari, BRM Cooper-Maserati, Eagle-Weslake and Honda in their undeveloped forms, and on sheer 'grunt' over such interim stop-gap cars as the nimble 2-litre Climax and BRM V8-engined Lotus 33s and BRMs.

Once this 3-litre Repco V8 had been proven in essence, all that MRD had to do was provide BRO with a suitable chassis to carry it, but the new incentive agreement which Tauranac demanded was not finalized until that November, with the first full-scale race under the new Formula, albeit a non-Championship event, mere weeks away in South Africa on 2 January 1966. In fact the V8 engine proved adequate throughout that season when mounted in Tauranac's 'ex-flat-16' BT19 lightweight spaceframe chassis and in the new BT20s later in the year.

Repco had named this Oldsmobile F85-based V8 their Type 620, engine numbers all being prefixed 'RB' ('Repco Brabham', of course) '620'. These numerals were themselves a two-part classification, '600' applying to the modified proprietary block and '20' to the duplicated sohc cylinder head design. Individual engine numbering actually commenced at 'RB 620-E1'.

The engine was extremely reliable through 1966 and its useable power was sufficient in the lightweight, good-handling Brabhams to prove extremely competitive. At Monza for the Italian GP an engine was delivered fresh from Melbourne, with *'Monza 350 hp'* stencilled boldly on its crate, thumbing its nose at the alleged '400-horsepower' opposition from Ferrari, Eagle-Weslake and BRM.

The truth of the matter is that engine 'E7' had produced a peak of 298 bhp on Repco's test bed and then, after further attention to its porting and a rise in compression ratio, BRO's ex-Climax engine specialist John Judd saw 311 bhp from it at 7250 rpm during a re-run in Climax's dyno shop at Widdrington Road, Coventry. He felt there was more to come but at this point the run ended as a piston burned out.

And the cars won four GPs in a row through that summer. It must have made BRM, Ferrari

Jack Brabham's 1966 World Championship-winning Repco Brabham BT19 on the pits straight at Reims during the French Grand Prix – the first Grand Prix to be won by a driver in a car bearing his own name.

and Cooper-Maserati weep, for these green-and-gold cars with the humble pedigree were slaughtering the thoroughbreds in the Championship chase.

While the Repco engine proved itself man enough to dominate the '66 World Championship, with the combination of Tauranac's chassis and the driving skills of Jack Brabham and his team-mate Denny Hulme, the opposition largely eliminated itself, and it was obvious that far stiffer competition would emerge in 1967. For a start the intrinsic deficiencies of the production Oldsmobile block, and the time-consuming and costly operations necessary to bring it up to scratch, now made production of a tailor-made Repco replacement inevitable since the basic idea had been proved sound. A new head design was also required, for the low-level exhausts of the 620-series had given Tauranac migraines while trying to weave pipes around the chassis tubes and away through his preferred suspension system.

On the crest of their World Championship wave, Repco pressed ahead with these developments for '67; an all-new block plus new heads with their exhaust ports exiting on top within the engine vee.

General Manager Frank Hallam headed a four-man design team working at Repco Brabham Engines Pty Ltd in Maidstone, outside Melbourne, with Phil Irving's influence as their guiding light. Norm Wilson headed this team, aided by John Judd from England, Lindsay Hooper and Brian Heard.

They redesigned the crankcase to improve rigidity. It was cast in aluminium alloy. Wet liners were adopted along with cross-bolted main bearing caps, and there was also a system of main bearing studs which distributed stress right through the new crankcase. These screwed into its underside and penetrated right through it with reduced diameter, relieving stress concentrations right through to the top of the new block where they were secured by nuts which were to be tightened after the main bearing cap nuts had been torqued down.

This purpose-built Type 700 block and crankcase saved some 30 lb weight compared to the converted Oldsmobile Type 600 which it replaced.

The redesigned cylinder heads now disposed their two valves per cylinder in line with the

cylinder axis, instead of at 10 degrees to it as before, and they also emerged flush with the head-face. Camshaft centres were changed to suit, and the original 20-series combustion chamber design was replaced by a bowl-in-piston arrangement to enhance 'squish' and thus improve burning of the incoming charge. This all-new head, with its reversed porting placing the exhaust outlets in the valley of the vee on top of the engine, was the Type 40.

OK, so what became of the Type 30 head?

Good question. There was a Repco Type 30 head design, but it mated the new bowl-in-piston combustion chamber arrangement with outside low-level exhausts. At that time it was felt that with parallel valves the burned gas had in any case to make quite a sharp turn as it left the cylinder and these pragmatic engineers felt it was surely immaterial to the gas which way they made it turn. However, test runs then indicated the fallacy of this argument, and when the chassis designer began to grumble about exhaust installation, so the 30-series design was held over and the centre-exhaust Type 40s took their place.

The 1967 season got under way, and the Repco Type 740 V8s proved themselves by giving Repco Brabham their second consecutive World Championship success. This time they took the title with perhaps a little more good fortune in face of much more potent, though crucially far less reliable, Lotus opposition. And Lotus used the brand new V8 Cosworth-Ford DFV engine.

By the end of that 1967 season, the Repco Brabham range of V8s included the now historic Olds-based 3-litre and Tasman 2.5- and 4.4-litre sports-racing RB620s, plus the new centre-exhaust purpose-built RB740s in both 3-litre F1 and 2.5-litre Tasman trim. New 4.2-litre and 2.8-litre Indianapolis track-racing variants were on the stocks, the latter employing Garrett AiResearch turbocharging.

Peak power from the World Championship-winning 740 centre-exhaust V8s had been only 330 bhp, but they had proved hugely efficient haulers in Tauranac's superb Brabham BT24 spaceframe chassis. Certainly Repco's Australian horses seemed hard workers. Cosworth claimed 408 bhp from their prototype batch of DFVs and Weslake credited their Gurney Eagle V12 with 417 bhp or so. Yet a study of the race, pole position and fastest lap record in the Appendix (page 335) shows how Repco Brabham now had to do something fairly drastic if they were to attain the unprecedented Formula 1 Constructors' Championship hat-trick beckoning them in 1968.

The Repco engineers studied two avenues of approach. One was for a short-stroke magnesium-block engine, the other for a daring new cylinder head design using a radially disposed 4-valve-per-cylinder layout.

Test experience with the held-over 30-series head had proved conclusively that there was a power advantage offered by crossflow gas paths and the stunning debut of Cosworth's DFV in Europe served graphically to emphasize it.

Repco's radial-valve disposition Type 50 heads now aimed to exploit this advantage to the full. The valves resided side by side in each half of a conventional pent roof combustion chamber, the exhausts and inlets being alternately placed, diametrically opposed across the chamber. They were operated from twin overhead camshafts in each head, alternate cam lobes on each shaft acting on inlet then exhaust valves. This layout allowed very simple valve actuation compared to Dr Ludwig Apfelbeck's notorious contemporary BMW Formula 2 head design in which a radial valve disposition was housed in hemispherical combustion chambers, with valve stems protruding radially like the horns on a sea-mine.

But the Australian team added complication enough as they had to lead their exhaust stubs out within the vee as a bunch of eight small-bore pipes, while four more stubs emerged below the heads outside the vee each side of the engine. One wonderful-looking test engine was built up using these heads with the snake pit of centre exhausts in the vee up top *plus* the banana-bunch side exhausts sweeping away down below like the old 620 system.

Fortunately, after such effort, results were most encouraging, but like so many engine men's flights of fancy, it would prove to be a chassis designer's nightmare due to virtually intractable installation problems. Sheer exhaust system weight would be another handicap to be tackled elsewhere. Tests with these Type 50 heads were promising, but they were shelved.

Alternative Type 60 heads were then drawn, using twin ohc and more conventional four-valve-per-cylinder layout. The exhaust and inlet valves were paired together this time to provide conventional crossflow gas paths. There were neatly tucked-away outside exhausts, and Lucas fuel injection was housed within the vee, where the valley space was now so restricted by the extra inboard camshaft housings that in-vee exhausts really would have been sorely cramped.

In parallel with all this cylinder head development, Repco had researched an ultra-light cast-magnesium block but eventually compromised, opting instead for the additional rigidity and stability of conventional cast aluminium, though the stroke was now shorter. This new block was fully 1¼ in. shallower than its predecessors from crankshaft centreline to head-joint. The completed engine would now be considerably lighter in consequence, despite its use of a nitrided geartrain to drive the new four-cam ohc system in place of the 600/700-series' chains. While both those early blocks had carried sufficient meat to offer that wide variety of capacities, the new 860 could offer only 2.5-litre or 3-litre versions. Redesigned crankshafts were used, with fewer balance weights, saving still more weight.

Time ran out on the team during these developments, and the first 800-series block to be raced was in fact magnesium, making its debut as a 2.5 during the 1968 Tasman Championship. Later that season, in 3-litre Formula 1 form, it eventually ran out of water and pulled out of line. The block survived with John Judd in his Rugby engine development concern, long after Repco had gracefully bowed out of racing.

One short-stroke test engine was also built up using a 2½-litre Tasman crankshaft combined with a wider bore and a 5-litre sports car head, developed for the 700-series Group 7 sports car V8. This hybrid test engine showed no power advantage, and so the definitive short-block 800-series engines appeared in 3-litre form with shorter con-rods, using 5.1 in. centres in place of the original F85-standard 6.3 in. type.

The time spent on these developments bit deep into the 860 programme for 1968 and the engines appeared in new BT26 Brabham cars only as very competitive units while they were running . . . which was rarely for very long.

By this time Repco's potential was being run ragged by the ferocity of European competition, mainly from the Cosworth-Ford DFV but also from Ferrari's latest V12s. The 12,000-mile gulf between Grand Prix battlefield in the northern hemisphere and engine development shop in Australia was just too big to bridge.

The problems which afflicted the four-cam Repco-engined Brabhams during 1968 included several dropped valve inserts, failed oil pressure, oil loss and water leaks. An honest assembly cock-up destroyed the drive gear for the right-side exhaust camshaft on Jack's car after only one lap at Brands Hatch. Then massive internal failures late-season included Jack's engine running its centre-main bearing and Rindt's breaking a gudgeon pin at Monza where it did not rain (very rare in that troubled season); continuous full-bore running simply overwhelmed Repco's lubrication system. When Brabham's engine was stripped down, one gudgeon pin was found in three pieces. As his oil pressure zeroed and the centre-main bearing ran he had switched off literally a split-second before those pieces ran amok and destroyed the unit as totally as had the less sympathetic Rindt's. No prizes to guess which driver was paying the bills . . .

After that experience, John Judd had Petter

diesel engine gudgeon pins machined to replace the originals. Constant and worrying wear had been found in the Alfa Romeo-made cam followers which had been used without trouble since 740 days. This now became the 860 units' latest bugbear. In the long Mexican GP excessive oil consumption dried out Jack's engine before the finish. In an effort to preserve those cam followers, which had broken behind his shoulders in the preceding US GP, some of the oil drains from the heads had been plugged to maintain more lubricant washing around the suspect followers. Unfortunately this simply caused extra leakage down the valve guides, and the BT26 oil tank just wasn't big enough to last the distance.

In between times there had been other dramas, and fleeting success which proved just how close Repco were to true competitiveness.

During practice at Spa, Jack had another valve insert detach, and Repco concluded that the material was shrinking to cause this problem. In a frantic trouble-shooting exercise, Jack Brabham flew himself home that evening while John Judd and Norm Wilson collected a fresh engine at Heathrow air-freight from Melbourne. It was stripped down overnight with the help of BRO chief mechanic Roy Billington, while team machinist Ron Cousins came in to fit the new parts. The modified cylinder heads were then cooked in Brabham's kitchen, and his wife Betty awoke to find her house filled with acrid fumes from the oven!

The BT26-Repco 860s showed their true potential in practice for the wet Dutch GP where Rindt qualified on the front row only 0.16 sec slower than Amon's pole-position Ferrari, and Jack Brabham himself was on row two in his sister car. But they nearly hadn't made it to that race, as immediately after their transporter had left their new Guildford race shop for Dover a telex had rattled through from Melbourne warning of an assembly error. The team's fresh 860 engines had insufficient static clearance between their valves and pistons, and the twain would surely meet should the engines be started.

The ever-practical Jack Brabham promptly bought a suitable wood chisel from a Guildford hardware store and at Zandvoort his mechanics lifted the 860s' heads and chiselled down the piston crowns to provide the necessary clearance . . . and only then did they produce that fine practice performance. This is why we should not compare this type of modern racing with the *alleged* hey-day of Daimler-Benz and Alfa Corse.

Yet in truth, the more we discover today of the way the giants of the past went racing, the less infallible they also seem to be. It is quite wrong to

The Repco Brabhams were nothing if not forgiving. Here on his way to victory at Monaco 1967 Hulme demonstrates his BT20's full opposite lock, those flat, deep-treaded Goodyears scrabbling for grip.

base high-flown technical judgements upon their racing records and design standards without also looking closer at the greasy-fingered background, often punctuated by similar last-minute panics and human errors. Racing cars and racing engines are made by man, and man is far from perfect, even when his efforts have been applied *en masse* by a 300-strong experimental department. Never swallow the legend whole, for legends are written by Public Relations men . . .

At Rouen for another wet race, the French GP, Rindt qualified on pole to prove conclusively there was nothing wrong in principle with the quad-cam BT26, but the car's fuel tanks split early in the race. Brabham's regular BT26 suffered a repeat fuel-feed problem which had dogged it in previous outings. Tauranac finally concluded that when its tanks were crammed full to the brim on race day an air vent became blocked and the fuel pump lacked sufficient suction to overcome the vacuum it was attempting to form within.

The Mexican GP of 1968 was the final works outing for Repco Brabham in Formula 1, although in 1969 Jack drove a Formula 3-based Repco Brabham BT31 fitted with a 2½-litre Repco 830 engine to third place at Sandown Park and subsequently first place in the Bathurst '100' at Mount Panorama, where he set fastest lap and won handsomely in his last road race for Repco.

It was the end of a three-season relationship which had yielded back-to-back Formula 1 Constructors' Championship titles for Brabham and Tauranac and Repco, and Drivers' titles for Jack Brabham himself and for his team-mate, Denny Hulme. It had been a triumph of elegant thinking and practical expediency over high-flown sophistication, and now – albeit with real power – Cosworth's V8 would follow where Repco's had led . . .

THE WORLD CHAMPIONSHIP BRABHAM CHASSIS

The availability of the BT19 spare chassis, tailor-made for the still-born flat-16 Climax 1500 cc engine, saved the day for the Brabham Racing Organisation when the new deal was finally forged with Motor Racing Developments in November 1965.

BT19 was a one-off multi-tubular space-frame chassis. Ron Tauranac persisted in his allegiance to this form of construction despite most contemporary opposition building stressed-skin monocoque cars. Multi-tubular frames were popular with MRD's paying customers because they were simple, well-understood and easy to set up. They were also straightforward and inexpensive to repair following an accident yet rigid enough to give competitive standards of handling, traction and braking. In Formula 1, Jack Brabham's BRO team put into practice what MRD produced by racing spaceframe-chassised cars.

BT19 had a well-triangulated frame of typical Tauranac design although the use of oval-section tube around its cockpit opening was unusual. Tauranac had found some was available and had used it simply to enhance beam strength around the cockpit – 'always the weak point in a racing design'.

The suspension was typically Tauranac, with unequal-length non-parallel front wishbones formed by a transverse link with a trailing radius rod jointed to it at the top, and a one-piece wide-based tubular wishbone at the bottom. Suitably modified Alford & Alder proprietary uprights were used (from the humble Triumph Herald saloon). Co-axial coil springs and Armstrong dampers were mounted outboard front and rear. At the rear, single top links, reversed lower wishbones and twin radius rods located specially cast uprights.

Initially, 13 in. wheels were fitted enclosing 10½ in. diameter disc brakes as had been standard on the 1½-litre cars. Later in the 1966 season 15 in. rear wheels were adopted housing new 11 in. discs and wearing the latest generation of square-shouldered flat-tread Goodyear tyres. Still later in its life BT19 was fitted with 15 in. wheels front and rear.

In original form this one-off car used a 1½-litre Formula Hewland HD five-speed transaxle, which really was not adequate for the 3-litre engine to which it was now mated. Early on, Jack Brabham always made gentle race starts, while Mike Hewland's Maidenhead-based transmission company developed a new and heavier gearbox, known as the DG, which was to become very popular in the 3-litre Formula. Both Brabham himself and his former team driver, Dan Gurney, who had now founded the Anglo-American Racers Eagle F1 team, had asked Hewland to produce a suitable transmission and Dan was delighted to see it carry his initials, 'DG'. Mike Hewland, however, told the author years ago that in fact someone now unremembered had leaned over his shoulder while he was working at his design and asked 'What's this, a different gearbox?', and 'DG' for 'Different Gearbox' it became.

This transmission featured a ZF limited-slip differential, and it drove to the BT19's wheels via one-piece solid halfshafts with inboard rubber couplings and outboard Hooke joints.

BT19 emerged as one of the very lightest true 3-litre GP contenders, and the economical engine, as already mentioned, enabled it to survive a full GP distance on no more than 35 gallons of Esso premium grade. Even so, BT19 was some 150 lb above the minimum weight limit of 1102 lb and Tauranac was far from happy with it, regarding it as 'a lash-up', even after it had won four consecutive GP races at Reims, Brands Hatch, Zandvoort and the Nürburgring, had given Jack himself the Drivers' World Championship for the third time in his career and brought MRD the Formula 1 Constructors' Cup World title.

Once BT19 was running, work had begun at New Haw on the true 1966 3-litre F1 cars which were intended first to support and eventually to supplant the lashed-up BT19. These BT20 cars used all round-section steel tube chassis members, mostly in 18-gauge stock but some from 16- and 20-gauge. The lower chassis rails were revised compared to BT19's and the cockpit area was double-braced with twin side tubes in place of BT19's oval members. Tankage was similar to BT19's although small scuttle and behind-seat tanks were now available for the long and thirsty Italian GP, but were not required.

The BT20s employed virtually identical suspen-

Jack Brabham's BT24, French GP, '67. Compact F2-sized package on F1 wheels and tyres has centre-exhaust Repco RB740 V8 engine, whisker spoilers on nose, deflector ahead of front wheel to extract radiator air and engine-bay side panel.

sion to BT19's, but geometry was revised from new to accommodate 15 in. wheels front and rear. In its first races, Hulme's BT20 used 12 in. diameter brake discs, but these were too large and 11 in. discs soon replaced them. Mechanically, BT19 and the BT20s were identical, but the later cars had front and rear tracks wider by 1 in. and ¾ in. respectively, and their wheelbase was 1½ in. longer. Externally the two BT20s built differed from BT19 in using vestigial two-piece engine covers in place of the duck-tail one-piece cowl of BT19, and their exhaust manifolding wrapped outside the rear suspension upper radius rods while BT19's were cramped inside the rods.

Tauranac was able to tackle the Formula 1 problem far more thoroughly in 1967. That season his new cars were based upon a highly successful Tasman Formula exercise raced in January/March that year. This had employed a production-type Brabham Formula 2 frame known as the BT23A, fitted with the prototype new centre-exhaust 2.5-litre Type 740 engine. Here, Tauranac used specially cast front uprights for the first time, replacing the Herald proprietary forgings which had done such yeoman service for so long on Brabham racing cars. The BT23's engine bay had been suitably reworked to house the V8 in place of the in-line four-cylinder Cosworth FVA unit which would appear in these production racing cars in European Formula 2 that summer. Three largely similar new BT24 Formula 1 cars would now be built.

Tauranac regards these as his 'first real go at Formula 1, apart from the BT3 in 1962. We looked at the existing cars from end to end, slimmed and pruned everything to the minimum, used our own cast uprights all round and generally spent a lot of time designing just enough car to do the job. The amount of thought and time that went into producing a car as simple and light as that was tremendous – probably a lot more than if we had gone all complex and sophisticated . . .'

These BT24s were delightfully compact, well-packaged cars, although based on the same relatively long wheelbase as the preceding BT20. Front track had narrowed by 1½ in. while rear track was wider by ¾ in. Apart from the new cast front uprights, suspension configuration was similar to the BT20's, but the whole car was extremely neat and the BT23-type front body panel was split

crosswise at the front suspension so that the nose cone could detach separately to ease freight and stowage. On the new type's debut at Zandvoort in the 1967 Dutch GP a Formula 2-type Hewland FT200 gearbox was used, saving still more weight, but it was not robust enough and so the hefty Hewland DG quickly replaced it.

These BT24s were very quick and forgiving, allowing their drivers to take liberties which the opposition could not look at. Denny Hulme narrowly beat Brabham himself for the Drivers' title while Jack had taken all new development testing upon himself, leaving the proven and reliable – and by the same token potentially slower – hardware to his rugged New Zealand team-mate.

The BT24s achieved three 1-2 victories during that season, in the French GP at the Bugatti Circuit, Le Mans, in the German GP at the Nürburgring and in the Canadian GP at Mosport Park, but in each of these races they had played second fiddle to the Lotus-Cosworth 49s until they broke, and in Germany to Gurney's Eagle V12 until it broke.

To finish first, you must first finish . . . and that was something at which the lithe little Repco Brabhams proved most adept.

The 1968 Tasman Championship saw Jack Brabham running another F1 prototype car in 2.5-litre form, this being the ultra-lightweight one-off BT23E powered by the latest Repco four-cam 830 magnesium short-block engine. Then, back home in England, Tauranac tried something new in his 1968 Formula 1 chassis design, the BT26: 'We tried to make a lighter but stronger frame by using alloy sheet panelling instead of tubular triangulation. This allowed us to use smaller-gauge, thinner section tubes for the basic frame, and the whole thing was built in a different way. Instead of making the bulkheads first and then joining them together in the jig, we laid down the bottom part of the frame on a flat bed, built the top deck immediately above it, and then put the side members in between. We used similar main rails to the earlier cars, but with ⅝ in. 20-gauge square-tube carrying stressed panelling on the floor and around the cockpit deck, on the sides and behind the seat, and in the dash panel frame, around the driver's thighs. It worked OK, but it might have been cheaper to build a monocoque in the long run.'

This BT26 was a bigger car than the BT24, 1½ in. longer in the wheelbase, 5 in. wider in front track and 5½ in. wider in rear track to apply longer lever moment on the Goodyear tyres and achieve better turn-in performance. Suspension and bodywork thinking was basically similar to that of the 1967 Championship-winning cars.

Although these hybrid-construction 1968 Repco Brabhams were unsuccessful in defending their predecessors' World Championship titles, they had their day, notably in the rain and mist-afflicted German GP – typically, where the four-cam Repco engine was concerned, in face of adversity.

One and a half hours before that race began a cracked titanium valve-spring retainer was discovered in Rindt's engine, and a mad scramble ensued to replace its cylinder heads with those cannibalized from the team's spare. The race V8 was reassembled with just 10 minutes to spare before the start and Rindt splashed around in the rain to finish third while Brabham himself was fifth in the team's finest race of that troubled year.

Most significantly, Ron Tauranac was one of the first Formula 1 car designers to think deeply enough about aerodynamics to adopt add-on tabs and vanes to minimize lift. Jack Brabham was himself an enthusiastic private flyer, and he recalled the Lotus 24 which he had driven in 1962 at Reims where he found it difficult merely 'to aim between the stands' when running flat-out along the undulating straight from Thillois towards Gueux. Although it had not been realized at the time, this was almost certainly due to aerodynamic lift unloading the front tyres and reducing steering reaction to a frightening degree.

It was noticed during 1966 that the BT19 and BT20 seemed to have a distinct advantage over the otherwise more sleek 2-litre Lotus-Climax 33 in very fast corners. One self-styled technical analyst has since attributed this to the relative torsional inferiority of the Brabham chassis, stating that Tauranac believed a little flexibility would ensure better-balanced tyre loading. Ron himself describes this theory in picturesque Australian. He has always been an advocate of chassis stiffness, 'the stiffer the better' and only remained faithful to the spaceframe as long as he did for other reasons, while being able to make his spaceframes 'stiff enough' to be consistently competitive.

In retrospect it would appear to be more the relative aerodynamic forms of the Lotus 33 and Repco Brabham nose cones which contributed to their relative high-speed behaviour. The Lotus nose cone was notably up-turned with a lengthy exposed undersurface in the direct airstream. The Brabham cone was more bluff with less curvature on both under and upper surfaces. It seems probable that this generated less lift than the Lotus cone, and when Tauranac enlisted aid from British Aircraft Corporation aerodynamicists at nearby Brooklands in 1967-68 genuine aerodynamic progress was made, even if this only revealed a fraction of its huge and as yet untapped potential.

At Spa in 1967, old BT19 driven by Hulme carried modest strip dive-planes either side of its nose cone in an exploratory attempt to kill front-end lift, which seemed quite effective on that very fast course. At Monza that year with BAC wind tunnel advice Brabham tried a bubble canopy and gearbox-fairing cowl to reduce his BT24's high-speed drag. These devices made little tangible difference, other than to distort the driver's vision through parallax and to overheat the gearbox oil, so they were discarded for the race.

Back at Spa in 1968, Brabham tied with Ferrari – following, as we shall see elsewhere in this volume, an unofficial wintertime Tasman Championship experiment by the Team Lotus mechanics – in introducing strutted rear aerofoils, mounted on the chassis, with their effect counterbalanced by broad dive-planes attached either side of the extreme nose. As the season progressed the wing era was upon us, and while the BT26s

suffered the mechanical problems of their new four-cam engines it was left to others to penetrate further into the new realm of aerodynamic research.

In 1969 the BT26s were reworked to accept Cosworth-Ford DFV V8 engines, and the Repco era had passed. The Repco Brabhams in all their various versions were never the spectacularly innovative technical gems which their major opposition might claim to have been, but they had in several ways shown the way ahead – not least in proving the intense value of a rigid regard for practical simplicity . . . a lesson many others would never, ever, learn.

Sheet-stiffened BT26-Repco 860.

Brabham and Tauranac took aerodynamic study very seriously in 1967-68. Here at Monza in '67 Jack tried this bubble canopy and engine bay-side, roll-over bar and gearbox-fairing panels to reduce drag. Unfortunately parallax distorted vision and gearbox oil nearly boiled!

Tauranac with help from aerodynamicist Ray Jessop introduced a strutted wing as early as the 1968 Belgian GP. Here at the Nürburgring Brabham demonstrates the BT26-Repco four-cam's chassis-mounted rear appendage plus balancing nose 'foils in his team's best race of the season.

Chapter 3

THE COSWORTH-FORD ERA 1967-85

Theo Page's original press-release cutaway of Cosworth-Ford's brand new DFV V8 was released with the original engine in June 1967.

The story of Cosworth Engineering and of its supremely successful Ford-backed V8 Formula 1 racing engine has often been told, notably in the John Blunsden and David Phipps book *Such Sweet Thunder* (Motor Racing Publications, London, 1971) and its sequel *The Power to Win* by Blunsden (MRP, 1983).

Briefly, the 'Cos' of Cosworth is Mike Costin, while the company's 'worth' is Keith Duckworth. Sometimes known derisively in their formative years as 'Cosbodge & Duckfudge Ltd', they matured from a small-time race engineering outfit operating from somebody else's premises to become the outstanding racing engine manufacturers of their day. Their production Ford-based Formula Junior, Formula 2 and Formula 3 racing engines dominated their respective classes with rare exception from 1960 to 1965, and then a new 1600 cc Formula 2 was promulgated to replace the existing 1-litre class from 1 January 1967.

Duckworth applied his now highly experienced designer's mind to production of a new dohc four-cylinder F2 engine, based on the Cortina 120E block. And at this point, Coventry Climax confirmed their customers' worst fears that they would indeed be withdrawing from Formula 1 racing at the end of the 1965 season, and would not be building engines to the new 3-litre Formula.

Duckworth had never designed a racing engine from scratch, but when Colin Chapman of Lotus asked him, first, if he thought he could design a new Formula 1 engine, and secondly, if he thought he should do so, the answer was affirmative. Colin asked him for a rough estimate of the cost of such a project, and the answer was 'around £100,000'.

Chapman wanted a new 3-litre racing engine for his team with an initial target output of 400 bhp. He considered this the minimum necessary to keep Ferrari, BRM, Eagle-Weslake and the rest in sight long-term. He had every confidence that Cosworth were capable of producing such an engine but now he needed someone prepared to finance it. He approached the British Society of Motor Manufacturers & Traders but, as he suspected, this proved a vain hope, the SMMT's representations to Government on his behalf drawing a blank. He also received a sympathetic hearing from Mr Macdonald, head of the BSR (British Sound Recording) company, and from David Brown of gear industry, tractor and Aston Martin fame. Neither produced much concrete result.

Chapman had been a long-time friend of dapper executive Walter Hayes, former Editor of *The Sunday Dispatch*, for whom Colin had once been freelance motoring correspondent. In 1961 Sir Patrick Hennessey, Chairman of Ford of Britain, had taken on Hayes as his new Director of Public Affairs, acting on the advice of veteran press baron – and proprietor of *The Sunday Dispatch* –

Keith Duckworth, Colin Chapman (part-hidden), Jimmy Clark and Graham Hill pose at Zandvoort with the spanking-new Cosworth-Ford DFV engine bolted into one of the tailor-made new Lotus 49s.

Lord Beaverbrook.

Largely under Hayes's direction, Ford espoused a new Total Performance image to lift them above the dull and rather tawdry 'minimum transport for the masses' image which they felt they were suffering from.

This new campaign involved them in motoring competition to an unprecedented degree. A strong Lotus-Ford link had already been forged with great success in Formula Junior and sports car racing, while the Lotus-Cortina saloon car was about to be launched and the Indianapolis 'Lotus powered by Ford' programme was also under way.

At dinner one evening in Chapman's home, Gothic Cottage, at Monken Hadley, Hayes was regaled with Chapman's thoughts and hopes for the new 3-litre Formula.

Ford of Britain's new Vice-President in Charge of Engineering was an American named Harley Copp, and Hayes found in him a racing enthusiast happy to support plans for a Ford-financed Grand Prix engine. Hayes brought Chapman and Copp together to discuss the former's concept of the perfect 3-litre racing engine. When Copp heard of Cosworth's pending intermediate plan to build a four-cylinder F2 engine based on the Ford Cortina cylinder block he was finally converted.

As John Blunsden has described 'From Duckworth's point of view, a two-stage project in which the successful production of a 1.6-litre four-cylinder Formula 2 engine could be followed by a "doubled-up" V8 power unit, with suitable modifications to the cylinder dimensions in order to bring its displacement within the 3-litre limit, made good sense. Most important of all it would mean that the cylinder head – in Duckworth's opinion the key component of any of his competition engines – could first be tested and proven on

the four-cylinder block before it was committed to a V8 . . .'

Of course, this was also very attractive to Ford as their PR people could then highlight the direct link between their production passenger cars and the Grand Prix machinery carrying their company's name.

Another American executive named Stanley Gillen had only been in England for six days as Ford of Britain's new Managing Director when his first meeting of the Ford Policy Committee was convened. It went predictably smoothly until Gillen reached the 'Any Other Business' section of the agenda, whereupon Hayes said: 'Yes, Harley and I would like to do a Grand Prix engine . . .'

The plan was to commit £100,000 minimum to the Chapman/Cosworth project, the Policy Committee voted it through and in the spring of 1966 a tripartite agreement was drafted between the Ford Motor Company, Cosworth Engineering and Keith Duckworth. For a payment by Ford of £100,000, Cosworth and Duckworth agreed to design and develop for Ford both Formula 2 and Formula 1 power units to be known as 'Ford' engines. The interim 1600 cc F2 Cortina-block unit would be known as the FVA – Four-Valve Series 'A' – and from it would be developed, as the contract put it, '. . . a 90-degree V8 3,000 cc engine using cylinder heads basically the same as/or developed from the above FVA suitable to race in International Formula 1 races under the regulations which started in 1966 . . .'

The Formula 1 engines had to be ready for use by May 1967, five engines to be available by 1 January 1968 and such engines would be maintained until 31 December 1968. Crucially, 'The choice of team will be at Ford's discretion, Cosworth being available in an advisory capacity if required'.

In effect, Team Lotus would have exclusive use of the engine in its first season, 1967, but rather to Chapman's dismay Ford would then offer it freely to other 'acceptable' customers from the start of 1968. This was a wise decision, and it

would do more than merely give Ford blanket coverage in Formula 1 racing for the next fifteen years. It would make contemporary Formula 1 both the best-supported and the closest-fought Grand Prix class in racing history. The upshot of all this would also be to make Formula 1 irresistibly attractive to outside sponsors and their interest would change the face of racing as we knew it. The ramifications of that decision to make the DFV generally available were very significant in shaping Formula 1's future character.

This historic initial agreement became effective on 1 March 1966, but Duckworth did not first set pen to paper until 23 June that year. Although the sum of £100,000 had been arrived at more by inspiration than calculation, it proved remarkably accurate, just like the rest of Duckworth's work.

FORMULA 2 THEORY AND . . .

In his initial design for the four-cylinder Formula 2 Type FVA engine, Duckworth had wrestled with the problem of enlarging valve area compared to his preceding 1-litre F2 SCA. The more gas one can persuade into and out of an engine, the more power it can produce from combustion of that gas – the old truism of 'the more you put in, the more you get out' which applies so widely in all our lives.

Restricted by the cylinder wall thickness in the 120E Cortina block, Duckworth could not increase the cylinder bore very much, so to obtain adequate valve area it was necessary to resort to four valves per cylinder. Both BRM and Climax had tried 32-valve V8s during 1964, BRM's failing to come up to expectations while Climax's was quite effective but not spectacularly better than the preceding 16-valver, as it should have been.

Only Honda's 1966 1-litre F2 engine had made really successful use of four valves per cylinder, Duckworth crediting this to their being 'the only people who had managed to get their detail work right; in itself the concept has always been sound, but only if the execution is up to the same standard as . . . a good two-valve layout'. Whereas the best 1-litre Cosworth SCA eight-valver had generated 143 bhp per litre, the 16-valve Honda 'four' was obviously over 150 bhp with its four-valve head.

After careful thought, Duckworth concluded that he should now aim for 200 bhp from a 16-valve four-cylinder 1600. He planned one layout using a pent roof combustion chamber with diametrically opposed inlet and exhaust valves, à la BMW and Repco, although the Repco RB50 head was unknown to him at that time. However, he then abandoned this scheme as it further demanded three spark plugs per cylinder for adequate ignition, while the inlet and exhaust systems on a V8 version would have been a major source of grief, as Repco would discover . . .

Consequently the FVA F2 unit emerged as a simple crossflow four-cylinder, intakes on the right, exhaust on the left, the narrow included angle between the pairs of valves being 40 degrees, the twin ohc driven by spur gears from the crankshaft nose and the standard Ford camshaft in the block retained to drive the water pump.

Talking to journalist David Phipps about his gas-flow philosophies, the always aggressively articulate Duckworth produced his classic quote: 'I have never believed there is any point in having a gas-flow rig and measuring the flow . . . A hole that looks nice and smooth and has no projections will generally flow easily . . . I would claim that I could arrive at something very close to . . . results from gas-flowing just by putting my finger down the hole and seeing what it feels like!'

He settled for the conventional pent roof combustion chamber and convinced himself that his particular design would burn most of the air he could get into it. The F2 chambers had a volume of 400 cc per cylinder; in the F1 V8 these would be reduced to 375 cc per cylinder since capacity per bank then had to be reduced to less than 1500 cc, as opposed to the F2 unit's displacement of just under 1600.

To achieve this reduction, either bore or stroke – or both – had to be decreased, and as the FVA's stroke was relatively long it was shortened for the DFV. This dictated keeping flat pistons apart from shallow valve cut-outs and decreasing the valve angle in the head. Since the F2 unit's combustion on test was clearly very good, Duckworth made this change with some trepidation. However, the valve angle reduction offered other advantages, in that it made the head rather more compact which helped minimize the danger of the V8 growing wider than might be sensible.

. . . FORMULA 1 PRACTICE

The fundamental decision in favour of a V8 had been made at a time when everybody else interested in the 3-litre Formula seemed to regard 12 cylinders as an absolute minimum. BRM had their fiendish H16-cylinder and there were even rumours of Honda building upon their multi-cylinder motor cycle expertise with a 24-cylinder! Repco, however, were demonstrating what could be achieved from the torque of even a humble sohc V8, while Cosworth had the valuable experience beneath their belts of having achieved over 140 bhp per litre from their four-cylinder F2 engine at a time when the 1500 cc Formula 1 V8 manufacturers were very pleased with themselves when they approached 150 bhp per litre.

Duckworth's train of thought further justified the choice of a V8 rather than V12 on grounds of greater mechanical efficiency, with fewer moving parts to foster friction loss, while in any case a V8 promised to be lighter than a V12. An advantage in mechanical efficiency also promised better fuel consumption.

However, Cosworth's four-cylinder experience had also proved that a simplified exhaust system could be achieved by adopting a flat-plane crankshaft. This crankshaft formation was a notorious vibration source in V8 engines. Duckworth admits he 'was not entirely happy about using a flat crank on such a relatively large engine', but when calculations suggested a 'maximum transverse shake . . . plus or minus 3-thou; we felt that this

should not be too serious . . . and it would certainly simplify the exhaust system'. For lightness' sake an alloy block was necessary, which at that stage of metallurgical development meant using some form of cylinder liner, since attempts to develop linerless engines in which the pistons ran direct in alloy blocks had not met with great success; the Repco V8 née Oldsmobile F85 being but one.

The bore spacing necessary to fit wet liners would have meant lengthening the block, unless bore dimension was considerably reduced from that proven on the FVA. Working with his detail draughtsman Mike Hall (whose BRM experience had included their F2 and prototype H16 units), Duckworth opted to retain the FVA bore. The stroke was decreased from 2.72 to 2.55 in., while con-rod length was then increased to avoid an unacceptable rise in piston acceleration which would bring greater stress and wear in its wake. Ordinary iron cylinder liners were adopted, sealed by two 'O'-rings at the bottom and by Cooper's mechanical joints at the top.

One great problem with a 90-degree V8 is how to achieve decent chassis design when such a square-cut lump has to be installed in the rear. Because of this it seemed logical to adopt BRM's (P83 H16) and Ferrari's (1500 cc flat-12 Tipo 1512) approach and to make the engine serve as a stressed structural member, mounted rigidly on the rear of a truncated chassis forepart, with the rear suspension carried either on the engine or gearbox, or on subframes attached to them.

Duckworth worked closely with Colin Chapman and Lotus chassis designer Maurice Phillippe on this, and they decided to mount the unit rigidly via two bolts passing through an alloy bottom beam at the engine's front end, with two additional strap plates on the cam-covers bolted into the upper hips of the monocoque. The intended Lotus 49 tub's side pontoons were only 9 in. apart at the rear, traditionally being matched to Jim Clark's physique at this crucial point. So the two lower bolts in that DFV front beam were spaced at 9 in. centres. Once Duckworth had drawn the cam-box mounting plate positions, the rear face of a suitable matching monocoque could be defined by these four mounting points.

Because the engine would expand as it heated up while running, they then had to ensure that the monocoque rear bulkhead would not be stretched by this expansion. Therefore, all shear was taken on the bottom mountings, while the two thin top strap plates linking the cam-covers to the monocoque pick-ups allowed 15-thou or so engine expansion without significant stress. Tyrrell designer Derek Gardner was not alone when he enthused about this mounting system as recently as April 1985, unequivocally describing it as 'a truly wonderful way of mounting a racing engine' allowing the car designer enormous freedom thereafter. Very hefty cam-carriers were provided in order to transmit chassis loads into the heads from the cam-cover strap plates and thence into the block without risking tappet seizure through carrier distortion. What's more, metal-to-metal joints were used throughout this assembly, since the loss of friction within the joints through use of paper gaskets might have allowed torsional loads to disturb the engine assembly.

From an early stage it was clear that little fuel could be carried alongside this engine due to its overall width including the low-swept exhaust system. This meant that all fuel would have to be carried within the monocoque forward chassis, and if wheelbase was not then to be exaggerated it was vital to minimize engine length.

This demanded that all ancillaries like the water and oil pumps should be fitted low down on the sides of the engine under the exhaust manifold curls, and items like the distributor should go on top within the vee. With an engine now strictly four cylinders long, a large-capacity fuel tank could be sandwiched in the rear of the monocoque between cockpit and engine, ideally situated near the car's overall centre of gravity, providing constant weight distribution as the fuel load diminished.

Duckworth's detail design showed equally deep thinking. He smoothed the crankcase's internal surfaces for aerodynamic efficiency, reasoning that since the crankshaft bob-weights would be rotating at some 170 mph it was reasonable to assume they would sweep the air within the crankcase round with them, so it might as well be given as smooth a passage as possible.

The flywheel was kept as small as possible to help keep the centre of gravity low, and this meant a special tooth form for the starter ring. It was impossible to mount a starter motor capable of meshing with this tiny flywheel alongside the crankcase, so it was turned about-face and bracketed onto the gearbox casing, driving forward to the starter ring. In any case it was useful to place the starter motor weight – and believe me it was a very heavy lump on these cars – as far back as possible.

Structurally, all major castings were in 'LM 8 WP' heat-treated aluminium alloy with cover castings in magnesium.

As in all previous Cosworth engines, the crankshaft was in nitrided 'M 40B' steel. Big-end bearing diameters were identical to the FVA's, which themselves matched Ford's production four-cylinder range although narrowed to minimize the block offset because Duckworth considered the production engine bearing areas excessive.

Main bearing diameter was enlarged to increase in-section overlap between the big-ends and mains, and to enhance crankshaft stiffness. Piston and con-rod design was along FVA lines, while the cam-drive geartrain of 14 spurs up the front of the unit incorporated a quill shaft on the crank nose, first found essential on the SCA. An injection/ignition pack slotted into the engine's vee, comprising a very heavy small-capacity alternator integrated with the distributor, injection pump and injection metering unit.

The bottom half of the engine carried the main bearing caps integral with the sump, enabling it to become a very strong beam in its own right, happy to transmit chassis loads.

In making such a short, flat-face engine, ancillary mounting was strictly confined to the sides and the vee. Only within the vee did this cause a major problem, as Duckworth had to leave more space there than he might have liked for that tubby alternator housing.

Mike Hall detailed the various pumps, metering unit and alternator assembly, Duckworth most of what remained. He worked mainly at home, often 15 hours a day, liaising with Hall and Mike Costin at the factory in St James' Mill Road, Northampton, one day a week. This went on for some nine months, manufacture then beginning of the first prototype DFV engine.

On its initial run in one of Cosworth's test cells, the DFV sounded terrific, hard and crisp as a Grand Prix engine should, but it pumped out its oil. The heads were drowning in lubricant which refused to drain down into the sump to be scavenged and pumped on around the system. A temporary fix was achieved by cutting holes in the cam-covers and tacking on collector boxes with external drain pipes to return this excess oil to the sump. The engines wore this system in the Lotus 49's first few races. It enabled the engine to breathe adequately, whereupon the Cosworth dyno recorded 408 bhp – Colin Chapman's 400 horsepower target had been met.

DEVELOPMENT TRIALS AND ERRORS

During one early dyno run a tooth snapped off one of the timing gears and on strip-down the gear bearings themselves showed distress. Clearly some strange torsional vibration was upsetting the geartrain, a problem which would afflict Cosworth for some time to come. Vibration was in fact a major characteristic of the new V8. Much of the rotating and reciprocating weight had been balanced out to minimize main bearing loads, but this dropped the natural frequency vibration period, which drivers would now have to pass through primarily at 8600 rpm, then secondarily at 9600 rpm.

This effect is the engine man's equivalent of out-

CAR
ATTACHMENT
POINTS

SUSPENSION
ATTACHMENT
POINTS

SCAVENGE
PUMP

TO MAIN
GALLERY

PRESSURE
PUMP

TO COOLER
& TANK

FROM
TANK

TO
RADIATOR

WATER
FROM
RADIATOR

of-balance front wheels. Any owner-driver of a 105E Ford Anglia will remember how desperately prone those pressed-steel wheels were to going out of balance, if indeed you had bothered to have them balanced at all. At certain speeds out-of-balance vibrations would build up which could set the steering wheel juddering uncontrollably in your hands. You could accelerate through it or brake out of it. Just imagine that same effect set loose within the DFV as the crankshaft passed through those critical speeds and you have some appreciation of what its main bearings and structure had to withstand.

Where the cam-drive geartrain torsional was concerned it seemed to pose only a long-term problem. The original test engine had completed several hours of trouble-free running before that tooth failure, far more than Grand Prix distance, so it was not deemed necessary to delay the engine's public debut.

While Cosworth were completing their first 'FORD'-lettered Formula 1 V8s, Team Lotus at Hethel near Norwich were completing two prototype Type 49 monocoque cars. Initial track testing was conducted by Mike Costin at Hethel aerodrome and Snetterton, before team driver Graham Hill was trusted to take over.

As is now genuine racing legend, the DFV powered Jim Clark to win the 1967 Dutch GP first time out in the new Lotus 49, after team-mate Hill had not only started from pole position, but also led convincingly in the early stages and set fastest race lap before being sidelined by cam-gear failure.

Post-race strip-down of Clark's victorious engine revealed that it too had stripped a cam-drive gear tooth. This was serious. One cure might have been to dispense with the geartrain and adopt instead internal-toothed rubber belts, but they would have compromised the direct mounting of engine to monocoque. Therefore the geartrain itself was tackled after various expedients had been tried with variable, and never complete, success. An analysis of the cam-lobe forms and their dynamic interaction across banks finally revealed very rapid torque reversals affecting the geartrain. Consequently new cam shapes were designed which minimized the torque demanded to turn the cam itself against the valve springs and to accelerate the valvegear. This modified cam form was to survive throughout the engine's competitive life although its initial purpose was purely to reduce shock loads on the cam-drive gears and so give them some chance of survival.

Still the geartrain failures occurred, despite improvements in gear design, strength, and support, until Duckworth designed a hub for the second compound gears which incorporated 12 slender quill shafts which could wind up under load to cushion gear and bearings against those still-savage torque reversals. The first of these cushioned compound gears was fitted in 1971, and despite occasional failures when run in conjunction with 'the more savage cams', or breakage of the gears below it due to crankshaft torsionals, geartrain trouble thereafter became effectively a thing of the past.

John Blunsden records that the scatter of geartrain trouble between different engines was very high. During a period when every other Cosworth runner seemed to be in constant timing gear trouble, Jochen Rindt's Lotus engine used the same set of gears and bearings in five races trouble-free! Duckworth told John they could never discover why certain engines 'would', while

These Autocar *sketches from when the DFV was unveiled in June '67 show* (top) *wide-spaced rear suspension pick-ups and, at front, engine mounts. V8 was stressed to accept chassis loads by that horizontal diaphragm linking cylinder banks and cast box sections along sides of sump.* Centre: *Oil scavenge and pressure pump flow was designed to maintain both banks' lubricant at even temperature.* Bottom: *Water system with pumps neatly packaged tight against crankcase.*

other engines 'wouldn't'.

The DFV undeniably had plenty of useable power throughout its life and this was particularly marked upon its introduction in 1967 for Team Lotus's use and in 1968 for other customer teams. But first-time Cosworth drivers were often caught out by the shattering way its power came in with an abrupt bang between 6000 and 6500 rpm. This made life difficult in the wet, and 1968 was a season studded with very wet races . . .

Initially, in 1967 Cosworth attempted to introduce artificially smooth throttle response by devising a cam control in which the throttle moved slowly through the first part of its opening, then very rapidly through the latter part. Tyre widths and sticky compounding progressed dramatically early in the DFV's career, and the proliferation of aerodynamic aids then added so much traction that the early embarrassment of too abrupt a power curve was minimized and the progressive throttle device was never used in anger. Duckworth in fact adopted closing springs on the injection system slides which went over-centre during their motion to provide a very high closing force, while relaxing tension as the slides were opened.

The Achilles heel of the DFV, as in so many racing engines, has been in its valvegear, particularly its valve springs. There is a natural antipathy between savage cam profiles used to gain performance and valve springs demanding adequate life. To give the valve springs a reasonable chance of survival, one trick was to use interference springs whereby the inner coil is a push-fit within the outer coil and the two rub together. Unfortunately this friction between the coils can itself cause damage and break a spring. It is better to reduce surge at source, but this solution essentially remained elusive throughout the DFV's active Formula 1 life. One problem with interference springs is that manufacturing tolerances are difficult to maintain, and different spring pairs often had differing rates of interference and therefore of reliable spring damping.

Towards the end of its frontline career, the DFV was offered with specially coated interference springs designed to prevent the scuffing which can lead to weakness and ultimate breakage.

One classic hiccup in operating DFV engines has been long-term storage of ready-to-run units, in more cases than might be considered comfortable due to F1 teams having engines rebuilt and ready but lacking the funds to pay for them upon collection as Cosworth and its licensed rebuilders normally required.

During their storage, unless they were turned regularly by hand, these engines would often damage their valve springs by keeping them trapped too long under compression. Almost inevitably, this would result in an early valve spring breakage soon after the engine had been installed and started up. If a valve dropped in, a very expensive shattering bang would ensue.

It was in 1979, after long investigation into the valve surge problems had yielded little of great value, that Duckworth initiated desmodromic, mechanically closing valvegear researches. By this time Cosworth were deeply involved in other programmes, particularly production of 2.65-litre DFV-derived DFX turbocharged V8s for American oval-track racing. When the research team encountered major problems (notably with their desmodromic valvegear test rig), the idea went onto the back burner and eventually was shelved.

From the beginning, the DFV's spark plugs had been buried deep within tubes cast into the heads, and cooling water had to divert around these tubes on its way to cool the adjacent exhaust valve areas. This obstructed coolant flow, and one day a damaged head was sectioned and Cosworth's trouble-shooters discovered that the cast-in water passage was totally blocked in places, creating local hot-spots. To prevent this happening in other engines the head castings were from that time bored out and thinwall plug sleeves were inserted which both provided better coolant clearance and enabled the interior of the waterway castings to be easily inspected to ensure

they were as drawn. These cylinder head plug tubes have since been a feature of all later DFVs.

Also from the beginning, Cosworth have had customer teams complaining to them that their DFV engines use/lose/overheat their oil. Cosworth have usually retorted in words of few syllables that it is the team's own silly fault, because many have consistently refused to use Cosworth's approved oil system. Engine manufacturers are much the same the world over.

Much more recently, when Porsche developed their TAG Turbo V6 engine in a *Typ 956* endurance car containing an oil tank the size of a self-respecting dustbin, they turned to McLaren on their first running of the engine in an F1 chassis and stated flatly: 'You've got a problem with your oil tank', because the engine threw out all its oil in three or four laps of Silverstone. In fact any more effective tank would have been quite impossible to install in a single-seater chassis, and the TAG engine's real problem was in its internal breathing, just like the DFV 16 years earlier. Since 1961, Formula 1 regulations have banned addition of oil during the race, so oil consumption problems are of crucial significance.

The first DFVs' steel liners had an unacceptably high rate of wear. Experiments with Tuftrided steel liners were unsuccessful. The problem was then exacerbated in 1970-71 by the adoption of induction airboxes which inevitably scooped in all manner of debris along with nice fresh air, and promptly dumped it into the rearmost cylinders, scoring the liners and causing rapid failure thereafter.

Special molybdenum-sprayed spheroidal graphite iron liners were tried, but they cost power and regretfully Duckworth reverted to cast-iron liners, which were tough as the proverbial old boot but which would shatter rather than merely dent or distort in the event of major mechanical failure from within, or from above, as when that perennial valve-surge problem might set a valve free.

Eventually Mahle Nikasil aluminium liners appeared, which at a stroke not only cured the oil consumption problems, but also saved 8 lb weight overall, reduced the number of expensive full engine rebuilds and obviated the need for lapping-in and fine-finishing rebuild time using less advanced liners.

Through the '70s Cosworth became the biggest supplier of forged pistons in the UK, having initially installed their own drop-forge to protect and supply their own requirements since the major piston manufacturer Hepworth & Grandage had opted out of the forged piston business as the British motor cycle engine industry finally laid down and died.

The DFV piston was changed in detail early on, but persistent oil control problems led Cosworth to study ring performance and occasionally question their supplier's consistency of manufacture. Formula 1 engine life is such that they are never adequately run in, and original manufacturing accuracy and tolerance is all-important if they are to give of their best. In 1983 Duckworth told John Blunsden 'the reason that we are not in ring trouble with the Nikasil liners is probably that the abrasiveness of the liner from new is such that it rapidly corrects any ring geometry imperfections!'

In its earliest days the DFV crankshaft caused much heartache. The original shafts were machined from bar, later they were forged, then forged from better material, with close scrutiny maintained of material cleanliness. This has always been a bugbear for serious Formula 1 constructors who too often find that their suppliers neither understand nor appreciate how vital material quality must be . . . not only to race success, but more vitally to driver safety.

Early on, Cosworth had a failure connected with the way in which the core plugs had been inserted to block the crank's internal drillings, and so an alternative plugging method was adopted. Then in 1970 came the celebrated 'bad batch' of Cosworth DFV crankshafts which had such a literally shattering effect upon many teams' hopes.

The shafts were toughened by the nitriding

Above: *Original neat Lotus 49-DFV installation impressed everyone. Note outside water rail from nose radiator, top of Lucas fuel-injection pump safe in its monocoque tunnel just ahead of lower radius rod pick-up, oil filter behind white Sperex VHT-painted exhausts. Right: Airbox era – here attached to Brabham BT34's DFV, 1971.*

process and then finish ground, and it was during this finish grinding process that somebody enthusiastically ground clean through the nitride-toughened upper surface of the crank in the corner of a radius. An entire batch of shafts was utterly ruined in this way, all breaking or cracking while on the dyno. The batch should have carried Cosworth through 1970 but they had to be scrapped, a replacement batch took several months to come through so Cosworth had to make do and mend wherever possible with old engines and salvaged cranks.

In 1977 Duckworth experimented with magnesium engines, having dabbled earlier with magnesium blocks in his company's experimental four-wheel drive Formula 1 car of 1969. Unfortunately, the main bearing housings were found to expand considerably in these units.

Duckworth wanted to restrict oil flow through the engine since it threatened to overwhelm the scavenge capacity of the pumps and lead to churning as the crankshaft dipped into excess oil accumulating within the sump. Consequently the crankshafts were redrilled to offer lower main bearing pressure. Whereas earlier engines had run never less than 85 psi oil pressure, the redrilled 'low-pressure crankshafts' now ran around 52 psi, and nearly all existing DFVs in serious use were converted at their subsequent rebuilds. After this, bottom-end bearing failures in the DFV became virtually a thing of the past except where other lubrication system failures or major leaks had occurred.

Meanwhile, Cosworth had sidestepped that original 1967 cam-box oil drainage problem and its stop-gap cure with those ugly external boxes and pipes by fitting an air pump. It lifted air and combustion 'blow-by' products – gas forced down the cylinder past the rings – from the bottom of the engine up into the heads, but this also transferred a lot of oil in the same direction.

The air pump was then employed as an additional oil pump, and now the total output of both scavenge pumps and the air pump was piped back to the oil tank. This ran the entire engine at an atmospheric depression, and what had formerly been a conventional breather pipe now served to draw air *in* from outside. Unfortunately this system then fed so much air mixed with the oil back to the oil tank that the tank's oil/air separation systems were overwhelmed, and some cars now blew up their engines soon after blowing all their oil overboard through the oil tank breathers!

The cure this time was to design enlarged-capacity Roots-type scavenge pumps complete with air separators, which drew air through the heads and pressured it to force-drain oil into the sump. The separation systems then split air from oil, blowing air from the top of the tank to atmosphere, while the oil was circulated to the cooler matrices and on round the system for another exciting ride through the pumps.

Ever-increasing cornering speeds and rising lateral G-forces posed increasing problems in the DFV's later life as the wing-car era developed from 1978, and ever-larger scavenge pumps were adopted to slurp away oil before it could accumulate on one side of the sump or the other under lateral G. The air separator itself also came in for considerable development. The in-drawn mixture of oil and air was separated by being centrifuged, the heavy oil being hurled outwards leaving the air in the centre. Initially the oil was thrown against a stationary canister wall, from which it tended to splash back and would froth. It was redesigned with a rotating outer wall travelling at much the same speed as the centrifuging oil, greatly diminishing the splash-back effect, separating the oil and air more effectively and also weighing less and being more compact than its predecessor.

Ignition systems originally used the dreaded Lucas-OPUS contact-breaker system to which this author had a great deal of less than happy exposure when involved in rebuilding Lotus 49 'R3' during 1982-83. One DFV specialist contacted for help at that time asked, 'What system is it you're having trouble with?' 'Lucas-OPUS', I replied.

DIANA STEVENS

The ultimate 3-litre F1 'Cossy' was the Cosworth-Ford (Ford preferred Ford-Cosworth) DFY V8, drawn by Diana Stevens when first announced in 1983. This shows revised heads, modified valvegear, block, drive-geartrain etc, and pound-for-pound still arguably the world's most powerful 3-litre atmospheric-induction engine.

'Aah well, you'd better make yourself comfortable then, because you're in for a looong, haaard, frustrating night . . .', he said, and he was absolutely right.

The OPUS pick-up was replaced early on by a magnetic trigger but heat build-up around the trigger site within the vee affected the pick-up magnet and it would all go awry.

The DFV originally required a rev-limiter to defend its conservative 9000 rpm safe limit. This was an electro-mechanical system, the mechanicals suffering terribly under the DFV's characteristic fierce vibration.

Capacitor ignition provided a great leap forward, led by Walter Scherag of Germany with their Contactless system first adopted by Tyrrell. It enabled use of surface discharge plugs with their greater heat range. The immense energy of the capacitor ignition's short-duration spark prompted drivers to comment on improved pick-up from corners although this improvement was quite impossible to quantify on the dyno. Monaco was tailor-made to show this ignition at its best.

Magneti Marelli from Italy had been anxious to break in on the DFV market and they produced a capacitor discharge system suitable for the DFV, as did Lucas of Britain, abandoning their now obstructive policy of only providing the racing world with adaptations of equipment already in commercial passenger car production. The amplifier box necessary for 'my' Lotus 49, for example, was identical to that used in the Jaguar XJS V12, right down to the same part number.

Where fuel systems are concerned, early 1967 problems were caused by dirt blocking the filters and slashing fuel pressure. Initial suspicion that the fuel bag material was breaking up saw larger filters inserted, and then a mod was made to the in-line filter 'O'-ring which was found not to seat satisfactorily and therefore allowed debris to pass through.

Initially the Lotus 49 and its imitators used an electric high-pressure pump to start the engine. A mechanical pump took over once the engine was running to build up to full power. These were subsequently replaced by a combined electro-mechanical pump incorporating a tiny electric motor and a one-way clutch assembly enabling the motor to drive the pump as long as the engine was running

at lower rpm than the motor in question. Once engine speed exceeded motor speed, mechanical drive took over.

In response to demand from ground-effects car designers in 1980, Cosworth introduced a new range of so-called 'slimline auxiliaries', moving everything as far forward as possible into the shadow of the car's monocoque out of the path of underbody air.

During the 1967 season Team Lotus's drivers began using 9500 rpm with relative impunity on their first DFVs, and only in face of Ferrari's new flat-12 cars in 1970 did serious DFV power development commence. Until that time it had offered the best all-round power/reliability/consumption/installation package since its inception in Formula 1; only now – in relative terms – did it have to begin to work hard for its living.

Ports were enlarged, trumpets shortened, revs and power rose. Subsequent developments included detail mods to pistons and connecting rods, one major machining change on the bolt-seat area of the con-rod caps alone greatly reducing stress at that point and dramatically improving component life. The original forged steel con-rods were themselves superseded by a vacuum remelted fat forging. The requirement for high revs led to detail investigation of big-end bolts and adoption of modified thread therein, spreading the loads over more thread surface.

As the DFV's power output was forced ever higher through the late-Seventies by the attentions of Ferrari, and then the emergent turbo engines, ever-increasing attention had to be paid to relieve stress concentrations in every component of the faithful old DFV. Nevertheless, Cosworth kept abreast of the problem and, with the chassis designers' help, abreast of all competition until 1982 when the magnificent 15-year win-

Top: *End of the line – for the 155th time a Cosworth-Ford V8 engine wins a World Championship Grand Prix as Alboreto acknowledges the chequered flag ending the 1983 Detroit GP, appropriately enough on Ford Motor Company's home ground. Tyrrell 012-DFY was just enough machine to do the job that day.*
Above: *Martin Brundle in the Cosworth-Ford DFY V8-powered Tyrrell 012 which through 1985 became Formula 1's last 3-litre V8 contender, culminating in the German GP, in which he finished tenth, then the Austrian GP, for which he failed to qualify.*

ning run of the DFV V8 engine finally reached the end of the road. For Cosworth Engineering, the greatest compliment that can be paid them is that they put a Grand Prix racing engine into quantity production and kept it at the top of the class for much more than a decade. The engine spun off variants which won the 24-hour race at Le Mans in addition to other, lesser sports car endurance events, and also came to dominate high-speed oval-track racing in the USA.

Emerson Fittipaldi's works Lotus 72 notched the DFV's 50th Grand Prix victory in Spain in 1973, while Jody Scheckter's Wolf took the engine past the 100 mark at Monaco in 1977. It was fitting that Elio de Angelis's works Lotus should just scrape home by mere inches to win the 1982 Austrian GP from Keke Rosberg's hard-charging

Williams-DFV, to achieve the engine's 150th *Grande Epreuve* victory, the last one that project catalyst Colin Chapman would see.

With that victory the faith which he had shown in Keith Duckworth and his fine company way back in 1965-66 had been more than merely repaid.

At the end of that season, despite the failure of fairly concentrated efforts to have the 2.0 equivalency factor changed between atmospherically aspirated and turbocharged F1 engines, there was still sufficient demand for Cosworth to embark upon a major modification of the V8 engine.

Throughout the major part of the DFV's life, Cosworth's licensed outside engine rebuilders, like John Judd's Engine Developments concern in Rugby, Nicholson-McLaren at Hounslow and Hesketh at Towcester, had built their own preferred tweaks into their engines, often aiming to improve cam profiles compared to Cosworth's age-old standard 'DA1' design.

Now, going into 1983, Cosworth offered an experimental design known as the 'DA12', offering 0.460 in. lift compared to the DA1's standard 0.410 in., with slightly steeper slope angle to make the valves open more rapidly. This DA12 went into production and some of the outside specialists then switched from their own designs back to the Cosworth product.

In Northampton, Keith Duckworth now re-examined the aerodynamic performance or

'windage' within the DFV crankcase in order to improve oil scavenging still further and reduce power loss. He found that oil was not being collected as intended and when redesigned collection slots were provided oil collection improved markedly, releasing several extra horsepower.

In parallel with this development, a new short-stroke version of the V8 engine to be known as the DFY was being designed. Two DFY programmes were in hand. To accommodate the largest possible valve area the 90 mm bore of the derivative 3.95-litre DFL long-distance sports car engine was adopted, and this was combined with a piston stroke of 58.8 mm for 2994 cc.

The initial DFYs emerged using cylinder heads broadly similar to DFV practice although recast to a new and distinctive design. Inlet and exhaust ports were enlarged and the head design enabled use of the 1.25 in. exhaust valves as fitted in later DFVs, but now the inlet valve size was also increased to 1.42 in.

These early DFYs used 0.432 in. lift 'BD4' inlet camshafts and 'DA10', 0.410 in. lift exhausts, valve angle being 16 degrees. With the latest head and crankcase mods the ultimate DFV version matched this initial DFY. The DFY added a shorter exhaust system and intake trumpets, and new magnesium inlet manifold and water pump plus various head modifications reduced overall weight from the 351 lb of the definitive DFV to only 307 lb, which wasn't bad with some 520 bhp available.

The first four DFYs were delivered to McLaren and the Williams team just in time for the 1983 French GP. The second DFY head design should have been available in time for Monaco that year. This was a completely new and entirely different design saving even more weight while offering greater long-term development potential. Cosworth's newly enlarged development team concluded that certain advantages were available from a more compact combustion chamber shape than was possible with the basic DFY's short-stroke dimensions and the 16-degree valve angle.

Consequently this second DFY head disposed its inlet valves at 10 degrees and its exhausts at 12.5 degrees. This narrow-angle DFY head also featured an integral instead of separate cam-carrier, contributing to a further 15 lb saving in weight, penetrating the 300 lb barrier for the first time and achieving a record low of 292 lb.

Valve diameters became 36.5 mm inlets and 32 mm exhausts, seating on bronze inserts and using inverted bucket tappets. A new forged-steel flat-plane crankshaft was employed; its shorter throw and the use of four instead of eight counterweights saved much weight. New enlarged-bore aluminium pistons were carried on 3 mm longer H-section machined forged con-rods. Each new head assembly saved some 3.5 kg (7.6 lb) over the DFV's. Ports were enlarged and revised and, still using Lucas injection and ignition, the power curve was improved virtually throughout the range, as was torque. The old torque surge around 6500 rpm was no more and now the DFY offered useable power right from 6000 rpm to the unchanged limit of 11,300 rpm. The reduced stroke cut piston speed and acceleration, minimized valvegear inertia and promoted quicker valve opening. Greater efficiency reduced the DFY's fuel consumption increase relative to gains in power and torque.

Although the short-stroke DFV and the definitive narrow-angle valved DFY both became known as 'DFYs', only seven of these true engines were built (for Tyrrell). This number was reduced to six as late as the 1985 German GP (the British V8's last World Championship race) when one blew up and was deemed to be beyond salvage.

During the DFV/DFY engines' long reign in Formula 1, some 382 of the V8s had been built.

Tyrrell's win at Detroit that year was Cosworth's 155th at World Championship level. The 3-litre engine which had revolutionized Formula 1 by opening it up to so many specialist constructors and teams had finally reached the end of the road but, as will be seen, its larger-capacity derivatives would continue to maintain bulk, if not quality, within the Grand Prix class.

Chapter 4

THE LOTUS-COSWORTH FORD DFV TYPE 49 1967-70

While Keith Duckworth, Mike Costin, Mike Hall and the Cosworth Engineering men were working on Ford's new Grand Prix engine, Team Lotus at Potash Lane, Hethel, in darkest Norfolk were finalizing detail design of their beautifully integrated Type 49 car intended to carry the new engine.

Lotus had made do through 1966 first with nimble little 2-litre V8 cars using specially modified Climax and BRM engines left over from the 1500 cc Formula. They had 3-litre BRM H16 engines on order which BRM's Chief Engineer Tony Rudd had designed to be attached to the rear closing bulkhead of a truncated monocoque forward nacelle in similar manner to the forthcoming DFV. Even earlier, the Type 39 Lotus designed by Maurice Phillippe to carry the still-born flat-16 Climax engine in 1965 would have used something close to this system, although that engine would have been steadied by aviation-style perforated angle-beams on either side.

There were two distinct Lotus monocoque chassis made for BRM's H16 engines. One was the Type 42 intended for the still-born 4.2-litre Indianapolis engine, and the other 'our' Type 43 for 3-litre Formula 1. Both used what was known at that time as 'full monocoque' construction, in that the stressed-skin scuttle sections completely encircled the driver's legs, while there was also a complete 360-degree stressed-skin fuel tank section behind his shoulders. The Formula 1 car was handicapped by the unreliability and gearchange difficulties which afflicted the BRM engine, until the US GP at Watkins Glen in October 1966, where Jim Clark's mechanical sensitivity actually managed to nurse the thing to the finish in first place using the BRM works team's spare H16 engine after Lotus's own had broken conclusively in practice.

The 43s were last driven in anger by Clark and his new team-mate Graham Hill in the 1967 South African GP. Two-litre V8s were used at Monaco and then came the Dutch GP at Zandvoort on 4 June 1967 and the stunning debut of the new DFV-powered Lotus 49s.

Colin Chapman had specified 'a simple car which wouldn't give us any problems, so we could sort out the engine' and it emerged as a very simple, essentially twin-boom, monocoque fuselage in general Type 42/43 style. There were full 360-degree stressed sections in the scuttle and behind the cockpit. At the front there was a rectangular footbox built around suspension-supporting square-tube frames. The centre tank's sloping forward-bulkhead formed the driver's seat back, while the tub terminated in that tank's rear closing plate, against which the fully stressed new engine snuggled up close.

This tub was skinned in 18-gauge L72 Alclad aluminium-alloy sheet shaped over internal mild-steel bulkheads to which the skins were riveted. The side booms carried circular access hatches on the outer scuttle sides, while large indented hatches in the cockpit inner skins gave the drivers elbow room and opened onto the internal tank space into which 15-gallon FPT rubber fuel bags could be inserted, then 'poppered' into position and piped up.

These two side tanks drained through non-return valves into a 10-gallon capacity centre tank behind the driver. Fuel pick-up was from a pot in this tank's base, which topped up with fuel from the side cells as the car accelerated, fuel surge in the side bags washing through one-way valves into the centre tank.

A tiny circular access plate on top of the scuttle opened onto the pedal assembly for service and adjustment, while ahead of the footbox – which contained the steering rack – there was a vee-planform oil tank attached by rubber bungees, and a light tubular subframe supporting what by modern standards was an immensely heavy brass radiator with twin cores, one for water, one for oil.

A detachable glass-fibre nose cone, swept well down hopefully to minimize lift, clothed this area and was the only detachable body panel in the piece, the rear-mounted engine being left entirely naked and unashamed. Hot air exiting the radiator was deflected by the shape of the oil tank out through the front suspension cut-outs. The underside of the tub was stepped to form pipeways on both sides for oil and water feed to the engine, although the large-diameter water return pipe was completely external, slung high on the left-side of the tub.

Suspension accorded with familiar Lotus practice, using robust fabricated top rocker arms to actuate inboard coil-spring/damper units tucked well out of the airstream each side of the footbox. A fabricated lower link was jointed to a radius rod leading from an inboard pick-up buried well back on the hull. New cast uprights supported thick ventilated brake discs mounted well inboard of the Lotus cast-magnesium wheels and thus exposed to direct airflow. Anti-dive geometry was built into this suspension system.

James Allington's artistry X-rays the first pair of Lotus 49s built in 1967, later cars from chassis 'R3 replacing the round scuttle-top hatch shown here with a rectangular type. Note also original heavily vented brake discs, shortly to be replaced by solids, and ignition units on tray above gearbox, also soon re-sited within engine vee. The ZF transaxle-cheek stiffening plates shown were fitted from the British GP. The bumper bars protruding from the gearbox tail-plate which were necessary only to make the tuned-length exhaust overhang legal have been omitted, so this is actually an illegal F1 Lotus. However, in 1967 serious protests were unheard of, a 'quiet word' being order of the day.

Top: *Colin Chapman and Jimmy Clark discuss their new toy at Zandvoort '67.* Above: *The object of their conversation, the Lotus 49, was merely a simple trouble-free 'bracket' to carry engine and suspension, fuel and driver. The external oil-drain boxes necessary on the earliest DFVs are visible on that right-side exhaust cam-box. Engine comprises rear of chassis structure, supporting gearbox and rear suspension.*

At the rear, triangulated tubular frames provided inboard pick-ups on the cylinder heads, with a cross-beam offering lower mounts bolted beneath a tailor-made, very light but uprated ZF 5DS12 five-speed and reverse transmission. This incorporated elegant sliding-spline joints within its output shafts on each side. Colin enthused about how 'ZF did us a beautiful job on those'. Others connected with Team Lotus were less sure . . .

Suspension location featured the usual top links, reversed lower wishbones, twin radius rods feeding drive and braking torques into the monocoque's rear corners, and an anti-roll bar. The inclined outboard-mounting coil/damper units were ahead of the axle, and the massive brake calipers were behind it, front and rear, clasping those thick ventilated discs.

As always, Chapman's touch was evident in the detail. Everywhere there was only just enough car to do the job – there was nothing staggeringly innovative about any part of it. The 49 was never another 25, nor 72, nor 78/79, but Chapman had wanted a simple car sufficient to allow Team to race a brand new untried engine, and this was it.

Ford had sensibly been wary of bad publicity from making too much promotional fuss too soon before the engine had proved itself, so the DFV's introduction was muted, without any great razzmatazz.

The first of the five V8s planned for Team that season was handed over on 25 April 1967, two days after completion and five months after commencement of manufacture. The original target debut date of 7 May, for the Monaco GP, was postponed, and much more sensibly the two extant Lotus 49s made their classical debut at Zandvoort, as had the Type 25 before them and as would the four-wheel drive Type 63 two years later.

Of course that was a fairytale debut. Hill's pole position practice time was fully 4.2 per cent faster than the existing Zandvoort record, an astonishing margin. By the end of the first race lap Hill's prototype car 'R1' led Brabham's Repco BT24 by some 200 yards, with Clark – who had done little testing since tax considerations kept him out of the UK – finding his feet in 'R2' in sixth place.

After 11 laps Hill's engine suffered its cam-gear failure, and Clark took utter command to win as he pleased.

In some ways this initial brilliant success flattered only to deceive, for Lotus reliability was dreadful through that mid-season. In performance terms, however, the 49-DFVs simply set new standards.

They were to take pole position for the next 11 consecutive Grands Prix, and while Hill often led races in his car it was always team-mate Clark's which would survive to win three more GPs; the British that July, and then, after a long hiatus, the end-of-season US and Mexican events.

While Chapman himself professed delight with ZF's specially tailored gearbox, Duckworth and Costin were unconvinced, judging it to be under-engineered for the job in hand. The French GP on the little Circuit Bugatti at Le Mans saw savage transmission torque reversals engendered by the stop-go racing there, causing casing flexure and crown-wheel and pinion failures which lost the Lotuses a dominant 1-2 lead, Hill's final-drive shattering after 14 laps and Clark's after 23.

The perceived advantage of the ZF transmission had been that it was considerably lighter than the alternative Hewland 'bunch of old mangle-gears', as Colin would affectionately dismiss them, then being used by most of the opposition. The Circuit Bugatti disaster, however, brought immediate ZF modification, with massive cross-bolted side plates being fitted as a temporary (British GP-winning) expedient before ZF came up with entirely redesigned – and inevitably heavier – casings. Thus one advantage over the bunch of old mangle gears was immediately forfeit.

More seriously, the ZF gearboxes had always featured fixed intermediate ratios and final-drives, so ratios could only be changed by near-total strip-down which was both time consuming and ill-advised in the often spartan and dusty race paddocks of those days. Ever since Team had first adopted ZF transmissions with their Type 21 car of 1961, they had taken a selection of ready-assembled 'boxes to each race to have a choice of final-drive and intermediate ratios. With the DFV's abrupt torque characteristics, Team was learning its circuits anew. The disadvantages of the ZF gearboxes could no longer be borne. Early in 1968 Hewland's easily gutted, omni-adjustable quick-ratio-change gearbox was adopted.

The original heavily ventilated brake discs were quickly abandoned since they over-cooled and glazed their brake pads, the pad losing its bite thereafter. Softer pad materials had been tried before thin solid discs offering more consistent temperatures were adopted.

The strength of those tapered front suspension top rocker arms proved suspect and they were strengthened twice, after the British GP and – surprise, surprise! – after the German race over the humps and bumps at the Nürburgring. Hill had led the British race at Silverstone until a rear suspension Allen screw worked loose and fell out, allowing one rear wheel to flop against the top rocker arm. Graham limped into the pits where the suspension link was put back in place and a fresh bolt wound home. After rejoining the race and tearing back through the field, his DFV engine blew up.

He was using a brand new 49, chassis 'R3', which had been frantically built up in an overnight panic after regular car 'R2' had damaged itself severely in practice due to another suspension failure. In the overnight construction panic at Hethel that vital Allen screw could not have been tightened adequately. The driver's comment in the paddock afterwards, 'Yeah – bugger innit', spoke volumes for the patience a World class driver can show when he knows that despite tribulation his is the dominant car of its time.

This third 49, 'R3', differed from its predecessors in that the tightly confined circular scuttle hatch opening onto the pedals in the first two cars had now been replaced by a much larger and more practical rectangular hatch, the side torsion boxes in this area being strengthened to compensate for the larger cut-out by inclusion of two extra internal bulkheads. Their inclusion meant shortening the main pontoon bag tanks, then adding two additional small-capacity bags ahead of these new scuttle bulkheads. All subsequent 49 tubs were built – or rebuilt – to this general structural form, though further modifications were made.

The top-link mount which had given trouble in the Silverstone incident was twice modified to prevent any recurrence of the fixing loss, and rear radius rod pick-ups on the monocoques were also reinforced – I have to say, from personal experience of having overseen restoration of 'R3', very crudely.

At the end of that first season stronger rear suspension subframes were adopted, bolting as they did onto the rear of the DFV engine heads and block.

Money availability has always dictated much of Formula 1 racing's technical development. At the 1967 London Motor Show the Esso oil company confirmed rumours that they were ending their motor racing sponsorship. Esso had been Team Lotus's financial mainstay for many years. Now Chapman's men beat the bushes for a replacement sponsor, and they came up with the Nottingham-based John Player tobacco company. Gold Leaf Team Lotus was born and, following their lead, national-colour Formula 1 racing teams would, apart from Ferrari, become a matter of history.

The fourth Lotus 49, 'R4', appeared for the South African GP opening the 1968 season and Clark promptly won in it to surpass Fangio's career record of 24 *Grande Epreuve* victories, setting the new record at 25. This race saw the first DFV engine appearance in another customer's hands as Ken Tyrrell's Equipe Matra International fielded its driver Jackie Stewart in a hybrid Matra-DFV special, and it initially led the race before Clark went ahead.

Special 2.5-litre versions of the DFV engine, known as the Cosworth-Ford DFW, were made for the Tasman Championship races in New Zealand and Australia from January to March that season, and 49s 'R1' and 'R2' were fitted with these units as 'Type 49T' cars, Clark contesting the entire series while Hill joined him in the Australian events. During their New Zealand tour, the Team mechanics experimented with a

silly idea – taking a scrap section of helicopter rotor blade, and mounting it on the tail of Clark's car to add aerodynamic download . . . Young Gianni Marelli, the Ferrari engineer caring for Chris Amon's Ferrari 246T V6 during that race-series, was fascinated by what most regarded as a Lotus 'try-on' and he photographed the device assiduously from every angle.

On 7 April 1968, Clark was killed in a piddling little Formula 2 race at Hockenheim. His passing marked for many the end of the sporting era of Grand Prix racing. This may well be true by pure coincidence, but from here on it became the highly commercialized big-business promotional 'front' which we know and perhaps simply try to ignore today. Irrespective of anyone's personal prejudice, commercial sponsorship could now support more teams interested in Formula 1 than ever before. The best-funded teams could also indulge in experimentation of a type only previously accessible to major industry.

During the early months of 1968 Team's experience with new-generation, ever wider tread Firestone tyres indicated that a more rearward weight bias would be advantageous. As tyre contact patches increased in size so loadings had decreased. Instead of finding greater traction with wider tyres, drivers found that in other than the most ideal track conditions these lighter-loaded tyres were more prone to slip and slide. The answer was obviously to load them more heavily to compensate. An analogy is to think of the girl wearing stiletto heels whose weight thus concentrated can pierce flooring, whereas the same girl, same weight, in carpet slippers can glide effortlessly across that same surface.

Initially this extra rearward loading was achieved by running the brand new so-called 'B-spec' car 'R5' at the Race of Champions with a huge oil tank wrapped saddle-fashion over its gearbox, carrying a small oil cooler perched on top, thus relieving the nose radiator of oil-cooling duty. Wider deep-cone wheels were fitted to carry the latest-generation Firestone tyres, suspension geometry being altered to suit by the adoption of new rear uprights with less projection above hub level, and lower top radius rod mountings. After this outing the new car was torn down to be comprehensively reworked as the true prototype

Lotus 49B.

Here Chapman and Phillippe lengthened the wheelbase by raking the front suspension arms 3 in. forward to put more load on the car's rear end. To limit rear-wheel toe-steer, tunnels were sunk into the lower rear quarters of the monocoque tub, and the lower rear radius rod pick-ups were resited well forward in them, closer to the car's centre-line axis. At the rear the engine still mounted in its classically simple fashion, while more substantial subframes on the back of it carried the rear suspension, oil tank and Hewland's latest 'bunch of old mangle-gears', the FG400. Now the DFV cylinder heads were relieved of carrying suspension loads direct.

The deep-cone cast-magnesium road wheels had grown from 8 in. to 10 in. wide front rims in the final two races of 1967, and now 12 in. wide fronts became standard with 15 in. diameters. The rear tyres were 15 in. wide across the shoulders and now presented such a major element in the car's overall frontal area that Lotus's traditional frontal area parsimony now seemed futile. Ron Tauranac of Brabham had experimented with vestigial trim tabs and spoilers to improve the handling of his Repco-engined cars at Spa the previous year, and now Chapman and Phillippe had evolved their wedge-elevation Type 56B turbine cars for the continuous high-speed regime of Indianapolis. From this exercise the new Formula 1 Type 49B inherited as near a wedge profile as was possible with a nose-mounted radiator.

The nose cone itself was largely unchanged, but a cuneiform glass-fibre engine and gearbox cowl was now adopted, incorporating a deck-top NACA duct feeding an oil cooler matrix buried beneath. Its expended air then exited through a vent in the cowl's rear transom. Whatever download this tail cowl hopefully imparted was trimmed out by a pair of airfoil-section fins or dive-planes projecting either side of the nose cone, so that the total download now acted about the car's centre of

Fairytale debut – Clark catches an incipient power slide out of the Hunzerug *on his way to winning the 1967 Dutch GP in Lotus 49 'R2, learning all about the new DFV's wicked power characteristics. Note neat cast front uprights and hefty top rocker arms.*

*Graham Hill in the German GPs of 1967 and '68.
Top: 'R3 in the* Karussel, *suspension thoroughly
loaded. Above: 49B 'R5 in GLTL livery '68, also in
the* Karussel, *showing off upright-mounted rear
wing and nose 'foils, swept-forward front
suspension, longer lower-rear radius rods
tunnelled into tub side, and tail-mounted oil tank.
Right: Hill won the '68 Monaco GP in 'R5's debut.*

gravity.

Hill had won the Spanish GP at Jarama in face
of mechanical mayhem amongst meagre opposition to notch the final success of the definitive
original Lotus 49 (actually using prototype/ex-
Tasman chassis 'R1') and now at Monaco in the
rebuilt 49B 'R5' he won another race most notable
for a staggeringly high rate of attrition. His new
team-mate Jack Oliver made an inauspicious
debut by destroying 'R1' early in the race. Back
home the wreck was stripped and rebuilt as a new
49B which would be numbered, in sequence at
that time, 'R9'.

This 'salvage and restore' policy became standard practice at Potash Lane, accounting for the
nine Type 49 'entities' using 12 individual chassis
numbers in their time.

The semi-wedge 49Bs ran two more races only,
as more ambitious aerofoil aids were on the way.
At Spa, where Oliver appeared in brand new 49B
'R6', strutted chassis-mounted rear aerofoil aids
had appeared on Ferrari and Brabham cars, their

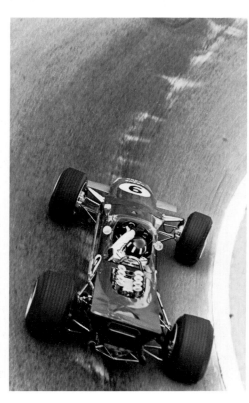

effect balanced by trim vanes on the nose cones.
Chapman was to take this new ploy further than
most, his Lotus 49Bs progressively developing
wings which were taller, wider and more powerful
than the opposition's and his drivers became test
pilots penetrating the unknown as surely as had
the Dukes, Yeagers and Lippitsches of aviation
history.

For the 1968 French GP at Rouen-les-Essarts,
Team emerged with its 49Bs carrying strutted
aerofoils acting direct upon the rear suspension
uprights to convert maximum download into pure
traction. Colin estimated 400 lb download at 150
mph, but in practice Jack Oliver edged his new
49B 'R6' into another car's slipstream on the rush
towards the pits and the winged Lotus simply
slithered away from under him and smashed into
a brick gate-post alongside the track at around
140 mph. The left-hand side of the tub deformed
grotesquely under impact, absorbing the shock
and enabling Oliver to emerge understandably
shaken but unscathed, while the gearbox and both
rear suspensions were torn bodily off the engine.

This incident simultaneously demonstrated the
dangers of toying with aerodynamic forces which
were not yet properly understood, and the
remarkable strength of the modern monocoque
single-seat chassis. We should also remember that
these were pre-seat belt days. Retention harnesses would not become mandatory until the following season, 1969.

These new wings were increasing drive-line
loadings quite dramatically. The introduction of
Firestone's sticky Y-construction, B11-compound
tyres aggravated the problem, removing a vital
element of slippage or drive-line cushioning which
condemned many a halfshaft UJ, and occasionally
the shafts themselves, to traumatic failure.

Heavier shafts were fitted, Mercedes-splined on
the first 49Bs, and a succession of ever-stronger
BRD and Hardy-Spicer joints followed until finally, for the 1968 US and Mexican GPs, the first
Lohr & Bromkamp 'Lobro' plunging CV joints
were adopted. They proved capable both of accepting the DFV engine's savage torque and the
extremes of suspension movement which the
Lotuses required.

Lotus 49B 'R7' appeared new for Rob Walker's
private team at the British GP in July 1968,
where Jo Siffert promptly won with it. The team
had begun the season with ex-49T 'R2' on loan.
Siffert crashed it at Brands Hatch in practice for
the Race of Champions upon its Walker debut. It
was destroyed by fire while being stripped prior to
repair.

In March 1969, strutted airfoil aids doubled up,
fore and aft, acting on both front and rear suspension uprights. Some called this a biplane arrangement, but 'biplane' to me suggests Sopwith
Camels and De Havilland Tiger Moth-style
arrangements with one wing above the other.
Hence my use of the term 'bi-wing' elsewhere in
this volume to describe cars with full-width aerofoils at both front and rear.

Passive mounts, with the wing incidence pre-set
on assembly, or by adjustment when stationary,
were normal; however, in Mexico City in the
Championship decider of 1968 – which Hill and
Lotus won – a feathering rear wing was employed.
This was actuated by a fourth foot pedal to the
left of the clutch, on which the driver would park
his foot along the straight, a Bowden cable feathering the rear aerofoil into a neutral position to
minimize drag. Entering corners the driver would
move his foot onto the clutch, releasing the wing
pedal; bungee cords in tension yanked the aerofoil
down into its maximum attack angle, adding drag
to help slow the car and download to assist traction away from the turn.

At Barcelona, for the Spanish GP on 4 May
1969, the two works 49Bs for Hill and Rindt wore
the largest, tallest, widest wings yet. They were
skinned in aluminium over too few section form-
ers and their mid-span surfaces were unbraced.
The struts themselves had been adequately
stressed to accept compression loads but could not
handle negative loading as the cars 'fell away'
from beneath them over the Montjuich Park cir-

cuit's notorious hump beyond the pits. Both Hill's and Rindt's cars suffered horrendous accidents due to wing collapses at this point. Graham's already once-rebuilt 'R6' would be rebuilt again but Jochen's horribly mangled 'R9', from which he emerged without serious harm, was fit only for the scrapman's skip.

This spectacular incident demanded action from the CSI and in the middle of practice for the very next GP, at Monaco, they announced a peremptory wing ban pending adequate definition of permissible aerodynamic aids. The teams fudged temporary expedient devices to see them through that street race, such as semi-wedge gearbox covers fashioned from the interior panelling of the Team Lotus transporter on the 49Bs, while the nose vanes remained unaffected.

There was a new B-spec car 'R10' there for Hill, Rindt's destroyed 'R9' having made its debut in the South African GP right at the start of the season, where it had been accompanied by another new 49B, 'R11', driven by guest driver Mario Andretti. This car 'R11' would be sold immediately thereafter to American privateer Pete Lovely, who would retain it into the 1990s.

At Monaco, Hill's stand-in team-mate Richard Attwood – deputizing for the injured Rindt – drove an old-style car. After the grievous damage to 'R6' and the loss of 'R9' this was actually a 49T with right-angle front suspension, being chassis 'R8' built specifically for Hill's use in the Tasman Championship the preceding winter. It had just returned from Australia buried under tons of rotting fruit in a delayed freighter, and the Lotus mechanics had hastily burrowed down to it upon their return from Barcelona and prepared it just in time to leave for Monte Carlo!

After the Barcelona upset and the sudden wing regulation change, Hill emerged to win his fifth Monaco GP, his second in a row in a Lotus 49B, the Swiss driver Jo Siffert was third in Rob Walker's private 49B 'R7' and Attwood was fourth in his old nail, having set fastest race lap.

Now at Monaco, relieved of those wing loadings, the 49s had emerged as case-hardened warhorses, strong and robust. For those who would still rubbish Lotus as manufacturers of fragile Grand Prix cars, Monaco 1969 proved a salutary lesson.

As already described, the CSI's new wing regulations were applied in time for the next Grand Prix race, at Zandvoort, imposing limits of 80 cm (31.50 in.) height above the underside of the car and 110 cm (43.31 in.) width overall behind the rear axle line. That Dutch GP witnessed internecine Lotus warfare between Hill and the recovered Rindt, and through the rest of that season the abrasive and outspoken Austrian established himself as much the faster of the two. The season saw some terrific battles between his Lotus 49B and the dominant World Championship-winning Matra MS80 of Jackie Stewart which we shall study shortly (see Chapter 5).

Team Lotus effort was split that season by the debut of their Type 63 four-wheel drive cars, and Chapman tried desperately hard to persuade his drivers to take the new model seriously, rather than concentrate upon their proven but now ageing 49Bs in their hunger to accumulate World Championship points. To force the issue he sold 49Bs 'R8' and 'R9' respectively to Jo Bonnier and to John Love in South Africa (who already had old 'R3'), leaving Team with only 'R6' in its umpteenth incarnation and the two 4WD Type 63s. For the British GP meeting at Silverstone Team's joint number one drivers complained bitterly about this move and Chapman was forced to relent, Bonnier's car being retrieved for Hill while Rindt took 'R6'. Bonnier was put into one Type 63 'on loan' to keep him sweet as possible – which was not a lot – and cadet works driver John Miles took over the other 4WD car.

The John Love sale was rescinded as the 4WDs failed to show any form, and Rindt eventually notched his long-awaited first Grand Prix victory at Watkins Glen that season, driving 'R6', while

The truncated Lotus 49 monocoque was an essentially simple riveted sheet aluminium affair with a square-tube framed sheet footbox, stepped underside to provide pipeways and front suspension bottom pick-up braced by that tube-stay up front.

Hill crashed 'R10' heavily and did himself serious injury when a tyre deflated. He had spun and stalled, push-started the car and drove on without being able to refasten his now compulsory seat belts.

So Team Lotus's third season with the 49s ended with two more GP victories to their credit, but their World titles had gone to Matra-DFV and to Jackie Stewart.

Now the Type 49s had run far beyond their expected life due to the failure of the intended replacement Type 63s. They had only ever been intended as short-term expedient cars in which the new Cosworth-Ford DFV engine could be proven, but learning first about the new age of aerodynamic aids and then the complex demands of the 4WD programme had prevented early development of an adequate replacement.

The cars were notorious for their fuel-system problems – repeatedly failing to scavenge the last few gallons from their now multiple bag tanks – and also for roasting their drivers with hot air from that nose-mounted radiator filling footbox and cockpit and heating the foot pedals.

In a determined effort to improve cooling and aerodynamic performance, top-ducted radiators had been adopted in time for the Italian GP, lipped and ramped vents in the top of the nose cone funnelling expended radiator air upwards along each side of the screen enclosure instead of 'hopefully' outwards low down on either side as before. The cars were improved but it was not a complete answer to the cockpit cooling question.

Add to these troubles the fierce, often instrument-wrecking natural vibration of the DFV engine and you have some idea of the conditions which those drivers endured.

The 49s were prone to marked pitch-down and tail-light wandering under braking – this being a trait which Siffert in particular enjoyed exploiting to the full when running in close company. He won himself the title 'Last of the Late-Brakers' and few friends amongst his fellow drivers by demonstrating the art at too close quarters.

Certainly the 49 was far from perfect, but it still had another season left in it . . .

Early in 1970, development of the latest Chapman-Phillippe two-wheel drive replacement car was lagging behind, and the old 49Bs were reworked yet again. Firestone developed a new 13 in. front tyre and four 49Bs – works team chassis 'R6', 'R8' and the freshly reincarnated 'R10', plus Walker's veteran 'R7' – were modified accordingly with new front uprights and front suspension geometry to accept 13 in. front wheels. These four cars were redesignated Lotus 49Cs. Meanwhile one final 49B had been built up as a display car for Ford of Britain, finished in GLTL livery and numbered 'R12'. It would not be used in anger.

Rindt was joined by Miles in the works team, while the barely recovered Graham Hill entered the twilight of his honoured career in Siffert's place with Walker. The old cars proved remarkably competitive until the startling new Type 72 made its debut, and when the new wedge-shaped car required an early partial redesign the works 49Cs were dusted down for a final frontline World Championship outing at Monaco. There Rindt triumphed over his own disinterest after stroking sulkily around until half-distance. Realizing he was in with a chance he took victory on the final corner of the final lap as race leader Jack Brabham made a rare mistake and slid off the road.

In the end, as late as April 1971, Tony Trimmer drove Rindt's Monaco-winning car – faithful old 'R6', which had had such a long racing history – in the Good Friday Oulton Park International. He damaged the car in a practice crash, and it was hurriedly repaired with parts cannibalized from 'R10' which fortunately happened to be on display in a garage not far away at Bradford. Yes, it was just like old times . . . Team Lotus in a last-minute panic.

Trimmer survived a pit stop and finished a distant sixth, four laps behind Rodriguez's winning BRM V12. It was the end of a classic Grand Prix design's International career.

Roll, bowl or pitch? The 49s were prone to pitch and squat and Rindt's 49B is in characteristic pose during the 1969 British GP. Those GRP nose cones rapidly wore through underneath. Here 'R6' displays state-of-the-art Firestone tyre sizes, top-ducted finned nose and end-plated rear wing.

Monocoque Chassis –
The First Two Decades

When Colin Chapman and Team Lotus successfully introduced 'monocoque' chassis to Formula 1 with their 1962 Type 25 they set new standards of weight:stiffness and set a new trend.

For 50 years monocoque construction had been standard practice in aviation. Credit for its introduction may go to Frederick Handley-Page for his aircraft shown at London's Olympia exhibition hall in 1911, or to Ruchonnet in France, but it was another French designer, Louis Béchereau, who produced the first streamlined fuselage deriving its stiffness and strength from its load-bearing stressed skin. Béchereau's Deperdussin racer of 1912 featured a skin formed from three 1.5 mm laminations of tulip-wood veneer glued together around a former. When cured, the structure was inherently rigid without internal framing. It was like an eggshell. Hence the nickname 'monocoque' was coined, mongrelized from the Greek *monos* and Latin *coccum* – 'single-shell'.

As early as 1915 a monocoque Cornelian light car raced at Indianapolis. In 1923 Gabriel Voisin built near-monocoques for the French GP, and in the UK around World War 2 Alec Issigonis and Laurie Bond both built monocoque sprint cars. Tom Killeen produced his monocoque-fuselage sports car for the early-1950s, Jaguar's famous D-Type used a stressed-skin monocoque centre-section with tube-frame engine bay, and the 1955-57 BRM P25s were part monocoque, using structural body-panelling around the cockpit opening. The lads at Bourne christened them the 'over-stressed skin specials'. They were light, stiff and very fast, but accessibility was 'barstorial'.

Six years later, Lotus tests with the prototype backbone-chassis Elan proved this structure immensely rigid for its weight. In planning lunches at a local Cheshunt restaurant Colin Chapman literally sketched on a table napkin his original scheme to apply a backbone chassis to a single-seater.

'I thought "Why not space the sides of the backbone far enough apart for a driver to sit between?" If we made the sides of the backbone as box-sections we could carry fuel inside them in rubber bags . . .'

So the Lotus 25 evolved, not a single-shell at all but instead two parallel D-section stressed-skin torsion boxes linked by bulkheads and a stressed-sheet floor panel, the open top being closed by clip-on glassfibre body-panelling. The 25/33 series tubs weighed around 70 lb, and with engine installed offered torsional stiffness around 2400 lb/ft per degree deflection along their length. This should be compared to around 1000 lb/ft per degree for a contemporary spaceframe chassis.

Tony Rudd and BRM then improved this open 'bathtub monocoque' with fully enclosing 360-degree panelling fore and aft of the cockpit in their 1963 P61 and 1964 P261 designs, while Forghieri of Ferrari developed their 'Aero' hybrid monocoque with stressed panels stiffening a sketchy internal tube-frame in 1963.

Chapman associate Len Terry produced a definitive full monocoque design in his superb Indianapolis-winning Lotus 38 and its Gurney-Eagle descendants. For 1966, it was Rudd and BRM again who developed the truncated three-quarter-length monocoque chassis which terminated just behind the cockpit in a bulkhead to which a fully stressed structural engine could be attached to support major rear suspension loads. Ferrari had supported their 1965 flat-12 engine in broadly similar manner on a 1965 truncated 'Aero' tub.

Robin Herd's 'Mallite' McLaren aluminium-balsa sandwich tub of 1966 attained unheard-of rigidity, around 11,000 lb/ft per degree, approximately three times stiffer than any preceding single-seater and better than some unitary-shelled production saloons.

Another Chapman designer/disciple Maurice Phillippe followed suit with the Lotus 49 of 1967, Maurice being an ex-de Havilland aviation engineer who had built his own monocoque-chassis MPS sports-racing car as early as 1955.

1968 saw Bernard Boyer of Matra introduce a more rigid highly subdivided monocoque carrying its fuel direct in spray-sealed side boxes, without bag tanks. Regulation changes for 1970 effectively made rubber-

bagged monocoques *de rigueur* in Formula 1, Brabham being the last refuge of the multi-tubular spaceframe.

In 1968, Honda had suspended their air-cooled V8 from a high-level projecting rear monocoque horn and two years later Ferrari adopted this idea in their supreme flat-12 312B package.

From 1973, deformable-structure tank protection measures saw McLaren's adoption of integral foam-packed moulded GRP hip radiator ducts to form the most complex monocoques yet. From 1976 Gordon Coppuck made extensive use of aerospace honeycomb lightweight panelling in his McLaren M26 design, and from 1978 Gordon Murray of Brabham began to use carbon-composite structural top panels in his otherwise sheet aluminium BT48-Alfa Romeo cars.

Ground-effect aerodynamics demanded ever-slimmer monocoques. The problem then was to achieve adequate stiffness despite the reduction in beam cross-section.

The 1977 Lotus 78s co-devised by Ralph Bellamy,

Martin Ogilvie, Peter Wright and Tony Rudd under the Chapman umbrella used aerospace aluminium honeycomb. Harvey Postlethwaite then popularized folded aluminium honeycomb sheet tub construction in his 1978 Wolf which begat the standard-setting Patrick Head-designed Williams FW07 of 1979-81.

Stiffness to resist ground-effect aerodynamic and suspension loads was still desperately needed. By 1979-80 torsional tests of new honeycomb and aluminium tubs commonly returned figures around 4500-5000 lb/ft per degree. With use this could fall to 3500 lb/ft, or less. Carbon-fibre and composite construction held the answer.

Peter Wright, the Lotus boffin so often mentioned in these pages, led Team this way, their Type 88 of 1981 being beaten to its public introduction by John Barnard's McLaren MP4/1. The essential difference was that the Lotus tub was built up from numerous flat precut composite panels, using the new material virtually as 'black aluminium', while McLaren tubs were true aerospace integral mouldings. Moulded-composite tubs into 1984 commonly returned 12,000-15,000 lb/ft per degree in torsional testing, and maintained it.

Yet into the mid-Eighties Brabham again became the last frontline refuge of an 'outdated' technology for their own excellent reasons, and still achieved Mallite McLaren-standard rigidity, I assume from Gordon's tacit nod, despite retaining sheet aluminium outer tubs. Meanwhile, his rivals adopted moulded carbon-composites, albeit tentatively in that until they gained experience they did not fully exploit their full weight-saving potential.

With the flat-bottom regulations of 1983, Gordon Murray and David North introduced a new form of 'modular' construction in their BT52, mounting the entire front suspension, steering etc as a sub-assembly on a one-piece aluminium front bulkhead machined from the solid, which in turn was inserted into the nose of a folded aluminium sheet – not honeycomb – outer tub. A complex moulded carbon-composite insert then stiffened the tub, forming scuttle top, cockpit accommodation, seat back and fuel tank top, a tall fully machined aluminium bulkhead closing the tub at the rear where the BMW engine attached with its tube stays. The tailor-made Brabham gearbox casing then provided basis of the rearmost module, carrying major rear suspension

elements. By juggling these ready-assembled modules the team could make rapid alterations or repairs in the field.

By the end of 1991, the Formula 1 car monocoque chassis had come a long way from Colin Chapman's original British patent application No. 21977/62, dated 6 June 1962. And, as related elsewhere within this volume, much further advance in line with ever-developing regulation requirements was to be made . . .

Above: *Sketch showing Colin Chapman's Lotus 25-style twin-pontoon monocoque, drawn to accompany his original Patent Specification filed 6 September 1963* (top left).
Centre: *Cooper's catamaran-style tub, 1968.*

Chapter 5

MATRA'S MAGNIFICENT HYBRIDS 1968-69

In 1969 Jackie Stewart proved virtually invincible behind the wheel of his Ken Tyrrell-managed, DFV-powered Matra cars carrying the 'Equipe Matra International' banner.

The French company Engins Matra is essentially a major aerospace, missiles and arms manufacturer. It was founded prewar by Marcel Chassagny, under the name CAPRA, as an aeronautical engineering sub-contractor. In Vichy France in 1942, Chassagny changed the name to *Mécanique-Aviation-Traction*, which was soon abbreviated to 'Matra'.

Postwar, the French Government was desperate to keep in touch with American and British missile development. Chassagny tendered for and won numerous contracts and Engins Matra's fortune was founded.

Chassagny had a friend named René Bonnet who built minor-Formula racing cars in conjunction with an aerodynamicist named Charles Deutsch. Their Deutsch-Bonnet ('DB') range of single-seater and sports cars often featured in the teeny classes at Le Mans using Panhard engines, and Chassagny put some capital into their company to help his friend. Financier Sylvain Floirat acquired a major shareholding in Chassagny's Matra concern and contributed greatly to its development.

In 1961 Deutsch and Bonnet split, and Bonnet decided to continue alone building Renault-powered competition cars, followed by a sleek little road-going Coupé named the Djet. He had a tough time, however, and with Floirat now controlling Matra's purse-strings Chassagny's backing could not be guaranteed. Soon afterwards, *Automobiles René Bonnet* went to the wall.

Chassagny, however, was able to buy Bonnet's assets and so Matra found itself in the motor manufacturing business. An engaging and dynamic young executive named Jean-Luc Lagardère became general manager of this new division, which they named Matra Sports. He recognized immediately the importance of promoting an image which would make the newly rechristened Matra Djet cars appeal to the moneyed youth market then emerging as much in France as elsewhere in the West. He concluded that Matra should pursue an energetic sports policy, and in 1965 the first Formula 3 Matra *monoplace* appeared, based on Bonnet's exploratory monocoque experience.

Lagardère would brook no half measures. The René Bonnets with Renault engines had lacked the power to be competitive. Ford engines were dominant in the class, so Lagardère's F3 Matra used a British-made Ford engine . . . no compromise.

Matra historian Jabby Crombac has highlighted the pragmatic approach of the former René Bonnet design team responsible for this F3 car. They arrived at its wheelbase and track dimensions simply by averaging those of every British F3 car at the 1965 London Racing Car Show: we all have to start somewhere.

What was unusual about the new car was the uncompromising aerospace construction of its monocoque chassis, for whereas Lotus and Lola in the UK were building stressed-skin punt-type tubs carrying their fuel within rubber bag tanks

inserted into the box-section pontoons on either side of the cockpit, Matra's new F3 carried its fuel direct in sealed pontoons, without the bag tanks.

This technique offered a major advantage in that the interior of each pontoon could be punctuated by numerous lateral bulkheads, greatly enhancing its torsional rigidity. If bag tanks were to be used this would have involved as many as eight or ten individual bags per side. That would have involved nightmares of plumbing and the strength-robbing necessity of providing a separate access hatch for each bag to be inserted, serviced and removed. To ensure fuel tightness within this 'bagless' sheet aluminium structure, its inner surfaces were treated with polymer resin. Construction was time-consuming and fiddly, but Engins Matra as an aerospace concern already employed similar techniques and had a labour force skilled in this technology.

The result was one of the most torsionally rigid F3 chassis, which, when properly set up, offered its drivers a narrow handling advantage which could make all the difference in such a tightly regulated and competitive class.

But in 1965 the cars were not very impressive in their first few outings, until at Reims-Gueux during the July speed weekend works driver Jean-Pierre Beltoise scrambled across the line first to win France's most charismatic F3 race of the season. The French enthusiast public was quite rightly elated. A race-winning new French-blue racing car had emerged after more than a decade

Stewart's Dunlop-tyred Matra MS80-01 during the team's 1969 French GP 1-2 features all-outboard spring suspensions, top-ducted nose radiator, podgy centre-section tankage and neat rear wing/oil-cooler duct/engine cowl moulding.

in the doldrums.

Meanwhile during that season in Formula 2, the British quasi-works Cooper team had been run by Ken Tyrrell with little success. Their spaceframe chassis were by that time relatively uncompetitive while their 1-litre BRM P80 four-cylinder engines proved highly unreliable. Tyrrell's 1-litre Formula 3 Cooper-BMCs had dominated both French and British Championship racing the previous year when lead driver Jackie Stewart had shot to stardom.

By the end of that season Stewart had signed a works BRM Formula 1 contract for 1965, and this brought Tyrrell the Formula 2 BRM engines for the Coopers which Stewart drove between Grand Prix commitments to BRM.

It was at the end of this season that Tyrrell made the trip to Paris for the *Trophées de France* F2 series prize-giving function at BP France's headquarters. There, journalist Crombac introduced him to Lagardère of Matra. He wanted his company to progress into F2 racing in 1966 but lacked the star name driver to make such an expensive step worthwhile. Now here was Tyrrell who had that driver. Stewart was to stay with

BRM for Formula 1 through 1966-67, and their Formula 2 engine was being improved that winter, so Tyrrell would continue to use it in the coming year. Having now abandoned hope of Cooper producing a decent chassis Tyrrell was looking for a competitive replacement.

Over dinner at Orly, Lagardère agreed with Tyrrell to supply an F3 monocoque Matra chassis fitted with an F2 engine for Stewart's evaluation at Goodwood circuit in Sussex.

Sylvain Floirat ran a string of race horses and owned a Bristol Freighter aircraft specially equipped to zoom them around Europe. Now it was used to deliver the Matra race car to Gatwick Airport not too far from Goodwood. Stewart had his doubts about this rather ugly little 'Frogmobile' before driving it hard, yet he emerged fascinated and very impressed by its sheer traction. It really did work well, so Tyrrell ran Matra-BRM Formula 2 cars through that 1966 season.

As it happened, the Brabham team had a better solution to that last season of 1-litre Formula 2 racing, for they had exclusive use of the 16-valve Honda four-cylinder power unit which left Cosworth's SCA and BRM's P80 gasping in its wake. The Brabhams used 'old-fashioned' spaceframes, but there was nothing that Stewart and the Matra's chassis could do about their horsepower.

A new 1600 cc Formula 2 took effect in 1967, and that season saw everybody of any significance using the new Cosworth FVA four-cylinder engine. Stewart now achieved considerable success in his Tyrrell-run Matra-Cosworth MS7 cars, as did the French works team itself, with drivers like Henri Pescarolo, Jean-Pierre Beltoise and 'Johnny' Servoz-Gavin.

Meanwhile in France the Government had become interested in the prospect of retrieving lost national prestige in Grand Prix racing. The publicity surrounding Matra's exploits in Formula 3 and Formula 2 had attracted influential attention, and the time was right. A new state oil company had just been created, under the 'Elf' name – some attributing this title to *Essence et Lubrificants Française*', while the company merely credits it to a marketing man's invention.

Another analyst found that sponsorship of motor racing at all levels would promote Elf more effectively than any mere advertising campaign employing less tangible devices. Elf therefore decided to back Matra in production of a Grand Prix car. These plans were finalized on 19 January 1967 at a meeting in Monte Carlo during the annual rally. Elf MD Jean Prada and Lagardère of Matra announced they would be co-operating technically and financially in design and development of an all-French GP car to be powered by a new V12 engine. Chief engine designer for Matra Sports was to be former Simca technician Georges Martin. Crombac tells how Martin saw a racing car for the first time in his life at that year's London Racing Car Show. They really were starting from scratch, but they had a lot of help.

In April that year the Government under Georges Pompidou announced a state grant of six million Francs – about £800,000 at that time – to assist the Elf-Matra Sports' Formula 1 programme. That June saw Ken Tyrrell present at the Dutch GP. He flew home determined to run Jackie Stewart in a Formula 1 car powered by one of these new engines in the coming season, 1968. The Scots star was very unhappy with his BRM Formula 1 equipment by that time and was not going to renew his contract with them. He had spent some very happy years with Tyrrell whose judgement and team he trusted implicitly, and he was willing to drive whatever halfway decent car Tyrrell could put under him in Formula 1. The only real opposition to Tyrrell's offer came from Ferrari, but that drive eventually went to a younger Tyrrell discovery – named Jacky Ickx . . .

Through that summer the ambitious Ken Tyrrell extracted a promise from Ford that he would indeed be able to purchase DFV engines for the coming season. Stewart agreed to join him for

both Formula 1 and Formula 2, with the British Dunlop tyre company paying the bill. All Tyrrell lacked now was a suitable chassis. He approached Lagardère and Matra, and again the timing was perfect.

With taxpayer's money involved, and a lot of premature publicity promising great things for it, the Matra V12 engine was in danger of causing more trouble than it was worth unless it achieved early success. Nobody but an opposition politician has any use for a state-backed loser.

Now here was Ken Tyrrell with potentially the world's finest driver under contract, asking if a Matra chassis might be available to use what was obviously the outstanding proven engine in Formula 1. If Matra would build a car to carry it, any success this hybrid might achieve could certainly offset bad publicity should Matra's own engine develop problems.

So Tyrrell got his cars. A specially modified version of the proposed V12 chassis would be produced to accommodate the British V8 engine, and Elf agreed to co-sponsor Tyrrell's new Formula 1 team which would operate under the name Equipe Matra International.

THE MATRA-COSWORTH F1 CARS

Tyrrell's first Formula 1 Matra was the MS9 test hack prototype. It used a Formula 2-type MS7 monocoque set up experimentally with fully adjustable suspension pick-up points to research systems proposed for the new V12 car.

At that time, in December 1967, Matra Sports' subsidiary long-distance team had already been campaigning 2-litre BRM V8-engined Coupés at Le Mans and other suitable events. The MS9 prototype was to have been tested with one of these V8s installed, but the Tyrrell deal was struck before the car had been completed and it was therefore modified to accept the fully stressed DFV engine hung Lotus 49-style on the rear of its truncated forward monocoque nacelle. This tub naturally used Matra's successful multiple-bulkhead so-called 'structural' fuel tank design.

The F2 MS7s had carried their unstressed Cosworth FVA engines on two pontoon horns extending either side of the engine bay from the rear cockpit bulkhead. The forthcoming V12 car was to use this engine mounting, which helped dictate its eventual 60-degree vee angle which was chosen to keep it narrow overall.

The stressed-block Cosworth DFV engine needed no rear chassis horns to sit upon. But its use fully stressed in Lotus 49-style meant that an engine-change in the field would necessitate removal and replacement of the suspension-supporting subframes on the rear of the engine. Matra's chassis designer Bernard Boyer felt he could save valuable resetting and brake bleeding time by including a lightweight tube frame extending from the monocoque's rear panel to a fabricated suspension pick-up diaphragm fitting round the gearbox. This device was not intended to accept suspension loads with the car in action, merely to keep the suspension undisturbed while the engine could be removed and replaced with relative impunity.

Otherwise this MS9 monocoque was very similar to its little-sister MS7s, even to the extent of sharing their short-race fuel capacity, for it was a test car and no more.

Either side of the cockpit, its two tank pontoons extended full length, linked at the front by a footbox housing pedals and inboard suspension elements, amidships by a box-fabrication dash-panel bulkhead in which the lightening holes doubled as instrument mounts, and behind the driver's seat by a robust third bulkhead section.

Rocker arm front suspension was broadly similar to Lotus 49 practice, as was the single top link, reversed lower wishbone and twin radius rod arrangement at the rear. Major suspension components, like the uprights and hubs, were borrowed from the company's MS630 sports-prototype cars. Cast-magnesium 15 in. diameter road wheels replaced the otherwise similar 13 in. wheels of the F2 cars, accommodating enlarged Girling disc brakes. Like the 49s, the

Matra MS9 employed a combination water/oil radiator core in the nose, slung ahead of a delta-form oil tank designed to cleave hot airflow exhausting from the radiator and fend it away through the suspension cut-outs on each side. The DFV engine, bolted on in its classical manner at the rear, drove via a Hewland DG300 five-speed and reverse gearbox. Rubber doughnuts and Hooke joints catered for halfshaft angularity and length variation as the road wheels rose and fell on bump and droop.

With Dunlop's backing, Tyrrell decided that an extended series of fine-weather tyre tests would form a valuable curtain raiser to his team's maiden Formula 1 season, and so a prolonged programme was undertaken at Kyalami in South Africa, following the South African GP there on 2 January 1968, which Tyrrell and Stewart had decided to enter despite Matra misgivings.

Matra had also sent a Formula 2 MS7 car with 1600 Cosworth FVA engine, ballasted up to Formula 1 minimum weight, for Jean-Pierre Beltoise to gain Grand Prix experience.

Matra themselves were so dubious about Tyrrell's ideas of actually racing MS9 that, as Crombac has recorded, Tyrrell was '. . . far from impressed when [his] car turned up – after a very short test at the Montlhéry track near Paris – painted in a coat of ugly green primer, just to make him feel this was not a proper racing car!'

At Kyalami the altitude rendered the cars' restricted fuel tankage slightly less of a problem although they would definitely have to make one refuelling stop if they lasted the distance. The MS9 hack's nose cone proved too restricted for adequate cooling and had to be cut back making this fungus-green ugly duckling even uglier, and an extra water tank and cooler were added under the roll-over bar. Stewart promptly qualified on the front row of the grid, led Clark's Lotus on the opening lap but fell back before his DFV engine dropped a valve. Beltoise survived race distance in the ballasted F2 car to finish sixth and add to this worthwhile Matra Formula 1 debut.

After its Kyalami race and test programme, MS9 would only run once more, in Albi testing.

The definitive Matra-Cosworth F1 car which followed was the MS10 in which Boyer introduced an extra tank cell à la Lotus 49 in the rear of the tub, between driver and engine bulkhead, raising the fuel capacity to a full 190 litres (41.8 Imperial gallons). Meanwhile, the MS11 chassis intended for the new V12 engine was to offer extra fuel capacity within its engine bearer horns. These extra tanks were obviously items which the DFV-powered MS10 neither required nor possessed. The hybrid MS10 weighed in at 560 kg (1234.5 lb), 20 kg (44 lb) heavier than the MS9 hack and 60 kg (132 lb) over the minimum weight limit.

Through 1968 the functional-looking pale-blue Matra MS10 brought Matra Sports the tangible success they required while their own MS11 V12 suffered, as predicted, its share of teething troubles while generating one of the most spine-tingling exhaust notes on the Formula 1 scene.

'MS10/01's debut came in the minor Race of Champions at Brands Hatch that March. And Stewart was appalled. It wandered frighteningly along the straights and understeered savagely in corners. As on MS9, Boyer had again adopted modestly lightened wheels and suspension uprights from his MS630 long-distance sports cars and they were still too heavy, seriously affecting the F1 car's sprung/unsprung weight ratio.

The offending components were further lightened. Titanium stub axles were used, but flexed, promoting brake pad knock-off as they tremored under brake reaction, giving the driver a dauntingly spongy pedal. Stewart hurt a wrist in an F2 Matra shunt at Jarama, Spain, and missed the subsequent Spanish GP held there. Beltoise took his place, crashing '10/01 mildly in practice due to this very brake problem, then leading the GP convincingly until an oil filter leak sent him into the pits. He rejoined, set fastest lap and was back in fifth place at the finish.

Beltoise drove the MS11 V12 for its ear-splitting debut at Monaco and, with Stewart still on the

Matra MS10 part-cutaway shows side-pontoon tank subdivision, monocoque stress-bridge bracing front suspension bay, oil tank and radiator ahead. DFV was only partly stressed; note engine bay truss-tubes visible alongside engine, supporting beefy fabricated rear diaphragm just ahead of halfshafts on which rear suspension hangs. MS80's DFV would be fully stressed.

Below: The F2-derived Matra MS10-02 at Nouveau Monde *hairpin during the wet 1968 French GP, Rouen-les-Essarts. Matra were surprisingly slow in developing aerodynamic aids. DFV engine mounting is well demonstrated here.*

sick-list, Servoz-Gavin drove MS10, qualifying on the front row and leading from the start only to brush a barrier in his excitement and break the car's transmission.

Steel stub axles and aerodynamic nose planes featured at Spa where Stewart returned and inherited the lead only for the high G-forces on this super-fast course to wash the car's final four gallons of fuel away from the pump pick-up and send him into the pits at the last moment, robbing Matra of a certain maiden victory.

A new, lighter 'MS10/02' with 2 in. wider front track was available for Zandvoort where Dunlop's wet weather tyre superiority assisted Stewart's maiden Matra-DFV victory and Beltoise's MS11 V12 second place. A lighter Hewland FG400 transaxle was fitted for the French GP at Rouen, where despite their aerospace pedigree Matra lagged behind in aerodynamic development, using only small and crude sheet foils fitted to the front suspension rocker arms. Poor tyre choice made this the first 1968 GP which a Matra-DFV did *not* lead . . .

A chassis-mounted midship wing was then tried at Brands Hatch but removed for the race in which Stewart's still-damaged wrist suffered terribly. Then at the Nürburgring the wing was used, Dunlop's wet tyres did their stuff and the streaming surface helped lighten the steering sufficiently for Stewart's wrist to hold up and he scored the most heroic victory of his entire career – simply leaving mere mortals as if for dead in appalling weather on the most demanding of all Grand Prix circuits.

Stewart's '10/02' then won the minor Oulton Park race; for Monza Servoz-Gavin took over the later MS10 with its midship wing to place second and Stewart used his older car now updated with a less buffet-prone cockpit and a rear wing mounted directly on the suspension uprights, but his engine broke its timing gears during the race itself.

At Watkins Glen, Stewart won in the spare car after his preferred mount had been set on fire by Mr Tyrrell (while fuelling it in the garage) and the World Championship title was then open going into the last race in Mexico City, between Stewart, Hulme and Hill – Matra, McLaren and Lotus – and all of them using DFV engines. Stewart's chance was lost, ironically by Matra's unique constructional method, as tank sealing polymer broke loose and partially blocked his car's fuel pump.

Winter development saw bi-wing airfoil aids developed in time for the 1969 South African GP, in which the two MS10s appeared with a front 'foil mounted on the chassis and a very tall rear 'foil on the suspension uprights. Stewart won both this race and the minor BRDC Silverstone event which followed with his 'MS10/02' in this form.

Matra had been extraordinarily slow to react in the aerodynamic war, considering the massive group expertise which should have been on call, and although they introduced a moveable 'foil actuated by a small aerospace electric motor, this was only available on Beltoise's factory V12 car, while the DFV-powered Tyrrell entries were demonstrably more competitive. Matra were in fact handicapped by the convulsion of social unrest which France suffered in May-June 1968, and developing their V12 had demanded close attention and massive effort. Dunlop tyre development, however, was extremely rapid. Matra wheel rims had grown through 1968 from 9 in. front/13 in. wide rear to 10 in./15 in. dimensions . . .

The Matra programmes were revised for 1969, the V12 engine now being reserved totally for sports-racing while Formula 1 effort was concentrated solely upon Equipe Matra International and their DFV-engined hybrids. Beltoise joined Stewart in this team and an all-new chassis design programme was initiated for them. There was also a plan for Jochen Rindt to be provided with a similar DFV-engined chassis which his Winkelmann Racing F2 team manager Alan Rees would operate for him. This deal did not materialize and Rindt signed for Team Lotus instead.

During that winter of 1968/69 there was much

Compare this shot with that on page 66 of Rindt, trying equally hard, same place, same race, in the Lotus 49. The MS80's anti-squat front suspension is working well, restricting forward weight transfer and reducing tendency of rear brakes to lock as the wheels 'go light'.

talk of the potential of 4-wheel drive in putting DFV power through to the road more efficiently than could existing rear-drive chassis and the tyres of the time, with or without aerodynamic aids. Stewart wanted a 4WD car available for wet races, of which there had been many in the '68 season. Matra could not afford to tackle endurance sports car racing as well as conventional F1 plus 4WD F1, so they arranged their budget to run to two new F1 chassis – the MS80s – for Tyrrell's team, plus an experimental 4WD car, the MS84. Tyrrell would supply both the DFV engines and the Ferguson 4WD transmission while Matra would be responsible for the chassis.

Meanwhile, Martin and his team revised their V12 engine design for a possible Formula 1 reappearance in 1970. At the end of the 1968 season the V12-engined MS11 car became purely an experimental hack, being fitted with engineer Caussin's hydraulic transmission system in a hasty conversion between 15 April and 18 May 1969. The original V12 engine, known as the MS9, had suffered from chronic overheating and Martin concluded that a complete redesign, with new block and head castings, was the only sensible remedy. MS11 was hill-climbed once during that season, refitted with conventional transmission and driven by Beltoise. For this outing it used a pre-production MS12 V12 engine destined for the forthcoming MS120 Formula 1 chassis.

Meanwhile, Boyer's 1969 MS80 design for the DFV engine was set out during the autumn of 1968, aiming to compensate for the known deficiencies of the MS10. Its afterthought midship fuel tank had been inadequately stressed, which compromised the monocoque's torsional rigidity. Front suspension offered more camber change than was comfortable on Dunlop's latest wide-tread tyres, tending to up-edge them on bump and droop with consequent sudden loss of contact area and hence ultimate grip. This manifested itself in too much inherent understeer and instability under heavy braking. The rear suspension was imperfect, allowing too much toe-steer for the rear wheels as the suspension moved through its arc. The inboard front coil-spring/damper mounting had also caused problems as the dampers overheated and extra cooling intakes had to be provided for their survival.

To improve rigidity, Boyer used his successful structural fuel tank system, Lagardère authorizing this feature even though it was already known that the CSI would be demanding rubber bag fuel tanks from 1 January 1970. As described earlier, this form of chassis structure prohibited use of bag tanks, so the new MS80 would be purely a one-season, one-shot car, ineligible for Formula 1 use into the '70 season. Consider the implications of this decision, and you will appreciate just how much faith Matra placed in their unique form of monocoque chassis construction.

Boyer concentrated his new car's tankage within its wheelbase in so-called 'Coke bottle' planform pannier tanks, concentrating the fuel load around the car's centre of gravity. To comply with latest regulations, these tanks were baffled by addition

of polyurethane foam, fed in through a row of small detachable access plates – far smaller than would be demanded if bag tanks had been used, even if the internal bulkhead layout had permitted. Boyer again used a fully stressed 360-degree scuttle section to stiffen the front end of his monocoque tub while the oil tank was moved from its MS9/10 forward mounting to a site between driver's shoulders and engine.

After the damper overheating problems of the MS10, outboard coil-spring/damper units appeared in the new MS80 front suspension, obviating the need for those strong but heavy and no less aerodynamically obstructive top rocker arms. At the rear Boyer took up the Len Terry/BRM-originated parallel link lower location. This offered much better toe-steer control than the preceding reversed lower wishbone with its single-point mounting on the chassis. It also eased provision of anti-squat geometry, to limit weight transference under acceleration.

Suspension geometry was dictated by needs of the latest-generation Dunlop tyres. Front wheels were now 13 in. diameter, rears 15 in., and Teflon-lined self-lubricating suspension ball joints were used since problems had been experienced with greased joints drying out on the MS10s. Unsprung weight at the rear was reduced by mounting the disc brakes inboard on the cheeks of the Hewland transaxle. Broad nose 'planes were fitted, trimming the effect of a tall strutted upright-mounted rear wing.

When it emerged, this podgily pregnant-looking MS80 scaled 535 kg (1179 lb) – 15 kg (33 lb) less than MS10. Its fuel capacity was enlarged to 210 litres (46.2 Imp. gallons) to cater for the greater thirst of the latest-tune so-called 9-series DFV engines, which were guaranteed to deliver 430 bhp at 9500 rpm.

The prototype MS80 tested briefly at Montlhéry before being flown out to Kyalami where it was used briefly in practice for the South African GP but not raced there, because Ken Tyrrell considered it as yet unproven. The old MS10 was indeed man enough to do the job, and driven by Stewart it won that race.

Stewart then gave 'MS80/01' its race debut in the minor Brands Hatch International, which it won. A flatter nose appeared for the Spanish GP where Dunlop's tyres proved inferior to those offered by Firestone and Goodyear, but when their runners struck trouble Stewart won by default and team-mate Beltoise in the number two MS80 – a brand new car at that meeting – finished third despite a delay when its gear linkage worked loose.

The celebrated Lotus wing-collapse accidents occurred in this race, and in mid-practice at Monaco two weeks later the CSI wing ban was

Cutaway of the Matra MS80.

applied, until new wing limitations could be introduced for the following Dutch race at Zandvoort.

Monaco was a catastrophe for the MS80s as both cars were found to have cracked transmission UJs on race morning and both broke these components on the same lap in the race itself. At Zandvoort, wingform engine covers and wider rear tyres appeared, Stewart winning comfortably; at Clermont-Ferrand Stewart, Beltoise and the MS80s placed triumphantly 1-2 before a French crowd – this splendid home performance doing promotional wonders for Matra Sports and Elf.

After a practice crash caused when a thrown-up piece of loose kerbing burst one of his MS80's front tyres, Stewart won the British GP – his fifth *Grande Epreuve* of the season – in Beltoise's usual car. The German GP was lost narrowly to Ickx's Brabham-DFV using the latest and now superior G20 tyre from Goodyear, while at Monza

the wily Tyrrell counselled use of an extra-high second gear to enable Stewart to make the final dash from the *Parabolica* corner to the finish line without having to change up. The last lap race situation was tailor-made for Stewart to exploit this advantage, and as main rival Rindt's DFV engine was bounced frantically on its rev-limiter, the wee Scot's Matra MS80 crossed the line first by inches, both to win the Italian GP and to clinch the World Championship titles for driver and constructor.

Team-mate Beltoise was also in that leading bunch, though without that specially cut long gear. His MS80 wore its rear wing, Stewart's ran low-drag configuration shorn of both nose planes and rear wing. Beltoise was able to enter that final corner first using the extra braking grip generated by his car's aerodynamic aids, but he was simply unable to exit as quickly with his standard gearing and finished third, merely 0.19 secs behind his team leader and 0.09 behind Rindt's Lotus.

Sure as eggs is eggs, the result of that thrilling Grand Prix had been decided pre-race, by Equipe Matra International's technical forethought and tactical vision. Most emphatically, Grand Prix racing is *not* all about drivers.

The 1969 season, and the Matra MS80s' racing

career, ended with the Canadian, US and Mexican GPs in which team and drivers were largely out of luck, but the operation had in any case lost a little incentive with the World titles already in the bag. And now the storm clouds had gathered . . .

Matra raced largely to promote its road-going Type 530 production car, successor to the Djet. Commercial success with this model had been hamstrung by Matra's lack of a proper dealer network. Although the car used the Ford V4 engine Ford refused to market it. Consequently Matra had begun planning a new production car powered by a proprietary engine from a more amenable source. Chrysler-France, building the Simca range, was now headed by Bill Reiber who, as former head of Ford-France, had made the original V4 deal with Matra! Now he was happy for them to use Chrysler engines but they would have to sever all links with Ford which meant the end of the Formula 1 Matra-DFVs. It made commercial sense, so for 1970 Matra refused even to consider modifying their World Championship-winning MS80s to suit the new bag-tank regulations, nor would they build chassis for any engine other than their own V12. They would race under the Matra-Simca name.

At Lagardère's request Tyrrell organized back-to-back tests for Stewart between V12 and DFV-engined cars at Albi, and the Scot was insistent that the DFV was a better proposition. Matra Sports would not compromise their Chrysler agreement by building new bag-tank chassis for the Ford-backed Formula 1 engine, so Tyrrell had to look elsewhere, turning initially to the upstart new March company while secretly having an MS80-like car of his own designed and built.

After a season's hiatus, Matra's reworked V12 engine reappeared in a rather weird-looking new MS120 works team chassis for 1970, but Matra Sports' cars would never win another Championship-qualifying F1 race. More years and more work would eventually see Ligier do the trick with the V12 engine, but it would never aspire to the heights of those Tyrrell-entered Matra-DFV hybrids of 1969.

Stewart's MS80, Silverstone, 1969 British GP. Now Matras were adequately be-winged with fences controlling airflow on nose and tail 'foils and nose-top. See how aerodynamically obstructive outboard suspensions could be.

Four-Wheel Drive

In search of improved traction to handle the new-found power and sudden torque of the Cosworth DFV engine in 1968-69, Cosworth themselves, Lotus, Matra and McLaren all experimented with four-wheel drive Formula 1 cars.

Much was made of these experiments both at the time and since but, after the final withdrawal of the 4WD Lotus 56B turbine car at the end of 1971, nothing came of these costly experiments in Formula 1 terms. Drivers could not adapt to the demands which the rather crude transmission systems employed placed upon their nervous systems and there was always a weight penalty.

Advances in aerodynamics and tyre development helped find solutions to the original traction problem which obviated the necessity for four-wheel drive. In retrospect, however, it is now apparent that devices such as the modern Ferguson Research viscous coupling, front-end limited-slip differentials plus modern racing tyre technology could have made the story's outcome completely different.

Essentially, four-wheel drive was a brief aberration in the story of Formula 1 development and was of *no* significance to the mainstream which followed, other than having indicated what not to do. For other reasons the March 0-2-4 and Williams FW07D six-wheeler projects employed four-wheel drive divorced from the steerable front wheels, which could have been successful had circumstances – and the regulations – been different. It was not until the Audi Quattro and Peugeot 4WD rally cars of the 1980s began rewriting the rough-road rallying record book that all-wheel drive was able to find its successful niche in ultra-high-performance motoring, most notably with Tony and Stuart Rolt's Ferguson concern in the van of development. It is in modern rallying and road-vehicle use that four-wheel drive has now proved its real value. The story of the 1969-71 4WD Grand Prix cars has been told most adequately elsewhere and in any case was, I believe, little more than an historic curiosity.

The story might have been different if 4WD had not finally been banned from Formula 1 in 1982, at a time when Williams had considered adopting a six-wheel design with the rear four driven, mainly for aerodynamic reasons. By 1985 so much power was available that, had 4WD still been an option, the leading designers would certainly have tried again, and into the 1990s its attraction remained obvious. But it had been left to production car engineering – and to the off-road rally world – to lead where the 'premier' Formula's rule-makers had feared to tread.

Top: *March's '0-2-4' experiment of 1977 pointed the way ahead but they had no money to capitalize upon it before F1 4WD was banned in '82 for '83.* Centre: *Matra's MS84 was a most effective 1969 4WD hack.* Above: *McLaren's M9A raced only once before being withdrawn as a costly failure.*

Chapter 6

LOTUS 72 – INTRODUCING NEW STANDARDS 1970-75

Tony Matthews' superb cutaway of a 1971 Lotus 72, showing car's multi-curvature tub skinning, all-inboard brakes, rising-rate suspension linkages and underwing oil tank and ducted coolers. Note ultra-low profile Firestone tyres, the new slicks at rear, virtual slicks at front.

During the Lotus 49's three-season life, Colin Chapman was increasingly irritated by this essentially simple design's inevitable deficiencies. He was particularly niggled by Graham Hill's habit of covering countless miles in race practice trying to find what he considered to be proper bump-stop settings.

Colin once told me, between laughter at the memories, 'My big dream for a car for Graham was one with rising-rate suspension so he could *never* get on a bump stop! Then he couldn't play around with it, and that alone would have made my season . . .'

Planning for the 1970 Lotus 49 replacement began as soon as the four-wheel drive Type 63 proved that approach to be a complete blind alley. Chapman and Maurice Phillippe discussed their new concept interminably and a specification was eventually drawn up. While the 49 concept hinged totally upon requirements of the new Cosworth-Ford engine, that for the new 72 hinged crucially upon two things – integration with a new Firestone racing tyre and optimisation of aerodynamic form to generate maximum possible download under the new wing regulations.

Basic tenets of the design included very low unsprung weight. Brake layout would reject the minimum possible heat into the hub/wheel/tyre assemblies. Combined with minimum overall weight and smooth, pitch-free riding characteristics, this would allow the new car to exploit softer – for which read 'faster' – tyre compounds than the opposition, without overheating and destroying them. This was the usual outcome when attempts had been made to race such tyres on vehicles not specifically designed for them. Now the forthcoming Lotus 72 was to give these virtual 'qualifying tyres' race-distance life.

The Lotus designers decided to achieve this aim by using rising-rate suspension, which would provide very soft springing free from the lack of control inherent in soft springs as such, and which normally allowed dangerous bottoming when the fuel tanks were full. Torsion bar springs were chosen as offering the neatest progressive-rate sys-

tem, and 'compound' torsion bars – explained shortly – would place the least demand on space.

Indianapolis track-racing experience with the Type 56 turbine cars in 1968 had proved that the wedge-shaped aerodynamic profile was very effective in generating negative lift – download – and to employ that shape on the 72 the nose radiator siting was dropped in favour of two radiators slung amidships on either hip. This in turn removed one heat source which had roasted drivers so often in the 49s. Resiting the oil tank in the tail also helped control cockpit temperatures and contributed to the 72's greater rearward weight bias, which extended the 49B philosophy of adding load on the rear tyres.

Mounting the disc brakes inboard on the footbox and transmission cheeks slashed unsprung weight and isolated a major source of heat from the wheels where experience had shown how much it could distress an already hard-worked racing tyre. Overall plumbing weight was considerably reduced and mass concentrated around the centre of gravity.

The whole design was centred upon an all-new wedge-section monocoque chassis, whose aerodynamic effect was to be enhanced and trimmed by a new design of three-tier tail wing and large nose planes.

The compound torsion bar springs used an outer tubular sleeve which was internally splined at one end to mate with an internal solid bar passing back through the outer sleeve. This outer was then mounted rigidly upon the chassis structure at its open end, from which the inner bar element protruded to pick up a linkage attached to the wheel upright and actuated by vertical movement of the suspension. The geometry of this linkage was such that the more the suspension deflected, the rate of twist on the torsion bar spring became proportionately greater still. This provided self-adjusting suspension to maintain virtually constant ride height and handling characteristics irrespective of changes in the car's fuel load as it was consumed during the race.

These compound torsion bars were so convenient because they were only half the length of conventional bars of similar rate, and they occupied far less inboard volume than conventional coil-springs. They were machined to very fine tolerances on equipment normally used for making gun barrels, and the bar's business end used crowded roller-race bearings to maintain minimum-friction clearance between outer sleeve and inner bar.

Suspension location was by conventional upper and lower wishbones, fabricated from nickel chrome-molybdenum sheet at the front and steel tube at the rear. The front wishbones were mounted on a front subframe, with their forward pick-up points lower than the rears to provide anti-dive characteristics. At the rear, forward pick-ups were higher than rearward ones to give pronounced anti-squat, preventing the car burying its tail under power.

This arrangement was intended to provide the required smooth-riding, low-pitch characteristics of the Type 56s upon which the Indy car drivers had commented so favourably, and to improve upon the 49s' notoriously acute nose-down-under-braking, tail-down-under-power pitching.

The new Type 72's inboard-mounted front brakes reacted on the wheels through specially made brakeshafts using Hardy-Spicer and Lobro driveshaft joints. The discs were solid, cooled by airflow entering via flush NACA ducts formed in the nose cowl, while expended air exited through moulded chimneys on the same cowl's upper surface.

The monocoque chassis itself was formed over steel internal bulkheads. Inner panels were in 20-gauge L72 Alclad sheet, while the outer skins were in softer, more malleable 18-gauge NS4 alloy to follow the necessary compound curves where the tub waisted in towards the hip-mounted radiator ducts.

The whole tub tapered forward in wedge form, and much was made of its external flush-riveting – aerospace style – to slash aerodynamic surface drag to an absolute minimum. Its inner panels sloped sharply towards the floor to provide necessary volume within the side pontoons for the FPT rubber fuel bags which fed a collector tank behind the sloping seat back panel.

A footbox structure projected at the front of the tub, fabricated upon a $^5/_8$ in. square-section tubular steel frame which carried pedals, master cylinders, front suspension and a fragile-looking forward frame to support the battery and body mounts.

At the rear the DFV engine bolted against the monocoque rear bulkhead, and suspension loads were carried on sandwich plates assembled into the Hewland FG transaxle casing. Since the suspension was relieved of major braking loads by the inboard disc mounting, only upper radius rods were fitted at the rear.

The Lotus 72's wing package was also a new development, in that its three-tier rear aerofoil enabled the wing assembly overall to run at a greater combined incidence than would have been feasible with a one-piece wing, which would have stalled at such a sharp angle of attack. This wing mounted above a three-gallon oil tank wrapped over the gearbox. Balance was provided by broad adjustable planes either side of the nose cone.

Upon the type's debut in the 1970 Spanish GP at Jarama, there were immediate problems. Rindt had an insulating spacer (which clamped between the front brakeshaft and disc to prevent heat-soak melting the drive-joint lubricant) overheat and disintegrate. This allowed the fixing bolts to fidget and stretch until they snapped, which left the driver with braking on only three wheels. Ventilated brake discs promptly replaced the solid originals on his car, chassis '72/2'.

Ambient temperatures in Spain were also too high for the new cars to cool adequately, so the radiator draught-includer ducts were enlarged by the simple expedient of outrigging them on spacers between pod and hull.

Type 49C wheel sizes were being used, 13 in.

Over the dune and far away – Rindt's Lotus '72/2' hammering on towards its first Championship round win in the 1970 Dutch GP. Just rebuilt sans anti-dive and anti-squat, the hip-radiatored 'doorstop' was possibly the only F1 car of that season to enjoy net aerodynamic download over its front wheels.

diameter fronts and 15 in. rears while rim widths were 10 and 15 in. respectively. Some 17 in. wide rears were tried by Rindt, but this set-up generated so much rear-end grip that the front end was utterly overwhelmed and understeer became excessive.

In fact, irrespective of wheel and tyre sizes, there were severe handling deficiencies. The 72s seemed to roll excessively and lift their inside rear wheels in cornering. Wet practice for the minor Silverstone race, however, showed them to be finding adhesion in conditions which essentially offered none. This would become characteristic of the 72s throughout their long frontline life.

After another poor showing in the race at Silverstone there was a major rethink. Only '72/1' was taken to Monaco, but as spare car, and Rindt astonishingly won there in his elderly 49C.

Meanwhile at Hethel, Colin Knight's fabricators tore down '72/2' to remove both anti-dive and anti-squat from its suspension systems. Removal of anti-squat was no great problem, merely requiring new rear subframes to be designed and made, but removing anti-dive was far more fundamental. Alteration of the front subframe and pick-ups meant that the original side skins would no longer fit so they had to be unstitched and scrapped and the monocoque completely reskinned around revised bulkheads to match the new front end requirements. In effect '72/2' was so extensively rebuilt that only the original rear cockpit bulkhead and engine mounts survived.

It had been considered necessary to remove both anti-dive and anti-squat because the former characteristic rendered the already light steering eeri-

Top: *Rindt's '72/2', Österreichring, 1970. Note wedge profile, wings, radiator ducts, rear torsion bars protruding at tail and new lop-eared engine airbox from which idea the tall 'snorkels' would quickly grow. Above: A 72's rear-end reveals anti-roll bar, vented inboard brake discs, and naked damper barrels with rising-rate geometry torsion bar linkages passing just behind.*

ly feelingless as the suspension stiffened under braking. Anti-squat was suspected of inducing a diagonal jacking moment across the car, causing that inside rear wheel to lift in corners.

The other extant Type 72, chassis '1', was less comprehensively rebuilt, the tub being unchanged and thus retaining anti-dive while the simpler rear end conversion was made to in-line pick-up frames removing anti-squat. This car was entrusted to Rindt's new team-mate John Miles, who was still finding his feet in Formula 1. A new parallel-suspension car, '72/3', became available for him at the German GP at Hockenheim in August. The old prototype '72/1' was then reduced and rebuilt as new with parallel suspension and it became Rob Walker's late-delivered replacement for his wonderful old Lotus 49C 'R7', driven by Graham Hill. This rebuilt car took the serial '72/4' and would have a very short active life.

Meanwhile the 72 had come of age after these extensive modifications. Rindt won on merit in his newly rebuilt '72/2' at Zandvoort and with luck at Clermont-Ferrand where the chassis had been further stiffened with cross-bracing in the rear of the tub and stronger suspension pick-ups. The rear dampers had also been resited as hot air

exhausting from the hip radiators had caused them distress.

For the British GP at Brands Hatch, Rindt's 72 introduced the engine airbox to modern Formula 1, gulping air into its injection trumpets from ducts situated either side of the roll-over bar. This at least would set new trends. Rindt was in luck once more and after Brabham's BT33 had left the Lotus for dead in second place, it ran out of fuel on the last lap and Rindt won again. At Hockenheim, Lotus could match Ickx's speed in the ever-improving flat-12 Ferrari and Rindt won on merit, by 0.7 second. Then the 72s hit trouble in Austria . . .

There the scrutineers spotted that the early-season Jarama radiator pod extension had taken the 72s' fuselage width beyond the 110 cm maximum. The pods had to be drawn in accordingly and the drivers promptly pulled 200 extra rpm along the straight! The lower ambient temperatures in the Styrian hills compared to the Jarama flood-plain enabled the cars still to cool adequately.

Rindt lost fourth place after a spin when his car's engine tightened, while Miles brought his car to a safe halt after suffering a front brakeshaft fracture. This was caused by an imperfection in the shaft's centre-drilling. John described the failure symptoms in the following way. '[It was] as though the moment I touched the brake pedal some enormous extra-terrestrial force had grabbed the steering and slammed it onto full lock. Fortunately I had room to sort it all out and go into the pits – very pale and utterly demoralized . . .'

The shafts were hollow to give some 'spring' to the brake-driveline, cushioning shock, and to save

a little more weight. In this case the drill had been run in from either end as usual, but the two drillings had not met perfectly in the middle, so leaving a stress-raiser ridge from which the shaft had fatigued. For the next race, the minor Gold Cup at Oulton Park, stop-gap solid brakeshafts were fitted to Rindt's '72/2'. The dark-blue Walker '72/4' made its muted debut there with Graham Hill driving. Rindt won the second heat; then came the Italian GP at Monza . . .

Rindt and Miles drove their usual cars while new team member Emerson Fittipaldi had a fresh works car '72/5'. In practice on the Saturday morning Rindt took out '72/2' running experimentally without wings, with standard brake ratios and on unscrubbed new tyres. Under braking from maximum speed into the right-handed *Curva Parabolica* his right-front brakeshaft almost certainly snapped, sending Rindt crashing into the left-side Armco barriers and stanchions. A barrier joint parted and the car's front end was demolished as the left-front suspension burrowed underneath and then hit an unyielding stanchion virtually head-on. The tub's forepart was first crushed, then ripped apart and Rindt was killed. Seven long years later an Italian court ruled that the initial loss of control was indeed caused by brakeshaft failure, but that poorly installed safety barriers were the crucial cause of the World Champion elect's tragic death.

At Watkins Glen new drivers Fittipaldi and Reine Wisell finished 1-3 in '72/5' and '72/3' to clinch the Drivers' title posthumously for Rindt and their fourth Formula 1 Constructors' Championship for Lotus.

THE LOW YEAR

Winter changes for the 1971 season included a new lubrication system and a return to drilled torsional front brakeshafts in place of the hefty solid components employed in the final North American races of 1970. Firestone were to introduce a new low-profile tyre in quest of more consistent contact area control due to the stiffer sidewalls which low-profile construction could offer. This involved suspension modifications to accommodate the new lower wheel/tyre centre-lines. The original magnesium uprights had been suspected of twisting. As cast-magnesium uprights robust enough to resist deflection would have been heavier than fabricated steel, the change was made to fabricated steel.

For the Good Friday Oulton Park meeting '72/5' used a new one-piece rear wing, and an in-line oil tank replaced the old saddle type to clean up airflow under it.

For the chassis number pedant, the Lotus 72 progression had been first to '72B' with the removal of anti-squat, followed by '72C' with the removal of anti-dive and its associated tub rebuild, and at Monaco in 1971 the '72D' emerged in Fittipaldi's regular '72/5' which now incorporated rear suspension geometry revised to match the new low-profile Firestones more efficiently. This new system featured twin radius rods, instead of single, on either side, while parallel lower links replaced the original bottom wishbone better to control toe-steer – a feature which BRM had espoused in 1967-68, and Matra in 1969. These changes helped tame a sudden changeover from understeer to oversteer which had troubled Team's drivers earlier in the season.

At Silverstone for the British GP, the original lop-eared style airbox was replaced by a tall single-scoop design. Maurice Phillippe left Lotus that autumn to design USAC and eventually Formula 1 cars – 72 derivatives in effect – for the Vel's Parnelli Jones Racing Team in the USA.

Prior to the 1971 US GP the 72s were further modified because rising-rate geometry no longer seemed advantageous. It was suspected of exacerbating the new low-profile tyres' chronic vibration problem, and was therefore removed from the rear suspension. Higher-profile tyres carried on smaller 13 in. diameter rear wheels were used brilliantly there by Fittipaldi to qualify only 0.017 second slower than Stewart's Tyrrell pole position time, but a multitude of problems then dropped him to

17th in the race.

This was in fact Team Lotus's worst Formula 1 season since 1959, for in every other season from 1960 to 1970 they had won Formula 1 races, yet in 1971 they won none. They had been handicapped by the morale after-echoes of Rindt's death, but more so by the relative inexperience of their two new drivers. Additionally, the faster of the two, Fittipaldi, had been injured in a mid-season road accident and, although he continued racing, team manager Peter Warr believed he had been more seriously affected than he was prepared to admit – a factor affecting car performance as surely as anything an engineer can do.

THE 72s' SECOND TITLE
New 1972 regulations demanded fuel tank protection in 16-gauge sheet, so the existing active 72s were reskinned in suitable material, while a sponsorship policy decision introduced the black-and-gold 'John Player Special' livery in place of the garish old red-gold-white Gold Leaf graphics.

Winter testing prior to the new 1972 season-opening Argentine GP proved a third-generation rear wing design, but this season witnessed a long succession of alternative oil tank, wing-mount and wing revisions made by Phillippe's successors, Martin Waide and Ralph Bellamy. Wheel diameters stabilized at 15 in. at the rear and 13 in. at the front, exhaust systems wove differing paths through ever-revised rear suspensions and Fittipaldi fulfilled all his huge promise.

The cars won World Championship GPs in Spain, Belgium, Britain, Austria and Italy plus minor F1 events at Brands Hatch, Silverstone and Vallelunga and the one-off major 312-mile Libre race back at Brands Hatch later in the season. By the time of the Italian GP that September, either Hulme of McLaren or Stewart of Tyrrell had to win all three remaining GPs without him improving on fourth place in any of those events to deny Fittipaldi and Lotus the World Championship titles. But he won at Monza, and so he became the youngest-ever World Champion Driver and Team Lotus took their fifth Formula 1 Constructors' Championship.

FOURTH SEASON – THIRD TITLE
Now the so-called 'super-team' syndrome prevailed for 1973, with Player hiring Ronnie Peterson to join the reigning World Champion in

Lotus's still-further developed Type 72s. Firestone's top management had dithered about whether or not to stay in racing, and consequently Colin Chapman – who never liked anyone messing him about – forged a replacement deal with the rival Goodyear concern. This necessitated considerable suspension retuning to match the different tyres, but Fittipaldi still won the first two GPs of the season untroubled in South America. In practice at Interlagos, Brazil, the elderly Lotuses were over a second faster than their opposition, and their advantage was so great that they were faster even on full tanks to demonstrate an awesome combination of chassis, tyre and driver power.

Chapman returned to Hethel after that race and briefed Ralph Bellamy to design – at last – a 72 replacement. 'All we need', he said, 'is a 72 100 lb lighter'.

From the European season-opening Spanish GP that year, new deformable structure tank protection regulations were to take effect, and Martin Waide drew the 72s' conversion. The ageing tubs were unstitched, rejigged and reappeared, initially at the Race of Champions, with double-skinned crush pads formed into integral radiator pods which replaced the earlier separate pod mouldings. New undertrays projected beyond the original tub sides to accept these additional structures.

Meanwhile, progressive development of the fabricated steel uprights had made them heavier now than comparably strong magnesium castings. Just as new castings were being made, Goodyear abruptly changed their tyre sizes, and consequently a stop-gap upright appeared which was very large and very ugly and in fact worked rather well.

During that 1973 season a series of alternative airboxes and far-overhung wing-mounts extending rearwards appeared, while Peterson's cars were progressively reinforced until they became strong enough to endure his driving style. He set the performance standards of the season but lost several races through car failure, until in July at the French GP he at last survived to the finish and won as we all knew he eventually would.

There was inevitably internecine rivalry between Peterson and his essentially senior partner Fittipaldi, but the reigning Champion's cause suffered at Zandvoort when a wheel collapse during practice effectively destroyed his faithful '72/5'

and a virtually new car had to be built up – slowly – to replace it.

The 72s' fiercest opposition that season came from the new ultra-short-wheelbase Tyrrells and the hip-radiatored McLaren M23s. Both these designs had more even weight distributions than the Lotuses, placing greater load on their front tyres, which were also produced by Goodyear. In an effort to load their front tyres more adequately, Lotus now experimented with wide-track suspensions necessitating stiffer torsion bar springs. These alone took ages to be made and delivered by Lotus's supplier. Magnesium rear uprights now proved overweight yet again, and another attempt was made with fabricated steel. The great expense in Formula 1 lies in the parts thrown away . . .

Although the Lotus 72 brought its manufacturer the coveted Constructors' title, neither of its drivers would take their competition's crown. Fittipaldi won three GPs, all early in the season, while Peterson won four, all later in the year. Meantime, Stewart won five in his Tyrrell to beat them both.

The Lotus 72s won their second Constructors' Championship in 1973. Here Fittipaldi leads Peterson at the Österreichring while (bottom) Emerson slams 72/5 round Barcelona on his way to scoring Lotus's 50th Championship GP victory, undeterred by a deflating rear tyre.

FINAL SEASONS AND SUCCESSES

Into 1974 the intended Lotus 72 replacement, the Type 76, was at last on the way. Goodyear reverted to 28 in. overall diameter rear tyres. Fittipaldi had joined McLaren, and Peterson was joined by Jacky Ickx in Team Lotus. In Brazil the 72s were fitted with year-old uprights to match the new 'tall' Goodyear tyres. Ickx won the minor Brands Hatch race against the odds in pouring rain, and as the new Type 76 cars failed dismally, the faithful if now positively geriatric 72s raced on.

Yet Peterson's prowess reaped victories in them at Monaco, Dijon-Prenois and Monza on three of the calendar's most widely divergent circuits. So effective did his car, '72/8', prove that a final all-new machine was built up at Hethel, chassis '72/9', but while it was still incomplete parts were cannibalized from it to repair '72/8' after a heavy practice accident at the Nürburgring. Wider front track – by just over 1 in. either side – appeared at Dijon. Drilled brake discs were adopted for the British GP at Brands Hatch. In favour of reduced frontal area promoting higher straightline speed, a reversion was made to narrow-track form for Monza and it continued into the US GP at Watkins Glen.

There, however, the 72s ran into a massive understeer problem on the latest-generation Goodyear tyres, which were better tailored to the front-end demands of the rival Ferrari, McLaren and Tyrrell cars which were in direct confrontation for those highly significant (discounting personal prejudices) Championship titles.

Now the Lotus 72 was in a minority of one. Goodyear could only afford to tailor tyres to the competitive majority and once the Lotus 72 slipped off that tightrope of success, it was all downhill. Major changes had to be made to match the old cars to the available tyres, for the tyres were no longer being tailored to these highly individual cars.

Lotus's 1975 season was thus catastrophically bad. Group Lotus was in trouble, Chapman's personal attention was often distracted. Money seems to have been short, there was insufficient to invest in serious development of that long-overdue Formula 1 replacement.

The so-called 'lightweight' chassis, '72/9', was still not ready for Peterson's use as the season began in Argentina. In Brazil his '72/8' and Ickx's long-faithful '72/5' ran with new rear uprights offering further revised geometry. Both cars used large front brake discs. Peterson's new car emerged in time for the minor Brands Hatch race where he finished third, but by this time he was very restless with the team.

A driver named Jim Crawford was brought in to handle Ickx's car at Silverstone but he suffered two major accidents, one in testing, the other in practice. Steel cable torsion bar actuation was being tried, operating only on bump when the cables came under tension. The new Goodyear tyres' radial rates demanded the heavier loadings imparted by cars like the contemporary Ferraris, McLarens, Tyrrells and Brabhams to achieve adequate working temperatures and Team Lotus suffered badly as the 72s simply would not heat these tyres adequately.

At Ricard-Castellet, Peterson's spare '72/8' featured helper coil-springs wrapped round the front damper barrels to assist the torsion bars because weight distribution had been radically altered by outrigging the engine some 5 in. aft of the tub on a tubular framework. A new oil tank was inserted 'twixt tub and engine to replace that over the gearbox, throwing more weight further forward. Ickx's '72/5' was rigged in a similar long-wheelbase form but without the helper coils. Peterson raced his regular short-wheelbase '72/9' and finished tenth while Ickx retired. It was his last race for Lotus, while Peterson was persuaded to persevere.

In the British GP he was joined by both Brian Henton and Jim Crawford, handling 72s '5' and '8' with pure coil-spring rear suspension in place of torsion bars. Conversely Peterson ran '72/9' in 1973 form – and that didn't work either.

John Watson had a one-off Lotus drive at the

By 1975 Goodyear had to tailor its tyres to more advanced cars than Team's old warhorse. Peterson's '72E/9', fourth at Monaco, sports deformable-structure tub shape, new wings and airbox.

Nürburgring, and in the US GP at Watkins Glen Peterson drove '72/9' and Henton '72/5'. They started the race 14-19 on the grid and finished it 5-12 in the results, Peterson stealing two final World Championship points in what was the Lotus 72's long-overdue swansong six seasons after its introduction.

During that period the classic Lotus 'wedge' had won no fewer than 20 Grand Prix races and had brought Team Lotus three Formula 1 Constructors' World Championship titles. At this point in the original edition of this book, I added 'By any standards the Lotus 72 was a truly great racing car'. Since the time I wrote those words further analysis of the admittedly great Type 72's story has left me a little less convinced. Those 20 GP wins were achieved from 76 GPs contested. The preceding Lotus 49s had won 12 GPs from only 41 started, the Lotus 25 series 14 from just

34 started. So while the Lotus 25s won 41 per cent of their GP races, the 49s won only 29 per cent and the 72s just 26 per cent. And then ten years later the McLaren-TAG Turbo MP4/2 family came along – against the fiercest Formula 1 opposition in years – and they won 48 per cent of their World Championship outings.

Do you see? Such analysis puts a different complexion upon the Lotus 72s' achievements. But what it cannot alter is the perception we all held at the time the 72s were current. They were the ever-present force to be reckoned with - the class of the field. And if that is what makes a Grand Prix car 'truly great' then the original copy I wrote for this section in 1986 must still stand. The only phrase I would unreservedly withdraw is 'By any standards' because that, quite patently, can no longer apply . . . The standards by which we judge have been upgraded, by McLaren International.

Of Wings and Things

Considered over our whole period, aerodynamic behaviour and effect has been the biggest single factor affecting the performance of the Grand Prix car from 1966-91, with design and performance of the racing tyre perhaps close behind.

As early as 1928 Fritz von Opel employed 50 in. span negative-incidence wings projecting either side of his Eugen Sander-built Opel RAK 2 rocket car, hopefully to keep him in contact with Berlin's AVUS speedway as, wreathed in smoke and trailing flame, he demonstrated its 120 mph performance.

In the 1950s Mercedes-Benz briefly adopted strutted wings on their racing 300SL Coupés, and at the Nürburgring Swiss engineer Michael May arrived with his Porsche sports car sporting an enormous strutted wing high above its centre of gravity just rear of 'midships. The scrutineers patted him on the head, expressed a hope the headaches would go away, and he was compelled to remove it.

At Daytona Beach in Florida an Indycar named 'Mad Dog' hurtled round the then-new banked superspeedway with Opel-like negative-incidence wings each side.

Then it became serious; by 1966-67 Texan Jim Hall's GM R&D-backed Chaparral sports-racing cars emerged with enormous strutted rear aerofoils acting directly upon their rear suspension uprights and thence directly loaded up the tyre contact-patch against the road.

An early GM-Chaparral inverted aerofoil-form body had pointed the way towards ground-effects aerodynamics as described elsewhere but flopped due to 'lack of correlation between actual high speed ground vehicles and simulation in a wind tunnel'. This failing would be repeated countless times by many other R&D teams.

GM-Chaparral further found that giant nose spoilers decreased drag, while tail spoilers increased it. Restricting airflow beneath the car cut drag. At the tail there was a tricky choice between either download or low drag. An experienced pilot, Hall promptly developed a deck-hinged feathering rear wing which gave download into corners, low drag along the straights.

But download on the body overwhelmed suspension travel in springs soft enough for good low-speed handling. So the ideal would be to react spoiler or wing loads direct into the top of the wheel uprights, acting directly through them to the wheel and tyre, leaving the car's sprung mass unaffected.

Thoughts turned progressively to fitting aerodynamic flaps on the suspension, then why not a strutted flap above the body, and logically thereafter why not a wing on tall struts running in clean undisturbed air?

In April 1966 the first wing was carved from solid pine, tested two feet above the rear of a Chevrolet Stingray and a foam-filled monocoque lightweight wing followed for the Chaparral 2E CanAm sports-racing cars. Once structural problems in the support struts had been corrected they were effective, still being driver-switched, high-drag/low-drag, high-download/low-download as required.

By the end of 1969 the ultimate strutted-wing Chaparral 2H ran in California with the biggest 'midship wing ever seen but meanwhile high strutted wings had run their course in Formula 1.

Following the Chaparral lead, Lotus World Champion driver Jim Clark had been interested enough to suggest a similar device to his mechanic Leo Wybrott and brothers Dale and Roger Porteous during their 1968 Tasman Championship tour of New Zealand.

Jimmy was driving a Lotus 49T and the Porteous boys knew about aircraft and at Teretonga, Invercargill, in the South Island race meeting they rigged Jimmy's car with a small airfoil standing on struts above its gearbox. The 'foil itself was in fact a sawn-off section of scrap helicopter rotor blade acquired from a nearby airfield dump.

Leo, in recent years works manager for McLaren International, described how Jimmy thought they had better not race the device after practising with it, because Colin Chapman back home in the UK did not know what they were up to, and if anything went wrong there would be 'hell to pay'.

But young Ferrari engineer Gianni Marelli, there with Amon's Tasman 246T car, was fascinated by the thing and painstakingly photographed it from every angle.

The Belgian GP at Spa that June was the fastest race in the calendar. Brabham had run small whisker nose spoilers there the previous year to minimize lift at speed, and this year Ron Tauranac and Ray Jessop arrived with strutted rear airfoils ready to fit on the cars, only to find Ferrari and Forghieri had thought along similar lines and their 312 V12 cars already had similar wings fitted.

Forghieri insists this development was sparked by conversation with fuel-injection and combustion expert Michael May, of bewinged Nürburgring Porsche fame,

who since 1962-63 had acted as a consultant to Ferrari, but the coincidence of Marelli's interest in that far-distant Lotus experiment at Teretonga is too great to be ignored.

Through 1968 and into 1969 strutted wings went forth and multipled. They grew higher, wider, shifted their feet from chassis to suspension uprights, appeared on both front and rear, while the Winkelmann Formula 2 Brabham team even ran a truly biplane device which would not have been out of place above the Western Front, 1914-18, in practice at Albi.

Fixed and feathering wings were developed until the Spanish GP 1969 Lotus accidents caused by wing failure persuaded the CSI to act and apply height and width and fixing rules to such devices.

For engineers in search of enhanced download to improve traction and cornering and braking grip, the strutted wing was a God-send, for it weighed merely a few pounds so, quite unlike four-wheel drive, represented very little additional mass to be accelerated, braked and cornered – yet in dynamic download it could generate a force of several hundred pounds which greatly improved lap speeds around a circuit.

Nose 'foils were used to balance out the loads of tail wings around the car's centre of gravity, and all manner of minor improvements and ploys would be used to gain ever more advantage . . . but that's another story.

The 1967 Belgian GP saw very high speeds as the new 3-litre cars came on song. Below: Clark's Lotus 49 leads Brabham's BT24-Repco, its bib spoiler minimizing front-end lift while Brabham ran separate cheek vanes in the race.

Just before the ban on strutted wings, Brabham's 1969 BT26-DFV won at Silverstone under this bi-wing arrangement.

Chapter 7

UNCOMPLICATED CRAFTSMANSHIP – THE CHAMPION TYRRELLS 1970-73

Tony Matthews drew 1971 Tyrrell 003 here for
Motoring News. *Note twin-disc front brakes, midships oil tank behind seat, unducted oil coolers under rear wing and roll-over hoop forward-braced in case engine should break away from tub in an accident.*

When it became clear that Matra were not prepared to build a DFV-powered Formula 1 chassis for the Tyrrell team's use in 1970, and both Ken Tyrrell and his World Champion driver Jackie Stewart were disinclined to accept Matra's offered V12 engine, Tyrrell had to find a viable alternative.

For the short term he ordered three Type 701 cars from the new March Engineering company . . . and while working hard to ensure the best possible back-up from them, he knew they could only ever be a stop-gap expedient. The only way ahead was to invest at long last in the design, development and construction of his own chassis. To do that he had to find a designer capable of creating a competitive car fit for Stewart's proven class.

His choice fell upon Derek Gardner, formerly with Ferguson, who had been responsible for the four-wheel drive transmission system used in Tyrrell's Matra MS84 experimental car during 1969. This quiet, precise Midlander with his gentle sense of humour had impressed Tyrrell as a very capable and well-qualified deep-thinker; perhaps just as important, he was not widely known in the racing world, and even if people did start asking him questions he was clearly very capable of keeping his mouth shut. This was most important, as nothing must be allowed to compromise the working relationship between Team Tyrrell and March Engineering.

Coincidentally, Gardner had just decided to leave Ferguson and to go freelance when Tyrrell telephoned with a proposition. They met in a pub at Henley-on-Thames, roughly halfway between Tyrrell's base at Ockham, Surrey, and Gardner's home in Leamington Spa, Warwickshire. Tyrrell asked Gardner if he felt capable of designing a Formula 1 car. After due – and typical – deliberation, Gardner jumped at the chance.

The new car had to be simple, it must need only minimal development before proving competitive. Tyrrell stressed the vital requirement for total secrecy then emphasized that the machinery of racing sponsorship demanded it be ready for the Oulton Park Gold Cup race on 22 August. If it

was any later 'you might as well chuck it in the Thames . . .'

In February 1970, at about the time that March were proudly unveiling their new Type 701s to the press, Gardner began work on what would be his first complete car design. He converted a bedroom at his home in Parklands Avenue, Leamington, into a drawing office and began his design study from a blank sheet.

He analyzed all contemporary designs and decided his own parameters for the best all-round aerodynamic form, minimum legal weight, and a low polar moment central mass concentration to promote the most favourable front/rear weight distribution. Acting ostensibly as a private individual, he began ordering forgings and castings for the new car and was amazed at the fine co-operation he received from the specialist suppliers concerned.

The first sacrifice of his racing career followed. He had to build a mock-up of the chassis and to make space for it he had to sell his beloved Mark VII Bentley, which he 'simply couldn't bear to leave outside in the weather'.

A local joinery firm built the wooden mock-up for him, which Derek completed with aluminium sheet, cardboard and a lick of blue paint. Now there was something tangible in existence, and Tyrrell's mechanics – who learned of the SP ('Secret Project') late in the day – offered comments and suggestions on its detail design. A DFV engine and Hewland gearbox were delivered to Derek's home and Stewart broke a Formula 2 test day at Goodwood to fly to Coventry to try the mock-up for size.

Derek's young daughter was a great Jackie Stewart fan, yet secrecy was such that she had no idea that the great man had been in her home until many weeks later . . .

By mid-summer the design finally seemed as painstakingly detailed as it could be. Only then was the first metal cut, but despite growing pressure upon time nothing was accepted without rigorous inspection and several made parts were rejected and had to be made again, acceptably.

THE PROTOTYPE EMERGES

Gomm Metal Developments of Old Woking, Surrey, only five miles from Tyrrell's Ockham workshops, made the prototype monocoque, which was an open-topped 'bath-tub' type for accessibility's sake, unlike the stressed scuttle design of the team's previous Matras. The tub was formed over fabricated steel bulkheads, with 18-gauge NS4 malleable aluminium-alloy skins. The forepart of the tub enclosed the driver's foot pedals, and a tubular subframe extended in front to carry the radiator and forward pick-ups for the lower front suspension members.

A massive front bulkhead structure extended into Matra-like 'wings' on each side, supporting tiny split upper wishbones and top mounts for the outboard coil-spring/damper units. Very wide-based fabricated lower wishbones were used and, despite Ken Tyrrell's desire to have unsprung weight reduced to the minimum, outboard front brakes were retained to keep the car simple.

The rear suspension hung on the DFV engine and Hewland FG400 transaxle via tubular subframes. Parallel lower links were used for toe-steer control, there was a single top link, twin radius rods and outboard coil/damper units. The rear brakes were mounted inboard on the transaxle cheeks, using 10½ in. ventilated discs similar to those in the front wheels, which were special centre-lock magnesium-alloy castings made by Aeroplane & Motor, as were the unusual and very lightweight suspension uprights and other castings. The stub axles were by Laystall, and most machining was performed by Jack Knight Engineering who were based not far from Gomm's sheet metal shop.

Gardner had tested a tenth-scale model of the car in the mechanical engineering department wind tunnel of the University of Surrey at Guildford. The result was an unusual-looking nose cowl with a wide blade-like airfoil span formed above an underslung 'shark-mouth' radiator air intake.

Hot radiator air exited through vents formed into the cockpit surround-cum-scuttle panel which was shaped in aluminium, and a broad central spine then diverted airflow around the cockpit sides and screen. Gardner intended this feature to feed relatively clean air back onto a two-tier tail wing which would be strut-mounted above the gearbox.

Fuel load was carried in four bags concentrated well within the wheelbase around the centre of gravity within a podgy Matra MS80-like 'Coke bottle' tub. When the prototype car was first assembled and weighed it scaled some 100 lb less than the team's proprietary March 701s, and was only 32 lb above the minimum weight limit. It had cost Ken Tyrrell £22,500, less engine and gearbox, compared to the purchase price of £9000 each for his March 701s. Now the new Tyrrell '001' had to prove its worth.

Its race debut at Oulton Park was indifferent during practice as the fuel metering unit drive failed, then the injection system blocked. Stewart elected to start from the back of the grid in this possibly recalcitrant new mount. On lap 2 of the first heat '001's throttles jammed and Stewart screamed into the pits to have the linkage freed off and loose bodywork re-attached. He then stormed out again and broke the lap record twice before an oil pick-up problem caused the engine to fail. Tyrrell then gave Stewart choice of either his familiar March 701 or the new Tyrrell '001' for the remaining World Championship GPs.

At Monza in practice for the Italian GP the new car's main tanks refused to feed the collector quickly enough to keep the engine running cleanly at sustained high rpm. There, Stewart was shattered by his friend Jochen Rindt's fatal accident in the Lotus 72, but he raced his March 701 hard and fast.

The Tyrrell's fuel system was improved for the trans-Atlantic trip to Canada, the USA and

Geoff Goddard's unusual Monaco shot shows wet practice for the 1971 GP, with Stewart's hammerhead-nosed Tyrrell 001 T-car lining up for the quayside chicane. It emphasizes the large proportions of frontal area occupied by tyres and by wings when set to high incidence for the wet on this low-speed circuit.

Mexico and '001' ran in each race driven by Stewart. They started on pole in Canada and on the front row at Watkins Glen and Mexico City. Stewart led both the Canadian and US GPs, and ran second before a minor delay, then hit a stray dog, in Mexico.

Thus in Stewart's hands the new car had shown terrific potential and had achieved more than enough to secure Tyrrell's sponsorship for 1971. There had been further teething troubles. Its wheels repeatedly worked loose during practice in Canada, then a much more serious left-front stub axle failure occurred when leading the race there. Gardner designed far more beefy replacement components which were machined from solid magnesium block by Jack Knight's craftsmen in time for the American race, which Stewart only lost when an oil-line retaining clip parted, causing the plastic line to fall against a hot exhaust manifold and burn through, which allowed the lubricant to haemorrhage away.

THE FIRST CHAMPIONSHIP TITLE

For 1971, Elf-Team Tyrrell was formed and Derek Gardner joined the Ockham team full time. Dunlop had withdrawn from Formula 1 tyre manufacture and Goodyear took their place supplying Tyrrell.

One most significant reason behind the team's success thus far had been that both Tyrrell and Stewart understood the immense value of prolonged tyre testing. January 1971 found them running '001' at Kyalami using 400 Goodyears specially flown out for the test programme.

1971 Race of Champions: Jackie Stewart heats up short-wheelbase Tyrrell 001's tyres. Scuttle-top spine deflected hot radiator air along each side away from driver's face; the cockpit surround bulge gave gearchange space.

Cosworth had decided to build only 15 new '11-series' DFV engines for that season, all of which they would maintain themselves while licensing approved outside concerns to service and rebuild the older units. Tyrrell were to have two of the latest engines, while JW Automotive – of Gulf-Porsche endurance racing fame – were to service their others.

Stewart ran one engine for no less than 986 miles at Kyalami before deciding it was due for a change. Tyrrell was confident that his new car's unreliability was now a thing of the past.

Certainly during the Stewart period, the Tyrrell team was in the box seat so far as supply of the finest Cosworth-Ford engines was concerned. But in appraising their success it would be asinine to ignore the superb workmanship and top-quality preparation which went into the cars which those engines powered, and which that driver drove. It was certainly a major factor in the success of cars which technically were perhaps regarded as more competent than sensational. Even so, few teams were as active in research and experimentation as Elf-Team Tyrrell under Derek Gardner's technical direction.

Continuing the Kyalami tests with a new engine, '001' went on through the 1400 mile mark until a pebble jammed between throttle pedal and bracket, and the dark-blue Tyrrell crashed quite heavily. Stewart jarred his wrist, while the monocoque's left-front corner was crushed back some four to five inches. The wreck was rushed back home where the damaged tub was unstitched, the skins beaten true and then reassembled.

Meanwhile, the new second car '002' – the first entirely Tyrrell-built vehicle – was progressing alongside this repair work in the Ockham workshop. The new car's tub was four inches longer than the prototype's largely to accommodate number two driver François Cevert's lanky frame. The new car's wheelbase was only 1½ in. longer than '001's but there were several other detail differences.

The cockpit offered more elbow room. Thicker 16-gauge NS4 alloy outer skins were now used instead of 18-gauge. The front bulkhead no longer used steel tubing within the tub. Now a more simple suspension-carrying frame was first made up on a jig, then slipped over the stressed-skin monocoque to which it was then riveted from outside.

A hefty 360-degree roll-over hoop encircled the rear bulkhead, being both spigoted and bolted through into the tub. The stressed DFV engine was also then bolted through this hoop, while forward radius rod pick-ups were carried on it. Other changes included new one-piece lower front wishbones, made from S514 aviation-spec material and chromed for protection from flying grit and debris; side fuel fillers replacing '001's central pot; and twin gearbox-mounted oil coolers in place of the single matrix which had been found deficient at Kyalami.

A new large-capacity Graviner fire extinguisher bottle lived in the stiffening panel under the driver's knees while the fuel collector, battery and oil tanks still tucked away behind his back. Solid brake discs appeared at the rear instead of ventilated and a stronger pedal assembly was fitted, all to improve 'feel'. Gardner was examining alternative body designs, but for the moment bodywork was unchanged, although glass-fibre cockpit surrounds were on the way, to replace the original aluminium type.

Returning to Kyalami for the season-opening South African GP on 6 March, Cevert mangled both ends of his brand new '002' while Stewart qualified '001' unchallenged on pole position at record pace – faster even than in tyre testing there. But he was then handicapped by indifferent performance from both engine and tyres during the race and finished a poor second. Three minor races followed with Stewart driving '001' as a lone Tyrrell entry while '002' was being repaired, and being beaten each time. The team was beginning to wonder just what kind of car it had, when '003' was completed in time for the Spanish GP at Barcelona. This was a new car specifically for Stewart's use, and with luck he was able to win with it in Spain, and then at Monaco, and in the French, British, German and Canadian GPs by season's end, while Cevert won the US GP in his regular car '002' and was second behind his team leader in France and Germany, and third in Italy.

Stewart won the Drivers' World Championship going away and Tyrrell became Formula 1 Constructors' Champion at their first attempt.

The only tangible difference between cars '002' and '003' was that Stewart's had adjustable foot pedals installed to compensate for his height deficiency compared to Cevert.

After the Spanish victory a new wedge-shaped nose cowl, rather like the contemporary Matra MS120's, was tested at Ricard-Castellet. It cancelled more lift with less drag than the blade nose but its effect was more than the existing rear wing could balance adequately, so Gardner

returned to the University of Surrey for further wind tunnel model research.

Cars '001' and '003' were then taken to the minor Silverstone race for Stewart to choose between, '001' wearing experimental Girling twin-disc front brakes. There were two solid discs on each hub, spaced by a double thickness of pad material, and with pistons on only one side of the caliper. The discs were given a degree of side-float which allowed them to move sideways, cramped by the pads, when the brakes were applied. The idea was to double pad and disc area and provide better heat dissipation plus the opportunity to reduce line pressures which permitted the use of smaller pistons and less deflection on pad wear. The problem had been that conventional discs were wearing the brake pads into a taper form. This in turn promoted 'knock-off' when the drivers braked hard, giving a spongy pedal feel and slashing driver confidence.

Stewart raced '003' at Silverstone, winning the first heat, but then he crashed heavily on the first corner of heat two. This appeared to have been caused by yet another jammed throttle, since the car powered straight on into the outside bank with its front wheels locked solid under heavy braking, but no cause could be found as the wreck was dismantled.

The whole front end of the monocoque had been wrenched to one side, grievously damaged with less than two weeks' grace before the Monaco GP. Yet flat-out work got the car to Monaco, where the Matra-like nose was tried in practice. The standard blade type was used in the race after Stewart had qualified on pole with it, fully 1.2 secs faster than Ickx's Ferrari, his closest rival.

Completing the warm-up lap, Stewart complained of locking front brakes. A Rose joint on the brake balance bar had come unwound and there was no time for it to be readjusted before the race began with the Tyrrell virtually brakeless at the rear.

The driver's personal genius shone as he came home regardless to a perfect win, having led all the way from pole and set fastest lap. He was violently sick as he climbed from the car, and the mechanics found its engine had consumed nearly two gallons of oil. That brilliant race had taken a lot out of both man and machine.

After Monaco, Gardner made his first real bodywork changes in time for the Dutch GP at Zandvoort where both regular cars appeared with double-disc front brakes and squat glass-fibre ram airboxes above the engine inductions. Lotus's 72s had been using small intakes to feed clean air since the previous year's British GP, while Matra used a rough snorkel-type intake which was really a mere airstream guide as it was not properly sealed. The idea intrigued Gardner, and now his properly sealed version really set the fashion. They worked well if kept clear of hot air from the radiators.

Also new in Holland, although only shown on '003' in scrutineering, was a bluff nose cone, reminiscent of a Porsche 908/3 sports-racing car's, which extended to the legal maximum width ahead of the front wheels and served to fair airflow over their tyres. This fairing killed a proportion of the aerodynamic lift which they – as, in effect, rotating cylinders interposed in a moving airstream – inevitably generated. Reducing that lift also reduced its inevitable companion, drag, and would yield great dividends.

The bluff nose made its racing debut in the French GP at Ricard-Castellet where its improved download and reduced drag helped make '003' quick through the corners and simply uncatchable on the long *Mistral* straight. The twin-disc brakes were removed there from both Tyrrells, after Stewart had a harmless practice spin into the catch-fencing, for Girling seemed happy with the lessons learned thus far. In the race, which Stewart won handsomely with Cevert second, the Frenchman's car lost an exhaust tailpipe. Safety keeps were fitted thereafter. At Silverstone for the British GP, both Tyrrells wore bluff noses and Stewart won so convincingly that '003's engine was sealed and its capacity checked and verified by the scrutineers post-race. In France fuel samples had been taken away for analysis. Neither check revealed anything illegal. The Tyrrell-DFVs driven by Stewart and Cevert simply had the measure of their opposition. The spare car, '001', received a bluff nose in time for the German GP, which yielded another Tyrrell 1-2 victory, and now Gardner had begun experimenting with an eye on 1972.

The later two cars' longer wheelbase seemed to make them more forgiving to drive than the original short-wheelbase prototype. Therefore '003' was rigged with a 4.3 in. long distance piece inserted between engine and gearbox, and incorporating a lengthened gearbox mainshaft, extended clutch release mechanism and lengthened rear subframes and radius rods. The whole rear suspension and gearbox assembly moved rearwards, altering weight distribution and raising polar moment.

The car was run in this form during first practice at the Österreichring, then returned to standard spec for second practice and the race, but lapped no faster. Gardner was interested in placing more weight on the rear wheels and cutting drag still further.

For Monza, '003' was set up with the long wheelbase kit plus a tray-type rear wing carrying the water radiators and oil coolers. The standard nose radiator remained in place, with a simple blanking plate to mask it off when running experimentally on the wing radiator system.

This worked well enough but temperatures were borderline by the standards of that time. Four years later similar temperatures wouldn't raise an eyebrow. Stewart raced '003' with the nose radiator in commission, though the tray-type rear wing and oil coolers were retained.

Both race cars reverted to standard trim with airboxes, bluff noses, front radiators and normal wheelbase for the money-making trip to Canada and the USA, winning both times. A third standard-wheelbase car '004' was completed right at the end of the season as a spare for Stewart.

BUILDING FOR THE FUTURE

Now Gardner had digested the results of his long-wheelbase experiments he believed that a driver of Stewart's perception and touch, or of Cevert's – for he had developed into a most capable *pilote* – could probably extract more from a skittish shorter-wheelbase car like '001'.

He had completed preliminary design sketches for a new Tyrrell to replace the relatively simple, short-life cars of the original series, '001-004'. While his team were racing in North America, Derek stayed at home, testing a full-scale mock-up of the new design in the MIRA wind tunnel at Nuneaton.

The new tub was low, broad and with a wedge profile, a chisel nose, midship water and oil coolers *à la* Lotus 72, and with a conning tower cockpit surround to compensate for the low tub height in defending the driver from the airstream. Steeply dihedral fins protruded either side of the nose cone and there were vertical fins on each radiator pod. The tall arching airbox had a radiused triangular air intake orifice derived from the tailfin engine pod of a BAC Trident airliner – which one of Ken Tyrrell's sons flew. Outboard coil-springs were retained on conventional rear suspension and with a new very wide-based wishbone system up front.

Derek Gardner had been intrigued by a finned Matra prototype. Fins, he felt, could be effective in cleaning up airflow to the rear wing with the car in yaw – sliding at a slight angle to its true direction of travel. Unfortunately, tunnel results indicated that the car would indeed be stable in a straight line but would be difficult to control in a slide. It wasn't worth the complication.

Stewart and Cevert concentrated upon their familiar '003' and '002' cars at the start of the 1972 season. Stewart would win the Argentine and French GPs in the ever-faithful '003', adding to his 1971 successes with the old car to make it arguably the most successful individual chassis in Grand Prix history, with no less than eight

Championship-qualifying victories to its credit. François's car ran new front suspension uprights integral with brake calipers in South Africa. These were subsequently adopted as standard. Derek's substantial makeshift uprights had been used throughout 1971, making him shudder whenever he saw them.

Stewart blooded the spare '004' at Monaco, but he was off form, and an ulcer was diagnosed soon after which meant he missed the Belgian GP at Nivelles. Immediately after that race the prototype 'series two' Tyrrell, chassis '005', was completed.

Gardner explained how he 'wanted to build a small car, a light, manoeuvrable, well-handling car. The type of car Jackie could make the most of . . .'

The new vehicle was as wide as its predecessors, but was lower and shorter, aiming at a more central mass concentration to reduce its polar moment of inertia, thus making it more swerveable and quicker to respond to steering and attitude inputs than its predecessors.

Its monocoque was a flat-topped, slab-sided bath-tub holding 41 gallons of Elf fuel in its pontoon bag tanks and raking down wedge-profile towards the nose. Deep cut-outs in the cockpit inner panels gave the driver elbow room, making this a difficult tub to build. Suspension followed Tyrrell practice though the top front wishbones were new one-piece fabrications. At that time only Lotus had adopted and remained faithful to all-inboard brakes, front and rear. This reduced unsprung weight, allowed the wheels to change direction more rapidly from bump to rebound – and thus reduced the chance of their bouncing uncontrolled clear of the road surface. No matter how sticky the tyres might be, they need to be in contact with something in order to stick to it . . .

In face of Stewart's misgivings, remembering his friend Rindt's death, Gardner considered that the bugbear of brakeshaft fragility had now been laid

to rest and he adopted ventilated discs and calipers mounted each side of a narrow pedal-box projecting from the tub's front end. They reacted on the wheels through solid GKN shafts equipped with double CV joints to cater for suspension and steering angularity.

Little '005' was very clean aerodynamically. Its nose was fully two inches lower than the 'series one' cars', its wheelbase two inches shorter. A nose radiator was retained, but the oil coolers were now in neat midships ducts which faired back into a flat rear deck combining with the airbox to encase the engine and feed clean air onto the tail wing. The conning tower idea emerged here in the plastic, with moulded horizontal strakes on each side to deflect hot radiator air away from the driver's face after exhausting through top ducts on the nose.

The new car was driven by Cevert in Silverstone tests, then more seriously in practice for his home GP at Clermont-Ferrand. After setting fastest time there he lost control and clanged into the Armco head-on. Because of the deep elbow cut-aways in the cockpit, the whole tub was found to have bent itself. It was not strong enough to endure that kind of mistreatment. Team Tyrrell was short of spares for its new baby, so the car was set aside to be repaired and strengthened with steel plates beneath its top skins.

Stewart won the Clermont race in '003' while Cevert finished fourth in '002' and cadet driver Patrick Depailler made an appearance in the spare '004'. He would drive it again in the US GP and would find a permanent place in the team 18 months hence.

New car '005' reappeared at Brands Hatch for the British GP, where Stewart set third fastest time in first practice and second quickest in the second session before a rear suspension Rose joint parted, releasing a radius rod which sent '005' into the bank again. This time the damage was minor. Chief Mechanic Roger Hill actually drove the car back to the pits but once again it would not be raced. During the GP Cevert crashed '002' heavily, ripping off its left-front wheel, and another car subsequently crashed into the wreckage, amputating both the Tyrrell's surviving suspensions. It was still repaired in time for the German GP, two weeks later at the Nürburgring, and

---

Below: *Stewart's Tyrrell 003 dominated mid-1971 GPs, thanks to new Cosworth exhausts, bluff nose to minimize drag-inducing front-wheel lift, and well-sealed engine airbox. Fenced rear wing showed further sophistication.* Left: *Girling's experimental twin-disc Tyrrell brake.*

Tyrrell's slabby but smoothly streamlined low polar moment 005 design of 1972 investigated here by Tony Matthews. Note all-inboard brakes, nose water radiator, hip coolers and tall airbox flowing into rear wing.

Cevert promptly crashed again in practice, doing it further major injury. Despite such treatment of '002', he disliked the spare car '004' so it was cannibalized and its entire rear end bolted to '002's hastily beaten-out monocoque in time for the race.

While these dramas afflicted '002', aspiring club driver Vern Schuppan was testing '005' at Silverstone, hacking up and down Hangar Straight with a mass of recording apparatus attached to investigate front-end vibrations as the inboard brakes were applied. Unfortunately vibration proved so severe it upset the test equipment so Gardner took the car to MIRA where its tremors were investigated on a rolling road. Inboard brakes clearly required further research, so '005' appeared in Austria with outboard front brakes and the Trident-type airbox. The original lower type had been gulping hot radiator air, and now he was climbing higher in search of a fresher draught.

Stewart raced the car at the Österreichring and built a spectacular lead until it began to vibrate and oversteer. He felt sure something had broken, but he persevered to finish seventh, after which nothing seemed to be amiss. In subsequent investigative testing at Silverstone '005' continued to misbehave, until the left-front tyre from the Austrian race was changed. Magically, it all came good. That tyre's inner shoulder had worn unevenly, possibly due to excessive suspension camber, and no other fault could be traced.

Monza followed, and either Stewart or Hulme of McLaren had to win there and in the final two GPs of the season to deny Fittipaldi and Lotus of the World Championship titles. Stewart drove '005' again while Cevert's '002' appeared with a large-diameter sleeve over each exhaust tailpipe, cowled from the oil coolers ahead of them. The intention was to harness exhaust gas energy to entrain air through the sleeve and so enhance cooling flow through the oil coolers. Sadly the whole panjandrum disintegrated after very few laps, the pieces bouncing and cartwheeling into history in the Tyrrell's wake. Gardner filed the idea for future reference . . .

For the North American trip, another 'series two' car, '006', was completed and it too used outboard front brakes although mounts were incorporated for the inboard type. Cevert took it over

happily and while Stewart won both races in Canada and the USA, Cevert followed him home for a Tyrrell 1-2 at Watkins Glen.

In late-season tunnel testing Gardner had tried another mock-up to investigate what he called a 'rectilinear structure' car, very short with a 91 in. wheelbase, and square cut with a long extended bluff nose. He toyed with eccentric-looking wing sections and also had a dry-sump gearbox lubrication system made which was used for the first time in the Canadian GP.

1973 – WINNING AND LOSING

Those dominant performances at the end of 1972 determined Elf-Team Tyrrell to retrieve Champion status in 1973. In Argentina to start the new season, both '005' and '006' appeared with inboard front brakes installed, coupled to the hubs via new large-diameter drive tubes in place of the original solid shafts. These provided instant indication of undue stress and impending failure.

The Brazilian GP was run at the long and bumpy Interlagos circuit. Tyrrell had tested there in December and found their short-wheelbase cars pitching and skipping in an unnerving fashion. Consequently the 1971 long-wheelbase conversion kit was reused. '005' ran first Brazilian practice in this form but was slower than Cevert's standard '006'.

A torsion-bar sprung rear suspension had been designed between these two South American races and a new wedge-shaped car with midship water radiators and a very stubby monocoque skinned in Mallite sandwich material was under study. This aerospace composite, sandwiching end-grain balsa wood in thin aluminium sheet, had been used by Robin Herd of McLaren back in 1966 but its manufacturers were astonished when Gardner visited them to order special sheets using Formula 1 regulation 16-gauge thick sheathing. The new car was initially to use coil-springs, because torsion bar delivery would take almost a year.

As late as the 1973 Italian GP, the new '74 Tyrrell was intended to be this very short car, narrow at the rear where the torsion bars would be fitted, with inboard-mounted rising-rate front suspension and hip radiators gulping air through a large NACA duct sunk into the top of the nose.

But it was not to be . . .

Meanwhile, in Kyalami practice Stewart had a rear brake-line chafe through, losing one brake circuit and crashing heavily, mangling '005's left side. Tyrrell had no spare car. The wreck had to be repaired with a set of outboard front brakes installed. Stewart took over Cevert's '006', set it up to his liking on race morning, and salvaged victory from that practice disaster.

On the Monday after the race, Cevert ran some Goodyear tyre test laps in the victorious '006'. A tyre overheated, so he stopped to have it changed. Unfortunately, wheels were stacked in the pits for both inboard and outboard brakes, and in error an outboard-brake wheel lacking the drive pegs necessary to lock it onto the inboard-brake drive tube was fitted. As Cevert entered Crowthorne Corner where Stewart had crashed, he braked hard, the brake tubes were retarded, but that unpegged front wheel revolved unhindered. Consequently, '006' spun viciously and smacked into the same wall which had mauled its sister. Fortunately damage was relatively minor.

Back home, a brand new 'series three' car was being completed for Stewart's use in Europe where the new deformable structure tank protection regulations would take effect in Spain. This new regulation had been published so late the previous year that '005' had been designed without foreknowledge. Had Gardner known beforehand, '005' would not have been built the way it was. However, it had more than proved itself, and since nobody wanted to change the basic design, separate crush pads were now added to these three Tyrrells as 38 lb afterthoughts.

The latest '006/2' had larger oil-cooler side pods to allow the water radiators to be moved there subsequently from the nose. Its older sister '006' was tested with a longer bluff nose to balance a rear wing outrigged further aft.

Using '006/2' Stewart won at Silverstone upon its debut, and then rewrote the World Championship record books. He won the Belgian and Monaco GPs to equal Jim Clark's career record of 25 Championship-round wins, then surpassed his late compatriot's total with further victories in the Dutch and German races. Cevert was second to his team leader at Zolder, Zandvoort and the Nürburgring to underline Tyrrell's

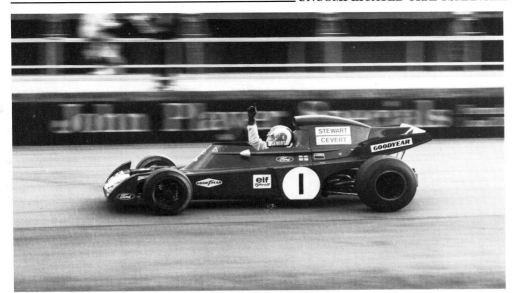

Left: Cevert testing stubby new Tyrrell 005 at Silverstone in 1972, see-through front wheels betraying inboard brakes in Gardner's well-faired prototype low polar moment design.
Below: Stewart equalling Clark's record 25 GP wins, Monaco '73 in deformable-structure '006/2'. Note tall 'Trident' airbox and brake cooling chimneys.

strength, but Lotus were able to accumulate more Constructors' Championship points with their Type 72 cars, both their drivers – Peterson and Fittipaldi – winning GPs during that year to foil Tyrrell's chances of a second Constructors' Championship title.

During that 1973 season, Tyrrell had encountered terrible trouble with overheating brakes at Barcelona and Zolder in Belgium, and new heavier, thicker Lockheed calipers and discs were fitted to '006' and '006/2' while '005' carried heftier Girlings for comparison.

This car had now become an experimental hack, and it practised at Zolder with hip water radiators, and a very sharp chisel nose with a NACA duct sunk into its upper surface feeding a front-mounted oil cooler. It then returned to bluff nose form for Monaco, chisel for Sweden, bluff for Ricard-Castellet and back to chisel nose thereafter, though it was bobbed slightly for the Dutch GP. In Canada and the USA '005' was entered for third driver Chris Amon.

Stewart's '006/2' was converted briefly to chisel nose form in Canada, and after Cevert's regular '006' was written off in that race a brand new car, '006/3', was completed for his use in the United States Grand Prix at Watkins Glen.

In practice there he crashed horribly and was killed, and the brand new car was demolished.

After the accident, towards the end of the afternoon practice session, Stewart and guest driver Chris Amon circulated briefly in their cars, and then Ken Tyrrell withdrew his entries that evening and the team sadly packed and returned disconsolately home.

Jackie Stewart had driven his last Grand Prix race, his 99th, in Canada and would not now reach his century. For Elf-Team Tyrrell it was the end of an era built around the greatest driver of that period. After Cevert's death they now had to plan and build anew for 1974, and Derek Gardner's plans for a highly strung thoroughbred car from which only the masters could extract an elusive potential now had to be set aside. With Stewart retired and Cevert dead, the new team drivers would be comparative schoolboys, and it was considered prudent to design completely different cars in keeping with their inexperience. Never again, within our period, would Tyrrell win the World Championship, but come 1987 they would have some consolation with a World title of a lesser hue . . .

The Tyrrell Six-Wheeler

In 1975 the Tyrrell Racing Organisation sought an unusual advantage over their fellow Cosworth DFV and Goodyear tyre users as engineer Derek Gardner evolved his remarkable six-wheeled Project 34 design.

The idea, as he tells the story, '. . . was to minimize induced drag by reducing lift at the front and to turn that small gain into the ability to enter and leave corners faster. It was a matter of trading downforce for cornering power and it seemed to work.

'Tyres stuck out in the airstream generate lift so one has to counteract that by adding downforce. If everyone else does more or less the same you all end up with very similar performance given that we all used the same engine and effectively the same tyres.

'If one can reduce lift it gives you extra effective downforce to play with and more downforce translates into more cornering speed.'

To achieve this aim he adopted a very broad bluff nose section masking two small-wheeled front suspension sets running 10 in. diameter front wheels and tyres. There was no advantage in car frontal area, since its value was still dictated by the huge standard-sized rear tyres, but this was not at all what Derek was seeking.

A rotating cylinder – such as that presented by a racing car wheel and tyre – introduced into a moving airstream will generate a force at right angles to its cylindrical axis, the magnitude of that force being related to the cylinder's radius. In the case of a rotating racing car wheel and tyre this force is exerted in an upward direction as lift. Appreciation of this effect is what led Tecno and BMW in Formula 2 and Gardner in Formula 1 – after Matra had introduced their full-width chisel affair at Kyalami '71 – to adopt the broad bluff wheel-fairing noses of 1970-71.

However, by reducing the front-wheel size in the P34 this lift was instantly reduced, enhancing cornering and braking forces, the actual reduction in overall diameter being from 21 to 16 inches.

Naturally, all four steerable front wheels were braked, and a further considerable advantage was found in using four front discs, offering increased mass of cast iron in the discs themselves which short-term reduced working temperatures; furthermore, an enlargement of the disc swept-area improved brake cooling by radiation. Increased rotational speed enhanced cooling airflow through the ventilated disc drillings and passages. Total pad area was also increased, which reduced working temperatures, and a gain of nearly 40 per cent in useable pad volume greatly extended pad life on certain demanding circuits.

Brake balance had to be achieved between the front two axles and the rear, and Gardner developed a triple

master-cylinder system, each feeding the brakes on one axle. The driver's brake pedal was attached to a balance bar acting at one end on the rear-brake master cylinder and at the other end onto a secondary balance bar which could be adjusted similarly to divide effort between the two front-axle master cylinders.

The team would set the balance first between the two pairs of front brakes, bearing in mind that if the first-axle brakes locked first then the effective wheelbase would be shortened, if the second-axle brakes locked first it would be lengthened, with consequent queasy changes in handling and driver 'feel'.

Disadvantages in the braking sense included the higher rotational speed of the small front wheels and discs for a given road speed, but since the discs themselves were smaller the critical rubbing speed at the pad surface was about the same as normal.

Once they had learned how to operate – and to drive – these unusual cars early in 1976, the Tyrrell team achieved significant success, as described in the Team Directory.

Taking contemporary tyre technology early that year, they had a distinct advantage in suitable conditions, but as the season progressed they encountered problems which outstripped Goodyear's development capabilities.

That was the season of Ferrari versus McLaren and quite rightly Goodyear concentrated development upon the needs of those cars, the 312T2s and M23s. When newly developed conventional front and rear tyres were introduced, the P34s could use the rears but there was no compatible new 10 in. front tyre for them. Consequently they had either to run unbalanced or to retain outdated rears.

To combat this small-diameter front tyre stagnation Gardner had only one option for 1977: progressively to increase the front track to load up available fronts to match latest compounds and construction. The small wheels' high rotational speeds in any case played havoc with the profiles of contemporary cross-ply racing tyres, the crown centre 'throwing out' to diminish contact area against the road surface.

The wider front track for 1977 necessitated bodywork changes in an attempt to retrieve aerodynamic advantage and the already overweight cars grew less and less competitive and became even heavier.

In retrospect, Gardner believes that radial-ply front tyres would have been the answer. 'If Tyrrell had been on Michelins the story might have been different' – and indeed Michelin were interested in assisting. However, by the time they had developed a new 10 in. size from scratch, Goodyear's conventional tyres for conventional cars would have leapt three or four stages further ahead.

Gardner had received an attractive offer to return to his first love of transmission engineering with Borg Warner and while an Elf-backed potential engine supply deal was being set up with Renault he had already taken on Maurice Phillippe to develop a Tyrrell chassis for a Renault engine.

After he had handed total responsibility to Phillippe and left the team, the Renault plan – which had included both a broad-arrow 3-litre nine-cylinder and a 1500 cc turbocharged V6 – evaporated. Maurice introduced a four-wheeled P34 replacement for 1978 and this was destined to win on conventional, competitive and untroublesome Goodyear tyres . . . only four per car.

Top left: Motor Sport's *Denis Jenkinson inspects 'P34/1' in 1976.* Top right: *Scheckter demonstrates the car's front-end grip into Monza's* Curva Parabolica *in that year's Italian GP.* Left: *Piola's exploded sketch amply illustrates the Tyrrell P34's complexity.*

Chapter 8

THE WEDGE-SHAPED McLAREN M23s 1973-77

Denny Hulme winning the 1973 Swedish GP at Anderstorp in McLaren 'M23/1' – a lucky win at the expense of Peterson's Lotus 72 though the McLaren also set fastest lap. This was the first of the long M23 series' 21 frontline race wins.

During the summer of 1972 all Formula 1 teams were thinking towards the deformable structure regulations which would become effective early in the new season. At Colnbrook, under the Heathrow flight paths west of London, Team McLaren thought more deeply than any other.

Not for them any afterthought tack-on crush pads in their new car. They determined to build a properly integrated tailor-made monocoque which would optimize their long-held tenets of strength, practicality and simplicity combined with sheer product quality.

Engineer Gordon Coppuck had been mainly responsible for McLaren's highly successful and innovative CanAm and Indianapolis cars during this period, but when ex-Brabham designer Ralph Bellamy – who had designed the M19s – left to return to Brabham at the end of 1971, Coppuck remained alone in charge of the drawing office.

He began work on the new 1973 Formula 1 car, drawing deeply upon his Indianapolis M16 experience with a wedge-form monocoque and hip-mounted radiators. McLaren's method of design had always pivoted around a workshop discussion which would include the team principals, drivers and mechanics in addition to the nominal designer himself. This system worked very well for the team for many years.

The basic M16 shape had followed the lead of the Lotus 56 and 72 wedges of 1968-70, to take full advantage of the constant high-speed regime prevailing at Indy. Now, during 1972, Coppuck recalls how 'we had taken an M16 tub and a Cosworth rear end from the M19, sat them down on the workshop floor, looked at them; thought about them, and weighed them, and all the answers told us the right thing. Do it. So we did, and the M23 came into being.'

The M19 in its final C-specification form had handled very well but was slow on the straight and overweight. The long and arduous development of its rising-rate suspension system had achieved a very efficient front end, but at the rear the team had admitted defeat and reverted to a constant-rate layout.

Eventually they could attribute the M19C's good handling to its big wings and rising-rate front end. Its poor straightline speed could be blamed on induced drag from those big wings and high profile drag from the bulbous, heavily riveted tub.

The new M23 was Gordon Coppuck's first Formula 1 design. Its tub was formed in 16-gauge aluminium sheet, shaped over a massive fabricated steel bulkhead at the front and a capacious tank section at the back, between the driver's seat back and engine bulkhead, which was itself a three-quarter affair, with separate steel fabrications for the top engine mounts. The dash frame consisted of steel bracketry rather than a conventional intermediate bulkhead, while steel pick-ups were built in for the rearward legs of the lower front wishbones, the front bulkhead itself extending back into the monocoque for eight to ten inches.

In the usual McLaren manner, which was unusual when originated by Robin Herd in 1968, all panel joints in these tubs were bonded with epoxy adhesive as well as being riveted – the riveting in effect securing the joint while the adhesive cured.

This new tub tapered in planform and also – at the front – in section where the front bulkhead was wider at top than bottom. Unlike the detachable radiator side pods of the Lotus 72 and the McLaren M16 Indycars, those of the new M23 were formed as an integral delta-form extension of the monocoque structure, the intention being to provide two-stage deformable protection under impact.

The tub's horizontal 16-gauge aluminium skins extended over and under these pods, shaping into their outer vertical panel while a glass-fibre insert section then slid into the pod intake, mating neatly with the aluminium skins and extending into the midship monocoque flank itself. Once the assembly had been drilled, countersunk and

Piola again, showing dimensional data of McLaren's multi-wedge M23 as modified for the 1975 season.

Hailwood's ill-fated Yardley M23 leaves Karussel at the Nürburgring prior to his career-ending 1974 German GP crash. Note centre-pillar rear 'banana' wing, deep-cambered nose 'foils and slender large-profile tall airbox.

flush-riveted this left a gap of about ³/₄ in. between GRP insert and aluminium skin, which McLaren's build crew under Don Beresford then filled with twin-pack aerosol foam. The foaming reaction began as soon as the two chemicals mixed at the injector nozzle, and precautions had to be taken to prevent the pressure created by the expanding foam then blowing out the GRP insert and distorting the aluminium. A shaped block was made up from the GRP mould to support the plastic against foam pressure, while the rest of the tub structure had similarly to be strapped and supported during this cavity-filling operation. A row of half-inch drain holes allowed excess foam to escape, and once the foam had set then the residue could be trimmed back, the holes capped and sanded smooth. The end result was a very good deformable crush pad built integrally into the hull and contributing towards its torsional rigidity without undue weight penalty.

Learning the intricacies of this new technique caused some heartache but, once the McLaren crew became accustomed to it, it worked well. One major drawback, however, was that it complicated damage repair.

Fuel tankage was concentrated amidships with relatively little capacity extending toward the dash panel on each side to promote Matra/Tyrrell/March-like low polar moment. All previous McLaren F1 tubs had carried their fuel right from front bulkhead to rear.

The M23's cockpit was as confined as possible to narrow the tub and ease airflow into the hip radiator ducts, which housed both the water radiators and oil cooler cores. Deletion of the nose radiator instantly reduced cockpit temperatures, further helped by the insulating effect of the large fuel tank between driver and hot engine bay. This set the driver further forward than ever before, with his feet ahead of the front axle line.

In the cockpit the Graviner fire extinguisher bottle sat crosswise beneath the driver's knees. For his protection the steering box was now inboard of the front bulkhead, just ahead of the dash panel and less than 12 inches from the steering wheel. All steering links and arms were behind the front uprights, leaving the front monocoque bulkhead extremely tidy with only the brake master cylinders and slender front anti-roll bar protruding.

A neat tray arrangement carried the lightweight Varley battery while a spidery tubular subframe extended further forward to accept the wedge-shaped detachable nose cone and its front aerofoil aerodynamic loadings. NACA ducts moulded into each side of this cone fed slots through the front bulkhead which played cooling air onto the inboard coil-spring/damper units buried just behind.

The rising-rate front suspension comprised wide-based lower wishbones and triangulated tubular top rocker arms whose inboard extremities compressed the spring/damper units via linkages with rising-rate geometry. With the new midship fuel tankage, variation in fuel load made much greater percentage difference to the load carried by the front wheels than by the rears. M19 experience showed that this allowed a much simpler system to be used there, with progressively wound coil-springs of the type which become coil-bound from the lower end as load increased.

Rear suspension location was by reversed lower wishbones, adjustable top links and twin radius rods. Some vital unsprung weight had been saved by dispensing with conventional sliding-spline driveshaft joints. These normally allow the driveshafts to telescope, so accommodating changes in length between their inboard anchorage on the final-drive outputs and their outboard anchorage on the wheel flange as the road wheels move through their suspension arc. Now Coppuck had adopted a floating axle system tried successfully on the M19s. It used two needle roller bearings in the upright instead of the conventional single needle roller and one fixed bearing. Two diameters were machined to suit on the fixed-length shaft, and it was allowed to float sideways in and out of the upright as the suspension rose and fell. The wheel face prevented the shaft pulling through one way, the fixed universal-joint yoke the other way. Shims fitted in assembly ensured the upright centred statically in the middle of the driveshaft bearing track provided.

This system worked very well, saving the considerable weight of a conventional sliding-spline joint, and a further saving followed when titanium driveshafts were adopted with steel yokes pushed onto them.

Lockheed CanAm-developed four-pot brake calipers were used, clasping 10.5 in. ventilated discs all round. At the front, where live stub axles were used, rotating within the cast-magnesium uprights, the discs were mounted outboard but not fully buried within the 13 in. diameter/11 in. wide wheels. At the rear, where road wheel sizes were 13 in. x 16-18 in. wide, the brake discs were inboard, further reducing unsprung weight. While the oil coolers sat right behind the water radiator cores within those integral side pods, the oil tank itself was buried in the left-rear corner of the monocoque, while the system catch tank formed a saddle over the bell-housing for the Hewland FG400 five-speed transaxle.

The oil cooler mounting tidied up rear-end plumbing to clear airflow beneath the working undersurface of the tubular-strutted rear wing.

At the time of its release in February 1973, the M23 was unusual in being so fully bodied, following Gardner's lead with Tyrrell 005 the preceding summer. The untidy engine induction was concealed within a shapely airbox cowl merging into the rear tub-cum-side pod form.

The M23 was an inch longer in wheelbase than the M19, at 101 in., and the tub was lower than its predecessor but the airbox extended taller than before in search of cleaner air, making the car noticeably higher. Front track was 65 in., rear track 62.5 in., overall length 170 in. and claimed weight 1270 lb distributed 34 front/66 rear.

In the next four seasons, thirteen McLaren M23s would be built – chassis number '13' being skipped for superstitious reasons so the final car took the number M23/14. The cars would bring their drivers two World Championship titles and their manufacturer one Formula 1 Constructors' Cup victory, and they would win no fewer than 20 Championship-qualifying Grands Prix, and arguably 21 if another on-the-road victory is counted from which car and driver were subsequently disqualified. The series was incredibly long-lived, like the Lotus 72, being in frontline use through four seasons.

In the first of those, 1973, four M23s were built, followed by four more in 1974 and two in 1975. No new M23s were produced in their second Drivers' Championship season of 1976, but two new works cars and the final private-entry car for American Brett Lunger followed in 1977 before the type was finally replaced by the slow-to-develop M26.

Of all these cars, chassis M23/4, M23/7, M23/8

and M23/9 were effectively written off in racing accidents. Only M23/7 would not be rebuilt at all, while number 4 was resurrected as a non-running promotional show car for Marlboro who were the team's sponsors from 1974 onwards, and number 8 was rebuilt as another show car, taking the chassis tag number '10'. Chassis 9 was rebuilt as a running museum piece in later years.

Meanwhile, the M23s had developed through B, C, D, E and F specifications. The modifications involved can be listed as follows:

M23B – 1974, chassis change around the front bulkhead to accept alternative progressive-rate or rocker arm front suspension – longer wheelbase – parallel-link rear suspension.
M23C – 1975, further revised suspensions – different airbox – driver-adjustable front anti-roll bar – short nose and side panel extension aerodynamics.
M23D – 1976, from 1 May, low regulation airbox – short-lived driver-adjustable rear anti-roll bar – air starter introduced – six-speed McLaren-Hewland gearbox – longer cockpit surround extending onto nose cone to accommodate James Hunt.
M23E – 1977, detail changes headed by redesigned front uprights to cater for new-diameter Goodyear tyres.
M23F – Category for McLaren-made parts intended for private-customer sale.

All of which sounds simple, but as we shall see the story was far more involved and the progression of development changes far more complicated and chronologically jumbled than this list records. In the real world, Formula 1 racing can be a confused and confusing business.

Back at the start, in 1973, the prototype chassis M23/1 was tested for some 65 laps at Goodwood before being flown to Kyalami ready for the South African GP there on 3 March. Even on its very first day at Goodwood it was faster than the extensively tested, two-year-old M19. Hulme commented on how unusual its far-forward driving position felt: 'you can almost lean out and touch the front wheels . . .'

For the first 10 laps or so he found it very difficult to judge rear wheel placing and to sense incipient oversteer. But with more practice he was able to induce oversteer at will and control it far better than was possible on the M19. The M23 would enter a stable and sustainable oversteer which the M19 had never offered. The cooler cockpit was also welcome, obviating a major cause of driver fatigue.

In the heat and altitude of Kyalami the twinned mounting of water radiators and oil coolers within the same pods proved to be a mistake, the coolers being resited either side of the gearbox, which also put more weight on the rear wheels.

The car was very quick, and Hulme took his first-ever GP pole position in it. He led the race, but an early-lap collision had sprayed the roadway with debris and he suffered a puncture. Rejoining with a fresh tyre fitted, Hulme was astounded to see a plume of smoke stream from the M23's left-front tyre on every right-hand corner. Presuming this tyre too was punctured, he stopped again to change it, but it was in fact intact. He finished only fifth after these delays but the M23 had shown terrific promise.

Through the rest of that season the works M23s would qualify regularly within the first three or four on the GP grids. A second car, M23/2 of course, was ready in time for Peter Revson to drive it in the minor Silverstone race on 8 April, in which he finished fourth while Hulme retired the prototype.

Three M23s were available in time for the first 'deformable structure' GP in Spain on 29 April, and at Zolder on 20 May Hulme's car carried a Graviner life-support system for the first time. This offered a breathable air supply piped into the driver's helmet and triggered in case of fire.

Revson crashed his car M23/2 in this event and the wreck was subsequently savaged as Jarier's March flew off on the same patch of disintegrating asphalt and crashed into the stricken McLaren.

Hulme won the Swedish GP with fortune on his side, though he also set fastest race lap, and when Revson was committed to a USAC race on French GP weekend, cadet driver Jody Scheckter made his European GP debut for the team by driving the latest chassis, M23/3. He qualified faster than Hulme, started from the front row and led the race until just 12 laps from the end when he and Fittipaldi of Lotus fell over each other in a corner.

All three M23s ran for the first time in the British GP on 14 July which has passed into history for 'Scheckter's shunt'. He lost control ending lap one between the pits and main grandstand and spun in front of the pack, causing a multiple accident which eliminated nine cars and stopped the race while the mess was cleared up. Revson won the restarted race in M23/2 while Hulme finished third.

Scheckter's M23/3 was still under repair one week later when the new M23/4 emerged as team spare at Zandvoort for the Dutch GP. This car was then driven by guest driver Jacky Ickx – a fugitive from Ferrari at this time – in the German GP at the Nürburgring, where his specialist circuit knowledge helped him finish third behind the dominant Tyrrells.

Coppuck meanwhile was developing a revised geometry suspension package for the cars but Silverstone testing was inconclusive so the M23s ran on unchanged.

The Canadian GP was another shambles, this time due to bad weather, but Revson won again, using M23/4 while Scheckter collided with Cevert's Tyrrell and mangled M23/2's left-front corner and side pod. The damage was repaired in McLaren Engines' facility at Livonia, Detroit, in time for the US GP at Watkins Glen, where Hulme and Revson finished 4-5 and Scheckter retired when a rear wishbone broke . . . fortunately this time without hitting anything hard.

1974 – FIRST CHAMPIONSHIP SEASON

For 1974, the Texaco-Marlboro McLaren team was born, with Hulme being joined by Emerson Fittipaldi since Revson had moved to Shadow and Scheckter to lead the Tyrrell team. McLaren's previous Yardley sponsorship continued into the new year with a one-car operation running an allegedly identical M23 for Mike Hailwood.

During the winter at Colnbrook, two brand new M23s had been built up, chassis M23/5 and M23/6. Lengthy winter testing at Ricard-Castellet had persuaded Coppuck and the McLaren team to modify their promising original design to compensate for the effects of the new rear wing overhang

McLaren experimented extensively: Hulme's 'M23/6' runs shortlived winkle-picker nose for 1974 Race of Champions. Whole car is neat, simple and exquisitely prepared. Clean airflow beneath rear wing was vital.

restrictions. The rear wing had to come forward some 10 in. from its 1973 position, but since this was measured relative to the rear wheels the answer was obviously to move the rear wheels further back. This would leave the wing in relatively clean air, well aft of the airbox. Airflow would also be improved by widening the rear track to minimize interference from tyre turbulence.

Consequently, wheelbase was lengthened by three inches with a bell-housing spacer extension between engine and gearbox setting the rear wheels further back. The front bulkhead structure was modified to accept either fixed-rate geometry rocker arm front suspension or the old progressive system. Rear track was widened by two inches and geometry changes were made to enhance traction away from slow corners.

New driver Fittipaldi did the lion's share of winter testing, Hulme as always being content to sit back and let someone else do the work.

Hailwood's Yardley-liveried prototype M23/1 was modified to similar specification and M23/4 in Marlboro livery became team spare when the 1974 season began in Argentina.

Fittipaldi took to team and car like a duck to water and did 97 practice laps in celebration at Buenos Aires! He was delayed there in the race by a stray plug lead, then inadvertently knocked off the electrical 'kill-switch' on his steering wheel. By the time he realized his mistake he had lost much ground. Meanwhile Hulme found his LWB M23 the fastest car present through the long fifth-gear loop at the end of the main straight and he closed on the leaders until Reutemann's dominant Brabham fell sick and Hulme took the lead on the penultimate lap and won. Hailwood finished fourth despite having a stone puncture in one radiator.

Optional higher radius rod pick-ups were provided on the chassis in Brazil where the bumpy Interlagos bankings demanded more suspension movement. Fittipaldi started from pole and led from lap 16 to lap 32, whereupon the race was flagged to a finish due to heavy rain, and Marlboro-McLaren's M23s had won two in a row. When Fittipaldi won the minor Brasilia race after Reutemann's leading Brabham blew up, the new M23 team had won the first three Formula 1 races of the season. The Brabham BT44 seemed clearly quicker, but McLaren preparation and reliable competitiveness had paid off handsomely.

Now the team began experimenting in earnest, searching for a decisive advantage, just as had

Reigning Champion Fittipaldi at Monaco 1975 in 'M23/9' showing its fabricated top rocker arms and exceptionally wide track rear suspension.

Derek Gardner with the Tyrrells in 1971.

Back in Europe for the minor Brands Hatch event, an ingenious new rear wing mounting appeared, copiously drilled on various arcs to enable a vast range of alternative wing incidences to be used at will. Another experiment involved a slender 'winkle-picker' wedge nose carrying longer-span, high-aspect ratio front 'foils, using a similar very exaggerated banana section to the tail wing.

At Kyalami, scene of the M23 prototype's very promising debut 12 months previously, Goodyear offered their new 28 in. outside diameter tyres.

For baseline purposes, Hulme's M23/6 was rigged initially in 1973 trim, complete down to the original wheelbase, rear track width, older-style wing sections and 26 in. outside diameter rear tyres. It simply ate the latest-compound Goodyears and Hulme reported it felt awful.

In the second day's practice, M23s 1, 5 and 6 all ran in Brands Hatch form, finding better stability and much improved traction on the new 28 in. tyres, as well as better download with the older-style broad nose cones which replaced the experimental winkle-pickers. Hailwood subsequently recorded the twin team's best finish, in third place.

The seventh M23 to be completed was ready for him to use in Yardley colours at the minor Silverstone race on 7 April, in which he lay briefly second before early retirement with clutch failure.

Five M23s were taken to Jarama for the Spanish GP, and Coppuck had them all set up in short-wheelbase form for more nimble response on the tight Autodrome circuit. Hulme's M23/6 had five alternative lower and three alternative upper pick-ups fitted for the rear radius rods to research optimum anti-squat characteristics, while Hailwood's spare M23/1 was in standard form as a comparative baseline.

There was considerable head-scratching about lessons learned from this exercise and at the faster Nivelles Autodrome for the Belgian GP all the M23s were delivered in long-wheelbase form, and Fittipaldi became the first driver of the season to win two GPs, staving off a strong Ferrari challenge to do so. Hulme was only sixth but set fastest lap, while Hailwood had run fifth before fuel pick-up problems slowed his car.

Short-wheelbase form might be considered most suitable for the tight street circuit at Monaco, but there Fittipaldi's regular M23/5 used a short spacer between engine and gearbox, while Hulme's M23/6 had a long spacer and Hailwood's a medium-length one! Each carried a winkle-picker nose with long-span front foils, while Fittipaldi's had the extra feature of tall vertical sighting masts on the foil tips to judge car placing better.

An unwell Fittipaldi inherited fifth place after a

M23 details. Top: Rigid plastic draught-excluder on the periphery of Mass's 'M23/9', 1976 British GP; that year's extended radiator ducts with oil cooler behind water cores; rear monocoque fillet, designed to coincide with DFV top mounting plate angle. Centre and above: Scheckter tested the M23's integral deformable radiator ducting in his 1973 British GP accident.

careful drive, to lead the World Championship standings.

New slimline airboxes with a much larger side profile appeared at Dijon-Prenois, extending further back towards the rear wing to improve airflow onto it. Vestigial plastic skirts around the under-periphery of the car were tried briefly at this meeting, in an attempt to exclude air from underneath and so minimize aerodynamic lift, thus allowing the wings to apply their download more effectively against diminished resistance. But the plastic skirting had only to touch the track surface to wear away. Any advantage seemed uncertain and slight.

Meanwhile a further modified brand new M23, chassis 8 in the series, was nearing completion at Colnbrook. It emerged at Brands Hatch, featuring low-offset front suspension with revised steering geometry, and parallel-link rear suspension which replaced the original reversed lower wishbone system. Fittipaldi liked the new car's reduced steering effort and used it in the race, inheriting second place.

Two weeks later, at the Nürburgring, the spare M23/5 appeared with parallel-link rear suspension and low-offset front end, while Hulme's regular car and the two Yardley chassis retained the earlier set-up.

During practice Hailwood crashed M23/1 heavily when it unaccountably turned sharp right out of the corner before the pits and smeared itself into the Armco. He continued practising in M23/7, convinced something had broken on the older car. In the race he then crashed chassis 7 very heavily after landing askew after a yump and hitting the barriers almost head-on. The steel feet carrying the bottom-front wishbone pick-up punched back into the monocoque and smashed the unfortunate driver's ankle and shin, ending his career and sparking a major reinforcement subsequently built into all M23s to prevent a recurrence. Chassis M23/7 was totally destroyed and uniquely amongst its family would never be rebuilt.

Fittipaldi had been stranded at the start, unable to find a gear, and he was rammed from behind by Hulme's sister car, so it was a bad weekend all round for the Colnbrook teams.

Since Phil Kerr's Yardley operation had lost both its chassis, M23/1 and M23/7, at the Nürburgring, the Marlboro team's spare M23/4 was resprayed to suit in time for the Österreichring, where David Hobbs was invited to drive it. This old car had last appeared in Hulme's hands at Jarama. Fittipaldi raced the latest-spec M23/8 while Hulme's older M23/6 still retained the reversed-wishbone rear suspension, though spare car M23/5 was to the latest spec. Fittipaldi's engine failed when running third. Hulme drove steadily to inherit second behind the winning Brabham BT44.

At Monza, Fittipaldi was second to Peterson's Lotus 72 by just 0.8 second, but McLaren displaced Ferrari at the head of the Constructors' Championship table. Only two Championship rounds remained: the Canadian and US GPs in North America.

Yardley took Jochen Mass there to drive their entry in these events where the cars ran in unchanged form other than the fitting of USAC team two-way radio sets for Watkins Glen, where Fittipaldi secured the Drivers' title, McLaren confirmed victory in the Constructors' Championship, and Denny Hulme retired from the race, and from racing, when his engine blew on the fourth lap.

1975 – UNSUCCESSFUL TITLE DEFENCE
The M23 entered its third season's racing in 1975, substantially unaltered from 1974 form although early in the season there were various suspension revisions tried to improve front-end adhesion and 'turn-in' performance. Four cars were used, two being written off during the season by Fittipaldi's new regular number two, Mass, both ironically on his home soil at the Nürburgring.

Ferrari had the most powerful and reliable cars of the season in their latest 312Ts, but McLaren's preparation managed by Alastair Caldwell gave the team a 74 per cent finishing record – 20 finishes from 27 starts – which Ferrari could shade only marginally with 75 per cent.

Another brand new car had been built for Fittipaldi's use, chassis M23/9, which made its debut in Buenos Aires. It carried Brabham-like front suspension in which the original tubular frame rocker arms had been replaced by substantial swept-back fabricated top arms with pullrods attached under their outboard extremities, pulling up a shaped actuating arm at the foot of gently inclined semi-inboard coil-spring/damper units. Mass's M23/8 retained the old fully inboard front suspension system, while Emerson's new car also used appreciably narrower rear track and both cars were fitted with abbreviated nose cones.

Fittipaldi promptly blooded M23/9 with first-time victory, the eighth World Championship round win for the M23 series, while in Brazil the team cars finished 2-3 behind Pace's victorious Brabham BT44B.

Chassis M23/9's Brabham-crib front suspension was modified in time for the South African trip with right-angle instead of swept-back arms, which served to lengthen the wheelbase and throw more load onto the front wheels. M23/8, meanwhile, had been brought up to South American specification, with swept-back pullrod front suspension and the shorter or standard wheelbase. When Fittipaldi's engine blew in practice, his spare car, M23/6, was prepared with the latest-style suspension and he raced it – unsuccessfully – in this form.

Back home for Brands Hatch, the old chassis M23/4 was prepared and offered a third variant front suspension layout, this time with the coil/dampers mounted totally inboard again, but this time vertically and actuated by conventional fabricated steel top rocker arms, the team being unconvinced by their pullrod experiments. After Silverstone's non-Championship race, non-rising-rate fully inboard front suspension was adopted as standard. The two regular cars at Barcelona – chassis 8 for Mass and 9 for Fittipaldi – used it, while chassis 5 last used at Kyalami retained the South American style rising-rate layout.

There at Montjuich Park, Fittipaldi was deeply unhappy with circuit safety and boycotted the race, while Mass competed and was declared the winner when a bad accident caused the race to be stopped.

The regular cars reappeared at Monaco, in 1974 medium-wheelbase form for agility, and Fittipaldi's carried a new cockpit-adjustable front anti-roll bar, enabling him to soften roll-stiffness as the fuel load diminished during the race. He finished second to Lauda's dominant Ferrari.

All these interminable changes and modifications owed more to practice than theory. You had a hunch, and you tried it, and if the car lapped faster you used it. This is race development in the real world, nothing like the academic engineering journalist's theorizing.

For Zolder, the long-wheelbase form returned and in mid-practice a rapid narrow-track mod was made to Fittipaldi's car and it promptly lapped faster, though the rival Brabhams and Ferraris

Fittipaldi demonstrates 'M23/10's' flat-topped deltaform at Monza 1975, with top rocker arm front suspension, steering behind the hubs, moulded front brake cooling ducts wrapping close inside the front tyres and low-slung tail oil coolers all visible.

were faster still. In time for the Swedish trip Coppuck developed further suspension mods but Fittipaldi was unimpressed. At Zandvoort the big articulated McLaren transporter disgorged its fleet of M23s with Coppuck smilingly claiming 'the Mark 197 arrangement' for M23/9, with its rear suspension modified this time, and with rearward side pod extension panels to improve airflow further beneath that vital rear wing.

Mass crashed M23/8 heavily in this race, mauling its front end, so for the subsequent French GP at Ricard-Castellet he raced M23/6 while Fittipaldi persevered with M23/9 in its Zandvoort form. As it happened Mass drove one of the best races of his life to finish third, close behind the second-placed Hesketh 308, while Fittipaldi was handicapped by poor handling and finished a distant – and fortunate – fourth.

At Silverstone for the British GP a new swallow-tailed rear wing was featured on Fittipaldi's car, and when the race was beset by heavy rain showers which sent cars spinning in all directions he emerged as lucky winner. McLaren always seemed to win the funny races – British and Canadian GPs '73, and now Spain and the British GP '75 . . . But Fittipaldi had kept his head while all around were losing their cool; it was a touch of class which made the most of his ageing car.

Mass's M23/8, damaged at Zandvoort, was rebuilt in time for the Nürburgring where the McLarens wore new contoured flairs on the trailing edges of the radiator pods and plastic vestigial skirt draught-excluders reappeared underneath. Fittipaldi's M23/9 had lost its driver-adjustable front anti-roll bar for this meeting.

Mass tried too hard in practice and wrote off his freshly rebuilt M23/8, then had a front tyre collapse on his spare car M23/4 in the race and destroyed this chassis as well.

Back at Colnbrook the intended M23-replacement M26 car was now being finalized but frantic work began to restore a full complement of M23s meantime. No spare car was available for the Austrian GP in which Mass took over the ex-Hulme M23/6, while a brand new car was built from the ground up in two weeks for Fittipaldi to blood in the so-called 'Swiss GP', a minor Marlboro-sponsored race at Dijon. This car was really number 10 in the M23 series, but there was no time to arrange new customs paperwork for it, so its chassis-plate carried the number M23/8-2 to inherit the Nürburgring write-off's carnets. When McLaren works manager Leo Wybrott later rebuilt the original M23/8 as a collector's car, it took the plate M23/10, which it retains in private hands to this day.

In the final race of 1975 at Watkins Glen, Fittipaldi again showed real fire. He was only narrowly bumped off pole by Lauda's Ferrari, and he finished an honourable second after being very badly baulked by the second-string Ferrari of Regazzoni. McLaren ended the season third in the Constructors' Championship, behind

Hunt's disqualification from the 1976 British GP caused much dispute. See the M23D-spec's new regulation airbox, forward roll-over bar within screen and undertray chevron air dam – the ground-effects era unwittingly dawns.

Ferrari and Brabham.

Testing at Ricard-Castellet in November, Fittipaldi crashed and broke a finger. Amid some acrimony he left McLaren at short notice later that month, but was replaced admirably by James Hunt whose former Hesketh team had just effectively closed down.

Hunt drove his first McLaren laps at a mist-shrouded Silverstone that December using the ex-Fittipaldi M23/8-2 with its pedals suitably moved forward to accommodate the Englishman's taller frame.

That winter saw the new Coppuck-designed M26 honeycomb car continuing its delayed development, while Alastair Caldwell had translated a personal pet theory into reality through the previous season. He felt there was room for a sixth speed within the existing Hewland FGA transaxle, and the team's Nicholson-McLaren tuned DFV engines could be tailored to a more peaky power curve which could be used to advantage with a six-speed gearbox. Caldwell was an abrasive character but he had played a major part in McLaren racing, insisting on quality in everything, and his pet six-speed gearbox project would now pay real dividends.

1976 – CHAMPION SENSATION

By the time the Brazilian GP opened the new season on 25 January 1976 some 30 lb weight had been trimmed off the existing M23s, in part by use of lighter body panels, stiffened with carbon-fibre filament. The parallel-link rear suspension had proved effective but heavy, and so reversed lower wishbones now reappeared, with toe-steer being adequately controlled by very accurate setting up of the radius rod lengths upon assembly – the joints at each end of the radius rod of course being screw-adjustable for length.

From the sponsor's viewpoint, this race also introduced the now familiar Marlboro dayglo red livery, to improve the cars' 'TV identity'. It was expensive but very effective.

The M23s were not ideal for Interlagos but the new six-speed gearbox, which the team kept quiet, served to plug some gaps around the course and Hunt promptly qualified on pole ahead of Lauda's Ferrari. He then ran second until a freak failure saw one of the fuel injection trumpets rattle

adrift, taking the screwed-in injector nozzle with it. Hunt continued on only seven cylinders until the errant trumpet jammed the throttle slides open and M23/8-2 spun off into the catch-fences, damaging its rear wing and oil coolers.

Another Caldwell development then appeared on the cars at Kyalami. The normal electrical starter motor was a heavy affair ill-suited to any racing car. Now he had developed a compressed-air starter system which appeared on the M23s, using an onboard reservoir chargeable from any air-line and activated by a small solenoid. An onboard battery powerful enough to turn over the normal electric starter was no longer necessary, saving another few pounds weight and unnecessary complication. This invention would be taken up by every other team in Formula 1.

Both cars practised at Kyalami wearing plastic aerodynamic underskirts, but they were removed after protest during a dispute over legal wing heights and what now constituted the 'underside' of the car.

Again Hunt started on pole and he was beaten by Lauda's Ferrari by only 1.3 secs after a hard race. The Hunt/M23 combination then scored its first victory at Brands Hatch one week later.

For Long Beach, California, the M23s wore CanAm brakes with 35 per cent greater pad area than normal. Hunt was barged out of the race by a Tyrrell but Mass placed fifth. Then at Silverstone Hunt won again, in a class of his own, the only driver in the 1;17 bracket in practice, starting his regular M23/8-2 from pole, leading all the way and setting fastest lap.

In Spain, where the new airbox regulations took effect, McLaren adopted an eared affair low behind the roll-over bar, forming the M23D variant. Mass took over the team's former spare M23/9 for this race, setting aside his usual M23/6 which he felt must be deficient in some inexplicable manner, having been quite unable to match his new team-mate's pace in the sister car. Unfortunately for him, Hunt promptly took out M23/6 and lapped just as fast as in his regular car, '8-2.

The two McLarens looked set for a 1-2 victory in this race until the luckless Mass's engine blew, leaving Hunt a winning margin of nearly 31 seconds over Lauda's Ferrari. But at post-race scrutineering the M23 was found to be 1.8 cm too wide across the rear wheel rims and the car was disqualified. McLaren protested and had the penalty reduced to a $3000 fine. This took time, and in the interim second place man Lauda's Ferrari had been declared winner, then demoted again as the original result was confirmed. This created an atmosphere of dissension which intensified as the season progressed.

Meanwhile, for the Belgian GP at Zolder the M23s' rear track was pulled back well within the new 215 cm limit – which itself had been based on the M23 dimension as it was the widest car in contemporary Formula 1 – by machining the inside wheel faces and adjusting the wishbone mounting points to match. Oil coolers had returned from the tail to the side pods, but early in practice Mass's M23/9 lost oil pressure so the coolers migrated back to the tail next day to reduce lubricant temperatures. Hunt led the Ferraris off the line, but his M23's handling was 'positively evil', the car began to smoke: he retired with dry transmission.

That hasty oil cooler move in the Zolder paddock had returned them almost, but not quite, to their South American siting. That 'not quite' proved vital. Suddenly the M23s seemed impossible to balance. The problem cost a month's competitiveness before being pinpointed. The resited coolers were robbing the wing underside of clean air and upsetting its performance.

Monaco gave little clue. Mass ran there with an additional new low-level rear wing in practice. In race morning warm-up they ran without the airbox, which improved airflow to the rear wing and enhanced download. But Hunt spun, and in Sweden he spun again, many times, before salvaging fifth place and another points-scoring finish at last.

Brainstorming the cause of their lost form, McLaren then resited the oil coolers precisely in their Spanish GP mounts. Testing commenced at Ricard, prior to the French GP, and as if by magic the old balance had returned. At that point in the season, halfway through the Championship, Hunt was a massive 47 points behind his main rival, Lauda of Ferrari.

How Hunt and McLaren fought back to win the French, British, German, Dutch, Canadian and US GPs – and were then disqualified from the British victory in Lauda's favour – and how Lauda then crashed near-fatally at the Nürburgring, is all part of recent racing history.

In Austria the prototype M23 replacement M26 emerged at last although it was not raced as Hunt again set M23/8-2 on pole position and led initially before running into mud and debris scattered onto the track by a Tyrrell accident. The car's handling deteriorated and he finished fourth. When his crew examined the car afterwards they found the left-front foil had been thumped from underneath and its angle of attack flattened slightly. Something had punctured its undersurface and the hole was stuffed with mud.

In the Dutch GP a flapping front brake cooling hose interrupted airflow over one of these sensitive nose foils, possibly causing excessive understeer which hampered Hunt until his opposition retired. Mass raced the M26 in this event, unhappily.

Spot fuel checks at Monza during Italian GP practice saw McLaren judged guilty of using illegally high octane Texaco mix, though this interpretation was subsequently overthrown. Short-term it still destroyed the team's chances as Hunt was forced to start from the back of the grid and went off the road trying to make up the deficit.

This dramatic season then reached its climax in the last three rounds – Canada, the USA (East) and Japan – and Hunt won the first two events in ever-faithful M23/8-2 and was third at Mt Fuji after a dramatic tyre change to steal the Drivers' Championship by one point from Lauda, though McLaren could not catch Ferrari in the Constructors' Championship. On the road Hunt had matched Jim Clark's record of seven GP wins in a season, only to be disqualified from two first

places, then reinstated in only one of them. But there was to be no second Constructors' Championship victory for the Colnbrook cars . . .

1977 – TWILIGHT

In 1977, the team played safe for the South American season-openers by fielding their trusty M23s although intensive winter development had seen the replacement M26 improving rapidly. Hunt drove his faithful M23/8-2, Mass M23/9 and M23/6 was team spare. Hunt crashed in Buenos Aires when a right-rear suspension bolt broke, while in Brazil Mass crashed heavily when under pressure from Andretti's new Lotus 78 'wing-car' and a spinning Tyrrell later did further injury to poor chassis 9. No M23 had suffered serious frontal damage since Hailwood's Nürburgring crash in 1974 and examination of Mass's wreck prompted detail monocoque reinforcement to the surviving cars prior to departure for Kyalami.

The remains of M23/9 were rebuilt years later by Leo Wybrott, using much of the original tub with new panels inserted. The M23 monocoques were so complex that no damaged ones were ever torn right down and reconstructed merely around the original bulkheads. Only one 'write-off' had proved total, and that was Hailwood's M23/7 whose mortal remains were indeed scrapped.

Due to slow development of the troublesome M26 replacement car, two brand new M23s were built for the first time since 1975 – chassis 11 for Hunt and 12 for Mass. Hunt put his new car on pole in South Africa, then won in old '8-2 with driver-adjustable rear anti-roll bar at Brands Hatch. This was the 21st and last race win for a works-entered McLaren M23 (including the 1976 British GP).

Mass's new mount made its debut at Long Beach but from the next race, the Spanish GP at Jarama, Hunt ran the latest M26 and it was left to Mass to tail off the M23s' frontline career up to the British GP at Silverstone when his own new M26 became available.

The Spanish private entrant Emilio de Villota campaigned old M23/6 during this period, attempting to qualify for World Championship GPs while also running in a British club-racing series. Bob Sparshott's BS Fabrications team ran the brand new customer M23F chassis 14 for their American customer Brett Lunger, replacing an old March which he had campaigned formerly. This little team later added ex-works car M23/11 as a second choice for Lunger.

Hunt's 1976 World Championship-winning car M23/8-2 was also dusted off and wheeled out again during the year, giving a little-known French-Canadian driver named Gilles Villeneuve his Formula 1 debut at Silverstone in the British GP, and then being handled by Italian Formula 2

star Bruno Giacomelli at Monza on 11 September 1977. This was the last M23 works entry, almost exactly 4½ years after the type's debut in March 1973.

Lunger subsequently ran chassis 14 privately on into 1978, competing in the Argentinian, Brazilian and South African GPs. This car was then sold to the British Melchester racing team for club driver Tony Trimmer's use, while Lunger failed to qualify his older chassis 11 in Long Beach before taking delayed delivery of a new M26. Trimmer failed to qualify M23/14 for the British GP while in the Austrian race a youthful Brazilian Formula 3 Champion named Nelson Piquet raced M23/11 and crashed it. He used the old car again in the Dutch and Italian GPs, finishing ninth in that latter event, on 10 September 1978, to mark the end of this remarkable McLaren model's World Championship career, 5½ years after it had begun.

Gilles Villeneuve airs his novice opinions upon his F1 debut with McLaren, British GP, 1977. Here the M23 shows off its bluff chisel nose, rocker arm front suspension, brake cooling scoops and regulation dash and rear roll-over bars.

Racing Tyres

Make no mistake, along with aerodynamic development racing tyre technology has been the ultimate arbiter of Grand Prix car performance throughout our period. Poor tyres, poor results . . . it has been as simple as that.

Through much of the 1961-65 1500 cc Formula, Dunlop held a tyre supply monopoly. They developed their racing tyres essentially to carry a 2000 lb car at around 180 mph round Le Mans for 24 hours, and that's what the Formula 1 people had to use on their 1200 lb cars screaming round Reims for two hours at a maximum 165 mph. During the 1963 season, Jimmy Clark's Lotus 25 completed – according to Colin Chapman, who told me so himself – four consecutive GPs on the self-same set of tyres . . .

Times changed. In 1964 Firestone entered the road racing fray and Goodyear followed earnestly in 1965. A three-way tyre war broke out on the Grand Prix circuits of the world.

In this history of the Grand Prix car I feel there can be no place for an adequate story of Formula 1 tyre development for it would by itself fill a sister volume.

But some significant points must be made. The contact-patches of the tyres are the *only* points of contact – conveniently disregarding the era of sliding skirts – between a car and the road. These small and ever-changing elliptical patches must transmit drive and cornering and braking reactions. Tyre technology has been engaged in producing carcass constructions and tread compound characteristics which enable the car using those tyres to transmit dynamic forces more effectively than its rivals.

At the start of our period tyres were relatively tall and narrow. Conventionally they were all of cross-ply construction, the casing plies being woven from variations of man-made textile cord and laminated one above the other, each ply carrying perhaps 30 cords per inch arranged four-ply deep.

Each cord layer would be moulded into the rubber compound devised by the manufacturers' chemists, the compound insulating each layer from the next to minimize internal friction which would overheat the tyre.

Wire cord controlled the tyre bead to keep it on the wheel rim, safety bolsters and bolts being adopted after instances – including Jimmy Clark's death – of a deflating tyre collapsing explosively and leaving the rim-ledges.

The tread compound was applied some 0.4-0.2 in. thick as the period progressed, across the tread, thickening to perhaps 0.6-0.32 in. in the shoulder. The chemists based their compound brews on synthetic styrene-butadiene rubber, polymer science flexing its muscles to offer compound mixes resisting abrasion and controlling internal heating because an under-heated tyre will not generate its full grip, and an overheating tyre will lose grip, blister, break up and fail.

The tyre compounder would add carbon black – for good tensile strength and wear – oils, waxes, vulcanizers, accelerators, decelerators, zinc oxide, sulphur . . . all with much the same enthusiasm as the three Witches.

Ever-softer compounds were tried by Goodyear, the giant, by Firestone and Dunlop as they sought ever-greater performance in all conditions. Some compounds proved too soft and sticky to endure race distance, but they produced prodigious lap times during their brief life. These race-distance failures became the great successes of qualifying, and 'qualifying tyres' had been born. The compounds in these tyres were very oily, heating up rapidly to pass through a level of optimum grip then equally rapidly lose performance. For 1981 only two sets of four qualifying tyres were permitted for each car, each set being marked with the car's number and scrutineered during official timed qualifying sessions to ensure nobody could literally 'pull a fast one'.

While this was a move to control tyre company costs and logistical pressures after a period during which the top three or four teams had access to a mountain of alternative tyres but the also-rans virtually nothing at all worthwhile, it also created some suicidal qualifying performances by drivers anxious to put in a quick lap before their precious and exhaustible supply of tyres 'went off', and Gilles Villeneuve died.

Tyre widths and heights and profiles altered greatly through our 26-season period, slick tyres coming into use in 1970-71 to offer greater contact area uninterrupted by tread pattern channels, and also to stabilize the ever-softer tyre tread compounds which with separate tread blocks had begun to overheat due to 'squirm' when in use.

Slick tyres at a stroke put more rubber on the road to enhance grip under all loads, while also enabling softer compounds to be used than ever before without serious danger of overheating and tread destruction since heat-

inducing squirm was now under control. Slots or drillings were the only blemishes remaining in the tread surface, being designed purely to enable tread wear and remaining depth to be measured by the tyre engineers. The slots were also a handy place to prod with their thermometer probes.

Tyre and rim widths grew progressively until regulations limited further development, while tyre height and sidewall height – profile – altered from one extreme to another during our period.

To limit movement within the tyre very low profiles were adopted by Firestone in 1971-72, running into severe vibration problems, and Goodyear then knocked Firestone out of competition – Dunlop having long since thrown in the towel – at the end of 1974. Progressive development of tall new 'wrinkle-wall' dragster-technology tyres had produced a taller-sidewall tyre which engendered a wind-up effect which heated the tyre very effectively and gave terrific traction away from the corners.

These taller-profile tyres had problems of lateral stability, however, as the car would roll and take up sidewall 'squidge' but the greater the tyres' overall outside diameter the softer compound it could preserve because its rotational speed was less than a smaller outside diameter tyre and therefore it asked less from its tread in terms of work.

Variation in manufactured size was always a major problem with cross-ply racing tyres. Racing cars and perhaps even more so racing drivers can be sensitive animals, and unequal overall dimensions between tyres on either end of a common driven axle could have both literally climbing the walls.

This difference was known as 'stagger' and the effect would be for the car to dive to one side or another consistently under acceleration, as the greater-circumference tyre on one side covered a greater distance during one revolution than did its partner – saving differential effect. Each team developed a 'tyre man' whose main task was solely to measure and carefully match sets of equal-sized, stagger-free tyres.

In certain cases stagger could be advantageous on certain circuits for which equally carefully mismatched tyres could be fitted, and very often painstaking tyre choices have been made which have won or lost races by running tyres of differing compound and construction on a car to match or combat given conditions.

In particular the left-front tyre of any racing car is especially hard-pressed on a conventional clockwise racing circuit in which the majority of turns are right-handers, and often harder, more durable compounds would be fitted there which would heat in sympathy with their three softer partners – four-wheeled cars these! – purely through the greater work they were asked to do.

Wet-weather tyres employed very soft compounds which would heat adequately even when douched continuously by standing and falling water, and were cut with continuous and interconnecting drainage channels and sipes to funnel water away, prevent aquaplaning, to squeegee the track surface near-dry and enable clean tread contact to be maintained.

In 1977 the French Michelin company entered the fray, first on Renault then Ferrari. Michelin had made their name on the 'X' range of radial-ply road tyres and now extended this technology into Formula 1.

Radial-ply tyre casings as the name suggests have their ply cords arranged – in theory – at 90 degrees to the direction of travel, i.e. on a line following the wheel

and tyre radius and passing through its hub centre.

In practice this was not quite true, for the bracing cords were more 'bias-belted' than truly radial, running for example at some 23 degrees across the tread although Michelin security was so tight and change so rapid one cannot be adamant.

The tyre tread section was then further braced by a steel or textile band moulded integrally into the rubber capping with the tread on top of that. The radial-ply tyre offered less tread distortion under load than a cross-ply, while its sidewalls were far more flexible, generating higher cornering force, better traction under power and braking and better straightline stability.

In practical terms the radial racing tyre, like the radial road tyre, offered higher ultimate grip than its cross-ply predecessor but was liable to give less warning of incipient breakaway. To run radial tyres suspension settings with more camber change became necessary as the suspension rose and fell through its arc. Radial-ply tyres also ran inherently cooler and had better squirm characteristics than cross-plies so again were capable of using softer, stickier and faster tread compounds.

The Italian Pirelli concern joined battle in 1981 also with radial-ply tyres, although they had little success and development seemed very half-hearted compared to the multi-million spending giants, Goodyear and Michelin.

Goodyear fought a terrific rearguard action for the cross-ply racing tyre throughout the height of the ground-effects era in which aerodynamic downloads of 3000 lb or more had to be endured and sustained.

A brief Goodyear withdrawal from racing in early 1981 set many teams a'screaming and brought in Avon tyres fleetingly just to keep the cannon-fodder teams mobile. The giant Goodyear company which had supported and often dominated Formula 1 for so many years subsequently returned in mid-season and progressively developed very effective radial-ply Formula 1 tyres of its own.

Racing tyre design and construction is an awesomely expensive business in which the technological development pace and staff learning curve is quite extraordinary.

Lessons learned in the crucible of Grand Prix racing have spun off into many other more mundane areas, worlds away from everyday road-vehicle tyre design and production, which has also benefited of course, and in this area at least Grand Prix racing really has, quite demonstrably, improved the breed.

At Goodwood '66 Goodyear's onboard recording equipment answered to the name Bert. While Gurney cornered his Eagle-Weslake V12, tyre designer Bert Baldwin watched his wares react.

Hewland Gearboxes

Of all racing gearbox manufacturers – and there are few – Hewland Engineering of Maidenhead, in the Thames Valley, is the best known and its range of transaxles used in Formula 1 has progressed throughout our period.

A beginner's guide to Hewland gearboxes shows that they offer very easy quick-change final-drive ratios and a range of good-quality, proven components which every Formula 1 team save Ferrari and Alfa Romeo has used at some time, if not throughout.

Their '3-litre Formula' involvement began with the DG300 ('Different Gearbox') five-speed of 1966, which soon became 'too heavy'. The Formula 2 FT200 developed for the 1600 cc Formula was, in comparison, 'too light' for Formula 1 power and torque, so the two were married together in a slightly different casing for 1968 and Mike Hewland named it the 'FG'.

In 1973 the FGA400 emerged, 'using a posher diff, Salisbury or cam and pawl' and its heavier casing provided mounts for inboard rear brakes.

The 'TL', introduced that same year, was essentially a 24-hour sports car box which Shadow adopted but it won itself a bad name because in its debut a bad batch of pinion shafts broke 'and the muck stuck and nobody liked them'. In fact only two TLs had bad shafts, and unfortunately Shadow had them both!

The 'FGB' emerged as 'a posh FGA' with integral oilways in its casing whereas the others had external piping.

Teams would adapt Hewland internals to their own requirements, having their own casings cast and adding many tweaks and modifications, using separate dry-sump oil systems, extensively filtering the oil, passing it over magnets to remove ferrous debris – anything to make what Colin Chapman described rather affectionately as 'Mike Hewland's bunch of old mangle-gears' survive race distance.

Into the mid-1980s most Formula 1 teams held a bigger Hewland part inventory than the Maidenhead company itself. McLaren began the six-speed Hewland conversion fashion in 1976, Hewland subsequently making their own six-speed FGAs which remained current into 1985 with some teams.

Regarding their price, Jimmy Buss, who ran Hewland's commercial side and had become a familiar figure to all racing people, recalls that the 1967 'FT' 'was the price of a Mini, £420, and today [1985] a Mini is over £3000 and our FT is only £2078. The DG in 1966-67 was around £480, an equivalent DG is now £2,420 and a DGB £4725... we offer good value, don't we?'

Towards the end of our period, although many F1 teams would be manufacturing ever more of their own transmission components, Hewland remained 'the original' – an honour hard won in such a competitive world.

Top: *Hewland's F1 dominance continued from 1963 until teams began making their own customized casings – still mostly with Hewland internals – in the late 1970s.*
Centre: *FGA specification side-elevation drawing.*
Right: *The basic gearbox unit internals for the FT200, FG400 and FGA were the basis for many specialized F1 team transmissions.*

Chapter 9

THE HAT-TRICK 'TRASVERSALE' FERRARIS 1975-77

Above: *Matthews dissects a 1975 Ferrari 312T, revealing within-the-wheelbase radiators and oil coolers, square-tube inner frame picking up front suspension and compact transverse-shaft spur-gear transaxle.* Right: *Niki Lauda barely had time to admire the Monaco view in 1975, when he won the GP in 312T '023'.*

During the 1974 season Ferrari re-established itself as a serious force in Formula 1 following two indifferent Grand Prix seasons. Their time- and money-consuming sports-racing car programme had now been shelved and Maranello's racing department concentrated its efforts totally upon Formula 1.

As we shall see later, during 1974 their *Tipo 312B3* flat-12 was developed into a very successful design which failed to bring Ferrari their first Formula 1 Constructors' Championship title in 12 years partly through the relative inexperience of its lead driver through most of the season, until the team failed him in the crucial deciding races at the end of the year.

The driver was Niki Lauda who was accompanied by the hugely experienced and capable – if not quite as quick – Clay Regazzoni. Ferrari's concentration upon Formula 1 and the completion of their own private test track just across the main Formigine Road from the factory, at Fiorano, enabled them to test interminably, and Lauda always made himself available for testing. He realized that his future and that of the team depended upon their exploiting every advantage they had, and having once created a new Formula 1 car they could literally 'throw everything at it' in their extensive tyre testing work for Goodyear.

If five alternative wing sets were available, then Ferrari would test each pair individually, then rear wing A would be tried with nose wings B, C, D and E, rear wing B with nose wings A, C, D, E – and so on, until every possible combination had been studied and extended to its potential in painstaking detail. Every conceivable minor alteration and change would simply be tested fit to bust, until the sun went down and the brief Emilian dusk settled over Fiorano.

Since they had this luxury of their own private and comprehensively instrumented test track, there was never a problem with booking public circuit time, while transporting the cars from factory to test venue took a matter merely of min-

utes. Once Ferrari had won their labour unions' support and they had got their own management act together, they were able to tackle Formula 1 racing more seriously than any other team.

In this way they could compensate for some distinct shortcomings particularly in chassis engineering, which would occasionally leap out of the bushes and beset them in coming years, notably once the aerodynamic area became increasingly sophisticated.

But for three halcyon years, 1975 to 1977, Ferrari were really on top of their game, and they became the first Formula 1 team in history to put together a hat-trick of three consecutive Formula 1 Constructors' Championship titles.

ENTER 'MODELLO 312T'

At the end of their 'so near yet so far' 1974 season, the racing department took stock. *Capo Ingegnere* Mauro Forghieri was able to reflect upon a year of adequate flat-12 engine reliability, although major failures at Österreichring and Monza had damaged their cause. The 312B3-74 chassis had survived without major modification other than detail aerodynamic changes but Forghieri felt that the basic concept still offered as yet unrealized potential. It was actually on 27 September 1974, before the team left home for the Championship-deciding US GP at Watkins Glen, that the new year's prototype 312T model was unveiled to the press at Fiorano.

Forghieri in effect was following the path which Derek Gardner of Tyrrell and Robin Herd of March had trodden in 1972, seeking further concentration of mass within the wheelbase to minimize polar moment of inertia and so produce a highly manoeuvrable, nimble car which might seem too nervous to the average Formula 1 driver but which with a Ronnie Peterson or Niki Lauda ensconced would prove to be a formidable weapon.

Whereas the preceding 312B3's front suspension coil-spring/dampers had nestled each side of the footbox, and used a spidery forward tube sub-

frame to pick up the leading elements of the lower wishbones, now the redesigned 312T tub carried all its major front suspension components on the forward face of its monocoque's front bulkhead.

Very long fabricated top rocker arms actuated steeply inclined Koni dampers with co-axial tapered wire rising-rate coil-springs whose feet were firmly anchored in a cast magnesium tray affair fitted to the bulkhead. The front end of the new monocoque was itself considerably narrower than that of the 'B3 which it superseded. Disc brakes were outboard at the front, inboard on the cheeks of the new lateral gearbox at the rear.

A system of links and levers actuated an exquisite little anti-roll bar which was bracketed to the centre of this assembly, and a trailing top link from the upper arm fed back into the meat of the tub, passing through an air duct section designed to feed water radiators slung either side just behind the front wheels.

Further aft, long side ducts fed air through oil coolers each side just ahead of the rear wheels, while beautifully moulded GRP body sections included a sharp-pointed shovel nose, with a strutted full-width airfoil wing perched on top. Side pods accommodated the regulation deformable structures, which overlapped the monocoque sides, the tub itself using Ferrari's familiar hybrid construction in which the stressed-skin structure was reinforced internally with steel strip and angle framing. The cockpit surround and engine cover-cum-tall airbox were in integral mouldings, smoothing airflow onto the centre-strutted rear wing while curled flip-ups moulded ahead of the rear wheels faired airflow around the broad Goodyear tyres.

Rear suspension was by reversed lower wishbones, replacing the original toe-steer restricting parallel link system in an apparently retrograde move, although it saved some weight. Like McLaren, Ferrari felt confident they could control toe-steer adequately by careful setting-up adjustment in assembly.

Wheelbase was increased to 2518 mm (99.1 in.) while front track was reduced to 1510 mm (59.4 in.) and rear track to 1530 mm (60.2 in.)

The most significant technical innovation however was the brand new *trasversale* – transverse – gearbox, which mounted on the rear of the flat-12 engine but with most of its mass now ahead of the axle line, within the wheelbase, to enhance that central mass concentration. The gearbox input was turned through 90 degrees by bevel gears to enable the gearbox shafts to be arranged laterally, final drive being via spur gears.

Franco Rocchi's engine development team had worked hard on the flat-12 engine and in its latest form 500 bhp at 12,200 rpm was being claimed. In Fiorano testing, Lauda immediately found the new car far more demanding to drive than the 'B3, as predicted, but equally its ultimate limits seemed much higher and with practice he was able to drive closer to those higher limits for longer than hitherto . . . he was maturing too. He was soon lapping Fiorano at 1 min 13 secs, compared to Merzario's best of 1;14.2 set in the original 'Forghieri 'B3' (see page 263) 15 months previously. At Vallelunga further testing saw Lauda down there to 1;07.5, a second inside the best 'B3 time of 1974; back-to-back tests between the 'B3 and the new 312T at Ricard-Castellet proved the new model's superiority.

When the team returned from racing the old 'B3s in South America at the start of the 1975 season, Lauda got down to 1;11.9 at Fiorano and two new 312Ts were then completed and available for the trip to Kyalami for the South African GP in March. Lauda drove the prototype car chassis '018' while '021' was available for Regazzoni. The intervening two chassis numbers '019' and '020' were, according to Ferrari, allocated to the last two 'B3 models. Neither of these was raced, '019' being heavily damaged in a testing accident and being broken up, while '020' simply went into store for potential future display duties before sale to a collector. Thus '018' remains rather isolated as the 312T prototype, and '021' then com-

mences the transverse-gearbox flat-12 series proper, which would encompass the future types 'T2 to 'T5 and would include no less than 26 further individual Formula 1 chassis in the six seasons from 1975 to 1980 . . .

1975 – THE FIRST CHAMPIONSHIP

This is not the place in which to relate the racing exploits of these cars and their drivers in any detail, but initially where the 312T is concerned suffice to record that Lauda won the minor Silverstone International to open the type's winning account early in the 1975 season. He then added victories at Monaco, Zolder, Anderstorp, Ricard-Castellet and Watkins Glen, while teammate Regazzoni won the minor 'Swiss GP' at Dijon-Prenois and the major German GP at the Nürburgring, to bring Ferrari their first Formula 1 Constructors' World Championship title since 1964 and Lauda his first Drivers' title. The team made 30 starts that season, including the 'B3 outings in South America and South Africa – where Regazzoni raced one of the older cars – and they recorded 24 finishes, eight of which were in first place. They added one second place, four thirds, two fourths, three fifths, two sixths, a seventh, eighth and ninth and one lowly 13th. Between them, Lauda and Regazzoni also amassed no less than nine pole positions and six fastest laps during that memorable Ferrari season, and they proved that the combination of their skills and the Ferrari's power, reliability and now handling was by far the fastest in contemporary Formula 1. Lauda in fact only failed to finish one race – the Spanish GP at Barcelona, in which he and his team-mate collided on the opening lap! Ferrari's first *trasversale* season was very much the more competitive Seventies equivalent of Mercedes-Benz domination in the Fifties.

Initially, however, the new car's debut at Kyalami had been indifferent, Lauda crashing '021' during practice when another car's engine blew up ahead of him and he slithered off on its spilled oil. Lauda's engine then lacked power dur-

ing the race, and it was subsequently found that its fuel metering unit drive belt had stripped some teeth and slipped because of that, restricting output to some 440 bhp, which was less than the rival Cosworth DFVs.

Lauda's Silverstone victory marked the debut of the third 312T to be built, chassis '022'. Another new chassis, '023', was ready for Lauda's use at Monaco and he won in it, despite falling oil pressure towards the finish caused by leakage through a defective pump seal. The engine was dangerously close to seizure in the final laps, with Lauda sensibly declutching and coasting through the corners, while Fittipaldi's McLaren closed rapidly just before the finish . . . one more lap and he might have got past.

Regazzoni crashed '018' heavily in this race, at the chicane, and both drivers had already crashed their cars in practice so the team mechanics were kept very busy indeed that weekend.

For Zolder new exhaust systems were fitted in search of improved low-speed pick-up. Normally the three front and three rear cylinders on each bank fed individual tailpipes. Now a balance pipe linked the front and rear set of manifolds each side, before they merged into twin exhaust megaphones, rolled from titanium sheet. One of these pipes split during practice, so the older system was refitted. Lauda had another manifold split on lap 58 of the race and he lost 300 rpm on the straights for the remaining dozen but he still won by a margin of fully 19 seconds from his closest pursuer.

Anderstorp saw a very lucky Ferrari win, for the strange Swedish circuit with its geometric semi-banked curves posed peculiar setting-up demands which few teams ever mastered, Derek Gardner of Tyrrell perhaps doing better than most. In this case Lauda had inherited second place when one Brabham faltered and he then took the lead in the last 10 laps when the other slowed due to track debris accumulating on its rear tyres, while the Ferrari's harder-compound rears were not so badly affected. Any good team makes its own luck

97

– Ferrari could claim a 'brilliant' tyre choice.

The fifth 312T, '024' made its debut at Ricard-Castellet for the French GP but its engine failed on the seventh lap, sidelining Regazzoni. In contrast Lauda drove '022' from the start right away into the Mediterranean heat haze and his rivals never had sight of him again as he led by two seconds ending lap one and despite late understeer as his tyres wore he won as he pleased, quite uncatchable.

The rain-swept British GP at Silverstone degenerated into a lottery but the Ferraris were never in genuine contention there once Regazzoni spun from the lead and Lauda suffered a bungled stop for rain tyres, being despatched with one wheel unsecured and falling off in the pit lane . . . *aah miseria!*

While Lauda had luckily won in Sweden at Brabham driver Reutemann's expense, Reutemann won at the Nürburgring at Lauda's expense as the Ferrari number one was leading handsomely until a tyre punctured. The Austrian GP was another rain-stopped farce, then for the major Italian GP at Monza Ferrari introduced new cylinder heads improving mid-range torque for the slow-speed chicanes which now despoiled this once super-fast speedway. Yet one of these new engines had failed in pre-race testing on Regazzoni's '024' so Lauda's '023' was fitted with a standard unit for the race. Regazzoni – the Italian-speaking member of the team – was given the 'high-torque' race engine. They started 1-2 on the front row of the grid and finished 1-3, Regazzoni victorious to a delirious reception from the *tifosi* while Lauda, handicapped by a minor damper problem, fell behind Fittipaldi's second-placed McLaren after holding the lead for 45 of the 52 laps. This success clinched the World titles for Ferrari and Lauda. Monza-headed engines were then used for the final race of the season at Watkins Glen.

Eleven days after that event, on 26 October 1975, Ferrari's new 1976 contender, the 312T2, was unveiled at Fiorano, but while its development progressed in similar fashion to that of the 312T the previous year's cars would run on into the first races of the new season.

In the 312T's case this involved the 1976 Brazilian, South African and US GP West at Long Beach and two minor British races before the new 'T2s took over, though their actual race debut came at Brands Hatch on 14 March in the Race of Champions. The Brazilian GP opened the new season at Interlagos on 25 January, with Ferrari

fielding 312Ts '023' for Lauda and '024' for Regazzoni, the Austrian winning from pole position while Regazzoni led before a stop to change a damaged tyre.

At Kyalami, Regazzoni's '022' broke its engine while Lauda's '023' was hampered in the vital final qualifying session when one of its tyres proved to be oversize causing queasy handling and leaving McLaren to steal pole position. Lauda led but from lap 20 his car's left-rear tyre began to deflate. His chosen brake balance reversed during the course of the race yet by judicious use of lapping back-markers he managed to hold off Hunt's McLaren long enough to win again, this time by 1.3 seconds. He also set fastest race lap but it was now evident that the Ferrari's 1976 advantage over the opposition was nowhere near so marked as it had been in 1975.

Consequently a new 'T2 made its debut at Brands Hatch while old '021' – the second 312T built – appeared there on loan to Scuderia Everest for Giancarlo Martini in a Fiat-Ferrari approved effort to bring on young Italian drivers. The unfortunate Martini qualified second slowest and then crashed on the warm-up lap when a brake snatched. He non-started.

The proven 312Ts '023' and '024' were used by Lauda and Regazzoni at Long Beach. It was the Ticinese's weekend as he qualified on pole, led all the way and won handsomely while Lauda settled for second place after flat-spotting a tyre early in the race then encountering gear selection difficulties – accompanied by horrible noises – in the closing stages.

This was the final appearance of the factory team 312Ts as the next race was the Spanish GP introducing the new regulations to which the 'T2 had been tailored. Before the Spanish race the Everest 312T again emerged in Martini's hands, at Silverstone. He both qualified and finished in tenth place, marking the end of the original *trasversale* series' racing career.

'MODELLO 312T2'

The 1976 model Ferrari was based upon a longer wheelbase than the perhaps over-sensitive 312T, nominally up some 1.7 in. to 2560 mm (100.8 in.) while track was cut to 1400 mm (55.1 in.) front and 1430 mm (56.3 in.) rear. These are works dimensions; actually both track and wheelbase were adjustable, the latter by fitting different top front rocker arms and lower front wishbones with alternative angles of sweep from chassis to wheel hub. Normally they swept rearwards for the standard wheelbase, but it was lengthened by right-angle items.

The new regulations due to take effect from the Spanish GP limited airbox height and rear wing overhang, and introduced roll-over protection at both ends of the cockpit. Overall width was now

restricted to 215 cm (84.65 in.)

The 'T2 had been designed in detail to meet these requirements, while the loss of the tall engine airbox was compensated for by provision of shapely intake nostrils moulded into the forward end of the cockpit surround, feeding air into trunkings formed integrally with the body panel and feeding plenum chambers low down on either side around the flat-12 engine's inductions.

The prototype car was first shown fitted with an experimental tube-frame de Dion rear axle system, sprung on coils and attached to the chassis structure beneath the *trasversale* gearbox by a Watt link. This parallel wheel movement system had been developed at Fiorano in conjunction with Goodyear as part of their 'vehicle dynamics' research programme, and it was intended to make optimum use of the American-financed, British-made racing tyres on very smooth circuits. It was easily interchangeable with the conventional 312T-derived, fully independent rear suspension system and in fact, save for a brief practice outing during the French GP meeting at Ricard-Castellet, the conventional system would always be preferred. At one stage, de Dion-framed front suspension was also tested, but this was not even practised in public.

As first shown, the 'T2 also wore streamlined front wheel spats which doubled as brake cooling ducts. They were designed to improve the flow of air off the nose wing and to act as fairings for the front wheels to minimize lift. But since they steered with the front wheels they would be deemed 'moveable aerodynamic devices' when Ferrari attempted to race them and would be rejected. Water and oil radiators remained in their 312T positions with suitable ducts moulded into each side panel as before.

The 'T2 monocoque was considerably lighter than the preceding designs, with aluminium internal framing replacing the previous steel infrastructure, while a true monocoque version was now also on the way. Apart from small triangular planform sections of the side cells, the whole fuel load was carried in three bags virtually line abreast across the tub behind the driver's shoulders.

Whereas the 312T had scaled 598 kg (1318 lb) dry, the new 'T2 weighed in at 575 kg (1268 lb) – right on the minimum weight limit, if Ferrari's public claims were to be believed.

Despite extensive testing, notably at Mugello in November 1975 and subsequently at Vallelunga and Kyalami in February 1976 in addition to the normal 'home' programme at Fiorano, the new 'T2 failed to show the kind of advance over its predecessor that the 312T had demonstrated over the definitive 312B3.

1976 – THE SECOND CHAMPIONSHIP

Lauda drove the prototype car '025' in the minor Brands Hatch race between the South African and Long Beach GPs. Conventional rear suspension was fitted, and after possibly setting fastest practice time (Scheckter's pole time for Tyrrell being considered suspect) Lauda ran an unspectacular fourth until a brake pipe parted after 17 laps.

The revised regulations then came into force at Jarama for the Spanish GP, so that race witnessed the 'T2s' serious debut. Lauda had injured his ribs in a domestic tractor accident yet he qualified on the front row in the new 'T2 '026' and led before running over a kerb and jarring his rib-cage; the understandable pause to wince and catch his breath allowed Hunt's attendant McLaren to go by and win, until the M23 was disqualified for being over-width in post-race scrutineering.

This latest 'T2 used a true monocoque chassis – in the Formula 1 sense – in that its hull was formed purely in stressed sheet shaped over internal bulkheads without the aluminium U-piece internal framing of the prototype '025'. Old 312T '018' was used as team spare, updated in line with the new regulations.

The two new 'T2s dominated in Belgium, Lauda-Regazzoni 1-2, and at Monaco the third new car

The name of the game – Lauda's 312T '026' wins the 1976 Belgian GP at Zolder, the tall '75-style airbox now replaced by those moulded cockpit-surround integral ducts, the full-width blade wing still working well.

was ready, its completion having been delayed by one of Italy's perennial metal-workers' strikes. This car, '027', was allotted to Regazzoni, while Lauda kept the structurally similar '026'.

During first practice there an interesting experiment involved use of a thin plastic-coated wire stretched across the leading edge of the rear wing to split the airflow and lower skin friction – or so they said. The 'T2s qualified 1-2 and Lauda scored Ferrari's sixth victory of the season, his third in a row counting the Spanish fracas, and eighth of the technically unbroken series which had begun at Monza the previous September.

Regazzoni's new '027' had lost third place when Hunt's McLaren blew up right in front of it at the harbour chicane, and Regazzoni slithered up the escape road on spilled oil. He rejoined fourth, fuming, stole third place and tackled Scheckter's six-wheeled Tyrrell for second. Just four laps from the end he pressed too hard and clanged into the guardrails, bending '027' quite extensively and ending Ferrari hopes of another spectacular 1-2.

Ferrari had never come to grips with Anderstorp, home of the Swedish GP. There they fielded the Monaco cars and experimented with cylindrical end 'plates' for the rear wings in place of the conventional flat aluminium sheet fences. The novel Tyrrells were uncatchable in the race, Lauda third, Regazzoni tenth, embarrassingly behind a flat-12-engined Brabham-Alfa Romeo . . .

The de Dion rear suspension was tried only briefly at Ricard, as were the quasi brake-scoop front wheel fairings, which the scrutineers rejected out of hand. The cars ran faster with standard scoops. The de Dion system had at one stage proved faster than the conventional kind at Fiorano, but Goodyear altered their tyres so often Ferrari were always having to catch up with what Goodyear did, rather than setting the pace and specifying the tyres which they required.

Now, at the end of Ricard practice, traces of oil were noticed issuing from the flat-12 engines.

Lauda built a three-second lead in the first three race laps, set fastest lap next time round and on lap nine '026' was shrilling down the long main straight flat-out at around 12,000 rpm when its engine cut with an abrupt crunch of shattering metal. The rear wheels locked momentarily and Lauda was lucky not to come to further grief.

The auxiliary drive flange pressed onto the crankshaft nose had been badly machined and fitted poorly. This initiated cracking, and the crank had broken, an identical failure later eliminating Regazzoni's '027' when in second place.

The third true-monocoque 'T2, chassis '028', was available for Lauda's use in the British GP. Regazzoni used '027' again and '026' became spare car. Lauda cut across his team-mate on the charge into the first corner and the Ferraris collided, sparking a multiple accident and a restart in which Hunt took part again. Ferrari consequently protested when he beat Lauda, who was handicapped by a badly fitted gearchange bush which tightened up during the restarted race.

Regazzoni had taken a spare car since '027's left-side water radiator and pipework had been torn up in the collision. He saved Ferrari further embarrassment when he switched off in face of plummeting oil pressure. The management blamed him for the collision – which seemed harsh. Hunt was disqualified by appeal to the FIA in Paris on 24 September, some two months after the event, and Lauda was declared winner.

His car '028' had by that time been destroyed in his ghastly Nürburgring accident, which seems to have been triggered by a rear suspension failure. Regazzoni's car led until an almighty high-speed spin on that opening lap dropped him way back,

Top right : 312T2 cross-section showing:
1, internal stressed-skin stiffened square-tube
base frame; 2, deformable structure crush pads;
3, water rails between radiators and engine;
4, seat moulding; 5, roll-over bar; 6, fuel tank
bay inner skin. Right: Regazzoni's 312T2 '027'
displays its podgy planform, Monaco '76. Flat-12
engine optimized overbody airflow towards
banana rear wing.

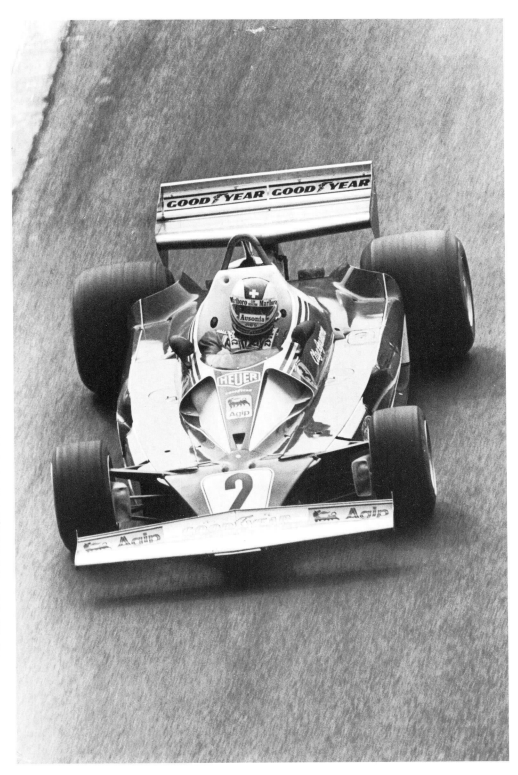

and perhaps he was willing to sit back and finish ninth after two pit stops following his team-mate's crash. Mr Ferrari obliquely blamed Goodyear for the team's set-backs at season's end.

How Lauda came back to race again in less than six weeks is all part of sporting legend. Ferrari reacted stupidly by cancelling their Austrian GP entries, rather then racing on to deny further Championship points to McLaren and their driver Hunt. They then saw sense in time to send Regazzoni to Zandvoort as a lone entry in '027' but he was unaccountably slow in practice. He then mounted a late charge in the race and finished a very close second to the McLaren. He was then in the dog-house again with Ferrari for having started his charge too late . . . Some people can't do anything right.

Ferrari proved as much by hiring former Brabham-Alfa Romeo driver Reutemann to take Lauda's place at Monza, but the spring-steel Austrian bounced back and returned to the fray, still with a chance of retaining his Drivers' title and assisting Ferrari to their second consecutive Constructors' Championship. Consequently the factory prepared three 'T2s for Monza: the heavyweight prototype '025' for new-boy Reutemann, '026' for Lauda and '027' for Regazzoni.

Ferrari reliability plus Regazzoni showing more fire than at any other time since Zolder yielded second for him, fourth for the singed Lauda and ninth for Reutemann, whose lofty frame was badly cramped in the prototype 'T2's cockpit.

Rest rather than test between Monza and Mosport Park then did nothing for Ferrari's chances as their end-of-season performances fell apart. In bitter Canadian cold the 'T2 lacked traction and oversteered badly, refusing to heat its tyres adequately. The oil cooler had been moved from its neat wing strut housing to sit on the gearbox casing itself, apparently at the CSI's insistence as it had been too outboard and vulnerable. This was only a tiny mass movement, but it could still transform the balance of such a delicate instrument as a modern Formula 1 car.

New rear top link suspension mounts were being used and they broke on both the Lauda and Regazzoni cars in the race, only Regazzoni salvaging one point for sixth place after barging Pace's Brabham-Alfa Romeo into the pit barrier . . .

Ferrari's continuous tyre test programme with

Top right and below: The 312T2's narrow nose cone cleared airflow into the radiator ducts at the front of each side pod, hot radiator air then being exhausted at sides above that tapered intake duct feeding cold air through hip-mounted oil coolers.

Goodyear had been badly disrupted by their mid-season dramas, while McLaren's had progressed apace. Now each team reaped the inevitable result. At Watkins Glen the gulf between Ferrari and McLaren was wider than ever before. Only Lauda was at all in contention and his '026' again oversteered as its fuel load burned down and the rear tyres in particular proved too lightly loaded to heat adequately. He placed third, and the Championship outcome depended on the inaugural Japanese GP.

At Fuji, Lauda's '026' was fitted with revised geometry front suspension supposedly promoting increased camber change but he muffed his start in heavy rain and after two laps retired in the pits, unwilling to race in such conditions. Hunt stole the World Drivers' Championship but Ferrari retained the Constructors' title for a second successive year as Regazzoni finished fifth for two points and the second McLaren failed to score, so Ferrari beat McLaren by nine clear points.

To Mr Ferrari this was everything but his backers might still have preferred Lauda to have taken the charismatic and more promotable Drivers' title.

During this fraught season, Ferrari's Formula 1 team cars started 31 times, achieving 23 finishes with 'six' firsts including those disputed results in Spain and Britain, four seconds, two thirds, a fourth and fifth, two sixths, three sevenths, an eighth, ninth and Martini's private-entry tenth at Silverstone in early season.

1977 – THE HAT-TRICK SEASON

The 'T2s ran on into the 1977 season but Ferrari developments were affected by the heart trouble which afflicted both engineer Rocchi and his colleague Salvarani that winter, and this following on the hiatus of the preceding autumn caused by the aftermath of Lauda's German accident.

A new 'T2 chassis '029' made its debut with Regazzoni's replacement Reutemann driving on home soil in Argentina to open the new season, while Lauda used '026' there with '027' in reserve. All three cars had been modified to feature the Fuji front suspension mod, while rear track had been increased marginally from the '76 spec. The engineers claimed 'twelve more horsepower' from the flat-12 engine but Lauda had been pointedly excluded from the winter test programme. Various body changes had been tested at Ricard-Castellet without his involvement and he had found it harder generally to arrange test miles. It was going to be a problem year for Maranello . . . again.

In Buenos Aires the little-changed 'T2s were

uncompetitive on race day. Reutemann's car handled poorly, skittering from understeer to oversteer, while Lauda retired with his engine misfiring and a furious vibration within the car. At Interlagos, Brazil, a new-section rear wing was available which Reutemann used and which Lauda claims was, significantly, not offered to him.

One might be forgiven for thinking we are discussing a team run by twelve-year-olds. This reversion to setting one driver against another was a grotesque throwback to less competitive times in the '50s and '60s when less than total team effort could still achieve results, and internecine rivalry paid Ferrari dividends. In the combative late 1970s they needed real luck on their side to get away with it.

On the long and difficult Interlagos track, Lauda's '026' was set up with too much castor, making its steering intolerably heavy. The inboard ends of the top rockers were binding against the fluid reservoirs on the front bulkhead. Consequently the car ducked and weaved dangerously on the bumpy bankings. That day saw Regazzoni, now driving in the tiny British Ensign team, lapping faster than both Ferraris!

Yet Reutemann was able to win a race dictated by broiling heat and a disintegrating track surface, while Lauda inherited third for the team on reliability alone, amongst just seven finishers.

Thereafter Lauda read the riot act to the powers at Maranello. He galvanized the team, jerking them back into gear. By force of personality – and an overdue dose of logic – he evidently made Forghieri drag out every extant 'T2 for comparative testing at Fiorano.

This programme then continued at Kyalami prior to the South African GP, which Lauda won in '030', brand new with revised rear suspension pick-ups, the top mounts being fabricated structures with integral brake ducts to cool the inboard brakes. Battery, oil tank, catch tank and gearbox oil cooler had been moved forward from their old mounting around the magnesium rear wing strut and they had lost their plastic fairing there, leaving the strut naked. A slimmer nose cowl was adopted, though retaining the now distinctive full-width front wing. 'The Old Lauda' re-emergence was confirmed as he took the lead from Hunt's McLaren on lap seven and won comfortably despite his car collecting some debris from the tragic accident which killed Shadow driver Pryce and a track marshal. The Shadow's detached roll-over bar wedged beneath the Ferrari's left side, puncturing its water system, and both Ferrari lower front wishbones were damaged. As coolant dribbled away so temperatures rose and oil pressure fell. Although the orange oil pressure warning light on the dash glowed brightly throughout the final laps Lauda was able to nurse it across the line to win by 5.2 secs before switching off immediately after the flag.

Lauda's 'T2 was then second and set fastest lap in the sensationally close US GP West at Long Beach which Andretti won in the new Lotus 78 'wing-car'. Jarama saw the Austrian break a rib during practice and he was unable to start, while a Ligier wheel coming loose rewarded Reutemann consistency with second place in Andretti's victorious slipstream.

The Ferraris achieved a reliable 2-3 finish at Monaco, but only after both flat-12 Brabham-Alfa Romeos had led them consistently before retiring. At Zolder the Lotus 78 was making the standards

Right: *All-round visibility is not an F1 car requirement – here's Regazzoni submerged in 312T2 '027', Zandvoort '76. Also noticeable are the mandatory electrical system cut-out switch, clearly marked as required since 1969, hex-nut, centre-lock wheel and purely functional Ferrari sponsors. Centre: Lauda's '030 flashing its flat bottom at Long Beach '77; underbody airflow had yet to be harnessed. Bottom: Trasversale – the 'T' of the World Championship-winning 312T series cars was provided, of course, by the transverse-shaft, spur-gear transaxle, concentrating compact mass as much as possible within the wheelbase and clearing rear airflow behind the obstructive flat-12 engine.*

of the time, Lauda was second to one. By the time of the Swedish GP the Ferrari team was again pulling apart, Lauda insisting the engineers should introduce a new car while Reutemann felt what they had was good enough. Ferrari disarray was perhaps exacerbated by Goodyear concentration upon the tyre requirements of the dominantly fast if fragile Lotus 78. With its underwing aerodynamic loadings it demanded more rigid tyre sidewall construction than hitherto. When Goodyear reacted accordingly, the Ferraris proved unable to heat these tyres adequately. It was the late-1976 syndrome all over again, only more so.

New chassis '031' – still a 'T2 – appeared at Dijon for the French GP, offering little new beyond restyled radiator air exits. The Ferraris finished 5-6. At Silverstone, Lauda patience inherited second place and another six points for himself and his team, then at Hockenheim for the German GP Ferrari's reliable power at last asserted itself and Lauda won after a Brabham-Alfa had retired and the leading Wolf slowed. This victory with six rounds still to run made the Drivers' Championship look like Lauda's, despite the team's problems.

Fairings were tried behind the 'T2s' rear wheels to reduce drag on this high-speed circuit but neither driver could detect any difference, so they were removed and quietly forgotten.

In Austria, Lauda was second and Reutemann fourth thanks to other competitors' failures and both Championship crowns were now clearly within reach. An F1 Constructors' Championship hat-trick had never before been achieved. It would be a Ferrari first.

At Zandvoort, '031' was fitted with a revised exhaust system to add mid-range torque but Lauda was convinced the advantage was as illusory as had been the after-wheel fairings at Hockenheim, and a standard system was refitted. Lauda won, again profiting from faster cars' failures. Reutemann was sixth after a wing damaging incident during the race.

By this time Lauda had arranged to leave Ferrari to join Brabham in 1978. It was an open secret by the time of the Italian GP at Monza, where Lauda paced home second behind Andretti's at last reliable Lotus 78. Now he needed just one more point to deny Scheckter's Championship ambitions with Wolf.

It came at Watkins Glen where Lauda placed fourth, for three points in fact, but the summary dismissal there of Lauda's Chief Mechanic, Cuoghi, in practice had decided him to withdraw from the team on the morning of first practice in Canada. He had driven his last race for Ferrari, and had left them as Formula 1 Constructors' Champions for the third consecutive season, and with a second Drivers' title under his own belt.

There was minimal 'T2 development for the last two races of that season in Canada and Japan, where Gilles Villeneuve joined Reutemann as team driver.

This turbulent but again undeniably successful season had seen Ferrari make 33 starts in the 17 World Championship rounds, Lauda scoring in every one of the 12 races which he finished – out of only 14 started. He won three times, took six second places on reliability and added a third, fourth and fifth. Reutemann's fourth place in the Drivers' Championship was achieved from 11 scoring finishes in the 13 events he finished from

17 started, including one win, two seconds, three thirds, two fourths and three sixths.

Since the birth of the *trasversale* series in 1975, Ferrari had raced cars built under 12 individual chassis numbers, five 312Ts built in 1974-75, and seven 'T2s built 1975-77. Chassis '023' started life as a '75 312T and raced on into the start of '76. It became the most successful individual chassis within the series, winning the Monaco, Belgian, Swedish and US GPs of 1975 and the Brazilian and South African races of 1976.

Now, at the end of 1977, Ferrari had taken their third Constructors' title with a design which was neither the fastest nor the most competitive, but crucially it was the most consistently reliable so their winning margin was a vast 33 points, with a total of 95 compared to Lotus's 62, McLaren's 60 and Wolf's 54. The team was to abandon Goodyear racing tyres in favour of Michelin in 1978, but they would not retrieve the World Championship mantle until the following year, 1979, with the model 312T4 whose story we shall trace shortly.

Ground Effects

Many years ago, a physicist named Bernoulli described the principle of velocity and pressure changes in a flowing fluid. Accelerate flow and pressure falls within the fluid. Now air is a fluid and if an airstream is introduced into a narrowing but otherwise open-ended tube or tunnel (a venturi) it is accelerated and its pressure falls.

This principle is harnessed in the venturi throat of a carburettor to suck in fuel, and having ventured into the area of wing form aerodynamics from 1967, Formula 1 engineering came to appreciate Mr Bernoulli very much some years later, in 1977-79.

As early as 1961 Texan oil-man, private flyer and intuitive race-engineering genius, Jim Hall, had beaten the hot British-built Cooper Monacos in an SCCA event at Elkhart Lake, driving his Troutman-Barnes built front-engined Chaparral 1 sports car with a Chevrolet V8 engine.

Chevrolet R&D sat up and paid attention. Some of their aerodynamicists then worked with Hall to produce an 'inverted airfoil' Chaparral body, with upswept undersides at nose and tail to form what was in elevation half a venturi tunnel between car underside and road surface. The car's passage through the air would then cause airflow to accelerate beneath the car, thus losing pressure and thereby sucking the car down against the road.

At least, they thought Mr Bernoulli had said it would . . . but it didn't.

When Hall tested the inverted-airfoil car at GM's Proving Grounds the front suspension reached full rebound at 120 mph as the nose rose, attempting to lift the front wheels clear of the ground. A massive snow-plough air dam was then fitted to *exclude* airflow running beneath the upturned under-nose section and this created so much downforce that Hall stopped half-way round his first lap with the front tyres grinding their way out through the front fender tops.

Had some form of skirting been suspended to seal that 'inverted airfoil' underbody against the road surface on each side, racing history could have been very different.

The modified Chaparral's problem stemmed from too much aerodynamic infill rushing in from ambient pressure between the wheels on each side, plus so much lift from the under-nose surface that enormous aerodynamic pressure under the nose attempted to flip the car over on its back. Perhaps only the weight of its hefty front engine saved the day until that air-dam was added with its consequent effect.

There followed a period when designers sought actively to exclude airflow from beneath their cars, to obtain downforce by harnessing airflow over the top of the bodywork and beneath their add-on airfoil wings.

Chaparral-Chevrolet continued to toy with wings and things, until in 1968-69 an anonymous race fan sent Jim Hall a sketch of a sports-racing car sucked down against the roadway by horizontal fans extracting the air from beneath it.

GM R&D engineer Paul van Valkenburgh, Chaparral's Don Gates and GM department head Charlie Simmons pursued the idea with test models which showed promise.

Gates worked out a fan and a skirt infill defence system while Don Cox, Ernie DeFusco and Joe Marasco engineered a chassis to match. The resultant Chaparral 2J 'sucker car' first ran in November 1969 and after considerable development was raced in the 1970 CanAm series where it created a sensation before being banned!

A 55 hp JLO snowmobile auxiliary engine had been adapted to run two extractor fans, reducing air pressure in a massive Lexan-skirted compartment around the car's centre of gravity and engine bay. The car proved blindingly fast, sucking itself to the road and exhibiting immense cornering power and traction – hence the ban, from which the restriction on 'moveable devices with a primary aerodynamic function' became entrenched.

Meanwhile, in England, BRM boffin Peter Wright had tackled the problem of cleaning up aerodynamic turbulence and obtaining some extra airfoil download area on the 1968-69 V12 cars. He conceived a bolt-on very high-aspect ratio wing-shaped pannier to mount each side of the slender monocoque hull of that period, projecting into the space between front and rear wheels. One BRM V12 was rigged in this manner with moulded glass-fibre wing panniers and was tested at Snetterton in 1968. Results were inconclusive, but promised enough for Peter and his boss Tony Rudd to produce a wind tunnel test model of a full-bodied 'wing-car'. It was tested briefly by them in early 1969 before the palace revolution which saw Rudd's resignation in mid-summer.

BRM's wing-car ideas were set aside. Rudd became Group Lotus Engineering Director for Colin Chapman; Peter Wright joined Specialised Mouldings, the racing car plastic body manufacturers, and set up their wind

tunnel R&D facility. Wearing an SM hat he suggested the BRM-clone March 701 pannier wing tanks to Robin Herd. These were raced in 1970, their shaped undersurfaces forming a half-venturi section with the road surface, but still high above it and lacking skirt sealing to prevent infill.

Then in 1973 Gordon Murray's pyramid-section Brabham BT42 punched a very small hole in the air, maintained good downforce from its upper surfaces and excluded most of the airstream from underneath. In his improved BT44s of 1974, Gordon ran a horizontal thrust-forward splitter or nose tray to exclude airflow. As the car pitched, however, so some of this sacrificial tray would wear away, some would survive.

That prompted him to consider fitting a dam amidships beneath the car's belly, near its pitch centre where the dam could never hit the road. He used a very thin, slightly flexible glass-fibre dam, divided to form a vee or chevron section beneath the car. Testing dictated 1.5 in. skirts for fast circuits, $\frac{7}{8}$ in. for bumpy courses.

Brabham's former BAC aerodynamicist and co-adoptor of the 1968 Belgian GP strutted wings, Ray Jessop, had taught Gordon how to use a manometer for air-pressure tests. Now Gordon fitted a liquid manometer clear U-tube on the car's side, with one end tapped to the site to be tested, behind the dam under the car for example, and using a coloured fluid and graduated pressure scale within the driver's vision.

Initially the driver would observe what level the liquid reached as he drove the car, and he would then report back. Subsequently they fitted an over-centre lever to clasp the plastic tube and hold the pressure difference for examination in the pit. This way they measured pressures on top of the nose, on the high airbox and beneath the car and when they found a pressure difference of perhaps 0.5 lb per square inch and multiplied that by the area of the car's underside over which that differential had been detected they were on their way to finding *several hundred pounds* useful download.

The under-belly air dam promoted an atmospheric depression which extended back for perhaps three or four feet. It was a practical expression of ground effect although the Brabham people did not really grasp its significance.

Fitting the skirts ahead of the centre of gravity enabled them to reduce wing incidence and that coincided with, as Gordon recalls 'an idea I pinched from Indy.

We saw some photos from David Phipps at the end of '73 showing the Liebeck lip on the back of a wing, a little curl now universal. It developed into the banana wing with its leading edge as high as the trailing edge, a wing with great camber but minimal frontal area. We had about 300 lb downforce from a wing like that plus, say, 150 lb from under the car – proved by the numbers we were seeing on the manometer . . .'

They attempted to keep it all secret through 1974 – though the belly dams were mentioned in the press – but McLaren had a good look and appreciated what was happening, and the McLaren M23s soon emerged with plastic appendages beneath their monocoques. An effect was noted, but it seemed impossible to persuade skirts to survive constant abrasion against the kerbs and track surface.

By 1976-77 Peter Wright headed Team Lotus aerodynamic research using Charlie Prior-made models in the Imperial College wind tunnel in Kensington, London. There he realized that the trick was to exclude airflow on either side of the car from infilling airstream-acceleration sections which could be formed by shaped underwing side pods on each side of the central chassis tub. The ground-contact aerodynamic skirt, *à la* Chaparral 2J of 1970, was adopted and rapidly perfected for Formula 1, and the ground-effects revolution was upon us.

The reduction of air pressure achieved in Wright's underwing venturi tunnels of course exerted its force in all directions, so not only did it suck down the car from below, it also sucked in the skirts on each side while accelerating air throughflow initiated by the car's passage.

In the sliding-skirt era from 1978 to 1980, it became vital to provide smooth, friction-free skirt travel to prevent these skirts from skewing and binding in their guides. Consistent contact with the ground had to be maintained to achieve consistent download as the awful bouncing or pitching effect known as 'porpoising' reared its ugly head. Intermittent skirt contact made and broke suction and, exacerbated by centre of pressure instability, in which the c.o.p. itself raced to and fro, the car self-excited and simply passed beyond suspension control.

The good cars did it well, most notably the Williams FW07 and Brabham BT49s, some others did it badly, particularly the Lotus 80, Arrows A2 and the dreadful Ferrari 312T5s.

Ground-effect aerodynamics, however, were here to stay, even after sliding skirts were banned, and despite the flat-bottom rule of 1983 banning venturi sections within the wheelbase. Useful ground effect was still to be obtained from low-set nose wings and end-plated diffuser surfaces slung beneath the gearbox.

Progress can never be un-invented . . .

Above left: *Peter Wright and Colin Chapman.* Left: *Wright tested wing tanks on this V12 BRM, Snetterton 1968.* Below: *Wright's BRM wing-car test model in the wind tunnel. Only the vital skirts were missing.*

Ferrari were just hitting new heights with their model 312T and McLaren were defending their World Championship titles with the M23s through the summer of 1975, when Team Lotus found themselves in really deep trouble. Their Type 72 cars were at last at the end of their long development, and their front suspension characteristics did not permit them to adapt adequately to the latest generation of Goodyear tyres.

Colin Chapman pondered the future. Sitting in his vast office at Ketteringham Hall three years later he told me how he had 'sat down and thought seriously about what we wanted, and decided the answer was a wing-car.'

This new concept in racing car design found its pioneering expression in the Lotus 78 of 1977 followed by World Championship domination in the Lotus 79 of 1978. The story of these two cars is virtually indivisible and so both will now be described in some detail, although only the latter achieved Constructors' Champion status.

Initially, Colin Chapman compiled a detailed concept document setting out his requirements and presented it to his engineering director, Tony Rudd, the former Chief Engineer of BRM. He was to establish a new research and development unit within the Lotus group.

As Rudd tells the story, that brief was far more than just an outline for a new car design – indeed a whole new car concept – it was a measure of Chapman's greatness.

'He realized that in racing we were down and out, and that we'd got it all wrong by the latest standards. And he made the right long-range strategic decisions while still involved in racing day-to-day. In his famous 27-page brief not only did he suggest the way to go, but he also listed all the things he didn't know, and then he left it to an old has-been like me and to a bunch of new boys to tell him all the answers . . .'

Rudd was anything but a has-been – he could not have held down his post with Lotus if that had been true – but he had not been closely involved with the racing cars until 1975, when research and development work began under his direction at Ketteringham Hall.

This was a rambling old country house folded within the woodlands close by the main Lotus plant at Hethel. During the Second World War it had been a Bombardment Group HQ for the US 8th Air Force, which flew Liberators from Hethel and the similar airfields dotted across the Norfolk plain nearby. The Hall later became a private boarding school before falling virtually derelict. Lotus acquired it, and former Brabham and McLaren designer Ralph Bellamy became one of its first inmates with a project to develop a new lightweight Lotus racing gearbox.

Rudd's Esprit production car design group arrived soon after, and with that project's conclusion Chapman put Rudd in charge of long-range Formula 1 research for Team Lotus. This new unit was to operate quite independently of Team and its everyday race commitments and pressures. It was to give Chapman the answers he wanted and to test the feasibility of the type of car which he had outlined.

His concept document was dated August 1975, one month before the release of the highly adjustable new Lotus 77 Formula 1 car (see page 286), Team's second serious attempt to produce a Type 72 replacement.

Ralph Bellamy became one early member of the Formula 1 R&D group, and a boffin named Peter Wright was another. He had been with Tony Rudd at BRM in 1969, and there they had laid down advance plans for a wing-car.

Chronic lack of success and eccentric management there had led to Rudd's summary dismissal in mid-season 1969. Tony Southgate had been appointed chassis designer in Rudd's place, Chapman had snapped up Rudd's services for Group Lotus and Wright had followed him there after a spell in charge of Specialised Mouldings' wind tunnel, for he was an aerodynamicist. After Rudd and Wright had left BRM, their wing-car programme was junked by the new regime. Wright had eventually joined Lotus to run their plastics research, and when that programme had been completed successfully his brilliant mind was applied to the new Formula 1 project.

The first BRM wing-car concept used stub wings sprouting either side of the central monocoque to clean up the aerodynamic turbulence between front and rear wheels and find some extra download. Robin Herd used a similar layout in his

Giorgio Piola's explanatory ground effects sketch is based on the Lotus 79 and shows (below): 1, nose fins; 2, venturi underwings; 3, expanding diffuser section; 4, suspension uprights well outboard to clear underbody airstream; 5, inboard spring/damper mounting for same reason; 6, inboard brakes (bad move); 7, end plate mounted rear wing. Bottom: 1, cambered nose fins; 2, improved 'Mosquito' leading-edge top-ducted radiator mount; 3, sliding skirt seal; 4, upswept exhaust efflux; 5, rear deck/engine cowl; 6, cambered rear wing.

March 701 design of 1970, but the idea was not then pursued to its ultimate conclusion since airflow management was not applied which would close off the underwing airstream from the general diffuse airflow around the outside of the car.

Wright joined Rudd and Bellamy at Ketteringham Hall – or 'Fawlty Towers' as it was known within Group Lotus – and through the autumn of 1975 this trio discussed Chapman's myriad questions of principle.

The philosophy was simple in essence: harness the car's entire form to generate advantageous aerodynamic effect, instead of merely using relatively tiny bolt-on wings at front and rear to load an aerodynamically redundant hull.

At that time every Formula 1 designer had studied in varying depth the effect of airflow around the sides and over the top of his car. Few, apart from Gordon Murray of Brabham and the McLaren boys, had tackled the potential embodied in the air flowing underneath it. Indeed, even then most had been trying various ploys to prevent too much air flowing under their cars at all.

Now the Lotus R&D group retained Charlie Prior, a first-class model and pattern maker from the Esprit team, to build quarter-scale model cars and aerodynamic devices for assiduous wind tunnel testing conducted by Wright at Imperial College, London.

A wind tunnel there was provided with a moving belt floor in the test section which mimicked the roadway passing at speed beneath a car. Little previous research had been conducted in this way. Normally test models sat on a stationary surface, or even less satisfactorily were suspended in space. This was fine for aviation testing but bore little resemblance to reality where land vehicles were concerned.

Questions were pursued in depth. If either bluff or chisel noses could be used, then both would be tested. If the chisel for example promised better, they would consider why; if it worked so well, should not other chisel sections then be used to gain more download somewhere else on the car?

Radiator siting is a vital cornerstone of any racing design. Rudd had been in charge of Rolls-Royce Merlin aero engine fault investigation during the war, and the inner-wing section radiator mounting of the De Havilland Mosquito aircraft came to mind. Its radiators were buried within ducts sunk into the inner wings' leading edges, air passing through the core and then exiting through conveniently sited ducts further back on the wing chord. Would side pods based upon this inner-wing section generate download when slung either side of a single-seat racing chassis?

A model mimic section was made and tested upside down in the wind tunnel to provide negative lift. Lift:drag ratio was the vital criterion – the best possible lift for the least possible drag being the target. Tony Rudd still recalls the message he received from Imperial College that Christmas. It read simply 'The Mosquito flies'.

Ducted radiators and pod sections of this type would be used to harness airflow beneath the pod underfloors – or underwings – to generate download. The low-pressure areas created by the acceleration of this airflow (see page 102) would be protected from infilling on each side by a skirt system which would extend from the pod side panels down to the road surface.

Now that overall concept, shape and principles for what would become the Lotus Type 78 had been decided, Bellamy settled down to draw the car while Wright delved further into its aerodynamics.

Mike Cooke set up and ran a test rig, simulating racing loads on every component as it was made. Unacceptable deflection brought immediate redesign until stiffness became adequate. The rig itself was rather crude, loading parts via cables passing over pulleys and attached to concrete-filled oil drums, but it was invaluable in building structural reliability into the new car. It also served to pinpoint some of the contemporary Type 77's deficiencies and helped bring that car to competitiveness by season's end, when Andretti drove it to win the Japanese GP.

Once Bellamy had finalized his layouts, Martin Ogilvie moved up from Team's base at Potash Lane to detail the new car's suspensions and other 'bits that moved', while Bellamy completed the chassis and they then combined on body design.

The prototype Lotus 78 – known in the curious sponsor-pleasing 'John Player Special' series then in use as chassis 'JPS/15' – was driven first time out at Hethel by Ketteringham's shop foreman, Eddie Dennis. Although a new Lotus racing gearbox was under development, it was not used on this prototype car 'to limit the unknowns' as Chapman put it.

Nigel Bennett, a former Firestone racing tyre engineer who had joined Team when the American company withdrew from racing at the end of 1974, conducted onboard instrumentation tests using borrowed Goodyear equipment while Andretti and his team-mate Gunnar Nilsson drove in extended circuit testing.

By the time Chapman decided to race the new car his R&D group had accumulated 2.2 miles of test-recording tape, had completed over 150 individual investigations, 54 rig tests and 400 hours of wind tunnel time at Imperial College. The statistics were impressive, but did the car work?

Tests indicated that it did, although aerodynamic values realized full-size were easily 25-30 per cent less than those predicted by wind tunnel model tests.

The new 'John Player Special Mark III' – alias Lotus 78 – made its public bow at a reception held in London's Royal Garden Hotel on 21 December 1976. Andretti was there, enthusing about its 'boulevard ride', and it certainly looked different . . .

The centre monocoque nacelle was slim, like the preceding Type 77's, but it had broad panniers slung either side between front and rear wheels. The tub was formed into a fully stressed tank section behind the driver's shoulders, while a structural scuttle panel passed above his legs up front. The new tub was light and very stiff through liberal use of Cellite sandwich material in its front bulkhead and side skins.

This material consisted of two thin dural sheets sandwiching aluminium honeycomb. It was very strong and stiff yet light and was borrowed direct from aerospace where the actual section employed by Lotus was used in Trident airliner flooring. Lotus's panels were actually made up for them by Technical Resin Bonders. The material had also featured in one panel on the Cosworth 4WD car of 1969 and had been studied closely by Derek Gardner during his Tyrrell researches of 1971-73.

Front suspension comprised swept-back front rocker arms and wide-based fabricated lower wishbones, carrying neat cast uprights with Lotus 77-style Lockheed twin-caliper disc brakes. These were a co-operative development between the two companies offering duplicated calipers clasping both leading and trailing edges of the ventilated discs. Originally they had doubled as structural members in the Type 77s, bolting on inboard, with the suspension elements in turn bolted onto integral lugs cast in the caliper bodies. An early modification to the Type 77 had seen the front brakes go outboard into the wheels, which is where the 78 now carried these 'balanced caliper' brakes.

Inboard coil-spring/damper units resided in neat niches recessed into the tub flanks. Massive fairings streamlined the tubular top rocker arm pivot supports which had been exposed on the Type 77s.

At the rear, the Cosworth DFV/Hewland gearbox assembly matched the 77's in all save two major details. Where the 77 had used a single bottom link, the new 78 used a massive fabricated wishbone, though the geometry was initially identical. On the 77 the inboard structural balanced brake calipers had been carried on special transaxle side plates which could be rotated to adjust anti-squat. Parallel top link suspension picked up on these inboard calipers. A neat innovation on the 78 on show (actually the second chassis, JPS/16) was the oil tank which was now integrated into the bell-housing spacer between engine and gearbox. This feature was to be widely copied, along with so many other features of the Type 78.

On JPS/15 oil had been carried in a tank accommodated within a four inch longer rear section of the tub. All subsequent 78s were built along JPS/16 lines, using the shorter tub and bell-housing tank. This gave them a 107 in. wheelbase against the prototype's original 110 in. type.

However, the new Lotus's magic ingredient lay within its side panniers. Essentially they housed wing fuel tanks towards the rear – around the car's notional centre of gravity – with the water radiators ahead of them in their 'Mosquito' mounts, exhausting expended air upward through shaped pannier-top vents. The ramp surface guiding this air out through the top vents was actually the upper face of the wing fuel tank panelling.

The tank undersides then curved upwards towards their trailing edges, terminating in line with the engine mounts to present what could be called an inverted wing section to the airstream. In fact it exerted its influence on the venturi principle described elsewhere (p.102).

Having generated an area of low pressure beneath these underwing sections, capable literal-

Andretti in the Lotus 78 at Monaco, showing off its broad flat side pods incorporating underwings within, top-ducted leading-edge radiators and nose-top oil cooler.

ly of sucking the car down onto the road surface, measures then had to be taken to prevent air infilling this depression from either side. This was the crucial step which had not been taken in the BRM experiment nor in the March 701.

Now Wright recommended that the 'tips' of these very long-chord, short-span pannier wings be closed off by Cellite end plates which extended virtually the full distance from front to rear wheel on either side. Furthermore, extending beneath the Cellite end plate, which might be better described as a 'side plate' in this instance, a bristle skirt extended down to road level. The hunt was on to discover an air-impervious material which could survive high-speed rubbing contact with the road surface, and a brush just seemed a reasonable expedient with which to start.

The panniers' upper decks, meanwhile, extended alongside the engine to terminate in flick-ups above the exhaust manifolding ahead of each rear wheel.

Conventional wings and fins provided trim and balance, but still there was more. Mounting the side radiators just aft of the front suspension gave more forward weight bias than hitherto, and this was further enhanced by the oil cooler being buried in a nose duct well ahead of the front axle line and by the far-forward driving position, forced there by the three fuel cells in line abreast behind the seat back. This concentrated fuel load around the car's notional centre of gravity and achieved Chapman's requirement for 'minimum change in handling and response as the fuel load lightens'.

After testing permutations with his highly adjustable type 77 – which was as much a research vehicle as a serious racing car – he decided that only three things really mattered: 'how long it is, how wide it is, and where the weight is! We'd tried seven different rear-suspension geometries on one occasion and the drivers were hard pressed to notice any difference. But when we increased the front track by an inch they raved.'

Consequently the 78's front track was extended close to the maximum limit, wider than the 77, so the new car could literally stick out a paw as its driver applied steering lock and the longer lever arm would give extra 'bite'.

Now Goodyear's contemporary front tyres were loaded as never before by a Lotus, and there was no problem in working them up to adequate temperature. Front-end grip was the greatest the drivers had ever known, and in turn it then allowed use of near zero-slip differentials to limit wheelspin, which in a design with less front-end bite would merely induce uncontrollable understeer.

This was partly at Andretti's request. He then prompted addition of a USAC-style driver-adjustable rear anti-roll bar, similar to that being introduced by McLaren from their Indy experience. He also recommended a preferential fuel drainage system, which would enable him to choose the order and degree in which his three available fuel cells drained down – thus further adjusting weight bias within the car during a race as its total fuel load burned away.

Andretti had forged a rare empathy with Chapman, rather similar to the relationship which this gifted engineer had once shared so successfully with Jim Clark. Andretti had the experience and innate sensitivity to trim his car into optimum balance on the fuel changeover tap and anti-roll adjuster. He worked unceasingly during that 1977 season to set up his Lotus 78s to an unprecedented pitch.

In USAC left-turn only track racing, 'stagger' – the use of unequal-circumference tyres giving the car a directional bias under power and braking – had become a highly developed practice, though still perhaps more art than science. Similarly, 'cross-weighting' – diagonal stiffness in the car adjusted on its spring platforms – was a familiar track-racing tweak to find optimum traction in the important corners on a circuit, and Andretti had the ability to appreciate when, where and how these finer points could be applied.

For Formula 1 he and Team Lotus took great pains to match sets of tyres. Manufacturing

Andretti and Nilsson in Team Lotus's two new Type 78s, chassis '3 and '2 respectively, Jarama, 1977 Spanish GP. Mario won, with Gunnar fifth. See the Tony Southgate-inspired Shadow-like nose oil coolers.

processes for cross-ply racing tyres inevitably produced variations within finished cover sizes and characteristics. Working with Chapman, Bennett and, briefly, Tony Southgate, another BRM refugee to come to Lotus (in his case via Shadow), even lateral tyre stabilities would be explored. This was done by altering wheel-offsets with the Speedline bolt-together sectional road wheels used.

The end result of this deep-thinking programme was that Andretti led more World Championship race laps than any other driver that 1977 season. He won four Grands Prix and his team-mate Nilsson won a fifth for the team in Belgium, in the rain.

But a string of five engine failures and three other mechanical faults kept Andretti, Lotus and the World Championship titles apart. Three new Cosworth development engines, using more radical cams and porting than the standard production units, failed behind Andretti's shoulders. Alternative Nicholson-McLaren rebuilt DFVs failed him twice more.

But Andretti won with luck and Nicholson power on his side at Long Beach and then from genuine merit, still Nicholson-powered, in the Spanish GP at Jarama. Luck gave him a third victory at Dijon when Watson's Brabham-Alfa Romeo faltered on the very last lap with Andretti and the Lotus 78 well beaten. Sweetest victory for this Italian-born American driver came at Monza in his 'home' GP where a revised Cosworth development engine with less radical valve timing survived to the finish, and the 78 was simply uncatchable.

The repeated engine failures were blamed by Cosworth upon a suspect oil tank in the car, causing aeration difficulties, but though Lotus changed the system as advised the precise nature of the problem was neither traced nor proved.

On the 78's debut in the heat of Buenos Aires, Andretti's 78/2 had its front end blown apart by an exploding onboard extinguisher bottle. Dangerous stuff, this safety equipment . . . In Brazil the same unfortunate car had then caught fire. Race retirements in both these events were mechanical, caused respectively by RHP/Lobro joint failure and then by a battery solenoid malfunction. In Sweden, having led 68 of the GP's 72 laps, Andretti's car ran low on fuel due to its Nicholson engine's metering unit having vibrated itself onto a full-rich setting, increasing its consumption.

These failures frustrated the unfortunate driver, while lapses on his part agonized the team. Despite his vast experience he would too often try to win his races on the opening lap, impetuously sparking first-lap accidents at Zolder and Fuji

which put him out.

During the season four Type 78 chassis were built, plated as 'JPS-15-16-17-18', all of which survived the year. Chassis '78/1' (i.e. 'JPS-15') would be sold to Mexican privateer Hector Rebaque for 1978 and he would also purchase '78/4' ('JPS-18') during that season. Team retained 78s '2 and '3.

The Lotus 78s' season was characterized as win or bust. By the end of it, the lack of minor place scorings left Lotus-JPS second to Ferrari in the Constructors' Championship, and Andretti third and Nilsson eighth in the Drivers' competition. Yet Andretti had still won those four GPs, while World Champion Lauda and runner-up Scheckter had won only three each, more reliable minor placings producing their greater points total.

The World Championship scoring systems rewarded consistency more than winning, and Chapman considered wryly 'merely driving for points just isn't the name of the game as far as I'm concerned'.

His Lotus 78 was undoubtedly the star of that 1977 season, but its performances had not been so clear cut as to convince the opposition – yet – that Lotus really had something in this ground-effects underwing business. Reliability had been poor, and while the car undoubtedly developed much download it also added much drag and was slow on the straights.

At that time several leading drivers would say 'Gimme a car that's fast on the straight, and I'll block 'em all off in the corners . . .'

Team Lotus was not unduly worried by the 78s' perceived straightline speed deficiency. They felt that other factors had intruded on the faster circuits, and in any case the car offered so much download that its drivers always wanted to use it *all*, not trim some out to diminish drag and so gain straightline speed. They loved its secure feel in corners, blinding round their opposition often on the outside line, with some adhesion still in hand.

Above all, the 78 excelled on turn-in bite into corners and on traction away from them. Its 'wing-car' aerodynamics worked and now for 1978 Team prepared a new design which would make the most of the 78's new technology.

1978 – THE BLACK BEAUTY

The existing Type 78s raced on into the new year with Ronnie Peterson joining Andretti to constitute perhaps the strongest driver pairing in Formula 1.

Andretti began the year by winning at Buenos Aires, while in South Africa Peterson won an extraordinary wheel-banging going-slow race from a Tyrrell on the last lap after Andretti's 78 had run low on fuel (again) and lost the lead.

Meanwhile, a much-refined Lotus 79, or JPS Mark IV, was on the way to capitalize upon experience with the 78, alias JPS Mark III. While the 78 had used relatively simple inverted side wings to generate its download, the new 79 went much further towards being a true ground-effects vehicle, in that its pannier underwings formed a far more sophisticated venturi section against the road surface and thus accelerated air passing beneath to reduce its pressure and so download the whole vehicle.

It was now hoped to find the missing 25 per cent of aerodynamic download which had been somehow misplaced between tunnel-testing the models for the Type 78 and running the real car full-size.

Lotus had claimed that the Type 78s had started out as heavy cars, and had shed weight during their racing career – the reverse of normality – but even so they were still too heavy for choice. One interesting suggestion in the Chapman concept document had been provision of onboard jacks to save time in testing and pre-race qualifying. The original cars had turned out too heavy to dare install them, but the 79 was to come that much closer.

Meanwhile, the Ketteringham R&D group had become diluted. Southgate returned whence he came to Shadow in mid-1977, and now Bellamy moved to Copersucar. Both embarked on new wing-car designs, the former more successfully than the latter. It appears that Bellamy had been the great advocate of using honeycomb in the 78

but towards the end of his time there his relationship with Chapman had deteriorated. Now 'The Old Man' took charge of the 79 project and, according to one member of his design team, 'decided perhaps to do it his own way, using sheet aluminium which he understood from the old days'.

There would be minimum use of honeycomb in the new chassis. This was arguably a retrograde step, and structurally the 78 would remain more advanced than its replacement.

But there were disadvantages with using honeycomb panels. Skin damage transmitted to the core was virtually impossible to repair short of total replacement and Team found major headaches achieving adequate strong-point mountings in the very thin aluminium skins. Consequently the 79 grew as a conventional sheet aluminium tub, with a high-set beam arrangement within its cockpit sides from which to hang the side pods and attendant structures.

Under the usual beady-eyed direction of 'The Old Man', the new Type 79 was drawn and detailed by Geoff Aldridge and Martin Ogilvie. One major objective was to improve airflow through the side panniers, and to achieve this the outboard fuel tanks and rear suspension spring/dampers of the Type 78 were deleted.

Formula 1 regulations had set an 80-litre maximum capacity for individual fuel cells, but now Chapman wanted to concentrate his entire fuel load in a single cell buried far from threat, deep in the rear of the tub. Application was made for the 80-litre limit to be waived, and the new 79 accommodated all its fuel in one single rear-tub cell between engine and driver. In an early design scheme, however, two tanks were drawn here.

The tub itself was made as slender as possible, to devote maximum width to those vital underwing panniers. The structural sections along either side of the cockpit were minimal. The forepart of the tub was strengthened by a perforated stress-panel bulkhead around the dash panel area, like the 77/78 series and very reminiscent of much earlier Lotus products from 1958 to 1962. An arched scuttle panel enclosed the driver's shins, tapering down into the shallow and slender nose. All structural panels were in aluminium sheet, apart from the tub floor which was honeycomb sandwich.

Front suspension was now squared up rather than raked back as in the 78, and the inboard coil/damper units were buried well out of the airstream within the tub sides. Top rocker arms and wide-based lower wishbones were spaced as far apart as possible to free air entry into the side pod radiator and underwing ducts. There was no sense in forcing a massive volume of air into these pods only for its free exit to be obstructed at the other end. For this reason the 78's outboard rear coil/damper mounting was replaced by an inboard variety, nestling the springs tight against the gearbox cheeks. New up-and-over high-level exhaust manifolds were introduced to remove another obstruction.

The now familiar double-caliper brake discs reappeared, outboard front and inboard rear. A single large water radiator hung raked steeply forward on the right side of the tub, within its side pod, while a smaller oil cooler was in the left-hand pod.

Without its bodywork the new Type 79 looked extremely gawky and spare, but with the large and voluptuous new body panels fitted it was transformed into by far the best-looking Formula 1 car of its time – Black Beauty indeed.

Peter Wright described the Lotus 78 as a car which tried out new ideas, while the Lotus 79 was the car designed around those ideas. Chapman had also long cherished plans for a lighter, longer-lived gearbox than the Hewland which would also allow two-pedal clutchless driving, which for many years had been one of 'Chunky's' hobbyhorses.

The prototype Lotus 79 (chassis 'JPS/19') was tested at Ricard-Castellet in December 1977. Wright reflects 'nobody fully appreciated what ground effect was going to do to loads and what those loads would do to a ground-effect car . . . all structures began to fatigue at an incredible rate!'

After some 150 miles of Ricard testing 'JPS/19's monocoque was shown to be woefully inadequate in torsional stiffness. There was also room for aerodynamic improvement, because the 79 had been intended as a 78 that was also quick in a straight line, and in this original form it just wasn't. Its original low-arch scuttle structure was also too confined for tall new Team driver Ronnie Peterson's comfort. The new Lotus-Getrag gearbox also showed room for improvement in these

Piola explodes the 1977 Lotus 78. 1, oil cooler; 2, extinguisher bottles; 3, Lotus-Lockheed balanced caliper brakes; 4, 'Mosquito' radiator siting; 5, primitive hinged skirt; 6, rear anti-roll bar adjuster; 7, side pod underwing floor behind wing tank; 8, rotating anti-roll bar blade; 9, Lotus-Lockheed balanced rear calipers; 10, Hewland FG400 transaxle.

initial tests. At first it felt like a real advance over the Hewland, being much lighter in weight, lighter to use and quicker-changing, but after a few laps running its selection mechanism would wilt under Formula 1 torques, having been far under-stressed in design. Chassis '19 was returned to Ketteringham's race workshop and dismantled. It would subsequently be rebuilt as a gearbox development hack – replacing an old Lotus 77 in that role – then later in the season would be rebuilt again to latest specification and pressed into service as a Team spare.

Meanwhile, the second Lotus 79, chassis 'JPS/20' (or, more logically, '79/2'), was completed in effect as a Mark 2 car with a stiffened monocoque featuring stronger cockpit sides, and a raised dash hoop and front scuttle panel to give the lanky Peterson some knee room. Rear suspension was also modified with a deeper upright and longer lower wishbones picking up beneath the gearbox on the car's centreline. The bolt-on moulded side pods retained carefully shaped top-exit cooler ducts and carried underwing floors below to offer higher download values than the interim style of the Type 78.

On the Ricard car these underwing sections had terminated at the front engine mounts, but in '79/2' they extended rearwards alongside the engine. The top body deck around the engine induction system was lowered and flick-ups were added to fair in the rear wheels and improve airflow under the end plate-mounted rear wing.

Andretti drove the car in this form in the Silverstone International, but after 58 practice laps – which was a long way – the new Lotus gearbox failed. A sister transmission fitted to Peterson's old 78 failed at precisely the same distance. Still the Swede qualified on pole with Andretti third fastest and loving every yard in his new car.

Team draughtsman Martin Ogilvie recalls Peterson going round lap after lap, proving the Lotus-Getrag gearbox, then suddenly going faster . . . 'And when he came in we said, "Ah, you've sorted out the selection problem", and he just smiled that slow smile and said, "No. I yust stopped you-sing the clutch." '

On race day it rained furiously. Peterson crashed during the warm-up while Andretti led briefly before aquaplaning off-course into an earlier victim of deep puddles at Abbey Curve and damaging '79/2' quite extensively.

Nevertheless, he commented: 'All in all, the 79 really gave us a message at Silverstone. Boy, that thing was good in the wet, really exceptionally good . . . but we had to have a Hewland gearbox in the car . . . with the Getrag I was having trouble hooking fifth even on the first lap . . .'

The car was rebuilt while 'JPS/21' ('79/3') was being completed and both emerged in a further-revised 'Mark 3' form. Chapman now reluctantly dropped the Lotus-Getrag transmission for further development – it would ultimately be shelved entirely – while Hewland 'mangle-gears' reappeared and over-the-gearbox exhaust systems were adopted to pull their profile closer to the rear cross-section of the tub. 'Clapper board' aerodynamic skirts were adopted, made from rigid Cellite sheet with an abrade-resistant lower edge, running in channels beneath the panniers. This would prove to be the rigid sliding skirt's definitive form, as only material and guide/control mechanisms improved further.

Lotus's lads rebuilt '79/2' so rapidly it appeared at Monaco as Team's spare car, and in practice there Andretti was stunned by its potential: 'It turned in as good as the 78, but the back end was at least as good as the front where on the 78 the front had always tended to overwhelm the back. It seemed like here was the perfect race car, with grip at the front, grip at the back, *incredible* traction . . .'

It was still considered unraceworthy, especially for the hurly-burly of Monaco, but then followed a Goodyear test session at Anderstorp in Sweden where Peterson drove the 79 and set times the opposition could not contemplate. He ran some 700 miles, then the car was taken direct to Zolder

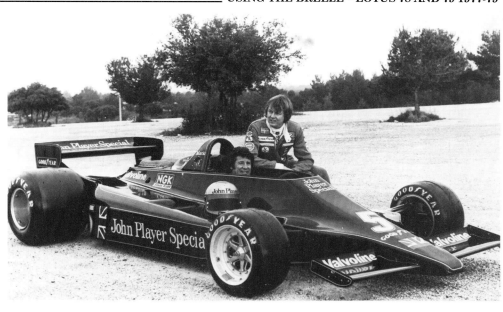

Birth of the John Player 'superteam': winter testing at Ricard 1977/78. Andretti and Peterson pose with '79/1' as Black Beauty belies its numerous teething troubles.

where it was intended to be Andretti's spare for the Belgian GP. Team engineer Nigel Bennett told Andretti he thought they could 'make a race car out of it'. Andretti talked to Chapman and they put $500 each into an encouragement kitty for the mechanics if the 79 survived race distance without a failure.

The rebuilt 'JPS/20' thus started its first Grand Prix . . .

By that time the old Lotus 78s had already proved themselves to be the cars to beat. Andretti had raced '78/3' and Peterson '78/2' in each of the five races from Argentina in January to Monaco in May. Their ten starts in these races yielded two first places – in Argentina and South Africa – one second place, two fourths, one fifth, a seventh (after leading), eleventh and two retirements – one mechanical, the other due to a collision in Brazil which broke the Peterson car's suspension.

At Zolder, in the sparkling rebuilt '79/2', Andretti qualified as he had done the previous year in the early Type 78, over a second faster than the rest of the field. He led from start to finish with little apparent effort and Peterson's sister 78 was delayed by a pit stop to change tyres but soared back through the field to finish second and so bring Team Lotus – two days after Chapman's 50th birthday – their fourth 1-2 result in a *Grande Epreuve*.

In the Spanish GP at Jarama, Peterson was out in the brand new '79/3' and the Lotus pair not only qualified 1-2 on the grid but again finished 1-2 in the race, while Andretti again set fastest lap. Mexican privateer Hector Rebaque had bought '78/1' and drove it sensibly before retiring. In the Swedish GP at Anderstorp the hastily completed Brabham answer to Lotus ground effects emerged as the controversial fan-car. Lauda won with it after Andretti had started from pole and retired, and Peterson was third, after being blatantly baulked by the Arrows in second place. Andretti's failure was put down to titanium valve spring caps dishing under load, allowing the retainers to fall out in three cylinders, whereupon a valve had broken.

The fan-car was ruled out of competition thereafter and the Lotus 79 was reinstated as the only ground-effects car of the season, although other teams like Wolf made valiant attempts to close the gap. Another Type 79 1-2 was scored in the French GP, while at Brands Hatch Peterson qualified his car on pole but both 79s failed after leading in the early stages. Andretti won the German race from pole. Peterson started alongside him on the front row, led and set fastest lap before retiring with gearbox failure. Rebaque was sixth in chassis '78/4', one of the two type 78s he had bought, and scored a Championship point.

Ever since whumping '79/3' over a kerb during qualifying at Ricard and losing pole there to Watson's Brabham-Alfa Romeo because of this error, Andretti had felt sure his chassis was some-

how out of true, despite having been back on the jig at Ketteringham; but Hockenheim dispelled his fears. Until then he had doubted the 79's straightline speed on such a fast circuit; 'Any doubts I had about the car were gone now. Really fast tracks I'd got to dread with the 78 but the 79 could run with anybody.'

The prototype '79/1' had been extensively rebuilt to the latest standard as a spare car for the late-season races, while Andretti regularly used chassis '3 and Peterson chassis '2. In Austria the 79s qualified 1-2 on the grid for the third consecutive time and set new performance standards, though not without problems.

Andretti's car ran new aerodynamic-section wishbones there in practice and with rear wing eased off to two degrees incidence for high speed the car felt 'really spooky through the quick turns'. The wishbones were the only new thing on the car, so they were replaced by the normal type, and it all came back as good as ever, indicating just how sensitive were these new-era cars.

Torrential rain then washed out the first attempt at running the GP after only seven laps had already seen Andretti – too anxious to clinch his World Championship – and Rebaque both crash. Peterson then won the restarted 47-lap second section of the Grand Prix from pole position in '79/2' and set fastest lap along the way.

In the Dutch GP at Zandvoort the 79s again qualified fastest in team order and finished 1-2 yet again, Andretti winning from pole in new car 'JPS/22' ('79/4') using parts salvaged from his wrecked Austrian '79/3' hung on a replacement tub.

The Italian GP followed at Monza. In race morning warm-up Peterson crashed his regular '79/2' following brake problems. No spare 79 was available so he fell back on his veteran '78/3' spare car for the race.

Andretti started from pole in his latest car '79/4' but a starting procedure muddle sparked a horrifying multiple collision on the charge into the first corner, and Peterson's Lotus 78 was barged head-on into a guardrail at high speed and its single-skin forward monocoque section collapsed upon impact, breaking both his legs. The chassis was demolished, its fuel system ruptured and the wreck caught fire, although Peterson was quickly pulled clear by fellow drivers. He was seriously injured but alive and in no apparent danger, only to die that night in hospital due to complications following fracture surgery.

Meanwhile the race had been restarted, Andretti won on the road but was docked a minute for jumping the restart and classified sixth. He still set fastest lap and clinched his

World title, but any joy Team might have felt was nothing compared to their loss.

They were committed to run two cars in the US and Canadian GPs ending the season and the French driver Jarier was taken on to accompany Andretti. At Watkins Glen the Italian-American qualified '79/4' on pole while Jarier drove '79/3', rebuilt since its Austrian crash. In race morning warm-up Andretti's car broke its right-rear stub axle and threw a wheel. He took over '79/3' for the race, guessing at correct adjustments to suit his needs while Jarier was strapped into old '79/1' – which had arrived from the UK only that morning – for its race debut.

Andretti led the Ferraris initially in the viciously oversteering spare 79 which also suffered spongy brakes and, after the Ferraris got by, his race ended with engine failure. Jarier meanwhile was plagued by tyre and fuel problems but after an early stop to replace a left-front tyre burned out by his inducing too much understeer on full tanks, he tore back through the field and challenged for second place until his tank ran dry with three laps to go. He set fastest lap, emphasizing the 79's superiority.

In Montreal for the Canadian GP, the Frenchman then took pole position in '79/3' and pulled out a huge 30-second lead by half-distance, only to drop back on lap 49 as brake fluid leaked from a defective line and he was forced to retire.

Andretti's '79/4' handled poorly throughout this meeting and its monocoque was found subsequently to have been twisted by the Watkins Glen incident. He could not use his spare car in this long race because its fuel capacity was too restricted. After a minor collision early in the race he could only finish a distant and disappointing tenth to end Lotus's trend-setting but bitter-sweet season.

The Type 79s had made 20 starts in eleven Grand Prix races, taking six first places, four seconds, a third, a sixth, one tenth, and a 15th (Jarier's final classification at Watkins Glen); there were six retirements. During that high summer of their success they accumulated 10 pole positions, the last seven in consecutive races – eight to Andretti, one to Peterson and one to Jarier. Only the French GP at Ricard broke their run, where Watson's Brabham-Alfa Romeo bettered Andretti's front-row time by a quarter of a second while the kerb-damaged Lotus 79 was being checked over.

The cars also set five fastest race laps – two

each to Andretti and Peterson, one to Jarier. When they were beaten for fastest lap they still set second and third fastest times, behind the Brabham fan-car, in Sweden; third and fourth at Ricard; second and third at Zandvoort, by 0.01 second behind Lauda's Brabham-Alfa Romeo; and fourth fastest (by Jarier) in Canada at the season's end.

After the 79's introduction into Championship racing at Zolder, the works 78s made only two more starts. Belgium yielded second place and fastest lap for Peterson in '78/2', while the Type's tragic swansong was at Monza where Ronnie was injured in '78/3', which of course was utterly destroyed.

So this remarkable if marred season saw Team Lotus take the Formula 1 Constructors' title by 86 points to Ferrari's 58, while Andretti took the Drivers' title from Peterson's tragically posthumous second place.

The 79s would run on into 1979 while the intended replacement Type 80 was being developed. Today this Lotus season tends to be recalled glibly as a total disaster. In truth it started quite well, although it was immediately clear that the opposition were not only following where Lotus had led into ground-effects aerodynamics but were immediately threatening to do a better job . . .

Team had new sponsorship from Martini in 1979 and appeared in British Racing Green livery with the red-and-blue Martini stripes made famous on so many long-distance racing Porsches. The prototype Lotus 80 would carry the chassis number 'ML23' following on from the John Player Special 'JPS' number system, but it was old 79s chassis '2-3-4' which began the season, with a brand new 79, chassis '5', out for Andretti at the third race, in South Africa.

Right at the start of the season it was obvious that Gérard Ducarouge's Ligier-Cosworth JS11 design was far more effective. These cars dominated the Argentinian and Brazilian GPs but Team's new joint number one driver Reutemann finished second behind the winning JS11 in Buenos Aires and Andretti fifth, so the 79s were still in contention. The Lotus drivers then qualified 3-4 behind the Ligier pair in Brazil, and Reutemann finished third behind them in the race. The Lotus 79 was still 'the best of the rest'.

At Kyalami the 79s finished 4-5 with Andretti capable of setting third fastest race lap in his new '79/5'. Reutemann qualified on the front row at Long Beach, while Andretti finished fourth and set fastest lap.

The new Lotus 80 made the first of its only three race appearances in Spain where it placed third, with Reutemann inheriting a distant second in old '79/2' despite the car suddenly proving unable

to match the race pace.

Thus far, Andretti had raced '79/4' in South America before taking on '5, then the 80, while Reutemann had used '79/2' everywhere but Brazil where he drove chassis '3. In Belgium the 80 was set aside and Andretti returned to '79/5' for the race. But he retired with brake trouble while Reutemann finished fourth, and in Monaco Reutemann drove '79/4' into a reliable third place after Andretti qualified slowly in the 80 and left the race with rear suspension failure.

At this point in the season, with seven races run and eight to go, the Williams FW07 came on song, the Ferraris were showing their sheer power and reliability, and the Ligiers were still very quick though they had lost their South American edge. Team Lotus toppled off the tightrope of competitiveness as surely as they had in 1975 with the old Type 72s.

In those first seven races of the '79 season, Team's entries had started 14 times and had finished in the Championship points 11 times. In contrast, the final eight races would see them start 16 times and achieve only four finishes, only one of which was in the points – Andretti's fifth at Monza, where he also set sixth fastest race lap and Reutemann finished seventh.

Two non-Championship race starts had also been made. Early in the year at Brands Hatch Andretti actually qualified '79/3' on pole and finished third, while at Imola in September, Reutemann qualified '79/2' third fastest and inherited second place in a sparse field. But that was a rare late-season highlight.

The 80 made its last race appearance in the French GP where its brakes, suspension and general aerodynamic misbehaviour caused Andretti despair, and thereafter Team had to campaign the 79s which were being run ragged by the opposition.

Team's nadir came in Austria, where Andretti's clutch failed at the start and Reutemann stopped to change tyre compounds and eventually gave up with 'handling problems'. After that third place in Monaco he seemed to have given up completely and was not in contention for the rest of the year. Some of Team's people nicknamed him 'Doris' . . . yes, it had got that bad.

Andretti did his determined best, but it was clear that whereas the Lotus 79 had been in a class of its own the previous year, times had changed since then and it could not withstand the pressure.

Peter Wright: 'In its day the 79 had been very effective, but then it had been the only proper ground-effect car around, and a lot had been compromised to make it effective . . . Now in 1979 it was up against second-generation ground-effect cars which showed up its deficiencies in cooling, brakes and also in structural stiffness, I am afraid. The 80 had been our second-generation car which had all the right capabilities in braking, cooling and structural rigidity but while we tried to find out what was wrong with its aerodynamic behaviour we had to go back to the 79 and with the pressures of the calendar preventing proper test and development it was no longer adequate into the second half of the season . . .'

The one-time pace-setting Lotus 79s' frontline racing career ended at Watkins Glen on 7 October 1979. Reutemann qualified remarkably well, sixth fastest in '79/3', and ran third in the rain-swept opening laps before being distracted by the fire extinguisher sensing unit which had come adrift and was bouncing around inside the cockpit. He lost control and spun off. Andretti meanwhile had '79/5's gearbox progressively strip teeth before jamming in fourth and causing retirement on the 16th lap.

The Lotus 79 was a classic beauty whose career shared enormous early success with subsequent mediocre failure. It represented both the pinnacle of Lotus's middle period at the top of the pile and the beginning of their dismal slump in the early 1980s. However, it is properly best remembered as the last of Colin Chapman's team's blinding flashes of brilliance – and one more which simply revolutionized all racing car design . . .

The gawky monocoque '79/2' being set up on travel wheels in Team Lotus workshops, early 1978. Note raised scuttle, shallow slender tail alongside cockpit, and water radiator laid bare without the side pod in place.

Brabham Fan-Car

During the early part of 1978 when Lauda and Watson were proving just how competitive the Brabham-Alfa Romeo BT46s could be against all but the new ground-effects Lotus 78/79 series, Gordon Murray and his right-hand man David North wrestled with the problems of designing a ground-effects car around the wide, low-level Alfa '115-12' flat-12 engine. Its heads projected obstructively into the precise area where ground-effect venturi tunnels should be sited.

They investigated mounting the engine in the front, then putting the fuel tank behind the engine, sandwiched ahead of the gearbox. It would have worked that way, but the multiple joints involved would have made it very heavy and handling changes between full and empty would have been spectacular.

In desperation they re-read the regulations, and spotted a loophole under which an extractor fan could be used to reduce air-pressure beneath the car so long as its 'primary function' was not 'aerodynamic' in the Formula 1 sense. In other words, it could be claimed that its primary function was to draw air through a radiator to cool the engine, rather than being intended to affect the performance of the car generated from its motion through the air.

They had already used a small fan in a panic attempt to cool the BT45C's horizontal oil matrices above the engine in South America, though there was no real link between the two ploys.

The fan-car device became a most celebrated case of rule-bending, for drawing air through a radiator is still literally an 'aerodynamic' function, unless my grasp of the English language is at fault, but even today its creator insists it was utterly legal. Indeed, it was declared so by the racing authorities, after its further use had been effectively banned by a change in their regulation wording.

So the famous Brabham BT46B fan-car came about. The initial idea had occurred around Kyalami time, which is very early in the season – hard evidence of Murray's remarkable perception. The team's 40-odd staff at Chessington set about building two cars for Monaco. All the bits were made and ready, but skirt and fan development delayed their race debut. At last, two cars – modified chassis 'BT46/6' and '4 – appeared in the Swedish GP which Lauda won while Watson also shone.

The BT46B emerged with a large horizontal water radiator above its engine, the whole engine bay area being sealed against ambient pressure infill underneath by flexible skirts extending down to the road surface with sections even sealing the slots in which driveshafts and suspension arms rose and fell. Massive effort went into finalizing skirt, fan and radiator.

Thermodynamics consultant David Cox calculated the number of fan blades, pitch and optimum rotational speed required. Typically, Murray and North agonized over potential problems and sought to design them out right from the start.

The fan drive was taken from the gearbox lower shaft,

Above: *Schematic drawing of the BT46B fan-car and fan mechanism.* Top left: *Fan, exhausts and engine-bay rear sealing skirt at Anderstorp, '78.* Top right: *The horizontal water radiator which justified the fan.*

but this would have created an H16 BRM-like problem if direct drive had been employed, since the inertia of the fan making the gearbox input shaft run on while the driver fought to slow it down sufficiently to find another gear could create some grief.

Therefore a sprag clutch was fitted at the back of the gearbox to uncouple the fan as the driver kicked out the clutch proper. To avoid a nasty pit accident a cut-out device was also added to enable the mechanics to disengage the fan with the engine ticking over.

A spur-gear drive train was necessary to raise the fan hub sufficiently to accommodate fan blades of reasonable radius. The problem of a racing start shock-loading the fan drive led to another friction-plate clutch going into the fan-hub assembly.

Brands Hatch testing then showed surprisingly there was *no* need for either the sprag clutch or pit disengagement devices, as the gearchange seemed unaffected even when the sprag locked solid.

But the original plastic fans disintegrated. Glass-fibre filled fans disintegrated as well. Within a week of the Swedish GP magnesium fan blades were cast and new hubs machined from the solid. Only three were ready in time.

Skirt sealing at the sides and rear had caused no problem, but the front lateral skirt ahead of the engine bay caused endless headaches until David North devised a brilliant system involving two stitched sailcloth sausage bags with a system of coinciding edged holes which enabled the 'bags' to be inflated by under-chassis airflow and then remain inflated against pressure and road surface changes which tried to force them clear of the roadway.

The first day's practice at Anderstorp wore away this complex front skirt, but Brabham's men fitted a skid on its leading edge for the second day and thereafter it worked superbly well.

Even sitting in the pit lane the cars would squat down when the throttle was blipped and the fan revved, but five teams protested its legality even before Lauda and Watson qualified 2-3 behind a Lotus 79. The Austrian won the race, showering dust and grit from the fan efflux in his car's wake.

Before the next race, the fabulous fan-car and any and all successors using that system were henceforth banned from competition, although the Swedish result was confirmed and the fan-car itself never declared illegal – indeed quite the reverse, for Gordon preserved a letter accepting its legality but frowning upon its future use!

And most regarded Gordon Murray and David North with reconfirmed, rather awed, respect.

BT46B, showing: 1, air-speed pitot; 2, underside ASI; 3, plastic skirts; 4, water radiator; 5, brake cooling; 6, rear upright air-seal slide; 7, engine-bay seal skirts; 8, exhaust efflux; 9, fan.

Centre: *The Dunlop puck-type carbon brakes pioneered in Formula 1 by Brabham in 1976.*

Chapter 11

THE FERRARI 312T4 – FLAT-12's CHAMPIONSHIP FAREWELL 1979

During 1978 the Ferrari 312T3 design, tailored to the team's new Michelin radial-ply tyres, had proved itself a deceptive beauty. The Italian team lost its coveted Constructors' Cup Championship title to Lotus's new breed of ground-effect Type 78/79 cars . . . and it hurt.

The Maranello engineers appreciated that Lotus had unlocked a new box of delights in using the underside of the car to generate so much aerodynamic download. But what was fine for Lotus and the other Cosworth V8 engine users was really bad news for Ferrari. Their otherwise superb flat-12 engine – with its remarkably low centre of gravity, excellent power and reliability – was too wide at a disastrously inconvenient low level to clear airflow adequately through underwing tunnels which would have to be crafted somehow on each side of the central monocoque spine.

Brabham had been in a similar bind with their Alfa Romeo flat-12 engine, but at Gordon Murray's request in August 1978 Alfa's Autodelta racing division under Carlo Chiti had buckled down and redrew their 12-cylinder as a narrow-based 60-degree vee, and the prototype such unit was out and running that December.

Although there may have been much to criticize in the Alfa Romeo engines, none could carp at such reaction time, for they had just designed and made an effectively new Formula 1 engine from scratch in only 15 weeks!

Just for once, Ferrari could not match their Milanese rivals. *Ing.* Forghieri's team had to devise their first real ground-effects chassis as best they could around their existing engine, as the decision had been taken not to ape Alfa and build one with a narrower base using flat-12 components. This was not penny-pinching; it was instead Mr Ferrari again proving his extraordinarily far-sighted ability to make the right long-term strategic decisions.

It seems he had listened to his engineers' thoughts on the potential of 1500 cc turbocharged engines for Formula 1, and had decided that future investment should lie there rather than in the short-term but costly expedient of building a new 3-litre which might be outclassed in 18 months.

The prototype Ferrari 312T4, chassis '037, was unveiled to the usual excited scrum of Italian pressmen on 15 January 1979. It was an ugly duckling of a car, one commentator derisively describing it as 'a motor mower', but it would prove itself every bit as practical . . . and decidedly faster.

It used the normal aluminium-sheet monocoque nacelle stiffened by internal aluminium angle-section fabrications bonded and riveted to the outer skins and the inner cockpit flanks. This was a reversion to pre-'T2 true monocoque practice, but stronger and far narrower than previous Ferrari

tubs following Lotus 79 style to offer a wide underwing area either side.

The large midships single fuel cell of the Lotus 79 looked to have been adopted, but in this case the tank section standing tall behind the seat back bulkhead actually accommodated three separate fuel bags. Due to the flat-12 engine's thirst the midship cell alone was insufficient so an extra cell was added in ugly 'step-outs' on each side. As so often in Ferrari chassis design, they looked like an afterthought, but to Ferrari the engine was all-important, the thing holding the wheels on always came second. In this case these step-outs intruded on available underwing tunnel area, but if they had not, there was always the flat-12 engine head and induction right behind them to form that obstruction. There, however, the effect would not have been so problematic, as the side-step tanks affected what should have been the shallow part of the underwing venturi.

A massive but light titanium roll-over bar stood on top of the main tank section, its rearward braces panelled in for rigidity and to provide convenient housings for the communications box, and emergency switchgear and triggers.

The front of the tub was tied together by a magnesium bulkhead casting, carrying the master cylinders, anti-roll bar and front leg pick-ups for the very wide-based lower wishbones. The dash panel was mounted within a front-braced titani-

Ferrari's 312T4 with its extensive overbody surfaces was not the prettiest thing around in 1979, but it worked well enough to win the Championship. 1, wing; 2, nose cone; 3, body top; 4, brake duct; 5, coil/damper; 6, steering rack on floor; 7, roll-over stiffening; 8, radiator; 9, engine-air intake; 10, rear anti-roll adjuster; 11, vents; 12, tub fillets; 13, oil tank; 14, sliding skirt; 15, intercom; 16, step-out tank; 17, main tank; 18, engine stay; 19, tailpipe; 20, battery; 21, tyre fairing; 22, upright; 23, brake duct; 24, top rocker; 25, tailpipes; 26, anti-roll bar; 27, gearbox; 28, wing pillar; 29, wing.

um forward roll-over bar, its front braces panelled in aluminium, with the familiar chassis plate riveted high. Cast-magnesium brackets fitted to the tub floor provided pedal pivots. Steel or magnesium insert strong-points provided pick-ups for other items hung on this rather untidy-looking tub.

It carried inboard front suspension along 'T3 lines, but the 'T4's nose box was narrower and the Koni dampers and co-axial coil-spring units nuzzled tight against the tub skins to clear airflow into the radiators and underwing tunnels. The lower wishbones were cross-braced to add rigidity. The inboard coil-damper units were actuated by fabricated tube-frame top rocker arms, pivoting on pins suppported by triangulated tube braces projecting from the heavily riveted front tub bulkhead. These braces were further supported fore and aft by long tubular members linking the pivot position to the meat of the tub at dash bulkhead level.

The rear coil/damper units were also inboard mounted, standing in channel sections against the transmission case casting behind the axle line. Tubular steel bottom wishbones located the typically Ferrari cast-magnesium wheel uprights. Fabricated-sheet top rocker arms actuated the coil/damper units, pivoting on cast-magnesium horns which projected each side of the familiar *trasversale* transmission housing.

The radiators were slung just behind the front suspension on each side of the tub, raked steeply forward to mate with ducting provided in the vast moulded upper body panels. Water radiator was on the left, oil cooler on the right, both fed from the engine pumps. Hot coolant was channelled through galleries in the bottom of the cam-covers into the water radiator piping, and cooled water then returned from the radiator through galleries in the tops of the same covers before being led away around the engine via the head waterways. The large oil tank further intruded into the right-side underwing tunnel, being slung outside the 'step-out' fuel tank structure there. A small gearbox oil cooler sat on top of the final-drive, exposed to the airstream above the rear bodyshell lip.

The body itself comprised a substantial one-piece removable top cover designed to generate as much download from above as from those improvised underwing tunnels down below. Its upper surface extended far forward into a projecting tray above the slender winkle-picker nose cone which faired in the front of the tub and supported a full-width Ferrari wing of the type familiar since 1973-74.

The cockpit surround was moulded as narrow and short as possible, ending in an abbreviated dorsal fin behind the roll-over bar to leave the smooth rear deck offering maximum airflow onto the underside of the centre-pillar-mounted rear wing. Pronounced moulded flip-ups faired the broad rear Michelin radial-ply tyres.

The radiator slings projecting each side of the monocoque doubled as body supports. Moulded into the body, behind the radiator ducting with its top exit louvres, the underwing floors of the side pod flared upwards to clear the low-level step tanks, oil tank and the flat-12 engine heads and exhaust manifolding. Integrally moulded intake trunks picked up cool air outboard of the radiator cores and directed it into plenum chambers sealed against the engine induction trumpets each side.

The outer flank of each side pod formed a box housing the sliding skirts, the skirts themselves riding on the track surface on single-length resistant strips which according to some reports were actually hard-wearing rubber, according to others ceramic, which seems more likely.

Brakes were by AP Lockheed, ventilated front and rear with single four-pot calipers. Steering was via a two-piece adjustable column passing down between the driver's shins to a Ferrari-made rack mounted on the monocoque floor.

Dimensions included a wheelbase of 2700 mm (106.3 in.); front track, 1700 mm (66.9 in.); rear track, 1600 mm (62.9 in.); length, 4460 mm (175.5 in.); width, 2120 mm (83.4 in.) The new 'lawn mower' weighed in, less fuel and driver, at around 590 kg (1301 lb), while Ferrari claimed that the further uprated 312B engines that year delivered a minimum 515 bhp at 12,300 rpm. The finished car was fully 10 in. longer than the preceding 312T3 to give sufficient aerodynamic surface for Forghieri's requirements, while the wheelbase was 6 in. longer than the 'T3 to provide adequate space for worthwhile venturi underwings before the various intrusive tanks, engine heads and manifolds were encountered.

In aerodynamic terms the car was a ground-effects start for Ferrari – though they had previously lashed up their 'T3s as quasi-underwing cars – but it was a poor compromise compared to the contemporary Williams FW07. We were all about to discover how aerodynamics wasn't everything . . .

The South African driver Jody Scheckter had joined the mercurial French-Canadian Gilles Villeneuve in the Ferrari team for that season, and they began their year in the old 312T3 cars uprated with makeshift underwings and sliding skirts which were notoriously ineffective and unreliable. The team was very conscious of these problems and 'T4 development included painstaking real-car test sessions in the huge Pininfarina wind tunnel near Turin.

In Argentina a multiple pile-up and a restarted race, in which the mildly injured Scheckter was not permitted to compete, fuelled vociferous condemnation of ground-effect skirted cars from this driver. Had all such Formula 1 cars felt as awful as his interim 'T3 he would have received more support from his fellow drivers.

The new Ligiers won in both Argentina and Brazil, before the new Ferraris were introduced to racing at Kyalami for the South African GP on 8 March 1979. Two new 'T4s were present, chassis '037 for Villeneuve and '038 for Scheckter on his native soil. Experiments were conducted in running without the front wing, but both cars not only felt less stable but were also slower on the straight.

The race was spoiled by a heavy rainstorm, which brought out the red flag. Villeneuve led the restart, still on a wet track, while Scheckter gambled by starting on dry tyres, believing the surface would dry out. He was right but he blistered his tyres after inheriting the lead as Villeneuve stopped to change from wet tyres to dry. Scheckter clung to his lead until a locking front brake flat-spotted a tyre and forced him into the pits for a change on lap 53. His delay handed the race back to Villeneuve who held off his teammate to the finish for a notable Ferrari 'T4 1-2 victory on the type's debut.

Equally good results would follow, for Villeneuve won in another Ferrari 'T4 1-2 finish at Long Beach, starting from the first Grand Prix pole position of his career and setting fastest lap along the way. In the minor Brands Hatch race he then completed Ferrari's hat-trick for the season by winning again in the old 'T3 chassis '033'.

In Spain the Ligiers were dominant, while Villeneuve's hopes of a Championship round hat-trick evaporated in a spin soon after the start when trying to pass Reutemann. Next time round he spun again. Scheckter's race deteriorated with his Michelin tyres and engine losing power, finally finishing fourth while Villeneuve was seventh.

Scheckter won at Zolder after the superior Ligier and Williams FW07 ran out of luck, driving the new 'T4 chassis '040 which would become his regular mount. Villeneuve set fastest lap in '039 after smashing its nose in a minor collision, rejoining the race 23rd and last and soaring back up the field like a homesick angel. He was challenging for third place in the closing stages when the hard-pressed 'T4 ran out of fuel.

At Long Beach the 'T4s had dominated with forward-mounted rear wings and brilliant traction on a circuit where ultimate download was not of prime importance. The forward-mounted rear wings were used again at Monaco, where Scheckter took pole from Villeneuve, the 'T4s again setting the standard. The South African led from start to finish for his second consecutive Grand Prix victory – this time on real merit – while Villeneuve lay second until his car's transmission failed around half-distance, probably due to a hurried engine change after the morning warm-up in which the unit had blown off an oil pipe.

Late in the race Scheckter had come under fierce attack from Regazzoni's Williams FW07, finally winning by less than a second. The 'T4 was not the class car of the season, in that others like the FW07 and the Ligiers could be quicker, but it had the strength and reliability to win consistently, which they lacked.

At Dijon-Prenois the turbocharged Renaults won their first Grand Prix and Ferrari were overshadowed after their terrific early season with the 'T4. In the four races from the French to the Austrian GPs, Ferrari's best performances were Villeneuve's wheel-banging with Arnoux's Renault – and second again in Austria, both times driving '041, which had made its race debut in France. Scheckter had scored points consistently, with fifth at Silverstone, fourth at Hockenheim and the Österreichring, and after taking second place at Zandvoort he was set to clinch the World Championship for himself in the Italian GP at Monza.

Both team drivers had a choice of two cars each for this event, a pair of conventional 'T4s plus alternative revised 'T4Bs, which featured outboard rear brakes, revised suspension geometry to suit and balanced calipers, one ahead and one behind the axle line to improve braking performance. The exhaust system was revised to tuck closer against the gearbox sides, the upper tailpipes flicking higher over the suspension arms to clear more underwing tunnel space down below. Villeneuve preferred his 'T4B configured chassis '038 and raced it while Scheckter raced his faithful '040 'T4. Once the leading turbo Renault had been halted by electrical failure the two Ferraris ran 1-2 from laps 13 to 50 for another outstanding 1-2 win on home soil, the Ferrari 'T4s' third double of the season.

In celebration, 'T4Bs '038 and '041 were taken to Imola for the Dino Ferrari non-Championship GP, Scheckter finishing third and Villeneuve seventh after a collision with the Brabham-Alfa Romeo which eventually won. It was an Alfa Romeo victory over Ferrari in a Ferrari Champion year – a unique occurrence.

Villeneuve was hell-bent upon winning the Canadian GP at Montreal and nearly did so, before being shouldered out of the way by a more nimble Williams FW07, which beat him into second place and lapped faster. Scheckter drove a subdued race and finished lapped in fourth place after a tyre-change stop. The season ended at Watkins Glen in the rain where Scheckter drove '040 and Villeneuve '041, the latter scoring the 'T4's sixth victory of the season, with luck on his side. Scheckter suffered a Michelin tyre disintegration after changing from wets to dries early on in a race dictated by rain.

Ferrari won the Constructors' Championship with 113 points to Williams's 75, while Scheckter was Drivers' Champion and Villeneuve runner-up.

Five Ferrari 'T4s had been built for the season, chassis numbers '037, '038, '039, '040 and '041, amongst which all but '039 had appeared in 'T4B configuration at the end of the year. They started 26 times in Championship Grand Prix races, returning six wins, seven second places, four fourths, one fifth, three sevenths, one eighth, and four retirements – although one of them yielded a 14th place classification. In addition the cars had run in the non-Championship event at Imola, finishing third and seventh.

This was the last Formula 1 season in which a compromise car could run strongly enough to take the World Championship titles and the Ferrari 'T4 had emphasized the wisdom of its manufacturer's long-term strategy. The following season's flat-12 'T5 would be an uncompetitive disaster, as the sliding-skirt ground-effects car era reached maturity. Ferrari meanwhile concentrated upon the next step forward, with their turbocharged V6 *modello* 126.

Chapter 12

THE WILLIAMS FW07-SERIES CARS 1979-82

After the Lotus 78s and 79s had so successfully introduced 'ground-effect' aerodynamics in 1977-78, the replacement Lotus 80 flopped and it was left to others to hone the ground-effects principle to its keenest edge. The most successful of these successors to the Lotus 79 was the long line of Patrick Head-designed Saudia-Williams FW07s.

He had become Chief Engineer of Williams Grand Prix Engineering upon its formation in 1977. They had campaigned a March-Cosworth that year to find their feet, while Head watched the exploits of the fast-cornering Lotus 78 with interest, noting its weaknesses, its slow straight-line speed and the unreliability of its special Cosworth 'development' engines.

He did not fully understand its aerodynamic approach and his fledgling team lacked the funds to invest in the wind tunnel test time which could have taught him what he did not know. Consequently, his first Williams Formula 1 design for 1978, type number FW06 in the Williams series, did not attempt to emulate the Lotus wing-car principles.

It was instead a conventional machine, elegant and simple as all Head's cars would be, arrow-head-shaped in planform. It proved itself amongst the best of the rest when driven so hard by Alan Jones during the Lotus-dominated season of '78.

That season over, Head then concentrated upon attempting first to match and then to improve upon Lotus's achievement. He appreciated that aerodynamics are the biggest single factor affecting the performance of a Grand Prix car.

'I was aware that Lotus did much of their wind tunnel testing at Imperial College in London, using quarter-scale models. Their tunnel incorporated a moving ground surface beneath the model being tested and I appreciated why that was important because racing cars do not fly through the air but roll along a road surface on their wheels.

'So I found the phone number of Imperial College, called them and asked for the head of the

department of aeronautics who turned out to be Dr John Harvey. We met, and he explained that Lotus did their work in the tunnel, he did some consultancy work for Arrows, and there was room for one other team. We wanted to be that other team . . .

'Having seen the Lotus 79 dominate that season we had a clear idea what we wanted to do. We didn't copy the 79 line-for-line, but it was undeniably the major influence upon the design of our new FW07, as it was on most other Formula 1 cars being built for 1979.

'We made a crude wooden model of what we wanted to test, put it in the wind tunnel, and found it was unbelievably bad!

'We ran several more tests with models of differing types – including one with very long ground-effect underwing surfaces which indicated the most prodigious downforces, but I shied away from using it because we were very new in this area, it would have been a very complex car and I wanted to set out with something fairly straightforward . . .'

He in fact designed something rather like the Lotus 79 in superficial appearance 'but I tried to optimize that layout'. When the new Lotus 80 flopped, however, Lotus developed their Type 79s further only to find them deficient in that year's company, while Head's optimization proved to be virtually everything he might have hoped.

In achieving this aim it was first important for Williams to have more engineering experience on hand. Head's first assistant, Neil Oatley, joined the team at this time, followed soon after by ex-Hesketh engineer Frank Dernie. He started at the tiny Didcot works in January 1979, by which time Head and Oatley were already halfway through the '07 design.

At Watkins Glen at the close of the previous season, Jones's FW06 had suffered a structural failure when a hub broke, throwing a wheel. It was not a design failure, but a material deficiency for the steel from which the hub had been made was

Williams Grand Prix Engineering certainly flew the flag in 1980, as here at Ricard-Castellet after Alan Jones won the French GP. In their FW07B cars WGPE paid as much attention to overbody airflow as ground-effects efficiency, exemplified by the low rear body clearing the deck ahead of the rear wing. The sliding skirt with its abrade-resistant edge rides on the road surface.

found to be full of 'inclusions' – impurities which compromised its integrity.

This failure both mortified and alarmed Head. It was a salutary reminder of the forces he was playing with in Formula 1.

'As Chief Engineer I felt it was my prime responsibility to see that things didn't fall off or come apart, and I took that very heavily . . . It was one of the major factors which made me rather slow in completing FW07. I purposely wanted to take a long time over it to ensure that every calculation was double-checked and confirmed, to be certain everything was sound and strong enough. What also delayed '07 was that we set out with a staff which was still tiny. Our manpower shortage definitely conditioned the rate at which we could make things . . .'

He and Frank Williams also considered, after finishing second and then running second in their last two races of 1978, that their existing FW06 cars could remain competitive in the early races of the new season. They were mistaken. Head had underestimated the development pace of most other teams, and his non-ground-effects '06s were completely outpaced by the new-generation cars as the season got under way in Argentina.

For the first time WGPE was fielding a full two-car team with drivers Alan Jones and Clay Regazzoni. They finished only ninth and tenth in Buenos Aires, 15th and a retirement in Brazil, ninth and another retirement in South Africa. Late sponsorship payment further delayed the FW07 project.

Eventually the first prototype Williams FW07/1 was ready in time to go to Long Beach, California, for the fourth Grand Prix of the season, but it lay in the Tech Center there, unused, covered by a dust sheet . . . except when an over-inquisitive rival team chief was caught under that dust sheet studying the goods!

By the end of April sponsorship money had been freed at last and two '07s emerged for the Spanish GP at Jarama. Both retired, though for those with the eyes to see it had been significant that in race morning warm-up Jones's '07 had left Andretti's Lotus 80 for dead, despite carrying a full fuel load. Andretti simply refused to believe that Jones's car was not running light; 'I couldn't stay with him,' he gasped.

In the race, Jones set the second fastest lap, bettered only by a Ferrari which was using sticky qualifying tyres to regain lost ground after a pit stop. The Williams men now began to appreciate FW07's enormous potential.

The type would evolve as the most successful of the ground-effects era Formula 1 chassis, winning two consecutive Constructors' Championship titles in 1980-81. It used an aluminium honeycomb sheet chassis structure, and since it was so typical of this type of late-Seventies/early-Eighties construction we will take a detailed look at its anatomy and manufacture.

A new FW07-series chassis began life as a flat sheet of aluminium honeycomb sandwich. The sheet itself was about 82 in. long, tapering towards what would become the tub's nose, and it was specially bonded to Williams's requirements with 22-gauge skins sandwiching 0.45 in. thick aviation specification honeycomb-cell filling.

Various aluminium inserts and dowels were fitted into drillings within the sheet to act as mounting strong-points, then two longitudinal slots were routed out by removing a sliver of inner skin while leaving the interior honeycomb intact. This then allowed the sheet to be folded along the slots like a child's cut-out card model to form the basic U-section tub. The various necessary brackets were then bonded and riveted into place.

The tub's general layout matched that of the Lotus 79; slender, with a large single-cell tank section behind the cockpit and a tall arched scuttle up front.

The basic channel structure was stiffened by added tank-top and seat-back panels, plus 20-gauge aluminium inner skins which were shaped over internal bulkheads either side of the confined cockpit. In original 1979 form this cockpit area flexed too much and in the 1980 FW07B develop-

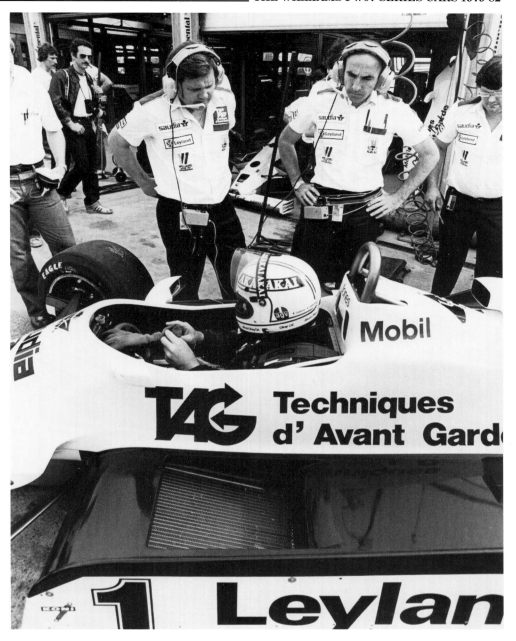

ment folded fillets were inserted around the driver's shoulder area where the original design had left a sharp angle between seat back and cockpit side.

The front end of the tub supported a very robust suspension pivot bridge. Pedal mounts were bonded and riveted to the tub floor with inserts passing through the front bulkhead to the master cylinders which protruded above an open topped sheet tray supporting the front wings and nose body.

The whole footbox/suspension bridge/driver's leg area was then enclosed by the tall arched scuttle panel, bonded and riveted to the dash hoop, the hoop in turn incorporating the regulation forward roll-over bar.

The tub structure was completed by addition of a closing plate at the rear, where the DFV engine would hang. Great care was then taken to grind off all intruding rivets to protect the American-made ATL 40-gallon fuel bag which was inserted through a bolt-on oval hatch in the top of the tank section, carrying an Avery-Hardoll aircraft-type non-spill filler.

As can be seen, the Williams FW07 'Lotus 79 clone' was in fact very different structurally. Its nearest similarity was in the tall arched scuttle panel, but just like the Lotus 79 this area proved far from satisfactory in torsional strength.

On the back of the tub, the familiar DFV engine hung on ³/₈ in. UNF bolts at four points; feeding in loads via multi-angular aluminium blocks under the conventional engine strap plates at the top,

Patrick Head (left) *and Frank Williams* (right) *built a remarkably successful team around Alan Jones from 1978 to 1981. In their second consecutive Constructors' Championship-winning season, they are at Hockenheim with 'FW07D/16'.*

and ready-inserted into the honeycomb underneath.

A complex cast-magnesium adaptor bolted between the engine and transmission, incorporating the oil tank as well as encasing a lightweight Desoutter air-starter motor and the clutch slave unit, thus performing four functions simultaneously. Furthermore, the adaptor to final-drive and final-drive to gearbox joint faces sandwiched two transverse plates which extended each side to carry the rear suspension pivots.

The Hewland FGB five-speed and reverse gearbox was bought from the Maidenhead manufacturer in virtual kit form and modified by all the customer Formula 1 teams to their own requirements.

As standard, the FGB gearchange entered the box at bottom right. Williams, however, converted it to enter top right, thus lifting the linkage rod clear of the airstream through the side pod and coincidentally shortening and stiffening it to improve the change.

Williams fed oil up the gearshafts and the gearbox oil cooler itself was fed with air from a duct sunk into the rear body deck. The engine oil catch tank was mounted above the gearbox. The rear wing pillar carried the regulation red rear light. On its left side there was an air-starter bayonet socket to connect with an external air-line. On the right was a jackplug socket which automatically retarded the ignition when connected for easy starting. Removing the plug returned the ignition to nominal setting.

The downloads achieved from the FW07 series' very effective underwing sections could be as much as 4-5000 lb. So the suspension had to be very stiff. Spring rates in fact varied between 600 and 1000 lb per cent per inch of deflection stiffness at the front, and between 800 and 1500 lb at the rear dependent upon the type of circuit and the downloads being generated. If the suspension was not rigidly controlled in places in which its designers did not want it to move, then flexure would compromise grip and traction and could also simply give the driver 'the willies'.

To help provide very rigid and well-controlled front rocker arm pivots, Williams's suspension bridge there consisted of two substantial but still elegant $^3/_{16}$ in. thick HE30 TF heat-treated aluminium plates up-edged above the driver's shins. Because both mounts fore and aft were in one piece, overhanging the chassis on both sides, crash damage to one corner could communicate itself to the other and repair was more difficult than it would have been if separate mounts had been used. Head considered that the rigidity of one-piece construction here simply outweighed the practical penalty.

Within the tub sides, below this bridge arrange-

ment, vertical channel sections enclosed the co-axial Koni damper/coil-spring units which stood on steel feet fitted into the honeycomb floor. Cutouts in the channels gave access for spring ride-height and damper adjustment.

Steel brackets braced the front corners of the 20-gauge aluminium skinned footbox, picking up the forward legs of the bottom wishbones down below and the bolt-on stays which braced the outboard tips of the front bridge-plate up top. The rear legs of the suspension wishbones picked up on either side of a steel crossbeam in the tub floor.

At the rear, the suspension-pivot crossplates extended the full width of the DFV cam-covers to carry the rear suspension pivots. Top links formed, in effect, a two-piece reversed upper wishbone whose adjustable-length rearward link served to adjust wheel toe-in/toe-out.

The rear suspension rocker arms themselves were mounted close against the foremost sandwich plate, that between the adaptor and final-drive, with their inboard crank arms reacting into vertical coil-spring/Koni damper units standing upon a magnesium casting bolted up beneath the gearbox.

Wide-based lower rear wishbones picked up on lugs in the front of the adaptor oil tank, and on an aluminium beam under the rear of the final-drive.

The magnesium spring/damper brackets were reinforced by vertical stress pillars, which spread their load high into the engine/transmission assembly.

The front rocker arms, front and rear wishbones and uprights were all beautifully fabricated from US aviation-specification '4130' steel alloy while the heavily loaded rear rockers were fabricated in 'S514'. Front uprights were exquisitely crafted magnesium castings. They supported outboard-mounted ventilated cast-iron brake discs, and the uprights featured cast-in cool air intakes and galleries designed to blow across both disc faces and into their internal ducts. Brake-cooling air intake trunks were fitted to the uprights, facing forward between the suspension links at the front, and over them at the rear.

The brakes used all-outboard 11 in. diameter discs, clasped on both leading and trailing edges by Lockheed aluminium twin-pot 'balanced' calipers, as originated in structural form for Lotus. Disc thickness varied according to circuit. For example, the team would employ 1 in. thick discs for Brands Hatch, but 0.9 in. thick discs for anywhere faster. Zolder's virtually unique braking demands were notorious, and Lockheed provided thicker and stiffer calipers for use there, but they mounted in the same way and had identical pad area. Slots routed into the disc faces swept away debris, to keep the pad-to-disc contact clean

and crisp.

The conventional brake balance bar was modified to accept a Smiths tachodrive connected to a knurled knob on the left-side dash frame, lower than the instrument panel. By winding this control to left or right the driver could juggle his brake balance as he pleased while in motion. With his front and rear anti-roll bar adjusters also available for fine tuning one could picture his controls as having more in common with an aircraft pilot's than a road car driver's.

This author has had a lot of exposure to historic racing cars made by Mercedes-Benz, Auto Union, Alfa Romeo and the like. Whenever a more jaundiced elder enthusiast says something like 'They don't make them like they used to', he may be technically right, but he is far off the mark as regards sheer quality. The Grand Prix car may have gone through a low period in the late 1950s and '60s, but by the late 1970s there was no room for slipshod blacksmithery by any team wishing to prove competitive. Frontline modern Formula 1 cars are all very well made.

Returning to the Williams FW07; both its front and rear hubs were machined from 'S514', the live axle at the front being fitted with Timken taper roller bearings fixed in the upright. All suspension pivots used ball races, the same size fore and aft at the front, but with larger races for the forward pivots at the rear where high tractive torques were applied.

In the suspension rod-ends, Williams normally specified NMB spherical bearings, falling back on Rose joints if NMBs were unavailable.

The rear anti-roll bar clamped against the rearmost suspension pivot plate and was driver-adjustable for stiffness from a left-hand cockpit control. An adjustable front anti-roll bar was also fitted during the 1980 season.

Steering was via a Jack Knight-adapted Lola magnesium rack housing with Knight gears and Williams's own outer housing ends. The assembly mounted above the driver's legs behind the front axle line and was foam-wrapped for his protection, being so close above his shins. The short steering column, universal joints and outboard steering arms were all Williams-made, while the steering wheel was a 10 in. diameter type by Personal.

Slung wide on each side of the slender central monocoque were the all-important side pods with their underwing 'floors' or diffusers. The '07 series cars' underwings were slung from aluminium strong-points inserted into the honeycomb tub sides. The underwings were initially in glass-fibre, but this material was insufficiently rigid, being too easily sucked out of shape by the downloads generated. Through 1980 the underwings would be in bent aluminium honeycomb retained for the '07 cars' life. They became carbon-composite in FW08. Moulded carbon radiator air intakes were used right from the start because their precise shape was so critical.

Along the outer edge of the underwing tray the vertical skirt box was attached. Its inner panel was honeycomb dotted with numerous inserts for it was very highly loaded. In comparison, the outer skin enclosing the skirts was a lightweight carbon-foam sandwich with solid glass-fibre inserts where bolt-on fixings penetrated. The skirts themselves were of carbon-glass, with three aluminium bottom-edge inserts containing ceramic skids on which the skirt rode against the track surface.

The skirts were of course free to rise and fall as the road dictated. There was a ball-race guide at the rear of each skirt to accept dragging loads, while a simple guide peg rode in a slot at the front. Their motion was smoothed by nylon rollers on aluminium axles fixed to the inner box skin and by nylon rollers on steel axle-pins on the skirts themselves.

Good skirt control, springing and guide systems were absolutely critical in maintaining a constant seal between skirt and roadway to ensure consistent download. As the underwing venturis accelerated airflow and reduced its pressure, so that low pressure area beneath the underwings acted not only on the underwings to draw the car down vertically, but also upon the side skirts to suck them in laterally. A skirt control system which allowed the skirt to skew and bind in its guides would compromise the aerodynamic seal against the track surface, download would be inconsistent and consequently both car and driver would suffer. Williams's skirt guide system was probably superior to any other team's (except perhaps Brabham's) from 1979 to 1981, and it showed.

Meanwhile, in 1977-78, the fashionable rear wing mounting had been via rigid end plates, mounted at their lower extremities on the ends of a lateral beam across the gearbox.

The formerly conventional centre-pillar mounting had interrupted airflow beneath the wing's working undersurface so end-plate support leaving the entire wing span uncluttered offered improved download. Unfortunately, on new-generation ground-effect cars the low-level lateral mounting beam for the end plates themselves then obstructed airstreams exiting from the underwing tunnels so designers reverted to centre-pillar support.

Williams's rear wings were of this type, aluminium skinned over alloy profile-formers, two in the middle and one either side, with aluminium and carbon-fibre end plates.

The team would race only one front wing shape. It used an aluminium pole as a main spar, with the wing sections formed over foam profiles which had been cut to shape by hot wire and template, and then clad with pre-made carbon skins. An aluminium trailing-edge flap was added and the wings were then mounted on the front tub horns.

Where ancillaries were concerned, an aluminium VW Golf diesel water radiator was adopted in the original FW07s. For 1980 a Citroën CX radiator would replace it. This unit, with its aluminium core and plastic header tank, was light and efficient and could have been produced no better and certainly no cheaper to special order. It lay at a shallow angle in the right-hand side pod, gripped between foam rubber pads.

The cooling system included a swirl-pot at the rear of the engine where steam bubbles could be centrifuged out of the coolant before hot water returned to the outboard side of the radiator. Pressure filling was available for rapid topping-up during qualifying or in the race when every split second saved could be vital. The pressure filler itself was actually a converted fire extinguisher canister, coupled to a high-pressure gas bottle.

Oil cooling was by a 44-row Serck aluminium radiator in the left-hand side pod of the 1980 cars, fed from the engine scavenge pumps by 'Aeroquip-16' braided flexible hose. The bell-housing oil tank carried two gallons of Valvoline oil when brimful. For Kyalami 1981 the water and oil systems would be modified, with the water radiator moving to the left side, oil cooler to the right.

Electrically, Williams tried both Lucas and Marelli ignition systems before opting in 1980 for the German Contactless brand which gave better-controlled sparking with less scatter. According to the drivers this gave them 'more power more consistently', although the advantage could not be proved on the dyno. The Contactless system lacked a rev-limiter over-ride for heroics, but the Lucas limiter was in any case considered to be 'a bit iffy'.

With an air-starter, only a tiny battery need be carried – in Williams's case a National Panasonic motor cycle type measuring only some 6 in. x 2½ in.

Several brands of dash panel instruments would be used, with variable success.

The fuel system drew from a collector box in the rear of the solitary bag tank. The system had changed at least twice during the car's original design period.

Initially in 1979, a toothed-belt-driven Lucas pump was used, suitably tucked in behind the tub section to clear airflow through the underwing side pod tunnel. Early in 1980 Williams fitted this pump – which is virtually a flat disc, smaller than the palm of your hand – onto the nose of the right-hand inlet camshaft.

Cosworth predictably objected, pointing out that ineffective pump seals could pass neat fuel into the cam-box and dilute the oil pumping through there with disastrous results. They specified instead an apparently Heath Robinson system, with an angle-gear drive from the tail of the left-side inlet camshaft, passing to a tacho-cable which ran forward to a tiny clutch device, then an electric motor, then the pump itself, perched on the tank top.

As described in the Cosworth chapter, the electric motor then powered the pump for starting, and once the engine fired the mechanical tacho-drive would take over.

All fuel lines had standard dry-break links to prevent leaks should an accident separate engine from tub.

Onboard safety systems included two Dreadnought extinguisher bottles, one 5 kg, the other 2.4 kg, mounted either side of the forward cockpit floor crossbeam. One bottle was piped around the cockpit, the other into the titanium tubing of the roll-over bar, down its bracing struts, and thence out through neat nozzles aimed into the engine vee. The Graviner life-support air bottle was mounted on the tank top, protected within the roll-over bar struts. Seat harness was by Willans.

Should the driver stall his engine on circuit, an onboard starter air-pressure bottle was carried, housed in one side pod. A right-hand cockpit lever opened the air-cock via a Bowden cable to give a 12-second churn on the starter. If the engine didn't fire, then it would be time to hop out and start walking . . . the race is over.

The bodywork had to be light yet rigid, and free of drag-inducing flutter. In 1980 Jones's number one team car would use a honeycomb resin cockpit section, the others glass-fibre. In 1979 the engine cover was aluminium honeycomb for the flat sections, with a riveted-in glass-fibre hump carrying the induction mesh. The 1980 engine covers were all glass-fibre with some foam and honeycomb stiffening.

Wheels were Dymag one-piece or Speedline bolt-together types, in 13 in. and 15 in. diameters with 11 in. wide front rims as standard and 17¼ in. or 18 in. wide rears.

Wheelbase was 106 in., front track 68 in., rear track notably narrower at 63¾ in., tailoring the wide rear rims to the overall width restriction. Overall height was 42⅞ in., until the tall Carlos Reutemann joined the team as Jones's team-mate in 1980, and his cars were fitted with a taller roll-over hoop to suit. Ground clearance was a nominal 3 in. under the monocoque.

At Zolder in 1979, Jones qualified third fastest in FW07/1 despite having broken a skirt. Regazzoni was shunted out of the race early on in '07/2 but Jones led the very potent Ligiers which had started the season so well. It was the first time since 1969 that a Williams-entered car had led a Grand Prix, but the spell lasted only until lap 40 when Jones retired with electrical failure.

The Australian was running in third place at Monaco in the new '07/3 until he clipped a barrier but Regazzoni finished second to score Williams's first FW07 points of the 1979 Championship. There followed a gap in the calendar before the French GP and Head used that breathing space to test at Dijon, where FW07 simply murdered the lap record. The Michelin-shod Renault turbocharged cars were to come good in that race, however, and they finished first and third, split by a Ferrari while Jones was fourth – the leading Goodyear runner home in his FW07 – and Regazzoni was sixth.

Then followed a simply stunning test session at Silverstone in preparation for the British Grand Prix. The lap record was 1;18 and Jones had already got down to 1;13.6 when a newly developed engine under-fairing was attached, and he ended that day clocking 1 minute 12.18 seconds. The sheer grip generated by the Williams cars in the race there enabled them to run 1-2 until the neck of Jones's engine's water pump cracked and dribbled away all the coolant. Out he went, leaving his popular team-mate to score the first victo-

The FW07C 'clearance car' of 1981 demonstrated here by Jones shows off its blade front wing, rocker arm suspension, top radiator ducts, high exhausts and brake ducting, here taped over, front and rear.

ry for both the new cars and the Williams team in chassis '07/2, adding fastest lap along the way.

Jones then underlined Williams superiority by winning the next three GPs in a row; Germany and Austria in the latest '07/4 and Holland in '07/1. In Austria the team cars finished first and second.

Jones and Regazzoni thereafter went on to complete this superb season with another superb 1-2 in Canada, using chassis '07/4 and '07/1 respectively but Jones lost a wheel after a fudged tyre change in the US GP at Watkins Glen. He finished only third in the 1979 Drivers' Championship despite having won – like Andretti in 1978 – more Grands Prix than any other driver.

Early-season disappointments with the old FW06 cars and late development of the '07s had clearly cost Williams dear . . . but it would all come right in 1980.

Patrick Head's engineering team now believed they needed a car which would be two seconds per lap quicker to continue winning. They developed the FW07B with composite undersides extending the underwing back through the rear suspension to generate greater downforce.

They tested extensively at Ricard-Castellet in the south of France and the development seemed very promising, but in practice for the Argentine GP at Buenos Aires Autodrome the new stiffened-monocoque FW07B – available as new chassis '07B/5 and '07B/6 – proved unstable due to 'porpoising'. Consequently, the B-spec components were hastily stripped off and Jones notched his sixth Grand Prix victory.

Jones was third in Brazil but retired the third new FW07B chassis '7 in South Africa where new team-mate Reutemann placed sixth to score his first point for Williams. Both FW07s were sidelined by collisions at Long Beach, while at Didcot the Williams engineers had developed an alternative B-spec package with modified undersides ending short of the tail and with modified cooling systems.

These definitive FW07B cars made their debut in the Belgian GP at Zolder. Pironi's Ligier beat Jones there, the '07B slowed by a blistered tyre, but Reutemann was third and Williams were now leading the Constructors' Championship table.

While the race team operated their cars in the Grand Prix calendar, engineer Dernie presided over a separate test team with its own chassis and engines which conducted the required research and development and reconnaissance testing at whatever venues matched the team's requirements.

The team held a float of 18 available Cosworth DFV engines, priced new at £22,600 each. Thirteen of them were raced regularly, four were earmarked primarily for the R&D unit, and one was maintained exclusively for experimental purposes.

Jones lost the Monaco GP with crownwheel failure in what had become his regular '07B/7 letting Reutemann through for his first Williams victory, in '07B/5. The Argentinian's luck then deserted him in Spain as he was tee-boned by another car and Jones managed to salvage a very lucky win in a very sick car. But this race was subsequently deleted from the Championship for political reasons, which robbed Jones and the team of nine valuable points.

At Ricard they utterly destroyed both Renault and Ligier with Jones first and Reutemann sixth in '07Bs '7 and '5 . . .

Jones and Williams consequently led their respective World Championship competitions into the British GP at Brands Hatch where, based on practice form, the Ligiers of Pironi and Laffite looked all set to do to Williams what Williams had done to them on their home soil. But this time the Ligiers encountered wheel problems and Jones won yet again, in '07B/7 this time with Reutemann third in '07B/5.

The South African girl driver Desiré Wilson drove FW07/4 at Brands Hatch but she failed to qualify. This car was subsequently written off in a testing accident at Donington Park, with Jones driving. Chassis FW07/5 became the test team car for the rest of the season before going on the North American tour as Jones's spare chassis.

On the fast circuits at Hockenheim and the Österreichring, the turbo Renaults were expected to show off their power. But in the German GP a Ligier won with the '07Bs second – Reutemann who had led before a tyre change in '07B/5 – and third – Jones in new car '07B/9 having started from pole position and setting fastest race lap. In Austria, Jabouille's Renault won at last with the '07Bs accumulating more points, second and third yet again. Reutemann's third place was taken in the debut race of new car '07B/8.

It still managed to go wrong for the Williams team at Zandvoort in Holland, where Jones crashed '07B/5 very heavily in practice when the throttle jammed open, and then in the race he broke a skirt in the spare car '07B/7 by sliding

carelessly over a high kerb and finished last. The practice crash damage was very bad and a replacement had been shipped out overnight, but within seven days the damaged '07B/5 was repaired and available. Nelson Piquet's Brabham won there in Holland and suddenly Jones's Championship lead over the Brazilian was cut to only two points.

There were three Championship rounds remaining, and at Imola Piquet beat Jones fair and square to take a one-point lead in the Drivers' Championship.

Williams arrived in Canada with four cars, eight Cosworth engines, 5.5 tonnes of spares and 26 people. They were taking it very seriously, but the effort looked like ending in farce as Jones and Piquet collided in the first corner of the race and the ensuing multiple pile-up caused the race to be stopped and restarted. Piquet took over his qualifying car with its special 'screamer' Cosworth engine for this restart and he led until the highly tuned V8 blew apart. This left Jones able to cruise home unconcerned to win the race in '07B/9 and the Drivers' World Championship title.

The team were determined to stay up on their toes for the final race of the season, the US GP at Watkins Glen which followed one week later, and Jones and Reutemann rewarded their efforts by promptly dominating the event and finishing 1-2 yet again, Jones winning his second consecutive GP in '07B/9, while Reutemann drove his regular late-season '07B/8.

Williams Grand Prix Engineering Ltd became undisputed Formula 1 Constructors' World Champion.

Frank Williams himself was still a wheeler-dealer at heart and because team finances were still quite tight he sold some of the obsolete 1979 FW07 cars, just as he had sold FW06s before them. John MacDonald's RAM Racing team bought the cars, FW07/1, '07/2 and '07/3 and they were driven by de Villota and more often by Rupert Keegan although it was always a struggle for them to qualify. Keegan's best finish was ninth at Watkins Glen, where Geoff Lees failed to make the race in the second car after a practice crash.

The service requirements of this private team added workload at the Didcot factory. De Villota managed to damage his car more severely than any works driver had so far achieved in a minor race at Monza, and RAM required a rapid rebuild to continue racing. It was good practice for the Didcot crew and kept the chassis shop busy when it was well abreast of works team needs.

The young American Kevin Cogan rented a RAM drive at Montreal but failed to qualify even after thirty despairing laps in the final practice session there, while Keegan crashed his car '02 heavily in practice and also missed the race. RAM were anxious to have both cars available for the Watkins Glen race one week later, and that Saturday evening they telephoned Didcot works

manager Dave Neal at his home – reversing the charges of course – to arrange a lightning monocoque rebuild.

The damaged tub was air-freighted into London and cleared through customs that Monday afternoon, the Didcot crew worked on it through Tuesday night into Wednesday, when it was flown back to New York ready for the start of Watkins Glen practice, and RAM's best finish of the season. This is typical of the pressures in Formula 1 . . . they demand special people to handle them.

During the following winter, Williams ran '07B/7 for Jones in his home Australian GP at Calder – a non-World Championship event which Alan's late father Stan had won many years previously. Now it was his son's turn.

During that winter of 1980/81 the war of the sliding-skirt ban was fought between the constructors and the FISA governing body. The constructors ran the South African GP without FISA sanction, using sliding-skirt cars. The so-called *Grande Costrutttori* or *Legalisti* teams – including Ferrari, Renault and Alfa Romeo – stayed away, while Reutemann won for Williams in the last brand new FW07B chassis (number '10) without Championship points being allowed.

The constructors had to accept the skirt ban and the 6 cm minimum ground clearance rule as well as the 585 kg minimum weight limit which went with it, so Williams rapidly produced an unskirted and ballasted 'clearance car'. This FW07C was ready in time for the official World Championship opening round at Long Beach, California, on 15 March 1981, using new chassis '07C/11 and '07C/12 built to the letter of the new laws.

They instantly finished 1-2 yet again, Jones in chassis '11 leading Reutemann in '12. Another 1-2 promptly followed, this time in reverse order in the same cars, in Buenos Aires but in the trick-suspension Brabham driven by Nelson Piquet proved uncatchable.

Although the Brabham's skirts were fixed to the chassis and its ground clearance was legal when measured stationary, the suspension included hydropneumatic jacking devices which lowered the car and therefore its skirts onto the roadway when running, thus regaining the ground-effect sealing which FISA had sought to outlaw . . . *and* the car was legal.

Consequently, Williams developed a lowering suspension set-up of their own, but at Imola Jones unfortunately rammed his team-mate, though Reutemann survived to finish third.

At Zolder, the Argentinian won in '07C/12, after Jones crashed '07C/11, and was running away with the World Drivers' Championship. Up to this point, Reutemann had had an incredible run of 15 consecutive GP finishes, every time in the points – thanks to Williams's competitive reliability. However, at Monaco his car's transmission failed and Jones inherited the lead briefly before losing it with fuel starvation in his new car '07C/15. The Australian driver then threw away a superb lead through driver error in Spain. In these two events alone a very likely potential 18 Championship points had been lost.

From the French GP the '07Cs wore revised side pods to cure an early-season tendency to porpoise, but they could not match Renault's pace. Reutemann raced '07C/14 for the first time at Silverstone, finishing second. The '07Cs were then further altered aerodynamically in time for the German GP and became truly competitive again,

Top right: *Secret of success, the WGPE wind tunnel at Didcot.* Below: *Reutemann at Silverstone, British GP, 1981 in 'FW07C/14' on his way to second place. See the hinged skirts used that season, fine air entry for side pods and overall smoothly integrated shape.*

but Jones's earlier mysterious fuel starvation fault reappeared and robbed him of yet another probable victory, and nine more points. In this race he gave the intended six-wheeler FW07D chassis '16 its race debut, in four-wheeled form.

This elusive fuel starvation fault was subsequently traced to a flow impediment through a pump union. An angle within the union was cut sharp instead of being radiused, and at that point swirl within the fuel flow promoted local vapourization and caused the problem. It was corrected by the most simple machining operation, merely cutting back that sharp angle into a smooth-radiused curve . . . end of problem, ironically at the cost of only a few pence.

This had taken months to locate and isolate, and had cost Jones Championship points and what could easily have been the first back-to-back double World Championship victory since his great compatriot Jack Brabham had last done the double in 1959-1960 for Cooper Cars.

Reutemann then suffered an uncharacteristic rush of blood at Zandvoort in the debut of the last FW07-series chassis, FW07C/17, where he triggered a collision which robbed him of more points, and which left him and Nelson Piquet now neck-and-neck for the 1981 Championship title on 45 points apiece. They raced on into the final round at Las Vegas, where Reutemann's always suspect psyche seemed to crack under the pressure and the Brabham driver was able to canter home to secure the Drivers' Championship, although Jones won the race outright in '07C/D/16 and Williams had long since secured their second consecutive Constructors' Cup victory.

Head's design team had been well advanced in the design of a new shorter and lighter replacement for the whole FW07 family. This new FW08 was intended originally to be a six-wheeler but would finally emerge in 1982 as a conventional four-wheeler built to run extremely light with an onboard reservoir for its 'water-cooled' brakes which would enable it to be brought up to legal minimum weight post-race for scrutineering, when the hitherto empty reservoirs could be filled with water. This perfectly admissible ploy enabled the team to compensate somewhat for the huge power advantage now being enjoyed by those teams with turbocharged engines, like Renault and Ferrari.

But, disgusted with the hard-ride torture handed out by the lowering-suspension cars fostered by the rules chaos of 1981, Alan Jones had retired from driving after his Las Vegas victory, and for the new season Carlos Reutemann was left heading the team, with the Finnish driver Keke Rosberg as his number two. Then Reutemann abruptly turned his back on motor racing and followed Jones into retirement in early season, and the '07Cs were campaigned thereafter by Keke Rosberg, Mario Andretti and Derek Daly, before the stubby new FW08s replaced the '07s in time for Zolder and the Belgian GP in early summer.

During the '07s' final races, Reutemann was second in South Africa with Keke Rosberg fifth; the Finn second but disqualified after a terrific performance in Brazil; then second again at Long Beach.

Rosberg would in fact end that season as WGPE's second World Champion driver in three years, but the Formula 1 Constructors' Championship would fall to Ferrari's new turbocharged cars which won more GPs and only failed to give one of their drivers the World title due to Gilles Villeneuve's ghastly fatal accident in Belgium and Didier Pironi's similar career-ending crash at Hockenheim.

During its long frontline run – beginning in the April 1979 Spanish GP and ending in the April 1982 US GP (West) at Long Beach – the Williams-Cosworth FW07 series included no less than 16 individual chassis (no number '13') and they won back-to-back Constructors' World Championship titles in 1980-81, plus 18 races overall, 15 of which were full World Championship-status Grands Prix. They proved themselves classic Grand Prix cars, of which Patrick Head and his men could be justifiably proud.

The Williams Six-Wheeler

In 1977 Robin Herd of March briefly – and cheaply – explored the low-drag aerodynamic advantages of an 0-2-4 six-wheeler layout for Formula 1 using front-size wheels and tyres with the rear four all driven. He simply added a third axle and final-drive behind the standard units but had no budget to develop the idea further.

Then during 1980-81 Renault and Ferrari began to set new performance standards with their turbocharged engines which the Cosworth brigade could not match.

At that time turbocharged engines simply were not available for client teams. Patrick Head of Williams Grand Prix Engineering approached Ferrari to use their V6 but the answer, predictably, was 'No'. Cosworth at that time had a rather negative attitude towards attempting to extract more than their usual 490-500 bhp from the DFV engine on which most specialist teams relied. Williams therefore began a development programme of their own with John Judd's Engine Developments concern of Rugby. Cam and valve specialist Chris Walters assisted, and they eventually saw 535-40 bhp from their DFVs.

Sheer straightline speed was the turbos' greatest single advantage, and they also had an edge on overall acceleration despite this being diminished by the extra equipment weight they carried.

Conventional rear tyres at that time were 29 in. outside diameter on ultra-wide rims, generating some 40 per cent of the car's aerodynamic drag. By using three axles, two driven at the rear, and running small front-size tyres on each, it was possible to reduce drag while at least maintaining, at best improving upon, aggregate rear contact-patch area and traction. And other advantages emerged.

Aerodynamic underwing skirts were restricted to the area within the wheelbase. With an extra axle, skirted underwings could be longer and their working area and total download therefore much larger. A six-wheeled model was made and tested promisingly in the Didcot wind tunnel.

The new 4x4 rear end was centred more or less around the conventional four-wheeled car's rear axle-line, the second-axle wheels now being some four inches ahead of the normal position with raked-forward driveshafts, and the new third axle outrigged just behind from an extension supplementary final-drive.

Hewland Engineering assisted on the transmission. The March 0-2-4 car was being hill-climbed by Roy Lane at that time and its FT gearbox first-gear often stripped because the normal wheelspin safety-valve had been removed by 4x4 startline grip. So Head was advised to use the more robust DG gear cluster, allied to smaller final-drives.

The FW07D monocoque was prepared for this rear end, and Jones first drove it one week after Las Vegas 1981, but stood by his decision to retire, despite two standing starts in which the new car took off like a bullet without wheelspin. Palmer tested at Silverstone in the wet and was very quick, the team suspecting they could actually run slick tyres on the third axle since the track was so well drained ahead of it by wet tyres on

the first two axles. Patrick was concerned however about tight corners, so a test was held at Croix-en-Ternois in northern France, where Palmer lapped as quickly as the new four-wheeled FW08 car. The '08's short tub had actually been tailored to match this 4x4 rear end with those vast underwings.

The six-wheeler was some 120 lb heavier and in this prototype form its aerodynamic download and drag were broadly similar. Because of their great length and considerable width, the underwings could get away with only a modest flare, rising towards the rear, but though this took them beneath the driveshafts, they still passed above the lower wishbones, which interrupted airflow in this crucial area.

Consequently a second-generation six-wheel conversion was then designed, in which fixed-length driveshafts would be used as lower lateral location members (as in the 1960 Lotus 18), leaving the six-wheeler's underwing tunnels completely unobstructed. In this design the conventional high rear wing on its pillar would be replaced by a simple rear-body trim-flap like the Lotus 80's.

Meanwhile water-ballast weight-saving ploys seemed more profitable short-term and Rosberg ultimately won the Drivers' Championship in the four-wheeled FW08, while calendar pressures only slowed progress on the six-wheeler update, tunnel tests suggesting 30 per cent greater download.

How well would it have worked?

With an outside consultant, Williams had by this time developed a very accurate lap-time-simulation computer programme. It predicted a Ricard-Castellet six-wheeler lap of 1;28. Prior to the 1985 Australian GP, on a circuit the team had never even seen, they set up this programme simply on the map provided. The prediction indicated an FW10-Honda best qualifying time of 1;20.4, actually clocking 1;20.5, and a best race lap of 1;23.1, actually clocking 1;23.7 . . . so the prediction programme really was incredibly accurate. By the end of 1985 the powerful Williams-Hondas, albeit flat-bottomed, were still lapping Ricard around 1;32 – four seconds *slower* than the far less powerful Cosworth-engined six-wheeled ground-effects car should have been.

But six-wheelers and four-wheel drive were both then banned for 1983 and perhaps it was as well, for this time everyone must surely have followed the six-wheeled lead and grids full of such exotica might have been too far removed from what the public and sponsors would understand to maintain credibility and interest.

But what a nice try . . .

Since the single most inefficient aerodynamic feature of the modern Formula 1 car has been its massively obstructive wide rear tyres, the use of six front-sized wheels and tyres on the enormously long-underwing Williams six-wheeler showed phenomenal straightline speed . . .

Chapter 13

THE GORDON MURRAY CHAMPIONSHIP BRABHAMS 1980-83

Nelson Piquet's first World Championship win came in 1981. His BT49C displays hydraulically adjusted pullrod front suspension and smooth overbody form feeding air beneath the rear wing. Bottom: Piola's BT49 sketch shows: 1, Girling 4-piston caliper; 2, carbon tub; 3, anti-roll bar; 4, steering rack end; 5, carbon skirt; 6, skirtbox inner; 7, dash; 8, machined aluminium tub insert; 9, water container; 10, gear linkage; 11, carbon underwing floor; 12, exhaust heat-shielding; 13, rising-rate geometry suspension pullrod; 14, bell-housing oil tank; 15, Girling 4-piston caliper; 16, rear wing-post; 17, gearbox oil cooler.

By September 1979 the Brabham-Alfa Romeo co-operative arrangement was drawing to a close, ending on a victorious note with Lauda's BT48 victory in the non-Championship race at Imola.

The decision was taken to revert to Cosworth power since Autodelta were spending more of their time concentrating upon development of their own rival Formula 1 project. A terrific effort by their Chessington workforce enabled Motor Racing Developments to present three still red-liveried BT49-DFVs (two race cars and a spare) at Montreal for the Canadian GP.

The cars used a lengthened version of Gordon Murray's existing BT48 slimline aluminium and carbon-panelled monocoque tub. The cars were 35 lb lighter than the BT48 when empty, 95 lb lighter when fuelled to DFV requirements.

Piquet ran 'BT49/2' third for a long time in the Canadian GP before retiring with gearbox trouble, while Lauda abruptly quit racing after the briefest of practice outings, much to his hard-worked crew's dismay. He was replaced immediately by Ricardo Zunino taking over 'BT49/3' for the race.

Second time out, at Watkins Glen, the new cars ran well, Piquet qualifying on the front row beside Jones's Williams and setting fastest lap before a driveshaft broke, while the novice Zunino qualified ninth quickest but spun off.

As 1979 ended, Brabham faced their first full Cosworth-powered season for four years. It would see Piquet growing in stature and experience while the team beavered away to develop their new DFV car to winning pitch. By the end of 1980 the BT49 was arguably the fastest Cosworth-powered car, despite Jones's Championship victory in the Williams FW07Bs, for Piquet had come within an ace of denying the Australian driver his title.

As a marque, however, Brabham could not challenge Williams for the Constructors' Cup because both cars in a team could score points in that competition and Brabham was effectively a one-star-driver team with the second seat filled normally by a driver paying for the privilege. Neither Zunino in early-season, nor his replacement Rebaque, could accumulate sufficient points to combat Williams's driver strength.

The two original late-1979 BT49s, chassis '2 and '3, appeared early in 1980. Seven more were built that season, chassis 'BT49/4-5-6-7-8-9-10'. In Argentina, '2 was team spare while Piquet and Zunino raced new cars '4 and '5 which wore revised rear suspension, modified side pod profiles and a new skirt system, and both radiator posi-

tioning and fuel system had been modified. They were the fastest cars on the straight, and Piquet finished second while Zunino drove carefully on the slippery track . . . at the tail of the field.

They had problems in Piquet's native Brazil, and a major development came at Long Beach where the BT49B variant emerged with its rear end modified to use a Weismann transverse-shaft gearbox which was narrow and tall and useful in altering weight distribution. The coil-dampers mounted on the rear of the gearbox side by side.

These mods appeared on chassis '3, the race cars '5 and '6 also using modified side pods, bodywork and rear suspensions though retaining the conventional Brabham gearbox. Piquet, in his regular car, was able to put in the perfect performance, starting on pole, leading throughout and scoring his first Grand Prix win.

New car '49/7 was ready for Zunino in Belgium fitted with the Weismann gearbox, though only in practice. The big Brabham-Alfa rear wing reappeared for the slow-speed circuit at Monaco, where both drivers crashed during first qualifying, damaging their cars' tubs. Piquet raced the spare while Zunino raced development car '3, hastily sent out from Chessington as replacement along with tub '6 unassembled. After a lot of work, the original Monaco cars were repaired in time for Spain, while a stiffened-monocoque new chassis '8 made its debut in France as spare and was finally raced by Piquet. It was very fast on the straight but lacked traction.

Larger 15 in. front wheels and the big Monaco wing were used for Brands Hatch, and for Germany reprofiled side pods appeared on Piquet's '49/3 (the team spare which he raced there), while at the Österreichring he crashed his own race car '7 very heavily in practice. Old '49/3 was again prepared for him and he finished in the points for the eighth time that season, as teammate Rebaque gave '49/6 the Weismann gearbox car's first finish.

Major change came in Holland. Gordon and his number two, David North, had developed a new front suspension sweep, lengthening the wheelbase by three inches, altering the relative positions of the centres of pressure and gravity, and new side pods were profiled to suit. Brabham could now run less wing, gaining on straightline speed while still retaining downforce. Both race cars – chassis '6 for Rebaque and '7 for Piquet – ran Weismann gearboxes and Piquet won after Jones slid over a kerb and damaged a skirt when leading.

Now the Drivers' Championship battle was joined in earnest between Piquet and Jones. A new chassis '9 was available for Nelson at Imola, and with its longer wheelbase and new side pods the BT49 was now superior to the rival Williams FW07B. Seeking reliability, the Weismann gearbox was set aside at this point and the trusty Brabham transmission reinstated, and Piquet won his second GP in a row.

Four cars were taken to Canada, Rebaque's spare '49/10 being brand new. Piquet rammed a Renault in early practice and set his time in his spare car '7. Both drivers preferred the smaller 13 in. diameter front wheels. After a first corner collision with Jones, Piquet had to use the spare car in the restarted race with its practice qualifying engine still installed, and this sprint unit broke when he was leading, losing him the World title.

Gordon told me: 'The car there was dynamite, but then it all went out the window which was really a bitter, bitter disappointment; not so much for me, as for all the effort our chaps had put in over such a long, long period . . .'

During that 1980 season Piquet finished ten of the 14 Championship rounds, placing 2-4-1-3-4-2-4-5-1-1, producing points every time. Zunino attempted seven GPs, failing to qualify at Monaco, retiring three times and placing 7-8-10 in his first three outings, Argentina, Brazil, South Africa. The Mexican, Rebaque, drove in the last seven races, finishing three times, 7-10-6 – scoring his solitary point at the scene of Piquet's and the team's bitter disappointment in Montreal.

Brabham placed third behind Ligier and Williams in the Constructors' Cup competition.

The application of a ban on sliding skirts marked 1981, which saw the dawn of the so-called 'clearance car' era. The rules insisted on a 6 cm clearance between their lowest suspended part and the road surface. Goodyear had pulled out of racing that winter, much development having been wasted by all teams on sliding-skirted cars, and Brabham turned to Michelin to use their radialply racing tyres.

The scene was set for a remarkable season.

Gordon described the situation after FISA's arbitrary application of the clearance rule. 'The hierarchy kept telling us don't worry. Skirts are in. You're OK. But we could see teams testing without skirts and we grew more and more nervous . . . we had been assured skirts were OK, we did absolutely no testing at all without them. Then it all exploded after Kyalami [run by FOCA as a skirted race, losing its Championship status accordingly] and suddenly the 6 cm clearance rule was in. That was a shaker. We had all discussed such a rule and rejected it as unenforceable . . .

'Now we had just a month to build clearance cars before Long Beach. So David and I took the rules and read them closely again . . .'

They were convinced that all teams would simply fit soft springs and allow the natural and inevitable vertical load upon the car at speed to force it down closer to the road surface whereupon its fixed-skirt ground-effect sections would begin to exert their download, despite the absence of sliding skirt seals against infilling around their periphery.

'There was no problem securely attaching any aerodynamic device to the entirely sprung part of the car but we could not have any device bridging the gap to the ground; fair enough. No part of our car when measured would be closer than 6 cm to the ground except wheels and tyres. Certainly no part would "systematically or permanently touch the ground" as had the old sliding skirts [and as the new rule now prohibited]. Even then, if the car hit a bump or kerb the skirt would leave the ground for a moment, and that would constitute "not permanently touching the ground".

'The rules were unenforceable . . . They said nothing about measuring the car at speed, and we understood the "correction of suspension height" rule to mean anything other than the normal loads experienced by a racing car.

'If you set a Ford Escort, for example, at 6 cm clearance stationary and then drive it on the road it's going to squat down and at some time it'll

clear only 5.99 cm, so did that mean we had to set cars at 7 cm static, so they would go no closer than 6 cm when loaded up at speed?

'That's not what the rule said. It was a stupid rule, we told them it would be unpoliceable . . . but we built a system which complied with it *to the letter*.

'We were confident everyone else would be doing exactly the same thing. We chose a soft air spring, storing the energy by compressing air in a central reservoir through a hydraulic piston, piped to cylinders on each suspension corner. By carefully choosing orifice sizes we could bleed fluid back to the cylinders to pump the suspension back up.

'This way, the car would in effect be blown down as it gained speed away from the pits or startline and download increased. Fluid would be forced out of the cylinders, load the piston and compress air in that central reservoir.

'Then if we got the bleed rate right, the car would stay down through slow corners without springing back up suddenly as download reduced. Once the car slowed on its way in, the compressed air would force back the reservoir piston, fluid would bleed back into the cylinders on each suspension corner and the car would rise to its 6 cm clearance for measurement.'

The lanky, quietly spoken South African told me this story at the end of that season, earnestly leaning forward to add 'No bullshit Doug – it was so *obvious* a loophole we thought everyone would be doing it.'

Brabham went to Long Beach with their latest BT49Cs, all agog to see who had the best lowering system, and they had several other tricks up their sleeve just in case. They confidently expected to see everyone running hydropneumatics, but nobody was!

This often happened to Gordon and his team.

At Long Beach they had their problems. 'The car went down and wouldn't come up, then it came up and wouldn't go down, then one end went down and the other jammed up. It was awful. We were using plastic hydraulic lines to save weight. They blew off or melted on hot parts, the fluid leaked, the car sank and stayed sunk. It looked as if Nelson wouldn't qualify so we took the system off his car and ran with conventional twin-rate coil-springs.'

In Brazil they were still in trouble but Piquet qualified on pole only for poor tyre choice to cost them the race. Both there and at Long Beach the BT49Cs had worn peripheral plastic skirts with thicker blocks of similar material protecting the bottom edge where it might touch the road.

These skirt devices were governed by the old rule which had applied in the days before sliding skirts. So the Brabhams ran the same fixed-skirt material used then without any complaints at the time. It would not survive if it touched the road surface, but once the car settled to its racing ride-height the skirt would prevent in-fill diminishing ground effect.

Williams and the opposition protested against the Brabham system to establish what was considered legal and what was not. They objected to the skirts' floppiness, enabling them to suck in

Top: *Piquet loads up 'BT49/8' through the S-bends at Ricard in 1980 when sliding skirts – visible here deeply extended between the car's right-side wheels as it rolls – were still legal. The diagonal links in the front suspension are the pullrods actuating levers at the feet of inboard coil-spring/damper units.* Above: *With DFV, Gordon Murray, Brabham's quietly innovative Chief Engineer.*

and run on an air-bleed bearing which kept them hovering just above the road surface. This was considered to contravene the requirement 'to remain immobile in relation to the sprung part of the car'.

Murray's reaction was natural: 'Everything moves to some degree. How rigid is rigid? Everything flexes to some degree, how do you define it?

'In Argentina everybody had some sort of skirt, bits around the rear wheels to seal them to the side pod, they bent when the wheel hit them, but not everybody had it round the edges of the car like us.'

Eventually he and team patron Ecclestone said they would gladly accede to the protests if everyone ran marker paint on the fixed skirts attached to their cars, and any one found to have touched the ground would be disqualified. Nobody would agree to that, for every car touched the ground or a kerb somewhere around the circuit at some time on a quick lap.

Still, the joke was that the Brabham BT49C lowering system was still troublesome. Gordon flew home between Brazil and Argentina to redesign it. In Argentina the Mark II system was better but still unreliable. It would not stay down out of slow corners. Fortunately Piquet picked up enough time round the quick curves to compensate, he won and Rebaque retired after running second in Piquet's wake.

A complete front spring and cylinder were stolen from the team's garage there and they were fascinated to see who would fit similar systems at Imola. There was still much ill-feeling about the Brabham ploy.

'It was a bad feeling – all the blokes you'd always chatted to, all your friends, suddenly not talking to you . . .'

They had redesigned the system again, put the cylinders on the suspension links instead of in the springs and changed the hydraulic lines from plastic to metal. This Mark III system was reliable at last until the race, when for the last ten laps Piquet screamed past the pits like a power boat with the car's nose jammed up and its tail still down.

The Imola scrutineers had examined the hydraulic system and approved it, but then dismissed the skirts.

'We said, "Fine, choose an acceptable material"; offered them a selection and they found one they couldn't bend and we put it on. It didn't make much difference to the downforce, just meant we had to make the suspension stiffer to maintain a more consistent ride-height. So we stiffened the springs, put more packers in the suspension to limit wheel movement and the car was the same – just no wheel movement.'

By this time opposition teams were working desperately to match the Brabham effect. Ligier were believed to have adopted a gearbox-switched lowering system which was clearly illegal under the regulation wording. Murray had told Ecclestone '. . . it wasn't right. All this struggling and work to make our systems operate properly, and now some teams were trying to take short cuts which we had avoided because we knew they were illegal.'

A Paris meeting of FISA then issued one of their famous rule clarifications specifying uniform skirts, not more than 6 cm deep and 6 mm thick. Although lowering switches were blatantly illegal they could not be policed, Murray contracted mumps and missed the Belgian race at Zolder and lay at home agonized as he received 'phone calls every day telling me "so-and-so's got a switch, the scrutineers have washed their hands of it, they say you can do what you like, we can't police it".

'At Monaco we put a switch system on one car

and kept the fully legal system on the other with a spare new system in the truck. I wanted to put a big notice on the switch saying "Suspension Height Correction Switch" but Bernie wouldn't let me.'

So the season developed in anarchy with every team running switched systems. Piquet threw a Monaco victory away when he crashed under pressure while leading, in Spain Brabham were off the pace but in the points, then when rain interrupted the French GP at Dijon Brabham dibbed out on tyres.

In the year the cars had gone from some 6.5 in. total wheel movement to 1.5 in. – half of which was provided by the tyres flexing. What had been brought about allegedly by a drivers' plea to ban sliding skirts so as to obtain slower, safer cars resulted in the cars actually shaking themselves and their drivers apart.

After Zolder, Goodyear had returned to the fray as Michelin were not prepared to service everyone much longer and would not give MRD a contract, so Brabham returned to the American company's tyres. But their temporary withdrawal had left them with no experience of these strange new-generation cars and that cost Brabham their chances at Dijon and Silverstone – the French race because at the restart Goodyear had no tyres soft enough for the final sprint, and the British race due to a tyre failure which put Piquet into the bank. In Montreal, for the Canadian GP, both hard and soft wet tyres were far too hard for the rainswept and bitterly cold conditions.

However, Brabham had only one mechanical failure on Piquet's car, a probable gudgeon pin failure which saw the engine blow up at Monza. However, 'the number of things broken, bent, cracked and shattered on his car after one race – which formerly would have survived several races under higher but more consistent loads with sliding skirts – was incredible. Lifing procedures had to be dramatically revised.'

During the season seven BT49s were used, chassis '7, '9-10-11-12 and '14-15. Piquet and Zunino ran 49B-spec chassis '10 and '7 at Kyalami last time out with sliding skirts, and the new BT49Cs for Long Beach then were '11 and '12 for Piquet and Rebaque, with '9 spare. At Imola, Piquet raced '9, otherwise running '11 until the British GP where it crashed heavily after that tyre failure. New car '14 was ready for him in Germany, and he used it until Canada where new car '15 made its debut and it was in this car that he clinched his Drivers' title at Las Vegas that October.

He had finished eleven of the 15 races, scoring points every time but one, winning in Buenos Aires, Imola and Germany, and elsewhere placing 3-12-3-3-2-'6'-5-5. Team-mate Rebaque attempted

all 15 Championship rounds after Zunino's one-off appearance at Kyalami, failed to qualify for Monaco and could only finish five times, 4-9-5-4-4, his fourth places coming in Imola, Germany and Holland.

Brabham ended the season second in the Constructors' Cup with 61 points compared to 95 for Williams.

Meanwhile, a new BT50 car had been completed in mid-season to track-test BMW's new four-cylinder turbocharged Formula 1 engine. In 1982, Brabham's year was dominated by turbocharged BMW engine development and the high spot was winning three races early in the year – two with the DFV and the Canadian GP with Piquet's BMW car leading Patrese's DFV home. That was a considerable feat because the team had to cater logistically for two entirely different cars, the BT49D and turbo BT50.

There was relatively little chassis development during the season apart from changes to their aerodynamic form, the centre of gravity and centre of pressure being in different places between '49D and '50.

The basic aluminium bathtub-cum-moulded carbon stiffening panel monocoque chassis was based still on the age-old Alfa Romeo V12 BT48 design which had been altered progressively in length and height. Brabham built many cars to maintain adequate stiffness, testing them for torsional rigidity at regular intervals and retiring old loose tubs, so 1982 was another hectic season for the Chessington build team.

The early-season DFV-powered BT49Ds used new tubs cut down to lower the bodywork which was new with swallow tail, carbon brakes (by the specialist American Hitco company) as standard, in addition to myriad detail improvements. Gordon described the BT49D as a bigger step from the BT49C than the BT49C had been from the basic BT49.

The team had to concentrate prematurely upon the still-troublesome turbocharged BT50 when BMW publicly insisted they do so. These demanded a 47-gallon race fuel load compared to 38 for the naturally aspirated BT49-DFV. BMW engine problems, which centred mainly on the electronic ignition and injection systems, largely ruined the rest of the year. The new engine was some 30 kg (66 lb) heavier than a DFV with all its radiators, heat exchangers and electrics but it was as well that Munich had a full inventory because Brabham consumed 7-8 engines in the French GP meeting. Even that was not a record; a test session at Ricard used up nine, though I understand that 'only about three of them were really big blow-ups'!

The new power and torque of the turbocharged BMW engines created problems with the faithful old Alfa Romeo-cased part-Brabham, part-Hewland transaxles, which had been designed originally for the flat-12 engine in 1976 and since used with V12, V8 and now in-line turbocharged four-cylinder units.

During the season Gordon developed the pit-stop ploy to start on soft, fast tyres and establish a sufficient time cushion for a stop to refuel and fit fresh soft-compound tyres. This also allowed fuel to be expended on cooling the turbocharger and engine, enabling greater boost and race-tune power to be deployed. But on balance Gordon felt that the tactic failed. That year it was only really successful in 'giving our sponsors exposure in races we weren't going to win . . .'

Using a BT49D-DFV, Piquet won at Rio but was disqualified after Renault protested against the use of 'brake-cooling' post-race water ballast and FISA upheld the complaint. His second and final DFV race of the season was at Long Beach where he retired. With the BMW engine he had started in the opening race at Kyalami, then returned to the fray at Zolder to finish fifth. He retired at Monaco, failed to qualify at Detroit, won at Montreal, was second at Zandvoort, then suffered four retirements before reaching fourth at Dijon, concluding the season with two more retirements.

New team-mate Patrese was third with DFV power at Long Beach, won with luck at Monaco

Piquet's 'BT52/3' at Rio, 1983 Brazilian GP. Lower monocoque is a folded aluminium sheet, black top is moulded carbon composite. Front suspension pushrods had to be more beefy under compression than pullrods which operate under tension.

and the DFV brought him second at Montreal. He made ten BMW starts, finishing only twice: 15th at Zandvoort and fifth at Dijon in the 'Swiss' GP. Brabham finished fifth in the 1982 Constructors' Cup.

The 1981 prototype 'BT50/1' had formed part of the new Brabham-BMW team at Kyalami, along with two new 1982 cars, '50/2 for Patrese and '3 for Piquet. When the BMW cars were then set aside for further development, much to BMW's public discomfort, 'BT49C/15' was used as team spare, being raced by Patrese at Long Beach. Two new BT49D chassis, '16 and '17, emerged new at Rio for Piquet and Patrese, the latter subsequently crashing his in practice at Long Beach. Chassis '17 was Patrese's Monaco winner, '16 his second-place car at Montreal where 'BT49D/18' was new as spare and not seen again thereafter. The latter was destined to be, with its ultra-low mileage, the last of the long Brabham BT49 line.

BT50 production proceeded with '4 new at Zandvoort for Patrese and the final 1982 car, 'BT50/5', new for Piquet at Dijon.

For 1983, Gordon and David North then designed a brand new BT51 pit-stop ground-effects underwing car with a small tank. However on 3 November 1982, only three months short of the first 1983 GP date, FISA announced an arbitrary ban on underwing devices within the wheelbase and placed a blanket flat-bottom ruling on Formula 1. Existing plans had to be torn up, the BT51 would be dismantled unraced and Gordon and David decided that the only proper approach to the new regulations would be to design and build a totally new car.

Thus the needle-nosed, spearhead-shaped, hip-radiatored, short side pod Brabham-BMW BT52 came into being. It used a typical modern-series Murray monocoque chassis, formed from a single aluminium sheet folded into a trough-section, tied together by very light but rigid one-piece aluminium bulkheads hogged out of the solid at front and rear, with moulded carbon-fibre scuttle and fuel tank top sections. Wide-track front suspension had inboard-mounted coil-spring/damper units operated by pushrods and rockers, and inboard rear suspension was supported on the slim internally webbed (giving a smooth exterior) Brabham transaxle casing. Delta nose fins trimmed out the effect of a big centre-pillar-mounted rear wing, and down below behind the back-axle line were neat underwing diffuser surfaces to add a little ground-effect download.

At the end of the year, Gordon reflected: 'We keep catching ourselves out. We convince ourselves that this is the obvious way to go, this is what everybody will be doing so we go flat-out to match them. And when we get to the first race everybody else has settled for the easy option, and we're out there on our own and already worn out by the effort.'

Yet Piquet won on the BT52s' debut at Rio, and thereafter Brabham-BMW had what Gordon describes as 'probably our most consistent season since 1974-75. We weren't uncompetitive anywhere, unless in the race we ran too little power or chose the wrong tyres. One satisfying thing was that after laughing at us in '82 when our cars often didn't last until the scheduled pit stop, everybody scrambled to follow us into the pit-stop routine.

'It was fun developing the new car too, but the low points were the stupid disappointments, like losing the lead with a puncture near the end, or a fuel fire near the end, or the driver falling off the road within sight of the finish . . .'

Early on, the gearbox proved a major weakness. American transmission designer Pete Weismann assisted in beefing it up to survive. In Rio the rear radiator concentration cooked the rear dampers. Rearranged ducting fixed that. Their only testing pre-Rio had been at Brands Hatch in the depths of an English winter, hardly ideal preparation for the height of the Brazilian summer!

Paul Rosche's BMW engine group, meanwhile, had progressed in leaps and bounds, the compact little turbocharged engine with its efficient Bosch electro-mechanical management system being

Above: *Piola's exploded BT52-BMW sketch shows wire-braced wing-plus-winglets, rear-end sub-assembly, tall moulded bag tank, stiffening webs on machined-from-solid rear monocoque bulkhead, and undertail diffuser ramp in moulded body panel.* Below: *Piquet's 'BT52B/3', German GP 1983, squats under BMW's power.*

competitive mainly in race-tune only until a major stride forward was made in time for the Dutch GP early in the second half of the season, when the 'turbo circuits' followed each other on the calendar.

With 42 or 43 gallons fuel capacity the BT52s could attack only the street-circuit races non-stop with confidence. They had been planned as pit-stop cars, complete with built-in pneumatic jacks and quick-change wheel fixings amongst other features.

Brabham used six BT52s and during the mid-season calendar gap a new BT52B-spec was developed with myriad detail changes including some to stiffen the tub with a more extensive carbon moulded inner 'bathtub'. Some weight was saved, lighter bulkheads being fitted. New bodywork introduced a revised underbody form and also smoothed out the original body's distinctive front suspension clearance blisters on top of the nose. The early-season dark-blue-on-white livery was also reversed, with white upperworks and dark-blue sides now to emphasize the sponsoring Italian dairy company's 'Parmalat' logos more vividly.

Three original BT52s had been readied in time for their debut in Brazil, in March, while 'BT52/4' was new for Patrese at Imola and was instantly badly bent about the nose moments after taking the race lead. It was repaired within days and raced again at Monaco, performed spare car duties in Montreal and became a show car thereafter.

Meanwhile, 'BT52/1' had been uprated to B-specification after Montreal and was the late-season spare car, being raced by Patrese at Brands Hatch.

The second prototype, 'BT52/2', was new for Patrese at Rio, and became the team's test chassis

after the French GP at Ricard which opened the European season. Piquet wrote it off testing at Brands Hatch on 31 August.

Chassis 'BT52/3' was also uprated (like '52/1) to B-spec after Montreal, acting as spare car at Silverstone and Hockenheim where it was raced by Piquet and effectively written off by the fire which ended his race there. BMW had used an off-the-shelf production type in-line fuel filter and this particular one just happened to have a casting imperfection in its alloy bowl; it split under engine vibration, dribbled fuel out into the airstream and this spray was then ignited by turbo flame on the over-run.

Meanwhile for Silverstone two brand new BT52Bs had been completed. Chassis '5 was Piquet's car, in which he won the Italian and European GPs and clinched his title at Kyalami, while chassis 'BT52B/6' appeared new in late-season for Patrese, in which he won the South African GP.

It had been a dramatic season, with the Brabham-BMWs suffering all kinds of niggling failures, Piquet twice going out with throttle linkage problems. At last at Zandvoort BMW's new-found power and a typically painstakingly prepared Gordon Murray lightweight qualifying special were enough to slam him straight onto pole position, but Prost put him off during the race in a minor collision. Prost had at that stage looked to have the Drivers' title sewn up, but the end of his season simply fell apart while the BT52-BMWs went from strength to strength.

Brabham and BMW had had their problems, but the Drivers' Championship is the one which the public at large know about, and Ferrari's Constructors' Championship title was small beer in comparison – unless you happened to be Italian.

Towards the Carbon Chassis

Roger Sloman of Advanced Composite Technology Ltd had been working hard to wean the motor racing world into using carbon-composites in areas other than simple detachable body panels when in 1977 Gordon Murray conceived and constructed his surface-cooled BT46 'arrowhead' Formula 1 car.

The surface cooling panels for the BT46 were highly sophisticated components which also served as structural sections of the monocoque skinning. They were specially manufactured for the job by Marston Excelsior – the British radiator specialists – using dip-brazing techniques to apply two lightweight skins of thin aluminium to an interior honeycomb of aluminium foil. Coolant was then to be passed through the finished sandwich, rejecting its heat via the vast fin surface area within, thence to external airflow licking the outer skins.

As it happened, the surface-cooling idea did not succeed in practice, but Gordon was hugely impressed by the combined rigidity and light weight of these finished structural sandwich radiator panels. They were attached as integral load-bearing sections of the BT46s' monocoque structure via 140 slip-nuts which permitted heat-expansion in one direction while locking solid under torsional loads. It was all very clever stuff . . . but now Gordon's fertile mind was making the next step.

'I was so impressed by those panels that I began looking closely at aluminium honeycomb composites as used in the aircraft industry, and then I read something about carbon materials and noticed their claimed stiffness modulus . . .

'This was something special. Here was a material which was half the weight of aluminium but *four times* stiffer. I thought if we could make a monocoque that light and even stiffer we'd be in pretty good shape – so I approached Advanced Composites to make us an experimental carbon panel for a racing car . . .'

He chose the important section through the scuttle area of an F1 tub – for the BT48 – extending from the nose to the forward cockpit lip. 'We commissioned a carbon section to fit there just experimentally and when it arrived we found it really was exactly as advertised – unbelievably stiff and light. Subsequently we began making more of the monocoque in carbon until only the external skins each side remained in aluminium. And that was because very early on we had seen an extremely poor reaction by that top front carbon panel in a relatively low-speed accident at Monaco . . .

'The car had just slid straight on into the Armco, relatively gently, but the carbon top panel simply shattered. I subsequently talked Bernie [team owner Bernie Ecclestone] into sacrificing a car to study just what would happen to its carbon panels in a more severe impact. We block-tested one BT48 – a real, raceworthy car – at the BMW test centre, with its tanks full of water and a dummy driver in place – and its carbon structure behaved very badly indeed, although in general the aluminium panels absorbed so much impact energy the damage really wasn't too bad. Its mildness surprised the BMW people, who had really feared for their dummy . . .

'So I then designed our new car with a full carbon interior, but with aluminium outside to provide adequate impact absorption and control. We then found that Kevlar could be mixed into the plies to hold the carbon together and prevent it shattering.'

The Brabham BT52 eventually emerged as a carbon interior/aluminium side-skin car, the same style tub then continuing into the BT53-54 series. Gordon developed a structural roll-over bar in carbon which proved effective and safe in tests with ACC/ACT, and eventually the Brabham BT55 of 1986 became his first all-carbon car.

'I had been bothered by the way some people were approaching carbon-composite tub manufacture. The problem was how to mould it adequately. John Barnard at McLaren used male internal moulding which demanded a large cockpit opening, simply in order to extract the tooling from within once the piece had been cured. Most others then adopted the two-piece or 'Easter Egg' method, moulding a tub in two sections which were

then seamed together either horizontally or vertically along the centreline. Lotus folded up their tubs from a flat sheet, and some moulded the sides and top of their tub in one piece, and then bonded in a separate floor afterwards to close the hole where the moulding had been lifted off the mould.

'These Easter Egg and top-moulded tubs had the joints cold-bonded and since I'd seen such cold-bonded seams popped open under impact they just terrified me. So I didn't want an Easter Egg car and made the BT55 entirely seamless instead.

'It was a very low, small tub, so we picked the tiniest guy in the factory and built a railway track which ran right into the tub and put him on his back on a trolley to go up inside the mould and lay up the plies in there by hand. It worked well, and was as well-integrated and strong as we could make it.'

When Gordon joined McLaren International from Brabham in 1987 he liked their by that time traditionally one-piece male-moulded form of carbon construction, apart from its use of cold-bonded internal panels and the aluminium 'horse's collar' front bulkhead left over from the days when it had carried rocker arm front suspension – long since superseded by a pullrod system. Consequently for 1988 the design was altered to dispense with the aluminium bulkhead and McLaren's MP4/4 emerged with a full carbon front end instead.

Top: *Gordon Murray's carbon-topped aluminium bathtub monocoque construction demonstrated in this 1983 BT52. Note inboard front suspension and onboard pit-stop jack at nose.* Above: *Derek Warwick in the 1986 Brabham-BMW BT55* showing off low-line aerodynamics permitted by its M12/13/1 inclined engine. The BT55 monocoque was Murray's seamless carbon/Kevlar moulding sandwiching thick honeycomb with inserted bulkheads machined from solid aluminium.

Carbon Disc Brakes

One of the major changes in Grand Prix car technology within our period has involved the replacement of the practical, traditional, effective but heavy cast-iron disc brake with the ultra-lightweight, high-friction carbon type.

This was another initially aerospace development adapted to motor racing use, the innovative designer who led the way here being Gordon Murray of Motor Racing Developments Ltd's Brabham team.

One day back in the mid-'70s he was reading about the technology featured in the Concorde supersonic airliner design, and he was fascinated by a passing reference to its carbon-carbon braking system, the description claiming a weight saving of 'around 1100 lb' compared to a then conventional metal disc/friction pad arrangement.

There are a lot of brakes on a Concorde's undercarriage, but even so such a massive weight saving promised entirely new possibilities for Grand Prix car design. Some who should know claim that every 10 kg excess weight on a GP car around an average 2.5-mile circuit can add two or three tenths of a second to a lap time. One accepts such a statement at face value, and does not ask what constitutes that 'average' circuit . . .

In any case Gordon contacted Dunlop, who made the Concorde brakes, and met their specialist engineers, discussed the possible application of carbon brakes to Formula 1 and Dunlop set about developing a suitable set.

Gordon Murray: 'Everyone was worried about using full plastic brakes, because the behaviour of the material *in extremis* was not thoroughly understood. Consequently we worked on a steel disc drilled to carry ten carbon 'puck' inserts on each side. Each puck had matching radii machined into it apart from the final one to be installed which had a flat on it one side – you fitted them all around the disc and then twisted the last one and it locked them all into place like a Chinese puzzle. It was a neat way of combining the lightweight, frictional and high-temperature-resistant properties of the carbon material with the known stability of a metal disc. We raced that system on the BT45 cars in 1976, and developed the system to its logical conclusion . . .'

But they encountered all kinds of problems, 'including writing off a car in Austria where poor Carlos Pace found there was nothing at home at all when he went onto the brake pedal and he flew straight into the Armco. That was due to overall diameter growth, the disc touched the caliper and its heat simply boiled the brake fluid, so that when he hit the pedal it simply compressed the vapour and the pedal went straight to the bulkhead without applying the brakes at all . . .'

In the late-1970s carbon-carbon brakes were gaining widespread acceptance in the aircraft industry. Landing aircraft effectively demand just one major braking application, after which taxying applications are normally intermittent and quite light despite the considerable inertia of a fully laden Jumbo jet. The operating regime demanded in Grand Prix racing is of course entirely different – repeated fierce applications in a most demanding environment in road races lasting up to two hours at a time.

Gordon heard of a specialist Californian company named Hitco – a division of Armco steel – manufacturing carbon-carbon brake materials for the aircraft industry, not only for undercarriage wheel brakes but also as rotor brakes in helicopters.

Aerospace-quality carbon-carbon is manufactured by superheating a web normally of carbonized rayon in a furnace charged with methane gas. The web accumulates carbon atoms forming upon it in what is known as a carbon vapour-deposition process. The base material is cooked and 'densified' over a long period of stepped thermal gradient build-up, finally emerging as a matrix of carbon-graphite built up around and locked together by carbon-graphite structural fibres – hence 'carbon-carbon'. The lengthy nature of this vapour-deposition process and the stringent controls necessary for successful manufacture explain the material's expensive price tag – particularly in the pioneering days of the middle- to late-'70s.

Gordon Murray struck up a productive working relationship with Dave Gibson of Hitco and they reached an exclusive co-development agreement for Formula 1, to perfect an 'all-plastic' disc brake rotor which would replace the Dunlop puck-type system in a steel disc which had foundered beneath both

thermal and mechanical problems.

'There were two main problems. One was excessive heat and how to control it. We did a mass of work on brake balancing, side to side, front to rear, cool-air ducting and so on – and we even had to control simple heat radiation. The carbon disc would heat up to a surface temperature of 1000°C – and at that level *anything* that could see it would suffer. Heat radiation alone would ignite bearing seals, grease in the hubs, boil fluid in the calipers, heat up the wheels and even cause the tyres distress.

'It wasn't enough just to duct cooling air onto the surface of the disc and over the caliper. We bled air into the interior of the disc through the hub so it also cooled the bearings and seals on its way through. We also made the wheels into fans, which eventually absorbed 2½ hp per corner just pumping air to control brake temperature and its effects. When we used the advantage of carbon brakes' light weight just for qualifying we also ran caliper water-cooling, a total-loss system sufficient for two or three qualifying laps only, just to prevent the fluid boiling. We'd then go back onto cast-iron discs for the race. We also passed air direct through the brake pistons themselves, and fitted insulating pucks behind the pistons to prevent conduction heating the fluid excessively.'

Initially in 1980, Brabham used 0.7 in. thick solid carbon-carbon Hitco discs, and quickly discovered it is not unusual for theory and practice to clash, as Gordon recalled: 'Theoretically, carbon-carbon should be good for 2½ thousand degrees Centigrade without degradation, but we found in practice that if we ran the material to just barely above 850°C in racing it would become oxidized in the cooling airstream we had provided.

'This had the weirdest effect. We could run 60 or

70 laps with negligible brake wear and perfectly adequate performance and then in just two qualifying laps the driver might exceed that critical temperature and the material would simply dissolve!

'We would see the effect around the exposed edges of the disc and the pad, never on the rubbing surfaces themselves. But if you let it continue both would end up like a piece of ragged, floppy cloth. It would just react with the air and oxidize.

'That triggered a lot of development work with Hitco, including anti-oxidant coatings for the carbon material, but we eventually found that cooling was the real key – you just had to control that temperature build-up, and attention to cooling in the finest detail really paid off . . .

'There were all the usual development problems, of course. Unequal wear, too much bite on one application, not enough the next – uneven temperatures producing a similar effect. And of course with carbon-carbon capable of generating such terrific heat so rapidly, and then capable of cooling just as rapidly, we had real headaches with differential expansion of materials. We eventually had to adopt silver-plated aerospace nuts which could withstand the temperature range ramping up and down so rapidly around a circuit without working loose, chattering, and eventually letting something vital come adrift.

'For some time we took the conservative option and ran conventional cast-iron brakes on the "heavy demand" circuits like Monaco, Montreal and Detroit, and only used carbon-carbon on the "light demand" circuits like Silverstone, Hockenheim and Monza. But the system developed quite rapidly, and by the end of 1983 we were sufficiently confident to rely exclusively upon carbon brakes . . .'

As also by that time were McLaren with the French-made SEP type – see page 185. Yet another technological advance had become established as a motor racing standard. Just another instance of the premier motor racing Formula doing its job.

Top: *The great challenge – perfecting carbon-carbon brakes was a painstaking (and painful) process. This is the 1984 McLaren layout with twin 'balanced' calipers to maximize pad area and extensive cooling drillings. There was much still to do . . .* Centre: *The superseded technology: engine/transaxle assembly of the 1985 Tyrrell 014 with inboard AP cast-iron rear brakes.*

Chapter 14

THE TURBOCHARGED FERRARI 126Cs 1981-83

While the Ferrari 312T4 was accumulating World Championship points so reliably during 1979, work began at Maranello on its long-term replacement – the first forced-induction Ferrari for nearly 30 years – and on 9 June 1980 the first prototype turbocharged Ferrari 126C was unveiled at the *Pista di Fiorano*. Renault's pioneering efforts to take advantage of the supercharged clause in Formula 1 had – as described in the Team Directory – gone off at half-cock in 1977-78 but, after winning Le Mans and ridding their system of that primary target in 1979, Renault Sport had concentrated its resources on Formula 1 and had begun winning by mid-season. As their turbo V6 became competitive so it became obvious that this was the way to go. Turbocharging, and construction of the specialized racing engines demanded by it for Formula 1, threatened almost prohibitive expense. Yet the potential for 650-plus horsepower when the very best atmospherically aspirated 3-litre could offer little more than perhaps 530 bhp (though Cosworth users talked of much less) was irresistible.

During 1979, Ferrari showed interest in building a turbocharged Formula 1 car, and, in collaboration with Brabham, BMW of Munich would soon follow suit.

Ferrari's engine group at Maranello was headed by veteran engineers Franco Rocchi and Walter Salvarani, assisted by Angiolino Marchetti, all answering to Chief Engineer Mauro Forghieri. Having studied the requirement in detail, they evolved a new 120-degree V6-cylinder engine, on which they tested three alternative forced-induction systems. Two involved conventional exhaust-driven turbochargers made by Kühnle, Kopp und Kausch of Germany, or by Garrett AiResearch of America, while the third featured a Swiss belt-driven mechanical pressure-wave supercharger developed by Brown Boveri & Co.

The new V6 owed only its 120-degree included angle between the cylinder banks to any previous Ferrari V6, while its double overhead camshaft four-valve-per-cylinder, single-plug cylinder heads derived from recent flat-12 practice.

The V6 offered several advantages over alternative V8 and four-cylinder studies. With each cylinder bank only 'three cylinders long' not only the block but also the crankshaft and camshafts could be shorter and much stiffer.

With fewer moving parts than a V8 it offered lower friction loss, while compared to a four-cylinder the reduced surface area of each individual piston promised less thermal trouble yet potentially provided greater piston area in total. The wide-angle vee provided plenty of space between inlet cam-covers to accommodate the turbochargers and electronic ignition and fuel injection equipment. In addition, the V6's relatively narrow base chamber left plenty of space each side for unobstructed ground-effects undersurface tunnels, quite unlike the old flat-12.

All engine castings were in light alloy and the four valves per cylinder were actuated by double overhead camshafts per bank, gear-driven from the crankshaft nose. Where the flat-12's bore and stroke dimensions at that time were 80 mm x 49.6 mm, the new V6 had a wider bore and shorter stroke, 81 mm x 48.4 mm, to displace 249.4 cc per cylinder, aggregating 1496.43 cc overall.

To accommodate the boost available from the prototype car's German-made Kühnle, Kopp und Kausch ('KKK') exhaust-driven turbochargers, compression ratio was low, at 6.5:1. Ferrari's published performance figures claimed only 540 bhp at 11,000 rpm, compared to the quoted 510 bhp (but probably more) at 12,000 rpm of the contemporary 'T5-tune flat-12. More significantly, at 7500 rpm the turbocharged 1500 delivered 100 bhp more than the flat-12 at that speed . . .

To provide the unit with accurately metered fuel/air charge throughout the revolution and turbocharger boost ranges, Ferrari had worked closely with Lucas and Magneti Marelli on their fuel injection and latest 'Digiplex' electronic ignition systems.

Renault had already made two major advances with their turbocharged Formula 1 cars. The first was the age-old step of intercooling the compressed charge before it entered the engine, to retrieve worthwhile density. The second was the adoption of two small turbochargers – one per bank – instead of one big one, to reduce each unit's rotating mass and inertia and so improve its response to throttle demand from the driver. This diminished the famous turbocharger problem of throttle lag – the delay between the driver opening the throttle and the turbochargers winding up sufficient boost to answer his call.

Brown Boveri's approach with their 'Comprex'

Arnoux at Hockenheim in 1983 with 126C3 '066', showing its abbreviated flat-bottom era side pods, pit-stop filler, in-line coolers, prominent front brake-ducts and massive rear wing.

Piola reveals the aluminium-honeycomb 1982 126C2: 1, bracketed blade wing; 2, footbox; 3, top rocker arm; 4, rocker pivot brace; 5, wide-based lower wishbone; 6, pedal access; 7, scuttle top; 8, brake duct; 9, protective high tub side; 10, side pod air-entry cowl; 11, honeycomb composite side panel; 12, intercooler; 13, inlet plenum; 14, fuel cell section; 15, skirtbox; 16, exhaust; 17, turbo intake; 18, KKK turbo; 19, wastegate vent pipe; 20, brake duct; 21, gearbox oil cooler; 22, rear anti-roll bar; 23, rear suspension rocker-pivot support plate; 24, suspension rocker; 25, brake caliper; 26, engine breather; 27, bell-housing; 28, wing-post.

pressure-wave supercharging system was quite different from these conventional turbochargers. Although the Comprex system was aimed mainly at diesel engines, Brown Boveri were at this time interested in promoting its use for small passenger cars, hence the promotional R&D link with Fiat-Ferrari.

The Comprex unit was driven not by exhaust gas flow but by an engine drive-belt and as such its output was directly proportional to instantaneous engine revs rather than exhaust gas flow. The Comprex system did however rely upon interaction with the exhaust gas pressure waves for the charge compression which it then delivered to the induction manifold. Its use by Ferrari was massively publicized, BB looking for widespread adoption of their system by production industry. It didn't happen.

This system displayed far better throttle response than the turbochargers during early testing, but the conventional KKK set-up always offered more power, more reliably, and in this form the car was generally quicker.

The first prototype 126C took chassis number '049' in the long Formula 1 Ferrari chassis series originated in 1969. The chassis monocoque was a slender nacelle skinned in riveted aluminium sheet in Lotus 79/Ferrari 'T5-style. To provide adequate stiffness with the smaller nacelle cross-section, a fairly hefty internal frame structure supported the external skins.

Fuel was carried in a single cell in the rear of this slimline tub, which had an octagonal section, elongated towards the top.

Heavily triangulated lower front wishbone pick-ups were built into the angles of the internal frame diagonal tubes which braced the side bays of the tub's forward section. A cast crossbeam built into the top of the tub provided forward pivots for the fabricated top rocker arms, while the rearward pivot bearings sat in tubular braces just behind.

The new V6 engine formed a fully stressed chassis member, while the *trasversale* transmission casing just behind accepted all rear suspension loads. Not even a radius rod reached forward to load the monocoque directly, although a steady bar on each side linked the rear suspension's forward top link pivot to the engine.

Rear suspension featured inboard coil-spring/damper units as at the front, here tucked tight against the gearbox flanks and actuated by

hefty fabricated top rocker arms. Location was by wide-based lower wishbones with the rocker arm and forward-mounted lateral link providing toe-in adjustment up top.

The gearbox itself was a beefed-up version of the immensely successful *trasversale*, now with a choice of five- or six-speed internals. The very short engine, only three cylinders long instead of six as in the flat-12, meant a lengthy spacer could be accommodated between engine and transaxle, in 'British style'.

Brembo – more familiar in the motor cycle world at that time but keen to break into Formula 1 – provided the heavily ventilated disc brakes, and were capable of lightning-fast reaction to Ferrari requirements. These were mounted all round to clear underwing airflow and were buried within the Speedline bolt-together split-rim wheels.

Bodywork comprised a one-piece top section-cum-cockpit surround, a detachable engine cover shaped as a semi-fin ahead of the centre-strutted rear wing, and a separate needle-nosepiece with the nose wing formed around it rather than sitting on top as had been Ferrari's style for 6½ years.

The side pods housed the water (on the left side) and oil coolers (on the right side) in similar raked-forward mounts to those of the 312T4 and 'T5, with the new turbocharger intercooler matrices set square behind them. The outer pod boxes housed fashionable spring-loaded sliding skirts with abrade-resistant bottom edges. Upper pod decks flared out from the nose and windscreen area to mimic the successful 'T4-originated download shape. They were relieved with neat hot air exit ducts serving the various coolers on each side, before running smoothly back alongside the engine to feed clean air beneath the rear wing. Moulded flick-ups did their best to fair in the rear wheels and their Michelin tyres.

Voluminous cool air intake ducts for the brakes protruded from the front wheels and up above the rear end of the pod upper decks.

Dimensions released at the time of the 126C's launch – Mr Ferrari insisting that the 'C' stood for *Corsa* ('Racing') not *Compressore* ('Supercharger') as would have seemed logical – were as follows: wheelbase, 2719 mm; front track, 1761 mm; rear track, 1626 mm; overall length, 4468 mm; overall width, 2110 mm; height, 1025 mm, weight, 600 kg (1322.76 lb).

In fact the prototype 126C, chassis '049, would

not appear in public until that September when it ran in practice for the Italian GP at Imola. By that time it had completed 10 weeks of serious testing between the Formula 1 team's race commitments with their sadly neglected 'T5 flat-12s. Chassis '049 was driven by Villeneuve during Imola practice, merely to keep him interested and to keep faith with the Italian *tifosi* because there was no intention of racing the car.

The irrepressible Villeneuve gave it all he had, lapping in 1;35.751, faster than in his flat-12 'T5.

The new car had by this time been modified with swept-forward front suspension arms lengthening the wheelbase and increasing rearward weight distribution. Its intercoolers were now mounted vertically rather than raked, a vertical rather than horizontal wastegate nestled into the turbocharger plumbing within the vee, and the original semi-fin engine cover had been replaced by a smoothly faired cover sloping down at the rear like the Boxers'.

During the winter of 1980/81, while the political squabbling between FISA and FOCA intensified, Scheckter had retired and Frenchman Didier Pironi took his place alongside Villeneuve.

Their Fiorano test programme proved that the 126C was extremely fast but hard on brakes, thirsty for fuel and still lacking mechanical reliability. Due to the political storm then raging it was unclear whether or not sliding skirts would be permitted in 1981. Scheckter's skirted Fiorano lap record in a 'T5 stood at 1;08.74, and Villeneuve's best unskirted 126C time, set on 11 January 1981, was 1;10.19. Using Comprex supercharging the French-Canadian clocked 1;10.61, before public testing commenced at Ricard-Castellet.

Ferrari boycotted the South African GP which was run by FOCA as a 'skirted' race, so the 126Cs' career commenced at Long Beach in March. Brown Boveri's Comprex R&D chief Tony Köllbrunner believed his supercharger could shine on this stop-go street circuit where crisp throttle response was more significant than peak power. The Comprex installation could be distinguished externally by its simpler exhaust system with a large oval-section megaphone emerging above a gearbox heat shield just ahead of the rear wing.

Bodywork design had been refined during this preliminary test programme, the 'T4-like forward tray being replaced by a slimmer cockpit surround

Left: *Villeneuve demonstrates Ferrari 126CK '052's dreaded bounce in 1981 at Jarama, Spanish GP, which he won by allowing potentially quicker pursuers no room to get by.*
Below left: *Villeneuve and '052' again, this time winning at Monaco. This uncomplicated car was intended to free engine development time; what Ferrari needed was a decent chassis to match their powerful and reliable new V6 engine.*

tion and lubrication systems.

By midway through 1981, the British brigade were looking enviously at the power and general reliability of the Renault and Ferrari turbo engines, and while they did not fear Renault's fragile organization, they knew how capable Ferrari could be should they climb back onto the competitive tightrope.

Just as Ferrari had caught up with British state-of-the-art Formula 1 chassis manufacture in 1963 by hiring John Surtees and Mike Parkes, so they did it again in 1981-82 by hiring Dr Harvey Postlethwaite, and the opposition's fears crystallized. 'All it needs', they were saying, 'is for Harvey Postlethwaite to give them a halfway decent chassis, and we won't see which way they've gone . . .' In Constructors' Championship terms, that is exactly what happened in 1982.

The Italians' troubled pronunciation of Harvey's surname as 'Pozelytwyte' was difficult for them so he became known in the factory as 'Harraveee', and quaintly elsewhere in nearby Modena as 'Mr Thompson' – his wife Cherry's maiden name.

With Wolf in 1978 he had introduced the folded aluminium-honeycomb sandwich form of construction taken up so notably by his former Wolf-Williams assistant Patrick Head in the Williams FW07 of 1979, and with his knowledge of British carbon-fibre developments and aerodynamic study he would bring Ferrari out of what one other English engineer rather dismissively described as 'the aerodynamic dark ages'.

The honeycombs used were to Ferrari specification: two thin sheets of aluminium stabilized by sandwiching internal foil honeycomb, to which the skins were carefully bonded. Postlethwaite's 1978 Wolf and the descendant Fittipaldi of 1980 had used honeycomb tub panels folded into channel sections like a 'U' laid on its side, the two reclining 'U's then being bonded together down a centreline joint to form the finished tub.

While the 126C series went through its progressive stiffening process, six months or more were spent just establishing facilities for the new technology at Maranello, designing and installing autoclave pressure ovens to cook and cure honeycomb bonds and carbon-fibre composites. The American Hexcel company's European division based in Belgium supplied materials and performed bonding operations on panels too large for Maranello to install the specialized press tools required. Once set up, production of the first 126C2 chassis at Maranello took about a month. Further into the 1982 season, Ferrari could crack out a new tub in 1½ days.

The 126C2 tubs emerged using the Postlethwaite form of construction, two channel-section honeycomb folds being united along the centreline, with carbon-fibre bulkheads inserted to stiffen it all.

Again the tub section was octagonal, as in the riveted-sheet 126C, but it was now lower and had a forward-sloping upper half to the rear closing bulkhead behind the central tank cell, whereas on the 126C this bulkhead had been vertical throughout its height. This minor reshaping enabled the heavy in-vee turbochargers and their plumbing to be moved forward.

The cockpit was high-sided, the sides merging into an all-enclosed dash panel surround and forepart which tapered smoothly into the integral footbox-cum-crush structure in the nose to protect the driver.

The various honeycomb panels were bonded together so this was a shiny aluminium Ferrari tub without a rivetline in sight. It was claimed to be 4.8 kg (10.58 lb) lighter than the 126C's.

At the rear the further developed 126C V6

with simple flares over the top front suspension pivots. The side pods were reprofiled, with top vents formed by three airfoil-section vanes either side of the cockpit before running back into smooth, unbroken decks midway along the tank bay. Unbroken top deck, side-vented side pods had already been tested and they would become standard from the next race in Brazil.

At Fiorano, Pironi established a 'T5 baseline time of 1;08.96, to which Villeneuve responded with 1;08.469 in a skirted 126C, and both drivers managed 1;10.2 in an unskirted Comprex car. Pironi lapped Ricard in 1;05.67 compared to the best time of 1;04.77 set by Giacomelli's skirted Alfa Romeo V12 179C.

Both Comprex and KKK variants were tried during practice at Long Beach, the quieter Comprex versions – known initially by Ferrari as the 126BBC but later reclassified as 126CX – proving slower than the KKK turbocharged 126CK version with its distinctively vicious overrun crackle. Both race cars, chassis '049 and '051, used the German turbos, and while the Comprex would appear again in practice for the Brazilian and Argentine GPs it would never be raced, Ferrari concentrating upon the KKK turbos thereafter.

From the start of practice at Long Beach it was evident that the KKK-turbocharged Ferraris would become a real threat once they were adequately sorted out. Reliability was poor in their first three races, the cars retiring each time, though on one occasion this was due to collision. They were also too heavy at 610 kg (1345 lb) and handling was poor, not matching the latest generation of Williams and Brabham 'clearance cars' which by this time were developing lowering suspensions to retrieve ground-effects download.

Six 126C-series cars would be built that season. The first trio numbered '049, '050, '051 were virtually identical in structure, but the follow-up trio of '052, '053, '054 were considerably modified around the front end, with an additional protective box section built ahead of the original pedal-box. Skinning around the inboard coil/damper housings was different and the top rocker arm pivot pick-ups were redesigned and fabricated in weight-saving titanium.

The first batch of three cars was then completely rebuilt, particularly around the front end, into a 'B-specification' which extended the new protective nose crush-structure the full depth of the tub, and raised a completely enclosed scuttle structure high above the driver's shins and feet, right up around the dash panel roll-over bar. Further to stiffen the chassis, sheet fillets were added along either side of the cockpit opening.

The front rocker arm pick-ups were faired into the tub fore and aft with sheet metal. At the end of the season, during final tests at Ricard-Castellet prior to the introduction of the all-new

honeycomb structure 126C2 design, the original cars' cockpit area was further stiffened and protected by the addition of higher built-up sides.

The new 126Cs had emerged as follows: '050 and '051 at Long Beach, '052 at Imola – where Pironi scored the type's first Championship points by finishing fifth while Villeneuve qualified on pole and led the race – '053 at Jarama and '054 at Silverstone.

More by luck, plus Villeneuve's intense application and irrepressible competitiveness, the underdeveloped cars actually won two Grand Prix races, at Monaco and in Spain after faster runners had dropped out. Though powerful and quick out of corners, the cars remained notoriously ill-handling and prone to bouncing as Ferrari's efforts to apply lowering suspension systems *à la* Brabham created untold problems. At Zolder, for example, Villeneuve's suspensions lowered correctly, but during the race the front end popped up and jammed there, the car hurtling round nose-high like a power boat. Its driver persevered apparently unconcerned, foot flat as ever . . . Nor was this problem confined to Ferrari: system-innovators Brabham had suffered similarly while winning at Imola.

The cars made 30 starts in that season's 15 World Championship GPs, winning two, and adding one third place, two fourths, three fifths, a seventh, an eighth, two ninths, a tenth and a fifteenth-place finish. The team's 16 retirements included five accidents and 11 mechanical failures – four apparent piston or other internal problems, two turbocharger failures, two driveshaft breakages and one each involving the electrical, injecengine was retained as a fully-stressed structural member accepting rear suspension loads. Suspension mounting was now lighter than before, using a shaped dural plate to pick up the rear ends of the rocker arm pivots and doubling as foundation for the rear wing post.

Front suspension was along broad 126C lines, with top rocker arm pivots sandwiched between lateral beams built into the honeycomb monocoque and braced forward to anchorages on the tub by jointed tubular rods.

Once again, water radiators and incoming-charge air-to-air intercoolers resided in the rear halves of the side pods, with shaped underwings moulded into a one-piece undertray – replacing the original two-piece design – underneath them. Hot air exhausting from the various coolers exited through louvred slots cut into the pod sides.

The nose treatment was new, with the full-width wing neatly strutted above the nose instead of being split by it as in the 126C. The *trasversale* gearbox again had provision for a sixth gear if necessary, and fairing panelling enclosed the bottom of the engine and extended either side of the transmission casing to the rear of the car, with neat slots in it to allow the driveshafts to emerge.

Dimensions released for the prototype 'C2 were as follows: wheelbase, 2657.8 mm; front track, 1787.4 mm; rear track, 1644 mm; overall length, 4333 mm; overall width, 2110 mm; overall height, 1025 mm; weight *c.* 595 kg (1311.74 lb).

The new car looked superb. It was quite neat and tidy compared to its predecessor and was beautifully made in most details. The team commenced their second full season of turbocharged Formula 1 racing using uprated 126C chassis '049B as spare in the first race at Kyalami, South Africa, where 126C2s '055 and '056 emerged brand new.

During the season, two of the cars were destroyed when Pironi crashed them in testing accidents at Ricard-Castellet, these being '055 soon after its Kyalami debut and its sister '056 later in the year. Both were heavy impacts in which the French driver escaped serious harm. Two new cars '057 and '058 appeared at Rio de Janeiro, the latter being tragically ill-fated. Chassis '059 emerged brand new for Pironi at Zolder and another new car '060 appeared for his use at Zandvoort. French driver Patrick Tambay joined the team in mid-season and he debuted '061 at Brands Hatch.

For the Maranello factory, the early part of the season was spent merely building cars. Engine installation changes were many and varied. Different radiator, heat-exchanger and ancillary mounts absorbed immense time and effort. The spark-box alone, Postlethwaite told me late in the year, 'chased around the cars like a frightened rabbit!'

The season was riven by a fatal accident to Villeneuve during practice for the Belgian GP at Zolder, 13 days after he and team-mate Pironi had fallen out at Imola. There, against meagre opposition – for the race was boycotted by ten FOCA teams in dispute with the FISA governing body – Pironi had won. However, Villeneuve had been leading before, as he saw it, his team-mate had disregarded team instructions and pit signals and taken over the lead and clung onto it, holding him off.

At Zolder, the still-smarting longer-serving *Ferrarista* was on his last qualifying lap, desperate to better Pironi's time when he collided with a slow-moving March. His 'C2, chassis '058, planed off the March's right-rear wheel and cartwheeled at high speed. Its first impact with the ground saw it jam its nose into yielding sand which trapped the tub's forepart and broke the chassis in two as the massive inertia of engine and gearbox flailed the tail over. The seat-back bulkhead ripped out, along with the unfortunate driver's seat harness mounts, and he was fatally injured.

Such chassis disintegration was widely criticized, but Postlethwaite and his Maranello study group subsequently attempted to reproduce similar damage on a tub section test rig, and the forces required to achieve it proved far higher

than had ever previously been considered possible in racing. The 126C2 design had already absorbed some extremely heavy, but conventional, horizontal-trajectory impacts at Ricard and what happened at Zolder was one of those killer-freaks which burst upon the scene perhaps once in ten years. It seemed unlikely that anything similar could happen again . . .

Critics of aluminium honeycomb construction held that, in order to save weight compared to conventional alloy-sheet, honeycomb sandwich skins had to be less than half as thick as the standard single-thickness panels. It was thought that these very thin skins would be likely to split and tear under heavy impact. Postlethwaite, Head, Murray and the other aluminium users emphatically believed otherwise . . .

After Villeneuve's death, Ferrari understandably non-started in the Belgian race, but reappeared at Monaco with a one-car entry for Pironi who raced '059 and almost scored a fortunate win, inheriting the lead on the penultimate lap before last-lap electrical failure then killed his engine and he was classified second. Then came Detroit and the Canadian GP and the debut of the pullrod suspension modification.

One major early problem with the 'C2s was sheer tyre consumption. The team had returned to Goodyear after four seasons with Michelin and initially the contemporary American-made tyres and the Italian chassis did not seem well matched. This was certainly not a weight-related problem as the new cars were tight against the new minimum weight limit, and with test miles accumulating the problems were rapidly resolved. Meanwhile Brabham and Williams amongst other teams had proved the efficacy of suspension systems in which the inboard coil/damper units were actuated by lightweight pullrods and rocker links in place of the hefty conventional top rocker arm system. Just before the Detroit GP in mid-season, Ferrari adopted their own pullrod system for the front suspension.

The sliding-skirt system ban of 1981 had produced cars in which tyre sidewall deflection was virtually the sum total of suspension travel. Massive aerodynamic forces had to be endured, and in cars of this type the rocker arms themselves had begun to act like undamped springs. They had in any case to be massive fabrications to support enormous downloads, and so they had become both bulky and heavy with their large frontal area generating wasteful aerodynamic drag.

At a stroke, the pullrod system removed the

need for this heavy, draggy component and also offered easy and useful rising-rate geometry. Now, upper location of the wheel upright could be entrusted to simple wishbones, which could be formed from aerodynamically efficient tube if required since there was no longer a massive bending load to be sustained only simple end loads. With these wishbones slim and light to save drag and weight, only the wheel and tyre remained as undamped springs worth worrying about within the suspension system.

This massive increase in front-end rigidity transformed the feel of the 126C2s. If Pironi had not stalled and become involved in a massive start-line accident at Montreal the team felt he would have 'walked the race, no problem'. Thereafter, the cars were redesigned around the pullrod suspension as an integral standard fitting rather than a bolt-on go-faster modification.

The first of these so-called 'B-specification' 126C2s was chassis '062 which was built pullrod from the ground up for Tambay in the Swiss GP meeting at Dijon-Prenois, while '063 and '064 followed by year's end.

Meanwhile the transmission study group had produced a new longitudinal gearbox to assist ground-effect underwing devices by replacing the wider but reliable and effective *trasversale*. This new longitudinal gearbox was used extensively in testing and practice late in the year but it was never raced.

Popular French driver Patrick Tambay joined Pironi in the team for the Dutch GP at Zandvoort where Pironi won handsomely in '060's race debut. The cars were consistently competitive now, finishing 2-3 in Britain and 3-4 in France, and Pironi looked to have the Drivers' Championship at his mercy when he suffered grievous career-ending leg injuries in wet practice at Hockenheim, in a near carbon-copy of Villeneuve's accident, which demolished 'C2 '061.

Tambay and the team responded brilliantly by winning the German GP next day, using chassis '060. The new-boy was then fourth in Austria but the G-forces in modern Formula 1 pinched a nerve in his neck and he was unable to start in the Swiss GP at Dijon-Prenois, which ran without Ferrari in consequence.

Mr Ferrari then invited Andretti to rejoin the

This 126C2's trasversale *gearbox was replaced experimentally by the in-line transmission here. Note brake-cooling ducts masking the wheels each side, carbon-composite underwings, rear suspension, 'top-heavy' V6 with turbos in-vee.*

team for the Italian GP at Monza, and the former World Champion repaid him handsomely by setting '061 on pole there and finishing third behind Tambay's second-placed '062B. The Frenchman was again unable to start the final race, at Las Vegas, where Andretti suffered one of the 'C2's too-prevalent suspension failures and retired in '061.

All development work on the cars suffered a major setback with Pironi's Hockenheim accident. Thereafter the direction changed and the priority was solely to play in the team's new drivers and generally salvage the best they could from this shattered season. Everybody responded superbly, from Tambay and Andretti to the most junior team member at Maranello, and the reward was Ferrari's fifth Formula 1 Constructors' Championship title in eight seasons, and the first ever for a turbocharged engine. They won the title with a total of 61 points to McLaren's 54 – modest consolation after the most bitter adversity.

Overall the team had made only 22 starts in the season's 16 World Championship Grand Prix races, running only a single car in the Monaco, Detroit, Canadian, German, Austrian and Las Vegas GPs and failing to compete at all in the Belgian and 'Swiss' events. Even so, they won three of the 14 GPs which they did start and added four second places, five thirds, two fourths, three eighths and one ninth-place finish. The team's four retirements involved three accidents and Andretti's rear suspension failure at Las Vegas but no engine failures.

During the winter of 1982/83 a major revolution took place within Formula 1. On 3 November 1982 the FISA Technical Commission voted through an instant ban on ground-effects underwing tunnel forms, and slapped a flat-bottom requirement on Formula 1.

Ferrari had been planning their Constructors' Championship title defence around a highly developed 126C3 design which was intended to replace the successful if ill-starred 'C2. Forghieri's engine group developed a water-injection system in conjunction with the AGIP fuel company, in search of more power. This proved a contentious ploy.

Compressing a gas, as in a turbocharger system, heats it up. Hot gas is less dense than cold, so it is normal for racing engineers to use an intercooler – either gas/air or gas/water – to lower the temperature of the newly compressed charge on its way into the engine. With water injection, evaporation of the water droplets within the incoming charge cools it still further. Density increases and charge capacity is enhanced. The more charge the engineer can force in and the more the engine can burn, the more power it will produce. By reducing the temperature build-up inevitable with boost compression, water injection permits higher boost

to be sustained and really substantial power gains result.

Ferrari and Renault would run their own versions of this system but BMW, whose turbocharged engines were now powering the Brabham cars, were doubtful of its legality, mindful of the Formula 1 regulation which banned fuel additives and regarding water as just that. Ferrari and Renault meanwhile counter-claimed that water injection was not a matter of employing water as an 'additive', merely as a 'coolant'. It was all a question of 'primary function' and Formula 1 had been up that particular path before in 1978 with the Brabham fan-car and the primary function of its 'engine-cooling' fan. Significantly, 'primary function' was a phrase which had been excised from contemporary Formula 1 regulations because of the arguable freedom it could admit on so many factors. The major manufacturers had some political clout, after all . . .

Quite apart from these controversial water-injection developments, Ferrari had built up a ground-effects interim test hack 126C3 prototype, based on an existing 'C2 aluminium-honeycomb monocoque, before the rule changes were confirmed.

This prototype used the longitudinal transaxle developed by the five-man transmission group during 1982. In Fiorano tests it proved 'an absolute *bomba*' according to Postlethwaite. Yet the flat-bottom rule change killed that concept stone dead, and the car was dismantled.

At this point the medium-range strategic decision was taken to modify existing honeycomb 'C2Bs to flat-bottom specification, while the forthcoming new 126C3 design was completely rethought and redrawn around an all-new monocoque which would be moulded in very light, very rigid, carbon-composite materials. Consequently the first half of 1983 saw Ferrari racing modified 'C2 honeycomb cars, while Postlethwaite's latest carbon-composite 'C3 was finalized.

Through 1982 Ferrari had adopted new technology to produce their honeycomb 'C2s. At Christmas they had moved their *Reparto Corse* – racing division – into its new purpose-built factory and headquarters building, partly on the old works car park directly across the main Formigine-Maranello road from the production car factory. There the administration and drawing office building was combined with its machine- and race-shop complex, while a covered walkway connected with a separate engine design and test house building across the courtyard.

Mr Ferrari had listened patiently to his engineers' requirements for carbon-fibre composite processing plant. To ensure even distribution of the matrix resins through the basic lay-ups of

Top: *After Pironi's Hockenheim practice crash in 1982, new team-mate Tambay won in 126C2 '061'. Note aerodynamic skirt running against road surface and low wing-incidence.* Above: *Villeneuve's 126C2 '058' with its Forghieri leg-pull full-width staggered wing at Long Beach 1982.*

woven cloth, vacuum-bags and pressurized ovens known as 'autoclaves' were necessary. When asked to authorize installation of an autoclave large enough to cook a Formula 1 monocoque, the octogenarian company founder again demonstrated his extraordinary far-sightedness. 'Make it big enough to house a 400', he ordered, specifying the largest of his company's production road cars.

Such an autoclave from a specialist manufacturer would have cost a considerable fortune. But Emilia, the region in which Modena and Maranello are situated, is rightly renowned for the broad spectrum of its industrial skills. An autoclave is essentially just a carefully monitored heated pressure vessel, and just round the corner from the new *Reparto Corse* was a pressure-vessel company by the name of Pannini. It was run by a kindred spirit to Mr Ferrari; they shook hands on a price and Pannini manufactured Ferrari's massive autoclave to the racing department's design in double-quick time. The racing department's staff then installed it in a corner of the workshop, with its computer-controlled heat-cycle system close by, and the oil-fired heating plant in an outhouse through the wall.

While supervizing completion of this enormous oven and learning how to use it and its smaller counterparts, necessary for minor composite components, they also began the new season with 126C2B chassis '063 and '064 modified to flat-bottom specification, alongside new 'C2B/83s '065 and '066 completed as flat-bottom cars from the ground up.

Patrick Tambay had been joined in the team by

continued on page 145

Final practice, Monaco GP, 1967. Lorenzo Bandini's low-frontal area Ferrari '312/67 001' at the Station Hairpin showing its in-vee snakepit of tuned-length exhausts, and the deep rear monocoque horns supporting the engine and accommodating fuel closer to the centreline than the podgy 1966 cars. Hot radiator air exits through the nose-top ducts, inboard front dampers are cooled from the intake just ahead of the suspension rocker arm, inboard rear brakes from the intake above the Modenese test plate number which allowed the car to be run on the road in Italy. Times have changed since then. Poor Bandini crashed fatally in the race next day, his car destroyed by fire, ostensibly due to driver fatigue after 82 of the 100 laps. The traditional Monaco race distance was shortened to 80 laps the following year.

Top: Ron Tauranac's 1967 Repco Brabham BT24s were light but not that light. Champion Denny Hulme yumps high over the 13.5 km hump at the Nürburgring, on his way to winning the German GP from his team chief. The BT24s were very much the minimum amount of car for the job, yet carried a lot of Goodyear tyre for the size of car. Note the out-turned lip ahead of the front suspension to create a low-pressure area and so extract hot radiator air sideways. The centre-exhaust Repco 740 engine and side-panelled engine-bay to minimize aerodynamic drag can also be seen. Nice cars. *Above:* Graham Hill's Lotus '49B/6' demonstrates the download power of its strutted rear wing at Watkins Glen during the 1968 US GP. Note waving front Firestone, and 49B's characteristic squat under power here increased by download. *Left:* The way it was – Grand Prix racing in a more genteel age: Jimmy Clark, the leading driver of his day, settles into his brand new Lotus '49/2' for the very first time ready for practice to begin at Zandvoort, Dutch GP 1967, with a crowd of 26 people to see it. On Sunday the new car and its Cosworth engine will win their debut Grand Prix, and a new era will have begun for Formula 1.

Formula 1 engines 1966-70 with (*above*) Gurney-Weslake
V12 in Dan's Eagle at Monaco 1967. Note the use of polythene
and rubber pipe, coiled capillary tube against rear cockpit
bulkhead and sinuous tubular rear anti-roll bar curled below
Lucas fuel injection metering unit; throttle linkage also
visible. The Hewland transaxle is protected by that robust
nerf-bar. *Right, from top left to bottom right:* 1967 Lotus 49's
Ford-backed V8 seen in later-season form, with ignition box
moved in-vee from top of ZF transaxle, cam-box external oil
drains still in place. Note beefy final-drive cheek plates added
after French GP distortion, also solid brake discs replacing
original ventilated type. The ultimate 3-litre box of tricks,
BRM's 1966 BRM H16 shows off its two-storey side inlets,
quad-exhausts and hefty starter ring on gearbox tail. Note
wafer-thin brake discs, copper brake pipes along radius rods
and copious polythene piping. Monaco '68 Matra V12's
Pan-pipe exhausts, inlets between cam-boxes and generous
oil de-aerating and catch-tank provision. 1966 wide 90-degree
Honda RA273 V12 deafening its custodians in the Monza
paddock. BRM H16 headaches continue, Monza '67. Honda's
1968 air-cooled RA302 V8 displays its rear-boom monocoque,
engine suspended beneath. BRM's V12 in McLaren's 1967
M5A at Monza, Aeroquip braided aviation hose is coming in.
Brabham's 4-cam 32-valve Repco 860 V8, Monaco '68.
Boxer: 1970-80 Ferrari 312B flat-12,
this is a 1974 unit with cast front tub mounting
instead of original over-boom pick-up. The gearchange tube
runs above right-side head, inlets on top; starter motor and
suspension pick-ups under gearbox on left.

Monaco 1969, strutted wings abruptly banned after first
practice, just as some teams were getting to grips with them.
Above: John Surtees shows off BRM's latest BAC-developed
aerofoil aids at Old Gasworks Hairpin; note slender cigar-
shaped 'P138/01' full-monocoque hull, centre-exhaust 48-
valve V12 and afterthought extra fuel tank. Wing struts act
on suspension uprights to load tyres, not suspension, direct.
Left: After the ban, Stewart hustles through *Mirabeau
Inférieur* in his Matra 'MS80-02' without its strutted rear
wing and featuring heavily riveted aeronautical monocoque
and bulged centre fuel tankage.

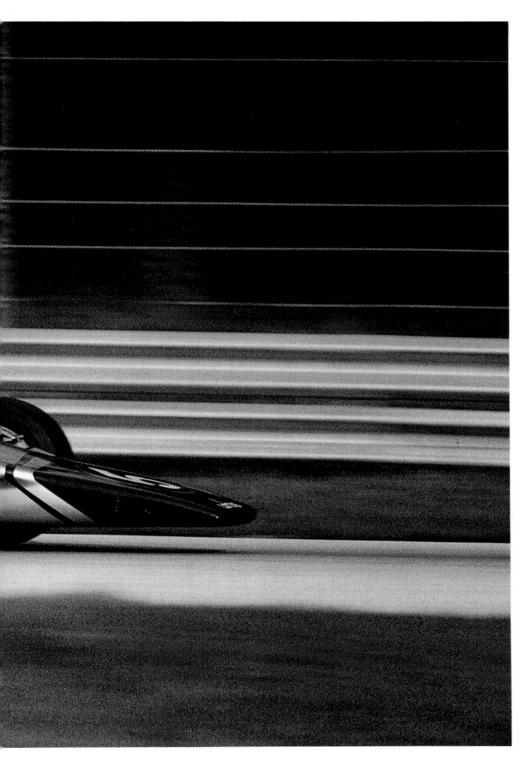

Left: Emerson Fittipaldi ran the Lotus 56B-Pratt & Whitney four-wheel drive gas turbine car in only one Formula 1 Grand Prix, at Monza in September 1971. Here he is, whistling into the *Curva Parabolica* at the end of the long straight which Colin Chapman felt would favour the heavy and fuel-bloated car's sustained high-speed preference. Bulged centre-section was necessary to gain GP duration fuel capacity – nearly 60 gallons. Indianapolis heritage is obvious in the door-stop aerodynamic form. The turbine exhaust chimney is behind Emerson's head, cool-air intakes for the sorely over-taxed rear brakes behind that. The car sports same-size Firestone tyres front and rear. *Below left:* Ronnie Peterson showing how in Colin Crabbe's March '701/8', 1970 French GP, Clermont-Ferrand. The car is rigged with the aerofoil-section supplementary 'wing tank' mouldings recommended to designer Robin Herd by Peter Wright of Specialised Mouldings, who originated the idea with BRM in 1968-69. They held handy extra fuel for the longer, thirstier races without added drag. This is the dawn of ground-effects car thinking eight years before Peter made it happen in the Lotus 78/79 underwing forms.

Left: The most successful individual Formula 1 chassis in history, Jackie Stewart's Tyrrell-Cosworth Ford '003' seen here on its way to winning the 1972 French GP, eighth and last of its Championship GP wins. Derek Gardner's impeccably executed design was a study in well-developed conservatism. Notable features include Matra MS80-like 'Coke bottle' tub with 'midships fuel, broad bluff nose minimizing front-wheel lift, moulded body top 'splitter' deflecting hot radiator air around cockpit, tall engine airbox, and fenced and flapped rear wing. Seat belts have been mandatory for three seasons. Arranging mirror visibility was a problem. *Top:* Classic profile – Fittipaldi's Lotus '72/5', winner of the race at Monza 1972, showing low-profile Firestone tyres, hip radiators, sculptured airbox and far-outrigged rear wing and oil tank giving rearward weight bias. The successful 72s were complex and are recalled by their mechanics as 'sods to work on'. *Above:* Changing circuits: Ricard-Castellet became home of the French GP in 1973 and was regarded at the time as 'utensilar'. In the snow-free south of France it became Formula 1's winter test home. Here, McLaren, Lotus, Tyrrell and Brabham nose treatments and frontal areas may be compared as Scheckter leads Stewart, Peterson (eventual winner), Fittipaldi, Reutemann and the rest from the start.

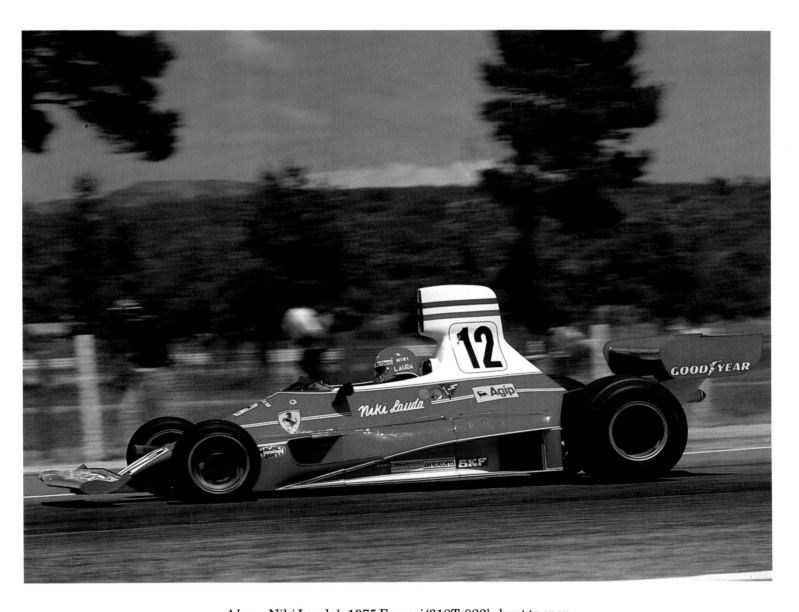

Above: Niki Lauda's 1975 Ferrari '312T-022' about to open out along Ricard-Castellet's one mile Mistral Straight. The dominant Ferrari displays its full-width nose wing, tall, well-sealed airbox and now regulation-overhang fenced rear wing with the mandatory bad weather tail-light beneath. Hot-air exit and cool-air entry ducts betray water and oil cooler positioning. *Left:* The angular planform of the McLaren 'M23/5' at Zandvoort 1974 as Fittipaldi clambers aboard. Note airbox form to clear optimum airflow onto large rear wing, flexible trunking to cool ventilated inboard rear brakes, and rear coil/damper and suspension pick-up frame. Goodyear slick tyres have been carefully selected, matched and marked for Emerson's use.

Following pages: Glorious start of an inglorious German GP at the Nürburgring in 1975. Tall airboxes and aerodynamic aids were in – compare Ferrari's full-width nose wings with white Brabhams' split-radiator noses, blue Tyrrell 007s' finned chisel nose with tyre-fairing end plates and the on-the-verge March 751's F2-derived full bluff nose. Flinty verges caused a puncture plague, Reutemann's Brabham (7) won, Laffite's Williams was second, ensuring the endangered team's survival to achieve greater things.

Derek Gardner's extraordinary six-wheeled Tyrrell Project 34s caused great excitement as they progressed rapidly towards their first GP win in 1976. Here at the site of the old Gasworks Hairpin at Monaco, Patrick Depailler's 'P34-2' leaps over the hump where new Rascasse circuit section joined the old. Note full-faired small-diameter front wheels, the wheel-sighting window let into the cockpit cowl, and enormous protrusion of the standard-sized Goodyear rear tyres. NACA inlet ducts on nose fed trunkings to cool first-axle brakes, the second-axle set being cooled from snorkel intakes just behind.

Above: James Hunt in his McLaren 'M23/8-2' on the charge, as he was throughout 1976, in the controversial Spanish GP at Jarama. He won the race, was disqualified then subsequently reinstated. New airbox rules have slashed its height, there is a forward roll-over bar ahead of the steering wheel, oil coolers are now in the side pods behind water radiators, and vestigial underbody draught-excluding skirts are just visible.

continued from page 128

former Renault driver René Arnoux. In most early-season races Arnoux drove '064, Tambay '065.

The interim flat-bottom 'C2Bs did not shine in pre-race testing at Rio, lacking rear-end adhesion and traction. In the Brazilian GP neither car impressed, seeming too heavy and not performing on their Goodyear tyres.

For Long Beach the team found adhesion by harnessing the download of enormous new rear wings with extra winglets projecting forward on both sides, supported by the full-width main air-foils' end plates. Snorts of disgust at this apparition soon turned to murmurs of admiration as the powerful V6 cars proved capable of hauling these high-drag/high-lift devices around the street circuit at a very competitive pace. The turbocharged engines simply had power to burn. Tambay qualified on pole and led easily, opting to conserve his tyres and adapt his pace to that of his pursuers. This was his undoing as he was rammed by Rosberg's Williams when it attempted to duck inside in one of the slow hairpins. Arnoux lacked the sensitivity to conserve his tyres and ruined two sets, changed twice, and was on his third set when the race finished with '064 actually placing third despite all these delays . . . it was that kind of race.

Arnoux ran '063 in the minor Brands Hatch International, the car using a new rising-rate rear suspension system in which the old familiar top rocker arms were replaced by triangular machined upper wishbones, with pullrods actuating the inboard coil/damper units. This proved too nervous for Brands Hatch, and the old system was refitted for the race. The Ferrari led before burning out three sets of tyres and being forced to retire as no more were available in the pit.

For Ricard-Castellet's long straight in the French GP the 'C2Bs were rigged with more modest rear wings, made now in carbon-fibre. The cars wore lighter bodywork and carried lightened starter systems. Ferrari followed Brabham's lead in adopting pit-stop race strategy, refuelling their car and fitting fresh tyres at around half-distance. A troubled race fell to Renault with the 'C2Bs finishing 4-7.

For the San Marino GP at Imola the pullrod rear suspension had been perfected and was fitted on '062, '064 and '065. Arnoux put his car on pole position but Tambay won with his team-mate third after the leading Brabham-BMW had crashed.

At Monaco, Arnoux had a collision and while the pit crew worked feverishly to put him back into the race, Tambay was waved away despite signalling frantically for a tyre change due to changing weather conditions. He had to run four long, slow laps on unsuitable tyres, Arnoux's bodged-up car retired while Tambay finally finished fourth in a race he might have won with better management. You can't win them all . . .

Arnoux's regular '064 was still being repaired after its Monaco collision when the team left for Spa-Francorchamps and the Belgian GP, so he ran old '062, bouncing wildly over the kerbs and losing a front brake cooling scoop before his engine broke a camshaft. Tambay qualified second fastest behind Prost's Renault and finished a strong second, splitting the French factory cars.

Arnoux felt at home in Detroit and qualified '064 on pole, with Tambay third fastest. But at the start Tambay's engine died due to fuel vapourization somewhere in the critically fine-balanced water injection system and zealous marshals pushed the silent car off course, far beyond the pit crew's reach and leaving no alternative to instant retirement. Arnoux, meanwhile, was running away, with the race apparently well won, until a wire came off a terminal in the Ferrari injection system. It was an uncharacteristic double failure for the reigning World Champion team.

In Canada, however, Arnoux was supreme, starting from pole again in his faithful '064 and leading throughout save for four laps around his scheduled refuelling stop. Tambay was third after

having to nurse an overheated rear tyre in the closing stages.

The author discussed the season with *Ing*. Postlethwaite the following week: 'The problem now', he observed, 'is convincing ourselves that the 'C3 is adequately better than the 'C2. After Canada, to be adequately better it'll have to win by a clear lap . . .'

Unusually, there was then a five-week break in the calendar before the British GP at Silverstone in July. This allowed the new carbon-composite 126C3 to be completed and prepared for a tyre test session at Silverstone in late June, the car having been unveiled to the press at Fiorano the previous week. Visually it was only marginally different from the preceding 'C2Bs, but in fact it was a very different beast indeed.

Known in the *Reparto Corse*'s thick drawing-office ledger as the *Tipo* 632, the new 126C3 used a unitary integrated tub moulded in carbon-composite reinforced with Kevlar. It was formed in two main sections, upper and lower mouldings, which were bonded together like a plastic construction kit, with machined magnesium bulkheads trapped in between.

While the external form of the 'C2 series had been provided by separate bodyshell mouldings, now the nose and cockpit surround shape of the 'C3 was achieved by the moulded tub itself. The only openings in it – apart from the fuel filler and various cable and pipeways – were the cockpit aperture itself, a hatch-covered nose bay containing the master cylinders and giving access to the back of the pedals, and a small circular access hatch enabling steering column and pedal-pad changes to be made.

Ferrari had a minor problem in the differing physiques of their two French drivers, for a spare car set up for Tambay had to be modified with pedal extensions to allow the diminutive, bird-like Arnoux to drive it properly. Observant journalists would check the spare-car pedal set-up in the race paddocks to see which driver was in favour! The mechanics, under burly, balding Vittorio Bellentani adored Tambay, and on balance he was usually ahead.

Initially the 'C3s' water radiators were housed in smaller, more rearward-confined side pods than those of the 'C2Bs, while suspension employed the proven 'C2B pullrod systems at front and rear.

The older style *trasversale* gearbox was preferred to the new longitudinal design now that the need to clear airflow from underwing tunnels no longer existed. In any case the *trasversale* helped give the required overall length for optimum rear wing overhang.

Forghieri would describe the Silverstone 'C3 as 'an evolutionary car intended to combine the good

points of the 126C2 with improved agility and handling'. Tambay reported that the 'C3 felt much more responsive and precise than the hybrid 'C2, but further development was required, and in that exploratory Silverstone outing the well-sorted 'C2Bs proved slightly quicker, despite Arnoux losing a wheel on his car due to an improperly fastened centre-lock nut, which fell off and sent him spinning harmlessly into the catch-fencing.

The 'C3s' turbochargers were still mounted in the vee above the engine, but they were now angled more rearwards to improve airflow to the compressor intakes. After early testing with the abbreviated side pods and rearward-mounted coolers, the longer 'C2B-type pods would be adapted to fit the new carbon tubs due to oil overheating problems.

These new 126C3 cars continued the established 126-series chassis numbering system which itself carried on from the 1969-originated 312 Boxer flat-12 line. For the British GP, Arnoux took over 126C3/066 and Tambay 126C3/067.

Goodyear had a very effective qualifying tyre at this time and Arnoux qualified on pole position with a best lap in 1;09.462, 151.9 mph – something close to the *maximum* speed of Gonzalez's 4.5-litre Ferrari 375 V12 which had first beaten the supercharged Alfa Romeos on this same circuit 32 years earlier . . .

But Goodyear's race rubber was no match for Michelin, and small rear wings fitted to minimize drag diminished rear tyre loadings, compromising the chassis's ability to put power down on the road. Goodyear's race tyre deficiency affected Ferrari and Williams most notably. As a rule of thumb, the 1983 Ferraris performed better the slower the circuit and the cooler the conditions, while they could lose that edge on the faster, hotter courses. At Silverstone, while Tambay's delicate touch nursed his car home third, Arnoux burned his tyres and finished a dispirited fifth.

It was after this race that Tyrrell officially protested against Ferrari's use of the AGIP water injection system. Eventually, and perhaps predictably, defendants Ferrari and Renault (who used a similar system developed in conjunction with Elf) won their case and the Tyrrell protests were dismissed, but it was a long drawn-out business.

Meanwhile the new 'C3s had qualified 1-2 for the German GP at Hockenheim, Tambay ahead, but in the race rough, tough little Arnoux stormed

Postlethwaite's 126C2 aluminium honeycomb tub of 1982 was notable as the first Ferrari monocoque without a rivet in sight. Features visible here in Austria are carbon cockpit insert, raked coolers, pullrod front suspension and long brake ducts.

Straightline speed would have been something to experience in the travel-wheeled Ferrari 126C2B here at Silverstone, 1983! Nothing very neat or tidy is apparent about the V6 turbocharged engine installation/rear suspension/transmission and wing mount.

away to win and set fastest lap, while Tambay's engine broke its valvegear – a now rare mechanical failure.

At the Österreichring the team achieved its third successive pole position with Tambay again fastest, but when he was baulked by a back-marker in the race, his team-mate chopped him off and then his engine failed again. Arnoux inherited the lead, only to be overtaken by Prost's Renault with six laps to run, having lost fourth gear. He finished second, and Renault regained the Constructors' Championship lead which they had just lost to Ferrari in Germany.

The Dutch GP at Zandvoort was usually lucky for Ferrari. The third new '3 to be built, '068, was available for Arnoux but he preferred his German GP-winning car and used it for the rest of the season. Until this time Ferrari's personnel were confident that they had the strongest engine, but during Dutch practice it became clear that BMW had taken a significant step forward. When Piquet's now faster Brabham-BMW was taken out of the race by Prost's sliding Renault, Arnoux inherited the lead then held to the finish, with Tambay second after a slow start and an exemplary recovery drive. This bad day for Renault left Ferrari leading the Constructors' Championship again.

The fourth 126C3 appeared in time for the Italian GP at Monza, '069 as spare car, but Patrese's Brabham-BMW took pole with the Ferraris only 2-3 in its wake. Rear suspensions had been modified slightly to prevent the tyres burning out their inside edges so quickly. Piquet's Brabham-BMW was uncatchable and Arnoux drove typically untidily into second place. Tambay's engine seemed down on power and he could not compete, finishing a distant fourth. Ferrari now led Renault by 17 Championship points but they were losing their grip.

At Brands Hatch for the European GP, Tambay crashed helplessly when his car's rear brake cir-

cuit failed leaving him with front brakes only, which locked. Arnoux spun repeatedly and staggered home ninth and dizzy.

In South Africa to decide the World Championship title, Tambay placed '069 on pole in his farewell Ferrari appearance, the announcement having just been made that Alboreto would replace him for 1984. Arnoux raced '066 in a despairing final tilt at the Drivers' Championship title, but the gulf between Goodyear race rubber and the Michelins used by the now dominant Brabham-BMW and Renault teams seemed wider than ever.

Back home in Maranello, Ferrari were sliding into one of their periodic bouts of internal political strife which would harm their performances in the field. At Kyalami, being pressed harder than ever before by the Brabham-BMWs' sheer pace, Ferrari reliability simply evaporated. Tambay retired with ignition failure while Arnoux gave up when a cracked head caused overheating. What had looked such a dominant season to follow the unfortunate but Championship-winning season of 1982 had ended in dismal failure.

This, however, is a relative judgement, for it applies only in the sense that any team is only as good as its last race, for cumulatively Ferrari still emerged from 1983 with yet another victory in the Constructors' Championship, having successfully defended their 1982 title, although their drivers again failed in their personal Championship chase.

During the year Tambay and Arnoux had qualified for every race, making 30 starts and finishing 20 times (Arnoux 11, Tambay nine), winning four GPs (Arnoux three to Tambay's one), taking eight pole positions (four to each driver), and setting three fastest race laps (two to Arnoux). Tambay had retired on six occasions, Arnoux on four, but every time Tambay finished he scored Championship points while Arnoux did not.

The new flat-bottom regulations had been intended largely to make racing safer and, unlike 1982, not one of the four 126C2B and four 126C3 cars built for use that year had been lost in accidents. Ferrari had come close to losing the Constructors' title at the last few fences but had hung on to make it their sixth victory in nine seasons – a record to beat and absolutely one to envy.

Turbocharging

The idea of using the exhaust gases of an internal-combustion engine to energize an air compressor which in turn boosted the engine's induction was devised by a Swiss engineer named Büchi around the turn of the century.

A turbocharger is a small centrifugal compressor driven via a common axle shaft by a radial-inflow turbine driven by exhaust gas flow. Pressurized air is then directed into the engine's induction. The denser air/fuel charge forced in, the more the engine can burn and the more power it produces.

Conventional turbochargers as commonly developed for diesel commercial vehicles and piston aero engines feature a drive turbine in high-temperature steel welded to its axle-shaft and housed within a cast-iron housing into which exhaust gas is directed. The axle-shaft runs on a plain inboard bearing and has an aluminium-alloy compressor impeller attached to its other end by end-nut, running within a light aluminium casing. The housings incorporate inducer and diffuser sections for the impeller, and collector and nozzle ring for the turbine plus the vital bearings, seals and lubrication feed for the shaft itself.

The complete assembly weighs as little as 15-20 lb, less in more recent years. The drive turbine has to survive in 1000°C-plus exhaust gas flow, while the impeller accelerates incoming atmospheric air by centrifugal force into the volute in which velocity falls and the air is compressed.

Turbocharger drive systems thrived in hot exhaust flow until material capabilities could be exceeded. Until Honda's IHI turbochargers adopted Inconel and then ceramic rotors, c. 1100°C was the maximum survivable. The new materials raised this threshold to 1300°, while the low-expansion material stability of ceramic enabled tighter rotor clearances to be sustained, improving efficiency.

The time delay between the throttle being opened, exhaust gas flow responding and the turbocharger itself accelerating to increase induction-manifold pressure produced the phenomenon known as 'throttle lag'. Moves to improve response included smaller, lighter, lower-inertia turbine wheels, the minimizing of induction tract and duct lengths between cylinder head ports and turbo installation, and also experimentation with variable-geometry intake scrolls – to enhance air velocity into the turbine entry – and pre-swirl to the airflow introducing it to the turbocharger's direction of rotation.

It was also advantageous to arrange extra fuel flow when first cracking open the throttle to produce an exhaust gas surge to spin up the turbine, and with time other similar ploys were developed to keep the wheels turning and maintain boost 'on tap'.

Early on, plain bearings had a hard time surviving in turbochargers, being both lubricated and cooled by high-pressure engine oil. If the bearing collapsed the turbocharger could shatter, pressure oil flooding the incandescent wreckage causing spectacular ignition and belching trails of blue smoke which signified 'a blown turbo'. With experience floating bearings were introduced and many complex fluid-dynamics tweaks were applied to the turbochargers' design both mechanical and aerodynamic to enhance their performance and characteristics. Wastegate systems to dump excess boost pressure were pre-set to open above certain levels which with the advent of ever-more sophisticated engine management systems became electronically controlled to maintain an optimum balance between engine rpm and boost.

As with mechanical supercharging, pressurizing the incoming air raised its temperature and a rise of as few as 10°C was quoted as costing 25 bhp since hotter air is less dense, defeating the object of the charge-boosting exercise. Consequently, as in many traditional supercharged racing engines, intercooler matrices were then used – in effect a radiator through which the charge was directed *en route* to the engine manifold to reject its heat to an outside medium – usually ambient airflow but in some cases water. Intercooling cut charge temperature from c. 240°C to c. 40°, the coolers themselves being painstakingly designed to cool effectively without reducing boost pressure by flow obstruction. Extra intercooling could be achieved for brief-distance qualifying by employing total-loss water sprays arranged from tube 'bars' directed onto the cooler cores. Butterfly-throttle valves were necessary since slide types normal with 'atmo' engines would be prone to jam due to the pressure differential directed across them.

Both Ferrari and Renault adopted water injection to increase further the density of their incoming charge, while BMW eschewed this approach, considering it use of a banned additive though FISA effectively kept out of the argument. In retrospect Ferrari came to believe they lost ground by the sideways step into water injection, retrieving it in 1986-88 by other avenues of development.

After setting out with adapted commercial turbochargers, turbocharged Formula 1 eventually came to demand tailored units – but not before the basically diesel turbos used initially by Renault, Ferrari and BMW had run as high as 180,000 rpm in reasonable security.

Since boost pressure itself provided a compression factor, turbo engine compression ratios were correspondingly lowered to achieve a sustainable effective ratio. Thus 6.5-7.0:1 compression ratios on 2.5-3.0-bar boost in 1981-82 equated to 12-13.0:1 in a contemporary 'atmo' engine.

Higher compression brought dangers of detonation. The

turbo engine's effective compression ratio varied with boost but increasingly precise ignition control and increasingly sophisticated fuel brews offset the detonation frontier despite effective compression ratios rising beyond 16.0:1.

To control turbine and combustion temperatures rich fuel mixtures were used with prolonged valve-opening overlaps until fuel quantity limitation was introduced in 1984. Until then black ropes of unburned hydrocarbon trailing from rich-running engines had typified turbocharged F1.

The name of the game was different from 1984. While Renault had pioneered the path towards mechanical reliability in turbocharged F1 engines in conjunction with Mahle pistons, Goetze rings and Schmitthelm valvesprings, their rivals would benefit by buying into the successful technology once proven at Renault's expense.

Piston crowns were particularly vulnerable. The heat path from internal combustion is from the piston crown, through the ring belt into the cylinder wall, thence to the coolant galleries. Renault introduced piston-crown cooling by oil spray onto the crown's underside. Mahle then developed an oil-gallery cooled piston which became widely popular and effective. Sodium-filled Nimonic high-temperature-resistant valves were used in ultra-hard Stellite seats and arduous valve-spring development was undertaken to survive radical cam profiles.

The four-cylinder turbo engines from BMW and Hart presented large piston crowns with associated heat-rejection problems compared to the smaller-crown V6s from Renault, Ferrari and Honda and Alfa Romeo's V8. The 'fours' also ran large single 110,000 rpm turbochargers while the V6s could run two smaller 180,000 rpm units – one for each three-cylinder bank. With lower inertia these multi-cylinders offered rather better throttle response and wider power bands, but the meaty 'fours' could often claim greater torque.

While electronic management system control of ignition and injection provided the key to maintaining turbocharged F1 engines just the right side of detonation and mechanical catastrophe, fuel chemistry played a primary role in shaping results.

Fuel chemistry itself helped delay detonation. While F1

fuel requirements specified maximum 102 octane, maximum 2 per cent oxygen and 1 per cent nitrogen by weight, the remaining 97 per cent to consist exclusively of hydrocarbons free of any alcohols, nitrocompounds or other power-boosting additives, there was ample scope for chemists to mix entirely legal brews of unimagined extra energy.

Turbo boost slowed flame spread within the combustion chamber after ignition. The chemists developed legal fuels which enhanced the rate of burning, generated greater heat energy and still resisted detonation.

In 1983 BMW worked with the Winterschall division of the BASF chemical combine to adopt high-density toluene-based fuels capable of all of the above. From 1984 this denser fuel made a nonsense of existing fuel restriction by volume – a gallon of toluene brew offering as much energy as more than a gallon of pump 4-star. To diminish volume even further fuel chilling was introduced. Toluene brews were heat tolerant, delaying detonation onset to permit compression ratios exceeding 8.0:1, enhancing both power and economy.

Into the final season of turbocharged Formula 1 racing in 1988, Honda were burning fuel consisting of 84 per cent toluene and 16 per cent n-Heptane, which tested at only 101.8 octane yet provided an immense energy bonus compared to the vast spectrum of variously adulterated petroleum fluids sold around the world as 'pump petrol'. Turbocharger sizes would be selected to generate required maximum boost pressure at medium engine speeds, and at high engine rpm excess boost pressure was then bled away to atmosphere, maintaining constant optimum pressure in the induction system.

The wastegate valve fitted with its own small tail-pipe on the exhaust manifold opened to bleed away excess boost when pressure reached a pre-set level.

This wastegate or 'pop-off valve' was pre-set – the famous 'turn of a screw' – to govern boost applied to the engine and hence potential power generated by it. From 1987 FISA specified pop-off valves pre-set at boost-restrictive levels.

From Renault's introduction of turbocharged engines to Formula 1 in 1977 to Brabham's introduction of pit-stop strategy in 1982 teams were restricted by car tank capaci-

ty in the amount of fuel they ran. With pit-stop strategy employed through 1983 by most teams, unlimited fuel was available and by running very rich the fuel's latent heat of evaporation could be employed to cool the turbos and cut the thermodynamic loads on the engines. Turbine entry temperatures were cut 80-100°C in this way.

This brought a vast increase in race power output from the turbocharged cars, and then the application of a 220-litre fuel limit for 1984 and the ban on in-race refuelling left the latest-generation turbocharged engines having to run harder, longer without benefit of such rich mixtures to minimize temperatures and stress.

At this point fuel management assumed vital significance, and it was TAG Turbo by Porsche and Bosch Motronic who found the best solution with their fabulously expensive MS3 system which offered the nicest balance between fuel consumption, temperature control and useable power output. It began to dominate World Championship Formula 1 in consequence.

Many extremely able engineers addressed themselves to all these problems in the early '80s and the rise in turbocharged 1500 cc Formula 1 power outputs from around 500 bhp in 1980, to 640 bhp minimum in the winter of 1983/84, to close on 800 bhp on race boost by that summer testifies to a soaring learning curve which roared on – thanks to 'rocket fuel' developments – until BMW's M12/13 engines outstripped the 1000 bhp limit of the Munich dynos and by extrapolation were considered to exceed 1300 bhp on 5.5-bar boost in 1986 – a shattering 866 bhp per litre.

With pop-off valve applied boost limitations of 4 bar in 1987 falling to 2.5 bar by 1988, in conjunction with reduction of fuel cell capacity from 195 litres to only 150, overall power outputs tumbled to Honda's best of 685 bhp at 12,500 rpm in the final season of turbocharged Formula 1 – 183 bhp per litre per bar boost against BMW's record 157 bhp/litre/bar boost just two short years before . . .

Few could deny that racing improves the breed.

Showing the turbocharged way forward – the Renault V6 series began it all in 1977.

Chapter 15

THE REMARKABLE McLAREN-TAG TURBO MP4/2s 1984-86

Niki Lauda just pipped his team-mate Alain Prost for the 1984 Drivers' World Championship title in McLaren International's extraordinary 12 GP-winning season. What was more extraordinary was Lauda's use of the same car, 'MP4/2-1', in all his races, winning five to Prost's seven. Note MP4/2's neat lines, pushrod front suspension, rocker arm rear suspension and vast rear 'foil with winglets.

McLaren International had achieved a remarkable resurgence in the fortunes of that honoured name since their formation – as described in the 'Team Directory' – in September 1980. Their John Barnard-designed Cosworth-engined MP4/1 cars had won the race to introduce carbon-fibre moulded monocoque construction to Formula 1. The new model made its debut in 1981 and, driven by John Watson, gained its maiden victory in that season's British GP. During 1982 he and Niki Lauda then won four World Championship Grands Prix in updated but still Cosworth-powered MP4/1Bs.

McLaren International – MI for brevity's sake – involved a partnership between former Team McLaren directors Teddy Mayer and Tyler Alexander with the ambitious, less experienced but highly talented former Project 4 team trio of Ron Dennis, Creighton Brown and engineer Barnard.

Early in 1983 their still basically 1980-designed MP4/1Cs with their Cosworth engines carried Watson to victory at Long Beach before the turbocharged engine domination really took hold. Through that late summer the McLarens proved themselves the best of the Cosworth brigade, until on 28 August the Dutch GP witnessed the race debut of a new TAG Turbo V6-engined McLaren MP4/1E driven by Lauda, while Watson ran the McLaren-Cosworth swansong race to finish a fine third overall.

In the next race, at Monza, both McLarens used the Porsche-engineered TAG Turbo V6 engines, and again in the European GP at Brands Hatch. Then came the South African event at Kyalami, where the new turbo McLaren showed real form as Lauda ran second and looked set to challenge Patrese's leading Brabham-BMW for the lead, only for its electrics to fail near the finish.

There followed a winter's development of all-new McLaren MP4/2 cars tailored to their custom-made turbocharged engine, and this completed the prelude to what would prove an historic Formula 1 season.

Misgivings about the long-term future of the 3-litre Cosworth V8 engine in Formula 1 had begun even before MI's formation. Renault's introduction of turbocharged 1500 cc engines in 1977 had been a faltering first step, though it was not until 1979 that they really performed. Ferrari, then BMW and Alfa Romeo all followed suit, as did the small British Hart concern, racing with Toleman.

Soon after commencing his carbon-fibre Formula 1 design for Project 4, Barnard had been approached by Heidegger, the Formula 2 BMW engine specialist, who was preparing an in-line six-cylinder turbocharged engine for Formula 1. Heidegger showed Barnard his plans but the hard-nosed Englishman said, 'Look, it might be great from the engine man's point of view, but when it comes to mounting it in a chassis it's a complete non-starter'. As an in-line six it was too long, the drive was taken from the middle of the crankshaft, it was canted to one side and it could not be used as a stressed member like a Cosworth. 'Engine people tend to worry about how to mount their engines on a dyno', Barnard explained, 'and thought stops there. The chassis designer is expected to bolt it in somehow – and that's not good enough.'

After MI's formation, the new board agonized over possible turbocharged engines to replace the ageing and increasingly outclassed Cosworth. Mayer and Alexander's huge experience was based upon building and operating competitive chassis around available proprietary engines. It was the same with Dennis and Barnard, but the engineer always chafed at such restraint because it meant compromising chassis design to match the engine. His idea of nirvana was to be able to dictate an integrated design including both engine and chassis. He wanted to be a Ferrari – or Mercedes-Benz – not merely what Mr Ferrari himself had so often disparaged as a mere *Assemblatore*, or, even more rudely, a *Garagista*.

MI's directors considered what engines were available. It came down to a choice between

Renault's V6 or BMW's in-line four-cylinder. Barnard dismissed the Renault as too much of a compromise, having begun life as a 2-litre sports-racing engine, subsequently converted to Formula 2, then turbocharged for Le Mans before being shrunk for Formula 1.

'It hadn't been designed seriously as a stressed member; pumps etcetera seemed untidy . . . There was talk of Cosworth producing them for Formula 1 but I honestly didn't think it was very good. BMW: . . . I personally didn't think an in-line four would do the job reliably. It was another iron block, production based, it wasn't useable as a fully stressed member – I just thought it was a big compromise . . .'

His discomfort with the available choice became one source of the dawning realization amongst MI's directors that their partnership had little future. Mayer was alarmed by the potential costs of turbocharged Formula 1, but he and Alexander pressed for a decision on available off-the-shelf engines. Barnard had been given technical control and he vetoed such haste. He disagreed that either a BMW or a Renault represented the limit of their options.

'But by that time', he told me, 'Ron was more used to the way I work, which is to start right at the top and work your way down until you get a breakthrough . . .'

It's not a bad philosophy.

They pondered on ways to avoid a compromise. Ferrari's V6 turbo was not available. The Alfa Romeo V8 had not yet been announced, and due to the small size of Brian Hart's operation they did not consider his four-cylinder turbo engine being developed for Toleman. 'No reflection on Brian', Barnard would explain, 'who's done a terrific job with limited resources – but essentially the same objections applied as to the BMW'.

So the question then was 'Who can build us a turbocharged engine?', and at that stage Porsche was suggested. They operated a customer design house and so Dennis arranged a meeting in the winter of 1981/82 with Porsche R&D chief engineer Helmuth Bott.

There had been many rumours of Porsche entering Formula 1 in their own right, but they preferred endurance racing as offering more direct spin-off for their production and customer R&D programmes. They had virtually unrivalled experience in turbocharged road-racing engine design, matched by a reputation for astronomically high pricing of R&D work.

Other Formula 1 teams had asked Porsche before if they would consider developing a turbocharged Formula 1 engine in Cosworth-Ford style for customer purchase. The answer had always been 'No'. Now Dennis asked a subtly different question: 'Would you build me a Formula 1 engine as my sub-contractor if I cover all costs?' – and the answer was a delighted 'Yes of course, step right this way Herr Dennis . . .'

Barnard visited Porsche's Weissach R&D centre outside Stuttgart with a rudimentary sketch of his engine package requirements and extensive specification notes.

At that time ground-effects underwing sections were the ultimate arbiter of racing car performance. He had a vision of a car with completely straight underwing tunnels extending unobstructed from front to rear, angled slightly inwards to avoid the rear wheels. This demanded a narrow engine with a small frontal silhouette, its exhaust plumbing raised high each side to clear the raised underfloors. He had wind tunnel-tested a model of such a car and it produced 30 per cent better lift figures than he had ever seen before. This promised enormous advantage which, with a custom-made engine of McLaren's own, would not have been available to their rivals.

Barnard set his requirements before Hans Mezger of Porsche's engine design unit, specifying maximum crankcase width and height, and maximum width across the cam-boxes. He utterly ruled out a four-cylinder and declared a preference for a compact V6, only three cylinders long of course, but he asked Porsche's opinion – might a V8 be better? Vee angle itself must certainly not

exceed 90 degrees, which would make the cylinder banks obtrude too far into his underbody, but it could with advantage be narrower. Pumps for oil and water had to go to the front of the engine within its crankcase silhouette. Exhaust pipes had to leave the heads horizontally, not down-swept, so as to lift the underfloors high on both sides.

The engine had to run as a stressed chassis member like the DFV, and he wanted it to pick up similarly on the chassis. The intercooler lines had to run up under the DFV-like mounting plates on the front of the cam-boxes, between engine and monocoque rear face, to keep within the silhouette.

He even specified a precise crankshaft height, the same as the DFV's, to offer the best design parameters for the whole car. It could have gone lower, but he wanted the ultimate ground-effects car and DFV height avoided potential piping and underbody problems.

Mezger – an excellent engineer in his own right – must have been rather startled by these bluntly specific demands. For years Porsche had rather dismissed Formula 1 as the province of dodgy motor traders and special-builders, not of 'proper' engineers. Their own Formula 1 foray had achieved meagre success before fizzling out in 1962, and they had not returned.

But the deal would go through, and he went away to prepare thoughts and costings. When Porsche's initial response favoured a three-year development programme, MI just laughed; 'They'll have changed the rules by then – do it in a year'.

Dennis came into his own in completing the deal. MI initially funded Porsche's design of the engine and prototype build, after which the design, its production rights, even its type number would be MI's property so that Porsche could not build it for somebody else if MI should fail to raise sufficient cash for more development and production. This six-month 'Phase I' gave Dennis time to raise production finance.

As the valued customer, Barnard was now in overall technical control. He was not too overawed by Porsche's reputation; it might be more in character to describe it as like a red rag to a bull. He would say 'NO' most emphatically when, for good reasons of their own, Mezger's group tried to ease their design straitjacket.

They produced draft layouts which Barnard vetted, and occasionally he would scream when they tried to slide something through his technical filter. One example involved some sump bolts which passed up through the crankcase. Initially Porsche sited the pumps at crank height on the front of the engine, which forced the sump bolts

Top: *Behold the conquering hero – Niki Lauda's World Championship-winning McLaren-TAG Turbo 'MP4/2-1' emerges to do battle. Uniquely, Lauda won his title using this sole chassis alone.*
Above: *John Barnard, creator of the unprecedentedly successful MP4/2s, quietly celebrates Championship victory in the Estoril garage after the 1984 Portuguese 1-2.*

out sideways for clearance so they added a little cast boss to accommodate them, and that boss exceeded Barnard's required silhouette. SCREAM! Bemused German design group amend their design and try again, keeping within the silhouette this time. The pumps dropped below crankshaft height and the offending bolts were brought in closer as required.

Barnard was most concerned with the overall package but he also closely followed its internal design. Decisions on optimum bore and stroke, valve angles, combustion chamber shape and so on were Porsche's alone.

Mezger's team also preferred a V6 to a V8 and produced studies of V6 primary and secondary balance curves at various included angles between 60 and 90 degrees. They could not go tighter than 60 degrees due to space demand for ancillary equipment within the vee, while Barnard would tolerate nothing wider than 90. The final angle of 80 degrees was Porsche's best compromise, identical to Honda's Formula 2 – and soon to be Formula 1 turbocharged – V6 racing engine.

The telling difference between the two units would be Honda's sprawling untidiness compared to MI-Porsche's tight compactness, prompting Barnard to observe: 'That's what will happen when engine men are asked to build a racing engine and there's no thought of asking what the car designers think. Car designers don't come into it . . .'

This was the key to the tight control of the project. MI were the customer and Barnard could state bluntly 'That's not what I want, do it again', and Porsche's design team would either have to convince him of the error of his ways, or do it again. The customer-contractor relationship proved very effective – both parties learned much.

Once the design was complete, the crunch came. MI had to produce the production money.

After approaching several potential backers, Dennis was finally successful in acquiring the support of Mansour Ojjeh's *Techniques d'Avant Garde* (TAG) concern to build and promote the engine. Ojjeh had enthusiastically sponsored the Williams team and when first approached by Dennis he asked its principals their advice. On balance they thought it was a good idea to be involved with a Porsche-engineered Formula 1 turbo engine, but they felt the financial burden could outstrip even such a wealthy private sponsor as TAG.

Porsche's services did not come cheap. Initial production of the engine would merely comprise initial investment. What would happen if it should prove barely competitive and require development of expensive new components like new heads for example? Overnight an investment of hundreds of thousands of pounds in obsolete heads alone could be written off, while new investment would be involved to replace them. A major commercial manufacturer such as Porsche racing on their own account, or Ferrari, or Alfa Romeo, could absorb such costs for the lessons learned, but it made less sense for a private sponsor backing a private customer. Had TAG thought this through?

Ojjeh intimated to Williams that they could have the engine as well as McLaren if he decided to finance it. I dread to think what Barnard and Dennis's reaction would have been to that offer had it been accepted, but Williams declined and eventually teamed up with Honda instead.

Ojjeh went ahead, forming a company named TAG Turbo Engines with MI personnel involved, and 'Phase 2' – the production contract – was signed between Porsche and TAG Turbo Engines in December 1982, by which time the prototype TTE-PO1 V6 unit was ready, running for the first time on a Weissach dyno on 18 December.

But by that time Barnard's vision of the ideal ground-effects car had been shattered . . .

The FISA ruling which insisted on flat bottoms for Formula 1 cars for 1983 had been announced on 3 November. Barnard was devastated. I vividly recall him spitting blood and venom at the time but didn't quite appreciate why. Overnight his 'no-compromise' engine had lost some of its reason to be.

Its specification '. . . would have been different if we'd been running flat-bottom rules from the start. The exhaust pipes would have swept down instead of sticking out, so we could tuck in the turbos closer, but otherwise because of the way we waisted in the sides of our car for other aerodynamic reasons it was pretty much the way we required, even under flat-bottom rules. I would have tried for a lower crank centreline though, and put the pumps on the sides to shorten it, that would have been useful – although it was already a very short engine . . .'

The prototype unit was shown to the press at the Geneva Salon in April 1983. Mezger explained: 'We consider the V6 configuration is the optimum for the current Formula 1, where we seek good fuel economy in addition to competitive power and a good package. The V6 is more compact, with less internal friction than a V8, and can rev higher than an in-line four-cylinder. We start-

ed straight away with six cylinders in mind. You need space in the vee for an intake manifold, injection equipment etc, so we rejected a 60-degree layout immediately as too narrow. A 90-degree offered good rigidity and is conventional, but this makes the engine too wide for our requirements . . . Our calculations on engine balance showed the 80-degree vee to be optimum. Honda has reached the same decision completely independently. Why have we not seen an 80-degree vee before? I can only guess nobody else has done the same calculations', he concluded, smiling broadly.

Few firm details of the engine have been released at the time of writing. McLaren International encouraged their employees not to say anything to anybody which might jeopardize technical advantage and in general they set an example from the top. The new TTE-PO1 V6's water-cooled block was cast in crisp aluminium alloy as were the heads, while the ribbed block itself, using Nikasil liners, was as neat and pretty as it was functional, a piece of technological art. It used a three-pin crankshaft with the pins phased at 120 degrees so when viewed from one end the shaft resembled a Mercedes-Benz three-pointed star. Each head, no wider than the average man's handspan, had two gear-driven camshafts actuating four valves per cylinder disposed at a narrow included angle. The same cam-drive geartrain also powered the water and oil pumps neatly packed into the front of the unit. At the rear, the tail of each exhaust camshaft drove a small three-plug ignition distributor, while the tail of the left-hand inlet camshaft powered the original mechanical fuel injection pump and metering unit via an internal toothed belt. The right-hand camshaft tail powered the fuel pump. A single KKK turbocharger and wastegate matched into each bank's simple but wide-flung exhaust manifolding.

Total weight of the package ready to go was 330 lb, and typical of the thought applied by Barnard was the integral tunnel cast into the left side of the crankcase into which the McLaren air-starter cartridge could be inserted, saving the weight of an individual casing of its own while the tunnel also provided a useful extra structural feature within the casting.

Mezger's preferred bore and stroke dimensions were 82.0 mm x 47.3 mm, displacing 1499 cc, and Porsche claimed 600 bhp, an immediate 75 bhp gain for McLaren compared to its Cosworth DFY V8s. Peak power was produced between 10,000 and 11,500 rpm, though the power band was claimed to be useable from as low as 8500 rpm. At the time of the press conference it was stated that the prototype units had completed some 4000 test miles.

The relationship between MI and Porsche was not without its problems. In some respects it was conducted rather at arm's length and was occasionally adversarial. Barnard's demanding nature and famously short-fuse temper sometimes caused the diplomatic, entrepreneurial Dennis some problems as he tried to hold it all together.

Porsche planned to endurance-test the pilot engine in one of their *Typ 956* Group C Coupé test hacks at Weissach. MI said 'Don't', wanting serious testing to begin instead in their Formula 1 mule, but Porsche went ahead regardless. They insisted they learned much from grinding round Weissach in the big Coupé, but the McLaren team drivers, Watson and Lauda, learned little, though Lauda drove very hard, ignoring the meagre safety facilities of the undulating test track. He revelled in the new engine's smoothness after the Cosworth V8's vibration, and there was no doubting its power; 'Incredible, fantastic!', he enthused, 'Just like being hit from behind by a bomb!'

Still, Barnard insisted that fitting the engine in a 956 merely delayed discovery of a more serious throttle lag problem than expected. The engine was mounted unstressed in the multi-tubular 956, so it was not running under the structural loads which would apply in Formula 1. The 956 was around 250 kg (551 lb) heavier than the Formula 1 McLaren, but Porsche's test team considered

throttle response was as good as on their standard turbo Group C flat-6. The McLaren drivers went to Weissach, tried the car and '. . . just looked blank and said "We don't know either way, funny old car, like a tank, you have to heave it round the corners" . . .' Irrespective, Watson completed some 540 km running, and Lauda around 300, and the embryo engine demonstrated good mechanical reliability.

Back in England, MI modified their old original prototype carbon-fibre Cosworth chassis, 'MP4/1-1', with 1982 straight-sided bodywork, into the turbo test hack model MP4/1D. When testing commenced with this far lighter car the drivers instantly recognized excessive throttle lag. The new engine also displayed an alarming oil breathing problem, emptying the Formula 1 hack's system in only 10 laps or so.

Porsche's men glared at McLaren's oil tank and remarked 'You've got a problem there', while MI's men pointed to the 956 Coupé hack which had a catch tank the size of a dustbin, quite out of the question in a single-seat open-wheeler.

Porsche responded very quickly, changing their KKK turbochargers and exhaust sizes to improve throttle response and investigating the oil-breathing problem. Testing progressed. Early on Lauda was thrilled to exceed 300 km/h (186 mph) at Silverstone. Although his Cosworth-engined car had been 36 mph slower than Arnoux's turbocharged Ferrari along Hangar Straight in the British GP meeting, now he was already within 12 mph of the Ferrari's speed with this heavy and extensively instrumented test hack. He pressed for the opportunity to race the engine as soon as possible, and the team's sponsors backed him, demanding that interim turbocharged cars should be built to replace the contemporary Cosworth race cars before the end of that season.

Barnard refused, but for once was over-ruled. His design philosophy could not contemplate such a rushed expedient. Whereas the late Bruce McLaren liked to 'build it early, build it well and develop it thoroughly before its first race', Barnard preferred to think deeply through the entire concept, research it in fine detail and only then build as late but as precisely as possible – the emphasis having been on extending the thinking time to a maximum.

Barnard believed the existing MP4/1Cs should complete the season, while background development could continue at a more thoughtful pace on the turbo test hack. Certainly McLaren would have finished the season with more Championship points that way.

But historically there is no substitute for race-testing a Grand Prix car. An hour's racing can highlight problems which could remain hidden despite weeks of private testing, but Barnard remained unrepentant. The test hack had been built merely to run the engine and no more, and when his arm was twisted to race the new engine short-term he simply could not bring himself to build two or three more such crude hacks.

'So in six weeks our blokes built two cars – well, one runner and the other 85 per cent complete – ready for Zandvoort. There Niki was unbelievably quick on the straight, but basically the Cosworth wing package download was way deficient with turbo power. We cooked the brakes in the race, a function of the turbo car going about 30 mph faster down the straight than the Cosworth . . .'

The interim turbo cars, chassis 'MP4/1E-01' and '02 were based on the former 'MP4/1C-05' and '06 monocoques, the latter becoming Lauda's regular mount, suitably modified to carry the new engines and their accompanying intercoolers and electronic gear.

Meanwhile, a frustrating new problem had intruded. Bosch had been asked by Porsche to develop an electronic management system to relate the new engine's ignition and fuel injection supply to demand. In 1984, fuel for a Formula 1 Grand Prix race was to be reduced from 250 litres to only 220, while refuelling stops would be outlawed. Consequently fuel economy matched to sheer power became vital, and the new management system was required to balance performance

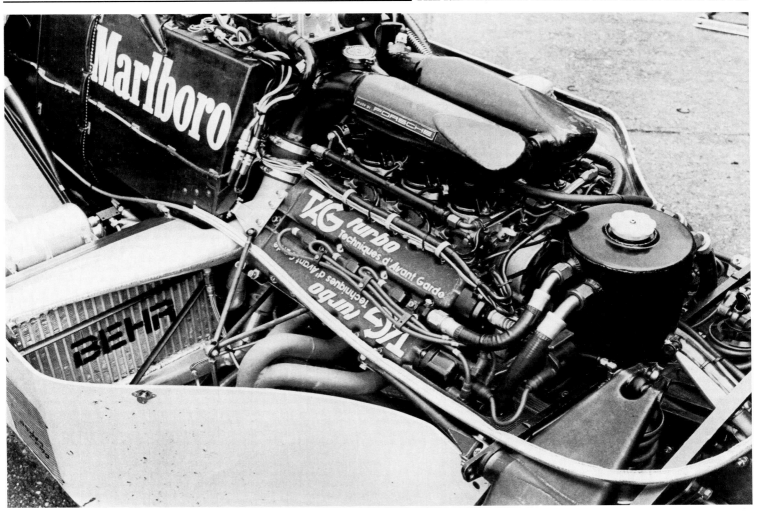

against economy in the most competitive and efficient manner. One Bosch development unit was already working closely with BMW on a semi-mechanical system based upon a Kugelfischer pump and metering unit, but now a separate Bosch team was to develop the 100 per cent electronic 'Motronic MS3' system exclusively for TAG Turbo Engines, via Porsche R&D. The system employed sensors and a processing unit to control solenoids which adjusted the fuel metering jets to govern fuel quantity and to time its delivery to each cylinder in line with demand. This was far from easy to achieve.

On initial test at Weissach the V6 had started perfectly every time, easy as a VW, but now at Zandvoort and on test it refused point-blank to start for hours on end.

The unfortunate Bosch technician would plug in his diagnostic electrickery and its monitor screen would merely flash up 'ERROR', whereupon hours of head-scratching could commence. And there was no communication between McLaren and Bosch, who made it clear they were working with Porsche and regarded McLaren's only function to be settlement of their bills . . . which of course set the veins bulging again on Barnard's forehead.

Very early in the programme this lofty attitude set MI looking for alternative contractors. They talked with Ford who were very interested in production car engine management systems, and also with Lucas and Marelli, but Porsche had age-old links with Bosch and eventually MI bowed to the inevitable.

Initially the engine had run on the Weissach dyno using mechanical injection. But once in the car Bosch decreed otherwise, understandably anxious to develop their own electronic system. Porsche's mechanical injection used a Kugelfischer pump, and Bosch own Kugelfischer, so it was a rather rueful Mezger who one day explained to Barnard that the next time they wanted a three-dimensional cam ground for the Kugelfischer mechanical system they could expect a six-month delivery delay . . .

So Bosch got their way, and the engine went into the cars on electronic management, and it caused untold heartache before coming good.

If anything, the individuals in the project had grown further apart. This was alarming, and it took Dennis's considerable skills – and then major technical problems – to force everyone to pull together. Something deep in the programming or function of the Bosch management system repeatedly prevented the engine from starting at all. Development of the cars was delayed while a third of total testing time could be wasted with silent engines.

Both new interim MP4/1E turbocharged cars raced at Monza in September, with a new double rear flap addition to the rear wing to seek extra download. There were starting problems in qualifying, while Lauda's car, '06, ran poorly in the race but Watson's '05 soared into seventh place before retirement. The V6 suffered its first mechanical failure when a locating pin in the cam-drive train sheared. It was a feature Porsche had used in many other engine applications without problem, but in the TAG Turbo V6 it failed so they rapidly developed an alternative.

Download was still inadequate. In haste before Brands Hatch a huge new rear wing was designed and made. It collapsed on Watson's car while Lauda had another valvegear failure, after which a subtle piston redesign went through. In practice both cars had starting problems and Bosch's men suffered severe earache in consequence.

Kyalami's South African GP ended the 1983 season, and a third interim MP4/1E was now available as spare, based on chassis 'MP4/1C-07'. MI were thankful for the two-day test session preceding official practice there. Barnard stayed at home to finalize his MP4/2 design for 1984, while race engineers Alan Jenkins and Steve Nichols wrestled with the interim MP4/1Es at altitude on the Rand plateau.

Again it was near-impossible to make the engines start or run properly, and little serious work was possible on the car set-up. Bosch's

The TAG Turbo V6 engine looked like a triumph of packaging, until it was installed in the car with all the necessary accessories attached. But it still set new standards. The low-slung KKK turbochargers are hidden in the side pods, drawing air through the gauzed intakes.

reprogramming of the management system for altitude proved wrong in practice but they reprogrammed it successfully for the race. The McLaren crew and Porsche engineers fitted the right turbos while the drivers and race engineers made a very fine tyre choice and the new rear wings were built properly this time. Poor Watson made a starting grid line-up error in the new spare car and was disqualified but Lauda was the fastest man on the track near the end of the race before his engine's electrics cut out and stranded him.

Hapless Bosch were blamed again. Their racing experience was very restricted, and they had fitted a humble production car regulator into the MP4/1E's alternator circuit. Its internals just vibrated apart, the alternator ceased charging and the management system was left with insufficient power to operate, so it simply shut down.

Lauda's performance before this failure was a massively morale-boosting high note on which to end the season but the repercussions of the continuing electrical problems were also valuable.

The Germans undoubtedly found their British customers demanding and blunt, but their own early tendency towards self-satisfied omniscience had been whittled away. Now they knew that Formula 1 really was tough and they could not relax.

In January 1984 the old interim cars were taken to Rio for the pre-season tyre test. The trip was catastrophic. The engines would neither start, nor run, nor perform adequately. Bosch returned to Stuttgart considerably shaken, Porsche and MI applied the pressure and a major re-examination began of the super-expensive management system. It paid real dividends.

Meanwhile the new MP4/2 tailor-made turbocharged cars were in production. The interim MP4/1Es' former Cosworth tubs had changed only in minor detail since the design's original inception in 1981.

Barnard's thoughtful approach to design before first cutting metal, or carbon cloth for that matter, had given remarkable stability to his creations. The original MP4/1 tub made by Hercules in 1981 was so successful that only minor modifications were made for the second and subsequent units. The large plan-area ground-effect '4/1s which raced through 1981-82 were hard to tell apart externally, and then the flat-bottom MP4/1C which replaced them with Cosworth power for 1983 retained that unmistakable family resemblance.

Barnard's MP4/2 tub redesign was governed by the TAG Turbo V6 being shorter than a Cosworth V8 and by the 220-litre fuel limit/refuelling ban preventing use of an undersized tank such as Brabham had used in 1983. The complex tub tooling was retrieved from the Hercules Corporation in Salt Lake City, Utah, where they made the McLaren tubs. It was part revised, part replaced, remachined and returned to Hercules.

New tub sections were moulded there, with a lower, longer tank section behind the cockpit. The lower sides of the chassis around the bottom wishbone rear pick-ups flared out to enhance airflow into the side pods, which themselves remained rather longer and more voluminous than was fashionable. The rear end of each pod curved in elegantly at the rear wheels, exposing a neat ground-effect diffuser panel like a horizontal fin, with both under and upper surfaces active, which swept up either side of the gearbox.

The lower rear wishbones lived beneath this panel, while the driveshafts and redesigned top rocker arms were all that interrupted airflow between wheel and vertical body side, the driveshafts projecting from neat holes in the side panelling which otherwise enclosed engine and gearbox completely. This was the soon-to-be-famous 'McLaren tail' which many other teams would copy with varying degrees of comprehension and success as the season progressed.

Barnard and Dennis impressed upon their team the need for design and technical security. For this reason few concrete details of the cars' construction were generally released and, with this and other considerations in mind, not one of the

carbon-composite McLaren cars was for years sold into private hands. Even the Marlboro-liveried MP4-series show cars used wooden mock-up 'SS' – 'static show car' – tubs rather than a production version which might allow detailed examination of the carbon-composite originals.

The carbon-composite tub, however, carried an aluminium nosebox for driver protection and neatly housed its front coil/damper units either side of his shins within the rigid moulded scuttle and forward tub structure. Where the side pod intakes extended amidships on the cockpit sides a neat slot intake sunk into the tub itself bled cooling air back into the engine bay.

The side pods were shorter, set further back than in the 1983 interim cars, but remained larger than most of the rival designs. Dual-purpose radiator cores lay raked steeply forward in each pod, each core's left side cooling water, the right side cooling oil. Two separate cores – set one behind the other, oil ahead of water – had been used in the interim '1E cars' longer pods.

Where the Bosch Motronic system boxes had been mounted in the front of the '1E side pods, they now moved to the top of the tank cell moulding, which itself sat lower and was some 6 cm longer than in the MP4/1-series tubs.

The TAG Turbo V6 engine hung neatly on the rear of this tub via its Cosworth-like four-point mounts. Where in the interim cars the KKK turbochargers hung out on either side at a shallow angle to the centreline to allow the exhaust manifolds to feed into them nicely without tight curves, this set them too far back towards the rear wheels for aerodynamic comfort. In the new MP4/2 Barnard wanted to bring the body waist further forward, so he shifted the turbochargers forward at a tighter angle with the manifolds cramping round towards them, then the tailpipes arching back close against the gearbox. He admitted, 'It's not ideal, and Porsche don't like it, but I think it's the car designer's job to juggle the best compromises, and that's *it*.'

The turbochargers drew their air through a horizontal duct under the high-pressure area on top of the side diffuser surface but this proved inadequate early on and an additional mesh-covered opening in the side panel was formed.

Plumbing passed pressurized air forward from the turbochargers into the bottom of the large Behr intercooler matrices housed at right angles to the tub within the side pod. Cooled compressed air was then ducted upwards through big-bore intercooler pipes into the round induction 'logs' on top of the engine. In the interim cars there had been too little space between the back of the old tubs and the front of the engine to pass the intercooler pipes under the cam-box mounting plates as intended. On MP4/2 space was allowed, so the pipes could tuck in neatly within Barnard's original silhouette.

The oil tank was incorporated into the engine/transmission adaptor plate, as on the interim car but now redesigned, while the gearbox itself was the familiar McLaren unit employing modified predominantly Hewland internals as on the old Cosworth cars, and now working overtime to cope with the 750 bhp of the TAG Turbo compared to the 550 bhp-plus of the ultimate Cosworth DFYs! Its oil system had been extensively revised to help, but by mid-season '84 Barnard would be working on an all-new transmission and the team was 'carrying eggs' all year where the gearbox was concerned.

Beneath the tail ramp, which generated valuable ground-effects download, the exhaust and turbocharger wastegate pipes exited in flush vents, playing their gases across the diffuser surface to entrain airflow. This created an early problem as the gearbox shroud suffered under exhaust heat. A metal-sided gearbox shroud was run for a while, which Barnard hated, until a heat-resistant carbon-fibre shroud became available, and survived happily with the exhaust gases playing across its outer surfaces.

His rear suspension redesign retained the same general layout as before, with wide-based flat-section lower wishbones, fabricated top rocker arms

actuating inboard coil/damper units and a single raked-back top link each side to control toe-in and camber. But now the rocker arms raked back from inboard, where the coil/damper mounts had moved further forward, as permitted by the shorter V6 engine. This allowed an even slimmer rear bodyline, hugging the engine up top and the gearbox down below and considerably enhancing airflow over both the lower ramp surface and the centre-pillared rear wing above it all.

As the new cars were being completed, just in time for the start of the season, so a production engine specification was frozen for the TAG Turbo unit. To save weight over the ten or so development prototypes used in 1983, it used titanium main crankcase studs and a lightweight cast-magnesium inlet manifold which replaced the hefty original bolt-together machined-section type used for shape experimentation.

MI's requirement was for a float of some 15 to 20 complete race engines with some five to ten extra sets of parts available at any time. By June 1984 they would have complete engines Nos. 21-35 in use.

True to Barnard's philosophy of extending the thinking time to the maximum before building late and building right, two new MP4/2s were completed in time for a brief three-day test at Ricard-Castellet before their Brazilian GP debut at Rio on 25 March. There the opening round of the 1984 World Championship was decided largely on fuel economy and most teams were in trouble towards the end of the hot, thirsty race. Porsche and Bosch had got their sums right, and Prost won after Lauda had looked likely to, profiting from the demise of some quick Ferrari and Renault opposition.

There were 16 Championship rounds in 1984 of which McLaren International won no less than 12, Prost winning the seven GPs at Rio, Imola, Monaco – rain-shortened, scoring half-points – Hockenheim, Zandvoort, *ersatz* Nürburgring and Estoril, Lauda adding five more victories, at Kyalami, Dijon-Prenois, Brands Hatch, Österreichring and Monza. Crucially, Lauda took four second places, at Montreal, Hockenheim, Zandvoort and Estoril, while Prost was second only once – at Kyalami – then third in Montreal and fourth in Detroit. Lauda accumulated 72 Championship points, compared to his faster team-mate's 71½, to clinch his third title in the final race of the season at Estoril, which Prost actually won with the Austrian second.

Little Prost could have tried no harder, having equalled Jimmy Clark's record number of GP wins in one season, yet he still only finished second to Lauda's reliable skills.

Meanwhile McLaren International scored the most convincing victory in the history of the Constructors' Cup competition with no less than 143.5 points to Ferrari's humble 57.5 in second place. It was a demonstration of crushing superiority unprecedented in modern Formula 1.

McLaren-TAG Turbo-by-Porsche MP4/2s had started 32 times in those 16 GPs and had won 12 of them – 75 per cent – and added five second places, four of them in team 1-2 finishes, plus one third, two fourths and one seventh, retiring 11 times.

The statisticians discovered that Prost had led 34.47 per cent of the season's race laps, Lauda ranking third in this respect behind Piquet of Brabham, leading 16.78 per cent. McLaren cars had led 51.25 per cent of the season's Championship race laps, totalling 1440 miles in the lead, against Brabham's 24.08 per cent – 714 miles.

Such were the pressures of race preparation upon the TAG Turbo project that special qualifying 'screamer' engines were not prepared to combat the Brabham-BMW speciality in this field. Even so, Prost took pole position three times against Piquet's nine which included a Brabham-BMW hat-trick of pole positions in the final GPs of the year. Lotus took two pole positions, one to each of their drivers, de Angelis and Mansell, Ferrari one with Alboreto and Renault one with Tambay.

The MP4/2 made its mark first time out with Prost at Rio, Brazilian GP, 1984. Here we can see the 'McLaren tail' with its aerodynamic diffuser ramps passing through rear suspension.

In comparison, however, the McLarens took eight of the season's fastest *race* laps using GP distance boost and power, and perhaps significantly while only two of these fastest laps came in the first half of the season, the other six were grouped together in the final eight races as Porsche's rebuild programme got into its stride and the team gained turbo experience. Against this octet of McLaren fastest laps, Brabham set only two unequalled, Ferrari two and these two marques shared a third between them; Renault set two, and Toleman one in the rain at Monaco with Senna driving his heart out.

Further examining the results, it could be argued that McLaren were lucky to win at Rio, where the opposition had problems, at Monaco, where Prost seemed set to lose his lead just as the red flag went out, and at Österreichring, where Lauda's gearbox broke but Piquet's pursuing Brabham was in tyre trouble and his team failed to appreciate that the leading McLaren was crippled.

But any team on the crest of a winning wave makes 90 per cent of its own luck. Part of the trick is simply sticking around, fuel-efficiently, until the race ends, and another part is to run fast enough to break the opposition before they can break you.

A new Gleason-type differential was introduced at Monaco and retained thereafter and at the same event the team obtained their first specially commissioned lightweight turbocharger housings from KKK. These allowed tighter internal clearances for higher boost and effectively were used for the rest of the year.

The team's biggest problem was simply to get parts made quickly enough. Porsche struggled desperately hard to come to terms with the frantic pressures of the Formula 1 calendar and McLaren's taut rebuild schedules.

The team tested different front uprights and other modifications during the year, but frequently found no conclusive advantage so no changes were made to the race cars.

At Detroit both MP4/2s broke their front anti-roll bars, which were not strong enough to withstand the bumps. Barnard had to re-stress the design and ordered new bars in titanium. They were long in coming, so heavier interim bars ran meantime, which grieved him.

In general then, the McLarens ran this fantastic season with incredibly little modification, evidence of how right had been the original thinking. There were in fact only two notable bodywork changes. One came in Austria where they ran a complete new front wing package intended to enhance ground effect and sensitivity although 'the length of time it takes to do the wind tunnel work and then to tool up the carbon-fibre wing itself' had delayed even this development.

In Holland came the debut of an enlarged turbocharger air intake on the rear bodywork side, square now in place of the original rectangular vertical slot. The team played around with an assortment of ducts and trunking to cool their McLaren-SEP calipers and carbon brakes, but they ended the season with effectively the same ducts as those they had started with, having never run iron brakes at all in either race or practice.

To make this remarkable team's achievement even more extraordinary, only four complete MP4/2s had been built, with a fifth tub held in reserve, but the fourth car had missed its target completion date in time for the Brands Hatch test just prior to the mid-season US tour, so instead of joining the race team for the trip it went direct into the test team.

Schedules were then so tight that after testing 'MP4/2-4' could never be rebuilt and race-prepared in time to join the race team, so it remained purely a test chassis for the rest of the year. Thus the McLaren-TAG Turbos' transcendant first full season was accomplished with only three race team cars. Lauda became the first driver in modern times to win the World Championship while driving the same car all season: this was chassis 'MP4/2-1'.

Meanwhile, 'MP4/2-2' was Prost's regular assigned car, but he was forced to race the spare chassis '3 in South Africa, and again at Imola and Hockenheim – winning both times – and finally at Monza. This car was also used in testing before the completion of chassis '4.

In Austria, where Prost spun off on oil and reported he had been holding in fourth gear, gearbox strip-down suggested from the condition of the selector mechanism that only fifth had been held in with any force. The car was not damaged by the spin so his inability to restart its stalled engine was infuriating.

The McLarens were by this time unusual in still carrying onboard starter motors with ring-gear teeth machined into the engine flywheel. But a stalled and hot turbo engine demands a much fiercer churn on the starter than a hot Cosworth before it will fire, and the team's old MP4/1-style aluminium pressure-air bottle had insufficient capacity for the job. However, an aluminium bottle large enough to restart the TAG Turbo would

Top: *Prost's 1985 Championship-winning MP4/2B at Imola where it won on the road but was disqualified for being underweight. The rear winglets of 1984 were now illegal; note the large ducts venting radiator/cooler air, louvred vents above turbos.* Above: *TAG Turbo's V6 shows off its 80-degree vee angle, high-swept exhausts and KKK turbochargers.*

be very heavy. Consequently, Barnard had asked Hercules to spin up some double-capacity half-weight pressure vessels in carbon-fibre. As Prost spun away the Austrian GP so the first batch of these vessels were sitting on Barnard's desk in Woking. They had not been fitted because when tested they leaked air . . .

Through this season the team still experienced engine problems, which fortunately were confined mainly to testing and practice. The V6 was dogged by mysterious water loss, Bosch's electronics eventually came under control, while most engine breakages involved burn-down failures, torching down the side of the piston after early valvegear misbehaviour had been corrected at the end of 1983.

Hans Mezger's team of three engineers, five design-draughtsmen and 27 mechanics divided into two groups for R&D and construction at Porsche Weissach had done a superb job on their demanding customer's behalf.

Rival team drivers raved about the TAG Turbo engine's superb pick-up out of slow corners, while McLaren's men continually bitched about inadequate throttle response and Prost recalled Renault's pick-up with affection. Mezger admitted, 'We can certainly win more easily on fast flowing circuits' but by the end of the season all circuits seemed to come much the same. The engine management system chip was set up for a specific quality fuel, which through a 'fuel company cock-up' was not supplied at Zolder for the Belgian GP. Practice there saw a series of shattering TAG Turbo piston failures, and other problems sidelined both McLarens in the race – a double retirement which would recur only once, in Dallas. Further piston failures punctuated practice for the French GP at Dijon, but Porsche had the fix, and in the race there Lauda won and Prost shone on newly built V6s flown down overnight from Weissach.

Barnard would admit to having some 750 bhp available in race tune, and only late in the season did McLaren adopt additional intercooler and radiator cooling for their qualifying shots, without besting Brabham-BMW let it be said. Michelin tyres were as consistent as ever while Goodyear's decision to adopt radial-ply construction had put them into a 'catch-up situation' all year. Late on, McLaren felt Michelin's development was lagging, and this was the only prior warning they would receive of the French company's sudden close-season withdrawal from Formula 1.

It is worth considering the context in which these remarkable McLaren-TAG Turbo cars shone so brightly. Were they making the best of 'a bad season' which simultaneously afflicted Brabham, Ferrari, Renault and the rest? Was it really the poor performance of others which made the McLarens look so good? Or was it the clear superiority of the Porsche-produced engine which would have achieved the same success in any other frontline chassis?

Where so many rival teams had an unreliable year I suspect that, excepting Ferrari which suffered other problems, they really had to run so hard just to keep McLaren in sight that they simply came apart at the seams.

In qualifying, and occasionally in the race, Brabham-BMW had an obvious performance edge and Piquet drove better than ever for them all season. He regularly out-qualified the McLarens and equally often led races before retiring. Some other cars arguably outhandled the McLarens, notably the Lotus-Renaults, but on The Day only Brabham-BMW posed them a consistent and serious threat. On the occasions when McLaren did not win from strength, they were always ready to win on reliability, fuel efficiency and driver wit. And of course they had the finest all-round driver pairing in competition.

It is interesting to ponder the crucial role still being played in the mid-1980s by the dismissively nicknamed *Assemblatori* teams in achieving success for the great constructors through their chassis engineering skills and simple racing wisdom. Where would Porsche have been without McLaren, BMW without Brabham, Honda without Williams, or indeed Renault – in what was for their works team a troubled season – without Lotus?

What wins races is possession of the best combination on race day. If any vital ingredient is missing, the chance is lost. The superbly integrated McLaren MP4/2 chassis/engine package proved good enough for its drivers to extract virtually everything the TAG Turbo engine had to offer, and that was plenty. Not only did it have lots of competitive horsepower, it also offered much useable mid-range torque. Bosch's super-expensive tailor-made management system made it the most fuel-efficient F1 engine of the year. The cars always finished with quite a lot of fuel left in their tanks. McLaren ran Michelin tyres at a time when they were the class of the field, and in the services of Prost and Lauda they had two of the top four drivers of their day. At most circuits on race day this combination proved just too hot for the opposition to handle.

Some observers, notably in the European press, doubted McLaren's contribution to the equation and put it all down to Porsche know-how. They were deluding themselves. Porsche did a superb job on TAG Turbo's behalf, no question, but McLaren had won the 'Cosworth class' in their last four outings with the DFV/DFY engines through 1983, and they simply continued that

dominance at a higher level after receiving their turbocharged engines.

And they were '*their*' engines, for McLaren International had commissioned the design in broad detail and policed the project without compromise while Porsche designed and manufactured the TTE-PO1 units so brilliantly for them.

At the end of 1984, the glory of McLaren-TAG Turbo and Porsche was truly indivisible.

For 1985, Barnard set out to build upon that incredibly successful season of '84, updating the existing MP4/2 design around the existing moulded carbon-fibre chassis with all-new bodywork, a new pushrod rear suspension, new front uprights and a new hub package.

The new year's major regulation change was the banning of the additional winglets on the rear 'foils which had enabled more download to be generated in '83-84. Winter tunnel testing enabled recovery of some lost download with even less aerodynamic drag. This meant an overall increase in aerodynamic efficiency, and with extra power found for '85 by all engine manufacturers, straightline speeds and lap times plummeted.

McLaren's major chassis work centred around Barnard's needs as follows: 'What I wanted to produce was a car which was totally predictable on the servicing side, so we could say this part does 500 miles and that part does 1000 miles; so we could accurately life all our components and then, apart from accidents, we could accurately predict how many parts we would need for the year's racing. I wanted a gearbox, engine and four suspension corners which we could completely ignore for two races at a time. With two pairs of races spaced only one week apart this was vital. I have nightmares about trying to race-prepare a car away from home in circuit lock-ups . . .'

McLaren MP4/2B cars were built up on chassis '3 (spare), '4 (Lauda) and '5 (Prost) in time for the first of the new World Championship series races at Rio, and old tub number '2 would join the team for Prost from Silverstone. An all-new chassis, '6, was completed for Prost in time for the South African GP at Kyalami, and had the distinction of being the first carbon moulding to be made in Woking rather than by Hercules in Salt Lake City.

Early in the season the new car proved itself as good as the team's 1984 Champion design had been, with Prost winning the majority of the races on the road, but losing on disqualification at Imola where his MP4/2B ended up underweight through over-consumption of fuel, oil, brake pads and tyres.

Then in the middle of the season the McLarens seemed to go off form, suffering especially in Montreal and Detroit, but came back with a vengeance on the fast circuits from the British GP at Silverstone forwards.

There were two main reasons for this. One was a suspension change, the other was the behaviour of McLaren's carbon-fibre brakes on the demanding American courses compared to their behaviour on fast circuits where they were not subjected to such intensive use.

John explained both the suspension and brake problems like this: 'Before we made the front suspension geometry change we were not really *plagued* by anything, no dreadful problems at all, but the drivers complained that the cars seemed to fall into an oversteer in/understeer out condition which was not very predictable and could be improved. They did not have total confidence in their cars' handling. So we just moved the suspension pick-ups and achieved a considerable improvement in feel.'

Prost tested the modification at Silverstone before the British GP, and a few days later Barnard told me: 'Just you wait and see what happens at Silverstone in the British GP, I think we will be in good shape there . . .' And they were, Prost dominant.

Subsequently the MP4/2Bs' rear suspension geometry was also modified to bring the cars into still better balance, Prost's assigned race car at Österreichring having the all-modified suspension though he actually raced and won in his spare car,

which lacked the latest rear suspension revision.

The team ran a new design rear wing and different flaps on the '84-style front wings, but most of the year was dominated by incessant work on the brakes. Barnard observed '. . . our blokes will probably remember 1985 as the Year of the Brake Duct!'

Throughout 1984 McLaren had run carbon brakes with their own design aluminium twin calipers, without problems. Nowhere did they run cast-iron discs. Ending that season John was happy with the brakes and felt they could remain unchanged for 1985 . . . But he was wrong.

They ran higher turbo boost in race trim in cars generating less aerodynamic drag, which meant they ran much faster at the end of the straights.

'The problem with brakes is that in effect they either work OK or don't work at all, giving all kinds of problems. Unless you reach their limit and run into problems you have no way of knowing how close to that limit you are. Although we had no trouble with them in 1984 I suspect now, looking back, that we were using 99 per cent of their capacity! But we had no way of knowing how close to the limit we had come.

'In '85, because we were going quicker between the corners, by mid-season we just lacked sufficient braking capacity.

'We had a real struggle in Canada, we had been on the limit in Monaco even though we won, and suddenly those teams using their Brembo calipers bought off the shelf from your friendly dealer looked in better shape than we were with our specially designed and made McLaren type . . . In Detroit we just ran out of brakes, simple as that, and at that time I got heavily into the braking side and looked at everything in the system.

'Ricard and Silverstone, of course, are no problem for brakes; then we tested at the Nürburgring and were really in deep trouble but by the time of the German GP I'd found the problem and fixed it and that made it all come right again. Before that we had been beaten in Canada and were a complete flop in Detroit, even Monaco was a terrible struggle, and we tried so many different types of brake duct our chaps were going crazy . . .'

During the winter there was evidently some alarm within the team at the apparent lack of direction within the TAG Turbo engine project. However, they got back into gear again, settled their 1985 engine spec in time for Rio and then made few further changes. In race tune on race day the Porsche-engineered power unit still offered the most consistent combination of power, reliability and economy in Formula 1.

New mirror-image, tailor-made turbochargers, were delivered in mid-season. The original interchangeable type demanded a slightly different exhaust system either side of the engine to feed them which slightly compromised the efficiency of one engine bank, so the new mirror-image KKKs put this right.

The persistent and mysterious water loss which had plagued the engines during 1984 had been cured, while the very compact and talented Bosch Motronic management system development team under Dr Udo Zucker had – in Barnard's words – 'Done a brilliant job of making that system perform really well . . . I think they really do deserve enormous credit for what they have done. Most races have seen us use all our fuel and the Bosch system has enabled us to do that perfectly while other teams have to carry extra fuel weight just in case their management system doesn't quite get consumption right. This allows us to start with a minimum load. We missed out at Imola when the car used more oil and more brake pad and more of everything than we expected, but everywhere else it's been very good.

'Bosch's management system is a marvellous piece of kit – it really has come good and people should be more aware that it's a Bosch development.'

This was a very different attitude to 1984's, but the early stormy days of the McLaren/Bosch partnership were now long gone and relationships were now marked by a healthy air of mutual respect.

Monaco 1986 – Alain Prost's McLaren MP4/2C's TAG Turbo V6 engine during final adjustment, showing off the car's balanced caliper carbon brake installation with beautifully moulded and matched cooling duct, pushrod-operated inboard suspension layout, KKK turbocharger and massive dry-sump oil tank. Engines No. '42' and '28' were used by Prost and Rosberg in that race. Highest TAG engine No. raced was '54', Johansson, Austrian GP, 1987.

ing two races due to a wrist injury suffered in a minor practice incident at Spa late-season, and he finished only three times, 4-5-1, at Imola, *ersatz* Nürburgring and Zandvoort – the last victory of his superb career as he announced his intention to retire at the end of the season. He retired after a minor crash in Adelaide caused by locking rear brakes, while leading handsomely.

For 1986 Barnard and McLaren International plus TAG Turbo Engines (by Porsche) found themselves aiming at a third consecutive Constructors' Championship title . . .

It proved to be quite a difficult year, not least because of John Barnard's increasing apparent disinterest in remaining a part of MI's growing empire. Ron Dennis and others prominent within the company came to appreciate the situation was untenable, and after five and a half successful seasons as technical director of McLaren International, John's MI career reached its end. In August he was gone, off to brainstorm a new Ferrari for 1988. He left the team midway through their spirited defence of the Constructors' title which had been their own in 1984-85. Engineers Steve Nichols and Tim Wright took over pending appointment of a new engineering director for 1987, and as expected they and the team did an effective job in bringing the season to a successful conclusion . . .

McLaren's 1986 MP4/2C cars looked superficially little changed from 1985's '2Bs or even 1984's supreme MP4/2s. They didn't even look far removed – unless you stood them side-by-side – from Barnard's original carbon-composite MP4/1s of 1981 . . .

At least John could joke about this long-lasting family resemblance, secure in its success having proved the quality of his basic concept: 'I now know, I'm absolutely convinced, that provided you put your finger on the right bits and pieces you can design a chassis which will go on for YEARS!' he told me.

McLaren's use of detachable body panels to provide aerodynamic shape, cladding a straight-edged structural inner tub, had always allowed the team total aerodynamic flexibility. Changing external shape did not dictate entirely new chassis mouldings. Equally, the tub's external shape posed no aerodynamic restrictions.

Even so, the new MP4/2C tubs moulded for 1986 were modified in detail from the 1985 '/2Bs, largely to take advantage of FISA's new 195-litre fuel cell restriction. The driver was seated lower, less upright than before, enabling subtle aerodynamic improvements which, coupled with a rear suspension change, plus repositioning of the turbochargers to improve inlet airflow, produced a faster car. The gearchange linkage was taken inside the tub instead of – as before – coming over the top of its right side at a 15-degree angle, which the drivers had never really liked. This move was dictated by Barnard's requirement to rearrange the turbocharger inlets.

This '/2C-spec configuration was actually the TAG Turbo V6's third turbocharger location. It was in-line, with the axis of the turbo fore-and-aft, drawing air from up front near the side pod radiator inlets. This change enabled MI physically to accommodate Bosch's latest engine management system air-sensing units, which measured actual mass-flow instead of merely volume, so monitoring changes in air density, a vital factor in fuel-efficient power production.

This was in theory the perfect method of regulating fuel supply, because once MI's latest Bosch Motronic MP1:7 management system computer had been told what air-fuel ratio was required, its

Apart from remapping engine performance profiles to match differing circuit demands, and the mirror-turbo introduction, there was little alteration to the TAG Turbo engine. It remained one which would not accept greatly increased turbocharger boost merely for qualifying, and the team was always at a horsepower disadvantage there against BMW, Renault and Ferrari. But in terms of race distance fuel economy on race day, the McLaren-TAGs were normally right there, leading the pace.

Although McLaren again won races consistently, Prost profited while Lauda's sister car was consistently unreliable, surviving once to beat Prost

narrowly at Zandvoort.

The team's change from Michelin to Goodyear for '85 initially found the Goodyear rear tyre was much less durable as a race tyre, which created problems of much less grip at the rear than in the front though that situation later reversed.

Prost's 16 1985 races yielded 13 finishes, all of them supposedly scoring points although his clear victory at Imola was disallowed as his car was underweight at post-race scrutineering. His finishing record read 1-(1)-1-3-3-1-2-1-2-1-3-4-3, including wins at Rio, (Imola), Monaco, Silverstone, Austria and Monza.

In contrast, Lauda's season saw 14 starts, miss-

Alain Prost was astonished and delighted to win not only the 1986 Australian GP at Adelaide but also to become the first driver to achieve back-to-back World Championship titles since Jack Brabham in 1959-60. Here he uncharacteristically bounces 'MP4/2C-5' over the kerbing.

new sensors could then tell it the mass-flow of air at any given moment, and it could compute how much fuel it needed to mix with that mass-flow to meet the required ratio. This was a continuous adjustment which promised the ultimate in best horsepower-cum-fuel economy under all conditions. The system would compensate automatically for changes of altitude, humidity, barometric pressure, everything. But for much of the year it was not raced, simply because its reliability compared to the old system was not yet proven, but as McLaren recovered from their mid-season dip, Bosch produced some definite management system improvements which triggered resurgence in time for Porsche's home race – the German GP at Hockenheim. But there the fuel level computer read-out was to go haywire instead . . .

Four revised new carbon-composite MP4/2C tubs were moulded at the Woking factory, using raw material supplied by MI's former sub-contractors, the Hercules Corporation.

A six-speed gearbox, based on the old five-speeder with a revised end plate assembly, became standard because terminal speeds were becoming so high that some rev jumps were now too big to keep within the TAG Turbo engine's most effective rev-band. These mods also allowed the gearbox to accommodate both reverse and an improved lubrication system.

The Porsche-engineered TAG Turbo engines themselves had been little modified. I believe only five new engines were produced to complete MI's

float of around 25 – at a reputed $100,000 a time – most changes being on Bosch's electronic side although some improved turbo compressors emerged which offered more boost without the old penalty in back-pressure.

Keke Rosberg replaced Niki Lauda as Prost's team-mate, and when he first applied his vast Williams-Honda engine experience to the TAG Turbo unit, he declared there was little difference in mid- to low-range torque, but at high revs the Honda seemed much stronger.

The new '/2Cs were indeed another stride forward from the twin-Championship winning '/2s and '/2Bs and as the new season progressed McLaren went swinging along, no big problems, until – as usual – the dreaded Detroit . . .

Prost was just being his usual staggeringly competent, cheerful self – arguably the most complete driver in the business – but meanwhile Keke Rosberg in place of the Prost-like smooth-driving Lauda caused McLaren some headaches. He quickly exhibited a problem with which the team eventually sympathised.

Typically, Ron Dennis was more inclined to accommodate the rugged newcomer than John Barnard, the hard man: 'I don't think he realised how different a McLaren was going to be to drive compared to what he'd had before because our car didn't respond to his driving style in the way the Williams had . . .'

John would not compromise his car merely to suit what he regarded as the new driver's uncultured driving style, until after Monaco when the Finn's car set-up was finally altered for him. 'It wasn't just oversteery . . . there's all sorts of degrees of entering a corner, how fast you apply the lock and how much weight transfer that application induces . . . he was then much happier with the car' . . . and he showed it by leading the race in Canada.

This wide new disparity between car set-ups for the team's two drivers then caused a considerable problem regarding the spare car, because it was no longer speedily adaptable to either man as it had been throughout the Prost/Lauda period.

After their strong finish to 1985, when they won the last three GPs in succession, the Williams-Honda team seemed set for top Championship honours in 1986.

McLaren ultimately deployed five MP4/2Cs against them, the first three being ready in time for the Brazilian GP at Rio, opening the season on 23 March, while chassis '4 made its debut as spare car at Spa for the Belgian GP on 25 May and '5 appeared new for Prost at Estoril on 21 September.

For the curtain-raiser at Rio in March, new boy Rosberg immediately out-qualified reigning World Champion Prost, but both new MP4/2Cs retired with piston failure, extending MI's losing run to four consecutive GPs. This was also the second consecutive race in which MI had not even managed to finish . . .

Was their once dominant edifice crumbling? The Brazilian piston failures were traced to engine management problems, and in Spain the cars then exhibited too much understeer during qualifying but in race morning warm-up Prost and Rosberg set quickest times. MI's race strategy was then ruined by misleadingly pessimistic fuel-state cockpit read-outs, causing both drivers to soft-pedal – finishing 3-4.

As always, the San Marino GP at Imola was to be all about fuel efficiency. In 1985 Prost had been disqualified after victory when his car ran out of fuel and proved under-weight when weighed. This time he ran out of fuel just before the finish but was able to stutter across the line, weighing-in legally at post-race scrutineering . . .

Rosberg ran out of fuel and lost second place two

laps earlier, having led for the first time in a McLaren from laps 29-33. Now he was classified only fifth.

Prost then started from pole in Monaco, led throughout and Rosberg drove luridly through the field to complete a fine McLaren 1-2. It was Alain's hat-trick of three consecutive Monaco victories in McLaren-TAG Turbo MP4/2-series cars.

At Spa for the Belgian GP, Prost was involved in a first-corner collision, driving on after replacing the tattered nose cone and wings in the pits and finishing sixth, setting fastest lap despite 'odd' handling. Rosberg seemed to ignore warnings to maintain low boost in order to stave off predicted piston problems, and after tigering through the field in the opening laps after the first-corner delay his engine predictably failed. Barnard was fulsome about the plus from Spa: 'Alain's comeback drive there was quite something, it was amazing, because after that first-corner shunt, the stop to fit a new nose and losing a lap he was blindingly fast even with a bent engine mount . . .

'When we got his car back . . . its top right-hand engine plate was bent like a banana . . . you can't bend one engine plate and leave the rest straight. The whole engine must have been skewed which means his car was literally bent in the middle!'

Despite which, Prost's post-race engine read-out revealed his use of normal race-boost throughout. Even in that situation the contemporary master had taken his lap times out of himself, not his car, the sign of pure class . . .

In Montreal, Porsche introduced a new fuel-feed system for the TAG engines with the fuel pump modified to provide a separate feed to each cylinder bank instead of a common feed as before. As so often, Barnard's concentration upon race tune in preference to qualifying saw Prost and Rosberg qualifying 4-6 before setting the quickest times in race morning warm-up. But in the race that afternoon Williams-Honda finished 1-3, McLaren 2-4 with everybody else resoundingly lapped. While still fuel-efficient and reliable, the McLaren-TAGs now clearly lacked the pace of the Williams-Honda.

At Detroit, never McLaren's favourite circuit, the MP4/2Cs qualified 7-9 after Alain had crashed into the wall at the exit from the chicane. The cars' lack of grip was so severe they even resorted to loading extra fuel in an effort to find some traction. Prost, with an intermittent cut-out problem, finished third; Rosberg's transmission failed.

The French GP then saw the Williams-Hondas dominant again, the McLarens preserving their tyres better but being clearly out-performed. The result mirrored Canada, Williams 1-3, McLaren 2-4, but Prost emerged heading the Drivers' table, with five points separating Williams from McLaren in the Constructors' Cup.

The performance gap between Williams-Honda and McLaren-TAG Turbo was underlined in the British GP at Brands Hatch, where Prost finished third but lapped! Rosberg had posted the first retirement with gearbox failure, a sobering day for McLaren International . . .

This mid-season slump had to be analysed. In Canada, Williams had demonstrated a sudden edge on fuel consumption, and Detroit was again a poor McLaren race, 'but we couldn't really see why'. At Ricard the cars ran well but the drivers had to back off to conserve sufficient fuel to finish . . . then at Brands Hatch despite being set up precisely in successful test-session form, they suddenly would not handle. The only possible explanation for this appeared to be some tiny external change, probably in the tyres.

For Hockenheim, revised TAG Turbo engines saw Rosberg suddenly dominant. He had never appreciated the stable inherent understeer designed into the McLarens and as preferred by the likes of Prost and Lauda. The Finnish former World Champion was a wholehearted racing 'animal' who loved an 'oversteery' car which would look into the corners early and respond to his hurling it about.

Such a driving style was effectively anathema to Barnard, but Rosberg considered that at Hockenheim for the first time he had a McLaren

which did not understeer. He admitted 'there's a touch of understeer in race trim, but the biggest problem I've had to deal with up to now is an acute "wash-out" understeer where you simply had to back off the throttle to regain grip at the front. Now it's mild by comparison, but the basic problem has been when I have talked about "less understeer", the McLaren engineers have been interpreting in terms of Alain's very fine margins. But I was talking about a very drastic change indeed. Now we're running a lot less rear wing at this circuit and I'm feeling really optimistic!'

The McLarens headed the starting grid line-up, but Piquet won for Williams by catching Rosberg just six laps from the finish after driving another two-stop race. The Finn in fact led most of the way, but after being caught and passed by Piquet he felt his engine die as he changed down for the chicane on the outward leg of the circuit, and he failed to complete the lap.

Prost actually entered the stadium section of the course on his last lap in third place before his engine also ran dry, the McLarens being classified 5-6, both victims of optimistic cockpit fuel level read-outs.

In Hungary a shambolic race for MI saw them suffer for lack of driver-to-pit radio as used by other leading teams, Prost and Rosberg both demanding attention in the pits at the same time, the World Champion for an engine management problem, the Finn for tyres. Prost eventually collided with Arnoux's Ligier, Rosberg retiring with a puncture and deranged rear suspension.

Come the Austrian GP, Prost had not won since Monaco and badly needed another nine points to defend his title. On the Styrian course his MP4/2C outran the Williams-Hondas and despite his TAG engine cutting out during the last five laps – 'In places I was freewheeling, then selecting a gear and trying to jerk it back into life' – he won by a clear lap from Alboreto's reliable but slow Ferrari. This was the 24th win of Prost's career, equalling Fangio's one-time career record, just one behind Jim Clark's and three behind Jackie Stewart's all-time career best.

Rosberg had seemed about to make it another McLaren 1-2 finish when his engine died due to an electrical short circuit.

This result left the Drivers' Championship nicely poised with Mansell – who had retired this time – leading on 55 points from Prost on 53. Williams retained 102 points from McLaren's 72, and there were four rounds remaining.

Before the next race, the Italian GP at Monza, John Barnard left McLaren International. Since he had sold his company shareholding he had been an employee, and he had already told Ron Dennis he intended to move on. What Dennis then saw as Barnard's increasingly open disloyalty in publicly talking terms with other potential employers spelled an abrupt end – 'It was a bad example for the staff'. John joined Ferrari, leaving Steve Nichols and Tim Wright to extend their control of preparation and race-engineering to complete this hard-fought season.

At Monza, Prost had to start from the pit lane in his spare car, and after an heroic drive through the field – punctuated to replace a disintegrating nose-cone assembly – he was tardily black-flagged for a starting rules infringement, only for his TAG engine to blow up before he could stop.

Rosberg fought against what he regarded as excessive understeer and daunting fuel-consumption warnings, and finished fourth.

After this race, Mansell of Williams-Honda led Prost by 61 points to 56 in the Drivers' table – while Williams had moved out of sight in the Constructors' Cup . . . there was to be no Ferrari-style hat-trick of Constructors' Championships for McLaren International . . .

The final European round followed at Estoril, Portugal, on 21 September. There Prost and Rosberg qualified 3-7, Alain running a new chassis 'MP4/2C-5', while Keke's car carried novel chrome-yellow livery to promote a new allegedly low-tar cigarette brand.

Prost finished second behind Mansell after Senna's Lotus-Renault ran low on fuel on the clos-

ing lap and Piquet's Williams had spun due to locking rear brakes – shades of Lauda in Adelaide the previous year! Rosberg's smoking TAG engine finally blew up.

The Mexican GP was then revived on 12 October. After Mansell's Portuguese *tour de force* he had Prost's title at his mercy as Prost qualified only sixth, Rosberg 11th, but an attack of Montezuma's Revenge suffered by the Englishman during qualifying persuaded the solicitous Frenchman to raise his hand at the drivers' briefing in response to the standard 'Any questions?', asking 'Yes, 'ave you a brown flag for Nigel . . .?'

Mansell then muffed his start and as the Williams-Honda team's race fell apart with almost grotesque tyre-wear, Gerhard Berger won, running his Benetton-BMW non-stop on Pirelli tyres. Prost's engine occasionally fluffed onto only five cylinders, and salvaged second place, closing the gap on Mansell who finished only fifth. Rosberg's race ended with a puncture after running in third position.

So the stage was set for a grand Drivers' Championship finale in Adelaide on 26 October. Mansell had totalled 72 points but now had to drop this Mexican pair as only his best 11 scoring finishes counted under contemporary rules. Alain Prost had leap-frogged Piquet's 63 points to regain second place, now with 64 of his total 65 points counting. Thus he was six points behind Mansell and needed a second place without Nigel scoring to become the first man since Jack Brabham in 1959-60 to achieve back-to-back Drivers' Championship victories.

In Australia Mansell did everything right, qualifying on pole with Prost fourth fastest. Rosberg in his farewell race – like Lauda there the previous season he was poised to retire – qualified seventh.

He was committed to helping his team-mate to the Championship if possible, and apparently throwing all caution to the winds he took an early lead, extending it with gusto. While Mansell and Prost both kept out of early trouble, Rosberg led at increasing speed until lap 62 of the scheduled 82. At that point Piquet was second, Mansell third and Prost fourth – four points to the Englishman, three to the Frenchman – the title would be Mansell's.

But on lap 63 Rosberg suddenly felt an awful vibration and rumbling from the rear of his car. Convinced the engine's bottom-end had let go he switched off and parked, giving his car only a cursory glance. Had he looked more closely he would have discovered that only the left-rear tyre tread had delaminated – the flapping section having caused all the noise.

Before the end of the following lap, a similar but more spectacular Goodyear tyre failure put Mansell out of the race. Williams called in Piquet for a precautionary tyre-change, leaving Prost leading, and anxious: '. . . for the last 15 laps my fuel read-out showed that I was five litres short, so I never reckoned there was any chance of making it. In other circumstances I would 'ave eased right back and tried to conserve things, but on this occasion I 'ad to win, so I forced myself to believe there was something wrong with the computer. I just pressed on, and as it turned out, I finished with it still reading five litres down. Obviously today the computer was wrong . . .' he beamed.

So he won the Australian GP, and joined the select band of only four men ever to have achieved consecutive Drivers' Championship titles in the 37-season history of the competition – Alberto Ascari, Juan-Manuel Fangio, Jack Brabham and now Alain Prost. With this 25th GP victory he had surpassed Fangio's career total and equalled Jim Clark's 1968-1973 record.

For three consecutive seasons the World Champion Driver had won his crown in McLaren International's dayglo red and white cars – but they would not make it four in a row come 1987. . . when not even an all-new MP4/3-series chassis could compensate for a TAG Turbo engine at the end of its useful life . . .

But what a story it had to tell.

Carbon-Composites

In the mid-'80s the phrase 'composite materials' assumed almost mystic significance amongst the racing media. Consider the term literally. There was nothing at all new about 'composite materials'. A composite of wattle and daub is an age-old material, just as was the plant fibre and chopped straw mixed into wet clay to prevent the Pharaohs' bricks cracking while they dried in the Egyptian sun. Papier mâché too – another composite material.

But composites in Formula 1 take on a diferent hue. Robin Herd introduced aerospace Mallite composite – a sandwich skinned in thin aluminium sheet bonded to end-grain balsa wood filling – in his 1966 M2B monocoque car. It offered great rigidity with minimal weight by the standards of the time.

Sandwich panels confining aluminium-foil hexagonal-cell 'honeycomb' infill between aluminium sheet skins had already become popular in the aviation industry during the 1950s. Such material offered light panels of outstanding stiffness. The Ford J-car of 1966 featured an incredibly strong, driver-protecting honeycomb chassis carried over into the Le Mans-winning 1967 Ford Mark IV, but as one crew member told me 'It was a sonofabitch to work with, and impossible to repair!'

Similar honeycomb panels were used occasionally in Formula 1, a little in Herd's Cosworth 4WD car of '69, a little more in Derek Gardner's experimental mid-series Tyrrells, more in the 1973-76 McLaren M23 and then with Kevlar and Nomex paper honeycomb infill in the 1977 M26.

In 1978 Harvey Postlethwaite made a Wolf chassis around a single sheet of aluminium honeycomb, folded up into a U-section trough, suitably stiffened by interior panels and cross-bulkheads, with the man in the middle and fuel in the back. Patrick Head's Williams FW07, built along similar structural lines, then became the finest aluminium honeycomb racing car ever built.

But others despised the stuff. To make a honeycomb lighter than a comparable-strength structure with simple aluminium sheet panelling, its skins had individually to be less than half the thickness of the simple aluminium panel to allow for the weight of the foil infill. Its critics claimed these thin surface skins simply tore like paper in heavy impacts, offering minimal driver protection, whereas heavier-gauge simple aluminium would absorb energy very effectively by progressive deformation.

Like so many contentious issues, much depended on where and how structural aluminium honeycomb was used. One proven designer told me how aluminium honeycomb was suspect in monocoque use as the epoxy bonding between honeycomb infill and outer skin would fail, allowing the tub to work and flex.

Yet one of his equally proven peers assured me the opposite is true, especially when more modern Redux glues have been used. The 1978 Williams FW06, for example, was bonded with Araldite which was attacked by brake fluid. The FW07s were Reduxed instead and one 1979 tub had covered 30,000 miles by 1985-86 and was still considered 'tight'.

Compared to old-style riveted aluminium tubs in which the rivet holes used to elongate, allowing the rivets to rattle around, and joints to chatter, properly bonded honeycomb monocoques were good news if made by a good team – production honeycomb tubs perhaps less so as quality control is necessarily less strict.

In the old days to re-rivet and reglue an aluminium tub was to give it a real treat . . .

Meanwhile, glass-fibre body panels as used in racing from the early-'50s were a composite more in line with the popular meaning of that term into the '80s.

Drawn fibres of glass spun into yarn, woven into mats and then set into a moulded shape within a cured resin matrix – this is what modern 'composites' are all about.

At this point let us consider Thomas Young (1773-1829) and his Modulus – which merely means a value describing the property of a material.

Young's Modulus puts numbers to the stiffness or otherwise of any material, and it is most illuminating in this context. The Modulus of steel is about 30 million lb per square inch, of wood about 2 million lb, of rubber about 1000 lb.

From around 1960 Government-backed aerospace development in the USA, Britain and Japan sought a new generation of super-stiff, super-light materials, and they came up with filaments of boron in the US – 60 million psi – and carbon in the UK, which I am glad to report had a Young's Modulus of a staggering 110 million psi.

The Americans' method of producing boron fibres – or the shorter form known as 'whiskers' – involved drawing a 0.013 mm tungsten wire through a reaction chamber part-charged with either boron trichloride or boron hydride. The wire was heated electrically like a light-bulb filament to more than 10,000°C whereupon a 0.05 mm layer of boron would build up on its surface.

Boron-composites in resin and aluminium matrices were then produced for aerospace use. They were certainly very light and stiff but boron-fibre cost some $700 a kilogramme – at early-'60s values – and was unsuitable for inexpensive fabrication processes.

Carbon-fibre was more practical. One primitive kind had been produced by Edison when he heated bamboo to make his electric light filaments, then in 1964 a team under Bill Watt at Britain's Royal Aircraft Establishment, Farnborough, succeeded in carburizing polyacrylonitrile (PAN) fibres – basis of the dress fabric Courtelle – under special conditions to produce a very practical fibre possessing very high Modulus and substantial tensile strength.

These fibres were a little weaker than glass fibres, but for their weight they were some eight times stiffer than both glass and conventional engineering metals, and resin-fibre composites made with carbon were extremely light and rigid.

DuPont in America then developed Kevlar which could be made much more simply, without need for the special conditions and intense heat applied in carburizing carbon-fibre. Kevlar comes from an organic polymer, similar to a high-grade cellulose like flax but Kevlar was four times stronger and unlike flax it could not rot, and its Modulus was about a third that of carbon. Compared by weight, Kevlar was not quite so stiff as boron or carbon, but it was quite close behind and was cheaper.

Commercially available carbon-fibre and Kevlar was offered ready-spun into thread then woven and usually pre-saturated in epoxy resin, as 'pre-preg' cloth. Apply a chemical catalyst or carefully controlled temperature and pressure in an autoclave pressure oven and the epoxy cures into a rigid matrix taking up whatever shape the mould containing the cloth might dictate.

The technique was similar to glass-fibre lay-up, but the end product far stronger and very much stiffer per unit weight.

The resin matrix was the key, locking the cloth fibres relative to one another. Fibre orientation within the structure could be aligned to take maximum advantage of their individual tensile strength and great stiffness, and minimize their weakness in compression, for the strength of composite materials of this type is extremely directional.

Once set within a well-cured resin matrix individual fibres could fracture without significant reduction in component strength because the resin matrix spreads the load throughout the cloth fibres, and where one might fail there's always another right alongside which will not. Fractures seldom propagate as extensive cracks because the plastic matrix does not transmit cracks, and fibres can be arranged as 'crack stoppers'.

Quite unlike steel or aluminium, any shape holes can be cut into a composite carbon panel or moulded monocoque with little danger of starting cracks from a sharp corner as you most certainly would if you cut a square hole in an aluminium or steel sheet.

Carbon-fibre became available on the open market in the '70s when Roger Sloman worked on R&D for Fothergill & Harvey of Rochdale who made carbon-fibre pre-preg. He recognized its potential in racing, but was alarmed by its misuse, as when he heard that carbon-fibre wheels were being made despite the material's poor compression performance.

He wrote to the specialist motor sporting press to say as much and soon received calls from Harvey Postlethwaite of Hesketh and John Horsman of Gulf-Mirage. The old Gulf-JW Ford GT40 team had first encountered the then very new – merely three-year-old – carbon material as early as 1967 when they 'won' some from aerospace contacts and used it to stiffen ultra-thin body panels around the wheel-arch edges and – as an open lattice – throughout the larger surfaces. Now Roger Sloman quickly produced stiff and light carbon-fibre wing end plates for Hesketh and airfoils for Gulf, then the Hill GH1 wing pillar followed but there was a breakdown in communication, and the inadequately braced pillar failed in Stommelen's 1975 Spanish GP accident.

Gordon Murray adopted flat carbon panels in the material's first use as a structural chassis element in his 1978 Brabham BT46 as Sloman set up his own Advanced Composite Components company in Heanor, Derby, mainly to produce carbon-fibre racing car wing and skirt components.

The extreme lightweight and high-rigidity combination of moulded carbon-composites attracted Formula 1 designers in 1979-80 as they sought to reconcile ground-effect car requirements for a very slim, low cross-section monocoque chassis with very high torsional rigidity to resist extreme aerodynamic and suspension loadings.

John Barnard blazed the trail as he joined the Project Four team in 1979-80 to design a new Formula 1 car which would become the McLaren MP4/1, and Peter Wright of Team Lotus almost simultaneously took them along a similar path for the Lotus 88, though techniques differed in detail. Similarly Carlo Chiti of Autodelta approached Sloman's ACC/ACT company to manufacture moulded carbon monocoques for Alfa Romeo.

While the Hercules Corporation in Nevada used internal moulding for the McLaren tub, so the 'good side' with a nice shiny surface finish was on the inside, Sloman used external moulding for his Alfa tubs – 'It was important they looked nice' – so the good side was on the outside. Lotus sought better material quality control by moulding flat panels, feathering the edges and bonding together a kit of flat parts to form their tubs – using the material as 'black aluminium'.

When Gordon Murray adopted a complete carbon inner moulding to stiffen his BT52-53-series aluminium outer tubs the interior seat moulding swept up to form an integral tank top, so in Brabham's case the 'good side' was on both the inside and the outside!

Carbon, as the stiffest of these new materials by weight, is used most extensively in these moulded monocoque tubs, while Kevlar is introduced as 'a tear-stopper', its percentage content progressively being reduced in some cases along with moulding wall-thickness as the teams gained experience and confidence, while Nomex foil cells appeared as void fillers to stabilize the finished structures.

A trend-setting major step forward was introduced in a low-key manner in the Gustav Brunner-designed 1983 ATS D6 in which the moulded forward fuselage's external surfaces provided integral outer body shape and cockpit coaming. A whole new era of motor car design and construction had dawned, and in ever more complex and sophisticated form remains with us ending our period.

The modern moulded carbon-composite: a Lotus 97T at Detroit, 1985.

McLaren MP4/1 – The First Moulded Carbon-Composite Monocoque

Below: 'Chassis built by Hercules' announces the labelling on the Barnard-designed McLaren MP4/1 moulded carbon-composite monocoque. Note the aluminium add-on nosebox, suspension pick-up extremities of the forward 'horse's collar' aluminium bulkhead . . . Right: Wingless Wattie – John Watson's McLaren-Cosworth 'MP4/1-5' dispensing with nose 'foils, Italian GP meeting, 1982. John placed fourth in the race.

The innovative McLaren MP4/1 carbon-composite monocoque was moulded by Hercules Inc. in Salt Lake City, Utah, using bolt-together internal – 'male' – tooling designed and machined in England, as described elsewhere.

One limiting factor in its design had been the need to retain a cockpit opening large enough to withdraw the dismantled tooling from within the monocoque once the moulding itself had cured. This quite large cockpit opening became an enduring feature of the McLaren MP4-series monocoques, and since the larger the aperture the weaker the surrounding structure threatened to become this attracted some criticism.

The original prototype tubs, moulded in 1981, featured a one-piece moulded external shell, a bolt-in machined aluminium 'horse's collar' forward bulkhead to accept rocker arm inboard coil-spring/damper front suspension units, and a separately moulded footbox and bonded-in inner side panels and cockpit seat-back panel to complete it.

To ensure maximum beam stiffness and driver protection, designer John Barnard compensated for the quite large, low-sided cockpit opening by strengthening that area with two quite massive integral solid carbon beams – each 10 mm thick – which curved down from the front edge of the rear fuel cell, down by the driver's shoulders, to run forward into the strong moulded 360-degree scuttle structure and dash area around the driver's thighs.

These solid carbon beams formed the out-turned horizontal top flange of a virtually Z-section inner skin panel

which was both bonded and through-bolted into each side of the basic U-section outer tub.

The forward fuel-cell closing panel was then bonded into place to complete this massively rigid and strong fully enclosed box section behind the driver's shoulders. Its rear closing panel of course incorporated integral engine mounting points.

Barnard employed eight plies of uni-directional carbon laid up around the mould tooling in a series of superimposed laminations, each successive layer being carefully angled – at plus or minus 45 degrees – relative to its underlying neighbour so that the wraps around the essentially hexagonal-section fuselage created the optimum load paths required. Anyone who has made a gum-strip model aeroplane fuselage or boat hull will appreciate exactly how complex it can be conceptually to start off a new strip at such an angle that it ends up at a predetermined place after wrapping entirely around the piece . . .

Extra strengthening layers of carbon were built up in 'difficult areas', corners of the structure, for example, while 14 layers of 'uni' ran full length through the floor 'at zero degrees', dead straight. This uni-directional carbon 'grain' through the length of the tub together with the cockpit strengthening beams provided robust crush resistance against a frontal impact, and also absorbed direct thrust from the driven rear wheels and rear suspension via the transmission casing, suspension radius rods and stressed engine block and mounts.

Each carbon laminate or ply was nominally 0.005 in. –

'five-thou' – thick, so the basic 8-ply skin was 40-thou thick, approximately 1 mm. Each finished monocoque panel for the new car actually comprised a ½ in. thick sandwich, in which ⅛ in. cell aluminium honeycomb of some 4½ lb/cu. ft density was contained between two finished 8-ply carbon skins.

This new McLaren MP4/1 carbon-composite monocoque emerged weighing some 90 lb, for a torsional rigidity along its length of a staggering 14,500-14,700 lb/ft per degree. In fact this original MP4/1 tub proved so strong – for approximately the same weight as a far less rigid conventional aluminium monocoque – that four laminations were deleted from later units, cutting weight to around 78 lb while still leaving them around 12,000 lb/ft per degree deflection in torsional stiffness, compared to 6000-7000 ft/lb for a good aluminium monocoque!

The extra rigidity of such a carbon-composite structure permitted the bottom of the new tub to be much narrower than the nearest comparable aluminium structure, minimum width at the rear tank bulkhead actually being dictated by the nine-inch spacing between Cosworth DFV lower engine mounts. Yet despite such slenderness these new nacelles offered greater rigidity than anything comparable which had gone before.

Almost simultaneously with all this pioneering work by MI Peter Wright and Team Lotus were evolving their fold-up flat composite sheet 'Kellogg's packet' construction method. Whichever approach one adopted, this was the way to go.

Chapter 16

THE TWICE CHAMPION WILLIAMS-HONDAS 1986-87

During the turbocharged era, Williams Grand Prix Engineering at Didcot had one of its formerly World Champion FW07-DFV cars returned for servicing. Some of the newer team members accustomed to turbo car complication – as seen here with the Honda V6 cars – gasped 'Half the bits are missing!' when they saw it.

The remarkable dominance of the McLaren-TAG Turbo-series cars was first challenged, and then broken, by the Anglo-Japanese Williams-Hondas in 1986-87.

In the 1985 Australian Grand Prix at Adelaide, the Williams team's Finnish former World Champion Driver, Keke Rosberg, completed the team's first hat-trick of GP victories since Alan Jones's Champion days with the FW07s back in 1980. His team-mate Nigel Mansell had won the two preceding GPs, at Brands Hatch in England and Kyalami in South Africa, as prelude to the Finn's Australian success and, having at last achieved both chassis and engine reliability, the Williams-Honda team seemed poised for a serious run at the 1986 World Championship.

But just before that new season began in Brazil, team chief Frank Williams was gravely injured in a road accident while driving to Nice airport from testing at Ricard-Castellet in the South of France. Some doubted his team's ability to remain on song without his dynamic leadership – Honda director Nobuhiko Kawamoto most significantly being

amongst them. But they all reckoned without the strength in depth which he and his engineering director partner Patrick Head had built into their company over their nine seasons together. In their lavishly equipped and sparkling purpose-built factory at Didcot – in Oxfordshire – they ran a well-drilled and immensely capable 100-strong team to back their new season's driver pairing of Nelson Piquet and Nigel Mansell. The test programme for the new year's FW11-Honda cars was well advanced and, as Piquet demonstrated when he won that season-opening race at Rio on the new cars' debut, none of the previous late-season's momentum had been lost.

In fact Williams-Honda ended that season with nine more GP victories, the team won the Formula 1 Constructors' Cup competition with 141 points against McLaren International's 96, and Nigel Mansell only lost the prestigious Drivers' crown to McLaren's Alain Prost in the very last qualifying round.

Quite simply, as installed in the impeccably pre-pared Williams FW11 cars, the Honda RA166 F-

Type V6 turbocharged engine offered the best combination of power-cum-fuel economy in contemporary Formula 1 . . .

The Williams-Honda FW11 was absolutely a state-of-the-art, high-technology Formula 1 car, carrying its twin-turbocharged four-cam 80-degree V6 Honda engine plus a mass of electronic micro-processing equipment to handle the power unit's boost, ignition and injection requirements, plus driver-to-pit radio communications, and car-to-pit in-race telemetry enabling the pit crew to 'watch the gauges' as well as monitor their driver's reaction to radioed instructions and advice.

Structurally, the car car was based upon a moulded carbon-Kevlar-aluminium-composite monocoque chassis.

The Japanese V6 was attached rigidly to the composite tub to form the rear part of the chassis's load-bearing structure. A six-speed Williams gearbox bolted rigidly onto the rear of the engine, its casing incorporating integral mounting lugs to provide rear suspension pick-ups.

Twin water radiators and induction air inter-

coolers were outrigged symmetrically on each side of the moulded monocoque within carefully shaped and ducted side pods, while oil cooling was entrusted to an ingenious 40 kw heat exchanger through which engine oil and cooling water were piped, one rejecting its heat to the other. This heat exchanger mounted low on the left side of the engine and was preferred to a conventional air-cooled oil radiator since it obviously created no extra aerodynamic drag, unlike a conventional oil/air cooler. The side pod matrices and ducts, plus the mass of engine management and monitoring electronics mounted high on the tub-top, were enclosed by exquisitely made and carefully tailored lightweight 'plastic' body panelling to provide the cars' aerodynamic external shape.

The fit between the engine cover panel and the mechanical parts enclosed beneath was superb, at least matching McLaren's admired standards with clearance beneath the panels being barely measurable in millimetres in some crucial areas. Such a close fit would have been practically impossible but for WGPE's use of computer-aided design/computer-aided manufacture (CAD/CAM) techniques. This represented an investment in technology typical of the uncompromising commitment to excellence in everything which was now essential for any team aiming to win consistently in Formula 1.

Williams's 1986 budget exceeded £7 million (exclusive of any engine costs), and it showed . . .

Their FW11 design was very much an evolutionary development of 1985's sometimes-troubled, subsequently dominant, FW10 series. That model had itself represented Patrick Head's first foray into moulded carbon-composite chassis construction. During 1984 his team's Williams-Honda FW09 cars had used chassis folded up from aluminium-skinned honeycomb sandwich-sheet. This manufacturing technique had served Williams brilliantly well, including the Alan Jones Championship-winning FW07 design of 1980 which went on in modified form to bring WGPE its second successive Constructors' Championship title in 1981.

But the new era of turbocharged Formula 1 had brought with it a whole new performance regime. Where the team's previous 3-litre naturally aspirated Cosworth-Ford V8 engines had produced perhaps 550 bhp, the new turbo V6s developed 850-900, and in early form their wicked torque characteristics made 'the power' come in with a murderous 'bang' as the drivers opened the throttle. They found themselves having to fight a car which one moment could be understeering into a corner with its engine dawdling, then almost instantaneously spinning its rear wheels and tail-wagging almost uncontrollably as the V6 erupted into ferocious life.

None of which exactly filled the drivers with confidence, or enabled the chassis to demonstrate any great virtue. The Japanese engineers of Honda R&D at Wako, outside Tokyo, had done an excellent job of producing one of the most powerful engines in contemporary Formula 1, but while it might have won any race run on a dynamometer test bed it wasn't yet a practicable proposition in a car driven around a road circuit by a mere human being . . . Honda had to learn what was required in terms of 'driveability' in Formula 1, and of course they would eventually learn fast once they had appreciated the problem.

Against this background, the winter of 1984-85 was a hectic time for Patrick Head and Brian O'Rourke, WGPE's specialist composites technology engineer. While rivals like McLaren, Lotus, Ferrari and Renault were all experienced in moulded composite chassis manufacture, WGPE under Head's typically rather conservative direction had refined aluminium honeycomb construction to a very high degree. Thus far he had staved off outside pressure to change to 'a black chassis', so why did he eventually change when he did?

He explained, 'I just decided that constructionally the time had come when it suited us best to have a chassis of the greatest possible cross section, which meant basically that it should form the outer periphery of the body, and that meant

moulding it in composite. I also wanted to make a stiffer chassis, but I didn't regard our '09 chassis as deficient or weak. It was actually a very strong aluminium chassis . . .'

In fact the moulded FW10 chassis was only 2 per cent stiffer wheel to wheel than the preceding aluminium '09 structure, and when Nigel Mansell first tested for the team at Ricard at the end of 1984 they ran a more responsive Honda engine with slightly modified exhaust and turbo installation in an FW09 and its times instantly improved by two seconds a lap, matching those set by any other car running similar tyres and normal boost. So the much-maligned aluminium FW09 had not in fact been as bad as it was contemporarily painted . . .

At that time most newcomer-teams to carbon chassis technology moulded their tubs in two clamshell halves which were then bonded together along a centreline, either horizontal or vertical. Head and O'Rourke instead, after much soul-searching, decided that the simplest production method for such a labour-intensive component (it involved laying up successive laminated plies by hand over a pre-shaped former or 'plug') would be to form the complete upper part of the tub as an inverted 'U', which could then be closed and completed by bonding in a separately moulded flat floor.

'We don't think there's anything particularly clever about doing it this way. It just seemed the least difficult way to do it – and the simpler you make the manufacturing process the more precise and better the finished article is going to be . . .'

Perhaps significantly several other teams subsequently adopted this Williams moulding method. Patrick admitted, 'I was fairly nervous of getting out of one chassis construction into another, and we were very, very late in building the prototype FW10 – the chassis mould was not completed until the third week of January 1985'. Fortunately, the opening Brazilian GP that season was late in March, and in that two-month interval two race FW10s could be completed for drivers Rosberg and Mansell, while an updated FW09 was prepared as spare.

These new-generation moulded tubs were made by a nine-man composites crew in WGPE's Didcot works. They found they could comfortably mould a new tub in four weeks, two weeks would be very quick, and the record 11-12 days. 'How fast can we make them?' Patrick grinned. 'It depends how hard I kick our blokes . . .'

After making the change to moulded composite tubs for 1985, Williams experienced no major problems at all. Head: 'We were very lucky. We hadn't organized ourselves to be able to repair them in the field, unlike some who took silicone rubber bags and vacuum pumps and repaired tubs on the spot if they were damaged. We would take a spare chassis with us instead, because quite honestly it doesn't really cause a big problem spacewise in the truck or costwise in overseas transport. So if we damaged one we would take that chassis out of service, send it back to the works and replace it with another chassis. We tend to repair them back here if they're damaged rather than in the field'.

The 1986 FW11 chassis looked very similar to a 1985 FW10, from which it was directly developed. It had laminated carbon double skins sandwiching Kevlar honeycomb in the upper sections of the tub while the lower, less curvaceous areas along the cockpit sides were reinforced internally with aluminium honeycomb foil. FW11's internal bulkhead arrangement and constructional method were much the same as FW10's.

Front and rear bulkheads in both FW10 and '11 were integral with the outer shell, but whereas in '10 the two small bulkheads sandwiching the inboard-mounted front springs and dampers were machined from aluminium, in '11 they were instead carbon-Kevlar-composite mouldings. The FW11 tubs had no aluminium bulkheads at all.

They were considerably lower than the '10, a little longer and about the same width, and whereas the '10's roll-over bar behind the driver's head was a bolt-on tubular affair, the FW11 had a com-

Nelson Piquet's 1986 Williams-Honda FW11 demonstrates the massive wing structures its excess of horsepower enabled it to employ, 'McLaren tail' rear waisting, pushrod front suspension and what – by 1990s standards – would be viewed as a grossly over-sized forward fuselage.

posite base-pyramid structure moulded into the chassis to carry fabricated steel roll-over protection on top, the actual height of the 'bar' itself being tailored to match the respective heights of Piquet and Mansell, dependent upon which driver had a particular chassis assigned to him.

For 1986, regulation race-distance fuel allowance was reduced to 195 litres from 1985's ceiling of 220. This made engine economy even more vital than hitherto while also, of course, enabling constructors to fit smaller fuel cells.

Essentially this permitted designers to adopt smaller tank sections than in 1985, but in both Williams's and McLaren's case they opted instead to recline the driver more – thus lowering his head within the car, in Williams's case by fully 4 inches. This enabled lower bodylines, further enhancing airflow to the all-important rear wing. Patrick's design team also concentrated the now 195-litre fuel load lower, and these moves combined to make the FW11 tub *c.* 1.5 inches longer than an FW10's.

The new driving position raised the driver's knees slightly to shuffle his backside further forward, his seat back then curling up through the shoulder area to give optimum support and enable him to hold his neck near-vertical. Some other teams had tried reclining their drivers more steeply, with an abrupt angular change between back and neck taken out in the neck joints rather than between the shoulder blades where the spine is nicely flexible. Forcing the drivers to angle their necks forward like that, instead of curving the seat back progressively through the shoulder-blade area as Williams were doing 'is sheer murder, drivers just can't stand it'.

Overall, the FW11's wheelbase was longer than FW10's – 112 in. against 109.5 in. – 'not because we particularly wanted a longer wheelbase but simply because the F-type engine was slightly longer than the previous year's E-Type, the gearbox length was unchanged but we also had that longer tank section in the tub behind the driver'.

The latest F-type Honda V6 engine hung on the back of the FW11 tub like an old-time Cosworth V8, via two large strap plates bolted down onto each cam-cover at the top and on two bolts running through a flange on the front of the crankcase down below.

There were few suspension differences between FW10 and FW11, largely because the '11 set-up was developed late in 1985 in the FW10B-spec cars which won consecutive GPs at Brands Hatch, Kyalami and Adelaide.

Pre-Brands '85, the cars now known retrospectively as the FW10As used a heavy-duty rocker-type rear suspension, in which movement of the wheel upright deflected the outboard end of a hefty upper rocker arm whose extended inboard extremity then bore down on the top of an inboard-mounted coil-spring/damper alongside the gearbox. This system was nicely rigid and effective if rather bulky, though it used a neat little hub carrier, whose cooling to the brake disc was 'a bit of an afterthought and not very good'.

Around May 1985, Head had decided that this rear suspension should be improved, and his staff produced a new rear upright for it which fed cooling air to the brake disc through integral tunnels instead of using strap-on external ducting. At the same time they drew a pullrod suspension, in which the hefty fabricated top rocker arms could be deleted and replaced by a slender diagonal link, passing from a pivoted spring/damper actuating lever sited at the foot of the inboard mounting up to an outboard pick-up high on the rear upright. With this system, as the wheel deflected over a bump, the upright's vertical movement would tug on the pullrod, which in turn would lift the inboard actuating link to compress the

spring/damper unit mounted above it up against a fixed top mounting.

One WGPE engineer worked on this new system on a fairly low priority, aiming for introduction on the new 1986 car, until in June '85 Head decided to accelerate the development.

At that point Honda had said they would modify the top of the engine with cut-down induction trumpets beneath a smaller induction 'log' to help aerodynamically by allowing the rear bodywork to be lowered, freeing greater airflow to the rear wing. Both the contemporary E-type engine and its predecessors had always been rather tall, and now Head saw the chance to gain experience in preparation for the FW11 design by running the new rear suspension with this modified engine on what would become the hat-trick winning FW10B.

It used the existing six-speed gearbox with casing patterns heavily modified to pick up the new pullrod suspension. Anti-squat angularity was built into this rear suspension system's geometry – whereas the '10A had none – to restrict the car's tendency to bury its tail under hard acceleration. This characteristic had caused problems, not least aerodynamic as the car's attitude changed so abruptly.

Since the introduction of the FW10B coincided with the team's victories at Brands, Kyalami and Adelaide, most pundits assumed that this new version must have been that much quicker than the preceding '10A, but at Spa for the Belgian GP the '10As had already been very competitive but their balance 'wasn't quite right enough to win'. Earlier, in the Italian GP at Monza, the '10As had been the fastest cars running until Mansell had an ignition system problem, after which he lapped as quickly as Rosberg until both cars stopped near the finish with mechanical problems.

Most crucially, the Williams-Honda FW10B might not have been much quicker than the '10A, but it was very much kinder on its tyres when setting similar lap times. The '10A had always been hungry, a tyre destroyer. This was in fact much of the reason for WGPE's pit crew becoming contemporary tyre-change champions, as demonstrated in Adelaide when winner Rosberg made no fewer than three tyre-change stops . . . and that was with the 'kinder' FW10B!

The '10As had already won at Detroit and took a strong second place at Ricard in the French GP, before Rosberg took pole position for the British GP.

Three races followed in a row – Austria, Holland and Italy – each spoiled for Williams by engine bearing failures after running competitively each time. But Honda R&D's engineers were now reacting quite quickly, and they finally fixed their bearing problems in the revised-top-end E-Type engines presented at Brands Hatch.

This background emphasizes how WGPE didn't just suddenly come good with the FW10B. In fact an improved and more reliable chassis had coincided with a more reliable engine to produce that successful late-season of '85.

Into 1986 the FW11 retained the pullrod rear suspension as introduced on those '10B cars, but with a 2-inch wider track and a tidied-up and better-integrated six-speed gearbox casing to support it all.

The FW11 front suspension used a pushrod system, with the diagonal link being based low outboard and rising to an inboard actuating link which depressed the inboard coil-spring/damper unit from above. A new-design front hub carrier was used which first ran in December testing at Rio, on a '10B. This new upright used the same bearing and hub arrangements as before but its brake cooling was improved.

Normally Williams ran French-made lightweight SEP carbon brake discs, clasped by carbon pads within AP aluminium calipers using titanium pistons. But there had been extensive experimentation with an Automotive Products carbon twin-disc system, offering roughly twice the friction and cooling area of a single-disc system plus several 'interesting characteristics'.

Pre-season testing included a hectic week at Estoril in Portugal, then two more Rio sessions,

one in mid-January, the other in February. The first of these Rio sessions saw the debut of the 195-litre fuel restriction F-Type – 'F for frugal' – Honda V6, mounted in an adapted '10B.

Honda R&D had few F-spec engines available at that time, and the Rio test '10Bs both wore the taller '10A bodywork because the team had a bigger new ECU central programming unit for the Honda engine's fuel injection plus a new tank-top position for the capacitor-discharge ignition box, moved from above the gearbox. With the tall original 220-litre '10A tank this demanded more room within the bodywork, so the old '10A engine cover was used to suit. Since this masked airflow to the rear wing, 'we knew that we were running slower than we could do, but we knew roughly by how much'.

In the subsequent February session at Rio, the team then ran one of these FW10Bs with '10A bodywork but F-spec engine for tyre testing, while the first of the brand-new FW11s made its debut there, at last combining all these winter developments . . .

Some of the new model's bodylines, especially its engine and tank-section cover, were designed on Didcot's newly installed General Electric CALMA CAD/CAM system, while the replacement FW11B-version under development for 1987 would be very largely designed on this system.

Three FW11s – all using F-Type engines upon which WGPE relied totally during 1986 – were ready in time for the curtain-raising Brazilian GP at Rio, which Piquet won after Mansell had come off second best in an opening-lap collision with Ayrton Senna's Lotus. Mansell's car at Rio raced with the AP twin-disc brake system installed, its only race thus being brief in the extreme, amounting to only one albeit fierce (!) application in anger.

These FW11-Hondas subsequently replaced the McLaren-TAG Turbos as the cars to beat, and while Senna of Lotus, Prost of McLaren and Berger of Benetton did just that it was generally very much a Williams-Honda season, with Mansell winning at Ricard, Spa, Montreal, Brands Hatch and Estoril and Piquet coming back at Hockenheim, Hungary and Monza.

Pondering the season that August, Patrick Head considered, 'Brands Hatch has been probably our best race, our only 1-2 so far, and a race run at enormous pace, continually setting new lap records and with both cars handling pretty well and neither driver complaining of anything; both in good nick after the finish. Nelson could have finished right on Nigel's tail, but I don't think, short of an error like missing a gear or something like that, he could have got past. We controlled the turbo boost they could run, using the radio from the pits. We have two race boost settings, high and low, and instructed them to use the lower boost setting, and the data we received in the pits told us that they were on the lower boost setting . . .'

Data received in the pits? In addition to having perfected a good audible radio link between pits and driver, WGPE with Honda R&D also used radio telemetry during the race, enabling pits-based engineers as well as the driver to read out fuel level, boost pressure settings and 'certain other data' throughout race distance. 'Oh yes,' laughed Head the engineer. 'The days have gone when drivers could *lie* to us!'

The actual telemetry processing and transmitting box on the cars, which kept the pit continuously informed of so many parameters, was no bigger than a Swan Vestas matchbox and weighed mere ounces, far belying its power and usefulness in race tactics and strategy when combined with the two-way radio link. Formula 1 had come to embody genuine team effort. It was no longer a case of the driver on his own once the lights flashed green . . .

The FW11s offered their drivers a four-position boost selector control, position '1' being a fuel conservation mode, '2' and '3' race boosts on higher or lower levels, and '4' providing an extra 50-60 bhp overtaking boost for very limited use only. It was not available to the drivers at every race. Of the two alternative race boost positions, '2' burned slightly too little fuel – hence producing less than optimum power over race distance – while '3' burned slightly too much, so the drivers would normally juggle between these two settings to survive race distance at the most competitive pace.

The team's worst race of 1986 was Monaco where they were handicapped by lack of hardware. Head had been concerned by gearbox longevity. In 1985 WGPE had run two alternative final-drive ratios, the lower of which had been very unreliable at Detroit and elsewhere, nearly always finishing a race fit to fall apart.

For Monaco therefore he decided to use the more reliable longer ratio but combine it with the lowest available first gear which could be cut. At Monte Carlo this final-drive soon proved to be not low enough and with a second new chicane included on the circuit this handicap was magnified, the engine being knocked down to around 4000 rpm, way off the cam, leaving engine pick-up and response 'just terrible', and giving the cars no chance against the better-geared McLarens and Senna's Lotus. Patrick had to admit to his drivers, 'Sorry, we just haven't got the bits', and thereafter he had new CWPs cut by a different company to produce a lower final-drive which worked perfectly, as at Detroit.

'Monaco was the only race we've gone to where we did not have the equipment to be competitive . . . and that was depressing, a drop-off by me', Patrick would admit. The only race where the extra pressures thrown onto him by Frank Williams's enforced absence caused real problems was Detroit, where under the pressure of contract negotiations and FOCA meetings he forgot to specify a brake caliper cooling adjustment which would have prevented Nigel Mansell's brake fluid boiling, as it did to cost him what could have been another win. In that case Nelson went by to lead handsomely, only to crash in one of the chicanes.

Changes to the six identical-tubbed FW11s built prior to the Hungarian GP were mostly in detail only, involving mainly the water and turbo-charge cooling systems. Chassis FW11/'1-2-3' were ready in time for the season-opening race at Rio, '1 being assigned to Nelson Piquet, '2 to Mansell and '3 performing spare car duties. Subsequently, chassis '4 was completed new for Piquet in time for the San Marino GP at Imola, and was subsequently written off in his heavy accident while leading at Detroit. It was replaced by chassis '5 at Ricard, and the Brazilian subsequently completed the season in this car. The final FW11 – number '6 – made its debut as Mansell's race car at the Hungaroring, and it was driven by him in the last six GPs of the season, including the Australian decider in which his World Championship-winning race lead was lost in that spectacular – and now historic – Goodyear tyre failure, while flat-out on the main straight.

Generally, these cars had all been progressively reinforced in certain areas to forestall potential problems, while Mansell's British GP first-start transmission failure centred upon an overloaded standard Lobro Porsche/BMW M1-type CV joint whose cage exploded under the Honda engine's startline torque. The English driver was very lucky in that case that a multiple accident caused a restart, giving him the chance to race again – and win – in his spare car. WGPE subsequently began making their own redesigned CV joint cages. Once bitten . . .

To defend their Constructors' Championship title in 1987, WGPE's new FW11B-Honda cars were improved in a multitude of fine details.

While the outer shell of the tub moulding remained much as before, both its internal bulkheads and the lay-up of its carbon-composite laminations had been altered. The major bulkhead redesign involved the seat back, which was raked more steeply to recline the driver even further and so lower his head.

Piquet had already been seated as low as possible within the FW11 while still being able to see over the coaming, but there was scope for Mansell to drop lower. Since he was willing 'to try it' despite Patrick's earlier stricture, the seat back

was realigned. Lower the head, lower the roll-over bar, freeing a cleaner airflow path onto the rear wing.

Major attention was paid to improved cooling, using different water radiators although still side-ducted as before. This arrangement offered aerodynamic advantages over the top-ducted system used previously by McLaren, for example, who had now adopted the contemporary Williams-led trend towards side-ducted radiators.

It is interesting to consider the rival cars of 1987 which followed WGPE's lead in various vital areas of design. The Williams FW11 series' engine installation was effectively copied by both Lotus and Ferrari in terms of cooling systems, turbos, and inlet 'log' configuration. The 1987 Ferrari F1/87 also mimicked Williams's general gearbox layout, ditto its moulded composite chassis and general car configuration. Ferrari were in fact also able to improve upon the Didcot product, by employing their lower engine and gearbox to some advantage.

Patrick Head explained rather wryly, 'Honda would not move the oil filter from underneath their engine despite continuous written and verbal requests from ourselves for them to do so. We were beseeching them to sit the engine 1½ inches lower and put the oil filter elsewhere which would mean we could lower the gearbox and the whole chassis as well, but Honda simply felt their engine was adequate as it was.

The Japanese – advised by Kawamoto, who was still sceptical of Williams's ability to maintain the pace following Frank's accident injuries – also decided that the best route to achieve the results they wanted was parallel engine supply to Team Lotus, for their star driver Ayrton Senna.

'It was because of this that I decided it was not worth doing an entirely new car for 1987 which is why we did the FW11B instead of an all-new FW12 which would have been smaller and lower, as planned. So I scrapped the FW12.'

Even this far into the era of moulded composite chassis technology, Patrick would tell me, 'We could quite happily construct a winning car out of aluminium right now – we don't have to have a carbon chassis and it's certainly not the prime reason why we didn't win as many races in 1984 as we did in '85 and '86.

'I was not really too impressed by the type of failure we saw in secondary components which were made in bonded composites. Things like wing support structures, wing end plates, skirts etc, we had seen a considerable number of them damaged and I'd also seen a considerable number of aluminium and aluminium honeycomb chassis damaged, and the way they reacted made a far better bet than carbon-composites. In '87 I would still regard the mode of failure of aluminium structures as better than of carbon components – but we've learned an enormous amount through mandatory crash testing of nose structures, a very good thing, and without that we might not have done as many 'load-to-failure' structure tests as we have. They have taught us a fair bit about failure of composites when overloaded. It is pretty catastrophic, so we made a nose structure designed to fail and to absorb energy during that failure process, and we then made a chassis designed effectively not to fail.'

As it happened, this structural design of the new FW11B was thoroughly tested 'live' by Nelson Piquet following an apparent tyre failure during qualifying for the San Marino GP at Imola.

'When Nelson crashed there at around 160 mph, the car went in backwards diagonally on the left-rear, after first hitting the left-front corner, which shattered the wheel and drove the upright clean through the side of the forward chassis. There was a shear failure of a large area at the side of the tub there and a shear failure on top of the chassis right through both the inner and outer skins. Fortunately the floor and right-hand side had no failure, but it would not have taken much more of a load for that front part to have come right off, leaving the driver's legs exposed . . .

'The rearward impact was then absorbed by the engine and gearbox, nothing on the tub apart

from the engine mountings actually failed there. But as it emerged a lot of people were patting us on the back for having built a car in which Nelson could survive a 160 mph shunt, whereas in fact if he'd been unlucky in only a slightly different way at a slightly different angle the story might have been very different, and a lot of people might instead have been vilifying us for building a brittle car!

'Having said that, I'm reasonably happy with the kind of structure we have now. I'm not aware of an alternative constructional method or material we could use which would give the driver a better chance in the event of an accident.'

Honda's winter R&D programme had pursued – as always – greater power and fuel efficiency, but this time with the added factor of making the most of FISA's mandatory new boost-limiting 'pop-off valves'.

Their new 1987 V6 engine for Formula 1 emerged as the RA168 'G-type' revving to 13,000 rpm and using a revised turbocharger installation. Both WGPE and new Honda client Team Lotus received these G-type engines, but the turbochargers for the Williams FW11B installation were initially angled further outwards than were Lotus's, the Ketteringham team subsequently matching Williams practice.

As the season progressed, an improved 'GE-type' Honda engine emerged – 'E' reputedly indicating improved fuel 'Efficiency' – and this unit reverted to the 1986 'F-type' rev limit of 12,000. That spec was then followed by a bewildering variety of GE2 – 'GE Phase 2' – and then GE2-1 or GE2-5 derivatives. Each specification state offered alternative tune and tailoring to optimize the engines for specific venues.

Eight FW11B-series chassis were built, each moulded new and none relying upon existing FW11 tubs from 1986. But only five of these new 1987 chassis were 'standard' FW11Bs since two late-season tubs specifically for active-cars were formed with the necessary hydraulic pipework moulded integrally into their structure.

There was also a one-off 'FW11C' tub built specifically for the expected Honda V10 3.5-litre naturally aspirated engine to come. This monocoque was number '7 in the FW11B series. It would never run with its intended power unit installed and would be modified instead after Honda abruptly broke its Williams contract to form the basis of the prototype Judd V8-engined test hack looking towards 1988 . . .

Nigel Mansell essentially retained chassis 'FW11B/3' all season, while Nelson Piquet lost his early-season chassis '2 at Imola and adopted '4 thereafter, while conventional chassis '1 continued to serve as team spare. When active-suspension car 'FW11B/5A' – 'A' for 'active', much to Group Lotus's disgust as they were in the noisy process of registering that word relative to their own active suspension system – was commissioned ready for the Italian GP, Nelson Piquet abandoned conventional chassis '4 for it. This car then replaced '1 as team spare. Chassis '6 became the test team's chassis, so at Estoril when Mansell appeared in an active-suspension car it was the final FW11B chassis, '8A.

Long before Lotus had become seriously involved in active suspension, the giant Automotive Products company in England had toyed, somewhat half-heartedly and – most significantly – without the motivation of racing pressures, with an active suspension system which was distantly related to Citroën ride-levelling systems.

Williams at Didcot had begun co-development of this AP 'active-ride' system in 1985, investigating its possible adaptation to Formula 1, mainly – it would appear – to achieve aerodynamic advantage through maintaining their cars in an optimum ride attitude.

Engineer Bob Pitcher had headed AP's active group. Now WGPE co-operated with him for a couple of years, before AP opted out and left the co-developers to go their separate ways, Pitcher continuing independently – largely for off-road and agricultural vehicles – while the F1 Williams

R&D group under Frank Dernie set about redesigning both the basic system and the way it worked.

They only began running their system in effectively the form in which it was ultimately raced as late as December 1986 – and even after Piquet's debut win with it at Monza in September 1987 Patrick Head admitted, 'We have still got an awful lot of work to do . . . One way of looking at it is that ideally we should begin racing promising R&D projects at the beginning of a year, not at the end. But the positive way of looking at it is that we have started early for next year'.

The Williams-Honda FW11B 'active-ride' cars used a lightweight hydraulic pressure pump driven off a camshaft tail to maintain pressure within an accumulator. Each suspension corner featured a strut and gas-spring mounted in series to handle all high-frequency bumps and ripples. They interacted with a valve allowing hydraulic fluid in and out of the strut under pressure to control its mean length. A rheostat connected to each strut signalled changes in its length to a central control computer, which could be programmed to trigger suitable responses from hydraulic valve blocks which fed gas-spring spheres in which pressurized fluid was separated from the gas by flexible diaphragms.

'We are not setting out to control the car as it goes over a bump, but on the back side of the bump the spring rebounds to maintain ride level. The system also handles anti-roll control' – like Lotus Active – 'and with four struts and a control system we are trying to exercise a degree of control over the plane of the car independent of what load is acting upon it – yes, we are attempting to maintain an attitude.'

That was how Head and Dernie explained the system at the time. Patrick was typically wary of making loud claims for it, beyond a cautious 'Drivers seem able to maintain very consistent lap times with it'.

Where Lotus made much of their active suspension reducing the motion stress and workload upon their drivers – which can pay dividends – the first question the down-to-earth Williams engineers asked was more 'Are we going quicker?' than 'Are you more comfortable?' although their car could of course be set up that way, and one could demonstrably affect the other.

The Williams active-ride system was simpler in hardware terms than Lotus Active, having fewer sensors around the car and being less compromised by any background of development for road cars with the vastly greater performance envelope that entailed. In other words Lotus Active was immensely 'over-capable' for Formula 1, while this less expansive Williams system was more finely

targeted, and perhaps 'capable enough'. Picking only the crucial areas to address had always been a Williams strength.

The system involved a weight penalty, but its power consumption was very small – less than 5 bhp – and had weight not become a matter of real priority in 1988 active development might have been pursued more rigorously.

Meanwhile, Patrick Head could observe of that 1987 season: 'It was quite clear from the start of the year that our opposition's new cars were either quick but not well sorted, or well sorted but unlikely to become threateningly quick; so essentially most of the opposition simply ran the same as before'.

Piquet finished second no fewer than seven times that season, in addition to winning the German, Hungarian and Italian GPs, finishing third in Portugal and fourth in Spain. Meanwhile Mansell won the San Marino, French, British, Austrian, Spanish and Mexican GPs but suffered five retirements. Even so, a second consecutive Formula 1 Constructors' title was secured for the team and the Drivers' Championship could be won only by one or other of their drivers into the penultimate round at Suzuka, Japan.

But there Mansell crashed heavily during practice, sustaining painful – if relatively minor – injuries which prevented him starting. Piquet thus became World Champion by default.

From the technical point of view, however, the nadir of Williams's season had certainly been in Hungary where Mansell lost a hard-won and handsome lead when his right-rear wheel's centre-lock nut worked loose and bounded away. Head admits, 'It was our fault. Tolerancing on the wheels had become too slack, and because the nut wasn't bedded firmly onto the wheel itself, the wheel fidgeted and progressively freed off the nut – which eventually just unwound and flew off. Previously, at Silverstone, we had found a wheel nut not quite tight on Nelson's car, but had misread it as a one-off event, rather than as a symptom of something more far-reaching'.

In practice, when wheels and tyres were being frequently changed, Williams always pinned their wheel nuts to ensure they had been properly tightened. But in the race itself they had become confident of running them unpinned to save time in a pit stop; 'we subsequently pinned our wheel nuts for the next three or four races before regaining confidence that we didn't need pins in the race any more'.

Throughout that 1987 season car set-ups remained virtually identical for each driver, and the simple active-ride system succeeded at Monza where Piquet won, despite permitting his tyres to overheat and blister.

Nigel Mansell's 1987 Williams-Honda FW11B shows off its shapely nose wing end plates, lengthy side pods enclosing side-ducted water radiator and intercooler cores, turbocharger periscope intake on pod top and tailored spine freeing airflow onto rear wing.

Highlight of the season was generally accepted to be the 1-2 finish in the British GP at Silverstone, in which Piquet and Mansell raced as hard against one another as if they had been representing rival teams, Mansell snatching the lead from the Brazilian in a memorable manoeuvre entering Stowe Corner after a terrific fight-back from earlier delay. 'As a car manufacturer,' Patrick remarked, 'it's always pleasing to see any race won by a car which has been driven absolutely flat-out for the entire duration without anything going wrong.'

Meanwhile, political clouds had gathered around WGPE's relationship – often tetchy – with Honda. It appears that the Japanese were culturally ill-equipped to handle a supposed satellite the minuscule (relative) size of Williams exercising its independence in driver selection. Between the engineers of Honda R&D and WGPE there had evolved mutual respect, but when Ayrton Senna agreed terms with McLaren for 1988, Nelson Piquet pre-empted his possible return to Lotus-Honda by signing a contract to replace him there. Having lost Piquet, WGPE refused to accept Honda appointee Satoru Nakajima. The Senna/McLaren deal involved supply of Honda engines, so the Japanese were faced with servicing three frontline teams. They abrogated the remainder of their contract with WGPE, reaching mutually acceptable terms in compensation, and Williams completed their Championship-winning 1987 season with minimal further technical feedback, and set about hasty design of a Judd V8-powered 'atmo' car to keep them in Formula 1 through 1988.

It was to be a sudden, heavy fall from dominance. Patrick Head reviewed the Williams-Honda period like this: 'Honda kept us pretty well in the picture through 1985-86, but became more secretive early in '87 and by the middle and end of the season had become very secretive indeed . . . We had a very good working relationship with many of their junior engineers, the chaps who worked closely with us, but higher management levels were often . . . inscrutable'.

Now Honda found a more profitable relationship with McLaren International, but after one season with Judd V8 power in 1988 Williams would eventually return to Honda-toppling competitiveness with power by Renault Sport.

Active Suspension

An active suspension system, in which wheel movements are controlled by a system onboard the car instead of being dictated completely by the inequalities of road surface upon which the car is running, first became a significant Formula 1 reality in the 1980s . . .

During 1987 Team Lotus ran computer-controlled active suspension on their Type 99T cars in which Ayrton Senna won the Monaco and Detroit GPs. It was a complex road car-orientated system – too complex for other teams to match, but it pointed the way ahead and other constructors would follow.

Senna first enthused over the prototype 99T with Lotus 'Active' (trade name) suspension during pre-season testing at Rio. Team consequently committed itself totally to running a pair of such cars that year – cynics suggesting that the 99T without Active suspension was so awful, Senna realized he had no choice . . .

Irrespective, victory followed on two of the most bumpy F1 venues, and the combination came close to winning the flat-out Italian GP at Monza too, only for Senna to slither wide at the *Parabolica*, enabling Nelson Piquet to

win in his faster Williams-Honda FW11B, fitted with Didcot's own 'reactive' system. So contemporary F1's two alternative computer-commanded suspension layouts finished first and second – an historic milestone which would not be followed by further significant success until 1992 . . .

Other self-levelling, self-damping suspension systems had appeared and been adapted for Formula 1, most notably the Citroën hydro-pneumatic system with which BRM had toyed in the 1950s and Ligier and Renault in the early 1980s.

Lotus interest in F1 ride control crystallized in 1981. Their ground-effect cars were uncompetitive in the era of lowering suspensions in which consistently shallow, pitch-free ground clearance was vital. Suspensions had become near-solid. Wheel travel fell from *circa* seven inches to less than one inch, mainly from uncontrolled suspension and tyre sidewall flex . . .

Interest grew in accurate onboard data recording to investigate. Peter Wright and Lotus R&D computer specialist Steve Green worked to develop a system with Dave Williams's Flight Instrumentation Group at the Cranfield Institute of Technology.

Coincidentally, Flight Instrumentation was developing

a variable-feel control system for the BAe Hawk trainer aircraft, to simulate the 'feel' of a wide diversity of other aircraft . . .

Williams showed Wright the mechanical heart of this computer-controlled mimic system, a compact variable-resistance hydraulic jack – in effect a synthetic spring, whose rate could be varied dynamically throughout its movement.

He suggested an active suspension using such 'actuators' would provide short-travel, pitch-free ride in Formula 1. They would allow no deflection whatsoever unless their controlling computer approved, and then only to a precisely defined degree. That could change continuously in response to whatever inputs the roadway applied to the car. All that was needed – apart from painstaking R&D – was a sensing system to monitor chassis inputs and requirements, and a processor with adequate computer software to make an hydraulic system operate the actuators as required.

Peter Wright described how 'The secret is to teach the brain to recognize the load and to tell the actuators to compensate for it in the most relevant manner for inputs ranging from a peak road shock of, say, 5000 lb, right down to somebody tapping on the body, applying a load of perhaps 1 lb. Obviously if you trigger 5000 lb-worth of compensation with a 1 lb input then something very uncomfortable is going to happen! Relating a suitable reaction to the relevant input is the tricky bit . . .'

Colin Chapman authorized this R&D programme. Within six months, a Mark I Active system was running in a Lotus Turbo Esprit test hack. Control was by a Cranfield Flight Instrumentation analogue computer, fed by accelerometers around the chassis. The car's only suspension medium was its hydraulic actuators which Peter describes as having been 'highly active, capable of producing accelerations of 10G vertically!' There were no back-up steel springs.

Team progressed rapidly to Stage Two. When they adopted Renault turbo engines in 1983, they had initially to retain a Cosworth V8 in their second car (for 'no-hoper' Nigel Mansell). The Chapman way was therefore to boost this car with 'something extra' – Active suspension . . .

Hence the Lotus 92's improved still-springless Mark II Active system, with hybrid analogue/digital computer offering finer-tune capability than the analogue-only Mark I.

This Active F1 Lotus ran only in Brazil and Long Beach '83. It was too heavy, under-developed and unreli-

A 99T

able, but was a real-car system accommodating 180 mph and 3G lateral load . . .

General Motors R&D was impressed . . . Active's wider potential for production car development promised profit, so Wright and Green transferred with the project to Lotus Engineering. A Mark III all-digital system superseded the two 'springless' exploratory systems, fitted to test road cars with stand-by fail-safe steel springs.

The interface between electronics and hydraulics was a battery of five Moog variable-flow valves, one on the pump output and one on each suspension corner, turning brief electronic commands into powerful hydraulic actions.

The clever technology was to prevent the car submitting to uncontrolled accelerations other than those required by the driver, i.e. increasing road speed, braking, or yaw (cornering). Peter Wright committed a memorable jargonism by reflectively describing the steering wheel as being 'really only a yaw velocity determinator . . .'.

The aim was to make the car stable – i.e. relatively unresponsive to random inputs. Once it was stable it became easy to drive. This was the plus which Senna appreciated first time out in the Active Lotus-Honda 99T.

Its Active system featured an hydraulic pump driven off the tail of the Honda V6's left-side exhaust camshaft. A valve-block on the pump's rear end controlled system pressure while an accumulator was mounted above the bell-housing oil tank to store pressurized fluid which could then be valved into the system in slow corners when engine revs fell too low. Pressure lines fed the hydraulic actuators on each suspension corner where a Moog valve dictated jack extension, damping action, etc.

The system computer was housed under the driver's seat, receiving continuous data on car and control motion from accelerometers, transducers and potentiometers around the car; those sensing accelerations laterally (as in cornering) and longitudinally (as in acceleration and braking) also being beneath the seat. A steering transducer monitored driver input.

By its very nature, 'active' suspension was more reactive, depending upon road or driver inputs to trigger response. The lag between trigger input and computed reaction had been narrowed through R&D – but the goal was (and remains) a genuinely active system detecting bumps ahead of the front wheels and correcting for them as they arrive . . .

Lotus's onboard computer could be attached by umbilical when stationary to a remote system through which logged data could be extracted, or the car system could be re-programmed to re-set ride heights, bump and rebound damping, anti-roll control, 'warp' (diagonal pitching) etc. As experience with the 99T grew so Team's regular race engineers – Steve Hallam on Senna's car and Tim Densham on Nakajima's – gained confidence in operating the Active system.

Their main problem was that more data derived from the Active F1 programme computer logs than an army of engineers could digest in the time available at a GP meeting.

Peter Warr: 'Vitally, Active gave the driver a very good and comfortable ride. It insulated him . . . and enabled him simply to concentrate harder for longer . . . At Monaco '86 in the 98T, Ayrton finished with a hole in his gearchange hand. That was common. At Monaco '87 in the Active 99T, he had such a smooth ride not only did he not damage his hand, he didn't even bother to tape it beforehand as a precaution . . .'

The downside? 'Concentration upon the system to the virtual exclusion of development in other areas cost something. Active added 10-12 kg weight, and driving the hydraulic pump absorbed some power and used a little more fuel so we had to run a little less boost to survive race distance . . .'

Meanwhile, Automotive Products had toyed, half-heartedly and – most significantly – without the motivation of racing pressures, with an active suspension related distantly to Citroën ride-levelling systems.

Williams Grand Prix Engineering Ltd at Didcot had begun co-development of this AP 'active-ride' as early as 1985, investigating possible adaptation to Formula 1, essentially to maintain an optimum ride attitude for aerodynamic advantage.

Engineer Bob Pitcher had headed AP's active group. Now WGPE co-operated with him for a couple of years, before AP opted out, and left the co-developers to go their separate ways, Pitcher continuing in his own right largely for off-road and agricultural vehicles – while a Williams R&D group under Frank Dernie set about redesigning both the basic system and the way it worked.

They began running in December 1986 – and even after Piquet's debut win with the system at Monza in September '87, Patrick Head observed, 'We have still got an awful lot of work to do'. In particular, former Lotus

Active user Nigel Mansell remained suspicious of the system.

The Williams-Honda FW11B 'active-ride' cars used a lightweight hydraulic pressure pump driven in the same way as Lotus's to maintain pressure within an accumulator. Each suspension corner had a strut and gas-spring mounted in series to handle high-frequency bumps and ripples, inter-acting with a valve allowing hydraulic fluid in and out of the strut under pressure to control its mean length. A rheostat connected to each strut signalled length-changes to the control computer, which could be programmed to trigger suitable responses from hydraulic valve blocks feeding the gas-spring spheres in which pressurized fluid was separated from the gas by flexible diaphragms.

With four struts and a control system Williams were seeking a degree of control over the plane of the car independent of what load was acting upon it, to maintain its most efficient and effective aerodynamic attitude.

Where Lotus made much of reducing motion stress and workload upon their drivers – which could pay dividends – Williams were more focused upon sheer competitiveness. They asked 'Are we going quicker?' more than 'Are you more comfortable?' although one could demonstrably affect the other.

The 1987 Williams reactive system used simpler hardware than Lotus Active, with fewer sensors around the car and being less compromised by any background development for road cars necessitating the vast performance and road surface envelope which that implied. While Lotus Active was immensely 'over-capable' for Formula 1, Williams 'reactive' was more finely targeted, and 'capable enough'. Picking the crucial factors had always been a Williams strength, and their simpler system was lighter and absorbed less than 5 bhp.

At the end of that season Peter Wright could report: 'We set ourselves several questions. Is Active useful in sorting out the aerodynamics of the car? Yes. Does it give an advantage in reduced driver workload? Yes. Does it improve grip by keeping the wheels on the road? Errr, we're not sure – the advantage in ride seems better so far. Could we make it reliable? Yes. Tyre wear? Again, not sure. There is a slight indication Active is easier on the tyres. It is definitely no harder . . .'

But Lotus Engineering road car programme demands dictated Active's removal from the F1 cars thereafter, and Williams too put reactive suspension development onto a back burner. Many teams researched and raced both attitude and ride-height control systems 1988-89 and through 1990-91 interest in more active systems accelerated, notably with Williams, Benetton, McLaren and Ferrari in the frame. Williams won the race with a minimalized but highly sophisticated system opening their season so memorably in 1992 – but that falls outside our period . . .

Key: 1, airspeed pitot heads sense true speed; 2, accelerometer sensors signal wheel deflection; 3, hydraulically length-adjustable wheel actuator units; 4, inertial platform motion-sensing accelerometers; 5, Central Processing Unit onboard computer; 6, electronically variable hydraulic Moog valves; 7, pressure fluid accumulator, rear with master-valve block and filters; 8, dual-purpose oil/fluid cooler handling gearbox lubrication and hydraulic systems; 9, engine-driven hydraulic system pressure pump; 10, hydraulic fluid reservoir.

Chapter 17

THE TURBOCHARGED McLAREN-HONDA MP4/4s 1988

The combined attractions of Ayrton Senna and McLaren International deprived Williams of Honda support in 1988 – and here at Monaco Senna scored one of the team's 15 wins in that year's 16 World Championship GPs in the flat-iron 'MP4/4-1'.

Nineteen eighty-eight has passed into history as perhaps the most peculiar motor racing season at premier level since the introduction of the FIA World Championship in 1950.

While the first two years of Formula 1 competition, 1950-51, had seen increasing parity between the two alternative forms of F1 car then accepted, the 1988 season proved there was little parity at all between the two divisions of Grand Prix technology which had been created – in their infinite wisdom – by the luminaries of FISA.

There were two really significant engine rule changes made to Formula 1 for this final season in which turbocharged 1.5-litre engines would be accepted. Firstly, the boost limitation allowed to 1500 cc turbo engines was slashed from 4 bar right down to 2.5 bar. Secondly their fuel tank capacity was diminished from 195 litres to just 150. Since in-race refuelling had been banned from the end of 1983, the power output of 1988's turbo engines should have been savagely restricted in two ways. Firstly, given no other mechanical development within the engine or chemical change within the fuel it burned, the 1.5-bar boost reduction – 1 bar representing ambient atmospheric pressure – would inevitably diminish maximum attainable power. This effect would then be amplified by the necessity to run more fuel-efficiently, in order to eke out that 45-litre lower fuel capacity to endure undiminished race distances.

This at least was the thinking behind the FISA governing body's decision to apply these changes, their intention being to force out turbos (which ironically they had so energetically once encouraged) before 1989, when Formula 1 was scheduled to become purely a 3.5-litre naturally aspirated class.

But, as so often, the engineers kept ahead of the rule makers, and Honda did this best – in conjunction with McLaren International's superb chassis and team organization. And what contemporary drivers could match MI's pairing of Alain Prost and Ayrton Senna?

Back in 1955, when Mercedes-Benz had hired young Stirling Moss to join Juan Fangio in their GP and sports car team, they were simply buying out potential opposition. Once Moss was with Mercedes rather than against them in a Maserati, whatever rare fragility their hardware might have suffered, driver ability could compensate. Equally, without a Moss in a rival car to force them on, Mercedes' cars would seldom be pressed hard enough to break.

Through 1988 this same philosophy was applied by McLaren-Honda. It was Ron Dennis's declared ambition for MI not merely to win Formula 1 World Championship titles but also to win every single qualifying race.

Honda's board had long since concluded that their production motor company was simply too small ever to challenge Toyota or Nissan in mass-production volume. So they opted instead to project a worldwide image of technical excellence, with domination of Formula 1 both its cutting edge and its most valuable promotional tool. They sank a reputed $50 million a year into reaping its rewards. Both partners in this particular relationship meant business . . . as had Mercedes-Benz before them.

Only the era and the names had changed; for Fangio – at this stage – read Prost, for Moss read Senna. This was an age-old way of GP business, and in absorbing the undoubted talent of Ayrton Senna to accompany the proven genius of Alain Prost McLaren-Honda armed themselves not only 'to do a Mercedes-Benz' but actually to improve upon the German company's once legendary Grand Prix record.

But the technical dice were resoundingly loaded in the Woking organization's favour. Only two frontline teams opted to pursue the 2.5-bar turbocharged F1 option for 1988, McLaren-Honda and Ferrari, and with their forced-induction engines displaying a 100 or more horsepower advantage over the very best of their 3.5-litre naturally aspirated opposition the season became broadly no contest. Add to this the fact that Ferrari took the long-term strategic decision to regard 1988 merely as an interim season in which only modified 1987 equipment would be deployed, and one can appreciate the uniqueness of McLaren International's position that year.

While Team Lotus also built Honda V6-engined chassis, MI was alone in building significant completely new cars for that final season of turbocharged F1 racing. Consequently, although MI deserve enormous credit for their logistical success in coming so close to winning every single Grand Prix of the year, it should be emphasized that any resemblance between genuine motor racing and the 1988 World Championship season is largely accidental.

For 1988, McLaren's armament had clearly improved from that of their final TAG Turbo-engined season in 1987, but as realistic people their engineers also understood just how much the opposition had either simply stood still, or had taken a great leap backwards.

Others' problems undoubtedly helped MI look so good. In the land of the blind, the one-eyed man will have the clearest view . . .

Steve Nichols had become MI's Turbo F1 Project Leader and at the end of that season he observed: 'We've worked very hard, and a lot of the reason for our success has been simply us and Honda doing a good job, but this has really been emphasized by the other teams being in such relative disarray'. A mature view from a realistic man.

The foundations for the new season had been laid during 1987 when Honda R&D's engineers at Tochigi, Japan, brainstormed the problem of which engine route to follow for '88. Should they remain with 1.5-litre turbos under the new year's harsh restrictions, or alternatively run their new V10-cylinder 3.5-litre 'atmo' instead? Their sums indicated that, despite the new restrictions, the 1.5 turbo retained greater potential.

McLaren's twice-champion TAG Turbo engine had been showing its age. MI needed a new engine supplier. Ron Dennis courted Honda, and

Left: The chassis moulding of the 1988 McLaren-Honda MP4/4 was new to comply with safety footbox and 'behind the front axle' pedal requirements, but aerodynamic form was still applied by separate detachable skin panelling. Right: Pure function – the cockpit of the most successful Formula 1 car design in decades, the MP4/4.

with the prospect of combining the talents of Prost and Senna under one roof the Japanese company abruptly switched horses for 1988 from Williams to McLaren International.

Before the F1 turbo era peaked in the days of the McLaren-TAG Turbo MP4/2 cars, Colin Chapman's classical Lotus 72s were the most successful Grand Prix cars of all time – having won 20 Championship GPs from almost 90 races, through 1970-74. Between 1984 and 1986, McLaren's MP4/2-TAG Turbo family rapidly overtook them, securing 22 wins in only 48 GPs.

John Barnard had left the team before the end of '86, joining Ferrari. McLaren's standards and work practices established during his regime were to be maintained and extended by his successors. The 1988 McLaren-Honda MP4/4 turbo car was created at short notice by a project group directed by John Barnard's former protégé, Steve Nichols. Meanwhile, Dennis had also brought in Gordon Murray, ex-Brabham, to soak up technical administration and management duties which previously had perhaps overloaded Barnard, now freeing MI's specialist design team to design.

Over preceding years, Formula 1 cars had progressively become too advanced and sophisticated for one man to create alone. As Turbo F1 Project Leader, Steve Nichols was responsible 100 per cent for the final decisions shaping the new McLaren-Honda MP4/4, but his team included Matthew Jeffreys (front suspension), Bob Bell Ph.D. (aerodynamicist – 'with a free hand to work up a shape and then try to fit the mechanicals inside it'), David North (Gordon Murray's former design partner at Brabham, now responsible for gearbox, rear suspension etc), Mike Locke (who

redrew the monocoque tooling for the new car) and Pete Burns, who created many of the fabrication jigs. Nichols himself 'handled some structural bits'.

Under 1988 safety regulations, the new tub's foot pedal position had to be drawn back some 20 cm from '87 spec behind the axis of the front-wheel centres, but even this inevitable lengthening of the chassis was compensated for by the shorter 150-litre fuel cell, which enabled the MP4/4's final wheelbase to be only 4 cm longer than a 1987 MP4/3's. The longer nose also housed an effective deformable-structure crush pad.

The free-air distance from faired roll-over bar behind the driver's head to the leading edge of the rear wing was shortened by 20-25 cm compared with the preceding MP4/3, while the arching peak line of the engine cowl was shorter but less steeply curved towards the rear.

Carbon brakes were drawn from 1986-87 stock, the bells etc being largely Steve's design, the calipers drawn long ago by Mike Locke to JB's thinking, since modified by Nichols.

'Just' drawing bodywork is an immense task. For years Colin Smith had been responsible for drawing McLaren's panels full-size, and the new '4/4s' were no exception.

The integration of fine details can make or break a great design. At one stage before manufacture the '4/4 front suspension geometry demanded a little 'ear' feature on the nose body panel to fair in the top wishbone pick-ups. That extrusive little ear 'bugged the hell' out of Nichols, so he and Matthew Jeffreys whittled away at their suspension geometry to angle the projecting wishbone pick-up inboard just enough to permit a smooth unbroken body curve which would flow cleanly, right through from nose to screen.

Eventually the concept gelled, a shape was decided which contained the smaller new 150-litre fuel tank and all Honda's mechanicals, and then came the luxury of the finer stylistic touches 'to make it look nice'. Perhaps 20 different A1 sheets of alternative windscreen possibilities were drawn

Gordon Murray had built low for Brabham – and his theme was perpetuated in the 1988 McLaren-Honda MP4/4 which dominated merely the most feeble opposition that season.

up before two were initially chosen, slightly different for each driver . . . tailored respectively to the compact little Prost and lanky Senna.

Meanwhile, at Tochigi, Honda spent the winter of 1987-88 developing effectively new turbo V6 F1 engines to 2.5-bar boost and 150-litres fuel economy. The resultant Honda 'XE2' and 'XE3' V6s offered respectively better economy or better top-end, for 'thirsty' or 'power' circuits, the 'XE3' reputedly revving to what was considered at the time a frantic 13,200 rpm.

Introduction of the latest small-diameter clutches enabled Honda to build lower, dropping their V6 crankshaft height fully 28 mm against 1987 spec.

It was to match this reduced crankshaft height that MI introduced a brand-new six-speed three-shaft gearbox, penned largely by David North with consultancy advice from veteran American transmission specialist Pete Weismann. It allowed the input shaft to enter from the clutch at low level, from which drive was stepped up into a conventional two-shaft gearbox section. This raising of the gearbox handily enabled the car's aerodynamic rear underfloor moulding to sweep up behind the rear axle-line – as permitted by the regulations – to generate useful ground-effect download. It proved far superior to the Lotus method of angling the entire engine/gearbox assembly up at the tail.

This crankshaft-lowering process permitted smaller block and sump castings, but their diminution would have left the old-style pumps projecting beneath, so they were redesigned and resited (wider) too. In search of ever-greater power/efficiency, Honda also redesigned their cylinder heads (for the umpteenth time), plus a mass of further R&D on the electronic management system.

Original spec first time out in Rio included a throttle system featuring six individual butterflies down below the intake log, beyond the pop-off valve. But it was found that on the over-run this allowed a pressure peak which popped the dump valve open, exhausting the pressure charge to atmosphere. When the driver floored the throttle again to accelerate – there was, relatively speaking, nothing at home. The instant cure at Rio was to run lower boost, but from Imola two single throttle butterflies appeared upstream of the pop-off valve, and the problem was cured.

Meanwhile, MI's late-struck deal with Honda meant the entire '4/4 programme had commenced

against the clock. After racing began in Rio a series of car-damaging incidents then left the team battling in 'a catch-up situation'. But against such feeble opposition it seldom showed.

None of the other turbo teams really counted, and on all circuits the McLaren-Hondas demonstrated a clear advantage over both turbo and atmo-engined challengers. But this was certainly not all engine, either, as Lotus failed dismally with similar Honda engines and service . . .

Despite its weak opposition, McLaren's MP4/4 chassis package simply shone.

Pure reliability problems were few. At Rio, Senna's gearchange linkage became disconnected, and at Imola and Ricard the gearshift reportedly felt 'sluggish and funny'.

Six MP4/4 carbon-composite monocoque chassis were moulded. The first was damaged in a shunt at Rio which revealed delamination in its front bulkhead due to a manufacturing problem which had to be eradicated. Another – chassis 'MP4/4-3' – was severely damaged in Monza testing and later rebuilt and consigned to Japan as a Suzuka-based Honda test car. At Monaco Senna suffered uncharacteristic apparent brain-fade while leading within a dozen laps of the finish and squidged '4/4-1's left-front corner against the sea wall at *Portier*. Even the McLaren twins' French GP duel which ended in another 1-2 triumph paradoxically also ended with two damaged chassis.

Prost had apparently thumped his winning chassis '4 over a tall kerb on, I believe, the opening lap, punching its front skid-plate up into the bottom of the tub and removing the gearbox skid-plate complete. Either that plate bounced back along the road beneath Senna's chassis '2, or he did the same as Prost a little later, they think at *Signes*, because in his case something smashed a crease right along his car's belly, penetrating right through the under-skins 'just ahead of his bum'.

That car had to be withdrawn from service to await convenient repair, not returning to the fray until season's end at Adelaide. Interestingly, every chassis but '4/4-3 won at least one Grand Prix, 15 of the season's total 16 falling before the Honda-powered cars, like this:

'MP4/4-1' – Senna won San Marino GP and Canadian GP.
'MP4/4-2' – Prost won Brazilian GP, Senna won Detroit GP and Japanese GP.
'MP4/4-4' – Prost won Monaco GP, Mexican GP and French GP.
'MP4/4-5' – Senna won British GP, German GP, Hungarian GP and Belgian GP.
'MP4/4-6' – Prost won Portuguese GP, Spanish GP and Australian GP.

At Hockenheim, internal turbo inlet ducts were used for the first time, replacing the prominent periscopes featured previously which had begun life purely as a 'hot-weather' or 'short-circuit' spec, initially for Rio. In fact the '4/4s proved to have so much intercooler capacity that their internal 'cool-weather spec' ducts (which demanded a shorter intercooler) were retained thereafter.

At Spa they found a minor improvement with a subtle front-geometry mod, and Prost tried to take off a wee bit too much wing in search of sheer speed and lost it, crucially, through *Eau Rouge*. In Hungary fuel economy became a problem under Mansell's pressure. Most circuits were tight on 150 litres of fuel, but Imola, Montreal, Portugal and Spain proved 'super-tight' – nail-bitingly so.

At Budapest Senna's car understeered badly in the top chicane. Prost's seemed superb but after qualifying badly he lost early places and finally fell back after one *banzai* attempt to displace Senna. A vibration was quoted as being created by a collapsed wheel bearing but this was not the case.

Early on at Monza, Prost and Senna raced each other too fiercely, too much boost, too rich, falling way behind on their fuel margins. A defective spark plug cut Prost's engine onto five cylinders before it blew. Senna radioed his parlous fuel state. Nakajima's Honda engine in the Lotus had already failed, and since Ayrton's Spa piston failure was known to have stemmed from running too lean he was advised to select rich mixture and low boost to preserve his engine, just in case. In fact this gave him the worst of both worlds, allowing Berger's Ferrari to close, too close.

In this context Senna had just enough fuel, and just enough time, to preserve MI's 100 per cent winning record, but any further unexpected anomaly would complicate the issue. That anomaly arose in the first chicane, as Jean-Louis Schlesser's Williams-Judd zigged while Senna zagged and the two cars collided. Senna was out of the Grand Prix, and McLaren had been defeated for the first – and only – time in 1988.

Steve Nichols recalled: 'I just sat there on the pits platform and couldn't help laughing when I saw the incident on the TV monitor. I never really expected we'd win *every* race. As the season progressed and we won more races the odds were increasingly against us. We were all a little disappointed to have got so far before it all fell through, but it's still a sport to me . . . I'm happy to see worthy competitors win too'.

In Portugal it was always necessary to trade wing for economy, 'and the drivers really start to earn their money'. There, MI agonized over economy before the start but Prost was brilliant while Senna suffered high-speed oversteer and poor economy. Both cockpit fuel read-outs were miscalibrated and in error – both cars finished with fuel on board and could have run faster, Senna's problem being greater than Prost's.

At Jerez the fuel prognosis was 'horrific – no way could we win'. Nichols has no doubt 'Alain's Spanish drive was just miraculous – I think the best performance of his entire career. That whole weekend, he got his car good, drove within his fuel – the atmos should have won that race but he just stole it from them . . .'

Again both cars finished with unburned fuel on board, but not as much as at Estoril. The read-outs were again in error, but this time within 'normal tolerance'.

And so the World Championship became a purely McLaren contest. And in England, their MP4/4B interim tub to accept Honda's naturally aspirated V10 3.5 had already commenced its painstaking programme of testing towards the season of '89.

And if that was not enough, consider now the Honda engineer who returned to Japan from their UK operation, and wrote to the effect that he was missing his work in England, 'as I am now working all day and far into every night trying to make current engine *reriable*'.

At that time they had won every race. Perfection, you see, was barely good enough . . .

Engine Management Systems

Traditional contact-breaker distributor systems struggle to supply sufficient, controlled ignition sparks at much beyond 6500 rpm. The problem is that they tend to bounce uncontrollably at higher speeds. In the 1960s, early transistorized ignition systems used contact-breaker points purely as a low-voltage trigger system, provoking a power transistor then to switch high-tension current from the coil – but mechanical bounce problems at higher rpm persisted . . .

Consequently, electro-magnetic pick-up systems were then adopted as low-voltage triggers. The engine fly-wheel carried pole pieces to induce a current pulse each time one of them flicked past a fixed pole on the crankcase. This pulse triggered an electronic amplifier to fire the main transistor's power pulse. These 'contactless' ignition systems proved more accurate than mechanical predecessors, enabling more powerful high-tension – HT – coils to generate up to 1000 sparks per second – enough to sustain 15,000 rpm in an eight-cylinder engine . . .

In the 1970s, capacitor-discharge systems emerged using a thyristor (switching) capacitor to store as much as 100 amps accumulating energy. A contactless trigger system could then fire the capacitor's high-tension current to the coil. Using voltage amplified from 12 to nearer 250, exceptionally high-energy sparks could then be achieved and hence the prominent warning upon such systems that 'high voltage can kill'.

Bosch, Lucas, Honda and Marelli all developed CD systems, and micro-electronics advances saw Buick develop a distributorless CD system in which a coil for each pair of spark plugs was triggered by an electronic control unit which monitored engine speed and load (boost) readings, adjusting timing relative to a programmed pattern and boost level.

As all major manufacturers embraced distributorless ignition combined with digital programming which also controlled fuel injection, so the modern micro-computerized engine management systems emerged. Individual cylinder control was achieved eventually by providing a separate coil united with each spark plug, sometimes a coil for each pair of plugs.

Formula 1 injection, meanwhile, had commonly delivered squirts of fuel to each cylinder timed by a mechanical shuttle-type metering unit to which fuel was pumped at constant pressure. By linking the slide throttle – a plate sandwiched into the induction system, sliding to coincide its holes with those of each ram-trumpet and each individual induction tract – by a fine-adjustable rod to a contoured cam, shuttle motion could be controlled. Its range then became variable with throttle opening to adjust the fuel amount metered to each injector nozzle. Within the metering unit, the cylinder in which the shuttle operated was rotated at engine speed, uncovering in turn ports through which the measured and now timed squirt of fuel was despatched to each nozzle.

When Renault launched its pioneering turbocharged engines, German Kugelfischer high-pressure mechanical injection was adopted, featuring a '3D' cam. This dumbell-shaped device offered control sensitive to both throttle position and boost pressure. While boost-level rotated the cam, a throttle-position linkage moved it axially. But since fuel quantity injected was adjusted relative only to load, not speed, each cylinder received the same amount of fuel in each injection pulse regardless of rpm.

Since mixture is critical in a highly stressed turbo engine, and fuel economy was always a factor, adjustment had to be lean not to waste fuel, yet rich enough to prevent overheating and possible piston damage.

As if these requirements were not sufficient spur for detail development of fuel injection control, the need to improve turbo engine 'driveability' – minimizing throttle lag and enhancing response – became imperative.

Micro-electronic advances enabled electronic control units – ECUs – to run a servo motor in an electro-mechanical system in response to inputs sensed from a variety of engine functions. The servo motor adjusted the injection metering unit cam as required in a pre-programmed menu of responses to given situations and demands.

All-electronic systems quickly followed with an ECU governing solenoid-operated injectors which triggered and timed duration of individual injection pulses.

Bosch in Germany led the way with electronic injection systems for production car use. By the 1980s digital converters were adopted enabling the ECU to incorporate a micro-processor, whose control of either electro-mechanical or all-electronic injection could be integrated with ignition control.

The micro-processor's Random Access Memory chip – RAM – and a plug-in Erasable Programmable Read Only Memory chip – EPROM – provided programmed responses to running conditions monitored by the various engine and driver-input sensors. The baseline RAM could be programmed during engine development running on the dyno, a coarse 'map' being created by the engineers writing in optimum ignition and injection settings determined over a range of engine speeds by painstaking manual adjustment. Once established, this initial 'coarse map' would then provide a series of marks on the programme graph to be in effect joined together to provide a fine-tune map of the engine's entire range. The management system EPROM, however, then provided an easy trackside adjustment facility – the chip being easily removed and plugged into a portable EPROM programmer to be 're-blown' and re-programmed.

In 1985, the British Zytek company introduced the first onboard re-programmable memory enabling comprehensive software map replacement in the field, transferred from pre-written discs via a portable computer.

Electronic 'spikes' induced by electro-magnetic interference from other systems within the car disrupted many a favoured ECU map, demanding painstaking insulation and isolation measures in response.

Electro-mechanical injection, meanwhile, commonly offered higher pressures than all-electronic systems. In 1983 both BMW and Renault used electro-mechanical injection with Kugelfischer's high-pressure pump. Working with Bosch, BMW adopted an integrated 'data logging' system with an extra RAM within the ECU which recorded digitized input signals and enabled them to be recalled into trackside computers for leisured analysis.

Initially this data log preserved only maximum and minimum values for each parameter – subsequently the duration spent at each peak, and eventually a continuous re-playable record within available time recording capacity.

It was also BMW who adopted telemetry, in which ECU signals were radioed direct into a trackside receiver while the car was in action.

Bosch held patents on the solenoid injector, and while Weber Marelli, for example, made their own under licence, the basic Bosch injector nozzle was restrictively small for turbo F1 requirements so two nozzles were consequently adopted by some constructors.

ECU engine control expanded rapidly to encompass electronically controlled turbocharger wastegate systems in order to maximize useable boost, while variable-geometry scroll turbo intake control was also explored.

From 1984, with fuel capacity limitations being applied, fuel economy became a vital consideration in Formula 1, placing added demand upon accurate injection, ignition and turbocharger boost control. Bosch simply did it best with their all-electronic system for McLaren-TAG Turbo.

The most ferocious of turbocharged F1 engines were aptly described as hand grenades liable to detonate at any moment, the safety pin being retained only by their management systems.

Much the same would prove true once 3.5-litre 'atmo' racing became serious from 1989, and as fuel chemistry and multi-valve timing have become ever more crucial towards the end of our period the science of electronic engine management has become all-embracing – though naturally the soaring development pace of its pioneering years through the mid-1980s has eased as advances become smaller, more elusive, and more costly to find and to exploit.

Electronic fuel injection and ignition management technology first made dominant impact upon Formula 1 in 1984 when Porsche brought in Bosch on the TAG Turbo V6 project for McLaren International – we can't resist the cliché, chips with everything, and here they are . . .

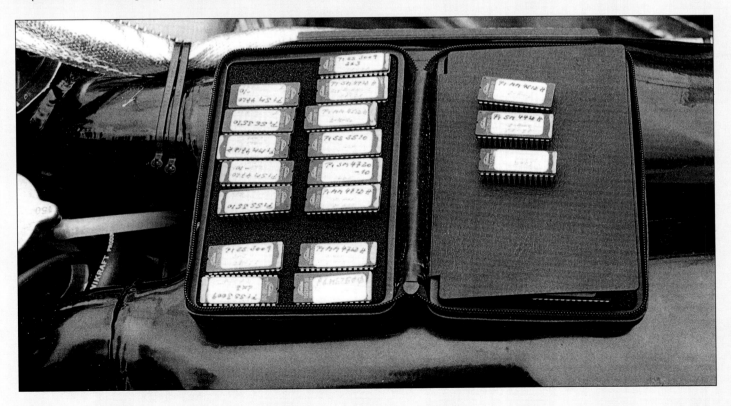

Chapter 18

THE 'ATMOSPHERIC' V10 McLAREN-HONDA MP4/5s 1989-90

Honda unveiled its new 3.5-litre naturally aspirated V10-cylinder Formula 1 engine at the Tokyo Motor Show of 1987, even before its 2.5-bar V6 turbo engines would enjoy their last dominant season with McLaren International.

Even while the McLaren-Honda MP4/4 turbo cars were winning 15 of the 1988 season's 16 World Championship Grand Prix races, the V10 'atmo' engine was out on test. It was installed in the stern of an interim MP4/4B test chassis, and was being test driven by Senna, Prost and stand-in test driver Emanuele Pirro.

As originally unveiled in Tokyo in 1987, the new V10 engine had produced barely 500 bhp. By the spring of 1988, 600 bhp had been achieved but early track testing revealed a potential lubrication problem which would recur during the 1989 racing season.

At McLaren's Woking headquarters, ex-Williams engineer Neil Oatley was Project Leader for the 1989 V10 car. Under the management of Osamu Goto, Honda were to supply a total float of eight of the RA109E V10-cylinder engines to McLaren at each Grand Prix meeting, two units for each race car and the spare, plus two extras as emergency back-up.

The MP4/5 was well advanced when Honda raised the possibility of changing camshaft drive from belts to gears. Honda asked McLaren to consider whether they could handle the inevitable weight penalty and installation problems this change would impose, emphasizing their belief that more accurate valve timing control could be achieved with gears rather than belts. McLaren accepted their decision, redesigning the MP4/5 to accommodate the reshaped power unit, and the race engines were gear-driven from the outset. This modification had a knock-on effect in terms of delaying the overall MP4/5 development programme by two crucial weeks which proved difficult to claw back.

The new car retained McLaren's traditional practice of separating chassis structure from aerodynamic body panelling in the interests of aerodynamic flexibility. The new monocoques were moulded in high-modulus material supplied on a world-exclusive basis by Hercules Aerospace. The MP4/5 emerged looking generically similar to its predecessors but with a greater number of aerodynamic changes than was customary. These alterations resulted from the team's intensive and continuous wind tunnel research programme, and

The 1989-90 McLaren-Honda V10 MP4/5-series cars impressed, as usual, with the Woking team's impeccable finish quality, superb body shut lines and overall sheer competitiveness. Compared to the turbocharged cars which went before, the 'atmo' machine offered more compact, neater lines, with abbreviated teardrop planform side pods, the most slender fuselage yet and relatively massive front wing area.

also reflected the greater air induction and cooling demands of the naturally aspirated V10 compared with the lightly stresed 2.5-bar Honda V6 of 1988. Dimensionally, the MP4/5 had a 114-inch wheelbase, and tracks of 71.6 and 65.75 in.

From the beginning of development a brand-new transverse-shaft six-speed gearbox had been necessary to shorten the overall power-train length. MI's engineers were determined to maximize this transmission's advantage before it was raced and consequently it was not introduced until mid-season.

The car began the year fitted with an evolutionary version of the David North-designed three-shaft longitudinal transmission from the MP4/4, in conjunction with McLaren twin-caliper brakes. The planned 'phase-two' specification was to include the new rear suspension, revised front uprights and single-caliper Brembo brakes in conjunction with the transverse gearbox.

In the opening race at Rio, Senna went out in a first-corner collision, while Prost's clutch trouble prevented him making a strategically crucial second tyre stop. The MP4/5 also displayed a fundamental handling imbalance, characterized by a nervousness on the entry to high-speed corners.

Both drivers also reported abrupt throttle response at the bottom of the rev range which exacerbated the handling problem.

An intensive eight-day test at Imola prior to the San Marino GP made progress on the handling imbalance, although traces of the problem remained throughout the season and it became normal to set up the chassis to accommodate this shortcoming.

But the driveability of the RA109E engine was improved for San Marino, where Senna shattered Nelson Piquet's outright lap record set with the unrestricted-boost Williams-Honda turbo in 1986 . . .

At Imola, Prost believed Senna to be in breach of a first-corner 'no passing' agreement which the Brazilian himself had suggested. Prost subsequently declared publicly at Monaco that Senna was 'not a man of honour', despite an apology from the Brazilian for the Imola lapse.

From that point forward the two McLaren drivers barely spoke, technical communication regarding the cars being conducted via engineers Nichols and Oatley.

For Monaco, the Honda V10 appeared in lightened form, while the single-caliper Brembo brakes

then being introduced in advance of the transverse gearbox saved further car weight. Senna won, driving around a stripped second gear.

In Mexico the two cars displayed different fuel consumption, feeding Prost's mounting paranoia that Honda were not providing him with equal equipment. In fact Honda and McLaren engineers spent two days filtering data during the run-up to the following weekend's Phoenix race, eventually concluding broadly that Senna used more fuel simply because he was working the engine harder than Prost, not that Prost's was less thirsty since it was set up to develop less power – as the Frenchman had apparently come to believe . . .

In fact the delicate footwork which had given him an edge in 150-litre limit turbocharged days now needed revision. Senna was simply spending longer at peak revs, using more fuel and developing more power, longer.

Prost then chose to alter the driveability of his engine following an early-season test at Jerez, having a different engine management chip installed in the units used in his cars. This richened the mixture slightly, improving the pick-up to complement his smooth and progressive throttle opening style. Senna, whose mid-corner throttle-blipping technique kept the revs up, did the same thing his own way.

Honda declared that engine power outputs in reality never varied more than 5 bhp between accepted units and maintained absolutely equal provenance to both drivers. Yet Prost was blasted off by his team-mate on the straight at Mexico City and remained sceptical. After a pit lane misunderstanding there his car was then fitted with the wrong tyre combination at his first pit stop, requiring a second stop to correct matters which dropped him to a distant fifth at the finish.

Alain Prost emerged desperately unhappy and soon afterwards decided to leave the team for which he had driven so long. By the time of the Italian GP at Monza he would be publicly accusing Honda of favouring Senna at his expense.

Meanwhile, after winning three races out of four, unreliability struck Senna at Phoenix, Montreal, Ricard and Silverstone.

At Phoenix a serious misfire cost him the lead. After the race that engine was returned to Wako where its electrical system was dissected without any fault being found. The car's electrical harnesses showed no problem either. Subsequent tests suggested that pits-to-car radio link signals in the confined streets of Phoenix had affected the engine management sensors by induction. This led to the transmitter/receiver aerials then being relocated on the chassis.

In Canada engine failure occurred, centring on the oil-ring package employed by Honda which highlighted a problem in the delicate and complex balance between low frictional losses and the need to retain compression and oil seal on the power stroke. This was aggravated by the wet conditions, water entering the engine, and by the necessarily intermittent throttle openings applied. This engine failure had thus been the product of a complex and unusual combination of circumstances.

As an intermediate step towards avoiding a recurrence of such problems, an oil condenser was added to the breather system before the French GP, further refinements to the car/engine oil system then following in time for the German GP.

On the longitudinal gearbox's last outing, at Ricard, Senna then had a spur gear break leaving the grid.

Installation at last of the transverse gearbox then brought the MP4/5 right down to the 505 kg 'TV ballast' weight limit – and in this configuration it made its debut at the British GP, at Silverstone. There the cars fell victim to a major oil tank malfunction but still qualified 1-2. Incomplete welding was the problem, located at a point where an oil scavenge pipe returned between the oil separator and the air catch tank – very difficult to discover since the tanks were manufactured from the inside out. It was finally traced on race eve using Honda's telemetry system to monitor pressure variations within the

Above: *Installation of the 3.5-litre Honda V10 engine in the McLaren MP4/5; note the raked radiator, monocoque fuel cell and cell-top electronics site.* Right: *The MP4/5's drivers were protected by the crushable forward footbox and 'behind-the-axle' pedals but still had coil/damper units by their shins.*

tanks themselves. This information was then passed to the factory staff who drilled inspection holes in the offending tanks, and were then able to pinpoint the problem by introscope examination.

Three replacement tanks were then prepared for the race, static tests being carried out before they were installed in the cars. Race set-up included a catch tank, the oil being recirculated by means of a cockpit-activated valve. The drivers were required periodically to press a button in response to pit signals during the race, an arrangement retained for the remainder of the season.

The transverse gearbox ostensibly performed well on its debut at Silverstone, although subsequent strip-down of that fitted to Prost's car revealed incipient bearing failure inconsistent with testing results. This was attributed to incorrect material specification but Senna had also obviously had problems as selection difficulties had seen him spin into the sand trap at Becketts Corner. In fact, revised and previously untested gearchange mechanisms had been used for the race, and marks on that in Prost's car implied a similar selection problem on the Brazilian's.

In Phoenix, meanwhile, Prost had wrecked his first monocoque in five and a half years' driving for McLaren. At Montreal he stopped early when his car's top-left front wishbone rear mounting point pulled out of the monocoque, a failure stemming from the reduced load-spreading properties offered by the higher-modulus carbon material from which the new MP4/5 tubs were being manufactured. Short-term interim repairs included an ungainly patched monocoque – which made perfectionist Ron Dennis wince – before more fundamental revisions to the structure were fed into the system as new replacement tubs were completed.

Senna wrote off another tub over a rock during

Hockenheim qualifying but won the race in what had originally been the spare car after Prost was slowed when a selector malfunction prevented him finding sixth gear.

Both cars then ran untroubled at the Hungaroring and Spa, but the drivers were again complaining of poor and abrupt throttle response from the Honda 'spec 5' engine in the wet Belgian race.

Honda invested hugely in developing different versions of the RA109E engine, aiming to optimize performance under widely differing conditions, taking into account potential fuel consumption, circuit characteristics and anticipated ambient temperatures.

Goto praised Senna's driving perception for contributing significantly to engine development throughout the year. 'We think it is now easier to take a Honda V10 off the line than a Ferrari F40!' was one memorable quote from the Japanese project chief.

At Rio for the engine's first race, Goto and his team had aimed for reliability with a slightly detuned version of the original V10 which had been tested initially with belt-driven camshafts. The definitive 'standard' engine was that known effectively as 'specification 3' and the potential power available at Rio but held in reserve was all offered in the engine tune taken to Imola. By the time of Monaco the ongoing commitment to weight reduction saw another 3 kg – a very considerable bonus – pared off the V10.

Prior to the Belgian GP at Spa two engines with further-revised specification were tested – 'spec 4' with more top-end power for use at Monza and possibly Suzuka and 'spec 5' offering improved low-speed driveability.

At Monza Senna's 'spec 4' engine suffered a major oil loss, ruining its bearings and causing his retirement from a commanding lead. But Prost came through to win, clinching McLaren-Honda's second successive Constructors' Championship with four of the 16 races still to run.

Eight of the MP4/5 cars were built, number '2 being that written off in Prost's practice accident at Phoenix. Numbers '1-2-3 had made their debut at Rio, '3 being most used subsequently as '4 appeared new as spare car in Mexico, later serving as test team chassis. Car '5 was new for Prost at Ricard, '6 for Senna at Silverstone – later severely damaged underneath by hitting the rock at Hockenheim – '7 was for Senna at Spa, and '8 new for Prost at Suzuka.

In 1990, the third year of the McLaren-Honda alliance, the team experienced a mid-season trough with drivers Senna and Gerhard Berger struggling to maintain competitiveness against the better-handling Ferrari 641s, as at Ricard and Silverstone. McLaren entrusted its Championship defence to an uprated version of the Neil Oatley-supervised MP4/5, the MP4/5B, powered by the latest version of the Honda V10 engine, now confusingly classified the RA100E in succession to the RA109E of 1989.

The MP4/5B featured a slightly enlarged fuel cell, altered front suspension geometry and a heavily revised version of the six-speed transverse gearbox which had been introduced into the race programme at the 1989 British GP. Significant changes had also been made to the profile of the side pods and radiator ducting. This research also produced a distinctive multi-arched diffuser panel beneath the tail which was incorporated into the new race cars from the start of the season.

The MP4/5B was based upon a wheelbase of 115.7 inches, with track widths of 71.8 and 65.7 inches front and rear.

From the outset it was clear that McLaren had set itself quite a task, its build programme for 1990 including not only the full complement of new MP4/5B chassis for the racing programme but also MP4/5C test cars and definitive race chassis to carry the forthcoming new Honda V12 engine for 1991. The first MP4/5B was then damaged badly when Senna bounced over a kerb during a pre-season test session at Silverstone, but the Brazilian considered that the revised chassis was considerably more responsive than its 1989 predecessor.

Prost's replacement within the team – Gerhard Berger, ex-Ferrari – started the season-opener in Phoenix from pole position but accidentally snagged the brake pedal while running second to Jean Alesi's Tyrrell in the opening stages of the race and slid into a tyre barrier. When the lanky Austrian had first tried a test car in the winter, he found he was banging his knees on the underside of the steering wheel bulkhead so the pedals were temporarily moved forward – and thus rendered illegal – for the purposes of pre-season development work.

The bulkhead was redesigned on all the subsequent MP4/5B race cars but despite these changes being carried out to the level both Berger and the team believed would solve the problem, there still proved to be inadequate room for the Austrian to prevent discomfort and cramp in a full-length

race. A succession of makeshift modifications then had to be made to the dashboard roll hoop to accommodate him. Only after a summer test session at Ricard for which the cockpit was altered to provide him with a more upright driving position was the problem effectively resolved.

The mid-season chassis crisis played right into Senna's hands, strengthening his bargaining position with the team as his first three-year contract was reaching its close.

Engineer Steve Nichols had left McLaren for Ferrari at the end of 1989. This move alone had apparently unsettled the Brazilian, and Neil Oatley's team did not seem able to provide him with the consistently good-handling chassis he had come to expect from McLaren. The sight of Senna wrestling the ill-handling MP4/5B around Silverstone before it got away from him and spun was a new experience . . . He recovered to finish the race but the car's underbody was damaged and a floor support stay broken by his excursion across the grass.

After these rather public Silverstone problems, a development blitz saw much of the chassis's apparent lack of sensitivity corrected with aerodynamic modifications which included abandoning the arched tail diffuser in favour of a more conventional and mild design. Although the arched diffuser created greater total download it made the car rather nervous on the entry to high-speed corners in a manner which left the design team pondering whether this was related to an aerodynamic problem or to lack of mechanical grip.

At Hockenheim Senna and McLaren-Honda at last came back into play to end three consecutive victories by Prost for Ferrari. The underfloor/diffuser package introduced post-Hockenheim then made the MP4/5B significantly more comfortable to drive, although lacking the downforce of its predecessor. Readying the parts, together with a high front wing development which was tested but not raced, had placed heavy demands on the Woking workforce and factory capacity.

Senna was by this time receiving the exclusive attention of race engineer Gordon Kimball, who from Hockenheim forward assumed responsibility for engineering support on the Brazilian's car. Neil Oatley concentrated upon design of the definitive new MP4/6 V12 car for 1991, Kimball taking over continued engineering development of the MP4/5B for the balance of 1990.

Significant geometry improvements were also introduced at Estoril and Jerez to alter the rising-rate characteristics of the cars' front suspension.

Under Goto's leadership, meanwhile, Honda development had continued apace, ultimately deploying a full 690 bhp from the naturally aspirated 3.5-litre V10s. Increased rev limits and low-density fuel for qualifying gave Senna up to 710 bhp for a string of sensational pole position runs which characterized the season.

The Honda engines burned lead-free Shell fuel mixes with no problems apart from Imola, where incompatibility between valve seat material and the fuel spec chosen for the race was blamed for

an unexpected power loss which left Berger unable to hold off Patrese's Williams-Renault in the closing stages. For the French GP a new low-friction-specification V10 was introduced but its worth was masked by the handling problems which beset the MP4/5B there and at Silverstone.

With the chassis restored to a reasonably competitive pitch at Hockenheim the German GP then saw the debut of the higher-revving and more powerful 'version 4' Honda RA100E V10, a slightly lightened power unit, and at Spa 'version 5' appeared on the scene with revised induction system in search of further-improved top-end performance.

The V10 proved prone to power loss during the season and it was not until Monza that Ayrton confirmed it had run a full Grand Prix distance without any perceptible drop-off in power. The sheer resources available to Honda and McLaren and their shrewd application had pulled the team through that nerve-racking mid-season crisis. What other team would have spent £9000 chartering a BAe 146 jetliner to fly a new floor section to Monza for only ten laps' testing before it was discarded?

Seven MP4/5Bs were built for 1991, the first, damaged in the pre-season incident at Silverstone, later becoming the spare second chassis at Montreal, Ricard and Silverstone. The three cars taken to Phoenix for the first race of the season were therefore '2-3-4, Berger's '2 only running again at Interlagos; '5 was new for him at Imola, '6 new for Senna at Montreal and '7 new for Senna at Suzuka, where it was damaged in the first-corner collision with former team-mate Prost's Ferrari 641 which ultimately clinched the World Championship for the aggressive – and in that case aggrieved – Brazilian. It would take a year but he would eventually admit that he intentionally drove into the Ferrari that day . . . the manoeuvre of an intensely competitive and totally motivated racing driver, but one which undoubtedly brought the 'sport' into disrepute and reflected no credit at all upon either Senna or the team for which he drove. It was an unsavoury end to McLaren-Honda's hat-trick season of World Championship honours, but one which should in no way detract from their engineering achievement. It merely reflected the frailty of man, in contrast to the capability of the machine.

Winning profile – Senna in the MP4/5-Honda V10 giving McLaren International's various suppliers full credit. The black-barred engine cowl 'TV logo' to those in the know read 'Marlboro' and was applied in nations where tobacco advertising is illegal.

Chapter 19
THE McLAREN-HONDA V12s 1991

Into 1991 – entering its fourth consecutive season – the McLaren-Honda partnership adopted its third configuration of Formula 1 racing engine – the latest Honda 3.5-litre 'atmo' V12. This RA121E 60-degree V12 superseded the RA101E 72-degree V10 of 1990 which was supplied instead for this one season to Tyrrell, on a fixed-specification basis.

Honda claimed 680 bhp from the new V12 at peak, exceeding the V10's best by some way, but after closed-season testing by Gerhard Berger, F1 cast-off Jonathan Palmer and F3000 hopeful Allan McNish, there was growing doubt that such a 'top number' was actually being realized, or was indeed useable, in the car . . .

Ayrton Senna had spent the winter of 1990/91 hibernating – as had become his habit – back home in Brazil, and when he returned to Europe for the final pre-season test session at Estoril he was loudly unimpressed with the new unit's performance. Both he and Berger in fact yearned for the V10's mid-range driveability, which the new V12 woefully lacked.

With such an engine shortfall it was relatively difficult to assess the latest MP4/6 chassis developed at Woking for the 12-cylinder engines.

Design of the MP4/6's new monocoque had been finalized by chief designer Neil Oatley's team before the appointment in June 1990 of former Ferrari aerodynamicist Henri Durand. The long lead time on the new V12 tub was partly the result of its featuring ultra-high-modulus carbon-fibre materials developed by Hercules in Utah. At least McLaren's traditional use of separate structural monocoque with *appliqué* external aerodynamic body skins had left Durand relative freedom to shape the finished car as he felt necessary.

While the monocoque nacelle itself was consider-

radiator consideration in addition to the larger fuel requirement exacerbated the lengthy V12 unit's prior demand for extra space within the wheelbase, increasing the MI design team's problems in minimizing weight.

The MP4/6's wheelbase was in fact kept to just 4 cm more than that of the preceding V10-cylinder cars' but its increased bulk overall gave Durand's wind tunnel team extra problems in maintaining adequate efficiencies in aerodynamic downforce and drag.

In fact the new model would make history in winning the first four consecutive rounds of the new season's World Championship 'right out of the box', but prime beneficiary Ayrton Senna was realistic enough to denounce the equipment roundly and to emphasize to both McLaren's and Honda's management that they had been incredibly – almost unbelievably – lucky.

According to both drivers the new V12 engine felt so under-powered and restricted in torque compared with the passed-on V10 that somebody, somewhere, could not be seriously considering further World Championship success . . .

Honda F1 project leader Akimasa Yasuoka explained 'We traditionally detune our engine for the first race of the season; we tend to go for reliability rather than power . . .' but Senna would not accept that without frank discussion.

This apparent engine deficiency was not too marked using the initial 'spec 1' V12 on the preposterous street circuit at Phoenix, opening the series, but three rivals lapped faster during the race and Ferrari and Williams-Renault unreliability assisted the Senna/McLaren cause.

At São Paulo, Brazil, he succeeded in winning his home GP at the eighth attempt but again thanks to semi-auto transmission problems with Mansell's Williams-Renault which took off the pressure when the leading MP4/6 would break its fourth gear in the closing stages and merely limp over the finishing line, finally jammed in sixth . . .

The MP4/6's transverse-shaft gearbox was a development of that used on the MP4/5B, revised and updated to save weight and provide faster gearchanging.

At Imola in winning round three Senna was plagued for the last 20 laps by diminishing oil pressure and an ever-brighter-glowing warning light, but again he was able to nurse an ailing MP4/6 to the chequered flag because all serious opposition had evaporated and there was nobody able to put pressure upon him, other than his team-mate Berger.

There in the so-called San Marino GP Honda's 'spec 2' V12 made its debut, with induction tailored to enhance mid-range torque.

At Monaco Mansell's Williams survived to the finish in second place, but mid-race problems with a throttle position sensor misdirecting his engine's management system had left him too far behind Senna to apply real pressure when the Honda V12 again began to lose oil pressure in the final 20 laps.

The Japanese engine was proving more fuel-thirsty than predicted and excessive internal friction and consequent higher cooling requirement robbed power. Uneven oil distribution through the crankshaft had contributed to serious main bearing wear and eventual failure.

After those four successive early-season victories, Williams's new semi-auto gearbox achieved reliability to match the power advantage of their French V10 engine and MI was rocked back on its heels from the Canadian GP through mid-season as the Williams-Renault FW14s dominated.

Engineer Yasuoka's engine group had suffered a tremendous blow to corporate pride during the Mexican GP meeting, during which the Renault V10 engine used by Williams was demonstrably superior in all departments, and Senna was pressured into trying so hard during qualifying he actually rolled his car.

In the French race at Magny-Cours, Senna's fuel-state read-out warned him to ease off and settle for a minor placing. Over-optimistic fuel read-outs then caused Senna to run dry in both the British and German GPs. In part these

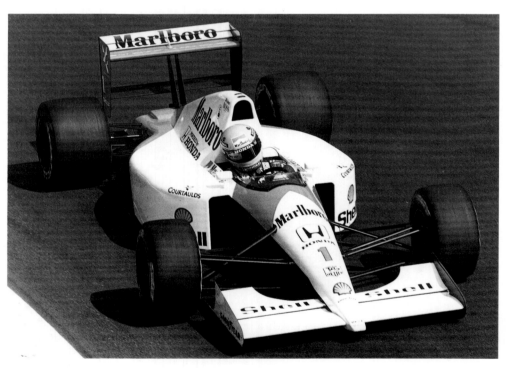

World Champion Ayrton Senna in his McLaren-Honda MP4/6, demonstrating its fashionably late-'80s/early-'90s pushrod front suspension, teardrop planform body form, biplane rear wing on blade centre mounts and the latest development of the 'McLaren tail' shape. Finish was of course exquisite, body fit superb . . . Above right: Into 1991, McLaren remained the sole significant constructor using a flat-sided inner monocoque with detachable appliqué *body panelling providing an easily changeable aerodynamic envelope.*

ably more rigid than its MP4-family ancestors, its construction minimized the specific number of separate components required and also featured the larger fuel cell considered necessary to feed the more fuel-thirsty V12.

Whereas the preceding MP4/5B front suspension had featured traditional vertically disposed coil-spring/damper units each side of the forward footbox, the new MP4/6 sited its dampers Ferrari-style on top of the scuttle, just ahead of the cockpit, where they were actuated by pushrods and bell-crank rockers.

This new coil/damper siting demanded a higher bodyline through the scuttle area than previously, while longer side pods were adopted to accommodate the V12's larger-area cooling demand. This

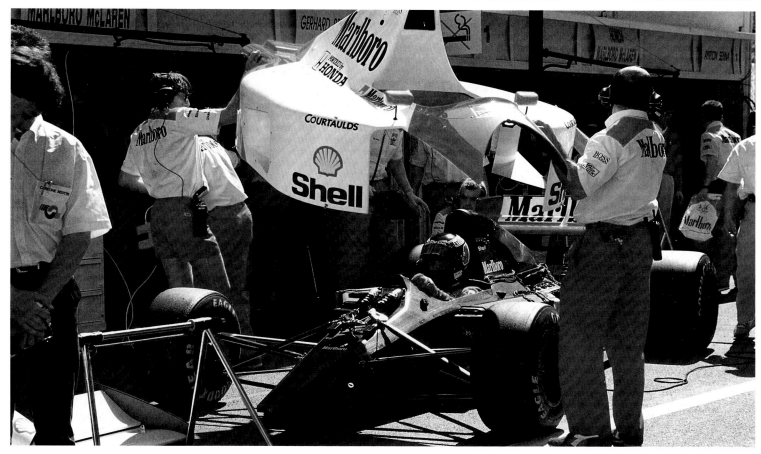

vagaries were attributable to programming difficulties in keeping abreast of Shell's alternative fuel characteristics altering consumption as fluid density, viscosity and vapourization-loss continually changed. MI's sister company TAG Electronics helped re-calibrate the Honda engine management systems to correct this distressing problem.

In addition to rewritten software for the management ECU, a sealed closed-circuit fuel system was developed, eliminating fuel vapour loss to atmosphere.

In time for the British GP at Silverstone, 'spec 3' engines became available with a shorter stroke to reduce internal friction, increase revs and release more power.

The MP4/6 was rigged for Silverstone with a short inter-link bar between the front suspension rocker arms to increase the system's roll-stiffness, while a driver-adjustable front ride-height control was also fitted.

After the French race, Honda R&D at Wako, Japan, rushed forward development of a dramatically revised V12 engine with new heads, crankshaft, rods and camshafts capable of sustaining 14,800 rpm in short bursts. The revised new engine was also to feature electronically activated variable-length injection trumpets, enabling intake tract length to be varied under command from the management system to optimize torque across the broadest possible rev-band.

Senna was provided with the first of these new-generation units for the Hungarian GP, in which he qualified on pole and was able to prevent the Williams-Renaults from attacking him successfully throughout race distance – using a new MP4/6 chassis number '8' lightened to compensate for its still overweight engine relative to the rival Renault.

There at the Hungaroring the MP4/6 also deployed an electro-pneumatic gearchange system for the first time at a race meeting, the result of joint MI/Honda developments building towards introduction of a raceworthy semi-auto gearchange à la Ferrari and Williams. This particular system – known as the McLaren '6Y' – comprised the six-speed transverse-shaft gearbox with pneumatic selector pressurized from a small gas reservoir mounted at the tail, the gearchange

system being triggered by electronic impulse from driver finger-tip flippers behind the steering wheel.

Another contemporary high-tech R&D programme involved the Japanese Showa damper-manufacturing company in researching competitive active suspension, MI employing Palmer, McNish and the experienced Stefan Johansson as test drivers throughout that summer. Michael Andretti – set to win the 1991 American CART Championship and son of 1978 World Champion, Mario – would also drive the McLaren-Hondas, though more on a driver than car evaluation basis . . .

Meanwhile, Senna's brilliance built on the Hungarian success by then nursing the MP4/6 to another victory in the Belgian GP at Spa despite a hardened spacer washer having failed in one of the gearbox clusters, lodging momentarily in the gearchange and causing a baulky 'change. Having warned the driver of impending trouble in this way, the errant fragment was trapped by the gearbox lubrication system's debris-trap magnets to prevent further intrusion. However, without an intact spacer the neighbouring gearwheels would normally have been free to slip out of engagement, but at Spa they rested firmly against one another. After feeling that initial baulkiness, Senna 'Grand-ma'd' the gearchange (as Dan Gurney used to put it) avoiding the lower ratios as far as possible, and the system again survived to the finish, thanks largely to his sensitivity.

Williams dominated at the Portuguese and Spanish events but MI's engineers revised the MP4/6 aerodynamic package in time for the Japanese event on Honda's test track at Suzuka, where Mansell fell off the circuit and Senna clinched the Drivers' title yet again.

There he backed off in the finishing straight to hand consolation victory to his team-mate Gerhard Berger – a noble gesture repaying the Austrian's unflagging support as number two.

The Constructors' title remained in dispute into the final GP of the season, at Adelaide, Australia, but there the race was rendered farcical by torrential rain – and Senna was declared winner with Berger third after the event was red-flagged, and McLaren International retained its title with 139 points to Williams-Renault's 125.

MI had manufactured more Formula 1 chassis than ever before during this 1991 V12-engined programme – the MP4/6 family embracing 11 individual car identities for race and R&D test-team duties. Senna's winning cars at Phoenix, São Paulo, Imola and Monte Carlo were 'MP4/6-3' (first two) and '5 (second two), and he also won three times in 'MP4/6-8' in Hungary, Belgium and Australia. Berger's regular mid-season car was 'MP4/6-6', which ran as '6Y with the electro-pneumatic gearchange in Hungary, while his late-season car, chassis '9, inherited that solitary victory courtesy of Senna's uncharacteristic generosity in Japan.

The full list of 1991 season public appearances by the MP4/6 cars is as follows:

'MP4/6-1' – spare Phoenix, Brazil, GB.
'MP4/6-2' – Berger Phoenix, Brazil, spare Imola, Berger Canada, Mexico.
'MP4/6-3' – Senna Phoenix, Brazil, spare GB.
'MP4/6-4' – Berger Monaco, spare Spain.
'MP4/6-5' – Senna Imola, Monaco, Canada, Mexico, France, GB, Germany.
'MP4/6-6' – Berger Imola, spare Monaco, Canada, spare Mexico, France, GB, Germany, ('6Y') Hungary, Belgium.
'MP4/6-7' – Berger France, GB, Germany, Hungary.
'MP4/6-8' – Senna Hungary, Belgium, spare Italy, Portugal, Spain, Japan, Australia.
'MP4/6-9' – Berger Belgium, Italy, Portugal, Spain, Japan, Australia.
'MP4/6-10' – Senna Italy, Portugal, Spain, spare Japan.
'MP4/6-11' – Senna Japan, Australia.

Above all this list demonstrates sheer commitment to success in the teeth of considerable adversity, McLaren International's reward being the team's eighth World Championship success in one or other – or both – available competitions for the seventh time in eight consecutive seasons. Which is not only an extraordinary record, but also one entirely unmatched in the entire history of Grand Prix racing.

McLaren International had proved itself a very special organization with a little help from well-chosen friends . . .

Semi-Automatic Transmissions

One of the most demanding restraints upon moulded composite single-seater chassis construction through the 1980s was the need to provide a rigid mechanical gearchange linkage between the cockpit gear-lever and the gearbox itself, mounted out behind in the breeze . . .

Not only did this linkage have to be sufficiently rigid to provide accurate selection – without twisting – in at least three different lateral planes, it also had to be strong enough to resist the attentions of an athlete with hyper-developed upper body strength yanking it to and fro longitudinally while in a highly stressed and often 'emotional' state.

In conjunction with the internal selector mechanism within the gearbox this linkage also had to provide high-speed gearchanges which would only interrupt the application of engine power or over-run torque for the most fleeting of milli-second time periods.

Naturally this speed of gearchanging could be enhanced by minimizing the mechanical movement range of the cockpit lever itself, but even with the minimum movement range achieved, the motion arcs of the gear-lever grip, and of the gloved driver's fist clutching it, demanded sufficient cockpit space to wave a fair-sized grapefruit two inches or more in all directions.

This demand upon space within the cockpit coaming, and the need to provide a gearchange linkage tunnel or external gearchange linkage clearance between cockpit and rear-mounted transaxle, was a major design headache which most F1 car designers took for granted until – after a number of false starts – John Barnard, at that time of Ferrari, addressed the problem determinedly in 1987-88.

Chaparral sports cars had most successfully employed GM automatic transmission in the 1960s. They performed well apart from initial lag on take-off from the start line. Driver Phil Hill caustically compared the Chaparral's getaway to that of a '52 Ford FluiDrive, but their 'autobox' undoubtedly saved driver load, and the two-speed GM system proved most effective in putting available horsepower down onto the road for the maximum period of time – which is the name of the game.

McLaren toyed with a similar sports car auto system but raced it only once – and in later years Porsche also tried one on their endurance cars, using a twin clutch system with concentric shafts which engaged the next required gear before the first would be disengaged. As the driver released one clutch, the system engaged the other . . . But no racing 'auto' – save Chaparral's – had made any significant impact until in 1987 Barnard detailed Maranello engineer de Silvestri to approach the problem taking full advantage of modern electronic micro-processing capacity to mate an electro-hydraulic clutch mechanism and gear-selection system within a version of the conventional mechanical gearbox.

During early discussions, much to Barnard's surprise, one Maranello old hand recalled previous in-house experiments with auto-selection once tested by Gilles Villeneuve. 'He apparently thought it was "OK, but not very interesting" . . . so they put it back on the shelf.'

To cater for the peaky power curve promised by the forthcoming new 3.5-litre V12 engine for 1989 'atmo' Formula 1 racing, a seven-speed transmission was developed, featuring electro-hydraulic selection to be triggered by finger-tip flipper switches mounted just beyond the steering wheel, absolutely to minimize driver movement while still permitting him positive command of the system. He would flip one switch to change up, the other to change down, while keeping both hands on the steering wheel all the time.

All that changed, in effect, was that the operating cylinder now had two pistons, the rear one controlled by a valve to open and close the clutch, while the forward piston remained conventionally linked to a driver foot pedal which had priority, over-riding the electro-hydraulic valved system. Each selector rod had its own actuating piston operating in a hydraulic system, each with two simple open/close valves. With both valves open the piston – and therefore its selector rod – would sit inoperative in neutral. When signalled electronically one valve would open and the other remain closed to present a pressure differential within the system, thus propelling the piston one way or the other as required, to select a suitable gear. The conventional clutch was operated by an electronically controlled Moog valve, sometimes by a proportional valve.

Once the driver took the car off the line in first gear using his conventional foot pedal, he would then change gear on the flipper switches, firing the selector system. To select reverse, a push-button control was provided on the dash panel. Since the conventional-layout mechanical

gearbox offered seven forward speeds, reverse was provided on one end of the 'box's fourth shaft.

The reverse-selector button was remote from the flippers, on the dash, to prevent accidental selection while driving normally. It still proved too easy to select as in the celebrated 1990 Portuguese GP incident when Mansell overshot his pit and instantly reversed into it, to disqualify himself. As Barnard recalled: 'Most systems would have required him to mesh nasty gears manually, which might have given him time to think better of it!'

Overall, 'The reduction in driver workload was a major plus. The bonus in car control by keeping both hands on the wheel also paid off in every race start when the entire pack is dodging around and jostling for position . . .'.

The timing of electro-hydraulic clutch release/gear selection/clutch re-engagement was handled by microprocessor programming upon the driver's command input. The system was marginally heavier than a straightforward manual-change transaxle, its electronic 'brain', the required hydraulic pump and the hydraulic fluid tank in the 'box being extras, but there was an offsetting weight saving on manual gearchange mechanism.

The prototype seven-speed semi-auto system was tried experimentally upon a turbocharged F1 Ferrari in the summer of '88, and the experimental Ferrari *Tipo* 639 was then designed for the new semi-auto system, but there was just about enough space within its tub to accommodate a conventional manual 'change. Despite many development problems Barnard then committed the new *Tipo* 640 design for 1989 to semi-auto, in that its new monocoque offered no space whatsoever for an alternative rigid gearchange linkage. The only linkage demanded by the semi-auto system between driver control and transaxle was a length of flexible electrical wiring . . .

One major feature differentiated the prototype 639 auto from the 640's – in the 639 system the ratio-changing drop gears were at the tail of the gearbox, behind the crownwheel-and-pinion; in the 640 they were moved

ahead of it to enable the underside of the gearbox's over-hanging section to be sloped quite sharply upwards, freeing the area for a gainfully upswept aerodynamic underfloor.

At one stage in early development, after Mr Ferrari's death, Fiat's Ferrari director Ghidella had a stand-up row with Barnard in the car park outside the Fiorano team HQ. Ghidella explained 'I cannot risk that gearbox – I personally cannot take that kind of risk in Italy . . .' to which the Englishman retorted, 'It's not your risk, it's mine . . .'.

The experimental 639 ran with auto transmission for the first time at Alfa Romeo's Balocco test track, which would hopefully be free of the spying press photographers resident at Fiorano. Then the test crew heard a low-flying helicopter approach! Since one of the *Tipo*

639's major features was its teardrop planform, the car was whipped out of sight into a building whenever the chopper reappeared . . .

Test driver Dario Benuzzi drove that day, with full automatic up-shifting. 'Under maximum acceleration it just went straight on through – beautiful'.

Co-ordinating engine and gearbox internal rpm upon downchanging was a more complex programming problem but the Ferrari system became reliable and accepted as state of the art into 1990.

For 1991, Williams quickly followed suit, developing their own version of the semi-automatic gearbox for their FW14 cars. In Williams's case again, as Patrick Head explained, 'Mechanically the transmission was totally conventional with normal gears and dogs – but while the Ferrari system uses a number of different selector rails with separate actuators on each rail to select each gear by moving the dogs into the gear-wheels, we instead have selector forks mounted on a barrel. The barrel is machined with a track upon it and we use a peg in a groove to index the barrel which then moves the rail to select the forks. Sequential gear-changing is imprinted in the barrel. We were initially very concerned about the possibility of selecting two gears at once – but after a few inevitable teething problems the system has proved very effective, and very efficient . . .'

While Ferrari's teething problems in 1989 attributed to the gearbox were largely created by electrical charging system failures – the low residual voltage stemming from which would first manifest itself as an inability to change gear adequately, if at all – Williams's teething problems early in 1991 were more involved with inadequate dimensional control within the gearbox causing problems once it got hot. 'By readjusting the cold settings we sorted out the early problems and slowly came to grips with it all . . .'

Certainly by the start of the 1992 season any driver who had to wrestle with an old-style manual gearchange could be considered to be driving an obsolescent Grand Prix car . . .

Office of a Barnard-series Ferrari with its gearchange flipper switches behind the horizontal spokes, right-hand to change up, left-hand to change down. Significantly, note the tightness of the cockpit moulding since there's no need for a manual gearshift and the space in which to manoeuvre it.

Aerodynamic technology, 1990s: 1, working under-surface of front wing generates downforce; 2, anhedral or strut-suspended front wing attachment to compensate for raised nose; 3, vortex stream from curled wing end plate directs flow to reattach at underside; 4, underside splitter also *fulfils flat floor regulations; 5, boundary layer developing, low pressure generated as underbody airflow accelerates due (6) to upswept underfloor; 7, windscreen tailored to driver directs airflow above and around his helmet; 8, highest-possible engine intake level seeking clean* *airstream; 9, downswept engine cowl cleans up airstream approaching (10) rear wing assembly; 11, internal flow side pod directs air through side-mounted radiator towards tail exit, minimizing turbulence within airstream approaching rear wing.*

Key: 1 and 2, front wings have longest chord at tip, providing peak download with peak leverage, slender root chord clears flow into radiator intakes; 3, rolled vortex-directing end plates keep underbody flow clean; 4, raised nose clears maximum airflow onto flat underfloor; 5 and 6, approximation of typical airflow pattern beneath underfloor; 7, upswept rear diffuser ramp with arched guides (8) harnesses exhaust energy (9) to entrain airflow in extractor effect; 10, titanium skid blocks protect underfloor from damaging *ground contact, generate spectacular spark showers on full tanks; 11, some designs employ side-exit radiator flow, side pod design seeking to prevent interference with airflow over body top; 12, waisting to clear airflow between rear wheels and body; 13, three-dimensional wingtip vortices, drag minimized and lift maximized by use of solid end plates; 14, brake duct moulding fairs entire inner wheel faces to optimize both passing airstream and cooling airflow pumped across brake.*

option. Those vertical vanes were a practical pain in the neck in any case, they always got in the way.'

A particularly impressive feature of his McLarens and of other 'Barnard cars' has always been the body fit, demonstrating microtight shut-lines to be proud of: 'Poor body fits always annoyed me. At Lola, in early-'70s production cars, getting anything like a decent body fit was an enormous problem. Specialised Mouldings did a good job on the fibre-glass panels but fitting them to the hand-made chassis was a nightmare; most times jointlines wouldn't match and the old "dobbers" would get at it with saws and resin and brushes, *eeugh*!

'At McLaren we built large body set-up frames and because of the way the car was made you could assemble complete bodies without the mono-coque so we were able literally to fit floor, side panels, rear end, engine cover, cockpit cover all on a jig, drill them through, and spend time making them really Fit. Because they were all done on the same jig they eventually became truly inter-changeable between chassis. That took a couple of years but we got there.'

Aerodynamically, the sidestep winglets used on rear wing structures during 1984 were particular-ly effective: 'When we had to take them off in 1985 we all lost a bit aerodynamically. The 1984 cars were very good, a lot of very controllable down-force until those sidestep wings were banned and we all had to start again . . .'

Broadly 'McLaren tail'-shaped cars then ruled Formula 1 until the next major change in configu-rative fashion, popularized by Jean-Claude Migeot and Harvey Postlethwaite in their high-nosed Tyrrell 019 of 1990.

'Once again there were numerous precursors but none went quite so far in exaggerating that high nose form with a splitter underneath, back towards the front axle-line. That Tyrrell nose opened the door to a small fork in aerodynamic thinking in the way it treats the flow going under-

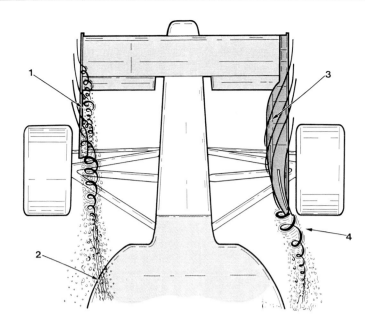

Above left: *Bent Sorensen's sketch of a Formula 1 nose section shows: 1, shaped end plate clearing wheel and fencing underwing depression against immediate infill by ambient-pressure atmospheric airflow alongside; 2, extended rolled plate section maintains download effect rearwards, controls and directs trailing vortices (3, 4 and 5); 6, titanium wearplate.* Above right: *Comparison between vortex trail of conventional front wing end plate (1) against modern rolled and extended end plate (3) showing how flow affects underbody at (2), clears it to reattach smoothly in (4).*

neath the car and around its sides. It's a case of controlling the flow where flow at the front affects performance generated at the back.

'That came along, and another less obvious device which had an important effect was the use of flaps on the front wings, with their inboard ends just cut away. At first glance you think, no end plate on them, just mounted off the main-plane of the wing ... but when you look at it that is very, very important. It's one of the most important things on the front end because the vortex they generate off the front wing is an effect you should use.

'You have to cut off the flaps on the front wing at just the right angle to get the vortex to pick up the side of the chassis and work to induce better flow along its underside. Today you can spend vast time in the tunnel moving the inboard end of that flap probably full-scale half an inch at a time, and tuning the angle of the end of it so you're literally pointing the vortex streaming away from it towards the side of the car, directing the airflow where you want it to go. It's almost like directing an air hose where it will do most good ...

'These are the kind of further ploys that the stepped nose unlocks. In itself it's an important feature to investigate. The stepped nose made that elegant and it throws open ways to do that. One way is just to end your flaps against the side of the nose, but suppose you get a gap there, and it generates a vortex, then what do you do with the vortex?

'Then somebody does the research, tackles a small deviation from the norm and there's an avenue opening up towards further improvement. The rolled-under, long end plates eliminate to a large extent any vortex coming off the front wing and they control what vortex there is – doing what the old vertical vanes used to do ... but a darned sight more efficiently.

'What Migeot and Postlethwaite did with their Tyrrell was to take the step a long way back in-chassis, to raise the nose even more. Now what most of us hadn't appreciated at first was what was the point with the flat-floor rule? If you had the chassis nose raised you still had to have the

flat floor coming forward to the rear face of the front tyre, so what was the point of taking the raised chassis over it? But if you looked at it in more detail you could see the advantages in controlling flow. It shortened the length of flat floor the airstream had to negotiate before reaching the working diffuser surface at the rear. This meant it maintained very high energy without it being diffused along the way. It was a good idea ...'

THE ENGINE QUESTION ...
Through the 1970s the Formula 1 engine question for most teams had been easily answered. They bought themselves a nice, relatively inexpensive Cosworth DFV off the shelf. Some might develop detail tweaks of their own in conjunction with a decent engine-preparation specialist like Nicholson or Judd, but essentially their engineers didn't really need to worry too much about that department – it was well understood, and well controlled, by others.

There were, however, tactical ploys which cost every active Formula 1 team member some worry lines ... Through 1982-83 pit stop race tactics paid off for some, their turbo engines demanding more fuel to survive race distance than the tanks could carry non-stop, and the Cosworth brigade followed suit. The mid-race break itself enabled a tyre change which in turn permitted softer-compound tyres to be used to recoup lost time. So what were the refuelling races of that period like from the pit row?

'I tell you, that was *frightening*! Oh boy. You could not *believe* what we were dealing with then. It never ceases to amaze me that we have consistently had fires in Group C just with gravity refuelling, while in Formula 1 we were consistently surrounded by these tanks bulging with petrol pressurized at 40 psi and there was hardly one fire. But *we* wouldn't just have had a fire, with flickery flames, a cheery little blaze – we would have had an explosion – BANG – it would have taken out the entire pit lane in one whacking great fireball! That was another case of getting around the rules as such, but it was such a risky ploy it was unbelievable ...

'In 1983, using what had been the Cosworth V8 chassis for the original interim TAG Turbo car, we only had 180 litres fuel capacity anyway, so we had no chance of surviving race distance unless we refuelled.'

It was during the brilliantly successful TAG Turbo V6 programme for McLaren International that Barnard's involvement with the concept, design and development of the Formula 1 racing engine became more fundamental: 'Initially it was a packaging exercise. We were the exclusive customer, Porsche undertook the work for us and what the customer asked for the customer was going to get. It wasn't always a comfortable rela-

tionship. They weren't at all used to being told precisely what the customer wanted, and there were very few changes from our specification that I was prepared to allow them to get away with'.

The same applied to Bosch, whose Motronic MS3 management system for the TAG Turbo engine was another project developed specifically to McLaren International's exclusive commission.

'Both eventually worked out well, because we were dictating terms and both Porsche and Bosch slowly came to appreciate that where F1 racing was concerned we had the experience to know what we were talking about. There was continual development of the Turbo – I made them do the handed turbo, the left- and right-handed turbo which formed quite a neat installation on the 1986 car – had the thing in line with the inlet from the front, ergonomically a very nice set-up, the air came in at the front, directly through the engine and straight out the back, goodbye ...

'I had argued for that precise mirror flow but mirroring the exhaust pipes like that probably didn't show up as much as I had thought. I had spent a long time talking to Udo Zucker of Bosch about it. I valued his opinion more than anybody else's and he said, "Look, because you can never guarantee you get two turbochargers the same we'll need to run the V6 like two in-line three-cylinder engines", and that's the way it ran, so we controlled each side, optimized the combustion process on each side and then the next step was to optimize airflow with airflow sensors. We ended up with the turbocharger and engine systems divided in two, and precisely matching one side to another was never really a factor. In reality it was impossible. But optimizing three cylinders at a time presented all sorts of options, like at one point towards the end we ran a big turbo on one side and a small turbo on the other, to give us pick-up at slow speed out of one corner, combined with top-end power for the long straight from the other ...

'Reliability was of course a huge factor throughout that period – we scored very heavily but we were lucky, you know. We had all kinds of failures in testing and practice but in the race it would all hang together.

'Fuel technology played a major role, especially in the turbo era, but also in recent atmospherically aspirated engine development. The amazing thing was that while Renault was getting upset about BMW having gone onto "chemical fuel" as they put it, so far as I can recall on the TAG Turbo project we used basically standard gas. We just mixed pump petrol and Avgas 60:40, then Shell Germany came along and effectively manufactured much the same sort of stuff by which time other people were getting into the heavy mixes, but it was only towards the end that Shell started making anything like that, the toluene fuel – it was ages before we had that.

'We were a long way behind on funny fuels – a really long way . . .

Eventually, by 1986-87, it was clear the costs of turbocharged engine technology meant there were simply not enough good turbo engines to go around. 'FISA began making noises about going back to naturally aspirated engines for the good of the sport, apparently in the belief it would revive the good old days of Cosworth versus Ferrari, when the racing was reckoned to be wonderful.

'So what happened? This transitional deal evolved with 4-bar boost and 195 litres of fuel for 1987 races, then 2.5-bar boost and only 150 litres of fuel allowed to turbos for 1988. Teams could change from 1½-litre turbos to 3½-litre atmo engines if they wanted, but could not swap back. Somebody had decided 2.5 bar was going to make an even match between the turbo engine and normally aspirated bumped up to 3.5 . . .

'Politically, I suppose, Formula 1 had to be seen to be taking a big drop in horsepower but what happened in 1988 was another bad joke. I just rule out the '88 season as a totally meaningless year in Formula 1. There were just two teams with competitive turbo engines, McLaren-Honda and Ferrari – and only McLaren built an entirely new car and Honda a new engine so they just walked away with it.

'Lotus had a Honda deal but how equal was their engine? It looked merely a contract filler, while everybody else was just staggering around with a hogged-out old Cossy or a cobbled-up BMW.'

After the success of the McLaren-TAG Turbos through 1984-86, Mr Ferrari wanted 'a Barnard car'. John's projected move to BMW, to create F1 cars there in-house, foundered when the board rejected the idea. And so he became Technical Director of Ferrari's *Reparto Corse*, and began work on what would be the new 3.5-litre naturally aspirated Ferrari for '89.

'By 1988-89, new safety regulations were pushing the steering ahead of the drivers' feet, his pedals back behind the front axle-line and so on – and I talked with Ferrari's engine people and decided to stick with a 12-cylinder. The feeling was that ultimately a 12 would offer the maximum power possible and at some point in time we were going to need maximum power. There was a contemporary argument that a good V8 might be 20-30 hp down on a good 12 but would be so much more driveable. Yeah, well forget it – at the end of the day the maximum power was going to count. We felt we must have maximum everything, maximum driveability, maximum rev range, maximum power, because for damn sure if we didn't then Honda would, and Renault, and anybody else who was serious. So even at the beginning we thought a 12 was the only way to achieve that.

'Then I set about packaging it and with Berger it was very difficult because he was so tall. But I came up with the compromise of wrapping some of the fuel around the side of the driver, I put the rads forward to get the weight distribution I wanted and it started off using an in-line gearbox which hung out the back in the conventional way as much as anything to allow me to get that long V12 in, because the transverse gearbox would have pushed the engine further forward.

'It all worked out – and the semi-auto gearbox thing was the next step in design if you like . . .

OF FERRARI, AND THE WIRE-GUIDED GEARBOX

'I'd been thinking for a long time about transmissions. One of the painful installations in a racing car is the gearshift. With the long engine we had to compact the fuel, spreading it around the sides and so on, and immediately this posed problems of having a nice gearshift. So the factors for me were (a) to make a slim cockpit where the guy didn't need all this room to waggle a stick around; and (b) to get away from the need to design in a complicated mechanism, passing right through various structures. If we could transmit gearchange commands through a length of wire flex instead of a rigid mobile rod there was a distinct packaging advantage.

'Right from the beginning I felt the possibility of going fully auto must be there. In conjunction with Bosch we'd run an electronic throttle at McLaren in 1985, but only in practice. It used a servo motor on the engine, a rotary encoder on the throttle and just an electrical wire connecting the foot pedal and the engine. With that coupled to a gearbox control and operating the clutch fully hydraulically, then I couldn't see why you couldn't make the fully automatic car.

'All of this time I was going along with the packaging process, the front of the monocoque was getting slimmer and slimmer, the footroom less and less so it was all fitting in the package.

'Old avenues are sometimes worth re-investigation, because modern technology might well make them viable in updated form. There was Forghieri's Ferrari de Dion axle system for '76 – I hadn't heard of it, and when I was with Ferrari it was never mentioned – yet it might have been one way to go in future. I'd be interested to know what happened to it. It was the same with the semi-auto gearbox. When I started talking about my ideas somebody said, "Yeah, we did something like that about five years ago . . ." and I discovered that *Villeneuve* had driven one they had tested!

For the first season of serious major-team 'atmo' Formula racing in 1989, Ferrari developed the Barnard-conceived Tipo 639 prototype *and* Tipo 640 race cars – *with their 60-valve V12 engines, teardrop planform, downward tapering side pods and vertically orientated radiator intake slots these cars went as well as they looked.*

'I got them to unearth the drawings. It was just a clever change, still with a lever – not the steering wheel toggle switches we adopted – but it had a drum on it like a motor cycle shifting drum . . . What had happened was typical – Villeneuve tested it and said, "Yeah, it's all right, but rather boring, I'd rather thrash it around," so they said, "Oh, all right then," and junked it . . .

'But yes, it was done, and Ferrari deserve credit for that. It's simply that if the situation's right for some kind of innovation it will happen. If the situation is not right then it'll be set aside . . .

'At that time Ferrari was thinking along the right lines but they just didn't have the electronics that could make the idea work – the time wasn't right. Just like a moulded composite monocoque – today you can build your monocoque to an ergonomic profile, fully structural and everything, but why? Because the manufacturing technology is now freely available, and is well understood . . . the time for it is right.

'In the case of the flick-switch gearchange, there was also a tremendous ergonomic advantage in the driver not having to take his hands off the wheel. The Ferraris shone in most of the race starts of 1989 because with both hands on the wheel they could jerk the car all over the road straight off the grid. In any case first gear in an F1 car is just a flash, *boomp* you need second, *boomp* third – the ability to buzz it up and still maintain full control was very evident at the starts.

'That ergonomic advantage was only slowly appreciated as the system got better and better and the drivers began to appreciate how much work it was saving. So it's now pretty much accepted as a necessary thing . . .

'I just remembered designs like the Chaparral, running ordinary torque converters . . . a much less efficient lump. Before that in 1981-82 I had a very long look to the point of someone actually working on it for me, at the old constant-velocity transmission based on a Van Doorne principle of expanding and contracting pulleys with a chain belt drive. We had a very long look at that . . . you'd keep the engine running within a band of maybe 500 rpm, pull it down for the start, then go up through the ratio range. Basically the engine would then run only within a very narrow rev band so there were obvious advantages in tuning the engine. But after a long look at that I decided really the drive principles at the time were just not good enough, chains not guaranteed enough. To work properly it would have required electronic control which at that time was not so easy to provide. Today it's so much easier to have a microprocessor built, and that's really what made the semi-auto box possible and practical.'

(RE-)ACTIVE SUSPENSIONS

Having delved deep into active suspension research with both Ferrari and Benetton, Barnard ransacked his experience of driver feedback from such names as Alain Prost, Niki Lauda, Gerhard Berger, Nigel Mansell and Nelson Piquet – three of them multiple World Champions – and emerged unconvinced of active suspension's true worth . . .

'It all comes back to what the driver wants. There's a load of geniuses out there who say, "We want the car to do this," but they don't really know what the car should be doing because they never drive one. You have to listen to a driver, not just any driver, but a good intelligent, capable driver, and really understand how he *senses* a car.

'I think a number of great-sounding schemes are non-runners. I think an active-suspension F1 car is never going to improve upon a really good passive car, but it does have to be a *good* one. Active is really just not necessary. I don't believe in it any more. I don't think it's a way to make a racing car quicker. It makes a racing car very comfortable, but not quicker. If you compare active work against a poor car – like they did at Benetton, and their '189 was a very poor car – it looks good but when you put it up against a really good conventional car it won't get up to it.

'That's how our test results looked to me. It comes down to the fact that the information the driver wants back from the machine to enable him to drive it quickly is different from what you want from a machine to go from here to Norwich comfortably and fast. It's the same with the engine: you start talking about constant velocity transmissions and the problem is that a driver needs an engine that works over a whole range because at different times when he's driving a car he wants to be able to put his foot in it and know what the engine's going to do for him. He needs to know he can kick it straight, or kick its tail out, or make it understeer – whatever his instincts might demand from split second to split second . . .

'If you sit there with 700 hp all the time and just the ability to move the throttle – what you're really doing is changing the ratio so you're just changing the speed of the car, and not directly its balance or attitude. I now feel – without driving F1 cars myself and without ever having driven them in anger – I firmly believe it will not give the driver the sensation he needs to be able to drive the car to its limit.

'It's too precise. The better the driver, the earlier he feeds the power in, and putting the power on the road is what it's all about. When a driver gets into a corner and he's loaded right up with sideforce, there comes the point at which his instincts tell him the time is right to feed in power. That cornering situation is changing the whole time. He's feeding in grip and it's changing all the time. Remember he's on the limit, and the grip level is changing all the time, the bumps in the road are changing, he's getting thrown around, and what it needs at that precise instant is to put his foot down at a point where perhaps the engine has got 500 hp perhaps at a time where it can only just handle 500 hp.

'Yet at the next given instant perhaps it'll handle 600 hp so he then wants 600 and then only the next moment does he want the full 700. So what he wants is the capability to say put the foot down now, and sit and wait and it's all coming together, it's all an unconscious act of the thing working together – that's why it's so important to have a good power curve on these engines. The maximum revs at which today's engines give top power are increasing all the time, but you can't do that at the cost of bottom and mid-range power. That's what Honda found in 1991 with the V12 – until they came along with the moveable trumpets they were ready to bin it, because it just wasn't as driveable or as good an engine as the old V10. It was only the ability to bring in the mid-range and to change the mid-range curve with the moveable trumpets and other bits, I guess, that they managed to save it. And I think if you look at that, these are the lessons which tell you that on a racing car things like constant-speed engines and transmissions aren't going to work.

'In theory the picture of the driver sitting there with 700 hp all the time is great. But then you're

After 'black chassis' came 'black brakes' – the high-friction, very lightweight revolution in racing car brake technology took place in the early 1980s but afflicted its pioneers with immense problems in insulating associated components – not least the wheel and tyre – from heat absorption.

actually there in this corner, the guy's personal computer tells him he has got to ease the pedal down just enough to maintain just the right grip level, and I think it's too big a job for him – he needs that cushion, that flexibility of power curve to enable him to do that as precisely as he wants. He needs the ability to control that precision. His personal computer is handling too much already – side load and so on, perhaps Senna up his tail – he's only driving on what he feels, nothing more. He's not going round watching G-meters, he's just driving on instinct and feel and ability, and that's a situation we engineers are never going to change . . . unless we take the man out of the cars entirely.

'Our test results persuade me that these active cars take away too much of the input the driver wants. And it's not just input – once he knows the car he will find situations in which he needs to trick it to make it do something unusual for him – something the engineer can hardly imagine. And if it's an active car he can't trick it . . .

'He might try to trick a front corner to dip and dig the front wing down to the deck to save a turn-in situation, say, but if there's an active system on that corner saying, "No, I'm going to pump that corner up, it's clearly hitting a bump", it takes away the driver's ability to overbrake his car here, or give it a big twitch and set it up diagonally and get the front to bite in there – once he gets to that point, the old rally driver thing, rush in and punch it out in a big oversteer – his options are being restricted. So I'm very much backing off a long way from active, as much as anything from the experiences I had at Benetton.

'So how much of it do you need? You can argue there's a need for some of it – a lot of people are running semi-active where you keep a spring and have a ram for active ride control more than anything – some are using jacked spring platforms, Ferrari did that in 1987, jacked the spring up and down and it enabled us to run a very soft spring unworried about ride height change due to load change. That's a long way from active suspension, but maybe that's all that's needed – and maybe you don't even need that. There's a lot of room left for development of more sophisticated mechanical spring and damper systems, and a lot we can get from it yet in terms of mechanical grip . . .'

MAKING THEM STOP

One really major advance in Formula 1 performance through the 1980s derived from carbon brakes. Before they came along, and until their considerable development difficulties had been overcome, the conventional F1 brake had been a 1-1.1 inch thick cast-iron disc. It was mounted on an alloy bell driven by the wheel pegs and was ventilated internally, normally with curved internal vanes cast integrally to pump air drawn into the disc centre via the suspension upright from the brake-cooling scoops, then centrifuging that air out radially through internal slots exiting from the disc edge.

Into 1983 AP Racing introduced a much improved, lighter cast-iron disc known as the 'sphericone' type with what were effectively stalagmites of iron grown into the interior cooling voids. 'Twin-pot' two-piston aluminium calipers were normal wear but turbo F1 car performance demanded four pistons per disc and pre-1983 that meant fitting 'balanced' calipers, one clasping the leading edge of each disc, and another the rear.

In 1983 the fast-developing Italian Brembo brake company introduced a new 'four-pot' four-piston caliper, quickly followed by AP Racing. One four-pot caliper per disc was usefully lighter than two balanced two-pots, but adoption of a carbon disc – in addition to the obvious advantage over cast-iron of the new material's higher coefficient of friction – could offer greater advantage still . . .

A set of carbon brake discs replacing a set of previously conventional cast-iron components could earn an immediate saving of 20 kg – and that was valuable unsprung weight too since most braking systems into the ground-effect era used all-outboard disc mountings. That saving of disc mass also slashed rotating mass, reducing inertia, giving the brake itself rather less to decelerate.

Murray's original Brabham carbon brakes had used Dunlop steel centres with carbon inserts. From 1980, Hitco of California supplied more sophisticated components, carbon-graphite composite discs, 0.7 inch thick but solid, slow to cool and impractical on twisty circuits where heat build-up would approach the level at which the carbon material could oxidize, creating an untenable wear rate. Destroying discs whose cost was ten times that of the conventional cast-iron type became distinctly unpopular at head office . . .

Even so, other leading teams became interested. Barnard recalls how Gordon Murray and Brabham had led the way, and how McLaren under his direction helped to establish carbon brakes as standard equipment for any serious racing car: 'I really began studying them in 1982.

'We were running the Cosworth-engined ground-effect car. I'd been looking at and talking for some time to Goodrich, an outfit in California who had carbon material for brake discs, and I vividly remember organizing a test at Donington with Niki driving. We had one set of each alternative to try. We were using the standard, small twin AP caliper, and there was a set of Goodrich solid, non-ventilated discs, a set of new SEP discs from France, and our normal iron disc as a baseline.

'We set up the car with the carbon discs and ran it and it was just *stunning*! It instantly shortened the braking distance at the end of the Donington Park straight from about 100 yards on the iron brake down to 60 yards on carbon.

'The crucial thing, you see, was that we were running a ground-effect car with lots of contact force through the tyre. When you stopped with that – provided you had the capability to dissipate the energy of the stop quickly (which the carbon brake did have) – you didn't actually stay on the brakes very long. Niki just stood on the brakes as hard as he could, because there was so much grip in the ground-effect car that he couldn't lock up the brakes against it. He could just stand on the pedal at the last possible moment, and the thing would just stop!

'That test really drilled it home, carbon was the way to go . . .

'Those Goodrich discs were made fundamentally – I believe – as a rotor brake for the Chinook helicopter. In France, SEP had started looking at carbon discs specifically for racing cars, but they were also just plain black discs with mounting holes drilled through them. I basically started working on them from that point forward – having a good, serious look – and we eventually ran SEP carbon brakes through 1983.

'They offered a far higher coefficient of friction than iron and their generation of heat and its sipation were both far quicker.

'With the conventional iron disc, once it was soaked with heat you then had to get rid of it. You could see it while testing on the circuit near dusk. You'd see the car coming down into the braking area, and with the carbon brakes you'd suddenly see this orange light bulb switched on inside the wheel . . .

'It literally looked just like that, the heat would build up so rapidly. And then they'd come off the pedal and *boomp* – literally just like that – the light bulb was switched out.

'With iron discs you'd just see a dull glow slowly build up, then dim down slowly after the brakes had come off as the heat was slowly dissipated. So this whole process of converting the car's kinetic energy into heat and then rejecting that heat to atmosphere was better and faster in the carbon/carbon brakes.

'Through 1983 we tried to run solid SEP discs (because the SEP seemed a slightly better material). We were still using the little AP twin-piston calipers, but for 1983 we had gone flat-bottomed so there had been a dramatic change of downforce and tyre grip under braking. That made the whole carbon thing difficult to cope with, because what you then had was a guy having to brake at 150 yards where previously he could have hung on down to 60 yards. Yet he was still rattling down the straight at the same speed so he was on the brakes a long time. That put us into problems of heat soak affecting the calipers, boiling fluid, calipers going over temperature, aluminium getting near its limits etc. We were still using just a solid disc, with only the two faces to get rid of the heat, so we had a real problem.

'We spent that year switching to and fro – iron to carbon, to iron, to carbon – then at Zandvoort we ran the TAG Turbo interim '1E car for the first time.

'As soon as we put carbon brakes on the turbo car, the higher top speed it offered compared to the Cossy made it almost undriveable under braking because the calipers just got far too hot. They could just about handle Cosworth performance – but no way would they look at the TAG Turbo.

'That car was not hugely heavier than the Cosworth – don't forget we had to ballast the

Cosworth car to meet the minimum weight in any case – and the turbo was only about 25 kg over, which was not enough to bother the brakes. But you just had to use the brakes longer.

'SEP were down near Bordeaux at that time – they later became "Carbone Industrie" – and they were quite helpful. We had been working more and more with the turbo in the latter half of 1983 and by that time were really more determined to make these brakes work.

'SEP had made the things for us but they hadn't been in racing long so were not "real racers". They had taken a disc, made it thicker than before, and drilled holes down into it to approximate a venti-lated iron disc. We made the mountings and leaned on SEP to get a full set here, NOW. We mounted a set for South Africa at the end of '83 and they were The Answer, *fantastic*. That clinched it for me and I made the decision to use carbon brakes exclusively through '84 . . .

'By that time we had also come to conclusions about the caliper requirement, and over that winter we made our own caliper set-up machined by us from higher-spec aluminium, and the 1984 McLaren-TAG ran the SEP ventilated discs and our own calipers. Gordon and Brabham had made their own calipers too, and we raced all-carbon brakes together from 1984. Again it was a case of having the commitment to do it which finally paid off.

'Like so many of these developments which are now taken for granted – any tuppenny ha'penny team can just buy the bits off the shelf, drop them on and they work straight away – you can only do that when somebody else has sorted them out. Somebody has to have said, "That is what is going to work". You don't just run into a problem and say, "OK – problem – chuck that idea in the bin, let's try something else . . ." For these things to be developed, somebody has to bleed . . .

'Turbo engine developments in F1 are a shining example – all those basic lessons were learned absolutely at Renault's expense, in public face if nothing else. They started racing in Formula 1 in 1977 and didn't even look like winning a thing until 1979. Time after time they boiled and broke and steamed and burned – but they were paying the price of being pioneers. Once they had sorted out the big problems with Mahle pistons and KKK turbochargers the rest of us could go to those suppliers and profit at Renault's expense by buying the kit whose development they had been paying for.

'On things like the moulded carbon monocoque and my bearings packages and CV and hub arrangements, SEP carbon brakes and the semi-automatic gearbox, that's why I get so frustrated when other people come along, pick up the technology and just take it all for granted . . . In Renault's case with the turbo engine even Keith Duckworth was saying the turbo 1½ would never make any more than 600-700 hp – but Renault went through that whole period and took all that ****, and won through. It's not easy to do, I tell you – it's bloody tough . . .

A QUESTION OF CLUTCHES

In the late 1940s, the embryo BRM team was looking at unprecedented power and torque from its 1½-litre centrifugally supercharged V16-cylinder Grand Prix engine. Lockheed was commissioned to produce a suitable clutch to handle that output, but when the result of their deliberations arrived at the team's Bourne HQ it was huge, heavy and quite impracticable for use in a racing car.

The BRM project's own engineers completely redesigned it, and devised an extremely neat and compact little clutch whose basic configuration formed the basis of the conventional competition clutch for years to follow.

The Cosworth DFV used as standard an AP Racing 7¼-inch diameter twin-plate diaphragm-spring clutch of broadly similar design. Its steel pressure plates had gear-toothed peripheries mating with internal teeth cut into a steel adaptor ring which, with the dished cover plate, were bolted to the engine flywheel. Once turbocharged

engines began doubling power and torque figures, the normal twin pressure plates had to be thickened to prevent the heat of a race start buckling them. Three- and four-plate clutches were tried. Real abuse – meted out in particular by four-cylinder turbo engines such as the BMW M12/13 – could split the adaptor ring, and – once compromised in this manner – centrifugal force could easily burst the entire clutch spectacularly asunder. Doubling the number of fixing bolts from six to twelve between ring/cover and flywheel contained this problem.

Aluminium clutch covers replaced steel and cut weight to around 9 lb, but meanwhile Honda F2 engines had found a better way, adopting an AP 5½-inch clutch which presented considerably less inertia, speeding engine response. With three plates and high spring pressures these compact clutches could handle 4-bar boost turbocharged F1 power and Honda used them on their V6s through 1987. These 5½-inch clutches used a lug-drive system instead of the toothed peripheral adaptor ring. This system enabled them to fling clear clutch-wear dust which was normally trapped inside the larger clutch's adaptor ring. This open assembly also improved clutch cooling, but where three- and four-plate clutches were concerned the drive lugs were tall and their junction with the cover had to survive enormous loadings.

Higher friction linings offered another advance. Brake-type carbon was attractive, but attempts to use Hitco material on the big 7¼-inch clutches had failed.

Barnard tells the story: 'Carbon clutches are also common now. Light weight, carbon's high coefficient of friction and its good heat characteristics all make it ideal. It was developed originally for inertia but you couldn't just make a conventional clutch in carbon, because the normal centre gear tooth system running on a splined centre is far from ideal for the material – the detail toothing was too fine for carbon, it splintered and crumbled. Then an ex-AP guy [John Lindo] working for Mac Tilton in California adapted a system of "posts" on the outside to drive a carbon-lined clutch, and that's pretty much how they are to this day . . .'

Hitco had developed a carbon material possessing stable friction properties at relatively low temperatures, and Tilton found its coefficient could double with only a modest increase in temperature – ideal for the ferocious start episode, then intermittent re-engagement use of a racing clutch.

'Temperature builds up on the surface of the clutch disc and as it rises so does the material's coefficient of friction, just briefly. While he's running, every time he changes gear there's that tiny bit of slip which keeps up the temperature and friction level but what you don't get is the plate distortion you experience with a metal clutch, so actual travel required for the clutch to engage and disengage is much smaller.

'The first thing we noticed with the carbon clutch was that you can actually do a quicker gearchange because all it needs is just the briefest tap on the pedal, and it's through.'

SEP under its new trading name of Carbone Industrie supplied suitable material to McLaren for an experimental 7¼-inch carbon clutch in 1985, but it was not raced. While Tilton's first carbon clutches were 7¼-inch assemblies, Lotus ordered a 5½-inch via Honda for the '87 season. Eager to save weight wherever possible to accommodate their active suspension system, a new small carbon clutch was immensely attractive – Tilton's scaled just 3.3 lb, and it sparked AP into producing their own 5½-inch lug-drive type, first with four plates, later three, and the new system became conventional into the 3.5-litre naturally aspirated formula years.

These lightweight, low-inertia, small-diameter clutches were also to have a profound effect upon engine architecture, enabling designers to build lower power units, reducing base chamber depths, lowering crankshaft centreline heights . . . further twists in the ever-continuing development spiral of the Grand Prix car . . .

FORMULA 1 RACING ENGINES – 1966-91

Apart from the extraordinary story of the Cosworth DFV, which is related in Chapter 3, we can examine here some details of the leading engines built and used in Formula 1 during our period. I make no apology for majoring on the BMW, BRM and Renault engines which played such a significant, if not always successful, role in the Formula 1 story from 1966 to 1991. Details of the minor engines of little real significance, such as the Coventry Climax 'Godiva' 3-litre hybrid, the Indy Ford, Serenissima and ATS V8s and the Tecno flat-12 are appended in the Shannon, McLaren, Cooper and Tecno sections of the Team Directory.

Alfa Romeo

Autodelta's basic *Tipo* 33 sports-racing V8 engine was first adopted for significant single-seater racing by Alec Mildren's Australian Tasman Championship Brabham team in 1968, two 2.5-litre versions being acquired for Frank Gardner's use. A similar 32-valve 3-litre Formula 1 engine was then to be developed for Cooper, but completed too late for that team's use, first being raced by McLaren in 1970 then March in 1971.

The V8 was an all-aluminium engine, with bore and stroke of 86.0 mm x 64.4 mm, displacing 2998 cc. With five main bearings and four overhead camshafts rotating in five bearings and driven from rear-of-engine chains, the 33/3 V8 had four valves per cylinder inclined at 39 degrees 30´, inlets 32 mm in diameter and exhausts 27 mm, delivering a claimed 400 bhp at 9000 rpm in sports car form. As uprated in 1970-71 with gear-driven camshafts for Formula 1 use, Autodelta claimed 430 bhp at 10,500 rpm when the Cosworth DFV was delivering some 440 bhp, the

Alfa Romeo's Tipo 1260 3-litre sports car-derived flat-12 was tipped as a challenger for the flat-12 Ferrari but didn't quite make the grade.

Matra V12 around 445-450 and the flat-12 Ferrari 460 at 12,000 rpm.

It was inevitable that *Ing.* Chiti should look enviously at his former employer Ferrari's engine and, with backing from the Alfa Romeo Board, his Autodelta design team produced a sports-racing flat-12 of their own for the 1973 World Championship of Makes season.

In sports car form this Alfa Romeo '115-12' engine was based on cast-magnesium blocks and aluminium crankcase, with aluminium or magnesium heads, carrying twin gear-driven overhead camshafts per bank rotating in seven bearings. They actuated four valves per cylinder inclined at the included angle of 35 degrees, inlets 30 mm and exhausts 25.5 mm diameter. The rear-mounted cam-drive gears also powered the 12-cylinder distributor and Lucas fuel injection pump and metering unit. Dinoplex electronic ignition was used, firing single 10 mm plugs per cylinder, and the balanced crankshaft revolved in only three Clevite main bearings, one fewer than Ferrari. Deep-skirted Mahle pistons were used.

Bore and stroke were 77 mm x 53.6 mm, displacing 2995.125 cc. Compression ratio was 10:1; Autodelta claimed 500 bhp at 11,000 rpm.

As developed for Formula 1 (described in the Brabham Team Directory entry, page 245) the engine ran increased compression – up to 11.5:1, valve sizes increased to 33 mm inlet and 26.7 mm exhaust, with a lift of 8.5 mm, and for a weight claimed to average 385 lb (175 kg) the units delivered a claimed 520 bhp at a raucous 12,000 rpm, plus 324 lb/ft torque.

But the flat-12 was an untidy engine apart from its overall dimensions of 30.7 in. long x 27.3 in. wide, and it took time for it to be more neatly packaged. By late 1977 it had become a potential winner with titanium rods and virtually every internal part altered from original sports-prototype form, saving 5 kg.

When Chiti's team rushed through their crash programme to develop the '1260' V12 engine from the flat-12 for Brabham's 1979 ground-effects car, they adopted bore and stroke dimensions of 78.5 mm x 51.5 mm so it was not a direct 'narrowing' of the flat-12 by any means. Compression ratio was quoted as 12:1, valves were as flat-12 and the engine weighed exactly the same – they say – 375 lb (170 kg). Power output was 525 bhp at 12,300 rpm, slightly more than the flat-12 and indeed the V12 engine would allegedly be the most powerful naturally aspirated engine ever seen in the Formula by 1982 when it was producing an apparently genuine 548 bhp.

By this time Chiti had turned to turbocharging, producing a compact but still characteristically rather untidy V8 Type 182T power unit. This

Alfa's V8 was like an untidy DFV and made little impression in the 1970 McLaren M7D and M14D.

engine had twin turbochargers specially made for it by Alfa Romeo Avio although KKKs and Garretts were also tried.

Bore and stroke were 74 mm x 43.5 mm, displacing 1496 cc and the engine was claimed to be delivering 600 bhp at 11,500 rpm in original 1982 form. But in Formula 1 terms it was a rather crude unit, Autodelta hurling fuel into it to cool it adequately and producing horrendous fuel consumption in return. The Alfa-engined cars were notoriously unlikely to survive race distance as fuel capacity restrictions were applied in 1983-84, although by 1984 the so-called '183T' V8 turbocharged engine was producing a claimed 670 bhp at 11,800 rpm, close to Ferrari's 126C but some 180 bhp behind BMW's fearsome little M12/13 turbo's claimed potential – if we believe all the figures in these days of variable boost – and demonstrably some 80 bhp behind the TAG Turbo Porsche in race trim.

Major modifications were made to the V8 engine for 1985, the main objective being to control its thirst for fuel. New Chief Engineer Gianni Tonti from Lancia worked closely with Bosch on fuel injection. Although Renault had left KKK in favour of Garrett turbocharging, Alfa took their place with the German company. Tonti's V8 modifications, which included redesign of both block and heads, were merely to see the Euroracing team through 1985 while an all-new replacement four-cylinder F1 engine was prepared for 1986 and its 195-litre GP-distance fuel restriction.

The Alfa *Tipo* 815-84T V8 in final form remained a 32-valve four-cam V8; bore and stroke was 74 mm x 43.5 mm, displacing 1497 cc, compression ratio 7.0:1, peak race-tune boost pressure 3.4 bar, peak revs (race) 11,300 rpm. Starting the year, Tonti specified peak power in race tune as 720 bhp at 11,000 rpm – which proved woefully inadequate as the season progressed. The engine, complete and ready to run, scaled 180 kg (396.8 lb) and Euroracing took 11 of them, including five qualifiers, to Rio for the first race. Bosch Motronic all-electronic engine management systems first appeared on the units at Imola, but the season was catastrophic, and, like Renault, Alfa Romeo announced they would not sanction another F1 car build programme for 1986, although Tonti's new four-cylinder engine would be made available for interested customers.

This Alfa Romeo *Tipo* 415-85T unit was unveiled in November 1985 as a neat 92 mm x 56.4 mm, 1498 cc in-line four aiming at 830 bhp in 1986 race-consumption tune. It was difficult to see any worthwhile teams who would be sufficiently impressed by Alfa's record to use it.

The new BMW-like Tonti engine was intended to use fully electronic injection unlike the V8's mechanical system, but its delayed development meant that its in-line four-cylinder configuration had been left behind by the sweeping tide of development. The large-area piston crowns presented by a 'four' exacerbated the potential for detonation which a 'six' or 'eight' helped avoid. Brian Hart (q.v.) had side-stepped the problem by reducing his four-cylinder engine's bore by 2 mm from 88 mm to 86 mm while the Italian unit's architecture looked suspect with its 92 mm bore – it offered a lovely short stroke, certainly, but those vulnerable piston crowns were too expansive for the boost pressures and temperatures normal by 1987.

The irony of this situation was that the 415T unit had been running on the bench for more than 18 months. It promised greater efficiency than the contemporary Motronic-injected V8, developing more power for less fuel at given boost. Fully electronic injection/ignition management was said to be working well on the unit, the engineers at Settimo Milanese claiming up to 820 bhp on 3.8-bar boost, with as much as 7 per cent better consumption.

The compact and light little block had been designed from the outset to be mounted as a fully stressed load-bearing chassis component. Benetton expressed interest for their Toleman chassis before opting for the BMW instead (q.v.). Ligier eventually adopted the 415T for 1987, Alfa by that time claiming 830 bhp at 10,500 rpm on 3.8-bar boost, with up to 1200 bhp (à la BMW) in qualifying trim with oversize single KKK turbocharger, 'rocket fuel' etc . . .

When FISA announced its 4-bar boost restriction for 1987, Tonti's team adopted a twin-turbo Garrett AiResearch induction system, one of each cylinder's two exhaust ports feeding separate manifolds to energize the 'chargers mounted low on the block's left side. With a common wastegate and single intercooler this 415T variant offered a claimed 900 bhp at 10,500 rpm at 4-bar boost.

However, once testing began in the new tailor-made Ligier JS29, driver Arnoux complained of inadequate response, improved by fitting smaller turbos which promptly curtailed straightline speed. As the opening race fast approached a manufacturing fault in a batch of turbos created further problems and after another fraught Imola test session late in March 1987 Arnoux bitterly criticized the engine on Italian TV. This compromised Alfa Romeo's public image, in direct contravention of a clause in the Ligier agreement, and next morning the Italian company announced cancellation of the deal.

It seemed suspiciously convenient, Fiat having just absorbed Alfa Romeo and now wishing to promote Ferrari as their only F1 operation while Alfa Romeo should handle saloon car racing and Lancia rallying. The four-cylinder turbo F1 project was dead.

Meanwhile Enzo Osella (q.v.) was desperate for an engine to maintain his fingertip hold on Formula 1, and Fiat smiled upon his shoestring efforts by authorizing loan of the turbo 890T V8 as a stop-gap until Osella could find funds to cover a new Motori Moderni *Tipo* 6VTC V6. The V8 engines were in essentially 1984 trim, barely capable of competing in 195-litre fuel ceiling races. With KKK 'chargers, Jofa-managed Spica injection and Marelli Dinoplex ignition, the Osella-Alfa Romeo became the late-'80s equivalent of Gordini in the later 1950s . . . makeweights, enthusiastic cannon-fodder filling grids as supporting cast to the superteams. Osella still even rebuilt engines in the paddock – unable to afford spares.

Into 1987 more funds became available, inadequate to secure a Motori Moderni V6 but enough for Osella to purchase the six or eight Alfa V8s and parts-kits his team already held. New 'Osella'-lettered cam-covers appeared and many consumable parts were re-manufactured by ex-Alfa original suppliers. As modified by Osella with re-worked induction and porting details, redesigned pistons and alternative-size KKK turbochargers, as much as 780 bhp at 11,500 rpm was claimed on 3.8-bar qualifying boost, plus 730 bhp at 11,000 rpm on 3.5-bar in race tune.

When FISA introduced its 2.5-bar/150-litre fuel limit ceilings for 1988, Osella developed the V8 turbo engine for one final season, reducing valve angle by 2 degrees from Alfa's original spec, improving cooling water flow in particular around the exhaust ports, adopting high-domed pistons to raise compression ratio to *c.* 10.5:1, and reducing valve and port diameters to assist fuel economy. Previous crankshaft cracking problems were obviated by redesign and remanufacture while smaller-sized KKK turbochargers were adopted for

optimum throttle response. Marelli-Weber full electronic management was fitted at last, combining electronic control of both the turbo wastegate and Marelli CD ignition.

Osella converted all eight of his V8 engines to this specification, claiming *c.* 600 bhp at 12,400 rpm at 2.47-bar boost for qualifying, little less in race tune. At the end of that final season of turbocharged F1 racing, Alfa Romeo's unsuccessful final period thus far of Grand Prix involvement finally petered out.

Only the flat-12 Alfa engines ever won Championship Grands Prix; one victory involved the Brabham fan-car and the other came after disqualification of the first two cars on the road which were Cosworth and Ferrari flat-12 powered. It is not an impressive record, though the engines were usually better than the works Alfas which carried them.

BMW

On 24 April 1980, the German BMW company from Munich announced their intention to supply engines for use in Formula 1. They had been very active, and highly successful, in Formula 2 and touring car racing since the late Sixties and after a brief foray in 1970 had introduced a turbocharged in-line four-cylinder engine early in 1977, mounted in 2002 saloons prepared and entered by the Schnitzer concern of Freilassing.

The performance of these cars persuaded BMW to back a co-operative deal with McLaren Engines of Livonia, Detroit, USA, to develop and race a turbocharged BMW 320 in American events to promote export sales.

Under technical direction of BMW Motorsport's Chief Engineer Paul Rosche and McLaren's Roger Bailey, the 2-litre unit was soon developing 550 bhp, then 600. It was not the most reliable racing engine but it showed what was possible.

Meanwhile, Renault had entered Formula 1 in 1977, both leading the turbocharged way and effectively making it 'respectable' for a major manufacturer to be involved in racing against the *garagistes*.

BMW development chief Karlheinz Radermacher and Sales Director Hans-Erdmann Schönbeck joined the enthusiastic Rosche, plus Motorsport's chief-elect Dieter Stappert and Press Department head Dirk Henning Strassl in advocating an entry into Formula 1, using a production-based turbocharged engine to emphasize the BMW 'M-Power' performance image. Strassl was particularly keen to advertize F1 success using a production block engine 'just like you can buy'.

Having developed his 2-litre four-cylinder BMW M12 Formula 2 engine from a 1972 output of some 270 bhp to over 330 bhp and having won six European Formula 2 Championship titles along the way, Rosche had the track record to back his predictions, and a deal was struck to develop a turbocharged BMW-powered Formula 1 Brabham, working closely with Gordon Murray of Bernard Ecclestone's Motor Racing Developments company.

Paul Rosche's engineering group sat down around a clean sheet of drafting paper in April 1980. They decided to use the standard 'small' BMW four-cylinder iron block and existing F2-type twin overhead camshaft four-valve-per-cylinder head. BMW Motorsport drew their blocks literally off the shelf from the main production plant. Bore and stroke dimensions were 89 mm x 60 mm displacing 1499 cc.

The finished cast-iron blocks weighed only some 7 kg (15.4 lb) once all machining had been completed. Cylinder bores were glass-polish finished direct into the block without any special surface treatment such as 'Nikasil' lining. But Rosche's men found that a brand new block casting was inadequately stress-relieved for their purposes and preferred well-run blocks with 100,000-odd road kilometres on them as ideally relaxed and stable. An artificial ageing process was therefore applied.

A flat-plane forged-steel, nitrided F2-type crankshaft was retained, carried in five plain Glyco main bearings and incorporating enlarged-flow oilways. It retained the standard production dimensions and bearing shells, 48 mm diameter mains and 45 mm diameter big-ends. The main timing spur gear was pressed onto its nose, a small toughened-steel flywheel bolted onto its tail.

Titanium 153.6 mm long con-rods were used, cut from plate, shot-peened for toughness and with big-ends closed by titanium bolts with steel nuts. Mahle's pistons were forged aluminium-alloy slipper-type – with very shallow skirts carrying two chromed-steel compression rings and one oil scraper. Hollow-steel fully floating gudgeon pins attached piston to rod. Each piston assembly complete with pin and circlips weighed only 365 grammes.

Rosche's proven F2-type cylinder head was cast in crisp aluminium alloy with four valves per cylinder inclined in pairs at 30 degrees included angle. They had beryllium-bronze valve seats, the steel-alloy inlet valves themselves being 35.8 mm

Factory cutaway of the BMW M12/13 turbocharged engine.

in diameter, Nimonic exhausts 30.2 mm. Double valve-springs were used, of course.

Copious water supply was galleried around the exhaust valves in particular, and BMW Motorsport were sufficiently confident of the standard production-type head-seal to retain a conventional gasket, tooth-ringed round the cylinders to resist boost pressure there. Head retention was by ten 10 mm bolts.

Cam-carriers were in aluminium alloy retained by long studs projecting from the camshaft bearing caps. Bucket-type tappets were used, with shims to set valve clearance. The twin overhead camshafts ran in five plain bearings, obviously less radical cam-lobe profiles being employed for the tighter circuits where mid-range torque was more vital than top-end flat-out power.

Camshaft drive was by geartrain from the crankshaft nose, gears running in needle-roller bearings, and also powering the oil pressure and scavenge pumps and alternator while rubber belt-drives were arranged from them for the water injection pumps.

The cast-iron crankcase base was closed by a cast-magnesium sump, with provision for oil/air separation. Four scavenge pumps were provided, two for the bottom end, one for the head and the fourth for the turbocharger lubrication system.

The exhaust manifold was stainless steel carrying a single KKK turbocharger and wastegate. The compressor housing was encased in a carbon-fibre moulding, and an induction tract plenum chamber was another carbon moulding housing the indirect fuel injector nozzles and feeding a cast-magnesium induction manifold.

A Bosch electric high-pressure pump was fitted for engine-starting, a Lucas mechanical pump taking over thereafter, driven from the inlet camshaft gear. A Kugelfischer-modified-by-Bosch metering unit was used, controlled by a digital electronic management system.

This sensed throttle opening from the main inlet butterfly position, plenum chamber boost pressure, block water temperature, filter fuel temperature, manifold air temperature and engine speed at the flywheel. This data was wired to a carefully chosen pre-set CPU chip whose programme continuously adjusted the injection pump and metering unit fuel flow to match engine supply to demand.

With a compression ratio of 6.7:1 and race boost pressure by 1983 of around 1.9 bar, this engine of relatively humble origin delivered over 650 bhp at 9500 rpm for a weight of 170 kg (374.8 lb) which figure includes the large single Behr intercooler used.

BMW brought Brabham into a more technological era of test and development, using radio link telemetry in track-testing to record and permit analysis of both engine and car performance.

Despite continuing unreliability, the early BMW M12/13 turbo engines were very powerful, delivering some 557 bhp at 9500 rpm in 1981-82 when Brabham began using them in anger at Kyalami. Initially, mechanical and turbocharger reliability was very poor and Brabham reverted to Cosworth power to accumulate some points before BMW insisted they bite the bullet and race the M12/13 seriously and soon, and they began winning in mid-season.

During 1982 the M12/13s were producing a genuine 570 bhp at 10,800 rpm in race tune. In 1983, when Piquet won the Drivers' Championship (the important one to BMW's customers), they were turning out a reliable 640 bhp at 11,000 rpm – 426 bhp per litre. In qualifying tune, with higher boost and additional intercooling capacity, there was talk of 750 bhp-plus – 500 bhp per litre. By 1984, when the little engine had become almost grotesquely unreliable in race form against the economical yet powerful TAG Turbo TTE-PO1 V6s, BMW salvaged some of their performance image with some scintillating pole positions, the engine running up to – and very possibly beyond – 850 bhp at 11,000 rpm (556 bhp per litre).

Paul Rosche's humble little in-line four-cylinder production-block BMW M12/13 made a wickedly potent Formula 1 engine into the mid-Eighties.

Top: The four-cylinder BMW M12/13 turbo engine in the 1984 Brabham BT53;
left: intercooler, right: radiator; exhaust could only 'blow' one side of undertail diffuser.

The 1983 World Championship victory with an engine 'based on the one you can buy' certainly brought a smile to Strassl's face – 630 days after the Bavarian project had begun.

Everybody sought more power, torque and economy from their engines for 1985. In qualifying tune BMW's 'specials' would run well into four figures. At Monza, for example, Piquet's Brabham-BMW exceeded 208 mph past the pits, and at Ricard 213 mph on the Mistral Straight, suggesting over 1140 bhp, while over 1270 bhp was extrapolated as Rosche's Munich dynos read to only 1000!

By the end of '85, 1000 bhp was virtually a minimum requirement for front-row qualifying – 666 bhp per litre – achieved by rapidly improving electronic engine management and highly classified internal engineering to burn specially mixed legal-octane high-aromatic fuel under 4 ata boost or more, with ever-increasing efficiency. BMW's fuels were specially brewed for them by a division of the BASF chemical company, with whom they had been conducting a lengthy development programme.

Only four years previously no more than a reliable 181 bhp per litre from Cosworth had won the Championship. In race-tune in 1985 533 bhp per litre was accepted as normal and the better heat-rejecting iron-block BMWs and Hondas were up around 566.

After the problems of 1984, BMW had tightened up quality control to retrieve engine reliability, and Brabham requested a lower inlet level permitting a lower intake box and new car body giving better airflow to both induction and rear wing. Their float of 25 'works' engines was clearly amongst the most powerful around, but output had to be tailored to Pirelli's available tyres for the Italian company was still learning through 1985.

Brabham-BMW ran higher race horsepower beginning the year than through mid-season because of this.

BMW's customer engines for Arrows were inevitably in more modest tune aimed at reliability, and were prepared and rebuilt under sub-contract by Heini Mader. That major success eluded BMW during 1985 was no fault of the German concern, for their apparently humble stock-block in-line four-cylinder remained the most potent engine Grand Prix racing had seen.

For 1986, BMW's Formula 1 development partner – the Motor Racing Developments 'Brabham' operation master-minded by Gordon Murray – requested a lay-down engine installation to reduce centre of gravity height and enable a low-line bodyform optimizing direct airflow onto a new car's rear wing surfaces. American transmission specialist Pete Weismann developed an offset-

input transmission tailor-made for the new engine installation which Murray pressed upon Paul Rosche's engine division in Munich.

Motorsport contracted to supply 30 of the new Typ M12/13/1 lay-down engines, with the block relatively unchanged from upright practice but now angled 72 degrees from vertical, offsetting the clutch to the right in the car, the head – induction on top of course – to the left. This lay-down project was initiated in August 1985 and some 100 lay-down blocks were cast, BMW taking the opportunity to trim a little weight from them.

Internally only oil gallery pistons and suitably adapted scavenge channels differed from 'upright' spec, and externally the unit was assembled into a beautifully crafted installation cradle. BMW eventually quoted qualifying output in excess of 1000 bhp and race power of c. 850 bhp but all within a tight power band from 8500-11,000 rpm. Once running began in the low-line, long-wheel-base Brabham BT55 astronomical water, oil and charge temperatures afflicted the programme. The lengthy induction tract apparently hampered pick-up away from corners, the chassis lacked traction and the project floundered. Murray believed the lay-down engine refused to scavenge its oil adequately, power loss from churning and windage being reflected by the heat rejected to oil. Rosche of BMW dismissed such claims of a scavenge problem, but in truth lack of development time before the race calendar commenced had simply killed the lay-down project on its feet.

The integral charge duct incorporated into the unit's mounting cradle proved too constricted and a separate duct adopted after the Hungarian GP improved matters. BMW's latest would attain only some 4.9-bar boost while the upright sister units used by Benetton were qualifying on up to 5.3 bar. Neither was the lay-down engine reliable, and Brabham reverted to an upright engine installation before season's end.

The upright M12/13 engine had been adapted in mid-'85 to use tailor-made Garrett turbochargers in place of the proprietary KKKs which had occasionally proved less than ideal. Customer-spec BMW upright engines for 1986 were then serviced by Mader in Switzerland, a float of 40 ensuring supply under a rental agreement to Arrows and Benetton in what was '85 works specification. Mader adopted a bumper turbo for qualifying and at Monza in September 5.5 bar was registered on Berger's slippery Benetton B186, running 20-nozzle intercooler water spray to control charge temperatures, producing 218.238 mph through the speed-trap on the main straight and widespread talk of the M12/13 developing 'over 1300 bhp'...

In contrast, race boost under the contemporary 195-litre fuel allowance was down to c. 3.7 bar, yielding some 850 bhp.

At season's end Mader's total stock of upright BMW M12/13 engines and equipment was retrieved by BMW Motorsport after the Munich Board's decision to withdraw from Formula 1. However, the United States Fidelity & Guaranty insurance company – which as 'USF&G' was the Arrows team's main sponsor – had a computer leasing subsidiary trading under the Megatron name. Megatron's Chairman John Schmidt was an influential member of the USF&G board and its involvement with Arrows was largely the result of his personal enthusiasm. Now USF&G confirmed continued support for Arrows through 1987 and concluded a deal with BMW Motorsport to take over the upright M12/13 engine programme, 38 such units plus 'kits' for a dozen more promptly being returned to Mader where they would be re-prepared and serviced and new 'Megatron'-lettered cam-covers fitted.

Ligier then suffered their celebrated last-minute rift with Alfa Romeo just before the opening race of the new season, and turned to Megatron in desperation. The extra load of servicing two more cars ran Mader ragged by the autumn of '87 and despite taking on extra staff and receiving extra blocks from Munich – to replace those wrecked in an epidemic of cracking – Megatron reliability proved poor.

For 1987 the 4 bar pop-off valve regulations came into effect and qualifying intercooler water sprays were banned.

MRD owner Bernie Ecclestone held BMW to their Brabham engine supply contract for 1987 but any attempt to revert to the upright engine was rebuffed as Munich had instead sold the entire stock to Megatron. Consequently the M12/13/1 lay-down engine reappeared in new Brabham BT56 chassis, by this time running fully electronic injection and a far more effective revlimiter.

Brabham's seven-speed Weismann gearbox had been tailor-made to make the most of the BMW 'four's admittedly narrow power band, but it made the lay-down unit excessively 'buzz-prone', the old mechanical rev-limiter's servo often proving too slow in winding the cam back to zero before mechanical damage had occurred. In contrast the limiting solenoid of a fully electronic system could cut instantaneously.

Under the new 4 bar pop-off valve regulations, the BMW unit suffered worse than the higher-revving rival V6s. Low-pressure injection was adopted to improve fuel efficiency by passing less during periods of valve overlap, since injection system valving proved variable and in any case to be competitive the four-cylinder demanded c. 3.9-bar race boost and inconsistent FISA pop-off valves often tended to blow open from as little as 3.7-3.8 bar as their springs weakened with race use.

In any case both engine and transmission reliability sagged through the '87 season, BMW finally bowed out of F1 involvement for 1988 and Ecclestone moth-balled MRD's Brabham operation to await a future buyer. But this was not quite the end of the line for the Bavarian Grand Prix engine...

During 1987, without major works involvement, and in particular due to supply of increasingly obsolescent ECU mapping chips from Munich, the upright M12/13 had lost its position as the most powerful unit in Formula 1. Engine failures were rife and reliability poor yet when FISA's 2.5-bar boost/150 litres fuel allowance regulations took effect for 1988, Arrows-Megatron opted to persevere for one more season, sensing the potential to achieve good results against the thinnest turbocharged field in years and a supporting cast of naturally aspirated 3.5-litre machinery...

BMW Motorsport finally bowed out completely after providing 40 new blocks to avoid the cracking problem of 1987, and Mader's Geneva opera-

tion assumed full responsibility for both mechanical development and management software mapping for '88. The finalized 2.5-bar Megatron units featured higher compression and reduced valve and port sizes in search of enhanced fuel efficiency, while piston form, con-rod length, camshaft profiling and fuel injectors were also revised. But as that final season of turbocharged Formula 1 unfolded so the Megatron engine's electro-mechanical injection system proved problematic, lean-burn combustion requirements demanding more efficient fuel atomization than the elderly system could effectively provide. The new blocks proved far more reliable under the more modest tune of 1988 than had their predecessors in '87, but in the field they were truly competitive only with 'atmo'-engined opposition, including the Cosworth DFZs also prepared by Mader.

And then the end of that season brought down the final curtain upon the era of turbocharged Formula 1 racing, and the BMW M12/13 engine family passed into history.

BRM

BRM entered the 1966 Formula with a terrific record behind them in the five seasons of 1.5-litre racing as described in the Team Directory.

The Chief Engineer at Bourne, Tony Rudd, and BRM's remote advanced projects study office attached to Harry Weslake Research in Rye, Sussex, had both studied proposals for a new 3-litre engine. At this time they worked quite well together, each evaluating the other's ideas, and the choice came down to either a 48-valve V12 promoted from Rye, or a two-valve-per-cylinder coupled twin-crankshaft H16-cylinder promoted by Rudd and his men at Bourne.

The more compact if frighteningly complex H16 was chosen as it could use proven 1500 cc V8 components, could be employed handily as a fully stressed chassis member mated to a monocoque chassis nacelle and had greater theoretical development potential (up to 600 bhp) than the V12. With an initial design target of at least 420 bhp, it should have cleaned up in its first season and should also have been well placed to repeat the performance in 1967.

While design progressed, BRM patron Sir Alfred Owen told his thunderstruck engineers he wanted to run the Formula 1 V8 cars in the 2.5-litre Tasman Championship in January/March 1966, representing important markets for his Rubery Owen industrial group. Rudd and driver Graham Hill argued that the 200-mile tankage Formula 1 cars were unsuitable for 100-mile Tasman races but Sir Alfred would not be moved, and BRM had hastily to enlarge their P56 1500 cc V8 engines to 2 litres.

As quick as they converted them, the enlarged V8s would break their piston rings on the team's test-bed at Folkingham aerodrome. This was thought to be connected with side loads on the piston due to the short con-rod coupled to the increase in stroke.

Matra had been using BRM P80 1-litre Formula 2 engines and they now ordered seven 2-litre V8s for use at Le Mans. Unlike the initial 1916 cc Tasman engines which would also be used in 1966 Formula 1 until the H16 became raceworthy, these were full 1998s. Bourne subsequently decided to go for broke and enlarged their works V8s to the maximum 2070 cc for the 1967 Tasman Championship and subsequent occasional Formula 1 use.

The 1916 cc engines of 1966 appeared with both side- and down-draught port heads, consistently recording 262-265 bhp and 258-260 bhp respectively on the dyno, yet Matra's full 1998s rarely did better and never got above 270 bhp. However, the 2070s shone, most giving 285 bhp and one (engine '5621', ex-Stewart) bellowed out a resounding 292 bhp!

Such is the reality of racing engine production and variation and the engineers were puzzled.

The interim V8s' longer stroke meant that BRM initially limited their drivers to 10,000 rpm in

Formula 1 racing but soon they were using 10,500 rpm unconcerned. At Reims, in the French GP, Hill's 1916 was towed along at 10,750 rpm by Parkes's Ferrari V12 and Graham told Tony Rudd, 'The thing was still going and still picking up power', until – inevitably – it broke a camshaft.

In retrospect, Tony told me: 'Had we known how successful the 2-litre was going to be it's quite probable we wouldn't have gone on with the H16 at the expense of the V12. We would have built a two-valve V12 first to get near 400 bhp, and it would have been light and reliable and we could have used a derivative of the very successful 1965 car which would have given us an excellent chance of the World Championship in 1966 and a good chance for '67 as well. We might never have built the H16 at all, in which case motor racing in the late '60s and early '70s would have been very different...'

Bourne committed itself to the P75 H16 early in 1965, and having extracted so much from the basic P56 V8 they were looking towards 146-147 bhp per litre from the H16, taking 440 bhp as a starting point.

The H-layout is really a slight misnomer; picture instead the 'H' laid on its side, two flat-eight boxer engines one above the other, their centre-line crankshafts geared together. It had been common in wartime aero engine design when Tony himself had headed a Rolls-Royce fault investigation department and was very familiar not only with such engines but also with their designers and trouble-shooters. The 24-cylinder R-R Eagle and Napier Rapier, Dagger and Sabre had all been 'H'-type engines.

Originally there was an idea to use only three camshafts each side of the engine, the centre shaft actuating the inlet valves in both the upper and lower 'eights'. Neat and weight-saving, it was found impractical, for extra space was needed between the cranks and Rudd and his assistant Geoffrey Johnson narrowed the angle between the valves and used a slightly larger cylinder bore to accommodate them. Now the H16's bore and stroke became 69.85 mm x 48.89 mm and there was no longer direct interchangeability with the 68.5 mm x 50.8 mm P56 V8's reciprocating components.

Tony had drawn upon Rolls-Royce Eagle H16 aero engine practice in adopting a crankcase cast in light alloy split along the main bearing cap line, with the coupling gears for the crankshafts in a separate pack bolting onto the back of the engine, connected to the cranks by two alleged quill shafts about an inch in diameter so not very flexible. The cylinder heads were from the 1500 V8s and timing packs from the F2 four-cylinder engines. The oil pumps were to a scaled-up V8 design, passing 32 gallons per minute. Tony himself describes the engine as 'an odd mixture of sophistication and the primitive'.

As an opposed engine, H16 bearing loads would be less than the preceding V8s and there was no reason to suppose individual components would not behave just as they had in those 1500s.

Tony Rudd: 'Of course we did not know there was a malevolent demon hidden in the middle of it.

'We had decided to use the long con-rod of the four-cylinder F2 engine, which had a cylinder block based on one half of the V8... We had terrible trouble with it in the first few F2 races of 1965 and the galling thing was that there seemed no way of coaxing it over 130 bhp. The first few all came out around 125-126...'

Very late in the day, they finally tried shorter con-rods on a lashed-up test engine. The first thing it did was break piston rings and the second thing it did was generate 140 bhp trouble free.

The shorter 1500 cc rods gave a 5.5 per cent reduction in side thrust, which yielded a 7.5 per cent increase in power output. Rudd's team now realized that the difference in piston velocity away from Top Dead Centre between the two rod lengths accounted for the F2 engine's lack of performance, which had always been greater at high rpm than low.

However, by this time the H16 engine was com-

BRM's H16 engine as originally laid out for 1966: above: planview emphasizes package size; below: front-end elevation shows compact coupling of two flat-8s with common vertical gear-pack.

mitted to the long F2-type con-rod and when it first ran the approximate 7.5 per cent loss of predicted power became apparent. Instead of the 440 bhp theoretically predicted they were lucky to reach 400, and when in mid-1966 the new 16-cylinder weighed 586 lb compared to the 1500 V8's 260 lb it was obvious 'we had got it wrong somewhere'.

Now there are several legends perpetuated about the shortcomings of the BRM P75 H16. It vibrated, its complex camshaft interconnections allowed drift causing valves to trip over each other, and so on.

Looking at the H16 its creator considers the first and biggest mistake was fitting the longer connecting rod, originally suggested by Charles Goodacre of the Ethyl Corporation, 'and I fell for it'. Hepworth & Grandage, the piston people, also checked the calculations and advised it would work 'but I was the one person who knew about the rate of burning and flame-spread after TDC, and I was the one who should have known better. It was not a good idea for a high-revving engine.

'The geared crankshafts were a mistake from a torsional vibration viewpoint but I don't think there's any evidence that it suffered from that vibration – as distinct from *experiencing* that vibration. It only suffered lack of inertia in its two crankshafts.

'And above all the main problem was that it was just plain 150 lb too heavy. We had calculated a weight of 460-480 lb since it was duplicating most parts of a 260 lb V8.

'The excess arose from castings designed around $^3/_{16}$ in. thick emerging well over $^1/_4$ in. thick, therefore 25 per cent thicker and 25 per cent heavier, accounting for 40 lb excess overall. Then modifications we added to strengthen the engine, like the flywheels and inertia weights, added another 40 lb and another 30 lb came simply from manufacturing expedience.'

The prototype H16 engine '7501' first fired at 10.45 a.m., 23 January 1966, and its weight quite shattered the engineers. It ran for seven minutes at 2000 rpm until the dyno prop-shaft seized. This was the precursor of a series of failures requiring a strip and rebuild costing a week on each occasion. Rudd suspected the inlet valves were trip-

ping over the exhausts but Geoff Johnson convinced him it was impossible by making a five-times full-size drawing with the valve paths plotted onto it.

'This theory', says Rudd, 'seems to have developed into a legend that this was one of the problems. There was never any evidence of it actually happening . . .'

It took more time to appreciate that the upper crankshaft had no flywheel of its own and relied totally upon the inertia of the gearbox and clutch to carry it from one firing cycle to the next, or upon the inertia of the lower crankshaft to which it was geared.

By April '66 there were still no raceworthy engines. When the inertia problem was recognized, they took large steel discs, split them and slipped them over the balance weights, bolting and tack-welding them together. Each one weighed 2 lb, there were four per crankshaft, another 16 lb in the engine. Now they could run to 10,000-11,000 rpm and the faster it ran the better the H16 looked.

Power remained disappointing, just under 400

bhp, but they were so relieved to find reliability they did not care, and the first engine went into a car for Monaco practice.

The gearchange was fearfully slow and wrecked all the dogs in the gearbox. Lotus had ordered one of the engines and their own was about ready when Colin Chapman had a look and said 'No wonder, you've put the clutch on the wrong way round!'

Instead of the clutch plates – which have negligible inertia – being connected to the gearbox layshaft, BRM had coupled the heavy outer drum with starter ring connected to it. Thus, when the driver changed gear he would disengage the clutch, the engine would die but the gearbox internals would run on under the inertia of the clutch drum and starter ring, hammering the engagement dogs as he fought to find the next gear. After a few changes the dogs would be damaged and the gearbox in need of a rebuild.

The H16s practised strongly at Reims and Rudd took a spare engine there in his company Rover, which took a poor view of the 500 lb lump in its boot.

Late in 1966 BRM's spare works team engine '7502' won the US GP in Clark's Lotus 43. It was not a heavily salvaged engine at that time, but became so after throwing its inertia weights during practice for the next race in Mexico. New 'eight-throw' two-pin crankshafts were fitted to provide a more permanent vibration cure, and from this point forward the engine fired and sounded like a true 16-cylinder, whereas originally it had fired two cylinders simultaneously so sounded like a loud eight.

Into 1967 the engine was reliable. Engine '7504' turned 400 bhp in March 1967 at 10,500 rpm and weighed some 580 lb with inertia rings on its crankshafts. It was never rebuilt as a two-pin engine. The highest power output recorded from an H16 was seen that March on engine '7506', just topping 420 bhp. Meanwhile, Sir Alfred Owen had authorized construction of a bet-hedging 3-litre V12 engine, not the Weslake 48-valver which in effect had become the Gurney Eagle unit but a sports-prototype oriented 24-valve design by Geoffrey Johnson.

This P101 unit was first employed by McLaren in the 1967 Canadian GP and would be taken up by the works BRM team to replace the H16 for 1968, and on to the end . . .

Bore and stroke were 73.8 mm x 57.2 mm, displacing 2998 cc, compression 12:1, and, after first running on 26 July 1967, engine 'P101-003' had peaked at 369 bhp at 9750 rpm on 14 August. On 3 November 1967, a 2.5-litre Tasman Formula 'P121-001' had its first dyno run, delivering 318 bhp at 10,250 rpm, engine '002' having run earlier

BRM's final serious season in Formula 1 was 1974 when new chief chassis designer Mike Pilbeam (seen here) developed the compact and quick P201s, but tight budgets and muddled management meant their P142 and P192 V12 engines were not man enough to realize the car's potential.

on 31 October, delivering 309 bhp at 9900 rpm.

As of 16 November 1967, six BRM V12 engines existed – three P101 24-valve 3-litres and three P121 2.5 Tasman units ready for Len Terry's new P126 monocoque cars and the 1968 Tasman Championship.

Meanwhile the ultimate, much-modified magnesium-block four-valve-per-cylinder H16 engine (yes, 64 valves, 128 valve-springs – imagine assembling it all) was completed and tested for 1968 but the policy decision was taken to set it aside and concentrate upon the simpler and lighter V12. The engine continued in test as late as from 13 December 1968 to 25 January 1969. It was number '7541' and the best of its eight runs peaked at only 378 bhp at 10,300 rpm; that was nothing like enough to compete with Cosworth's DFV, which was already beyond 430 bhp.

In comparison, P101 V12s were running as high as 404 bhp at 10,000 rpm (number '019 on 11 January 1969), and Johnson then developed a four-valve-per-cylinder chain-driven camshafts 48-valve P142 unit for 1969; units '142-001' and '002 were available for Oliver and Surtees in the Spanish GP on 4 May.

The first 48-valver had run on 28 February on the Folkingham bed, recording 453 bhp at 10,350 rpm and '002's first run on 26 March yielded an instant 455 bhp at 10,750 rpm. This was almost 50 bhp more than the best P101 24-valvers and through the season the six P142 engines available to the team averaged 440 bhp at a time when Cosworth were claiming 430 at 10,000 rpm.

In 1970, the P142s powered more adequate Southgate-designed chassis and began winning races, but power was not destined to improve dramatically in the years left to BRM and its V12 engines. After Rudd had gone to Lotus, Aubrey Woods took over engine development. He considered the chain-driven four-cam centre-exhaust P142 overheated both its water and oil too easily, and suffered badly from detonation. Its relatively long stroke was a limiting factor, new pistons were required and they took a long time to make. He designed new cylinder heads lowering engine CoG with outside exhausts and in-vee inlets with improved ports and enlarged cooling waterways. The crankcase was now cross-bolted and stiffened to allow use as a semi-stressed chassis member.

The BRM V12s would always retain their camshaft chain-drive as the system's last refuge in Formula 1.

Woods subsequently left to join Amon Engines, Peter Windsor-Smith taking over with Rubery-Owen also consulting Walter Hassan and Harry Mundy. Windsor-Smith produced a new P192 V12 for 1974, which carried new heads with narrower-angle valves and altered porting, while the pistons were flatter and lighter, and there were bottom-end improvements. Some 13 lb was saved and a shorter stroke and wider bore were mentioned. With minor modifications the lighter short-stroke crankshaft was also intended to fit old P142 crankcases, but ex-BRM staff seem to doubt if the short-stroke crankshaft was ever in fact produced – certainly not in any numbers.

As the team entered its final serious, if even then barely significant, season in 1974, Bourne quality control records indicate that engines '142-008', '009, '017, '018, '021 and '022 as prepared for the Nürburgring on 31 July 1974 peaked respectively at 454, 444, 430, 444, 435 and 439 bhp. This displayed little, if any, progress over the previous five years, for all engines were run on the same Folkingham dyno, unless that too was growing weary with age.

P192 engine '002 peaked at 453 bhp at 10,750 rpm prior to the British GP at Brands Hatch that season. At 7000 rpm this V12 delivered 284 bhp, at 8000 rpm 352, at 9000 rpm 433 and at 11,000 rpm 447 bhp. Peak torque was 236 lb/ft at 9000 rpm.

A final further Aubrey Woods-revised P202 engine was developed for the Stanley-BRM car of 1977 delivering a claimed 480 bhp at 11,200 rpm but it looked neither conspicuously powerful nor reliable and it failed dismally – a sad and demeaning postscript to the story of a once honoured name. At its peak, BRM had been a superb outfit – an incontrovertible fact which Bourne's many detractors too easily forget.

Anyone who has never made a mistake hasn't done very much and BRM never fell into that category.

Ferrari

The Maranello concern's 1966 V12 F1 engine was a 77 mm x 53.5 mm 60-degree light-alloy V12 with four overhead camshafts. Of modest sports-racing provenance, it was claimed to deliver 380 bhp at 10,000 rpm (probably nearer 360 bhp), with Lucas fuel injection and Marelli coil and distributor ignition.

The elderly but now fuel-injected 2.4-litre four-cam Dino V6 engine used briefly in 1966 was well suited to the more tortuous circuits, but the Ferrari 312 V12s were Maranello's frontline armament.

Major V12 developments have been described in the Team Directory and by the end of its long run in 1969 it had become a roller main-bearing power

unit with Lucas electronic transistorized ignition, Lucas fuel injection, compression quoted around 12.0:1 and an output of some 410 bhp at 10,500 rpm. While the DFV V8 had the narrow included valve angle of 32 degrees at this time, the Ferrari V12's valves were still disposed at 50-55 degrees, and BRM's at 61 degrees.

In 1970, the Forghieri/Rocchi/Bussi engine design team produced their splendid *Tipo 312B* flat-12 power unit which in ever-developing form would power their Formula 1 cars for a decade.

The horizontal 'boxer' layout (some people calling it a 180-degree vee!) was adopted to enable a very low centre of gravity to be achieved. It also cleared airflow beneath the rear wing and saved a little weight compared to the V12. Dimensions were 78.5 mm x 51.5 mm, displacing 2991.01 cc. Four-valve-per-cylinder heads borrowed late-series V12 experience.

In initial form piston and crankshaft problems caused a string of testing failures, not least involving lubrication problems solved by the provision of a tilting dyno bed at Maranello to reproduce cornering surge conditions.

The flat-12 was a very high-revving unit and to minimize friction losses its crankshaft revolved in just four main bearings, two plain shell bearings amidships and ball-bearing races at nose and tail. This left the crankshaft with rather dubious support and, after initial breakages, crankshaft torsionals were controlled by the addition of a Pirelli cushion coupling between crankshaft and flywheel, achieving reliability to match 460 bhp between 11,500 and 11,700 rpm power. By 1974, power was up to 495 bhp and by the end of the engine's useful life it was delivering nearer 510 bhp at 12,000 rpm – which few doubted.

The light-alloy block-cum-crankcase was cast in two parts, united on a crankshaft centreline bolted flange. The heads were cast in crisp aluminium alloy disposing four valves per cylinder actuated by double overhead camshafts per bank powered by geartrain from the crankshaft nose.

Light-alloy cylinder liners were used, cooled by water circulation at their upper ends, by oil circulation down below. The crankshaft was machined from a steel forging, each of its six crankpins carrying two con-rods. The crankshaft nose gear drove alternator, ignition distributor and fuel metering unit via gears and pinions. The crankshaft tail drove the valvegear train. A tiny flywheel assembly incorporated a rubber vibration damper. Forged titanium con-rods were used, with plain big-end bearings, although rollers were apparently used experimentally on occasion.

Mahle forged aluminium pistons were used, pocketed for valve clearance and 'squish'.

A single oil pressure pump driven off the rear of the right-hand cylinder-head timing gear fed the oil filter mounted behind the fuel metering unit, then on into the front of the block. The scavenge pump resided in the same housing as the pressure pump, returning oil to the tank which chased around the car in the various 312B, 'B2, 'B3, 'B4, 312T and 'T2-3-4-5 models in which variations of this power unit featured.

The two cars, the 1973 *Spazzaneve* 'B3 prototype and a 1977-spec 'T2, which were in my care briefly seemed to have nothing interchangeable between their two engines.

The 1979 Championship unit featured an ancillary scavenge pump driven from the exhaust camshaft in one head to clear excess oil from the head chambers into the block. A complex magnesium casting on the front of the engine encased the ancillary drive gears and a solitary water pump.

Water fed into the heads through channels cast integrally into the block covers. The left-side exhaust camshaft drove a high-pressure fuel pump. Engine mounting to the chassis was via lugs on the early units suspending the flat-12 from the rear beam of the 312B and 'B2 series cars, then via four studs in the head covers from the 'B3 model forward.

Internal dimensions of the 312B series engines varied enormously, as did the precise design of their castings and internals, and layout of their ancillaries. Only overall configuration and dimensions, within an inch or so, remained constant through their 11 seasons of competition.

Ferrari listed late-series dimensions as 80 mm x 49.6 mm, giving a unit cylinder capacity of 249.31 cc, or 2999 cc overall. The 1979-80 engine was 650 mm long, 680 mm wide and 300 mm tall and weighed 180 kg with accessories attached.

The turbocharged 120-degree V6 126C power unit developed for 1981 had bore and stroke dimensions of 81 mm x 48.4 mm, displacing 1496.43 cc. With its KKK or Comprex BBC pressure-wave supercharging (although the latter was over-publicized and really hardly significant), this unit had a compression ratio of 6.5:1 and delivered a claimed 560 bhp at 11,500 rpm in 1981 form, rising to 580 bhp at 11,800 rpm in 1982, 620 bhp at 11,500 in 1983 and 680 bhp at 11,500 rpm in 1984. It weighed 175 kg (375 lb), as do nearly all Italian Formula 1 engines, if we believe their manufacturers' figures. The flat-12 in final form was lighter, not carrying turbocharging ancillaries nor having to resist 126C temperatures and pressures, at 160 kg (353 lb).

Ferrari pursued rapid development of their engine, evolving a turbocharger run-on fuel-burning system to keep them wound up on boost ready for the driver to open the throttle again after decelerating on the over-run. With AGIP, an atomized-water injection system was also developed to enhance already intercooled induction charge density, and power output rose progressively to 580 bhp at 11,800 rpm in their first turbocharged Constructors' Championship season of 1982, then 620 bhp at 11,500 rpm in 1983 and finally an alleged 680 bhp at 11,500 rpm – presumably in race trim – in the fuel-conscious season of '84. Subsequently, effort expended upon water injection would come to be regarded inhouse as harmful to potentially more profitable development elsewhere, and as the 1984 Ferrari season fell apart major changes took place, including the dismissal of *Ing.* Forghieri from direct *Reparto Corse* involvement.

Ing. Ildo Renzetti and Luciano Caruso redesigned the V6 engine for 1985, producing new heads with reversed ports to place the inlet ports

Right: The 120-degree V6 turbocharged Ferrari contrasts with (below) a Maranello factory section of the 312B flat-12 engine showing its deep base chamber, roller-bearing mains, narrow included valve angle, induction tracts above the heads, exhausts below and extensive cross-bolting of the split crankcase castings.

in the vee, exhausts outside, manifolding sweeping away through KKK turbochargers low either side. This enabled chassis designer Postlethwaite to create a far neater, lower-bodied car than hitherto, the best-looking in Formula 1. A new digital electronic management system had been developed for the new 156/85 by Weber-Marelli, combined with an AGIP Petroli water-suspension *emulsistem*, and upon release in February '85 Maranello claimed 780 bhp at 11,000 rpm. Development continued rapidly with a quad-turbo engine being tested early in the year but remaining unraced. An electronically controlled wastegate adjustment, to give fine-adjustable boost while running, was adopted during the season, however.

Nevertheless the V6 engine was near the end of its development life, its original 1980-81 design having itself been trimmed to the bone around an ultimate requirement for perhaps only 700-750

bhp. Forghieri's planned four-cylinder replacement was tested through the 1984-85 winter, but Ferrari's chassis section disliked its slant design as this posed installation problems, and it then proved mechanically unreliable on Caruso's test beds. With Forghieri removed from F1 responsibility, his slant-4 engine was set aside; the V6 went into its fifth racing season with a quoted 780 bhp and at Estoril its times suggested 793 bhp in race tune. German GP qualifying required a calculated 988 bhp to achieve Ferrari's times, while race tune there gave around 839 bhp, ostensibly little more than TAG Turbo and BMW, the latter perhaps anxious for reliability and tyre-conservation on home ground. In Austria, the Ferraris had to run some 881 bhp in race tune to face BMW, Honda and TAG Turbo and mechanical reliability began to falter.

Thereafter Ferrari's season collapsed as the high boost pressures necessary to keep competitive

Ferrari's 126C turbocharged 120-degree V6 1.5-litre engine made its debut at Long Beach, 1981. This is the KKK twin-turbocharged version; see the underwing floor curving up beneath the side induction 'log'.

overwhelmed the 120-degree V6's mechanical reliability. It became obvious that they no longer had the most powerful engine in Formula 1 and by the end of 1985 a major rethink and redesign had become necessary.

For 1986 a French engineer arrived at Maranello, ex-Renault Sport. Jean-Jacques His and the Maranello engine division were to begin work on an all-new 90-degree V6 engine to replace the long-faithful but now creaking 120-degree unit which in effect was entering its sixth season of competition, further uprated with 7.5:1 compression and a race output of around 850 bhp at 11,500 rpm from 3.8-bar boost.

To tailor this ageing unit to the new 195-litre fuel allowance involved digitized electronic injection with new solenoid-operated valves to enhance fuel economy by avoiding wastage during valve overlap in the transitional rev ranges. The unit also featured lighter reciprocating mass, improved materials throughout, reduced fuel input timing, and the injection system itself was uprated to sustain nozzle pressures above 10 bar and capable of opening the injectors for as little as 0.6 milliseconds only – both improving atomization of the heavy fuel mixes then being recognized as the way ahead, and further restricting fuel wastage. More sophisticated electronic control was provided by sequential phased ignition offering more flexibility in programming ('mapping'). It is claimed that Ferrari achieved a specific fuel consumption of 210 grammes per hp/hr in this programme.

During the '86 season, a cylinder head modification programme produced altered combustion chambers and ports, followed by a new exhaust system at Imola, while a triple exhaust tailpipe and wastegate vent assembly was introduced in Canada, feeding its high-velocity gases onto the underwing to energize airflow beneath that surface and so enhance aerodynamic download. In an attempt to reduce throttle lag a new butterfly throttle was tried ahead of the turbos. Ferrari also developed an electronic wastegate control, and Garrett turbochargers progressively replaced the German KKKs – in race trim from the Belgian GP, while KKKs were retained for qualifying only until the British GP.

Garrett offered greater individuality of specification and also improved reliability. The induction system was further modified with new 'charger casings from the Austrian GP, plus improved intercoolers from the Italian GP. Actual horsepower achieved seems to have been closer to 820 than the 850 sometimes claimed, but in qualifying at Ricard for example no less than 1070 bhp was calculated after a top speed of 342.2 km/h had been recorded.

By the end of that season what had long been feared was confirmed – Ferrari simply needed an all-new block, the alloy V6 was no longer man enough to contain and control the awesome forces being unleashed within it. Blocks were distorting, friction losses were uncontrollable as bearings phased out of line, oil temperatures were high, structural cracks were appearing.

What was essentially engineer His's rather

Renault-like new 90-degree F1/87 engine was first tested in the *Reparto Corse* dyno cells in September 1986.

A narrower vee configuration had been evaluated but the Cosworth-like 90 degrees offered a practical compromise in terms of installation and ancillary accommodation, plus structural integrity. Nominally at least, the new unit retained the old 120-degree V6's bore and stroke of 81 mm x 48.4 mm, displacing 1496.4 cc. Improved rigidity was provided in part by the narrower vee but mainly by the adoption of Renault-style thin-wall cast-iron block manufacture. It was the first Ferrari engine in this material. To contain and control similarly high internal pressures and dynamic forces within another alloy block would have meant resorting to balance weights and dimensions which added so much weight it would be heavier. *Ing.* Ildo Renzetti, erstwhile head of Ferrari's race engine section, had in recent months been co-opted by Fiat to develop the company's new FIRE engine using thin-wall iron casting alloys and techniques developed by the group's Teksid subsidiary. Now he was brought back to Fiorano, and Teksid metallurgy and casting techniques were applied to the new F1/87 turbo V6.

This thin-wall, fine-tolerance manufacture enabled the new iron engine to emerge lighter than its alloy predecessor. Architecturally, its timing gear train moved to the front of the unit from the rear, driving the usual twin overhead camshafts in aluminium heads. The cylinder bores were linerless, the three-pin steel crankshaft ran in four main bearings, and carried titanium con-rods and Mahle light-alloy pistons with Goetze rings, plus a vibration damper.

There were four valves and a single spark plug per cylinder, in 8.0:1 compression combustion chambers, included angle between the inclined valves being 32 degrees. The digital electrical system featured Marelli ignition, Weber injection now rated above 10-bar pressure, and the latest-generation Ferrari/Marelli/Weber management system. An individual coil was provided in the cap to each spark plug – another Renault Sport feature – enabling the normal HT loom to be discarded and the plugs to be triggered instead by simple low-voltage signals, minimizing high-tension volt leakage, and optimizing control with instant correction in each cylinder as the management system software might demand.

Ferrari claimed some 880 bhp at 11,500 rpm for this new unit, 588 bhp per litre. Unit weight was only 150 kg, and thermodynamic efficiency was high, a specific consumption below 200 gm per hp/hr – 198 gm – being claimed. Such frugality would be essential for the new year's 4-bar boost/195 litres fuel allowance Formula.

This engine was mated to a new longitudinal gearbox replacing the old faithful *trasversale* unit for aerodynamic reasons. Little engine modification seems to have been made during the year save for turbocharger and induction system variations. From the first race a single plenum chamber was fitted to enable just one pop-off valve to be used, while modest head changes to the combustion chambers and inlet ports followed Spa. At Imola one analysis suggested a true F1/87 output of 874 bhp for qualifying and 791 for the race. At the German GP in more top-endy tune for the very fast Hockenheim course, up to 932 bhp was suggested for qualifying and 867 for the race, then 950 bhp in Hungary, 900 for the race.

By that time new-material Garrett turbocharger internals had arrived – with silicon nitride ceramic coating, ultra-light rotating parts and low friction bearings – enabling Ferrari to flutter their pop-off valves open, matching the 4.1-4.2 bar levels against which Honda had been knocking most of the year.

Intensive research and development centred upon the fuel system configuration and electronic controls, atmospheric air sensors and a rev-counter on the large turbos employed in Mexico. Garrett's new turbos were available only in left-hand configuration, Ferrari compensating by providing different exhaust systems side for side.

At his final press conference that December, Mr Ferrari declared 'we faced the last competitions of the year with 910-920 bhp and we ended up qualifying at 960 bhp' but he was already urging development of a re-headed 90-degree V6 for the 2.5-bar/150 litres Formula to follow in 1988.

That would be a meaningless season for Formula 1 as in effect only McLaren-Honda built all-new for the year. Ferrari dabbled half-heartedly with a 'B-spec' '87 chassis and mildly modified engine – and the result was a foregone conclusion save for the Maranello team's lucky but joyously received one-off victory in their home race at Monza.

Approaching that year's problem of diminished boost, tighter fuel restriction, Ferrari's engineers considered that with a notional loss of 25 bhp per 0.1 bar reduction in boost, the 1.5 bar boost reduction for '88 would mean a loss of c. 375 bhp.

So they would initially be looking at ways to improve upon 525-555 bhp. Higher rpm was attractive, and alternative turbo dimensions, rotational speed and electronic control were explored, seeking an extra 40-50 bhp for every extra 1000 rpm.

Aiming at 12,000 rpm and 620 bhp, compression ratio was pushed to a marginal 10.0:1, and by the time of the first race, in Brazil, the V6 was running to 12,200 rpm. Piston velocity rose from 18.5 to 19.4 metres/sec, but once again FISA's pop-off valves initially proved variable, blowing open just below the 2.5-bar threshold to promote sudden power loss. Electronic wastegate control was then introduced to provide automatic boost pressure control, smoothing delivery despite the FISA valves' inconsistency.

Valves, valve springs, camshafts and pistons all came under scrutiny, a useable 12,600 rpm was available in Canada, some 650 bhp in qualifying, and the original throttle system of six individual butterfly valves (one per port) was replaced by a single butterfly near the pop-off, which was itself sited like Honda's over a venturi throat, effectively to falsify the true boost pressure regime. To eke out the 150 litres fuel allowance as AGIP provided high-density toluene mixes, 590-615 bhp proved Ferrari's effective limit in race tune during this final season of turbocharged Formula 1 racing, but considerable effort was expended in an unsuccessful attempt to match Honda's finest, injection pressures soaring far above 10 bar, induction-charge intercoolers having to be enlarged and from the Hungarian GP a by-pass system being included with automatic control to smooth out the charge temperature graph.

And after just two seasons Ferrari's 90-degree iron-block turbo V6 had reached the end of its useful life...

Meanwhile, John Barnard had joined Ferrari from McLaren and had concentrated largely upon development of an all-new naturally aspirated 3.5-litre F1 car for 1989. After investigation of many possible engine configurations, a 65-degree V12 was chosen as offering the greatest power and development potential in conjunction with ease of installation.

The new 12-cylinder block was a similarly thin-wall iron casting to that used in the 90-degree V6 turbo engines, running linerless bores and with published bore and stroke dimensions of 84 mm x 52.6 mm, displacing 3497.96 cc. Heads were in light alloy, initially described as featuring a compression ratio of 11.5:1. Four valves per cylinder were attributed to the unit, although it was known that five valves per cylinder were under development, both four- and five-valve configurations actuated by twin gear-driven overhead camshafts per cylinder bank. Weber-Marelli digital electronic injection was adapted to the 12-cylinder configuration, together with Magneti Marelli's static electronic ignition with individual coils in unit with the plug caps.

The uprated 60-valve engine emerged towards the winter of 1988/89, Ferrari claiming 635 bhp for it at 12,500 rpm in original form, though at the expense of a poor mid-range torque curve. This was anathema to engineering director John Barnard and in its second phase of development

Slimline packaging of the 3.5-litre Ferrari V12 'atmo' engine began with its 65-degree vee angle, opened up from Maranello's traditional 60-degree configuration just enough to accommodate vital ancillaries within the valley. Spark plugs feature coil-in-cap ignition. Note also rear suspension configuration and careful fairing provided around suspension links by body side panel.

the new 60-valve engine had its 'top number' lopped back to 600 bhp while its useable power curve from 8000 rpm was considerably improved. Barnard's seven-speed semi-automatic longitudinal gearbox had been equipped with so many ratios specifically to accommodate the peaky power curve of a high-revving V12, but with the engine section working hard to improve the unit's overall driveability the team would eventually find itself able to save the weight of an extra gear ratio and run the 'box as a pure six-speeder.

Once racing began in 1989 Ferrari suffered from attempting to develop its semi-automatic transaxle in the midst of a racing season due to managerial timidity in committing to the system early enough in pre-season testing. Power from the new V12 was always disappointing, and in attempting to improve the dyno charts' top numbers the engine section again tended to overlook the practical necessity of providing a broad and useable mid-range curve.

When the *Tipo* 640 made its race debut in Brazil, broader cheek intakes were provided in the headrest fairing which doubled as an intake airbox, lateral vents were added for cooling air exit and a larger cooling system header tank fitted to combat high ambient temperature. For Monaco six-into-one exhausts were fitted to find extra low-speed torque, and for Mexico a 1971-style engine airbox was re-invented with a semicircular intake ringed by the roll-over bar. This necessitated re-siting the engine management ECU, while the original single oil cooler in the engine vee gave way to twin lateral coolers. In Canada an airbox duct was introduced which was separate from the body panelling, sitting within it more as an integral part of the engine.

An 'Evolution 3' engine was available for the French GP, contributing towards a 5 kg weight saving overall and claimed by Ferrari to provide 640 bhp in qualifying tune. Electrical problems affecting the transaxle's semi-automatic operation had been blamed by Barnard on the alternator suffering unnecessary heat stress due to its siting

in the vee, then by the left-side exhaust bank. For the British GP it was provided with its own improved cooling duct, and more effective heat shielding.

Some 650 bhp was then being claimed, a new engine oil reservoir was sandwiched beneath the gearbox and the preceding twin oil cooler matrices were replaced by a single core right-side mounted in the side pod above the water radiator and a gearbox oil cooler was also sited there.

Major modification followed for the Italian GP, despite factory denials a short-stroke version with dimensions of 86 mm x 50.2 mm against the hitherto standard 84 mm x 52.6 mm apparently being used. For the first time the engine could run well beyond 13,000 rpm and 660 bhp was reputedly exceeded for the first time – 645-650 in race tune.

Through 1990 the Ferrari engine went through a staggering series of modifications and sub-types. Those used in anger included the '036', '037', '037B' and a modified '036'. The season-opening engine was the '036' succeeded by the higher-revving '037' with altered bore and stroke dimensions. Development was slower than expected so the '037B' was used first, the '036B' being an interim unit incorporating elements of the forthcoming '037' design within the original engine.

The definitive '037' engine eventually made its bow in Hungary and towards the end of the season the Ferrari V12 was claimed to be producing a genuine 680 bhp at 13,000 rpm but it notably lacked the major advantage of meaty mid-range torque displayed by Honda's contemporary V10.

In 1991 the latest-version Ferrari V12 was revving to 14,600 rpm but still lacked mid-range torque compared to Renault and Honda. In Monaco and Canada throttle-sensitive butterfly valves in the exhaust system were tried to increase torque and variable-length induction trumpets were evaluated from Hockenheim forward...

Just like Renault, Ferrari's engineers tended to look for the highest possible horsepower number in their dyno test-house running while ignoring the self-evident truth that wide-ranging mid-range torque is what wins road races. But the Italian engineers took this search further than their French counterparts and until mid-season the Maranello chassis engineers – and drivers – were tearing their hair out demanding greater mid-range punch, never mind ultimate horsepower.

A change of direction came with the introduction

of the new stepped-nose Ferrari 643 at Magny-Cours, when a new-sanction 60-valve V12 engine accompanied it and the fortunes of drivers Prost and Alesi both took an upturn. It would all go bad again before season's end. AGIP seemed to lag behind Shell, Elf and Mobil on all-important fuel chemistry to liberate real power from these 3.5-litre naturally aspirated engines. Marelli seemed to be off the pace in the electrical engine management war. And Ferrari fortunes suffered accordingly.

It was notable how Ferrari for the first time made a customer-spec F1 engine available to an outside team – Minardi – who deployed these units slightly more effectively on occasion. The curious manner of Ferrari's new management was demonstrated, however, when the sponsor who would have financed Minardi's use of the engines – Pioneer – was then lured to back Ferrari's works team . . . Fiat had far to go to manage its Ferrari F1 division adequately.

Into 1991 a comprehensive engine redesign was completed, aiming at ever-higher crankshaft speed, which it achieved by adopting an ultra-short stroke, and with AGIP fuel chemistry being applied to permit compression ratio to be raised as high as 13.5:1 without encountering destructive detonation problems. With this redesign, the old in-house engine classification system which had yielded variant identifications such as '036' and '037' was changed, reverting to the traditional system whereby the unit volume of one engine cylinder identified each model. In this particular case 3500 cc divided by 12 cylinders = c. 291, so the 1991 60-valve Ferrari V12 F1 engine became the *Tipo* 291 unit, various '.?' suffix numbers then being added to indicate further design variations.

Midway through the season, Ferrari's *motoristi* were looking at 15,000 rpm from extensive study of materials employed, lightening rotating and reciprocating parts, and seeking to save power loss in the cooling and lubrication systems.

The *Tipo* 291.2 engine was introduced at Imola beginning the European F1 season, and from the very sound analytical computer programme used by Italian technical writer Enrico Benzing it appeared to be developing a genuine 718 bhp in qualifying tune, and 706 bhp from what data was recordable in the brief race of the one car to reach the startline . . . Prost having spun his car into the sand traps on the warming-up lap, and Alesi following him there in the opening laps.

For Monaco special versions of the '.2 engine

were prepared with the 84.0 mm x 52.6 mm bore and stroke of the 1989 '036'-series units, instead of the preceding season's 2 mm larger bore, 2.4 mm shorter stroke '037'-spec to boost mid-range torque for the street circuit. It appears these engines were used only in Monte Carlo qualifying.

A mildly refined '.3 variant followed, from which the 15,000 rpm '.4 was developed, followed by the '.5 which featured experimental variable-length induction trumpets and was first deployed in qualifying at Mexico City. Testing at Hockenheim and at the Hungaroring in preparation for their respective GPs proved a further sophisticated variable-length induction system, using the 'slash-five' top-end V12s in Germany and 'slash-fours' for enhanced mid-range torque in Hungary. The telescoping variable-length trumpets were actuated by an electronically controlled high-pressure oleo-pneumatic system, triggered by throttle pedal position and engine rpm sensors. To add 'meat' low-down in the rev range the high-velocity induction favoured by lengthy inlet trumpets is required. For optimum engine performance at ultra-high rpm, very short intake tubes are favoured. Within a working range of some 100 mm, the Ferrari system looked promising, but Honda were attacking the same problem simultaneously on their RA121E V12, and starting from a higher baseline they would shine before that season's end . . .

With fixed-length induction, the German GP engines at Hockenheim developed around 733 bhp for qualifying ('.4 units) and 715 in race tune (on '.3s). A further-developed engine variant combining both variable-length induction and major internal revisions – the '.6 unit – was then developed in a feverish attempt to bring Ferrari onto some kind of competitive level against Renault's latest RS3B V10 and Honda's V12s, this new Italian unit having the ultra-short stroke of 47.9 mm (reduced by 2.3 mm from '037' standards), and a 2 mm wider bore, at 88 mm. This unit reputedly offered a broader power band, sustaining 735 bhp at best over a spread of 500 rpm instead of 300 rpm as hitherto – while peaking at an ear-splitting 14,800 rpm.

It appears that the *Tipo* 291.5 V12 was raced for the first time on just one car at Estoril, then appeared with variable exhaust throttling at Barcelona to promote bottom-end punch, this system having been tried previously at Monaco and Montreal. The finalized 291.6-specification engines then emerged for qualifying in Japan, combining all the most promising of the season's developments in one engine spec.

Considering the 65-degree Ferrari V12 engine family's overall development 1988-1991, its progress could be tabulated as follows:

	1988	1989	1990	1991
Tipo No:	'036'	'036'	'037'	'291.6'
Bore:	84.0 mm	84.0 mm	86.0 mm	88.0 mm
Stroke:	52.6 mm	52.6 mm	50.2 mm	47.9 mm
B/S ratio:	0.63	0.63	0.58	0.54
Output (bhp):	c. 620	c. 665	c. 700	c. 735
RPM:	13,000	13,600	13,800	14,800
Compression:	11.5:1	11.9:1	12.5:1	13.5:1

But by the end of 1991 the inescapable fact remained that Ferrari had not won a single race that season, and despite all the best efforts of the Maranello *motoristi* their V12s were nowhere near matching Renault and Honda step for step. Perhaps more damagingly, too much of Ferrari's potential was being dissipated in team management and personality problems at the top . . .

As one disillusioned Italian enthusiast put it 'To judge if a fish is bad, you examine the head . . .'. Into 1992 Ferrari's Fiat overlords tried hard to put that right.

Ford

To survive in Formula 1 Cosworth Engineering and Ford had to address the 1.5-litre turbocharged option after 1986. Assured of the Formula's long-term prospects by FISA President Balestre, Ford Detroit – as opposed to Ford of Dagenham who had originally backed the Cosworth DFV programme independently of its American parent company – was persuaded to expect a class of racing guaranteed to survive until at least 1989 and probably into the 1990s.

Former Ford Cologne touring car team chief Mike Kranefuss was by this time head of motor sport Detroit, and upon receiving his report the board authorized a five-year programme under which Cosworth in England would produce a suitable power unit, two years for test and development, three years for frontline racing.

Ford's own Motorola electronics division was to develop the all-important tailored management system for the new engine. Initially a four-cylinder research programme was evaluated, *à la* BMW or Zakspeed, using a block derived from the 1600 cc BD block, trimmed to 1497 cc by fitting a short-throw crankshaft. Run up to 3 bar boost in initial dyno tests, six successive catastrophic failures were encountered, attributed to crankshaft vibration following excessive loading. Cosworth considered that on standard-grade pump fuel the idea could have sufficed, but with toluene fuel mixes rapidly being developed by all potential F1 rivals it became clear the four-cylinder approach was inadequate.

In September 1984 Ford had authorized development of an all-new pure-bred racing engine, Cosworth's only restraints being use of the Ford Detroit management system and of Ford-designed cam-cover logos.

Keith Duckworth and chief engine designer Geoff Goddard produced the neatest and most compact 120-degree V6 turbo unit yet seen, in their TEC Turbo which began dyno testing in Northampton just 12 months later. Contemporary flat-bottom F1 car configuration enabled the low CoG potential of the 120-degree layout to be adopted, saving the installation problems posed by engine mounts and exhaust system runs in a 180-degree or 'flat' six-cylinder layout. The low-lying engine offered a chassis designer optimum airflow potential to a rear wing while the broad valley of the 120-degree V6 provided plenty of space for a compound turbo-supercharging system which Cosworth considered using. This was a combination exhaust gas-cum-mechanically driven compressor device which Lotus R&D also had

in view for the still-born Toyota F1 V6 engine which they drew – they in fact built a prototype batch of six or so units – at around the same time.

FISA was still making noises about further reducing turbo engine capacity to just 1200 cc while this work was in progress, so two alternative-capacity versions were studied.

The TEC Turbo V6 emerged with an aluminium-alloy block with three-pin crankshaft running in four main bearings, the bottom end being robustly located by both vertical and horizontal cross bolts. Nikasil liners were used, with 'O'-ring seals, while the heads and cam-carriers were integrated into single castings, also in aluminium alloy. Cosworth had an exceedingly valuable asset in its specialist foundry at Worcester in which they were able to 'cast exactly what we draw', endowing their crisp castings with a control and precision which enabled them to match the strength of the thin-wall iron V6 block castings which Renault and Ferrari both considered necessary to withstand turbo loads.

Camshaft drive was taken off the nose of the short crankshaft and was entrusted to a revival of the hoary old timing chain. It could be made as thin as a timing gear, it was light and to some extent self-damping and a twin-chain system was adopted to provide smaller sprockets and shorter chain runs. Ancillary belt drives powered the water pump, oil pressure pump and alternator along the left side of the block, and three oil scavenge pumps – one for the turbo, two for the engine base chamber – and a centrifugal oil/air separator on the right side.

Oil-cooled flat-topped pistons were adopted, initially of Mahle manufacture, later Cosworth's own, and the cylinder heads featured an identical 40-degree included valve angle to the old FVA F2 engine of the late 1960s, offering plenty of space between the valves for the cooling so vital in a turbocharged system.

Cosworth became a development partner of Garrett in the turbocharging department while a long-lasting relationship with Marelli-Weber led to adoption of the Italian Raceplex capacity-discharge ignition and solenoid-actuated injectors. Since the injectors – like Bosch's – were too small to supply the needs of a high-revving turbocharged V6 racing engine, two were fitted to each cylinder.

The Ford TEC 120-degree V6 turbocharged engine was a triumph of compact packaging despite the inevitable complication of turbo manifolding, intercooling and management electronics. Here's the installation in a 1987 Benetton B187.

No mistaking the Cosworth DFV-series family background of the company's 75-degree Ford HB Series V 3.5-litre Formula 1 engine deployed by Benetton in 1991. Using Ford electronic engine management systems and revving to 13,000 rpm, this was another compact power unit, like the TEC turbo V6 before it.

Detroit's Motorola EEC IV production engine management system was at that time considered to be the world's most advanced, commanding timing of both ignition and injection, plus injection duration, and also capable of running an electronically controlled turbo wastegate.

The new engine's compression ratio was listed as 7.0:1, its weight just 128 kg, and peak rpm 10,500. It first ran on the dyno in the summer of 1985, Cosworth testing mechanically in Northampton while Ford US mapped its management system in Detroit. On 20 February 1986 the engine was track-tested for the first time in a Haas-Lola, running on Ford's Boreham test track in Essex. It was to be devoted exclusively to the new Haas team for that season, but was intended to be made available off the shelf – DFV-style – in later seasons.

However, there was a growing perception that it had been presented to the wrong team: new in Formula 1, with a new chassis, new engine . . . but old ex-McLaren management, and drivers who were almost as elderly.

The TEC was not available until Imola, when the new V6 was cleared to run 11,000 rpm and 3.6-bar boost on 'souped-up' AvGas rather than toluene-loaded 'rocket fuel'. Three engines serviced one car there, while the other entry retained the team's stop-gap Hart power (q.v.). By Monaco time five engines were available and both cars were TEC-equipped.

Like so many underpowered engines, the TEC was described by the drivers as being 'nice, progressive and smooth', its characteristics obviating the sharp pitch-change which had dogged the

more rumbustious Hart-powered Haas chassis. But it lacked snap, and punch and top-end too.

Naturally these were early days, as in mid-season 'rocket fuel' was adopted and 3.8-4-bar boost, 7.5:1 compression ratios from Brands Hatch until Monza, where an experimental 8.0:1 appeared with even more volatile fuel brewing, and the TEC proved measurably superior to the Hart it had supplanted. The 8.0:1 variant reappeared in Australia, and over 4-bar boost was recorded, over 1000 bhp at 12,000 rpm . . .

Sufficient parts for 25 engines had been produced by that time, 20 having been assembled, but the Haas team had lost its sponsor and its assets were sold. It had not been the proper team for Ford to entrust its new engine to.

Benetton then concluded a leasing deal for 1987 while Ford extended its Cosworth backing to underwrite development of a new 3.5-litre naturally aspirated F1 engine. Cosworth provided 22 TEC engines fitted with twin FISA 4-bar pop-off valves, one to each bank. This immediately handicapped the team in that they could not over-boost their engine with the same facility as their rivals who had just single valves to beat. Mobil replaced BP as fuel chemist, Ford Detroit provided an improved turbo package and a superbly successful Cosworth throttle response programme eventually rendered lag immeasurable on the ECU recording log. Despite being restricted to a genuine 4-bar boost in qualifying, the TEC V6 performed brightly in race tune but the cars were unreliable.

The TEC was touching on a genuine 1000 bhp in both qualifying and race tune by the end of that season but despite the rash FISA promises which had influenced Ford Detroit's programme authorization in the first place, turbocharged F1 was to be further restricted for what would be one final season in 1988, and Ford had no interest in further flogging their dead horse – just as it was promising to knock Honda off their pedestal . . .

Meanwhile, the naturally aspirated 3.5-litre Formula 1 parallel class introduced in 1987 had

been dominated by Tyrrell cars powered by another Cosworth-Ford engine – the DFZ V8.

This unit was offered purely for customer sale off the shelf, a makeweight grid filler capable of maintaining a foothold in Formula 1 for the teeny teams, safeguarding their sponsorship and prize fund incomes. In creating the DFZ, Chief Racing Engine Designer Goddard concentrated upon minimizing costs, using as much existing componentry as possible from the long line of DFV, Indy DFX, DFY and enlarged-capacity DFL V8 stock as possible.

The short-stroke 90 mm block was selected, with a new crankshaft featuring eight balance webs since the 'Cozzy' had always been regarded as 'a real old shaker' and the 3.3-litre DFL had been notoriously and destructively vibrant in operation. Standard DFV head castings were machined to accept enlarged ports and valves, and new 12.0:1 compression pistons were carried on H-section DFX stock con-rods. Cosworth added its own in-house management system originally intended purely for Formula 3000 DFV/DFY use. It combined Bosch solenoid injectors with Lucas capacitor discharge ignition and housed both the ECU and injector drives in one box. Cosworth provided its own maps for the unit and while simple it was also extremely practical and as customer-friendly as any management system could be, and easily programmable from a portable micro computer.

The DFZ peaked out at 565 bhp at 10,500 rpm with a safe rev limit of 11,000 and a broad, meaty torque curve ending in a virtual plateau from 10,250 to 10,750 rpm.

For that pilot season of 3.5-litre naturally aspirated F1 racing in 1987, Mader in Geneva undertook a hectic schedule of F1 DFZ servicing and preparation for the AGS, BMS-Dallara, Coloni, EuroBrun, Larrousse-Lola, Rial, Minardi and Tyrrell teams.

Tyrrell dominated the naturally aspirated Championship and for 1988 new Cosworth collaborator Brian Hart produced a new front cover and resited pump mountings for a specially lowered DFZ provided exclusively to the Tyrrell team. This unit was matched to the latest-type 5½ in. AP competition clutch which had recently become available to replace the traditional 7½ in. diameter type. The smaller clutch enabled the engine to be lowered 25 mm, using a base chamber casting performing a similar function on Cosworth's latest DFR V8 works engine, thus handily increasing casting quantities to achieve an economy of scale. This lowered bottom-end provided useful benefits in CoG height and aerodynamic packaging of the rear end of Tyrrell's 017.

In the DFR, Cosworth was developing its own next-generation naturally aspirated V8 for the Formula 1 customer market. The Benetton team had reached an agreement with Ford for exclusive use of this new-type V8 through 1988 to co-operate in an R&D programme which would build towards an all-new Ford engine for '89, when the DFR would be available for general sale to outside customers, leaving Benetton exclusive use of the new works engine.

The original DFR employed the 90 mm Cosworth block, like the original DFZs, but with the Tyrrell DFZ-type lowered sump and small clutch as standard. Yamaha-patent cylinder heads with five valves per cylinder were produced for the first five DFRs, but Cosworth's dyno testing showed no advantage for this 40-valve engine over the conventional 32-valve and the Yamaha heads were set aside before the float of 20 units provided for Benetton eventually raced.

The definitive 32-valve Cosworth DFR V8 finally emerged with the lowered DFZ bottom-end allied to better breathing heads, and for public consumption it was considered to produce 'around 600 bhp' at just under 11,000 rpm. The latest Ford engine management system derived from the very sophisticated outfit developed with the TEC Turbo V6 featured data logging and telemetry facilities plus a particularly well publicized continuous fuel consumption read-out.

Unfortunately Benetton's men found these first-series DFRs developed '30 horsepower less than expected' in addition to vibrating so badly 'it just began shaking many of the smaller parts to bits'. Benetton's computer predictions for their B188 car had been based upon a 680 bhp/540 kg power/weight ratio, which proved to be nearer 650 bhp/560 kg in practice once the chassis had been made man enough to absorb the DFR's vibration. Cosworth (ever conservative) would only talk pessimistically of '600-620 horsepower'.

For 1989 the Witney-based team's DFRs were replaced by the all-new 75-degree Ford HB V8 'by Cosworth'. Ford had given Cosworth complete design freedom to select what it might consider the optimum configuration to meet the needs of a race-winning F1 team. Keith Duckworth, Geoff Goddard, Martin Walters and Dick Scammell evaluated alternative engine forms at great length before dismissing possible V10 and V12 programmes in favour of another but this time more compact, narrower-vee V8. Folding up the previously traditional 90-degree V8 into the narrower 75-degree angle minimized some of the '90's classically severe horizontal vibration, transforming some of it into a vertical component. Chief designer Geoff Goddard: 'We explained this to Rory Byrne of Benetton by saying that where his drivers had previously come past the pits with their eyes wobbling side to side, they would now come by with them wobbling up and down, on an elliptical path!'

When Ford announced their new Cosworth-created 3.5-litre 'works' engine for the naturally aspirated Formula races of 1989, they were extremely sparing with hard factual information. The new 75-degree 'HB' V8 was tailor-made for the favoured Benetton team's B189 car. Cosworth packaging of course made the new unit extremely compact, approaching the high standards set by their 120-degree TEC Turbo V6, 595 mm long, 591 mm wide and just 521 mm tall. To achieve significant weight savings over the 140 kg of the 1988-spec DFR 90-degree V8, lightweight aluminium alloys were selected for the block, head

and sump castings, magnesium alloy for the non-structural cam-covers and carbon-composite for the induction intakes.

The new narrow-angle works V8 had a 12.0:1 compression ratio, four valves per cylinder operating by twin overhead camshafts per cylinder bank and would be burning Mobil fuel. The Ford EEC IV electronic engine management system had been adopted – according to Ford's publicity machine being 'capable of processing more than 1.0 million commands per second'.

The fuel system was also totally new while new oil and water pumps and additional auxiliary drives for an active suspension system hydraulic pump were also provided.

Ford Electronics had designed a new-generation EEC IV engine management system, while a new data logging system capable of recording information at the rate of 100 readings during each 0.001 second had been added.

At 595 mm the new HB would be slightly longer than the DFR to accommodate slightly larger-bore pistons, but it was also usefully narrower, and lower. Cosworth's initial target was said to have been a minimum of 600 bhp. It was nearer 650, but it was not enough.

The green light had been given for the project in April 1988, the prototype engine first ran on the dyno just before Christmas but Cosworth warned Benetton not to expect a useable engine before the end of March '89.

Remarkably few problems were encountered on the test bed, but once installed in the latest B189 car the new HB suffered a sequence of mysterious crankshaft failures, the first in a test at Pembrey, a second at the Imola test session where driver Nannini saved a third just as it was going.

Consequently the engine's race debut was delayed until the French GP, round 7 of that year's Championship. Cosworth concluded unpredictable secondary torsional vibrations were damaging the engines, and their crankshaft and its drive take-off gears were redesigned to rectify the problem.

Even so, by the end of that season the new Ford HB was able to establish itself as the best of the V8 runners – which unfortunately is virtually to damn it with faint praise, for all that counted were the V10s of Honda and Renault and Ferrari's V12.

Through 1990 Benetton continued to enjoy exclusive use of the Ford HB, starting the year with a third-generation version with redesigned exhaust system and new low-friction crankshaft bearings, developing – according to Cosworth's conservative claims – '625 bhp at 12,500 rpm'.

Benetton's new engineering director John Barnard became most unhappy with the slow pace of development, until a Series IV version was supplied in time for the British GP with power up to 650 bhp at 13,000 rpm. This new spec included modified pistons, con-rods, heads, valves and valvegear in addition to re-mapped programming for the Ford EEC IV electronic management and injection system. From that point the latest B190 Benetton cars became seriously competitive in race tune and succeeded in winning the last two races of the season in reasonably meritorious manner.

Meanwhile the DFZ and DFR had continued to support midfield and makeweight runners. In 1989 Cosworth would update the earlier DFZ stop-gap engine for about half the £48,000 asking price of a new DFR, and this route was taken by several teams as demand for the latest DFR outstripped Cosworth's ability to supply.

These 'conversion kits' included new cylinder heads, manifolds, injection trumpets and camshafts and servicing of customer DFRs and DFZs was carried out by Brian Hart for Onyx, Arrows and Tyrrell, and by Mader for Scuderia Italia, Minardi, AGS, Coloni, Osella and Rial with Tyrrell's engines being cared for by Langford & Peck.

According to Cosworth 'a really good DFR would produce a little under 600 bhp, depending on dyno variations' and despite a handful of unexpected failures afflicting the second main cap bearings

these engines could usually be depended upon for up to 500 miles' reliable running between services. They were also durable. Brian Hart observed, 'Everybody over-revs them, and as a rule they survive. Missed shifts take them through their electronic limiter; we generally only take them out of the car if they have exceeded 12,300 rpm . . .'

The 1989 Cosworth DFR had bore and stroke dimensions of 90 mm x 68.65 mm, a displacement of 3494 cc, and ran a nominal compression ratio of 12.5:1. It weighed 315 lb (142.8 kg), which looked very good compared to the 75-degree Yamaha OX88 V8's 319.6 lb (145 kg), but against the 90-degree Judd CV V8's 284.4 lb (129 kg) and the 76-degree Judd EV V8's 275.5 lb (125 kg) that particular statistic lost its lustre . . .

For 1990, the Hart-prepared DFRs used by Tyrrell's latest raised-nose configuration Type 019 cars were said to offer over 625 bhp at 11,500 rpm and driven by Alesi they several times shone at a level really way above their proper station.

Hart-prepared and serviced DFRs also powered the Arrows A11B while Langford & Peck DFRs powered Ligier, Mader DFRs Minardi and Scuderia Italia and Osella switched its units from Mader to Tickford during the season. By this time 450 miles was considered a prudent interval between rebuilds, and Hart was looking towards 12,000 rpm for 1991, and an evergreen DFR output approaching 640 bhp.

Only the fingertip teeny teams of Formula 1 remained as DFR users into 1991, and all struggled even to pre-qualify for most events. The ex-Osella Fondmetal team and Larrousse-Lola used Hart versions, AGS used Mader, while the hapless Coloni one-car team achieved a 100 per cent failure to pre-qualify record, first with Mader engines, then Hart around mid-season, and finally Langford & Peck – changes reflecting financial trauma rather than specific preference on the ailing little team's behalf.

Meanwhile the Ford HB used by Benetton became the only engine other than McLaren's Honda V12 and Williams's Renault V10 to win a 1991 Grand Prix. Specifically to fit the latest Barnard-designed Benetton B191 the Series V HB featured matching tailor-made cam-covers with leading-edge lugs which, combined with corresponding lugs on the leading edge of the engine base, mated with the forward monocoque. The latest-version HB also incorporated an ancillary balance shaft built in to damp out vibration which it was anticipated would affect electrics associated with the car's electro-hydraulic and projected active suspension systems.

The engine was used in both the B190B and B191 cars but units were also supplied for the first time to a client team, this being the new Jordan équipe for use in their 191 cars as second-string. For the HB and for Benetton it was a hard year. Cosworth pursued a continuous development programme but it certainly was neither rapid nor energetic enough for Barnard's liking – before his mid-season split with Benetton – and the programme demonstrably lagged behind Ford's main rivals – Honda and Renault. The greatest strides were made with Mobil's fuel chemists, high-energy fuel brews being the name of the game in modern Formula 1.

The Series V used for most of the year revved to 13,000 rpm, while with the introduction of pneumatic valve-closure systems similar to Renault Sport's in the Series VI for the last two GPs, drivers Piquet and Schumacher could deploy a crescendo of 13,500 rpm at last – a truly amazing speed for a 3.5-litre short-stroke V8. Just imagine the reversal loads on such large pistons . . .

Performance modifications were made to Benetton's engines 4-6 months ahead of going onto Jordan's – while reliability mods went onto both team's engines simultaneously. By the end of that season, some 70 Cosworth-Ford HB V8 engines were in existence.

Later in the year the further-modified Series VI unit emerged, with its pneumatic valve closure extending this remarkable V8's rev range beyond 14,000 rpm to close our period.

Gurney-Weslake

Engineer Aubrey Woods had vast BRM experience when he was seconded to the BRM 'think-tank' development group based at Weslake Research in Rye, Sussex. In effect this had been a BRM political device to shuffle their former Chief Engineer, Peter Berthon, sideways away from their Bourne factory, but the Weslake proposal for a 3-litre 48-valve V12 was considered most seriously for 1966 before being rejected in favour of the H16.

This rejected proposal then formed the basis of the Weslake Type 58 V12 engine which appeared in Gurney's Eagle at Monza in 1966. Successful gas-flow specialist Harry Weslake aimed to maintain good power and torque over a very wide speed range by use of a compact combustion chamber mated to carefully chosen port sizes. These had to be large enough to maintain good flow but sufficiently tight for high gas velocities to be maintained, contributing an internal ram effect.

Such theories had worked well on the 2-litre BRM V8 engine with which Woods was familiar, with internal dimensions of 73.3 mm x 59.2 mm; the new Type 58's measurements were 72.8 mm x 60 mm.

The new V12 was very reminiscent of BRM V8 practice, with similar ribbed crankcase castings, seven main bearings instead of the V8's five, the crankcase sides extending below the crankshaft centreline to support two-bolt bearing caps. As in the BRM V8s only the rear main cap was cross-bolted.

Cylinder design was standard BRM, with thin-wall cast-iron wet liners secured by a top flange nipped between cylinder head and the closed block top face. Con-rods were identical in length and design to BRM's and piston mechanical design below the crown was the same, with narrow slipper skirts and only two rings.

Valvegear was pure BRM, incorporating twin coil-springs, cup-type tappets above, bolted-in ferrous carriers for each tappet and camshafts rotating in crowded roller bearings, though Woods made both head castings identical to ease manufacture and servicing.

A very narrow included valve angle was adopted, enabling one-piece twin-cam-covers to be provided, minimizing weight and width and pre-dating the Cosworth DFV heads to come.

Valve sizes were 1.2 in. and 0.985 in. for inlets and exhausts respectively, valve lifts being 0.375 in. and 0.312 in. Short stub manifolds within the vee connected the inlet ports to a single throat fed with fuel from a Lucas injector nozzle. Camshaft drive was from a train of gears carried in a separate split magnesium casing at the front of the engine. Block and heads were cast in aluminium alloy, and all-up weight was only 390 lb.

The water pump and pressure and scavenge oil pumps were gear-driven from the crankshaft nose, and other accessories were driven from the timing gears; the alternator and twin Lucas distributors. Woods had to move some ancillaries back on the V12 to allow it to fit the space dictated in the Eagle tub by the alternative Indy Ford V8. The left-side exhaust camshaft tail drove the mechanical fuel pump, the right exhaust camshaft tail operated the Lucas ignition trigger and the fuel injection metering unit was driven by a cogged belt from the right-side inlet camshaft.

The V12s were built for Anglo-American Racers Inc. by a Weslake crew under Michael Daniel's direction. Prototype assembly in August 1966 occupied 1200 man hours and on 18 August it ran for the first time. Within a week it was claimed to produce 364 bhp at 9500 rpm but, as described in the Eagle section of the Team Directory, it suffered numerous problems of overheating, quality control and rebuilding, and ultimately the project collapsed in recrimination – fortunately not before Gurney had won a minor Formula 1 race and the classic Belgian GP with it in 1967.

The basic design was subsequently revived in 1970 when Harry Weslake discussed a potential long-distance sports car and Formula 1 engine

The Gurney-Weslake V12 of 1966-68 (above) was the most glamorous Formula 1 power unit of its time, all trumpets, tailpipes and oil filters.

with Stuart Turner and Len Bailey of the Ford Motor Company. The new engine was much modified and revised but in 1972 proved a dreadful flop, despite Weslake and an independent dynotester – yes, they had to prove it – recording 464 bhp at 10,750 rpm. One engine was installed in a BRM P160 (it fitted rather nicely!) and run at Ricard without impressing while Brabham built a special car for it which was not considered worthy to be raced and the project petered out.

This was a pity because, apart from anything else, it was a superb-looking power unit.

Hart

Brian Hart, former racing driver turned engine manufacturer, established his fine engineering reputation with a long and successful series of Ford-based engines, most significantly for Formula 2. He followed on from this by manufacturing his own unit from the ground up and aspiring to Formula 1 with a 1500 cc turbocharged 'Hart 415T' version of this unit in conjunction with the Toleman team in 1981. Toleman had used Hart engines to win the previous season's European Formula 2 Championship and it was a bold move for both to plunge into Formula 1.

The alloy-block four-cylinder in-line Hart turbocharged engine had bore and stroke dimensions of 89.2 mm x 60 mm, displacing 1499 cc. Compression ratio was 6.7:1 and with a single KKK turbocharger the unit delivered a claimed 557 bhp at 9500 rpm, compared to the Cosworth DFV V8's contemporary *circa* 500 bhp, the Renault V6's 540, Ferrari's 560, BMW's 557 and Matra's 510 bhp.

But the 415T and its Garrett turbocharger proved fragile as the team pursued a painful and frustrating development programme. The in-line four-cylinder, as BMW proved, had some advantages in fewer bearings and piston rings, and smaller friction area hence lower friction losses which in turn meant less thirst for fuel.

In 1984 form, Hart claimed 600 bhp at 10,750 rpm at 2.1-bar boost in race tune and the engine was mechanically very reliable if still a little outclassed by its multi-million budget opposition. It came very close to winning that year's Monaco GP in Senna's Toleman in pouring rain and other good Toleman performances in better conditions proved the Hart 415T a potential points-scorer if

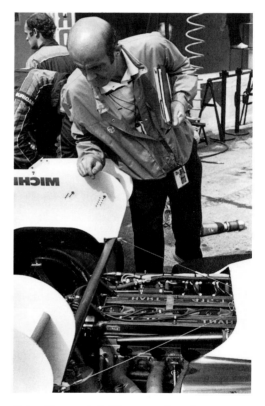

Brian Hart made brilliant use of a tight budget by enabling several smaller teams to compete in turbocharged Formula 1 from 1981 to 1985.

not a natural front-runner.

Development had included introduction of what Hart calls a 'monobloc' engine configuration, although more properly this is a *testa fissa* (fixed head) design in which there is no separate head joint to be sealed against coolant, boost-pressure and combustion leaks, the head and block being cast in one integral unit. Hart also adopted British Holset turbocharging to benefit from that small and enthusiastic company's flexibility and willingness to pursue special development on his behalf.

There have been any number of small enthusiast chassis builders involved in Formula 1 since 1966 but none can compare with the ability and application necessary to manufacture and develop successfully specialist Formula 1 engines. In this respect the popular Brian Hart was unique and very welcome.

The ultimately integral-headed Hart 415T engines sadly ran out of reliability as numbers in use and competitive pressure grew.

Throughout 1984-85, considerable advances in Formula 1 power output were made possible by improvements in engine management systems, cylinder filling and combustion, enabling the restricted amount of fuel then allowed to be burned with increasing efficiency. However, these strides were led by the major manufacturers and the tiny Hart concern was unable to keep pace. When their development partner, Toleman, was unable to run early in 1985, Hart's progress was hampered. Hart engines were also being used by RAM, Spirit and the new Beatrice team. Hamstrung development combined with tight-stretched rebuild capacity, and the need to run ever-higher boost to keep in touch, created very poor reliability. Hart-engined cars were placed healthily only four times from 33 starts in '85: eighth, 12th (twice) and 14th.

Development had picked up rapidly once Toleman's tyre-supply problems had been overcome by buying Spirit's contract as the smaller team bowed out of Formula 1. British Holset turbocharging and Hart/ERA digital management was used, with Marelli CD injection. At 2.5 ata boost Hart quoted 740 bhp at 10,500 rpm which even in Toleman's good TG185 chassis was inadequate until the German GP where the car qualified on pole after second-session times were hampered by rain. There the Hart seemed to be delivering some 822 bhp in qualifying tune, falling to 728 for the race. This was the lowest in Formula 1, but even so reliability had been lost and as Toleman adopted BMW engines for 1986 the respected Brian Hart's brave foray into Formula 1 seemed to be ending.

The Carl Haas Beatrice-sponsored FORCE team kept the British four-cylinder turbo engine in competition into 1986, pending delivery of the new Ford TEC V6 with which they had been entrusted. As the Cosworth-engineered six-cylinder engine was slow appearing, Hart modified the 415T for the start of the 1986 season with improved cooling, a new water pump, improved electronics and single-box Zytek (formerly 'ERA') management system. The block was shortened by 12 mm demanding revised chassis mounts. The small-bore 86 mm engine was chosen with simple single-plug head, 34-degree included valve angle (16-18), a new crank, new rods and pistons and with split exhaust tracts designed for twin turbocharger induction. With an 8.0:1 compression ratio and burning toluene fuel the 86 mm engine could complete a 195-litre fuel limit race on 3.7-bar boost, generating over 800 bhp.

FORCE leased 88 mm Hart engines to fill the gap before the Cosworth TEC V6 should become available, with '86 mods, revised cooling system but smaller '84 standard turbo slightly modified. Once the V6 engine became available to FORCE, with the RAM team dead and no takers for the 86 mm engine, which looked a good 4-bar unit, Hart was left with no customers, the cost of turbo technology having put his 415T beyond the means of those who might have been interested. Brian Hart Ltd was subsequently absorbed by Cosworth Engineering, developing and servicing their naturally aspirated 3.5-litre V8s . . .

Honda

The Japanese motor cycle colossus had entered production of cars and light vans in 1962, and within two years began promoting its new models by building an ambitious transverse V12-engined 1500 cc Formula 1 car.

It was a motor cycle-type engine in its extensive use of roller bearings and Honda used similar technology in a crushingly successful four-valve-per-cylinder 1-litre four-cylinder Formula 2 engine for 1966, used by Brabham.

That September their monster new Formula 1 four-valve-per-cylinder roller-bearing RA273 V12 appeared in the Italian GP at Monza, as described in the Team Directory. This mighty engine with drive taken from the centre of its crankshaft had dimensions of 78.0 mm x 52.2 mm, displacing

2992 cc. Its published specification included 1.16 in. diameter inlet valves, and 1.02 in. exhausts disposed at an included angle of 75 degrees, 35 degree inlet and 40 degree exhaust. Valve lift was 0.325 in. With Honda timed fuel injection and transistorized electronic ignition this incredibly raucous unit delivered '400-plus' bhp at 10,000 rpm.

As described, development went at best sideways and sometimes backwards in the two seasons' racing which followed. By 1968 Honda were claiming 430 bhp from their RA301 V12 with the narrower included valve angle of 65 degrees, still the most powerful engine in Formula 1.

The ill-fated air-cooled RA302 used a 120-degree V8 with dimensions of 88.00 mm x 61.40 mm, displacing 2987 cc and producing an estimated 380 bhp at 10,500 rpm.

Honda withdrew from Formula 1 at the end of that 1968 season and would not return to four-wheeled single-seater competition until 1980 when they produced their new 80-degree V6 iron-block 2-litre four-cam racing engines intended for contemporary Formula 2.

They were successful in Ron Tauranac's Ralt cars and in 1981 Honda supplied Ralt's works F2 team with 20 updated V6 engines claiming 10 per cent more power than the rival 315 bhp best BMW and Hart units. Team and drivers had their problems but Lees won three races and took the European Championship title for the Honda engine.

The new Spirit team joined Ralt in the Honda camp for 1982 Formula 2 but the anticipated Honda domination failed to materialize, picking up only three race wins. Johansson's Spirit-Honda was on pole for five of the first eight races and there was at least one Spirit on the front row in each of the first nine events. Ralt-Honda suffered development problems on their cars, yet in 1983 they steam-rollered the Formula 2 Championship, with drivers Thackwell and Palmer utterly dominant, the latter winning the last five Championship rounds successively to clinch the title.

Part of the thinking behind the V6 F2 engine concept was to employ the same cylinder bore as the then dominant 2-litre four-cylinder BMW engine, but combined with a shortened stroke to permit Honda two more cylinders within the capacity limit. This was, as technical director Nobuhiko Kawamoto explained, 'so theoretically we could get one and a half times the power'.

The six-cylinder engine was arranged in an 80-degree vee – unusual at that time – inherited from the company's CX500 motor cycle engine. Since they were creating a pure-bred racing unit without a road-going application, smooth-running considerations were subordinated to sheer power.

Honda's 1967 centre-exhaust V12 as raced by John Surtees.

Top: *The unfortunate air-cooled Honda V8 slung beneath the RA302's rear boom at Monza, 1968; and* (above) *the 80-degree F2-based turbocharged unit in the Spirit, 1983.*

This enabled adoption of a crankshaft configuration which ran the engine as two three-cylinder units with opposing cylinders sharing common con-rod journals, and exhaust interference tuning possible. Firing was simultaneous between the cylinders forming each pair of 'vee-twins', the 80-degree vee angle between the cylinder banks meaning in effect that the right-hand bank cylinder was phased to fire 80 degrees of crankshaft revolution before the left-hand. There would then be a further 240 degrees crankshaft rotation before the next firing cycle.

This produced an uneven firing sequence and an engine which was powerful, but which never ceased to amaze first-time drivers with its harsh vibration.

Engineer Nobuhiko Kawamoto's design team, with Nakamura consulting, also favoured finger cam-followers rather than the widely conventional inverted bucket type. While most engine designers considered that the compact bucket cam-follower system provided the most direct, and hence most precisely controlled, valve-actuating method, Honda's experience in high-rpm engines persuaded them that valvegear weight and oil drag could both be minimized, and much greater freedom given for alternative valve-closure coil-spring developments, by using separate finger followers.

In this system each valve was accompanied by a corresponding remote-pivoted finger, the end 'knuckle' of which was shaped as a profiled follower, lying beneath the conventional camshaft lobe, close above the head of the corresponding valve-stem. The lobe above could force the finger down by bearing on top of the knuckle, the finger tip then opening the valve beneath it. As the camshaft continued to rotate, on the closure slope of the lobe, the valve was returned to its seat by the rebound of conventional co-axial coil-springs.

As developed by Honda this system permitted higher sustained rpm. Its disadvantages involved extra space demands high in the head, evidenced by the new unit's tall and voluminous cam-boxes.

Other than its finger-type cam-followers, and unusual vee angle, this F2 engine seems to have been broadly conventional, right down to its plain bearing bottom-end as Honda had now dropped the heavy and space-demanding roller bearings of their old 1966-68 racing designs.

Honda confirm no dimensions, but bore and stroke were reported as being 90 mm x 52.3 mm, giving a stroke:bore ratio of 0.58:1. Early F2 engines ran to 10,500 rpm, later development yielding 11,500.

Meanwhile, Honda had announced a renewed interest in Formula 1, and modified the basic and rather untidy 80-degree four-cam V6 F2 engine to 1500 cc turbocharged F1 form for Spirit to test as described.

The Honda RA163-E F1 V6 was shrouded in secrecy, no details of internal dimensions being published, merely claiming 600 bhp with twin KKK turbocharging, though Japanese IHI units soon replaced the German turbochargers. Honda all-electronic engine management was adopted, and at the end of the season the units were used by new purpose-built Williams FW09 cars in the final race at Kyalami. In 1984, the IHI turbocharged RA163-Es proved wickedly powerful but with abrupt power curves which made them very hard to control and were demanding on chassis performance.

The crankcase and block did not seem adequately stressed for use as an integral chassis component while local cooling hot-spots were blamed for a crippling series of piston collapses.

The bore and stroke of the 1984 D-engines appeared to be massively over-square, at 90 mm x 39.2 mm according to one unconfirmed source, giving a displacement of 1495.5 cc accompanied by the huge piston area of 381.7 cm^2, compared to the Renault EF4B's 348.5, Alfa's 344.1, Porsche's 316.9, Ferrari's 309.2, the Renault EF15's 302.3, BMW's 250.0 and Hart's 243.3 cm^2. These large-area piston crowns were fragile under turbo stress and often failed, while the stroke/bore ratio of 0.44 promoted the very narrow useable rev band of which Williams's drivers complained so much. The new E-engine introduced in June 1985 seemed less over-square, 82 mm x 47.2 mm, giving 1494.8 cc and a piston area of 316 cm^2. At Silverstone it was independently calculated that Rosberg had at least 1077 bhp during qualifying and 815 bhp in race tune, not as much as the rival BMW 'fours' but useable over a wider rev band, and the team admitted those figures were 'about right'. In fact the engines peaked at Ricard, and when bearing problems intruded boost was wound back. Race power was some 850 bhp, however, by late-season.

Some observers believed ceramics were being used by Japan's 'Yellow Peril', but team members hotly denied this, pointing out that the poor conductive qualities of ceramics meant unacceptable combustion chamber heat build-up, which would aggravate pre-ignition to destroy pistons even more rapidly . . . perhaps significantly, as had been seen in the old D-engines.

Honda's power advance, first with the D-engine through the winter of 1984/85, then with the replacement E-engine in mid-1985, was attributed more to improved filling and burning thanks to combustion chamber design and injection system development. This promoted more complete burning of the fuel/air charge, simultaneously improving both fuel consumption and power output, while Honda's close co-operation with IHI had improved turbocharging efficiency.

Like other teams, William-Honda used dense high-aromatic fuel (in their case produced for them by Mobil), aromatic being heavy hydro-carbon like toluene to optimize performance, and they ended 1985 by comfortably winning the last three races in succession.

Honda required a more useable power curve, improved mechanical reliability and better structural rigidity within their basic iron block. It is possible – although precise details of recent Honda racing technology have always been notoriously difficult to confirm – that a less radical stroke:bore ratio was adopted, nearer TAG Turbo's alleged 82 mm x 47.2 mm, a ratio of 0.57:1.

In this form Honda had unlocked great power, around 810 bhp in the British GP race at Silverstone and over 1070 bhp for qualifying there, figures also confirmed (from the information supplied to Williams engineers).

Williams had been nagging at Honda to reduce the powerful but still untidy V6 engine's overall height, and lower inlet manifolding finally appeared in time for the Brands Hatch race. The engines had also fallen foul of a run of bottom-end bearing failures, but the revised top-end E-spec units delivered to Brands Hatch also had improved bearing arrangements.

Honda Kikaki – the Japanese company's carburetion section – had freed more power through painstaking development of their all-electronic management system to improve distribution, atomization and combustion. The key to fuel-efficient power production was to persuade the variable-orifice injector nozzles to atomize the fuel more thoroughly, ensuring rapid evaporation as it picked up heat upon entry to the combustion chamber, dispersing into the oxygen available there to burn completely with minimum waste.

In June 1985 a lavishly equipped engine service and rebuild 'shop had been opened adjoining the Williams factory at Didcot. All race engines up to the 1986 Brazilian GP were Japanese-built, subsequent units up to the end of that year being rebuilt and serviced at Didcot.

For the 195-litre fuel restriction of 1986 Formula 1, Ichida's engine group introduced the further-developed RA-166E 'F-spec' V6 series – 'F' for 'Frugal'. An 82 mm Honda bore has been quoted for 1985, the '86 units reputedly shrinking the bore still further to just 79.0 mm with a stroke of 50.84 mm.

In conditions of ever-increasing boost, large-area piston crowns were bad news. At high rpm and high boost rapid and efficient combustion was vital, as was speedy heat rejection from the vulnerable piston-crown centre via the rings and cylinder wall to the coolant.

Williams's sponsoring fuel company, Mobil, compensated for energy lost through FISA's fuel quantity restriction by following the BMW-Winterschall and Elf route into toluene-bearing higher-energy heavy fuels. These brews demanded great encouragement to ignite at all, prompting development of high-pressure injection systems for thorough atomization and high-squish piston-crown and combustion chamber shaping to encourage efficient combustion once the incoming charge had been sparked off. Compression ratio was apparently up to 7.4:1.

Honda's electronics included a new and enlarged ECU central programming unit, while car-to-pit telemetry was developed to give the pit-based engineers a continuous up-date on the health of their charges out on circuit. These F-spec engines carried new lowered plenum chambers at the front of the unit, with double inlets, the turbocharger air inlets themselves were lowered and the injectors relocated.

An intercooler by-pass sent charge air direct to the plenum to improve throttle response. Honda's turbo development was of course continuous, including variable-geometry turbine scrolls to vary the engine's torque characteristics. They toyed with turbocharger water cooling, while a more successful development provided the driver with an engine boost control which selected completely new engine management software maps for each required characteristic. The four selectable positions were summarized as follows: *1* - fuel saver; *2* – low race boost; *3* – high race boost; and *4* – overtaking superboost (triggering an extra 100 bhp . . .). Over 5-bar boost could be harnessed in qualifying tune and no rival could match Honda's race power.

For 1987, Honda discovered the services of Ayrton Senna and signed to supply Team Lotus for him in addition to Williams, subsequently breaking their contract with the Didcot team at the end of 1987 to take on McLaren in their place, for whom Senna had just signed. Consequently, Honda had moved into a new engine preparation base at Langley, near Slough, at the start of the '87 season. Honda's F1 engine team had been supervised in the field by engineer Sakurai while project design leader Ichida ran affairs at Honda

R&D's new Tochigi complex some 60 miles north of the Tokyo waterfront. Engineer Osamu Goto had been running the UK engine shop, and he was appointed as 1987 F1 Project Leader, replacing Yoshitoshi Sakurai. At Langley his team now prepared some 60 4-bar-restriction pop-off valve engines for Williams and Lotus, each carrying a single pop-off valve in a venturi throat mounting.

These 1987 G-spec units with a revised 'charger installation revved to 13,000 rpm. Both Williams and Lotus received 'G-spec' engines although the Didcot team's turbochargers were initially angled further outwards than were Lotus's, the Ketteringham team later matching Williams practice.

As the 1987 195-litre fuel restriction season progressed an improved 'GE'-spec engine emerged – 'E' for fuel 'Efficient' – which reverted to the 1986 rev limit of 12,000 rpm. With flat-top pistons, four-valve per cylinder pent roof heads with twin ohc and finger-type cam-followers, single-plug ignition, and a four-main-bearing three-pin crankshaft, these latest variants of the all-conquering Honda V6 also carried IHI turbochargers with a lightweight aluminium compressor wheel and a turbine impeller in Inconel – an ultra-high-temperature-resistant alloy which was difficult to work but excellent in such an application.

Individual ignition coils were incorporated into each spark plug mounting in a distributorless or 'static' system new for '87 , Honda like Ferrari following Renault Sport's lead. This system offered closer ignition control, enabling the engine to run closer to its detonation threshold.

While the basic 'G-spec' proved more refined, powerful and reliable than its predecessors, from it Honda rapidly developed the GE2 ('GE Phase 2') then a bewildering series of type-serials like GE2-1 or GE2-4. Overall that year, the 'GE2' engine spec seemed most effective and became standardized later in the season. Each spec offered alternative tune and tailoring to optimize the engine to differing circuits. Compression ratio was increased progressively to reach 8.2:1 by the summer of '87, by which time Honda were burning an 84 per cent toluene fuel.

Atomization had become really problematic at that level, and to improve the situation an engine management system-controlled intercooler bypass was introduced so that under suitable conditions uncooled pressure air could be directed straight from the turbocharger's compressor section to the induction plenum, where its higher temperature promoted better atomization of the

incoming charge. As a by-product it also improved throttle response so at a stroke driveability and fuel efficiency were both improved. There had to be a downside, and there was – outright power decreasing and internal heat-stress rising; but as long as the engines would hold together mechanically, the mid-range performance bonuses outweighed the peak power deficit. Lap times kept coming down . . .

Also in that season of '87, Honda's management system made use of a Bosch-developed exhaust gas analysis probe. By sensing excess oxygen within the exhaust tract this 'Lambda probe' could signal incomplete combustion, the management system software then ordering corrective action from the injection system to supply the optimum fuel:air ratio under given conditions.

In German engineering practice the Greek letter *Lambda* symbolises the ratio of the quantity of air supplied to that actually required for complete combustion of any fuel, hence Bosch's 'Lambda probe'. Every fuel mix requires a given mixture ratio of air for complete combustion. This 'stoichiometric ratio' is expressed as a Lambda of 1.0. In comparison to normal pump petrol's stoichiometric ratio of around 14:1 (that being equivalent, therefore, to the Lambda of normal pump petrol), Honda's *c.* 84 per cent toluene fuel for '87 had a ratio of around 13.7:1 and the latest RA167E engines developed peak power from it by running some 23 per cent rich – i.e. the required Lambda being 1.23:1, which was what the probe's signals would constantly be directing the Honda management system to achieve.

For 2.5-bar boost/150-litre fuel allowance racing in 1988, Honda abruptly dropped Williams despite their contract having another year to run, and the Japanese adopted McLaren and the services of Ayrton Senna alongside Team Lotus in WGPE's place.

Still the public achievement of engineering excellence remained the aim. As ever the philosophy amounted to winning at any price. Consequently Honda developed a new engine version and McLaren a brand new tailored chassis for this one solitary season's racing – and they

Honda's turbocharged V6 Formula 1 engines developed from a cobbled-together variant of the basic 2-litre Formula 2 power unit of the early 1980s. They would never achieve good looks, but their performance rewrote the record books. This 2.5-bar boost RA168-E unit is installed in one of the near-unbeatable McLaren MP4/4s of 1988.

The 3.5-litre Honda V10 'atmo' engine of 1989-91 perpetuated the Japanese manufacturer's winning ways in McLaren chassis but could do little for Tyrrell in that last season of '91, prior to the Mugen re-badging for '92. Ten cylinders in a 72-degree vee were judged the best compromise between demands for mid-range torque and top-end peak power.

won every Championship round but one in what would have been a Formula 1 *tour de force* had there been any credible opposition – but there was not, even Ferrari using an old updated chassis and a relatively simply detuned engine . . .

Honda's 2.5-bar RA168E V6 for '88 used an iron block with wall thicknesses as narrow as 2.0-3.5 mm, Nikasil wet aluminium liners and flexible 'O'-ring sealing (allowing free expansion at the bottom of the liner to cater for the difference in expansion rates between their aluminium and the ductile cast-iron block). McLaren specified the latest small-diameter clutches, prompting Honda to lower crankshaft centreline height fully 28 mm from 1987 spec. This permitted smaller and lighter block and sump castings but this would have left the old-style pumps projecting underneath so they were redesigned and resited (wider) too.

The A1-Si6Cu4 aluminium-alloy heads featured pent-roof combustion chambers, forged aluminium-alloy three-ring pistons were oil-spray cooled, con-rods were I-section in forged titanium alloy and the exquisite steel three-pin nitrided crankshaft rotated in four Vandervell plain bearings. Honda numbered the cylinders front to rear, right bank before left and firing order was sequential along the engine, 1-4-2-5-3-6.

Up in its alloy heads, the four steel camshafts ran in four plain bearings carried in a detachable cam-carrier/tappet block. Finger-type cam-followers were retained, and this season would prove

their value as the Honda units were allowed to scream to 14,000 rpm before their pre-set rev-limiters cut in. Camshaft drive was by spur gears from the crankshaft nose, where take-offs also powered the resited twin water pumps and a six-section (two pressure, four scavenge) oil pump.

Honda PGM F1 fully electronic injection and CDI ignition obviated the need for both a metering unit and distributor. There were two solenoid-adjustable injectors and a single NGK M10 spark plug (fired by its own associated coil) per cylinder.

The twin IHI RX6D turbos now used ceramic rotors on a ball bearing-supported shaft. Interestingly Honda disclaimed any suggestion they had pursued serious development of either two-stage turbocharging or compound turbo/supercharging.

This RA168E engine measured 517 mm in length, 672 mm tall and 626 mm wide, while Honda – ever coy – admitted only to 'over 600 bhp at 12,500 rpm'.

The inevitable loss of power under the new restrictions served to emphasize throttle lag inherent with the turbocharger in contrast to the instantaneous reponse of the better 'atmo' engines. Above all fuel-efficiency was vital, which meant a major hyke in compression ratio, from 8.2 to 9.4:1, and the reduction in available combustion chamber volume then dictated a further narrowing of the included angle between the overhead valves, from 39 degrees to 32.

Any increase in compression ratio runs the danger of overstepping the fine line between peak efficiency and destructive detonation. Honda tested 30, 60 and 84 per cent toluene fuel brews, cutting them with suitable proportions of normal iso-octane and heptane to arrive at the required 102 (RON) octane rating to satisfy the regulations. They published test-house results in which at 2.5 bar and 12,000 rpm the 84 per cent toluene mix permitted 10 degrees more ignition advance than the 30 per cent mix, purely thanks to

increased resistance to detonation. Such an ignition advance promoted better thermal efficiency – more power produced per unit of fuel burned.

Burning 84 per cent toluene fuel at a Lambda value of 1.15 – 15 per cent rich – the RA168E in 2.5-bar form developed a Honda-confirmed 685 bhp plus 43.2 kg/m torque. ECU logging had revealed that in race driving the throttle spent by far the majority of its time wide open, or entirely shut off. Honda therefore concentrated upon restricting fuel consumption at full throttle. In the course of this work they found that as boost rose from 2.2 to 2.5 bar not only power but also fuel consumption improved, thanks to better charging efficiency promoting better thermal efficiency.

While the qualifying-tune engine developed its 685 bhp on a charge air temperature cooled to 40°C, race tune 1988 demanded a 70°C charge temperature, a mixture set only 2 per cent rich and fuel temperature of 80°C. Peak power in this tune was no more than 620 bhp at 12,500 rpm, and specific fuel consumption was 200 gm per bhp per hr, matching Ferrari. Fuel consumption in this race tune was no less than 13 per cent better than in qualifying tune.

Between the qualifying and race engines there was little power-curve effect up to 8000 rpm but thereafter the race-tune unit's curve flattened markedly, power loss totalling 9.5 per cent.

In original form at Rio the throttle system used six individual butterflies down below the intake log, beyond the pop-off valve. On the over-run this allowed a pressure peak which popped the dump valve open, exhausting the pressure charge to atmosphere. When the driver floored the throttle pedal, there was nobody at home . . . The instant cure in Brazil was to run lower boost, but from Imola two single-throttle butterflies appeared upstream of the pop-off valve and the problem was cured.

Three broad specifications of engine were deployed for varying circuits, the 'XE2' and 'XE3' forms most used offering respectively better economy or better top-end power. For 'thirsty' or 'power' circuits the 'XE3' revved to 13,200 rpm. Generally, lower boost permitted quicker-responding turbos, and by adroit fuel chemistry and very high injection pressures Honda succeeded in properly atomizing the heavy toluene fuel despite the reduced induction manifold pressures.

And so at the peak of its development under turbocharged F1 regulations in their final form, Honda's dominant V6 engine could achieve 183 bhp per litre per bar boost.

Honda's approach was characterized by one of their engineers who returned to Japan from the UK operation, and wrote to the effect that he was missing his work in England 'as I am now working all day and far into every night trying to make current engine reliable'.

At that time they had won every race. Perfection, you see, was barely good enough . . .

Even while their RA168E 1.5-litre turbo engine was barking its way through that final victorious season, Honda was well advanced with development of the replacement 3.5-litre naturally aspirated V10 unit for 1989. This 72-degree vee configuration unit had first been unveiled at the 1987 Tokyo Motor Show when dyno testing registered little more than 500 bhp. By the late summer of 1988, V10s were on test in a McLaren MP4/4B test chassis and 600 bhp had already been exceeded.

Under Goto's F1 stewardship, Honda would provide a float of eight of these RA109E V10-cylinder engines to McLaren at each GP – two for each race car and the spare, plus two extra as emergency back-ups. Design of the MP4/5 chassis for this engine was well advanced when Honda raised the possibility of changing camshaft operation from belt to gear-drive. The Japanese engineers asked if McLaren could handle the associated weight penalty and installation problem, while emphasizing their feeling that valve timing accuracy would be better with a gear-drive rather than belts. McLaren agreed and the V10 raced in this form from the outset, though car development lost time which the team subsequently struggled to recoup.

An effectively 'spec 3' RA109E V10 offered more driver-friendly characteristics at Imola '89, and by the time of Monaco that year a valuable 3 kg had been pruned off its weight. In Mexico a disparity in fuel consumption between the Senna and Prost V10s fed the Frenchman's increasingly paranoid belief that Honda was favouring his team-mate. Honda and McLaren engineers jointly spent two days combing their race data during the run-up to the following weekend's Phoenix race and concluded that Senna used more fuel simply because he worked his engine harder.

The delicacy of control which had served Prost so well during the years of turbo fuel rationing was now being usurped by Senna simply running his V10 longer at peak rpm, using more fuel, developing more power for longer.

Prost then chose to alter his engine's characteristics after an early-season test at Jerez, seeking improved driveability. A tailored management chip was adopted, richening the mixture slightly, improving pick-up to complement his naturally smooth and progressive throttle-application technique. Senna's mid-corner throttle-blipping style required no such change.

Honda maintained publicly that the variation between accepted engine outputs was never greater than 5 bhp. An inexplicable misfire in Phoenix was finally attributed by guesswork to the pits-to-car radio signal somehow affecting the engine management sensors. The chassis aerial was relocated in consequence. In Canada an engine failure centred upon the oil ring package, highlighting a problem in the complex balance bteween low frictional losses and the need to retain pressure gases and oil on the power stroke. An oil condenser was added to the breathing system before the French GP to avoid a recurrence of this problem.

Before the Belgian GP two engines were tested, 'spec 4' with extra top-end power and 'spec 5' for

mid-range driveability. At Spa the drivers complained of very poor and abrupt throttle response from one while at Monza Senna had a catastrophic bearing failure with the other, due to oil loss. Still the Championship was totally McLaren-Honda's.

For their second-generation V10 engine, confusingly reverting to the RA100E classification, Honda R&D sought a 30 hp power improvement over the preceding RA109E, sufficient reliability to prevent engine-created race retirements, and to improve driveability 'through the achievement of more driver-friendly characteristics'.

The RA100E emerged for 1990 revving 800 rpm higher than the preceding RA109E and developing 40 more bhp – eventually averaging around 690 bhp in race set-up, while brief period over-rev and specially low-density fuel for qualifying could boost that peak to nearer 710 horsepower.

A new throttle system greatly enhanced combustion particularly during the part-open phase. After the bearing failures due to poor lubrication suffered in the 1989 Canadian and Italian GPs, a completely revised dry-sump system had been developed with more effective scavenging and pressure feed, which Honda claimed was fully capable of resisting lateral cornering loads of 4G and above, an acceleration force of above 1G and a deceleration force of up to 3G. Continuous testing would prevent a single engine-orientated retirement throughout the 1990 season.

They were not so successful where what were regarded as engine ancillaries were concerned. In the British GP Berger's McLaren retired after a throttle linkage pullrod had broken.

The initial RA100E 'version 1' unit made its debut at Phoenix, Honda rating its power output as little better than the RA109E's but both reliability and driveability being considerably improved.

From rounds 2 to 5 'version 2' engines were deployed with improved combustion unleashing an extra 10 bhp, the power curve now peaking 500 rpm higher than had the RA109E's. Meanwhile Shell was developing an unleaded F1 fuel for Honda which was used for the first time in the Brazilian GP. At Imola for round 3, an unexpected power loss was encountered and for Monaco the unleaded fuel was dropped in favour of a conventionally leaded mix. A joint Honda/Shell development programme pinpointed the problem, the

lead-free fuel apparently causing erosion of an ill-chosen valve-seat material, and the use of improved unleaded fuel resumed in Canada for round 5, the investigation having also yielded valuable improvement to the engine system itself. The engines ran unleaded for the remainder of the year.

Meanwhile 'version 3' spec was used in rounds 6-8 (Mexico to the British GP), a major effort to reduce internal friction by saving on bearing areas freeing another 8 bhp. This proved to be a usefully more responsive engine offering improved fuel economy but Honda complained of a chassis shortcoming in McLaren setting-up their cars to make the most of Goodyear's latest tyres compared not only to Ferrari but also to Leyton House . . . 'It wasn't possible to make good use of 100 per cent of the engine's capability . . .'

The Tochigi design team then introduced new valve return mechanism and lighter pistons for 'version 4', gaining another 300 rpm and an extra 7 bhp on average, thus 800 rpm and 25 bhp more than the previous year's RA109E. This spec made its bow in the German GP and was also used in round 10 (Hungarian), and rounds 13-14 (Portuguese and Spanish GPs).

From this work a further developed 'version 5' evolved aimed mainly at a further increase in outright horsepower. A Cray super-computer had been used to simulate broad band induction conditions, leading to a new induction system releasing a further 5 bhp – 30 more than the old '109E's best. 'Version 5' V10s were consequently used on the pure power circuits at Spa and Monza (rounds 11 and 12), winning both times.

A final 'version 5' RA100E V10 then emerged for round 15, the Japanese GP, and was used for the second and last time in round 16, at Adelaide, Australia. This version combined 'version 4's new induction system offering unmatched power at low and mid-range engine speeds, the new Shell fuel and reduced internal friction. Without any sacrifice in low-speed and mid-range torque, this version 5 offered a 40 bhp advantage over the

_____

Ending our period, McLaren relied upon Honda's latest V12 3.5-litre 'atmo' development, which unit proved to be not only a mixed blessing for the team but also Honda's Formula 1 swansong, leading to the manufacturer's withdrawal at the end of 1992.

1989 '109E unit.

For 1991, the new RA121E 60-degree V12 was introduced in search of greater potential power than the V10 could provide. Honda R&D had begun work on the V12 in the spring of 1989 and the prototype unit had commenced testing that October. After nine months' dyno-testing the first track tests had been run at Silverstone in June 1990.

Early on, the V12's power output exceeded that of the 'version 6' V10 and Honda claimed enhanced driveability too. The new engine was to equip McLaren for 1991 but the V10 programme was extended in parallel to provide Tyrrell with an uprated RA101E version for '91.

This unit was a direct development of the 1990 RA100E tuned to promote a wider useable power band as urged upon Honda by test and race driver Nakajima. Tyrrell's first technical contacts with Honda had been made as early as February 1990.

To deal with the V10 programme's 1991 season first, it initially shone brightly – the McLaren drivers looking wistfully at Tyrrell's engines during the early-season races until the initially less impressive V12 became adequately well developed. There was considerable early-season rivalry between the two groups of Honda service engineers, those running the V12s for McLaren and those handling the V10s for Tyrrell. The latter shone at Monaco until a catastrophic internal failure burst incandescent V10 internals clean through the Tyrrell's carbon-composite underfloor panel. But later in the year the Tyrrell-Honda combination faded fast – and eventually foundered, barely noticed.

The 60-degree V12s supplied to McLaren, meanwhile, offered greater piston area than the V10 and the potential for still higher crankshaft speeds. They topped 680 bhp to eclipse the V10s' best, but the drivers were profoundly disappointed after their first race experience of the engines – recalling the V10 as having been more torquey, more driveable, 'just quicker'. New Project Leader engineer Akimasa Yasuoka countered, 'We traditionally detune our engine for the first race of the season; we tend to go for reliability rather than power . . .'.

But the new RA121E was inherently heavier than its sister V10, more fuel-thirsty and beset by unexpectedly high internal frictional losses. The heat rejected to its oil was evidence of the latter shortcoming and a spate of main-bearing failures triggered an investigation which concluded uneven oil distribution was the cause.

Thanks to rival teams' unreliability, McLaren still won the first four GPs of the season, the 'spec 1' V12 being used at Phoenix, Interlagos and Monaco, the 'spec 2' – with revised induction offering better mid-range torque – at Imola. A shorter-stroke 'spec 3' engine was introduced at Silverstone seeking reduced internal friction, higher rpm and still higher power – aiming towards 710-720 bhp.

Senna ran out of fuel at Silverstone and Hockenheim, Shell's experimentation with fuel mixes of differing densities and viscosities making consumption prediction a tricky task. McLaren's associated company TAG Electronics helped recalibrate the management system software, installing the appropriate correction factors for differing fuel brews. Since the fuel mixes' enhanced vapourization was held responsible for some of the shortfall, thanks to evaporation out through the tank breathers, a closed circuit fuel system was adopted on the cars, sealed from outside atmosphere.

In mid-season, from the Mexican GP, the rival Renault V10 was demonstrably superior to the Honda V12, and an accelerated programme at Wako delivered an extensively modified 14,800 rpm V12 in time for the Hungarian GP. With actively controlled variable-length induction trumpets the early hole in the torque curve's mid-range had been adequately filled, and from Spa forward the RA121E in its latest form regained superiority over Williams's Renault engine – securing Honda's fifth successive share in the Formula 1 World Championship title.

Ilmor

Engineers Mario Ilien and Paul Morgan met when both were employed by Cosworth Engineering. Ilien, a Swiss, had created the ROC Chrysler Formula 2 engine in 1972 and later accumulated experience in designing a sidecar racing power unit and working on diesel engines before joining Cosworth on their Cosworth-Sierra and DFY engine projects. British production engineer Paul Morgan had meanwhile been intimately involved with the Indy racing DFX turbo engine, but he and Ilien joined forces in November 1983 to form their own independent company, Ilmor Engineering Ltd.

They were convinced that a business opportunity lay in producing a more modern Indycar engine of higher power potential than the ageing but hitherto utterly dominant DFX. To an extent, Cosworth paid the price of that virtual monopoly upon success and its own conservatism in losing these two engineers, who would now topple Cosworth pre-eminence in the American track-racing market.

They took their proposals to CART Indycar team patron Roger Penske in Philadelphia who agreed to under-write their original design and development of a truly up-to-date V8 which would out-perform the DFX. Penske then concluded a deal with General Motors, under which the new Ilmor engine would be promoted, marketed and labelled as the 'Chevrolet Indy V8'. Ilien began design work on 3 January 1984, the partnership built a well-equipped modern factory at Brixworth, Northamptonshire, and the prototype engine first fired on 16 May 1985 – having missed Penske's scheduled target date by just one day.

The unit found its feet in Indycar racing during 1986 and began beating the DFX-powered opposition in '87. By 1988 Chevrolet's name was winning the only race which really mattered – the Indianapolis '500' – and through the following three seasons the British-built engines became standard wear for any team wanting to compete seriously in Indycar racing, no fewer than 187 of the turbocharged V8s having been produced by the start of 1992 – output having averaged 36 a year.

However, Ilien and Morgan were very conscious during this period of having all their eggs invested in one potentially fragile basket. 'We wanted to diversify', Paul Morgan admitted, 'and since the new 3.5-litre naturally aspirated Formula 1 looked set fair and stable we decided to attempt a design to supply demand there . . .'. Penske had become a director of the company, and again he declared his willingness to under-write design and development, while Ilien created a suitable F1

unit, and Morgan looked for a potential client to race it.

Meanwhile, March had been back in Formula 1 competition from 1987, sponsored by Japanese entrepreneur Akira Akagi's Leyton House organization. Team manager was Ian Phillips, former Editor of *Autosport* magazine and a very shrewd and effective operator in the racing world. He had begun negotiations with Ilmor Engineering to secure a tailor-made new F1 engine for the team, but fell foul of company politics in mid-1990 and left the team together with chief engineer Adrian Newey – who would build his reputation with Williams-Renault for '91, while Ian joined the embryo Jordan team.

But Akagi agreed to purchase badging rights in return for development of the new Ilmor F1 engine project '2175A', which materialized as a Leyton House-dedicated unit known as the 'LH10' since it was a 72-degree V10-cylinder, to power the latest CG911 Leyton House car.

Unfortunately the revamped F1 team had bitten off more than it could chew, and its car development capability was overwhelmed for much of 1991 by the need to perfect not only a new chassis but also a new transmission and engine, all at once.

Gearbox manufacture problems bit deep into pre-season engine development track test time. Lubrication problems arose and had to be resolved, and it was not until mid-season that the chassis and transmission situation was sufficiently stable to allow practical engine development to proceed.

It's natural for engine manufacturers to demand ideal cooling and lubrication systems from car designers, who naturally want to optimize these systems within restraints of aerodynamic, structural and systems packaging. It's regrettably common, therefore, for an engine manufacturer's recommendations to fall upon deaf ears. Such differences are a standard fact of F1 life, and have been so for years. Ultimately it is the chassis designer's job to choose which compromises he makes, but often engines simply will not survive X cooling area or oil flow against Y demand – and it will always be the team which suffers, killing engines and losing race finishes.

This applied to the Leyton House-Ilmor season of '91, but the *coup de grace* was applied in September when Akagi was arrested in Japan for alleged financial malpractice, and his entire

The Ilmor 72-degree V10-cylinder engine produced initially for Akira Akagi's ill-fated 1991 Leyton House team was a neat and light yet quite sophisticated Formula 1 power unit from the British specialist company founded upon CART Indycar 'Chevrolet' V8 success.

Leyton House organization – including the Formula 1 team – was seriously compromised.

Ilmor consequently bought back the engine design and operating rights from Leyton House, and before the end of the season the 'LH10' was being known again by its original project number – the Type 2175A – and the 'Leyton House' lettering had been removed from its cam-covers . . .

The 40-valve short-stroke V10 had been completely overshadowed by Judd's rival – perhaps more humbly specified – V10, as used by the BMS-Dallara team. It was a completely new design, inheriting nothing save experience from the line of turbocharged Indycar V8s which preceded it. Main castings, block and head were all in aluminium alloy, it featured a structural sump (reminiscent of Cosworth practice) and its four overhead camshafts were gear-driven off the crankshaft nose. The crank itself ran in six main bearings and carried titanium con-rods and Ilmor's own in-house pistons. One oil pressure pump and five scavenges were mounted alongside the sump, driven by internal-toothed belt from the crankshaft nose, the water pump being tucked in similarly to the left side of the block. British-made Zytek engine management was adopted, a static distributorless system with coil-in-cap plugs, and Ilmor's own inlet tract etc. Predictably, bore and stroke dimensions remained classified, but the engine was 592.5 mm long and exceptionally light – scaling just 126 kg.

It had some way to go, but the development potential was there, and while the Chevrolet Indy engine had taken a while to find its feet, Ilmor were looking forward to a regular top-third-of-the-grid position in Formula 1 come 1992 . . .

As it was, the highlight for Ilmor of their V10's maiden season had been inheriting just one single, solitary, World Championship point in Hungary . . .

Judd

John Judd learned the ropes in racing engine development and manufacture with Coventry Climax, before working on the Australian Repco V8 project from 1966-68 on behalf of Jack Brabham. With Sir Jack's support he subsequently established his own Engine Developments Ltd company in Rugby and produced race-developed versions of proprietary power units for various production-based minor race Formulae. These customer racing engines included a very successful Formula Super Vee unit, followed by a water-cooled Volkswagen-derived Formula 3 unit. John's company also established a fine reputation as one of Cosworth's recognised list of DFV Formula 1 and DFX Indycar engine preparers/rebuilders.

Former Brabham designer Ron Tauranac's modern Ralt company then reintroduced Honda to European Formula 2 racing in 1980, using engineer Kawamoto's new V6s. Engine Developments was commissioned as a UK rebuild and preparation base for this programme, and from that association the company co-operated in production of an Indy V8 engine in the mid-1980s, the unit being largely designed at Rugby and its block cast in Japan.

This 90-degree 2.65-litre Type AV V8 engine was first raced in 1986, and a Type BV 3-litre F3000 naturally aspirated version was developed from it. The next logical step was then to enlarge this basic design still further to encompass new 3.5-litre naturally aspirated Formula 1. Honda remained interested in Engine Developments' programme and, partly in order to keep Formula 1 grids full for '88, the Japanese company supplied block casting patterns for AV, BV and the new Formula 1 Type CV engines all to be cast in the UK.

Where both the AV and BV engines had employed Honda-type finger-follower valve actuation, the 'Brabham-Honda'-lettered AV Indycar engine had introduced the Judd-inspired camshaft gear-drive at the rear of the engine, taking its drive from the tail of the flat-plane crankshaft where it was considered that the flat-plane

V8 shaft's inherent vibration was less severe than at the nose. All three of the 1988 all-British-made Engine Developments power units featured new cylinder heads carrying conventional valvegear, replacing the Honda-type finger-follower configuration.

In preparation for the 1988 Formula 1 season, Leyton House March and Ligier had both ordered the new 'Judd'-lettered Type CV V8, the intention being for March to operate as favoured-status development partner. But when Honda abruptly announced its decision to renege on the remainder of its Williams contract, dumping the Didcot team in favour of McLaren, Judd found himself supplying the Williams team as well.

Compared to the contemporary Cosworth DFZ, the new Judd V8 was claimed to be lighter, with usefully lighter reciprocating mass – in part thanks to a very short stroke – a lighter non-structural sump pan, its cam-drive gears at the less vibratory rear end of the unit instead of at the front à la Cosworth, and – thanks to its short-stroke/larger-bore architecture – particularly large valve area for better breathing.

The aluminium-alloy block extended below the crankshaft centreline, permitting a lightweight non-structural sump. The low crankshaft centreline, permitted by a 5½ in. clutch, allowed overall height to be minimized, and saved further casting weight. The sump pan was itself cast in magnesium as were the detachable tappet blocks and cam-covers, while the heads themselves were in aluminium.

While the cam-drive gears drove off the crankshaft tail, a pinion on its nose provided a power take-off to pumps each side of the block and to an intermediate shaft running back through the vee, belt-driving the distributor and alternator on a subsidiary shaft there.

Fully electronic fuel injection was adopted, the client teams applying their own pressure pumps. Zytek provided engine management. Dimensionally, the CV V8 was 590 mm long, 670 mm wide and 550 mm tall. The units weighed barely 127 kg (280 lb). Some 50 CVs were fielded during the 1988 season.

Seeking higher rpm, an apparently even shorter-stroke V8 was under development for 1989, and March chassis designer Adrian Newey suggested a new engine should also adopt a tighter vee angle which would offer aerodynamic benefits in installation. The result was the new narrow-angle 76-degree Judd EV V8 engine which was supplied exclusively to the Leyton House-backed March team for use in the latest CG891 cars. Although driver Capelli had finished second using Judd CV power in the late-season Portuguese GP the previous year, Judd carried over barely 5 per cent of the old CV internals into the new EV engine. The unusual included angle of 76 degrees

Workmanlike, affordable, ultra-light and quick enough to ensure survival for a number of teams up to and including the calibre of Williams 1988 – the Judd series of V8 engines provide a shining example of what can be done on modest budgets by the best of the specialists . . .

was chosen on pure practicality. An angle of 75 degrees would have been the norm, like the Cosworth-Ford HB – but at that stage Judd's blocks were being machined on an early CNC tool which was only adjustable one whole degree at a time, not a half-degree. Since a 75-degree vee demands machining at 37½ degrees from the vertical, and a 76-degree at 38 degrees, the latter vee angle was the one selected!

The tighter valley between the cylinder heads left no room for the distributor and alternator which had previously lived there, and this was one factor in the adoption of Marelli static ignition which dispensed with a distributor altogether, instead using eight coil-in-cap spark plug components.

John Judd explained: 'Although the length of the engine is largely dictated by the cylinder bore and spacing, we managed to achieve quite a considerable increase in bore diameter for an effective length increase of only 8 mm over the CV. The weight is also reduced by 4 kg, and maximum power is up by 15 bhp with a 500 rpm increase in maximum engine speed . . .'

For reasons largely unconnected with the new dedicated engine, the Leyton House March team's fortunes took a sharp down-turn that season, and as Adrian Newey pointed out at the time 'Most of the engine-related problems have been ancillary malfunctions. We've had a few piston and valvegear problems admittedly, but mainly electrical gremlins'.

The 90-degree CV engines had been modified for the new season, featuring new camshafts and an improved piston-ring combination to improve oil consumption which had proved problematic during the '88 season. Team Lotus adopted the CV unit for its latest Type 101 cars, as did the revived Brabham team for its new-beginning BT58s, and the struggling EuroBrun outfit.

In an attempt to find something extra from the engine Team Lotus commissioned the Tickford R&D subsidiary of Aston Martin to develop special five-valve-per-cylinder heads for the unit, but in a reflection of Cosworth's own experience with Yamaha 5vpc heads on the DFR V8 the 40-valve engines showed little obvious advantage over the standard 32-valve type. They were also more complex and involved to service and rebuild, and their valvegear complexity threatened reliability problems. In consequence the standard CV was generally preferred to the 40-valve Judd-Tickford hybrid. Neither Lotus nor Brabham were top teams any more, and the CV completed its second season in low-key manner.

For 1990 the narrow-angle EV V8 used by Leyton House was more reliable, but the season was hardly under way before the Japanese sponsor announced a long-term agreement with Ilmor Engineering for a new V10 in '91. Although Leyton House remained nominally the 'works' Judd team for 1990, narrow-angle EVs in their latest form were also sold to the Brabham team, while EuroBrun struggled on with old CVs. Following the failure of Franco Rocchi's ill-conceived W12 engine, the Italian Life team had one final twitch of life when patron Ernesto Vita swapped horses to the Judd CV but his Life car remained unable to pre-qualify.

Only two teams ran Judd engines in 1991, Dallara and Lotus. Beppe Lucchini's BMS-Dallara team had taken up the new Type GV 72-degree V10-cylinder customer engine developed by Judd 'as a flyer' for the new year. It was a unit designed to a price, without any pre-agreed sponsorship or client, simply building sensibly upon all the experience hard earned through the V8 period. It was a sensible unit, compact and no-nonsense, aimed at keeping a foothold in Formula 1. Initially run with a Zytek management system, when BMS-Dallara took it up their system was replaced by Magneti Marelli.

Judd initially claimed a power output of 660 bhp at 13,500 rpm, the unit offered a wide power band and was hailed by Dallara's drivers for its driveability. Looking back on the season Judd would observe he was 'On the whole quite pleased . . .'. In its maiden season the new engine had gone quite well in the Dallara cars. It generally proved very reliable – certainly when compared to Ilmor's rival V10 – but perhaps because Dallara *listened*, and matched their car cooling and lubrication systems to the engine as Judd recommended.

The combination then lost reliability in mid-season partly due to Judd relaxing requirements to change engines over-revved in practice or qualifying. The team wanted to minimize such changes, and it cost them dear. Judd then stiffened over-rev limitations and requirements to change 'buzzed' engines, and race reliability returned. Twenty-one of these 40-valve GV V10s were used, 'No. 22' being built fresh for winter testing at season's end.

Highlight of the season was Dallara's third place at Imola. The biggest disappointment was Japan where both cars qualified strongly without problems, only to collide on the second lap.

Meanwhile Team Lotus only just escaped closure during the winter of 1990/91 by the skin of its teeth, and when the salvaged organization was quite unable to afford renewal of the Lamborghini engine deal for the new season, its new directors fell back instead upon the Judd EV, which provided sensible and well-understood motive power at a price the struggling team could afford. In fact, Judd's role was once more that of a safety net, just as it had been when the company's first in-house F1 engine had kept Williams in competition through 1988 . . .

At the end of 1991 there were some 40 EVs in circulation, and apart from possible conversion to F3000 there were no plans to build more. Within Lotus capabilities that season they had performed respectably and, like Brian Hart before him, John Judd worked wonders on the kind of budget which would hardly have kept Honda in cam-covers for a season . . .

Lamborghini

After the American Chrysler Corporation took a controlling interest in Nuova Lamborghini, the Emilian supercar manufacturer based at Sant'Agata Bolognese, they sought to capitalize upon the marque's charismatic name by setting up an advanced projects division entitled Lamborghini Engineering to take it for the first time into serious competition, producing a new 3.5-litre naturally aspirated Formula 1 engine. Former Ferrari technical director *Commendatore*

Mauro Forghieri ran the project, and the Lamborghini 3512 power unit emerged as the first Formula 1 12-cylinder 'for the '90s'.

Forghieri had tailored the new power unit for client team use, describing it as being 'simple, easily useable by *clienti* – conceived above all to minimize its external dimensions'.

In fact there would be much smaller and far more compact F1 V12s produced but when first launched in April 1988 the 3512 was greeted by the Italian press with such accolades as 'incredibly small and easily adaptable – thanks to a transverse gearbox – in the same actual chassis which have formerly used 90-degree V8 engines'.

The 80-degree V12 was 720 mm long and weighed a claimed 160 kg, 5 kg more than Cosworth's contemporary makeshift DFZ. To save weight Forghieri made extensive use of magnesium castings and titanium internal reciprocating parts, and he was aiming at rotational speeds of 12,500 rpm and more. The engine was not truly Emilian – as Modena-based enthusiasts were quick to point out – in that major castings were supplied by Flan e Flambo, a former sub-contractor of Autodelta and Abarth in Lombardy. Crankshaft and camshafts were manufactured and the blocks machined by Montepilli, also near Milan, the V12s finally being 'merely assembled structurally by Lamborghini Engineering'.

Four valves per cylinder were adopted in the original unit, Forghieri reserving his position on possible 5vpc developments. Bore and stroke were quoted as 85 mm x 51.3 mm, displacement 3493 cc, and although Marelli-Weber electronic injection and ignition appeared on the prototype at the press launch, this was replaced by a Bosch MP 1.8 management system into the 1989 season. Pistons and rings were by Mahle and Goetze, and development weight was reduced to a quoted '146-150 kg', while power output was claimed merely as '600 bhp-plus' at 13,000 rpm.

The cam-covers significantly carried 'Chrysler' and 'Lamborghini' cast lettering, and for that maiden season the unit was taken up by the

Larrousse-Lola team – others having rejected it because they deemed it excessively heavy. That season witnessed a running battle between shedding weight and gaining reliability, a major improvement being achieved mid-season by the change from Marelli to Bosch injection and management.

For 1990, Team Lotus took on the expensive Lamborghini engine option in addition to the continuing Larrousse-Lola effort, and at Ketteringham Hall a new Lotus Type 102 chassis was designed to accommodate the chunky 3512. To maintain a reasonable wheelbase a transverse gearbox was required, and this was designed by Lotus and largely made by Lamborghini at Sant'Agata. The engine was equipped with the latest-version Bosch 1.8 management system, and was claimed to offer not only increased power but also improved mid-range torque. However, it was the Lola which would complete the season looking the more promising of Lamborghini's two *clienti* teams.

All four drivers agreed that the 3512 delivered its considerable power in a smooth and progressive manner, but it remained both bulky and heavy amongst contemporary company and it was undeniably demanding in terms of fuel consumption, lubrication and cooling. The Lotus-Lamborghini partnership got off on the wrong foot with designer Frank Dernie failing to pay sufficient heed to Forghieri's advice concerning the engine's oil capacity requirements. This resulted in new oil tanks having to be designed and adopted for the 102 between testing and the first race.

In the autumn of 1990 it was announced that Ligier would receive Renault V10 engines for 1992, and for the interim season of '91 had arranged supply of the latest-specification Lamborghini 3512s. In addition, Lamborghini Engineering had designed its own F1 chassis initially for the still-born Glas venture backed by a Mexican entrepreneur named Gonzalez Luna – 'Gonzalez Luna e Associati' hence 'Glas'. However, he disappeared in mysterious circumstances in

Life

Ernesto Vita's optimistic little Life F1 team based at Formigine, just down the Modena road from Ferrari's familiar home at Maranello, hoped to race their one-car team entry in the 1990 World Championship season, using a dedicated in-house engine designed for them by former Ferrari engine specialist, *Ing.* Franco Rocchi.

He chose the unusual 12-cylinder layout of a 'broad-arrow' or 'W' configuration, arranging the unit in three banks of four cylinders each, a basic vee with an additional vertical centre bank cast into the light-alloy block casings. The unit had bore and stroke dimensions of 81 mm x 56.5 mm, displacing 3493cc and with a quoted compression ratio of 13:1 it revved to c. 12,500 rpm. The broad-arrow arrangement had been popular in WW1 vintage aero engines, such as the magnificent Napier Lion 12-cylinder which was adopted between the wars for the Campbell *Bluebird* and Segrave *Golden Arrow* Land Speed Record cars. It offered a particularly compact package, only four cylinders long unlike the normal six-cylinders-long V12, but it complicated big-end and crankshaft packaging and the triplicate exhaust runs it demanded were a considerable headache for any chassis designer interested in optimizing his car's aerodynamic form.

Above all, it was a configuration which cried out for painstaking development, and although Vita invested quite heavily in his little F1 team it was never up to the task of making Rocchi's engine competitive.

At the beginning of 1990 Rocchi was talking of 600 bhp from the W12, which was already insufficient to compete. So it proved during that season's pre-qualifying sessions, drivers Gary Brabham (for the opening two GPs) and subsequently Bruno Giacomelli (for the next ten) never managing to get through them to qualifying proper. Finally the W12 was replaced by a Judd CV V8 for the Portuguese and Spanish GPs, without improvement. Life was extinguished by season's end – an unfortunate little postscript to Rocchi's otherwise honoured career . . .

But at least he had tried.

Maserati

The Maserati V12 engine was an enthusiastic update of a decade-old 60-degree four-cam design as described in the Cooper section of the Team Directory. From new it was already antiquated in many respects and after its maiden season of 1966 when everyone was struggling to develop new cars and engines it was never genuinely competitive.

The 1966 *Tipo* 9 four-cam V12 had bore and stroke dimensions of 70.44 mm x 64 mm, displacing 2989.48 cc, and on Lucas fuel injection, with a mixture of either Lucas or Marelli coil and distributor ignition, delivered a healthy 360 bhp at 9000 rpm in 1966 although very heavy and thirsty. Maserati also, strangely, record a 68 mm x 68 mm 'square' version of this engine displacing 2693.7 cc, delivering 340 bhp on carburettors.

The *Tipo* 9 engines had intakes between the camshafts, while the modified *Tipo* 10 of 1967 featured new Heron heads with three valves per cylinder, twin inlet and one exhaust, and the inlets in-vee.

The *Tipo* 10 Heron-head engines had a shorter stroke and bigger bore (75.2 mm x 56 mm) to permit and take advantage of this three-valve-per-cylinder design and with a compression ratio listed as 11.8:1 power output increased to a claimed 380-390 bhp at 9800-10,000 rpm.

But neither Cooper nor Maserati could sustain development pace, there was no money available to finance engineer Giulio Alfieri making a new start with a really modern power unit, and Maserati's interest in Formula 1 ended after the opening race of 1968.

Mexico in 1990 and Italian industrialist Carlo Patrucco stepped in with his Modena Team SpA to take over the in-house 'Lambo' F1 car programme and run the new cars through their first season . . .

Larrousse-Lola then lost its major Japanese sponsor when the ESPO Corporation collapsed, and during the winter of 1990/91 Gérard Larrousse himself was held by FISA to have lied in his 1990 World Championship entry by presenting his team's chassis as in-house Larrousse products, rather than admit they were really made by Lola as a sub-contractor. Since F1 teams were all required by that time to manufacture their own chassis, FISA took a seriously dim view of this bureaucratic failing (any enthusiast knew perfectly well who produced Larrousse's tubs) and the unfortunate former works-Porsche driver's team lost all its travelling cost concessions etc for the coming season. Thus he could no longer afford the Lamborghini engine, and only just survived by adopting Cosworth DFR V8s instead.

Simultaneously, Team Lotus was in a similarly parlous state. It had run out of cash, and was only just rescued from the very brink of closure at Christmas 1990. For 1991 the British team adopted relatively inexpensive narrow-angle Judd V8 engines, leaving Ligier and the new Modena Lambo teams as Lamborghini's representatives.

The latest-variant 3512-007-E V12 engine used a redesigned block, and two different bore/stroke configurations were available, with revised head machining to suit new valve and porting arrangements, plus new Bosch/Lamborghini electronic engine management. The still bulky V12 was accompanied by a modified version of the in-house 6T-009 transverse gearbox previously cased to their own requirements by Lotus and as supplied to Larrousse.

Forghieri was moving onto an electric car project within Lamborghini Engineering, but the 3512 in its latest form with more input from Chrysler US was said to be approaching 700 bhp at 13,800 rpm – though it still scaled some 145 kg. Forghieri was

That's right, this is a big photograph of a big engine – the Mauro Forghieri-originated Lamborghini 3512 proved to be a hefty, bulky, thirsty and expensive but demonstrably powerful 'atmo' Formula 1 contender 1988-90 before development impetus fell away . . .

always at pains to emphasize that Lamborghini's F1 engine programme was a very small one. Despite working with Elf for Ligier – and AGIP for the Lambo team – he would maintain 'our fuel chemistry was not always to the same order as that available to Renault from Elf and Ferrari from AGIP. We have always been – since I started the V12 project just in a flat here at the end of 1987 – a small team. Development of the engine has always been dependent on the difference between what the teams will pay, and what the actual cost of manufacture was . . .'

Some 50 of the 3512 engines had been built by the end of 1990, and only 20 of the '91-spec units followed, the difference being that they could rev ultimately to 13,500-14,000 rpm. There was talk of them developing 700 bhp in latest form, Forghieri commenting 'we saw 690 genuinely on the dashboard units in time for the last races . . .'

But by that time the Renault RS3B engine was said to be wailing out 770 bhp at 14,200 rpm and the Honda RA121E V12 780 bhp at 14,800 rpm. And they weighed c. 139 kg and 150 kg respectively . . .

The Ligier chassis was poor, and into 1992 Lamborghini Engineering supplied its next-generation versions of the 3512 to Minardi – after the Faenza team's solitary season with Ferrari V12 engines in 1990 – and also renewed its old association with the now re-invigorated and renamed Venturi-Larrousse team. But neither could be considered natural front-runners. In its three seasons of Formula 1 competition, the Chrysler-Lamborghini V12 family had achieved precious little – and few signs appeared of it ever receiving the wholehearted factory backing necessary for it to make the grade as a natural race winner.

Matra

Much of the Matra V12's development is related in the Team Directory entries for Matra and Ligier. Suffice here to record that Georges Martin's design team sought to maximize piston area and achieve high revolutions to achieve power.

The original 60-degree Matra MS9 V12 emerged in 1968 with inlets between the twin camshafts on each head. In this early form it was not capable of being mounted fully stressed as an integral chassis member; it was also over-thirsty, unreliable and prone to overheating while its average output of some 390 bhp at 10,500 rpm was inadequate in DFV and Ferrari V12 company.

Initially it had produced as much as 420 bhp using a six-tailpipe exhaust system with each six-cylinder bank regarded as a separate in-line engine with cylinders 1 and 6 feeding one tailpipe, 2-5 another and 3-4 the third, each side. But this system had a poor power curve making the car difficult to drive, so a more conventional four-tailpipe system was then adopted, robbing it of some 30 bhp.

After a lay year in 1969 during which the MS12 engine was developed in sports car racing, Matra Sports raced their V12 again in Formula 1 in 1970. The crankcase had been redesigned as a stressed chassis member, and completely new narrow-valve-angle (31.5 degrees) heads were fitted. Inlet ports were now in the valley of the vee and one-piece cam-covers concealed both camshafts per bank. The new valve angle provided a shallower and more efficient combustion chamber, and enabled less deep-crowned and hence lighter pistons to be fitted. Inlet valve area was increased, fuel injection revised and each bank fed a single tailpipe, MS12 output rising to a claimed 450 bhp.

In mid-1971 Martin's team introduced further-redesigned heads, with still narrower-angle valves and further-flattened, lighter pistons. Now Matra adopted year-by-year type numbering, and this type MS71 V12 was used in the MS120B cars that season but oil scavenging problems intruded. Revised lubrication arrangements produced the MS72 engine used in the 1972 MS120B-C and sports-prototype cars, and from 1973 to 1975

Matra concentrated upon long-distance sports car competition.

Further redesigning of cylinder head and internals for 1974 sports racing achieved around 480 bhp at 11,200 rpm. This MS73-74 V12 was retired from endurance racing in 1975 but reappeared in the Formula 1 Ligier in 1976-77. In 1978 its crankcase was shortened by 27 mm to fit the Ligier JS7/9, before the units were again withdrawn at the end of that season.

Low priority development continued behind the scenes, and Ligier returned to Matra power for 1981-82, the MS81 unit having been tailored to ground-effects chassis requirements, its crankcase and sump assembly having been narrowed as much as possible with ancillaries repositioned within the cross-section instead of hanging out in the breeze on either side.

The series of Matra V12 engines were based upon a developing design of cast-aluminium block, with a two-part crankcase-cum-sump down below. The earliest 'Type 6W' crankshaft induced vibration problems and the bearing suppliers

Vandervell recommended a redesigned shaft, the '4W', which was lighter yet still very stiff, benefiting from the engine's low bore:stroke ratio, 79.7 mm:50 mm, displacing 2993 cc.

In this form the engine won the Le Mans 24 Hours race of 1971, proving itself extremely reliable, but by 1978, as they sought a target of over 12,000 rpm, the 4W crankshafts over-stressed the centre main bearing and blocks began to crack. Matra reverted to the original 6W crankshaft, which had identical bearing diameters, and cracking ceased, the engine running its final races operating normally outside the 6W's critical vibration period.

The crankshafts were machined from solid steel billets, nitrided, and slung in seven main bearings with caps both vertically and cross-bolted for 24-hour reliability. Two titanium or steel con-rods were carried side-by-side on each crank-pin. The crankshaft nose carried a press-fit main pinion driving the cam-geartrain, which also powered the oil pressure pump and two scavenge pumps down below and the water pump immediately above. Each gear ran on needle or roller bearings. The seven plain-bearing camshafts actuated the valves via bucket-type cam-followers, with shim clearance adjustment. The entire cam-drive was enclosed by a cast-magnesium cover bolting onto the front of the engine.

Forged steel press-fit liners were used, sealed by 'O'-rings at their base, with individual head sealing rings for each cylinder. Piston design evolved as described into a near flat-head form save for valve clearance indents. Heads themselves were cast in the same AS19KG (French norms) as the crankcase and block, incorporating aluminium-bronze/cupro-nickel valve seats, and bronze valve guides. Inlet valve heads were 33 mm diameter, exhausts 27.2 mm, and valve lift around 9 mm, the four valves per cylinder surrounding central threaded bronze inserts carrying the single 10 mm spark plug per cylinder. Slide throttles were used with fuel injectors screwed into the induction trumpets. Lucas injection was used with a mechanical pump identical to the DFV's driven by the left-side inlet camshaft. The mechanical Lucas metering unit was subsequently replaced by an electronic metering control system.

Unusually, Ligier did not use a high-pressure starting pump, preferring instead a small fuel reservoir within the tanks, gently pressurized, feeding the injection system upon command from a dash-panel button. Ligier retained this system on both Cosworth and Matra-engined models.

The French V12s ran a compression ratio of around 11.5:1, and in 1981 form delivered some 525 bhp at 12,200 rpm with peak torque of 33 m/kg at 10,000 rpm. The engine weighed 170 kg (374.78 lb) including starter motor, and despite its relatively modest Formula 1 success will always be remembered with affection by all who heard it perform.

MGN

The French engineer Guy Negre produced a broad-arrow or W12 engine for 3.5-litre naturally aspirated Formula 1 racing, but was unable to gain sufficient backing to develop the engine to raceworthiness. A prototype unit was tested in the stern of an elderly AGS chassis, but went no further, Negre then searching for a significant customer in Group C, but failing . . .

Motori Moderni

Early in 1984 Alfa Romeo's managerial unease with their Euroracing satellite team's performances in Formula 1 finally resulted in the dismissal of their long-serving former Ferrari, then Autodelta, Chief Engineer, 61-year-old *Ing.* Carlo Chiti.

In partnership with Piero Mancini, the indefatigable Tuscan promptly set up a new company in Milan named Motori Moderni. The intention was to build pure-bred racing engines for the forth-

Top: *The Matra-Simca MS12 V12 engine cross-section reveals flat-head lightened pistons and narrower valve-angle modifications made in 1971. Above: Cutaway of MS12 as originated for 1970.*

coming new three-litre Formula 3000 (using the Lamborghini Jalpa V8 as a base) and for 1500 cc turbocharged Formula 1.

For the premier class he laid out a Ferrari-like KKK twin-turbocharged four-cam V6, and worked as usual with blinding speed, progressing from a blank sheet of paper to running prototype in less than five months. Two engineers, Nicolazzi and Bernardoni, and seven draughtsmen, Villa, Degan, Bollati, Colleta, Pastori, Boldrini and Vigini, made this possible, but Motori Moderni aimed at a potential 800 bhp and even as racing recommenced at the beginning of 1985 this was far from sufficient to perform respectably, never mind competitively.

The F1 engine was to be built in a new factory at Novara and emerged as a 90-degree V6, 80 mm x 49.7 mm, displacing 1498.8 cc, revving to 12,000 rpm and delivering a claimed peak 720 bhp at 11,300 rpm, with peak torque of 46 kg/m at 9000. Compression ratio was 7.0:1. It used Bosch-Kugelfischer electro-mechanical fuel injection and two KKK turbochargers gave 2.2 ata boost in race tune. Marelli Raceplex electronic ignition was used. Four valves per cylinder were disposed at an included angle of only 14 degrees and the aluminium-block V6 weighed in at 147 kg (324 lb) less clutch, but including other ancillaries and the two heavy turbochargers.

Giancarlo Minardi's new team took up the Motori Moderni engine for their small-budget 1985 Formula 1 programme, giving the new V6 its race debut at Imola. The new engine was under-developed, the car and its driver, Martini, unknown quantities and jointly this optimistic Italian venture achieved nothing significant during the season.

Carlo Chiti's *Tipo* 6VTC V6 engine had been designed entirely new from a clean sheet of paper and the roly-poly Tuscan engineer's old association with Enzo Ferrari paid off as *Il Drake* authorized Motori Moderni's use of an elderly but still invaluable Lucas-Ferrari electro-mechanical fuel injection system. But while this system made the unit feasible in Formula 1 it remained light years behind the increasingly sophisticated major teams' latest electronic management systems from Bosch, Honda and Marelli-Weber. Chiti sweet-talked Mr Ferrari once more and Maranello's Marelli-Weber system was shared with the tiny Novara concern for 1986. Using this equipment, uprated KKK turbocharging and toluene-bearing fuel mixes the 6VTC's qualifying-tune output rose to *c*. 950 bhp on 4.3-4.4-bar boost.

Minardi continued to use the engine through 1986-87 with little tangible success and little evident development other than normal attention to the turbocharging and induction systems to tailor the unit to 4-bar pop-off valve and 195-litre fuel allowance restrictions. Ultimately the Minardi team took the naturally aspirated 3.5-litre engine option for 1988, buying Cosworth DFZ V8 power units, and the Motori Moderni 6VTC was thereafter confined to Group C2 endurance racing, enlarged to 1.8-litres displacement to power an Argo car run by the Dollop team . . .

Motori Moderni's Formula 1 involvement would only continue in partnership with Subaru (see page 213).

Neotech

Swiss Formula 1 team owner Walter Brun had long experience of Group C endurance racing, and in 1989-90 he was instrumental in backing development of a new 3.5-litre naturally aspirated V12 racing engine which could have potential as a customer unit in both forms of competition. Austrian businessman Manfred Pehr's Pehr Holding Group had established the Neotech company with the intention of developing it into a kind of Continent-based Cosworth, Judd or Ilmor.

Pehr explained that he had made the decision to build a suitable engine as early as August 1987 with the 1988 subsidiary class of 'atmo' Formula 1 imminent. The plan for 1990 was for an engine to

be tested in Oscar Larrauri's Group C car, while engineer George Ryton was developing a new EuroBrun chassis specially made for the engine in England. A Judd engine was to power the F1 car early in the new year, modified by Roberto Ori, who had also designed a new transverse gearbox to accommodate the Neotech V12 engine.

The 70-degree V12 itself was designed by former Porsche and BMW Motorsport engineer Rolf-Peter Marlowe. Like the forthcoming Footwork-Porsche V12, the engine featured a divided crankshaft with central power take-off, a train of spur gears driving twin overhead camshafts per cylinder bank. Running the engine as two tandem V6s with the divided crankshaft was claimed to avoid vibration and torsional problems inherent in a necessarily lengthy one-piece 12-cylinder camshaft, thus permitting ultra-high rpm. Marlowe was aiming to achieve 640 bhp at 12,400 rpm, plus 455 Nm torque at 9000 rpm, and a system safe up to 14,000 rpm – an astronomical figure in 1988-89, although it was soon to be achieved by Renault, Honda and Ferrari.

Both block and 4vpc head castings were in aluminium alloy, the cam-covers interestingly in carbon-composite. Considering its Germanic parentage, the engine was equipped with Porsche Group C-derived Bosch Motronic MP 1.8 electronic ignition and injection, the ignition system being of the static or distributorless type, with coil-in-cap spark plug connectors and low-tension signal wiring.

Published dimensions included bore and stroke of 84 mm x 52.5 mm, capacity 3491 cc, compression ratio 11.8:1, length 660 mm, width 457 mm and weight 137 kg, but essentially the unit disappointed and never appeared in anger in Formula 1, EuroBrun remaining faithful to the ageing 90-degree Judd CV V8, and struggling even to pre-qualify through the 1990 season . . .

Osella

See entry for Alfa Romeo, pages 186-7.

Porsche

Really one of the tragedies of the young 3.5-litre 'atmo' Formula years, and telling evidence of Weissach's apparent loss of grip upon technological reality – the 1991 Footwork-Porsche V12 engine began life as a Weissach design centre project which was offered to McLaren International in 1987 as the turbo era was nearing its end, and 'atmo' racing had been confirmed for 1989.

MI's new Technical Director Gordon Murray was astonished as he first unfolded the elevation drawing of the new four-cam V12 with power take-off from the centre of its low-level crank via spur gears to an output shaft above. His first reaction was that the engine had been drawn larger than lifesize. In fact – it was simply huge;

Sad postscript to the serious racing activities of a once hallowed name – the tragic Footwork-Porsche centre power take-off 80-degree V12 of 1991.

an already antiquated, obsolescent concept which was absolutely an engine man's production, not a chassis designer's preferred package. In short the engine was everything which the TAG Turbo had not been, while effectively coupling two of the 1500 cc V6s in tandem.

As MI instead did a deal with Honda which combined both an immediately available low-line turbo V6 engine for 1988 and a new 3.5-litre 'atmo' V10 for 1989-90, the Porsche engine concept remained available, and it was eventually taken up in the summer of 1990 by Wataru Ohashi's Footwork company, which had absorbed the former Arrows Formula 1 team under its own corporate title.

The Porsche V12 thus emerged as the wholly sponsored 'Footwork' engine. It was presented in effect in the same way as the TAG Turbo V6 programme, only here it seems the chassis engineers had precious little effective influence upon the power unit's initial conception.

The engine remained Porsche-labelled when first unveiled during the 1990 Japanese GP meeting in the stern of an interim Arrows A11C chassis – the A11B 'renewed from the dashboard back . . .'.

Concept of this 80-degree 3499 cc four-cam V12 was credited to engineer Hans Mezger – who had a glittering track record thus far. Its central power take-off offered the advantage of minimizing torsional vibration problems as it united in effect two very short V6 cranks in tandem, promising higher rpm in mechanical safety. It was also – as Honda had found in their similar-configuration 3-litre V12 of 1966-68 – a factor which made the engine big, bulky, and heavy in contemporary company.

Despite optimistic forecasts, the Footwork-Porsche project proved itself a predictable disaster looking for somewhere to happen. The engine simply did not perform. It neither developed the power nor showed the reliability and compatibility with Alan Jenkins's FA12 Footwork chassis which it needed to come even close to being competitive.

The intensely disappointed and dismayed team opted instead to fall back on Cosworth engines early in the summer as the costly Porsche V12 was returned to Weissach 'for further development'. After a decent period it was quietly shelved. One cannot help but believe that such a disaster following upon the failure of Porsche's American CART racing project would not have been allowed to happen in Dr Piech's day at Weissach.

Demonstrably, the accountant-led Porsche company of the late '80s/early '90s was no longer the technological force it had become under the old-time family regime . . .

The Footwork-Porsche V12 story is sad indeed.

Renault

The enormous *Régie* Renault is one of the world's largest production motor vehicle manufacturers and it returned to Grand Prix racing in 1977, having won the very first Grand Prix in 1906. Its comeback was built around an iron-block four-cam (belt-driven) V6 engine originated in 1972-73 as a conventional 2-litre for Alpine-Renault to contest the European Championship for 2-litre sports cars. It was known as the Renault-Gordini Type CH1, apparently initialled in honour of Usine A. Gordini's late Technical Manager Claude Haardt (Gordini was Renault's competition and high-performance engine development subsidiary). However, its finalized design was credited to a team headed by the division's contemporary chief, François Castaing.

The compact new V6 powered the Alpine-Renault A440 *Barquette* built for the 1973 European Championship but the combination disappointed, the team withdrawing from the last two rounds without having scored a single point.

A winter's work brought both car and engine on song. The CH1 V6 delivered a claimed 305 bhp at 10,800 rpm and revised A441 *Barquettes* powered by it dominated the 1974 2-litre Championship. They won all seven races, placing 1-2 four times and once 1-2-3, and driver Serpaggi won the Championship title from team-mates Larrousse and Jabouille.

Inset: *Renault Sport's early EF1 turbocharged V6 engine in 1979; from left to right, chassis designer Michel Tétu, team directors Jean Sage and Gérard Larrousse and engine specialist Bernard Dudot. Main illustrations: For 1980 Renault Sport produced this twin-turbocharged, twin-intercooled version of their powerful and now reliable V6. These detailed drawings reveal the four-valves-per-cylinder dohc heads, belt-driven ancillaries tucked against the crankcase flanks, complex KKK turbochargers and wastegate, intercoolers, exhaust pipework and induction path piped from turbochargers to the 'logs' on top of the unit.*

Meanwhile, the national oil company Elf fostered the development of French driving talent by backing an extensive Formula 2 programme, which eventually embraced the Renault-Gordini V6 engine when the regulations admitted racing-block engines in 1976.

More significantly, on 23 March 1975 a new turbocharged A442 V6 *Barquette* shared by Larrousse and Jabouille had won the World Championship of Makes round at Mugello. It was subsequently third at Monza, fourth at the Nürburgring, third at Watkins Glen and third overall in the Championship.

Engineer Bernard Dudot was instrumental in the development of this turbocharged engine which was the first step in a planned Renault assault upon the great promotional prize of the Le Mans 24 Hours classic.

Dudot had graduated as an engineer from the CESTI institute in Paris – 'Like the *Institut des Arts et Métiers*', he says, 'and then I started work with Citroën. But there I was a very small gear in a very big machine so after only one year I joined Alpine at Dieppe, and at the end of 1973 I moved to join Castaing who at that time was still Technical Manager of Usine Amédée Gordini where I started work on 2-litre Formula 3 and rally car engines for him . . .'

Soon after his arrival the then Renault Competitions Manager, Jean Terramorsi, suggested a plan to attack Le Mans in earnest. Alpine-Renault had never been there with a hope of winning outright.

Terramorsi galvanized his technical team. Dudot recalls: 'He was a very futuristic thinker, and he looked at what we were doing already in rallying and Formula 3, and the new V6 was about to begin for 2-litre sports car racing and he wanted to take it to Le Mans. We had just this one real racing engine, and the only way to use it for Le Mans would be to fit a compressor to it and he saw that turbocharging seemed the best way.

'So I was sent off to California – this was still in 1973 – to learn all I could about turbocharging, talking to Garrett AiResearch and other specialist people. While I was there I got a telegram. The project was stopped. Come home. But I had all the information ready for when we could go again and, after five months of no turbocharging,

Terramorsi came in and said, "OK, we are all go again now". So Jean-Pierre Boudy and I began work seriously, first on a four-valve four-cylinder as used in the production Alpines and Renault 17.

'It was a very long-stroke engine, the volumetric efficiency was not very good, because in the narrow bore there was no space for an adequate inlet valve.

'After that development, which taught us quite a lot, we started work properly in July 1974 on the racing V6 in the 2-litre *Barquette* for the '75 World Championship. The A442 installation had a Garrett turbocharger and wastegate. It looked quite good in testing, we started racing with this engine in Mugello, and we *won*!

'We did two seasons in the Championship 3-litre class with this engine but won no more.'

They had changed the basic V6's compression ratio, pistons, lubrication and injection, having to use an injection system compatible with the boost pressure within the cylinder. The German Kugelfischer pump was used as it could adapt fuel flow relative to boost which the contemporary alternative Lucas pump could not. Water flow was increased to improve exhaust valve-seat cooling and sodium-filled valves were used to keep them cool and hopefully ensure survival.

'Always we had problems with the cars and the engines, but we were learning all the time and Terramorsi's ideal was still Le Mans . . .

'In 1976 we race-tested a European Championship-specification car at Le Mans for the first time. It was a normal 2-litre and it ran nine hours in a good place until a piston problem. Running full-throttle on the long straight caused detonation; it was a temperature problem . . . but we were happy. Now we were sure that a turbocharged special car for Le Mans could win it.

'In 1977 we prepared very hard for Le Mans. We tested very thoroughly at Ricard which has another long straight and three special cars ran in the 24 Hours but again we had a piston problem. They were cracking on the long straight. We were running with Porsche and led them for three hours early on, but our last car stopped at 21 hours, though Mirage ran Renault engines and finished second.

'Now we knew we could win but we had to test the engine at high revolutions on a very long

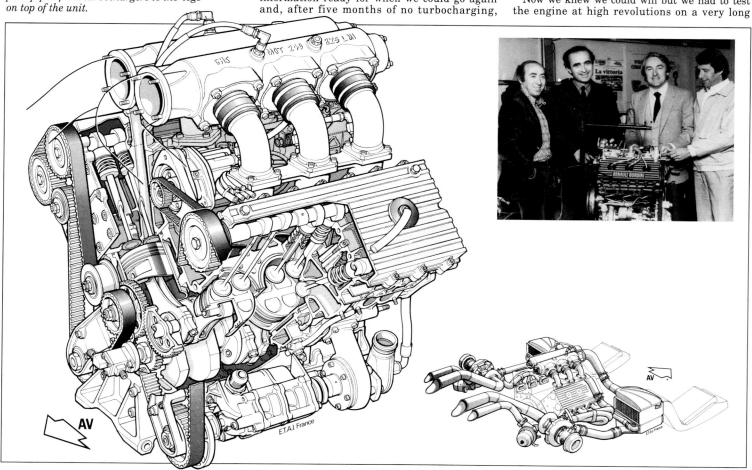

straight. Ricard was not long enough, you cannot test at Le Mans since it is a public road and there was no other track suitable in Europe. So we went to the GM testing ground at Columbus, Ohio, and ran two tests successfully with only one car and one engine, and we learned that we should change a little the height of the block to keep sufficient height above the pin in the piston – to reduce compression ratio the piston had been shaved – we had only 6 mm depth of piston above the pin . . . was too little.

'In 1978 we won Le Mans', he says simply, but it took massive effort. After the 1977 disappointment some 30 modifications had been made to the V6 engine, from valve-springs to the position of the plug cable supports. Three marathon tests were run – 3500 km at Ricard, 3000 km in Ohio and another 7000 km at Ricard. A test rig reproduced the stresses of 3 *miles* a minute on the Mulsanne Straight. Valve-springs were changed to improve reliability; a change of turbocharger widened the power range. The engine now delivered some 500 bhp at 9900 rpm, the Le Mans A442As and 1978 'Bs running 1997 cc units, the new A443 an enlarged 2140 cc engine. The A442s finished first and fourth, with Pironi and Jaussaud winning.

It was slap in the middle of this vast, lengthy and publicly high-profile programme, two years before their eventual Le Mans victory, that Renault's Formula 1 project had begun.

'We were working maximum effort to win Le Mans when the management said, "We are going into Formula 1", and we said, "But what about Le Mans?", and they said, "Yes, we are going to win Le Mans *as well*!" This was not really possible.

'In 1976 we actually started the Formula 1 project with just four people, Boudy and two or three mechanics and sometimes part of my time. I was Technical Manager of the Le Mans project. That was vital. Castaing was General Manager of Renault Sport overall. De Cortanze was on chassis and he designed the original Alpine *Laboratoire* test car – a *monoplace*.'

Régie chief executive Bernard Hanon had asked Dudot if he could make a Formula 1 engine of sufficient power to be successful: '. . . and I said "Yes it is possible" – I knew the potential was there but it was more difficult to have good throttle response with a small 1500 cc engine because the boost has to be higher.

'There was also a big problem because the only engine we could use as a basis was the 2-litre iron-block. We only needed the stroke for 1500 cc. At the beginning, to get one raceworthy engine we had to build three: two would break and one survive.'

Initially, they tested the Le Mans 2.1-litre Type CHS and putative 1500 cc Formula 1 Type EF1 – 'E' in honour of Elf support – turbo engines back-to-back in a pair of *Barquettes* at Ricard.

'Jabouille found the small engine very good but there was still a lot of work to do. Then we took the new *Laboratoire* to Jarama where there are only short straights between the corners and Jabouille found he could not get back on the boost before having to brake for the next corner. We found we had a BIG disaster about response. Boudy and I were desperate. To go racing we had to reduce boost a little. Boudy went to that first race at Silverstone, not me. At Le Mans we ran about 2-bar boost and in Formula 1 we ran about 2.7 bar and on the test-bed 2.8 bar.'

They learned rapidly. Mahle and Goetze, their piston, liner and ring suppliers, learned with them, as did Garrett, for their original production turbochargers were made to inadequate tolerances for Formula 1. Compressor wheels, turbines and axle bearings all failed: 'At this time they were running 130,000 rpm on plain bearings'.

Then after Le Mans '78, 'everybody worked on Formula 1 and from August '78 we were in Formula 1 seriously'.

The first step of course had been a single Garrett turbocharger engine 'and we made big progress by introducing the smaller twin-turbochargers by KKK at Monaco '79 although the race was a big disaster when intercooler cracks

lost boost.

'We could buy small turbochargers easier from KKK while Garrett had to make special small ones for us and now we knew in Formula 1 you have no time to wait.

'The twin-turbocharged engine also used a water intercooler to reduce the temperature of the pressure air. We had tested this at the end of 1978 and the improvement in piston life was very large. Response was also very much better with the two small turbos instead of one big one, though we also improved injection, length of the intake pipes, the turbine wheels, housing and compressor, all to reduce this lag, and for '79 we began spraying oil up under the pistons to help them cool.

'In a turbocharged engine compression ratio is lower but combustion temperatures 500-600 degrees higher. A 1500 can give over 750 bhp and is so small there is little area to lose heat.

'We had our big win at Dijon and through the rest of 1979 worked on reliability. We had a little problem with valve-springs – also in 1980 – due to the cam acceleration being very big because we had very large valve opening and the springs were breaking. We worked out an improvement with Schmitthelm and from 1981 our valve-springs have been reliable.'

The EF1 engine was based upon a fine-cast block in Renault's GS (Spheroidal-Graphite) iron. The original design involving Castaing had specified this material to offer strength and rigidity plus thermal resistance and stability. The *Régie*'s foundry was adept at casting very thin iron sections, enabling weight savings which made the finished block comparable with an aluminium component of similar strength, which would have required thicker sections.

The EF1 iron block had wall thicknesses of 3.5-4.0 mm. See the BRM H16 section to compare technologies (pages 189-91).

The block carried cast-aluminium-alloy heads and crankcase with integral main-bearing supports. Design changes were made to the crankcase stiffening ribs during the EF1's life, the basic architecture otherwise being little changed.

Nitrided steel wet-liners were inserted, fixed at the top of the block where thermal stress was most intense, free to expand axially at the bottom, where sealing was by two 'O'-rings. Oil and water passages were sealed by Viton 'O'-rings at head and crankcase joints.

The crankshaft – like all modern racing engine crankshafts – was an almost disappointingly modest-looking 'bit of bent wire'. Nevertheless, it was elegantly machined from a steel billet, including integral bob-weights and was nitrided for toughness. Its three crank-pins were typical V6, spaced 120 degrees from each other; end-on the shaft resembled the Mercedes-Benz three-pointed star symbol. Each pin carried two con-rods, one from each cylinder bank of course.

Nitrided forged steel con-rods were fitted, titanium coming later. Plain bearings were used throughout. The forged aluminium-alloy pistons were by Mahle, with a shallow crown and four valve clearance indents. Three rings were used.

The aluminium heads featured a very shallow pent-roof combustion chamber form with narrow-angle valves, inlets at 10 degrees to the cylinder axis, exhausts 11° 30′ for an included angle of only 21.30, seeking what Renault described as 'a more flexible combustion'.

Cam-carriers, like Cosworth's, were in cast aluminium alloy, supporting the double overhead camshafts in four plain bearings each. Internal-toothed rubber belt drive powered them from the crankshaft nose, the belts also driving such ancillaries as the water and oil pumps and alternator *en route*. This belt-drive system saved the weight of a complete cascade of spur gears and allowed easier replacement in the rare event of failure, or normal course of maintenance and rebuild.

A single oil pressure pump circulated lubricant at 8-10 kg/cm², and a simple scavenge pump returned it through the oil cooler matrix to the dry-sump system tank.

There were individual centrifugal water pumps

for each cylinder bank, all pumps being tucked against the crankcase flanks and driven by the cam-drive belts.

Ignition was by Magneti Marelli electronic system, and injection employed the Kugelfischer plunger-type pump already mentioned. There was a throttle device in each of the twin KKK turbochargers, which slung low on the trailing stainless steel or titanium exhaust system and which had their own lubrication arrangement using carefully filtered engine oil.

Bore and stroke of this 90-degree V6 were 86 mm x 42.8 mm, displacing 248.6 cc per cylinder, 1491.6 cc overall. The unit was 680 mm (26.7 in.) wide, 650 mm (25.5 in.) tall and 480 mm (18.8 in.) long *sans* clutch. Weight was listed as 180 kg (396.8 lb). It was designed to be mechanically safe to some 12,000 rpm and the 1980 version would deliver a quoted 500 bhp at 11,000 rpm, plus 38 m/kg (275 lb/ft) torque at 9600 rpm.

Major change came quietly in 1981 when the original thin-wall cast-iron block was replaced by a redesigned and lighter cast-aluminium unit.

'We had to change the thickness of the casting but it was generally the original Castaing design' – Castaing himself having gone to work in Detroit at the end of '79, and Dudot becoming Technical Manager for both engines and chassis in his place.

Whereas the iron blocks had come from Renault's own foundry which had considerable experience with good-quality thin-wall iron castings, the new aluminium blocks were contracted out to Messier who could deliver more quickly.

Dudot rightly considers 1981 to have been 'generally successful, while 1982 was our best year but we had a problem . . .'

In developing an engine management system for the V6 the original pneumatic device used to adjust the Kugelfischer injection pump's mixture cam was replaced by a microprocessor-controlled 'cheap Japanese electric motor', the system sensing boost, intake temperature, throttle position etc and the motor then continuously adjusting the mixture cam as required.

The system was introduced at Monaco which Renault led but the electric motor simply could not survive in the heat and vibration of the engine vee. 'Vibration broke the motor's winding, we tried desperately to damp it out but we lost the Championship that year for sure because of this. At Zeltweg and Zandvoort, Prost and Arnoux broke these motors, while it took four months to get a new motor designed and made by an aviation company working with the Renault laboratory.'

In 1983 reliability was much improved by the new Renix management system motors and water injection. Dudot and Jean-Pierre Boudy adopted bigger turbo casings and wheels and Boudy developed his water injection pack on his company Renault 18 saloon!

'But the rest got more power from their engines, specially BMW whose power in the second half of the season left us behind.' Engine performance proved inconsistent after rebuilds; then, 'at Monza we had the first reliability problem, in the turbocharger – the turbine wheel got too hot and broke up, losing Prost the race. The power problem was really about the adaptation of the turbocharging, and in the final race at Kyalami it was worse. It was necessary to improve power. We were running 3.2 bar in the race, 3.4 in practice – no more – we had about 650 bhp at 10,500 rpm in '83, compared to about 550 at the same speed in 1980.'

Through the winter of 1983/84, Dudot's team changed horses again from KKK back to Garrett: 'We felt sure we could use greater potential from Garrett now because they are a bigger company than KKK with the ability and will to develop special turbochargers for our needs . . . At the last race of 1984 we could match the TAG engine on power and after starting the year with a problem on fuel consumption we were now very close to TAG and Ferrari.'

They ditched the heavy water intercooler in favour of an air-to-air intercooler, which also improved aerodynamic performance.

The French Régie *Renault and Elf oil company both invested heavily in Renault Sport and with whole-hearted commitment by both French engineers and the British Williams team's technicians their 3.5-litre 'atmo' 67-degree V10 engines would ultimately topple Honda's long domination of Formula 1.*

In 1983, customer V6 turbo engines were supplied and maintained for Team Lotus and in 1984-85 also for Ligier. Only the works Renault Sport team's engines were made and serviced by the Gordini plant's 85 staff at Viry-Châtillon, the customer units being handled by a sub-contracted concern named Mecachrome, based near Bourges, where some 15 technicians handled strip and rebuild. Renault Sport maintained a float of 15 works engines, each client team in theory having 12 to choose from to service two cars. These units were drawn from a float at Bourges so that an engine might appear in a Ligier one weekend, a Lotus the next, the British team making by far the better use of them that season.

Asking Dudot what he believed to have been the most significant single steps in the story of Formula 1's first turbocharged engine he thought hard before replying: 'We made a lot of progress – a *lot* of progress – on turbocharger lag, and also on thermal problems with pistons and rings, and Mahle and Goetze who make our pistons and rings learned with us . . . which was good for Ferrari and BMW . . .', he added with a mischievous grin. 'But the obvious big steps were twin turbochargers, intercooling improvements and the improved management system.'

Renault displayed remarkable courage in taking the first pioneering steps into this new Formula 1 technology, and in some ways they paid the price of pioneering while always handicapped by their own labyrinthine management systems. Second-generation turbo engine manufacturers, like Ferrari and BMW, and third-generation, like TAG Turbo-Porsche, benefited from lessons learned at

the *Régie*'s expense.

For 1985, Dudot's engine team developed a new EF15 variant V6 so as to improve on the existing EF4's fuel consumption at high power outputs. The new engine mounted differently, like a Cosworth DFV this time with cam-box strap plates up top and two points down below, while the EF4 still attached beneath its heads at the front and in Lotus's case was stayed by additional tube-members for additional rigidity. While the EF4B unit's internal dimensions were 86 mm bore x 42.8 mm stroke, displacing 1492 cc, the EF15's were less over-square, with narrower bore and longer stroke at 80.1 mm x 49.4 mm, 1494 cc. Claimed power minima for these units were respectively 760 and 810 bhp. The EF4Bs were more amenable to accepting high qualifying boost than the EF15s, and would seem to have exceeded 1000 bhp in this tune. Lotus made better use of the engines than Renault's own works team which was by this time in final run-down. When customer EF15s became available in quantity from Mecachrome, Lotus regularly qualified on EF4Bs then fitted the more economical EF15s for the race. It paid off, and by late-summer 1985 Viry-Châtillon concentrated upon EF15 production, with Dudot's team studying 195-litre race consumption options for 1986.

In preparation for the 1986 season, sporting director Jean Sage joined the Viry-Châtillon engine operation from the race team, which was closed down. Renault Sport had been reorganized, Bernard Casin taking over as general manager, Pierre Tiberghien as President, and the division became more closely integrated into the *Régie*'s central organization. Jean Sage had attempted to secure backing for an effective management buyout of the team, without sufficient success to bid successfully. AGS acquired most of the plant from the race-team workshops at Evry and the racing operation's main personnel dispersed to jobs elsewhere. Most notably chassis aerodynamicist Jean-Claude Migeot went to Ferrari, accompanied by engine designer His from Viry-Châtillon.

Dudot's division there, meanwhile, was to continue development, production, service and supply of turbocharged F1 V6 engines for Team Lotus, while Tyrrell and – after some furious politicking – Ligier would race engines serviced and rebuilt by the Mecachrome sub-contractor at Bourges. Meanwhile, development work on the originally Renix engine management system was taken in-house at Viry-Châtillon, the *Régie*'s mainstream electronics subsidiary fading into the background.

It had, however, already developed an onboard data log capable of monitoring ten parameters for a restricted period of running, or two throughout race distance. Both the RS engineers and Lotus had made great use of this system, and the normal race-distance logs of revs and boost pressure had much to reveal when related to lap times . . .

Major development for the '86 engines to be used by Ayrton Senna's Lotuses was the low-inertia, lightweight DP valve-closure system. *Distribution pneumatique* had been born of long-lasting valve-spring problems which were the limiting factor to ever-higher rpm. Studies emphasizing the added weight and complexity of fully desmodromic – mechanically closing – valvegear indicated research into alternative systems and in 1984 work had begun to develop an 'air-spring' system.

New valves were designed and made, featuring a flange machined on the stem, the flange acting as a piston crown within a neat chamber charged with nitrogen gas from a piped circuit and central reservoir. This gas system was pressurized static to around 1.8 bar and as the cam-followers opened each valve so the stem-flange would compress the gas within its co-axial 'spring' cylinder. As the cam rotated into the closure phase, so the compressed gas within the cylinder would act against the valve stem flange, lifting it back into closure. Dudot's men found that increasing gas pressure within the system was tantamount to fitting stiffer valve-springs, with none of the accompanying weight and vibration penalty that would have entailed with conventional coil-springs of stiffer rate. Good news for the chassis engineers was that the DP system saved some 2.5 kg high in the engine, providing a lower centre of gravity. So far as the driver was concerned, an inadvertent over-rev could more easily be survived as there was no mechanical spring to over-stress or break. DP thus opened the door to an entirely new regime, 13,000 rpm was within Renault's grasp, and the DP-equipped EF15*bis* V6 turbo was cleared to 12,500 rpm in 1985 and to 13,000 rpm from the start of 1986, replacing the EF4*bis* as the Renault-powered teams' favoured big gun for qualifying, in which it ran – like its predecessor – without an over-boost dumping wastegate.

The Renault Sport engineers also abandoned the traditional mechanical-type rotary ignition distributor, adopting individual HT coils integral with the cap of each spark plug, the engine management ECU then triggering each coil/plug in the necessary sequence via simple – and reliable – low-tension wiring. Without the old problems of current leakage and 'scatter' from lengthy HT plug leads, plus the potential imprecision of wearable moving parts, this 'static' ignition enabled each individual cylinder's ignition to be more finely controlled, and the ECU's management mapping to be that much more precise. Another door had been opened.

It was now possible to control ignition well enough to run closer than ever before to detonation, which permitted a hike in compression ratio, theoretically yielding an immediate bonus in enhanced fuel consumption. However, this increase in compression would bite Renault hard, as head cooling inadequacies around the combustion chambers would be found out . . .

The driver fuel read-out system had been further developed and was claimed to be more accurate for '86. Elf provided toluene-inclusive heavy fuel brews, adding 10 kg extra mass to a cell full, and thanks to that better control on the very threshold of detonation Renault proved capable of keeping the pin in their grenade better than most. They ran 3.7-4.0-bar boost in race tune, while in qualifying for the Portuguese GP a new turbocharger gave Senna 5 bar, and in time for the final GP in Australia the EF15*bis* works Lotus engine hit 5.2 bar – a genuine 1100 bhp and more . . . Eight pole positions for Ayrton Senna, but the more conservatively tuned EF15*bis* race engines – though very good units – still could not match Honda's fuel efficiency. Local overheating in the heads was identified and re-cast heads emerged in the EF15C variant (available in time for the French GP), which proved better – but still not quite a match for the latest Honda, and the EF15Cs proved prone to an elusive misfire, often dictating their replacement by a normal EF15*bis* in search of race reliability.

Before year's end, at Senna's urging, Lotus ignored its Renault contract's remaining year to gain Honda power for '87. Renault could hardly complain, having been in breach of its agreement with Team in '86 by supplying two other teams instead of one, so spreading its resources more thinly than promised. But Renault Sport needed a top-line team, a potential race winner, to justify further effort into '87. McLaren seemed a possibility – the TAG Porsche V6 nearing the end of its development – but Shell vetoed a deal. Early in the new year Ligier's planned association with Alfa Romeo's four-cylinder turbo collapsed in acrimonious disarray but a plea to Renault for re-supply fell this time on deaf ears. Renault Sport had bowed out of turbocharged Formula 1 – Bernard Dudot and his talented team had set their eyes on a longer-term target . . .

The opportunity for Renault to return to Formula 1 was provided by the new 3.5-litre Formula of 1988, when Frank Williams found himself searching for a factory engine to replace the Judd V8 with which Honda's betrayal had left him. Dudot's group had been authorized to develop a 3.5-litre F1 engine as early as April 1987. The new RS01 unit emerged as a 67-degree V10-cylinder and agreement with Williams was announced in June 1988. The first FW12B-Renault V10 then ran in Riccardo Patrese's hands

at Ricard in October 1988 and by the summer of '89 WGPE was being serviced by a float of around 30 units.

The camshaft drive pulley caused early problems but a minor pulley redesign resolved them.

For 1990, after a maiden season's occasionally successful, often disappointing racing with the original RS01 V10 engine – around 40 of which had been produced – Renault Sport built their hard-earned experience into what was in effect an entirely new RS2 unit, which otherwise inherited little more than the common 67-degree vee angle and the number of cylinders. Bernard Dudot and Jean-Jacques His – returned to Renault Sport after his spell at Ferrari – were aiming at higher power, lower weight and more compact packaging to facilitate installation within the car. During 1989 the RS01 engine's speed had been raised by 1000 rpm between Rio and Adelaide. Most obvious change was the Honda-like replacement of the troublesome internal-toothed camshaft belt-drive by a spur-gear train, aiming at adequate timing control for rotational speeds of 14,000 rpm.

To compensate for the extra weight of the camshaft gear-drive, a comprehensive weight-saving programme addressed the rest of the system. The new RS2 unit emerged weighing only 139 kg, 2-3 kg lighter than the RS01 despite the cam-drive change. To provide a cleaner, neater unit, the ignition, in addition to the cooling and lubrication systems, were all encased, impressively packaged into a unit which was not only 48 mm shorter than its predecessor, but also 15 mm lower.

The alternator, once housed within the vee, was now mounted to the left of the clutch.

Great attention had been paid to block material, Dudot's team eventually opting for lightweight aluminium-alloy castings rather than magnesium or thin-wall iron, in view of considerable progress achieved by Renault in perfecting both light and rigid high-quality castings in such light alloys.

The induction system was completely redesigned to achieve optimum results from Elf's available fuel. Pneumatic valve closure was retained.

Renault Sport director Bernard Casin talked at the new engine's release of the V10 concept being 'Our engine for 1990 and '91', as he considered it offered an ample margin in both power and development potential. An alternative V12 was being studied, but as Dudot declared 'The V10's potential is enormous. In percentage terms we made as rapid progress with the 1989 engine as we had with the turbo engines of the early '80s . . .'

Where the 1989 RS01 engine had been 'just an engine offered to any potential customer for Formula 1', the new RS2 was tailored to WGPE's individual requirements. Two distinct development steps were taken: 'evolution 1' introduced at Imola had new intakes and a revised combustion chamber form, while 'evolution 2' at Spa featured radical new camshafts and an entirely remade crankshaft/con-rods rotating assembly to raise the engine's useable rev range to *c.* 12,800 rpm. Quality control problems with con-rod bolts from an outside supplier were the only major mechanical problems during the year, afflicting the team during practice for the French and British GPs.

Similarly giant strides were made in the replacement RS3 for 1991. Despite retaining the now classical 67-degree V10 configuration, this latest variant was again described as 'a new engine', differing from the preceding RS2 in its bore and stroke dimensions, a new cylinder head design, new camshaft drive, new induction, provision of a more rigid 'front timing end', a new oil sump arrangement with redesigned lubrication system and new Magneti Marelli electronic engine management system which was not only more powerful in ECU terms but also significantly smaller and lighter. The RS3 was also 14 mm lower still than its predecessor. Length of the new unit was 620 mm, width 550 mm and height to the heads 425 mm and again it was claimed to weigh in at only 139 kg. Using this engine, Renault Sport strode ever closer to the World Championship title desired – and they would at

last reverse the march of Honda, and Japan . . .

This RS3 unit was at least the equal of Honda's V12 until three-quarters of the way through the season. Elf's fuel development played a major role in such success.

A further-developed RS3B unit with new valve-gear and redesigned induction and combustion chambers, developing well over 750 bhp at 14,000 rpm, was available in time for the Italian GP at Monza, but its performance advance was not as great as expected and it was not used extensively. The Renault engines suffered not one major breakage in a race – Patrese retiring at Imola after an electronic sensor failed, Mansell at Spa due to a faulty voltage regulator. All would come good in 1992 . . .

Subaru

At the Italian GP meeting of 1988, a modest press conference was convened by *Ing.* Carlo Chiti's Motori Moderni company in conjunction with the Japanese Subaru concern to announce a collaborative deal involving a 60-valve flat-12 3.5-litre 'atmo' engine as a potential customer power unit for the new Formula.

The tiny Motori Moderni concern run by Chiti and his industrialist partner and backer Piero Mancini had experienced tough times in turbocharged Formula 1 with its initial 1500 cc V6 units (see pages 208-9), and even the Italian press expressed surprise that a Japanese production company like Subaru should commission a Formula 1 engine from Italy.

In fact the first contact between the two concerns had been made at the 1987 Japanese GP, and within twelve months Chiti's tiny staff of only 15 at Motori Moderni had completed their *Tipo* 1235 Boxer – not only a unique flat-12 solution to the 3.5-litre Formula question, but quick to follow Yamaha's lead into five-valve-per-cylinder technology.

Subaru was interested in the horizontally opposed configuration since they had remained faithful to it over 30 years' production. Chiti explained he was initially sceptical but after discussion with leading British chassis designers, who had assured him it would be feasible to arrange decent aerodynamic packaging around such a flat, broad unit, he embarked upon design and development at his customarily breakneck speed.

Initially three 1235 units were built. They were entirely Italian-made using the same specialist sub-contractors as Alfa Romeo and Lamborghini Engineering. At least one engine was initially intended to power a Dome 'supercar' aimed at the Japanese market, and a parallel Group C Dome for endurance racing. Plans declared included a move for Motori Moderni from Novara closer to Subaru's European Technical Centre in Milan. Minardi was cited as an F1 home for the 1235, to run as the Minardi-Subaru by the end of '89. Engine price to outside customers would be around 140 million *lire*, and 30 units were to be produced.

Chiti cited a target of 13,500 rpm for this 84 mm bore x 52.6 mm stroke, 3497 cc aluminium-alloy-block engine, an output exceeding 600 bhp 'with minimal vibration', and a weight of 159 kg (350 lb). While the Cosworth DFZ was 684 mm wide, the new 1235 was 54 mm wider. Weber-Marelli injection was used with a more sophisticated Bosch system envisaged for the future, with Marelli static ignition.

Development proved rather slow, the engine eventually making its Formula 1 bow in the stern of the already woefully uncompetitive Coloni C3B in 1990. Mated to a Subaru transverse gearbox the car was makeshift, overweight and ungainly. In time for Imola some 21 kg (!) had been trimmed off the package, but to no avail. Bertrand Gachot attempted to pre-qualify the flat-12 in each of the first eight GPs of the season, Phoenix to Silverstone, failing every time.

Subaru read the runes – and their engine was withdrawn from Formula 1 thereafter.

TAG Turbo

Background to the TAG Turbo by Porsche TTE-PO1 engine is described fully in Chapter 15. The engine statistics included a bore and stroke of 82 mm x 47 mm displacing 1482.18 cc. Compression ratio was 7.5:1, block cast in aluminium alloy with Nikasil cylinder lining, pistons and rings were by Mahle and Goetze, bearings by Glyco, and engine management by Bosch Motronic MS3 system. Twin KKK turbochargers were fitted, alternative smaller units with closer clearances permitting higher boost pressures and improved throttle response being developed to McLaren's commission. For a weight of 145 kg (319.61 lb) the 80-degree V6 unit delivered 750 bhp on race boost at 11,500 rpm, a genuine 500 bhp per litre.

Into 1985, TAG Turbo were caught by the opposition as the project seemed frozen by complacency. A new engine spec was decided just in time for the season-opener at Rio, after which few changes were made. TAG Turbo still did not resort to the high-boost, lightweight-car qualifying ploys used by some, but come race day the V6's race-tune output was always very competitive in the latest MP4/2B car. This was thanks largely to the Bosch Motronic management system which had now reached reliable maturity.

Dr Udo Zucker's system had emerged at a time when neither Bosch nor any other electronics company had reached that level of complexity on road cars. It is very difficult indeed to match injection and ignition requirements to a turbocharged engine across such an immense range of airflow from idling on zero boost up to 11,500 rpm on full boost. 'Mapping' engine performance across such a wide range is a very complex business and Bosch achieved this brilliantly during most of the '85 season to help McLaren win their second consecutive Formula 1 Constructors' Championship.

Hans Mezger having been seconded now to other projects, Porsche engineer Rolf Hahn took his place working closely with McLaren on the engines. Overall the TAG Turbo V6 remained the most consistent combination of power, reliability and economy in Formula 1.

The engines remained averse to accepting high boost for qualifying, partly because as boost was raised so back-pressure increased to the point where no further advantage could be gained. TAG Turbo also seemed to be lagging on fuel technology until Shell supplied a newly developed high-aromatic fuel for the abortive June meeting at Spa. Engine failures resulted and the fuel situation was reviewed as a high priority, properly tested new recipes being rapidly developed.

Very few details of TAG Turbo engine performance have been released, and Italian press calculations suggesting 890 bhp in qualifying at *ersatz* Nürburgring, falling only marginally to 821 bhp for the race, are scoffed at by the team as being 'exaggerated'. Certainly they said they would have been very happy if published Österreichring figures of 956 bhp (qualifying) and 866 bhp (race) had been anywhere *near* true!

In relative terms, however, the TAG Turbo's fifth place in the qualifying power league improving to a close third place in race tune would seem supportable. For 1986, a hat-trick of Constructors' titles became the immediate target and, generally speaking, the German-engineered V6 remained the engine to beat.

Throughout the TAG Turbo engine's life, the continuing philosophy of progress through evolution rather than revolution again produced engines which might well be beaten for peak power in qualifying, but which would offer a most competitive combination of performance, driveability, fuel-efficiency and reliability on race day. McLaren continued to prepare impeccably competitive chassis, but the inescapable truth was that the organization was still very much the customer, and its backers had to pay Porsche for every pencil lead, sheet of drafting paper, every minute in the dyno test that the Weissach concern devoted to the F1 engine programme.

Against this background, McLaren's thoughtful and intelligent conservatism really shines, and again they would excel when it most mattered, on race day.

Various problems were encountered, as at high altitude at Kyalami in '85 where smaller turbochargers were required to match ambient conditions before the engines would perform adequately. Subsequently three sizes of impeller turbine and two sizes of compressor were used. The larger turbos increased power at the cost of throttle response, while smaller, lighter, lower inertia turbos provided just the opposite.

Specially commissioned KKK turbo casings came on-line in time for Monaco, becoming standard on the team cars from then on. Lighter thin-wall turbine housings followed. From the German GP onwards, mirror-image KKK turbos were available to optimize performance bank to bank within the engine, but as John Barnard recalls – see page 182 – this objective was not only unattainable, but unnecessary. Improved engine management and advances by Shell in fuel quality enhanced performance as the season progressed.

During qualifying for the French GP at Dijon a number of engines were severely damaged by piston failures, the result of unexpected detonation problems melting down the piston crowns. This sudden plague was ascribed to a sub-standard fuel batch supplied by the nearest local Shell establishment. Until halfway through the 1985 season, the engines had been burning nothing more sophisticated than a 40/60 AvGas/pump fuel blend. After the French experience all McLaren's fuel was provided by Shell Germany, and a dense toluene-bearing mix was formulated to keep pace with BMW Winterschall and Renault Elf developments.

Meanwhile Dr Udo Zucker was improving the Bosch electronic management system which played such a decisive role in making the TAG Turbo engine the pre-eminent factor in contemporary fuel-restricted turbocharged Formula 1. Drivers Lauda and Prost were assisted by a dash panel read-out including fuel state in the form of the number of laps possible on current boost.

It appears that the engine's genuine performance involved development of around 3.3 bar in race tune, c. 800 bhp allied to mid-range torque peaking at some 497 Nm. Up to 890 bhp was available for qualifying, it was said.

For 1986, Barnard relocated the turbochargers as part of his chassis re-packaging programme, drawing in air from a new position close to the radiator inlets. The old problem of the engine refusing to accept higher boost due to exhaust back-pressure within the turbocharging system led KKK to offer newly developed turbines. During one test of the earlier system, boost had been wound up to its practical maximum, and lap times showed no improvement.

At Hockenheim Bosch deployed the latest version of their management system, the MP1:7, and KKK yet another new turbocharger, known as the HHB. The engines responded by generating 3.9 bar in qualifying which projected both Prost and new team-mate Keke Rosberg onto the front row of the grid. The race then turned sour for them as the fuel read-outs proved inaccurate and both engines coughed dry when the McLarens seemed set to finish 2-3.

At this point the relationship between McLaren team chief Ron Dennis and technical director John Barnard had effectively broken down, because John was publicly discussing his future with rival teams. He left to join Ferrari, but his deputies left behind at McLaren filled the gap admirably and kept the TAG Turbo-powered operation moving forward against their main rival – Williams-Honda . . .

Prost was able to secure back-to-back Drivers' Championship victories although McLaren-TAG Turbo lost their coveted Formula 1 Constructors' title to Williams-Honda. At that point the TAG Turbo engine had won an incredible 22 GPs from the 48 contested in three seasons' endeavour.

In preparation for the forthcoming 195-litre fuel restriction season of 1987, the Porsche engineers

had been experimenting with higher compression ratios in search of improved fuel consumption. Rosberg's engines in the last three races of '86 had featured 8.0:1 compression pistons, with the fuel chemistry and engine management refinements necessary to keep them on the right side of the detonation barrier.

The 1987 season was in fact this historic engine family's last. The V6 unit was said to develop the same normal race boost of 3.3 bar as in '86, and power output was claimed to reach 850 bhp at 12,800 rpm. But in addition to the new and lowered fuel restriction, this was the 4-bar FISA pop-off valve season. The German V6s' configuration with non-interlinked cylinder banks, running as two in-line three-cylinder units in effect, required two FISA pop-off valves. During 1986 the non-pop-off TAG had hit 3.9-4 bar for the first time in qualifying tune when it punched Rosberg onto pole position at Hockenheim, but normally it ran out of gain at 3.6-3.7 bar.

Now it was using Bosch's mass air-flow induction sensing in qualifying to help map race-tune requirements, but this system was capable of being confused by a leak in the system – and twin FISA valves if over-boosted and blown open provided twin leaks in the system . . .

In testing the McLaren and Porsche engineers tried running the pop-offs blown open and saw 4 bar-plus but – as engineer Steve Nichols put it – 'it puts a massive strain on the turbos . . .'.

The ageing power unit was rapidly approaching the limit of its practical development, and to promote and handle the fuel-efficiency pre-requisite of its raised compression ratio the new higher-crowned pistons were heavier, and so were their gudgeon pins and con-rods. This increase in reciprocating mass took the engine into vibration problems, creating failures in other areas. Weissach had made a rare miscalculation at this late stage of the TAG Turbo saga, and pre-Hockenheim a solution had to be provided by re-balancing the crankshaft. After leading the German GP, Prost and the veteran engine were cheated out of yet another well-deserved victory when the alternator drive belt snapped, permitting the battery to run flat, killing the engine's life-giving electrics.

At Imola a similar belt failure had been experienced, the first such breakage after around 100,000 miles' running with the engine. It was deemed a random failure at the time, 'not significant'. Then another snapped in Silverstone testing, and another at Ricard. At that point the pulley size was changed to reduce load, only for the 'shattering experience' of that Hockenheim race failure, while leading.

The American Gates company rapidly produced a redesigned twin-belt drive, introduced in Hungary, and with the rebalanced crank the old reliability seemed to have returned. Although MI's new engine supply agreement with Honda for '88 was announced in September '87, as late as the Mexican GP that year new features appeared on the TAG Turbo-powered works cars – in this case telemetry aerials transmitting data from the Bosch ECU log.

The 1987 Australian GP then saw the TAG Turbo V6s' swansong, but both cars sadly retired with carbon brake system failures, while their engines remained healthy . . .

Still the unit had given Prost three more race wins and could easily have made that four but for the Hockenheim disappointment. They had placed 1-3 in Brazil, 1-2 in Belgium, and then above all Prost's new record-setting win in Portugal when he surpassed Jackie Stewart's career best of 27 GP wins.

In its four-and-a-bit-season life the TAG Turbo engine had provided its creators with three World Championship titles and 25 GP victories. It had been a costly project, but it had repaid the investment in pure gold, and had demonstrated what Porsche could produce with an intelligent, practical and gifted customer making the rules.

This splendid engine came within a whisker of making that four consecutive World titles in 1987 – a remarkable achievement indeed, but one which Honda would yet match . . . But the fact that both engine manufacturers achieved such success allied to the same team – McLaren – is no mere coincidence . . .

Yamaha

Yamaha's name is of course world-famous in motor cycle competition and the company's experimental department's clients included, amongst others, the giant Toyota concern. They came to four-wheeled competition via a 2-litre engine known as the OX-66 which ran effectively in Japanese Formula 2 in 1986. A Cosworth DFV-based V8 Formula 3000 engine then followed – also campaigned in the national Japanese class series – known as the OX-77, and in 1988 driver Aguri Suzuki won the Japanese Championship title on Yamaha power. The company promptly stepped up into Formula 1 for 1989, for which season a three-year agreement was announced with the German Zakspeed team.

Their research work had gone far into perfecting – as they claimed – a five-valve-per-cylinder combustion chamber form which they duly patented. Under Engine Technology Director Norio Shimizu they initially devised a 40-valve competition V8 upon a Cosworth base, but for the Zakspeed 891s they produced a promising-looking 3.5-litre 75-degree V8 which was new from the ground up.

This narrow-angle 40-valve unit was designated the OX-88. It used in-house Yamaha injection matched to the 5vpc combustion chamber requirements and with major castings in aluminium alloy it scaled a quoted 145 kg. Its twin overhead camshafts per cylinder were driven by individual internal-toothed flexible belts per cylinder bank, driven off the crankshaft nose. Pumps were neatly tucked tight alongside the crankcase in Cosworth style, and static CDI ignition was employed. Yamaha kept internal dimensions to themselves but declared a displacement of 3489 cc and claimed peak power exceeding 600 bhp at 11,000 rpm and peak torque in excess of 43 kg/m at 9000 rpm. Safe rev limit was 12,000 rpm and the OX-88 unit measured 560 mm in length, and 570 mm in width.

However, the Japanese manufacturer suffered an appalling maiden F1 season with Zakspeed. The engines failed with monotonous regularity, repeatedly preventing the team drivers from even managing to pre-qualify. The record brevity of life for an OX-88 was said to be just 49 seconds between ignition and disintegration in the Silverstone pit lane . . . Before the end of the year it was clear that Zakspeed was dead in the water as an F1 team, and Yamaha withdrew for a season to lick their wounds and regroup around a tailor-made new V12-cylinder aiming to stage a fighting comeback in 1991.

The Japanese concern badly needed a major team to carry its banner, but none was available. Eventually they fell into a deal with Dennis Nursey's reincarnated Brabham team which itself had much to gain from such an association.

Shimizu put together an engine project team including engineers Hiromitsu Matsumoto, Takaki Kimura, Kengo Nishi and Hiromitsu Matsumoto and their labours produced Yamaha's new OX-99 70-degree V12 engine which was officially unveiled virtually simultaneously with Porsche's similar unit for Footwork (Arrows) just before the 1990 Japanese GP.

By long by-gone standards the Porsche unit was compact, but the Yamaha was smaller, showing by how much Weissach had missed the modern mark. The new Yamaha unit naturally featured 5vpc heads, and to minimize weight extensive use was made of aluminium alloys, titanium, magnesium and carbon-composite mouldings. The unit emerged 725 mm in length, 540 mm wide and 504 mm high and was claimed to weigh 'less than 140 kg' which put it on a par with the Renault V10.

Yamaha took over the former Proteus Technology Aston Martin Group C facility in Milton Keynes, England, and established a new satellite company there named Ypsilon Technology Ltd to act as an F1 engine service

Yamaha made an appalling debut in Formula 1 with these 3.5-litre Type OX-88 75-degree V8 engines used by the Zakspeed team in its fatal season of 1989. Yamaha would persevere, but their motor cycle racing quality was not apparent in Formula 1.

base and in which a new Yamaha road-going 'supercar' would be developed around a detuned version of the V12 engine.

However, once pre-season testing began, a string of top-end valvegear failures forced a careful re-think of its high-speed capabilities. Conservatism thereafter ruled the rev limits applied and in a Formula in which maximum rotational speed had become the ultimate arbiter of competitive power production, the new Yamaha was hamstrung. Before the end of the season the V12 launch-function words of senior MD Takehiko Hasegawa – 'I look forward to building a Brabham-Yamaha dynasty in which we both merge our efforts towards a common goal' – looked simply high-flown phooey, although his follow-up – 'I promise that we will pursue our goal steadily and relentlessly' (which isn't easy for any Japanese to pronounce) – remained true in that a move was arranged for the Jordan team for 1992, Yamaha sticking with Formula 1 despite its grave disappointments.

Even so, its latest F1 engine had shown little sign of truly competitive performance. Yamaha's World Championship form within the motor cycling world seemed to have suffered in translation to Formula 1 – and more significantly Yamaha's public image had suffered severely too . . .

Zakspeed

The German engineer Erich Zakowski set up his Zakspeed tuning company in 1968 and made its name with a long series of very effective competition Ford saloons. They became increasingly Zakspeed, less and less Ford, and the company accumulated vast experience of highly specialized turbocharged racing engines. Just like Brian Hart in Britain, Zakowski finally decided to build engines of his own from scratch instead of modifying Ford units virtually beyond recognition, and against this background he made the ambitious move into Formula 1 for 1985.

Although ambitious, he took this step cautiously with distinctly Germanic logic and practicality. A state-of-the-art carbon-composite Formula 1 car was built as described in the Team Directory, while Zakowski and his engineers designed and built a neat, broadly BMW-like, in-line four-cylinder turbocharged F1 engine for it.

Through the summer of 1985 continuous devel-

opment saw the compression increased to 7.0:1, more radical camshafts enabling the engine to be run faster – up to 11,000 rpm – and the fitting of a crankshaft damper to control a cam-drive gear destructive vibration period.

Zakspeed was handicapped by lacking either a qualifying-tune engine or even a qualifying-only bumper turbo, until for the Portuguese GP Bosch electronic injection became available in place of the original mechanical system.

For 1986 a fully mapped low-pressure Motronic system was ready, derived in part from Porsche experience, in part from the system developed for Alfa Romeo's stillborn four-cylinder turbo unit (q.v.). Fuel-efficiency, mechanical reliability and competitive horsepower under all conditions remained often conflicting targets. A single-turbo four-cylinder was by nature a peaky unit, its power characteristic 'sudden' and 'driver-unfriendly'. Work was required to spread this band, to smooth the curve, to enable the driver to use every horsepower the neat little unit could offer, yet higher peak power was always demanded, and lower fuel consumption too.

Keenly conscious of the thermodynamic stress to which any four-cylinder turbo unit's large pistons were to be exposed, Zakspeed's featured twin cooling oil sprays and painstaking attention had been paid to cooling throughout the unit's development. By this time the team claimed 850 bhp from 3.5/3.6 bar in race tune and the ability to sustain 4.5 bar in qualifying.

In search of improved driveability plus more power, alternative KKK turbo sizes became available from Monaco and from the British GP heavy BMW-type toluene fuel by Winterschall AG was adopted, better-atomized by triple injectors per cylinder to permit a further compression ratio rise to 7.5:1.

Since KKK interest in F1 turbo development had diminished following BMW's scaling-down, Zakspeed adopted American Garrett compressors from the Portuguese GP, and through 1987 the little German constructor's four-cylinder engine attained a full 4 bar on some circuits. But while it displayed adequate midfield power and reasonable throttle response it remained too peaky, lacking competitive mid-range torque and as money was scarce the project marked time.

The brave – or capricious – decision was then taken to adapt the engine to 2.5-bar/150-litre tune for the final turbo F1 season of 1988. Compression rose to 8.0:1, smaller ports and valves were adopted but both the engine and the chassis to carry it proved inadequate and could hardly qualify, never mind race successfully. At the end of that year Erich Zakowski's organization bowed out of Grand Prix engine manufacture. It had been a brave try – but doomed by the organization's modest size and lack of any outside customer . . .

TEAM DIRECTORY

In this section we cover the marques which have not won the Formula 1 Constructors' World Championship, in some cases despite many years of trying, and we also provide some detailed background to the less successful cars built by those teams whose Champion designs are fully described elsewhere in this volume.

In effect, the cars whose story is outlined here divide conveniently into winners, losers and no-hopers, but such clear-cut distinctions are often unfair. Many a slow car has been slow simply because there was insufficient money within its team to provide a competitive engine or a good enough driver. Some very nice-handling chassis never achieved a thing for that very reason, while occasionally a real 'old dog' of a car has won races despite its inferior design, helped towards success by more money in the team, perhaps a better driver and with infinitely better luck.

There is no divine right to be lucky, nor is there any rule which says life will be fair to you; such a brutal truism is seldom more apparent than in Formula 1 . . .

AGS

Henri Julien's *Automobiles Gonfaronaise Sportive* concern was based at Gonfaron in southern France and had built a series of notably wide-track/low overall height Formula 2 and F3000 cars which had performed respectably over several years. Their design was by engineer Christian Vanderpleyn and by the summer of 1986 he was well advanced on the team's new Formula 1 project, which had been commissioned by the Italian Jolly Club late the previous year, in support of the Florentine 'Arno International' F3000 team. Vanderpleyn had his prototype carbon-composite F1 fuselage moulded by the military manufacturer MOC in France, reputedly taking a short-cut by employing redundant Renault Sport mould tooling while other necessary fabrication was by AGS themselves to the decent standard already seen in their minor-Formula cars. MOC had indeed moulded the admirably high-quality composite underfloors, noses etc for Renault's RE60 cars and had tooled up to produce their subsequently shelved RE70 monocoque.

The lower portion of the subsequent AGS JH21C F1 prototype tub was effectively Renault RE70, with the upper sections of the mould tooling adapted to suit Vanderpleyn's Brabham-style ultra-low CoG theories. Arno's Carlo Giorgio was seeking sponsorship to run driver Mario Hytten in the new car, which was to be powered – at that stage – by the Motori Moderni V6.

Giorgio was unsuccessful on Hytten's behalf, the car being debuted instead by Ivan Capelli in the Italian GP at Monza, backed by the Jolly Club and 'Charro'-lettered. The new AGS JH21C – chassis '01' – was long and heavy and was nicknamed 'The Auto Union' by some better-heeled and less sympathetic teams . . . It was considerably lower than the similarly engined contemporary Minardi, and considerably longer since its designer's T-section fuel tank demanded a considerable extension to the rear of the tub. Capelli qualified on the penultimate row and retired with tyre failure after 31 laps. The bulky car reappeared low-key at Estoril, again driven by Capelli, only to be sidelined by gearbox trouble after six race laps. A second JH21C was available but not used.

Following this tentative first step into Formula 1, the Gonfaron-based team built two completely new JH22 chassis numbered '32 and '33, for 1987, servicing a singleton entry for Pascal Fabre. The cars were completely new, sharing only their rear uprights with the original Renault-based model. They were very reminiscent of March practice with curvaceous, narrowing bodywork. Fabre contested 14 GPs from Rio to Mexico, while Brazilian driver Roberto Moreno took over the ride for Japan and Australia completing the season. The cars proved remarkably reliable, if unimpressive – Fabre's record in the first seven events reading 12-13*-10*-13-12-9-9 before his first retirement, at Hockenheim. He was then 13th and 16th in Hungary and Austria before failing to qualify in both Italy and Portugal, retiring again at Jerez and then failing to qualify after the long trip to Mexico City . . .

Moreno qualified successfully for his GP debut at Suzuka and then again in Adelaide, and after retiring in Japan he finished sixth amidst mayhem in Australia to score his own and the French team's maiden World Championship point! They had fared more respectably within the 'atmo'-only Colin Chapman Trophy competition for Constructors, and in fact ended the season third behind Tyrrell and Lola, with 41 points against Tyrrell's 169 and Lola's 50, and bettering March's total of 38.

In 1988 three JH23s were used, developed from the previous season's cars and powered by production Cosworth-Ford DFZ engines, again servicing a lone entry to be driven by Philippe Streiff who had had previously shown promise if a somewhat hot-headed nature in Tyrrell and Ligier cars. Under his hard driving the team's reliability subsided, and he was classified only six times – 10-12-12-9-8-11* at Imola, Mexico, Spa, Estoril, Suzuka and Adelaide.

But right at the start of 1989, poor Streiff was grievously injured and paralysed in a pre-season testing accident at Rio. The shocked team continued with one uprated 1988 car, chassis '34 for Joachim Winkelhock – brother of Manfred, killed in a Group C Porsche at Mosport Park – at Rio, Gabriele Tarquini joining him at Imola in 'JH23B/33'. Chassis '36 would also be used by Tarquini at Mexico, Phoenix and Montreal after which two new JH24s then emerged, three being built and raced by Tarquini and Yannick Dalmas who replaced Winkelhock from the British GP forward.

The JH24 featured a stiffened monocoque carrying lower, shorter side pods with leading edges flared back from the monocoque fuselage instead of square-cut as hitherto.

Winkelhock's record had comprised seven dismal failures to pre-qualify. Dalmas's was no better, five pre-qualifying flops followed by exclusion from the meeting for a rules infringement at Estoril, then three final pre-qualifying failures to complete an appalling year. Tarquini provided the team's only Grand Prix starts, qualifying for Imola and the next five rounds, but inheriting a cheering sixth place in Mexico and seventh at Phoenix. Even so, it was a costly season with precious little return.

For 1990, AGS design was directed by Claude Galopin, Vanderpleyn having taken a post with BMS-Dallara. The Gonfaron team used three JH24s, chassis '37, '38 and '39 at Phoenix and Interlagos opening the season. These developed cars featured completely new front suspension with single central damper, but they were still far too heavy – some 35 kg above the minimum limit. The team then introduced its lower, leaner replacement JH25 at Imola, distinctive for its confined side pods pinched in tightly at the tail to expose broad aerodynamic platforms and with a sweeping tail diffuser surface down below. The single transverse damper of the JH24 was retained, actuated via rocker arms topping pushrods each side.

Four JH25s would emerge, numbers '41-'44 for the same drivers. Dalmas was able to pre-qualify ten times, only to fall at the next hurdle – official qualifying – at another five GPs. He actually made it to the race only at Interlagos and Estoril (retired both times), Monza (too far behind to be classified as a finisher), Ricard (17th) and Jerez (9th). His entry was withdrawn at Imola.

Meanwhile Tarquini failed to pre-qualify for the first six consecutive GPs, then got through for the seventh, at Ricard, only to fall in official qualifying. He then made the race for the first time at Silverstone, but retired. After not pre-qualifying in Germany, Tarquini finished 13th at the Hungaroring, then failed to qualify for four of the final six GPs, retiring at Jerez and Adelaide. Out of a possible 32 starts, AGS made it to the grid on only nine occasions and were classified as a finisher only three times.

It was not particularly impressive.

Through the winter of 1990-91, team owner Cyril de Rouvre negotiated energetically with Gérard Larrousse suggesting a merger between their two troubled organizations. Michel Costa had a new JH26 car designed but no funds were

The AGS JH23 at Monaco 1988, driven by Philippe Streiff – a good-looking Cosworth DFZ-powered no-hoper, out on the opening lap here . . .

available to build it. Still AGS fielded updated versions of the JH25 to be driven by Johansson and Tarquini in '91. It retained Mader-prepared Cosworth DFR V8 power, of course, but suspensions and aerodynamic packaging had both been revised. Immediately after the Brazilian GP de Rouvre applied for receivership and a controlling share in the team was acquired by Italians Gabriele Rafanelli and Patrizio Cantu – the latter owning the Crypton F3000 team. Christian Vanderpleyn returned to replace Costa and Johansson was replaced as driver by Fabrizio Barbazza.

Vanderpleyn set about improving the existing JH25 hardware and put ex-Modena Team engineer Mario Tolentino onto designing a new JH27, Costa's still-born JH26 programme being abandoned. The new ownership succeeded in filing a long-term plan with the French authorities which released AGS from financial control, but the season proved a litany of failures even to pre-qualify. The JH27 emerged at Monza with similar result, its engine failing on Tarquini's opening lap. Talks reopened with Larrousse, Tarquini moved to Fondmetal and was replaced by Grouillard but after failing to qualify in Spain the team opted out of the last two long-haul races, in Japan and Australia. Three JH25s and the twin JH27s had appeared during the season. But AGS's time had run out . . .

Alfa Romeo

Alfa Romeo is a name rightly revered by racing enthusiasts for its classical years of competition dominance prior to 1952. After a false start with Cooper in 1968, the Milan company returned to Formula 1 in 1970. A 3-litre V8 sports-racing engine was supplied to McLaren 'just to keep in touch', and this engine was also used by March in 1971 before being dropped. By 1975 another sports-racing engine, the 3-litre flat-12, had been developed for use in Formula 1, and after being fitted initially in one of Graham Hill's Embassy team Lola T370s, it ended up with Brabham instead.

Alfa Romeo's modern racing endeavours were handled by a satellite company named Autodelta, which had been founded at Udine in 1963 by ex-Ferrari, ex-ATS* engineer Carlo Chiti in partnership with Ludovico Chizzola. They prepared and modified Alfa Romeo cars for competition, moved to Settimo Milanese in 1964, and became an integral part of Alfa Romeo there in 1966. From 1967 they built and raced the long series of Alfa T33 sports-racing cars; making chassis, bodies, engines, gearboxes, everything – with help where needed from the Alfa production plants.

The Brabham flat-12 relationship was close but largely unsuccessful. As early as 1977 Autodelta were preparing their own Formula 1 car design around the flat-12 engine. This *Tipo* 177 hack was driven by Vittorio Brambilla at Alfa's Balocco test centre during '1978, while Gordon Murray of Brabham had sparked Autodelta's crash programme to redesign the flat-12 as a narrower 60-degree V12 for a new ground-effects Brabham chassis to race in 1979. In parallel, design work began in Milan for a new Alfa Romeo V12 Formula 1 'wing-car'.

Despite Alfa's poor financial state, the Board decided to authorize a factory race programme in Formula 1, essentially for 1980, with race development being pursued during the summer of 1979.

The podgy prototype 177, with its hefty riveted aluminium chassis and bulbous bodywork, made its debut in the Belgian GP at Zolder, driven by Giacomelli and tended by engineers Chiti and Marelli plus ten mechanics and a tatty borrowed transporter. The car had originally been developed on Pirelli tyres, but the Italian tyre company felt unready to enter Formula 1 at that time, so

Automobili Turismo e Sport, not to be confused with the German ATS Wheels company of later date.

the new team made its bow on Goodyear. Giacomelli was quicker than the Renaults at one time and the car ran reliably until a collision caused retirement in the race.

The unique 177 reappeared at Monza alongside the first new V12-engined 179 'wing-car'. With aerodynamic design by Robert Choulet of the SERA wind tunnel facility in Paris, this car was notable for its far-forward cockpit, lateral radiators instead of in-line in the pod sides as on the 177, and for its retention of inboard rear brakes, which impeded airflow from the underwing tunnels. Its oil tank was unusually high on the sloping rear of the monocoque rather than low down between engine and gearbox as conventional. The bulbous bullet nose and general shape were similar to the Arrows A2.

Two 179s ran in Canada with new Williams-like nose sections, slim and finned, and though Giacomelli didn't start, Brambilla was very nearly in the points.

Marlboro sponsored the team for 1980, when the 179 design was revised with outboard rear brakes and new rear suspension with the uprights buried deeper within the wheels to clear underwing airflow. Giacomelli was joined by Depailler to drive the cars, with new 179s chassis '3 and '4 racing in Argentina. The team lacked organization – a wheel change in Brazil costing 53 seconds – while much work was done on side pod aerodynamic development and stiffening the monocoques early in the year, adding 7 kg (some 15 lb) chassis weight, although new partially carbon-fibre body panels saved 30 kg (66 lb). Titanium suspension parts were introduced and at Long Beach chassis '3 and '4 appeared with reinforced footboxes, while at Monaco the fifth chassis emerged as spare with a new 12 kg lighter V12. In Spain, Brambilla joined the team as third driver, though the team reverted to a regular two-car entry thereafter.

New car '179/6' appeared at the British GP where Giacomelli raced it, this tub having carbon-fibre panels in the front of the tub and on top of the fuel cell section. Rear suspension mounts were more robust following breakages at Ricard and extra oil cooling was provided. The team had suffered several apparent suspension failures during the season, and on test at Hockenheim one seems to have been responsible for the death of Depailler, believed to have been in chassis '4.

Giacomelli ran alone in Germany and Austria until Brambilla joined him in Holland, the 179 producing something over 520 bhp. At Zandvoort chassis '7 emerged, numbered as chassis '4 to use existing paperwork, and featuring a lowered

engine. At Imola the new 1500 cc V8 turbo engine was on show in a corner of the Alfa Romeo garage while on circuit Giacomelli disputed second place in chassis '6, proving the 179s' increasing stature, now running flat rear body sections without flip-ups in front of the rear wheels. In Canada, Williams-like underwings were adopted and in the US GP at Watkins Glen 'Panda' Giacomelli qualified on pole and led convincingly until the ignition 'black box' failed.

Having just come to grips with sliding-skirt ground-effects, Autodelta suffered most from the sliding-skirt ban applied for 1981, following superbly fast winter testing at Ricard using skirts.

Andretti joined Giacomelli that season and the existing 179s were updated as lighter 179Cs, although Autodelta were always wary of disclosing chassis details and at best individual car identities are supposition. However, informed Italian sources consider Andretti normally raced '02, Giacomelli '03 early in the season though he took '01 for the Belgian race; a new car '04 became Andretti's regular mount for Monaco and Spain, where Giacomelli drove '02.

The team experimented hopelessly with hydro-pneumatic lowering suspensions and the immense jounce loads sustained by cars of this type proved too much for the 179Cs which were retired for rebuilding in mid-season. Old cars were raced at Dijon, Andretti taking '03 while Giacomelli was in old '06.

At Silverstone the revised 179C/D emerged, 5 cm lower overall and with new freeflow rear suspension. By the time of the Dutch GP, engineer Gérard Ducarouge had joined from Ligier, and the 179s ran Ligier-like side pods moving the centre of pressure rearwards. In Italy these underwings extended back to the driveshafts, but the cars showed little better form. A new carbon-fibre tub was now under development to add much-needed torsional rigidity.

This emerged at the start of 1982, largely designed and completely made by Roger Sloman's Advanced Composite Components company of Derby, England. Built in just three months the new *Tipo* 182 weighed only 535 kg (1179 lb) less ballast. The tub's underbelly was shaped into a venturi form and the bottom of the V12 engine had been narrowed by pump and pipe relocation to improve aerodynamic performance.

Ducarouge – working now in conjunction with engineer Pierluigi Corbari – had also redesigned the gearbox to place the gearchange on top out of the airstream, but the three new 182s in Brazil were troubled by oil surge. At Long Beach, new driver de Cesaris qualified on pole to widespread astonishment, but wrote off his car '182/01' against a wall after leading.

Extra oil tank baffling was added subsequently and a new tub, chassis '4, appeared for de Cesaris at Imola, demanding 40 kg ballast to reach the minimum limit. On the eve of Imola practice, a 179 fitted with the prototype V8 turbo engine was tested for the first time at Monza, driven by

Left: *One of racing's longest-serving engineers, Autodelta's Carlo Chiti's designs were impressive for speed of execution though rarely for competitiveness.* Top: *Giacomelli's new Alfa Romeo 177 flat-12 at Zolder 1979.*

Giorgio Francia. An oil pipe broke and it caught fire . . . Alfa Romeo luck.

The tub was still too wide, and a 20 cm narrower 182B moulding appeared in Belgium. This B-spec included revised bodywork and underwings but the parts were very slow to make due to demands on time by race preparation and turbo development. Eventually the team reverted to running the 192s in near-original form. Chassis '4 was written off by de Cesaris in Canada, where a new '182/5' emerged, tailored to the V12's now-reduced fuel consumption with 195 litres capacity instead of 200, but in this long, thirsty race it ran short.

The expensive Signor de Cesaris wrote off chassis '5 in France and '6 replaced it in Austria, where both Alfas were damaged in a startline fracas. By this time the Alfa V12 was clearly the most powerful normally aspirated 3-litre engine around, but a 1500 cc turbocharged unit was necessary to win.

The long-awaited Alfa Romeo 182T finally emerged at Monza, featuring a taller tank section behind the cockpit containing 250 litres of fuel instead of 195-200 litres. The oil tank moved at last from the tub top into the bell-housing adaptor, between engine and new turbocar gearbox. The team had achieved so little, however, that there were rumours it would fold at the end of that year.

It didn't quite happen that way. Instead, Paolo Pavanello's private Euroracing team of Milan took over from Autodelta, which would continue to manufacture their hardware. It was ailing, however, and would be absorbed at the end of 1984 though it continued to produce Euroracing's Formula 1 engines and gearboxes at Settimo Milanese.

Three ACC carbon-composite chassised 183T turbocars ran in Brazil driven by de Cesaris and Baldi, the engines using Italian-made Sylo turbochargers and the cars running on Michelin tyres. There had been little winter testing but they were of course revised to match the new flat-bottom rules, with shorter side pods.

The fourth new turbo chassis appeared at Ricard for Baldi after he creased '3 at Long Beach. When qualifying times were forfeit at Ricard due to an empty extinguisher – illegally saving weight – being discovered in one of the cars, Ducarouge was fired, moving to Lotus amid dark mutterings that his dismissal had been engineered by upstaged enemies within the team . . .

Luigi Marmiroli took his place under Chiti while

engine development forged ahead. At Monaco the Alfa V8s were running 2.2-bar boost at 11,500 rpm, and new engine heads appeared in Detroit – four engines at Montreal one week later being to the new specification. A brand new chassis '5 emerged at Silverstone, while parallel reduction in engine thirst and the adoption of pit-stop race strategy to refuel enabled chassis '3 and '4 to have their fuel cells literally cut down to 225 litres capacity. This lowered the centre of gravity and eased airflow onto the now vital rear wing. Rear suspension was revised and new turbo wastegate pipes emerged from the side pod tops. This 183T B-spec was applied to the latest chassis '5 by the time of the Dutch GP at Zandvoort.

For the European GP at Brands Hatch a pneumatically adjustable wastegate blow-off valve – controlling the pressure at which turbocharger boost vents to atmosphere instead of charging the engine – was introduced. De Cesaris crashed chassis '5 heavily in practice there but it was repaired for the race. Revised radiator designs appeared in South Africa, improving aerodynamic performance, while the latest chassis '6 remained at home, testing its new pushrod suspension at Balocco.

The cars had shown new promise, taking second places in Detroit and at Kyalami, while de Cesaris

had led at Spa for 18 extraordinary laps. For 1984 Euroracing Alfa Romeo reappeared with their cars wearing Benetton knitwear's green livery on new Luigi Marmiroli-designed carbon-chassised 184T cars. These slim, rounded-nacelle machines were driven by Patrese and Cheever. Two were available for the opening race at Rio, with '183T/6' as spare, the cars all featuring pushrod front suspension, pullrod rear. A 3-litre water tank for water injection into the engine was carried but there was no sign of the carbon-fibre head and sump covers which had been much remarked upon at the new model's Italian press debut. Ten 183T turbo engines were available to the team in Rio, and they looked determined to do well.

A new car, chassis '3 was available for Cheever at Zolder and a fourth car emerged at Hockenheim, but third place for Patrese at Monza and fourths for him at Kyalami and for Cheever at Rio were the best of another indifferent season.

Pavanello engineered Chiti's removal from the team with Alfa Romeo president Massacesi's approval in mid-season, his place being taken by *Ing*. Giovanni Tonti, fresh from the Lancia endurance team, but fortunes did not greatly improve.

For 1985 Euroracing Alfa Romeo lured British designer John Gentry away from the Toleman team whose 1984 car had handled notably well when driven by Senna. Gentry produced a new suspension layout in what became the Alfa Romeo 185T design, two of these new cars going to Rio for the start of the new season, accompanied by an old 184T, chassis '1, as spare. By that time Gentry had already moved on to join his former Toleman team driver Warwick at Renault Sport, and it was left to Tonti to develop the 185Ts towards competitiveness, and that proved impossible.

Three 185Ts were built, the third chassis making its debut for Cheever at Imola, but by mid-season Euroracing gave up in despair, junked the first two 185Ts, rebuilt the third to 184T-spec and wheeled out old 1984 chassis '2 and '3 for Cheever and Patrese to complete the season.

They achieved very little. Both drivers started all 16 Championship rounds, but Patrese finished only four times and Cheever only three, and these placings respectively were 9-9-10-11 and 10-11-17 so Alfa Romeo abjectly failed to score a single World Championship point.

Patrese enhanced his already ugly reputation for dangerous driving during this sad season, Cheever was unable to rise above the quality of

---

Top: Using side pods and skirts 'borrowed' from Williams, Giacomelli put Alfa 179 V12 '003' on pole for the 1980 US GP and led the race. Alfa had got it right – then sliding skirts were banned. Right: De Cesaris's moment of glory, Belgian GP '83, leading in Alfa's 183T V8 turbo '02'.

Chris Amon's torsion-bar suspended AF1 in the 1974 Spanish GP, Jarama, using conventional nose aerofoils instead of the nose-top wing originally intended.

Southgate had completed design work for a new Shadow DN9 before leaving that team. Inevitably his new Arrows FA1 was very similar because design thinking cannot change overnight. Southgate was a designer of vast experience – ex-Lola, Eagle, BRM and Shadow – and he had also worked with Team Lotus in 1976-77 at the height of their Lotus 78 development. Consequently, and inevitably, his new DN9/FA1 designs would be ground-effect 'wing-cars', though subtly different to the Lotus concept in using double venturi wing sections bolted one above the other on the flanks of their slim centre-tanked monocoque, although the air exit from the pods was hampered by outboard rear suspension and inboard rear brakes.

As it was, the first Arrows FA1 emerged before the remaining personnel at Shadow managed to complete their first DN9. Patrese easily qualified 'FA1/1' for the Brazilian GP and second time out in South Africa he qualified seventh on the grid and led for over 30 astonishing laps until his Cosworth engine failed. He notched Arrows' first Championship point with sixth place at Long Beach, and was sixth again at Monaco – the Arrows performing well on street circuits – followed by a rough and tough second in Sweden, holding off Peterson's delayed Lotus 79.

However, Shadow patron Don Nicholls had his revenge over Arrows that midsummer when Mr Justice Templeman found in his favour in the London High Court and declared that it would not have been possible for Arrows to complete their car within 60 days without the use of drawings which were Shadow's copyright. He declared 40 per cent of the components to have been copied and banned the FA1 from racing, causing the four FA1s built to be dismantled.

Southgate, meanwhile, had designed a replacement Arrows A1 in June and the first of the three built was completed at their Milton Keynes factory in less time than the original FA1! It appeared in Austria and Arrows did not miss a race.

Patrese was vilified by his fellow drivers for some rough tactics, although the assertion that he caused Peterson's fatal accident at Monza was proved groundless. He was still banned from the US GP, so responded by finishing strongly and placing fourth in Canada to end a hectic first season. The cars had won Warsteiner beer sponsorship and were finished in gold livery. From Kyalami, Stommelen had driven the second car, though with very poor results, often non-qualifying. Yet Arrows finished their maiden season ninth-equal in the Constructors' table, tied with Williams on 11 points.

his car and more than once the two drivers took each other off the road. The once mighty Alfa Romeo name had been back in Grand Prix racing on its own account for six full seasons by the end of 1985 without winning a race... two pole positions and one fastest lap representing their only superlative performances in all this time. And now they withdrew from Formula 1.

In World Championship terms, the Alfa Romeo team understandably scored no points in their 1979 part-season, but in 1980 they placed eleventh with only four points; in 1981 they were eighth with ten points, tied with the mere *Assemblatori* teams of Tyrrell and Arrows; in 1982 they were ninth with seven points, in 1983 improved to sixth with 18 points, but in 1984 dropped back to eighth with 11 points and in 1985 scored no points at all and so did not feature in the Formula 1 Constructors' Championship table – results which, in all conscience, were hardly worthy of the risk to Alfa Romeo's once revered name.

Amon

New Zealand driver Chris Amon made his name with Ferrari in 1967-69. He was almost legendarily unlucky, and his fortunes scarcely improved with March in 1970, nor Matra-Simca in 1971-72, nor Tecno in '73. While with Tecno he had insisted upon an improved chassis for their flat-12 engine, which sponsors Martini commissioned from Gordon Fowell and Alan Phillips's 'Goral' concern. Amon was impressed with engineer Fowell's work, despite the car's performance not being worth a light, and with backing from wealthy enthusiast John Dalton he commissioned a new Formula 1 car for 1974, to be 'like a Lotus 72'.

It was to use a slimline aluminium monocoque chassis with the fuel load concentrated between cockpit and Cosworth DFV engine, hip radiators, simple torsion bar suspension using de Carbon gas-filled front dampers and inboard brakes front and rear. Aerodynamic form was developed by a Professor Tom Boyce, with a scalloped nose profile topped by a shallow-strutted fuselage-width wing, claimed to prevent boundary layer build-up and enhance download, while a broad rear wing was supported by vast swept-back end plates.

One complete car and a spare tub were manufactured by John Thompson in Northampton and assembled in Amon's Reading workshop by former McLaren and Rondel team mechanic Richie Bray.

In an early test at Goodwood a titanium front stub axle broke and the car lost a wheel, crashing quite heavily. Amon was in any case unhappy with intense vibration under braking, possibly connected with torsional flexion in the front brakeshafts, and Amon AF1 chassis '01's only race would be the 1974 Spanish GP at Jarama in April, where it ran a conventional nose cone but broke a brakeshaft in the race. Using a new full-width bluff nose and outboard front brakes, Amon

qualified at Monaco, but opted not to start when a hub showed signs of incipient failure. The car was later taken to the Nürburgring for the German GP, where both Amon and Larry Perkins drove it in practice and the latter crashed, knocking off a wheel. Amon had a final try at Monza but failed again; by that time he felt uneasy whenever he sat in it, nothing was going right and the luckless project was abandoned.

Apollon

Swiss driver Loris Kessel, a former Brabham client, arrived for practice at Dijon during the 1977 French GP with the Apollon, which proved to be an elderly Williams FW03, rebodied and sprayed yellow. He was not allowed to run... See entry for Williams, pages 324-5.

Arrows

The Arrows Racing Team was founded by refugees from the Shadow Formula 1 project (see page 315) in the winter of 1977/78. Team manager Alan Rees, sponsorship entrepreneur Jack Oliver, designer Tony Southgate and draughtsman Dave Wass set up on their own with backing from Italian financier Franco Ambrosio. Anxious to qualify for membership of the Formula 1 Constructors' Association for 1979 they could only miss one non-European GP in '78. Since the Argentine and Brazilian races opened the calendar, they had to design and build their first car in just two months, in time for Rio on 29 January.

Piola's sketch of Tony Southgate's original Arrows FA1 shows its twin ground-effects sidewing attachments amongst other details. This was the design subsequently judged to infringe Shadow copyright.

The existing cars were modified as A1Bs for 1979, chassis '3 for Patrese, '2 for Mass, with new rear suspension, side pods, wings, skirts and larger brakes, but as the year progressed the thinly financed team was under strain, their cars heavy and out of date while Southgate developed a new second generation ground-effect car, the A2.

This remarkable heavily faired-in, bullet-nosed device had its engine and gearbox angled upwards to allow full-width aerodynamic underfloor sections to be fitted. The A2s appeared at Dijon, 'A2/1' for Patrese, 'A2/2' for Mass, but they never handled well. In Holland the A2s used revised front suspension and modified rear wings. Patrese crashed '1 heavily and its tub had to be rejigged, while the cars were simply uncompetitive. Mass drove a modified 'A1/5' in Canada in preference to his A2, but failed to qualify in any case.

The drastic measure of angling the entire engine and gearbox, so the gearbox end plate was some 3 in. higher than conventional, had raised the car's centre of gravity. This move coincided with the insertion of tight chicanes on many circuits to slow the cars and the A2, tailored to high-speed

courses, proved reluctant to change direction tidily. Like the Lotus 80, the Arrows A2 porpoised badly and the experiment had to be abandoned. During the year three more A1Bs had been produced, followed by the unloved brace of A2s, and Arrows again finished ninth in the Constructors' table but with only five points against the 11 of their maiden season. The miscalculation of 1979 was put right with the A3 wing-car introduced in Argentina, 1980, when Patrese was second quickest in the unofficial Saturday morning session and everyone sat up and took notice. The A3 had the shortest wheelbase in Formula 1 and the narrowest rear track after the Ensign, its gearbox was shrouded-in to reduce drag and ease airflow away from the underwing tunnels, but Arrows never seemed to appreciate fully the necessity for a skirt system which sealed adequately both against the road surface and within its own skirt-box, to prevent spillage infilling the low-pressure area which the venturi surfaces were struggling to create to download the car.

In South Africa a new 'A3/3' emerged for Mass, with a 4 cm wider front track to ease airflow into the side pods, and at Long Beach 'A3/4' appeared, with angled suspension for a longer wheelbase, though this handled poorly and the team refitted standard suspension. Patrese shunted chassis '1 in Belgium and chassis '5 was completed for him to race at Monaco, Southgate altering its weight bias by moving the extinguisher bottle and other components.

The team appreciated its aerodynamic prob-

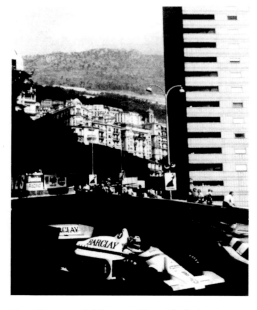

lems. The A3s understeered all season, and in midsummer Dave Wass spent time at the Imperial College wind tunnel, testing quarter-scale models to find an answer. At the British GP the A3s tested under-nose skirts *à la* Lotus 80 to find more front-wheel adhesion, but the work was rushed and failed in its purpose. Longer wheelbase form was tried again to load up the front end, but late in the year Southgate left abruptly, leaving Wass as chief designer. A sixth A3 was completed for the North American tour ending the season and Arrows found themselves seventh-equal in the Championship with 11 points, just like 1978. But now all eyes were on 1981, and the skirt ban regulations.

Over the winter Wass decided the best fix within the team's now very restricted budget would be 'to destroy the rear suspension, make its adhesion as poor as the front's so that at least the car would come back into balance'.

He reduced rear camber change by some 60 per cent, and in South Africa in FOCA's last skirted race – refused Championship status by FISA – Patrese qualified on row three and finished sixth, while at Long Beach for the first 'clearance car' race, with everyone running on similar Michelin tyres following a temporary Goodyear withdrawal, he promptly qualified on *pole* and led the race until his fuel pressure faltered.

The car was now in balance and competitive, Patrese finishing third in Brazil but as hydro-pneumatic suspension lowering devices became *de rigueur* following Brabham's lead, Arrows found themselves back with skirt problems and fell off the tightrope once more.

Second driver Stohr was unable to contribute much and at Zolder he rammed his stalled teammate's car at the start, crushing chief mechanic Dave Luckett between the two cars in a gruesome startline misunderstanding, though Luckett happily recovered. In France Patrese ran chassis '5 with a new Arrows-cased gearbox which was some 10 cm narrower with high change linkage out of the airstream, and there were new flatter uprights.

By this time Goodyear were prepared to return to racing, Michelin became alarmed at the prospect of servicing too many teams to remain competitive, so attempted to palm off Arrows to the Ecclestone/Avon tyre supplies company. Rees and Oliver of Arrows responded by refusing the offer they had been made and going to Pirelli instead, starting with the British GP.

For the rest of that season Arrows were handicapped by poor grip, and by Pirelli's physical weight penalty, each tyre scaling 12 kg (26 lb) more than the comparable Michelin, and 15 kg (33 lb) more than Goodyear. In Holland each of three Arrows A3s on hand had different rear suspension sets to make their tyres work and by the end of the year, when Jacques Villeneuve (Gilles' brother) failed to qualify in Canada and the US, there seemed little point in going to the races with so

Top: Unsuccessful Arrows A2s, with distinctive aerodynamics, Zandvoort '79. Centre: Patrese's Dave Wass-developed Arrows A3 clearance car (with dislodged nose wing) at Jarama, 1981, during the team's period of greatest promise. Above: Boutsen's Wass-designed turbocharged BMW-engined Arrows A8 at Monaco 1985.

little chance of success. Even so, the good start to the season gave the team 10 Constructors' Championship points, eighth-equal with Tyrrell and Alfa Romeo.

Wass designed new A4 cars for 1982, three being ready in time for Brazil, where they were driven by Henton and Baldi. Arrows were living hand to mouth, picking up often local sponsors wherever they could. Wass aimed for ultimate downforce in his A4 wing-car 'but we still ignored the necessity for really sophisticated sealing systems and we ran into constant porpoising troubles'.

New Pirelli tyres, 6 cm narrower than before, improved the cars in Holland, where they were driven notably by Surer and showed higher top speed and lighter steering, but a new A5 – effectively a Williams FW08 copy – emerged at Dijon in the 'Swiss' GP, using an aluminium honeycomb tub and pullrod suspension, very small and light enough. Wass consciously designed it with some 30 per cent less download than the A4 and in practice it proved far easier to control, so lapped faster, Baldi and Surer taking turns to drive it.

Five A4s had been built, chassis '2 being written off in Surer's Kyalami accident, while the A5 remained unique. The team placed tenth in the Championship, with five points from Baldi's two sixth places, in Holland and Austria, plus Surer's fifth in Canada and yet another sixth in Germany . . . very much the poor men picking up crumbs from the rich man's table.

The winter of 1982/83 saw the flat-bottom rule change and Wass designed new A6 cars to suit, having returned to Goodyear tyres. They would perform better but now the age of the Cosworth engine had passed and a turbocharged engine was vital for success, and Arrows on their slender financing had none available. 'We lost on horse-power, everywhere . . .'

Former World Champion Jones drove for them briefly at Long Beach but they could not afford him long-term. At Imola, shorter underwings appeared in an effort to save the gearbox too much heat embarrassment and at the end of the year a new pullrod rear suspension was tried. Arrows were again tenth in the table, with four meagre points from Surer's early-season fifth at Long Beach, and two sixth places at Rio and Imola. Chico Serra drove the second car in early season, replaced subsequently by Thierry Boutsen who finished seventh in both Detroit and Montreal.

The unique A5 from 1982 had been updated to A6 specification and was used up to Montreal, while four true A6s, numbered '2-5', were built.

In the winter of 1983/84 Oliver negotiated use of BMW four-cylinder turbocharged engines for the coming season, but Arrows had to accept them direct from BMW Motorsport rigged with ATS team standard radiators, intercoolers and turbochargers, far behind Brabham quasi-works team specification. This was a disappointment which severely constrained design of the A7 turbocharged cars, and since the engine deal had only been completed at the last minute, design was rushed and aluminium honeycomb monocoques were used again, though with a carbon-fibre inner moulding. Wass and the team were now entering an entirely new world of turbocharged power and loadings, and with more time a moulded carbon tub would have been developed, as it was in fact for 1985.

In the A7-BMW cars they tried to keep the A6 suspension, because it had worked well, 'but a Cosworth isn't a turbo' and this proved another enforced misjudgement which would not have happened given more time to test and to think. The A7s ran with pullrod front suspension, rocker rear, and made great use of Italian Brembo brakes before AP balanced calipers reappeared.

Arrows finished ninth in the Championship with six points, all but one from Boutsen's Cosworth-powered sixth in Rio and fifth at Imola, and his A7 turbo fifth in Austria. The faithful Surer was sixth behind his team-mate at the Österreichring and earlier in the season, when still Cosworth-powered, he managed three consecutive finishes in the first three GPs, 7-9-8.

Arrows A6 chassis '2 was written off in a start-line shunt at Detroit, '4 and '5 being the others raced in this year, while four A7-BMWs replaced them during the season. Dave Wass embarked on a new moulded carbon-composite A8-BMW design for 1985, using pushrod front suspension, pullrod rear, the Heini Mader-prepared BMW four-cylinder turbo engines' exhaust system rising through the rear suspension à la Brabham.

Three A8s had been completed by the time the season opened in Rio, chassis '4' following for Boutsen in Portugal, '5' emerging as a spare, raced by Berger in Austria. Both drivers started all 16 GPs, and Arrows' reliability was quite good, Boutsen finishing 12 times and Berger nine. Boutsen inherited second place in the fuel-consumption derby at Imola, was fourth in Germany and sixth in successive races at Brands Hatch and South Africa ending the year. His other finishes were 11-9-9-7-9-8-9-10. Berger scored points at the end of the year with fifth at Kyalami and sixth in Australia, placing 13-11-8-7-9-7-10 elsewhere, so Arrows' improvement came just as the season was ending. Until that time BMW had been disappointed that the Milton Keynes-based team had not performed as well as they felt their customer engine merited and it was touch-and-go whether they would retain use of the German unit for 1986.

In fact Arrows continued to run its A8 cars, chassis '2', '4', '5' and '6' through 1986 and introduced a new 'A9/1' at Hockenheim. The new A9 was designed by Dave Wass to suit new 195-litre tank regulations. A gearbox inboard of the final-drive was adopted for the new car, aiming at a well-balanced long-wheelbase chassis – 100 mm longer than the A8's. The gearbox was based on Hewland DGB components and Wass developed it as an easily detachable assembly to permit easy ratio-changing, its oil feeds incorporating dry-break quick-release couplings. The gearbox itself was integral within the otherwise conventional unified oil tank/spacer. Wass's A9 carbon-composite monocoque was designed with access to British Aerospace facilities and it was intended that BAe should make it. However, industrial trouble at BAe Wythenshawe delayed the programme, and the prototype tub was finally moulded instead by Advanced Composite Technology, Roger Sloman's ACC company's new racing subsidiary – which explains the appearance of references to both ACC and ACT in these pages. Pushrod suspension featured front and rear, slatted radiator side ducts were a prominent feature as was the tall head-fairing immediately behind the cockpit, which fell away most abruptly into a much lower engine cover to clear airflow towards the rear wing.

The team's 1986-season drivers were Thierry Boutsen and the unfortunate Marc Surer, whose F1 career was ended in an horrific rally accident in Germany, while driving a Ford RS200. His navigator was killed and the popular Swiss badly burned. He was replaced at Arrows by Christian

Reminiscent in profile of a Soviet nuclear submarine, the turbocharged Arrows-BMW A9 on its debut at Hockenheim, 1986, driven by Thierry Boutsen. Designer Dave Wass adopted an inboard gearbox betwixt engine and final-drive to clean up rear-end aerodynamics, resulting in a long wheelbase.

Danner, who had started the season with Osella.

Boutsen had the frustrating experience of finishing no fewer than four times in seventh place, just outside the World Championship points, at Jerez, Imola, Monza and Mexico City. His only other classified finishes were eighth in Monaco and tenth at Estoril – no points at all for himself or his team. Marc Surer competed only in the first five GPs, retiring at Rio and Jerez, then achieving a modest hat-trick of ninth places, at Imola, Monaco and Spa. Danner then took over the second Arrows from Canada forward, and the best of his four finishes was sixth – in the points! – in Austria, highlight of a desperate year for the USF&G-sponsored team.

The A9's inboard gearbox proved troublesome upon its debut at Hockenheim and was replaced by a conventional transmission for the stub-end of this very poor season, in which Arrows had scored just that single, solitary Championship point.

Ross Brawn – ex-FORCE, the Haas-Lola team – took over Arrows chassis design for 1987, the team having been reinvigorated with extra sponsorship. His new A10 tubs were made by Arrows themselves at Milton Keynes, with mouldings reinforced by aluminium-honeycomb filler. A redesigned DGB-internals transmission bolted up to the latest Megatron-BMW upright four-cylinder turbo engine, a redesigned semi-load-bearing sump casting permitting the power unit's bearer cradle to be simplified and lightened.

In planview the A10s had a pronounced 'McLaren tail' feature with the side pods waisting in sharply to fair through the rear suspension. The prototype A10 was shaken down at Donington in March, just before departure for Rio. Hitco carbon disc/carbon pad brakes were replaced by French SEP discs from Imola. Five chassis were built for new drivers Derek Warwick and Eddie Cheever, a strong and reliable pairing, not quite from the top drawer but both dependable journeyman drivers of great experience and high ability.

Cheever would be classified as a finisher seven times, including fourth at Spa and two sixth places, at Detroit and Estoril. Warwick had six finishes, his best being fifth in the British GP and a sixth in Hungary. He was also lucky to escape without serious injury in a heavy accident at Mexico City, which destroyed chassis 'A10/4'. Arrows ended the season sixth-equal in the Constructors' table, tied with Tyrrell on 11 points.

Updated A10B-spec chassis were used in 1988, chassis 1-4, the team falling back on the old 1987 chassis A10/2 and '5 after Ricard as spare cars.

The 1990 Footwork Arrows A11B – seen here at Montreal – combined the Cosworth-Ford DFR V8 engine with an updated 1989 chassis design in what was merely a transitional season awaiting delivery of the team's promised Footwork-Porsche V12.

Cheever and Warwick drove again for their second full season together. Cheever finished seven times, 8-7-6-11-7-8-3 – best results being the Championship points-scoring sixth in Mexico and third at Monza. Warwick's record, meanwhile, was 4-9-4-5-7-6-6-7-7-4-4 – those four fourth places at Rio, Monaco, Monza and Estoril being backed by fifth in Mexico and sixth at Silverstone to give Derek 15 points, seventh-equal in the Drivers' Championship. This good, consistent season was rewarded by a shared fifth place for the team in the Constructors' Cup. Remember, this was the no-competition 2.5-bar final year of turbocharged Formula 1 racing . . . but otherwise it was a very sound season for the USF&G-sponsored team with its BMW-derived four-cylinder Megatron turbo engines reaching the end of their life.

Winter weight-saving of *c.* 23 kg included carbon-fibre clutch and aluminium flywheel, titanium axles, carbon plies removed from Kevlar body panels, and smaller radiators (possible since reduced 2.5-bar boost rejected less heat), together with titanium axles and other measures.

Heini Mader's Swiss concern prepared the Megatron engines with Gerhard Schuman, ex-BMW, supervising. But, with mechanical and electronic parts being made no more, supply became a problem.

Under 1.5 bar less boost than '87, the engines' mechanical reliability improved, 'til a mid-season compression hike reintroduced occasional failures. The elderly Bosch-BMW electro-mechanical injection and management systems could not be mapped so thoroughly as more modern rivals, but efficient vapourization from very high pressure PI gave good economy.

The A10B proved better than the old A10. For much of the year the four-cylinder engine consistently popped its 2.5-bar preset FISA valve prematurely – at around 2.4 bar. A pressure pulse generated within the plenum chamber was to blame. The pop-off valve was so placed as to coincide with this pulse-wave's peak, hence its premature opening. Discovery and correction instantly gave an extra 20-30 bhp for Monza. Starting practice for the first time with full-power, well-sorted cars, drivers Cheever and Warwick had done well.

Marc Surer at Ricard-Castellet, 1980, in Brunner-Wardrop designed ATS D4 '03' – a Williams FW07 lookalike, sliding skirts clearly visible against the road surface.

The team ended the Constructors' Championship level with both Williams and March on 20 points, their best total for years . . .

For 1989, Arrows joined the ranks of customer 3.5-litre Cosworth DFR/DFZ V8 engines, in their case prepared by Brian Hart – in parallel with those for Tyrrell and Onyx. The Arrows A11 looked impressive early in the new season powered by the DFR but fortunes slumped as the year progressed.

Five of the new Cosworth-engined A11s were produced, the first three new at Rio with chassis '1 spare car, '2 for Warwick and '3 as Cheever's regular race chassis, while number '4 emerged new for Cheever at Ricard and '5 for Warwick at Suzuka. Martin Donnelly drove 'A11/2' in the French GP in place of Warwick, finishing 12th.

Warwick was fifth in both the first two GPs at Rio and Imola, but then followed a string of four retirements. Cheever's record in those same events read R-9-7-7-3-R, his third place at Phoenix thanks to attrition ahead. Later in the season Warwick achieved three sixth places – at Hockenheim, Spa and Suzuka, while Cheever's best was fifth in Hungary, but he also failed to qualify when troubles beset the team at Monza. Seventh place, with 13 points, in the Constructors' table was an indifferent result.

For Arrows, 1990 was to be a bridging season. In January it was announced that the team had been acquired by its major sponsor, the Japanese Footwork Corporation, and in February a $40 million contract was confirmed by Porsche to build an exclusive new V12 F1 engine for Footwork Arrows' 1991 programme. Consequently, with efforts concentrated towards the season of '91 they relied upon developed versions of their 1990 cars and tried to achieve results by simple reliability.

Design of the revised A11B cars was credited to James Robinson, working with ex-McLaren and Onyx engineer Alan Jenkins and Paul Bowen. A taller central fuel cell was now incorporated behind the cockpit, replacing the previous multi-tank system involving cells around and beneath the driver's legs. Taller, narrower side pods featured in an aerodynamic re-suiting, and rear suspension had also been revised.

Drivers were to be Michele Alboreto – now in rapid decline – and Alex Caffi, although his place was taken by Bernd Schneider in the opening race at Rio. Alboreto actually failed to qualify three times, in succession at Imola and Monte Carlo, and finally at Adelaide ending this poor season. He retired five times and his finishing record otherwise read 10-17-10-12-13-12*-9-10 – no points scores. Caffi missed Rio and Jerez (after crashing heavily at Estoril). He also failed to qualify for three races, at Imola, Mexico and Adelaide (where no Arrows made the race to justify the long trip). However, Caffi retired only twice, and finished fifth in Monaco to notch the team's only Championship points of the season, securing Arrows' last place in the 1990 Constructors' table – ninth-equal with Brabham. Caffi's other eight classified finishes were 8-7 (at Silverstone) 9-9-10-9-13*-9. Clearly the Caffi/Arrows A11B combination's rightful level was ninth or thereabouts . . . and the Arrows story effectively reached its low-key end . . . See entry for Footwork, page 273.

ATS

This team bears no relationship to *Automobili Turismo e Sport*, also known as ATS, which flopped in Formula 1 in 1963. This ATS is a German specialist wheel company headed by one Hans Gunther Schmid. An enthusiastic but autocratic man, he decided to promote his wheel company by entering Formula 1 in 1977, buying the Penske PC4 cars upon the American-managed team's withdrawal from Grand Prix racing.

One car, chassis 'PC4-002', was driven by Jean-Pierre Jarier on the team's debut at Long Beach in April '77, qualifying comfortably in midfield and immediately scoring a Championship point by finishing in sixth place.

The three Geoff Ferris-designed PC4s completed

Right: *Up with the action – Alan Jones in the 1985 Beatrice-Lola at Monza, Teddy Mayer beyond him, Hart turbo engine behind.* Below right: *Silvio Moser's 1970 Bellasi-Cosworth special.*

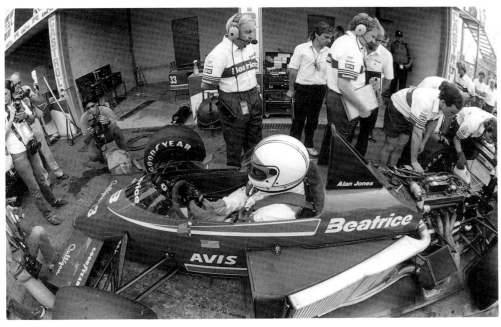

a staccato season with a variety of drivers, but Schmid determined to have his own cars built for 1978. He bought March's Formula 1 interests and their membership of FOCA, and Robin Herd of March developed the existing Penske PC4 design for the German to form the ATS HS-1, later further modified by John Gentry who also evolved a new wing-car design known as the ATS D1. Team drivers included Mass, Jarier, Bleekemoelen and Rosberg but the Bicester-based team found it difficult even to qualify and had a pitiful year, even worse than March's swansong effort in 1977.

Shortly after the D1's debut in practice at Zandvoort, Mass broke his leg testing it at Silverstone, but Rosberg subsequently gave the team some hope with better performances in the D1 in the North American races ending the season.

For 1979 Fred Opert took on team management, and ex-Ferrari aerodynamicist and engineer Giacomo Caliri designed D1 revisions in his Fly Studio bureau. One car would be entered for H-J Stuck to drive. Schmid had rapidly established a reputation as a hire and fire merchant, making few friends. Caliri was out by the time of the Belgian GP but Stuck wrestled his ill-handling car throughout the year, best placing being fifth in the wet final race at Watkins Glen, where the tall German's wet-weather skills did the team proud and they found the reliability for him to finish.

For 1980 ATS confirmed their position as one of the real 'no-hoper' teams. Gustav Brunner and Tim Wardrop were responsible for design and construction of two D3 cars, followed by six D4s which were effective Williams FW07 look-alikes. They were driven notably by Surer and Lammers; Surer broke his legs at Kyalami but Lammers qualified third quickest at Long Beach to widespread amazement. When Surer returned, Lammers moved to Ensign and ATS ended the season as consistent midfield qualifiers but scored no Championship points.

In 1981 the Hervé Guilpin-designed HGS1 appeared, in which the ABBA-backed Swedish drummer-cum-racing driver Slim Borgudd managed to finish sixth at Silverstone!

Schmid persevered in 1982 with two HGS models modified by Don Halliday and now known as the model D5. Two entries were made regularly for Manfred Winkelhock and the Chilean Salazar who was fifth in the small-field race at Imola, while Winkelhock was fifth at Rio.

For 1983 Schmid won use of the BMW four-cylinder turbo engine through BMW's interest in his driver Winkelhock who had formerly shone on BMW power in Formula 2. Gustav Brunner designed a neat new moulded carbon-fibre monocoque pioneering integral outer body shape and cockpit coaming to take the engine, designated D6 in the ATS system, and three such chassis would be built. Winkelhock always showed promise but the team's destructively capricious management repeatedly ruined his chances, making less of the car than it was clearly capable of. Again they scored no points.

For 1984 BMW stood by ATS but it was an even worse year and the team withdrew after BMW refused to support them again in 1985. 'D6-03' had been team spare until written off by Winkelhock in Monaco practice, and two new D7s followed for Winkelhock and Berger.

In Championship terms, Schmid's team had scored no points at all in 1978, 1980 and 1983; they managed two points for eleventh place in the 1979 table, one point for twelfth-equal (with the far less ambitious Theodore team) in 1981, and four points for eleventh place in 1982. It had been an expensive exercise, with minimal return for the intense effort which Schmid's ever-changing staff had unstintingly expended over eight virtually fruitless seasons.

Beatrice-Lola

After relinquishing his interest in McLaren International, American Teddy Mayer developed a CART track-racing operation for the US, using proprietary March cars with Cosworth DFX turbocharged V8 engines. The team performed quite well, technical preparation and direction being controlled by the other former American McLaren director, Tyler Alexander. They missed Formula 1, however, and during 1984 developed plans to return to the World Championship series with a new British-based operation and massive US backing. This came from entrepreneur Carl Haas – for many years Lola Cars' US concessionaire – and from the major Beatrice Corporation, a fast-growing conglomerate with interests in foods, various types of manufacturing and also owners of the Avis car rental empire.

Mayer set up FORCE (Formula One Race Car Engineering) to build the new car, designed by ex-Williams engineer Neil Oatley. Haas's Lola interests emerged in Team Haas-Lola who were to race the car, although Lola Cars had virtually no part in its design. Long-term it would employ a new 1500 cc turbocharged Ford engine developed by Cosworth Engineering in Northampton, England. Short-term, just to get the show on the road in '85, Hart four-cylinder engines were employed.

Former World Champion Alan Jones was persuaded out of retirement to drive for the team and two slender carbon-monocoque Beatrice-Lola-Hart THL-1 cars emerged in the final four GPs of 1985, '001 being the spare car raced by Jones – very briefly – at Monza and Brands Hatch, and '002 being his race car for Kyalami, where he non-started, and Adelaide. Hart engine fragility prevented any serious progress, the three races ended in three retirements, and into 1986 the project remained an unknown quantity. See entry for Haas-Lola, page 273.

Bellasi

The Italian Formula 3 constructor Vittorio Bellasi was approached by Swiss owner/driver Silvio Moser to build him a Cosworth-engined Formula 1 car for 1970, when a rule change demanding metal fuel tank sheathing logically dictated use of a monocoque to replace the old tubular spaceframe cars. Moser had performed quite well in Charles Vogele's ex-works Brabhams, and now Bellasi made him a bulky, heavy but workmanlike riveted aluminium monocoque to pick up suspension based on his old Repco Brabham BT24's. The new car was undistinguished, Moser failing to qualify in its debut at Zandvoort 1970 and not making the race until Austria on 16 August,

where he started last on the grid and retired with a holed radiator. At Monza he failed to qualify again and did not reappear until the Italian GP 1971, when the podgy Bellasi again failed to qualify. It survives intact today, in the Donington Collection, near Derby, England.

Benetton

The renamed Toleman team's drivers for 1986 were Gerhard Berger and Teo Fabi, and three new cars were ready for the start of the season, the final chassis being completed during the week prior to the opening Brazilian GP and tested by Maurizio Sandro Sala. Ultimately, seven of these B186 cars would be built, chassis '4 being written off during practice at Montreal. And the season saw Benetton begin to soar . . .

Initially the short-notice, minimum testing time change from Hart turbo to upright BMW M12/13 power created problems, despite both turbocharged engines being simple in-line four-cylinder designs.

Engineer Rory Byrne: 'We only started designing the B186 in the last week of October '85, wind tunnel research, everything.' The early part of the season was devoted merely to making sufficient parts to go racing, while the cars ran as built until after Ricard.

The powerful, top-endy BMW's chassis demands were quite new, as evidenced at Rio where the cars were quickest on the straight, but only midfielders on lap time. The team had exclusive use of the MoD wind tunnel at Shrivenham, and a subtle but total reworking of chassis and aerodynamic configuration was evolved there. Only then could aerodynamic and fundamental set-up changes be phased in; new underbody, front and rear wing systems and front and rear suspensions were all redesigned to harness BMW's power, and it was not until the Österreichring that they could all be combined into one complete package.

There Benetton could at last use all the available power, their Pirelli tyres proved best and at

Above: *Gerhard Berger's Benetton-BMW B186, fifth in the 1986 Italian GP.* Below right: *The replacement Benetton-Ford TEC B187 at Jerez, 1987, demonstrating its far-forward driving position, centre fuel cell, engine location etc.*

last a Rory Byrne Formula 1 design really showed world class.

So much in fact that the B186s seemed set for a stunning 1-2 until Fabi ran over a bump leaving the chicane, and the engine over-revved as his rear wheels bounced clear. Then Berger agonizingly suffered a battery fault due to porosity in a plate-to-terminal connection.

In contrast, Benetton's least competitive race had been Montreal.

Seven tubs were built, '04 being written off at Montreal, two others being rebuilt after serious damage, one in a fire at Silverstone and the other during brake-testing at Croix-en-Ternois.

With Brabham crippled, Benetton carried Pirelli hopes high. The Italian tyre company's pre-season testing was wrecked by Brabham problems and Benetton's lateness, but the Witney team caught up fast. Pirelli were competitive early on, and Byrne felt that if his chassis had been sorted out that early in the year, they could well have excelled. The Pirellis were most effective on rough surfaces; smooth tracks were not their *forte*. But Pirelli made fine constructional changes to assist Benetton's escape from handling troubles, and while there were some problems with having sufficient tyres available to service the team's needs, what was at that time Pirelli's farewell season in Formula 1 saw them perform very well . . . but in effect for the *wrong* teams.

Berger's season began 6-6-3-R-10, then came five retirements interrupted by tenth at Hockenheim. After his superb showing in Austria he then finished seventh, was fifth at Monza, retired in Portugal and then won non-stop in Mexico City to notch the team's maiden Grand Prix victory. Retirement followed in Adelaide but the Benetton-BMW had proved its promise.

Little Teo Fabi, meanwhile, had a record ruined by 11 retirements, his finishes reading 10-5-7-5-10 at Rio, Jerez, Spa, Estoril and Adelaide respectively. The team took sixth place in the Constructors' Championship, with 19 points, behind Williams, McLaren, Lotus, Ferrari and Ligier.

The deal for Benetton's F1 team to convert from upright BMW four-cylinder to Cosworth-Ford V6 for '87 was not done until mid-October '86. They came immediately under intense pressure to have a team of all-new cars ready for Rio opening the new season, but in one respect at least it was a real pleasure to make the change.

During 1987, the fine form shown by Rory Byrne's always distinctively different-looking F1 cars seemed to emphasize the mistake Ford had made in 1986 by entrusting their Type TEC V6 turbo engine to the ill-starred FORCE Haas-Lola team. That largely wasted season was one they could ill afford as their brilliantly packaged (for a 120-degree) little engine suddenly found its life abbreviated by FISA rule changes.

After years with in-line four-cylinder engines from Hart and BMW, now they were dealing for the first time with a proper ground-up racing engine concept. It offered the great advantage of symmetry, a block properly stressed to act as a load-bearing chassis member. At last here was an engine tailored to integrate perfectly into a modern F1 chassis design. For the second time in two seasons, the Witney team had to build new relationships with a new engine supplier but it worked well and jointly they made rapid progress.

Very little even in detail could be carried over from the Benetton-BMW B186 into the new Ford-powered B187. Four cars had been built and run in time for the Brazilian GP – including 'B187/1' sadly written off in the pre-GP Rio test. As the season progressed, nine subtly T-section B187 tubs were built, their noses 15 cm narrower than any other contemporary car's. Chassis '8 was written off at Monaco while two more were withdrawn from service under the team's normal component-lifing programme.

After the Monaco shunt had identified a rather brittle area in the unusually slender tub, the laminate-spec was changed to add strength to subsequent mouldings. An all-round – front and rear – suspension geometry change was introduced at Ricard, the system running effectively unchanged thereafter.

In horsepower terms Cosworth-Ford's turbo V6 was always quite competitive but early on its throttle response was relatively poor. This was improved in time for Detroit when the Garrett turbocharger system was altered. Ford maintained a float of about 25 of the engines, including development units, but several were damaged early in the year and in mid-season, with some races only a week apart, Benetton had barely sufficient V6s to do the job.

A change of Mobil fuel in time for the Austrian GP helped greatly improve engine reliability, and the cars then became most competitive. They nearly always qualified very strongly, despite their engine's configuration as two individual in-line three-cylinder units – with exhaust systems not interconnected bank-to-bank – which dictated use of two separate FISA pop-off valves, with their doubled leakage area, 'which meant we couldn't run the valves open in qualifying, because that would simply over-speed the turbos . . .'.

Interestingly, the other 'two-valve' V6 team, McLaren, had been looking enviously at Benetton's qualifying pace, wondering how they could possibly wangle such horsepower with twin pop-off valves! That considered, the Benetton-Ford's qualifying ability looks even more impressive . . .

Their qualifying form dipped at Monaco, where the early-season throttle-delay really bit, but the improved system became available next time out on the similar circuit at Detroit, where they shone. On medium-speed circuits like the Hungaroring and Estoril they struggled to maintain adequate tyre temperatures, being always notably light on their tyres, and although Goodyear's control covers quite impressed they would have run softer compounds if they'd had the choice.

Thierry Boutsen was teamed with Fabi for the year. The Belgian's record included eight retirements, his finishes reading 5-7-4-4-5-14-5-3, while Fabi retired nine times, otherwise finishing 8-5-6-3-7-4-5. Boutsen's third place was in Adelaide, his two fourths in Hungary and Austria. Fabi's third came in Austria, his fourth in Portugal.

Benetton placed fifth in the final 1987 Constructors' Championship table with 28 points, behind Williams, McLaren, Lotus and Ferrari.

Tragically, Ford compounded its error of placing

continued on page 241

Previous page: The right racing line demonstrated by three very different designs at Monaco 1976: Lauda's Ferrari 312T2 leading the rush from *Mirabeau Inférieur* into *Le Portier* from Ronnie Peterson's shoe-string budget F2-based March 761, Regazzoni's second Ferrari and the Tyrrell-twin P34 six-wheelers of Depailler and Scheckter. *Above:* Gordon Murray's Brabhams were all beautifully built, few more popular with the team than the 1975 BT44B seen here, showing off its broad nose with horizontal sacrificial 'air-splitter' protruding forward which prompted early Brabham ground-effects experiments, split water radiators inside, rising-rate pullrod suspension, and pyramid section tub. Black grip on tub side was a hand-hold so the driver could lever himself out of cockpit, otherwise his hands would just slide down the sloping surface! Goodyear treaded tyres are unusual in such a sunny scene. The air-hose is evidence that compressed-air power tools were gaining popularity. *Right:* The Right One – in this case Lauda's Ferrari '312T2-030' hounding Hans Stuck Jnr's Martini-backed Brabham-Alfa Romeo 'BT45/1' down into the Old Station Hairpin at Monaco, 1977. The Martini-Brabham's flat-12 Alfa engine demanded a lot of fuel and cooling.

Above: New dawn, Mario Andretti's Lotus 78 'wing car' heralded the harnessing of ground-effect aerodynamics in Formula 1 during 1977. Here, with the improved Type 79 (*right*) under development back home, Mario is on his way to winning the 1978 Argentine GP at Buenos Aires in '78/3'. The 78's underwings generated their download rather far forward due to protruding wing tanks, engine exhaust and outboard rear suspension obstructing side pod air-exit, and grip from its wide-track front end always overwhelmed the rear. The Lotus 79, seen here with Andretti at home and the Guv'nor, Colin Chapman, alongside, had over-the-gearbox exhausts, all its fuel in a single tub tank, centred its download further aft and went as well as it looked in 1978. The following year showed up its system and stiffness inadequacies.

Tony Matthews 1981

Left: Scheckter's 1979 Ferrari 312T4 'lawn-mower' which made effective use of overbody air to achieve aerodynamic performance when Ferrari were increasingly confused by new ground-effects technology. Note clean airflow onto front wing, around cockpit and over low rear deck to that highly cambered, low frontal area wing. Some pressure loss was inevitable on the wing centre due to masking by high cowl ahead, hence Ferrari's increase in wing-chord there to increase active area in the blind spot. *Below:* Ultimate expression of the ground-effects car era, Alan Jones actually unsticking his Williams 'FW07/7' for a change, Long Beach 1980. Over the hump here the left-side skirt with its abrade-resistant edge can be seen just clearing the dipping roadway. The aerial is a timing trigger. *Below left:* Tony Matthews' artistry unveils some of the secrets of the 1981 Williams FW07C 'clearance car'.

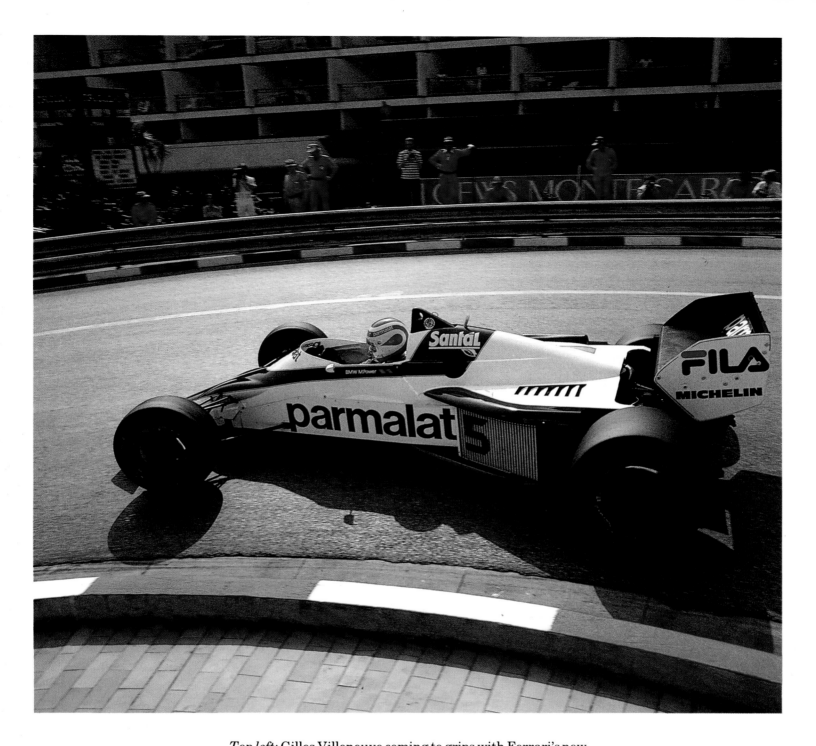

Top left: Gilles Villeneuve coming to grips with Ferrari's new 1.5-litre 126C2 turbocharged cars, in this case '055, at a rainy Kyalami, South African GP, 1982. The Postlethwaite-designed aluminium honeycomb cars gave Ferrari the handling to match their turbocharged power. The fixed skirt should be noted, with its resistant edge running against the road, and clean over-body airflow. *Left:* 'All Ferrari need', the British said, 'is a half-way decent chassis and we won't see which way they've gone'. Dr Harvey Postlethwaite was imported to deliver the goods which he did with the carbon-composite mid-1983 'C3, as seen here at Silverstone with René Arnoux installed. Flat-bottom regs have led to abbreviated side pods, mid-ship tub tank forces driver forward, pullrod front suspension is used, tub moulding forms external 'body'. *Above:* Gordon Murray's approach to flat-bottom rules was the all-new spearhead Brabham BT52 BMW turbo. Nelson Piquet is seen here at Monaco — despite a draggy rear end it was a striking and Drivers' title-winning package. Michelin radial-ply tyres were inherently consistent in manufacture, and the bad old days of team tyre specialists painstakingly selecting and matching inconsistent covers were a fading memory.

The second half of our period has seen a fascinating variety of engines appearing in Formula 1. *Opposite, top left to bottom right:* Lotus 79 stripped out, 1978, showing spidery tub, up-and-over exhausts, inboard brakes and rear coil/dampers tucked within DFV section, Aeroquip everywhere and the red-cased rear anti-roll bar adjuster cable clearly visible. Brabham's Alfa Romeo V12 was produced with incredible speed for 1978 but reliability suggested as much. Underbody floor is visible sweeping up in that left-side pod, Alfa still demanded a lot of cooling. BMW's M12/13 turbo made its Brabham bow in 1982 and became the most potent unit in Formula 1, with over 1270 bhp in 1985 test-trim. Heat insulation was copious, and vital. Renault pioneered the turbo option from 1977 – here's an EF4 V6 in the 1984 Lotus 95T. Left-side manifolds feed one 'charger, pressure air then passing through the intercooler ahead, into engine-top induction log. Note seamed carbon tub, waisted-in 'McLaren tail', rear ground-effects diffuser moulding 'blown' by exhaust below, and sidestep winglet ahead of axle line up top. In Renault's cars the V6 displays its array of electronics, vital for mid-1980s 950 bhp. Ferrari's 1981 126C V6 shows off its in-vee twin turbochargers, centre wastegate with vertical flue, hip-mounted intercoolers feeding side induction logs direct. Water radiators recline out ahead, underwing floors below. The curved-tube rear suspension truss would have done Cooper credit. Note tiny rear anti-roll bar on top of the excellent *trasversale* gearbox.

Above right: Dominant 1984 engine: McLaren's Porsche-engineered TAG Turbo V6 was reliable, powerful and, thanks to John Barnard, stringently well-packaged. Just two hand-spans cover the cam-box length, V6 mounts in the DFV strap-plate manner; note McLaren tail, inboard rocker arm rear suspension, large de-aerating oil tank, low-slung KKK turbocharger, carefully sealed intercooler and carbon tub.

Finally, the magnificent 3.5-litre Honda RA109E V10-cylinder 'atmo' engine of 1989 as installed in McLaren's MP4/5 cars.

Alain Prost gave Marlboro-McLaren and Unipart maximum exposure at Zandvoort '84. Here the standard-setting MP4/2-TAG Turbo-by-Porsche shows off its beautifully conceived and well-packaged low-drag, high-download form, diagonal front suspension pushrod links, hip turbocharger air intake just ahead of that rear wheel and well-fenced rear winglets and wing. Prost's carbon-composite chassis 'MP4/2-2' led 61 of the 71 laps after qualifying on pole and beat team-mate Lauda's 'MP4/2-1' by 10 seconds into second place.

Inset opposite: Honda's lowered RA168E 2.5-bar V6 turbo engine was matched in 1988 by the low-line McLaren MP4/4 monocoque owing much to Gordon Murray's BT55 concept. Pure high-modulus Hercules carbon-fibre – without Kevlar-type tear-stopper additives – skinned the moulded seamless structure.

Overleaf: As usual with Ferrari, the team's fortunes were inextricably entwined with the heart displayed by its drivers and the unity within the team created by its engineers and management. Here at Monza in 1990 much of both was in evidence, Nigel Mansell trying his hardest – as always – in the 3.5-litre V12 *Tipo* 641, demonstrating its Barnard-conceived teardrop planform and handsome functionality.

Anglo-Japanese World Champions both – Ayrton Senna in the dominant V10-engined MP4/5B at Suzuka in 1990, and the Woking team's replacement MP4/6 with Honda RA121E V12 engine being race-prepared in the Suzuka garages, 1991. Honda would bow out of Formula 1 at the end of 1992 with a glittering record.

continued from page 224

the TEC V6 with the wrong team upon its introduction in 1986 by then withdrawing it from competition a year too soon at the end of '87. Benetton found itself 'going atmo' for '88, and ditching its Ford V6 turbo engines which still seemed so promising in testing in favour of twenty full-spec 3.5-litre Cosworth-Ford DFRs. These lower, lighter V8s were planned initially to use Yamaha-derived five-valve-per-cylinder heads, but they were never raced, Benetton's DFR engines being delivered instead as conventional 48-valvers.

Eight new B188 chassis were produced, to be campaigned by Boutsen and Fabi-replacement Alessandro Nannini.

Designer Rory Byrne's first problem in converting to the big V8s was simple chassis re-engineering merely to resist the Cosworth-Ford V8s' notorious vibration. Partly because of this – plus a new gearbox and chassis each exceeding design-weight – the new B188s emerged 20 kg too heavy, and worse the 48-valve DFR gave 30 bhp less than predicted.

Nannini damaged one B188 beyond repair in Jerez testing. The cars which ended the season were far developed from those which started it. Initially the team had underestimated the 3.5-litre V8's cooling requirement. But at least one car finished almost everywhere after painstaking testing over race distances to locate and cure problems in private . . .

But Byrne had no illusions: 'To consider we'd done a worthwhile job we had to be competitive with McLaren. Nobody managed to do that . . .'

Reliability was good enough for Boutsen to fail to finish only twice, at Ricard and Silverstone in mid-season, while Nannini's cars failed to finish seven times. Boutsen scored no fewer than ten times, with a commendable six third places, one fourth, one fifth and two sixths. Nannini was undeniably quick, but less reliable, scoring six times – two thirds, a fourth, a fifth and two sixths. He was also seventh – just outside the points – in Mexico. This all contributed to Benetton's best Constructors' Championship performance yet, third to McLaren and Ferrari, with 46 points.

Into 1989 four of the B188s were uprated for the start of the season, and entrusted once more to Nannini, now backed by the young Englishman Johnny Herbert, who was not yet fully recovered from severe leg injuries suffered in an F3000 collision at Brands Hatch the previous summer. New B189 cars eventually emerged in time for the French GP at Ricard, by which time Emanuele Pirro had been signed to replace Herbert, who returned to convalescence.

For the new year the Cosworth-Ford DFR engine with its DFV-derived 90-degree V8 configuration had been replaced for Benetton as Ford's favoured 'works' team by a completely new 75-degree V8 known as the HB. To carry this new unit Rory Byrne produced a pencil-slim Benetton B189 chassis, but it was to be delayed by a series of problems . . .

Cosworth had been given complete freedom by Ford to select the most practical configuration they might want for a new generation of engines capable of winning in Formula 1. The project was authorized in April 1988, and the first HB engine fired into life on the Northampton dyno just before Christmas that year. Cosworth then informed Benetton that March would probably be a realistic target date for the engine's first run in a car.

The narrower new V8 engine enabled Byrne to produce a slimmer car than hitherto, presenting greater clean aerodynamic surface to direct airstream and by Benetton standards proving notably sensitive to aerodynamic set-up.

The Ford V8 looked good on the test bed, running quite reliably considering its novelty, but Nannini shunted the prototype B189 at Snetterton during its initial shakedown running, and then in further testing at Imola between Rio and the San Marino GP Nannini crashed again, this time after a wheel rim had cracked.

By this time, however, the team was about to find itself in serious trouble with the new engine. While testing at Pembrey a crankshaft broke, and in another Imola test a second failed, and Nannini caught a third just as it was beginning 'to rumble'. While Cosworth wrestled with the problem, the new cars' debut had to be postponed until round seven, the French GP at Ricard – the old 90-degree V8-engined B188 cars being raced meantime.

Cosworth's engineers concluded that secondary torsional vibration periods were creating the problem, and redesign of both the crankshaft and its take-off drive was necessary to correct it.

Since the old cars and engines were being kept in harness longer than planned, the team's manufacturing programme for the new cars was badly obstructed as B188 service parts had to take short-term precedence.

Against this background it was ironic that it was a rear suspension failure – right under the beady eye of an overhead TV camera – which then sidelined Nannini from his first race with the brand new B189 . . .

Even so, the Benetton B189 with its new 75-degree Ford engine was firmly established by the end of the season as the best V8 contender behind Honda, Ferrari and Williams-Renault.

Four B188s were used in the early part of the 1989 season, serials '4, and '7-8-9, followed by six new B189s from Ricard forward, chassis '4 emerging at Hockenheim, '5 new for Pirro at the Hungaroring – but not raced – and '6 new for Nannini at Monza.

Nannini's full season with the team yielded nine finishes, six retirements and a disqualification (in Montreal). He scored eight times, including an inherited maiden victory – after Senna's disqualification – in the Japanese GP at Suzuka, second in Adelaide, thirds at Imola and Silverstone, fourths at Mexico City and Estoril, fifth at Spa and sixth at Rio.

The walking wounded Johnny Herbert finished well, fourth at Rio, fifth at Phoenix but only 11-14-15 in between and he then failed to qualify at Montreal whereupon he was replaced by Emanuele Pirro. He then finished five times in the last ten races, but only 9-11-8-10 before fifth place in Australia ending the year. Benetton slipped a place in the Constructors' table, placing fourth on 39 points to McLaren, Williams and Ferrari.

For 1990, Benetton director Flavio Briatore signed up former McLaren and Ferrari engineering director John Barnard to build Benetton into a dominant Formula 1 force. At least, that seemed to be the intention, but it did not work out that way . . .

When Barnard joined the team from Ferrari, the B190 was about as far advanced as had been

Nelson Piquet's Benetton-Ford HB B191 at Phoenix, 1991, showing off its bulkhead-free truly monocoque moulded fuselage nacelle, pushrod front suspension and braced rear wing at high incidence on this street circuit.

Brunner's Ferrari F1/87 when he had first moved in to Maranello. Consequently the car was not a Barnard conception, but it had much Barnard detailing built into it by the time it entered service.

Initially, Benetton used stop-gap B189B chassis '4, '5 and '8 at Phoenix and Interlagos, then began the season's serious business at Imola with the first three new B190s for drivers Nannini and newcomer Nelson Piquet. Five more B190s would be built to complete the season.

In the B190s, the latest carbon-composite Benetton monocoque complied with new dimensional regulations concerning cockpit opening and internal size and Barnard was changing the team's emphasis from the Rory Byrne-style of ultra-pitch-sensitive design towards his own favoured packaging which promoted greater purely mechanical grip than some designers. Consequently, weight distribution and suspension geometry of the Benetton B190 both differed from its immediate predecessor. And it worked, the car proving less sensitive to small setting-up changes than the B189s.

Ford continued exclusive supply of the 75-degree Cosworth HB engine to Benetton, beginning the new season with a third-generation version of the V8 unit producing some 625 bhp at 12,500 rpm. A fourth-generation version of the engine was then provided in time for the British GP at Silverstone featuring redesigned pistons, connecting rods, cylinder heads, valves and valvegear plus remapped Ford EEC IV electronic engine management and fuel system.

This proved to be a considerable leap forward, but Barnard became increasingly restless since the Ford engine programme appeared to him to regard this kind of six-monthly progress step as sufficient, while he could see Honda, Ferrari and Renault making progressive steps almost every other race, and he believed them to be drawing further away each time.

Still the B190 proved itself the fastest V8 of that second half-season, and Nannini's duelling with Berger's McLaren-Honda for third place at Spa emphasized just how well its overall aerodynamic and chassis package could operate when the V8 engine package was itself being regarded as outmoded.

Nannini was joined in this 1990 team by Nelson Piquet, ex-Lotus with a cloud over his head as the former triple World Champion's performances had been sadly under-par for two full seasons. Now he was engaged on a payment-by-results basis and with a better car than he had enjoyed for so long, and massive financial incentive, he would shine for the Witney team.

Piquet suffered only two retirements in the entire season. He was disqualified at Monaco, but otherwise failed to finish in the points only once, at Monza (seventh). Otherwise his impressively consistent finishing record read 4-6-5-2 (Montreal) 6-4-5-3 (Hungary) 5-5-1-1, these last two successive race wins being achieved with a fine race set-up and profiting by others' problems in Japan and Australia to complete the season.

Nannini meanwhile retired from only four events, but finished in the points only six times – 3-4-2 (Germany) 4-6-3 – before suffering a terrible injury in a helicopter accident, his right forearm being severed but reconnected by micro-surgery. The team replaced him with Piquet's Brazilian friend, Roberto Moreno, who rose excellently to the opportunity by finishing second behind his new team-leader in Japan, then seventh in Australia. Considering he had previously failed to pre-qualify nine times during the season in the uncompetitive EuroBrun here was evidence of just how important a role the engineers and the equipment they provide really plays compared to driver ability . . .

Benetton had recovered to place third in the Constructors' Championship, on 71 points to Ferrari's 110 and McLaren's customarily victorious 121.

While Barnard was perfecting design and manufacture of the new B191 cars for 1991, four uprated versions of the B190 were used in the first two GPs of the new season, at Phoenix and Interlagos, these appearing as B190B chassis '2, '7, '8 and '9. The new Barnard-designed car made its bow – relatively untested – at Imola and despite its relatively conventional appearance with the now fashionable 'Tyrrell-type' raised nose aerodynamics, it was stucturally innovative.

A new carbon-composite manufacturing process enabled Benetton to dispense with load-carrying internal bulkheads and bracketry, relying upon the integrated monocoque shell to perform that duty. Unlike previous Barnard cars the monocoque moulding was external-finished and formed the forward aerodynamic skin, the old development freedom of separate cover body panels having been sacrificed for structural integrity and light weight. Although intended originally to run from the outset with semi-automatic transmission and active suspension, the car began its career without either and would run in that form throughout the season.

Barnard needed 'some plus' to capitalize upon the B191's potential with the latest Cosworth-Ford HB Series V V8 engine, and Benetton took the gamble of signing with Pirelli to combat the leading teams on Goodyear. Sadly, Pirelli's 1991 F1 tyres proved a liability rather than a bonus, and on occasion Benetton played second fiddle to the brand new Jordan team using customer-status Ford HB engines.

The new Series V works units meanwhile were tailored for B191 mounting, and its internal balance shaft had been adopted to damp out vibration periods which could affect the electronics of the car's intended semi-auto gearchange and active suspension.

However, Barnard found himself increasingly at odds with the Benetton management. He felt unable to put his signature to the company's 1990 accounts, was unhappy with Cosworth's commitment to F1 engine development and Benetton abruptly discarded him just after the Canadian GP. His longtime assistant Gordon Kimball was made technical director in his place, but the team made little further progress on B191 developments before the end of the year.

Just before the British GP TWR Jaguar Group C team owner Tom Walkinshaw took a 35 per cent interest in the company, introducing his own personnel, including Ross Brawn ex-Arrows, and bringing back Rory Byrne, Dave Wass and Pat Symonds from work on a stillborn Reynard F1 project.

Nelson Piquet finished 11 of his races, winning in Canada when Mansell's leading Williams failed on the very last lap. Otherwise Nelson's finish record read 3-5-8-5-3-6-5-11-7-4. Moreno drove in 11 races for the team, finishing six times, 7-4-5-8-8-4. The new regime's management style saw Piquet estranged and abandoned, and Moreno dropped before Monza in favour of new German *wunderkind* Michael Schumacher – stolen, in their view, from Jordan. In his five late-season outings he finished three times in the points, 5-6-6.

Despite the introduction of the latest Series VI pneumatic-valved Ford V8 in time for the Japanese GP and Piquet's inherited last-lap victory in Canada, for Benetton-Ford 1991 was a troubled season largely worth forgetting . . . Six of the B191s had been deployed during the season.

Boro

See entry for Ensign (pages 258-9).

Brabham

The detailed story of the twice Constructors' World Championship-winning Repco Brabhams is told in Chapter 2. Their relative failure in 1968 with the four-cam Repco Type 860 engine has also been described.

The first two seasons of the new Formula inevitably saw the use of a number of former 1.5-litre or *Libre* Brabham spaceframe chassis (built by Motor Racing Developments Ltd) with various engines in Formula 1. During 1966 – especially in the early events before the new Formula got into its stride – six of these hybrid cars competed. They were all BT11 chassis of original 1964-5 manufacture; 'F1-1-64' being the works car with 2.7-litre Climax four-cylinder FPF engine entered for Hulme in early-season. Chassis '2-64 was a rechassised car with this serial originally entered by the South African Scuderia Scribante in the November 1965 Rand GP, which it won driven by Brabham himself, using another big FPF engine. Aldo Scribante subsequently ran the car in South African events, including the International GP, for Dave Charlton. 'F1-4-64' was a BRM V8-engined car originally entered by Bob Gerard, and later David Bridges, for John Taylor, who sadly sustained fatal burns in this car following a German GP collision at the Nürburgring. Rhodesian former motor cyclist Bob Anderson's DW Racing Enterprises team ran his immaculate bright-green BT11 'F1-5-64' with 2.7 FPF power with great success until his fatal testing accident at Silverstone in August 1967. Rob Walker's 1.5-litre BRM V8-powered 'F1-6-64' appeared right at the start of the 1966 season in South Africa, while the final BT11 of this interesting but obscure sextet was the production *Libre* car 'IC-5-64' owned and entered by South African Otelle Nucci for Pieter de Klerk.

At more significant level, in 1969 Jack Brabham and Ron Tauranac bowed to the inevitable, cut their Repco engine ties and adopted the Cosworth DFV V8.

The existing BT26 hybrid-construction chassis with their part stressed-skin stiffened spaceframe chassis were altered to accommodate the British engine. Two existing ex-Repco BT26s were uprated as DFV-powered works team BT26As, chassis '2 for Brabham himself and '3 for new team driver Ickx.

Old ex-works 'BT24/3' had been sold to Frank Williams and fitted with a 2.5-litre Cosworth DFW V8 engine for Courage's use in the Tasman Championship. After that tour this car was sold to Swiss privateer Moser who fitted it with a 3-litre DFV as a replacement for the Charles Vögele-owned BT20 which he had campaigned previously. Williams replaced this car with ex-works prototype 'BT26/1' which he also had converted to DFV power for Courage to contest the World Championship GP series.

Jack himself destroyed 'BT26/2' in a pre-French

GP testing accident at Silverstone – where he had earlier won the International Trophy in '26/2 running new Goodyear G14 wet-weather tyres and wearing twin strutted wings. He broke an ankle and so missed the mid-season GPs leaving Ickx to uphold team honour alone. A replacement 'BT26/4' was completed in time for the British GP in which it was driven by Ickx to finish second. Subsequently, he won the German GP in this car and the minor Oulton Park Gold Cup race in his early-season regular '26/3. Brabham returned to take over chassis '4 from the Italian GP, these two works cars finishing 1-2 in the Canadian GP at Mosport Park.

The BT26As were arguably the best-handling cars of the 1969 season but they suffered on reliability. Jack himself qualified on pole for the season-opening South African GP at Kyalami and ran second until his car's wing fell off. Ickx also lost his wing. Brabham broke an engine at Barcelona and Ickx broke a wishbone but he was classified sixth. Wing trouble persisted. Courage broke a valve spring.

At Monaco, Brabham collided with a BRM and Ickx disputed second until a rear upright broke, leaving Courage a splendid second place in his private Brabham. Ickx and Brabham placed 5-6 in Holland, Courage suffering clutch trouble.

Ickx shone as he always did when he was undisputed team leader. He was third in France after running second most of the way, second at Silverstone with Courage fifth, as well as adding a new lap record to his win at the Nürburgring where he started on pole. He bent his car during pre-race filming at Monza when he found a barrier erected across the road! A spate of engine failures wrecked his Italian GP practice and race though Brabham himself ran high until a fuel pipe pulled out. Courage drove another fine race and led briefly until fuel starvation began.

Jack qualified on pole before the Canadian 1-2. Courage retired with a fuel leak but at Watkins Glen he was second after holding off both works cars in a spirited duel, Jack having to stop for fuel and finishing fourth, while Ickx was second and set fastest lap. In Mexico, Goodyear tyres shone again; Brabham took pole once more but finished only third after injection problems while Ickx gained second and set fastest lap. Courage bounced his car off Siffert's Lotus and finished tenth.

During the season the Kyalami wing failures had been traced to the omission of a washer on the stays, the bolts subsequently being overtightened, while those at Silverstone and Barcelona were due to extra loading caused by the adoption of end plates. After Kyalami, Jack's '26/2 was fitted with 2 in. wider track long wishbones, '26/3 being updated accordingly while '26/4 had the wider track from new.

After the Barcelona wing collapses on the Lotus 49s and Brabham BT26As, Ron Tauranac was largely responsible for framing the new wing regulations which took effect at Zandvoort, but he felt chassis-mounted wings were bad in principle as they caused the car to run nose-up under acceleration. The Brabham marque finished second behind Matra-Ford in the Constructors' Championship. 'BT 26/4' went to Tom Wheatcroft, founder of the Donington collection, for 1970, when it would be driven briefly by Bell.

For 1970, fuel tanks had to be metal-sheathed, so Ron built his first monocoque Formula 1 cars,

Graham Hill in Ron Tauranac's 1971 'lobster claw' Brabham BT34 at Brands Hatch (opposite page) *contrasts with the BT37* (left), *cobbled together around BT34 bag tanks to keep the team racing in 1972-73. This BT37 is in 1973 form with deformable structure side pods. Below left: Gordon Murray, who succeeded Colin Chapman as the most innovative F1 design engineer, ponders his BT44's pullrod front suspension.*

The cars were lucky at Silverstone where Graham won in the BT34 with Schenken third in '33/1, but at Monaco Graham bent '34/1 and Schenken came tenth after bursting a tyre.

The British GP at Silverstone saw Schenken run as high as third until his gearbox failed; in Germany he was sixth in '33/3, then in Austria Schenken and Hill placed 3-5 for the team's first two-car score of the season. They ended the season ninth and last on the Constructors' table with just five points.

At Brands Hatch in the minor final race of the season Schenken finished fifth in '33/3 while the modified '33/1 was driven by Reutemann, making his serious Formula 1 debut, finishing ninth just behind Hill's still-unique '34/1.

During the winter of 1971/72 Tauranac sold MRD to Bernie Ecclestone, businessman, former Formula 1 Connaught private entrant and more recently Rindt's business manager. 1972 was a formative season for the revamped company.

They retained 'BT33/3' and the BT34, while Ralph Bellamy from McLaren handled technical development – which was modest. The BT34 ran in Argentina with revised bodywork and narrower rear track for Reutemann, Hill driving the ex-Schenken BT33 updated with 16-gauge regulation outer skin, strengthened bulkheads, revised bodywork as seen at the end of '71 and new Girling four-pot brake calipers. Reutemann ran Goodyear's latest G52 soft-compound tyres there to qualify on pole.

The Bellamy-designed BT37 ran at Silverstone; in effect a BT34 with conventional nose radiator and regulation deformable structure tank protection. Front track was 1.5 in. narrower and it was some 25 lb lighter. Parallel-link rear suspension was adopted on the cars in mid-season.

Ecclestone also backed a test programme, building a one-off BT39 to accommodate the Ford-financed Weslake Type 190 V12 engine which had been intended for sports car use and was based upon 1966-68 Gurney-Weslake V12 experience. The project had similarities with the contemporary March 721G in that it used a basic F2 tub – a BT38 design – completely reskinned with 47-gallon fuel capacity. Hill tested the Brabham-Weslake briefly at Silverstone prior to the Italian GP but the claimed '445 bhp' engine was underpowered. The brief test told the team all they wished to know and Ecclestone was not afraid to write off the investment and put the project down to experience.

Brabham made 35 starts in 14 races in 1972, finishing 20 times, winning the minor Interlagos event and adding third there, but had only one fourth, a fifth and two sixths at Championship level.

Ending that year Bellamy moved to Lotus and his quiet young assistant, Gordon Murray, was offered the chance to take his place.

Gordon had been a great fan of the svelte little Lotus 25s of 1962-63 and had an image of a small, light and simple Formula 1 car which Ecclestone allowed him to build. Since the rather pathetic BT37 had been restricted by the decision to use existing BT34 bag tanks, no compromises were to stand in the way of the new 1973 deformable-structure BT42. Nothing current was to be used which could possibly limit it.

Gordon wanted to gain on top speed by making a smaller hole in the air than the preceding BT33-34-37 cars, so adopted a triangular pyramid-section monocoque design. The idea for this had been 'kicked around' with Bellamy before he left, and the intention was to keep centre of gravity low, maintain airflow on top of the chassis and to match the DFV cam-cover slope, thus providing

---

the BT33s.

Three of these handsome, podgy-tubbed machines were built, each slightly different from its predecessor and many detail modifications were made during the season. Jack's turquoise-and-gold 'BT33/2' works car was joined by newcomer Stommelen's sister 'BT33/1' in German magazine livery from the start of the season. Jack's car was consistently the fastest conventional-layout Cosworth-powered car but due to unreliability and some team mistakes his last driving season collapsed as defeats were snatched from the jaws of victory.

He won the South African GP on 'BT33/2's debut. He led the Race of Champions before suffering electrical trouble and was close behind Stewart at Jarama when '33/2's crankshaft broke. At Monaco, Jack made his famous mistake on the very last corner, losing the lead and limping home a thoroughly disgusted second. Punctures hampered his progress at Zandvoort and he crashed Stommelen's car heavily in practice. Clutch trouble was the problem at Spa, while at Clermont he finished a tardy third.

He dominated the British GP only to run out of fuel on the last lap. Thereafter the Brabham season fell apart. At Hockenheim there was an oil leak, in Austria a stone pierced his radiator and in Italy he went off the road when his engine cut. A massive oil leak ended his run in Canada, at Watkins Glen he spun and stalled, losing much time, and in Mexico – his farewell outing – his

engine failed, losing third place. He had scored 25 points in the first part of the season but added none in the second half.

Meanwhile, Stommelen failed to qualify at Monaco but was fifth at Spa, missed the Dutch GP after Jack had bent his car in practice, and then himself wrote off 'BT33/1' in practice at Brands Hatch. A new 'BT33/3' was ready for him to finish fifth in Germany, third in Austria and fifth again in Italy. Brabham placed fourth-equal with McLaren in the Constructors' table.

In 1971 they fell to the foot of the Championship. Jack had gone back to his native Australia, and Tauranac seemed to miss him badly as he ran the team alone on a tight budget. Driver Graham Hill was past his best and number two Schenken's best was not good enough.

Ron's latest 'lobster-claw' BT34 design was little better than the BT33, whereas Hill thought it worse. Its monocoque was squarer in section and to minimize front end lift Ron divided the conventional nose radiator and slung two small cores in faired pods ahead of each front wheel, a tub-width nose wing bridging between them.

Jack's 1970 '33/2 was sold to private entrant Alain de Cadenet for Chris Craft to drive late in 1971. Stommelen's wrecked '33/1 had been rebuilt to accompany '33/3 in the new works team, Hill and Dave Charlton driving them at Kyalami, doing nothing. Schenken managed to reach fourth at Brands Hatch in '33/1 where '34/1 made its debut, Hill encountering engine trouble.

nice straight load paths for the top engine mountings.

Gordon adopted a short wheelbase and very simple fuel system, employing only three tanks – a large one amidships pushing the driver quite far forward plus one on each side. He used Tauranac's BT34 split-radiator position just ahead of the front wheels which faired into a full-width nose, streamlining the front wheels and minimizing lift. These split radiators in the nose could be made some 50 per cent smaller than mid-mounted radiators because they received cleaner direct airflow, and could also be made any shape.

The BT42 emerged some 10 per cent smaller on frontal area than some cars but was still not the quickest along the straight. There were also shortcomings in stiffness and geometry which would later be corrected on the BT44.

During 1973 the team campaigned 'BT37/1' and '2 in early events before the first 'BT42/1' was written off on its Race of Champions debut by the unfortunate Watson, its throttle jamming open at Stirling's Bend. Ceramica Pagnossin-sponsored Italian driver de Adamich destroyed '37/1 in Spain. Five more BT42s were built that year: chassis '4 was destroyed by the luckless de Adamich – neither of his write-offs really being his fault – in the Scheckter collision during the British GP at Silverstone, '3 became Reutemann's usual mount, '2 and later '5 allocated to Wilson Fittipaldi, while '6 appeared late in the year driven by Stommelen and then the recovered Watson.

After brief elation and final disappointment when Reutemann led in Barcelona, Brabham's results showed Reutemann third at Ricard and Watkins Glen, fourth in Sweden and Austria, and sixth at Silverstone and Monza. Wilson Fittipaldi was fifth at the Nürburgring to add to his sixth in Argentina, and de Adamich was fourth in Belgium and seventh at Monaco in the remaining BT37. Brabham cars had made 42 starts in the 15 GPs and scored nine times, taking fourth in the Constructors' table.

For 1974, Murray began work on the improved BT44 and the prototype emerged just in time to be shipped to Argentina for the first race, not turning a wheel in England before it left. Gordon, Team Manager Herbie Blash and their long-serving team members rate the BT44 as one of his 'nicest' cars – a honey both to work on and to drive.

Gordon recalls: 'I tried to keep the good points of the 42 in the new car. What I wanted to do really necessitated starting with a new tub. I built in rising-rate suspension, while the wheelbase was one inch longer . . . it was generally a neater car in detail, simple and without a great deal of fabricated work, the kind of stuff which gives trouble.'

He introduced pullrod rising-rate front suspension linkages in this BT44, using semi-inboard coil/dampers standing on pivoting feet, tensioned by rods attached to the outboard front wishbone tip. This obviated the need for massive top rocker arms, 'beams in bending', which Gordon called 'Nasty, horrible things'.

Subsequently, pullrod suspensions would be widely adopted, as were pushrods which Gordon also evolved – 'Pullrods the other way up, they needed to be heavier of course, being in compression rather than tension'.

In his native Argentina, Reutemann shone again and led until the airbox ripped away around its retaining bolts, losing 200 rpm on the straight. Five laps from the end while still leading handsomely, a plug lead came loose so the engine ran on seven cylinders, before finally stopping during

Four Murray Brabhams: opposite top left: _1973 BT42 which introduced the pyramid-section, low frontal area, low centre of gravity tub;_ top right: _1974 BT44 retained split nose radiators but added aerodynamic improvements;_ bottom left: _the much-maligned surface-cooled 1978 BT46 which became such a fine car with its Alfa Romeo flat-12 engine;_ bottom right: _Piquet in his 1985 BT54-BMW turbo at Rio, racing for the first time on Pirelli tyres._

the last lap . . . out of fuel. 'We had had a panic on race morning with a wheel seized on, and although 39 gallons of fuel should have gone in the tanks, one churn didn't go in . . .'

Many Grand Prix races, much prize money and an awful lot of glory have been squandered this way.

The four surviving BT42s, chassis '2-3-5-6, were raced early in the year, four new BT44s '1-2-3-4 replacing them.

The BT44s had a new, less drag-inducive nose and smoother cockpit area cleaning up airflow onto the rear wing. BT44s '1 and '2 ran for Reutemann and rent-a-driver Robarts in Argentina, with 'BT42/3' spare, while motor trader John Goldie's Hexagon of Highgate team ran the ex-Fittipaldi 'BT42/2' for Watson in its chocolate livery. 'BT44/1' used the underbelly chevron air dam discussed on page 102.

In South Africa, new tapered-wire progressive-rate rear springs were introduced on Reutemann's car. In Spain, old 'BT42/5' and '6 appeared for Swiss driver Moser, entered by Bretscher Racing, but did not run as he had been fatally injured in the Monza 1000 Km. These cars subsequently raced under the Scuderia Martino Finotto banner for Larrousse.

In Sweden, the '44s toyed briefly with 12 in. diameter front wheels and in Holland Goodyear tried their latest 24 in. outside diameter rear tyres on 10 in. diameter rims against the normal 26 in. OD on 13s. This was an attempt to combine smaller frontal area with contemporary deep and soft sidewall construction, improving straightline speed and incidentally driveshaft angularity, but after a brief run in practice the BT44s reverted to normal trim.

These rims and tyres were tried again at Dijon and in Austria, while at Monza 10 in. rims were tested with 18 in. wide rear tyres, 2.5 in. wider than normal. Spare chassis '3 was used, then returned to standard for Watson to race after crashing his own Hexagon 'BT44/4'. This car had made its debut in Germany, replacing old '42/2 which Ian Ashley failed to qualify in the USA at the end of the season.

Von Opel had briefly replaced Robarts as second MRD driver but was superseded from mid-season by Pace.

The Brabham BT44s at some stage led each of the season's first five races. Suspension geometry and stiffness deficiencies were corrected to enable Reutemann to score the Ecclestone and Murray team's first victory in the South African GP, then winning again in Austria and the US where Pace and Watson completed a works team 1-2 and Brabham 1-2-5 result.

Reutemann finished nine of his 16 GPs, placing 7-7-1-12-6-3-1-9-1, while von Opel's neat if brief MRD career comprised two non-qualifications, two retirements and two ninth places. Pace had an unlucky debut, non-qualifying at Brands Hatch due to a car problem, and thereafter started six races, finishing five of them – 9-12-5-8-2. Brabham ended the season fifth in the Constructors' table.

For 1975, Martini and Fina sponsorship coloured the formerly virgin-white Brabhams' flanks, and Gordon developed his successful BT44s as BT44Bs with stiffened tubs, revised narrower front suspension though still rising-rate, and redesigned bodies with greater-downforce nose sections.Chassis '44B/1 was new in Argentina, 'B2 was built from '44/3, 'B3 from '44/1 and 'B4 from '44/4.

The underbelly air dams reappeared for the partly high-speed circuit of Kyalami and in Spain small 'whisker' foils appeared on the nose sides, greater downforce now balanced by deeper banana-section rear wings offering minimal frontal area. Pace tried the underbelly air dam in Holland and thought it was terrific; Reutemann tried it and preferred to run without.

At Ricard, cycle-type front wheel mudguard fairings were attached, ostensibly to deflect flying grit and gravel. Gordon always loved a try-on. After first practice they were removed.

Pace crashed '44B/2 in the rain at the British

GP, though nevertheless was classified second, and '44B/4 which had been completed earlier in the year made its race debut under him at the Nürburgring.

Reutemann scored in eight of the year's 14 GPs, won in Germany and was third in the Drivers' Championship. His record included only two retirements from 14 GPs, placing 3-8-2-3-9-3-2-4-14 before his first failure in Britain, then 1-14-4 at the end of season. Pace won his home GP in Brazil, being classified as a finisher six times, 1-4-3-8-5-2. Brabham finished second to Ferrari in the Constructors' table.

It had been their best season but could have been better still, for the BT44Bs' development stagnated as Gordon concentrated upon a new Alfa Romeo-engined project. Ecclestone had first made contact with Autodelta (Alfa's competitions wing) as early as June 1974 to discuss use of their 3-litre flat-12 sports car engine. The deal was agreed late that year and Gordon spent much of the summer of '75 engrossed in designing a new car around this large, heavy and thirsty but powerful unit.

It could offer some 510 bhp, compared to the DFV with perhaps 480 bhp, but as a sports car unit it had untidy ancillaries and was some 40 kg (88 lb) heavier. Additionally it needed 8 to 12 gallons more fuel depending on the circuit, greater cooling surface and more oil; it was also 11 in. longer than a DFV and some 3 in. wider.

Consequently the 1976 Brabham-Alfa Romeo BT45s were hefty brutes. Gordon had to abandon his preferred pyramidal tub section to accommodate sufficient fuel and the flat-12 engine in a broader, more squared-off tub. Autodelta fought to reduce consumption and weight, while MRD developed the chassis.

As early in the season as Kyalami, weight was being saved by using more titanium in the tubs and more magnesium in the engines. Chassis '45/3 emerged at Long Beach, 10 kg (22 lb) lighter than '1 and '2 with still more weight saved in the engine. In Spain, Reutemann bent '45/2 badly in practice; it was rebuilt for Belgium but there Pace demolished the latest '45/3.

At Monaco, the latest Brabham-Alfa Romeo six-speed gearboxes appeared, though raced only by Pace. The RAM Racing team fielded 44Bs '1 and '2 for Nelleman and Kessel, though without luck, '42/2 being their spare.

In France, a stride was made with modified front suspension rising-rate geometry, deep skirting all round the bottom of the chassis, new airbox design, brake fans and streamlining wheel discs in the front wheel centres. Rear suspension settings were also revised and Pace was timed at 177.36 mph on the Mistral Straight. Power was never a problem.

A new 5 kg (11 lb) lighter '45/4 emerged for Pace at the British GP, using lighter gauges and more titanium, and in Germany it used an air-starter like McLaren's, plus experimental Dunlop disc brakes with carbon-fibre insert pucks as friction surfaces, potentially saving weight and offering better retardation as they could endure higher temperatures than conventional brakes. Reutemann moved to Ferrari, unable to cope with the BT45s' development, RAM driver Stommelen taking his place in '45/1 with carbon-fibre brakes. Meanwhile, RAM ran into litigation with driver Kessel and did not start.

Stommelen finished sixth, but Pace ran the carbon brakes in Austria and had the discs expand on the straight – the fluid boiled as he touched the pedal and he entered the _Glatzkurve_ brakeless at 180 mph, destroying '45/4. The carbon brakes gave endless trouble with boiling fluid, vibration, wear, inconsistency and snapping bolts. However, the system's day would come.

In Holland, lower rear wishbones were tried instead of parallel links in practice, reverting to normal for the race, but the new centre-pivot suspension was used throughout in Italy (where Pace qualified faster than the Ferraris!) and in America. Perkins joined Pace in the American races and a new '45/5, lighter still by 6 kg (14 lb), made its debut.

Patrese demonstrates pit-stop race strategy in 1982. The ploy worked for the first time here in Austria but three laps later BT50/4's engine broke.

Initially, communication with Autodelta was poor: without warning such vital items as engine mountings could vary by up to half an inch from one engine to another, causing nightmares in assembly and preparation.

During 1976, the cars had been quite reliable, Pace finishing nine of his 16 GPs, 10-9-6-9-8-4-8-4-7, his fourth places coming in France and Germany. Reutemann had a miserable time in contrast with nine retirements in his twelve races, finishing 12-4-11, Spain providing his best placing, where there was a promising Brabham-Alfa 4-6 finish. But Brabham tumbled to ninth in the Constructors' Championship.

Into 1977 the Brabham BT45s scaled some 620 kg (1366.8 lb), though a lighter B-spec was on the way and with Pace's unstinting faith the team were showing real progress.

Pace damaged '45/1 heavily in Argentine practice and it was rebuilt as the first BT45B in time for Kyalami with its engine lowered by 1.5 in., parallel-link rear suspension and Brabham-Alfa six-speed gearbox, saving around 55 kg (122 lb). Pace qualified second, Watson was on pole for the Race of Champions but news of Pace's death in a flying accident broke later that day and there was no joy in Watson's third place.

Stuck joined Watson at Long Beach where three BT45Bs ran, Watson qualified on pole at Monaco and in Sweden – where the last new 'BT45/6' emerged for Watson – he might have won but for a collision. In France, again in '6, he led only to run out of fuel within a mile of the finish, and in the British GP in '1 he led again until another fuel system malfunction.

He qualified on the front row in Germany, but the second half of his season slumped. Stuck raised morale with third in Germany and Austria and led the flooded US GP before crashing.

Pace had run only three races before his tragic death, finishing second in Argentina, going out in Brazil and 12th at Kyalami after again showing well. Watson finished only five of the 17 GPs, 6-5-2-8-12, while Stuck finished eight of his 14 Brabham-Alfa GPs, 6-6-10-5-3-3-7-7, scoring more points. Brabham-Alfa finished fifth in the Constructors' table.

In mid-season '77, Gordon had begun work on a pyramidal monocoque replacement for the BT45s, using surface cooling to minimize aerodynamic drag, and featuring greater driver protection. The tub sides rose to shoulder height, while nose box and wing occupied a separate foam-filled monocoque structure. A double-skinned panel went up to the dash panel and supported the now mandatory front roll hoop. Dunlop carbon-fibre brakes reappeared after a year's absence and sophisticated instrumentation was adopted. Digital displays enabled the driver to select read-outs on whatever function he required, including instantaneous lap times, saving reliance upon pit signals which are inevitably one lap out of date upon reception. The BT46 also had integral air jacks to facilitate speedy tyre changing in practice and race, activated by an external pressurized air supply. More weight was saved on the six-speed Brabham-Alfa gearbox, and rising-rate Murray suspensions appeared front and rear.

Unfortunately, the surface coolers towed still air with them and overheated, the digital instrumentation vibrated itself into failure and the BT46 was not raceworthy as the new season began. So Brabham raced new BT45Cs chassis '7 and '8 with shallow full-width nose radiators. The BT46 was redesigned with nose radiators and chassis '46/3 and '4 made the model's debut at Kyalami. Chassis '2 became team spare, replaced by '5 at Monaco where they qualified 2-3 and Watson led – having started from pole the previous year only to lose the lead into the first corner. But his brakes faded, Lauda set fastest lap and Gordon twigged the significance of Lotus 79 ground-effects and told Ecclestone they were finished

unless they did something drastic to keep in touch.

As the Lotus 79s came on song, Gordon and his assistant, David North, developed the legendary Brabham BT46B fan-car (see page 109).

In Spain, '46/6 emerged for Lauda while Watson retained '4 and these machines were reworked as fan-cars for their unique victory in Sweden. Following the British GP, Watson drove '5 and in Holland Lauda took new car '7, while for the American trip Watson used chassis '8.

The fan-car was banned and a second-generation BT47 which had already been designed had to be shelved, so BT46s completed the season. The BT46C variant for the Austrian GP had its water radiators faired into the monocoque just behind the front wheels, thus enabling the original needle nose to return and improving weight distribution. They placed 1-2 at Monza after the on-road 1-2 Lotus and Ferrari had been penalized for jumping the start.

Both Lauda and Watson ran all 16 GPs, the Austrian finishing excellently the seven times he managed to finish at all: 2-3-2-1-2-3-1. Watson was overshadowed, finishing ten times 8-3-4-5-4-3-7-7-4-2 and the marque reached third place in the Championship. This was more encouraging.

Autodelta had made a bewildering range of changes to their flat-12 engine. Only the basic head and block castings remained unaltered; all the internals were different from the original 1976-spec, the layout was more tidy, there were titanium rods and exhausts, and the flat-12 was within 25 kg (55 lb) of the Cosworth DFV.

But after the Lotus 79s' dominance, Gordon knew that ground-effects showed the only way to go; to arrange underwing tunnels the flat-12 engine must be replaced by a V12. Autodelta built a suitable Alfa Romeo '1260' engine within three months of MRD's request. By the end of 1978 Gordon felt robbed of probably two Drivers' titles. The Italian engines had been strong and reliable in '78. Take the Lotuses out of the equation and Brabham would have won many races.

The new Alfa 1260 was available a few weeks ahead of the BT48 Brabham chassis designed to accept it. With 525 bhp at 12,300 rpm it was slung as a stressed engine on a narrow and neat aluminium sheet tub which incorporated moulded carbon-composite structural panels in the scuttle and around the fuel cell, forming some 30 per cent of the tub. Pullrod suspension used totally inboard coil/dampers and there were full-length underwing side pods.

Gordon and David North had felt it was vital to build a second-generation ground-effects car rather than merely copy the Lotus 79 layout, simply to keep contact with Lotus themselves. Consequently they developed a full-length under-

wing car with low-level rear wing in Lotus 80 style. At this stage Gordon still did not use a wind tunnel, his work was intuitive.

Like the Lotus 80, it was a disaster, but Brabham instantly recognized it as such during practice in Argentina and hastily ripped off the offending surfaces, cut back the underwings and were soon able to run – at Kyalami – in aerodynamic balance without nose foils.

Gordon Murray: 'We didn't understand centres of pressure. In Argentina the springs were far too soft and the skirts sticking up. Any dynamic input – acceleration, braking or cornering – simply upset the whole thing and the centre of pressure went rocketing up and down the car two or three feet one way or the other!'

Like the Lotus 80 the Brabham BT48 in original full-length underwing form suffered the dreaded 'porpoising', and at one point in Argentine practice Lauda felt the front wheels lift off as it attempted to fly . . .

Thus began a miserable Brabham season. Four BT48s were built, '48/1 and '2 appearing in Buenos Aires as spare and race car for Lauda, while new team-mate Piquet drove old 'BT46/7'. At Kyalami, Piquet used '48/3 with '1 spare and Lauda took over chassis '4 in Belgium where Piquet qualified faster. However, the Austrian crashed '4 at Monaco, the rebuilt car being used as spare in France where Lauda raced '2 but returned to the latest car at Silverstone. At Monza, Piquet tore '48/3 in two in an almighty accident, while in the Dino Ferrari GP at Imola Lauda won in '48/2.

Not only was this the Alfa Romeo 1260 V12's only victory, it also marked the end of the Brabham-Alfa relationship, for at Chessington three brand new BT49-Cosworth DFVs were being completed hastily for the trip to Canada and Watkins Glen. Autodelta would be concentrating upon their own Formula 1 cars hereafter, and the Brabham BT49s' story is related in Chapter 13.

During 1979 Lauda had started an unlucky thirteen GPs in the Brabham-Alfa BT48s, finishing only twice, sixth in South Africa and fourth in Italy. Piquet made four finishes from his 13 Brabham-Alfa starts, placing 7-8-'12' and fourth in Holland.

Brabham ended the season eighth in the Constructors' table but now at last they were beginning their run towards World Championship success, as described in Chapter 13.

With first Cosworth DFV and later turbocharged BMW power the team rode their World Championship-winning wave to the end of 1983, until reliability sank in 1984.

For that season, extensive winter testing of BT52C and then BT52D development specs finally formed the basis of a shapely and still essentially spearhead-form BT53. The prototype chassis 'BT53/1' was retained as test car, while five new BT53s were built during the season, employing a folded aluminium outer tub skin with moulded carbon-composite inner-cum-tank top and fully machined solid aluminium bulkheads.

Drivers for the season were Piquet and the Fabi brothers, usually Teo, sometimes Corrado. Chassis 'BT53/2' was new for Teo at Rio and was raced by him at Kyalami, Zolder, Imola and Dijon, then driven by Corrado at Monaco, Montreal and Dallas, returning to Teo for the middle of the season until Hockenheim.

Spare car duties were performed by 'BT53/3' from Rio to Monza, being raced by Piquet at Detroit after the startline collision and restart.

Piquet's usual car was 'BT53/5', new at Rio, though he raced '4 in the autumn from Brands Hatch to Monza, then took over new car '6 at *ersatz* Nürburgring.

Gordon described 1984 as '. . . a disaster for Brabham results, really worse than when we were using Alfa Romeo engines, but on the other hand, though exasperating, it's been quite satisfying to see your car on pole and leading races against such serious opposition.'

The Brabham-BMWs were the only cars to challenge McLaren seriously that year but the pattern of failures was frustrating, each one being different, without an established pattern. Perhaps it was symptomatic of overstressing an engine near the limit of its possible development. BMW uprated their engines for Brabham's 25-unit pool, claiming 770 bhp in race tune, ending the season with more than 850 bhp in qualifying.

An early spate of turbocharger failures abated for the American mid-season tour when the BT53s' weight distribution was changed with the relocation of 'hot elements', siting the oil cooler in a nose-top duct. The team had bearings fail, seals go, bad welding, wrong fuel, timing problems, an overheating turbo. At Zolder, bad fuel destroyed ten engines.

A revised BT53B aerodynamic package for Brands Hatch was a disaster because it refused to heat its tyres adequately despite handling well. The B-spec was shelved although its underwing and rear suspension modifications were retained.

BMW attributed early-season turbo troubles in part to running too hot in the new car layout. Non-engine failures included a pinion-bearing collapse stopping Piquet in Germany and an oil union coming undone at Zandvoort. At Monza a radiator punctured, possibly due to Piquet hitting a kerb early on.

Piquet finished only seven of the season's 16 GPs, winning twice in Montreal and Detroit, finishing '9'-7-2-3-6 otherwise. Teo Fabi drove 12 GPs between CART commitments in the USA, finishing four times (9-3-4-5) and scoring three times, while younger brother Corrado drove at Monaco, Montreal and Dallas, finishing just once – a pointless seventh in Texas.

Brabham finished the season fourth in the Constructors' Championship.

At the end of 1984 Michelin withdrew from Formula 1, and Ecclestone signed with Pirelli, who had hitherto been uncompetitive, instead.

That change, combined with the need to improve BMW engine reliability, involved some 12,000 miles winter testing, much of it in the heat of Kyalami. This was like finishing one race season then immediately doing another, only more concentrated, through the winter.

They emerged with a more reliable engine but it was not enough and the team's gearboxes would also be unreliable through '85. Brabham had asked Pirelli to develop a competitive race tyre first, then qualifying tyres later. They had competitive hot-weather tyres for Rio only for a gearbox to fail.

The 1985 Pirellis were always very weather sensitive. If the appropriate tyres for whatever ambient conditions happened to be available, the Brabhams ran well. It was like that at Ricard, with a new tyre good in very hot weather. That new tyre was a big change, and from half-way through the season a competitive Pirelli qualifying tyre also emerged. Tyre testing proceeded continuously, and the Brabhams were very quick in a cold test at the Nürburgring and quickest in a freezing test at Zandvoort, then looked potential winners at Brands Hatch on a cool grey day . . . contradicting a popular impression that Brabham's Pirellis only performed in a heatwave.

Gordon Murray's BT54 design was the last in Formula 1 to retain an aluminium outer skin, stiffened by a complex moulded carbon-composite inner-cum-scuttle-and-tank-top. Like the BT52s/53s, it used modular construction with the entire front suspension hung on a machined-from-solid nose bulkhead plugged into the front of the tub structure, and a similar engine/gearbox/rear suspension module at the rear. Continuous torsional tests throughout the season monitored each chassis's health, weakening ones being retired, which explains why no less than nine BT54s were built.

Whereas in 1983/84 it had become standard Brabham practice to produce a B-spec update mid-season, their intensive winter testing for '85 left the BT54 broadly settled all year. Gordon at last abandoned the American Hitco carbon brakes for French SEPs with modified Girling calipers which tested well and whose manufacturers offered 'a good deal'.

Three of the longer-side pod BT54s were new in Rio for Piquet and new driver Hesnault, but the young Frenchman was replaced by Surer from Spa in June when the Belgian GP was postponed due to the relaid road surface breaking up. Chassis '4 was new for Piquet at Estoril, round two of the series, '5 new as spare at Monaco and later burned up in a fire at *ersatz* Nürburgring testing, '6 new for Piquet on the return to Spa, '7 a new spare at Silverstone, '8 emerging for Surer in Austria and '9 new for Piquet at Brands Hatch.

Piquet started all 16 races, finishing only seven: 8-6-1-4-8-2-5. The win came in blistering heat – hence the Pirelli legend – at Ricard, placing second at Monza, fourth at Silverstone, fifth at Spa and sixth in Detroit.

Hesnault had only three races, retiring each time and failing to qualify at Monaco, while Surer did well in his 12 races, being placed eight times: 15-8-8-6-6-10*-4-8. His points scores, in sequence, came at Silverstone, the Österreichring and Monza, while he looked a likely winner at Brands Hatch until his car caught fire.

The Brabham-BMWs were handicapped mainly by their tyres which were generally inferior to Goodyear all season. They ran higher race horsepower beginning the year than through mid-season in deference to the tyre situation. A computer failure at Imola saw them burn all their fuel while at Silverstone 'We cocked up completely and were just utterly uncompetitive and finished with a lot of fuel left over'.

The end of that season was also the end of a Brabham era, for Nelson Piquet left the team which had brought him two World Championship titles to join Williams-Honda in place of Keke Rosberg.

For Brabham, 1986 became a nightmare. The team's drivers were Elio de Angelis and Riccardo Patrese, but on May 14 the unfortunate former Lotus driver lost his life in a testing accident at Ricard-Castellet. His BT55 – chassis '2 – rolled onto a barrier and caught fire in the very fast outward-leg esses, and with no effective help nearby the popular Roman was lost.

This awful incident deeply affected Gordon Murray, and the production of his low-line BT55 with its 72-degree lay-down BMW M12/13/1 engine became a case of too many eggs being jeopardized in one basket. Pre-season testing was grossly disrupted by problems with the new Weismann transmission and chassis, which left team, BMW and Pirelli alike all in trouble. Under calendar pressures they could not catch up, and Elio's death – the first driver Brabham had ever lost – was an extra, crippling, blow.

In retrospect Brabham had suffered most from the loss of rear-wing sidestep winglets when they were banned for 1985. The quite tall upright BMW engine masked the rear wing centre, so something had to be done to clear airflow to the wing. Gordon's lay-down engine idea would achieve this, while also slashing frontal area and lowering centre of gravity. It should have worked.

But back in 1958 Colin Chapman had laid the Climax four-cylinder engine on its side in his first Formula 1 Lotus 16, and it encountered problems, winding its own oil round in the crankcase and letting it pool in the head and cam-box. Similar problems beset the 72-degree Bee-Emm, scavenging had to be improved to release power otherwise being absorbed, and its induction also seemed constricted. All season it ran very hot indeed. All these problems offset the low-line BT55's low frontal area advantages. BMW could not improve their engine while chassis problems masked evidence of progress. Reclining the engine dictated

The 'low-line' Brabham-BMW BT55 in the Rio garage 1986, Patrese pondering its seven-speed gearchange, his mechanics the car's M12/13/1 slant engine.

Sergio Rinland and John Baldwin's 1989 Brabham BT58 design employed the Judd CV V8 engine and Pirelli tyres on which it shone in such early-season events as the Monaco GP. The BT58 featured one of the slimmest fuselages of its day.

bevel-drive transmission, which made the car long, compromising nimble response in search of straightline speed. It was consistently slow out of corners, yet was often fastest by the end of the straight. It was dogged all season by this poor traction.

By British GP time when Patrese drove an upright-engine BT54, Brabham was happy to go all-upright but BMW lacked the engines, as they were fully committed to Mader for Benetton and Arrows.

Two major rear suspension revisions were made in search of traction, and the front suspension was reworked to move the wheels rearwards, so applying more weight to the rears. Rising-rate changes were also made, but Brabham were so far behind it proved impossible to close the gap mid-season. They were on the treadmill where so many others had suffered before. Yet morale within the team remained remarkably high to face adversity.

Eight BT55s were built, each tub being slightly different in carbon lay-up, but having started with such a radically different car they were crippled once problems interrupted the development programme. The Chessington team brought an old BT54, chassis '9, out of retirement in the Donington Collection for Patrese to race at Brands Hatch. Three new BT55 cars had been readied for the start of the season, '1 being a test chassis found unsuitable. The design was then considerably modified to produce the spec to which chassis '2-'8 were then developed. Chassis '5 was written off in a Donington testing accident.

Elio de Angelis's four races for the team yielded only eighth place at Rio, then three retirements before the accident between the Monaco and Belgian GPs. Patrese drove in all 16 GPs, and retired 11 times, otherwise being classified sixth after retirement at Imola, then 8-6-7-13. Derek Warwick took de Angelis's place from Montreal for the final 11 events, although he non-started at the Österreichring. His four finishes make poor reading: 10-9-8-7. It was an appalling year for the formerly trend-setting team, and they managed merely ninth place in the Constructors' standings, ahead of Arrows and doubling the Milton Keynes team's score – by scoring two points . . .

Gordon Murray was determined not to end on a low note, even though he had by this time had enough of the pressures of Formula 1 design and engineering direction. For 1987 David North produced the BT56 chassis design, converted from an upright BMW-engined concept to accept the lay-down engine with a shortened transaxle, one ratio having been removed since power with 4-bar boost was hardly a problem. Unfortunately, a more complex dry sump lubrication system necessary to feed the redesigned gearbox with its relocated shafts then demanded an additional scavenge pump, which replaced the weight saved. Sergio Rinland, ex-Williams, detailed the new carbon tub which was made in Williams style with a separate floor bonded into a one-piece upperworks moulding. The separate front suspension module previously favoured by Murray was replaced by a conventional front end with the dampers inside the scuttle. Having taken over the FORCE team, Brabham now adopted their THL-2 type rear uprights and full-length diffuser, both wing and underwing profiles being FORCE forms and the BT56 emerging in this respect sharing many features with the contemporary Arrows A10 designed by ex-FORCE engineer Ross Brawn.

Compared to the unfortunate BT55, the new year's BT56 weighed about the same – too much by some 15-20 kg – but its 40/60 weight distribution was better and its shorter wheelbase encouraged weight transference to enhance mechanical grip and promote good traction out of slow corners.

Brabham fielded BT56s chassis '1-'4, driven by the all-Italian pairing Riccardo Patrese and Andrea de Cesaris until Stefano Modena replaced the former – who had been engaged by Williams to replace the injured Nigel Mansell – in Australia at the end of the season.

It was a pathetic swansong season for the old Brabham team as both Gordon Murray and David North left the team they had made so great. De Cesaris finished only twice, but he was third at Spa, eighth in Adelaide. Patrese's 15 outings for the team yielded five finishes – 9-9-5 (Hungary) 13-3 (Mexico) and once classified as a finisher, a distant 11th in Japan. F3000 hopeful Stefano Modena looked good before his retirement in his one-off outing at Adelaide, ending the season. Brabham took eighth place in the Constructors' table, with their 10 points, ahead of Lola, Zakspeed, Ligier, March and AGS.

For 1988, the Motor Racing Developments Ltd Brabham team bowed out of racing and did not re-emerge until the company had been acquired from Bernie Ecclestone by Swiss financier Joachim Luhti, Walter Brun also being involved. The team was consequently re-formed to return to racing in 1989 with all-new BT58 cars, designed by Rinland and John Baldwin. Looking distinctively Brabham in their slender, pointed lines with short side pods, five BT58 chassis were produced for drivers Martin Brundle and Stefano Modena, powered by the Judd CV V8 engine and running Pirelli tyres.

On tight circuits these tyres gave the revived Brabham marque a distinct edge – particularly

vividly demonstrated at Monaco – but the BT58 proved slow on long straights and yielded its position as the quickest early-season Judd runner to Team Lotus's rival Type 101s.

Brundle finished sixth at Monaco and Monza and fifth in Japan, but otherwise retired from seven GPs and failed to pre-qualify at both Montreal and Ricard. Modena shone at Monte Carlo, finishing third, but his only other finishes of the year were 10-11-14 in Mexico, Hungary and Portugal while he was excluded from his own Italian GP. Otherwise he at least qualified every time. The team ended the year eighth-equal with Dallara in the Constructors' Championship, both with eight points. But on the Wednesday prior to the Belgian GP, money-man Luhti had been arrested in Zurich on embezzlement charges, and the team's future was again in the melting pot.

In 1990 Brabham was rescued from eternity through last-minute acquisition by Nakauchi-San's Middlebridge Group just before the season-opener at Phoenix. They obtained Judd's new 76-degree EV V8 engines which Leyton House were using as nominal 'works' team and development partner. Sergio Rinland developed the BT59 logically from his 1989 car, mouldings being suitably modified in line with latest cockpit regulations. The cars were campaigned through the first half of the season with BT58 rear ends, suspension and longitudinal gearbox, a new transverse gearbox then being adopted progressively in mid-season. Considerable teething troubles were immediately experienced and the car did not look quite so good thereafter.

The team actually ran BT58 chassis '1, '3, '4 and '5 in the first two GPs at Phoenix and Interlagos, before completing new BT59s from Imola, five of these cars being produced. Gregor Foitek drove in the first two GPs, qualifying both times before retirement from the races themselves. He then moved to Onyx/Monteverdi, while his Brabham place was taken by Sir Jack Brabham's son David, who failed to qualify six times, failed to finish in seven of the eight races he did actually start, and finished only 15th at Ricard . . .

Meanwhile, Stefano Modena ran the entire season for the team, qualifying every time, finishing fifth in Phoenix and otherwise 7-11-13-9-17*-12 while retiring from his other nine races. With two World Championship points, the revived team finished last – ninth-equal with Arrows – in the Constructors' Championship.

Brabham and Yamaha then joined forces for 1991 – both with much to prove. The new OX-99 V12 engine was unveiled at Suzuka before the 1990 Japanese GP, and Brabham produced modified BT59Y chassis to accommodate it, three of which raced at the start of the 1991 season, serials '1, '3 and '5. Pre-season testing failures were rife on the engine, and it was to be constrained in ultimate crankshaft speed throughout the following year. The BT59Y was only ever a stop-gap design, an unwieldy and overweight compromise car until Sergio Rinland's tailor-made BT60Y replacement became available at Imola, strikingly profiled with a missile-sharp nose, underslung front wing, initially irregular-planform side pods and pushrod suspension all round. A problem surfaced with the original foot pedal positioning as the pedal pads moved ahead of the front axle line safety threshold when fully depressed. This had to be corrected, delaying the BT60Ys' debut, and another mid-season delay involved manufacture of stronger composite underfloor panels.

The season was punctuated by an unnerving series of 'finger trouble' failures, not least wheels working loose or being lost altogether at Mexico City, Spa and Monza. Drivers Martin Brundle and Mark Blundell maintained reasonable morale despite such problems, plus a series of other structural and installation failures. Brundle was excluded from the Monaco GP after a minor rule infraction, and failed to qualify at Adelaide. But he finished fifth for Yamaha at Suzuka, his other finishes reading 11-12-11-11-9-13-12-10. Blundell showed real talent, still failing to qualify for both the Canadian and Japanese GPs, but finishing five times, 8-12-6 (at Spa) 12-17.

In mid-season John MacDonald – of former RAM Racing fame – replaced Dave Price as team manager, then Rinland moved out and the project faltered rapidly as funds diminished.

Yamaha had to inject more money than they had planned and the relationship rapidly soured, the Japanese eventually forging their alternative deal with Jordan for 1992, leaving Dennis Nursey's team to fall back on Judd GV V10 power – and another year's increasingly desperate battle for survival. Five BT60Ys had been fielded during the season, number '5 only for the last two GPs, in Japan and Australia.

BRM

Founded as a trust intended to organize a co-operative industrial Grand Prix car venture in 1945-46, British Racing Motors – BRM – had been a subsidiary of the privately owned Owen Organisation since 1952. From its base at Bourne in Lincolnshire it had campaigned Formula 1 cars in three Formulae from 1950 and finally won the World Championship with its 1500 cc V8-engined cars driven by Graham Hill in 1962.

BRM was, in effect, a British Ferrari, making its own chassis, engines and gearboxes while all around were specialist 'kit car' teams buying engines from one supplier (often BRM itself), buying gearboxes from another and merely engineering and operating their own chassis.

Through the last three seasons of 1½-litre racing, 1963-4-5, BRM was a magnificent team with not a weak link in the chain. It was immensely consistent and Hill came within an ace of winning a second title in 1964 but had actually scored too many times. To comply with contemporary rules, he had to drop his lowest-scoring finishes, allowing Surtees and Ferrari to pick up the titles instead. BRM was second in the Constructors' table in each of those three seasons.

For the start of the new 3-litre Formula in 1966, Chief Engineer Tony Rudd opted to build an H16-cylinder engine. It began life as a pair of the successful P56 1500 V8 engines with their cylinder banks laid horizontal, mounted one above the other with their crankshafts geared together, though it did not quite emerge like that after development. Until it became raceworthy, BRM ran Tasman 1.9-litre versions of its highly successful P261 1964-65 Formula 1 cars. Engine development is outlined on pages 189-91.

These very neat cigar-like full-monocoque cars were on the minimum weight limit and had available some 275 bhp at 9750 rpm. Chassis '2616' and '2617' were driven by Hill and Stewart as the European season began seriously at Monaco, Stewart winning and Hill finishing third. Both crashed in the first-lap rainstorm at Spa in which Stewart broke his collarbone and destroyed chassis '7; Hill, however, later ran high in the French GP until a camshaft broke.

Stewart returned for the British GP, in '2614', but the V8 BRMs were slower than the Repco Brabhams and even Gurney's merely four-cylinder Eagle. Hill was third; a week later he came second in Holland with Stewart fourth, they achieved 4-5 at the Nürburgring, but after this the 2-litre cars were pensioned off as the H16s took precedence.

The BRM used a bulky P83-design forward-monocoque nacelle with the compact but heavy P75 H16 engine and gearbox bolted rigidly onto its rear bulkhead as a load-bearing structural member. In this respect, it anticipated the Cosworth DFV but was itself pre-dated by the 1965 flat-12 Ferrari model 1512.

The factory H16 did not actually race until September 1966, although it had made one very brief appearance at Reims in a Lotus 43 and was given practice runs at Monaco, Spa and Reims – where it had first shown promise. A variety of mechanical problems, mostly with clutch and gearchange, made it unraceworthy until Monza.

Both works H16s ('8302' for Hill and '8303' for Stewart) retired early, Hill's engine disintegrating internally and Stewart's car developing an incurable fuel leak. Clark's Lotus 43-H16 ran strongly between pit stops, and the hope which this engendered seemed justified two weeks later when first Stewart then Hill led the Oulton Park Gold Cup before engine trouble intruded.

The US GP at Watkins Glen followed, where the spare works H16 engine, '7505', won, but as it was fitted in Clark's Lotus 43 Chief Engineer Tony Rudd had a little explaining to do when he returned home . . .

The works engines also ran well – for a time – until Hill's car broke its final-drive and Stewart's its engine. Mexico was an anti-climax, as Clark's US-winning H16 exploded in practice and the substitute failed to perform in the race. Stewart's ran third until its engine grenaded, throwing a crankshaft counterweight, but Hill's refused to run properly and this was worrying for it had the latest eight-pin crankshaft intended as frontline armament for 1967.

That formative season also saw a private Tasman P261 '2615' with former 1½-litre 1960 cc V8 engines entered by Bernard White, notably for Bondurant. Other BRM V8 engines powered Lotus 25/33, Brabham BT11 and even old Cooper

Above: *At Reims '66 Graham Hill has BRM P83 '8302' really growling in practice.* Below: *Stewart deemed his ancient 2.1-litre Tasman P261 V8 '2614' more suitable in the 1967 French GP.*

and BRP chassis during the season for Ireland, Siffert, Hobbs, Bonnier, Wicky and John Taylor.

The Bourne works team made 19 starts and finished seven times, all with the Tasman V8s; placing 3-1, 2, 2-4 and 4-5, scoring 22 points for fourth place in the Constructors' Championship.

Had BRM's planning worked out, 1967 would have been the year of the H16. In dyno testing before Monaco, '66 engine '7504' had delivered 395 bhp at 10,250 rpm and it remained consistently the most potent unit, exceeding 400 bhp that winter. But Rudd planned a new four-valve-per-cylinder unit and Geoffrey Johnson was designing a new P101 24-valve 3-litre V12 which BRM hoped to market for sports car racing. McLaren ordered the prototype for Formula 1, while running Tasman V8s in their own chassis in the interim.

The H16 cars' main problem was excessive weight. Except at Monaco where Stewart led for a time in '2616' V8, BRM was handicapped by the H16 being nearly 300 lb overweight, even in magnesium-skinned P115 lightweight form, while the earlier conventional skin cars were 350 lb overweight. After the Race of Champions a wide-based upper rear wishbone replaced the original single link system, and it was some time before the solitary '1151' handled as well as the P83s.

The season began badly when Stewart's engine in '8303' blew up on lap 2 in South Africa, and new team-mate Spence ran 32 laps in '8302' until an oil pipe broke. At Monaco, Stewart's 2.1-litre uncharacteristically broke its final-drive (having already won three Monaco GPs) but Spence's '8302' finished sixth, albeit four laps behind.

At Zandvoort, Stewart practised '1151', which was three inches narrower and incorporated a top-ducted radiator, and raced '8303' but lost brake fluid; Spence, meanwhile, was eighth. However, Stewart showed his class by leading at Spa until the car started jumping out of gear and finished second in '8303', with Spence's '8302' fifth. Stewart's car was geared for 198 mph at 11,000 rpm.

Stewart preferred '2614' for the French GP at Le Mans, finishing third. Irwin's '8302' placed fifth despite a last-lap engine cut but Spence retired '8303' early with the gearbox output shaft broken. Stewart's new '8304' broke at Silverstone, where Spence had ignition failure. At the Nürburgring, the cars chewed up five crown-wheels and pinions – Irwin having finished seventh in the Parnell team-entered '8301'. Mosport saw McLaren's debut for the new BRM V12 engine, while Stewart spun '1151' out of its maiden race, Irwin spun '8302' clogging its throttle slides with mud and

Spence finished fifth in '8303'. Stewart and Irwin retired at Monza and all three BRM H16s failed at Watkins Glen, though Spence was able to salvage some pride with fifth in Mexico. As Stewart departed for 1968 and V12 engines were introduced, BRM would start anew, leaving the lightweight magnesium 64-valve H16 to be abandoned, unraced.

Spence drove the H16's farewell race at Kyalami on New Year's Day 1968, but both his '1151' and team-mate Rodriguez's new P126 V12 were dogged by fuel vapourization.

In its entire career the BRM H16 engine started only 20 races, 16 at Championship level, winning once in a non-works client's car. BRM's 1967 record included 32 works-car starts but only 12 finishes; their 17 points gave them sixth place in the Constructors' table.

The new P126 V12 cars used elegant monocoque tubs stress-skinned 360 degrees through the scuttle area and carrying the V12 mated to a Hewland DG300 gearbox. They were designed and built by freelance Len Terry's consultancy to ease pressure on Bourne. Three of the cars were built by Terry's Transatlantic Automotive Consultants concern and used his parallel-link rear suspension layout.

Chassis '126/03' used a Formula 1 3-litre V12 engine for Kyalami, chassis '01 and '02 using 2.5-litre V12s for the 1968 Tasman Championship, later being re-engined to Formula 1 form for the European season. The Bourne-built version of the P126 was known as the P133; '01 made the type's debut in Rodriguez's hands at the minor Brands Hatch meeting in March, '133/02' being written off by him at Monaco. A lightweight full-monocoque P138 emerged with BRM gearbox for the Italian GP but had hardly been used by the season's end.

Early on, Rodriguez's '133/01' was second in the Race of Champions after Spence qualified '126/03' on the front row, but bottomed through an oil pipe in the race. Spence was second fastest again at Silverstone, the engine timing chain breaking as he was in second place. Just over a week later, Spence was killed in a Lotus turbine car at Indianapolis, devastating his friends at BRM.

Rodriguez drove '133/01' at Jarama, led 11 laps and was fighting to retain the lead when he crashed, while Courage's quasi-works 'B-team' Parnell-entered '126/01' broke its metering unit drive belt.

Attwood joined the team at Monaco, finishing second and setting fastest lap in '126/30'. At Watkins Glen, Indy star Bobby Unser drove the P138 which had first appeared at Monza with a new BRM gearbox in place of the Hewland and with the rear suspension mounted on extended monocoque rear horns, but its engine blew. From Rouen, top-ducted nose cones were adopted McLaren fashion, and a variety of wings arose.

They made 38 starts that season, finishing 19 times, and after that early-season promise in the non-Championship races and at Monaco, Rodriguez placed second in Belgium, third in Holland and Canada, and fourth in Mexico – all in '133/01' – but the cars never challenged on equal terms and the relatively modest 24-valve V12 engine was no match for the 32-valve Cosworth V8s. On 18 February 1969, the prototype 'P142-001' 48-valve engine had its first run, delivering 441 bhp at 9300 rpm, while P101 24-valve units '003, '006 and '009 gave respectively 390, 393 and 383 bhp at 9750 rpm when tested at about the same time.

Surtees joined for the 1969 season but the 48-valve V12s lacked reliability and torque. The trouble began at Kyalami where the new engine broke a valve guide in practice and did not even race in Surtees's '138/02'. The 48-valve units were still

Top right: BRM's 3-litre V12 emerged in works cars in 1968 but Bourne was losing its grip by this time. Left: Richard Attwood during his brilliant 1968 Monaco GP drive in '126/30'. Below: The V12 came good in Tony Southgate's 1970 P153 design, here with Rodriguez's '02 winning at Spa.

not ready for Silverstone and the works cars were withdrawn, but at Barcelona Surtees finished fifth with engine '142-002' and team-mate Oliver retired '133/01' with engine '142-001'.

While concentrating on combating Cosworth engine power, BRM lost its way over chassis design. Their monocoque cars were always beautifully built but were dated, featuring slim low-frontal area forms in an era when aerodynamic demands dictated flatter, broader shapes.

Alec Osborne was responsible for the circular-section P139 which incorporated new-geometry suspension, low rear-mounted oil coolers, reduced weight, and 45 instead of 38 gallons fuel capacity – as in the P138 but now contained in a multitude of small cells. It appeared in practice at Zandvoort but was not considered raceworthy. Oliver retired '133/01' early with gear selector trouble and Surtees trailed round in '138/01' to finish ninth. At this point there was a great upheaval at Bourne and Rudd was dismissed, Tony Southgate having been brought in from Eagle as chief chassis designer.

BRM missed the French GP but reappeared at Silverstone for the British race. Surtees drove '139/01' modified with one of his own Surtees TS5 F5000 nose cones to improve aerodynamic performance, increased fuel capacity and revised exhaust system to find more mid-range power, but after qualifying sixth a front wishbone broke when third on the opening lap and Oliver retired soon after with another transmission failure. At the Nürburgring, Surtees's '139/01' was withdrawn after practice failures and Oliver retired '138/01' which had bottomed so badly that it had holed its sump.

A complete redesign of the lubrication system finally brought Surtees third at Watkins Glen but the cars were obsolescent and Southgate's new broom would make a clean sweep for 1970.

During this sad 1969 season, BRM made 27 starts, finishing nine times, with only seven points for fifth-equal place with Ferrari in a Constructors' table which included only six scoring teams.

Work on a new P153 chassis began on 1 October 1969, and the prototype was completed in three months. Its shallow 'onion-shaped' aluminium-skinned forward tub carried the engine in a tubular rear truss. Testing was limited to around 150 miles at a damp Silverstone before two P153s went to Kyalami for the South African GP. There a rear axle broke and Southgate rushed out with bolt-on modifications; Rodriguez finished ninth in '02.

Larger, redesigned back axles were introduced at the Race of Champions, where the BRMs ran sponsorship livery for the first time – the white, gold, russet and black of Yardley cosmetics – and Oliver led in '153/01' until a rear axle sheared again. The forging cores were soft, not having been heat-treated properly due to a sub-contractor's error.

New rear axles had been fitted in time for the Spanish GP, and new car '153/03' for Canadian driver George Eaton had also been provided with redesigned front axles although thus far they had given no trouble – whereupon Rodriguez's '02 broke a front stub-axle in practice! Eaton didn't qualify, so his car's new-design stubs were fitted one each to the left-front of the Rodriguez and Oliver cars. Oliver apparently had one snap on the first lap, '153/01' being consumed in the ensuing fire, as was the Ferrari which it had rammed.

By 1971 BRM's latest Southgate-designed P160s were true front-runners; however, Bourne's management were being tempted to run too large a team. Here is the 'onion-monocoque' Southgate car sporting aerodynamic nose aerofoil end fences.

A major engine development came at Monaco where Marelli ignition replaced the original Lucas system, and new car '153/04' appeared for Oliver. Southgate and the team were confident for Spa where their top-endy V12 and good aerodynamics should count; Rodriguez promptly won in '02.

At Zandvoort the BRMs suffered three punctures and Rodriguez wrote off his Spa-winning '02 in a practice accident. One Dunlop tyre actually jumped the four bolsters fitted to retain it, so BRM fitted eight in their wheels thereafter. Rodriguez raced new car '05 after his crash, a sixth P153 emerging as spare at Hockenheim. Reliability was poor mid-season with oil surge, indicating that a new lubrication system was needed, which unfortunately increased drag. At Monza, where great things were expected, Rodriguez's '05 threw a rod and Oliver's '04 popped off its watercap – both after leading. Eaton had a new bifurcated-port engine, '142-007', which went well there until it overheated due to porous casting.

At Ste Jovite in Canada fuel consumption proved a major problem, having fallen from some 6 mpg to only 4.8 mpg; the P153s had insufficient capacity to survive race distance and were forced to make a pit stop. Despite this handicap, Rodriguez finished fourth in Canada, second at Watkins Glen where he had looked set to win before his enforced pit stop, then sixth in Mexico, where Oliver was seventh.

BRM had finished 16 times from 37 starts and placed sixth in the Constructors' table, with 23 points.

Southgate produced the finest 3-litre BRM in 1971: the definitive chisel-nosed P160, a cleaner, lower, lighter development of the P153, though actually incorporating few interchangeable parts. At the end of 1970, a seventh P153 had been completed, to race early in '71. Four new P160s would be built that year: '01 making its debut with Rodriguez at Kyalami, '02 for new team member Siffert at Ontario in March, '03 for Rodriguez at Zandvoort and '04 for new driver Ganley in Austria.

The P160s were very fast and proved it by winning the Austrian and Italian GPs; they handled very well and also became reliable. There were chassis problems early on and the Firestone tyre vibration that season also caused coil failures which were not avoided quickly enough. But in mid-season the team lost Rodriguez – killed in an insignificant little German sports car meeting – and the year ended with their other star driver, Siffert, dying in BRM's first, and only, fatal accident – at Brands Hatch, in which '160/02' was burned out.

During that season, BRM had run a regular three-car team, which expanded to four at the Nürburgring, while in Canada and the USA they ran five cars, all five finishing at Watkins Glen, 2-4-9-13-14. The season's record showed 59 starts yielding 43 finishes, with Ganley failing to qualify at Monaco and non-starting in Canada. The team won two minor races in addition to their two GPs, adding five second places, a third, five fourths, three fifths and a sixth. They were second in the Constructors' table, with 36 points, their best result since 1965 and the end of 1½-litre Formula 1. From here on it was all downhill.

Successfully running those five cars at Watkins Glen influenced the thinking of team Chief Executive Louis Stanley, the self-styled patrician husband of Jean Owen, part-owner of the Owen Organisation itself.

He concluded a new sponsorship deal with Marlboro for 1972-73, and planned a full season with a five- or even six-car team, magnifying the team's potential earning power and the exposure it could offer its sponsor.

Stanley told Southgate: 'If you can run one car you can run ten, you just employ ten times as many people'. In motor racing, it doesn't work like that. His *diktat* demonstrated a lack of understanding of epic proportions.

BRM launched no less than 63 starts overall, 50 in Championship races, from which they finished in the points on only four occasions. Compared, for example, to McLaren's 16 places from 25 starts, such return was dismal. No fewer than ten different drivers appeared. Team manager Tim Parnell had the task of running four and five cars at a time and everything suffered. The V12 lost its edge as both engine and chassis preparation was over-stretched.

Southgate recalled: 'Tim and I kept losing our way. There'd always be two cars in the pits so I'd talk to the drivers, make changes to the cars and by half-way through the session I'd be having hysterics. We'd lose track of which car was which. I'd say to this white helmet: "Ah Pete, er, no – it's not Pete, it's Howden isn't it? Now then, what did we do to your car last time you were in . . . ?" I took a tape recorder with me eventually so I could note all the changes down at the end of the day.'

The initial driver line-up included Beltoise, Gethin, Ganley, Marko and Soler-Roig, with Wisell and Schuppan in reserve. Soler-Roig left, Wisell won a more established place, then poor Marko was blinded in one eye by a flying stone at Clermont, ending his career. Redman, Oliver and Canadian Bill Brack all drove and a motley selection of old P153s, 1971 P160s and the two latest Southgate P180s was campaigned.

Beltoise's heart gave the team a rare high-spot in pouring rain at Monaco where he won in '160B/01'; at Brands Hatch at the end of the year

Tony Matthews' skill unveils the 1971 BRM P160. Note the large oil tank and ducted oil coolers beneath the rear wing; rearward weight bias was increasing.

Right: *Beltoise's P180 with its extreme rearward weight bias and Southgate 'ladybird-section' hull at Monza, Italian GP, 1972. Below: BRM's 3-litre zenith, autumn 1971: Siffert's '160/03' (top) and Gethin's '160/01' (centre) win consecutive Austrian and Italian GPs. Bottom: Beltoise again, this time winning at Monaco, 1972, handling '160B/01', tail light aglow. Far right: Significant swansong: Mike Pilbeam's angular 1974 P201 design.*

in changeable weather Parnell made the right tyre choice, helping Beltoise to win in '180/02', Schuppan coming fourth in '160C/05' and Gethin fifth in '160C/06'. The P160s had been built new for the season along with the two Southgate 'ladybird section' P180s.

These dragster-like cars experimented with more rearward weight bias, 30:70 front:rear, with radiators hung under the tail wing. They made their debut in Spain, but Ganley retired '02 at Monaco and Wisell at Oulton Park. Their handling was poor and they were shelved because, as Southgate admitted: 'we got the 160 going better which only made the 180 look worse; we fitted 180 suspension parts to the 160s and later in the season got it running, but the drivers wouldn't look

at it. Didn't want to know . . .' – until Beltoise was eighth in '180/02' at Monza and ran it thereafter.

Parnell and Southgate went over Stanley's head to Marlboro to persuade them to reduce the team to three cars. Five days before the British GP Stanley relented, but although he approved the move there was insufficient time to prepare those three cars properly. Two retired, Beltoise was 11th and Stanley asked coldly, 'If running three cars means none of them finish, why don't we run five?'

Engine man Aubrey Woods had been replaced by Peter Windsor-Smith, who struggled to keep the V12 competitive and at the end of the year Southgate moved to Shadow. This left gearbox designer Alec Stokes as the sole survivor of the old-time BRM senior engineers, Mike Pilbeam taking chassis responsibility.

Throughout 1973, the P160's third season proved it was still as good as any of its rivals. A new deformable-structure P160E version appeared, with new chassis '07 first running in Spain, '08 in Belgium and '09 in the British GP.

They braked and handled as well as any but the V12 engines could no longer compete with Cosworth. BRM development had stagnated. They were hard-pressed to reproduce 1972 times on some circuits. Fifty starts were made in Formula 1, yielding 26 finishes; Regazzoni third at Silverstone in the minor meeting, sixth in Austria and Brazil and seventh in Argentina; Beltoise fourth in Canada, fifth in Spain, Austria and Holland, and new-boy Lauda fifth at Silverstone and in Belgium.

BRM predictably lost its major sponsor for 1974, the Owen Organisation was itself in trouble but French Motul oil support secured drives for three French drivers: Beltoise, Pescarolo and Migault – the first being past his best, the latter not having a best and Pescarolo ranking somewhere in between. Amon joined at the end of the year and cheered the Frenchmen by assuring them the cars really were as gutless as they believed, then proving his own ability by qualifying in mid-grid at Watkins Glen.

Stanley had been trumpeting about 'regaining one's self-respect', running 'British Racing Green' and being 'unsponsored' for 1974 and criticizing major sponsors for the power they were attempting to wield in Formula 1. His tune had changed so often, with little reduction in volume, few took any notice.

Still, Bourne was staffed by some excellent people who made the best of limited funds and eccentric management. Pilbeam produced a new pyramid-section, mid-radiator, short-wheelbase chassis in the new P201, which handled excellently. Four were used that season but they were too heavy and under-powered with the now much-patched and ancient V12 engines.

Old P160Es '05 and '09 were joined by a new car, '160E/10', while '201/01' made a superb but flash-in-the-pan debut at Kyalami where Beltoise finished second on 'qualifying' tyres. Beltoise had two P201s available at Monaco, '03 emerged for Pescarolo at the Nürburgring, and at Monza Beltoise drove this car, while Pescarolo debuted '04 and Migault inherited '01. Running engines '008, '021 and '007, they each retired – Beltoise and Migault on the opening lap and Pescarolo surviving three laps. Beltoise demolished '03's front end in practice at Watkins Glen and non-started, while Amon's run home ninth in '201/04' may be regarded as the end of the long and sometimes noble BRM saga.

Irrespective, Team BRM had made 42 starts that season, with most of their 24 finishes in the early part of the year. Beltoise added fifths in Argentina and Belgium to his second in South Africa, while Pescarolo and Migault were 4-5 in the minor Silverstone race. Thanks to Beltoise's results, BRM finished seventh in the Constructors' Championship with the last ten points they would ever score.

Promises of ever more power had proved empty on track and, ending the year, Stanley publicly blamed Bourne's loyal and highly competent staff for 'shoddy' work, making many redundant after years of service. Parnell resigned in disgust, his men having been asked to make bricks without straw.

The ailing Owen Organisation divested itself of Team BRM for 1975, Stanley taking it on and entering the old P201s one at a time as Stanley-BRMs, initially with Mike Wilds retiring '201/04' from his two races in South America, then Bob Evans persevering in the now feeble '201/05' – except in Belgium where he ran '02 – failing to qualify at Monaco but finishing four of his other eight races, 15-9-13-17, plus sixth in the Race of Champions and tenth at Silverstone.

Starting 1976, Stanley-BRM sent their re-nosed P201B, '04, to Brazil with Ian Ashley strapped into the cold seat; they retired. The team then retreated to Bourne until the following winter when Stanley announced plans for a grand return in 1977. It happened, linked to the extraordinary story of the Stanley-BRM P207, a bulky, vaguely Ferrari-like vehicle designed by freelance Len Terry.

Two were built, with revised P200 V12 engine by Aubrey Woods and an improved Alec Stokes gearbox. Stanley-BRM were sponsored by Rotary Watches, who had been foolish enough to believe prophecies of Grand Prix-winning glory. The tiny remaining Bourne staff under Alan Challis and Alec Stokes were happy just to be back. Larry Perkins was to drive. He was in Buenos Aires awaiting his car's arrival by air when he was told it was not coming, because it proved too big to fit through the freight-plane's door at Gatwick Airport – the fault of the shipper, who had subsequently to compensate Stanley-BRM.

The team did get the car to Brazil where, amongst other problems, it was unable to run more than two consecutive laps without overheating – Interlagos being rather hotter than Lincolnshire in January! Perkins drove old '201B/04' at Kyalami, finishing 1fifth, but '207/01' non-started the Race of Champions and Perkins walked out in disgust.

Conny Andersson was unable to qualify for the Spanish, Belgian, Swedish and French GPs, Edwards could not even pre-qualify for the British race, and Teddy Pilette failed in Germany, Holland and Monza. This was a rather different picture to that painted for Rotary, and their partnership with Stanley-BRM collapsed amid acrimony and litigation.

Even so, Stanley-BRM stumbled on into 1978. Though out of serious Formula 1, a P207C was run for Pilette in glorified club racing, and was uncompetitive even there.

Activity ceased during 1979 but in 1980, and then again in 1982, the enthusiastic John Jordan, who had bought much BRM material, entered cars under the Jordan-BRM name in bush-league Formula 1 'clubbies'. British Racing Motors had been founded by ordinary enthusiasm and it was there in the early Eighties that it all ended . . .

Coloni

The enthusiastic Enzo Coloni's tiny Italian organization, based at Passignano sul Trasimeno, outside Perugia, attempted Formula 1 for the first time in 1987, their prototype FC187-Cosworth DFZ V8 chassis appearing at two late-season races only, in Italy (failing to qualify) and Spain (retired), driven by Nicola Larini. The car was designed by Roberto Ori, a former Dallara engineer, and was broadly conventional with carbon tub but short 2800 mm wheelbase considering its foot pedals were already back behind the front axle line as would become mandatory in the following year.

For 1988 the little team did its best for driver Gabriele Tarquini with three improved type FC188-Cosworth chassis. He did his best to pre-qualify, qualify and hopefully race in Formula 1, but the entire team suffered from all-round inexperience . . . All had to learn under the intense pressures of their first full F1 season, and as money ran short they struggled on only some 50 per cent of the pre-planned budget. A lighter Coloni-Cosworth 188 was produced for Spa, and one with greatly improved slimmed-down aerodynamic configuration for Monza, but they always seemed to be trying to do just too much, with too little . . . and seemed well out of their depth at Grand Prix level.

Tarquini in fact qualified comfortably for the first five GPs of the season, finishing the last two of them 14-8, but then followed four consecutive failures to pre-qualify as the opposition forged ahead. The Hungarian, Belgian and Portuguese GPs were also started, finishing 13-R-11, but Tarquini failed to qualify at Monza, and to pre-qualify for the final three races – a costly way to travel the world.

In 1989 Enzo Coloni attempted to run a regular two-car team. Chassis FC188/1 and '2 appeared early in the year, the replacement C3s emerging in Canada – chassis '1 – and then Ricard – chassis '2, for drivers Roberto Moreno, Pierre-Henri Raphanel and later Enrico Bertaggia. Engineer Christian Vanderpleyn had joined the team from AGS but despite his efforts even Moreno was unable to qualify for five races, and even to pre-qualify for seven subsequent events. He started

the Monaco, Canadian, British and Portuguese GPs, but failed to finish every time.

Meanwhile Raphanel in the team's second entry managed to clear pre-qualifying for the first time in the third race of the season, at Monaco, where he won a place on the starting grid along with his team-mate Moreno but like him retired. Seven successive failures to pre-qualify followed, Raphanel moving to Rial for the last six GPs from Spa – for whom he consistently pre-qualified, but equally consistently then failed to qualify during official timed practice. It must have been a demoralizing experience; as it was for Bertaggia who replaced Raphanel in the Coloni team from Spa to the end of the season and never pre-qualified successfully.

In 1990 the Subaru (read Motori Moderni) flat-12-engined Coloni C3B – chassis '2 – appeared at Phoenix and ran through the first half of the season, followed by three C3C Cosworth DFR-powered cars, using chassis '1, '3 and '5, making four Colonis in all, Bertrand Gachot being the Perugia team's sole driver. The Subaru-engined car used a Motori Moderni-designed transverse gearbox but the car was still ungainly and markedly overweight.

Eight successive early-season failures to pre-qualify the Subaru-engined version led the engine's long-optimistic Japanese backers to withdraw it, the loss of face being too much to bear. By that time, however, they had already – in May – bought out Enzo Coloni's 49 per cent share and he was no longer involved in the team which continued to bear his name.

Following the flat-12 engine's withdrawal, the team bought Cosworth DFR V8 replacements, but the cobbled-up car still failed to pre-qualify in the next two races at Hockenheim and the Hungaroring. Gachot then succeeded in clearing the pre-qualifying hurdle for the last six GPs of the season, only to set times – heartbreakingly – still too slow in official qualifying to take a place on the starting grid . . .

For the teeny teams, merely attempting to start a Grand Prix with a grid restricted to only 26 cars had become a mighty mountain to climb . . . and in modern Formula 1 Coloni was the teeniest of teenies.

After the débâcle of 1990 and the so-called Subaru flat-12 engine, there was talk of running a two-car team for '91. It didn't happen, and Coloni re-emerged instead with a so-called C4 chassis whose design was credited merely 'to the Coloni technical department with assistance from the University of Perugia', Cosworth DFR power and Portuguese driver Pedro Chaves, supported by Japanese sponsorship. Chaves never succeeded even in pre-qualifying and at Monza on the team's home ground came the ultimate humiliation – the engine refused to start, and despite the desperate mechanics feverishly hunting the cause the session ended without the Coloni ever setting a tyre on the circuit. For Chaves's home GP at Estoril a new Langford & Peck DFR was adopted but blew up almost immediately. Without a spare, Chaves was left disconsolate in the pits. He quit the team thereafter. Coloni sought another driver for Barcelona, but found none, declaring instead the sale of a majority shareholding to the Italian shoe maker Andrea Sassetti to enter 1992 F1 under the title 'Andrea Moda'.

To qualify for that entry Coloni had to contest the last two long-haul races of 1991, and managed to scrape together the readies to pay for the trip from enthusiasts' contributions. Japanese driver Naoki Hattori tried to pre-qualify where Chaves had failed . . . and he failed too. Coloni was the only F1 team with a 100 per cent record during 1991, or 0 per cent, depending upon one's viewpoint . . . Perhaps all their money could have been better spent?

Young Belgian hopeful in Italian no-hoper, Bertrand Gachot in the 1990 Coloni-Cosworth DFR C3B, failing to qualify on his home circuit at Spa; notably low side pod profiles, pushrod front suspension . . .

Connew

Peter Connew was a draughtsman working for Team Surtees when they entered Formula 1 racing in 1970 and he developed ambitions to have a go himself. With absolutely zero finance, he designed a single-curvature riveted aluminium monocoque to take a Cosworth/Hewland power pack. He built the tub with help from some friends in an Essex lock-up and was gratified to find component suppliers as helpful as they were. This was probably the most under-financed of all true Formula 1 specials, and perhaps 'Connew' itself was an unfortunate name when seeking sponsors.

A pilot-build tub and one complete car, '002', were completed and with French Darnval seafood sponsorship the team entered the 1972 British GP at Brands Hatch, only for François Migault to fail in qualifying due to a suspension collapse.

The damage was repaired in time for the German GP but although they arrived at the Nürburgring they could not gain an entry due to Migault's inexperience. They started in Austria but rear suspension problems retired Migault after 22 laps.

David Purley qualified the PC1 for the end-of-season Brands Hatch race but was unable to start due to electrical trouble. It was then converted to Formula 5000 trim with a 5-litre V8 engine. It had been fun while it lasted . . .

Cooper

Early in 1965 John Cooper sold his Cooper Car Company to the Chipstead Motor Group. One of their executives was the Italian Mario Tozzi-Condivi. He was an old acquaintance of Adolfo and Omer Orsi who owned Maserati, and when Cooper's existing engine suppliers Coventry Climax refused to support the forthcoming 3-litre Formula, Tozzi-Condivi approached the Orsis instead.

They were keen to sell Cooper a Formula 1 engine but Tozzi-Condivi would not commission Maserati development at Chipstead's expense. Instead he proposed Cooper becoming sole concessionaires for a 3-litre engine to be developed by Maserati, which would be sold to private owners in custom-made Cooper cars. The Cooper works team engines would remain Maserati's property and they would commit themselves to providing sufficient units for three works cars, to competitive development and to all necessary servicing, for which Cooper would pay a flat rate per rebuild . . . of around £700 a time.

Cooper paid seed money to launch the project and *Ing.* Giulio Alfieri began to update and enlarge his nine-year old 2.5-litre V12 engine which had been introduced in the front-engined era.

Cooper completed their T80 spaceframe chassis – built for the still-born flat-16 Climax engine – as a V12 test hack. It was completed late in 1965 and during that winter Cooper's ex-Connaught, ex-Jaguar chassis engineer Derrick White designed a robust and practical monocoque chassis – Cooper's first – to carry the hefty, thirsty and bulky V12.

He noted that it would take '14 weeks to design and build. 15 weeks to develop design & build 5 [cars].' Cooper took on ex-BRP team engineer Tony Robinson, who had been building aluminium monocoques since 1963, to oversee the work and the new Cooper T81s were beautifully made.

The prototype made its debut at the London Racing Car Show in January 1966 as the first fully fledged British 3-litre F1 car. By 1500 Formula standards it was enormous. Its twin-boom tub was skinned in duralumin for rigidity and housed 50 gallons of fuel to satisfy the big V12 engine. Front coil-spring/damper units were inboard, rears outboard and an ingenious inboard-of-the-upright front disc brake system exposed them to direct cooling airstream. The Maserati engine drove via a heavy ZF 5DS25 transaxle identical to the Ford GT40's.

Private entrant R.R.C. 'Rob' Walker bought chassis 'F1-2-66' for Siffert's use, French owner/driver Guy Ligier bought 'F1-4-66' and Swedish veteran Bonnier had 'F1-5-66'. Chassis '1, '3 and '6 were retained as works cars for Rindt and Ginther, the latter loaned by Honda pending completion of their own car.

In mid-season Surtees joined from Ferrari, new chassis '7 being completed to accommodate him although he would regularly race chassis '6, while Amon had a one-off drive in '7 at Reims, finishing eighth.

The big cars handled indifferently until sorted out after the arrival of Surtees but they were fast enough, Rindt finishing second to a Ferrari at Spa after leading. In Germany, Ligier wrote off chassis '4 while Surtees and Rindt finished 2-3 in cars '6 and '3 and Surtees clocked fastest lap.

With something like 360 bhp the hefty Coopers were now manageable and handling well, nicely built, very strong. Surtees might have won the US GP but was barged off course by a back-marker and could only finish behind Rindt in another good team 2-3, having set fastest lap.

The V12 ran well at altitude in Mexico City. Surtees qualified chassis '6 on pole and won, Bonnier sixth in chassis '5.

The big T81s had made a total 39 starts, winning once, with three second places, two thirds, three fourths, three fifths and three sixths in 23 finishes. Surtees and Rindt finished 2-3 in the Driver's Championship, Cooper second in the Constructors' Cup, their best season for four years.

Surtees moved to Honda for 1967 but Rindt had to serve another year with Cooper. Rodriguez had a one-off drive in South Africa in Surtees's Mexican-winning chassis '6 and won on reliability with local driver John Love second in his old ex-McLaren Tasman Cooper-Climax 2.7 four-cylinder T76, 'FL-1-65'. From this point it was all downhill . . .

At Monaco, Alfieri's latest engine emerged, using the 1966 *Tipo* 9 bottom end with new *Tipo* 10 three-valve-per-cylinder Heron heads. A new narrower valve angle permitted lighter single covers enclosing both camshafts. Inlets were resited within the vee in true crossflow form with the exhausts outboard. Twin spark plugs per cylinder lay beneath the exhausts in the side of the combustion chamber, rather than more conventionally. Three-plug heads were also tried. Internal-toothed flexible belts drove from the front of each inlet camshaft to 12-pole distributors fed by Lucas transistors.

White and assistant Bob Marston had developed an experimental lighter and smaller radiator as well as new fabricated magnesium disc wheels but they remained unused at Monaco.

A new lightweight T81B car had been completed using aluminium instead of duralumin skins and a Hewland instead of ZF gearbox, plus the new disc wheels. This chassis, 'F1-1-67', was first used by Rindt in this finalized form in the Dutch GP. While the Lotus 49s set new standards there, the Cooper-Maseratis of Rindt and Rodriguez lined up on row two. But reliability faltered that summer.

For the British GP the new T86 appeared, chassis 'F1-2-67' with magnesium-elektron skinned shallow monocoque to compensate for the still massive overweight of the engine and fuel load. Suspension was T81B-style, while the flat-scuttled car had quite the ugliest nose treatment ever seen in Formula 1! It used a *Tipo* 10 36-valve engine mated to a Hewland gearbox, saving some 112 lb compared to the T81.

For the Nürburgring, both this T86 and its T81B sisters used Hewlands, but the engines suffered a plague of disintegrating starter rings, which damaged engines, gearboxes and tubs. In testing, the T86 lifted its nose at speed and after adding 30 lb of lead (!) a chin-spoiler was fitted for Monza. Ickx made his Formula 1 debut there in the T81B, both machines using 36-valve engines with revised combustion chambers, Hewland gearboxes and rear suspension which now placed the rear brake discs inboard of the uprights, as at the front. Rindt finished fourth, Ickx sixth, both ahead of Ferrari to delight Maserati's men.

In America, both 36-valve 24-plug and 36-valve 36-plug engines were in use, prompting Keith Duckworth, the designer of the 8-cylinder, 8-plug Cosworth DFV, to remark that if one spark wasn't

---

Above left: *Peter Connew's special, British GP, 1972.* Below: *The Beast – Cooper-Maserati T81 at Brands Hatch, 1967, driven by Rodriguez and demonstrating its beefy shape, front brakes exposed to direct airstream and cranked lower wishbone-ends.*

enough to set fire to the charge then something was radically wrong. It was really the technology of the 1950s breathing its last. Not only was the 36-plug engine heavier than the 24-plug, it also required extra ignition coils, room for which had to be found on the already crowded cars.

The privateers, Siffert and Bonnier, soldiered on to the end in their T81s, while Ligier had replaced his wrecked 'F1-4-66' with ex-works chassis 'F1-7-66' before buying a Repco Brabham BT20 after the 1967 French GP.

Two elderly spaceframe Cooper Specials ran in some 1966-67 events: Pearce's 'F1-1-64' with a two-cam Ferrari 250GT V12 for Chris Lawrence, and Fritz Baumann's 'F1-1-65' with an ATS V8 sports car engine for Bonnier in France '66 and for Moser later in 1967.

By the end of that season the Maserati deal had run its course and would not be renewed. In the South African GP on 1 January 1968, Siffert drove Walker's faithful old 'F1-2-66' – affectionately nicknamed *Torrey Canyon* after the wrecked and oil-oozing Land's End supertanker – into seventh place. Scarfiotti and Redman respectively retired the works team's T86 'F1-2-67' and T81B 'F1-1-67'; Bonnier retired his T81 '5-66 and local driver van Rooyen had the Climax four-cylinder engine break in the even older T76 Tasman car, 'FL-1-65', to mark the end of Cooper's penultimate Formula 1 season.

Tony Robinson had left after the original T81 build programme but now returned at John Cooper's invitation to supervise construction of the latest T86B cars for the new BRM V12 engine. Cooper had wanted to use the Cosworth-Ford V8 but was unable to because of his BMC/BMH tie on the Mini-Cooper saloons.

The new T86B tub was skinned principally in 18-gauge NS4 malleable aluminium sheet formed over three mild-steel bulkheads fabricated around 22-gauge tube. The BRM engine was smaller, narrower and lighter than Maserati's and was less thirsty, so there was no need for magnesium skinning to save weight. Over 40 gallons of fuel was still carried, however, alongside the cockpit, in the rear horns supporting the engine and in a 6-gallon scuttle tank. Suspension used many T86/81B parts, with pronounced front anti-dive. The BRM V12 cooled better than the Maserati, so the T86B's nose was slimmer.

Chipstead's marketing interests extended to Alfa Romeo. A deal was struck with Autodelta (Alfa Romeo competitions) to run a 3-litre Alfa T33 sports car-based V8 in Formula 1, copying the Maserati deal. The third T86B-style tub was actually classified T86C (serialled 'F1-3-68') and was prepared with 4 in. shorter rear booms for the V8. Bianchi tested it at Silverstone with a 2.5 V8, but the 3-litre would never come.

Meanwhile the T86B-BRMs were still some 118 lb overweight. Three of the cars were built, Redman giving the type its debut at Brands Hatch in March where he placed fifth in the prototype 'F1-1-68'. Two cars, chassis '1 and '2, were driven by Gardner and Scarfiotti at Silverstone, placing reliably 3-4, and the same cars then inherited consecutive Championship GP 3-4 finishes at Jarama and Monaco, driven by Redman, Scarfiotti and Bianchi. Bianchi was sixth for another point at Spa where Redman's chassis '2 was destroyed when a lower front wishbone snapped.

A new chassis '4 was driven by Elford into fourth place at Rouen – his single-seater debut – but in the team's final 11 starts that year they only finished once in the points, Elford fifth at Mt Tremblant in Canada.

The T86Bs had been modified with stronger wishbones after the Spa accident, and for the British GP chassis '5 used a top-ducted radiator to kill nose lift. At the Nürburgring both T86Bs had strutted rear wings. Elford's circuit knowledge gave him fifth spot on the grid but he crashed heavily in spray on the opening lap, ripping two wheels off chassis '4. The repaired car was fitted with a spring-loaded trimming rear wing for Monza where he crashed again, due to brake failure.

The team simply faded away at the end of that season, their final appearance being in Mexico where Elford finished eighth in 'F1-4-68' while Bianchi retired '1-68.

Cooper never really recovered from the loss of their BP sponsorship in 1967. Although they abandoned the BRM engine as underpowered at the end of 1968 and a new Cosworth car was designed, negotiations for Wilkinson Sword sponsorship failed and this famous team withdrew.

The old Cooper-Maserati T86 'F1-2-67' survived in Colin Crabbe's Antique Automobiles team in early 1969, using a 36-valve 24-plug engine. Elford finished 12th in it at Silverstone, while historic racer Neil Corner was fourth in the F1/F5000 Madrid GP at Jarama amongst a thin field. At Monaco there was no need to qualify and Elford started last on the grid, 8.2 seconds slower than Stewart's Matra on pole, finishing seventh, six times lapped. This was Cooper's last outing in a Grand Prix, the team's assets being auctioned off on 11 June 1969 to end a noble story.

Copersucar

See entry for Fittipaldi, page 272.

Cosworth

In 1969 Cosworth Engineering set out to produce an advanced four-wheel drive Formula 1 car of their own design and manufacture which would overcome the traction problems which so many of their client teams were experiencing with the abrupt power delivery characteristics of their DFV V8 engine.

Design had commenced early in 1968 when youthful McLaren Chief Engineer, Robin Herd, had been invited to join the Keith

the body with broad-set monocoque tub to generate aerodynamic download which was trimmed out by wedge-section nosepieces ahead of each front wheel and a modest strutted wing above the tail. The nose radiator was top-ducted and a unique lightweight magnesium-block DFV was used to compensate for 4WD system weight, turned about-face to drive to front and rear axles.

In extensive testing with drivers like Costin himself – no mean performer – and Redman, it became clear that putting worthwhile power through the front wheels overwhelmed the capabilities of contemporary tyres. The massive understeer which this induced could be minimized only, it seemed, by reducing the torque-split bias to that end. The message was that more power should be transmitted through the rear wheels; ideally they should use rear-drive only, which made the entire system redundant.

Robin told the author: 'Bruce McLaren described it best when he said driving a four-wheel drive Formula 1 car was like trying to sign your autograph with someone jogging your elbow all the time'. He considered a limited-slip front differential was needed, but effectively the requirement for four-wheel drive had in any case been overtaken by far more effective aerodynamic develop-

ment, 'so what was the point?'

The one complete Cosworth car was sold unraced to collector Tom Wheatcroft and survives today in his magnificent Donington Collection at Donington Park near Derby, while its uncompleted sister pilot-build is in a museum in Australia.

Duckworth/Mike Costin company in Northampton. Robin recalls how thrilled he was to be offered 'the chance to sit at the feet of Duckworth and learn' and in that respect it was a valuable exercise reaching ultimate fruition in his March cars.

Short-term, however, the advent of strutted wing aerodynamic aids during the summer of '68 sidestepped the very problems to which the excess weight and complication of four-wheel drive had been addressed.

Robin's strikingly unconventional design used

Above: *Brian Hatton's* Motor *drawing of Robin Herd's 1969 Cosworth tells all.* Top: *Mike Costin testing the stillborn but fascinating 4WD car at Silverstone. A low-level rear wing was later fitted.*

Dallara

The BMS-Dallara team made its Formula 1 bow in 1988 fielding a former 1987 F3000 tub at Rio, then from Imola running three new FA188B F1 cars as singleton team entries for the promising former Osella driver, Alex Caffi.

Millionaire historic car collector 'Beppe' Lucchini had created the team, and he made perhaps the wisest choice of all his ilk by backing GianPaolo Dallara's (ex-De Tomaso) return to Formula 1. Caffi repaid their support repeatedly with good performances in both qualifying and on race day. The F188 was the longest car in contemporary Formula 1 at 2880 mm overall, powered by the Cosworth DFZ V8 engine and with all its fuel confined in the tub's rear cell, behind the driver. Of all the small Italian teams, Scuderia Italia aptly – with such a patriotic title – did the best job in impressing race engineers at the head of the field, the Nichols, Heads, Byrnes and Barnards. The common word from them was that 'with the material and money available, Dallara did a damn fine job . . .'.

However, very little in the way of concrete results was achieved. The new team's 1988 record saw Caffi failing to pre-qualify twice, at Rio and Montreal, but he started every other race, and regularly showed well despite finishing seven times only, 8-12-11-15-10-7-10, and thus failing to secure a single World Championship point. A new tub – number '3 – was flown out to Canada to replace '2 severely damaged in Caffi's collision with Arnoux's Ligier in Mexico. The damaged car would be returned to service as Caffi's spare ending the season in Japan and Australia. March-like airbox and front wing sections were adopted later in the season.

For 1989 the now two-car Dallara team used Heini Mader-rebuilt Cosworth DFR V8 engines in new B189 cars evolved logically from the B188s by GianPaolo Dallara himself and his colleague Marco Tolentino. They were notable for their nose profiles whose undersides now rose towards the rear. But Caffi again failed twice to pre-qualify – this time at Rio and Silverstone – while his new team-mate de Cesaris failed in official qualifying at Ricard. Caffi finished seven times, 7-4 (Monaco) 13-6 (Montreal) 7-11-9, and de Cesaris's record of nine finishes was poorer, 13*-10-13-8*-3 (Montreal) 7-11-7-10. The Brescia team finished the Constructors' Championship eighth-equal with Brabham on eight points.

Designer Dallara was joined by Christian Vanderpleyn, ex-AGS, in developing the 1990 B190 cars, still DFR-powered, and Emanuele Pirro joined de Cesaris in the Brescia team after Caffi had signed for Arrows, Gianni Morbidelli standing in for an unwell Pirro at the first two races.

De Cesaris was excluded at Ricard and missed qualifying in Germany, but started every other race though finishing only twice, 13-10 at Mexico City and Monza.

Morbidelli failed to qualify in Phoenix and was then 14th at Interlagos, while Pirro made the starting grid in all 14 of his appearances but retired 11 times, finishing 11-10-15 in Britain, Hungary and Portugal. Dallara had again failed to score a single Championship point.

For 1991 the new Judd GV V10-engined *Tipo 191* car was designed by ex-Minardi engineer Nigel Couperthwaite and featured the latest in high-nose aerodynamic form with pushrod suspension front and rear and an in-house transverse six-speed gearbox. Six BMS Dallara 191 chassis were deployed as the season unfolded.

A close relationship developed between the British engine supplier and the Italian team, and drivers Lehto and Pirro enjoyed the new V10's broad power band and enjoyable driveability. Pirro had been a McLaren test driver in the early days of the Honda V10 programme, and he considered the Judd unit superior for that relative stage in development.

Dallara ran Pirelli tyres and suffered badly through the latter half of the season as the tyres

Alex Caffi's Dallara F189-Cosworth DFR at Estoril during the 1989 season in which he and Andrea de Cesaris did well enough in these effective division three cars to establish Beppe Lucchini's team firmly in Formula 1.

proved inconsistent and prone to serious deterioration over race distance. Lehto qualified for every race, but finished only five of them, a good third at Imola (after many front-runners had retired), then 11-13-8-12. Pirro was outfumbled in pre-qualifying three times, but finished nine GPs, 11-6 (at Monaco) 9-10-10-8-10-15-7.

In mid-season team owner Lucchini had arranged supply of Ferrari customer V12s for 1992, and Judd again had the galling experience of a solitary get-by season with a team capable of doing the job quite well.

De Tomaso

Argentinian entrepreneur Alessandro de Tomaso made his name as an amateur racing driver in the Fifties, with OSCA, Maserati and Ferrari cars. He subsequently set up a specialist company manufacturing high-performance cars in Modena, Italy. By 1969 *Automobili de Tomaso* was building a Ford V8-engined mid-engined Coupé named the Mangusta for US sale, and development began on a new US-oriented Coupé, the Pantera.

To promote the company name and indulge his own enthusiasm, de Tomaso authorized production of a monocoque Formula 2 car in 1969, designed by *Ing.* GianPaolo Dallara – co-creator of the remarkable Lamborghini Miura – and for 1970 he agreed with British private entrant Frank Williams to enter Formula 1. Dallara was briefed to design a new chassis to carry the standard Cosworth-Hewland power pack.

A single-car entry would be made for Piers Courage who had scored two second places in Williams's private Brabham BT26 the previous season. Three de Tomaso *Tipo 308* cars were built, chassis serials '505/1-2-3'. Initial outings showed promise, though at least 120 lb too heavy and track initially too narrow. Engine shortages slowed development. Courage had to retire chassis '1 at Kyalami after hitting a kerb too hard, and at Jarama he wrote it off after qualifying on the third row of the grid, being unable to start.

A lighter chassis '2 ran at Silverstone, where Courage finished third; Stewart drove it in practice and declared 'It's quite good'. At Monaco, Courage ran seventh before the steering tightened and at Spa his engine failed. A still lighter third chassis was now available as spare but, while

lying seventh in the Dutch GP at Zandvoort, de Tomaso '505/2' crashed and burned furiously, Courage losing his life. This was shattering.

De Tomaso totally lost interest and the tiny team missed the French GP but returned at Brands Hatch with '505/3' driven by Redman. A hub failed after qualifying and he non-started. He then failed to qualify at Hockenheim with more car trouble, and due to his sports car commitments Schenken then took over, retiring from the Austrian GP with engine trouble, finishing in Canada after a long stop to change a damper, having the suspension break at Watkins Glen and being refused an entry for Mexico. De Tomaso took chassis '3 back to Modena, and still has it, derelict, today, while Williams would buy March cars for 1971, before beginning to build his own (see page 324).

Eagle

American driver Dan Gurney and his fellow former Le Mans winner Carroll Shelby – creator of the Cobra sports car project – formed All-American Racers essentially to win the Indianapolis 500 Miles on Goodyear tyres.

The team began its career by entering a Lotus and two Halibrand Shrikes in the 1965 Indy race, while Gurney was still driving Brabham cars in Formula 1 and AAR's new purpose-built factory was being completed at Santa Ana, south of Los Angeles in California.

Gurney wanted to fly the All-American flag in Formula 1 with the start of the new Formula in 1966, so to design his new cars both for Indy and Formula 1 he hired Lotus engineer Len Terry, whose Type 38 had just won at Indy driven by Clark.

Terry designed a Lotus 38-like Indycar for AAR, to be named the Eagle and to carry a handsome beak-like nose treatment. He then adapted this design to Formula 1 road racing, with less fuel capacity. In fact the Indy design was compromised slightly to enable conversion to road racing, low roll-centre heights featuring in the suspension geometry, though Terry believed a higher roll axis would suit Indy better. Furthermore, despite asymmetrical suspension offset being common at Indy, Terry adopted symmetrical suspension for the track car to generate development experience for the road racer.

Four Type T1G Formula 1 monocoques would be completed in 1966, skinned in 18-gauge aluminium unlike the 16-gauge skinned track cars, saving 50 lb weight. These were full monocoque tubs, with 360-degree stressed-skin scuttle and seat-back sections either end of the cockpit opening.

In his suspension and other tube component design Len Terry went up in diameter and down in wall thickness compared to the Lotus 38 to gain strength without weight penalty. He also planned fitting a second brake disc and caliper on the inboard end of each live front stub-axle to add braking power at the front, but this idea would be shelved.

AAR adopted the 'Anglo-American Racers' title for Formula 1 and were to use an all-new 3-litre V12 Eagle-Weslake engine, built by Weslake & Co., of Rye, Sussex, on England's south-east coast. The design was by ex-BRM engineer Aubrey Woods, who had worked with Gurney when he was a BRM team driver in 1960. A Weslake V12 design with four-valve-per-cylinder heads had been rejected by BRM in favour of their own H16, yet by the summer of 1965 a twin-cylinder test engine to this design was giving good results, so Gurney became interested. An engine contract had been signed in October 1965 for six engines, and space for AAR's British base was provided beside Weslake's premises.

The new V12 would not be available for the start of the new season so AAR bought four stop-gap 2.75-litre Coventry Climax FPF four-cylinder engines to put miles on at least one chassis. Outputs ranged from 190 to 235 bhp, and the best of these 'old nails' was dropped into chassis 'AAR-101' and tested at Goodwood on 8 May 1966. Gurney was stunned by the four-cylinder engine's frantic vibration.

Maiden race was in the Belgian GP at Spa, Dan qualifying last for this power circuit and finishing seventh after a mid-race stop to relieve himself in the roadside ditch, wedging a rock under the Eagle's wheel and leaving the engine ticking over! 'The vibration got to me', he explained, 'I was fearful something was going to burst inside . . .' At Reims, in a more continent performance, he finished fifth in the French GP for his new marque's first World Championship points.

The need for better steering lock had led to the rear lower wishbone legs being kinked to give space, anti-dive was taken out of the front geometry and at Brands Hatch Gurney qualified third and held second place until broken piston-ring lands retired '101. Engine problems grounded the Eagle again at Zandvoort where Gurney both qualified and ran fourth.

AAR engine specialist John Miller rebuilt and developed at least one of the Climax units at Santa Ana with American forged pistons to produce 255 bhp. Gurney ran fourth at the

Top: *Heyday: Dan Gurney takes '102 off from pole position alongside team-mate Richie Ginther's new '103 in the 1967 Race of Champions at Brands Hatch, which the Eagle pair dominated.*

Above: *Deep monocoque, beak nose and gorgeous finish typified the AAR Eagle-Weslakes; 'T1G-102' at Le Mans 1967.* Below: *Bill Bennett's drawing of the 1966-67 Eagle-Weslake.*

Dying days: Dan Gurney sports his new-fangled Bell Star helmet in his only finish with the aerodynamically modified Eagle-Weslake '104, Nürburgring, 1968.

Nürburgring using this engine but a broken condenser bracket dropped him to seventh at the finish.

At Monza he qualified with the Climax engine but raced the first Weslake Type 58 V12-powered car instead. A week after first dyno test the engine gave a claimed 364 bhp so, with Monza only one week away, it was rushed to Italy and installed in 'AAR-102' in the paddock there. Phil Hill practised Eagle-Climax '101, while Dan found problems with the new car's fuel system and with oil temperature soaring in the race he switched off after 17 laps.

Both Climax and V12 cars ran in the US and Mexican GPs – the V12 overheating and throwing out its oil at Watkins Glen, then being retired by Bondurant in Mexico because of fuel feed problems. Bondurant's '101 had been disqualified for receiving outside assistance in the USA, and Gurney drove it into fifth place in Mexico with its Climax engine ailing.

Old '101 appeared once more in Gurney's hands, in the 1967 South African GP where it was retired again, before being sold to Castrol for Canadian Al Pease to drive.

Castrol support for 1967 replaced AAR's original sponsor Mobil, whose departure left the Formula 1 team grossly under-financed. Oil blow-by in the engine had been traced to excessive clearance in cylinder liner fit.

Gurney had a new '413 bhp' engine in '102 for the minor Race of Champions at Brands Hatch, accompanied by new team-mate Ginther in chassis '103 with its prototype V12 claimed to be capable of producing 409 bhp. They ran 1-2 in the final before experimental brake pad trouble retired Ginther, and Gurney won narrowly from a Ferrari.

The Eagle had landed . . .

Though undeniably beautiful, it was a heavy car, some 180 lb over the minimum limit. The cars were lettered 'Harvey Titanium' after California's Harvey Aluminum company had advised replacement of the design's aluminium skins with magnesium and substituting titanium for steel components to save weight in a new chassis.

Ginther failed to qualify at Monaco and Indy; at Zandvoort he felt unable to compete in modern racing and abruptly bowed out of the sport. Gurney, meanwhile, ran third briefly at Monaco only for '103's Lucas fuel metering unit drive belt to break.

Chassis 'AAR-104', nicknamed the 'mag-ti Eagle', was visibly different from its sisters with its close-spaced magnesium skin riveting. All suspension links were titanium, leading to a reduction in weight for the top front wishbone alone from 3³/₈ lb in steel to under 2 lb in titanium. Exhaust manifolds in titanium saved 20 lb; a total 88 lb being saved as '104 scaled 1192 lb. Chassis '103 was subsequently fitted with a titanium suspension set and some of Weslake's V12 castings were changed from aluminium to magnesium to reduce weight still further.

In '104, Gurney was fast at Zandvoort only for the metering unit to fail again, but at Spa he set a new lap record despite low fuel pressure causing a

top-end misfire and won the Belgian GP in grand style, one week after winning Le Mans for Ford. It was the zenith of Dan's fine career.

McLaren joined the team as second driver for the French GP, driving '102 and Dan using '104 on the front row, but both retired with minor failures. In Britain massive engine failures intruded, three V12s breaking that weekend. In Germany Gurney nearly won. With three laps to run, a 45-second lead and a new lap record to his name, a UJ cross sheared – McLaren having already retired with another engine failure.

In Canada Dan was third in '103, and at Monza three Weslake V12s failed, one in practice, one in Gurney's '104 while leading and one in guest driver Scarfiotti's '103, within the opening six laps. Gurney ran '104 as a lone entry in the US, where its suspension failed, and Mexico, where he holed its radiator at the start.

By this time AAR were dubious of Weslake's ability to sustain manufacturing and assembly quality under Formula 1 pressures. AAR hired ex-Vanwall fitter Doug Orchard to assemble engines drawn from Weslake parts on a new monthly basis for 1968.

In South Africa Gurney retired with oil leaks and overheating, quite uncompetitive, and a spare engine installed for a post-race Goodyear tyre test then proved in poorer shape than the race engine! Gurney severed his Weslake tie thereafter and set up a new shop in Ashford, Kent, to build and test the engines. Woods joined them, and from 1 May AAR's entire UK operation, engine and race shop were concentrated there. One V12 was tested on the BRM dyno at Folkingham where it gave no more than 390 bhp – another rude shock after Weslake's claims, for the BRM dyno was hardly considered pessimistic.

An improved Eagle Mark 1A V12 was under development, the team missing Spain and appearing at Monaco, where Gurney started from the back of the grid and was an early retirement. More races were missed before reappearance at the British GP, but although running quicker Gurney again retired. He was ninth at the Nürburgring, having run third early on before a tyre was damaged. Monza was hot, and fast, and the V12 wilted under the strain of climbing from 13th to seventh as oil pressure disappeared.

There, Gurney tried a works McLaren M7A with Cosworth engine, and next day he arranged to drive it for the rest of the season, setting aside the never completely developed Eagle-Weslake.

At Santa Ana new ex-Lola designer Tony Southgate was drawing the 1969 Formula 1 Eagle, with all-magnesium skins. It was to be a neat slim car with outboard front suspension aiming at minimum limit weight and, in view of the V12's continued problems and insufficient budget for further serious development, they thought of building a similar alternative Cosworth car.

But funds were very short, Gurney was not too happy at the fire risk in a magnesium car – mindful of Schlesser's death in the air-cooled magnesium Honda at Rouen – and in November 1968 further Formula 1 plans were abandoned. Henceforth, All-American Racers would concentrate upon US racing, Anglo-American Racers as such being wound up. Woods returned to BRM and a buyer was sought for the V12, Honda expressing brief but unfulfilled interest, and the most gorgeous of all 3-litre Formula 1 cars would be raced no more.

Ensign

Former Lotus sports and Formula 3 driver Morris Nunn built the Ensign F3 cars before being approached by one of his customers, wealthy Liechtensteiner Rikki von Opel, to produce a Cosworth/Hewland Formula 1 car for 1973.

Ensign-Cosworth N173 chassis 'MN01' made its debut in the French GP at Ricard, using a simple made-out aluminium monocoque clad in strikingly styled Specialised Mouldings glass-fibre bodywork with a full-width chisel nose, hip radiators and a spectacular rear wing supported on its end plates.

It was all finished in bright green with yellow pin-striping and was beautifully made and well prepared. Peter Gethin helped with initial development.

Von Opel was little more than a cheerfully amateur driver and placed 15th in France, 17th in Britain and ignored the Dutch and German GPs. He then returned for the Austrian, Italian, Canadian and US events, finishing only in Canada, 20th and too far behind to be classified. Never mind, it was fun, Mo Nunn had a taste for Formula 1 and they were learning fast.

But into 1974 von Opel considered his car uncompetitive and he drove briefly for Brabham before leaving motor racing altogether. Despite having lost his banker, Nunn was determined, somehow, to stay in Formula 1. A second chassis, the more conventionally bodied N174 'MN02', had been completed and guest driver Redman tried both at Silverstone before racing '02 and finishing eighth.

Having abandoned Formula 3 customer car production, all Nunn's eggs were in the Formula 1 basket. He needed an angel to finance survival and one appeared in the diminutive form of Hong Kong/Macau millionaire Theodore 'Teddy' Yip, who injected finance to give his Australian driver Schuppan the ride.

He drove 'MN02' five times and failed to qualify twice, from the Belgian to German GPs. Yip then withdrew, and Nunn arrived in Austria with F5000 driver Mike Wilds and old 'MN01' with revised cockpit section and altered engine cover and airbox. Poor Wilds had little chance, and failed to qualify three times, eventually making the grid at Watkins Glen, where he was 14th, unclassified.

For 1975 the Dutch HB Bewaking alarm systems company bought the Ensign drive for Roelof Wunderink. Wunderink first drove '02 at Brands Hatch in March, qualified for the Spanish GP, but failed to qualify at Monaco and missed the Belgian and Swedish races. Wunderink had hurt himself in a Formula 5000 accident and Gijs van Lennep drove in the Dutch GP, comfortably finishing tenth, while a new Bewaking-financed Dave Baldwin-designed LNF75 – or N175 – model 'MN04' appeared there as unused spare.

It used rising-rate front suspension and inboard brakes all round and again was very nicely made, belying the Walsall team's humble facilities.

Lennep drove it in the French GP, Wunderink failed to qualify it in Britain, then Lennep was sixth in Germany to score Ensign's first Championship point.

Meanwhile, Amon joined Nunn to drive 'MN04' in Austria alongside Wunderink in '02. After his misfortunes in his own Amon AF1 the previous year, the newcomer had reservations about the LNF75's inboard front brakes but he ran well in the car, without worthwhile results, for the rest of the season.

Nunn fell out with HB Bewaking, so for 1976 they took 'MN04' away and he was left to race two-year-old 'MN02' which was updated as far as possible for Amon at Kyalami, Long Beach and in two minor British events, finishing fifth at Brands Hatch. At Long Beach, '02 – which had been advertized for sale for £4000 in the winter – ran 12th fastest in first practice and was eighth in the race, which proved either how good a car it was or how brilliant Amon could be.

Meanwhile, a new Dave Baldwin-designed LNF76 chassis 'MN05' was being completed to conform to the latest airbox and roll-over bar regulations in force from the Spanish GP. Again, it looked beautifully made with AP Lockheed balanced caliper front brakes mounted outboard partly in deference to Amon. At Jarama he qualified tenth and finished fifth for two Championship points, and at last Ensign seemed to be going somewhere. HB meanwhile allowed Australian driver Larry Perkins – who acted as his own mechanic, transporter driver, chief cook and bottle washer – to enter their old 'MN04' under the 'Boro' name, and he finished 13th.

Amon drove well at Zolder, running fifth until 'MN05's left-rear suspension broke and it crashed

Left: *Clay Regazzoni in the Ensign N177 during the 1977 Swedish GP, showing off the neat car's shallow rectangular-section tapering tub, hip radiator pods, separate cockpit shroud and massive roll-over protection.* Below left: *Regazzoni in the neat Ensign-DFV N180 'MN11' on its debut at Buenos Aires, 1980. Later that year he would crash badly at Long Beach to end his fine career.*

Theodore-sponsored '179/01' or 'MN11' which emerged in South Africa. It incorporated a huge radiator built into the scuttle ahead of the cockpit but this proved a miscalculation and the radiators were split back into the side pods for Long Beach. For Spain, Nunn modified old '06 with ground-effect side pods lashed on, since the new 179 was late returning from California.

179 as a wing-car ran at Monaco but it had become a regular non-qualifier by this time. In France Patrick Gaillard drove, then qualified for the British GP but Surer replaced him at Monza. There, Nunn announced new plans for 1980 but, overall, Ensign had only qualified for two races with Daly, two races with Gaillard and one with Surer, while the only finishes had been one 11th and two 13ths . . . a literally pointless season.

Regardless, Nunn had won Unipart backing for 1980, running Regazzoni again in an all-new 180 car designed by former Lotus engineers Ralph Bellamy and Nigel Bennett. The riveted aluminium monocoque car was a virtual Williams FW07 copy but differed in its side pods and its ultra-narrow rear track. At Kyalami a spare car '02 became available but in Long Beach Regazzoni crashed very badly when apparently assured of fourth place, ramming another car parked in an escape road. He was paralyzed by his injuries, ending his career and ruining Ensign's hopes of a bright future; chassis '180/01' was destroyed.

In the remainder of the season first Tiff Needell, then Lammers drove; Ensign failed to qualify for six GPs and placed 14th and 12th in only two finishes. There was no 'MN13' but 'MN14', the third N180, was completed in time to be Needell's spare at Monaco. Gaillard drove in Spain . . . no joy.

Into 1981, Nunn clung onto Formula 1 by his fingernails, 'MN14' was updated to B-spec and renumbered N180B 'MN15', to be driven by Surer. A second N180B tub was brought to Hockenheim and was on its wheels by Österreichring but was never actually completed. Surer drove six times and saved the team at a time when Nunn was staring down the gun barrel in Rio.

There the car felt comfortable in heavy rain and Surer drove very competently to place fourth, remarkably setting fastest lap as well as earning Ensign precious survival money. He did it again with sixth at Monaco, but Chilean Eliseo Salazar then rented the drive for himself in the last nine races, failed to qualify once and finished sixth in Holland on reliability. This compensated for other shortcomings and Ensign ended the season 11th in their Championship, with five points.

The final season under the Ensign name came in 1982 when 'MN15' was updated while waiting for new car N181, 'MN16' (a Brabham look-alike wing-car), to be completed. Roberto Guerrero drove 'MN15' at Kyalami then took the new 'MN16' at Long Beach. A second N181 was started but never finished, while Guerrero failed to qualify five times, his only finish placing him eighth at Hockenheim. The earnings from this season had been minimal but a faint glimmer of hope came when Guerrero qualified respectably for the last race, at Las Vegas. That hope was cruelly dashed when a jubilee clip on a cooling system hose worked loose, gushing water, just before the start and they could not race.

Nunn's old sparring partner, Teddy Yip, had for some time held an interest in the team, and after that unfortunate finale to 1982 he combined his recently acquired Shadow team with Nunn's, using the Ensign cars and his own Theodore Racing title, and persevered for '83. See entry for Theodore, page 318.

very heavily. Perkins finished eighth. Amon finished at Monaco in his repaired car, while Perkins was unable to qualify on his minimal budget.

In Sweden Amon was sensational, qualifying third, but when challenging for third place in the race the Ensign's left-front wheel broke loose, causing another heavy accident, painfully bruising Amon who was lucky to escape so lightly.

While he recovered, Patrick Neve drove the rebuilt 'MN05' in France, hopelessly off the pace and finishing 18th. Amon was back for the British GP but in Germany he withdrew from the race and from the team after witnessing Lauda's crash. Roland Binder drove in Austria, Ickx joining the team at this point, though without result beyond qualifying comfortably. Subsequently, he destroyed the car in a massive accident at Watkins Glen, apparently caused by another structural failure, which tore 'MN05' in two and injured the Belgian's legs and feet.

Perkins meanwhile crashed 'MN04' at Zandvoort but rebuilt it in time to qualify strongly in the middle of the Italian GP grid, only for the engine to disintegrate, ending his season.

Nunn, indefatigable, now planned to rebuild his car and his team for 1977 with sponsorship from Tissot and Castrol. A brand new N177 chassis 'MN06' was completed for new driver Regazzoni who ran it in the first six races, finishing sixth for another point in Argentina and apparently surviving the culture shock of changing from Ferrari to Ensign quite well. After qualifying on row four of the 2-by-2 grid in Spain, Regazzoni damaged the car in a race collision. He went off to Indy in the midst of Monaco practice, Ickx racing '06 in his place, finishing tenth, while new car 'MN07' was

available as spare in the paddock.

Regazzoni was seventh in both Sweden and France, while at Silverstone for the British GP two Ensigns appeared, '06 for Regazzoni and new car '08 entered by Yip's Theodore team for Patrick Tambay, who qualified easily while Regazzoni did not.

Both Ensigns completed the season, Regazzoni driving '07, Tambay '08; the works driver fifth in Italy and the US, Tambay showing promise with sixth in Germany, while third place was in the bag at Zandvoort when the Theodore Ensign ran out of fuel. Tambay was fifth in Canada and Ensign ended the season tenth in the Constructors' Championship, with ten points.

This marked the high tide of Ensign fortunes.

For 1978 Nunn had to do his best with his basically three-year-old cars, using chassis 'MN06-7-8' with a variety of rent-a-drivers, including Lamberto Leoni and Danny Ongais but settling finally on Ickx and Daly. British-based entrant Mario Deliotti bought old 'MN04' for Geoff Lees's use in British national Formula 1 races, and it was also handled by Giancarlo Martini and Desiré Wilson. Piquet and Harald Ertl featured in late-season events as did Lunger, but Daly was Ensign's most regular pilot. An 'MN09' car was built for David Price Racing for Val Musetti to drive in national Formula 1, both this car and old '04 subsequently coming under the Deliotti umbrella. Only in the final race of the season, at Montreal, did it all come good for Nunn, Daly finishing sixth to score a point at last.

This struggle for survival continued in 1979; construction of 'MN10' was started but later abandoned, followed by an extraordinary new

EuroBrun

In the EuroBrun team, millionaire enthusiast Walter Brun invested in Formula 1 with Paolo Pavanello of previous Euroracing Alfa Romeo fame. Founded ready for the 1987 season, the team was based at Senago, Milan. Like Coloni they used Cosworth DFZ V8 engines in three model ER188 cars for drivers Oscar Larrauri and Stefano Modena, the latter having shown great promise in his F1 debut in 1987. But Formula 1 seemed to prove more expensive than either principal had calculated. They had the money to race but not to test, which is self-defeating in the crucible of the Formula 1 World Championship. They experimented with Weber-Marelli injection in place of Lucas, seeking more consistent performance under changing weather conditions, but EuroBrun made little impact amongst critical observers at the other end of the grid – the front, the only place which matters.

The bulky, heavy EuroBrun ER188s were designed by Marco Tolentino and Bruno Zava. Poor Larrauri failed to complete the parade lap and so did not start his debut race in the car at Rio, while team-mate Modena raced there but retired. Larrauri failed to qualify next time out at Imola, and then at Silverstone, and then failed to make the grid in six consecutive races from Hungary, not pre-qualifying on three of those occasions. Larrauri retired five times, his two finishes being 13-16 at Mexico and Hockenheim.

Modena, who had looked quite good in the Brabham team, suffered as he failed official qualifying five times, was not classified at Imola, was excluded from both Monaco and Mexico, then clocked four retirements and finished only 12-14-12-11-13 with depressing symmetry reflecting accurately on the quality of the equipment.

For 1989 the EuroBrun design was revised to accept Judd CV engines, and Walter Brun ran a single-car entry for young Swiss driver Gregor Foitek, later replaced by Larrauri. Modified chassis '4 and 5 were used again, followed by two ER189s, none of which ever made it to a Grand Prix starting grid . . .

Foitek's record was sad, non-qualifying in Rio, then failing even to pre-qualify for the next ten GPs. Larrauri then failed to pre-qualify for the final five races of the year.

Still EuroBrun continued, taking on former Barnard associate George Ryton to develop their three Judd V8-engined ER189s to be driven by Roberto Moreno and no-hoper Claudio Langes. The latter amassed a 100 per cent record of 14 failures to pre-qualify while the worthy Moreno emerged from the experience with two non-qualifications and nine failures to pre-qualify against his name, plus being excluded from the meeting in Mexico City. He started for the team in Phoenix, finishing 13th, and Imola, retiring, before being offered the injured Alessandro Nannini's place in the Benetton team up at the other end of the grid to complete the season . . . He jumped at the chance, and EuroBrun went under . . .

See entry for Neotech in the Engine Directory.

Above left: The EuroBrun F1 cars were never beautiful – Oscar Larrauri's ER188-Cosworth DFZ at Imola 1988. Below: Lorenzo Bandini, Monaco, 1966, in the hybrid Ferrari 246T 2.4-litre Tasman V6 'special' with which he began the season in support of Surtees's full 3-litre V12 cars.

Ferrari

Maranello's first 3-litre Formula 1 car used a four-cam 24-valve V12 derived from their 3.3-litre 275P sports-prototype unit, uprated with Lucas fuel injection. Ferrari claimed 360 bhp at 10,000 rpm but, upon first acquaintance, driver Surtees was unconvinced – it felt like 'no more than 270'!

The engine was also thirsty, demanding a voluminous monocoque chassis which used Ferrari's 'Aero' hybrid construction, with a tubular internal frame stiffened by riveted-on aluminium stressed skins. It was a full-length tub with projecting rear horns supporting the engine, transaxle and rear suspension. Front suspension used top rocker arms and inboard springs, rear suspension outboard springs but inboard disc brakes.

Three of these model 312 cars would be built, numbers '0010-11-12. The latter was a special long-chassis/long-cockpit car for the tall Mike Parkes after Surtees left in mid-season, having just won the Belgian GP in '0010.

Chassis '0011 raced only once that year, in the Italian GP at Monza, where Ferrari fielded three 312s powered by reheaded 36-valve V12s offering perhaps 370 bhp and which dominated thoroughly. Bandini had led at Reims in '0010 until a missing throttle stop caused the cable to break, wrecking Ferrari chances.

In addition they used a 1965 monocoque, '0006, fitted with a 2.4-litre four-cam Dino V6 engine early in the season, the engine as used in Formula 1 from 1958-60 and in the 1961 246SP sports-prototypes, now modernized with fuel injection. This light, nimble and powerful special had been intended for Surtees's use in the winter Tasman Championship but injuries prevented him from going.

He won at Syracuse and Spa in '0010, while Scarfiotti won the Italian GP at Monza – imagine the noise! – in '0011, with Parkes second in '0012. The hybrid Dino 246T was second at Syracuse and Monaco then third at Spa driven by Bandini. It reappeared unsuccessfully in Scarfiotti's hands at the Nürburgring – for which it should have been very well suited – and finally as a private Parnell Racing team replacement entry at Monza, driven by Giancarlo Baghetti. It was ideal for Monaco and Surtees should have driven it there, but it was handed instead to Bandini, contributing towards the departure of Surtees from the team.

Thereafter Ferrari concentrated upon sports-prototype development to beat Ford at Le Mans in 1967. Bandini drove '0010 as a lone team entry in the US GP, therefore, and led before either a spark plug electrode smashed a piston, or a piston smashed the spark-plug electrode. He retired and the team cancelled its Mexican GP entry.

In essence Ferrari should have walked the 1966 Championship, and would surely have done so had they looked after Surtees. The engineers were doing their job but the team's internal politics simply threw it all away. They experimented with both Dunlop and Firestone tyres during the season, opting for an American dollar contract in the end. They would use Firestone tyres until changing to Goodyear for 1974-77, to Michelin for 1978-81, returning to Goodyear thereafter.

Into 1967, despite their heavy endurance racing commitment, Ferrari ran a three-car Formula 1 team for a choice of four drivers – Bandini, Parkes, Scarfiotti and new-boy Chris Amon.

Franco Rocchi uprated the V12 with new reversed-flow cylinder heads. The inlet ports were still between the camshafts but the exhausts now exited in the vee, gathering the pipework within the roll-over bar cross-section, clearing the airstream either side. A new lightened magnesium-zirconium alloy crankcase was on the way, while Walter Salvarani completed a new weight-saving five-speed transmission, based on his latest 1600 cc Formula 2 design.

The 312-67 prototype car '0001 used 1966-block engines with centre-exhaust heads in original form, installed in a slim new 'Aero' type pseudo-monocoque chassis whose engine bay horns rose taller and stiffer than before. They carried fuel now displaced from what had been the bloated centre section of the 312-66 model tubs. This low-frontal area Ferrari looked superb and an output of 390 bhp at 10,000 rpm was claimed from its revised 36-valve engine, though the drivers again suggested this was optimistic . . .

Ferrari missed South Africa due to sports car commitments, their Formula 1 season commencing instead in the minor Brands Hatch meeting where Bandini drove '0001 into second place just 0.4 second behind the winning Eagle-Weslake V12, Amon had a road accident so non-started old '0010 and Scarfiotti was fifth in his Monza-winning '0011.

Parkes won at Silverstone using his long-cockpit 312-66 '0012 with centre-exhaust engine; two 312-67s ran at Monaco, where Bandini qualified second fastest but crashed '0001 fatally late in the race, and Amon was third in brand new '0003 after a pit stop to change a punctured tyre had lost him a certain second place.

Ferrari then scored a dead-heat victory at Syracuse, where Parkes started on pole with '0012 centre-exhaust engine, and Scarfiotti set fastest lap in his '66-specification '0011.

There was to be no longer-cockpit 312-67 car for Parkes so at Zandvoort he again raced his '66 special, finishing fifth sandwiched between Amon's '0003 and Scarfiotti's brand new '0005. In Belgium, Parkes destroyed his elderly special in a first-lap accident which ended his own Grand Prix career, Scarfiotti saw it all and subsequently opted out while Amon again soldiered round to finish third.

In the following six races Ferrari made singleton entries for Amon, normally in chassis '0005 with '0003 spare.

Once they had got the endurance races out of their system, Ferrari could concentrate more effort upon Formula 1 in the second half of the year. Their new lightweight-block V12 and F2-based gearbox appeared at the Nürburgring, and for Monza the all-new lightweight car '0007 emerged with the latest block and gearbox plus four-valve-per-cylinder heads. The four valves

were disposed at a slight radial angle in planview, giving a semi-hemispheric pent-roof combustion chamber though the angle between the valves was narrow, cramping the camshafts too tightly together to allow the inlets to remain between them. They were moved to outside the heads, therefore, while exhausts remained within the vee and single spark plugs fired the mixture.

Now Forghieri's claims of 390 bhp seemed realistic, and since the chassis, according to Amon, was already 'an absolute dream' to drive, Ferrari were set to win races again. It could have happened at Watkins Glen, where the Lotus 49s proved fragile, but Amon's engine blew up 12 laps from the finish and the limping Lotuses finished 1-2. In Mexico, Amon qualified second to Clark's Lotus 49 in '0007 but ran low on fuel, finishing ninth behind his once-only team-mate, Jonathan Williams in '0003.

A low-key finale to the season came at the new Jarama Autodrome, in Spain, where Andrea de Adamich drove '0005 quietly into a lowly ninth place in the Madrid GP.

In 1967, Ferrari had made 22 Formula 1 starts, 15 of them in Championship GPs, winning none but taking four third places. Bandini's death and Parkes's injuries had coincided with excessive pressure upon the racing department and so made this an indifferent season.

For 1968 Ferrari abandoned endurance racing in displeasure over a rule change and concentrated upon Formula 1. It paid off. The 48-valve engines now gave around 410 bhp but compared to the minimum 408 bhp Cosworth DFVs they lacked mid-range torque, with 'nothing at home below 9800 rpm' according to Amon, who was joined by Ickx and de Adamich.

The cars suffered high water and oil temperatures, and associated power loss. The V12 was still thirsty, Ferrari having to start most races carrying 8-10 gallons (56-70 lb) more fuel than their Cosworth rivals.

Three 1967 chassis, '0003-5-7 (Ferrari's system skipped even numbers at this time), were used in South Africa and at Brands Hatch, where the unfortunate de Adamich crashed '0005 very badly, hurting himself and ending the car's career.

A new 312-68 chassis '0009 appeared for Ickx at Silverstone with its engine lowered in the chassis. Amon was third there in '0007 and Ickx fourth in the new car. Amon raced '0007 in the first six events of the season, before taking new chassis '0011 at Rouen and using it in the next five events, eventually destroying it in a heavy race crash at Monza. Ickx used '0009 in his summer races, apart from Spa where he drove old '0003, but in Germany he put new car '0015 – even the Italians missing out '0013 – on pole position.

For the American races Amon drove '0009 while Ickx crashed '0015 heavily in Canadian GP practice, breaking his leg and ruining his chance of

Amon at Spa in his Ferrari 312/67 during the 1967 Belgian GP, these low-frontal area centre-exhaust V12s now being mouth-watering collector's items.

the Drivers' Championship.

At Spa, as described on page 79, Forghieri introduced a strutted aerofoil mounted above the gearbox and the cars handled superbly well there. Forghieri subsequently moved the aerofoil forward, closer to the centre of gravity to distribute download more evenly front to rear but the drivers found it less effective, preferring sheer traction to this theoretically better balance.

Amon built his legendarily unlucky reputation this season. He qualified on three consecutive pole positions – Spain, Spa and Zandvoort (the team having refused to enter Monaco after Bandini's death there) – and he led the first two handsomely until fused fuel pumps and a holed oil cooler respectively robbed him of victory. It rained in Holland, where Firestone's wet-weather tyres proved no match for Dunlop, and the peaky V12 rev band made the Ferrari tricky to control. Amon was worse affected than Ickx in these conditions, and when it rained again at Rouen, Ickx won unconcerned.

Ickx and Amon qualified 1-2 on the grid at the Nürburgring but by this time the Cosworth cars were far ahead aerodynamically and were quicker away from slow corners. Derek Bell joined the team in the minor race at Oulton Park, driving '0007, while Forghieri devised an ingenious moveable wing system for Monza, energized by engine oil under pressure. The wing dropped into a high attack-angle for maximum download in first, second and third gears, but feathered for low-drag, high-speed with the throttle open in fourth and fifth. It returned to the download position in those gears when the brakes were applied. An over-ride switch was also provided, which Amon preferred but which Ickx disliked and had it removed from his car.

Amon qualified on the front row at Monza with this system but an oil leak onto a rear tyre caused an almighty accident which destroyed his '0011 in the race. Ickx was third and was still in contention for the World Championship title before having '0015's throttle jam open, breaking his leg in the Canadian accident. Amon was able to dominate that long race imperiously in '0009 running with extra fuel tankage outrigged alongside its engine bay, despite losing the clutch as early as lap 12. Sadly the final-drive suffered under clutchless gear-changing, and failed with 17 laps to run, robbing the New Zealander and Ferrari of their third probable victory that season.

Ferrari had made 30 Formula 1 starts, winning just one Grand Prix, taking one second place and three thirds. But their cars were on the front row

The shaded area shows the structural form of the 1970-71 Ferrari 312B semi-monocoque chassis, with its flat-12 engine suspended beneath the protruding rear horn, after the style of the 1968 Honda RA302.

nine times, eight to Amon, and they took four pole positions, three of them his. Three of the six cars used were effectively written off, while unreliability robbed Ferrari of those three probable GP wins and the title.

The company encountered financial crisis in 1969 but still returned to endurance racing, if low-key, while Mr Ferrari took the long-term strategic decision for Forghieri's men to develop the new 312B flat-12 for 1970 while *Ing.* Stefano Jacoponi took Formula 1 team responsibility to do his best with the obsolescent V12. Only three cars would be used in the new season: '0009 from 1968, plus two new cars '0017 and '0019.

They used very similar monocoques to the successful 312-68 cars, but new flattened nose cones gave them a totally different, more podgy appearance.

Despite protestations that the further-revised 48-valve V12s now delivered 435 bhp, Amon could not believe they had even 1968 power. New heads reversed the porting once more, returning the exhausts to the outside of the vee, lowering the car's centre of gravity and reducing airflow turbulence around the rear wing. Inlets were in the vee, more radical new camshafts were fitted, and disastrous efforts were made to reduce internal friction by reducing main bearing area.

Except for the minor Silverstone meeting, where Bell drove '0009, Amon raced alone until the British GP, initially with new 312-69 '0017 introduced at Kyalami, then taking '0019 brand new at Monaco. At Barcelona, the Ferrari was equipped with a low-reciprocating mass V12 featuring new titanium con-rods and further revised valve timing. Amon found difficulty in gearing the car properly due to a massive flat-spot in the engine's output between 9800 and 10,400 rpm, but still qualified second quickest in practice. After the works Lotus 49Bs had crashed due to wing collapses, '0017 led by over 30 seconds only for its engine to seize. At Monaco, Amon was second when the diff failed. Pedro Rodriguez joined him for the British GP but gearbox and engine failures sidelined them both.

Ferrari withdrew from the German GP to prepare the new 312B for a debut at Monza, but the new engine failed repeatedly in testing and this was the final straw for Amon, who left in disgust. Rodriguez ran out the stub-end of the season, easing '019 home sixth in the Italian GP, then driving '017 within its capabilities in Canada, the US and Mexico, finishing latterly fifth and seventh.

Ferrari had made only 13 Formula 1 starts and achieved just six finishes, three of them by Rodriguez at the end of the year when it didn't matter. Amon finished only one race, with a good third place in Holland, but he had been in a winning position in Spain and was well placed at Monaco before it all went wrong . . .

The 312B came on song in 1970. Its flat-12 engine is discussed elsewhere, but when the car first appeared its 'Aero' style chassis suspending the engine beneath a rearward-projecting beam – reminiscent of the air-cooled Honda V8 – was the best-integrated 3-litre Formula 1 package yet created. It would remain the best packaged of all Ferraris until the Postlethwaite 156 appeared in 1985.

Five 312Bs were built that first season; chassis '002 being destroyed by fire at Jarama and replaced by a completely new car taking the same number.

Ickx returned as number one, and 312B development may be judged by results: the new design's first finishes occurred in its fourth race, placing 4-8 in the Belgian GP; then qualifying on the front row and setting fastest lap in its fifth race, in Holland; able to take pole position for its sixth race, in France; followed up by qualifying on pole for four of the next seven races while placing on the front row in *all* seven.

The cars set fastest lap in six races, including five of the season's last six. From 25 starts in 1970 they recorded 17 finishes, won four of the last five races of the year and were first and second in three of them, 1-2-7 with their three-car entry in Austria.

It rocked the Cosworth brigade to the last locknut and washer but the new cars had come on song just too late that season to win the World Championship titles. Ickx, who won the Austrian, Canadian and Mexican GPs in '001, had a chance of the Drivers' title until a fuel pipe broke at Watkins Glen, where Rindt's posthumous crown in the Lotuses was assured. Regazzoni won the Italian GP in '004 while the other team driver was another newcomer, Ignazio Giunti.

For 1971, three revised new 312B2 models were built, serialled '005-6-7, while existing 'B1s '001-2-3-4 would appear in 1970 form before at least one was modified to 'B2 trim, if we believe the chassis numbering. Since such a total conversion would have entailed one of the new squarer-section monocoques replacing the rounded 312B section, we can take the numbers with a pinch of salt – never mind the history, let's make the customs carnets fit . . .

The definitive 'B2 tub had a reduced frontal area and adopted a more wedgy flat-topped, vertical-sided form. The inboard front suspension of 1970 was retained, but at the rear Forghieri mounted the coil/dampers above the gearbox, actuated by bell-crank extensions of the upper suspension links. Engine improvements were made in search of better combustion.

Ickx, Regazzoni and Andretti drove, and Ferrari won the first three races – Andretti the South African and non-Championship Questor GPs in

Tony Matthews' drawing of Regazzoni's 1971 British Grand Prix Ferrari 312B2 shows its aero-style internal-tubed monocoque chassis with its inboard semi-rising-rate rear springs. Firestone's slick racing tyres were first tested during practice for the early-season Questor Grand Prix at Ontario, California, and were introduced to Championship racing in the Spanish GP. They were in response to Goodyear's introduction of a slick tyre in the South African Grand Prix which had opened that season.

'002 and Regazzoni at Brands Hatch in the new 312B2 '005. Later, Ickx ran a minor Hockenheim race in '003, but the new 'B2's only win other than at Brands Hatch would be Ickx's masterly wet-race performance in the Dutch GP.

Overall, the flat-12 Ferraris made 31 starts in 1971, finishing 16 times and notching five wins but only two at Championship level, one each for 'B1 and 'B2, while their three non-Championship wins split 2-1; 'B1, 'B2.

Yet in that first half-season the Ferraris had won five of the seven races held, qualifying on the front row every time, on pole three times and setting four fastest race laps.

In the second half they made 17 starts in seven races and finished only five times, though achieving 3-4 in the German GP. They were four times on the front row, took one pole position – at Silverstone – but Ickx was responsible for the only fastest lap, in the US GP.

So a season which had started so well simply fell apart in ill-handling and unreliability. Had Ferrari's run been concentrated in one calendar season, instead of being split back-end of 1970/front-end of '71, the cars would have made history indeed!

The 'B2's ill-handling, especially upon bumpy surfaces, was exacerbated by Firestone's development of new ultra-low-profile tyres which encountered harmonic vibration problems shaking the cars to pieces, both Ferrari and BRM losing races for this reason (see page 94).

For 1972 the 'B2s' inboard-mounted rear coil/dampers were resited outboard with conventional linkages, and wider tracks were adopted at the front and rear. Aerodynamic changes were made to nose section and wings but only one new chassis was made, namely 'B2 '008. The 1971 drivers were retained but Andretti missed much of mid-season with other commitments, then Regazzoni broke his wrist, so Galli and Merzario ran as stand-ins until The Men reappeared in Austria and Italy.

The 1972 Ferrari record shows 29 starts, 19 finishes, only one victory – though a most convincing one – and 10 more finishes in the points. Team achievements included 2-3 in Spain, 3-4 in Argentina, and second at Monaco. Ickx drove '006 in five early races, '005 for seven races thereafter including the German GP at the Nürburgring in which he was inspired, qualifying on pole, setting fastest lap and winning so handsomely. But the 'B2 was heavy, aerodynamically ineffective and could not match Lotus 72 handling that year.

Ferrari then ran aground on internal bickering. Forghieri completed a prototype deformable-structure car aimed at the forthcoming 1973 regulations, using a very brief wheelbase, low polar moment central weight concentration and side radiators fed through NACA ducts cut into a full-width snowplough nose. It would never be raced. It lived with the author for some weeks in 1983, still looking horrible, its aluminium body panels were incredibly heavy, but nevertheless Forghieri was on the right track with this central mass concentration, and would still have the last laugh . . .

Short-term, driver criticism of this 'Spazzaneve' (snowplough) prototype, '009, plus relative failure through 1972 saw Forghieri assigned to future project development, out of the racing team as in 1969 when his group had developed the 312B to revive Ferrari's racing fortunes.

Ex-Innocenti engineer Sandro Colombo was given technical charge of Formula 1, now running Goodyear tyres for the first time. Ferrari began the year with the obsolescent 'B2s '005-6-8, and a new deformable-structure 312B3 was completed. Due to continuing metal-working union unrest, Ferrari sub-contracted John Thompson's TC Prototypes company of Weedon, near Northampton, England, to build three bare aluminium-sheet monocoque chassis to Maranello drawings. The engine-suspending rear beam was now dispensed with, the revised flat-12 engines instead bolting fully stressed onto a cast-magnesium sandwich plate fitted against the tub's rear bulkhead. The tub itself was broad, rectangular in

Left: *Team Manager Peter Schetty wears Regazzoni's helmet to test an interim 312B2 at Modena, October 1971. Note rear springs now outboard.* Below: *Classical beauty: Ickx's Ferrari 312B '003 on its way to second place in the 1971 Spanish GP, Barcelona. This car is preserved today in Britain in the Donington Collection. Bottom left: Ferrari 312B2s under preparation, showing the squarer tub shape of these cars (background) and the suspended mounting of the flat-12 engine beneath that rear monocoque horn. Bottom right: Ickx at Monaco 1972 in the 312B2 with rear spring/damper units conventionally outboard again.*

section and slightly wedge-form towards the nose. Inboard front coil/dampers were retained, actuated now by fabricated rather than forged top rocker arms; the rear was conventional, feeding major loads into a cast-alloy bridge bolted over the transaxle.

The three 'Thompson monocoque' 'B3 Ferraris were chassis '010, '011 and '012 in the 312B series. Ickx tested '011 with side radiators at Fiorano just before the Spanish GP at which the new deformable-structure regulations would take effect. It overheated and the team fell back on '010 rigged with a conventional nose radiator. Both cars ran in Barcelona practice, Ickx concentrating upon '010, as a lone entry. He ran alone in Spain, Belgium, Sweden and the British GP; Merzario, his early-season team-mate in the 'B2s, rejoined him at Monaco and in France. The only worthwhile results were sixth at Anderstorp and a 5-7 finish in France but the cars were uncompetitive and Ferrari withdrew entries for the Dutch and German races.

Reputedly under Fiat pressure to improve fortunes, Ferrari had summoned Forghieri to return to Formula 1. He reworked '312B3 010' in 20 days in time for Merzario to drive it in Austria, the car now using lengthy radiators raked forward in the hull sides, air being ducted through them from underneath and out through vents on the side pod upper decks. The oil tank was sited at the rear of the tub to the right of the engine, the oil cooler on the opposite side, and Forghieri had applied his low polar moment theories as in the hapless *Spazzaneve* to transform the 'B3 into a more raceworthy proposition by season's end.

Merzario was seventh on the revised car's debut in Austria. Ickx returned to run '010 suitably modified at Monza, finishing eighth while Merzario shunted '011; then the Italian driver completed the season in Canada and the USA, driving '011 in singleton entries, 15-16. Meanwhile at Maranello work progressed on an all-new Forghieri 312B3 for 1974.

This agonized season had seen Ferrari make only 19 Formula 1 starts, with 14 finishes but only four in the points, all with the 'B2s in the three early-season races at Buenos Aires, São Paulo and Kyalami. Ickx had driven '005 home fourth and fifth in the former pair, qualifying on the front row in Brazil, while Merzario's results were 9-4-4 in '008 and (at Kyalami) in '005, while Ickx crashed '006 in the South African race.

There was little joy in the rest of the season, the best 'B3 finish being 5-7 in France, never looking competitive.

For 1974 the team was reorganized under the management of Luca di Montezemolo, Forghieri in charge of technical direction, and with drivers Regazzoni and new-boy Lauda. The 312B3s were developed with tubs remade though initially retaining the interim 'B3 chassis numbers for paperwork convenience. The revised monocoque had the cockpit moved forward some five inches within the wheelbase, revised cylinder heads boosted flat-12 output to some 495 bhp at 12,600 rpm, and with Lauda and Regazzoni forming an excellent driving team they would return to the winner's rostrum.

Six 1974 312B3s were produced, under the numbers '010-11-12-14-15-16, recording 32 starts, 30 of them in Championship GPs, 20 finishes, 18 in GPs, and returning three wins – Lauda in Spain and Holland, Regazzoni in Germany – seven seconds, two thirds, three fourths, two fifths and a lowly 11th in Championship events. All but one

Grand Prix finish scored points, while in the minor Brands Hatch race they finished 2-5.

In addition, the new car's pace was emphasized by its nine pole positions, eight to Lauda, including six in a row from the Dutch to the Italian GPs . . . they were *quick*.

Driver immaturity and an extraordinary race organizers' error in the British GP caused Lauda to become boxed in by a scrum of hangers-on after a late-race pit stop and he was unable to rejoin a race which he had been leading, foiling Ferrari's best Championship hopes since 1970. But the record would be put right in 1975-76-77 (see pages 96-101).

For 1978, aiming at a fourth consecutive World

title, Ferrari ran existing 312T2 cars '027 and '031 for Reutemann and Villeneuve in the South American races before introducing all-new model 312T3s at Kyalami, chassis '032-033. These had been specifically tailored to the team's new Michelin radial-ply tyres, which demanded more camber change in the suspension geometry. Tubular front rocker arms actuated coil/dampers, which were larger than before and were now mounted outside the tub footwell. The body was completely redesigned, with a shapely spearhead planform shell, full-width wing and smooth flow onto the delta-form rear wing.

This was the season of the Lotus 79s and ground-effects, which Ferrari could not harness comfortably due to the width of their flat-12 engine. Considering this handicap, they had another very good season, making 32 starts in the 16 GPs, finishing 21 times, with five victories – Reutemann in Brazil with 'T2 '031, Long Beach in '032, Britain '033 and the USA '035; Villeneuve won in great style on home soil in Montreal, driving '034 with Reutemann third in '035 behind him. They had two pole positions, Reutemann on the street circuits at Long Beach and Monaco, and were four times on the front row, that at Long Beach seeing the 'T3s side by side.

Ferrari ended the season second in the Constructors' Cup, but in 1979 they would win it again (see pages 110-11).

In 1980 the hapless 312T5 was a makeshift ground-effects flat-12 car which was never adequately developed, and which in truth was run virtually as a spare-time effort while everyone who mattered (excluding the drivers) concentrated upon development of a new turbocharged engine and car for '81.

The result was Ferrari's worst season in many

years. They made 27 starts in the 14 GPs, Scheckter actually failing to qualify for his penultimate race, in Canada, and they were classified as finishers 18 times. Their only points were scored from three fifth places – Scheckter in Long Beach, and the irrepressible Villeneuve in Monaco and Canada. Additionally, Villeneuve finished sixth in Belgium and Germany.

The 'T5 chassis were '042-43-44-45-46-48, '047 never being raced if it existed at all.

The ungainly cars simply destroyed their Michelin tyres and pit stops to change tyres were a normal part of their days' racing. It was like the old days of tortoise and hare – unblown cars versus thirsty, refuel-stopping, supercharged machinery – but in relative terms the unfortunate 'T5s were never capable of haring anywhere. The long-term investment in turbocharged development of the new 126C, however, would pay off handsomely – and the failures of 1980 must be seen as Ferrari's investment in a brighter future.

Ferrari fell apart as a Formula 1 force with a terrible season in 1984. The new 126C4 cars were effectively revised 1983 Constructors' Championship-winning 'C3s (see Chapter 14). The bottom of the 'C4 moulded carbon tub was identical to the 'C3's, although the upper section was a little different, the two sections went together differently and were a little stiffer. Some 10 per cent was trimmed off engine weight, eight per cent off gearbox and the centre of gravity was slightly lower.

Nine 'C4s were built, the team taking four to most races but only seven ('071-077) were used, the eighth tub being ready for build-up just before the penultimate race and the ninth at that time fresh out of the tooling but not bonded together.

An early arrowhead shape was tried with the radiators upright and angled back but this discharged hot air against the tub and boiled the fuel. Changes were made, while at Maranello the senior engineers were restless and Forghieri's highly personal theorizing had left him in an isolated position. In-house politicking would play a major part in this poor season (by Ferrari stan-

dards), with a fall to *only* second place in the Constructors' Championship, accumulating a measly 57.5 points to McLaren's 143.5.

Worst thing of all, perhaps, was Ferrari's win at Zolder, which led to an assumption that everything had come right. The drivers had been on form there, Goodyear's tyres had excelled in heat *and* a rogue fuel batch had decimated the opposition, while the troublesome electronic ignition had been replaced by a Lucas-Ferrari mechanical system. But then the team slipped into the abyss.

In the first 13 GPs up to Zandvoort, Arnoux finished nine times: 3-2-4-3-5-2-6-6-7. This was acceptable, but Alboreto finished only four times: winning in Belgium, then 6-5-3. If the cars finished they scored (all but once) but what was so serious was that they no longer looked likely winners that mid-season.

Just before the British GP, crisis management prevailed. At Brands Hatch two of their four 'C4s, '075 and '076, were revised with new radiators and intercoolers in top-ducted side pods. Pushrod suspension then replaced pullrod as development progressed. In Austria these 126C4/M (for *Modificato*) cars tried a 13 cm (5.1 in.) wheelbase stretch with altered underwing, but if run in anything other than high-download tune they just did not perform.

At Monza, '075 had been testing a side-ducted body. A similar 'K4 solution was tried in Austria but abandoned. In the Italian race, Ferrari were out-performed by *green* Alfa Romeos but salvaged a lucky second place.

There two McLaren-waisted 'C4/M2s appeared, on chassis '072 and '074 but 'C4/M1s '076 and '077 raced. The 'M2s ('074 for Alboreto, '077 updated for Arnoux) ran far more effectively in the final two races. Alboreto's final three GPs of the year yielded 2-2-4 finishes, while Arnoux clocked up a retirement, a fifth and a ninth in the same period.

In the vast and clinical new *Reparto Corse* at Maranello, *Ing.* Renzetti had joined Tomaini's race team, while long-serving Forghieri had been removed from racing and seconded to the *Reparto Ursa (Ufficio Ricerche Studi Avanzati)* to develop

Shapes of the Eighties: top: *Alboreto in the Ferrari 126C4 at Monaco 1984, Postlethwaite carbon-composite tub, pullrod suspension, twin-turbocharged V6 engine and huge rear wing with abbreviated side pods;* above: *backs to the wall at Monza 1984; note reshaped side pods.*

long-term advance projects.

That winter, work progressed on Forghieri's last hurrah, a slant-four 1500 cc turbo engine which gave the chassis engineers installation nightmares. As 1985 approached it appeared to be stillborn as the most complete team in Formula 1 looked towards a new 1200 cc turbocharged Formula 1 for the late Eighties.

For Ferrari 1985 was a season much like '83

Alboreto's 1985 Ferrari 156/85 in Austria when the team suffered several engine failures but salvaged third place.

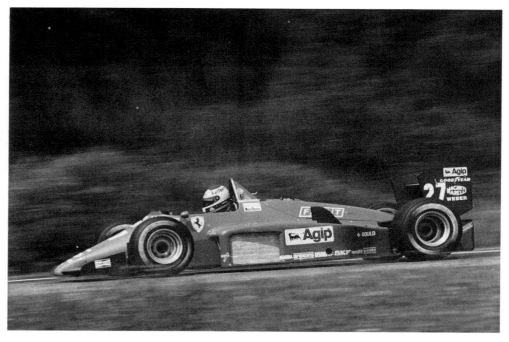

with one exception. This time they lost the Constructors' Championship *as well as* the Drivers' title when their form fell apart at the year's end.

Nine new 156/85 chassis were built, numbered '078-086, each one a little different from its predecessor, but '078-082 were more similar to each other than to chassis '083-086. Design and construction used CAD-CAM computer-aided design and modelling technology with co-operation from Aermacchi aeronautics and Gould computers. New low-mounted turbochargers were adopted instead of the earlier in-vee layout. The smooth, long-tailed, low-slung 156s were the year's best-looking cars and performed well for two-thirds of the season. For Monaco rear suspension geometry was modified, and the front was revised for the first fruitless visit to Spa, where electronic wastegate control was also featured. Still chassis balance was not quite right and new tubs at Ricard had revised front suspension but events suggested a team in increasing trouble. Intercooler, oil radiator and water radiator positions were all revised for Germany but this was the last occasion on which Ferrari had competitive horsepower.

Chassis '078 had been the winter test car then team spare raced by Alboreto at Spa; '079 was new for the Italian at Rio and was raced by both drivers subsequently; '080 was new for Arnoux's swansong at Rio; '081 new at Imola for Alboreto; '082 new for newcomer Johansson at Spa in June;

As cockpits became confined so detachable steering wheels were standardized, as in this 1986 Ferrari F1/86. Note the digital dash display. Years later Stefan Johansson was asked by a waffling F1 car collector, 'Tell me, Stefan, the 1986 turbo Ferrari was notably difficult to start wasn't it?' 'Not at all', the Swede replied, 'I just waved my index finger like that' – circling it above his head – 'and away it went . . .'.

'083 new for Alboreto at Ricard; '084 emerged for Johansson there in practice only, later becoming team spare; '085 was new for Alboreto at Monza and finally '086 made its debut for Johansson at Brands Hatch.

Balancing race-tune power against fuel consumption had always been a nice trick which Ferrari seemed to have well under control. McLaren regarded the 156s as their TAG Turbo engine's equal in race-tune economy, but the pressure of the new E-Type Honda engine and also Brabham-BMW's four-cylinder late in the year simply broke Ferrari's heart.

The awful realization that they were beaten on sheer horsepower hit Maranello like an ice-cold shower. It was a difficult, *difficult*, thing to swallow. In the later races their attempts to match even Renault and TAG-Porsche power saw Ferrari having to run boost-levels which blew their alloy-block V6 apart. It had become thermodynamically unreliable, and it looked as if a formerly excellent 1982 engine designed for, say, 700 bhp, was now being asked to contain 850-900 bhp or more.

From the mid-season American tour forward, the 156 chassis seemed not to perform as well as previously. It was very efficient but much too sensitive to different types of track; fine at *ersatz* Nürburgring, in trouble at bumpy Zandvoort and Brands Hatch. It seemed suited best to circuits which were like Ferrari's Fiorano test track, but modern Formula 1 had outgrown Fiorano, which lacked very high-speed corners.

The 156s for Monza were extensively reworked, Harvey Postlethwaite's section having swapped downforce generated by ground-effects for downforce generated by wings. They ran minimum download, minimum drag in qualifying and even then were demolished by BMW and Honda and even struggled against Renault. That was the point, on the holy ground of Monza, at which the cold shower hit poor Ildo Renzetti's engine section.

Team leader Alboreto contested all 16 GPs, finishing nine of the first 11, then significantly being merely classified after retirement at Monza and subsequently failing in each of the last four races of the season. His finishing record read 2-2-2-1-3-2-1-3-4-13*, which was good enough to give him the Drivers' Championship lead for most of the season, until Prost forged ahead for McLaren. Alboreto's victories were in Canada and Germany. Team-mate Arnoux was fired after Rio (where he finished fourth) and his replacement Johansson did the remaining 15 GPs, finishing ten of them – 8-6*-2-2-4-9-4-5-4-5 – looking set to win at Imola before running out of fuel and generally doing a fine job.

Until their late-season slump, Ferrari had led McLaren comfortably in the Constructors' Championship, but they were unable to resist the British team's pressure, and a major rethink began in the *Gestione Sportiva* for 1986.

The 1986 season saw Ferrari struggling. In hindsight it seems as if at least 80 per cent of their problem was paying the price for failing to invest in their own wind tunnel four or five years earlier.

The Fiorano tunnel was not commissioned until October 1986. The faster the circuit, the better the Ferraris showed, but their overall F1/86 package was clearly deficient in that year's company. The '86 chassis were demonstrably better than '85's but the opposition had progressed so rapidly they were still not good enough . . .

Drivers were Michele Alboreto and Stefan Johansson. The former retired nine times in the 16 GPs, his best finish being second in Austria. Johansson retired six times, and finished third four times – at Monaco, Budapest, Austria and Adelaide.

Type 156/85 chassis serials '085' and '086' were the first-built, '085' appearing only once as spare at Rio while '086' was found to have a structural problem within the moulding and was broken up for testing. It was later replaced by a new moulding to form a new-spec F1/86 under the same chassis serial, used by Johansson only at Detroit to replace '091' crashed at Montreal. The definitive F1/86 chassis '087'-'094' inclusive appeared as follows: '087' and '088' new for Johansson and Alboreto respectively at Rio, '089' new at Jerez as spare car, '090' new for Johansson at Imola, '091' new spare at Spa, '092' first seen as a bare tub taken to Monaco but not required, then raced by Alboreto at Montreal, '093' new for Johansson at Ricard and '094' new spare at Estoril, eventually raced by Johansson in Adelaide – eight new cars in all.

In search of more reliable braking Ferrari replaced proprietary Brembo brake calipers with a new design of their own early-season, but after two hydraulic leaks – one of which caused Johansson a tremendous head-on smash at Jerez – it was set aside and Brembos re-adopted. At Rio a disc bell failed, while other problems centred elsewhere. Three cars were lost in crashes, '087' at Jerez, '090' at the Österreichring and '091' at Montreal – all with the luckless but irrepressible Johansson at the wheel.

Ferrari finished fourth behind Williams, McLaren and Lotus in the Constructors' Cup, with only 37 points to Lotus-Renault's 58, McLaren-TAG's 96 and Williams-Honda's 141. Johansson's ten classified finishes read 4-10-3-11*-4-3-3-6-12-3, while Alboreto's seven read 10*-4-8-4-8-2-5. The Swede finished fifth in the Drivers' Championship, the Italian eighth-equal with Laffite and Arnoux of Ligier-Renault.

For 1987, the longest-established team in

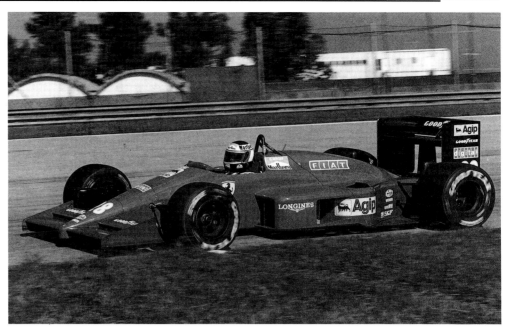

Win or lose, Italian racing red Ferraris have always been the most exciting-looking cars in Formula 1 – Berger's F1/87 at Rio, 1987, demonstrating its flapped front wings, neat, side-ducted rearward side pods and the massive rear wing which turbo power allowed the car to tow.

Formula 1 entered its fortieth consecutive season with something to prove. Ferrari had last won a Grand Prix in August 1985 at *ersatz* Nürburgring, and had then endured a pretty disastrous season of '86. John Barnard had joined from McLaren International as Engineering Director, essentially working remote at his satellite GTO Ltd – 'Guildford Technical Office' in England – with special responsibility for design and development of a new long-term F1 car for 1988. The F1/87 project had already begun by the time he took office, essentially the work of design engineer Gustav Brunner, but he oversaw its finalization and development and GTO-made parts were incorporated.

Early on, Barnard's long-term '88 project had seemed destined to be powered by a 3.5-litre naturally aspirated engine, but by mid-season '87 he was not so sure. 'The way it looks at the moment', he said, 'if we have to choose between a 2.5-bar turbo for next year or 3½ litres naturally aspirated, we've got to go for the turbo because as it stands at the moment it looks as if it's going to have a clear 100-horsepower advantage, and in effect that's only this week's figure. Next week's might be higher. You can go a fair way towards compensating for maybe 30 or 40 horsepower in the chassis, but no way can you compensate for 100 . . .'

Views altered a little later in the year, but on balance development of the new atmo engine project was extended longer range to be proven during the second half of 1988 and not raced until '89. The 2.5-bar turbo option would indeed be adopted for '88.

Meanwhile, the *Reparto Corse* prepared the F1/87, regarded by some as a Williams FW11 look-alike. Maranello design hierarchy at that time included honorary Italian Harvey Postlethwaite, Gustav Brunner and two ex-Renault specialists, engine man Jean-Jacques His and aerodynamicist Jean-Claude Migeot, the latter subsequently being joined by another Frenchman, Henri Durand, ex-Ligier.

It seems that by November when Barnard joined, the team was partially committed on chassis shape, its rear-end treatment and suspension detailing being finalized subsequently. It emerged as something of a committee car, with a few weak areas of compromise. They were tackled, but some items – such as a new wing set – were apparently slow in appearing.

By the time of the Mexican GP, the team's seven F1/87 cars had been built, numbered from '095' to '101' in Ferrari's long series which had begun with the prototype 312B flat-12 late in 1969; 101 F1 cars in 17 seasons – a average of six a year.

Of those latest F1/87s, chassis '095' was introduced at Rio as the team spare (raced by Berger), '096' was new there for Alboreto and subsequently

destroyed in his violent qualifying crash at Monaco, '097' was Berger's assigned car new at Rio, '098' new spare at Monaco raced there by the bruised Alboreto, '099' new as spare at Imola and first raced by Berger at Ricard, '100' made its debut for Alboreto at Budapest, and was severely damaged on the Saturday morning in Spain, while '101' was new for Alboreto in Mexico.

Chassis '100' was subsequently repaired but probably not to be raced again, being devoted instead to R&D rig-testing, while chassis '099' was devoted to R&D use as what Postlethwaite called 'a genuine *muletto*', developing the Barnard-suggested, *Ing.* de Silvestri-drawn, semi-automatic transmission and electronics towards the future. Initial objective of this system had been manifold, partly to speed gearchanges, partly to ease the physical load upon the driver, but largely just to free chassis design from the restraints of accommodating a rigid-rod gearchange run as opposed to simple, flexible lengths of electrical flex.

During the 1987 season Ferrari made no great single leap forward in engine development, it was more a process of steady and continuous performance improvement. Sadly, reliability did not keep pace. Maranello seemed to regard its V6 as having been no more or less competitive than anything else in face of the Hondas, but it was crucially unreliable.

Chassis failures also occurred – suspension components, CV joints and gearboxes – there was little pattern to the problems, until the ultimate consistency of the Mexican GP in which both F1/87s retired with the same failure – 'a top-end combustion problem'; holed pistons and shattered rings.

The cars' Marelli-Ferrari electronics came to include engine-data radio-telemetry from Monza, where high-power qualifying tune was adopted, after a test-session at Imola in which the system worked really consistently for the first time. Perhaps sadly it enabled the pit crew at Jerez to look on helplessly while the read-outs revealed Alboreto twice over-revving his engine (inadvertently) – hitting some 14,000 rpm – on the lap before it blew asunder.

There also, Berger slid over a kerb and smashed the bottom of his car's oil-tank casting. The team had begun to employ two-way driver-to-pit radio communications at the beginning of the season, so presumably the 'talk-back' was colourful . . .

A revised aerodynamic package emerged at

Maranello's first victory after Enzo Ferrari's death came romantically in the Italian GP at Monza, where Gerhard Berger inherited the lead from Senna's stricken McLaren-Honda with just two laps to go in this F1/87/88C – chassis '102'.

Hockenheim, coinciding with Postlethwaite's regular reappearance on the race team. Gordon Kimball from GTO had been running Berger's car, but from Hungary as developments towards '88 became crucial Mr Ferrari agreed with Barnard that they should concentrate on the future project back in England, leaving others to race the current cars.

They were competitive in Hungary, less so in Austria and Italy, perhaps due to being not quite set up correctly. But on a mixed-type medium-speed circuit like Estoril they were fine, and again – pre-failure – in Mexico. Car-spec was basically unchanged from Hockenheim, and the drivers responded superbly. Once engine-specs were equalized between the two drivers Berger really made his mark. He inevitably took criticsm in Italy for spinning away the Portuguese GP lead, but the fact he recovered to finish second after giving Ferrari's fortunes such a massive boost was a major plus both for him and the team . . . And then he won the last two races in fine style. All Italy loved him.

Under Goodyear's control-tyre policy, the *Reparto Corse* seemed to have learned a great deal about the interaction between various tyre parameters and their chassis, and by late-season they might perhaps have preferred Goodyear to do things a little differently in terms of chosen constructions. Perhaps, for example, a marginally different tyre in Spain could have assisted their cause, but generally speaking everybody started equal and they were fairly happy with that.

As for the opposition, the feeling seemed to have been 'There's only Williams-Honda – if we had got our act together earlier in the year we should have been right with them . . .'. But fluttering their FISA boost valves, Ferrari had proved they could do it, but for most of their 40th year they could not sustain the impetus. Whenever this extraordinary organization really pulled together it took under beating. It is significant therefore, that for too much of 1987 the team was eminently beatable . . .

For five consecutive mid-season GPs, Ferrari achieved no finishers. Berger made it to the chequered flag seven times, 4-4-4-4-2-1-1. Alboreto finished only five of the 16 Grands Prix run, his season including a litany of failure which extended for ten successive retirements through the

heart of the season. His finish record read 8-3-3-4-2, at Rio, Imola, Monaco, Suzuka and Adelaide respectively.

Ferrari ended the year fourth in the Constructors' Championship, behind Williams-Honda, McLaren-TAG and Lotus-Renault. Berger was fifth in the Drivers' Championship, Alboreto seventh.

Once the decision had been taken to continue running the V6 turbo engines for one final 2.5-bar season in 1988, delaying the new 3.5-litre design until '89, the existing chassis were updated for the new year's regulations as the F1/87/88C.

Chassis '102', '103' and '104' were the only tubs produced new, all making their debut at Rio commencing the season ('102' as spare) while old '101' acted as team spare in the Americas tour, Mexico, Montreal and Detroit in mid-season. The drivers continued unchanged, Alboreto and Berger.

They should have been right there. Simple as that. After Berger's two great wins at the end of 1987 Ferrari seemed poised for great things in the new year. But McLaren-Honda had built entirely new, dedicated 2.5-bar cars for this one fleeting season. Ferrari's 1987 victory on Honda's home ground at Suzuka had seemed the equivalent of the Japanese strike on Pearl Harbor. 'I fear we have awoken a sleeping giant . . .' read Japanese warlord Yamamoto's quote from 1941. Now Honda awoke, Ferrari faltered, and were *stamped* into the mud.

The season became one of their most troubled – quite typically for all kinds of political reasons broadly unconnected with racing itself . . .

Certainly Mr Ferrari's diminishing grasp and ultimate death was reflected by this lack of firm control. But lack of adequate direction from senior team members embroiled in Maranello politics cost dear. In turn this condemned the season to mediocrity; McLaren's steam-roller faced little but meagre opposition.

During the politicking, John Barnard concentrated upon finalizing his V12 atmo prototype car for '89 at GTO Ltd in England. Only after Piero Lardi-Ferrari had been promoted broadside out of racing and chassis engineer Harvey Postlethwaite, engine specialist Jean-Jacques His and aerodynamicist Jean-Claude Migeot had departed too did the situation settle, with Barnard finally technically directing under manager Capelli of Fiat as chief executive, assuming much of the former Mr Ferrari/Piero Lardi-Ferrari role.

Former 156 turbo V6 engineer Renzetti was restored to command over the engine programme, while another Fiat appointee, Restelli, took over

management monitoring.

At Monza, like a Hollywood script, Berger and Alboreto were able to pressure Senna, and when he collided with a Williams-Judd which he was attempting to lap they scored a stunning Ferrari 1-2 victory on home soil in the first Italian classic to follow Mr Ferrari's death.

Maranello had tried to match Honda turbo power within the new 2.5-bar boost/150 litres fuel restrictions at all costs. And this cost them dear in mid-range torque, reliability and fuel economy.

Once Barnard became 're-involved' around the time of the French GP, he and Renzetti changed course, adopting milder cams, altered compression ratios, reverting to an '87 intercooler set-up and seeking magnified mid-range grunt rather than top-end numbers.

New side pods and bodywork were introduced in August, slightly smaller than before with some internal flow from the radiators instead of all-external flow as hitherto. A new rear wing was also developed to match the revised engine package, introduced at Spa. Before Monza the entire revised package had been tested and showed promise – swapping some qualifying edge for improved race performance. Electronic, driver-controlled ride-height adjusters were introduced to enable fine-tuning in motion – the cars performed adequately in Portugal but Jerez's twists demanded greater downforce which compromised efficiency and knocked Ferrari's resurgent turbos off the pace.

By that time the final turbo F1 Championship was already lost. The turbo cars were not worth much more investment in money and time.

By this time, back home in Maranello, Barnard's GTO-designed Ferrari 'atmo' V12 was amassing thousands of miles' experience with both the new engine for '89 and its associated automatic gearbox. An old turbo chassis was also adapted as an atmo hybrid to put further miles on the new V12 60-valve engine, factory test driver Dario Benuzzi being assisted by Roberto Moreno plus Berger and Alboreto when available.

Ferrari's hurts of '88 were sadly self-inflicted, and if in public perception they reflected badly upon Fiat's technology it was largely Fiat's own fault for allowing such drifting to have occurred at all. And doubts remained whether Fiat appreciated that Formula 1 participation needs unified control. Running Ferrari by committee must surely fail. The awful warning was already there in recent history – remember Renault Sport . . .

Berger had eleven finishes to his name – 2-5-2-3-4-9-3-4-1 (the sensational surprise win at Monza) 6-4. Alboreto had nine finishes – 5-3-4-3-

17-4-2 (Monza) 5-11. They placed third and fifth respectively in the Drivers' table while *La Ferrari* as a team took second place to McLaren-Honda in the Constructors' Cup.

For 1989, the new atmospheric-induction 60-valve V12-engined *Tipo* 640 Barnard car emerged, chassis '107' to '112' being followed by one delightfully numbered '112*BIS*' to avoid the superstitiously adverse '13'. These seven cars were driven by new recruit Nigel Mansell ex-Williams, teamed with Gerhard Berger.

The first 640 – chassis '107' – made its debut as spare at Rio and was first raced, and destroyed, by Berger at Imola. Chassis '108' had been new for Berger at Rio, and later served only as spare at Imola and Monaco before reverting to test purposes. '109' was Mansell's Rio winner, '110' made its debut for Berger in Mexico, '111' was the new spare at Ricard raced by Berger, '112' made its first appearance at Spa for Mansell, and '112*BIS*' was new for Berger at Monza.

The elegant *Tipo* 640 represented over a year's intensive work by Barnard's group. He had picked his way through the political turbulence left at Maranello in the wake of Mr Ferrari's death in August 1988, and he had even had a high-level confrontation with senior Fiat management over the adoption of his ambitious electro-hydraulic gearchange mechanism, a potential resignation issue.

The 640 or 'F1/89' was a logical development of the two *Tipo* 639 'F1/88' prototypes which had been tested at Fiorano throughout the previous year, while the F1/87/88C turbo cars had carried Ferrari into battle in the last year of turbocharged 1500 cc Formula 1.

Visually similar to the 639 though different in many details, the 640's distinctive tall and narrow radiator inlets and side pod forms which were deep at the front then tapered rearwards, plus its new teardrop planform, all demonstrated a new direction in the search for peerless aerodynamic efficiency. The car was able to race with relatively small wings at most circuits, dissipating less horsepower without the need to pull barndoor wings through the air. The 640 chassis was narrower than that of the exploratory 639, its fuel tank and wheelbase longer.

The new Barnard-conceived/de Silvestri-detailed electro-hydraulic semi-auto gearbox was fundamental to the new car. A conventional foot-operated clutch was used only for the start, and leaving the pits, gearchange thereafter being commanded and operated from butterfly flick-levers behind the steering wheel. The right-hand flick switch changed up through the 'box, the left-hand flick switch changed down. A potential disadvantage was that the driver could only change down sequentially, through each gear in succession, missing none, but the clutch would not be disengaged for a millisecond longer than was necessary to save the gearbox internals from being battered, and changes themselves were significantly faster than by any manual system.

This transmission and its related systems caused much soul-searching and repeated early-season problems. At Rio the car proved very fast in a straight line when its 65-degree V12 engine was really developing little more power than the contemporary Cosworth DFR V8! The combination of Barnard's chassis and Ferrari's drivers proved capable of handling Prost, Senna and their McLaren-Hondas on medium-speed courses. But at Rio the team had so much trouble during qualifying they felt certain neither Mansell nor Berger would ever survive race distance. New team director Fiorio even suggested to Barnard starting Mansell on half tanks 'just to put up a show' before the inevitable failure. The Englishman was disgusted at the very idea – they gave it a go, Mansell ripped into the race win-or-bust, and the new 640 didn't bust . . .

All Italy went wild.

Subsequent transmission-related failures included hydraulic pump, broken wires and major vibration problems which shattered the alternator. When it stopped charging the battery progressively flattened, and once it reached a level where

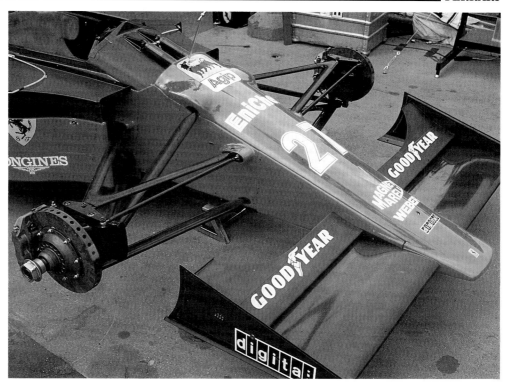

not enough current was available for the electro-hydraulics to function properly it was always the gearbox which shut down first. But the actual auto-clutch mechanism proved very reliable, and these peripheral problems took too many races to resolve. Once the team had got its technical act in gear, Mansell finished in the top three from the French to the Belgian GPs.

The 640 tub saved Berger's life in a massive impact and fiery aftermath at Imola. To maintain a minimum wheelbase with the long V12 engine, the fuel cell behind the cockpit had been confined, with additional wing tanks low down on each side. In the Imola crash, one of these had been ruptured. Now Barnard changed laminate 'lay-up' of subsequent carbon-composite tubs, and retained the wing tanks with anti-peel bolts penetrating both outer and inner monocoque skins to trap a plate within, minimizing any danger of another fuel cell separation.

Changes to the front anti-roll bar and the addition of a rear bar accompanied a change from Koni to Penske dampers to improve ride control over bumpy surfaces, and by the end of the

Top: *Droop-snoot – Concorde-like aerodynamics of the 1989 Ferrari 640 in its slender duckbill nose cone with flapped canard wings, and rocker arm-actuated scuttle-mounted spring/damper units behind.* Above: *Alain Prost's 1990 Ferrari 641 at Suzuka where he got the better of pole-man Senna at the start only to be driven off the road in the first corner – thuggery which clinched Senna his second World title. This shot emphasizes the rearward downslope of the 641's side pod topsides; TV camera 'wing' is also visible on the airbox.*

European season the Ferraris had won three GPs and were clearly McLaren-Honda's main opposition.

Mansell's 1989 season saw him disqualified at Montreal and Monza, excluded from the Spanish GP for allegedly ignoring the black flags shown him at Estoril where he had overshot his pit and reversed into it for a scheduled tyre change, and retiring from seven other events. His finishes were 1-2-2-3-1-3 – winning at Rio and Budapest, second at Ricard and Silverstone, and third at Hockenheim and Spa.

Jean Alesi leaning into one of the Phoenix street circuit turns in the disappointing 1991 Ferrari 642. These cars' revised side pod air entry shape is apparent.

Berger, however, suffered terribly – missing Monaco due to his Imola burns, and finishing only three times – 2-1-2 – in consecutive races at Monza, Estoril and Jerez.

While Ferrari placed third behind McLaren and Williams-Renault in the Constructors' Cup, Mansell was fourth in the Drivers' competition, and Berger seventh.

Engineer Barnard left Ferrari to join Benetton upon completion of his three-year contract. He was replaced by his former lieutenant, Steve Nichols from McLaren International. He assumed his new responsibilities in foggy Emilia in November 1989, dovetailing in with ex-Williams engineer Enrique Scalabroni, already there as nominal chief chassis designer. Nichols was inheriting a Barnard design for the second time in his career. As at McLaren there was no advantage in immediately starting anew.

In fact the revised 1990 Ferrari *Tipo* 641 featured a new 220- (instead of 205-) litre fuel cell, faired within redesigned bodywork, a new diffuser panel beneath the tail and other aerodynamic improvements. The larger fuel cell demanded significant structural changes in Ferrari's carbon-composite methodology, and although the wing fuel tanks were retained they were better protected, with heavier carbon sections around them and more thorough through-bolting.

World Champion Alain Prost joined Mansell ex-McLaren on the driver strength, and for their use seven of these improved *Tipo* 641s were produced, numbered '115'-'116', then '116*BIS*' to avoid the Italian unlucky number '17', with numbers '118'-'121' following on. The first 641 chassis '115' was

new as spare car at Phoenix, where Mansell gave '116' its debut and Prost '116*BIS*'. At Imola '118' made its bow driven – and spun mightily at very high speed – by Mansell. Prost was assigned '119' brand new at Monaco but was rammed by Berger's McLaren on the opening lap there and it was replaced by the spare '116' in the restarted race. Chassis '120' became Mansell's new spare at Ricard and was first raced by him at Hockenheim while '121' emerged new for Prost at Spa.

Valving for the electro-hydraulic gearchange was changed for the new model to improve reliability and accessibility. For Imola the 641/2 variant featured revised bodywork to which the drivers initially objected due to increased cockpit buffeting. The 641/2 also increased cooling capacity with revised radiator ducting to satisfy new demand from the ever more powerful V12 engine.

This Imola-specification car was regarded as the definitive Ferrari 641. Again it proved fine-handling albeit critical to setting-up in qualifying trim, both drivers complaining it was difficult to make their soft-compound qualifying tyres survive a full lap during early season race preliminaries.

Further gearchange development included programming to enable non-sequential downchanging. Prost was more enthusiastic than Mansell, who preferred the security of changing down gear by gear, rather than risk selecting, say, first from fifth while really seeking third. The selection programme could in fact be changed in minutes, and a dual programme system permitting either option to the drivers became available at Estoril.

The 1990 season became a battle royal between Senna of McLaren-Honda and Prost of Ferrari. Prost was able legendarily to conserve his tyres in the early stages of a race, then use their remaining performance profitably to the full during the vital closing stages. He could run fractionally less

wing than the more 'animal' Mansell, and his tireless commitment to test and development work made Prost very popular at Maranello, where he built a profitable relationship with his former McLaren colleague Nichols – and others – advancing his cause in a manner deeply disenchanting to the the the more abrasive Nigel Mansell.

Prost retired four times, including the Japanese GP at Suzuka in which he collided with Senna's McLaren-Honda entering the very first corner to end his challenge for the Brazilian's World Championship crown. He won five GPs, Brazil, then the Mexican, French and British in mid-season succession, followed by the Spanish GP at the end of the European season. His other placings were 4-5-4-2-2-3-3 for second place in the Drivers' competition.

Mansell had more than his fair share of mechanical disappointment, finishing only nine times, winning in Portugal, and otherwise placing 4-3-2-18-17*-4-2-2 for fifth place in the Drivers' table.

Ferrari were runners-up to McLaren-Honda in this hard-fought season's Constructors' Championship, beaten by 11 points. It had been a close-run thing . . . decided by Senna of McLaren so blatantly punting Prost into opening-lap retirement in the deciding race at Suzuka.

Considering Fiat-Ferrari's immense potential and excellent facility access, its fall from competitiveness during the 1991 season demands investigation . . .

From being a front-running team in 1990, Ferrari failed to win a single race in '91 and never really looked capable of doing so. To understand Ferrari's failure, one had to examine the season within the context of the company's recent history, because the cycle of cause and effect in Formula 1 is fairly long. Panics of February '91 could be traced to problems initiated or errors made during the summer of 1990.

Immediately after that year's Mexican GP, Ferrari's technical side was headed by engineers Enrique Scalabroni and Steve Nichols. Scalabroni had little experience of 'race engineering' on circuit. Nichols had vast experience from his long period with McLaren, working on Lauda's regular cars before becoming deeply involved in conceptual design.

Consequently, at Ferrari, Nichols ran circuit work with the drivers and cars, and back at the works concentrated upon longer-term research and development, analyzing active-ride systems, for example.

Scalabroni, meanwhile, ran day-to-day chassis design, drawing a new car for the forthcoming season of '91. However, Nichols had explained to the Fiat-Ferrari management executives that he would like more influence upon the new car's basic design. They ruled that Scalabroni and Nichols should work together on the new design programme, which appeared acceptable to both.

But the team's French aerodynamicist Henri Durand was unhappy. He had personal problems with both Scalabroni and with team director Cesare Fiorio, and when McLaren offered him a good position he accepted it . . .

Scalabroni then decided he was unhappy with the methodology and management practices at Maranello/Fiorano and gave the management a 'change it or I leave' ultimatum. He left, barely 2-3 weeks after Durand.

His 1991 car layouts were partially complete. However, Durand's parallel aerodynamic developments in the Fiorano wind tunnel had followed an entirely different direction.

Steve Nichols and the surviving Maranello technical team were left with a part-complete 1991 design created by a designer who was now working for Team Lotus, and with part-complete 1991 aerodynamic studies created by an aerodynamicist who was now working for McLaren . . .

Neither car design nor aerodynamic studies were compatible with one another – more depressingly, neither would prove particularly good . . .

Scalabroni's concept for the '91 car owed more to the 1990 Williams FW13B than the existing Ferrari 641. Since the FW13B had not performed particularly impressively for most of 1990, the surviving Ferrari team were reluctant to follow Scalabroni's design path. Meanwhile late-season developments with the 641 worked quite well and so the strategic decision was taken instead to develop that theme further for '91, refining and improving areas in which some weakness remained detectable.

Scalabroni's departure and this revised strategic thinking meant that the six months' work he had put into his preferred project was wasted. Now Ferrari started again with the *Tipo* 641 but an otherwise clean sheet of paper. Yet they had no specialized aerodynamicist on the staff until December, when Jean-Claude Migeot returned to Ferrari from Tyrrell, having previously worked for the Italian team alongside Harvey Postlethwaite after making his name with Renault Sport in the early 1980s.

Effectively then, Ferrari made an alarmingly late start upon design and manufacture of a definitive 1991 F1 car, the *Tipo* 642 being in effect a straightforward 'tidy-up' of the preceding 1990 *Tipo* 641 design. Its major modifications resulted directly from key changes in FISA's fuel accommodation and aerodynamic regulations.

Where previous 3.5-litre 'atmo' Ferraris had contained chassis length by compensating for the extra length in their V12-cylinder engines by wrapping some fuel tankage each side of the driver, such outrigger cells were now banned. Consequently the new 642 was given a more capacious central cell without the wraparound, while its nose wings were reduced from the previous 1990 150 cm span to 140 cm for 1991 and the rear wing brought 100 mm further inboard, reducing its leverage around the rear axle line, and thereby diminishing its total downthrust potential.

Engine developments concentrated largely upon new electronic management and high technology, aiming to relate fuel economy to enhanced all-round performance and fuel efficiency.

Ferrari's second place in Phoenix – although distant behind Senna's winning McLaren-Honda – proved nothing amidst such attrition, but clearly Ferrari were not as competitive as they had hoped. Both McLaren-Honda and Williams-Renault had drawn away.

Nichols: 'There was talk in the press of there being a major front suspension problem on the 642 but that wasn't true. It was effectively the same system which had worked well on the 641, with only detail modifications for the new year. The real problem was that in altering our aerodynamic package to match the new regulations we had lost perhaps 15 per cent total downforce, and although we quickly regained perhaps half of that in Migeot's wind-tunnel developments we found the cars had become relatively unstable under load . . .'

In the new *Tipo* 642's first tests at Ricard it had seemed acceptable, but in a subsequent pre-season session at Estoril in Portugal problems surfaced.

After the experiences of Phoenix and Brazil, a major improvement programme yielded revised suspension to compensate for the aerodynamic inadequacies. This looked promising in testing at Imola. Migeot then added aerodynamic changes with revised wings and tail bodywork, but Imola proved a Ferrari disaster as Prost slid off on the warming-up lap and Alesi went off in the opening laps.

Fiat-Ferrari management was hyper-sensitive to media criticism within Italy. It was always difficult for the race team at Maranello/Fiorano to maintain a logical sense of proportion . . . to keep their eyes on the targets of McLaren-Honda and Williams-Renault and to ignore the press . . .

The aerodynamically repackaged Ferraris from Imola were known as the 642/2, and for the Canadian GP a new front suspension was adopted with interlinked rockers effectively reacting against each other, similar in concept to the mono-shock system some others had adopted. Penske dampers and new extended front wing end plates – similar to Benetton's – were also employed, the latter directing vortex-free airflow to re-attach smoothly around the hull centre-section. Experiments were conducted with a bevel-disc system co-axial with the dampers. Bilstein gas dampers, with no remote gas reservoir, were tested on Alesi's car at Monza and became standard from Estoril.

Meanwhile, post-Imola media hysteria focussed even greater effort upon the decision which had been taken immediately after Brazil to accelerate development of a 641/642 replacement design – the high-nosed *Tipo* 643. There was no time available to create a completely new car, but an extensive redesign – mainly around the front end of the monocoque – would suffice.

In only 12 weeks from a clean sheet of paper to running the prototype new car, changes were only possible in restricted areas. Since the tooling around which the 642 monocoques were moulded split naturally at the steering bulkhead, only that part of the mould-tooling which shaped the section ahead of that point was modified, the section rearwards surviving unchanged. A new high-nose profile and under-chassis splitter wing system were developed, together with new front suspension.

The engine, rear suspension and automatic gearbox assembly then survived – like the rear half of the tub moulding – in 'Imola' specification.

Between the two types of cars, the relegated 642s and the replacement high-nosed 643s, the rear ends – engine/gearbox/suspension – plus all pedals, controls, instrumentation, fuel cells etc were interchangeable, but neither bodywork nor monocoques were common to both designs. Front wings also differed, although the old 642-type rear wings could fit the 643s if expedient.

The new *Tipo* 643's first test at Imola revealed a dramatic improvement, as did the French GP where Prost was only narrowly beaten by Mansell's Williams-Renault in a genuine motor *race*. At Silverstone Ferrari had the problem of

having not tested the new 643 there, where the varied demands of the revised circuit were much greater than those at Magny-Cours. Consequently Ferrari struggled to compete. They tested the new cars at Hockenheim, and their subsequent failure to be really competitive in the German GP was a great disappointment to them.

'The Hockenheim race just proved to us that although we had made great steps, Williams-Renault and McLaren-Honda were still one step ahead of us . . . In the race we were demonstrably in better shape than the McLaren-Hondas, but we couldn't touch the Williams.

'However, qualifying was another case, because both Williams and McLaren-Honda were out-performing us there. Once Senna has beaten your guy in qualifying and starts ahead of him on the grid, he's virtually impossible to overtake. That's what really upset Alain at Hockenheim, because the new 643 in race trim felt quicker almost everywhere than the McLaren was going ahead of him . . .'

Into the autumn races, Ferrari considered their V12 engine to be marginally behind Honda's, further behind Renault. Engine driveability was 'OK' but the cars still lacked aerodynamic stability, and consistency. The cars 'jumped about a lot on bumpy surfaces'. Attempts to improve the aerodynamic situation by using harder damper settings explained the bump-sensitivity. Download varied hyper-sensitively to changes in speed, ride height and rake. Hiro Teremoto, an ex-Showa damper technician formerly with Benetton, was engaged to pursue a development programme in this area.

Alain Prost had developed a good working relationship with his race engineer, Luigi Mazzola, and his skills in car set-up remained arguably as good as, if not better than, Senna's at McLaren. The same could not be said of Prost's '91 teammate, Alesi, who was still very inexperienced, like so many graduates of recent F3 and F3000 racing.

Alesi's approach was, however, intelligent, conservative and mature. The Ferrari V12 was revving to 14,600 rpm but had a notably hollow mid-range torque curve. At Monaco and Montreal throttle-sensitive butterfly valves were installed in the exhaust system in an attempt to improve torque. Variable-length induction trumpets were tried from Hockenheim forward but meanwhile Prost was increasingly at odds with the Fiat hierarchy, publicly critical of policies and personalities. After the Japanese GP this led to his dismissal, and Morbidelli drove in his place at Adelaide.

Four Ferrari 642s were built earlier in the season – serials '123-'126, the older '122 joining them as spare for the opening two races. Four new 643s followed, '127-'128 making their debuts at Magny-Cours, '129 emerging as spare at Silverstone and '130 for Prost at Monza. All the monocoques were moulded by Ferrari's UK facility, GTO Ltd at Shalford, Surrey.

Prost finished the season fifth in the Drivers' table after failing to win a race, but finishing eight of the 14 GPs he actually started, all in points-scoring positions – 2-4-5-2-3-3-2-4. Alesi was also classified eight times but from all 16 races – 12-6-3-4-3-5-3-4. The team ended the season third in the Constructors' Championship with 55.5 points (the abbreviated Australian GP having counted half points and Morbidelli being placed sixth in the flood) to Williams-Renault's 125 and McLaren-Honda's victorious total of 139.

Major management changes were to take place during the winter of 1991/92. Cesare Fiorio had long since been removed as *Direttore Sportivo*. Now Luca di Montezemolo replaced him, Harvey Postlethwaite returned as *Direttore Tecnico*, the British GTO operation was closed and the facility sold to McLaren Cars' road supercar project, and Niki Lauda was called in as a consultant. Could matters improve? Only time would tell . . . but Barnard was on his way back.

FIRST

See entry for Life, page 279.

The Caliri-styled Copersucar-Fittipaldi F5A worked reasonably well in the former double World Champion's hands, here leading de Angelis's Shadow DN9B, Buenos Aires, 1979.

In Fittipaldi's case there was life after death. They floundered through 1982, making a one-car entry for Serra, stripping their 1981 cars, rebuilding '3 and the latest '5 to F8D specification, while '4 remained in their Reading works as a spare tub. One Richard Divila/Tim Wright-designed F9 emerged at the British GP to be driven subsequently by Serra as the team's swansong. The Cosworth era was gone, and a turbocharged engine was vital for success. Serra fought his qualification battles well, starting in nine races, finishing six and placing sixth for a point at Zolder and seventh, just out of the points, in Austria.

Through the winter of 1982/83, the brothers tried to raise new sponsorship, but failed; early in the new year the author bought a DFV from them and it seemed like the kiss of death, for they took the money and closed their Reading works within the hour . . . was it something I said?

See entry for Wolf.

Fittipaldi

After an indifferent career as a Formula 1 driver, Wilson Fittipaldi – the elder of the Brazilian brothers – set up his own team to build a car sponsored by Brazil's Copersucar sugar marketing organization, which he would drive in 1975. There was much money involved and, with former mechanic Richard Divila, the elder Fittipaldi developed a Cosworth-powered 'special' built in São Paulo.

The prototype Copersucar-Cosworth FD01 had a deep, shapely monocoque, nose radiator ducted under a full-width blade wing and rear-mounted radiator, and was regarded pretty much as a joke through '75. Wilson tackled 13 GPs, failed to qualify twice, non-started once and finished six times with tenth as his best at Watkins Glen. The prototype crashed heavily on its debut in Buenos Aires, and '02 ran in Brazil, now with twin rear radiators and more robust rear suspension to obviate the cause of the Argentinian crash. New chassis '03 appeared in France and was used for the rest of the year.

The car was quite hopeless, Wilson mediocre, and for 1976 his double World Champion brother Emerson was persuaded to join him, reputedly for a ton of Copersucar money. All Brazil held its breath . . . but to no avail, for the Copersucar team achieved less than Emerson's potential.

Four Divila-designed FD04 types were now produced, using in-line hip radiators cowled into shapely flaring side pods and featuring a full-width chisel nose with wide airfoil ahead of it, like the Hesketh 308B. Emerson was sixth on luck and reliability at Long Beach and Monaco but failed to qualify in Belgium. Another sixth came in the British GP but hopeful Brazilian teammate Ingo Hoffman had only four drives, failing to qualify in three of them and reaching 11th in his home GP, driving 'FD01/3'. Emerson drove 'FD04/2' in Spain, '1 again until France where '3 appeared, and '4 from Holland to the end of the season.

The FD04s ran on into 1977 before ex-Ensign designer Dave Baldwin produced his replacement Fittipaldi F5 (no 'D' for Divila here), three being built. They looked like developed Ensign LNF75s, but Baldwin left abruptly just before his first F5's debut in the French GP and development stalled. Emerson's driving and the cars' reliability won fourth places in Argentina and Brazil as well as fifth at Long Beach; later another fourth came in Holland but he failed to qualify in Germany and Italy. Poor Hoffman ran only in South America, retiring and finishing seventh. They drove old 'FD04/3' and '1 in those races, Emerson using 'F5/1' from France and 'F5/2' from Germany on.

The brothers hired Giacomo Caliri's Fly Studio consultancy to update the Baldwin design as the F5A wing-car for 1978. At last Emerson became almost competitive – second in Brazil, fourth in Germany and Austria, fifth in Holland and the USA and sixth in Sweden, gaining 17 points and seventh place in the Constructors' Championship – although the car never looked a potential race winner.

For 1979 the Fittipaldis hired ex-Lotus designer Ralph Bellamy to build them a second-generation wing-car and he produced the rearward-podded needle-nosed F6A for them in São Paulo, which looked sensational but flopped. It was discarded and the old Caliri aerodynamic-pack F5As were updated instead. Subsequently, the two F6As built were modified for use later in the year. Emerson started all 15 GPs, retired from seven, his only score being sixth in Argentina, though he was eighth in Italy and Canada, and seventh in the USA. Alex Ribeiro failed to qualify the second car in the North American races.

For 1980 Fittipaldi Automotive merged with the remnants of Wolf with Harvey Postlethwaite designing new F8 cars for Emerson and Rosberg, after beginning the season with ex-Wolf honeycomb cars. The new year's 'F7/1' was ex-Wolf 'WR8' and 'F7/2' ex-Wolf 'WR7' while chassis 'F7/3' was completely new. Emerson normally raced '1, Rosberg '2, with '3 the spare car raced by the Finn at Long Beach.

The completely new, long-podded, short-nosed 'F8/1' made its bow in the British GP driven by Emerson, was crashed by Rosberg at the Österreichring and quickly rebuilt around a new tub. Chassis 'F8/2' was new in Germany, Rosberg racing it twice, Emerson five times. Rosberg placed third in Argentina and fifth in Italy, while he was also seventh at Zolder but non-qualified for three other races. Emerson, meanwhile, inherited third at Long Beach and was sixth at Monaco, starting all 14 GPs and retiring from six.

Emerson hung up his helmet at this point; sponsorship was drying up and Postlethwaite joined Ferrari. Gary Thomas developed the F8C for 1981, three chassis running for Rosberg and Chico Serra; 'F8C/2' using a 1980 tub, 'F8C/3' being built new and a third chassis, 'F8C/4', first appearing as a spare tub at Kyalami and later completed for Serra to drive from Long Beach. With poor backing, poor engines and poorer tyres Fittipaldi stood no chance. Rosberg retired from six of the first nine GPs, finished 9-12 and non-qualifying in the others. In the last six races his entry was scratched once, he non-qualified four times and was tenth at Las Vegas to end the year. Serra had two finishes, 7-11, retired from his three other races and non-qualified eight times, non-started once and was scratched from the Austrian GP.

Fomet

Italian industrialist Gabriele Rumi's Fondmetal wheel manufacturing company had been the Osella team's major sponsor before taking it over at the end of 1990. Enzo Osella and former ex-Ferrari chief engineer Tomaini both left the team, which Rumi moved into new premises at Palosco, near Bergamo. Rumi went even further and established a separate design and composite manufacturing facility in England, at Bicester, where under the name Fomet 1 it was run by engineer Tino Belli.

No suitable frontline engine deal was available at such short notice for 1991, so Rumi instead arranged supply of Hart-developed Cosworth DFR V8 engines, and the old Osella FA1Me chassis was updated for the start of the new season. Grouillard was retained as driver, and Belli, Riccardo Rosa and Tim Holloway created a new Fomet 1 chassis for him which made its debut in testing at Imola.

Richard Divila – recently sacked by Ligier, which is no disgrace – had previously worked with Grouillard for Osella, and he now joined the Fondmetal project. His efforts in conjunction with Grouillard and the rest of the team paid off when the new car was persuaded to qualify quite handsomely in Mexico. It became harder to make the race later in the year, and a new Fomet 1 chassis was desperately required as the original began to delaminate. The new car qualified well at Spa, finishing tenth – which by the team's standards was a triumph – but meanwhile Divila and Rumi had split, and the Brazilian was once more out on his ear, Tim Holloway replacing him as race engineer.

The new chassis was then written off in Monza testing, and when Grouillard struggled with the older version Rumi fired him and hired Tarquini instead. Grouillard had qualified for only four GPs, finishing only at Spa, while Tarquini finished 12-11 in Spain and Japan before failing to pre-qualify in Australia.

Fomet-Cosworth DFR F1, Olivier Grouillard failing to qualify for the 1991 Hungarian GP.

Footwork

Prior to the 1991 season, the Arrows team was rechristened, reflecting its acquisition by the Footwork Corporation of Japan in December 1989. Footwork boss Wataru Ohashi reputedly committed $35 million to the Porsche 3.5-litre naturally aspirated F1 engine project for 1991, but the programme developed into a spectacular fiasco which nearly ruined the Milton Keynes team and certainly dealt Porsche's battered image of technical excellence a further devastating blow to add to the relative failure of its CART racing engine for the US.

The engine saga is further detailed in the relevant engine section here, but to accommodate the bulky 80-degree V12 designer Alan Jenkins created the FA12 chassis to replace the early-season, very unwieldy FA11Cs from Imola forward. The FA12 was notable for its knife-edge vertical prow raised nose form, but Alboreto wrote off the prototype during pre-race testing at Imola to set the tone for what would follow. As the Porsche V12 failed disastrously to approach even the team's minimum expectations the agonizing decision was taken to replace it with Hart-prepared Cosworth DFR V8s from the French GP forward.

In practice the transfer gears necessary to mate the team's transverse six-speed gearbox to the different crankshaft height of the Cosworth V8 broke repeatedly. These failures caused a string of non-qualifications and from the German GP the Footwork-DFRs had to pre-qualify, so the old FA11C-DFR rear assembly was adopted in its entirety to achieve some kind of reliability.

Despite some late-season tests, the Footwork-Porsche agreement was formally dissolved on the eve of the Japanese GP and replaced by a deal for the team to run Mugen-labelled Honda V10 engines for '92.

The team had used four A11Cs at the start of the season, with chassis '2 acting as team spare until Monaco. Four Porsche-powered FA12s replaced them, the prototype being destroyed at Imola, and Caffi damaging chassis '2 – and hospitalizing himself – at Monaco. The Italian then sustained facial injuries in a road accident and Johansson replaced him for four mid-season GPs, two Porsche-powered, two DFR. He qualified for just one race, in Canada, and retired from that. Caffi's only starts were in the last two races of the season, placing 10-15, while Alboreto made it to the grid nine times, his only finishes being 15th at Estoril, 13th in Australia! Chassis '3 and '4 began life Porsche-powered and were converted to DFR power from the French GP forward, '5 and '7 being V8-engined from new . . .

Glas

See entry for Lambo, page 278.

Haas-Lola

The 1986 season would see the end of the American-backed team established by Carl Haas and Teddy Mayer under the Beatrice-Lola banner (see page 223) as the Beatrice Group's enthusiastic President was ousted and his replacement viewed Formula 1 with little favour . . .

Three Neil Oatley/Ross Brawn-designed THL-1 chassis – numbers '001-'003 – were used early in the season, subtly revised to accept the latest-spec Hart four-cylinder turbo engines which were half-an-inch shorter overall and with redesigned exhaust runs. Drivers were Alan Jones and Patrick Tambay, both excellent in so many ways but both by 1986 long past their sell-by dates . . .

Five improved THL-2s followed from the same creative stable, first introduced at Imola where '001 served as spare while '003 was used by Jones, and featuring the brand new Ford TEC V6 turbo engine. The Ford engine was designed from the outset as a stressed-block unit, and it was shorter and lower than the Hart in-line 'four'. This

allowed the rear end of the THL-2 tub to be revised, its 195-litre fuel cell was shorter and its cockpit sides taller to enhance rigidity. In section the fuselage was also more rounded for aerodynamic advantage.

An extra-long spacer between engine and transaxle maintained the THL-1 wheelbase despite the shorter engine, enabling the body to be fashionably waisted and neatly cowled inboard of the rear wheels.

The latest 'THL-2/002' made its debut for Jones at Monaco, where Tambay crashed '001 so heavily it would not be raced again. The unfortunate Frenchman then also wrote off '002 in his injurious accident at Montreal, while '004 was deployed for the first time at Spa, driven by Jones. Chassis '005 became Tambay's regular car from the French GP at Ricard-Castellet. Neil Oatley introduced a wide-ranging suspension redesign at Monza introducing both anti-dive and anti-squat characteristics. In Mexico another change was introduced, after testing had shown benefit from a longer wheelbase with 50 mm spacer between engine and transaxle to limit pitch-change, throw more weight onto the front wheels and make the cars more 'driveable'.

Jones retired from both his Hart-powered outings in the THL-1, Tambay retiring his at both Rio and Imola, but finishing eighth in Spain. Jones raced the Cosworth-Ford TEC-powered THL-2 in 14 GPs, officially retired from nine of them while his classified finishes read 11*-10-9-4 (Austria) and sixth (Portugal).

Tambay's THL-2 record included his non-start in Canada following that heavy practice accident which also sidelined him for Detroit, being too far behind to be classified at Estoril and otherwise retiring seven times, leaving just three finishes – 8-7-5, all in successive mid-season GPs, Germany, Hungary and Austria.

Although the team finished eighth in the 1986 Constructors' Championship, ahead of Brabham and Arrows, this was not quite what either Ford or Beatrice had envisaged. Losing both their sponsor and the engine, Carl Haas and Teddy Mayer sold the FORCE operation and its hardware to Bernie Ecclestone for incorporation where possible into the Motor Racing Developments Brabham operation . . .

Top: The Footwork-Porsche FA12 of 1991 flattered only to deceive. Designed by Alan Jenkins the chassis had a distinctive boat-bowed nose but engine problems foiled any worthwhile development. Above: The combination of a new team, a new car, a new engine and old drivers proved too much for the 1986 Haas-Lolas to shine: Jones's THL-2 at Monza, 1986.

Above: *The Postlethwaite-designed Hesketh 308, in 1974 form with nose radiator and hip oil cooler, was subsequently modified to run with in-line hip water radiators.* Below right: *James Hunt's Hesketh 308 at Zandvoort, Dutch GP 1974, shows off its flat-topped, curve-sided tub form, bluff nose with large horizontal splitter and rear wing.*

Hesketh

Lord Alexander Fermor-Hesketh was a very young, very wealthy enthusiast who entered Formula 3 racing with a Dastle car in the early Seventies, his little team full of knock-about if rather juvenile fun, but run by the experienced Anthony 'Bubbles' Horsley. They provided James Hunt with Formula 2 and Formula 1 Surtees experience in 1972, and he made their name in 1973 driving a new F1 March engineered by Dr Harvey Postlethwaite, previously with March.

The team was based at Hesketh's stately home, Easton Neston, near Towcester, Northamptonshire, within earshot of Silverstone circuit. Elated by their March success, Hesketh Racing built an all-new Postlethwaite-designed Cosworth/Hewland car for 1974. He drew on his considerable aerodynamic knowledge and produced a shapely wedge-elevation, Coke bottle planform monocoque car known as the Hesketh 308. In initial form it used a nose radiator but would subsequently be revised, introducing in-line hip radiators and a wide blade nose with full-width wing ahead.

Hunt tested '308-1' in Brazil early in 1974, it qualified on pole at Brands Hatch but retired with bad handling in the race. At Kyalami a driveshaft joint failed but on home ground at Silverstone Hunt put '308-1' on pole again, set fastest lap and won the International Trophy on merit. In the next five GPs he drove '308-2', finishing only once, third in Sweden. This car was badly damaged in the French GP and was rebuilt around a new tub in late 1974 with rubber-controlled front suspension and new bodywork.

The 308s were competitive in Hunt's hands but the question became 'Is it the car, or is it the driver?', for they seldom qualified well at GP level and were unreliable. Chassis '308-3' was used from the German GP, finishing third in Austria but chassis '2 with blade nose raced in Canada and the USA, finishing fourth and third respectively.

This promising debut season left Hesketh sixth in the Constructors' Championship with 15 points, and for 1975 Postlethwaite further developed the 308B, while a replacement all-new 308C was under development. He had experimented briefly with rubber cone suspension medium but would alternate with conventional coil-springs after the 1975 season had begun. Hesketh sought

reliability in '308-3', Hunt finishing second and sixth in Argentina and Brazil, using rubber suspension medium, while he usually raced '308-2' thereafter.

Hesketh had no external sponsor and now – despite the continuing parties and high jinks – money was very tight. For the Spanish GP, '308-1' was sold to private entrant Harry Stiller for Alan Jones to drive; both Heskeths, works and private, crashed. Rob Walker entered the Jones car later, while Horsley rented '308-3' to Torsten Palm for Monaco (non-qualifying) and Sweden (tenth).

Jones showed promise but achieved little. Hunt's '308-2' was the sole Hesketh representative at Zandvoort and Horsley's team actually won on tyre-change strategy in a wet-dry race, after qualifying on row two. Hunt qualified there again in the next race, the French GP, finishing second, but was out of luck until Österreichring where he qualified on the front row and finished second. In the latter race, rent-a-driver Brett Lunger was 13th in '308-3'.

The all-new shallow-chassis, in-line hip radiator 308C made its race debut in the 'Swiss' GP at Dijon, but rigidity, in suspension as well as chassis, was deficient. Hunt could only finish eighth. The car felt queasy under him; despite this, he finished fifth at Monza, where Lunger reached tenth in '308-3', and at Watkins Glen, where Hunt always went well, the 308C finished fourth but Lunger crashed.

Meanwhile old '308-1' had been sold to German privateer Harald Ertl, who performed most respectably on a tight budget, eighth in Germany, ninth at Monza.

Lord Hesketh decided to cut his losses and withdrew from Formula 1 at the end of '75, selling the 308Cs to Walter Wolf who also took some of the staff and Dr Postlethwaite's services. Hunt went to McLaren, becoming World Champion but Horsley preserved the Easton Neston company as Cosworth DFV engine-preparation specialists and continued to prepare and enter the old 308B or updated-spec 308D cars for paying customers.

Ertl raced '308/3' throughout 1976 achieving reliable results, including seventh in the British GP and eighths in Austria and Japan. Hesketh Racing ran Guy Edwards in '308/2', without distinction, until it was written off in the Lauda crash at the Nürburgring. New chassis '308/4' was used by Stommelen in Austria, then by Edwards, and Alex Ribeiro in the USA.

The irrepressible Horsley found new rent-a-

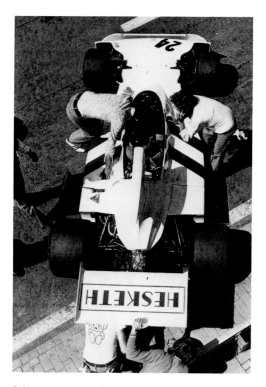

drive customers for 1977 and young engineer Frank Dernie produced five distinctively tapered new 308Es for them. Hopeful drivers included Rupert Keegan; Ertl, who was going no further after a good run and who left in mid-season; Hector Rebaque, who had great difficulty qualifying; and Ian Ashley, who suffered similarly and was badly hurt in a terrible practice accident in Canada, which destroyed '308E-3'. Keegan demolished 'E-1' in the race there, ending Hesketh's season.

Into 1978 Divina Galica, the girl driver, non-qualified for the South American GPs and crashed at Silverstone, as did Daly in old 'E-1'. Cheever qualified 'E-5 for Kyalami but had an oil pipe fail after only eight laps, and Daly tried and failed to qualify chassis '5 at Long Beach and Belgium, and 'E4 in Monaco. By May, chassis '5 had been sold to John Cooper, already owning an ex-Wolf-Williams 308C, for national British Formula 1, and Hesketh's racing days were over.

Hill

Former double World Champion driver Graham Hill had established his Embassy Racing team in 1973 driving a Shadow DN1 and in 1974 commissioned construction of the Lola T370s. During the 1974/75 winter he then backed design and construction of a developed version of the T370, known initially as the Lola T371 but which was very quickly and more logically renamed the Hill GH1.

It was Lola-like, with water radiators podded just behind the front wheels à la Ferrari, but the monocoque was slightly triangular in section with inward-sloping side panels. It was Cosworth-powered of course. Design was by youthful Andy Smallman, a former Lola employee who had been seconded to the team. The new cars' tubs were made by John Thompson's TC Prototypes company, four being completed. The prototype 'GH1/1' made its debut in South Africa '75, where Stommelen finished seventh.

Hill himself was no longer driving seriously and for the Spanish GP at Barcelona Migault drove 'GH1/1' and Stommelen took brand new 'GH1/2'. This car ran a new experimental carbon-fibre rear wing post, against its manufacturer's recommendation on this rugged circuit, and after an early field-decimating multiple accident Stommelen actually led under heavy pressure. Over the severe hump into the first corner where the famous Lotus 49B wing collapses had occurred in 1969, the Hill's wing post failed, pitching Stommelen into a huge accident which killed five bystanders, demolished the car and caused the race to be abandoned.

Graham failed to qualify in his swansong outing at Monaco, and thereafter ran his cars for newcomer Tony Brise, Jones, Migault, Schuppan and – later in the year – the recovered Stommelen. Brise ran nine races, finishing five times, 6-7-7-'15'-15. His sixth place came second time out, in Sweden. The car by no means set the world on fire but it was a competent design while Brise showed great promise.

Jones drove four times, with a 100 per cent record of finishes, 13-16-10-5. His fifth place in Germany added two more team points, giving an aggregate of three to put the Hill team into 11th place in that season's Constructors' Cup competition. Migault drove only once more after Spain, at Zolder; Schuppan retired in Sweden and Stommelen was 16th in Austria before retiring in Italy.

Smallman designed a new part-pyramid section tub for 1976, the Hill GH2. It reputedly had many problems in initial testing at Ricard that November, and Graham flew Brise, Smallman and other team members home that evening contemplating some weeks of hard work to put it all right. Arriving over London in fog, their private aircraft struck the grasping branches of a tree on Arkley golf course and crashed – all on board were killed. 'GH2/1' rests today in the National Motor Museum at Beaulieu, Hampshire, as a memorial to one of Britain's best-loved racing drivers and his unfortunate team.

Honda

The Japanese Honda Motor Company had rapidly spreadeagled all opposition in motor cycle racing after a tentative start, and in 1964 set out to do the same in Formula 1 with an unusual transverse V12-engined spaceframe-chassised RA271 design. A regular two-car works team then ran improved RA272 machines during 1965 and by the end of that season they had clearly the most powerful engine, and Ginther easily won the Mexican GP for them.

Unfortunately for Honda, this was the final race of the 1500 cc Formula, so their potentially dominant RA272 was left obsolescent, all dressed up with nowhere to go.

Undismayed, indeed greatly encouraged, Honda R&D headed by engineer Yoshio Nakamura concentrated intense effort upon 3-litre development for 1966.

The new 3-litre RA273 V12 was late appearing and made its debut in the Italian GP at Monza in September, where it instantly impressed as the largest and most powerful car in Formula 1. Ginther drove bravely, the car may have been rather slow and unwieldy through the corners, but it accelerated fiercely and was very fast at the end of the straights.

The V12 engine had its power take-off amidships, geared down to an output shaft, so in effect it was actually two V6 engines in tandem. If it had used the conventional 60-degree vee angle, the take-off shaft under the crank would have made it uncomfortably tall, but Honda chose a 90-degree angle (unusual for a V12) instead, which made it uncomfortably wide. They then applied their motor cycle engine experience to the full, by using roller bearings everywhere rather than plain bearings, which offered theoretical advantages in decreased friction but which physically made the engine uncomfortably big and heavy. Motor cycle practice also extended to the four-valve-per-cylinder combustion chamber design, which itself was being tried very successfully in their contemporary 1-litre Formula 2 racing engine, which would dominate the class in Brabham's factory cars.

Overall, the Honda RA273 V12 is a classic example of 'an engine man's engine', with little practical thought devoted to the kind of chassis necessary to carry it.

Also in accordance with motor cycle practice, in which low all-up weights and multi-speed gearboxes were common, the V12's peak power and torque were confined to a narrow band at the top of its rev range, making the five-speed gearbox inadequate for the driver to keep the engine working at its optimum speed on the tighter road circuits. Power circuits like Spa, Reims and Monza were an increasingly endangered species, yet with the massive excess weight which the Honda had to brake and accelerate in every corner these would be the very circuits to which it was best suited.

The full-length aluminium monocoque had to carry a huge fuel load and was stiffened by a fully stressed scuttle section above the driver's legs. The completed car when dry weighed no less than 740 kg (1631 lb) – nearly 40 per cent more than the legal minimum. It was claimed to possess 420 bhp at 10,000 rpm, yet that was only some 25 per cent more than the average of its opposition, all of which were at least 15 per cent lighter. In fact it seems doubtful if in Monza form the engine had more than 380 bhp and though the V12s seemed to begin life with great power, they then deteriorated markedly with age despite Honda's best rebuild efforts.

At Monza the prototype RA273 chassis 'F-101', with its spectacular snake pit of exhausts within the engine vee, qualified on the second row of the grid and was running second in the race – deafening everyone present – when a rear tyre deflated and pitched Ginther into an almighty accident in the high-speed *Curva Grande*. Chassis 'F-101' was used up . . .

Two new cars, 'F-102' and 'F-103' appeared in the next race at Watkins Glen, driven by Ginther and Bucknum, '102' featuring a 7.75 in. wider track. In Mexico, Ginther led for the first two laps in this car but progressively lost power – a habit typical of the old RA272 transverse V12 cars – and finished fourth.

For 1967 Honda R&D ceded racing responsibility for their cars to former multiple motor cycle World Champion, and 1964 motor racing Champion Driver, John Surtees. He set up Honda Racing in Slough, England, to campaign the developed V12s. Unfortunately, his faith in Honda doing to the Formula 1 world what they had done to motor cycling was misplaced. His two seasons with them coincided with a major expansion in their production car programmes which diverted attention from Formula 1 development, at Honda Racing's expense.

During negotiation, he had recognized limitations of their existing design, as they themselves had, and the 500 lb engine plus the giant chassis needed to carry it just had to go.

Modern advances in lubricant and plain bearing technology made roller bearings unnecessary. Honda had an all-new 360 lb plain-bearing V12 on the drawing board but it would clearly be a long time coming. Meanwhile, by using elektron castings in place of aluminium 90 lb was saved, while power was allegedly up to 412 bhp and 450 was considered within reach. A further 50 lb was saved by design of a two-shaft gearbox to replace the original three-shaft version.

Surtees began 1967 race-developing old 'F-102' with any worthwhile results regarded as a bonus. He took two third places although the car was slow in '67 company, while passenger car demands siphoned off Honda's best R&D men, leaving him with an untried, inexperienced crew and the Formula 1 programme suffered while they learned. For example, at Kyalami two engines disintegrated in practice because fragments of broken file had been left inside them during assembly, Surtees finishing third with a

---

Ginther's Honda RA273 V12 challenges Parkes's Ferrari 312 V12, Monza 1966.

bitsa engine lashed together from salvaged parts.

High-mileage chassis 'F-102' was rested at Monaco where Surtees raced 'F-103' but a wrong-specification and inadequate hose burst on the grid. 'F-103' was retired from further competition, having run only three races in its life, as Surtees concentrated development upon '102'.

Honda power showed at Spa, but there the engine blew up; then in its last two outings, at the British and German GPs, despite running poorly, Surtees was able to salvage sixth- and fourth-place finishes on mechanical sympathy.

This was the Formula 1 car with everything – excessive weight, indifferent road-holding, what Surtees described as 'hellish differential trouble' causing serious tyre wear, and chronic difficulties with Honda's own low-pressure fuel-injection system.

On slower circuits Surtees could gear it to keep between 8750 and 10,000 rpm in the meat of the narrow torque band, though it was marginal even then. On faster circuits a higher top gear increased ratio gaps so at various points around the circuit the Honda was right 'off the cam' with poor response until it came back into its working range. And at low engine speeds, fuel was drawn so slowly through the injection system that it was prone to heating up and evaporation, which caused the unmistakable and characteristic Honda misfire.

At Spa in 1966 Surtees had geared his Ferrari 312 for 176 mph and in 1967 there he geared the Honda for 190 mph at its peak power engine speed of 9500 rpm. It steadfastly refused to pull more than 8000 in practice . . .

Due to chassis structure limitations it had not been possible to change suspension pick-up points and the 1967 RA273 suspension was a compromise demanding spring rates some 30 per cent higher than ideal. This caused wheel patter at high speed when the car would wander and skip on Spa's super-fast straights. The two-shaft gearbox was successful but the elektron engine tried at Monaco and Zandvoort had expansion and pressurization problems, blowing out its oil, while the original-spec V12s were down to 408 bhp at Monaco and 385 again thereafter. In Germany the fuel mixture became over-enriched, giving 4.5 mpg consumption, thereby using nearly 46 gallons for race distance or some 460 lb of fuel . . .

Surtees had gained approval to build a lighter chassis at Slough. He raced Lola CanAm cars in between Formula 1 commitments and had a close engineering relationship with the neighbouring Lola company and its founder, Eric Broadley. Now he drew heavily upon Lola's T190 Indianapolis car design. Honda chassis designer Sano came to Europe to assist and, to rush the car through, they adapted existing T190 tub sections wherever possible. The tub terminated behind the cockpit, where the engine would be slung in a multi-tubu-lar subframe also supporting the gearbox and rear suspension.

This hybrid Honda RA300 was skinned on Lola's chassis jig, modified to Honda Racing requirements. The front bulkhead was identical, as were certain pressings, while radiator, pedals and so on came off the shelf and they also used the Lola T190 nose cone mould. But from the front bulkhead back the tub matched Sano's and Surtees's suspension requirements, quite different from the offset Indy Lola layout.

Every conceivable corner was cut to get the car ready but the team had to miss the Canadian GP and aim for the Italian at Monza in September. The car emerged weighing 1340 lb dry – a saving of 228 lb, 150 lb off the chassis alone – and the old system of six fuel tanks and six separate pumps was simplified to just three tanks and one pump, arranged to drain completely in contrast to the old system which always left four gallons unuseable. Because the car was lighter, consumption would be less, so tank capacity was cut from 50 gallons to 44. Back in Tokyo 'Naka-San' made the elektron engine reliable, got power back to 395 bhp (more than since Monaco), and by playing with exhaust pipes on the dyno improved power down around 8000 rpm.

The new car 'RA300/1' – dubbed the 'Hondola' by the press – won on its debut in a sensational finish at Monza.

It was used again in the US, with stronger wishbones, but fuel injection problems persisted; yet, despite diff trouble, Surtees finished fourth in Mexico.

Through the 1967/68 winter Honda decided to continue although Surtees had lost his major sponsor when BP pulled out. The RA300 was raced for the last time in South Africa but was now two seconds off the pace and could only finish eighth.

Honda's promised new lightweight RA301 chassis 'F-801' emerged at Jarama, flatter and lower than the RA273 but now with outboard front springs à la Brabham. But it was 90 lb heavier than the RA300. The revised engine used Formula 2 type valvegear with torsion bar valve springs, the inlets were in the vee, exhausts now outside, handling and fuel injection troubles persisted, yet Surtees ran third before gear selection failed. However, when we talk of anyone running in high-sounding positions in 1968, one must remember how thin the grids were that year. Only 13 cars started the Spanish GP.

At Monaco the RA301 gearbox broke again; at Spa Surtees had the power to lead until the rear suspension broke. He was second in the French GP, fifth in the British after a newly fitted strutted wing collapsed and third in the US, but with whole-hearted factory involvement it would surely have been so much better.

A second RA301 chassis, 'F-802', was assembled at Slough, redesigned by Len Terry with parts made at his Poole works. It was skinned in magnesium instead of '801's aluminium to save precious weight, and the rear suspension was improved. Hobbs drove it at Monza, running sixth until a valve dropped, wrecking the engine. Surtees used '802' as his training car in the US and Canada but it was afflicted by various problems. It ended its career fifth in Mexico driven by Bonnier.

Meanwhile in mid-season an entirely new Honda RA302 had appeared, chassis 'F-801', tested by Surtees at Silverstone just prior to the French GP. He found it not yet raceworthy, but Mr Soichiro Honda himself was on a trade mission to France at that time and both he and the GP organizers wanted it to run, driven by Jo Schlesser.

The RA302 was extraordinary. It used an *air-cooled* 120-degree V8 engine with four valves per cylinder, all torsion-bar sprung. The engine was slung beneath a high-level extension boom protruding from the rear bulkhead of a truncated magnesium-skinned forward monocoque and driving via a new five-speed gearbox. Suspension was the only conventional part of this wholly Japanese designed and built newcomer.

Surtees still felt it was too new to be raced but Honda's visiting management insisted. The twitchy-handling RA302 was misfiring from the start, possibly due to rain being drawn into its gaping induction and cooling intakes and finding a way into the electrics, and poor Schlesser lost control when the V8 cut completely; the car climbed a bank and somersaulted, exploding into a furious magnesium blaze which killed its unfortunate driver.

A replacement RA302 chassis 'F-802' emerged in time for the Italian GP at Monza, lacking the oil-mist cooling of the prototype though the engine itself was still air-cooled. But Surtees used the V12's top end power to the utmost in practice to qualify on pole position only to go off the road in the race when Amon crashed the Ferrari in his path.

Honda withdrew from this enforcedly half-hearted and ultimately tragic Formula 1 programme at the end of 1968 but would return as a supplier of turbocharged 1500 cc engines in 1983.

Jordan

Eddie Jordan made his name in Formula 3 and Formula 3000 racing before declaring his intention to make the giant stride into Formula 1 for 1991. The loquacious Irishman not only succeeded in securing valuable sponsorship for the new project but also won supply of customer-status Cosworth-Ford HB V8 engines.

Former race mechanic Gary Anderson drew a neat and workmanlike raised-nose chassis and aerodynamic package in conjunction with Andrew Green and Mark Smith, deploying a particularly distinctive form of drooping-flanked rear diffuser which would operate extremely well when run in close contact with the road surface, and a monoshock suspension system à la Tyrrell. Jordan signed drivers Bertrand Gachot and Andrea de Cesaris, and after a low-key debut in Phoenix the Jordan team did a superb job – putting together one of the finest new team debut seasons in modern Formula 1 history.

They had to pre-qualify, of course, and barring misfortune proved capable of doing so quite comfortably. Low-speed understeer was a problem, but Anderson chose to trade it for exceptional stability in extremely high speed curves. If anything the Jordan 191s were handicapped in qualifying by an inability adequately to heat Goodyear's qualifying rubber. The new cars' notably good traction would overwhelm their front-end bite.

Seven of the Jordan 191 chassis were produced

weeks before the opening race, Ligier turned at effectively zero notice to Megatron for the supply of alternative BMW M12/13 engines. Tétu and Michel Beaujon were faced with revising their brand new tailor-made JS29-Alfa Romeo design to accept the German engine, which was taller, longer, had a 20 mm higher crankshaft and which lacked a fully stressed crankcase, thus demanding some kind of support cradle at the rear of the monocoque moulding.

This entailed an immense crash programme, including returning the carbon/Kevlar fuselage mouldings to their manufacturer, Advanced Composite Technology in England, where they were modified around the rear. The team's new transaxle tailored to the Alfa engine had to be matched to the Megatron unit's higher input, and since that year's normal Megatron structural sump was an exclusive Arrows item, Ligier had to adopt instead simple tubular-steel A-frames to co-support the engine which was to be supplied to them with a conventional sump pan. This major change wrecked the JS29Bs' prospects, leaving them some 35 kg overweight, untidy and aerodynamically compromised.

The team understandably missed the opening race at Rio, but subsequently appeared with four JS29B cars – numbered '2-'5 – later uprated to 'C-spec with new side-vented side pods and new nose and tail diffuser configuration from Ricard. The chassis were progressively stiffened and lightened as the season developed and number '6 was introduced new as a JS29C at Jerez.

René Arnoux was joined by new signing PierCarlo Ghinzani. His new Ligier-Megatron broke on the warm-up lap at Imola, retired nine times, including failures in the last five successive GPs, he salvaged sixth place at Spa and then four more finishes – but merely 11-10-10-10. Ghinzani similarly retired from the last five successive GPs, also failing to finish four more times, being excluded in Britain, then finishing 7-12-12-8-8 elsewhere. The team finished 11th-equal and last in the Constructors' Championship, with Arnoux's Spa point.

For 1988, Ligier had no turbo alternative, and concluded a supply agreement instead with Judd for the new Ligier CV V8 3.5-litre 'atmo' engine. Michel Tétu adopted a most unusual fuel tank arrangement – once considered but rejected by Gordon Murray for a ground-effects Brabham – in which a 70-litre fuel cell was sited behind the engine, augmented by twin 60-litre cells in the fuselage, each side of the driver. He could select which tank to drain to alter the balance of the car, and a Citroën-derived power steering system was used experimentally on Arnoux's car at Rio. The oil tank was inserted between the engine and the rearward fuel cell. Four of these over-complicated, under-performing and hefty JS31 cars were built for drivers Arnoux and Stefan Johansson – who joined the French team ex-Ferrari and McLaren.

Ligier's old glory days were long gone. When their drivers qualified – which was nowhere near often enough for an outfit of their former stature – Arnoux and Johansson were way down the grid, and when they raced they seldom rose above mobile chicane status, their cars unmanageable, uncompetitive and worse still showing negligible improvement as the season progressed; much of the time, in fact, quite the reverse.

They could not blame Judd. They had so many chassis problems they could contribute little to the Rugby engines' development. Williams consequently bore the main Judd installation development load upon their broad shoulders until March – who had been in similar difficulties to Ligier early in the season – came to grips with their problems around July and showed the Frenchmen how. A new JS31 body emerged at Monza, but the old type reappeared at Estoril. This seemed to typify Ligier design development '88 – often surprising, too seldom logical. By season's end the only direction left to Ligier seemed to be up – or out.

Arnoux twice failed to qualify, retired nine times and did not reach a Grand Prix finish until the British race in July.

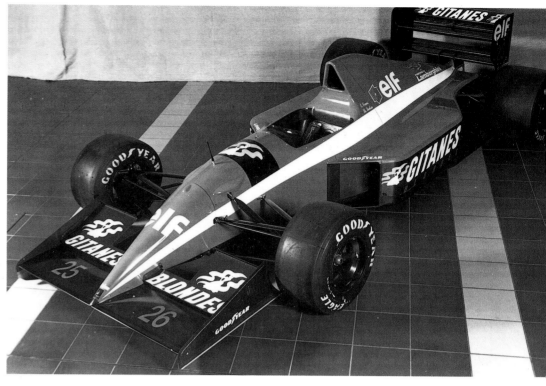

His finishing record then read 18-17-13-10-17. Johansson non-qualified six times, retired from seven events and placed 9-10-9* in the other three. Ligier had scored not a single Constructors' Championship point.

Michel Tétu moved on, and for 1989 Cosworth-Ford DFR engines were adopted for new Ligier JS33 chassis hurriedly conceived and designed by Michel Beaujon with former Penske engineer Ken Anderson and the Fittipaldi brothers' former technical associate, Richard Divila, more recently ex-FIRST team.

They seem to have had a practical grasp on what not to do and the errors of 1988 were avoided in a neat carbon-composite tubbed design with short side pods and pushrod suspension front and rear and longitudinal six-speed Ligier transaxle with Hewland internals.

Six JS33s were built, for the long-faithful René Arnoux's swansong season and new signing Olivier Grouillard. But still they suffered, Arnoux missing out in qualifying seven times, retiring from three races and finishing 12-14-5-11-9-13 elsewhere, his fifth place being scored in Montreal. Grouillard had a better qualifying record, only failing four times, and although he retired from seven GPs his five finishes were 9-8-6-7-13, scoring that single point in the team's home race at Ricard.

Ligier featured again in the Constructors' table, placing 13th-equal with Rial at season's end.

The team soldiered on into 1990, awaiting new state-of-the-art V12 power from Lamborghini agreed for 1991. Consequently this became a bridging season for Ligier – as it was for Arrows – relying merely upon uprated JS33Bs developed by Beaujon and Divila for new drivers Philippe Alliot and Nicola Larini, powered by Langford & Peck-serviced Cosworth DFR engines. The chassis revisions saved a claimed 35 kg, front suspensions had been redesigned and in mid-season a transverse gearbox built jointly with X-Trac created reliability problems. Additionally, Alliot continued his spectacularly destructive Formula 1 career, one assessment concluding he had 'written off' *eleven* Ligiers before the European season ended.

Certainly the JS33Bs were most severely used, a classic case of 'crying themselves to sleep each night'. Alliot was excluded from the opening race in Phoenix, he failed to qualify at Spa and was disqualified at Hockenheim, but otherwise confined most of his car-damaging incidents to practice and qualifying, and recorded nine finishes – 12-9-18-9-13-14-13-10-11 – and only four retirements. Larini qualified consistently for every

The 1991 Ligier-Lamborghini JS35 was intended to serve as a stopgap car until the Magny-Cours-based team could expect Renault V10 engines for 1992. The JS35 design was originated by Michel Beaujon, later amended into the JS35B by Frank Dernie. Neither design endeared itself to Ligier's drivers.

race, and failed to finish only three times. He notched two seventh places, in Spain and Japan – just out of the points – five 10ths, three 11ths, two 14ths and a 16th. And not a points-score in sight. Ligier had been merely going through the motions, pinning their hopes of revival upon Lamborghini's promised power for '91.

Guy Ligier had been able to announce supply of Renault V10 engines for 1992, which left 1991 as one of his generously financed team's all-too-regular 'interim' seasons.

The Lamborghini 3512 V12 engine was adopted, installed initially in JS35 chassis penned at Ligier's lavish Magny-Cours works by a design committee consisting of Michel Beaujon, Claude Galopin and Richard Divila. Frank Dernie arrived ex-Lotus too late to have much influence on this design, and the Lamborghini engines immediately demanded an enlarged oil tank. After poor performances in Phoenix and Brazil both Galopin and Divila were fired, and Dernie began serious work on a replacement JS35B which made its debut in the FOCA test at Silverstone, pre-French GP. Even so, it almost proved too little too late, Ligier only narrowly avoiding demotion to pre-qualifying status after the British GP. Just before the Hungarian race Ligier hired Gérard Ducarouge ex-Larrousse to develop the '35B, freeing Dernie to concentrate upon a JS35R interim chassis to test the forthcoming Renault V10, a definitive new JS37 V10 chassis for 1992, and upon complete restructuring of the team in preparation for a return to major-league contention come the new year. Six of the JS35 chassis were deployed during the season, serials '2 to '7, the latter being built to B-spec as new and deployed for the first time at Monza, while all other chassis save serial '3 were modified to B-spec during the season.

The Ligier drivers were glumly outspoken about their cars' deficiencies. Boutsen was placed nine times (never in the points), 10-7-7-8-12-9-17-11-16-9, and Comas qualified for only 13 races, his record reading 10-10-8-11-10-11-11-18. Precious little joy for *Les Bleues* there. Overall, Guy Ligier's 'witch hunt' mentality in times of trial continued to separate what had become – in effect – France's national F1 team from success . . .

Lola

Eric Broadley's Lola Cars company built space-frame Climax V8-engined Formula 1 cars for John Surtees's Bowmaker team in 1962 but did not return to Formula 1 until 1974. In that year, they were commissioned by Graham Hill to build Cosworth/Hewland cars to replace his Embassy-sponsored team's Shadow DN1 of 1973.

Edwards hurt his arm in a Formula 5000 crash so Gethin drove the second car in the British GP at Brands Hatch. However, its engine broke on the warm-up lap so he took over the spare, set up for Hill, but after rattling around the cockpit like a pea in a drum for one lap, he quit. By the Austrian GP, Hill admitted: 'The more we experiment the more we come back to Lola's original design!' Edwards' replacement, Stommelen, crashed chassis '1 when a tyre deflated. They drove for the rest of the year, Hill eighth in Italy and the US, Stommelen 14th in Canada and 12th in the US.

Hill almost pulled off a deal to use the Alfa Romeo flat-12 engine in 1975, spare chassis '1 being fitted with a slave unit before negotiations collapsed and the engines went to Brabham instead.

The Lolas were reliably uncompetitive. A new Hill GH1 was built for 1975, but the old T370s appeared at the start of that season, Hill and Stommelen 10-13 in Argentina, 12-14 in Brazil, while Stommelen inherited seventh at Kyalami where Hill crashed in practice and did not start. Thereafter the ill-fated team concentrated upon their own Hill chassis. See also entries for Beatrice-Lola, page 223, and Haas-Lola, page 273.

Following the defection of the Haas team at the end of 1986, former driver Gérard Larrousse in conjunction with Didier Calmels put together a Formula 1 operation for the 1987 World Championship series based in Antony, France, to race Lola chassis, and the Huntingdon company's design team under Ralph Bellamy created the new LC87 for them, three 3.5-litre Cosworth DFZ V8-powered chassis being built. The team missed the season-opening race at Rio but then ran a one-car entry for Philippe Alliot until the last three races, when a second LC87 was fielded for Yannick Dalmas. Chassis '1 was reserved as regular spare, chassis '2 being introduced for Alliot from Imola and '3 making its debut for him at Hockenheim.

Alliot retired from nine of his races, but scored three World Championship points with sixth places in Germany, Spain and Mexico. His other three finishes were 10-8-12 and the infant team ended the season ninth in the Constructors' Cup, with its three points . . . but second to Tyrrell in the Colin Chapman Trophy restricted to 3.5-litre 'atmo'-engined cars, with 50 points to Tyrrell's towering 169.

In 1988 the Lola LC88 was produced, five being built. Ralph Bellamy, Chris Murphy and Lola Cars of Huntingdon building, rebuilding, and rebuilding again (and again) four of their LC88 cars according to the factory, five according to the chassis numbers sighted. Bellamy left the team after a disagreement over policy following the Rio season-opener.

Generally the Larrousse team had quite a hectic year with TV producers fascinatedly following Philippe Alliot's progress around the circuits, poised for what at one stage seemed to be his inevitable spin or accident. His less experienced team-mate Yannick Dalmas promised to make a real mark in Formula 1, but the Lolas never quite managed to assert themselves in the atmo class and had their work cut out to match the pace and sheer class of Benetton, March and Williams through this season.

These same drivers were retained until the Japanese GP at Suzuka, where Aguri Suzuki replaced Dalmas, and in Adelaide Pierre-Henri Raphanel was teamed with Alliot. Chassis '2 was withdrawn from service after being crashed heavily in practice in Hungary, by Dalmas.

The LC88s were logical developments of LC87

practice, with the front dampers mounted on top of the monocoque, unusually vestigial engine cover and exhaust tucked in close to the gearbox flanks.

Alliot qualified comfortably every time, failed to finish eight times, was classified as a finisher (10th*) in Adelaide and placed 17-10-14-12-11-14-9 in his other seven GP starts. Dalmas failed to qualify at Montreal, retired four times and placed seventh at both Monaco and Detroit, just missing out on the points. His other finishes were 12-9-13-13-19-9-11; nothing remarkable. He was replaced by local rent-a-driver Aguri Suzkui in Japan (16th) and by Pierre-Henri Raphanel who failed to qualify the second-string car at Adelaide ending the season. A pointless year for the French team, but supply of the Forghieri-designed Chrysler-Lamborghini V12 engine had been arranged for the coming year.

Initially two LC88 chassis were cobbled together with the Italian 12-cylinder engine, installation height being 6 cm higher than possible purely to mate the existing transaxle input shaft level. The six-cylinder long Lamborghini engine compared to the four-cylinder long Cosworth DFZ dictated a 30 cm wheelbase stretch which did nothing for the car's overall weight, nor its manoeuvrability . . .

The LC88B chassis used were numbers '3 and '4, replaced by the definitive LC89-Lamborghini from Imola, designed by a Lola project team led by Chris Murphy. They exhibited contemporary slen-

The Larrousse Lola-Lamborghini V12 LC89 drew heavily upon the Huntingdon production competition car company's recent Indycar experience and combined the hard-to-accommodate Italian engine with this lengthy but handsome fuselage and body form.

der fuselage forms, widening through the cockpit with damper units in line on top of the monocoque, offset pushrods acting upon the rear of the leading damper and front end of the rearward unit. To limit wheelbase Forghieri had produced a new transverse gearbox for the cars which also featured a very low engine cowl and distinctive delta-form diffuser panel.

Four of these LC89s were produced, '1 for Alliot and '2 for Dalmas at Imola, '3 new for Alliot from Mexico and '4 new at Ricard as spare. Alliot was entered for all 16 GPs, failing to pre-qualify in Hungary, failing to finish ten times, once too far behind to be classified though still running at the finish, and placing 12-16*-9 before a Championship point-scoring sixth place in the Spanish race at Jerez. The team greeted that success as a major victory . . . 15th-equal and last with AGS in the year's Constructors' Championship.

Dalmas's first four 1989 outings were sad and sorry, non-qualifying each time and eventually moving to AGS, while Larrousse replaced him with Eric Bernard for the French and British GPs, in which he was classified 11th and retired respectively. Michele Alboreto then became available, having fallen out with Ken Tyrrell, and he completed the season with Lola-Lamborghini from Hockenheim on, notching four retirements, 11th at Estoril, then two failures to pre-qualify and one at the next hurdle in the final three GPs. Not very impressive, but the French-entered Anglo-Italian cars were big, unwieldy and unreliable.

Despite being beset by fraught financial troubles throughout much of 1989-90, the Larrousse team pressed on with Eric Bernard and the Japanese Aguri Suzuki as drivers. Bernard went well and Suzuki respectably, the Frenchman's record being marred by eight retirements, five in the last five consecutive races. His finishing record in the other eight GPs read 8-13*-6-9-8-4-6-9, scoring points in order at Monaco, Silverstone and Budapest. Suzuki non-started once, retired from nine starts, but his six finishes read 12-7-6 (GB) 14-6 (Spain) then third in his native Japan. The car showed off the Lamborghini engine's straight-line grunt to good effect but it was still rather large and thirsty. The LC89 chassis '3, '4 and '5 were used at the start of the season, followed by the Larrousse-Lola L90 with 3 cm longer fuel cell and redesigned airbox of which five were produced, chassis '1 new at Imola as team spare, '2 there for Suzuki, '3 for Bernard, then '4 new for Bernard in Montreal and '5 new for him at Ricard. A tailor-made new gearbox casing by Montupet was introduced on these cars during the year.

The Larrousse-Lola team had survived all kinds of vicissitudes during its young life – not least the jailing of Gérard's initial partner Didier Calmels for the *crime passionel* fatal shooting of his wife. But despite continual financial traumas and repeated rumours of the team's imminent demise they managed somehow to continue, and their 1990 results were the best yet – securing sixth place in the Constructors' Championship, with 11 points, ahead of such fallen names as Leyton House, Team Lotus, Arrows and Brabham . . .

Gérard Larrousse's modest team somehow survived a traumatic winter into 1991. FISA ruled that points and qualifying status hard-won through 1990 were forfeit owing to a perceived infraction, and although Larrousse salvaged his team's right not to pre-qualify in subsequent negotiations his points were wiped from the record, though FISA still recognized his sixth place in the 1990 Constructors' table. His major sponsor – the ESPO Corporation in Japan – then failed, yet still Larrousse soldiered on, and his team survived thanks to great forebearance by such suppliers as Lola Cars and Brian Hart, who agreed to provide DFR V8 engines for the new year.

Chris Murphy's Lola L90 design was neatly updated into the new year's L91 by Eric Broadley himself, working with Larrousse's Gérard Ducarouge and Lola staffmen Mark Williams (normally running their F3000 programme) and Bruce Ashmore (CART car programme). There was insufficient finance available to pursue any kind of serious L91 development, but drivers Bernard and Suzuki pronounced themselves very happy with the latest chassis's good balance, improved turn-in bite and general driveability.

Suzuki failed to qualify four times and was unable to start in Brazil, but otherwise finished just once – sixth amidst the mechanical mayhem of Phoenix. Bernard finished 9-6 (in Mexico) in his 13 outings before the Friday morning free practice crash in Japan which broke his leg. Gachot then failed to qualify in Adelaide.

Reliability problems centred upon the Larrousse-designed, Lola-manufactured six-speed gearbox with its Lamborghini internals, and save for modest wing revisions by the end of the season the Larrousse-Lolas were virtual starting money specials, limping off the startline with time-expired components – the team simply seeking survival.

It succeeded, Larrousse winning new sponsorship from the Japanese Doi Group and continuing in Formula 1 into another season.

Lotus

Colin Chapman's Team Lotus entered the new Formula in 1966 with little hope of defending successfully their 1965 World Championship titles, which had been won with Clark. The BRM H16-engined Type 43 which they slowly developed through 1966 is described in the Lotus 49 chapter (4), Lotus 72s are covered in Chapter 6, while the 78s and 79s are described in Chapter 10.

Meanwhile, early 1966 saw several elderly Lotuses competing, not least in Team's own hands, for they ran their monocoque Type 33s 'R9' and 'R11' with 2-litre BRM P56 and Coventry Climax V8 engines. Spence, Clark and Arundell drove them, while a completely new 33, 'R14', was completed for Clark in the British GP, pending raceworthiness of the 43-H16.

The private Parnell team's own built-from-parts 25/33, nicknamed *Percy*, was fitted with a 2-litre BRM V8 and performed well in Spence's hands, while their older 25s, 'R3' and 'R7', appeared briefly with 2.7 Climax four-cylinder power and even unmodified 1500 cc V8s from the old Formula.

Spence won the non-Championship South African GP in Team's 'R9', powered by the first of two stretched 2-litre Climax V8s specially built for Clark. Arundell was fourth in this comeback race after grievous racing injuries, driving 'R11' with a 1500 Climax V8.

For the British GP, a BRM V8 went into 'R11' for Arundell but the mechanics left a rag in an oil-line and it blew up as soon as it started. The 2-litre Climaxes were reserved for Clark's spanking new 'R14', which finished fourth after losing brake fluid. In Holland he challenged the Repco Brabhams hard until a coolant leak left him third, and Spence was fifth in *Percy*. Clark set 'R14' on pole at the Nürburgring but crashed, and at Monza he drove '43/R1' while Spence was fifth in Parnell's 'R13', Arundell eighth in the outclassed 'R11'-BRM and local man 'Geki' ninth in 'R14'. Clark was third in the Gold Cup, Arundell sixth in 'R14' at Watkins Glen and seventh in 'R11' at Mexico City.

A second 43-H16 was ready for the 1967 South African GP when Hill joined Clark in what would become the Cosworth-powered superteam. Both 43s failed. *Percy* was driven by Irwin in the Race of Champions and by Courage in the Oulton Spring Trophy, before Irwin took him back for Silverstone to finish seventh.

Team Lotus reappeared at Monaco where Clark ran 'R14' for the last time, retiring with a broken damper mounting, and Hill finished second in 'R11'-BRM.

Next time out, at Zandvoort, the Lotus 49 legend was born. Irwin was seventh there in *Percy*, Parnell concentrating on quasi-works BRM P261 and P83 H16 cars thereafter. Old 'R11', meanwhile, had been sold to Craig Fisher in Canada, placing 11th at Mosport but non-starting in Mexico due to a faulty fuel metering unit.

While the Lotus 49s ran their successful course, Colin tried to replace them in 1969 with a sophisticated four-wheel drive design, the Type 63. Traction had become a problem early in 1968 with Cosworth V8 power and abrupt mid-range torque, and four-wheel drive was considered the cure-all.

Coincidentally, the wing era dawned, solving the traction problem more cheaply, with less complication and significantly less weight.

The engineers interested in 4WD were unconvinced, Colin and his people amongst them. Two Type 63s were built, using a broad, shallow, full-length monocoque tub, whose DFV engine was turned about-face and drove thence to front and rear final-drives. The experiment flopped, though Rindt was finally persuaded to take it seriously enough to place '63/1' second in the minor Oulton Park Gold Cup, which would be the best performance of the 1969 4WD crop.

Cadet driver John Miles made most of the 63, while Bonnier drove one briefly at Silverstone. But putting power through the steerable front wheels overwhelmed contemporary tyre technolo-

gy, and Formula 1 4WD evaporated in terminal understeer, excess weight and complication.

Meanwhile, in 1968, Hill had qualified fastest in practice for a USAC road race at Mosport in Canada driving one of the Indianapolis 4WD Lotus 56 turbine cars. He enthused about how fabulous the smooth-riding turbo car felt for road racing.

Colin discussed a plan with Pratt & Whitney to produce 3-litre equivalency gas turbine engines for Formula 1. Three cars would have been built for 1969 but P&W's prime interest was Indy, rather than European Formula 1, and development lagged.

At Monaco in 1970, Colin had a chance encounter with his P&W contact and heard that a 3-litre equivalent turbine was nearly ready at last. The fourth Indy Type 56 tub was lying in store at Hethel, and it was rigged with the prototype '3-litre' engine and tested that autumn. It was hoped to startle the opposition on the high-speed track at Monza but braking and throttle lag were still problematic for road racing, so the Type 56B as it was known was held back for '71.

Its debut came at the Race of Champions, Fittipaldi driving. It bottomed very badly and finally wiped off its right-rear suspension. Wisell ran briefly fifth at Oulton Park, then Fittipaldi qualified on the front row at Silverstone (using bigger brakes) and finished third in heat two.

The taper-sided hull was then bulged to carry extra fuel for full-length GP racing. Dave Walker drove at Hockenheim in June but the engine failed in practice and it did not race.

A replacement engine was available for the Dutch GP; it rained and Walker had a real chance in the smooth 4WD car, only to crash. Wisell ran in the British GP, then for Monza the 56B was sprayed gold and black to form Lotus's sole entry since legal problems following Rindt's fatal crash there in 1970 prevented them entering under their own name and livery.

Fittipaldi drove, ambient temperatures were too high for the turbine to generate peak power and he soldiered home eighth. One week later, in the *Preis der Nationen* F5000 race at Hockenheim, Fittipaldi qualified on the front row and finished second after setting fastest lap – end of experiment, on a fairly high note.

The Type 72s remained centre-stage and their remarkable performance on new Goodyear tyres in Brazil '73 persuaded Chapman that all they needed to stay ahead was a '100 lb lighter 72'. Ex-Brabham and McLaren designer Ralph Bellamy was detailed to design it, which involved 72-type suspensions and geometries being attached to an all-new tub incorporating some innovations.

The new Type 76 tub's shape was a shallow and slender delta-form. Initially, electro-magnetic clutch operation featured, controlled from a gear-knob button. The idea was to enable the driver to brake with his left foot and maintain engine revs with the other, Lotus having learned the value of such techniques at Indianapolis. Driver Peterson was particularly enthusiastic but the system proved more trouble than it was worth and was scrapped.

The Type 76 was the first Lotus to be designed and built entirely under the John Player Special sponsorship regime and a new numbering system was henceforth used for this 'Mark I' chassis type. Chassis '76/1' carried a plate reading 'JPS/9', to follow on from the existing Lotus 72 series after '72/8' (which was plated 'JPS/8') . . . still with me? The second new car, '76/2', became 'JPS/10' but the specialist press would not play ball and preferred to use their own, more logical manner of indicating who did what with which.

The 76s' systems played up and Peterson eventually persuaded Chapman that the proven old 72s would be more effective; so they were. The 76s were relegated to spare-car duties at Monaco and Anderstorp, though on the way home from Anderstorp, Team tested at Zandvoort where Peterson crashed '76/1' heavily, knocking himself out when some experimental brake pads gave trouble.

For the Dutch GP there, Ickx's spare '76/2' ran

with its water radiators far forward behind the front wheels, shrouded in new side panelling. Colin told me: 'When we got the 76s their systems didn't work – fuel, oil, cooling and brakes didn't work, and the steering wasn't very good. Nothing very serious . . . half-way through the programme neither Ronnie nor Ickx would drive them and then we put one on the scales and it weighed the same as the old 72! Its rear hubs were cracking and I had this terrible fear of a wheel coming off. I just couldn't live with that so I said to Ralph, "Look there's no point in sorting it all out; if we do, all we've got is a car the same weight as the 72 with fifty new problems . . ."'

The repaired '76/1' went to North America as spare at the end of 1974, Schenken qualifying it as second alternate and taking off after the field at Watkins Glen. He was disqualified on lap 6: a fitting finale to the Type 76's brief career.

Early in 1975 a new design team was set up at Hethel under Team Manager Peter Warr, including Mike Cooke, Geoff Aldridge and Martin Ogilvie, briefed to translate Colin's latest Formula 1 concept into metal, while in parallel Ralph Bellamy worked on a new Lotus 'queerbox' transmission for Chapman's pet theories about two-pedal driving.

He wanted to learn about the effects of long and short wheelbases, wide and narrow tracks, and the Type 77 was designed in effect as an experimental interim car, working towards the Type 78 which would hopefully put Lotus back on top in 1977.

The new Type 77, or John Player Special Mark II, featured an Aldridge-designed slender aluminium tub, to which Martin Ogilvie attached a structural caliper inboard brake system in which the calipers doubled as pick-ups for the suspension links and wishbones. Hip radiators appeared in neat side pods.

Brazil opened the World Championship, Peterson crashed '77/2' ('JPS/12') after coolant leaked onto a rear tyre, and after an overnight rebuild it developed steering trouble. Andretti had a one-off drive in '77/1' ('JPS/11') and in the race the two collided, as had the luckless 76s on their Kyalami debut two years before.

Peterson heeded the omen and joined March, Team Lotus engaging the inexperienced Bob Evans and Gunnar Nilsson for South Africa, Brands Hatch and Long Beach; Nilsson drove alone at Silverstone.

Like the 72 before it, the 77 failed to heat its front tyres adequately, so freelance Len Terry did a quick redesign to outboard front brakes, using production Ralt F2/F3 uprights. The first set fitted to '77/2' became standard.

Andretti joined full-time from the Spanish GP onwards and Tony Southgate moved to the team from Shadow immediately that race was over. He found himself being flown by Colin straight to the Chapman holiday home in Ibiza where he was grilled for three days solid by the Lotus boss.

Tony described the experience: 'After the steady plod at Shadow it was like being dragged from a convalescent home and dropped in the middle of a mad 'ouse . . .'

Lotus thinking on weight distribution, for example, was very outdated. Nevertheless, they caught up, stiffened the 77's structures and Andretti won the Japanese GP in 'JPS/11' ending the year.

Although 'JPS/14' ('77/3', there being no '13' in the JPS numbering series) had been crashed heavily in testing at Anderstorp by Andretti, he qualified on the front row for the Swedish GP and led 45 laps until his engine exploded. The damaged car was rebuilt with more forward weight bias, a Southgate nose oil cooler mount like the Shadow's, while, later, a cockpit-adjustable rear anti-roll bar (Andretti Indy practice) and a lightweight air starter like McLaren's became standard.

Revised front suspension geometry appeared at Monza, as did deeper aerodynamic skirts to control airflow beneath the hull. In North America the 77s ran a 4 in. shorter wheelbase and brush skirts as a Type 78 development. Andretti's win at Fuji was supported by Nilsson finishing sixth; Team were back in business.

The Type 78/79s set new performance standards and began the ground-effects car revolution through 1977-78 but in 1979 the opposition raced ahead as Lotus became bogged down in development of their Type 80, which flopped.

The thinking behind the 80's design was to maximize underwing area to capitalize upon the download generated by ground-effect side pods fringed with sliding skirts. In the 80, the underwings extended back through the rear suspension to the car's tail, download acting around the car's notional centre of gravity in order to dispense with conventional nose and tail aerofoils to trim it out.

Gordon Murray of Brabham had anticipated this Lotus development in his original BT48-Alfa V12 design but encountered immediate 'porpoising' problems in practice for the Argentinian race, then ripping off most of the underwing. At Kyalami, the BT48s ran safely without nose fins and found the way ahead, while Lotus's Type 80 had yet to emerge.

This was based around a slim honeycomb aluminium monocoque tub, with side pods curving inside the rear wheels and the sliding skirts rashly following this curve. Additional skirts hung beneath the nose section, and air passing underneath was encouraged to exit upwards through a duct with an adjustable trim-tab sitting inside. In this way the tab was masked by the nose section in frontal area, yet could trim the car front to rear. The whole Type 80 rear end was new, the gearbox/clutch/oil tank casting being beautifully made, like the rest of the car.

The prototype, known as '80/1' to enthusiasts or 'ML23' in the new Martini-sponsored team's latest system, gave trouble in testing. Its under-nose skirts could not survive pitch, which ground them off against the road surface as the car porpoised. They were removed and conventional nose fins appeared each side. It had been intended that when the original nose section became effective, the separate rear wing between its tall end plates could be deleted, leaving just the full-width rear trim-tab on the bodywork to do the job alone.

The 80 made a decent race debut at Jarama, where Andretti finished third and set fastest lap. However, in testing at Dijon, Peter Wright recalls: 'we suddenly encountered the most dreadful bouncing problems', possibly exacerbated by the S-bend main skirts skewing and jamming in their slides to break suction against the road, then freeing and remaking the seal to slam on high download again. Stiffening the suspension to control this pitch made the car skittish and again uncontrollable in an agonizing descending spiral of failure and frustration.

At the height of the season the 80's problems could not be solved, so it was set aside after the French GP and another Team Lotus failure passed into history. Three Type 80s had been built.

For 1980, the 'ML' Martini-Lotus prefix became 'EL' for Essex-Lotus after another sponsorship change, and tests during the winter with a heavily modified 79X, which was a cross between the 79 and 80, led to construction of a new Type 81. The prototype was run by new team driver de Angelis in Buenos Aires, while '2 ran there driven by Andretti.

Three more Type 81s emerged during the season: '3 was new in South Africa as spare before being crashed mightily by de Angelis at Long Beach and subsequently completely rebuilt; chassis '4 emerged new in Monaco as spare and was promptly written off by Andretti in practice.

Lessons learned were incorporated in the Type 81B which used a new monocoque and '81/4's chassis-plate. It was completed in the paddock at Hockenheim, being raced first by newcomer Mansell in Austria and Holland, then crashed by him in Monza practice.

These tubby short-nosed Type 81s did not

Left: *The complexities of the 1969 Lotus 63 4WD car uncovered in the Silverstone pits.* Below: *The Lotus 76 as unveiled to the press in 1974 with multi-wedge forms, twin rear wings, hip radiators and two-pedal control beneath the skin. As a '100 lb lighter 72 it was an abject failure.*

Above: *Piola's sketch shows the troublesome Lotus 80 with its curved sliding skirts: 1, nose supports; 2, pedal access; 3, Lotus-Lockheed balanced calipers; 4, inboard spring/dampers; 5, rear anti-roll bar adjuster; 6, radiator air ramp; 7, roll-over bar; 8, 9, brake ducts; 10, rear uprights; 11, driveshaft; 12, rear wing side plates; 13, two-piece wing; 14, wing side plates.* Below: *The Essex-Lotus 81s at Long Beach 1981 after the storm had broken around the 'twin-chassis' 88. Here de Angelis's '81/3' leads.*

and hard against their intention being construed in this way.

This 'primary' chassis was actually suspended on four coil/damper units coupled to the bottom of the wheel uprights. Dynamic loads were handled by the conventional rocker arm/wishbone layout of the inner monocoque which was by the same token insulated from high aerodynamic loading. It was claimed to be the inner or secondary chassis.

This novel layout had much to commend it, as it harnessed ground-effect download yet protected the driver from its worst effects.

The prototype '88/1' was used by de Angelis in between vociferous protests at Long Beach, Rio and Buenos Aires, but was eventually ruled illegal and the rules changed to make it clearly so.

Had the 88 been accepted, at least one great driver might still be alive today and another's career might not have been ended . . .

Faced with the rejection of the 88 concept, Colin gained the support of the British RAC who said they would accept the concept in modified 88B form for the British GP at Silverstone. Consequently Type 88Bs were produced, but Ferrari, Talbot-Ligier and Alfa Romeo protested again, and FISA horned in from Paris by stating flatly that the 88 concept and all derivatives *were* illegal and the RAC had no option but to agree, sending Team's mechanics into a 12-hour conversion job to strip the 88Bs and return them to 87 'single-chassis' specification.

Team had introduced these effective stand-by Type 87s '1 and '2 for Mansell and de Angelis in Monaco, '87/3' running at Silverstone for de Angelis, and '87/4' converted from '88B/4' for Mansell in the autumn fast-circuit races. New '87/5' was spare car at Monza. Meanwhile '88B/2' was converted from '87/2' for Mansell at Silverstone and then converted back to 87 form for second practice, while '88B/4' was completed for de Angelis at Silverstone but converted to '87/4' for Mansell at Hockenheim.

Amidst all this controversy, de Angelis put together a decent season, being withdrawn from Imola but otherwise starting all 14 GPs, and finishing ten times, 5-6-6-5-5-6-7-7-5-4-6, all but twice in the points in a consistent display of the Type 87's natural level.

Mansell was less consistent, failing to qualify at Silverstone after all the practice hullabaloo, finishing five of his 13 races, 11-3-6-7-4, three times scoring points. Team's seventh place in the Constructors' table was their lowest since 1975, but their 22 points showed an improvement over 1980.

The old Type 87s '2-3-4-5 appeared at Kyalami in 1982, '5 becoming a pullrod-suspension car. The new much-tidied Type 91 emerged at Rio and followed on from the 87-sequence chassis numbers, the prototype tub '6 going to de Angelis, with '7 for Mansell. In tidying up the design, Peter Wright told me, 'We tried to take ten per cent weight off *everything*.'

Car '91/8' was new as spare at Zolder and '9 new as spare at Monaco, though the latter was not a successful tub and suffered relegation to show car duties (Team nicknaming it 'The Flexi-Flyer'). Chassis '10 was new, therefore, for Mansell ending the season at Las Vegas. Chassis '91/5' was a conversion from old '87/5' which had last been seen at Kyalami and served as team spare in midseason.

The Type 91 was a handsome, stub-nosed car with a long downswept engine cover behind the far-forward cockpit, and it featured variable front track and wheelbase like the old Type 77s from the last period when Team had lost their way and were floundering about, in 1975-76.

De Angelis missed Imola in the FOCA boycott,

impress and Lotus struggled all season. Andretti was classified as a finisher only five times, 12-7-7-8-6, his only point being scored in the USA as the season ended. De Angelis was finding his feet in Formula 1 after his move to Lotus from Shadow amidst litigation and he did better, similarly being classified only five times but inheriting second in Brazil and placing fourth in Italy and the USA. Cadet driver Mansell retired in Austria and Holland, learning about the 81B but failing to qualify after his accident at Monza.

From their fourth position in the Constructors' table with 39 points in their troubled 1979 season, Team Lotus slipped to fifth with just 14 points in 1980.

Faced with the problem of massive ground-effects download now demanding ultra-stiff suspensions to support it, making both cars and drivers prone to physical failure, Team experimented late in 1980 with a Type 86 hack using a Type 81-like aluminium monocoque chassis. Colin's team conceived an effective twin-chassis design which would form the basis of the controversial Lotus 88.

Initially, Wright, Ogilvie and the other engineers appreciated that very light yet stiff bodywork was required and therefore used carbon panels with Nomex honeycomb sandwiched between. In search of further weight saving without compromising stiffness in a very confined cross-section monocoque hull, they made the next logical step – discarding aluminium sheet or honeycomb tub construction in favour of inherently stiffer but lighter, moulded carbon-composite.

Whereas McLaren was having its carbon tub set up for moulding at this time, Lotus formed their version from flat moulded sheets, the flat panels then being cut to shape, edges feathered, then seamed and bonded together to form the monocoque. The whole thing was done in about 12 weeks from start to finish, to form the basis of a conventional Type 87 and alternative 'twin-chassis' Type 88. This was the plot . . .

The 88's primary chassis consisted of the bodywork, supporting side pods, wings and radiators while riding independently within that structure was a secondary chassis composed of the monocoque tub, engine, gearbox and front and rear suspensions.

The outer or primary chassis could be seen as a massive one-piece, full-length, full-width enveloping wing acting direct upon the suspension uprights at all four corners. This was the way FISA would see it . . . though Lotus argued long

Top: Team's 1981 substitute for the 88 was the carbon-tub Lotus 87. Piola shows: 1, wing; 2, nosebox/wingframe; 3, carbon tub; 4, fairings; 5, mirrors; 6, radiator 'airflow activator'; 7, radiator; 8, exit louvres; 9, rear diffuser; 10, engine; 11, side pod; 12, wing. Left: The sketches of the Type 88's two 'chassis' fail to show how the crossbeams fitted around the tub.

Above left: *The big idea – the 'twin-chassis' Type 88 shows its quite handsome if bulky lines at Long Beach '81, enveloping de Angelis, while* (above) *in Brazil '84 his new Gérard Ducarouge-designed Lotus-Renault 95T showed real signs of coming very good indeed, back on Goodyear tyres.*

but his 15 races yielded eight finishes, 8-5-4-5-4-4-6, and he actually won the Austrian GP in '91/8' after a fearsome final dash to the line, just 0.05 second in front of Rosberg's Williams after the turbocharged cars had all struck trouble.

This was also the 150th GP win for the Cosworth DFV engine, and the last Lotus race victory which Colin Chapman would see.

Mansell again was fated, missing both the Dutch and French GPs with minor injury, and his 13 races saw six finishes, 3-7-4-9-8-7. Team's total of 30 points gave them sixth place in the Championship between Brabham and Tyrrell. Things were improving, but slowly.

For much of 1982 the Lotuses suffered two main problems – porpoising over bumps and understeering on slower circuits. In practice for the British GP they toyed with pullrod suspension, but raced rocker arms to the end of the year. The cars were more effective on fast circuits than slow. It proved difficult to set them up, demanding many miles of testing before they were considered 'right there' and in a race it was then hard to maintain the car within its competitive 'working area' between full tanks and empty.

Before his tragically premature death that winter Colin had signed a deal with Renault Sport to use their turbocharged V6 engines in 1983. Peter Warr was now in sole executive charge of Team Lotus. Until sufficient French engines became available Team began the new year with two Cosworth cars, known as Type 92s but based on '91/5' and '10 which had been converted to the recently introduced flat-bottom rules. Chassis '5 was used as a spare until Montreal then pensioned off, while '10 was raced by Mansell from Rio to Montreal before his turbocharged Type 93T appeared.

The prototype Lotus-Renault 93T chassis '1 appeared for de Angelis at Rio and was retired at the conclusion of spare car duty at the Österreichring having been replaced by the much improved Gérard Ducarouge-designed 94Ts. Chassis '93/2' ran from the Race of Champions to Silverstone, where it was a spare, being retired thereafter. The 93Ts had been far too great, gormless and cumbersome to be successful and early active-suspension experiments were shelved.

Chapman had been impressed by Ducarouge ever since his Matra-Simca sports car team days and the French engineer was taken on in June after being dismissed by Alfa Romeo. He used old rocker arm suspension Type 91 tubs as the basis of his new 94Ts, and the revised weight bias of this much lighter model gave the Pirelli-shod cars hope at last.

The two 94Ts at Silverstone were '1 for de Angelis, which used '91/7's tub, and '2 for Mansell, using '91/8's, while '3 appeared for the Italian dri-

ver at Zandvoort.

De Angelis ran 14 Renault-powered races but finished only twice, reaching ninth at Spa and fifth at Monza for two meagre Championship points. Mansell raced the Cosworth car eight times, finishing 12-12-'12'-6, the point being scored at Detroit in Lotus's penultimate race with the engine which they had introduced 16 years earlier to Formula 1.

Mansell drove the revised and much-improved 94Ts seven times, sparkling in the British GP to make fourth place for the type's debut, then adding fifth in Austria, eighth at Monza and third at Brands Hatch to show some real form at last, scoring ten points and boosting Team's Constructors' Cup total to 12, seventh-equal with Tyrrell.

Ducarouge and Team then did a fine job on their 1984 Lotus 95T, only four being built, all brand new and set up to clearly defined specifications, and operating well now that Lotus were back on Goodyear tyres after their sorry Pirelli period. Old '94T/1' was used in Rio as spare, while '95T/1' was a test and spare chassis, raced only at Imola by Mansell. Chassis '95T/2' was new for Mansell at Rio and was his regular car thereafter, de Angelis drove '3, while '4 was a new team spare, raced by de Angelis at Montreal, Detroit and Estoril after its introduction at Dijon-Prenois.

The 95T was arguably the best-handling chassis of 1984. Only one tub was lightly damaged all year (by hitting a kerb) and Team had never lost one of the 17 carbon-composite tubs made since 1981. Ducarouge introduced a slow-speed aerodynamic package and a high-speed one and these were effectively the only changes to be made.

With both Ferrari and Williams in trouble, Goodyear gave Team terrific testing commitment, but their American-made race tyres could never match Michelin's grip so the Lotuses were unable to compete on even terms. In part this was due to tyres, in part the effect of Renault's fuel consumption problems.

Renault engineer Bruno Mauduit was attached to Team and he had a lovely time with his cars consistently out-performing Renault's own . . .

De Angelis might have won Rio but for a misfire, Mansell could have won when leading Monaco in heavy rain but lost control and crashed; at Detroit de Angelis had a gearbox failure when catching the leader at a second a lap, and at Dallas more gearbox trouble and another driver error wrecked bright Lotus hopes after another fine qualifying performance. At Hockenheim, de Angelis was leading the McLarens when the car failed again. A new gearbox was ready for the end of the season, carbon brakes were tried but not raced seriously.

At one stage de Angelis looked as though he

would win the Drivers' title on reliability, as McLaren's two star drivers split the winning between them. He finished 12 of his 16 GPs, the first ten consecutively: 3-7-5-3-5-5-4-2-3-4. With his fourth in Holland and fifth in Portugal, he was able to accumulate 34 points to reach third in the Championship. Mansell in comparison finished only five times, but actually scored every time, 3-6-6-4-3, for another 13 points. This gave Lotus third place in the Constructors' Cup with 37 points, compared to Ferrari's 57.5 and McLaren's staggering 143.5.

For Lotus 1985 was only satisfying in that every year since Colin Chapman's untimely death their results had improved. Four of Ducarouge's latest Type 97T-Renaults were built for the new year, closely based upon the promising 95T of 1984, the Type 96 having been a stillborn Indy project. The 97T had small winglets on the rear of each side pod to compensate for the banning of rear wing extensions as used in '84, and also adopted the CART-racing idea of vertical vanes in the front suspension to clean up turbulence and reduce drag. Others would copy where Ducarouge led with varying degrees of comprehension and success.

Once again, Team's tiny car inventory was sufficient as not one was written off and each of the 21 carbon-composite series tubs built over five seasons had survived.

They used a mixture of Renault's old EF4 and revised new EF15 V6 engines. The EF4s were in qualifying-boost tune which the customer EF15s would not accept to the same degree. After qualifying, EF15s would be fitted for warm-up and the race, along with new drive trains/rear ends to replace those freshly compromised by qualifying loads. Essentially the spare car was EF15-powered throughout, being used in practice to assess appropriate race-tune consumption. An average 270 miles went onto each engine before it was due for service.

The 97Ts saw more changes than the 95Ts, partly due to 1985 Goodyear tyre development. First they improved rear tyres, then fronts, and so on, to-and-fro but generally moving forward all the time.

Three of the new cars had been ready in time for Rio: '97T/1 acted as spare but raced by de Angelis at Imola and Monaco and becoming the test car thereafter; '2 was new driver Senna's regular mount up to Detroit, then spare raced by de stopped a third of the way round the last lap, 2.5 litres short . . . He was rightly deeply disappointed after driving what he felt was the race of his life . . .'

Through the season Team had deployed only their normal complement of four chassis, Ducarouge's aerodynamic package basically remaining very stable all season although continuous suspension development made the cars better latterly on rear-tyre consumption.

The qualifying ploy seemed to reappear at Estoril, but the key to Senna's startling closing-minutes charge onto pole there was his stopping a half-hour earlier to have an experimental turbocharger pair fitted. They had been run only on a Viry-Châtillon dyno but showed considerable extra power, so Team took the gamble . . . and it paid off spectacularly.

It was another moment which, as Peter Warr said, 'the Old Man would have loved'.

In fact Senna stole a string of pole positions, failed to finish six times, won at Jerez and Detroit and otherwise took four second places, two thirds, a fourth and a fifth for fourth place in the Drivers' Championship. Dumfries struggled – inevitably – in the second car, failing to qualify at Monaco, retiring from nine other races, and finishing 9-7-7-5-9-6 in the balance. His fifth place came at Budapest, the sixth in his farewell outing for the team in Adelaide. Team finished third in the Constructors' Championship with 58 points to Williams-Honda's massive 141, and McLaren's 96.

Now Peter Warr had finalized a deal to use Honda engines for 1987, and took on the Japanese company's hugely experienced test driver, Satoru Nakajima, as Senna's new team-mate.

The technical story of Team's 1987 season centred upon their Active suspension as described in detail elsewhere (see pages 166-7). However, there were constructional changes concerning the Lotus carbon-composite tubs. For years they had been formed from a single flat sheet, routed out along the fold lines, folded up 'like a Kellogg's packet' and then taped and bonded along its edges. In the 1986 Type 98T car, Gérard Ducarouge had temporarily abandoned this system and instead adopted individual sandwich panels of carbon-Kevlar-composite with aluminium honeycomb filling, which were then bonded together along their edges like a plastic kit. Meanwhile development went on to perfect a folded single-sheet structure which would not compromise the aluminium-foil filling in the folds, and this refined 'Kellogg's packet' system was introduced in the 1987 Type 99T-Hondas.

Internal bulkheads machined from solid aluminium provided mounts for suspension and engine. Front and rear suspension geometries were revised to match 'Active' requirements.

Apart from its manufacturing method, the 99T differed from its successful 98T predecessor principally in the engine attachment system for what was now an 80-degree Japanese V6 compared to the previous 90-degree French V6. A brand new six-speed Lotus gearbox and final-drive was necessary to exploit the Honda's wide rev range.

What really surprised Team initially was the powerful Japanese engine's incredibly harsh vibration compared to the smoother but less potent 90-degree Renault. This vibration was so intense that the first time Senna drove the car – in pre-season Rio testing – he quickly returned to the pits and reported imminent engine failure! Nakajima had already done many miles testing earlier Williams cars, so he tried the 99T and asked simply 'What's all the fuss about – that's perfectly normal . . . Don't F1 engines *always* vibrate like that?'

Lotus now discovered what Williams already

Angelis in Austria; '3 acted as the Italian's regular race car; while '4 came in new at Monaco and was Senna's race car from Ricard onwards.

Newcomer Senna was Team's greatest attribute, taking seven pole positions, leading 10 of the 16 GPs for a total 270 laps, 38 more than his nearest rival, Rosberg of Williams, but only winning two, often hitting trouble. Between victory at Estoril and at Spa and good placings elsewhere, Senna's first eight retirements effectively broke down as: two due to Team's chassis, five to Renault's engine and its ancillaries, and one driver error.

De Angelis did his usual reliable job and was given first place at Imola after Prost's McLaren disqualification.

Senna's season included nine classified finishes from 16 starts, placing 1-7*-16-10*-2-3-3-1-2; while de Angelis finished from 11 of his 16 starts, once being unclassified and once disqualified, placing 3-4-1-3-5-5-5-5-6-5 – as usual scoring every time he finished.

For Peter Warr one significant landmark was reached at Monza. 'There in 1970', he said, 'Team used a 200 mph final-drive for the first time, in a Lotus 72 running low-drag configuration. It's taken us 15 years, but this year at Monza we were back up to 200 mph again'. And in safety.

Team had begun to win again; Colin Chapman himself would have been delighted.

For 1986 Lotus built four Type 98T cars for Ayrton Senna and young Johnny Dumfries. They were aiming high, anxious to provide Ayrton Senna with his first World Championship title. Gérard Ducarouge's new Lotus Type 98T abandoned Team's original 'folded-up Kellogg's packet' form of carbon-composite chassis construction in favour of a system of separate mouldings bonded together. Like his Type 96 Indy and 97T 1985 Formula 1 tubs, aluminium foil was used as the void-filling sandwich between the 98T's moulded composite skins. Its bulkheads were machined from solid aluminium. The smaller 195-litre fuel cell reduced tub height behind the cockpit, enabling the management system black box to be mounted there, giving easier access and simplifying the wiring loom. For the first time Lotus had a continuously monitoring fuel level read-out dash display.

Their Renault V6 engines were prepared and rebuilt by Renault Sport themselves at Viry-Châtillon, whereas the other client teams – Ligier and Tyrrell – drew their engines from Mecachrome in Bourges. Despite the extra length of the 1986 Renault engine package, Ducarouge maintained his preferred 2720 mm wheelbase, locating new pullrod rear suspension on a new one-piece magnesium transaxle casing with six-speed Hewland DGB-type internals. Senna would avoid the six-speed 'box, preferring five speeds in the new casing. A ride-height adjuster was introduced to compensate for lightening fuel load – a

cockpit control governing hydraulic rams on top of each spring/damper.

Renault Chief Engineer Bernard Dudot's new weapon for 1986 was the EF15*bis* engine, which inevitably became known popularly as the 'EF15B'. It was available in two forms, standard or 'DP' – *Distribution Pneumatique* – see engine section.

The combination of DP valvegear and revised ignition saved 5.51 lb in the upper part of the engines, while the induction logs and pipes on top were lowered and curved inwards to allow a neater, lower or tighter body-panel shape in this crucial area.

While the EF15*bis* – DP-spec or otherwise – was intended for economic racing, the older high-boost EF4*bis* was no longer compatible with the new 1986 chassis, it was too big, so EF15s with water injection and no wastegates were used instead.

However, when Senna finished at Rio in round one on near-dry tanks, Piquet's Williams-Honda won easily with fuel to spare. For Lotus-Renault, the writing was clearly on the wall . . .

To give the Brazilian every possible advantage short of a Honda engine, Ducarouge developed a low-ground clearance, high-download qualifying ploy with a dropped underfloor which helped pop Senna onto pole at Jerez and Imola and caused a terrific stir which Colin Chapman himself would have *relished*. At Imola a bad UJ batch ruined Lotus hopes, and at Monaco Senna had to settle for second behind an uncatchable McLaren.

On circuits where consumption was no problem, like Detroit, Senna could shine, and did. At that point he still led the Drivers' Championship, and a further improved C-spec engine emerged with a redesigned lean-burn top-end for more economical power.

Team hoped to compete again in the horsepower-versus-fuel economy battle, but at Brands Hatch the new engine misfired and they had to race the old one. At Hockenheim the new engine ran well but Piquet's Williams-Honda ran better. In Hungary the new engine again misfired, they had to run the old so Senna inevitably used all his fuel again. This misfiring problem intruded intermittently, when it mattered most, in Austria and only extensive subsequent testing traced its certain cure to careful, painstaking selection of all-compatible electrical components. There was no apparent difference between them, simply some would work in harmony and others would not. It was trial-and-error to match a misfire-free set.

For Monza they at last felt confident they had gripped this problem. They had, so a bad clutch batch bit them instead . . .

Peter Warr: 'By this time it was the last chance to keep our Championship hopes alive. Renault's onboard computer had been superb, very accurate, all season, until in Portugal Ayrton had 1.4 laps still showing on his gauge when the engine knew, that every ancillary mounting on a Honda-powered F1 car had to be man enough to withstand a terrible shaking. Even exhaust and undertray stays and intercooler mounts were affected. During the Brazilian GP the vibrations sheared the bonded joint between the bottom of the oil tank and the carbon swirl tube inside it through which oil centrifuges to remove air bubbles. This allowed still heavily aerated oil both to blow from the breather and return to the engine, which began to seize – retiring the car.

Before the Hungarian GP, Gérard Ducarouge redesigned the 99T's body to improve aerodynamic efficiency, lowering the engine cowl and cockpit coaming to clear the rear wing.

Six 99T tubs were built, three race programme cars, two more for the UK test programme and the sixth going to Honda in Japan for test driver Hoshino's R&D work. No doubt Honda's chassis men also took a very close look 'for future reference'?

Some 100 G-Type V6 engines were in circulation, low-mileage qualifying units being serviced and rebuilt by Honda's special single-test cell UK facility at Langley, Buckinghamshire, while long-distance race engines were analyzed and rebuilt in Japan. Team regularly put 1000 km-plus on an engine, the Honda proving far more serviceable than the preceding Renault turbo V6s in this respect. Race power outputs around 900-950 bhp were suggested.

Senna retired from three of the year's 16 GPs, was disqualified in Australia for having oversized brake cooling ducting attached to the car, and otherwise won twice – at Monaco and Detroit where the Active suspension system eased much of the physical load upon the driver – and added three second places, two thirds, a fourth, two fifths and a seventh place. He thus scored points in 11 of his 12 race finishes and ended the season third in the Drivers' Championship behind Piquet and Mansell of the Williams-Honda team.

Nakajima retired five times, was unclassified once, and scored points at Imola (sixth), Spa (fifth), in Britain (fourth) and his homeland (sixth). His other six finishes were 7-10-13-11-8-9.

Team Lotus finished third in the Constructors' Championship behind Williams and McLaren.

Unfortunately, this was not as good as Senna had clearly hoped, and he signed for McLaren for 1988, taking Honda with him, although they would continue to supply Team Lotus too throughout the year. To replace Senna, World Champion Nelson Piquet signed on to move to Lotus from Williams . . . who had lost their Honda engine supply at short notice, and would be falling back onto Judd V8 power.

With reigning World Champion Nelson Piquet and *identical* (Lotus boss Peter Warr's word) Honda engines to McLaren, they should have been in fine shape to challenge Prost and Senna. Like Ferrari, it didn't happen. Unlike Ferrari, Lotus just flopped miserably. Team endured what was perhaps their most disappointing season – in relative terms their Type 100T cars just lay down and died.

Before season's end, chief engineer Ducarouge had departed, aerodynamicist Frank Dernie (ex-Hesketh, ex-Williams) was engaged to replace him and Team had realized that much of their direction through the year had been misdirected by fundamentally flawed information received by the development programme. What confused the team so badly was relative performance between their car and McLaren's on different circuits. There was no consistency nor pattern. One weekend the Lotus might be quicker on the straight, so they would work at improving its speed through corners. Next weekend it could be blinding fast through certain corners, but pathetic on the straights, and slower still through different corners. Piquet – his reputation on the line – found he could balance the Lotus either for fast corners, or for slow, but he could seldom achieve an acceptable compromise between the two. Nakajima it was hoped would handle c. 850-900 bhp better in his second GP season than he had 1000 bhp first time round. Instead he could show no progress.

During 1987 some suggested that Lotus committed themselves so totally to Active suspension that season because the basic 99T was so bad without it. In 1988 Lotus R&D withdrew their

Active system from Formula 1 to concentrate upon its full development for production cars. Perhaps this left Ducarouge's 1988 design dangerously exposed. Some blamed variable engines. At one stage Honda project engineer Goto – in charge of common engines available to both Lotus and McLaren – said simply 'There's the truck full of engines, pick whichever one you want'. The Lotuses lapped no quicker.

Their worst outing was probably Mexico where Warr confidently expected to do well, at altitude with the atmos handicapped and the turbos unaffected. But they had two engine failures, unsuitable fuel creating pre-ignition which holed pistons.

Five Lotus-Honda 100Ts were built. They will not be recalled as classic racing cars, least of all by their dejected drivers. Piquet retired from seven races, and although his results look quite good by most standards they were unimpressive in the unique situation of Honda turbo v. atmo cars in 1988; three thirds, a fourth, two fifths, one sixth and two eighth places. Nakajima twice failed to qualify on street circuits – at Monte Carlo and Detroit – he retired six times and scored only once, sixth at Rio. His other finishes read 8-11-7-10-9-7-7. Lotus-Honda were beaten into fourth place in the Constructors' Cup by Benetton-Ford, best of the atmo teams, Piquet finished an outclassed sixth in the Drivers' competition, and Nakajima 16th-equal with PierLuigi Martini – and last.

Team Lotus lost its Honda contract and for 1989 fell back upon Judd CV8 engines fitted with Tickford-developed five-valve-per-cylinder heads. Frank Dernie and Mike Coughlan designed new Type 101 cars, very slender and compact with a distinctively waisted front end and unusually tall cockpit profile matched to Nelson Piquet. Bilstein cockpit-adjustable disc-springs were mounted low down in removable blisters on the fuselage flanks. The monocoque swelled around the cockpit and fuel cell and the exhaust manifolding snuggled in along the chassis lines. A very slender longitudinal six-speed transaxle permitted a wide diffuser panel beneath the tail, with vertically mounted

Lotus-Lamborghini Type 102 – chassis '3' – run by Martin Donnelly in Hungary, showing off its slender forward fuselage, wide-track pushrod front suspension and slender airbox. The design's strength saved the driver's life in his awful accident at Jerez.

rear spring/dampers just ahead of the gearbox section.

Unfortunately, Dernie's tenure at Team Lotus started poorly and barely improved. The Lotus-Judd CV was overshadowed in early season by the similar-engined Rinland/Baldwin-designed Brabham BT58, before benefiting from better straightline speed in the later races. Drivers were Piquet and Nakajima again, both non-qualifying in Lotus's nadir meeting, the Belgian GP at Spa. Nakajima non-qualified twice elsewhere, was not classified once and retired seven times, as did his team leader. But Piquet's finishes read 11-4-8-4-5-6-8-4 against 'Nakajap's' 8-8-10-7-4 – that fourth place being achieved in a memorable swansong drive in torrential rain at Adelaide. This fortified Team's opinion that Nakajima was simply too slightly built to have displayed his true talent in Formula 1, lighter steering and handling in the wet permitting it all to shine through . . .

However that may be, he was very much the more popular driver within the team, the detached, often morose Piquet establishing zero *rapport* with his crew. Team finished sixth in the Constructors' Cup, with 15 points, sandwiched between Tyrrell and Arrows.

For 1990, Team had high hopes for their new Lamborghini V12 factory engine agreement – forged by new chief executive Tony Rudd's age-old acquaintance with the Italian concern's engineering director, Mauro Forghieri. Much was expected of the latest Dernie-designed Type 102, tailor-made for the latest Lamborghini 3512/90 V12 engines, with taller, wider fuel cell to feed the thirstier multi-cylinder engine, tidied front suspension, and larger side pods accommodating enlarged water radiators to cope with the 3512's greater cooling demand.

Derek Warwick – ex-Arrows – and the promising Ulster Formula 3000 driver Martin Donnelly were engaged for the new year but the programme began badly as Lotus failed to heed Forghieri's recommendations on feeding the new

engine's lubrication system. New oil tanks had to be designed and made even before the cars made their race debut, and then the 102s showed a dispiriting lack of grip and handling problems which were to dog them all year, despite moves to stiffen the monocoques. A front suspension failure was experienced second time out and for most of the season the Lotus-Lamborghinis were deeply overshadowed by the shoestring Larrousse Lola-Lamborghini operation, as they were even struggling to qualify.

Warwick suffered nine retirements, including each of the last five GPs, while Donnelly did not start at Rio but contested 12 other races before suffering an appalling accident in qualifying at Jerez. It seems a front suspension component had failed, but the car totally disintegrated as the mass of the big V12 engine powered straight through, the carbon fuselage shattering under impact against the trackside barrier. The fact of Donnelly's survival – though grievously injured – bore testimony to the inherent impact absorption provided by the contemporary Grand Prix car.

Before his accident, Donnelly had finished five races, 8-8-12-7-12. His place was taken by Johnny Herbert – set aside by Benetton and himself a survivor of severe leg injuries suffered in a racing accident. He retired his Lotus from the last two GPs on the calendar. Meanwhile Warwick finished fifth in Hungary, sixth in Canada and 7-10-11-8-11 elsewhere, and emerged from a massive first-lap accident at Monza to race his spare car in the restarted Italian GP.

Of the five unloved Lotus-Lamborghinis built, numbers '1 and '2 had been introduced at Phoenix, '3 was new for Donnelly at Imola and written off – utterly – at Jerez, '4 made its debut for Warwick at Imola and '5 was new as spare at Ricard, being heavily savaged only third time out – but in its maiden race – at Monza.

Long before the end of the season, Team's Camel cigarette brand sponsors had announced they would be taking their money elsewhere for 1991, Dernie was gone to Ligier and into that winter Team was virtually bankrupt, its friends rallying round to offer some way out – some path to survival in some form into the new year. All the old strength and dynamism had leaked away . . . and in the deserted workshops at Ketteringham Hall only the sentimental could detect the last vestiges

of that old Lotus magic . . .

Team Lotus barely scraped into 1991 as a viable entity, being rescued at the classical 'one minute to midnight' from what looked around Christmas time to be certain collapse. Salvation came from Peter Collins and Peter Wright, backed by German GM dealer and F3 team owner Horst Schübel. They could not afford the Lamborghini engine and fell back instead upon John Judd's trusty EV 76-degree V8s. The new Lotus 102B version of the old Lambo-powered design was considerably revised, Team claiming over 4800 components had been changed, rendering over 90 per cent of the car completely new.

Three of the new monocoques were moulded from the latest available composite materials – advised by the Russian Sukhoi aerospace concern – and featuring a mixture of high-modulus and high-strength unidirectional fibres.

The 102Bs' rear bulkhead was completely redesigned to accept the Judd EV engine, and a new bell-housing, oil tank and six-speed transverse gearbox were adopted. Aerodynamic form was revised after a series of tests in the 'Honda' tunnel at London's Imperial College, but in mid-season Team acquired the old Williams quarter-scale moving-ground tunnel as its own.

The new car had completely new nose, body top, undertray and wing sections, plus redesigned fuel, oil and engine cooling systems. Suspension was new-geometry and throughout the season the Lotus 102Bs clung on against far more potent, modern and better-funded equipment. Drivers Häkkinen, Bailey, Bartels and Herbert gave of their best. Häkkinen finished eight races, 9-5-(Imola) 9-12-14-14-14-19 and only failed to qualify once (in France). The unfortunate Bailey failed to qualify for three of his four GPs, but finished sixth at Imola behind his team-mate. Herbert's spasmodic season yielded eight entries, failure to qualify upon his comeback in Canada, then being classified five times, 10-10-14-7-11. The young German, Bartels, was thrown in at the deep end, and sank, failing to qualify in all four attempts.

After a brief and not particularly serious test of an Isuzu 3.5-litre V12 engine (discovered in Japan by Elan and McLaren F1 road car styling consultant Peter Stevens), a customer Cosworth-Ford HB V8 engine deal was agreed to take Team forward into 1992 . . .

Lyncar

This was another Cosworth/Hewland 'kit-car', built in 1974 for McLaren engine builder John Nicholson to drive as a private entry and sponsored by the enthusiastic Bruno Drury's Pinch Plant hire company. Amongst his other racing designs, manufacturer Martin Slater had built a highly successful Formula Atlantic car which Nicholson raced, and the Formula 1 car became chassis '007' in his Lyncar series – which was named in his wife's honour.

Nicholson made his debut in '007' in the 1974 Race of Champions at Brands Hatch, being classified 16th, but at Silverstone he finished as high as sixth in the International Trophy. The British GP meeting then saw him up against the big guns and he failed to qualify. He brought the car out again in 1975, retiring from the Race of Champions, finishing 13th at Silverstone in the non-Championship meeting but qualifying successfully for the Grand Prix there in July, where he was classified 17th after crashing in the downpour which caused the race to be cut short. Thereafter he concentrated upon power boat racing while continuing his highly successful Nicholson-McLaren engine business.

Maki

This tiny, enthusiastic and rather misguided Japanese Formula 1 project was the brainchild of Kenji Mimura who designed a bulkily unconventional-bodied Cosworth/Hewland 'kit-car' in conjunction with Masao Ono. The F-101 was unveiled with considerable fanfare and was to be driven by former McLaren and BRM driver Ganley. He was unable to qualify for the British GP, and in the attempt to qualify for the German GP at the Nürburgring where he said the car was 'actually feeling very good' he suddenly found himself wildly out of control at high speed as something in the suspension apparently broke. The car rammed the guardrail and its entire front end, including suspension and pedals, was ripped away, Ganley's legs and feet being injured as they were dragged along the ground while the wreck spun to a halt.

The opinion was expressed that most Formula 1 teams 'wouldn't even make a water tank that way', and the car was seen no more that season.

It returned, however in 1975 when the much modified 'F101-02' was entered for ex-Lotus driver Dave Walker for the Belgian and Swedish GPs. However, it did not appear, then did not start and was way off the pace in Holland driven by Hiroshi Fuchida. The Japanese driver failed to qualify for the British GP at Silverstone, and Tony Trimmer then tried and failed to qualify it in Austria and Italy. Nevertheless, he started the non-Championship Swiss GP at Dijon-Prenois, five seconds off the pace, and finished 13th, six times lapped.

Maki's last chance came in the 1976 Japanese GP, when an allegedly new car, serialled 'F102A-1' and driven by Trimmer, again failed to qualify.

Enthusiasm alone was never enough . . . exit the Maki.

Above: *Howden Ganley braving the Maki at Brands Hatch, British GP 1974, before the ill-fated trip to the Nürburgring.*

March

March Engineering was formed in 1969 by Max Mosley, Alan Rees, Graham Coaker and Robin Herd to build production racing cars. It was a fine time to begin, for in addition to a healthy market for Formula 2 and Formula 3 chassis several teams were also at a loss to find chassis for Formula 1, including Ken Tyrrell's World Champion team. What's more there were several sponsors seeking involvement.

March won backing from the American Granatelli brothers' STP Corporation for a two-car works team plus a single sister car for STP's own driver Andretti. Tyrrell bought three cars for Stewart and Cevert and Crabbe's Antique Automobiles team would run another car for works appointee Peterson's Formula 1 debut.

Herd had to design a simple, easy-to-build car which would perform respectably without lengthy development. His March 701 featured a simple straight-sided aluminium monocoque, with a cast-magnesium front bulkhead and two smaller castings providing suspension pick-ups at the front. The nose radiator, fire extinguisher and battery lay in a projecting forward tray, and the Cosworth/Hewland DG300 pack bolted on conventionally at the rear. Suspension was conventional, outboard all round. Robin reflects, 'There was hardly time to build the cars let alone use inboard suspension and do it properly'.

However, in conjunction with ex-BRM engineer and aerodynamicist Peter Wright – at that time running the Specialised Mouldings wind tunnel at Huntingdon – Robin adopted moulded glass-fibre low aspect ratio wing-shaped auxiliary tanks bolted on either side of the tub; a precursor of Wright's later ground-effect underwing side pods introduced on the Lotus 78/79s.

'At that time', Robin explains, 'there was a terrific differential in the amount of fuel required from race to race so add-on tanks were a good idea. Peter recommended this idea, and it worked – we might have found a little extra downforce and it certainly carried extra fuel without a drag penalty.'

March had to build at least six 701s in three months, and they succeeded. The car was initially effective, but there were so many fundamental compromises in its design that once Lotus and Ferrari sorted themselves out the 701s could no longer cope.

Tyrrell bought 701 chassis '2-4-7 for his drivers Stewart and Servoz-Gavin, though the latter abruptly opted out of racing at Monaco and was replaced by Cevert. Works drivers Amon and Siffert drove '701/1' and '701/5', the former machine receiving a new tub under the same number in mid-season, thus setting a March fashion which has confounded and confused those who try to keep track of these things ever since. History mattered less than retaining the same chassis number as the available customs papers when a car had to be rebuilt and another race was

Robin Herd's 1972 March 721X was intended to set new standards but passed into history as a flop. Its low polar moment design concentrated mass within the wheelbase.

looming next weekend.

Andretti's STP team car was chassis '3 – wrecked in Austria and seen no more – and Peterson's Crabbe car '701/8'.

March made a fantastic start to their Formula 1 career with five cars running at Kyalami and Stewart on pole alongside Amon; only Stewart and Siffert finished, 3-10. Stewart won the minor Race of Champions from pole in '701/2' – the cars looking awkwardly high-set when they ran without the wing tanks on their rolled-under tub sides. In Spain, he qualified on the front row and won March's maiden Grand Prix victory, Andretti and Servoz-Gavin 3-5 behind him, though Siffert had not qualified. Amon then took the International Trophy at Silverstone on aggregate, winning from pole and setting fastest lap; Stewart won his heat and was placed second overall.

Thus, March won three of their first four Formula 1 races . . .

It was extraordinary and it could not last, even though Stewart and Amon qualified 1-2 at Monaco and Spa, where Amon set fastest lap and finished second behind a BRM. Stewart put '701/4' on the front row in Holland and was second again, but thereafter the 701s fell off the pace, with Amon coming second in the French GP and Stewart second in Italy. By this time the chance had passed as Tyrrell built his own cars for 1971 and March thereby lost a customer.

Robin 'had a proper go at Formula 1' in 1971 with the model 711 design, an unconventional device with its aerodynamic form based on advice from Frank Costin; an elliptical centre-strutted nose wing, compact hip-radiator aluminium monocoque, and all-inboard brakes to minimize unsprung weight. The distinctive nose wing proved incredibly incidence-sensitive. As they attempted to reduce incidence to minimize drag and find better straightline speed at the Österreichring, the 711s would exhibit terrific understeer and lap slower, marring Lauda's maiden GP.

The 711s lost much of their originally extensive aerodynamic bodywork early on, and outboard front brakes were fitted after a brakeshaft snapped on the Williams car '711/3', driven by Peterson at the minor Brands Hatch meeting. Subsequently, there were few structural faults, except to the private Williams cars for Pescarolo. The experiment of playing Alfa Romeo's V8 off against Cosworth's was unprofitable in results.

Old 701s ran on into the first part of 1971, in the Williams team for Pescarolo, Bell and others using chassis '6; new chassis '11 in the new Mordaunt-Guthrie team for Beuttler, while chassis '10 had been sold to John Love for use in southern African Formula 1. Car '701/9' emerged, owned by Hubert Hahne and driven by Jarier at Oulton Park late in the year, and entered for the Frenchman by the Shell-Arnold team at Monza.

Six 711s appeared, Peterson heading the works team in '711/2', for most of the season in '6, and finally in the Brands Hatch Victory race in '4. Normally his car was Cosworth-powered but March toyed with Alfa Romeo's V8; sponsored rides for Galli and de Adamich, normally in chassis '711/1'. Peterson wrote off this car at the minor Silverstone meeting when the Alfa V8's throttles jammed open but it was rebuilt around a refabricated tub. The top-endy Alfa engine was fitted in '711/6' – if we believe the numbers – for the French GP at Ricard. However, Peterson retired and thereafter ran DFVs exclusively.

All four 711s in Spain ran outboard front brakes and nose-mounted batteries were provided for the STP works entries to improve their sprung:unsprung weight ratio. For Monaco, Peterson's '711/2' was provided with strengthened rear suspension, and the Alfa-engined car which Galli failed to qualify there was a brand new replacement for Ronnie's Silverstone write-off, albeit still wearing '711/1's chassis-plate. A low-drag nose was tested at Monza but the 711s raced with standard nose cones shorn of their elliptical wings. In Canada, the Gene Mason Racing '711/5' appeared for American club driver Skip Barber.

Peterson drove brilliantly all year, placing sec-

Formula 2-derived F1 March cars: top: *James Hunt making his name in the 1973 British GP at Silverstone in the Postlethwaite-developed Hesketh team 731.* Above: *British GP 1975 – Mark Donohue in Penske's March 751.*

ond at Monaco, Hockenheim, Silverstone, Monza – just 0.01 second behind the winner! – and Mosport Park; as well as achieving a third at Watkins Glen, fourth at Zandvoort and finishing second in the Drivers' Championship behind Stewart. March Engineering were third-equal in the Constructors' table, tied with Ferrari behind BRM and Tyrrell, maintaining their 1970 position.

Now Herd was determined to win the Championship in 1972, and invested much time and effort in a highly mass-concentrated low polar moment March 721X.

Initially, a lighter 711 development known as the March 721 contested the early-season races, losing its 711-like nose-top wing after Argentina and adopting a bluff nose form with moulded-in planes ahead of the front wheels either side. Peterson drove '721/1' and new team-mate Lauda took '721/2' which did only two races before being withdrawn. Meanwhile, an Alfa Romeo sports car drive had been arranged for Peterson in the 1971 Watkins Glen 6 Hours race. He used a car fitted with Alfa's gearbox-ahead-of-final-drive transmission which pushed the engine far forward to concentrate mass within the wheelbase, whereas a conventional gearbox like the Hewland waved in the breeze out behind the back axle. Peterson found the Alfa T33 to his liking, encouraging Robin to make his biggest mistake.

Alfa Romeo provided gearbox components for the 721X, which also introduced new rear suspension with inboard coil/dampers at the rear. But the 721X's weight distribution did not suit the Goodyear tyres which March had just adopted, having previously run Firestones. Space was very tight and restricted the differentials useable; the 721X was dogged by understeer when entering corners and suffered vicious oversteer leaving them, though otherwise handling well on fast curves. Although Peterson quite liked the 'X, team-mate Lauda tried it for the first time and grunted 'No vay', and he was right.

March talked to Firestone who felt they could provide tyres which would improve behaviour, but races were being lost, the season was passing by and an instant 'fix' had to be found.

Consequently, the two 721X cars were withdrawn after contesting only the Spanish, Monaco, Oulton Gold Cup (where Peterson's '721X/2' used a conventional Hewland FG400 transaxle) and Belgian races, and hastily built production Formula 2-chassised 721G cars replaced them for

the French round.

The first 721G had been built in just nine days prior to the Spanish GP for Beuttler's private entry, the 'G' standing for *Guinness Book of Records* because it had been devised and built so quickly. He liked it, and works 721Gs, chassis '2 initially for Lauda and '3 for Peterson, rapidly followed; the team leader finishing fifth at Clermont. He was third in Germany, qualified on the front row in Canada but was disqualified for reversing in the pit lane having overshot his marks, Lauda being disqualified from the same race in '721G/4' for receiving outside assistance. Few F1 teams share with March the distinction of having had both entries disqualified in the same Grand Prix . . .

At Watkins Glen Peterson was fourth, and he qualified on the front row for the final race of the year at Brands Hatch, where Migault debuted the Ecurie Volant Shell '721G/5' intended for hillclimber Daniel Rouveyran, and bent it badly.

Meanwhile, private entrant Frank Williams had run '711/3' for Pace and '721/3' for Pescarolo. The latter had a hectic time as he crashed the long-suffering car at Monaco, Clermont – where it was badly damaged so the Frenchman instead wrote off the new Williams FX/3 in the next race at Brands Hatch – then at the Nürburgring, (writing off '721/3' again), Austria (writing it off a third time) and at Monza. In the last race the car appeared with a unicorn nose wing, possibly indicating that it was the ex-Lauda '721/2' revived under '3's serial. Between destructive accidents, '721/3's tub had been remade in Williams's own workshops, then replaced by a brand new tub from Bicester.

Of more eccentric note was the 'Eifelland-Cosworth Type 21' *née* March '721/4'. The German driver Stommelen's long-time sponsors Eifelland Wohnwagenbau (Caravans) backed walrus-moustached artist Lutz 'Luigi' Colani to style florid body panels including an integral periscope mirror on the centreline ahead of the cockpit but most were quickly replaced by standard panelling. Stommelen had nine outings, finishing seven times, 13-10-10-11-16-10-15, which record tells its own story. Stommelen sold the car to the London Hexagon car dealership and they entered it for Watson at the final Brands Hatch meeting, where he finished sixth in a promising Formula 1 debut.

After this 1972 season, March Engineering merely toyed with Formula 1. Robin explains: 'After that season we merely converted our production Formula 2 designs to Formula 1, providing cars where drivers or sponsors wanted to pay us for the privilege and generally tackled Formula 1 on Formula 2 budgets.

'Our bank had got whingy, telling us "You must take life more seriously".'

Team manager Rees had left to create Shadow while Mosley and Herd ran their 'team', such as it was, alone as March's production Formula 2 and 3 cars dominated their classes. The outstanding March of 1973 was the Hesketh entry for Hunt, developed and tended by former March engineer Harvey Postlethwaite, which made its debut at Monaco, then finished 6-4-3-7-2 in its next five successful GP outings in France, Britain, Holland, Canada and the USA. There, at Watkins Glen, Hunt challenged hard for the lead, set fastest lap and was beaten by just 0.312 second.

With such a driver there was little wrong with a well-developed converted Formula 2 car. In fact the 1972 works 721G chassis numbers were used in these updated 1973 '731' versions which looked totally different with their deformable structure tank-protecting side pods and narrower rear tracks.

Beuttler ran his original '721G/1' into the new season at Kyalami, then returned it to the Bicester works, taking over a new 731 numbered '721G/2'. David Purley acquired a sister 731, reputedly based on the ex-Beuttler '721G/1' tub. The Hesketh car carried ex-works plate '721G/3' but was definitely all-new; Dr Postlethwaite made sure of it – no tired, stretched old tub for *his* driver.

Jarier, March's 1972 Formula 2 star, normally

drove a solitary works-entered 731 numbered '721G/4', though newcomer Roger Williamson took over for the British and Dutch GPs, being involved in the Schecter collision through no fault of his own at Silverstone before crashing fatally at Zandvoort after a suspension failure.

For 1974 the F2 monocoque 741s emerged with hip radiators angled almost in-line each side of the engine, sheet magnesium end plate-mounted rear wings and spatular bluff noses derived from 1973 F1 and F2 experience. Stuck and Ganley drove in early-season, Vittorio Brambilla replacing Ganley with Beta Tools' orange livery on his often-battered tubs thereafter. Stuck showed terrific car control almost in the Peterson mould and was fifth at Kyalami fourth in Spain, while Brambilla was sixth in Austria to highlight a season which saw the Marches performing respectably, all things considered.

Brambilla wrote off his '741/2' at Jarama when the rear wing swayed forward under braking, its stays cramped a brake hose against a disc, which sawed through it, leaving Brambilla with front wheels locked and no retardation at all on the rear. A new tub replaced the damaged original on '741/2' in Belgium. A second new tub went into the car for the German GP but, like George Washington's axe, it was still 'the same car'.

The same happened to Stuck's '741/1' after it was heavily damaged at Monaco. Both 741s had begun the season painted British Racing Green. Brambilla brought orange *Beta Utensili* livery and Stuck's car progressively changed colour to match, appearing as a green and orange patchwork at one stage 'as he progressively wrote off the green panels'.

An F2-derived extra-long nose section appeared in Sweden, adding download leverage, while narrow track gave good straightline speed on the fast end-of-season courses.

In 1975, Brambilla began the season alone in an old 741 modified with new regulation engine-bay extinguisher and battery moved from tail to nose, but in Spain his lighter '751/3' was supported by Lella Lombardi's new '751/2' and they finished 5-6 for the best March result in years. Better would follow.

Brambilla was very quick at Zolder until the circuit burned out his Formula 2 brakes – 'because we literally couldn't afford to buy proper

Formula 1 brakes'.

At Anderstorp for the Swedish GP nearly all the geometric corners suited the 751, where the team ran Brambilla on new 20 in. wide rear wheels to add tyre stability and stripped all excess weight out of the car. In a meteoric qualifying shot on extremely stiff springs making the car handle like a kart, he qualified on pole and led the race until a UJ failed.

Penske bought '751/5' new for Donohue in time for the British GP where he was classified fifth and Brambilla sixth after accidents in the rainstorm which stopped that race. The works 751 there had new geometry suspension and horizontal rear winglets projecting from the side plates low down just behind the rear wheels. They were judged legal and gave 200 rpm more along the straight by cleaning up turbulence from the wide rear tyres. They were a forerunner of the rear diffuser underwings used in 1983-84 but, again, Herd did not pursue the idea.

The Penske car was rebuilt after its Silverstone crash with new bulkhead castings and some reskinning, but in morning warm-up in Austria Donohue was fatally injured as its left-front tyre collapsed at speed. The race was stopped by torrential rain, at a time when Brambilla's narrow-track '751/3' was leading, so he was declared winner, subsequently celebrating by smashing the nose cone in a victory-lap incident.

The Italian GP was a disaster, as Brambilla's clutch failed and both Stuck (whose '751/2' sported a new tub following a crash in Austria) and Lombardi crashed again; however, in the USA Brambilla and Stuck finished 7-8.

For 1976 Peterson left Lotus after the season had begun and returned to his old friends at March, whom he loved and where he was immensely popular. They ran the whole season that year on a budget of just £35,000. The developed 761 cars were very agile, quick on the straights, immensely fast in damp conditions but unreliable.

At Ricard a speed trap on the long Mistral Straight showed Peterson quickest at 182.56 mph, with Brambilla next up at 179.43 mph, in the two March 761s . . .

Peterson ran 15 races for the team, being classified as a finisher only six times but featuring prominently – crashing out of second place on

spilled oil at Monaco, leading in Austria, starting from pole and heading the field in Holland and surviving 43 laps in the lead to win the Italian GP at Monza, where spasmodic rain showers cooled the car's brakes just enough to finish.

He started on the front row in Canada and led eight laps, then at Watkins Glen qualified on row two but started the race with a fractured front bulkhead allowing the suspension mounts to move about, and understandably did not feature. His sixth in Austria was Peterson's only other points score.

Brambilla finished five races but his only score was sixth in Holland; Lombardi was 14th in her solitary race in Brazil; while Merzario finished twice out of five starts before moving to Wolf-Williams for the end of the year, never finishing another race.

One Karl Oppitzhauser failed to practice for the Austrian race, while in contrast the reliable Stuck finished five of his 16 GPs, 4-12-4-7-5, his placings in Brazil, Monaco and the USA bringing him and the team eight points.

March ended the season seventh in the Cup table, the neat rounded-arrowhead tub 761s with their in-line hip radiators and bluff nosepieces with forward-thrust splitter tray doing wonders on such a tight budget.

For 1977, improved 761B and nose-radiator 771 cars were produced by Herd and his assistant Martin Walters, three of each running during the season. Mosley (law graduate son of Sir Oswald) acted as field engineer that year because March's Formula 2 programme backers BMW had threatened to withdraw if Herd, the real engineer, 'did not stop playing around with Formula 1 and concentrate upon their Formula 2 programme. So I had to do Formula 2 and Max set up the Formula 1 cars for Ribeiro and Ian Scheckter, and that was it.'

Frank Williams bought an ex-works March tub – said to have traces of orange paint on it – for Neve to drive in Williams Grand Prix Engineering's maiden season. Eight GPs were started, finishing 12-10-15-9-7-18 and failing to qualify in France, Germany and Holland. Merzario ran his private car seven times, failing to qualify in Monaco, Germany and Holland, his only finish being 14th in Belgium. Other private March drivers that year included Michael

Think of March in Formula 1 and most enthusiasts call to mind the distinctive shape of the 1971 Type 711 with its Frank Costin-advised aerodynamic form and unicorn nose wing.

Adrian Newey set new standards for slimline fuselage construction in the Leyton House-sponsored March 881, the footbox being no more than 10 inches wide. Having made his reputation in Indycar design, Newey was bound for the top in Formula 1.

Bleekemoelen, Bernard de Dryver, Boy Hayje, Brian Henton, Brett Lunger, Stuck (one race only in South Africa before joining Brabham) and Andy Sutcliffe – jointly achieving nothing. Seven cars had been built.

The Rothmans-sponsored Mosley team for Ribeiro and Ian Scheckter meanwhile started 22 times, finishing six races whose best placings were eighths for Ribeiro in Germany and Canada. They non-qualified nine times.

At the end of that season March sold their FOCA membership to Schmid's ATS team and left Formula 1 to continue their highly successful minor-Formula production programmes. March cars raced on in bush-league Formula 1, with drivers like Guy Edwards, Jurg Zaborowski, Bruce Allison, Gerd Biechteler, Geoff Lees and Dennis Leech.

The 1978-79-80 seasons saw March racing elsewhere. Then in 1981 they returned, being commissioned to build customer cars for the RAM team. These modest March 811 wing-cars with Cosworth power were driven by Daly and Salazar, failing to qualify twelve times with 16-7-11-8 representing their only finishes, seventh being in the British GP. No less than six of these new March 811s, numbered 'RM01' to 'RM06', were built and for 1982 RAM updated chassis '05 as spare car to support new 821 models, chassis '07-08-09-10-11 for drivers Mass and Boesel. As would become characteristic of RAM, they suffered a series of accidents.

Boesel destroyed 'RM08' testing at Snetterton, '09 was written off in the startline collision at Detroit and '10 featured in Mass's potentially horrifying high-speed accident at Ricard during the French GP when it hurdled the catch-fences and somersaulted into a spectator area and caught fire, miraculously without anyone being seriously harmed. This accident perhaps was the last nail in the coffin of the clearance ground-effect wing-cars, making the latter-day March significant in at least that unhappy respect.

For 1983 RAM Automotive manufactured their own new Cosworth cars, initially retaining the March tag (see entry for RAM, page 308).

In 1985, Formula 3000 had replaced Formula 2 as the 'schoolroom class' subsidiary to Formula 1, using 3-litre racing engines primarily from Cosworth – their age-old DFV V8s. Italian enthusiast Cesare Gariboldi's Genoa Racing team ran a new DFV-powered March 85B for a promising driver named Ivan Capelli. The car was derived from the final F2 March, the 842, developed by Ralph Bellamy and Ian Holloway to

F3000 requirements.

Capelli's continuing exploits in the class through 1986 won him drives in Japanese F3000 in cars owned by businessman Akira Akagi and backed by his 'Leyton House' industrial property companies. Akagi began to support Gariboldi's operation in Europe and showed interest in stepping up into Formula 1. Gariboldi made the introduction to March where Robin Herd had decided the time was right to return to the fray at Grand Prix level. And so March returned to Formula 1 in 1987, initially running an interim car, a modified Formula 3000 Type 87B dubbed the 87P – chassis '1 – pending completion of a pure-bred Formula 1 design, the March 871. The 87P was powered by the latest 3.5-litre Cosworth DFZ engine driving through a March six-speed gearbox. It had the new rear suspension intended for the definitive F1 871 – of which three would be produced – and its F3000-sized fuel cell gave it no chance of surviving a full GP distance.

Gordon Coppuck – that fine ex-McLaren and Spirit engineer – had worked on March's customer single-seaters before running the company's 1986 sports car programme, and now he and Tim Holloway were committed to the Formula 1 project.

The definitive March 871 emerged at Imola, noted for its tall (and trend-setting) airbox, longer wheelbase and enlarged fuel capacity relative to the 87P. Cosworth was over-committed on engine production and DFZs were scarce, March even running a 3.3-litre DFL sports car V8 at Spa. Even so, Capelli led the 'atmo' class there until the engine's oil pressure sagged – perhaps understandably.

The 87P had non-started at Rio, and Capelli later suffered nine retirements in the 871s, often when running well. But he finished six times 6-10-11-13-9-12 and that sixth place at Monaco was a tremendous fillip, a Championship point so early in the new team's career . . . and 11th-equal place in the Constructors' Championship, tied with AGS and Ligier . . .

For 1988, Adrian Newey designed a striking new March 881, pioneering a new F1 shape with the slimmest fuselage yet seen, waisting in to a 10 in. wide footbox and with some of the lowest side pods yet seen, tightly squeezed towards the tail where a large and powerful underbody diffuser was provided. Its 112.4 in. wheelbase was one of the longest in the class, and after unsatisfactory service from the Mader Cosworth DFZs in 1987 team manager Ian Phillips was able to secure the new Judd CV engines on a development-partner basis for 1988. This close relationship was diluted somewhat by Williams's subsequent short-notice fallback onto John Judd's new Honda F3000-derived engine as the Japanese giant pulled its turbo V6s from the Didcot team to supply McLaren instead.

A two-car team of these new 881s was to be run,

in Leyton House's Florida green livery, for Capelli and Brazilian Mauricio Gugelmin. Six were built, chassis '4 being destroyed in Capelli's practice shunt at Detroit, and chassis '6 not raced after being damaged by Gugelmin in a practice accident first time out, brand new, at Suzuka.

With the ultra-slimline 881, engineer Adrian Newey confirmed a reputation founded in CART racing, the cars toppling Benetton as consistently the quickest of the atmo cars late-season, but lacking their reliability.

Early-season Judd engine installation problems combined with gearbox troubles and general inexperience, Newey for example 'seeing many of the circuits for the very first time'. There was no time spare to detail the engine programme, March gratefully sharing Williams experience. With only a dozen or so of Judd's 46 Type CV engines on strength, March were too short to test as much as they might have liked. Judd's rebuild programme came under constant pressure to rebuild and turn round V8s ever faster.

The team's nadir came at Imola, where March lost four nose cones in as many laps, the fixing loadings being exceeded by the downforce generated. At last, at Silverstone – one circuit they all knew well – they really took F1 by the scruff of the neck. Drivers Capelli and Gugelmin both impressed, especially the former once the race began while the Brazilian gave Newey considerable technical feedback.

Capelli retired six times, his finishing record reading 10-16-5 (Canada) 9, then three successive fifth-place finishes in Germany, Belgium and Italy, followed by a fine second in Portugal, then sixth in Australia.

Gugelmin retired eight times, was fourth at Silverstone and fifth in Hungary, his other six finishes reading 15-8-8-8-7-10. March Racing ended up fifth-equal in the Constructors' Cup competition, sharing their score of 20 points with Williams-Judd and Arrows.

This tight-knit, friendly and fast-growing team had established an excellent springboard of experience, knowledge and perhaps most important confidence and credibility ready for '89.

Giuseppe Gariboldi, to whom March Racing owed so much, was killed in a road accident in December 1988, and Newey's further developed CG891 design for the new year bore his initials *in memoriam*. The new car was packaged to make the most of a 76-degree narrow-angle version of Judd's V8 engine, suggested by Newey when he heard Judd was planning a short-stroke version of the CV and considered more advantageous aerodynamically. These engines became exclusive to the Bicester team. The programme represented a considerable financial investment, but until the first could be made race-ready four developed 881s reappeared, chassis '3-'6 (repaired), before being replaced by the CG891 of which five were deployed during the year.

Newey wanted to employ a full-width arched diffuser panel at the rear of the CG891, adopting an inboard gear cluster ahead of the final-drive to provide the space. Unfortunately this transaxle's casing proved inadequately rigid during the season, flexure causing a series of early-season failures. The narrow-angle Judd EV engine had its share of teething problems and unfortunately the 891 proved unreliable during a year which also saw business problems between Akagi of Leyton House – who had been buying the team – and the March parent company in Britain, which did not help programme delays.

Capelli's season was riven by 14 retirements, finishing only at Monaco and Spa, 11th and 12th. Gugelmin once failed to qualify, was once disqualified, once unclassified as a finisher and eight times posted retirements, but his five finishes included a fine third at Rio, then 7-10-7-7 – three times just missing the points in Belgium, Japan and Australia. From fifth in the Constructors' Cup in 1988, March tumbled to 12th, on just four points, in 1989.

From 1990 the now wholly Leyton House-owned team operated under that title. See entry for Leyton House, page 278.

Martini

Unrelated to Martini & Rossi, Tico Martini was a Channel Islander who made his name hill-climbing a kart-like special in the early Sixties before settling down as a French-based Formula 3 and eventually European Championship-winning Formula 2 manufacturer, with workshops at the Magny-Cours circuit.

For 1978 he built a one-off Cosworth/Hewland monocoque car, its slim arrow-head chassis reminiscent of the contemporary Williams FW06, to be driven by Arnoux. It featured inboard top rocker arm front suspension with a parallel link system at the rear and used a six-speed FGA gearbox. The project was sponsored by RMO, a temporary-staff agency, Silver Match, manufacturers of lighters and pens, and by Elf, the French oil company. It was known as the model MK23 in Martini's system, MK being the initials of Martini-Knight – the Knight family running the Magny-Cours driving school – rather than an abbreviation for 'Mark'.

The MK23 made its debut at Kyalami where Arnoux failed to qualify. Loss of oil pressure prevented him starting at Silverstone and at Monaco he failed even to pre-qualify. In Belgium he finally made the race, finishing a reliable but uncompetitive ninth, and he was then 14th in his home GP at Ricard. The fast circuit at Hockenheim saw him fail to pre-qualify again but in Austria he was ninth. The car's only race retirement came at Zandvoort where its wing mount failed but that was the end and Martini opted out of Formula 1 thereafter.

Matra

The emergence of Matra Sports as a Formula 1 force and their World Championship victory of 1969 is related elsewhere (see pages 68-72). They experimented rather half-heartedly with a space-frame four-wheel drive car named the MS84. It was the cheapest and simplest of the 1969 crop and the only one to score a Championship point with Servoz-Gavin's sixth place in Canada. For the last race in Mexico the engineers split torque 100 per cent to the rear wheels and the driver reported a great improvement in handling and 'feel'! After that Championship season Matra Sports had to shelve their Cosworth-Ford interest in view of their own takeover by Chrysler's French subsidiary Simca.

For 1970 Georges Martin revised his V12 engine, stiffening its crankcase sufficiently to act as a stressed chassis member like the Cosworth DFV, and designing new cylinder heads with a narrower valve angle and shallower combustion chamber, offering enlarged inlet area while demanding less deep-crowned, and therefore lighter, pistons. Inlet ports were now within the vee instead of between the camshafts, which were themselves closer together, thanks to the narrower valve angle, and that permitted generally narrower and hence lighter head assembly castings. This new MS12 engine's bottom end was unchanged. A Boulogne company named *Moteur Moderne* helped in this development.

Bernard Boyer had to design a new monocoque to comply with 1970 regulations, and he chose a rectilinear configuration, heavily riveted with sloping upper faces on fuel tank panniers each side, offering downthrust planes to the airstream. Wheelbase was longer than the Champion MS80 but suspension geometry was similar with a narrower-track front end. Citroën power-assisted steering was tried but not raced, while the car carried a large rear wing and wide spatular nose cone with canard fins either side.

The first two chassis, 'MS120-01' and '02, were raced by team drivers Beltoise and Pescarolo in South Africa, finishing 4-7, but at Brands Hatch for the minor International Beltoise crashed '01 in practice, amputating two wheels and damaging the tub. It was repaired for Pescarolo's use in Monaco practice and was then crashed by him back at Brands in the British GP. It was repaired again in time for the American tour as spare and was retired from competition thereafter.

Meanwhile Pescarolo normally drove '02 and his 11 starts in it yielded nine finishes, including third at Monaco for Matra's first four 1970 Championship points, and fifth in the French GP at Clermont. There it was dogged by low oil pressure, then crashed mildly, as well as suffering a damper failure – after all of which fifth place was a terrific bonus. The tub was in fact distorted in this accident and after being straightened it finished sixth for another point in Germany and seventh in Canada.

The glorious-sounding French V12 cars were far more difficult to work on than their Cosworth-engined opposition, a Matra engine change taking seven or eight hours against the DFVs' ninety minutes.

Beltoise concentrated upon chassis '03 in which he started 12 races, finishing six times; third in Belgium and Italy, fifth in Holland and Mexico and sixth in Austria. This vehicle was an improved car which first appeared in Spain with 13 in. front wheels instead of the 15 in. type, better brakes, wings and lightweight titanium rear hubs. Integral front upright calipers appeared on both '02 and '03 there while V12 development extracted more power, now claimed to be around 435 bhp at 11,000 ear-splitting rpm. The 13 in. wheel experiment was unsuccessful as the smaller new brakes were cooking, so 15 in. wheels reappeared for Monaco. Nevertheless, Spa saw another outing for the low-drag 13 in. type. The 15 in. wheels and better-cooled brakes would be used for the slower, tighter courses but the cars were dogged all season by persistent understeer so revised anti-roll bars and camber angles were adopted at Clermont, where Beltoise was able to lead his home race until a puncture and fuel starvation spoiled France's day.

At Monza, a new MS12T engine with further stiffened crankcase and 'special' (presumably titanium) lightweight rods appeared, but reliability suffered in Canada and the USA.

Much of the cars' handling deficiency was attributed to torsional flexion in the chassis structure. Certainly now that Matra had to use bag tanks instead of carrying their fuel direct in the hull boxes they were robbed of the extreme monocoque sub-division which had made their 1968-69 cars so rigid.

For 1971, Pescarolo was replaced by Amon, who drove '02 in the minor Argentine GP that January and won on aggregate! This was to be Matra's one and only Formula 1 victory.

The winning car became team spare before final retirement when '06 was completed for that year's Monaco GP.

Meanwhile, Amon drove '03 – wearing a new full-width wheel fairing nose – to finish fifth at Kyalami, fourth at Ontario and California, and third in the Spanish GP.

In the latter race, Beltoise drove the revised new MS120B prototype '05, using Boyer's latest stiffened tub design with laterally down-sloping side tank upper surfaces. Martin's latest engine mods included a new exhaust system, more radical camshafts and a modified crankshaft.

For Beltoise this was a difficult season as he had been judged culpable for a fatal accident in an early-season Argentine sports car race, being suspended until Spain, and later in the year suffered a further suspension. He would make only eight starts, all in '05, and his only Championship point came in Spain, though he finished five times and

The 'Matra-Matra': Beltoise in the MS10 V12 at Rouen during the 1968 French GP meeting, showing off the car's F2-derived cigar shape and its Georges Martin-designed wailing multi-piped V12 engine.

was seventh in France and England.

Chassis '06 – last of the MS120Bs – appeared as Amon's spare at Monaco. In time for the Dutch GP it was fitted with the latest MS71 reheaded V12 but was used only in practice, Amon then racing it in France where he finished fifth despite breaking several valve springs. In face of continuing MS71 troubles Amon persevered in the German GP but crashed the car, which there included the entire rear end assembly of '04 bolted onto '06's tub.

Tyre deflations were traced to wheel problems; the team tried running on higher pressures which caused excessive understeer. Matra development had slowed as their long-distance sports-racing programme gained precedence. They missed the Austrian GP to catch their breath, '06 being modified with extra chassis stiffening between driver and engine, while engine porting was again altered to find more power. At Monza, Amon promptly qualified '06 on pole and led before his visor was ripped off and he dropped back to finish sixth.

Matra achieved nothing more that season but through the 1971/72 winter, Martin, development chief Loze and engine test manager René Fortin succeeded in boosting the MS71 V12 from 440 to 450 bhp at 11,500 rpm.

Boyer further modified his cars' front suspension to suit the latest-generation Goodyear tyres, and a smoother wide nose was adopted with twin top ducts to vent hot radiator air instead of the broad single duct of '71, these changes forming the MS120C specification.

Now they would enter just one car, for Amon, but the MS120C changes proved insufficiently radical to remain competitive. A preparation problem forced Amon to non-start in Argentina. By Kyalami the oil tank was moved to the rear, altering weight distribution, while 35 kg (77 lb) was pruned away in time for the Spanish GP by using titanium exhausts in conjunction with a lighter honeycomb core rear wing and new light alloy wheels. All this work was carried out on chassis '06, but at Monaco Amon found he preferred his old spare MS120B '04 so the latest

engine and other parts were transferred from '06 and he raced the older car, finishing sixth after four stops to clear a misting visor in the heavy rain which marred that race.

The new MS120D chassis '07 finally appeared in the French GP, using a totally redesigned tub, scrapping the original rectilinear form in favour of a rounded centre section more reminiscent of the old MS80. Weight was concentrated further rearward, the oil tank was permanently in the tail, its old housing behind the seat in the back of the tub now being taken by fuel. Amon promptly qualified on the front row and for 19 laps the French crowd believed in miracles, Amon leading in the blue Matra. Unfortunately, road work in preparing the Clermont course had left the verges strewn with sharp stone chippings and many competitors suffered punctures; Amon was one, falling back to ninth before charging through the field to finish third.

He then crashed '07 in practice at Brands Hatch, racing '04, and finishing fourth after an early collision. Thereafter '07 suffered various

mechanical *ennuis*, but ended the season with a fifth to its credit in Germany and sixth in Canada.

Meanwhile, Matra-Simca had won Le Mans, a victory provoking immense adulation in France, and the management decided sports car racing like this offered far better value than Formula 1, so the Formula 1 programme was abandoned forthwith. They would return as an engine supplier – experimentally to Shadow in 1975, then more seriously for Ligier in 1976, and again in 1981 – but would build no further Formula 1 cars of their own.

Left: *The Matra MS10 V12 set everyone's spines tingling upon its debut at Monaco 1968.* Below: *At the other end of the Matra story, Chris Amon's brand new rounded-tub MS120D '07' at Clermont, French GP, 1972 – their final F1 season.* Above: *Cam-drive geartrain of the French V12 in 1968 form.*

McGuire

Australian amateur driver Brian McGuire made the long trip to England with fellow hopeful Alan Jones in the early '70s to race Formula 3 cars. Jones made his name and fortune, McGuire did not. In 1976 he bought ex-'works' Williams FW04 chassis '1 and won the Thruxton Shellsport club race in it. For 1977 he had the old car updated in a vain attempt to make it competitive enough to run in serious Formula 1. He called it the McGuire BM1 and entered for the British GP at Silverstone. He failed to pre-qualify, lapping nearly 3.5 seconds slower than the quickest of those who also failed to pre-qualify.

No other GPs were entered, and later that year, while practising in 'BM1-1' for the August Monday meeting at Brands Hatch, a mechanical failure caused an awful accident in which McGuire himself and two unfortunate marshals were killed as it somersaulted onto their post at Stirling's Bend.

McLaren

New Zealand racing driver Bruce McLaren left the Cooper Car Company after seven seasons as team driver to go his own way with the start of the new Formula in 1966. He based his tiny team at Colnbrook, near London's Heathrow Airport, and ran it in partnership with American Teddy Mayer.

Robin Herd, a youthful but brilliant engineer previously at the Royal Aircraft Establishment in Farnborough, Hampshire, designed an advanced monocoque F1 chassis for that first season, known as the M2B and skinned in Mallite-composite sheet, an aerospace sandwich material comprising end-grain balsa filling between thin sheets of aluminium. The Mallite McLaren full monocoque tub possessed almost legendary torsional rigidity, around 11,000 lb/ft per degree deflection at a time when conventional tubs claimed perhaps 4-5000 lb/ft per degree, and the otherwise very rigid Eagle achieved 6200 lb/ft.

Sadly, McLaren's choice of a modified Indy Ford four-cam V8 centre-exhaust engine was catastrophic. It was over-valved and over-ported and had a very narrow useable rev band. For the record, it was a 95.3 x 52.4 mm unit, 2999 cc, and producing 300 bhp at 9000 rpm. McLaren hastily adopted a humble Serenissima sports car V8, cutting down the rear chassis horns of 'M2B/2' to accommodate the Italian unit's side exhausts. The 'M166' engine's dimensions were as follows: 91.5 x 57.0 mm, displacing 2996 cc and giving an alleged 350 bhp at 8600 rpm. This gave them their first point-scoring finish, sixth at Brands Hatch, the team then concentrating upon their CanAm sports cars while the Italian V8's actual output was only some 260 bhp.

Three M2Bs had been laid down and two completed, the Serenissima car failing to start after practising in Holland, 'M2B/1' then being prepared with a revised Ford V8 engine fitted with Chrysler 'Hemi' induction tracts coaxing output to some 321 bhp at 9500 rpm for the US and Mexican GPs. Bruce finished fifth on reliability and retired with engine failure respectively, his team's four starts having yielded two finishes, both in the points, though not as securely as it may sound.

McLaren used BRM's new V12 (intended for use in sports cars) in 1967, starting the year with a 2.1 Tasman V8 until the new V12 was ready. The V8 mounted in a Formula 2 McLaren M4A aluminium bathtub monocoque, rigged with extra fuel tankage, known as the M4B — not to be confused with the Trojan-built production McLaren M4Bs for American 'Formula B' racing at that time. The rear of the tub had been cut away to accommodate the V8.

Bruce tackled five races in 'M4B/1', three of them non-Championship; fifth at Oulton Park and Silverstone, fourth for three Championship points at Monaco (for which the little car was admirably suited) and then crashing heavily in the Dutch GP, the car subsequently being burned out when testing.

Through that mid-season Bruce accepted an Eagle team drive and the prototype BRM P101 V12 engine became available enabling the new monocoque M5A to be completed as a runner in time for the Canadian GP in August. Mallite had been abandoned as too complex and heavy in favour of sheet aluminium, the rounded M5A having a fully stressed section enclosing the driver's shins for'ard, leaving the area above his knees open for maintenance. Behind the seat back two rear horns carried the V12, claimed to deliver 370 bhp at 9750 rpm, driving via a Hewland five-speed DG gearbox.

The engine as delivered was a little longer than anticipated, with water pump and distributors encroaching upon the cockpit. To save weight the alternator was omitted. The Varley battery lay on its side under the seat back and the oil tank.

During the Canadian race, the hot oil tank cooked the battery. It was a rainy race and Bruce gained on the leaders before spinning but recovered to run second until the road began to dry. A Lotus 49 retook second place, then the new BRM engine began to misfire as the cooked battery ran flat. Without an alternator to recharge it Bruce had to stop for a fresh battery, finishing seventh.

At Monza, McLaren flew. Having qualified on the front row and with 20 laps to go he and Surtees's Honda were wheel-to-wheel ready for a final dash to the flag when a BRM cylinder liner collapsed. They had found another 19 bhp and both McLaren car and driver shone. But M5A then retired in both the USA and Mexico, the four starts having yielded just that debut finish.

Old 'M5A/1' was driven by new team driver Hulme in South Africa to start the 1968 season, finishing fifth, and subsequently was sold to Bonnier to replace his Cooper-Maserati. The McLaren-BRM was outgunned even in the dry there by the Repco Brabhams supposedly producing 340 bhp. The new Cosworth-Ford DFV now offered customers a minimum 408.

Backed by Gulf Oil sponsorship McLaren had ordered five DFVs and Herd designed a new M7A bathtub aluminium monocoque to match. Shortly afterwards he left to join Cosworth, leaving assistant Gordon Coppuck to complete the new cars.

Chassis 'M7A/1' driven by McLaren and '2 for Hulme made a terrific debut, winning the Race of Champions from pole position and setting fastest lap, 1-3, followed by 1-2 at Silverstone with Hulme winning from pole. He was second in Spain, fifth at Monaco where Bruce crashed '1 heavily, leading up to a sensational Belgian GP where Bruce won after last-lap fuel shortage had felled the leaders.

Hulme won the Italian GP with Bonnier sixth in the M5A-BRM. Hulme and McLaren were then 1-2 in Canada, where Gurney rented 'M7A/3' but retired with overheating, and in the USA Gurney and McLaren placed 4-6 while Hulme crashed 'M7A/2' heavily after a halfshaft broke. The wreck was rebuilt frantically in time for Mexico where the Championships would be decided between Hulme, Stewart and Hill – McLaren, Matra-Cosworth and Lotus.

The rebuilt car's suspension broke early in the race and it crashed again, leaving Bruce to finish second in 'M7A/1'.

In all, the M7s started 29 times that season, 25 of them at Championship level, finishing 20 times, 16 at Championship level, winning five times (three GPs), and taking four seconds, a third, two fourths, two fifths and two sixths.

These simple, competitive cars continued racing throughout 1969 when old 'M7A/1' was sold to South African privateer Basil van Rooyen. Bruce experimented with wide pannier tanks to reproduce the better handling of his sill-tanked CanAm sports cars – and failing. This pannier car was 'M7A/3', also known as model M7B, which Bruce drove in South Africa and at Brands Hatch before taking over the Formula 5000-chassised M7C chassis 'A/4 at Silverstone.

This car featured a tall structural monocoque rear bulkhead rising behind the driver's shoulders, unlike the shallow tubs of the true M7A. Where the production F5000 M10A tub supported its American V8 engines on rear horns, M7C had these horns amputated to provide the conventional Cosworth mounting.

The M7B was sold to Colin Crabbe's Antique Automobiles team for Vic Elford; reaching tenth in Holland, fifth at Clermont, sixth in the British GP and then being written off at the Nürburgring.

McLaren's major effort for the early part of the season involved the hapless M9A four-wheel drive car. It would race only once, in the British GP, being driven by Bell until its suspension collapsed. This Jo Marquardt-designed car was one of the better 1969 4WD cars but like the others it did nothing but absorb time and money.

Tyres were decisive in Formula 1, as Firestone and Dunlop were both ahead of Goodyear (which McLaren used) until the latter rounds of 1969, when the latest G18 and G20 compounds excelled, allowing Hulme to win handsomely in Mexico, racing faithful 'M7A/2' for the 26th time.

McLaren's 1969 F1 record totalled 26 starts, with one victory, one second place, four thirds, four fourths, four fifths, three sixths, a seventh and an eighth comprising their 19 finishes. It

Bruce McLaren himself in his F2-based M4B with 2.1-litre BRM V8 engine at Oulton Park early in 1967. This hybrid special did well before being burned out in a testing incident.

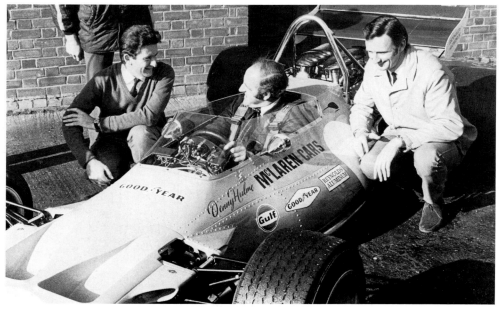

Top: *Denny Hulme winning the 1968 Italian GP at Monza in his wingless M7A, rigged here with a supplementary right-side fuel tank for this long race. These cars initiated McLaren's F1 reputation for outstanding workmanship and preparation.*
Above: *Unveiling the Coke-bottle rising-rate suspension 1971 M19 outside the Colnbrook factory are (l to r) Ralph Bellamy, Denny Hulme and Team Manager Phil Kerr.*

should be noted that although Bruce McLaren finished fourth at Monza, his time was only 0.14 second behind the winner. *That* was a motor race . . .

In January 1970 the expected rear-wheel drive replacement for the now obsolescent M7-series was introduced. Known as the M14A it was improvement by evolution, not revolution. Where the M7s' front suspension had rearward legs demanding extra internal bulkheads within the monocoque sides to provide an anchorage, the M14 front suspension was forward braced to offer both better steering lock and enabling longer fuel tanks to be housed within the tub. The monocoque wrapped round 360 degrees in the scuttle.

Two M14As were built, plus an M14D tailored to accept the Alfa Romeo V8 sports car-based Formula 1 engine which appeared at last, having first been mooted for Cooper in 1968. Alfa's driver de Adamich handled this car and an older M7D tub similarly converted. The McLaren-Alfa never matched the McLaren-Cosworth. Old 'M7A/2' still survived in works hands.

Bruce McLaren was killed in a CanAm car testing accident at Goodwood that June, Gurney replacing him as works driver with Hulme and Gethin. Surtees had bought the M7C, chassis '4, making four starts but never finishing before his own new car made its bow.

Best performances were Hulme's second in South Africa in 'M14A/2', McLaren's second in Spain in '14A/1', while Hulme was third in the British GP, driving 'M14D/1' fitted with a Cosworth in place of the Alfa, third in Germany in his usual 'M14A/2', and third in the same car in Mexico to end this sad season.

For 1971, ex-Brabham designer Ralph Bellamy produced his new 'Coke bottle' monocoque M19A design with geometrical linkage rising-rate suspensions at front and rear. This encountered severe development problems after a promising debut at Kyalami where Hulme led handsomely in chassis '1 until a bolt fell out of its rear suspension with only four laps to run, finishing sixth. In Championship races that season, the two regular cars '1 and '2 carried Hulme to fifth in Spain, fourth at Monaco and 12th at Zandvoort, where the second car emerged for Hulme and where Gethin in 'M19A/1' was 15th though not classified.

Gethin was ninth in France, then Oliver drove '1 for ninth in Austria, and Donohue used it to gain a tardy third place behind Hulme's chassis '2 in Canada. The Donohue car was painted in the Penske team's Sunoco dark-blue and yellow livery; Hobbs was tenth in this car at Watkins Glen,

while Hulme crashed '2. The best showing even in minor races was Hulme's third in the Questor GP at Ontario and after those heady early races the season fell apart.

Bellamy told me: 'The rising-rate suspension offered many theoretical advantages but in practice worked well enough at the front end of the car and less well at the back. Trying to sort it all out and set up the system so the driver felt happy and could understand what was going on proved rather tricky . . .'

Tyre vibration troubled everyone that season; by fitting far stiffer rear springs this was controlled but grip alas then destroyed. Donohue, the master car-developer, came to conclude later in the year that the M19s' problems were more to do with poor wing forms than trick suspension. Irrespective, Bellamy left the team during the 1971/72 winter to return to Brabham, thence to Lotus.

The M19s were modified for 1972, featuring improved wings and conventional rear suspension. Hulme's chassis '2 in new Yardley livery then won at Kyalami, as if in compensation for 1971.

A new lightened 'M19C/1' – ostensibly the last of the series – was completed for Hulme in the Race of Champions. Redman later deputized for new team driver Revson (absent at USAC races in America) and he crashed 'M19A/2' heavily at Clermont after which it was rebuilt around a new tub. The damaged original was subsequently rebuilt as a show car, renumbered 'R4' as a replica. The M19s' best result followed in the Austrian GP with Hulme and Revson 2-3 in pursuit of Fittipaldi's dominant Lotus 72; Hulme in 'C/1 and Revson in the re-chassised simpler and lighter 'A/2. Old 'M19A/1' was reworked with 49 gallons fuel capacity for the 312-mile Rothmans 50,000 *Libre* race at Brands Hatch, Redman finishing second.

Scheckter made his Formula 1 debut in 'A/1 at Watkins Glen. It had been a better year and the M19s would reappear in the early races of 1973 – Hulme and Revson 5-8 in Argentina, third and retired in Brazil and then, while Hulme gave the new M23 its debut in South Africa, Revson and Scheckter placed 2-9. Scheckter finally crashed 'M19C/1' in the minor Brands Hatch meeting, the Coke bottle cars' farewell appearance.

The new M23s' story is detailed on pages 87-93, and it in turn was replaced by the extensively honeycomb-chassised M26 designed by Gordon Coppuck as a lower, lighter, hip-radiator version of the M23. It made its debut during 1976 but was set aside as McLaren concentrated upon its M23s.

Second team driver Mass had given 'M26/1' its race debut at Zandvoort that August, placing ninth, then retired it from the Italian GP. The brief closed season prior to the new 1977 season saw extensive M26 testing. However, McLaren continued to run its faithful M23s until the Spanish GP because as 'M26/1' was being tested by Hunt at Kyalami a bolt on one of the balanced front brake calipers backed out and machined its way through the wheel rim, deflating the tyre and causing a comprehensive accident which virtually wrote off the car.

A new 'M26/2' was ready for Hunt at Jarama but it handled erratically and retired. M23s were raced at Monaco, then the M26 returned at Zolder with revised wings and an oil cooler in a nose duct to improve balance. It was well suited to the constant-radius corners at Anderstorp, qualifying third and running second before a stop for fresh tyres. The M26 was improving with every race and at Dijon Hunt put 'M26/2' on the front row and finished third. The Kyalami-damaged 'M26/1' was rebuilt for Mass to drive at Silverstone, Hunt placed '2 on pole and won luckily after the leading Brabham-Alfa faltered.

Mass ran a new 'M26/3' at Zandvoort, Hunt won again in 'M26/2' at Watkins Glen and was thundered out of the race in Canada by Mass! Poor 'M26/2' was bent severely against a wall. Hunt took over Mass's '3 in Japan and at one stage the two M26s, Mass in '1, ran 1-2 before the German's engine failed and Hunt won comfortably; the third improved; Nichols admits 'we were quite shocked to win at Rio but the engine people really had made big improvements...'.

Rosberg having retired, Stefan Johansson was signed on to run as McLaren's number two to World Champion Prost through 1987. The first three races were good for McLaren, then engine development seemed to lose its way. Between late 1986 and early '87, three successive increases in compression had been made in search of enhanced fuel efficiency. These changes, such as higher-crowned, heavier pistons, needing more rugged gudgeon pins etc, added reciprocating mass high in the unit. Weissach's feeling seems to have been that the increases were insignificant, but their cumulative effect subtly upset the V6's balance. Just pre-Hockenheim Porsche's people re-calculated and re-balanced the crankshafts with the effect seen as Prost dominated, until that alternator drive-belt snapped.

I suspected at the time that something more fundamental had failed, seizing the belt-drive inside so that the belt itself snapped as symptom rather than cause. Not so. MI had previously had an alternator belt snap at Imola – the first for around 100,000 miles' running with the engine, a random failure, 'not significant'. Another then parted in Silverstone testing, and another at Ricard. Now the pulley size was changed to reduce load – only for another belt to part, 'a shattering experience', as Prost led in Germany. A redesigned, new-spec belt was promptly adopted from Gates in the USA... it first ran in Hungary, and appeared to be the cure.

Five of the new MP4/3 tubs were moulded, plus a sixth interim version modified to accept the Honda V6 as a pre-'88 test hack. Two tubs were severely damaged during the Österreichring weekend, one being repaired promptly and the other held in reserve, and when another was dinged at Estoril, the Austrian tub's repair was brought forward. Johansson's Mexican tee-bone then entailed despatching the test-team's chassis to Japan. This was greater damage than MI had experienced since their earliest days with de Cesaris.

MI had very seldom been able to derive much advantage from applying extra boost to the TAG Turbo engine, the penalty in increased back-pressure always negating any gain. The German V6's configuration with non-interlinked cylinder banks required two FISA valves. In 1986 the non-pop-off TAG engine ran just on 3.9-4.0 bar for the first time at Hockenheim when it punched Keke Rosberg onto pole position, but normally it ran out of gain around 3.6-3.7 bar.

For 1987, development at last enabled it to accept more boost, but Bosch's mass air-flow induction sensing used in qualifying to help map race-tune management could be confused by a leak in the system and the twin FISA valves if blown open provided twin leaks in the system! Also, the higher the boost the greater the throttle lag, so particularly for the McLaren-TAG Turbos there was a point where added boost ceased to add useful power, and beyond which lap time improvements fell away. They tried running the pop-offs blown open in testing and saw 4 bar-plus 'but it puts a massive strain on the turbos...'.

In any case McLaren's philosophy, proven many times, has always been to concentrate on race-tune rather than qualifying and 1984-86 this had paid off in spades. Through 1987, there just wasn't quite enough power left in that ageing but now legendary engine as it headed towards honourable retirement.

High points of the season? 'Prost's three wins, 1-3 at Rio, 1-2 at Spa, although admittedly that was somewhat hollow after Williams, Ferrari and Senna's Lotus had all dropped out – but above all Estoril, which was extremely exciting for all of us. It wasn't really a bad season, though inevitably disappointing to have lost both Championships. However – discount the vibration problems and those belt failures and Alain clearly would have been right there, again...'.

Five new MP4/3 cars had appeared, and in them Prost suffered five retirements, was classified

ninth after retirement at Monaco, but won at Rio, Spa and – after an agonizingly long drought by his standards – Estoril to break Jackie Stewart's career record of 27 World Championship-qualifying GP victories. Otherwise his record read 3-3-3-6-15-2-7.

Johansson had quite a torrid time, reaching its nadir in Austria where he was lucky to escape uninjured in a high-speed practice collision – which was more than could be said for his car, and for the unfortunate deer he hit. He failed to finish five times, otherwise placing 3-4-2-7-8-2-7-6-5-3-3. With Prost placing fourth in the Drivers' Championship, Johansson sixth and MI second again to Williams in the Constructors' Cup the Swede was unfortunate to be 'aced out' of his drive by the advent of Ayrton Senna and a Honda engine deal for 1988. But Formula 1 is a hard taskmaster, and anything short of excellence receives short shrift at the top...

Now McLaren International was back in Championship-winning form, as related in Chapters 17-19.

Merzario

The Italian Arturo Merzario was primarily a sports car and road racing ace, but he was also competent in Formula 1. When the offers of drives dried up he promptly built a car of his own based on the old March 751.

This was in 1978, and he attempted to run the complete season with his Merzario A1 specials, chassis '01 and '02. They were very hefty-looking cars, the effect heightened by the spindly Merzario's extraordinarily low driving position, the top of his head barely visible over the high cockpit coaming. He tried wider tracks at Kyalami and had a fright in Long Beach qualifying when the steering column dropped loose. Chassis '02 appeared in Austria, finished in the paddock with revised front suspension and many titanium parts. He qualified for eight of the 16 races but finished none.

Merzario pressed on in 1979, first with his updated A1B then with the new A2 designed in conjunction with his mechanic Simon Hadfield. Neither were proper wing-cars, though by Kyalami the A2 had everything necessary bar the slender tub. A new '03 car appeared at Long Beach which was too fragile to race, and after Merzario fell down the stairs at his workshop and broke his right arm Gianfranco Brancatelli attempted to pre-qualify at Monaco, following the withdrawal of his Kauhsen team. He failed, but Merzario had bought some of the Kauhsen hardware.

For the British GP, the remarkable Merzario

ran the Kauhsen-based A4 co-designed by GianPaolo Dallara of Lamborghini and de Tomaso fame, this being a proper wing-car with single fuel cell behind the cockpit, underwing side pods and slender, high scuttled riveted aluminium monocoque, rocker arm suspensions and outboard brakes, but it was not enough.

At Monza, Merzario became probably the first Grand Prix driver to be sponsored by an undertaker but his hopes had been buried by the season's end. He tackled 14 GPs, non-qualified for 12 of them, and retired in Argentina and Long Beach.

There was no longer a place for 'specials' in modern Formula 1 and the tyre supply situation, with hot 'qualifiers' rationed for the major teams and only 'wooden' tyres left over for the non-FOCA teams, negated the last chance the little men might have had.

Minardi

Giancarlo Minardi had been running various Formula 2 teams for several years when he decided to make the step into Formula 1 for 1985. It was a product more of enthusiasm and available sponsorship than of technical excellence, and team driver would be a wealthy newcomer, former Italian Formula 3 Champion, PierLuigi Martini.

A Giacomo Caliri-designed F3000/F1 car was built by Minardi in their Faenza plant, the prototype being intended for Alfa Romeo V8 turbo power. However, during 1984 Carlo Chiti was dismissed from Alfa Romeo and set up his own Motori Moderni concern to build an all-new turbocharged V6 intended for customer sale à la Cosworth DFV. Inevitably, with Chiti's reputation, there would be few takers, and Minardi emerged as the initial and, for some time, only customer.

Four carbon-composite M85 chassis were built and Chiti's new V6 was not raceworthy in time for the opening races at Rio and Estoril, so chassis 'M85/1's engine mounts were revised and a shorter spacer inserted between engine and gearbox to carry a Cosworth V8 engine without disturbing the designed wheelbase. The car ran near-horizontal rear dampers over the gearbox, and unfortunately looked as hopeless as its driver.

Both its 3-litre races ended in retirement; the new Motori Moderni V6 emerged at Imola after

Must be all that pasta – the hefty-looking Minardi M85B cars of 1986 were powered by the Motori Moderni turbocharged V6, but from this modest beginning the Faenza team would improve. Driver here is Andrea de Cesaris.

PierLuigi Martini's Minardi-Ferrari M191 heading towards fourth place in the 1991 Portuguese GP. Despite this success, the first works team ever to obtain Ferrari customer-spec engines did not, overall, impress.

700 km trouble-free testing, but it proved desperately underpowered and Martini retired again. He failed to qualify at Monaco and in the next 12 GPs retired or crashed nine times, was classified 11th in Germany though not running at the finish, and took the chequered flag 12th in Belgium and eighth and last in Australia. Nevertheless, Minardi announced plans for a two-car team in 1986.

The Italian Formula 2 manufacturer continued in Formula 1 with Motori Moderni V6 turbo engines in 1986, and two regular entries for drivers Andrea de Cesaris and Alessandro Nannini. Nominally, they used chassis 'M185-4' and 'M185-1' and '2 early in the year before one new M186 appeared in Hungary for the final third of the season. A fifth M185 tub was reputedly built up as a replacement race car, taking the plate from 'M185-3' crashed at Monaco and written off. These re-used 1985-season monocoques featured Caliri's preferred method of composite construction, combining carbon/Kevlar inner skins and aluminium outers, sandwiching aluminium honeycomb in between. They were rigid, and perhaps more resistant to penetration damage than contemporary pure carbon-composite mouldings, but they were also rather heavy.

The early-season M185s had smaller fuel tanks, and Mr Ferrari had personally authorized Weber/Marelli to supply Motori Moderni with engine management systems co-developed with Ferrari for Minardi's 12 leased engines. The revised 1985-86 cars featured new front suspension geometry, the upper wishbones were relocated and pullrod linkages had been changed. They were also still overweight. Ex-Ferrari designer Caliri was now joined by Tommaso Carletti ex-Ferrari and Renault, but although the M185s showed competitive midfield form in qualifying Motori Moderni unreliability cost them dear.

De Cesaris failed to qualify at Monaco, retired 14 times and finished eighth in his only finish, at Mexico City. Nannini also failed to make the Monaco grid, retired 13 times, was unclassified at Estoril and 14th in Mexico, where the V6 turbo engine seemed more comfortable at altitude since both cars finished.

Minardi did not have the funds to complete Caliri's latest re-tubbed, all-carbon/Kevlar M186 until Budapest, but the team suffered badly from lack of the necessary funds to pursue a sensible wind tunnel programme. The 10 kg lighter M186's front suspension, lightweight Agusta-cast transaxle and side pod configuration were all used

on the M185s before the new all-composite-tubbed car emerged. Its monocoque was in fact moulded by ATR of Teramo in the Abruzzi, with 195-litre fuel cell and Toleman-type aerodynamic step beneath the nose, although this was soon deleted due to insufficient wind tunnel time to explore its effect.

The carbon/Kevlar-fuselage M186 prototype of 1986 spawned three new, slightly lighter mouldings for '87, clad in lighter bodywork and featuring developed front suspension and five-speed transaxle. The Minardis began the season as the last refuge of metal brake discs in Formula 1, but at Ricard SEP carbon-carbon brakes appeared for the first time, cutting weight to c. 555 kg.

Nannini had become number one driver with Adrian Campos his number two. But Nannini's season record included 14 retirements and his only finishes were 11th in Hungary and Portugal – the latter result merely being official classification after yet another failure to finish. Campos did not start at either Spa or Monte Carlo, he retired 13 times and his only finish of the year was 14th at Jerez.

For its fourth season of Formula 1 in 1988, Giancarlo Minardi's Faenza-based team at last progressed thanks to the acquisition of naturally aspirated Cosworth engines in place of their previous Motori Moderni V6 turbos. They ran a regular two-car team, but regarded the season rightly as an evolutionary period, finding their way into the Cosworth DFZ V8 fold, learning to absorb the British engine's ferocious car-breaking vibration periods and aiming first to qualify in the upper half of the grid, second to secure Championship points. Luis Perez Sala, Campos and PierLuigi Martini drove for the team, Campos losing his drive to the very promising Martini after Montreal.

Five new M188-Cosworth cars were used, co-designed by Caliri and Aldo Costa, and some 12 kg lighter than their turbocharged V6 predecessors, with fuel cells wrapping around the driver on each side. Rear suspension was derived from the M187, while the front suspension was new and novel with torsional damper activating links. 'M188/1' was new for Sala at Rio, '2 for Campos, chassis '3 followed new for Sala at Imola, '4 made its debut in his hands at Ricard and '5 was new for Martini at Estoril.

Campos's brief five-race record read R-16 then three failures to qualify, his last attempt being at Montreal before his replacement by Martini from Detroit where he delighted his team by finishing sixth to secure their first-ever World Championship point! It was a startling return and despite non-qualifying at Hockenheim and Spa and four retirements, he finished four more times, 15-15-13-7. Sala also failed to qualify on the two high-speed circuits at Hockenheim and Spa, and

was too far behind to be classified at Ricard, but he finished seven times, 11-11-13-10-8 (Estoril) 12-15, once more than his retirements. Martini's Detroit point was good enough to place Minardi for the first time in the Constructors' Cup, tenth and last – but it was a breakthrough after years of faithful, relatively shoestring endeavour.

In 1989 Minardi again used Mader-prepared Cosworth engines, by this time the DFR variant, and on ever-improving Pirelli tyres the team showed better form as the season progressed. Ex-Lotus engineer Nigel Couperthwaite joined Aldo Costa in charge of design. Five developed M188B cars started the season, the race cars uprated with new rear suspension featuring dampers mounted on top of the transaxle. These cars were used from Rio to Monaco, followed by definitive Couperthwaite/Costa M189s from Mexico City forward – where numbers '1 and '2 ran, '3 then making its debut driven by Sala at Ricard, '4 written off by him on its debut at Monza and '5 new for Martini at Estoril. Paolo Barilla replaced Martini at Suzuka, retiring in the prototype M189.

These new-generation Minardis featured very slender fuselages in which the fuel load was now concentrated entirely behind the driver, and flanked by long, low side pods. Pushrod suspension was broadly similar to that of the M188Bs but the coil-spring/damper units now mounted within recessed cells above the driver's legs.

Meanwhile Martini failed to finish nine times, but his finishing record was the best yet for the Faenza team – 5-9-9-7-5-6 – his two fifth places being taken in Britain and Portugal, sixth in Australia. Sala failed to qualify four times, had eight DNFs and four finishes – 6-15-8-12 – sixth place at Silverstone making the British GP a real joy day for the Italian cars. They ended the season tenth-equal with Onyx in the Constructors' Cup, on six points.

Early in 1990, Minardi pulled off a terrific coup – or so it appeared at the time – by becoming the first Formula 1 team ever to secure supply of factory Ferrari engines. The arrangement was not to take effect until 1991, but meantime Minardi could run a bye season with interim Cosworth cars effectively filling in time, and showing great dependence upon the competitiveness of Pirelli tyres. Couperthwaite had gone, to be replaced by René Hilrost.

Barilla replaced Sala alongside Martini but he did not impress and was himself replaced by Gianni Morbidelli for the Japanese and Australian GPs ending the season. Chassis M189 '3-'6 were used early in the season, followed from Imola by five new M190s, which were slimmer, lighter and stiffer than their predecessors, and featured upturned noselines, similar to the Tyrrell 018s.

Barilla's poor season included six non-qualifications, a crash at Spa and three retirements. His four finishes read 11-14-12-15 and Jerez saw his final appearance for the team. Martini did not start at Imola, retired eight times and finished seven – 7-9-12-15-11-8-9 – never quite in the points. As Morbidelli retired from both his late-season GPs, Minardi completed this literally pointless interim season, looking forward to greater things with Ferrari V12 power for '91. Their high hopes would be sadly dashed . . .

Minardi's pull with Fiat-Ferrari was based upon driver Martini's strong performances in having out-qualified Ferrari's works entries at Phoenix in 1990 driving an elderly M189. This feat had suitably impressed Fiat boss Gianni Agnelli – opening discussions which led to agreement. Ex-AGS engineer Aldo Costa designed the new M191 chassis with aerodynamicist René Hilrost, but the Ferrari alliance dictated a switch from Pirelli tyres to Goodyear and the old-series, basically 1989-spec '036' V12s supplied for much of the season, without the latest in AGIP fuel brews as available to the works entries, prevented the team from shining. Later in the season 1990-spec '037' V12s showed some improvement, but Minardi was finding it hard to meet Ferrari charges and only six engines were provided for each event.

Martini finished fourth at Imola after front-runners had retired, then on merit at Estoril, otherwise being classified seven times – 9-12-7-9-9-12-13. Morbidelli started 15 races for the team, being classified seven times – 8-7-11-13-9-9-14 before his one-off appearance for Ferrari in Prost's place at Adelaide. His Minardi seat was taken there by Moreno, who finished 16th in the rain-shortened fiasco which passed for a Grand Prix race.

Finances allowed only six Minardi-Ferrari chassis to be built, only five of which (excepting chassis 'M191/2') ran in anger.

Early clutch problems triggered gearbox failures which interrupted the new chassis's planned development. A new aerodynamic underfloor contributed to a considerable mid-season improvement from the French GP forward, and in Portugal late in the season Martini challenged Alesi's works Ferrari fiercely for third place, and finished fourth.

By the end of our period Minardi was in considerable financial difficulty – the future lying in a Lamborghini V12 engine deal, so not looking especially rosy . . .

Onyx

Mike Earle's British-based Onyx team made its name running works-supported March cars in Formula 3000 before aspiring to Formula 1 in 1989. Designer Alan Jenkins – ex-McLaren and Penske – had a growing reputation to enhance and his Cosworth DFR-engined ORE-1 cars emerged as nicely made and handsome machines, though criticized by some for being perhaps overcomplicated. Pushrod-operated front spring/damper units mounted in cells above the driver's feet, while at the rear pushrods acted upon spring/dampers accommodated within guides cast into the casing of a costly six-speed transverse gearbox developed by the X-Trac concern, a daring investment by the new team . . .

Five of these Onyx ORE-1s would be built, chassis '1 and '2 making their bow for Stefan Johansson and Bertrand Gachot to drive at Rio, '3 new for Johansson at Imola, '4 for Gachot at Ricard and '5 for Johansson at Monza. The team was sponsored by Moneytron – a financial body run by a somewhat eccentric but expansive Belgian who would subsequently fall foul of the law. Johansson drove the entire season for Onyx, failing to pre-qualify eight times, retiring from four races but finishing 5-8-3 at Ricard, Spa and Estoril and being disqualified in Montreal. His team-mate for most of this first season was Bertrand Gachot, who failed to pre-qualify for the first six races, then finished 13-12 at Ricard and Silverstone, missed out in official qualifying at Hockenheim and then retired from each of the following three GPs. He was replaced by the Finnish F3 star J. J. Lehto for the last four races, and he then failed to pre-qualify at Estoril and Suzuka, and retired at Jerez and Adelaide. Onyx ended its first Constructors' Championship tenth-equal with Minardi on Johansson's six points.

With the collapse of Moneytron, Onyx found itself in grave jeopardy into 1990, the Swiss enthusiast and prestige car manufacturer Peter Monteverdi taking an interest in the company which kept it going, running barely changed ORE-1 chassis '1 to '6, followed from Imola by the replacement ORE-2 chassis '5, '6 and '7. Neither Johansson nor Lehto could qualify at Phoenix and Interlagos. The Swede left the team, to be replaced at Monteverdi's behest by fellow Swiss Gregor Foitek for the next eight GPs up to the Hungarian event, which proved to be Onyx-Monteverdi's swansong. The team did not appear at Spa for the Belgian race and Monteverdi announced its closure, an alleged outstanding debt of $400,000 to Goodyear merely in tyre charges being much publicised at the time.

Lehto missed out in qualifying at three more events after his early-season DNQs, started five GPs but finished only once, 12th at Imola. Foitek missed qualifying only three times, at Ricard, Silverstone and, like his team-mate, in that final, fatal meeting at the Hungaroring, and his five

Grand Prix starts ended in three retirements, a good-looking seventh (not running at the finish after colliding with Bernard's Lola) at Monaco and 15th in Mexico.

Onyx had campaigned some promising-looking cars but times were hard and the task they had faced proved harder.

Osella

In the 1970s Italian Enzo Osella bought the Abarth company and made a series of small-capacity sports-racing cars which achieved considerable Italian national success; then from 1976 he embarked upon Formula 2, winning three races in 1979 with Cheever driving. Osella and Giorgio Stirano then designed and built a bulky Cosworth-powered FA1 wing-car which initially weighed over 650 kg (1433 lb) but which was trimmed down subsequently, for Cheever. Neither team nor driver had an easy time, failing to qualify four times through 1980 and finishing only once, 12th, with a new FA1B car, at Imola of course!

Two FA1s had been built in Osella's Turin factory, using Ferrari 'Aero' hybrid monocoque construction, with a tubular-steel internal frame stiffened by the aluminium stressed skins. Chassis 'FA1/1' ran most of the season, chassis '2 appearing brand new as Cheever's spare from Monaco. The revised FA1B had a much lighter and 8 cm (3.1 in.) narrower aluminium tub allowing larger-area underwings and Cheever drove this in the last three events.

Osella ran a proper two-car team in 1981. Beppe Gabbiani became regular driver, with a notable string of 12 non-qualifications to his name and he finished not one of the three GPs he did start. Giorgio Francia had one outing, failing to qualify in Spain, PierCarlo Ghinzani two outings, finishing 13th at Zolder after his only qualification. Angel Guerra failed to qualify three times and retired at Imola, before Osella hired the experienced and able Jarier for the last seven GPs, for which he qualified 100 per cent and finished four times – 8-8-10-9.

Two new regulation 'clearance cars' had been built under *Ingegnere* Giorgio Valentini's direction, namely FA1Bs '3 and '4. The prototype 'FA1B/1' was uprated and retained as spare, while a new FA1C model emerged at Monza for Jarier.

This was lighter and stiffer, like an Arrows A3

up front, Brabham BT49 at the rear, and it dispensed with the 'Aero' hybrid structure, using aluminium sheet with honeycomb outer skins for driver protection. It had the shortest wheelbase in Formula 1, its aerodynamic form developed by *Ing.* Beccio in Fiat's Orbassano wind tunnel.

Osella retained Jarier for 1982; he started 13 races, failed to qualify at Monaco and Österreichring, and did not start in Las Vegas. He finished three times, placing 9-4-14, the fourth place being at Imola where there were only a dozen starters due to FOCA's boycott.

A young Italian Formula 2 driver, Riccardo Paletti, was given his Formula 1 chance, but anyone with a Cosworth engine could have only limited hopes in '82 and he failed to qualify five times. He raced in the thin Imola field but failed to start due to a practice accident after qualifying in Detroit. A week later he qualified on the back of the grid at Montreal but at the start he was unsighted by the pack ahead and smashed flatout into the stalled pole-position Ferrari, dying later while 'FA1C/002' was destroyed. This tragedy left Jarier to race alone thereafter.

Osella's season began with FA1Cs '001-2-3, Jarier damaging '001 heavily during Las Vegas practice at the other end of the year, '003 being bent at Detroit in practice and not reappearing, and '004 being Paletti's warm-up crash car at Detroit, repaired for Jarier's use in Montreal and subsequent races.

For the German GP Osella perversely adopted new wide-track rear suspension – odd, because most people tried to run narrow track on the faster circuits to find more speed – and with engine and gearbox undertrays the cars became known as FA1Ds.

Osella persevered into 1983, starting with FA1Ds, updated by Giuseppe Petrotta to conform to flat-bottom rules with very abbreviated hip radiator pods exposing slender forward tub nacelles and numbered as new, awaiting a new Alfa Romeo 1260 V12-engined car in mid-season. This FA1E prototype was actually a Cosworth tub converted for the longer Alfa unit, and it was driven by Ghinzani from Imola onwards, a second FA1E '02 emerging with Alfa power for team-mate Corrado Fabi and a third car following.

These later FA1Es were designed by Tony Southgate and built by a company he had formed with John Thompson, the well-known jobbing monocoque specialist, named Auto Racing Technology Ltd, originally set up to build the aborted Ford C100 endurance cars. Their Osella chassis used a slender aluminium-sided, carbon-topped tub with unusual pushrod front suspension in which the rods fed direct into the feet of coil/dampers mounted high on the scuttle spine, reacting either side of a common mounting.

PierCarlo Ghinzani demonstrating the flat-bottom regulations needleform of Enzo Osella's Southgate-designed FA1E '003' at Kyalami, 1983.

In the early-season Cosworth cars, Fabi posted three non-qualifications and five race retirements, while Ghinzani simply non-qualified in his three Cosworth outings. In the Alfa cars Fabi non-qualified three times more, and his four races included two finishes, 10-11. Ghinzani's Alfa-powered races included five non-qualifications, six retirements and just one finish, 11th at the Österreichring. By this time Autodelta were concentrating upon their 183T turbo V8 engines for the Alfa Romeo 'works' team and the V12 was a forgotten quantity, hardly any better than a decent off-the-shelf Cosworth.

Chassis used were 'FA1D/001' and '002 for Fabi and Ghinzani respectively early in the year, then the Alfa-powered FA1Es '001 from Imola, '002 new for Fabi at Silverstone and '003 new for Ghinzani there.

The Alfa V8 turbo was available to Osella with the prospect of being competitive at last in 1984. Osella actually took over an ACC British-made ex-Alfa Romeo 183T carbon-composite chassised car, slightly remodelled and repainted in their 'Kelémata' sponsor's colours for Ghinzani. He survived an almighty accident in it pre-race at Kyalami, which cannot be said for the car . . .

After 'FA1F/01's demise in this manner, three more 'proper' Osella-Alfa V8s emerged, with design credited to Enzo Osella and Southgate no longer consulting: '02 was new for Ghinzani at Zolder, '03 new at Monaco as team spare and '04 new at Brands Hatch for new team number two Jo Gartner. He had driven old Alfa V12 'FA1E/02' at Imola and retired, then ran the last seven races, retiring four times and finishing 13-5-'16'. The points-scoring fifth place was achieved on Osella's home soil at Monza where the aces ran out of fuel in the closing laps and Gartner was too slow to be that thirsty, despite the Alfa engine being a desperately dypsomaniac unit.

Ghinzani, meanwhile, understandably did not start at Kyalami and failed to qualify at Imola – which stung – but his 14 races yielded five finishes – 12-7-5-9-'7' – his fifth place being at Dallas where the disintegrating state of the track, the heat and fuel economy decimated the field and again the slow Osella survived when most around had not.

For 1985 Osella engineer Nino Petrotta modified the 1984 FA1F chassis '01 and '02 for Ghinzani's lone-entry use as spare and race cars in Rio and Estoril, opening the new season, then introduced his improved FA1G design at Imola. It weighed in at 568 kg, 10 kg lighter than the '1F, with altered aerodynamic form, side radiator and vertical intercooler like a Toleman, a wider front track and now an '85-spec Alfa Romeo V8 turbo engine.

Ghinzani subsequently took the second Toleman driver's seat, making room at Osella for Dutch driver Rothengatter from the German GP.

Both drivers did seven races for the team (based in Volpiano, Turin), Ghinzani failing to qualify at Monaco and Rothengatter at Brands Hatch. The Italian finished three times, the Dutchman only twice; placing respectively 12-9-15 at Rio, Estoril and Ricard, and 9-7 in Austria and – very much on inheritance – in Adelaide.

It was always difficult to understand what a team like Osella could gain from Formula 1, particularly as they were always handicapped by their uncompetitive Pirelli tyres; nevertheless, it has always been good for racing that such teams will contribute colour and quantity, and cheerful enthusiasm.

The little Torinese team struggled through 1986 with its Giuseppe Petrotta-designed FA1F, '1G and '1H cars, powered by the Alfa Romeo 890T turbocharged V8 1.5-litre engine. As part of Enzo Osella's original deal with Alfa Romeo in 1983, he had been supplied with an ex-Euroracing carbon/Kevlar monocoque which provided the basis of Petrotta's first turbo FA1F. That prototype chassis '1 had been destroyed in Ghinzani's Kyalami crash, Osella's 'FA1F-02' – using an aluminium honeycomb-filled carbon/Kevlar fuselage moulding by CMA, *Composite Material Aeronautic* – replacing it and saving some 10 kg weight. CMA was well regarded for its high-quality Renault and Ligier F1 body panelling. Hamstrung by a

virtual petty cash budget, the team had introduced its FA1G development late in 1985, lighter than '1F but still too heavy, its mechanically injected Alfa V8 engine still too thirsty. Petrotta's FA1H was then tailored to the Motori Moderni V6 in the hope of Osella raising sponsorship to afford it. This did not transpire, the car was not readied until Imola '86 and without finance to run Chiti's V6 engines Alfa Romeo came up trumps again, allowing Osella to retain its V8 engines and spares to complete that season.

The one-off Osella FA1H had to be manufactured from the existing FA1G tooling to save expense. Consequently Petrotta simply cut down the top of the fuel cell section to match new 195-litre requirements, handily clearing airflow to the centre of the rear wing. To revise weight distribution the wheelbase was extended 30 mm.

Still Osella attracted drivers with backers prepared to pay for an entry into Formula 1. A two-car programme was prepared for the new season, Ghinzani continuing alongside newcomer Christian Danner. Alfa Romeo's Jofa management system was offered to the team in an attempt to match the new 195-litre fuel capacity to race distance survival, but boost had to be so restricted Osella had no hope of running competitively. Fiscal considerations also meant minimizing qualifying mileage to maximize reliability come the race . . .

Ghinzani failed to qualify at Monaco and did not start at Brands Hatch after destroying the one-off '1H, but his 14 races produced only one meagre finish – 11th in Australia.

Danner drove in the first six GPs, missing out in qualifying at Monaco and retiring each time he started, before moving to Arrows from the Detroit race forward. He was replaced by the Canadian Allen Berg for the last nine races excepting Monza, writing off his FA1H in the start accident at Brands Hatch, not being classified in Australia, retiring four times and otherwise placing 12-13-16. Alex Caffi drove the car at Monza, finishing too far behind to be classified.

Three CMA-moulded FA1Fs were produced, numbered '2-'4. Petrotta moved to Alfa Romeo at the end of the year, Osella recruiting Ignazio Lunetta in his place. Alfa offered some quiet support and for the first time in years proper wind tunnel research and even track testing became feasible for the team. Alfa sold Osella the remaining V8 turbo stock – enough for eight units – at a

price they could afford, the Motori Moderni V6 still being beyond their means. New cam-covers were cast with 'Osella' lettering in place of 'Alfa Romeo' and Lunetta developed a much lighter (c. 540 kg) FA1I car to carry the engine into battle through '87.

Lunetta drew the FA1I in the winter of 1986-87, developing its aerodynamic form with consultant specialist Sergio Beccio in Dallara's moving-floor tunnel facility. But results had to be compromised in order for the new '1I tub to be moulded from the existing tooling modified as much as possible. Lunetta reversed much of Petrotta's thinking, shortening the car to save weight, and replacing Petrotta's rear suspension in which rocker arms and pullrods compressed both ends of the spring/damper units with a conventional pullrod layout.

In 1987 '1F-01 '1G and '1I were used by Gabriele Tarquini, Alex Caffi and Franco Forini, Caffi failing to qualify in Spain and Australia and not starting the GP proper after the green-light collisions in Austria. He retired 12 times and was only classified as a finisher after failure – 12th at Imola. Tarquini appeared just once, in his maiden GP outing, at Imola, and retired, while Forini drove three times, retiring at Monza and Estoril and failing to qualify in Spain.

Osella drew in its horns and confined itself to a one-car entry for the 1988 season, Nicola Larini handling chassis '1I and two new '1L chassis. By mid-season, Enzo Osella himself was readily admitting he had made a grievous error in choosing to continue development of his Alfa-derived F1 turbo engine. The investment in developing the engine to suit 2.5-bar turbo limitations swallowed funds much needed elsewhere. To achieve 600 bhp simply cost a fortune, and there were the 3.5-litre atmo cars running probably 620 minimum . . . it would have made so much more sense to buy Cosworth V8s from England.

Really the tiny team from Volpiano, Turin, had hoped to qualify well on turbo power but desperately late delivery of too many parts knocked them completely out of their planned stride. What should have been new at Rio could not appear until Monaco. Osella remained way behind and off the pace all season. Only their fantastic and praiseworthy enthusiasm kept them going.

Larini only twice failed to pre-qualify – at Budapest and Adelaide – but he fell at the next hurdle – qualifying – at Rio, Mexico City and Montreal. The new '1L car then failed scrutineering amongst much arm-waving on home soil at Imola!

FISA's regulation dispensation that season enabled last-year turbo teams to run existing chassis without the requirement to have their foot pedals drawn back behind the front axle line to enhance driver safety, a regulation enforced for all atmo cars and any new-build turbos. Osella's new ex-Ferrari engineering director – *Ing.* Antonio Tomaini – had altered the existing tub mould yet again to lower the fuel cell, and the scrutineers also considered the engine mounts and other details had been so altered the FA1L should be considered a new design. Consequently, with its foot pedals still ahead of the front axle line, it was unacceptable. Osella felt sore that the rival Rial had been permitted to run at Rio with an illegal oil cooler mounting, but with minimum further fuss sought a clarification of the regulations from FISA, to which the car was subsequently modified, its 1987 fuel cell and engine mounts both being reinstated.

Larini's ten GPs of the season finally resulted in seven retirements and a 9-19*-12 finishing record.

For 1989 Osella returned to running a full two-car team for Ghinzani and Larini, using FA1I-89 chassis '4-6, three cars in all, new Cosworth DFR V8-engined machines designed by Tomaini and by some way the neatest F1 Osellas yet seen. Side pods were short and compact, front dampers were mounted at driver's thigh level within the cockpit actuated by pullrods and a linkage system and the rear dampers were sited alarmingly close to the engine exhausts, demanding neat NACA ducts on the engine cover to cool them. Despite

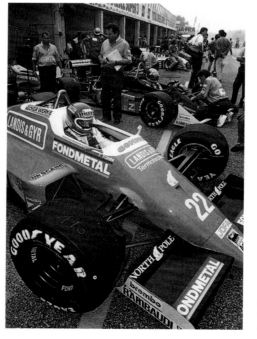

Osella on home soil – Franco Forini making his F1 debut in the Alfa Romeo 185T turbo-engined FA1I at Monza, Italian GP, 1987. He qualified last and retired with turbo failure.

their attractive looks, Ghinzani still failed to pre-qualify the cars 13 times, retiring from his only two GP starts, in Hungary and at Jerez. Larini missed out seven times in pre-qualifying, was disqualified at Rio, excluded at Estoril and retired from six events, only being classified 12th at Imola.

In 1990 it was back to a one-car team, the driver being Olivier Grouillard, using chassis FA1L '05 and '06, replaced by Tomaini's latest FA1Me – after sponsor Fondmetal – chassis '08 and '09 – two cars – from Imola. They were noted essentially for having their front suspension spring/dampers now mounted on top of the monocoque rather than longitudinally each side of the cockpit. Side pod form was taller and shorter than hitherto, but the DFR rear end was identical to the FA1Ls'.

Grouillard continued to struggle – being bumped from the GP grids twice in pre-qualifying, five times at the next hurdle, and retiring from five of his nine Grand Prix starts. His finishing record read 13-19-16-13. But still the little team struggled on, adopting the Fomet name for 1991 . . . see page 272.

Parnelli

Serbo-American Velco Miletich, together with his former Indianapolis-winning USAC Champion driver friend Rufus Parnelli Jones, had formed Vel's Parnelli Jones Racing in 1969 after the track Champion's retirement from driving. They were very successful in USAC and also embraced drag racing, Formula 5000 and even off-road events like the Baja classic. They were heavily backed by Firestone tyres and for 1974 decided to enter Formula 1 by building a Firestone-shod car to be driven by Andretti.

This was a natural step, for VPJ had a number of ex-Team Lotus Formula 1 personnel who would include Chief Engineer Maurice Phillippe, Crew Chief Dick Scammell and Team Administrator Andrew Ferguson.

Their new Formula 1 Parnelli VPJ4 was a development of Phillippe's work on the Lotus 72; wedge-form, hip radiators alongside its Cosworth engine, rearward weight bias, torsion bar suspension and all-inboard brakes. The debut of the car (carrying Viceroy cigarettes livery) came in the late-1974 Canadian GP, where Andretti finished seventh. It also qualified third quickest at Watkins Glen, only for an electrical problem to intrude at the start.

The sophisticated new car showed great promise but Firestone abruptly withdrew from racing, leaving Vel's Parnelli to rely on outdated stock tyres for 1975, without hope of competitive devel-

opment. Worse, Jones had no interest in Formula 1 and was not carried along by Miletich's enthusiasm.

Andretti began the new season in Argentina with 'VPJ4/002' on Firestones, but for the second race in Brazil it was Goodyear-shod. He placed third in 'Team USA's entry in the minor Silverstone race and led the Spanish GP in '002 after the field had been decimated by an early collision. Sadly his car had also been damaged in that shunt and as its rear suspension progressively failed he eventually crashed. He missed the Belgian race (away at Indianapolis) and the Dutch GP; his 12 Championship outings saw four proper finishes, 7-4-6-12, which was not bad, all things considered . . .

His consecutive fourth- and sixth-place points scores came in the Swedish and French GPs. He had shunted '001 during practice in Sweden, new noses were tried in France and outboard front brakes appeared at the Nürburgring to load up the latest-generation Goodyear tyres – the same problem afflicting the 'genuine' Lotus 72s at that time. Chassis '001 was also on outboard brakes at Monza, and one of the two cars at Watkins Glen ran coil-spring rear suspension in place of torsion bar, so curing a much-criticized tendency to spin the inside wheel under power. Andretti had driven '002 in early-season races until new car '003 appeared at Monaco, then took charge of '001 in the French and British GPs, '002 at the Nürburgring, '003 in Austria, '001 in Italy, '002 in the USA. But his team owners had quite lost interest: winning was not easy, there was minimal return and they had other business problems in the USA.

Early in 1976 Andretti carried the project on his shoulders, while young English ex-McLaren designer John Barnard did what work he could on the car. Chassis 'VPJ4B/002' appeared with coil-spring suspension all round and redesigned rear bodywork to finish sixth at Kyalami. The same chassis, with '75-style rear body, shorter nose and 'All American Racing Wheels' lettering, retired at Long Beach. Vel's Parnelli abandoned Formula 1 thereafter, and the team was disbanded.

Only the crew and that beautiful car would be missed, and Andretti was outspokenly bitter at this wasted opportunity.

Pearce

Wheeler-dealer J. A. Pearce, based in Southall, West London, was a skilled welder who had built Chris Lawrence's Deep Sanderson chassis, before emerging as head of a considerable wheel and tyre and motor trading business. He built a Formula 1 Cooper-Ferrari 250 GT V12 special in 1966 which

Mario Andretti in the Vel's Parnelli Jones VPJ4 in the 1975 French GP at Ricard, showing off the car's Maurice Phillippe-originated Lotus 72-derived lines and far rearward hip radiator pods.

Lawrence raced for him. Following this relative success – it earned some start money – Pearce manufactured two new Formula 1 spaceframe chassis to be powered by the Martin V8 engine, manufactured by Ted Martin's tiny engineering and tuning workshop in Haddenham, Buckinghamshire.

Most of the circuit development for this two-cam light-alloy V8 had been done by Roy Thomas of Lucas Engineering. This Formula 2 team fitted one in a Lotus 35 F2 chassis, which was raced at Mallory Park on Boxing Day 1966, driven by Roy Pike and finishing third. Courage then drove it at Brands Hatch in March 1967 but an overnight head change had been botched and a rocker bent as it was started just before the race, forcing it to non-start. Sadly Courage then crashed heavily in Snetterton testing and it was seen no more.

Meanwhile, the prototype Pearce Formula 1 chassis had been exhibited at the London Racing Car Show, for which the Ferrari engine from the older, heavier Cooper had been earmarked. However, three more compact cars were to be built, only two of which were ever completed, tailored to the more compact Martin V8. Lawrence lapped the Brands Hatch short circuit in the 52 second bracket in an early test, only to crash heavily, severely damaging the prototype car. The two complete Pearce-Martins and the old Cooper-Ferrari, all in the team's metallic pale-green colours, were in the team transporter parked at Silverstone on the Wednesday before the International Trophy meeting when the vehicle caught fire. Everything was totally destroyed.

Penske

The patrician Philadelphian businessman Roger Penske made his name in SCCA sports car racing in the early Sixties, before concentrating his sporting interests upon running CanAm, long-distance sports, TransAm and Indycars, mainly for the very accomplished engineer-driver Mark Donohue.

After winning the 1972 CanAm Championship in his Penske-entered turbocharged Porsche 917/30, Donohue retired from driving. During 1974, however, Penske laid plans to enter Formula 1 and Donohue was tempted back into the cockpit.

Penske appreciated that he could not tackle Formula 1 from a US base, and he took over the former McRae Formula 5000 workshops in Poole,

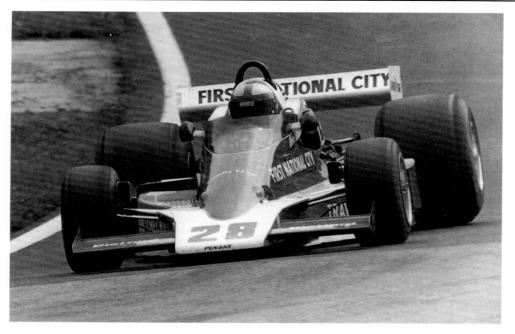

John Watson's drive in the Penske PC4 here at the Österreichring in 1976 cost him his beard, as he won! All Penske cars have been beautifully built and prepared, and this Formula 1 winner was no exception.

Dorset, on the south coast of England, to have his cars designed, built and prepared. Even after his Formula 1 team's eventual demise, this facility would continue to produce highly successful Penske track racing cars for years to come.

The prototype Penske PC1 made its debut in the 1974 Canadian GP at Mosport Park. It was designed by former Brabham draughtsman Geoff Ferris, featuring a very clean wedge profile with hip radiators. Front suspension had semi-inboard springs actuated by rocker arms extending from large planform faired-in fabricated top links, parallel links were used at the rear and there was talk of fitting cockpit-adjustable anti-roll bars for 1975, as planned by March in 1972 but not used.

Donohue easily qualified for the race and finished 11th, then retired from the US GP.

For 1975, a second PC1 was completed, with a wider track than '01, new rocker arm inboard front suspension and modified airbox and wing. Donohue was seventh in Argentina but retired in Brazil with handling problems.

The PC1 was not really competitive and Donohue was unhappy with both his own form and the car's. He was a distant eighth at Kyalami where 'PC1-02' ran a 3 in. wider rear track and 5 in. spacer between engine and gearbox, lengthening its wheelbase. He crashed at Brands Hatch but was sixth at Silverstone.

Some progress was clearly being made but then Donohue crashed at Barcelona. At Monte Carlo, where '01 ran a 5 in. narrower front track and short wheelbase for the tight circuit, he crashed heavily yet again in practice. Nevertheless, it was rebuilt in time to race once more uncompetitively, finishing 11th.

The Swedish GP saw a decent result at last, Donohue reaching fifth to gain his first two Championship points. A new chassis '3 appeared at Zandvoort in narrow-track form, but eighth place there and retirement with driveshaft joint failure in France convinced Penske – used to success – to cut his losses in the short term by dropping the PC1 and trying a March 751 customer car instead.

One of the works 751s was tested by Donohue at Silverstone, instantly some two seconds per lap quicker than the PC1, so a brand new Penske March was built up. Donohue crashed fatally due to a front tyre failure on race morning at the Österreichring in August.

After the March's destruction, Penske missed the Italian GP but Ferris was joined at Poole by the team's American engineer Don Cox and between them they developed a new PC3 design based on the March, though the PC3 retained the successful PC1 rear end and Hewland FGA gearbox unlike March's preferred FG.

When questioned on the PC3's similarity to the March 751, team manager Heinz Hofer remarked sagely: 'When you don't know the neighbourhood, you don't stray many streets away from home . . .'

New team driver Watson qualified 'PC3-01' safely in mid-field at Watkins Glen, but a severe misfire on the warm-up lap caused the PC1 prototype to be hastily substituted. Watson's reliable ninth came as a surprise, because the car had not been race-prepared, having been merely a sponsor's display-piece in the paddock.

This was the prelude to a much better year for Penske's Formula 1 hopes in 1976, with Watson starting 16 races, 15 of them Championship rounds, and finishing 11 of them. Three PC3 chassis were built and results included fifth at Kyalami in chassis '1, while Watson crashed '02 in the minor Brands Hatch meeting, was seventh in Belgium and 10th in Monaco in '01. The PC3 still wasn't quite 'there'.

A new PC4 appeared at Anderstorp in June, but its throttles jammed open on the first lap and it crashed. This machine had a very low-built tapered-planform monocoque. Its Ferrari-like nose wing used in Sweden was replaced by a slim chisel affair with side fins for the next race at Ricard, where a longer wheelbase was used. PC4 featured in-line hip-mounted radiators and a very slim and neat cockpit surround and engine cover, intake ducts for the engine induction being moulded into its shoulders.

It proved fundamentally better than the PC3s. Watson was third at Ricard – only to be disqualified because the leading edge of the rear wing side plates proved to be a centimetre above the legal maximum height, the whole assembly having bent backwards on its mounting during the race.

Repositioned oil coolers improved balance for Brands Hatch, Watson finishing fourth, then seventh in Germany and winning on merit after qualifying on the front row in Austria.

In Holland, Watson qualified on the second row and duelled for the lead until gearbox trouble intervened. Local driver Boy Hayje rented old 'PC3-02' there but suffered driveshaft failure. In the US GP, Watson finished sixth and in Japan qualified on row two but retired with engine failure.

Chassis 'PC4-02' had been raced in Canada and the US and was then returned to Poole for stripdown while only '01 went to Japan. Penske had decided to withdraw from Formula 1 and concentrate upon American track racing, which promised a better return. The Penske PC4 cars were bought by Hans Gunther Schmid for his ATS

team's Formula 1 programme in 1977 (see page 222), while the old PC3s went into other hands.

Pilbeam

See entry for LEC, page 278.

RAM

John MacDonald and Mick Ralph's RAM team entered Formula 1 with immaculately prepared Brabham and March cars from 1976, but they were run for no-hoper drivers and achieved nothing significant. RAM persevered regardless, always with support from FOCA supremo Bernard Ecclestone, who is generally very good to the smaller teams. In 1981 they brought March back into Formula 1 and then began building their own cars for 1983.

Initially they retained the March name for their Dave Kelly-designed Cosworth-engined RAM model 01. Three such chassis were built, '01-2-3 of course, and they were campaigned through that season by drivers Salazar, Jean-Louis Schlesser, Jacques Villeneuve and Kenny Acheson.

They achieved little. Schlesser placed sixth (second to last) in the minor Race of Champions at Brands Hatch in '02's debut, Salazar was 15th in '01 at Rio and Acheson 12th at Kyalami to end the season. They failed to qualify 12 times, their car simply not up to the job.

For 1984, however, MacDonald obtained Hart 415T four-cylinder turbo engines as proven by Toleman, and the still impecunious team converted RAM '01/01' from Cosworth to Hart power as a pilot exercise while new carbon-composite chassised RAM 02 cars were built.

The prototype RAM '02/01' made its bow at Rio driven by Philippe Alliot, hybrid '01/03' running there for his team-mate Jonathan Palmer. Alliot drove '02/01' regularly until effectively writing it off in Dallas practice and therefore non-started in the race. RAM '02/02' was new for Palmer at Zolder, crashed heavily following a chassis failure thereby stopping the British GP at Brands Hatch, and was then rebuilt for the final races of the season.

RAM '02/03' made its debut in the British GP for Alliot and was badly bent by a multiple accident – with little blame attaching to its unfortunate driver – within its first mile of racing there.

After its Dallas wounds had been repaired, '02/01' re-emerged as '02/04' in time for Alliot to race again in Austria.

The sum total of this demanding and fraught season included 13 starts for Alliot yielding only three finishes, 10-11-11, and 14 starts for Palmer, with six finishes, 8-10-9-13-9-10, which impressed nobody, unlike the preparation of these pretty little cars. Alliot failed to qualify twice and was unable to start after the Dallas crash, while Palmer failed to qualify only once but too often proved a baulky back-marker when the leaders were lapping him. Mike Thackwell qualified for his lone race with the team in Montreal, but failed to finish.

RAM Automotive girded its loins and prepared regardless for 1985 . . .

For 1985, RAM produced four new 03-series carbon-monocoque cars designed by Gustav Brunner, but they suffered a desperately uncompetitive and unhappy season culminating in dire financial straits and missing the last two races, which left the Oxfordshire team in jeopardy.

Initially, two new Hart-powered 03s were ready for drivers Alliot and Winkelhock in Rio, chassis '3 being introduced for the German at Imola, and '4 for him at Silverstone. Tragically he would be killed in a Canadian Group C endurance race and his death seemed to sap team morale even more than their dreadful reliability and accident record.

Alliot did 13 races for the team, failing to qualify at Monaco; RAM opted out of Kyalami and Adelaide at season's end. He finished only once: eighth in the 03's Rio debut.

Poor Winkelhock started eight GPs, also failed

to qualify at Monaco, was unclassified in Portugal but finished 13th at R o and 12th at Ricard.

Kenny Acheson took his place for Austria, Monza and Zandvoort retiring at the former races and failing to qualify in Holland.

By the end of 1985 the indefatigable RAM team had lost its sponsor (Skoal chewing tobacco) and the future of the now-uncompetitive Hart engine itself seemed in doubt. They were heading into the dark . . .

Rebaque

Wealthy Mexican privateer Hector Rebaque bought Lotus 78s and a 79 from Team Lotus and ran them with variable success into 1979. The cars were always immaculately prepared for him by Ian Dawson's organization but Lotus had little in the way of spares and less development to offer as 1979 progressed.

Rebaque normally raced his 79 with the 78 as spare, but at Zandvoort for the Dutch GP a new Lotus 79 clone was delivered on the Mexican's transporter as spare car. It was the Rebaque HR100, chassis '01', using a Lotus-like slender tub flanked by Williams-copy side pods and skirts, with modified suspension, a water radiator in the right-hand side pod and oil coolers for engine and gearbox in the left.

Design and construction was by Penske Racing at Poole, Dorset, the project supervised by Geoff Ferris and Derrick Walker. Rebaque talked of a second all-new design which would appear for 1980.

He drove HR100 at Monza but failed to qualify, then made the race in Canada only for the engine mounting to fail. He failed to qualify at Watkins Glen, the season ended and through the following winter, after John Barnard had tried briefly to help the team, the project was shelved. Rebaque drove the number two works Brabham in the last seven GPs of 1980 and nothing more would be heard of the first, and so far the last, Mexican Formula 1 car.

Renault

The nationalized French *Régie* Renault became the largest motor manufacturer involved in Formula 1 when they took the brave decision to enter the first 1500 cc turbocharged contender, in 1977. Renault had a long competition involvement behind them, notably with Amédée Gordini's engine development programmes and with Jean Redelé's Dieppe-based Alpine concern.

Once the *Régie*'s chief executive Bernard Hanon authorized Formula 1 research, an experimental Alpine *Laboratoire* single-seater was built at Dieppe, designed by André de Cortanze. Aerodynamicist Marcel Hubert developed a sleek body with Ferrari-like full-width nose wing, while the sheet aluminium tub itself was slab-sided Coke bottle in planform, carrying in-line hip radiators either side of its engine bay.

At the Gordini workshops, technical head François Castaing with Bernard Dudot and Jean-Pierre Boudy developed a turbocharged version of their existing essentially 2-litre Formula 2 and sports-racing V6 engine (see pages 210-11).

Michelin had achieved considerable competition success with Renault and Alpine and now decided to support their Formula 1 venture, so as to promote their radial-ply tyre technology internationally and steal some of Goodyear's glory. Consequently, the *Laboratoire* Alpine Type A500 turned a wheel for the first time on Michelin's Ladoux test track near Clermont-Ferrand on 21 May 1976. Works F2 and sports car driver Jabouille ran an extensive A500 turbo test programme that summer, and approval was given to go racing in 1977.

Meanwhile, in April '76, Alpine had been absorbed as a Renault subsidiary, while Renault Sport was founded to handle the *Régie*'s wide-ranging competition interests, run by ex-driver Gérard Larrousse. Renault-Gordini at Viry-Châtillon, south of Paris, would prepare the new Formula 1 car and develop its turbocharged engine.

Renault announced their Formula 1 plans in December 1976; but the finalized car itself would not appear until the following May.

This yellow-liveried Renault RS01 was neatly packaged, reminiscent of the Formula 2 Alpines, its Hubert body remodelled and developed from its A500 basis in the St Cyr wind tunnel. The aluminium tub was folded from two large alloy panels, stiffened by internal steel strap plates. It was designed as a simple car, minimizing potential chassis problems to enable engine and tyre development to proceed unhindered. Turbocharger plumbing was neater than on the A500 jury rig, and included a block-type intercooler nestled between engine and rear of the tub to cool the boost charge between turbo compressor and the induction 'log' on top of the engine. Oil and water radiators by Chausson were slung in-line just ahead of the rear wheels, and transmission was via a six-speed Hewland FGA400 gearbox. Bodywork was elegantly styled, made by Moch in moulded Kevlar.

The new car's debut came on 16 July 1977, at Silverstone, which was well suited to the characteristics of the turbo engine. A maiden outing public failure in France would have been hard to justify and in some respects Renault still had more to lose than gain by participation, for they could only be beaten by far smaller concerns.

Jabouille qualified 21st and retired early after the induction manifold split, venting boost to atmosphere and leaving him with a simple low-compression 1500 in a 3-litre race.

After a break for further development, Jabouille ran in four more GPs that season – Holland, Italy, the USA and Canada, failing to qualify in Canada and never finishing.

Renault Sport were still trying to win Le Mans with their turbocharged sports-prototype cars so their 1978 Formula 1 effort was still confined to a single car for Jabouille, commencing in South Africa after ignoring the South American overture. Jabouille normally drove 'RS01/2', racing '3 instead only at Long Beach and Zolder. The car's qualifying record reads 6-13-12-10-11-10-11-12-9-3-9-3-9-22 as development progressed – note the late season improvement after Le Mans.

It was of course most at home on fast circuits, and at altitude as at Kyalami. The first finish came at Monaco, tenth, but in France the engine failed after one lap. At Watkins Glen, Jabouille finished fourth to score Renault's first points, then in Canada he was only 12th but reliability was improving. In all the RS01s made 14 starts, being classified as a finisher five times.

At Kyalami, revised bodywork placed the oil cooler in a nose duct and Jabouille did few laps at

Turbocharged monocoque tubs had to be strong. Renault's primitive-looking heavily riveted early-series chassis is under assembly at Viry-Châtillon in December 1979. In the preceding season the Régie's team at last came good and proved that turbocharged 1500 cc engines were essential in Formula 1.

René Arnoux's RS12 in the rain at Watkins Glen, 1979, demonstrating the shape of French Formula 1 thinking at that time, the turbo engine pulling big wings plus sliding-skirted ground-effect loads.

full speed. When he did, he was quick. At Long Beach, an old-style airbox had been attached just to cool the single large Garrett turbocharger, while mixture adjustments had unlocked more power. One early problem had been overheating the left-rear brake caliper, simply because it was close by the turbo. For the Monaco race, Jabouille made the best of his Michelin tyres and good brakes, despite the low-revving engine keeping him busy on the gears, and achieved 12th on the grid by a fine effort.

Jabouille was fifth fastest in first qualifying at Anderstorp, looking more stable than the Ferraris on the same tyres, but his final practice was spoiled by engine problems in one car and a flat battery in the spare. In France he said: 'Throttle response, power, everything has to be better before I can challenge for the front row . . .' It would come . . . However, the RS01s were encouragingly less destructive of their tyres than the Ferrari 'T3s.

In qualifying at Hockenheim, the radiators were packed with ice to combat hot weather, and in Austria a new water-cooled intercooler was introduced. Jabouille tested his two cars back to back, one with water intercooling, the other without, and the new system was consistently faster as the engine no longer lost power when it got hot.

At Monza many drivers were shaken by the Renault's straightline speed. Villeneuve reported, 'It's incredible, it passed me on the straight like you can't believe. It must be 10 km/h faster than anything else here.' Both Renaults there were fitted with improved intercoolers and new pistons and rings.

But the season ended mutedly in Canada where Jabouille only just made the grid after rain prevented him setting up the chassis adequately, then finding himself with pick-up problems out of the slow corners. Renault Sport still lacked race-wise experience compared to their rivals, most of whom expected to set up their cars fairly accurately in the factory before revisiting a circuit.

Now Renault made their serious debut in Formula 1 with a proper two-car team for 1979, Arnoux joining the veteran Jabouille, who now had by far the most experience of turbocharged engines of any road racing driver in the world.

Chassis designer Michel Tétu, previously with Ligier, completed a new RS10 ground-effect car in time for the Spanish GP, featuring a slender aluminium centre monocoque, extensively top-louvred side pods and an elegantly designed rear wing supported on curvaceous end plates.

Spain followed a disappointment at Long Beach where Arnoux's 'RS01/3' broke a driveshaft on race morning after Jabouille had crashed at 170 mph following a similar practice failure. Rather than risk a repetition, team manager Jean Sage wisely withdrew from the race.

Both drivers were equipped with RS10-series wing-cars for Monaco, but Renault changed their system so that while 'RS10' was driven by Arnoux, Jabouille's broadly similar sister car was chassis 'RS11'. It was slightly lighter with a new front wing and other detail changes. Both cars used twin KKK turbochargers, one per bank instead of relying upon a single large 'charger feeding both banks. This greatly improved both throttle response and mid-range punch; at last the Renaults were to become competitive and could set new standards. After Monaco there was a month's break before the French GP at Dijon-Prenois.

During this hiatus a general tyre test session was held at Dijon, during which Harvey Postlethwaite of the Wolf team was watching a speed trap on the top straight, while a Renault was running.

'I'll never forget it', he says. 'Suddenly it read out a speed about 20 mph faster than anything we'd ever seen before . . . That was it, the Renault was coming good. Soon we would all need turbos . . .'

In 1977 at Dijon Andretti had taken pole in the Lotus 78 at 1;12.21; now, two years later, Jabouille took it in 'RS11' at 1;07.19, while Arnoux in the new 'RS12' qualified alongside him to make it a bright-yellow Renault turbo front row.

In Monaco their intercoolers had leaked, here at Dijon they were strengthened and Sage and his men merely hoped for a cool race day; they got it, Jabouille winning while only Villeneuve's combative driving in the Ferrari could bundle Arnoux back into third place for a 1-3 finish, Arnoux setting fastest lap.

Jabouille qualified on the front row at Silverstone but misfortune and mismanagement wrecked his race before a valve-spring failed while Arnoux finished second in 'RS12'. The Renaults were on pole for the next four races in Europe, but rather fell off the tightrope in North America where their only finish was Arnoux's second at Watkins Glen. In Italy it was an all-Renault front row, which mightily concentrated Ferrari's mind on turbocharger plans for 1980-81! But reliability continued to handicap the *Régie*'s team.

A fourth wing-car, 'RS14', ran in North America. Water-spray brake cooling was employed at Montreal for that circuit was very hard on brakes

and the turbo engine's relative lack of overrun braking gave the brakes a hard time. At Watkins Glen where the weather was cold and wet the Renaults, traditionally light on Michelin's rubber, were unable to heat the tyres adequately and grip was lacking.

Renault Sport ended this first successful Formula 1 season with a record of 28 starts in 14 GPs – discounting the non-starts in Long Beach – and they finished only eight times, the 1-3 in France backed by seconds in Britain and the USA, sixth in Austria and one each 8-9-10. They did not finish in the Dutch, Italian and Canadian GPs, making it a fruitless autumn; reliability was still poor.

For 1980 Renault devoted a massive budget to their World Championship quest, and began brilliantly with Arnoux winning in Brazil and South Africa – both times thanks in part to team-mate Jabouille's grotesque misfortune when leading – but fortunes declined as the season progressed. Michelin tyres caused some headaches and a bad batch of valve-springs ruined mid-season, while Jabouille's sole reward in a season of disappointment and frustration came when he won in Austria. Arnoux had performed brilliantly in practice at Long Beach, Zolder and Ricard.

A new RE20 chassis design emerged, featuring improved new side pods, new skirt system, gearbox spacer, new intercoolers and a modified cooling system. The 'RE' signified 'Renault-Elf' in honour of the main external sponsor.

In Argentina the team ran new car 'RE22' for Jabouille, '21 for Arnoux with '20 spare. In Brazil victory should have been Jabouille's but for a broken turbo; in South Africa the cars featured cable clutch linkage for the first time, lighter and more sensitive in operation, and while a puncture deprived Jabouille of victory, Arnoux won again in 'RE21'.

For Long Beach, Arnoux had a new 'RE24' fitted with Italian Brembo brakes, Jabouille's '23 featured integral bodywork around the tail and a wider rear track in search of improved traction. The spare 'RE22' had hydraulic servo brakes, tested by Arnoux as a continuation of a Ricard test programme. But the Brembos were dropped due to disc cracking, AP Lockheed being used instead. Further brake problems handicapped their race.

For Zolder, larger discs and bigger Girling instead of Lockheed calipers were tried, necessitating 15 in. instead of 13 in. diameter front wheels. Jabouille's clutch broke at the start and Arnoux finished fourth. Monaco did not smile on the *Régie*, while the FOCA/FISA battle saw the Spanish GP run without 'Grandee' team participation, Renault being one to opt out.

Michelin's tyres did not work well in France and engines began breaking; at Brands Hatch a big new rear wing appeared, proof of the power the French V6 turbos could now afford in search of download. A new 'RE25' emerged at Hockenheim, driven by Arnoux, but both cars there were sidelined by valve-spring failures. Some weight was saved by lighter carbon-fibre side pod end plates on both cars.

For the Italian GP at Imola, brakes would again be crucial and different types of standard discs, AP ventilated discs and special brake pads were tested. Large cooling ducts were fitted, and there was also a new engine cover on each car. In Canada, Jabouille crashed 'RE23' very heavily, injuring his legs, and Arnoux was left to run alone at Watkins Glen in 'RE25', finishing seventh after a skirt had broken and thereby diminished download.

Through 1980, the Renaults had made 27 starts, being classified as finishers 12 times, winning three GPs, placing second (Arnoux in Holland), fourth (Arnoux in Belgium) and fifth (Arnoux again, in France), which was little concrete result compared to their five pole positions and three fastest laps. The two Renaults had filled the front row at Kyalami early in the season, then consecutively in the Austrian, Dutch and Italian GPs in the autumn.

Now they were provenly competitive, Renault looked seriously towards 1981 as being their sea-

Above: A new tub form for Renault in the 1981 Belgian GP where Michel Tétu's simplified, lighter RE30 made its unfortunate debut, Arnoux failing to qualify.

son. Sliding skirts which had enabled the Cosworth teams to maintain competitiveness against the turbos had been banned, power would surely tell. However, FISA's variable rulings embarrassed Renault Sport just as seriously as any of the British teams.

Renault set out with the long-wheelbase RE20B models, developed from the 1980 RE20 to run without sliding skirts while the new RE30 design, tailor-made for the new regulations, was being completed. Renault would have been happy to continue with skirted ground-effect side pods to harness their power, but in the first fixed-skirt 'clearance car' races Brabham introduced their hydropneumatic suspension lowering devices. Renault felt certain FISA would ban such a ploy but in April it was declared legal, and Renault were horrified.

Now the cars could run fixed skirts against the ground, the new RE30 had been tailored as an unskirted car and they were instantly behind the field.

They ignored FOCA's unofficial sliding-skirt South African GP, testing at Ricard instead with enlarged side pods and even bigger front and rear wings. Chassis 'RE26B' was driven by Jabouille's replacement, Prost, and 'RE27B' was used by Arnoux without success at Long Beach.

In Brazil, the servo-assisted brakes gave trouble, contributing to practice incidents, and the system was removed from the race cars, both having suffered race collisions. A new monocoque was flown out to Buenos Aires to replace Arnoux's damaged tub. The cars were fast but the Brabhams were faster; Prost and Arnoux placed 3-5 on reliability but both were troubled by vibration due to a flat-spotted tyre and imperfect wheel rims.

Where the RE20 had been a simple development of the original RS10, the new RE30 marked a new beginning for Renault Sport. Michel Tétu had to save chassis weight to compensate for the extra poundage of turbocharger ancillaries such as the intercoolers and increased fuel load. Where there had been five fabricated bulkheads in the RE20, there were three machined castings and two fabricated bulkheads in the RE30. The latter was still aluminium skinned since Renault fought shy of carbon-composites, mistrusting their impact resistance. The RE30 also featured lighter bodywork, with a new gearbox enclosing FG400 internals in a Renault casing which incorporated the oil tank (formerly located in the spacer between engine and gearbox, which had now been dis-

pensed with). The wheelbase was 13 cm (5.2 in.) shorter and the rear dampers which had previously been hung on the spacer now picked up on the gearbox.

Intercoolers raked forward behind the radiators in each side pod, while Bosch electronic fuel metering had been adopted. The AP brake servo and hydropneumatic suspension systems were driven from gearbox pumps, the suspension circuits not interconnecting all four wheels. They were instead paired front and rear to combat differing aerodynamic loadings fore and aft. The car generally was lower than the RE20-series, its side pods lower and the revised centre tank cell longer and lower than before, while the winkle-picker nose was more slender.

However, at Zolder Arnoux failed to qualify after numerous problems while Prost broke old 'RE22's clutch as the race was stopped and restarted – it could not endure two turbocharged standing starts.

Post-Zolder testing of the new cars produced raceworthy 'RE31' and 'RE32' at Monaco, these cars and the spare using servo brakes, and seven new engines were made available, revving to 11,500 rpm. Prost's new 'RE32' had hydropneumatic suspension, which also went onto Arnoux's car during practice, but the extra pump load affected the gearbox so the system was removed again. Both race cars were damaged early on and retired later.

Two RE30s ran at Jarama: 'RE33' was new for Arnoux in place of his '31 shunted at Monaco, 'RE32' being used again for Prost after he had demolished '30 when a wheel broke during Dijon testing.

The Monaco-damaged '31 was repaired in time for the French GP at Dijon, all three Renaults there having modified side pods with undersurfaces around the gearbox like the unsuccessful Williams FW07B at Buenos Aires '80. Air venting was tidied up with superfluous flaps removed, and rear wings of a new design appeared on the race cars. Prost in 'RE32' won on aggregate after a rainstorm stopped the race, and he took the restart on soft tyres with turbo boost wound up.

New, narrower rear wing stays appeared at Silverstone, Prost took pole and the Renaults dominated until fuel feed trouble stopped Prost and burned valves deleted Arnoux from the race.

At Hockenheim new side pod end plates merging into the rear wing appeared, Arnoux's rear tyre was punctured by another car's nose wing on the first lap, and a skirt damaged in the drag back to the pits caused bad handling thereafter. Prost was handicapped by his engine's rev limiter cutting in 600 rpm too early. After running 2.7 ata boost at Hockenheim, they fell back to 2.6 at the Österreichring. Underwing extensions then appeared at Zandvoort, where Prost's 'RE34' sported further-revised bodywork with one-piece nose wing support and he won from pole, whereas Arnoux crashed after starting from the front row alongside his team-mate.

For Monza, Arnoux's 'RE33' was in similar trim to '34 as at Zandvoort and he took Renault's fourth consecutive pole position but Prost led throughout, saying his car's handling on race tyres was better than on qualifiers. Arnoux spun and stalled.

In Canada changes included new injectors, intercoolers, lightweight honeycomb side pods, 13 in. front wheels, different brake ducts and new carbon-fibre front and rear wings, taking the Renaults below 600 kg for the first time. Prost's 'RE34' scaled 595 kg (1311.6 lb) Arnoux's 'RE33' 598 kg (1318.4 lb).

At Las Vegas, 'RE30' replaced Arnoux's 'RE33' crashed in Montreal, and the team was fresh from full-size wind tunnel testing in the Lockheed facility at Atlanta, Georgia. The long-awaited new electronic ignition system disappointed during

The bulky but powerful Renault RE40 carried Alain Prost within sight of the Drivers' World Championship in 1983, but turbo failure in the deciding South African GP here at Kyalami left him sitting in the pits. Nelson Piquet won the title in his Brabham-BMW amidst Renault complaints about BMW's 'funny fuel'.

Renault's swansong as a Formula 1 chassis constructor came in 1985 with the RE60, driven here by Patrick Tambay. Notable are its more wedge-shaped aerodynamics, accentuated by the paint scheme and pin-lining, and still massive rear wing sections.

practice and was set aside.

Just one more win would have given Prost the Championship but they had had that win within their grasp and had lost it at Silverstone due to their faulty valve batch; at the Österreichring due to a broken suspension rocker; and in Spain, where Prost had been faster than eventual winner Villeneuve but fell off. The Renaults had none the less dominated for sheer pace in the UK, Germany and Austria, but could not finish until Holland. At least the car was now competitive on all kinds of circuits.

They had made 29 starts in the 15 1981 GPs, finishing 14 times, winning three, with three second places, a third, a fourth, a fifth, two eighths, two ninths and one 13th. They sat on pole for six consecutive races: France, Britain, Germany, Austria, Holland and Italy – four times to Arnoux, twice to Prost. Renault were setting standards, but still not winning that elusive Championship.

In 1982, Prost and Arnoux set off 1-3 with RE30Bs at Kyalami. Lighter underbody panels and SEP carbon discs were tried on the T-car, new carbon wing mounts being replaced by metal after Arnoux and Prost both broke them pre-race. Water ballast was added to a hollow seat moulding at Long Beach where the cars were allegedly underweight for the first time. At Imola, Prost had new chassis 'RE30B-8' (the system being restyled). Then new side pods appeared for Monaco.

In Holland, new wastegate ventilation appeared after turbo failure had been caused by lack of it in Canada. New front suspension appeared at Ricard and hydraulic suspension provided at Brands Hatch, both being removed for Zandvoort, where Arnoux crashed '7. Chassis '8 was badly damaged by Arnoux at Dijon and a new chassis '9 was brought to the UK, with reinforced lower front wishbones to prevent another wheel loss as at Zandvoort. In Germany, chassis '10 was new and carbon-fibre brake discs were tried briefly.

Overall, this was another disappointing season, riven by failure of a tiny electric motor within the injection system which combined electronic control with a Bosch-Kugelfischer mechanical pump to produce a considerable performance advantage.

When the new system came on song at Monaco,

Prost led to within two laps of the finish when he crashed due to brain-fade when under pressure, destroying his favourite chassis '4. Thereafter the electro-mechanical fuel injection system repeatedly betrayed the cars. Running conventional injection cost two seconds per lap at the Österreichring, the electro-mechanical system was refitted for the race and its tiny motor failed again. It was a humble proprietary unit which was being expected to survive in the heat and vibration of the engine vee, and could not. They tried alternatives without success before finally issuing a custom specification to a specialist subcontractor who tailor-made what they wanted. This was used in the last race of 1982 at Las Vegas and ran reliably through '83.

Renault also suffered a series of accidents and had to use four replacement chassis. While much effort concentrated upon the EF1 engines, the cars were surprisingly conventional, with all-aluminium tubs, some carbon-fibre side pod panels to save weight, but no raceworthy carbon-fibre brakes (unlike Brabham), nor pullrod suspensions, and the wheelbase was unchanged all year. Track was enlarged 6 cm (2.4 in.) to the maximum 215 cm. Porpoising at speed was a problem, Renault's fore-and-aft split hydraulic damping system controlling this effect with variable success. Sage felt that the 150 km/h wind tunnel at St Cyr was perhaps a contributory factor; it might have been better to use a 300 km/h tunnel.

During 1982 they had made 32 starts in the 16 GPs, finishing only 12 times, but winning four GPs – Prost two, Arnoux two (including the French GP in which he held Prost out of a victory which might have won him the World Championship) – plus three second places, a third, a fourth and one sixth place.

Having come so close, Renault had two goals for '83: more power and adequate reliability. Tétu drew a new RE40 carbon-composite chassis but the management decided that an interim flat-bottomed RE30C would suffice for the opening races. Time had been short since the imposition of the new rule and they felt confident everyone would be running interim cars, reckoning without the reaction speed of teams like Brabham who built all-new. So Renault entered 1983 with a disadvantage and the RE40 programme had to be accelerated.

Engineer Jean-Pierre Boudy wrung more power from the ageing V6, adopting bigger turbo casings and impeller wheels and developing a water injection pack to use their extra boost. In the winter of 1982/83 he developed water injection on his company Renault 18 saloon.

Three interim RE30Cs ran at Rio. The prototype RE40 emerged at Long Beach. The logistics of running two different types caused Sage deep grief, while electrical problems wrecked the new model's debut. It was new, it was carbon-composite and 'we just couldn't find a good earth'.

Renault got a grip until Zandvoort and by the penultimate race Prost seemed all but assured of the Championship. Six RE40s had been built, the prototype retiring to static test and mock-up duties.

Prost's engine suffered significantly at Imola, Montreal and Monza. They had problems with inconsistent performance quality after rebuilds. The 700 rpm rev loss from the normal 11,000 rpm to only 10,300 at Imola was never explained, even the works' strip-down report finding nothing amiss. At Monza there was no mystery, the device regulating turbo heat build-up was faulty when fitted, allowing the turbos to overheat and damage the impeller wheels, thereby losing boost.

Three wing forms were run, plus a fourth barndoor like Ferrari's at Brands Hatch, the penultimate round. It was ironic that the team should again miss out on the Constructors' Championship where both cars could score points, for new team driver Cheever's misfortunes in the second car cost the largest motor manufacturer in Formula 1 dear indeed.

At Rio, the RE30C chassis '11 and '12 were new, using cast-magnesium front uprights and fabricated rears ready for the RE40. Italian Brembo brakes were tried again, the inlet manifold had been redesigned and Boudy's water injection made its debut. For Long Beach the 12 kg (26.5 lb) lighter RE40 prototype chassis '00 made its debut, the tub moulded by Hurel-Dubois at Vélizy.

Three RE40s went to Ricard for the early-season French GP: '00 the spare, now superseded by '01 for Prost and '02 for Cheever, the latter two both equipped with rapid-refuelling non-spill fillers for pit-stop race strategy. 'RE40/03' was new at Imola for Prost, a higher carbon content in its composite moulded tub making it distinctively darker in colour than its predecessors. Cheever ran radially drilled carbon discs there, as at Ricard, saving 7 kg (15.4 lb) weight.

For Monaco a greatly extended full-width rear underwing or 'diffuser' was fitted, terminating below the trailing edge of the rear wing. It lay beneath the rear suspension and had four-pipe exhausts playing across the underside to entrain airflow across the diffuser undersurface and add useful extra download. Renault actually claimed the device was to reduce local exhaust heating of the tyres, but their rivals grumbled . . . and at Spa protested that the system harnessed a moveable aerodynamic device, the engine internals, to entrain air. FISA declared the system legal and everyone adopted it subsequently.

New tubs '04 and '05 appeared at Silverstone, to '03 standard but saving 10 kg (22 lb). The four-pipe engines had been found to overheat during Hockenheim testing so for Silverstone they reverted to the original style. Shorter rear bodywork was adopted for Hockenheim where ultimate download is less important than low drag and top speed.

Prost had to drive T-car '03 in the race there with longer rear bodywork after his assigned race car overheated on its way to the grid. In Austria, '03 had short bodywork fitted. Overheating persisted, apparently due to poor separation of steam entrained in the water flow, a problem which also affected other users of Renault engines.

By Holland, '03 had been lightened to the standard of the later cars. Chassis '05 was damaged there in Prost's accident, new chassis '06 replacing it for Monza. A single spray-nozzle intercooler 'super-cooler' system was used there in qualifying, and at Monza a twin-nozzle system cooled both sides of the matrix to find still more power. New car '06 was down to 545 kg (1201.5 lb) and first run in Brands Hatch tyre testing. At Brands, '05 returned, and they sent to South Africa four Renaults instead of three as well as nine engines in a vain effort to clinch the Championship which

Prost had dominated for so much of the year. Running the big Brands Hatch rear wings and special qualifying engines for the first time with larger turbochargers, the Renaults were still over 5 mph slower than the Brabham-BMWs on the straight. They tried narrow near tyres to gain speed but nothing would work. Prost retired '05 with turbo failure, while Cheever finished a distant sixth in '04 . . . and Renault's best-ever chance of the Championship title had gone.

Prost left to be snapped up by McLaren for 1984, Warwick joining Tambay in the rebuilt Renault team to drive a new Tétu-designed model RE50. After prototype '01 had completed initial testing it then, unraced, became a show car. RE50s '02-3-4' were new at Rio, the latter pair being race cars for Tambay and Warwick. '05 was new for Tambay at Zolder and was written off like its new sister '06 in a first-corner collision at Monaco, when the two collided!

Chassis '07 was new for Warwick as a spare at Montreal, where he raced '04 repaired after a heavy accident at Dijon, '08 was new at Brands Hatch and was raced by him late-season, while '09 was new for Tambay at Hockenheim and completed the season in his hands, save for one drive by Warwick at *ersatz* Nürburgring.

These eight carbon-Kevlar race cars were a profound disappointment. After reservations about their KKK turbochargers in 1983, Dudot adopted large American Garrett AiResearch 'chargers for the new season. Plans were laid for a spring-time split in Renault Sport's factories, Dudot's engine plant with its 100 employees taking over the whole of the original premises at Viry-Châtillon, while Jean Sage took his chassis and gearbox race shop and its 70-odd staff down the road to new premises at Evry.

The alloy-block engines were now standard, initially suffering some flexion problems which were corrected, though costs soared as the alloy blocks had to be changed twice a year whereas the old iron blocks ran for ever. The latest 'EF4' power unit featured revised heads.

Warwick gave the team a strong start by nearly winning in Rio. The main problem under the new 220-litre fuel restriction was sheer consumption. This was especially serious at Imola but they did much work with the latest Marelli-Weber injection system and with the Renix ('Renault Electronics') management system so that by the end of the season the cars could run race distance without the drivers progressively reducing boost pressure.

Early on in Rio, Warwick's new RE50 was struck by a McLaren and bent a wishbone, which broke and robbed him of a potential win near the finish. Stronger wishbones were adopted thereafter but at Monaco and Dijon they proved so strong that they transmitted shock-loads direct into the carbon-Kevlar tub and punched the pick-ups straight through into the cockpit, injuring the drivers. Thereafter the tub pick-ups were reinforced, adding weight until 'RE50/08' emerged redesigned in carbon – they said without Kevlar – from Brands Hatch.

The greater engine power compromised gearbox reliability which became very marginal by season's end. Intensive SEP-Renault carbon-fibre brake tests continued all year but they were not raced until Monza, when management prevailed upon the drivers to race them despite their lack of progressive feel and tendency therefore to lock. Both drivers quite liked them in the race, where revised high-compression engines proved strong.

Overall, Renault Sport felt they had not achieved their potential for they failed to win a single race and were often struggling to match Lotus performances with their V6 engine.

They started 31 times and were classified as finishers only twelve times. Warwick's finish record read 3-2-4-2-3-11, and Tambay's 5-7-2-8-5-6-7, aggregating 34 points for just fifth place in the Constructors' Cup. From 1978 to 1983 Renault Sport had placed in sequence 12th, sixth, fourth, third, third and second in the Constructors' competition, so the drop to fifth in 1984 was indeed a fall from grace.

The mighty French *Régie*'s decline accelerated into 1985. The production company had been suffering huge trading losses and had to shed many employees, so the Board decided that their expenditure on Formula 1 should be closely scrutinized in light of poor results. Gérard Larrousse was shouldered aside and a new man, Toth, put in his place; the popular former Le Mans winner moved to Ligier and, significantly, chassis designer Tétu went with him, leaving his new RE60 design allegedly complete but the cars unbuilt and obviously undeveloped. The team's labyrinthine management practices had always handicapped progress and now things merely seemed to get worse.

At Viry-Châtillon, Bernard Dudot was completing his new EF15 V6 engine to complement the existing EF4s, while drivers Tambay and Warwick were unchanged. But Renault Sport 1985 was a shadow of what had gone before, and it would be left to Lotus and Ligier to make the best use of Dudot's fine engines.

One test RE60 chassis had been completed and three new team cars then followed in time for Rio where chassis '2 was the spare raced by Tambay, '3 new for Warwick and '4 Tambay's originally assigned car. Chassis '5 would follow as spare at Monaco where Tambay again raced it first time out, this machine being updated to modified RE60B-spec in time for the German GP. New RE60Bs, chassis '6 and '7, had appeared at Ricard for Tambay and at Silverstone for Warwick.

They were down to the 540 kg limit, using RE60 chassis mouldings but with the electrics moved from above the fuel cell into the cockpit to allow a 15 cm lower engine cover. Smaller radiators permitted shorter side pods, the nose cone was slimmer, new uprights and wishbones were fitted, and brake calipers moved ahead of the rear discs. An EF15 qualifying engine had to be developed since the normal EF4B 'qualifier' would not mount on the '60B tub. Renault's qualifying showed little notable change.

Chassis '7 was written off in a practice accident in Holland. Chassis '8 was new as spare car in Austria, raced by Warwick at Zandvoort and then, after creasing '6 in practice at Monza, Tambay took over '8 as his regular mount for the balance of Renault's final Formula 1 season.

The team boycotted Kyalami on political grounds, so both drivers contested 15 of the 16 GPs. Their cars were not very reliable, and even less competitive; it was pathetic to see, agonizing to experience.

Tambay notched eight finishes, scoring points 5-3-3-6 at Rio, Estoril, Imola and in France, 7-10*-7-12 elsewhere; Warwick finished only seven times, 5-5-6 at Monaco, Silverstone and Spa, 10-7-10-7 elsewhere, which was poor. Evidence that Renault were losing all intent of retrieving Formula 1 competitiveness came at the *ersatz* Nürburgring where 'RE60/4' was prepared as a TV camera car for ex-Brabham Elf protégé Hesnault, inevitably diverting attention from the 'serious' race cars. Thus it was no surprise when Renault's F1 withdrawal was announced soon after, and the team merely went through the motions for the few GPs left to them.

Their defection was a serious blow not only to company and national pride, but also to Formula 1 itself, which could ill-afford to lose the support of such an industrial giant. Fortunately Renault would continue to supply Lotus, Ligier and Tyrrell with engines and into 1986 it remained to be seen if they could achieve the Championship victory on Renault's behalf which in nine seasons' competition had eluded the *Régie* itself. They could not . . .

Renault Sport had always been forced to fight its war with one arm tied behind its back, for French labour laws and social requirements forced them to observe rigid working hours and for overtime and weekend working to be tightly controlled. Even with enthusiastic union support, they could never exploit the seven days a week, 24 hours a day commitment of the British teams' people, nor their flexibility and speed of response. The speed at which urgently required modifica-

tions can be made can win or lose the next race, and neither did Renault have on hand the myriad small specialist sub-contractors available in the UK, or on the Emilian plain in Italy.

Nothing is easy in Formula 1, but right from the start it had been harder for the largest manufacturer in the business. Renault's decision to take on the specialists with a largely untried engine concept and to pay the price of their pioneering was a brave one which had changed the face of Grand Prix racing.

Rial

Gunther Schmid's reincarnated Rial wheel company – see the entry for ATS – backed this 1988-89 Formula 1 effort, which made more impact in its first season than most of the hopeful Cosworth DFZ-powered brigade. Schmid used former Ferrari chassis engineer Gustav Brunner's services, and he produced a neat and shapely carbon-composite monocoque unmistakably reminiscent of his Ferrari F1/87 and stillborn Maranello Indycar work.

The Rial ARC1 would be described by some as 'the blue Ferrari'. Brunner adopted a novel front suspension configuration with its pullrod-operated dampers lying longitudinally at floor level. Rial's own gearbox was produced and three ARC1s were built, '1 new for de Cesaris at Rio, '2 becoming available as team spare at Imola and '3 being completed in time for Hockenheim. Brunner had mounted the prototype's oil coolers at the trailing edge of the rear diffuser panel. The team was warned in pre-season Imola testing that such a mounting infringed the regulation requiring cooler protection within the car, but Andrea de Cesaris was still permitted to run at Rio with this mounting, working his way into sixth place before a routine tyre stop, then having a rear disc bell work loose and finally over-revving the engine when he missed a gear. Still the car impressed and de Cesaris's career was saved . . .

He retired 11 times but was classified as a finisher in five GPs, 9*-4-10-13-8*, his fourth place in Detroit earning the little team three valuable Championship points and 13th-equal place alongside Ligier in the Constructors' Championship.

Some of 1988's Cosworth DFZ-powered F1 teams would hardly have looked threatening in Formula 3000 company. This was not one of them. As had been the case with ATS, money was tight, but the quick if accident- and temperament-prone de Cesaris was regularly amongst the very quickest Cosworths. A good car, not badly run – in comparison to some of its Cosworth brigade peers.

Rial continued into 1990 as a more ambitious two-car team, Brunner's ARC1 concept being developed after his departure by aerodynamicist Bob Bell – ex-Brabham – Martin Goodrich and Stefan Fober to form the new ARC2 model. A fashionable step was inserted beneath the nose and the monocoque's fuel cell enlarged to *c.* 200

The 1988 Rial ARC1 was a notably neat and elegant example of that season's new breed of Cosworth DFZ-engined 'atmo' Formula 1 cars. Its Gustav Brunner design declares his previous Ferrari experience loud and clear.

litres. Three Rial ARC2s were produced, '1 and '2 making their debut at Rio, '3 emerging at Imola.

Drivers were Christian Danner and Volker Weidler and their problems effectively killed the team. Danner failed to qualify for nine GPs, Weidler for eight early-season, and then a ninth at Budapest. He was excluded from the German GP. Danner finished four times 14*-12-4-8 – his fourth place being amongst widespread mechanical mayhem at Phoenix. His last outing was at Estoril.

Weidler was replaced by Pierre-Henri Raphanel for the last six races, but the result was unchanged – successive failures to qualify. Gregor Foitek tried the sister car in Danner's place at Jerez. No better. Bertrand Gachot then joined Raphanel for the season-ending races in Japan and Australia, and he couldn't make the grid either. Rial withdrew from Formula 1 forthwith.

Safir

See entry for Token, page 318.

Shadow

American entrepreneur Don Nicholls founded his Advanced Vehicle Systems company to build and race an extraordinary small-wheeled CanAm sports car known as the Shadow in 1970. He subsequently turned his attention to Formula 1, having won major sponsorship from the huge Universal Oil Products (UOP) company, in part to publicise their lead-free fuel products. Former March team manager Alan Rees was interested, as were former BRM driver Jack Oliver and chief chassis engineer Tony Southgate. They would form the nucleus of Nicholls's British-based AVS Shadow company which would build brand new Cosworth/Hewland Formula 1 cars for 1973.

Southgate designed the first car largely in his home at Bourne near BRM. It was his first non-V12 Formula 1 car and he misjudged the destructive vibration of the Cosworth V8. When the first shapely, chisel-nosed, hip-radiatored, squared-off 'Coke bottle' Shadow DN1 appeared – chassis 'DN1-1A' – it literally shook itself apart.

Team drivers were to be Oliver and the American Follmer, whose enormous sports car experience included the 1000 hp Porsche 917 turbocharged cars so Formula 1 held few fears for him. Follmer enjoyed all the luck going in his Formula 1 debut, for his chassis '2A survived race distance while Oliver's prototype retired to place sixth at Kyalami – immediately scoring a Championship point – and at Silverstone, and then third at Barcelona. At Zolder, for the Belgian GP, the newly laid track surface disintegrated and Oliver wrote off '1A. Follmer, meanwhile, had crashed '2A in practice; it was repaired for the race but sand jammed the throttle slides open and he went off and was stranded in a sand trap. At Monaco, '2A's luck ran out and it was written off in a collision.

Oliver ran a new car, 'DN1-4A', there and finished 10th, but he was dogged by misfortune, becoming involved in the multiple pile-up which stopped the British GP and crashing again in Holland. Follmer drove 'DN1-5A' to replace '2 but achieved little despite five more finishes that season. Oliver took 'DN1-6A' home eighth in Germany and third in Canada where he led that chaotic race during changeable weather, a flurry of tyre-change stops and muddled lap charting. Redman drove chassis '4 in Follmer's place at Watkins Glen. For 1974, new team drivers Revson and Jarier took over as Oliver retired to management duties while the much improved Shadow DN3 made its debut.

Jarier drove 'DN1-7A' in Argentina but destroyed it on the first lap in a collision with Revson's prototype DN3. He then raced '5A in Brazil, where this last DN1 works entry ended with a seized wheel bearing.

One other DN1 had been built in 1973, chassis '3, bought as a kit by Graham Hill for his new Embassy-backed one-car team. The car fell to bits at Monaco, and Hill furiously strengthened it subsequently, ending the season with seven finishes. However, none was worth a candle and the 9-10-12-13-14-16-13 finishes were sad to see.

Hill bought Lolas for 1974, while Shadow's new DN3 proved competitive. Southgate learned from the mistakes of DN1, stretched DN3 with a spacer between engine and gearbox, revised its aerodynamics with a long nose (top-ducted to enclose the oil cooler) and provided a slimmer engine airbox and centre-strutted 'banana' wing.

Revson qualified 'DN3-1A' on row two in its debut at Buenos Aires, ran sixth in Brazil, finished sixth at Brands Hatch, but then in pre-race testing at Kyalami crashed fatally due to failure of a poorly machined titanium suspension part.

Jarier drove 'DN3-2A' for the rest of the season, finishing nine times, including thirds at Silverstone and Monaco, with a fifth in Sweden. Redman drove 'DN3-3A' in Spain, Belgium and Monaco but could not endure the 'bullshit' of Formula 1 and opted out. Bertil Roos drove once in Sweden, followed by ex-Token driver Pryce, who joined Shadow from the Dutch GP. There he damaged '3A in a startline collision, and in France he qualified on the second row and had another startline accident. A new tub had just been finished in Shadow's Northampton factory, which was hastily completed, taking '3A's chassis-plate to keep the customs paperwork tidy.

Meanwhile, 'DN3-4A' had been in use since Monaco as a spare car until Pryce wrote it off in Austrian practice. Since the original '3A had been repaired in time for the Italian GP, where the 'fake' '3A was also to run, the obvious thing to do was to put '4A's plate on the French GP-damaged chassis (the original '3A). The proper plate would be restored to this car for the South American trip at the start of 1975 . . .

Chassis '5A (currently numbered '3A) carried Pryce to his first Championship point, sixth in Germany.

For 1975, Southgate further modified his original DN1 concept, which had been fine-tuned in the DN3, to an even more refined state in the DN5. In this, he sought improved aerodynamic form and cooling, different weight distribution and less weight.

Old 'DN3-3A' had been updated with some DN5 bits to form a '3B interim car which Pryce drove in South America alongside Jarier's new DN5. Five DN5s would be built, and the first shone brilliantly in Argentina and Brazil. Jarier qualified on pole both times, only for 'DN5-1A' to shear its final-drive on the warm-up lap in Argentina, then

The luckless Tom Pryce showing off the fine lines of the Tony Southgate-designed Shadow DN5 in the 1975 Dutch GP in which he finished sixth. Far outboard wings front and rear and towering airbox typify the period.

have its fuel metering unit fail after leading for 28 laps in Brazil.

Despite suspicious muttering about UOP's special lead-free fuel supplied for these cars, the new DN5 was clearly very competitive, with excellent handling. Pryce had 'DN5-2A' at Kyalami after crashing his DN3B in Brazil, and at Brands Hatch he qualified on pole and won handsomely – Shadow's first Formula 1 victory.

Pryce and Jarier qualified 2-3 at Monaco, where Jarier crashed '1A heavily, but he reappeared in a new car, '4A, in Belgium. Pryce qualified sensationally on pole at Silverstone for the British GP but both he and Jarier crashed when leading.

The fast circuits like the Österreichring and Monza came in the autumn, and Nicholls arranged use of Matra's MS71 V12 engine in a new tailor-made DN7 chassis. It was driven by Jarier in Austria, who reported: 'It's very smooth; it will pull strongly from low in the range, from about 6000 rpm, up to 11,900'. Fuel-injection problems sidelined it in the race, and at Monza the DN7 again retired with fuel pump problems as well as proving to have insufficient fuel capacity to survive race distance in any case.

Matra preferred to supply Ligier for 1976, so 'DN7-1A' was set aside.

It had not been a rewarding season despite the great promise shown. Jarier finished only once in the points, fourth (for half-points) in the red-flagged Spanish GP; Pryce salvaged third in Austria, fourth in Germany, and three sixths in Belgium, Holland, and Italy for eight Championship points. Shadow finished sixth in the Constructors' table.

Unfortunately, UOP abruptly decided it did not appreciate Nicholls's methods and withdrew sponsorship for '76. This was a body-blow which crippled Shadow's chances of building on the DN5's undoubted promise.

The old cars were updated as '5Bs for '76 and remained competitive early on, Pryce reaching third in Brazil where Jarier fought hard for the lead, only to crash 'DN5/6A' heavily and write it off. He never tried as hard again for Shadow. Jarier normally drove chassis '4A while Pryce's mount was '5A until Holland when the new Southgate-conceived, Dave Wass-completed 'DN8-1A' made its bow, qualified third on the grid and finished fourth in the race.

Had finance been available, DN8s would have raced from the start of the year, but Southgate had walked out to join Lotus R&D, leaving Wass in technical charge. The DN8 was a neat, lightened and further-refined example of Southgate thinking with a notably low new monocoque tub, high-sided cockpit surround and new AP Lockheed balanced twin-caliper brakes. The nose cone was still distinctively Shadow with the familiar oil cooler in its duct, the car retaining neatly cowled hip radiators.

Jarier ended the season without a single Championship point but Pryce was third in Brazil and fourth in the British and Dutch GPs, the team eighth in the Constructors' Cup.

Finances were still desperately tight-stretched at the start of 1977. Renzo Zorzi in 'DN5-5A' joined Pryce in the DN8 in Argentina and Brazil, finishing sixth in the latter event but proving as slow as his car. A new sponsor enabled a second DN8 to be completed for Kyalami where Pryce was killed in 'DN8-2A' in a stupid accident after Zorzi's car stopped beside the main straight smoking around the tail. A teenage marshal ran across to him carrying a heavy extinguisher just as Pryce arrived flat-out; he struck and killed the marshal and lost his own life when the extinguisher hit him in the face.

After this appalling incident, Alan Jones, driving 'DN8-3A', joined Zorzi at Long Beach, while Riccardo Patrese subsequently replaced Zorzi. Oliver returned from retirement to handle '8-1A' in Sweden while Patrese returned to the team from France to Germany, Merzario driving in Austria, then Patrese at Monza and Jarier joining Jones in the USA when Patrese was engaged in Formula 2.

Southgate returned in mid-summer and development instantly accelerated. A new 'DN8-4A' ran in practice at Hockenheim with slimmer centre section and flared in-line radiator pods ahead of the rear wheels, plus an oil cooler back in the nose, from which it had earlier been removed. Jones had already accumulated places – sixth at Monaco and fifth in Belgium – but his drive in Austria was rewarded by a win in '4A after the team had chosen the right set-up and the opposition faltered. New car '5A was driven by Merzario and was then bent at Monza by Patrese. Jarier drove 'DN8-6A' brand new at Watkins Glen.

Shadow ended the season seventh in the Constructors' Championship with a very respectable 23 points. This was despite parting company with prime sponsor Ambrosio after the German GP, just before the revised DN8 came good, so earnings from the Austrian victory and Jones's subsequent third in Italy and fourths in Canada and Japan were very handy.

During that winter, however, team principals Rees, Oliver, Southgate and Wass abandoned ship to form Arrows, thus leaving virtual absentee landlord Nicholls to pick up the pieces and to pursue them to the High Court...

A new DN9 Southgate wing-car design was completed for 1978 by John Baldwin (see entry for Arrows, page 219). New drivers were Regazzoni and Stuck, the Ticinese finishing fifth in Brazil and Sweden but otherwise having a dreadful season, non-qualifying five times. Stuck only non-qualified once – though he failed to start at Long Beach – but he retired ten times and only had one worthwhile finish, namely fifth in the British GP. Danny Ongais drove Ted Field's Interscope team 'DN9-3A' at Long Beach and the Österreichring, failing to pre-qualify both times. Five DN9s and the three early-season DN8s were employed during this awful season.

For 1979 Shadow struggled with updated DN9s driven by young hopefuls de Angelis and Lammers. Richard Owen and John Gentry had modified the cars to B specification, three B-spec cars appearing in the early-season races, de Angelis ramming the new Alfa Romeo at Zolder, bending '3B in the middle, and having a new tub for Monaco.

Shadow DN9B chassis '3 and '4 were available for de Angelis as race car and spare in the British GP, '2 and '5 for Lammers, one car with revised rocker arm suspension which went onto both cars at Hockenheim to stop de Angelis whining about

his team-mate being favoured. But the Shadows were heavy and never able to make best use of the second-division Goodyear tyres to which they were entitled. At Monza '3B and '4B were fitted with new side pods to little effect.

De Angelis qualified for 14 of the 15 GPs, retired from seven of them but finished fourth at Watkins Glen, having been seventh, just out of the points, in Argentina and Long Beach. Lammers qualified for 12 of the races, retiring five times and returning no worthwhile finishes. Shadow were 10th in the Constructors' table, with de Angelis's three points from that last race of the season.

John Gentry initiated design of a new DN11 for 1980, which was completed by Vic Morris, three being built for Stefan Johansson, David Kennedy and Geoff Lees as the season developed. But the cars were never developed, and only Lees managed to qualify for a race, at Kyalami, being classified 13th after writing off chassis '2. Johansson failed to qualify for both the Argentine and Brazilian GPs, and Kennedy for the first seven races on the calendar.

But the DN11 was recognized early on as a flop and a new little DN12 was designed by Morris with help from Swiss specialist Chuck Graemiger. It had the shortest wheelbase in Formula 1 but was a hefty-looking device and again its preparation and development left much to be desired. The prototype DN12 emerged in Belgium, and chassis '2 in Spain.

Just before the Belgian GP, Teddy Yip, who was already an Ensign shareholder, bought Shadow in partnership with enthusiasts Jack Kallay and John Cooper (no relation to the John Cooper). Nicholls disappeared into the shadows whence he came. The team was renamed Theodore Racing but Yip felt there was little sense in throwing good money after bad. When both Lees (in 'DN12/1') and Kennedy (in 'DN12/2') failed to qualify for the French GP on 29 June 1980, the team returned sadly to England and quietly closed down. Yip was to use its nucleus as the basis of his Theodore team for 1981, when Lees would race 'DN12/2' for the first and last time at Kyalami – where he crashed again to end his own serious Formula 1 aspirations. See entries for Arrows and Theodore.

Shannon

Veteran racing mechanic Aiden Jones joined forces with even more experienced inveterate special-builder Paul Emery to produce an obscure little no-hoper Formula 1 car which ran once only at this level, in the 1966 British GP at Brands Hatch.

Jones produced a spidery-looking, exceptionally slim, riveted aluminium monocoque chassis, into the rear of which he and Emery persuaded an enlarged version of one of the rare, hitherto unraced and supposedly stillborn 2.5-litre Coventry Climax FPE V8 engines. These had originally been produced for the start of the then-new 2½-litre Formula twelve years before.

Climax had believed media reports of the fantastic power then being obtained by Mercedes-Benz, Ferrari and Maserati and with a remarkable lack of self-confidence – or even of practical research on their own part – shelved their plans, believing that 264 bhp at 7900 rpm on fuel injection was inadequate – which it was not.

Now the remaining FPE stock, said to include four complete engines and many spares, had been sold to Emery, who proposed to fit Tecalemit-Jackson fuel injection. The V8s had meaty wet liners facilitating easy conversion to larger capacity, but they had been designed and developed to run on alcohol fuel rather than straight pump petrol.

Emery and Jones forged ahead regardless, otherwise redundant former Lotus and BRP driver Trevor Taylor took the cold seat, and the ratty-looking little Shannon retired on the first lap of the race, with a split fuel tank – or so they said. The car was seen again, but not with the V8 engine installed. End of story.

Spirit

Ex-March Formula 2 team manager John Wickham and ex-McLaren and March designer Gordon Coppuck – of Championship-winning McLaren M23 fame – formed Spirit Racing to tackle 1982 Formula 2 with the 2-litre Honda 80-degree V6 engine.

After some success they aspired to Formula 1 in 1983, bringing Honda with them. They converted one of their Spirit 201 chassis, number '4, to accept a prototype 1500 cc turbocharged Honda engine and, after promising tests in California in the 1982/83 winter, they entered the hybrid car at Brands Hatch for their Swedish driver Johansson. It was a modest effort with a slender budget, but Johansson raced it again in the British GP at Silverstone, and at the Österreichring, Monza and Brands Hatch. He also drove another converted F2 Spirit, '201/6', at Hockenheim and Zandvoort as the improved model 201C, while the small team's first pure Formula 1 car, '101/1', was spare for the European GP at Brands Hatch.

Spirit finished three of those six GPs, 12th at

Thin end of a mighty wedge – Stefan Johansson driving the F2-derived Spirit 201C at Zandvoort, 1983, powered by the turbocharged Honda V6.

Hockenheim, seventh at Zandvoort and 14th at Brands Hatch, but effectively proved the Honda F1 turbo engine.

It was therefore a bitter blow when Honda pulled the rug from under Spirit to support Williams for 1984. To sweeten the pill they helped finance Spirit's survival in Formula 1 using Hart 415T four-cylinder turbo engines. The 101 chassis was converted to '1B spec for the Hart unit and tested by Emerson Fittipaldi who was considering a return to Formula 1. He thought better of it, Italian driver Baldi's sponsors then buying the drive at Rio, Kyalami, Zolder, Imola and Dijon. Baldi finished eighth at both Kyalami and Imola. At Monaco, Baldi failed to qualify a new car '101/2B', Dutch driver Huub Rothengatter taking the drive mid-season but non-qualifying at Montreal, Brands Hatch and the Österreichring. A Cosworth had to be used in Detroit due to a Hart engine famine but Spirit non-qualified again, best finishes for Rothengatter being tenth at Hockenheim in '1B and eighth at Monza in '2B. Baldi returned for the final races at the Nürburgring and Estoril, finishing 8-15 but Spirit had barely survived a thankless season.

For the little teams it is as hard merely to qualify as it is for the major teams to qualify on pole or win the race. Spirit ended 1984 virtually *sans* hope and future.

They persevered into 1985 but finances were stretched crucially taut. The 1984 chassis were remodelled as Spirit-Hart 101Ds, chassis '2 and '3, featuring resited radiators and intercooler in new side pods, plus a change to pushrod front suspension. Mauro Baldi drove '2 in Rio and Estoril, where he crashed, then retired '3 at Imola. Spirit then sold their tyre contract to Toleman, their 1985 results being 'unclassified' at Rio, then twice retired. Spirit survived the rest of the season rebuilding '70s F1 cars for private collectors, but their Formula 1 aspirations had ended and the team eventually disbanded.

Surtees

After a long and brilliant career as a racing motor cyclist John Surtees took up motor racing in 1960, became World Champion with Ferrari in 1964 and subsequently drove for Cooper, Honda and BRM. As early as his third season, in 1962, he commissioned construction of a special Lola in what was virtually his own team. He was never a man to suffer fools gladly and never delegated if he felt he could do the job better. Ultimately this perfectionism proved counter-productive.

He maintained a close association with Lola into 1967-68, running his own Team Surtees sports car team, and in 1969 Team Surtees built a series of Len Terry-designed TS5 full-monocoque cars for this class while Surtees himself was serving his unhappy season with BRM. At the end of that year he determined to take up Cosworth power for 1970, buying an ex-works McLaren M7 to tide him over.

The new Surtees-Cosworth TS7 design was by Surtees himself, building on experience from the TS5. Chassis '001 appeared at the British GP, using a distinctively small and neat arch-topped, vertical-sided aluminium tub, with inboard front suspension, outboard rear. Surtees held seventh before the engine ran its bearings. Cosworth problems in fact ruined that first half-season, but at Oulton Park Surtees dominated, winning heat one and overall.

A second TS7, lower and lighter with titanium hubs, was available at the Österreichring and at Monza, where '001 suffered a rear suspension failure in practice and the rear end of '002 was grafted on for the race, but electrical trouble and a bad fuel leak sidelined the car after only one lap.

Surtees scored his first points in his own cars at Ste Jovite, Canada, fifth in '001, and he was sixth when the flywheel disintegrated at Watkins Glen, and in Mexico finished a clutchless eighth. Bell drove '002 at Watkins Glen, scoring a point for sixth place.

Early in 1972 new rent-a-driver Stommelen led Heat One of the non-Championship Argentine GP from start to finish in his TS7 but retired after a collision in Heat Two. The type had its farewell race at Kyalami where a new TS9 appeared. This was a still lower, more robust car generally similar to the TS7 until side radiators were adopted later in the year, together with a full-width bluff nose, pierced to allow cooling air through the front suspension area into the side pods. It used a Hewland FG400 instead of DG300 transmission. Surtees ran second in 'TS9/001' on its debut before a gearbox oil cooler pipe parted and the transmission seized. New 'TS9/002' was ready for Stommelen for the Spanish GP, '003 was sold direct to Team Gunston in South Africa for John Love's use in national Championship racing, while '004 emerged at the French GP as a spare. For the Italian GP at Monza that September, new car 'TS9/005' appeared with side-mounted radiators, but these were replaced by a conventional nose radiator after practice. The side radiators were made to perform satisfactorily in time for the US GP and retained thereafter.

At Monza, Surtees's old motor cycling chum Hailwood came into the team and he promptly finished fourth in '004, just 0.18 second behind the winner . . . it was a close finish. Surtees had won the Gold Cup race again in this same chassis.

For 1972, Hailwood became a regular team driver, Surtees went into virtual retirement from driving and cars were also entered for de Adamich and Schenken. Hailwood came second in the minor race at Brands Hatch and in the Italian GP, as well as fourth in the Belgian and Austrian races, driving 'TS9/005'.

Pace joined in Schenken's place for the final Brands Hatch race and was second, in Schenken's former regular mount 'TS9/006'. This car raced only once more, when it was hired to Hesketh for their driver Hunt's Formula 1 debut in the 1973 Race of Champions, where he finished strongly in second place.

Surtees made his last appearance as a driver at

Monza in 1972, handling his brand new prototype TS14 car built to 1973 deformable-structure requirements, with the tub skinned in a sandwich of aluminium, foam and glass-fibre, side radiators, broad pierced nose but now having outboard suspension at the front as well as the rear. Surtees retired '001 with brake trouble and tyre problems – their Firestone tyres would remain a problem throughout 1973, when vibration caused much grief.

Early in 1973 Hailwood led the Race of Champions majestically in '001 until either a tyre or suspension failure hurled him into the bank near the end of the main straight. The car was repaired in time for Mass to drive it in the British GP where all three Surtees cars were heavily damaged in the legendary 'Scheckter shunt' ending lap one. '001 was repaired again for Mass to finish seventh in the German GP.

The second TS14, '002, had been ready for Hailwood in Argentina and was written off in the Regazzoni collision at Kyalami in which Hailwood won the George Medal for rescuing the Swiss BRM driver from his blazing car. New regular team member Pace appeared in 'TS14/003' from Argentina, and after serving occasional spare car duties this machine was totally written off in the Silverstone collision. Chassis '004 was Hailwood's mid-season car; it was unreliable and in the US GP its rear suspension collapsed, and Hailwood would leave to drive for McLaren in '74. Chassis '005 was driven by Pace at the Nürburgring to set

Top: *Mike Hailwood enters one of the Monza chicanes in Surtees TS9 '005', 1972 Italian GP, on his way to second place. Car retains TS7-style angular tub but has hip radiators, pierced bluff nose.* Above: *Surtees's distinctively angular monocoque structure dominates this view of Alan Jones's TS19 at Ricard, 1976.*

fastest lap in the German GP, finishing fourth, and he was third in Austria, but the tail-end of the season slumped and like Hailwood he suffered a suspension collapse at Watkins Glen.

For 1974, new TS16 cars emerged, similar to the TS14s in configuration but some 60 lb lighter. Five were built and raced by Pace and Mass, while Leo Kinnunen handled the prototype for AAW Racing mid-season, non-qualifying and getting nowhere. Pace abruptly walked out on Surtees after the Swedish GP, joining Brabham to Surtees's intense disgust, and as the team slid down the tubes Dolhem, Bell and Jabouille all variously tried the cars and failed to qualify. BMW's Austrian veteran Dieter Quester drove 'TS16/005' in Austria and finished ninth, but Bell, Dolhem and Kinnunen all failed to qualify at Monza where Surtees is a folk hero and that really hurt.

Austrian F2 driver Helmuth Koinigg was given a drive alongside Bell in Canada and though Bell again failed to qualify, the uncomplicated newcomer drove very well in 'TS16/005' to finish 10th. Next time out, at Watkins Glen, poor Koinigg crashed '003 – apparently due to a tyre failure – and was killed, and Delhem's sister car '004 was withdrawn when the sad news reached the pits.

This was a tragic end to a season in which Team Surtees had almost sunk without trace. Earlier, Pace had finished fourth in his native Brazil, Mass was second and set fastest lap in the minor Silverstone meeting, but from the Belgian GP, where Kinnunen non-qualified, the cars recorded 16 race starts, 11 non-qualifications, only four finishes (9-10-11-14) and no points.

Surtees was spent as a serious force. In 1975 he ran modified TS16s as a one-car team for Watson, who started 14 races including the Race of Champions and the minor Silverstone event, (the team not going to Germany, Italy or the USA). He finished 10 times, reaching second in the Race of Champions in 'TS16/004' and fourth at Silverstone, fifth in the 'Swiss' GP but never scoring a Championship point.

For 1976 the Edenbridge works developed new TS19 cars, featuring a double-angle pyramid-section chassis reminiscent of the Brabham BT42-44 series. Very small and very nicely made, two works cars with different sponsors were run, essentially for Jones and Lunger, and fortunes improved.

The American gave 'TS19/001' its debut alone in South Africa and Jones was second sensationally in '002 on its debut at the Race of Champions. Thereafter a new '003 appeared for Lunger in Sweden while Pescarolo occasionally raced '001 under Team Norev Racing colours. The cars made a total 37 starts, Lunger non-qualifying at Long Beach and Jarama, Pescarolo at Monaco and the Nürburgring. The revived team achieved remarkable reliability as the cars finished 26 times and their last four GPs – the Italian, Canadian, US and Japanese – saw 11 Surtees starts and no retirements. Lunger, Pescarolo and Jones ran cars '002, '004 and '001 in the first three events, Jones taking '004 in Japan while Lunger and Pescarolo stayed home and Noritake Takahara drove '002. Best results were Jones's fourth in Japan and fifths in the British and Belgian GPs.

Surtees was one of the teams picking up crumbs in 1977, when TS19s were campaigned for Brambilla, supported most often by Binder but also occasionally when rent was offered by Perkins, Tambay, Trimmer, Divina Galica, Schuppan and Leoni. The gritty Perkins finished fourth in Belgium to score the team's first points of the year, Brambilla and Schuppan 5-7 in Germany and Brambilla sixth in Canada.

With improved Beta Tools and British Air Ferries backing in 1973, the TS19s were at last superseded by the improved TS20 – another distinctive pyramid-section Surtees – in mid-season, drivers Brambilla and Keegan setting out to do the whole season, never scoring a point and

Brambilla being injured in the Monza collision which led to Peterson's death.

Arnoux and Gabbiani drove 'TS20/003' and '001 in the final US and Canadian races of that season, which marked Surtees's swansong, for without Championship points his team's FOCA membership was in jeopardy along with travel savings this entailed outside Europe. John was in any case also unhappy with the handling of Formula 1 finances where the minor teams were concerned, and when he could find no adequate sponsor for his new TS21 design he withdrew from World Championship racing.

Some recent Surtees cars raced on in bush-league Shellsport Formula 1, but drivers like Phillip Bullman, Claude Bourgoignie, Robin Smith, Richard Jones, Gordon Smiley, and Branco Abdul-Halik were hardly expected to build any legends.

Tecno

The Pederzani brothers of Bologna made their company's name with a long line of highly successful racing karts, followed by a series of ultra-short-wheelbase spaceframe Formula 3, and eventually Formula 2, cars. By 1971, they felt sufficiently confident in their own capabilities to embark upon a comprehensive and costly Formula 1 project, developing a flat-12 *boxer* engine broadly similar to Ferrari's superb 312B. The brothers won backing from Martini & Rossi, and after many delays their prototype *Tipo* PA123 chassis 'T-001' made its public debut in the Belgian GP at Nivelles-Baulers. The ugly flat-topped, tumble-home-sided aluminium monocoque used similar hybrid construction to Ferrari, with a tubular infra-frame stiffened by the riveted-on aluminium stress skins. The Tecno engine was stressed and bolted rigidly to the monocoque's rear bulkhead, whereas Ferrari's was still suspended from an overhead beam at that time.

The Pederzanis had planned to use side-mounted radiators, but testing proved the flat-12's cooling demand was so high that a huge nose radiator was necessary, cowled by a full-width bluff nose.

Suspension was unusual only in placing its coil-spring/dampers almost vertically, while track was the narrowest in Formula 1.

Two spare engines were in the Tecno truck at Nivelles and snide comments upon the car's untidy appearance faded as driver Galli hurtled past the pits, the flat-12's exhaust howling a higher, more piercing note than Ferrari's. The green anodized induction trumpets added an unusual sartorial touch, while Galli qualified second to last and ran respectably before spinning in front of a Ferrari causing a collision.

The Tecno reappeared in the minor race at

Vallelunga, Rome, Galli finishing third amongst five finishers from only seven starters. Great race, that one . . .

Second driver Bell ran '002 at Clermont-Ferrand but did not start as the chassis cracked in practice. Galli tackled the British GP with '002 which had a new rear suspension cross-beam over the gearbox and coil/dampers more conventionally angled to improve their working efficiency, redesign being by Ron Tauranac of Brabham fame.

Nürburgring expert Bell drove '002 in Germany, the car having widened front suspension and revised oil tankage. Its engine failed. Suspension development continued but in Austria Galli was '17th' (unclassified) and for the Italian GP at Monza a second chassis '005 [sic] emerged with neater front suspension and Matra-like full-width chisel nose for Galli alongside regular '002 for Bell, who failed to qualify, while Galli completed only seven laps before the engine failed again.

Only '005, for Bell, was taken to North America but this was a wasted journey as it crashed on the warm-up lap in Canada, while at Watkins Glen the engine failed after only eight laps.

The project had made little progress but continued into 1973 with continued Martini & Rossi support. Ex-McLaren mechanic and F2 Tui constructor Alan McCall was commissioned by Luciano Pederzani to design a new state-of-the-art chassis for the car. Meanwhile, Martini & Rossi racing consultant David Yorke had commissioned the Goral consultancy formed by engineer Gordon Fowell and enthusiast Alan Phillips to produce a new chassis to be built in England by monocoque specialist John Thompson of Northampton, intended to make better use of the Italian engine.

Luciano Pederzani had commissioned McCall in December '72 to create a chassis for him personally – as distinct from the Martini & Rossi race team – to prove it could be done in his Tecno factory. Allan came to think the world of Pederzani who 'was a brilliant machinist and just loved machines. As they had no sheet metal equipment we hand-cut all the aluminium and did all the bends over wood with mallets. I used Tauranac's rear end and did a front end using Tui uprights . . . The front rockers weighed 4 lb each against Ferrari's 16 lb. The motor weighed 84 lb more than a Cosworth and needed 50 gallons to do 200 miles, yet the car weighed in only 38 lb over the limit . . .'

It was built in just ten weeks by McCall, Luciano Pederzani, Swiss mechanic Eddie Wiess and 'the apprentice, Savio'. Pederzani asked McCall to find a driver to run it as the 'Tecno Tui', distinct from Martini & Rossi. Allan contacted fellow Kiwi Chris Amon but his services were then taken up by Martini, along with McCall's new chassis since the rival Goral was not yet ready.

The McCall Tecno 'PA123 T-006' was tested in the wet at Misano-Adriatico at the end of March, but Pederzani then apologized to Allan 'for leading me on, paid me in full a hell of a lot of money and with my contract completed I left . . .' Amon disliked the new chassis but felt the engine had potential – like the flat-12 Ferrari on which he had turned his back in 1969 . . . Interestingly Luciano Pederzani and Allan McCall had parted on good terms, and in 1992 Allan would still declare emphatically, 'For me he was one of the greats in motor sport and I felt privileged to have known him . . .' From a man who had worked with Colin Chapman, Jimmy Clark and Bruce McLaren this is praise indeed . . .

The McCall car then made its public bow in the Belgian GP at Zolder. It employed a triangular planform monocoque tub, with a fenced twin-entry bluff nose, tubular rocker arm front suspension and wishbone rear end. It still looked unfinished, the suspension neither plated nor painted, and the engine was tired after extensive testing. Amon's ex-BRM engineer Aubrey Woods

Chris Amon shone on his debut with the Allan McCall-built Tecno PA123 at Zolder, 1973, finishing sixth despite roasting in the cockpit.

was present, fresh from Amon's catastrophic Formula 2 engine project – everything Amon touched seemed to turn to dust.

Yet he finished that race, utterly exhausted, but in sixth place to score Tecno's first-ever World Championship point. At Monaco he qualified comfortably in mid-field, but retired with brake and chassis problems after running seventh before a front tyre punctured.

Thereafter Tecno withdrew, pending completion of the new Goral E731 chassis, causing Amon to miss the Swedish and French GPs before he reappeared at Silverstone for the British race.

There, both McCall and Goral chassis were available, the latter being a remarkably low, parallel-sided, wedgy affair with a rounded-off flat nose and top-ducted radiator fed from an intake underneath. It was so new that Amon could not even fit properly into its cockpit and its tired old engine made it clearly unraceworthy. Accordingly, he started the race in '006 and retired with fuel pressure problems, which recurred in the next, very poor, downfield performance in Holland.

Both cars were present for the Austrian GP, the McCall device arriving in Tecno's transporter while the Goral was towed in on a trailer behind Fowell's road car. Amon qualified both – just – but flew home before the GP in disgust, opting out of the team. The project simply petered out in acrimony and back-biting and the flat-12 Tecnos would not race again. Martini & Rossi's Formula 1 money found a far more sensible home with Brabham for 1974, while Amon again demonstrated his appalling judgement by commissioning Fowell to build a Cosworth Formula 1 car of his own for that season.

Theodore

The Macau-based millionaire Theodore 'Teddy' Yip had sponsored several teams and drivers before launching his own Formula 1 project for 1978. The little team would be managed by Irish former racing driver and entrant Sidney Taylor, and former Brabham creator Ron Tauranac was commissioned to design and build them a Cosworth/Hewland kit-car which would be called the Theodore TR1.

Ron designed quite one of the ugliest contemporary cars, reasoning that airflow between the wheels of any racing car will be turbulent, so one might as well fill that space with bodywork. He pursued this theory very successfully with his Ralt production cars built in Snelgar Road, Woking, Surrey, and now Theodore Racing took

over those premises while Ralt moved to Brabham's – and Tauranac's – old home at New Haw, near Byfleet, Surrey.

Theodore-Cosworth 'TR1/1' made its debut in Argentina '78 where driver Cheever failed to qualify. The same thing happened in Brazil. Rosberg then took the drive in a new second chassis 'TR1/2' for the minor Silverstone race, qualifying 12th on the 17-strong grid and *winning* in torrential rain which decimated the field and made the most of his car control.

This freak result was really just reward for Yip's years of racing support. The second chassis was used for Long Beach, Monaco and the Belgian GPs but now Rosberg and the team came down to earth with a bump, for they never once managed to qualify. By the time of the British GP, Yip had abandoned the car and was negotiating to buy Wolf machines instead.

Three years later, in 1981, Yip commissioned another Formula 1 Theodore-Cosworth, to be designed by Tony Southgate, having since bought the moribund Shadow team. The season began at Kyalami with ex-Shadow equipment, chassis 'DN12/1' being renumbered 'TR2' for Lees to drive, but he had a collision and later crashed.

Southgate's new 'TY01/1' was a distinctive new wing-car with centre pylon-mounted full-width nose wing, which Tambay debuted in Long Beach, qualifying easily and finishing sixth for an immediate Championship point. Two more chassis were built, modified during the season with progressively abbreviated side pods to make download more manageable, lowering suspensions and eventually sporting conventional canard wings each side of the nose. When Tambay joined Talbot-Ligier in mid-season, Surer took his place. Tambay's seven Theodore races included one non-qualification at Zolder and four finishes apart from Long Beach, his best place being seventh at Monaco. Surer drove eight times, failing to qualify only for the Italian GP, while he finished five times, best placing eighth in Holland. Having scored a Championship point, Theodore placed 12th in the Constructors' table, tied with ATS.

Yip entered a TY01 for Daly at Kyalami opening the 1982 season, while two new aluminium-honeycomb monocoque TY02 cars were built, to be driven by Daly – before his entry into the Williams team – then by Lees, Lammers and, ultimately, the promising Irish newcomer Tommy Byrne.

They achieved nothing. Daly had three races, finishing once, at Kyalami, 14th. Lees's entry was withdrawn at Imola in concert with other FOCA teams, and he retired from the Canadian GP, his only other appearance. Lammers failed to qualify

five times, made the Dutch GP on his native soil but retired, and Byrne failed to qualify three times late-season, and retired in both Austria and Las Vegas.

Yip's struggling Theodore team and Morris Nunn's moribund Ensign outfit then combined for 1983, using the former's name and the latter's cars, continuing the Ensign type and chassis numberings, the uprated cars – see 'Ensign' – becoming N183 variants of the original N181 design. Chassis 'MN16' was an uprated '82 car, while 'MN17' was the uncompleted spare tub that season. The third car, 'MN18', was brand new for Rio '83, both these later cars using carbon-fibre cockpit-stiffening inserts in honeycomb tubs. Team drivers starting the season, and paying for their drives, were Roberto Guerrero and former motor cycle star Johnny Cecotto, while Henton had a one-off drive in '18 at the thinly supported Race of Champions, finishing fourth.

Cecotto tackled all but the last two races of the season, failing to qualify for four, finishing six with a best of sixth at Long Beach for the team's only point.

Guerrero tackled every race but the Championship decider at Kyalami, failing to qualify only once but failing to finish seven times, being too far behind to be classified as a finisher on two occasions and placing 12-13-12 in his last three outings.

At the end of the year it was obvious a turbocharged engine was necessary to survive in Formula 1. Theodore could hope for none, designer Nigel Bennett had already moved to Lola to help design a US CART Championship-winning track-racing car so Yip and Nunn turned to CART racing in search of a smaller pond in which to be big fish . . .

Token

In the early Seventies former Brabham Formula 1 mechanics Ron Dennis and Neil Trundle founded their own Formula 2 team, named Rondel Racing. During 1973 they laid ambitious plans to graduate to Formula 1, building a car designed by Ray Jessop, a former BAC aviation engineer who had worked closely with Brabham in earlier years. Coincidentally, the oil crisis frightened many major companies away from sports sponsorship. In that commercial atmosphere Rondel shelved their plans, but the project was taken up thereafter by businessmen enthusiasts Tony Vlassopoulo and Ken Grob – hence the name Token.

Their Cosworth/Hewland RJ02 'kit car' used a slim, parallel-sided monocoque faintly reminiscent of a Lotus 63 4WD car's, and after a prototype pilot-build, chassis '02' was prepared for racing, making its debut with Pryce driving in the early-1974 Silverstone meeting. It showed quite respectably before its gear linkage went awry. Pryce qualified for the Belgian GP but crashed there, subsequently being taken into the Shadow team.

An entry for Laffite in the French GP was withdrawn and Purley (of LEC fame) then attempted to qualify the car for the British GP but failed. Ian Ashley was another hopeful to drive the Token, finishing 14th and last in the German GP, and being classified 13th in Austria.

Early in 1975 the old car reappeared, entered for fun by John Thorpe's Safir Engineering company which specialized in Range Rover conversions and eventually manufactured the Mark V Ford GTs. Trimmer drove the car twice, being classified 12th (and last) in the Race of Champions and 14th (and last) at Silverstone, after which the RJ02 raced no more.

Derek Daly made three appearances in Teddy Yip's Theodore-Cosworth TY01 in the opening races of the 1982 season, his only finish being 14th at Kyalami. The car was a wealthy enthusiast's hobby, not a serious attempt to get anywhere in Formula 1.

Toleman

Ted Toleman had built up the largest car-transporter company in Britain and indulged his wealth by racing power boats and entering motor racing. He set up his racing team under the management of Alex Hawkridge to campaign and then to build and race cars under his own name. They won the European Formula 2 Championship with Hart power in 1980, using self-built chassis designed by Rory Byrne and John Gentry, and for 1981 took the immensely bold but perilous step of embarking upon Formula 1, not only using untried new Toleman TG181 chassis of their own design and manufacture, but also commissioning a new Hart 415T turbocharged engine based on the successful F2 four-cylinder unit, and untried new Pirelli tyres.

That maiden season was fraught and frustrating. Both team and engine manufacturer operated on tight budgets, though in their Formula 2 star drivers Brian Henton and Derek Warwick they had at least one known quantity. But the pair qualified only once each and only Henton finished his race – tenth in Italy. They joined Formula 1 at Imola with new chassis 'TG181-01' and '02, '03 subsequently appearing for Warwick at Jarama, '04 for him at Silverstone and '05 for Henton at Zandvoort.

In 1982 Toleman continued with their ungainly and ugly TG181C aluminium monocoque cars, now sponsored by Candy, the Italian domestic machinery manufacturers, and drivers were Warwick and the Italian Teo Fabi. One 1981 B-spec car '05 was retained, and two new C-spec cars '06 and '07 were completed. An all-new carbon-fibre TG183 emerged at Monza for Warwick. The carbon moulded tub was reinforced by Kevlar rods, used pullrod suspension in place of the '181's familiarly awful tube-stayed rocker arm system, and was a far nicer package. The nose-mounted oil cooler was retained within much prettier bodywork and the steadily improving Hart engine was now semi-stressed.

It was hoped this car would be a great improvement over the old 'Belgrano' as the TG181s had been dubbed, but first time out at Monza it was appalling. Warwick's season included three non-qualifications, two withdrawn entries (Detroit and Montreal) but 11 starts, much better than '81 despite only two finishes – 15-10 in France and Germany. Fabi's year saw seven non-qualifications, the two scratched entries in North America and only seven races, never finishing.

After two years of barely relieved struggle, Toleman became established in 1983. Unfortunately their Hart engine turbochargers gave more trouble than the engine itself, Garrett were disinclined to assist adequate development so Brian Hart adopted British Holset turbochargers instead, pursuing vigorous development with them.

New flat-bottom TG183B cars were developed for that season, the prototype '01 being updated and '02-3-4 appearing new as the season progressed. Giacomelli and Warwick drove. Warwick qualified for all 15 GPs, finishing six and came eighth in Rio and seventh at Spa. Then, with reliability and the driving ability he had always displayed, he finished 4-6-5-4 in the season-ending series of GPs at Zandvoort, Monza, Brands Hatch and Kyalami. Giacomelli was less successful overall, failing to qualify at Monaco, but his 14 GPs included five finishes, reaching seventh at Monza and sixth at Brands Hatch to place both Tolemans in the points.

Toleman were unable to progress properly in 1984, however. They ran the four TG183Bs, '02-3-4-5, into early-season for new drivers Senna and Cecotto, and Senna more than compensated for the loss of Warwick to Renault Sport. Cecotto destroyed '04 during practice in South Africa, and the all-new TG184 then emerged; three being built ('01-2-3) ready for Dijon. A new car '04 was ready for Cecotto at Brands Hatch but within its first lap it was utterly demolished as the throttle jammed open and Cecotto was severely injured

when the carbon tub shattered against the barriers. Final car '05 was new for Senna at Hockenheim, the young Brazilian star being joined by Swede Johansson for season's end.

Cecotto made nine starts for the team, before his British accident, but finished only once, ninth in Montreal. Senna non-qualified at Imola but started 14 other GPs, being suspended from the Italian race after breaking his Toleman contract option by signing with Team Lotus for 1985. He finished six times and made the most of his car, with a rousing second place in pouring rain – coming within an ace of winning – at Monaco, third at Estoril and Brands Hatch, sixth in both Kyalami and Zolder, then seventh at Montreal. Johansson finished fourth at Monza and 11th at Estoril from his three late-season starts.

While Senna began winning GPs for Lotus in 1985, Toleman found themselves in a dreadful tangle after Michelin pulled out of Formula 1 at the end of '84. Hawkridge's raucous criticism of Pirelli in the past hung about the team's neck like an albatross.

Goodyear were fully extended and would service no more teams and while Rory Byrne had a very promising new TG185 Hart-powered chassis ready there were no serious tyres on which to run it. This was a body-blow to both team and winter development of the Hart engine, agonizing for signed-up drivers Watson and Johansson. It was only corrected when they bought out Spirit's F1 tyre contract as that tiny team's exit gambit, and with Benetton sponsorship Teo Fabi emerged to drive a single Toleman entry from Monaco. Watson was left without any drive, while Johansson had been summoned to Ferrari.

Four TG185s were ready in time for Monaco, Fabi racing '3, then '4 being damaged in practice at the Nürburgring before becoming new number two Ghinzani's car, while '5 was new for Fabi at the Österreichring, completing the season thereafter.

The Byrne cars again operated very effectively relative to the restricted power of their Hart engines, a stepped tub underside generating useful extra aerodynamic download and creating great interest. Fabi took a popular pole position in Germany, but the cars were unreliable, being classified only twice in 13 starts – 12th at Monza, 14th (not running) at Ricard. Ghinzani did not start in his Toleman debut at the Österreichring,

Stefan Johansson driving the Toleman-Hart TG184 in Ayrton Senna's place in the 1984 Italian GP – note the massively effective rear wing with its 'side-step' outrigger winglets, banned come 1985.

then contested the next six GPs, retiring each time.

It has always been hard for such a small team using such an effectively shoestring engine but the promise of BMW power for 1986 made the future look brighter, for in recent years Toleman's chassis had promised better results than could be achieved without reliable horsepower. The acquisition of the team by the Benetton family (which would prompt a change of name prior to the new season) also suggested that better times lay ahead. See page 223.

Trojan

Peter Agg's Trojan group of companies built production McLaren racing cars until McLaren abandoned minor-Formula design at the end of 1972. Ron Tauranac, late of Brabham, was then hired to redesign Trojan's basically McLaren M21 Formula 2 monocoque to form the Trojan T101 Formula 5000 customer car for 1973. Agg was keen to enter Formula 1 and, after completing a T102 F5000 design for 1974, Tauranac was asked to produce a Cosworth-engined T103 Formula 1 car for Schenken to drive that season.

Tauranac produced a very simple, ugly car, with split nose radiators fairing the front wheels and a broad centre-section filling the area between the wheels 'where the air's going to be all messed up and turbulent anyway'. Oil coolers were suspended behind the rear wheels to provide a radiator at each corner of the Suzuki motor cycles and Homelite chainsaws-logoed car.

Budget was minimal and 'T103/1' ran in nine of the season's European GPs, being refused an entry in Sweden and failing to qualify in Holland and Germany. It finished three of its seven starts, 14-10-10 in Spain, Belgium and Austria, and was withdrawn thereafter. It was not a design to be proud of but as a car that had been built very quickly and very cheaply indeed it actually did rather well for itself.

Tyrrell

After Stewart's retirement and Cevert's tragic death at the end of 1973, Tyrrell Racing Organisation designer Derek Gardner abandoned a new very short wheelbase, low polar moment car for 1974 and substituted instead a longer wheelbase car, still advanced with torsion bar suspension, all-inboard brakes and hip radiators slung on a slender monocoque – the Tyrrell 007. New drivers Scheckter and Depailler began the season in the ex-Stewart '005' and '006-2' cars (see Chapter 7), making six starts in Argentina, Brazil and South Africa, and finishing five times, including Depailler's 6-4 placings at Buenos Aires and Kyalami.

'007/1' made its debut at Jarama with Scheckter fifth. At Zolder, two 007s ran, Scheckter on the front row, fifth in the race. Depailler reverted to '006-2' for Monaco and also at Dijon mid-season after crumpling his 007 in practice, otherwise it was 007s throughout.

In all, four were built, and Scheckter used the prototype until Canada. There, as he drove '3, its right-front inboard brake straps broke one by one; he felt the first go but pressed on because he was racing and crashed only when the last finally parted. Chassis '007/2' was flown out for the final race at Watkins Glen. Depailler's normal mount was '2 until new car '4 ran in North America.

At Monaco the cars had run with doubled straps on the inboard brake disc mountings to control a recent spate of breakages. At Zandvoort, experiments on Depailler's car tested different rear suspension geometry and extended radiator pod cowling in an attempt to enhance airflow through the cores, which was unsuccessful. New '007/3' made its bow at Brands Hatch, where Scheckter suffered failures of a rear suspension top link and a front brake strap in practice, before winning the race to compensate.

Car '007/4' emerged at the Österreichring with the revised rear suspension, but it did not run, Gardner explaining that its geometry would show better on a bumpier course.

At Monza he experimented with in-line water radiators, parallel to the car's longitudinal axis. They were fitted to Depailler's car in addition to the standard face-on podded cores, and piped separately during practice. March had worked towards this mounting with shallow-angled radiators in their 741, and Postlethwaite's Hesketh would run in-line hip radiators in the next race, in Canada. They would become common. Scheckter's car featured an adjustable sliding windscreen to arrive at the most comfortable height without cutting.

The Tyrrell 007s made 21 starts, finishing 15 times, including Scheckter and Depailler achieving 1-2 at Anderstorp. Scheckter finished a lucky first in the British GP, was second in Monaco and Germany, third in Belgium and Italy, fourth in France, fifth in Spain and Holland and could have won the Drivers' title at the last round at Watkins Glen, only for a fuel system fault to dash his hopes.

The 007s continued through 1975, though now with an outboard front brake conversion to load up Goodyear's latest-generation tyres; after Kyalami, coil/dampers replaced the difficult to adjust torsion bars, being mounted inboard front, outboard rear, and making the cars more comfortable to drive.

New chassis '007/5' for Scheckter at Kyalami introduced abbreviated delta pods with angled radiators, a new airbox and rear coil-springs. Depailler's '007/2' sported a similar system. Stronger lower front wishbones were fitted after a failure to Depailler's car at Interlagos. In Spain both race cars ran slanted radiators.

At Ricard new chassis '007/6' emerged, whose use of thinner gauge in places saved some 30 lb, which allowed the team to run a third entry for Jabouille. Scheckter crashed this car in the rainstorm at Silverstone, and a new chassis was hastily completed for the Nürburgring, taking the same number '6 even though it was actually the

eighth 007 tub built. A tyre deflated and Scheckter crashed again, the third '007/6' emerging brand new in Austria! At Watkins Glen the 007s ran glass-fibre under-skirt strips as pioneered by Brabham and McLaren, Leclère driving a third entry, retiring with engine failure.

Scheckter and Depailler made 28 starts in the 1975 Championship rounds – all 14 GPs – but were inconsistent, though reliable. Scheckter finished 11 times, results running 11-1-7-2-7-'16'-9-'3'-8-8-6; winning at Kyalami, second at Zolder and classified third after crashing at Silverstone. He placed seventh in the Drivers' table, with 20 points. Depailler also finished 11 times, 5-3-5-4-12-9-6-'9'-9-11-7, his first four finishes scoring points in Argentina, South Africa, Monaco and Belgium but tailing off thereafter. Depailler was ninth in the Drivers' table while Tyrrell came fifth with 25 points in the Constructors' Cup.

Through 1976 Gardner developed his remarkable six-wheeled Project 34 design detailed elsewhere, but the team began the season with 007s '4 and '6. Both chassis were started in three GPs, then one (chassis '6 for Scheckter) was used at Silverstone, and again in Spain where Depailler gave P34 chassis '2 its debut.

Scheckter and Depailler finished 5-2 in Brazil, 4-9 at Kyalami and, respectively, retired with suspension failure and placed third at Long Beach in 007s. Scheckter was third at Silverstone and suffered an engine problem at Jarama, where the six-wheeler's debut ended with a crash due to brake problems, after qualifying third.

Both Tyrrell drivers had P34s for Zolder – Scheckter taking '3, Depailler in '2 – and they would run these same cars until Österreichring in August where 'P34/4' appeared as spare and Scheckter destroyed '3 after suspension failure. A replacement '3-2 was completed but Scheckter drove new chassis '4 late-season, Depailler driving '3-2 for the first time at Fuji.

In all, the new P34s made 27 starts and finished 19 times, making remarkable early-season progress. Their results included, consecutively: fourth and engine failure at Zolder, 2-3 at Monaco, and 1-2 at Anderstorp where Tyrrell had achieved similar success with the 007s two years before. Thereafter, from the French to the Japanese GPs, the six-wheelers' results read 6-2, 2-R, 2-crashed, crashed-R, 5-7, 5-6, 4-2, 2-R, R-2.

Meanwhile, old '007/4' had been sold to the Italian Scuderia Gulf-Rondini for Alessandro Pesenti-Rossi, who made his debut in the German GP finishing 14th, last and lapped. He placed 11th in Austria, where '007/6' had been entered by OEASC Racing for Otto Stuppacher who was not allowed to start. Pesenti-Rossi failed to qualify at Zandvoort but was 18th at Monza. Stuppacher did not start in the latter race, packing up and going

Jody Scheckter shows off the clean lines of Derek Gardner's 1974 Tyrrell 007, challenging hard for the World Championship title.

home before it began. He then made the long trip to non-qualify in Canada and the USA. Chassis '007/5' emerged in Japan, entered by Heros Racing for Kazuyoshi Hoshino, and retiring as weather conditions changed and no spare tyres were available to the little local team.

The Tyrrell P34s had given Scheckter 12 races and ten finishes, 4-2-1-6-2-2-5-5-4-2, finishing third in the Drivers' table, while Depailler's 13 P34 drives yielded only seven finishes, 3-2-2-7-6-2-2, building his reputation as the eternal second in Sweden, France, Canada and Japan. He was fourth behind his team-mate in the Championship, and Tyrrell third in the Constructors' Cup.

Depailler was probably the strongest 'number two' in the Formula. He could have won in Canada where he was challenging for the lead until intoxicated by a fuel leak and in Japan he led briefly until tyre trouble intervened.

For 1977 it all went wrong: the updated P34s were bulkier, heavier and unwieldy, while their tyres were off the pace, lacking development and ignored by Goodyear who had to concentrate upon their more numerous four-wheeled clients. Peterson joined Depailler as Scheckter had moved to Wolf. New chassis '5 emerged for Peterson at Kyalami, '7 being raced by Depailler from Spain and the Frenchman pressing spare car '6 into active service from Austria to season's end.

They made 34 starts, finishing only 15 times, the best being Depailler's second in Canada after qualifying sixth quickest, while Peterson qualified third there but retired with a fuel leak. Depailler was also third in Japan, Argentina and South Africa; Peterson came third in Belgium in the wet, Depailler reached fourth at Long Beach and in Sweden, Peterson was fifth in Austria and sixth in Italy. The Swede ended the year and his brief Tyrrell career with fastest race lap and fifth on the grid at Watkins Glen, before being rammed up the tail by Villeneuve's Ferrari at Fuji.

Otherwise reliability and competitiveness had gone out the window. It was a sad Tyrrell season, with the drivers 8-14 in their Championship and the team placed fifth with only 27 points in its Championship.

The cars had been heavy and difficult to drive, and the drivers became frustrated and disappointed. Derek Gardner returned to the motor industry and Maurice Phillippe took over as Tyrrell's Chief Designer.

In 1978 Phillippe produced a typically minimum-limit four-wheeled P34 replacement, trimmed to the bone but beautifully built. It was

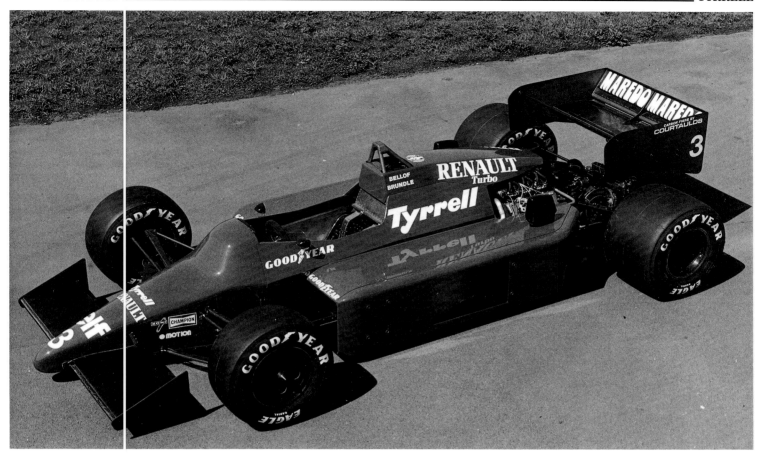

'1 in the original opening-lap collision at Spa, and '4 – which was brand new at the time – following Streiff's brake problem at Monaco. The first three DG016s had all made their debut at Rio, '3 as spare, chassis '5 was introduced for Streiff at Detroit, '6 for Palmer at Hungaroring, and '7 for Streiff at Monza.

One major problem beset the team early in the season, an unaccountable and apparently incurable misfire. Cosworth's management system boffins eventually traced and eradicated it during lengthy tests at Donington Park. Once the problem was cured this once-great team never looked back – top of the B-stream class . . .

After demolishing his car against Streiff's spinning sister machine in the initial start at Spa, Palmer was unable to take the restart, but otherwise he contested every race and finished all but two of them, fourth overall in Adelaide, fifth at Detroit and Hockenheim and seventh at Ricard, Hungaroring and Mexico City. His other finishes overall were 10-11-8-11-14-10-8 and he won the Jim Clark Trophy 'atmo' class drivers' championship with no fewer than 95 points to team-mate Streiff's 74 in second place. Overall the Tyrrell twins placed 11th-equal with Nakajima and 14th-equal with Andrea de Cesaris in the 'big boys' Championship. Streiff's own record included a non-start in Austria after losing his car in an abortive start, and otherwise he retired from only three of his 15 GPs, placed fourth at Hockenheim and sixth at Ricard, seventh at Jerez and 11-8-9-10-9-12-12-8-12 elsewhere.

For 1988 – with more major teams turning to 3.5-litre atmo engines – the World Championship was obviously going to be a harsher, colder environment for the still small and now underfinanced Tyrrell Racing Organisation. Five new Brian Lisles-designed 017 cars were produced for Palmer and newcomer Julian Bailey, who never quite made the grade. The new chassis '1 and '2 had been introduced respectively for Palmer and Bailey at Rio, '3 followed new for Bailey at Monaco, '4 for Palmer at Montreal and '5 for Palmer at Suzuka, although it would not be raced either there or at Adelaide to complete the season.

Tyrrell used a kind of half-way-house Cosworth engine, based upon the new DFR-style lowered crankcases in what were otherwise their Hart-

Tyrrell have built some of the most purposeful and no-nonsense of Formula 1 cars and their 014 model of 1985 was no exception, tailored to match the demands of the Renault V6 turbocharged engine, with narrow aluminium-sided monocoque, rectilinear side pods and large rear wing.

rebuilt DFZ V8s. Cosworth simply needed to increase casting quantity of their DFR crankcases in order to minimize unit cost, and Tyrrell understandably were happy to oblige by having them built into engines for their cars. But to any outsider with his heart in the right place, Tyrrell's struggles of '88 were painful to see. They suffered a heavy fall from the somewhat artificial relative heights of 1987 . . .

Palmer twice failed to qualify and he failed to finish eight races. His results record read 14-5-6-5-4-11-12 – high spots obviously being those fifth places at Monaco and Detroit and sixth in Montreal. Bailey unfortunately failed to qualify ten times, his six races yielding three true finishes – 16-12-14 at Silverstone, Monza and Suzuka and he was also classified ninth after late retirement in Detroit.

The team finished eighth in the Constructors' Championship, with five points, beating new-boys Rial and Minardi.

Hope was breathed into the team by the appointment of Harvey Postlethwaite and aerodynamicist Jean-Claude Migeot fresh from Ferrari to pull Tyrrell away from the precipice in 1989.

For 1989 017 chassis '3, '4 and '5 were uprated as 017Bs for the start of the season – featuring inboard six-speed gearboxes mounted ahead of the final-drive and intended for the new 018s, five of which replaced them progressively from Imola forward.

The new 018 featured a 'mono-shock' front suspension damper, with both front suspension pushrods activating a single Koni damper mounted against the 'scuttle' ceiling within the monocoque moulding. Side pods were small, compact and confined and a neat engine airbox rose behind the cockpit, enclosing the roll-over bar. The prototype Postlethwaite/Migeot 018 made its debut at Imola where new team driver Michele Alboreto failed to qualify and old hand Palmer took it over for the race. Chassis '2 was introduced for

Alboreto at Monaco, '3 for Palmer at Ricard, '4 for him at Hockenheim and '5 new as team spare at Monza, first being raced at Jerez – by newcomer Jean Alesi.

While Palmer and Alboreto began the season with the team, the Italian was later replaced by Johnny Herbert at Spa and Estoril, and more permanently by the Formula 3000 star, Jean Alesi – who proved to be Formula 1's find of the season.

Alboreto drove only the first six races before splitting from Tyrrell to join the Larrousse-Lola team after missing three mid-season races. For Tyrrell he had failed to qualify at Imola, retired twice at Phoenix and Montreal but finished third in Mexico, fifth at Monte Carlo and tenth in trouble at Rio. Palmer's third complete season with the Ockham team saw him contest all 16 races, failing to qualify for the last, in Adelaide. He failed to finish seven times, though classified ninth in Phoenix. He placed sixth at Imola and Estoril but otherwise seventh at Rio, then 9-10-13-14-10 was an indifferent record.

Herbert's two Tyrrell outings at Spa and Estoril ended in retirement and non-qualification respectively, but Alesi electrified everybody in Formula 1 with a battling fourth place upon his debut in the French GP at Ricard, a result he repeated at Jerez, adding fifth at Monza, his other races ending in ninth and tenth places and three retirements.

Tyrrell ended this transitional season fifth in the Constructors' Cup, their best result for years, with 16 points in the wake of Benetton and the big three – McLaren, Williams and Ferrari.

The definitive 1990 Tyrrell was the all-new Postlethwaite/Migeot-designed 019, seven chassis being produced, but the team actually began the new season with three old 018s, chassis '2, '3 and '5, to be driven at Phoenix and Interlagos by Alesi and Satoru Nakajima, ex-Lotus and a player in the manoeuvrings which promised Tyrrell Honda V10 engines for 1991, by which time McLaren would be running the new 3.5-litre Honda V12s.

The Cosworth DFR-engined 019 offered a major stride in enhanced ground-effect aerodynamic performance. The car complied with flat-bottom regulations by provision of a flat underfloor extending forward to the trailing edge of the front wheels, ahead of which the underside of the fuselage

Satoru Nakajima in his final season of Formula 1 with the Honda V10-engined Tyrrell 020 which proved such a disappointment after a promising start in 1991. The Migeot/Postlethwaite raised-nose feature pioneered in the preceding 019 is clearly visible.

forepart reared steeply to a raised needle nose cone. This raised nose section moulded round into an aerodynamic splitter where it met the regulation underfloor and with distinctive anhedral front wings clearing airflow onto this splitter a significant increase in download was harnessed without resort to an oversized rear wing. The Tyrrell 019 emerged with a notable edge on straightline speed.

The quality of the Postlethwaite/Migeot package was proven by the ease with which it could be set up for differing circuits, leaving maximum time for the team to test, develop and select its Pirelli tyres.

A single coil-spring/damper unit reclined longitudinally within the fuselage, disc springs at each end of the torsion bar connecting the upper ends of the suspension pushrods.

The first raised-nose 019s replaced the 018 at Imola, chassis '1 for Nakajima, '2 for Alesi (unraced) and '3 the spare which the French-Sicilian took over for the GP. Nakajima's prototype car was wrecked in a violent first-corner accident during its debut there and never raced again. Tyrrell-Cosworth '019/4' followed at Montreal, '5 had a brief life as spare at Ricard and Silverstone, '6 made its debut for Alesi at Monza and '7 for Nakajima at Jerez. Tyrrell had adopted Pirelli tyres just before Phoenix and the manner in which Alesi led there in the old 018 despite zero pre-race testing on the Italian tyres had raised terrific optimism.

When Brian Hart produced 'a sensational 625 bhp at 11,500 rpm' development DFR, the Tyrrell 019 proved a most competitive package for a team still operating on limited finance, though the edge went off performances – and team harmony – in the last third of the season.

Alesi did not start at Suzuka – by which stage of the season his relationship with the team was very strained – and he was classified 11th after failing to finish at Hockenheim. Otherwise he retired from five races and his finishing record read 2-7-6-2-7-8-8-8-8, demonstrating his and his team's decline as the season passed its height. His second places in Phoenix and Monte Carlo demon-

strated his tigerish qualities as a street racer, his sixth place being scored at Imola.

Meanwhile Nakajima was unable to restart at Estoril and he suffered worse reliability, failing to finish ten times, and otherwise placing 6-8-11-6-6 – scoring his points one by one at Phoenix – a fine weekend for the team, finishing second and sixth, although there had been handy attrition amongst natural front-runners – Monza and Suzuka (of course).

Tyrrell finished fifth again in the Constructors' Championship, with 16 points, and looked forward to V10 Honda power for 1991.

The Ockham team looked resurgent in preparation for the 1991 season, having secured the works Honda V10 in revised RA101E form just replaced by the V12 at McLaren, and with a suitably revised version of the often impressive Postlethwaite/Migeot-conceived 1990 019 car to carry it. After early promise, however, the new George Ryton-designed Tyrrell-Honda 020 was to prove a considerable disappointment, in part due to the team's failure to come to grips with the V10 engine's own physical disadvantages, in part due to the woeful inconsistency of the Pirelli tyres they had agreed to use.

The Honda V10 was quite a bulky – rather typically untidy – engine and despite Tyrrell producing a new transverse six-speed gearbox (around X-Trac internals) to maintain the old Cosworth V8 car's wheelbase, the former weight distribution was adversely affected. Essentially the 020 fuselage retained the general form of the 019 with an evolutionary nose form, inverted gull-wing canard wings and the same mono-shock suspension.

Early gearbox problems had to be cured but with its altered weight distribution the 020 quickly proved to have lost the 019's outstanding turn-in performance. Tyrrell's associated Honda V10 engine crew thoroughly enjoyed early-season performances which repeatedly showed the in-house rival V12 used by McLaren in a poor light, and at Monaco Stefano Modena shone in his 020 – running second behind Senna's McLaren until a catastrophic engine failure in the tunnel sent shrapnel ripping clean through the car's carbon-composite underfloor.

When Harvey Postlethwaite's contract expired at the end of July, he bowed out of Formula 1 for the time being, joining the Sauber/Mercedes-Benz Group C operation with a re-entry to GP racing a future target. When the Daimler-Benz board

voted otherwise, he would return to Fiat-Ferrari as their new technical director for '92.

Meantime, Pirelli's tyres seemed super-sensitive to ambient temperature changes, introducing another wild card variable into the already difficult task of pinpointing handling deficiencies. Driver Nakajima was effectively going through the motions in his last season before retiring, and after mid-season Modena apparently lost heart. Nakajima finished only seven times, 5-10-12-8-15-13-17, which was not particularly impressive, while Modena's record included nine finishes, second in Canada, fourth in Phoenix, 11-7-13-12-16-6-10 elsewhere. The drivers felt that Benetton's Pirelli tyres were superior to the covers provided to them, and it was not until a late-season Silverstone test just prior to the last two GPs that a modified chassis ('020/8' – last of the 1991 series) with revised suspensions proved a great improvement. It was too late, however, as Honda's V10 would be Mugen-labelled for use by Footwork in '92, and sponsor Braun was abandoning Formula 1 . . . Tyrrell's 1991 great leap forward had stumbled on take-off.

Williams

Frank Williams, sometime Formula 3 racing driver turned racing car dealer-cum-team patron, graduated very successfully from running a Formula 2 Brabham into Formula 1 in 1969, entering a Cosworth-powered Brabham BT26 for his great friend Piers Courage. For 1970 he ran de Tomasos – Courage losing his life in one – and in 1971-72 March cars. There were many disadvantages in running proprietary cars, so when FOCA began organizing charter travel and race promoters introduced sensible start and prize money, the time was clearly ripe for Williams to build his own Formula 1 cars.

One of his sponsors, the Italian Politoys toy company, put up £40,000 towards the construction of a Len Bailey-designed car. Bailey had worked formerly on the Ford GT40 project, and his new 'Coke bottle' aluminium tub was made by Gomm Metal Developments of Old Woking, Surrey. Williams based his team in Bennett Road, Reading, Berkshire.

Former Brabham constructor Ron Tauranac acted briefly as Williams's technical consultant and the Politoys-Cosworth FX3 made its debut in the 1972 British GP at Brands Hatch. Like all

Bailey creations, it was very pretty with shallow bulbous tub and chisel front-radiator nose, but Pescarolo destroyed it early in the race. Amon drove the rebuilt car back at Brands Hatch for the final Formula 1 race of the year but retired, misfiring.

For 1973, Williams cars were backed by Piero Rivolta, of Iso-Rivolta, and Marlboro, being known as Iso-Marlboros. Three of these modified FX3s were completed, drivers initially by Ganley and Galli, then by other rent-a-drivers paying for the privilege. John Clarke, ex-March, designed new Iso-Marlboro IR cars to match the new deformable-structure regulations, in force from the Spanish GP. These were nice cars and handled well but suffered oil system problems which broke many engines. Williams called in de Tomaso designer GianPaolo Dallara, who changed the rear suspension geometry; Clarke left in an understandable huff, for the cars' results reflected budget more than design quality.

During 1973 the early-season FX3s made nine starts, finishing only four times, the best being Trimmer's fourth in 'FX3B-3' at Brands Hatch. The IR cars made their debut at Barcelona, chassis '3 in Austria, totalling 24 starts with 12 finishes, including sixths in Holland and Canada, driven by van Lennep and Ganley. Ickx was seventh in a guest drive at Watkins Glen, commenting favourably on the car.

Merzario joined for 1974, making a vivid impression in Buenos Aires as he blew two DFVs, leaving the tachometer needle lodged at 13,000 rpm! Since the rev-limiter made this impossible under normal acceleration he must merely have changed down as he would normally have done in his previous flat-12 Ferrari, thereby punching the V8 through the roof on the over-run . . .

Williams ran modified Iso-Marlboros in this season. Driving alongside Merzario were Tom Belso, Gijs van Lennep, Richard Robarts, Jabouille and, ultimately, Laffite, the latter winning a regular place in the last five races. Merzario gave new heart, qualifying brilliantly in South Africa, finishing sixth and going well until a crash at Jarama damped his ardour. He was his old self again at Monza for fourth in his home GP. Overall, the team tackled 16 races, failed to qualify four times and finished only six times, placing 3-6-14-8-9-4, which was not too bad.

Ex-McLaren engineer Ray Stokoe updated the ageing cars and designed a square-cut new monocoque for 1975 designated 'FW04', old IR's becoming FWs. IR02 was rebuilt on a new tub as FW02. With shoestring finance, in part from a tough Swiss businessman named Ambrozium, Williams ran two cars for Merzario and Laffite, though when they had sports car commitments with Alfa Romeo, alternative drivers included Flammini, Brise, Damien Magee, Ian Scheckter, Ian Ashley, Jo Vonlanthen, Renzo Zorzi and Signorina Lella Lombardi.

Williams survived, buying discarded wings and bits from other teams, like Hesketh, to keep running. During 1975 they made 24 starts and finished ten times. It looked hopeless, finishes being 11-7-7-14-12-11 up to the German GP. However, punctures decimated the field there and Laffite finished second – Williams's best finish since 1969 with Courage and the Brabham BT26.

That was worth some £5500 and assured Williams of continued FOCA membership for 1976 with the travel savings that this involved. Frank had met an Austro-Canadian oil-man named Walter Wolf, and when Wolf looked for a Formula 1 team to buy into, Williams gave him 60 per cent in return for liabilities of around £140,000 (see entry for Wolf, pages 329-30).

Late in 1976 Frank was shouldered out of Wolf's racing plans. Ex-Lola engineer Patrick Head had joined him in Reading just before the Wolf takeover, and had stayed on under Dr Postlethwaite through the catastrophic Wolf-Williams season of '76. When Frank left, he took Patrick with him to be Chief Engineer in his new team, Williams Grand Prix Engineering, based in tiny premises in Didcot, Berkshire.

With backing from the sponsors of Belgian driver Patrick Neve, he bought a much-used March 761, chassis '7, for £14,000, and added four Cosworth engines.

WGPE ran the March through 1977, and for 1978 Head designed his first Formula 1 car – the Williams FW06. This arrowhead shaped car was small, light and simple, with in-line hip radiators, nose-duct oil cooler and full-width front wing. Backing came from Saudia Airlines, it was driven by ex-Shadow man Jones, and the Head car worked.

Through 1978 Williams built three FW06s, Jones starting all 16 GPs, finishing nine; fourth at Kyalami, seventh (after running second until a nose wing collapse) at Long Beach, fifth at Ricard, and second on merit in the US GP at Watkins Glen. Before retiring, Jones also ran fourth in Sweden, second at Brands Hatch, third at Hockenheim and looked set for another second place end-of-season at Montreal before suffering a puncture.

WGPE placed ninth-equal in the Constructors' table with this one-car entry and clearly had one of the best non-wing-cars of the year. This assured backing for Head to build the FW07 wing-car for 1979 (see pages 112-17). After ten seasons trying, Williams was about to dominate Formula 1.

At the end of the FW07 period in 1981, Head set out to design a six-wheeler but had also developed reservoirs which helped save startline weight as they could legitimately be topped up after the race to meet the legal minimum weight requirement in scrutineering.

The six-wheeler ploy would continue development but only slowly.

Consequently, the FW07 replacement FW08 emerged at Zolder in 1982 as an ultra-short wheelbase, short chassis car designed around a weight-limit water tank and incorporating a short, tall fuel cell abaft the cockpit.

From the back of the tub it was virtually pure FW07, little changed from 1979 form. Six FW08s were run, a mid-season misfiring problem in Rosberg's car being cured by moving the fuel tank outlet. Rosberg built a good working relationship with the team, and his number two, Daly, was very popular as well as a super race driver but qualified poorly and therefore was prone to startline collisions.

Now Williams were aiming at their third consecutive Cup title. Apart from the change from FW07C to FW08 after Long Beach, little new was tried. Only two different side pod profiles were used, effectively one for fast circuits and one for slow. Later in the year, the wheelbase was lengthened 1½ in. by raking the front suspension forward, altering weight distribution by around 1.5 per cent. Generally, the cars felt more at home on the faster circuits, and for the final race at Las Vegas they reverted to short wheelbase form.

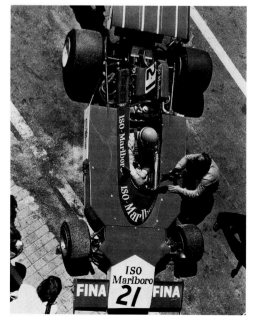

There was experimentation with skirt materials and spasmodic trials of carbon-fibre brakes, but wear rate with the French SEP-made brakes and heat-soak boiling the fluid when the cars stopped precluded their use in anger.

All aerodynamic study was undertaken in Williams's own wind tunnel at Didcot. Much of the expense of Formula 1 disappears into parts never used and some idea of this 'wastage' can be gained from experimental engineer Frank Dernie's wind tunnel programme. Of all the underwing profiles designed, developed and tested, only Marks 1, 4, 6, 7, 13, 18 and 24 were actually raced; the rest just 'weren't good enough'. Mark 18 formed the original FW08 spec, the late-1982 Mark 24 underwing matching a smaller rear wing for faster circuits. The Mark 24 wing gave a four per cent shift in the centre of pressure and by the end of the season Mark 31 was already under test.

Four FW07Cs were used early in 1982, numbers '14-15-16-17, the latter effectively written off by Rosberg at Rio.

The new 'FW08/1' was normally spare, being raced by Rosberg in Montreal, Hockenheim and the Österreichring. Chassis '2 was essentially Dernie's test-team car, spare at Monaco, and performing show and spare car duties at Las Vegas. Chassis '3 was Rosberg's new mid-season race car introduced at Zolder, and he raced it three times to Montreal. Chassis '4 was Daly's debutante at Zolder, and he raced it to Ricard, after which it was retired. Chassis '5 was new for Rosberg at Zandvoort and he raced it eight times, winning the 'Swiss' GP (a Championship round that season) at Dijon. Finally, chassis '6 was new for Daly at Hockenheim.

Rosberg won the World Drivers' Championship, but Williams failed to secure their potential Constructors' Cup hat-trick, placing only fourth in the table behind McLaren and Renault with 58 points. Constructors' Cup success requires not only a fast and reliable car but also two potential winners to drive them.

Rosberg's season included 15 of the 16 GPs as Williams had joined other FOCA teams in the ill-advised boycott of Imola. He finished 12, his record running 5-2*-2-2-4-3-5-3-2-1-8-5 (*disqualified). He scored in every finish save that eighth place in Italy when the rear wing pillar snapped.

In contrast, the record for Daly, who had joined Williams after Reutemann's abrupt retirement from racing, included only the last 12 races, and he was classified only eight times: 6-5-7-5-5-7-9-6. Although five of those finishes scored Championship points, it was not good enough and Williams did not retain him for 1983.

The new year saw Head's design team rejig FW08 to suit new flat-bottom regulations, one 1982 chassis 'FW08-6' being updated while two were completed brand new to C-spec for Rio, chassis 'FW08C/7' and '8. Chassis '9 emerged new at Ricard as a spare car, old chassis '2 was brought to Brands Hatch as a spare following a practice accident to Rosberg, and tubs '10 and '11 were also completed but not required.

Laffite joined Rosberg, but by now the age of the Cosworth had passed.

Early in the year the FW08Cs showed the other Cosworth cars the way, but later McLaren forged ahead on the faster circuits. Extended footbox protection was grafted on to the original tubs to match new 1983 requirements and these early tubs also retained the attachment inserts originally demanded for the old side pods and underwings (which the true 1983 FW08C tubs lacked while featuring integral footbox protection).

One major development programme produced a new Williams six-speed gearbox.

The cars worked quite well wherever they could run a lot of wing, which means slower circuits, but Head admitted 'it was pretty mediocre' elsewhere.

Tyres, again, were dominant, Goodyear's bias-

Frank Williams struggled to keep his team afloat during the early 1970s. His essentially John Clarke-designed 1974 FW-ex-IR-series cars like this one had much to commend them.

The stubby Williams FW08's tub was originally intended for a six-wheeler, hence its brevity. Rosberg (here at Hockenheim) brought the team their second Drivers' World Championship success.

belted 'radials' causing heartache because without turbo power the team could not afford the aerodynamic loads to prevent them 'going doughnut-shaped' at high speed. Towards the end of the year, Laffite's form caused serious concern as he was a shadow of his former self, though prospects looked rosy for the new turbocharged Honda FW09 cars which were prepared hastily for the finale race in South Africa.

These FW09s retained the Head folded aluminium honeycomb chassis form of the FW07-08 series, and in 1984 no less than nine would be used.

Williams had originally concluded a deal with Honda in the winter of 1982/83 for a development car, but Honda wanted to see how the Spirit Formula 1 venture for which they were providing engines would evolve. In mid-summer '83 Head began FW09 design and the prototype was tested at Donington Park prior to the Italian GP. At the time there was no thought of racing a Honda-powered car that season but at Monza Patrick remarked to Frank Williams that if they were to challenge seriously for the Championship in '84 they should race FW09-Hondas in South Africa.

First time out on test both drivers commented how nicely the new Williams-Hondas handled, but initially they had insufficient intercooler capacity to handle full boost at Kyalami, despite qualifying well.

That November, WGPE moved into a stunning new custom-built factory at Didcot, and began stiffening FW09, and producing a complete new gearbox with pullrod rear suspension. In South Africa, the car was quick but showed the dominant understeer which would dog it in 1984.

Starting the new year in Rio, Rosberg fulminated about this understeer, but WGPE could not revert to the old set-up because parts were not available. The pullrod rear end cars had to run unhappily up to Dijon, the new gearbox gave trouble due to a crown-wheel cutting problem, and Head now wished to waist in the rear bodywork *à la* McLaren MP4/2 to seek a useful download advantage without additional drag. This layout demanded rocker arm rear suspension which the new gearbox could not accept, so the tailored

FW09 gearbox had to be set aside and replaced by the old, basically Hewland, FGB as used on the FW07-08 cars.

They ran in this rear rocker arm form from Monaco. An FW09B used the new bobbed-in tail on test prior to the mid-season American tour, one such running in Canada but suffering an engine failure related to exhaust pipe form so everything was then hurriedly modified to original.

The definitive FW09B emerged thereafter with a five-inch longer wheelbase, long rear adaptor, new exhaust system, altered bodywork and side panels, FGB gearbox and FW08-like wider track rocker arm rear suspension. The cars ran essentially in this form for the rest of the year while a new FW10 began design for 1985, nine 1984 cars having been built.

Understeer dominated the season. Some of this appeared to be traceable to the Goodyear radial tyres, but normal palliatives destroyed traction. This was aggravated by the Honda engine's vicious power curve.

Through these problems, Laffite had a miserable season. He retired 11 times and his five finishes (8-8-5-4-14) were the worst WGPE record since the team's first cars ran in 1978. Rosberg fought harder, retiring on 10 occasions, but winning the very hot race at Dallas on personal fortitude and car control, aided by team forethought as he had been provided with a driver cooling device. Elsewhere he placed 2-4-6-5-'9' (having retired but

being classified as a finisher) in the other five GPs, and always running in the top four.

Williams-Honda ended the season sixth in the Constructors' Championship, after a difficult first turbocharged season.

Late in '84, Patrick decided to adopt moulded carbon-composite chassis construction for his 1985 FW10-Honda, the first 'black Williams'. After one pilot-build prototype shell, eight more followed, seven being completed. Chassis '1 and '2 were new at Rio, '3 for Rosberg at Imola. 'FW10/2' was effectively written off at Detroit by new driver Mansell, then a tyre explosion at Ricard destroyed his new 'FW10/5' on its debut. Chassis 'FW10/4' went to Japan for Honda's engine development test programme, driven by Satoru Nakajima.

Chassis '6 was new for Mansell at Silverstone and would win two late-season GPs in his hands, while '7 emerged for Rosberg in Austria and would win the Australian GP season finale.

In early 1985 Williams ran modified D-Type Honda V6s, then from Montreal the revamped E-Type. D engines were given the improved engine mounts of the forthcoming Es to match the FW10 tubs, and were further modified to sidestep early IHI turbocharger problems. A new transmission, still six-speed, had been adopted for the D's narrow rev-band where power was enough ' . . . to break traction in second and third . . . [sigh, then a rather rueful chuckle] . . . and fourth and fifth as well . . .'

The E engines emerged at Montreal where Rosberg finished 25 seconds behind the winning Ferrari despite two stops; Mansell had a boost problem and effectively ran a 185-litre consumption race. Rosberg won the next race, in Detroit – the Williams-Honda had come good. It would fall back briefly with engine bearing problems, then dominate the end of the season.

The FW10s were mechanically acceptable at Ricard but the heat and speeds there aggravated their ferocious hunger for tyres. A spell of unreliability followed – the car at Silverstone, largely the engine bottom-end subsequently – until Spa's team 2-3 finish. Before Brands Hatch, the engine induction and rear of the body were lowered to improve airflow to the rear wing with redesigned transmission and new pullrod instead of rocker arm rear suspension. Now the FW10 could handle Honda's reliable power well enough for a convincing team 1-3 in Mansell's maiden GP win, and he then led a team 1-2 at Kyalami, and Rosberg was victorious in Adelaide.

Rosberg started all 16 GPs, finishing nine, 8-4-1-2-12*-4-3-2-1; Mansell started 15 (missing the French after his monstrous practice accident) and finished ten, 5-5-7-6-6-6-11*-2-1-1, scoring points eight times.

The irrepressible Keke Rosberg as always working the Williams-Honda FW10's suspension hard on his winning way in the 1985 Australian GP. The Adelaide circuit was notoriously hard on brakes, hence the primitive extra cooling trunks lashed onto the front hubs here.

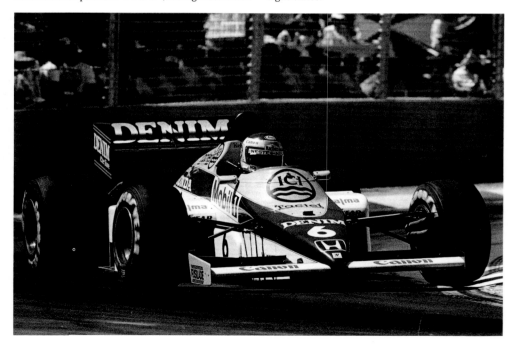

Williams used French SEP carbon brakes everywhere but Detroit and Adelaide where they ran iron, with supreme success.

Their three successive victories in the last three 1985 GPs left Williams looking best-placed for the 1986 season to come.

After their Constructors' World Championship double of 1986-87 – described in Chapter 16 – Williams lost Honda engines for 1988 at desperately short notice.

Having been dumped so abruptly, WGPE had precious little time to prepare a sensible programme for '88. At very short notice their old associate from Cosworth DFV days, John Judd, agreed to supply his new Honda-derived 3.5-litre Type CV V8 engines. Didcot then spent a hectic winter producing suitable new FW12 'atmo' cars from a clean sheet of paper.

To compete with the turbos, any new atmo car had to be right down on the class's minimum weight limit to exploit that 20 kg advantage against the 1500 cc turbocharged opposition. At decision time, all testing experience pointed to Williams's version of active suspension – which they described as 'reactive' in deference to Group Lotus sensibilities – being the way to go. Having opted to use it, mass had to be pared everywhere to achieve minimum weight despite its presence. In retrospect Patrick Head is adamant 'We should have built two-way cars which could carry either reactive or steel-spring suspension – but after an Estoril test with the reactive '11C in which Riccardo Patrese was very quick, then another at Jerez where Nigel said, "This is really good", we thought we were right to commit ourselves entirely to reactive.'

By mid-season, experience proved otherwise. Looking back at Williams's seven sets of redundant reactive-ride components at the end of the year, the magnitude of their '87-88 winter manufacturing programme could be appreciated. These ride systems alone involved almost as great a production programme as the rest of the cars combined. Argentine engineer Enrique Scalabroni also developed an all-new transverse gearbox within a lighter case, packaging gears ahead of the axle into a smaller space.

Feeling they were popularly discounted from any chance in '88 after the Honda débâcle, they reacted spectacularly to qualify second quickest alongside Senna at Rio, well inside the previous atmo record. But precious little joy followed.

Engine installation and systems problems intruded while reactive suspension misbehaviour completely confused and deterred the drivers. The electrical system rectifier seemed unable to cope with heat and vibration. The reactive system broke three top rear wishbones – only once in a race (Mansell at Ricard) – by hammering against its end stops. FW12s abandoned over spreading pools of hydraulic fluid or stricken by electronic glitches became commonplace.

Such ride system problems were not unforeseen, but combined with the team's engine unreliability, manpower became too tight-stretched to cope.

'Running a reactive ride car is a very big deal, you have to take a lot of extra equipment, back-up and people to look after the spares etc. If the car itself had run well we could have handled it, but as it happened we got into a hole and did not exhibit the capability to get out of it. At Silverstone it became bad enough to make the change worthwhile. The result was a cobble-up which worked quite well . . .'

There were few problems converting the cars' rear end overnight from reactive to steel-spring suspensions, but the front end – exceptionally tight on space – was a major headache. Patrick Head left Silverstone at 2.30 Friday afternoon, contacted the Didcot works on his 'Yuppeephone' while driving there and specified disc springs: 'Look up in the catalogue something with the right rates!' Suitable springs were finally located in Worcester only some five minutes before closing time. The proprietor was persuaded to take them home, WGPE collecting that evening. Through the night the standard FW12 front struts were modified to accept a piston now fitted

Seen here with side pod panelling removed, Nigel Mansell's Williams-Judd CV V8 FW12 with active suspension raised many eyebrows here at Rio, 1988, by qualifying second to Ayrton Senna's new McLaren MP4/4, which had inherited what had previously been the Williams Honda engine deal. Williams-Renault's eventual defeat of McLaren-Honda in 1992 was sweet revenge . . .

with a damper valve, while the reactive system bump stop was replaced by the new disc spring. Around 6 a.m. Saturday morning the first units were completed at Didcot, run up on their damper test-rig and seemed 'about right'. Head returned to Silverstone with them around 8 a.m., found the spare car stripped ready for conversion and after practice the drivers pronounced the difference 'Like night and day . . .'. And Mansell staged his customary terrific drive on home soil to finish second.

In Hungary the FW12s were again competitive and could conceivably have won. Patrese's ECU faltered, leaving his engine on seven cylinders. In Jerez again they were 'reasonably competitive', but by that time it was the stub-end of a long, hard season, one 'terribly disappointing for the workers who put in double effort throughout . . .'.

Six FW12 tubs were built, of which only the first five were raced. Chassis '1 emerged for Mansell at Rio and promptly qualified on the front row there. Chassis '2 was Patrese's Brazilian mount, '3 the spare. 'FW12/4' made its bow in Mexico as spare car and served as such for the remainder of the season, while chassis '5 was new for Mansell's use in Japan and Australia, but was not raced at either venue.

Mansell was incapacitated for the Belgian and Italian GPs – Brundle, then Schlesser taking his place – but he finished only two of his other 14 GPs in the Williams-Judds, second in both his home event at Silverstone and the Spanish race at Jerez. Otherwise he regularly starred until his Williams faltered, 12 retirements in 14 Grand Prix races being an appalling record for any top team. But while Mansell was unhappy with the situation, WGPE were unhappier . . .

Meanwhile Patrese nursed his sister car to the finish in half his 16 outings – fourth in Adelaide, fifth at Jerez, and sixth three times, at Monaco, Budapest and Suzuka. He was also seventh at Monza and eighth at Silverstone.

Williams-Judd finished fifth-equal with Arrows and March in the Constructors' Cup, with 20 points to their name.

While the Judd engine had kept Williams racing through 1988, a team of such size and capability required a major manufacturer engine supplier, a

no-holds-barred programme to take on Honda and Ferrari's best. The Judd V8s had suffered from excessive oil consumption amongst other inevitable teething troubles for such a small engine supplier, and, added to the reactive suspension headaches, Head confessed it would be a relief to regain engine supply from a major manufacturer. Such an arrangement was reached during that summer with Renault Sport, WGPE to use the new 3.5-litre RS01 V10-cylinder engine which Bernard Dudot's engineers had developed for the new Formula 1.

In fact the sixth Williams FW12 chassis was completed as a Renault V10 test car-cum-potential racer for 1989. The new V10 had first run on the Viry dyno in January '88 but Renault's top brass had demanded a deal with a major team before approving full resumption of an F1 engine programme. Renault Sport thus became as anxious to attract a major team as WGPE were to re-establish support from a major engine supplier.

For 1989 the FW12C emerged, five being used of which the first three were 1988-built. These and the subsequent 1989-built cars would all be replaced by the new re-tubbed FW13 late-season, of which three were built. 'FW12C/1' made its bow at Rio as team spare, '6 was deployed there for Boutsen's debut, '7 for Patrese. Boutsen crashed chassis '8 during testing just prior to the season-opener at Phoenix. Subsequently, 'FW12C/9' appeared new for Boutsen at Imola, and '10 new at Monaco as spare, first being raced by Patrese at Hockenheim. In the absence of any available established star drivers, Riccardo Patrese was teamed with Thierry Boutsen, ex-Benetton, both good professional drivers, yet to prove any superstar status.

At Phoenix WGPE ran one new chassis and two uprated 1988 cars for the race. The new monocoque's internal bulkheads had been designed to accept pullrod front suspension from the outset, older cars had bulkheads modified from their original pushrod location. The cooling systems featured an electronically controlled by-pass to recirculate coolant through the radiator cores if it proved to be insufficiently cooled before re-entering the engine.

Patrick Head had decided to produce an integrated chassis and engine package around the Renault V10, but he was equally convinced that the FW12 concept retained plenty of development potential. The Renault RS01 V10 test car was based upon the FW12B with vertically mounted inboard spring/dampers which had been taken to Japan but not raced at the end of 1988. The French V10 engine's power drove through a revised version of the Williams transverse six-speed gearbox now magnesium-cased to save c. 10 kg against the original aluminium version.

Early-season transmission problems with the FW12Cs were traced to wavering manufacturing tolerances. Revised gearchange mechanisms were researched, developed and tested. The Renault V10 engines proved generally quite reliable. Amongst a series of development steps the induction system was altered for Monza and WGPE also had to fit larger radiators then to cope with cooling demand. The bodywork needed significant revision, and all this work took time away from the replacement FW13 project.

The first new FW13 cars finally entered service at Estoril, both cars overheating into retirement after rubbish accumulated in the side pod intakes.

The FW13 was a logical development of the FW12C, employing an entirely new monocoque which was very slender, with all suspension anchorages on its exterior and nothing at all intruding into the footwell. It was much lower at the front with pushrod-operated spring/dampers housed above the driver's knees, covered by a detachable access panel. Fuel tankage wrapped around the driver's hips and the water radiators were housed well back in brief side pods without side air-exits. The new carbon-composite tub was mated initially to the proven FW12C rear-end assembly.

It was planned to re-adopt reactive suspension on the 1990 FW13 car, so WGPE retained an

The Adrian Newey-masterminded 1991 Williams-Renault FW14 became truly competitive once transmission reliability had been achieved in mid-season, and with active suspension it would dominate 1992. Here Nigel Mansell is heading for second place behind Senna's McLaren in Hungary.

FW12 with Judd engine for continued reactive system development, F3000 competitor Mark Blundell serving the R&D team as its test driver.

Through 1989 Patrese finished ten times, taking four second places, in succession at Mexico, Phoenix and Montreal, and finally at Suzuka. He added two thirds, at Ricard and Adelaide, fourths at Hockenheim and Monza, a fifth at Jerez and 15th at Monte Carlo.

Boutsen also finished ten GPs, but he shone in the rain and won both the Canadian and Australian races, took three third places, at Budapest, Monza and Suzuka, placed fourth at Imola and Spa and sixth at Phoenix. Otherwise he finished tenth at both Monaco and Silverstone.

Patrese finished third in the Drivers' Championship – ahead of his former team-leader, Mansell, now with Ferrari – and Boutsen was fifth.

The same pairing was retained for Williams's second Renault V10-powered season in 1990. The existing FW13 design demanded considerable revision to accept the 1990 Renault V10 which nestled lower in the chassis than its predecessor, with a reduced crankshaft height. It demanded different engine mountings, a modified casing for the six-speed transverse gearbox to match the lower crankshaft input and also a different cooling system, housed in lengthened side pods. The pushrod front suspension had been altered, with the rockers mounted rather higher on top of the monocoque fuselage, now faired beneath distinctive – and ugly – blisters. Relocation of such ancillaries as the fire extinguisher improved cockpit accommodation and long-range fuel cells appeared each side of the seat for heavy-consumption circuits.

Two late-'89-built FW13Bs and one new car

were deployed at the Phoenix curtain-raiser, starting the new season: 'FW13B/5' for Patrese, '6 as spare and '7 for Boutsen. Chassis '8 followed new for Boutsen at Imola and '9 was introduced for Patrese's use at the Hungaroring.

In mid-season the R&D team experimented with a 'mono-shock' single spring/damper system *à la* Tyrrell, without a front anti-roll bar. It was intended for the 1991 FW14 project but Patrese enthused about it after a trial run at Silverstone and wanted to race it at Ricard in the French GP. Patrick was not sufficiently confident of its true race-distance potential when car weight would vary from full tanks to empty, and the only prudent answer was 'no'.

Head's engineering group at WGPE was reinforced during the summer as Adrian Newey joined from Leyton House after the controversial failure of his latest CG901 design in the early-season races, culminating in non-qualification for the Mexican GP. For 1991, Patrick set out to correct the errors he felt he had made on the FW13B and Adrian those he had perpetrated on the Leyton House CG901. This 'don't get mad, get even' approach would pay off.

In particular, during long, hard races the FW13B had worked its tyres more destructively than its major rivals. Above all 'it just wasn't quick enough . . .'.

Yet again, Boutsen finished ten of the season's 16 GPs for Williams, winning from pole position at Budapest after leading all the way and holding off an entire boiling mob for the duration. He added one second place (Silverstone), one third (Phoenix), two fourths (Monaco and Jerez), and four fifths (Brazil, Mexico, Japan and Australia) plus sixth at Hockenheim – thus scoring every time.

The loyal Patrese – by this time the most experienced Grand Prix driver in the history of the World Championship – finished 12 times, happily winning on home ground at Imola, but otherwise finishing 9-13*-9-6-5-4-5-7-5-4-6 – scoring seven times.

Boutsen and Patrese finished sixth and seventh in the Drivers' table with 34 points and 23, while

Williams-Renault trailed McLaren-Honda, Ferrari and Benetton-Ford – fourth in the Constructors' Cup. For 1991, Boutsen was replaced in the team by the return of Nigel Mansell – and the Anglo-French WGPE-Renault partnership was poised for a ferocious assault upon McLaren's two World titles in the coming year . . .

By 1991, WGPE was back on the road to true competitiveness. Nigel Mansell was recruited to join Patrese in new FW14 cars co-designed by an engineering team led by Patrick Head and Adrian Newey. The new chassis emerged as the 'car of the year', an outstandingly effective package aerodynamically, powered by a very fine engine in the latest-version Renault RS3 V10. Williams had developed a semi-automatic electro-hydraulic version of their six-speed transverse gearbox, and it was largely this system's unreliability at the start of the season which prevented Mansell from achieving his life's ambition and the Williams team taking another World Championship title. The Williams semi-auto transmission had completed around 1000 km testing in the stern of an FW13, plus many hours running on a static test rig, and the FW14 was designed exclusively around the system – without provision for a conventional rigid rod gearchange mechanism – from the outset.

The FW14 fuselage adopted Tyrrell 019-like raised nose aerodynamic form and was moulded in carbon aramid epoxy composite, being external-finished with the forward section providing the aerodynamic surface of the nose. Pushrod suspension was carried, with the front coil-spring/damper units mounted on top of the nose section, beneath an access cover.

Newey had joined WGPE from Leyton House in the summer of 1990. He had extensive test experience of a raised-nose configuration model and using the in-house Williams tunnel at Didcot he made considerable progress upon optimizing that configuration.

After debut gearchange system failures at Phoenix, the FW14s used only five of their six speeds at Interlagos where Mansell was able to pressure Senna's McLaren until another gearchange system problem caused him to spin. It was not until Monaco that the FW14s really began to show their class. For the first seven races of the season Patrese out-qualified his English team-mate – largely since minor problems made Mansell spend much time in his spare chassis which was not fitted with Renault Sport's contemporary qualifying-specification engines. At Montreal Mansell then dominated the Canadian GP and was savouring impending victory on the closing lap when he apparently found neutral into the hairpin corner; before he could catch the engine on the throttle its revs had died away, it stalled and, with insufficient electrical charge left in the system to re-engage a gear hydraulically, he was unable to bump-restart the V10.

The Renault engine with Elf's latest state-of-the-art fuel technology was demonstrating a clear edge over the Honda V12 used by McLaren. Apart from the early gearchange problems, a persistently long and soft brake pedal beset the team all season, something a switch from Brembo to AP Racing calipers at Monza helped rectify. A new half-scale wind tunnel was commissioned at Didcot in mid-summer and, although the closing stages of a dramatic World Championship season were enlivened by a considerable Williams charge, Renault had sat back on their laurels and were overtaken by Honda developments. A botched wheel-change in the Portuguese GP compromised Mansell's already slender hopes of taking the title chase down to the wire in Adelaide, and a recurrence of the brake vagaries in Japan finally ended his chase, in the sand traps at Suzuka.

During the season only five FW14s had appeared in anger, the prototype 'FW14/1' being confined to spare car duties in the first three GP meetings, while chassis '2 was Mansell's regular race mount from Phoenix to Mexico, his spare thereafter. Patrese swapped between chassis '3 and '4, while Mansell completed the season from the French to Australian GPs in chassis '5.

Nigel's season was marred by three consecutive early-season retirements, plus two more at Spa and Suzuka, and his disqualification after the pitstop débâcle – in which he was signalled to rejoin the race before his car's right-rear wheel had been tightened – at Estoril. His results in the other ten GPs read 2-6*-2-1-1-1-2-1-1-2, and he ended the season second to Senna in the Drivers' Championship, on 72 points to the Brazilian's 96.

Patrese was third in the Drivers' table on 53 points, his 16 outings having yielded five retirements, and a finishing record of 2-3-1-5-2-3-5-1-3-3-5. Mansell had won the French, British and German GPs in mid-season succession, plus the Italian and Spanish events. Patrese won in Mexico and Portugal, and the team was only just pipped to the year's Formula 1 Constructors' Cup title, second with 125 points to McLaren-Honda's 139.

Wolf

Austrian-born Canadian Walter Wolf made a fortune in the oil equipment business. He part-sponsored Williams until at the end of 1975 he bought Hesketh's equipment and plant for a reputed £450,000. He then took on Williams's liabilities for a 60 per cent share in the business. At a stroke he had gained full FOCA (Formula One Constructors' Association) membership for two cars which he would not have had with Hesketh alone, worth around £150,000 a year in saved travelling expenses outside Europe. His Hesketh material and some personnel, including designer Harvey Postlethwaite, moved into Williams's workshop in Bennett Road, Reading, Berkshire.

Marlboro money came into this new Wolf-Williams team, bringing driver Ickx and F2 hopeful Michel Leclère. But the Wolf-Williams season of 1976 was a catastrophe.

The Hesketh 308C – known now as the Wolf-Williams FW05 – was aerodynamically and structurally mediocre, and as it was strengthened and continuously modified so it became some 120 lb

Jody Scheckter's Postlethwaite-designed Wolf WR1 notches Cosworth-Ford's 100th GP victory, Monaco, 1977.

overweight, creating a built-in penalty of a second a lap. Ickx was quite incapable of sorting it out and was fired after non-qualifying for the British GP. Poor Leclère was utterly bemused by the desolation around him, Merzario filled in for the last seven GPs but whereas the first part of the year saw the cars qualify for nine starts and retire only once, Merzario never finished at all. Warwick Brown was 14th in the second-string car at Watkins Glen. Three FW05s were campaigned, two originally built by Hesketh. In September, Williams was dismissed from what had been his team, Peter Warr joined from Lotus to manage affairs for 1977 and Postlethwaite designed an all-new car for a one-driver team built around Scheckter, previously with Tyrrell.

The new Wolf-Cosworth 'WR1' emerged as a neat and attractive arrow-head car, with curvaceously wedgy bodywork enclosing the rugged monocoque. Postlethwaite concentrated upon reliability. Three of these cars were built that season, 'WR1-2-3', and while most rivals concentrated upon twin-caliper balanced brakes, Postlethwaite relied upon a fully floating conventional system, which performed superbly. Whenever Scheckter finished, Japanese GP aside, he was never lower than third. He started 17 races, won – luckily – on his Wolf debut in Argentina, and again at Monaco and in Canada, was second at Kyalami and Hockenheim and third at Long Beach, Jarama, Zandvoort and Watkins Glen. He retired seven times, but never due to mechanical failure on the chassis. A perpetual fuel pressure problem bothered the team but paradoxically it profited from being too new to qualify for Cosworth's hot 'development' engines, which wrecked the Lotus 78's season. At Monaco, Scheckter scored the DFV's 100th victory on a Hesketh-built unit, rejecting Ford's offer of support. All wins were in 'WR1' and Scheckter was runner-up in his Championship; Wolf fourth in their own, with 55 points.

In 1978 Lotus completed their ground-effects car revolution and the old 'WR1-4' series – a fourth car having since been completed – were patently outclassed in South America. Postlethwaite rushed out his own wing-car design, the unusually ugly Wolf 'WR5' and 'WR6' duo.

The new wedge-monocoque 'WR5-6' design with its massive cooler sunk into the front cockpit fairing made its bow in practice at Monaco and was first raced at Zolder, 'WR6' being ready in time for the French GP. Old cars 'WR3-4' were sold to Theodore for Rosberg. Scheckter led the British GP for a while and raced through the field to claim second at Hockenheim. He raced 'WR6' for the first time in Holland, but destroyed it at Monza, a total rebuild producing another car using the same number for the US GP where he finished third and Canada, placing second. Bobby Rahal drove 'WR5' at Watkins Glen finishing 12th, then raced elderly 'WR1' in Canada where – that's right – the fuel system played up, just as it had done with Scheckter in '77. Wolf finished fifth in the Championship, with Scheckter's 24 points; Rosberg achieved nothing in the Theodore cars.

Scheckter signed for Ferrari for 1979 as Walter Wolf progressively lost interest in his team. Hunt joined them as driver but seemed equally disinterested and quite suddenly retired from racing after seven races which yielded only one place, eighth at Kyalami.

Three new cars, chassis 'WR7-8-9' were built, introducing Postlethwaite's folded aluminium honeycomb sheet construction. 'WR7' caused uproar in Buenos Aires when it featured clutch impeller vanes drawing air through the oil cooler. Rivals construed this as a moveable aerodynamic device now excluded by the 'anti-fan-car' regulations and its ducting had to be altered to prevent download advantage being gained. Wolf then had to mount a secondary oil cooler behind the water radiator.

After Hunt's defection, Rosberg briefly breathed new life into the team, proving the car could perform by running fifth for some time at Zandvoort, but ambition was draining from the team despite the best efforts of Postlethwaite and Warr.

Reliability slumped and Rosberg non-qualified in Canada and only finished on his team debut, ninth in France.

During the winter of 1979/80 Walter Wolf agreed to a team merger with Fittipaldi, the Brazilian brothers putting their name on both Postlethwaite's cars and the team's Reading premises, 'WR9' becoming the basis for the 1980 Fittipaldi F7s (see page 272).

Zakspeed

The German tuning wizard Erich Zakowski had made his name with all manner of Ford-based racing saloons and had extensive experience of turbocharging in them when he decided to enter Formula 1 for 1985. His Niederzissen-based team developed a neat little four-cylinder alloy-block turbo engine of 1495 cc, claimed to deliver 700 bhp at 11,500 rpm, intended to match an exceptionally well-packaged moulded carbon-composite chassis designed for them by ex-Chevron engineer Paul Brown. They made their debut at Estoril in round two of the Championship series, with Dr Jonathan Palmer driving Zakspeed 'ZAK841/1', while chassis '2 was ready for him to adopt as his regular car at Ricard. After the Dutch GP he unfortunately broke a leg in a Group C Porsche crash at the Spa meeting in which Tyrrell driver Bellof lost his life, so Zakowski invited Formula 3000 driver Christian Danner to take his place for the Belgian and Brands Hatch races, the little team not travelling outside Europe.

In all they contested nine races, Palmer non-starting at Imola, while his only finish was 11th at Monaco. Both Danner's outings ended in retirement, so the little German team had little to show for their first foray into Formula 1. But they impressed many not only with their tightly financed car's neat design but also its turn-out.

For 1986 three Paul Brown-designed Zakspeed 861 cars were built and raced in a two-car programme by Jonathan Palmer and Huub Rothengatter. The new 861 logically benefited from the smaller 195-litre regulation fuel tank compared to the preceding 841 design, and overall design philosophy for the car was to make it simpler, lighter and more practicable to run. Above all the Niederzissen team had to acclimatize properly to the tempo of Formula 1 racing. The 861 inherited the 841 transaxle and two cars were ready for the start of the new season, two entries being made regularly from Imola and the third 861 chassis emerging at Monaco. New carbon brakes appeared with that car but were not raced until the German GP. Chassis '1 was eventually written off after Rothengatter crashed it in Mexico.

Palmer retired from eight GPs, his finishing record being an indifferent 12-13-8-9-10-12-10*-9 – that best eighth place coming at Spa. Rothengatter meanwhile missed the opening two races then failed to qualify at Monaco, and non-started at both Detroit and Mexico City – after breaking down on the parade lap in the American event. He retired from nine of his 11 races, finishing 12th in Canada and eighth in Austria. No points for the German turbo team . . .

It had quickly become evident that the 861 was still too big and heavy, and as a Motronic-controlled engine variant was developed the four-cylinder unit's customarily vicious power curve finally overwhelmed the basically 1983 chassis concept's capabilities. Paul Brown left the team towards the end of the year and Chris Murphy replaced him from Zakowski's IMSA sports car programme.

His brief to produce a lighter car with much better aerodynamic capability resulted in the replacement *Typ* 871 for 1987. The capacious 861 tub's upperworks were slimmed and lowered, and lowering the engine's plenum chamber permitted a finer rear deck line. The new 871 scaled 565 kg and its aerodynamic form – developed by engineer Heinz Zollinir in the Aachen University and BMW factory wind tunnels – proved more efficient with higher downforce and lower drag.

For 1987 861 chassis '2 and '3 were used early in the season, replaced by the new 871 from Imola, three of which emerged, '2 appearing at Spa and '3 at Ricard for new drivers Martin Brundle and Christian Danner.

Brundle retired ten times, but he finished fifth at Imola to score two World Championship points, then 7 (Monaco) 11-8-14-11 in the other five races he completed. Danner meanwhile was excluded from the Monaco GP after triggering a violent qualifying collision with Alboreto's much faster works Ferrari, then failed to start in Portugal and retired from eight other events. His six finishes read 9-7-8-9-9-7, just missing the points at both Imola and Adelaide. Zakspeed finished the season tenth in the Constructors' Championship with Brundle's two points from Imola.

The German team continued to persevere with its turbocharged four-cylinder engine into the 2.5-bar boost season of 1988 – beating their heads against an impenetrable wall. The revised engines were installed in four updated 1987 chassis, as permitted by this interim year's regulations, to save the expense of all-new construction for just one fleeting final turbo season. The intercoolers were resited in very much narrower side pods and a new engine cover adopted, all in search of minimum drag matching reduced power. Chassis '1 and '3 ran at Rio for drivers Bernd Schneider and PierCarlo Ghinzani, '2 served as spare. Zakspeed struggled, badly, Schneider failing to qualify ten times, Ghinzani eight. While the Italian started eight GPs, retired from five and finished three, Schneider started six, retired from five and finished 12th in his home event at Hockenheim. His last start came in Japan, as he failed to qualify again in Adelaide. Ghinzani's three finishes read 15-14-14, in Mexico, Montreal and Hockenheim. At least in their home GP, both the team's cars

Cooling demands effectively dominated the turbo era, as is obvious in this stripped Zakspeed, revealing its water radiators and turbo-charge intercoolers, and the complex – and hot – pipework and plumbing draping around the engine bay.

survived to the flag . . .

For 1989 Zakspeed's luck seemed to have changed. The Japanese Yamaha company's OX88 3.5-litre 75-degree V8 engines with patented 40-valve head design were supplied to them on an exclusive basis, perhaps in reflex action to Cosworth having dismissed the Yamaha five-valve-per-cylinder concept as being no better than their own four-valvers for the new DFR engine. For Yamaha this 1989 season with Zakspeed featured a steep learning curve and a catastrophic loss of face back home. New *Typ* 891 cars were tailored to the Japanese engines by consultant designer Gustav Brunner, ex-Ferrari, ex-Rial and so many other marques. The carbon-composite tubs used were very similar to his previous F1/87 and Rial ARC1/2 designs, with pullrod suspension all round, mounted vertically at the rear and longitudinally along the lower plane of the monocoque at the front. The Japanese engines were mated to Zakspeed mag-alloy-cased transaxles and the new cars featured a notably low side pod form. Four of these cars were built and obstructed as they were by a litany of engine failures they failed to *pre-*qualify for all save two Grand Prix starts, both by the faithful Bernd Schneider, who retired both times – at Rio and Suzuka. His Japanese team-mate, Aguri Suzuki, had a 100 per cent record, being bumped from the field in pre-qualifying for all 16 races.

No team attempting to operate at such major manufacturer-supported level could survive such a season. Erich Zakowski withdrew from F1.

Formula 1 Factory Drawings

General Arrangement

LOTUS TYPE 49

Previous page:
Simplicity which set the standard: Maurice Phillippe's general arrangement for the Lotus 49, dated 5 May 1967.

Right: *Extremely shallow and broad aluminium monocoque tubs became popular in the late Seventies. Phillippe's Tyrrell 008 tub is typical. 1 August 1977.*

Above: *The ground-effects aerodynamic revolution was born in Ralph Bellamy's Lotus 78 general arrangement drawing, dated 13 June 1977.*

Below: *Formula 1 rear suspension, in this case Patrick Head's 1978 Williams FW06, 20 January 1978.*

Above: *The sliding skirt itself had to be rigid as well as precisely controlled within its guides. Williams did it better than most – this FW07 skirt drawing is dated 8 April 1980.*

Left: *Towards the future: Ferrari's CAD/CAM modelling for their 1985 126C. Gould computers and the Piaggio aerospace design company co-developed a system which created and cut patterns from resin block without a line being drawn on paper.*

The Racing Record

Within these pages it is quite impossible to reproduce in full results of all Formula 1 races held between 1966 and 1991. However, here we do our best, listing the first six in each of the events held, and adding details of pole position, fastest lap and a brief summary of the event. This allows us to record fine performances which failed to achieve solid results. The bald record book itself can never reflect credit on those who led, perhaps from start to penultimate lap, only for some often obscure failure to rob them of victory so close to the finish. This listing begins with the non-Championship Rand GP at Kyalami circuit, outside Johannesburg, on 4 December 1965, which was run to the new regulations although they did not formally take effect until 1 January 1966.

The listing to the end of the 1991 season includes 427 individual races, 375 Championship GPs and 52 non-Championship events, and it gives us all the bare statistics of success, failure, and relative performance from 1966 to 1991 inclusive.

Driver, engine capacity, car-engine manufacturer, type and individual car chassis number are all listed, and we hope that the enthusiast will browse happily in this unique record of 26 hectic years of motor racing's premier Formula. A magnifying glass is recommended . . .

4-12-65 Rand GP,
Kyalami, ZA – 50 laps, 127.20 miles
1. Jack Brabham (2.7 Brabham-Climax FPF BT11 F1-2-64/2), 50 laps in 1:18;11.2, 97.69 mph.
2. Pieter de Klerk (2.5 Brabham-Climax FPF BT11 IC-5-64), 50, 1:18;17.1.
3. Paul Hawkins (2.7 Lotus-Climax FPF 25 R3), 50. 4. John Love (2.7 Cooper-Climax FPF T79 FL-1-65), 49. 5. Jo Siffert (1.5 Brabham-BRM V8 BT11 F1-6-64), 49. 6. Innes Ireland (1.5 Lotus-BRM V8 25 R4), 49.
PP – Brabham, 1;30.8; FL – Brabham, 1;31.5, 100.11 mph.
Fine race dominated by effectively Tasman Formula cars with Brabham and Love battling wheel-to-wheel until the latter's rear suspension gave trouble after he had often led.

1966

1-1-66 South African GP,
East London – 60 laps, 145.98 miles
1. Mike Spence (2.0 Lotus-Climax V8 33 R11), 60 laps in 1:29;39.4, 97.75 mph.
2. Jo Siffert (1.5 Brabham-BRM V8 BT11 F1-6-64), 58, 1:29;59.8.
3. Peter Arundell (1.5 Lotus-Climax 33 R9), 58. 4. Dave Charlton (2.7 Brabham-Climax FPF BT11 F1-2-64/2), 58. 5. Sam Tingle (2.7 LDS-Climax FPF LDS 3), 57. 6. John Love (2.7 Cooper-Climax FPF T79 FL-1-65), 56.
PP – Jack Brabham (Repco-Brabham V8 BT19 F1-1-65), 1;25.1; FL – Brabham, 1;25.2, 102.91 mph.
Jack Brabham led from lap 2 in his brand new Repco V8-engined car until lap 51 when he spun and engine refused to restart because injection pump drive belt had snapped.

1-5-66 Syracuse GP,
Sicily, I – 56 laps, 195.27 miles
1. John Surtees (3.0 Ferrari 312 V12 0010), 56 laps in 1:40;08.3, 114.67 mph.
2. Lorenzo Bandini (2.4 Ferrari Dino 246 V6 0006), 56, 1:40;32.9.
3. David Hobbs (1.9 Lotus-BRM V8 25 R13), 54. 4. Vic Wilson (1.9 BRM V8 P261 2615), 53. 5. Jo Bonnier (1.9 Brabham-BRM V8 BT11 F1-6-64), 52. JNC '6th'. Guy Ligier (3.0 Cooper-Maserati V12 F1-4-66), 39.
PP – Surtees, 1;42.3; FL – Surtees, 1;41.4, 118.99 mph.
Surtees took the lead from Bandini on lap 4 and the Ferraris won virtually unopposed.

14-5-66 BRDC International Trophy,
Silverstone, GB – 35 laps, 102.45 miles
1. Jack Brabham (Repco-Brabham V8 BT19 F1-1-65), 35 laps in 52;57.6, 116.06 mph.
2. John Surtees (3.0 Ferrari V12 312 0010), 35 in 53;05.0.
3. Jo Bonnier (3.0 Cooper-Maserati V12 T81 F1-5-66), 35. 4. Denny Hulme (2.7 Brabham-Climax FPF BT11 F1-2-64), 35. 5. Jochen Rindt (3.0 Cooper-Maserati V12 T81 F1-3-66), 34. 6. John Taylor (1.9 Brabham-BRM V8 BT11 F1-4-64), 33.
PP – Brabham, 1;29.8; FL – Brabham, 1;29.8, 117.34 mph.
Small entry but Surtees's new Ferrari could do nothing against Brabham, who led throughout.

22-5-66 MONACO GP,
Monte Carlo – 100 laps, 195.41 miles
1. Jackie Stewart (1.9 BRM V8 P261 2617), 100 laps in 2:33;10.5, 76.50 mph.

2. Lorenzo Bandini (2.4 Ferrari Dino V6 246 0006), 100 in 2:33;50.7.
3. Graham Hill (1.9 BRM V8 P261 2616), 99. 4. Bob Bondurant (1.9 BRM V8 P261 2615), 95. UNC '5th'. Richie Ginther (3.0 Cooper-Maserati V12 T81 F1-6-66), 80. UNC '6th'. Guy Ligier (3.0 Cooper-Maserati V12 F1-4-66), 75.
PP – Jim Clark (2.0 Lotus-Climax V8 33 R11); FL – Bandini, 1;29.8, 78.35 mph.
Stewart duelled with Surtees's Ferrari until its diff failed, then led from lap 14 to finish.

NOTE – *All cars listed hereafter are 3-litres unless otherwise marked.*

13-6-66 BELGIAN GP,
Spa-Francorchamps – 28 laps, 24.8 miles
1. John Surtees (Ferrari V12 312 0010), 28 laps in 2:09;11.3, 113.39 mph.
2. Jochen Rindt (Cooper-Maserati V12 T81 F1-3-66), 28 in 2:09;53.4.
3. Lorenzo Bandini (2.4 Ferrari Dino V6 246 0006), 27. 4. Jack Brabham (Repco-Brabham V8 BT19 F1-1-65), 26. 5. Richie Ginther (Cooper-Maserati V12 T81 F1-6-66), 25. UNC '6th'. Guy Ligier (Cooper-Maserati V12 F1-4-66), 24.
PP – Surtees, 3;38.0; FL – Surtees, 4;18.7, 121.93 mph.
Field decimated by opening lap accident in torrential rain, Rindt led Surtees's fuel pump-afflicted Ferrari until Cooper's diff played up five laps from finish.

3-7-66 FRENCH GP,
Reims-Gueux – 48 laps, 247.58 miles
1. Jack Brabham (Repco-Brabham V8 BT19 F1-1-65), 48 laps in 1:48;31.3, 124.55 mph.
2. Mike Parkes (Ferrari V12 312 0012), 48 in 1:48;40.8.
3. Denny Hulme (Repco-Brabham V8 BT20 F1-2-66), 46. 4. Jochen Rindt (Cooper-Maserati V12 T81 F1-3-66), 46. 5. Dan Gurney (2.0 Brabham-Climax FPF T1G 101), 45. 6. John Taylor (2.0 Brabham-BRM V8 BT11 F1-4-64), 45.
PP – Lorenzo Bandini (Ferrari V12 312 0010), 2;09.1; FL – Bandini, 2;11.3, 142.09 mph.
Bandini's Ferrari led for 31 laps until throttle cable broke, Brabham scored first *Grande Epreuve* victory for driver in a car bearing his own name. Gurney's new interim Eagle scored its first points.

16-7-66 BRITISH GP,
Brands Hatch – 80 laps, 211.92 miles
1. Jack Brabham (Repco-Brabham V8 BT19 F1-1-65), 80 laps in 2:13;13.4, 95.48 mph.
2. Denny Hulme (Repco-Brabham V8 BT20 F1-2-66), 80 in 2:13;23.0.
3. Graham Hill (1.9 BRM V8 P261 2616), 79. 4. Jim Clark (2.0 Lotus-Climax V8 33 R14), 79. 5. Jochen Rindt (Cooper-Maserati V12 T81 F1-3-66), 79. 6. Bruce McLaren (McLaren-Serenissima V8 M2B M2B/2), 78.
PP – Brabham, 1;34.5; FL – Brabham, 1;37.0, 98.35 mph.
Brabham led from start to finish, superb drive by Clark spoiled by stop to top up brake fluid.

24-7-66 DUTCH GP,
Zandvoort – 90 laps, 234.54 miles
1. Jack Brabham (Repco-Brabham V8 BT19 F1-1-65), 90 laps in 2:20;32.5, 100.10 mph.
2. Graham Hill (1.9 BRM V8 P261 2616), 89 laps.
3. Jim Clark (2.0 Lotus-Climax V8 33 R14), 88. 4. Jackie Stewart (1.9 BRM V8 P261 2614), 88. 5. Mike Spence (1.9 Lotus-BRM V8 25 R13), 87. 6. Lorenzo Bandini (Ferrari V12

312 0010), 87.
PP – Brabham, 1;28.1; FL – Denny Hulme (Repco-Brabham V8 BT20 F1-2-66), 1;30.6, 103.53 mph.
Great race between the Brabhams and Clark's Lotus which took lead, then lost it in a stop to add water.

7-8-66 GERMAN GP,
Nürburgring – 15 laps, 212.69 miles
1. Jack Brabham (Repco-Brabham V8 BT19 F1-1-65), 15 laps in 2:27;03.0, 86.75 mph.
2. John Surtees (Cooper-Maserati V12 T81 F1-6-66), 15 in 2:27;47.4.
3. Jochen Rindt (Cooper-Maserati V12 T81 F1-3-66), 15. 4. Graham Hill (1.9 BRM V8 P261 2616), 15. 5. Jackie Stewart (1.9 BRM V8 P261 2614), 15. 6. Lorenzo Bandini (Ferrari V12 312 0010), 15.
PP – Jim Clark (2.0 Lotus-Climax V8 33 R14), 8;16.5; FL – Surtees, 8;49.0, 96.45 mph.
Long duel for lead between Brabham and Surtees decided when the latter's clutch failed.

4-9-66 ITALIAN GP,
Monza – 68 laps, 243.44 miles
1. Ludovico Scarfiotti (Ferrari V12 312 0011), 68 laps in 1:47;14.3, 135.93 mph.
2. Mike Parkes (Ferrari V12 312 0012), 68 in 1:47;20.6.
3. Denny Hulme (Repco-Brabham V8 BT20 F1-2-66), 68. 4. Jochen Rindt (Cooper-Maserati V12 T81 F1-3-66), 67. 5. Mike Spence (1.9 Lotus-BRM V8 25 R13), 67. 6. Bob Anderson (2.7 Brabham-Climax FPF BT11 F1-5-64), 66.
PP – Parkes, 1;31.3; FL – Scarfiotti, 1;32.4, 139.19 mph.
Ferraris uncatchable on home soil, Scarfiotti leading from the Ferraris. Honda written off in its debut race.

17-9-66 International Gold Cup,
Oulton Park, GB – 40 laps, 110.44 miles
1. Jack Brabham (Repco-Brabham V8 BT19 F1-1-5), 40 laps in 1:06;14.2, 100.04 mph.
2. Denny Hulme (Repco-Brabham V8 BT20 F1-2-66), 40 in 1:06;14.2.
3. Jim Clark (2.0 Lotus-Climax V8 33 R14), 40. 4. Innes Ireland (1.9 BRM V8 P261 2615), 40. 5. Chris Lawrence (Cooper-Ferrari V12 Spl T71 F1-1-64), 38. No other finishers.
PP – Brabham, 1;34.2; FL – Brabham & Hulme, 1;36.6, 102.89 mph.
BRM H16s fought exciting battle with Brabhams, Stewart led but both he and team-mate Hill retired.

2-10-66 UNITED STATES GP,
Watkins Glen, NY – 108 laps, 248.40 miles
1. Jim Clark (Lotus-BRM H16 43 R1), 108 laps in 2:09;40.1, 114.94 mph.
2. Jochen Rindt (Cooper-Maserati V12 T81 F1-3-66), 108 in 2:11;26.9.
3. John Surtees (Cooper-Maserati V12 T81 F1-6-66), 107. 4. Jo Siffert (Cooper-Maserati V12 T81 F1-2-66), 105. 5. Bruce McLaren (McLaren-Ford Indy V8 M2B M2B/1), 105. 6. Peter Arundell (2.0 Lotus-Climax V8 33 R14), 101.
PP – Jack Brabham (Repco-Brabham V8 BT20 F1-1-66), 1;08.48; FL – Surtees, 1;09.67, 118.85 mph.
Bandini's Ferrari led and broke, Brabham's Repco V8 broke its cam-followers, Surtees spun while lapping a back-marker to spoil Cooper's great chance and Clark won using BRM's high-mileage spare works H16 engine. It would prove to be the H16's only victory.

23-10-66 MEXICAN GP,
Mexico City – 65 laps, 201.93 miles
1. John Surtees (Cooper-Maserati V12 T81 F1-6-66), 65 laps in 2:06;35.34, 95.72 mph.
2. Jack Brabham (Repco-Brabham V8 BT20 F1-1-66), 65 in 2:06;43.22.
3. Denny Hulme (Repco-Brabham V8 BT20 F1-2-66), 64. 4. Richie Ginther (Honda V12 RA273 F-102), 64. 5. Dan Gurney (2.7 Eagle-Climax FPF T1G 101), 64. 6. Jo Bonnier (Cooper-Maserati V12 T81 F1-5-66), 63.
PP – Surtees, 1;53.18; FL – Ginther, 1;53.75, 98.33 mph.
Ginther's Honda led briefly until Surtees's Maserati V12 engine warmed up and he proved unbeatable. Rindt was third behind Brabham in second Cooper until sidelined by suspension failure.

1967

2-1-67 SOUTH AFRICAN GP,
Kyalami – 80 laps, 203.52 miles
1. Pedro Rodriguez (Cooper-Maserati V12 T81 F1-6-66), 80 laps in 2:05;45.9, 97.10 mph.
2. John Love (2.7 Cooper-Climax FPF T79 FL-1-65*), 80 in 2:06;12.3.
3. John Surtees (Honda V12 RA273 F-102), 79. 4. Denny Hulme (Repco-Brabham V8 BT20 F1-2-66), 78. 5. Bob Anderson (2.7 Brabham-Climax FPF BT11 F1-5-64), 78. 6. Jack Brabham (Repco-Brabham V8 BT20 F1-1-66), 76.
FL: Formula Libre (Tasman car).
PP – Brabham, 1;28.3; FL – Hulme, 1;29.9, 101.88 mph.
Works Brabhams dominant in practice; Hulme led majority of race until Repco's brake fluid boiled. Love took lead in private Tasman Cooper only to stop for fuel 6 laps from finish, Rodriguez inheriting another Cooper victory.

12-3-67 Race of Champions,
Brands Hatch, GB – 2 x 10-lap heats,
40-lap Final, 26.49 miles/105.98 miles
HEAT ONE: 1. Gurney; **2.** Surtees; **3.** Ginther; **4.** McLaren; **5.** Spence; **6.** Scarfiotti.
HEAT TWO: 1. Gurney; **2.** Ginther; **3.** Surtees; **4.** Scarfiotti; **5.** Rodriguez; **6.** McLaren.
FINAL:
1. Dan Gurney (Eagle-Weslake V12 T1G 102), 40 laps in 1:04;30.6, 98.66 mph.
2. Lorenzo Bandini (Ferrari V12 309 0001), 40 in 1:04;31.0.
3. Jo Siffert (Cooper-Maserati V12 T81 F1-2-66), 40. 4. Pedro Rodriguez (Cooper-Maserati V12 T81 F1-6-66), 40. 5. Ludovico Scarfiotti (Ferrari V12 312 0011), 40. 6. Chris Irwin (2.1 Lotus-BRM V8 25 R13), 39.
PP – Heat One, Gurney, 1;32.2; Heat Two, Gurney (result of first heat); Final, Gurney (ditto). FL – Heat One, Gurney, 1;32.6, 103.02 mph; Heat Two, Gurney 1;32.6, 103.02 mph; Final, Jack Brabham (Repco-Brabham V8 BT20 F1-1-66), 1;34.4, 101.06 mph.
Gurney's Eagle V12s uncatchable in heats but pressed hard in final, first by Brabham until ignition wire came adrift, then by Bandini who closed right up in new 24-plug, 36-valve 1967 Ferrari.

15-4-67 Spring Trophy,
Oulton Park, GB – 2 x 10-lap heats,
30-lap Final, 27.61 miles/82.83 miles
HEAT ONE: 1. Hulme; **2.** Surtees; **3.** Spence; **4.** Hill; **5.** McLaren; **6.** Oliver.

HEAT TWO: 1. Hulme; **2.** Surtees; **3.** Brabham; **4.** Stewart; **5.** McLaren; **6.** Spence.
FINAL:
1. Jack Brabham (Repco-Brabham V8 BT20 F1-1-66), 30 laps in 47;21.4, 104.94 mph.
2. Denny Hulme (Repco-Brabham V8 BT20 F1-2-66), 30 in 47;21.8.
3. John Surtees (Honda V12 RA273 F-102), 30. **4.** Jack Oliver (1.6 Formula 2 Lotus-Cosworth 41B), 30. **5.** Bruce McLaren (2.1 McLaren-BRM V8 M4B M4B/1), 29. **6.** Mike Spence (BRM H16 P83 8302), 29.
PP – Heat One, Jackie Stewart (BRM H16 P83 8303), 1:32.2, Heat Two, Hulme (result of Heat One); Final, Hulme (ditto). FL – Heat One, Brabham, 1:32.4, 107.57 mph; Heat Two, Hulme/Spence 1;32.8, 107.11 mph; Final, Brabham/Hulme, 1;33.4, 106.42 mph.
Brabhams dominant in charity event; Stewart's practice pace in BRM H16 not reproduced in race – he crashed in Final when running fourth.

29-4-67 BRDC International Trophy,
Silverstone, GB – 52 laps, 152.20 miles
1. Mike Parkes (Ferrari V12 312 0012), 52 laps in 1:19;39.2, 114.65 mph.
2. Jack Brabham (Repco-Brabham V8 BT20 F1-1-66), 52 in 1:19;56.8.
3. Jo Siffert (Cooper-Maserati V12 T81 F1-2-66), 52. **4.** Graham Hill (2.1 Lotus-BRM V8 33 R11), 51. **5.** Bruce McLaren (2.1 McLaren-BRM V8 M4B M4B/1), 51. **6.** Mike Spence (2.1 BRM V8 P261 2614), 50.
PP – Jackie Stewart (BRM H16 P83 8303), 1;27.8; FL – Hill, 1;30.0, 117.08 mph.
Tiny 12-car field, Parkes led from start to finish for his first F1 victory.

7-5-67 MONACO GP,
Monte Carlo – 100 laps, 195.41 miles
1. Denny Hulme (Repco-Brabham V8 BT20 F1-2-66), 100 laps in 2:34;34.3, 76.69 mph.
2. Graham Hill (2.1 Lotus-BRM V8 33 R11), 99 laps.
3. Chris Amon (Ferrari V12 312 0003), 99. **4.** Bruce McLaren (2.1 McLaren-BRM V8 M4B M4B/1), 97. **5.** Pedro Rodriguez (Cooper-Maserati V12 T81 F1-6-66), 96. **6.** Mike Spence (BRM H16 P83 8302), 96.
PP – Jack Brabham (Repco-Brabham V8 BT19 F1-1-65), 1;27.6; FL – Jim Clark (2.0 Lotus-Climax V8 33 R14), 1;29.5, 78.60 mph.
Stewart's 2.1-litre BRM led briefly, otherwise entirely Hulme's race; Bandini sustained fatal injuries in horrific Ferrari accident when closing in second place.

21-5-67 Syracuse GP,
Sicily, I – 56 laps, 194.77 miles
1. *DEAD-HEAT* – Mike Parkes (Ferrari V12 312 0012) and Ludovico Scarfiotti (Ferrari 312 V12 0011), 56 laps in 1:40;58.4, 113.73 mph.
3. Jo Siffert (Cooper-Maserati V12 T81 F1-2-66), 54. **4.** Chris Irwin (2.1 Lotus-BRM V8 25 R13), 53. **5.** Jo Bonnier (Cooper-Maserati V12 T81 F1-5-66), 53.
No other finishers.
PP – Parkes, 1;41.6; FL – Scarfiotti, 1;41.0, 121.82 mph.
Staged finish, only seven starters!

4-6-67 DUTCH GP,
Zandvoort – 90 laps, 234.45 miles
1. Jim Clark (Lotus-Cosworth V8 49 R2), 90 laps in 2:14;45.1, 104.49 mph.
2. Jack Brabham (Repco-Brabham V8 BT19 F1-1-65), 90 in 2:15;08.7.
3. Denny Hulme (Repco-Brabham V8 BT20 F1-2-66), 90. **4.** Chris Amon (Ferrari V12 312 0003), 90. **5.** Mike Parkes (Ferrari V12 312 0012), 89. **6.** Ludovico Scarfiotti (Ferrari V12 312 0005), 89.
PP – Graham Hill (Lotus-Cosworth V8 49 R1), 1;24.6; FL – Clark, 1;28.08, 106.49 mph.
The fairytale debut of the Cosworth-Ford DFV V8 engine in the Lotus 49s, rewriting the performance standards of their day. Hill led for 10 laps until timing gear failure, trimming 3 secs off lap record before team-mate Clark took over to score a truly historic triumph.

18-6-67 BELGIAN GP,
Spa-Francorchamps – 28 laps, 245.36 miles
1. Dan Gurney (Eagle-Weslake V12 T1G 104), 28 laps in 1:40;49.4, 145.74 mph.
2. Jackie Stewart (BRM H16 P83 8303), 28 in 1:41;52.4.
3. Chris Amon (Ferrari V12 312 0003), 28. **4.** Jochen Rindt (Cooper-Maserati V12 T81 F1-1-67), 28. **5.** Mike Spence (BRM H16 P83 8302), 27. **6.** Jim Clark (Lotus-Cosworth V8 49 R2), 27.
PP – Clark, 3;28.1; FL – Gurney, 3;31.9, 148.85 mph.
Clark led 12 laps before plug trouble after making first 150 mph Spa lap for pole in practice, Stewart's BRM H16 led until lap 20 but was slowed by gearbox problem, Gurney won despite fuel pressure problem with his Weslake V12.

1-7-67 FRENCH GP,
Circuit Bugatti, Le Mans – 80 laps, 219.20 miles
1. Jack Brabham (Repco-Brabham V8 BT24/1), 80 laps in 2:13;21.3, 98.90 mph.
2. Denny Hulme (Repco-Brabham V8 BT24/2), 80 in 2:14;20.8.
3. Jackie Stewart (2.1 BRM V8 P261 2614) 79. **4.** Jo Siffert (Cooper-Maserati V12 T81 F1-2-66), 77. **5.** Chris Irwin (BRM H16 P83 8302), 76. **6.** Pedro Rodriguez (Cooper-Maserati V12 T81 F1-6-66), 76.
PP – Graham Hill (Lotus-Cosworth V8 49 R1), 1;36.2; FL – Hill, 1;36.7, 102.30 mph.
Lotus 49s briefly dominant until final-drives failed due to case flexion, allowing new F2-based Brabhams to take command.

15-7-67 BRITISH GP,
Silverstone – 80 laps, 234.17 miles
1. Jim Clark (Lotus-Cosworth V8 49 R2), 80 laps in 1:59;25.6, 117.64 mph.
2. Denny Hulme (Repco-Brabham V8 BT24/2), 80 in 1:59;38.4.
3. Chris Amon (Ferrari V12 312 0003), 80. **4.** Jack Brabham (Repco-Brabham V8 BT24/1), 80. **5.** Pedro Rodriguez (Cooper-Maserati V12 T81 F1-6-66), 79. **6.** John Surtees (Honda V12 RA273 F-102), 78.
PP – Clark, 1;25.3; FL – Hulme, 1;27.0, 121.12 mph.
Lotus 49s dominant, Hill's a replacement car built overnight after practice crash, still led until rear suspension bolt dropped out, leaving victory to Clark.

6-8-67 GERMAN GP,
Nürburgring – 15 laps, 212.60 miles
1. Denny Hulme (Repco-Brabham V8 BT24/2), 15 laps in 2:05;55.7, 101.47 mph.
2. Jack Brabham (Repco-Brabham V8 BT24/1), 15 in 2:06;34.8.
3. Chris Amon (Ferrari V12 312 0005), 15. **4.** John Surtees (Honda V12 RA273 F-102), 15. **5.** Jo Bonnier (Cooper-Maserati V12 T81 F1-5-66), 15. **6.** Guy Ligier (Repco-Brabham V8 BT20 F1-2-66), 14.
PP – Jim Clark (Lotus-Cosworth V8 49 R2), 8;04.1; FL – Dan Gurney (Eagle-Weslake V12 T1G 104), 8;15.1, 103.15 mph.
Clark's Lotus led until suspension failed, Gurney's Eagle led dominantly until halfshaft UJ broke with two laps to go.

27-8-67 CANADIAN GP,
Mosport Park, Ontario – 90 laps, 220.50 miles
1. Jack Brabham (Repco-Brabham V8 BT24/1), 90 laps in 2:40;40.0, 82.65 mph.
2. Denny Hulme (Repco-Brabham V8 BT24/2), 90 in 2:41;41.9.
3. Dan Gurney (Eagle-Weslake V12 T1G 104), 89. **4.** Graham Hill (Lotus-Cosworth V8 49 R3), 88. **5.** Mike Spence (BRM H16 P83 8302), 87. **6.** Chris Amon (Ferrari V12 312 0005), 87.
PP – Jim Clark (Lotus-Cosworth V8 49 R2), 1;22.4; FL – Clark, 1;23.1, 106.53 mph.
Rain-swept race, Clark's Lotus took lead from Hulme before his ignition drowned, allowing two Brabhams another 1-2 victory. McLaren made fine debut in new M5A car introducing BRM V12 engine.

10-9-67 ITALIAN GP,
Monza – 68 laps, 243.44 miles
1. John Surtees (Honda V12 RA300 RA-300/1), 68 laps in 1:43;45.0, 140.50 mph.
2. Jack Brabham (Repco-Brabham V8 BT24/1), 68 in 1:43;45.2.
3. Jim Clark (Lotus-Cosworth V8 49 R2), 68. **4.** Jochen Rindt (Cooper-Maserati V12 T81 F1-2-67), 68. **5.** Mike Spence (BRM H16 P83 8302), 67. **6.** Jacky Ickx (Cooper-Maserati V12 T81B F1-1-67), 66.
PP – Clark, 1;28.5; FL – Clark, 1;28.5, 145.35 mph.
Sensational race, Clark led until puncture, Hill until DFV engine failed, leaving Clark set to win, having regained a whole lap deficit from 15th place after pit stop. Clark's engine starved on last lap, leaving Surtees and Brabham racing side by side to the line.

16-9-67 International Gold Cup,
Oulton Park, GB – 45 laps, 124.25 miles
1. Jack Brabham (Repco-Brabham V8 BT24/1), 45 laps in 1:10;07.0, 106.37 mph.
No other F1 finishers in first six – all 1.6-litre F2 cars.
PP – Brabham, 1;30.6. FL – 1;31.6, 108.51 mph.
Wholly inconsequential minor event.

1-10-67 UNITED STATES GP,
Watkins Glen, NY – 108 laps, 249.40 miles
1. Jim Clark (Lotus-Cosworth V8 49 R2), 108 laps in 2:03;13.2, 120.95 mph.
2. Graham Hill (Lotus-Cosworth V8 49 R3), 108 in 2:03;19.5.
3. Denny Hulme (Repco-Brabham V8 BT24/2), 107. **4.** Jo Siffert (Cooper-Maserati V12 T81 F1-2-66), 106. **5.** Jack Brabham (Repco-Brabham V8 BT24/1), 104. **6.** Jo Bonnier (Cooper-Maserati V12 T81 F1-5-66), 101.
PP – Hill, 1;05.48; FL – Hill, 1;06.0, 125.46 mph.
Staged 1-2 by Lotus 49s went wrong as Hill suffered clutch problems and Clark's rear suspension partially collapsed, Amon's Ferrari passed Hill but lost oil pressure, Clark limped home to win.

2-10-67 MEXICAN GP,
Mexico City – 65 laps, 201.95 miles
1. Jim Clark (Lotus-Cosworth V8 49 R1), 65 laps in 1:59;28.70, 101.42 mph.
2. Jack Brabham (Repco-Brabham V8 BT24/1), 65 in 2:00;54.06.
3. Denny Hulme (Repco-Brabham V8 BT24/2), 64. **4.** John Surtees (Honda V12 RA 300 RA-300/1), 63. **5.** Mike Spence (BRM H16 P83 8302), 63. **6.** Pedro Rodriguez (Cooper-Maserati V12 T81B F1-1-67), 63.
PP – Clark, 1;47.56; FL – Clark, 1;48.13, 103.44 mph.
Clark led lap 3 to finish, unchallengeable.

12-11-67 Spanish GP,
Jarama, Madrid – 90 laps, 190.35 miles
1. Jim Clark (Lotus-Cosworth V8 49 R1), 60 laps in 1:31;10.4, 83.60 mph.
2. Graham Hill (Lotus-Cosworth V8 49 R2), 60 in 1:31;25.6.
3. Jack Brabham (Repco-Brabham V8 BT19 F1-1-65), 60.
No other F1 finishers in first six – all 1.6-litre Formula 2 cars.
PP – Clark, 1;28.2. FL – Clark, 1;28.8, 86.40 mph.
Only four F1 cars in hybrid F1/F2 field, de Adamich's Ferrari retired, elderly works Brabham not man enough to trouble the Lotuses.

1968

1-1-68 SOUTH AFRICAN GP,
Kyalami – 80 laps, 203.52 miles
1. Jim Clark (Lotus-Cosworth V8 49 R4), 80 laps in 1:53;56.6, 107.42 mph.
2. Graham Hill (Lotus-Cosworth V8 49 R3), 80 in 1:54;21.9.
3. Jochen Rindt (Repco-Brabham V8 BT24/2), 80. **4.** Chris Amon (Ferrari V12 312 0007), 78. **5.** Denny Hulme (McLaren-BRM V12 M5A/1), 78. **6.** Jean-Pierre Beltoise (1.6 Matra-Cosworth FVA MS7-03*), 77.
*Ballasted Formula 2 car complying with Formula 1 regulations.
PP – Clark, 1;21.6; FL – Clark, 1;23.7, 109.68 mph.
Most significant race, marking Clark's 25th GP victory, breaking the Fangio record, and also the dawn of the general Cosworth-Ford DFV V8 engine era, with customers like Tyrrell Matra now using them in addition to Lotus. Clark led from lap 2 to the finish at record pace, circuit improvements assisting his record-breaking.

17-3-68 Race of Champions,
Brands Hatch, GB – 50 laps, 132.45 miles
1. Bruce McLaren (McLaren-Cosworth V8 M7A/1), 50 laps in 1:18;53.4, 100.77 mph.
2. Pedro Rodriguez (BRM V12 P133 133-01), 50 in 1:19;07.6.
3. Denny Hulme (McLaren-Cosworth V8 M7A/2), 50. **4.** Chris Amon (Ferrari V12 312 0007), 50. **5.** Brian Redman (Cooper-BRM V12 T86B F1-1-68), 50. **6.** Jackie Stewart (Matra-Cosworth V8 MS9-01), 49.
PP – McLaren, 1;30.0; FL – McLaren, 1;31.6, 104.15 mph.
McLaren led from start to finish in his new Cosworth-powered car; BRM V12s showed good pace.

25-4-68 BRDC International Trophy,
Silverstone, GB – 52 laps, 154.49 miles
1. Denny Hulme (McLaren-Cosworth V8 M7A/2), 52 laps in 1:14;44.8, 122.17 mph.
2. Bruce McLaren (McLaren-Cosworth V8 M7A/1), 52 in 1:14;55.7.
3. Chris Amon (Ferrari V12 312 0007), 52. **4.** Jacky Ickx (Ferrari V12 312 0009), 52. **5.** Piers Courage (BRM V12 P126 126-01), 51. **6.** David Hobbs (BRM V12 P261 Spl 2615), 50.
PP – Hulme, 1;24.3; FL – Amon, 1;25.1, 123.82 mph.
The new McLarens dominant again, BRM V12s competed fiercely but did not last long.

12-5-68 SPANISH GP,
Jarama, Madrid – 90 laps, 190.35 miles
1. Graham Hill (Lotus-Cosworth V8 49 R1), 90 laps in 2:15;20.1, 84.41 mph.
2. Denny Hulme (McLaren-Cosworth V8 M7A/2), 90 in 2:15;36.0.
3. Brian Redman (Cooper-BRM V12 T86B F1-1-68), 89. **4.** Ludovico Scarfiotti (Cooper-BRM V12 T86B F1-2-68), 89. **5.** Jean-Pierre Beltoise (Matra-Cosworth V8 MS10-01), 81.
No other finishers.
PP – Chris Amon (Ferrari V12 312 0007), 1;27.9; FL – Beltoise, 1;28.3, 86.67 mph.
Beltoise's Matra led early on until oil leak developed, Amon's Ferrari led until lap 52 when fuel pump failed, and Hill then inherited victory, Hulme falling back affected by fumes and McLaren retiring when well placed.

26-5-68 MONACO GP,
Monte Carlo – 80 laps, 155.33 miles
1. Graham Hill (Lotus-Cosworth V8 49B R5), 80 laps in 2:00;32.3, 77.82 mph.
2. Richard Attwood (BRM V12 P126 126-03), 80 in 2:00;34.5.
3. Lucien Bianchi (Cooper-BRM V12 T86B F1-1-68), 76. **4.** Ludovico Scarfiotti (Cooper-BRM V12 T86B F1-2-68), 76. **5.** Denny Hulme (McLaren-Cosworth V8 M7A/2), 73.
No other finishers.
PP – Hill, 1;28.2; FL – Attwood, 1;28.1, 79.86 mph.
Servoz-Gavin's Tyrrell Matra led opening lap – in Stewart's absence – but hit barrier, Hill leading thereafter to take his fifth Monaco victory; debut win for the modified Lotus 49B.

9-6-68 BELGIAN GP,
Spa-Francorchamps – 28 laps, 245.32 miles
1. Bruce McLaren (McLaren-Cosworth V8 M7A/3), 28 laps in 1:40;02.1, 147.14 mph.
2. Pedro Rodriguez (BRM V12 P133 133-01), 28 in 1:40;14.2.
3. Jacky Ickx (Ferrari V12 312 0009), 28. **4.** Jackie Stewart (Matra-Cosworth V8 MS10-01), 27. **5.** Jack Oliver (Lotus-Cosworth V8 49B R6), 26. **6.** Lucien Bianchi (Cooper-BRM V12 T86B F1-1-68), 26.
PP – Chris Amon (Ferrari V12 312 0007), 3;28.6; FL – John Surtees (Honda V12 RA301 F-801), 3;30.5, 149.83 mph.
Aerofoil appeared on Ferrari and Brabham; Amon's Ferrari and Surtees's Honda fought early battle until stone punctured Ferrari's radiator, Honda chassis failure on lap 10, Hulme/Stewart battle for lead then resolved when Hulme had UJ failure. Stewart's Matra ran short of fuel on penultimate lap and McLaren inherited sudden victory!

23-6-68 DUTCH GP,
Zandvoort – 90 laps, 234.45 miles
1. Jackie Stewart (Matra-Cosworth V8 MS10-02), 90 laps in 2:46;11.26, 84.66 mph.
2. Jean-Pierre Beltoise (Matra V12 MS11-01), 90 laps, 2:47;45.19.
3. Pedro Rodriguez (BRM V12 P133 133-01), 89. **4.** Jacky Ickx (Ferrari V12 312 0009), 88. **5.** Silvio Moser (Repco-Brabham V8 BT20 F1-2-66), 87. **6.** Chris Amon (Ferrari V12 312 0009), 85.
PP – Amon, 1;23.54; FL – Beltoise, 1;45.91, 87.56 mph.
Stewart took wet-race lead from Hill's Lotus on lap 4

and lapped entire field before two-thirds distance, later allowing Beltoise to unlap himself. Triumph for Dunlop rain tyres on the Matras.

7-7-68 FRENCH GP,
Rouen-les-Essarts – 60 laps, 243.89 miles
1. Jacky Ickx (Ferrari V12 312 0009), 60 in 2:25;40.9, 100.45 mph.
2. John Surtees (Honda V12 RA301 F-801), 60 in 2:27; 39.5.
3. Jackie Stewart (Matra-Cosworth V8 MS10-02), 59. **4.** Vic Elford (Cooper-Maserati V12 T86B F1-4-68), 58. **5.** Denny Hulme (McLaren-Cosworth V8 M7A/2), 58. **6.** Piers Courage (BRM V12 P126 126-01), 57.
PP – Jochen Rindt (Repco-Brabham V8 BT26/2), 1;56.1; FL – Pedro Rodriguez (BRM V12 P133 133-01), 2;11.5, 111.28 mph.
Heavy rain, Ickx superb in Firestone rain-tyred Ferrari, Rodriguez second in BRM until lap 46 retirement, Surtees also on intermediate tyres. Race marred by Jo Schlesser's fatal accident in new air-cooled Honda V8.

20-7-68 BRITISH GP,
Brands Hatch – 80 laps, 211.95 miles
1. Jo Siffert (Lotus-Cosworth V8 49B R7), 80 laps in 2:01;20.3, 104.83 mph.
2. Chris Amon (Ferrari V12 312 0011), 80 in 2:01;24.7.
3. Jacky Ickx (Ferrari V12 312 0009), 79. **4.** Denny Hulme (McLaren-Cosworth M7A/2), 79. **5.** John Surtees (Honda V12 RA301 F-801), 78. **6.** Jackie Stewart (Matra-Cosworth V8 MS10-02), 77.
PP – Graham Hill (Lotus-Cosworth V8 49B R5), 1;28.9; FL – Siffert, 1;29.7, 106.35 mph.
Lotus 49Bs dominant, Hill's works car leading for 23 laps, Oliver in sister car for further 17 laps until retirement, Siffert in Rob Walker's new private 49B taking over to hold off Amon until the end. Tall strutted aerofoil aids proliferate.

4-8-68 GERMAN GP,
Nürburgring – 14 laps, 198.64 miles
1. Jackie Stewart (Matra-Cosworth V8 MS10-02), 14 laps in 2:19;03.2, 86.86 mph.
2. Graham Hill (Lotus-Cosworth V8 49B R5), 14 in 2:23;06.4.
3. Jochen Rindt (Repco-Brabham V8 BT26/2), 14. **4.** Jacky Ickx (Ferrari V12 312 0015), 14. **5.** Jack Brabham (Repco-Brabham V8 BT26/1), 14. **6.** Pedro Rodriguez (BRM V12 P133 133-01), 14.
PP – Ickx, 9;04.0; FL – Stewart, 9;36.0, 88.67 mph.
Yet another rain-swept race, mist adding another hazard, Dunlop tyres and Jackie Stewart triumphant, extending their lead throughout. A classic performance.

17-8-68 International Gold Cup,
Oulton Park, GB – 40 laps, 110.44 miles
1. Jackie Stewart (Matra-Cosworth V8 MS10-02), 40 laps in 1:00;39.0, 109.29 mph.
2. Chris Amon (Ferrari V12 312 0011), 40 in 1:00;43.6.
3. Jack Oliver (Lotus-Cosworth V8 49B R2), 40. **4.** Pedro Rodriguez (BRM V12 P126 126-03), 39. **UNC '5th'.** Tony Lanfranchi (2.1 BRM V8 P261 2614), 34. **UNC '6th'.** David Hobbs (BRM V12 P261 Spl 2615), 34.
PP – Graham Hill (Lotus-Cosworth V8 49B R5), 1;29.2; FL – Stewart and Amon, 1;30.0, 110.44 mph.
Stewart led start to finish amidst great mechanical carnage.

8-9-68 ITALIAN GP,
Monza – 68 laps, 242.95 miles
1. Denny Hulme (McLaren-Cosworth V8 M7A/2), 68 laps in 1:40;14.8, 145.41 mph.
2. Johnny Servoz-Gavin (Matra-Cosworth V8 MS10-02), 68 in 1:41;43.2.
3. Jacky Ickx (Ferrari V12 312 0015), 68. **4.** Piers Courage (BRM V12 P126 126-01), 67. **5.** Jean-Pierre Beltoise (Matra V12 MS11-02), 66. **6.** Jo Bonnier (McLaren-BRM V12 M5A/1), 64.
PP – John Surtees (Honda V12 RA301 F-801), 1;26.07; FL – Ickx, 1;26.6, 148.52 mph.
Only six finishers from 20 starters, Surtees's Honda dominated practice, McLarens more competitive on new Goodyear rubber, slipstreaming battle punctuated by Amon crashing Ferrari heavily on oil; McLaren and Siffert both featured prominently before retiring.

22-9-68 CANADIAN GP,
Ste Jovite-Mont Tremblant – 90 laps, 238.50 miles
1. Denny Hulme (McLaren-Cosworth V8 M7A/2), 90 laps in 2:27;11.2, 96.96 mph.
2. Bruce McLaren (McLaren-Cosworth V8 M7A/1), 89 laps.
3. Pedro Rodriguez (BRM V12 P133 133-01), 88. **4.** Graham Hill (Lotus-Cosworth V8 49B R6), 86. **5.** Vic Elford (Cooper-BRM V12 T86B F1-4-68), 86. **6.** Jackie Stewart (Matra-Cosworth V8 MS10-01), 86.
PP – Jochen Rindt (Repco-Brabham V8 BT26/3), 1;33.8; FL – Jo Siffert (Lotus-Cosworth V8 49B R7), 1;35.1, 100.32 mph.
The luckless Amon's Ferrari equalled Rindt's pole time in practice and dominated race despite inoperative clutch, until lap 72 when final-drive failed after strong challenges by Rindt and Siffert ended in their retirement – McLarens running 1-2 for final 17 laps.

6-10-68 UNITED STATES GP,
Watkins Glen, NY – 108 laps, 248.40 miles
1. Jackie Stewart (Matra-Cosworth V8 MS10-02), 108 laps in 1:59;20.29, 124.89 mph.
2. Graham Hill (Lotus-Cosworth V8 49B R6), 108 in 1:59;44.97.
3. John Surtees (Honda RA301 F-801), 107. **4.** Dan Gurney (McLaren-Cosworth V8 M7A/3), 107. **5.** Jo Siffert (Lotus-Cosworth V8 49B R7), 105. **6.** Bruce McLaren (McLaren-Cosworth V8 M7A/1), 103.

PP – Mario Andretti (Lotus-Cosworth V8 49B R5), 1;04.20; FL – Stewart, 1;05.22, 126.96 mph.

Andretti's Lotus debut on pole sensation of practice, but Stewart took lead from him on lap 1 and held it thereafter.

3-11-68 MEXICAN GP,
Mexico City – 65 laps, 201.94 miles
1. Graham Hill (Lotus-Cosworth V8 49B R6), 65 laps in 1:56;43.95, 103.80 mph.
2. Bruce McLaren (McLaren-Cosworth V8 M7A/1), 65 in 1:58;03.27.
3. Jack Oliver (Lotus-Cosworth V8 49 R5), 65. 4. Pedro Rodriguez (BRM V12 P133 133-01) 65. 5. Jo Bonnier (Honda V12 RA301 F-802), 64. 6. Jo Siffert (Lotus-Cosworth V8 49B R7), 64.
PP – Siffert, 1;45.22; FL – Siffert, 1;44.2, 107.26 mph.

Stewart's Matra failed in duel with Hill's Lotus for World Championship while third contender Hulme's McLaren, hastily rebuilt after US GP crash, broke suspension and crashed again. Siffert's private Lotus very fast before and after pit stop to repair throttle linkage, shattering lap record by 2.9 secs in climb back through field.

1969

1-3-69 SOUTH AFRICAN GP,
Kyalami – 80 laps, 203.52 miles
1. Jackie Stewart (Matra-Cosworth V8 MS10-02), 80 laps in 1:50;39.1, 110.62 mph.
2. Graham Hill (Lotus-Cosworth V8 49B R6), 80 in 1:50;57.9.
3. Denny Hulme (McLaren-Cosworth V8 M7A/2), 80. 4. Jo Siffert (Lotus-Cosworth V8 49B R7), 80. 5. Bruce McLaren (McLaren-Cosworth V8 M7A/3), 79. 6. Jean-Pierre Beltoise (Matra-Cosworth V8 MS10-01), 78.
PP – Jack Brabham (Brabham-Cosworth V8 BT26A/2), 1;20.0; FL – Stewart, 1;21.6, 112.50 mph.

Stewart's bi-winged Matra led from start to finish, set new lap and race records. Brabham's new Cosworth-powered BT26A took pole, ran second early on until wing collapsed, team-mate Ickx suffering similarly.

NOTE – *From this point only non-Cosworth DFV engines are specified.*

16-3-69 Race of Champions,
Brands Hatch, GB – 50 laps, 132.50 miles
1. Jackie Stewart (Matra MS80-01), 50 laps in 1:13;10.4, 108.65 mph.
2. Graham Hill (Lotus 49B R6), 50 in 1:13; 17.4.
3. Denny Hulme (McLaren M7A/2), 50. 4. Jo Siffert (Lotus 49B R7), 50. 5. Jack Oliver (BRM V12 P133 133-01), 48. 6. Pete Lovely (Lotus 49B R11), 46.
PP – Hill, 1;28.2; FL – Jochen Rindt (Lotus 49B R9), 1;26.8, 109.91 mph.

Stewart start to finish again, this time in new Matra MS80 and, in freezing weather, he and Hill set faster race average speed than old lap record. First four same as in South Africa, but only 12 starters.

30-3-69 BRDC International Trophy,
Silverstone, GB – 52 laps, 154.49 miles
1. Jack Brabham (Brabham BT26A/2), 52 laps in 1:25;20.8, 107.00 mph.
2. Jochen Rindt (Lotus 49B R9), 52 in 1;25;23.0.
3. Jackie Stewart (Matra MS10-02), 52. 4. Jacky Ickx (Brabham BT26A/2), 52. 5. Piers Courage (Brabham BT26/1), 51. 6. Bruce McLaren (McLaren M7A/4), 51.
PP – Stewart (driving Matra MS80-01 took spare MS10 for race, starting from tail of grid), 1;20.1; FL – Rindt, 1;30.6, 116.30 mph.

Brabham's new Cosworth car came of age and led start to finish, running before Stewart practised MS80 but raced older MS10 in awful weather due to more suitable rim availability, starting from back of grid. Brabham's engine cut out due to low fuel on final lap which allowed Rindt's Lotus to close in exciting finish.

13-4-69 Madrid GP,
Jarama, E – 40 laps, 84.63 miles
1. Keith Holland (Lola-Chevrolet V8 T142 Formula 5000), 40 laps in 1:03;29.8, 80.0 mph.
2. Tony Dean (BRM V12 P261 Spl 261-5), 39 laps.
3. Jock Russell (Lotus-Ford V8 43 Spl 31 Formula 5000), 38.
4. Neil Corner (Cooper-Maserati V12 T86 F1-2-67), 38.
No other serious finishers.
PP – Peter Gethin (McLaren-Chevro V8 M10A Formula 5000), 1;31.9; FL (F1) – Dean, 1;34.2, 3.78 mph.
The most minor and inconsequential of 'F1' races.

4-5-69 SPANISH GP,
Montjuich Pk, Barcelona – 90 laps, 211.98 miles
1. Jackie Stewart (Matra MS80-01), 90 laps in 2:16;53.99, 93.89 mph.
2. Bruce McLaren (McLaren M7C M7/4), 88 in 2:17;40.0.
3. Jean-Pierre Beltoise (Matra MS80-01), 87. 4. Denny Hulme (McLaren M7A/2), 87. 5. John Surtees (BRM V12 P138 138-01), 84. '6'. Jacky Ickx (Brabham BT26A/3), 83.
PP – Jochen Rindt (Lotus 49B R9), 1;25.7; FL – Rindt, 1;28.3, 96.03 mph.

High-winged Lotus 49Bs dominant but both crashed mightily due to wing collapses; Amon's Ferrari inherited lead until lap 56 when engine failed, a lucky win for Stewart. Ickx's Brabham second for while until wing failure, ran third after stop until wishbone broke five laps from finish.

18-5-69 MONACO GP,
Monte Carlo – 80 laps, 155.33 miles
1. Graham Hill (Lotus-Cosworth V8 49B R10), 80 laps in

1:56;59.4, 80.18 mph.
2. Piers Courage (Brabham BT26 Spl BT26/1), 80 in 1:57;16.7.
3. Jo Siffert (Lotus 49B R7), 80. 4. Richard Attwood (Lotus 49B R8), 80. 5. Bruce McLaren (McLaren M7C 'M7A/4'), 79. 6. Denny Hulme (McLaren M7A/2), 78.
PP – Jackie Stewart (Matra MS80-02), 1;24.6; FL – Stewart, 1;25.1, 82.67 mph.

Hill first man to win five Monaco GPs after Stewart's Matra led until UJ broke and Amon's new Ferrari then led until diff failed. CSI ban on high wings came abruptly during practice.

21-6-69 DUTCH GP,
Zandvoort – 90 laps, 234.45 miles
1. Jackie Stewart (Matra MS80-02), 90 laps in 2:06;42.08, 111.04 mph.
2. Jo Siffert (Lotus 49B R7), 90 in 2:07;06.60.
3. Chris Amon (Ferrari V12 312 0019), 90. 4. Denny Hulme (McLaren M7A/2), 90. 5. Jacky Ickx (Brabham BT26A/3), 90. 6. Jack Brabham (Brabham BT26A/2), 90.
PP – Jochen Rindt (Lotus 49B R6), 1;20.85; FL – Stewart, 1;22.94, 113.08 mph.

Stewart took lead on lap 16 when Rindt's Lotus broke UJ, Hill's Lotus having led the opening two laps before handling deteriorated. Great drive through field by Siffert and close battle for third won by Amon's Ferrari.

6-7-69 FRENCH GP,
Clermont-Ferrand – 38 laps, 190.19 miles
1. Jackie Stewart (Matra MS80-02), 38 laps in 1:56;47.4, 97.71 mph.
2. Jean-Pierre Beltoise (Matra MS80-01), 38 in 1:57;44.5.
3. Jacky Ickx (Brabham BT26A/3), 38. 4. Bruce McLaren (McLaren M7C 'M7A/4'), 37. 5. Vic Elford (McLaren M7A/3), 37. 6. Graham Hill (Lotus 49B R10), 37.
PP – Stewart, 3;00.6; FL – Stewart, 3;02.7, 98.62.

Stewart's most convincing victory thus far, leading from start to finish, Beltoise making it Matra 1-2 after desperate race-long duel with Ickx.

19-7-69 BRITISH GP,
Silverstone – 84 laps, 245.96 miles
1. Jackie Stewart (Matra MS80-01), 84 laps in 1:55;55.6, 127.25 mph.
2. Jacky Ickx (Brabham BT26A/4), 83 in 1:56;36.1.
3. Bruce McLaren (McLaren M7C 'M7A/4'), 83. 4. Jochen Rindt (Lotus 49B R6), 83. 5. Piers Courage (Brabham BT26 Spl BT26/1), 83. 6. Vic Elford (McLaren M7A/3), 82.
PP – Rindt, 1;20.8; FL – Stewart, 1;21.3, 129.61 mph.

Great Rindt Lotus/Stewart Tyrrell battle until lap 62 when wing end-plate cut into Lotus rear tyre and Rindt had to make a stop, Ickx coasted across finish line out of fuel.

3-8-69 GERMAN GP,
Nürburgring – 14 laps, 198.64 miles
1. Jacky Ickx (Brabham BT26A/4), 14 laps in 1:49;55.4, 108.43 mph.
2. Jackie Stewart (Matra MS80-02), 14 in 1:50;53.1.
3. Bruce McLaren (McLaren M7C 'M7A/4'), 14. 4. Graham Hill (Lotus 49B R10), 14. 5. Jo Siffert (Lotus 49B R7), 12. 6. Jean-Pierre Beltoise (Matra MS80-01), 12.
PP – Ickx, 7;42.1; FL – Ickx, 7;43.8, 110.13 mph.

After slow start Ickx broke lap record, caught Stewart, duelled for three laps then won as he pleased while Matra allegedly lost all gears but third. Only four F1 finishers, Siffert being classified despite having crashed heavily and Beltoise retiring with suspension failure.

16-8-69 International Gold Cup,
Oulton Park, GB – 40 laps, 110.44 miles
1. Jacky Ickx (Brabham BT26A/3), 40 laps in 1:00;28.6, 109.57 mph.
2. Jochen Rindt (Lotus 63 [4WD] R1), 40 in 1:01;50.8.
3. Andrea de Adamich (Surtees-Chevrolet TS5 Formula 5000), 39. 4. Trevor Taylor (Surtees-Chevrolet TS5 Formula 5000), 39. 5. Mike Hailwood (Lola-Chevrolet T142 Formula 5000), 39. 6. Alan Rollinson (Brabham-Cosworth FVA BT30 Formula 2), 38.
PP – Jackie Stewart (Matra MS80-02), 1;27.2; FL – Stewart, 1;28.6, 112.19 mph.

Second successive win for lone works Brabham, but Stewart's Matra took lead from lap 2 until broken battery terminal caused pit stop which cost him three laps.

7-9-69 ITALIAN GP,
Monza – 68 laps, 242.95 miles
1. Jackie Stewart (Matra MS80-02), 68 laps in 1:39;11.26, 146.96 mph.
2. Jochen Rindt (Lotus 49B R6), 68 in 1:39;11.34.
3. Jean-Pierre Beltoise (Matra MS80-01), 68 in 1:39;11.43. 4. Bruce McLaren (McLaren M7C 'M7A/4'), 68 in 1:39;11.45. 5. Piers Courage (Brabham BT26 Spl BT26/1), 68. 6. Pedro Rodriguez (Ferrari V12 312 0019), 66.
PP – Rindt, 1;25.48; FL – Beltoise, 1;25.2, 150.96 mph.

Classic race to decide 1969 Championship, eight cars in slipstreaming battle for lead thinned to four in final charge, Rindt, Beltoise and Stewart in turn led during final half-lap – study the first four finishing times above!

20-9-69 CANADIAN GP,
Mosport Park, Toronto – 90 laps, 221.31 miles
1. Jacky Ickx (Brabham BT26A/3), 90 laps in 1:59;25.7, 112.76 mph.
2. Jack Brabham (Brabham BT26A/4), 90 in 2:00;11.9.
3. Jochen Rindt (Lotus 49B R6), 90. 4. Jean-Pierre Beltoise (Matra MS80-01), 89. 5. Bruce McLaren (McLaren M7C 'M7A/4'), 87. 6. Johnny Servoz-Gavin (Matra [4WD] MS84-01), 84.
PP – Ickx, 1;17.4; FL – Ickx, 1;18.1, 114.78 mph.

Stewart just led Ickx until lap 33 when their cars collided and both spun, Ickx quickly regained track but Matra would not restart, excellent Brabham 1-2 result, Rindt's Lotus held initial lead, first points for 4WD.

5-10-69 UNITED STATES GP,
Watkins Glen, NY – 108 laps, 248.40 miles
1. Jochen Rindt (Lotus 49B R6), 108 laps in 1:57;56.84, 126.36 mph.
2. Piers Courage (Brabham BT26 Spl BT26/1), 108 in 1:58;43.83.
3. John Surtees (BRM V12 P139 139-01), 106. 4. Jack Brabham (Brabham BT26A/4), 106. 5. Pedro Rodriguez (Ferrari V12 312 0017), 101. 6. Silvio Moser (Brabham BT24/3), 98.
PP – Rindt, 1;03.62; FL – Rindt, 1;04.34, 128.69 mph.

Season's sixth pole and first-ever GP win for Rindt in Lotus 49B, Stewart led just briefly before engine failed, fierce battle between works Brabhams and Courage's private entry sister car. Wet practice proved 4WD approach delusory.

19-10-69 MEXICAN GP,
Mexico City – 65 laps, 201.94 miles
1. Denny Hulme (McLaren M7A/2), 65 laps in 1:54;08.80, 106.15 mph.
2. Jacky Ickx (Brabham BT26A/3), 65 in 1:54;11.36.
3. Jack Brabham (Brabham BT26A/4), 65. 4. Jackie Stewart (Matra MS80-02), 65. 5. Jean-Pierre Beltoise (Matra MS80-01), 65. 6. Jack Oliver (BRM V12 P139 139-02), 63.
PP – Brabham, 1;42.90; FL – Ickx, 1;43.05, 108.53 mph.

New compound Goodyear G20 tyres dictated race, Hulme took lead from Ickx on lap 10 in veteran McLaren chassis and held it despite record-breaking Brabham lap.

1970

7-3-70 SOUTH AFRICAN GP,
Kyalami – 80 laps, 203.52 miles
1. Jack Brabham (Brabham BT33/2), 80 laps in 1:49;34.6, 111.70 mph.
2. Denny Hulme (McLaren M14A/2), 80 in 1:49;42.7.
3. Jackie Stewart (March 701/2), 80. 4. Jean-Pierre Beltoise (Matra V12 MS120-01), 80. 5. John Miles (Lotus 49C R10), 79. 6. Graham Hill (Lotus 49C R7), 79.
PP – Stewart, 1;19.3; FL – Brabham & John Surtees (McLaren M7C 'M7A/4'), 1;20.8, 113.61 mph.

New March 701s performed well, Brabham in his first monocoque F1 car took lead from Stewart's 701 at quarter-distance to win unchallenged.

22-3-70 Race of Champions,
Brands Hatch, GB – 50 laps, 132.50 miles
1. Jackie Stewart (March 701/2), 50 laps in 1:12;51.8, 109.11 mph.
2. Jochen Rindt (Lotus 49C R6), 50 in 1:13;28.0.
3. Denny Hulme (McLaren M14A/2), 50. 4. Jack Brabham (Brabham BT33/2), 49. 5. Graham Hill (Lotus 49C R7), 49. 6. Peter Gethin (McLaren M7A/2), 49.
PP – Stewart, 1;25.8; FL – Brabham, 1;25.8, 111.19 mph.

Brabham's fine BT33 set for dominant win when ignition failed three laps from finish. Stewart's win rewarded hard drive in ill-handling March, Oliver's new BRM P153 led sensationally before falling back to eventual transmission failure.

19-4-70 SPANISH GP,
Jarama, Madrid – 90 laps, 190.15 miles
1. Jackie Stewart (March 701/2), 90 laps in 2:10;58.2, 87.21 mph.
2. Bruce McLaren (McLaren M14A/1), 89.
3. Mario Andretti (March 701/3), 89. 4. Graham Hill (Lotus 49C R7), 89. 5. Johnny Servoz-Gavin (March 701/7), 88.
No other finishers.
PP – Jack Brabham (Brabham BT33/2), 1;23.9; FL – Brabham, 1;24.3, 90.33 mph.

Stewart led throughout while field delayed by new flat-12 Ferrari/BRM collision and fire on first lap. Brabham caught Stewart and seemed set to pass when his engine failed. Fine but fortunate result for March. Poor debut of new Lotus 72.

26-4-70 BRDC International Trophy
Silverstone, GB – 2 x 26-lap heats, 154.49 miles
HEAT ONE: 1. Amon; 2. Stewart; 3. Courage; 4. McLaren; 5. Rindt; 6. Hulme.
HEAT TWO: 1. Stewart; 2. Amon; 3. Courage; 4. Hill; 5. McLaren; 6. Wisell.
AGGREGATE:
1. Chris Amon (March 701/1), 52 laps in 1:13;32.2, 124.19 mph.
2. Jackie Stewart (March 701/2), 52 in 1:13;42.2.
3. Piers Courage (de Tomaso 308 505/3), 52. 4. Bruce McLaren (McLaren M14A/1), 52. 5. Reine Wisell (McLaren M7A/2), 51. 6. Denny Hulme (McLaren M14A/2), 50.
PP – Heat One, Amon, 1;21.4; Heat Two, Amon (result of first heat). FL – Heat One, Amon, 1;22.1, 128.35 mph; Heat Two, Stewart, 1;23.3, 126.50 mph.

In absence of BRM, Matra and Ferrari, works March roundly beat Stewart's in Heat One and kept pace with it in Heat Two for aggregate victory.

10-5-70 MONACO GP,
Monte Carlo – 80 laps, 156.33 miles
1. Jochen Rindt (Lotus 49C R6), 80 laps in 1:54;36.6, 81.84 mph.
2. Jack Brabham (Brabham BT33/2), 80 in 1:54;59.7.
3. Henri Pescarolo (Matra V12 MS120-02), 80. 4. Denny Hulme (McLaren M14A/2), 80. 5. Graham Hill (Lotus 49C R10), 79. 6. Pedro Rodriguez (BRM V12 P153 153-02), 78.
PP – Jackie Stewart (March 701/2), 1;24.0; FL – Rindt,

1;23.2, 84.56 mph.

Stewart's March led convincingly but failed on lap 28 leaving Brabham to hold off strong challenge from Amon's works 701 until its suspension failed. Rindt in old Lotus 49C started racing near half-distance, caught Brabham and pressured veteran into final corner mistake, stealing classic win.

7-6-70 BELGIAN GP,
Spa-Francorchamps – 28 laps, 245.32 miles
1. Pedro Rodriguez (BRM V12 P153 153-02), 28 laps in 1:38;09.9, 149.94 mph.
2. Chris Amon (March 701/1), 28 in 1;38;11.0.
3. Jean-Pierre Beltoise (Matra V12 MS120-03), 28. 4. Ignazio Giunti (Ferrari 312B 002/1), 28. 5. Rolf Stommelen (Brabham BT33/1), 28. 6. Henri Pescarolo (Matra V12 MS120-02), 27.
PP – Jackie Stewart (March 701/2), 3;28.0; FL – Amon, 3;27.4, 152.07 mph.

Super-fast circuit permits 12-cylinders to overturn usual Cosworth domination, though Stewart's Matra and Rindt's Lotus 72 both led briefly before engine failures, strong BRM uncatchable thereafter; Matras and Ferraris also shone.

21-6-70 DUTCH GP,
Zandvoort – 80 laps, 208.80 miles
1. Jochen Rindt (Lotus 72 R2), 80 laps in 1:50;43.41, 112.95 mph.
2. Jackie Stewart (March 701/2), 80 in 1:51;13.41.
3. Jacky Ickx (Ferrari 312B 001), 79. 4. Clay Regazzoni (Ferrari 312B 003), 79. 5. Jean-Pierre Beltoise (Matra V12 MS120-03), 79. 6. John Surtees (McLaren M7A 'M7A/4'), 79.
PP – Rindt, 1;18.50; FL – Ickx, 1;19.23, 118.38 mph.

Revised Lotus 72 proved its class, Ickx's Ferrari delayed by puncture.

5-7-70 FRENCH GP,
Clermont-Ferrand – 38 laps, 190.19 miles
1. Jochen Rindt (Lotus 72 R2), 38 laps in 1:55; 57.00, 98.42 mph.
2. Chris Amon (March 701/1), 38 in 1:56;04.61.
3. Jack Brabham (Brabham BT33/2), 38. 4. Denny Hulme (McLaren M14D/1), 38. 5. Henri Pescarolo (Matra V12 MS120-02), 38. 6. Dan Gurney (McLaren M14A/1), 38.
PP – Jacky Ickx (Ferrari 312B 003), 2;58.22; FL – Brabham, 3;00.75, 99.68 mph.

Ickx's flat-12 Ferrari led 14 laps until engine failed, Beltoise's Matra 11 laps until tyre punctured; Lotus 72 inherited second win in row.

19-7-70 BRITISH GP,
Brands Hatch – 80 laps, 212.00 miles
1. Jochen Rindt (Lotus 72 R2), 80 laps in 1:57;02.0, 108.69 mph.
2. Jack Brabham (Brabham BT33/2), 80 in 1:57;34.9.
3. Denny Hulme (McLaren M14A/2), 80. 4. Clay Regazzoni (Ferrari 312B 002[2]), 80. 5. Chris Amon (March 701/1), 79. 6. Graham Hill (Lotus 49C R7), 79.
PP – Rindt, 1;24.8; FL – Brabham, 1;25.9, 111.06 mph.

Ickx's Ferrari left field for dead but broke transmission after only six laps; Rindt's Lotus led narrowly until lap 69 when constant shadow Brabham easily took lead, only to have engine starve of fuel on last lap, handing another lucky win to Lotus.

2-8-70 GERMAN GP,
Hockenheim – 50 laps, 210.89 miles
1. Jochen Rindt (Lotus 72 R2), 50 laps in 1:42;00.3, 123.90 mph.
2. Jacky Ickx (Ferrari 312B 003), 50 in 1:42;01.0.
3. Denny Hulme (McLaren M14A/2), 50. 4. Emerson Fittipaldi (Lotus 49C R10), 50. 5. Rolf Stommelen (Brabham BT33/3), 49. 6. Henri Pescarolo (Matra V12 MS120-02), 49.
PP – Ickx, 1;59.5; FL – Ickx, 2;00.5, 126.02 mph.

Race-long sheer speed battle between flat-12 Ferrari and Lotus 72 resolved in latter's favour.

16-8-70 AUSTRIAN GP,
Österreichring – 60 laps, 220.39 miles
1. Jacky Ickx (Ferrari 312B 001), 60 laps in 1:42;17.32, 129.27 mph.
2. Clay Regazzoni (Ferrari 312B 003), 60 in 1:42;17.93.
3. Rolf Stommelen (Brabham BT33/3), 60. 4. Pedro Rodriguez (BRM V12 P153 153-05), 59. 5. Jack Oliver (BRM V12 P153-153-04), 59. 6. Jean-Pierre Beltoise (Matra V12 MS120-03), 59.
PP – Jochen Rindt (Lotus 72 R2), 1;39.23; FL – Ickx & Regazzoni, 1;40.4, 131.70 mph.

Total Ferrari domination, Ignazio Giunti also featuring in third 312B, only one V8 in top six.

22-8-70 International Gold Cup,
Oulton Pk, GB – 2 x 20-lap heats, 110.44 miles
HEAT ONE: 1. Surtees; 2. Oliver; 3. Rindt; 4. Hailwood; 5. Ganley; 6. Taylor.
HEAT TWO: 1. Rindt; 2. Surtees; 3. Oliver; 4. Gardner; 5. Ganley; 6. Taylor.
AGGREGATE:
1. John Surtees (Surtees TS7-01), 40 laps in 59;48.2, 110.8 mph.
2. Jochen Rindt (Lotus 72 R2), 40 in 59;51.6.
3. Jack Oliver (BRM V12 P153-04), 40. 4. Howden Ganley (McLaren-Chevrolet M10B 400-05 Formula 5000), 40. 5. Trevor Taylor (Lola-Chevrolet T190 F1/7 Formula 5000), 38. 6. Fred Saunders (Crosslé-Rover V8 15F 70-04 Formula 5000), 36.
PP – Heat One, Surtees, 1;36.2; Heat Two, result of first heat. FL – Heat One, Surtees (Tyrrell 001), 1;26.6, 114.78 mph; Heat Two Rindt, 1;27.6, 113.47 mph.

Surtees able to pace himself in Heat 2 after comfortable win in Heat 1 when Rindt's Lotus handicapped by gear ratio choice. Stewart gave new Tyrrell-Cosworth fine debut despite minor troubles – note his record lap.

6-9-70 ITALIAN GP,
Monza – 68 laps, 242.95 miles
1. Clay Regazzoni (Ferrari 312B 004), 68 laps in 1:39;06.88, 147.07 mph.
2. Jackie Stewart (March 701/4), 68 in 1:39;12.61.
3. Jean-Pierre Beltoise (Matra V12 MS120-03), 68. 4. Denny Hulme (McLaren M14A/1), 68. 5. Rolf Stommelen (Brabham BT33/3), 68. 6. François Cevert (March 701/7), 68.
PP – Jacky Ickx (Ferrari 312B 001), 1;24.10; FL – Regazzoni, 1;25.2, 150.96 mph.
Hectic race followed sombre practice in which Rindt died when Lotus 72 crashed; BRM V12s and Ferrari flat-12s most prominent in initial 12-car slipstreaming leading bunch.

20-9-70 CANADIAN GP,
Ste Jovite-Mt Tremblant – 90 laps, 238.50 miles
1. Jacky Ickx (Ferrari 312B 001), 90 laps in 2:21;18.4, 101.27 mph.
2. Clay Regazzoni (Ferrari 312B 004), 90 in 2:21;33.2.
3. Chris Amon (March 701/1), 90. 4. Pedro Rodriguez (BRM V12 P153 153-06), 89. 5. John Surtees (Surtees TS7-001), 89. 6. Peter Gethin (McLaren M14A/1), 88.
PP – Jackie Stewart (Tyrrell 001), 1;31.5; FL – Regazzoni, 1;32.2, 103.47 mph.
Stewart established dominant 17 sec lead in new Tyrrell 001 until stub axle failed after 31 laps, flat-12 Ferraris uncatchable thereafter.

4-10-70 UNITED STATES GP,
Watkins Glen, NY – 108 laps, 248.40 miles
1. Emerson Fittipaldi (Lotus 72 R5), 108 in 1:57;32.79, 129.79 mph.
2. Pedro Rodriguez (BRM V12 P153 153-05), 108 in 1:58;09.18.
3. Reine Wisell (Lotus 72 R3), 108. 4. Jacky Ickx (Ferrari 312B 001), 107. 5. Chris Amon (March 701/1), 107. 6. Derek Bell (Surtees TS7-002), 107.
PP – Ickx, 1;03.07; FL – Ickx, 1;02.74, 131.97 mph.
Stewart's Tyrrell dominated until lap 62 when oil-line burned through on exhaust, Rodriguez's BRM looked set to win until lap 100 when he had to add fuel, Fittipaldi's maiden Lotus win clinched their own and Rindt's World titles.

25-10-70 MEXICAN GP,
Mexico City – 65 laps, 201.94 miles
1. Jacky Ickx (Ferrari 312B 001), 65 laps in 1:53;28.36, 106.78 mph.
2. Clay Regazzoni (Ferrari 312B 004), 65 in 1:54;13.82.
3. Denny Hulme (McLaren M14A/2), 65. 4. Chris Amon (March 701/1), 65. 5. Jean-Pierre Beltoise (Matra V12 MS120-03), 65. 6. Pedro Rodriguez (BRM P153 153-05), 65.
PP – Regazzoni, 1;41.86; FL – Ickx, 1;43.11, 108.49 mph.
Ferrari/new Tyrrell battle evaporated when Stewart's steering column worked loose, he later hit stray dog; race marred by crowd encroaching on track. Jack Brabham third in his farewell race when engine blew, 13 laps from finish.

1971

24-1-71 Argentine GP,
Buenos Aires – 2 x 50-lap heats, 211.90 miles
HEAT ONE: 1. Stommelen; 2. Siffert; 3. Pescarolo; 4. Amon; 5. Wisell; 6. Reutemann.
HEAT TWO: 1. Amon, 2. Pescarolo; 3. Reutemann; 4. Prophet; 5. Spice; 6. Marincovich/Young.
AGGREGATE:
1. Chris Amon (Matra V12 MS120-02), 100 laps in 2:08;19.29, 99.18 mph.
2. Henri Pescarolo (March 701/6), 100 in 2:08;41.15.
3. Carlos Reutemann (McLaren M7C 'M7A/4'), 100. 4. David Prophet (McLaren-Chevrolet M10B 400-04 Formula 5000), 96. UNC '5th'. Derek Bell (March 701/1), 88. 6. Jo Siffert (March 701/5), 86.
(Drivers not featured overall but named in first 6 in heats drove the following cars: Rolf Stommelen, Surtees TS7-002; Reine Wisell, Lotus 72 R3; Gordon Spice, McLaren M10B 400-05 Formula 5000; Carlos Marincovich/Greg Young, McLaren M10B Formula 5000.
PP – Heat One, Stommelen, 1;15.85; Heat Two, result of Heat One, FL – Heat One, Wisell, 1;15.10, 101.68 mph; Heat Two, Amon, 1;15.05, 101.75 mph.
New Tyrrell driver Stommelen dominant until pushed off in Heat Two by rather desperate Amon's Matra, Siffert having led Heat Two until suspension failure – first F1 win for Matra V12.

6-3-71 SOUTH AFRICAN GP,
Kyalami – 79 laps, 203.52 miles
1. Mario Andretti (Ferrari 312B 002[2]), 79 laps in 1:47;35.5, 112.36 mph.
2. Jackie Stewart (Tyrrell 001), 79 in 1:47;56.4.
3. Clay Regazzoni (Ferrari 312B 004), 79. 4. Reine Wisell (Lotus 72 R3), 79. 5. Chris Amon (Matra V12 MS120-03), 78. 6. Denny Hulme (McLaren M19/1), 78.
PP – Stewart, 1;17.8; FL – Andretti, 1;20.3, 114.32.
Regazzoni led initially for Ferrari until wheels lost balance, Hulme took over in brand new McLaren M19 but suspension failure four laps from finish gave Andretti and Ferrari victory.

21-3-71 Race of Champions,
Brands Hatch, GB – 50 laps, 132.50 miles
1. Clay Regazzoni (Ferrari 312B 005), 50 laps in 1;13;35.0, 108.04 mph.
2. Jackie Stewart (Tyrrell 001), 50 in 1;13;58.6.
3. John Surtees (Surtees TS9 001), 49. 4. Tim Schenken (Brabham BT33/1), 48. 5. Howden Ganley (BRM V12 P153 153-03), 48. 6. Ray Allen (March 701/6), 48.
PP – Stewart, 1;24.6; FL – Graham Hill (Brabham BT34/1), 1;26.7, 110.03 mph.

Wet/dry weather decided minor event. Stewart's Tyrrell led on 'semi-wet' Goodyears until track dried and dry Firestone-tyred Ferrari took over from lap 25. Tyrrell with new 11-series DFV engine clearly the faster car; debut of Lotus 56B turbine car.

28-3-71 Questor GP,
Ontario Speedway, California – 2 x 32-lap heats, 204.42 miles
HEAT ONE: 1. Andretti; 2. Stewart; 3. Siffert; 4. Hulme; 5. Ickx; 6. Amon.
HEAT TWO: 1. Andretti; 2. Stewart; 3. Amon; 4. Rodriguez; 5. Hulme; 6. Schenken.
AGGREGATE:
1. Mario Andretti (Ferrari 312B 002[2]), 64 laps in 1:51;48.410, 109.70 mph.
2. Jackie Stewart (Tyrrell 001), 64 in 1:52;04.324.
3. Denny Hulme (McLaren M19A/1), 64. 4. Chris Amon (Matra MS120-03), 64. 5. Tim Schenken (Brabham BT33/1), 63. 6. Peter Gethin (McLaren M14A/1), 63.
PP – Heat One, Andretti, – Heat Two result of first heat. FL – Heat One, Amon, 1;43.088, 111.54 mph; Heat Two, Pedro Rodriguez (BRM V12 P160-01), 1;42.777, 111.88 mph.
Stewart's Tyrrell led both heats, and was passed in both by Andretti's Ferrari, while Amon's Matra challenged the Tyrrell strongly in both heats but punctured tyre in the first.

9-4-71 Spring Trophy,
Oulton Park, GB – 40 laps, 110.44 miles
1. Pedro Rodriguez (BRM V12 P160-01), 40 laps in 57;33.4, 115.11 mph.
2. Peter Gethin (McLaren M14A/2), 40 in 57;38.0.
3. Jackie Stewart (Tyrrell 002), 40. 4. Howden Ganley (BRM V12 P153-03), 39. 5. Allan Rollinson (March 701/5), 36. UNC '6th'. Tony Trimmer (Lotus 49C R6), 31.
PP – Stewart, 1;25.8; FL – Rodriguez & Gethin, 1;25.06, 118.93 mph.
Latest BRM led throughout, Gethin and Stewart fought fierce duel in its wake, lap record shattered, despite only 11 starters.

18-4-71 SPANISH GP,
Montjuich Pk, Barcelona – 75 laps, 176.62 miles
1. Jackie Stewart (Tyrrell 003), 75 laps in 1:49;03.4, 97.19 mph.
2. Jacky Ickx (Ferrari 312B 003), 75 in 1:49;06.8.
3. Chris Amon (Matra V12 MS120-03), 75. 4. Pedro Rodriguez (BRM V12 P160-01). 5. Denny Hulme (McLaren M19A/1), 75. 6. Jean-Pierre Beltoise (Matra V12 MS120-05), 74.
PP – Ickx, 1;25.9; FL – Ickx, 1;25.1, 99.64 mph.
Ickx's Ferrari led first five laps before Stewart dominated, Ickx closed up at finish, lowering his pole practice record time; 12-cylinder cars all looked strong.

8-5-71 BRDC International Trophy,
Silverstone ,GB – 2 x 26-lap heats, 150.80 miles
HEAT ONE: 1. Stewart; 2. Rodriguez; 3. Hill; 4. Surtees; 5. Beltoise; 6. Gethin.
HEAT TWO: 1. Hill; 2. Amon; 3. Fittipaldi; 4. Gethin; 5. Pescarolo; 6. Hailwood.
AGGREGATE:
1. Graham Hill (Brabham BT34/1), 52 laps in 1:11;03.2, 128.50 mph.
2. Peter Gethin (McLaren M14A/2), 52 in 1:12;37.0.
3. Tim Schenken (Brabham BT33/3), 52. 4. Pedro Rodriguez (BRM V12 P160-01), 51. 5. Mike Hailwood (Surtees-Chevrolet TS8-005 Formula 5000), 51. 6. Henri Pescarolo (March 711/3), 51.
PP – Heat One, Chris Amon (Matra V12 MS120-04), 1;20.0; Heat Two, result of first heat. FL – Heat One, Jackie Stewart (Tyrrell 003), 1;20.5, 130.90 mph: Heat Two, John Surtees (Surtees TS9-001), 1;20.6, 130.73 mph.
Stewart crashed Tyrrell 003 first corner Heat Two, Rodriguez's BRM punctured on debris from blown Matra engine, Hill inherited popular win for new 'Lobster Claw' Brabham.

23-5-71 MONACO GP,
Monte Carlo – 80 laps, 153.33 miles
1. Jackie Stewart (Tyrrell 003), 80 laps in 1:52;21.3, 83.49 mph.
2. Ronnie Peterson (March 711/2), 80 in 1:52;46.9.
3. Jacky Ickx (Ferrari 312B2 006), 80. 4. Denny Hulme (McLaren M19A/1), 80. 5. Emerson Fittipaldi (Lotus 72 R5), 79. 6. Rolf Stommelen (Surtees TS9-002), 79.
PP – Stewart, 1;23.2; FL – Stewart, 1;22.2, 85.58 mph.
Staggering Stewart/Tyrrell performance, driver superb as car lost rear brakes before start yet he led start-to-finish and set new record lap on this demanding circuit. Peterson's driving put March 711 in second place.

13-6-71 Rindt Memorial Race,
Hockenheim, 35 laps, 146.64 miles
1. Jacky Ickx (Ferrari 312B 003), 35 laps in 1:10;11.7, 126.20 mph.
2. Ronnie Peterson (March 711/2), 35 in 1:11.05.5.
3. John Surtees (Surtees TS9-001), 35. 4. Howden Ganley (BRM V12 P153-07), 35. 5. Nanni Galli (March 711/1), 35. 6. Skip Barber (March 711/5), 34.
PP – Ickx, 1;56.8; FL – Ickx, 1;58.8, 127.82 mph.
Easy win for Ickx's Ferrari, both team-mate Regazzoni and Wisell in Lotus 72 held second early on before suffering electrical and brake trouble respectively.

26-6-71 DUTCH GP,
Zandvoort – 70 laps, 182.70 miles
1. Jacky Ickx (Ferrari 312B2 006), 70 laps in 1:56;20.09, 94.06 mph.
2. Pedro Rodriguez (BRM V12 P160-01), 70 in 1:56;28.08.

3. Clay Regazzoni (Ferrari 312B2 005), 69. 4. Ronnie Peterson (March 711/2), 68. 5. John Surtees (Surtees TS9-001), 68. 6. Jo Siffert (BRM V12 P160-02), 68.
PP – Ickx, 1;17.42; FL – Ickx, 1;34.95, 98.78 mph.
Wet race dominated by acknowledged wet-weather drivers in smooth 12-cylinder cars, new Firestone rain tyres on first eight cars home. Dave Walker's Lotus 56B 4WD turbine car crashed after five fast early laps climbing through field, 4WD's last great chance wasted.

4-7-71 FRENCH GP,
Ricard-Castellet – 55 laps, 198.22 miles
1. Jackie Stewart (Tyrrell 003), 55 laps in 1:46;41.68, 111.66 mph.
2. François Cevert (Tyrrell 002), 55 in 1:47;09.80.
3. Emerson Fittipaldi (Lotus 72 R5), 55. 4. Jo Siffert (BRM V12 P160-02), 55. 5. Chris Amon (Matra V12 MS120-06), 55. 6. Reine Wisell (Lotus 72 R3), 55.
PP – Stewart, 1;50.71; FL – Stewart, 1;54.09, 113.91 mph.
Tyrrells pulverized opposition, Regazzoni's Ferrari and Rodriguez's BRM both held second place but failed to maintain the pace.

17-7-71 BRITISH GP,
Silverstone – 68 laps, 199.04 miles
1. Jackie Stewart (Tyrrell 003), 68 laps in 1:31;31.5, 130.48 mph.
2. Ronnie Peterson (March 711/6), 68 in 1:32;07.6.
3. Emerson Fittipaldi (Lotus 72 R5), 68. 4. Henri Pescarolo (March 711/3), 67. 5. Rolf Stommelen (Surtees TS9-002), 67. 6. John Surtees (Surtees TS9-002), 67.
PP – Clay Regazzoni (Ferrari 312B2 005), 1;18.1; FL – Stewart, 1;19.9, 131.88 mph.
Ferraris led from chaotic start but Stewart's Tyrrell again uncatchable once in front; strong pursuit by Siffert's BRM foiled by severe low-profile Firestone tyre vibration.

1-8-71 GERMAN GP,
Nürburgring – 12 laps, 170.27 miles
1. Jackie Stewart (Tyrrell 003), 12 laps in 1:29;15.7, 114.46 mph.
2. François Cevert (Tyrrell 002), 12 in 1:29;45.8.
3. Clay Regazzoni (Ferrari 312B2 005), 12. 4. Mario Andretti (Ferrari 312B2 007), 12. 5. Ronnie Peterson (March 711/6), 12. 6. Tim Schenken (Brabham BT33/3), 12.
PP – Stewart, 7;19.0; FL – Cevert, 7;20.1, 116.07 mph.
Stewart took lead at second corner, Ickx spun Ferrari out of second place, Siffert's BRM looked capable of catching Stewart but vibration ruined ignition coil leaving only Ferrari close to Tyrrells' speed and durability. Cevert took 20 secs off lap record on modernized circuit.

15-8-71 AUSTRIAN GP,
Österreichring – 54 laps, 198.34 miles
1. Jo Siffert (BRM V12 P160-02), 54 laps in 1:30;23.91, 132.30 mph.
2. Emerson Fittipaldi (Lotus 72 R5), 54 in 1:30;28.03.
3. Tim Schenken (Brabham BT33/3), 54. 4. Reine Wisell (Lotus 72 R6), 54. 5. Graham Hill (Brabham BT34/1), 54. 6. Henry Pescarolo (March 711/3), 54.
PP – Siffert, 1;37.44; FL – Siffert, 1;38.47, 134.39 mph.
The perfect performance from Siffert's BRM – pole, fastest lap, led throughout – deflating tyre allowed Lotus to close at finish. Tyrrells both retired, Stewart became Champion by trackside.

22-8-71 International Gold Cup,
Oulton Pk, GB – 2 x 20-lap heats, 110.44 miles
HEAT ONE: 1. Pescarolo; 2. Ganley; 3. Surtees; 4. Gardner; 5. Gethin; 6. Hailwood.
HEAT TWO: 1. Surtees; 2. Ganley; 3. Gardner; 4. Rollinson; 5. Craft; 6. McRae.
AGGREGATE:
1. John Surtees (Surtees TS9-004), 40 laps in 57;38.6, 114.96 mph.
2. Howden Ganley (BRM V12 P153-06), 40 in 57;50.0.
3. Frank Gardner (Lola-Chevrolet T300 300-F1-1 Formula 5000), 40. 4. Alan Rollinson (Surtees-Chevrolet TS8-007 Formula 5000), 40. 5. Chris Craft (Brabham BT33/2), 40. 6. Mike Walker (Lola-Chevrolet T192 192/F1/26 Formula 5000), 40.
PP – Heat One, Peter Gethin (BRM V12 P160-01), 1;24.6; Heat Two, result of Heat One. FL – Heat One, Henri Pescarolo (March 711/3) & Surtees, 1;25.0, 116.93 mph; Heat Two, Surtees, 1;24.8, 117.21 mph.
Gethin's BRM and Pescarolo's March collided in Heat Two removing Surtees's likeliest rivals as he won poorly supported race at record speed.

5-9-71 ITALIAN GP,
Monza – 55 laps, 196.35 miles
1. Peter Gethin (BRM V12 P160-01), 55 laps in 1:18;12.60, 150.75 mph.
2. Ronnie Peterson (March 711/6), 55 in 1:18;12.61.
3. François Cevert (Tyrrell 002), 55 in 1:18;12.69. 4. Mike Hailwood (Surtees TS9-004), 55 in 1:18;12.78. 5. Howden Ganley (BRM V12 P160-04), 55 in 1:18;13.21. 6. Chris Amon (Matra V12 MS120-06), 55.
PP – Amon, 1;22.40; FL – Henri Pescarolo (March 711/3).
Five cars in final leading bunch and while Peterson and Cevert eyed each other Gethin slammed past both to steal BRM victory, 0.61 sec covering first five home! Stewart, Ferraris and Amon's Matra all had troubles after featuring strongly.

19-9-71 CANADIAN GP,
Mosport Park, Toronto – 64 laps, 157.38 miles
1. Jackie Stewart (Tyrrell 003), 64 laps in 1:55;12.9, 81.96 mph.
2. Ronnie Peterson (March 711/6), 64 in 1:55;51.2.

3. Mark Donohue (McLaren M19A/1), 64. 4. Denny Hulme (McLaren M19A/2), 63. 5. Reine Wisell (Lotus 72 R6), 62. 6. François Cevert (Tyrrell 002), 62.
PP – Stewart, 1;15.3; FL – Hulme, 1;43.5, 85.53 mph.
Wet, misty race dominated by Stewart although Peterson led twice before nudging a back-marker and having to settle for second.

3-10-71 UNITED STATES GP,
Watkins Glen, NY – 59 laps, 199.24 miles
1. François Cevert (Tyrrell 002), 59 in 1:43;57.991, 115.09 mph.
2. Jo Siffert (BRM V12 P160-02), 59 in 1:44;32.053.
3. Ronnie Peterson (March 711/6), 59. 4. Howden Ganley (BRM V12 P160-04), 59. 5. Jackie Stewart (Tyrrell 003), 59. 6. Jacky Ickx (Ferrari 312B2 006), 59.
PP – Stewart, 1;42.642; FL – Jacky Ickx (Ferrari 312B2 006), 1;43.474, 117.50 mph.
Stewart led until lap 14 when understeer allowed team-mate ahead to win, the Champion falling back; Ickx's old B1-model Ferrari was closing on Cevert mid-race until alternator failed.

24-10-71 Victory Race,
Brands Hatch, GB – 40 laps, 105.96 miles*
*Race stopped after Siffert's fatal BRM accident on lap 15, results declared at 14 laps.
1. Peter Gethin (BRM V12 P160-03), 14 laps in 19;54.4, 111.82 mph.
2. Emerson Fittipaldi (Lotus 72 R6), 14 in 19;54.6.
3. Jackie Stewart (Tyrrell 003), 14. 4. Jo Siffert (BRM V12 P160-02), 14. 5. Tim Schenken (Brabham BT33/3), 14. 6. John Surtees (Surtees TS9-002), 14.
PP – Siffert, 1;22.8; FL – Fittipaldi, 1;24.0, 113.57 mph.
Tragic minor event to celebrate Stewart's title. BRMs dominant in practice with Gethin equalling Siffert's pole time, Gethin led throughout.

1972

23-1-72 ARGENTINE GP,
Buenos Aires – 95 laps, 201.40 miles
1. Jackie Stewart (Tyrrell 003), 95 laps in 1:57;58.82, 100.33 mph.
2. Denny Hulme (McLaren M19A/2), 95 in 1:58;24.78.
3. Jacky Ickx (Ferrari 312B2 006), 95. 4. Clay Regazzoni (Ferrari 312B2 005), 95. 5. Tim Schenken (Surtees TS9-006), 95. 6. Ronnie Peterson (March 721/1), 94.
PP – Carlos Reutemann (Brabham BT34/1), 1;12.46; FL – Stewart, 1;13.66, 101.59 mph.
Stewart led throughout but newcomer Reutemann challenged strongly on home ground until sticky Goodyear tyres on which he gambled deteriorated and he had to make tyre-change stop, Fittipaldi's Lotus held second place until its suspension failed.

4-3-72 SOUTH AFRICAN GP,
Kyalami – 79 laps, 201.45 miles
1. Denny Hulme (McLaren M19A/2), 79 laps in 1:45;49.1, 114.23 mph.
2. Emerson Fittipaldi (Lotus 72 R5), 79 in 1:46;03.2.
3. Peter Revson (McLaren M19A/1), 79. 4. Mario Andretti (Ferrari 312B2 007), 79. 5. Ronnie Peterson (March 721/1), 79. 6. Graham Hill (Brabham BT33/3), 78.
PP – Jackie Stewart (Tyrrell 003), 1;17.0; FL – Mike Hailwood (Surtees TS9-005), 1;19.8, 116.35 mph.
Fine race – Hulme led lap 1 before Stewart opened a lead; Hulme/Fittipaldi/Hailwood (Surtees) battle then closed gap, Surtees looking set to take lead for Surtees when rear suspension bolt broke. Hulme eased off to cool engine and Fittipaldi pressed Stewart until Tyrrell gearbox seized on lap 44. Lotus inherited lead but oversteered on light tanks and Hulme went by on lap 57 to win; Hill just held off March newcomer Lauda for 6th by 0.3 sec.

19-3-72 Race of Champions,
Brands Hatch, GB – 40 laps, 105.96 miles
1. Emerson Fittipaldi (Lotus 72 R5), 40 laps in 56;40.6, 112.22 mph.
2. Mike Hailwood (Surtees TS9-005), 40 in 56;54.0.
3. Denny Hulme (McLaren M19A/2), 40. 4. Peter Gethin (BRM P160-03), 40. 5. Tim Schenken (Surtees TS9-006), 40. 6. Jean-Pierre Beltoise (BRM P160-05), 40.
PP – Fittipaldi, 1;23.9; FL – 1;23.8, 112.84 mph.
Effortless 13 sec win by Fittipaldi's Lotus, another fine Surtees performance by Hailwood, Gethin prominent throughout but lost places as race progressed.

30-3-72 Grande Prêmio do Brasil,
Interlagos – 37 laps, 182.02 miles
1. Carlos Reutemann (Brabham BT34/1), 37 laps in 1:37;16.248, 112.91 mph.
2. Ronnie Peterson (March 721/1), 37 in 1:38;43.904.
3. Wilson Fittipaldi (Brabham BT33/3), 37. 4. Helmut Marko (BRM P160-01) 36. 5. Dave Walker (Lotus 72 R6), 36. 6. Luiz Bueno (March 711/6), 35.
PP – Emerson Fittipaldi (Lotus 72 R7), 2;32.4; FL – E. Fittipaldi, 2;35.2, 119.74 mph.
Moral victory for Emerson Fittipaldi who led until suspension failure, 4 laps from end. Only 11 starters, three retiring with dust jamming throttles in first corner.

23-4-72 BRDC International Trophy,
Silverstone, GB – 40 laps, 117.08 miles
1. Emerson Fittipaldi (Lotus 72 R7), 40 laps in 53;17.8, 131.81 mph.
2. Jean-Pierre Beltoise (BRM V12 P160-01), 40 in 53;19.6.
3. John Surtees (Surtees TS9-006), 40. 4. Denny Hulme (McLaren M19C/4), 40. 5. Peter Revson (McLaren M19A/2), 40. 6. Peter Gethin (BRM V12 P160-03), 40.

PP – Fittipaldi, 1;18.1; FL – Mike Hailwood (Surtees TS9-005), 1;18.8, 133.72 mph.
Hailwood's Surtees led until engine failure 10 laps from end, lowering lap record en route, after BRMs led opening laps.

1-5-72 SPANISH GP,
Jarama, Madrid – 90 laps, 190.15 miles
1. Emerson Fittipaldi (Lotus 72 R7), 90 laps in 2:03;41.23, 92.35 mph.
2. Jacky Ickx (Ferrari 312B2 006), 90 in 04:00.15.
3. Clay Regazzoni (Ferrari 312B2 008), 89. 4. Andrea de Adamich (Surtees TS9-004), 89. 5. Peter Revson (McLaren M19A/2), 89. 6. Carlos Pace (March 711/3), 89.
PP – Ickx, 1;18.43; FL – Ickx, 1;21.01, 90.00 mph.
Fittipaldi qualified on front row, passed Stewart's leading Tyrrell on lap 19 and dominated thereafter.

14-5-72 MONACO GP,
Monte Carlo – 80 laps in 156.32 miles
1. Jean-Pierre Beltoise (BRM V12 P160-01), 80 laps in 2:26;54.7, 63.85 mph.
2. Jacky Ickx (Ferrari 312B2 006), 80 in 27;32.9.
3. Emerson Fittipaldi (Lotus 72 R7), 78. 4. Jackie Stewart (Tyrrell 004), 78. 5. Brian Redman (McLaren M19A/2), 77. 6. Chris Amon (Matra V12 MS120-04), 77.
PP – Fittipaldi, 1;21.4; FL – Beltoise, 1;40.0, 70.35 mph.
In heavy rain Beltoise and BRM triumphed, leading from start to finish, only Ickx's Ferrari in same class that day.

29-5-72 International Gold Cup,
Oulton Park, GB – 40 laps, 110.44 miles
1. Denny Hulme (McLaren M19A/1), 40 laps in 57;15.6, 115.17 mph.
2. Emerson Fittipaldi (Lotus 72 R5), 40 in 57;53.0.
3. Tim Schenken (Surtees TS9-006), 39. 4. Brian Redman (Chevron-Chevrolet B24 72-01 Formula 5000), 39. 5. Vern Schuppan (BRM V12 P153-06), 39. 6. Ray Allen (McLaren-Chevrolet M18 500-05 Formula 5000), 39.
PP – Peter Gethin (BRM P160-03), 1;24.6; FL – Redman, 1;25.8, 115.85 mph.
Comfortable McLaren win at record pace against thin F1 field, Fittipaldi's Lotus handicapped by poor tyre choice.

4-6-72 BELGIAN GP,
Nivelles, Brussels – 85 laps, 196.68 miles
1. Emerson Fittipaldi (Lotus 72 R7), 85 laps in 1:44;06.7, 113.35 mph.
2. François Cevert (Tyrrell 002), 85 in 1:44;33.3.
3. Denny Hulme (McLaren M19C/1), 85. 4. Mike Hailwood (Surtees TS9-005), 85. 5. Carlos Pace (March 711/3), 84. 6. Chris Amon (Matra V12 MS120-06), 84.
PP – Fittipaldi, 1;11.43; FL – Amon, 1;12.12, 115.38 mph.
Regazzoni's Ferrari led first 8 laps then the Lotus 72 was simply driven away from everyone else – the Ferrari went out in collision with the new flat-12 Tecno.

18-6-72 Gran Premio Republica Italiana,
Vallelunga, Rome, I – 80 laps, 159.04 miles
1. Emerson Fittipaldi (Lotus 72 R5), 80 laps in 1:37;31.9, 97.85 mph.
2. Andrea de Adamich (Surtees TS9-004), 80 in 1:38;04.7.
3. Nanni Galli (Tecno flat-12 PA123-F-001), 79. 4. Mike Beuttler (March 721G/1), 79. UNC '5th': Howden Ganley (BRM V12 P160-05), 79.
No other finishers.
PP – Fittipaldi 1;9.82; FL – Fittipaldi, 1;10.06, 99.98 mph.
Inconsequential race, fodder for Fittipaldi's Lotus which led start to finish.

2-7-72 FRENCH GP,
Clermont-Ferrand – 38 laps, 190.19 miles
1. Jackie Stewart (Tyrrell 003), 38 laps in 1:52;21.5, 101.56 mph.
2. Emerson Fittipaldi (Lotus 72 R7), 38 in 49.2.
3. Chris Amon (Matra V12 MS120-07), 38. 4. François Cevert (Tyrrell 002), 38. 5. Ronnie Peterson (March 721G/3), 38. 6. Mike Hailwood (Surtees TS9-005), 38.
PP – Amon, 2;53.4; FL – Amon, 2;53.9, 103.61 mph.
Stewart and Tyrrell back on form but superb Amon performance in new Matra leading 20 laps until tyre deflated. Eight cars delayed by punctures.

15-7-72 BRITISH GP,
Brands Hatch – 76 laps, 201.32 miles
1. Emerson Fittipaldi (Lotus 72 R7), 76 laps in 1:47;50.2, 112.06 mph.
2. Jackie Stewart (Tyrrell 003), 76 in 1:47;54.3.
3. Peter Revson (McLaren M19A/1) 76. 4. Chris Amon (Matra V12 MS120-07), 75. 5. Denny Hulme (McLaren M19C/1), 75. 6. Arturo Merzario (Ferrari 312B2 005), 75.
PP – Jacky Ickx (Ferrari 312B2 005), 1;22.6; FL – Stewart, 1;24.00, 118.84 mph.
Ickx's Ferrari led 48 laps until oil cooler punctured, Fittipaldi had won duel with Stewart and led until finish.

30-7-72 GERMAN GP,
Nürburgring – 14 laps, 198.64 miles
1. Jacky Ickx (Ferrari 312B2 005), 14 laps in 1:42;12.3, 116.60 mph.
2. Clay Regazzoni (Ferrari 312B2 007), 14 in 1:43;00.6.
3. Ronnie Peterson (March 721G/3), 14. 4. Howden Ganley (BRM V12 P160-06), 14. 5. Brian Redman (McLaren M19A/1), 14. 6. Graham Hill (Brabham BT37/1), 14.
PP – Ickx, 7;07.0; FL – Ickx, 7;13.6, 118.81 mph.
Ickx took 12 secs off record in practice, led race throughout; Fittipaldi's Lotus lost 2nd place late in race when gearbox broke, Stewart collided with Regazzoni and crashed on last lap.

13-8-72 AUSTRIAN GP,
Österreichring – 54 laps, 198.34 miles
1. Emerson Fittipaldi (Lotus 72 R5), 54 laps in 1:29;16.66, 133.32 mph.
2. Denny Hulme (McLaren M19C/1), 54 in 1:29;17.84.
3. Peter Revson (McLaren M19C/2), 54. 4. Mike Hailwood (Surtees TS9-005), 54. 5. Chris Amon (Matra V12 MS120-07), 54. 6. Howden Ganley (BRM V12 P160-06), 54.
PP – Fittipaldi, 1;35.97; FL – Hulme, 1;38.32, 134.50 mph.
Stewart's new Tyrrell 005 led until lap 24 when Fittipaldi went by in spare Lotus 72, Tyrrell's handling deteriorated and McLarens closed on leader near end.

10-9-72 ITALIAN GP,
Monza – 55 laps, 196.35 miles
1. Emerson Fittipaldi (Lotus 72 R5), 55 laps in 1:29;58.4, 131.61 mph.
2. Mike Hailwood (Surtees TS9-005), 55 in 1:30;12.9.
3. Denny Hulme (McLaren M19C/1), 55. 4. Peter Revson (McLaren M19C/2), 55. 5. Graham Hill (Brabham BT37/1), 55. 6. Peter Gethin (BRM V12 P160-05), 55.
PP – Jacky Ickx (Ferrari 312B2 005), 1;35.65; FL – Ickx, 1;36.3, 134.14 mph.
Fittipaldi and Lotus clinch titles, after tense battle with Ickx's Ferrari faded 10 laps from end due to Ferrari electrical fault.

24-9-72 CANADIAN GP,
Mosport Pk, Toronto – 80 laps, 196.72 miles
1. Jackie Stewart (Tyrrell 005), 80 laps in 1:43;16.9, 114.28 mph.
2. Peter Revson (McLaren M19C/2), 80 in 1:44;05.1.
3. Denny Hulme (McLaren M19C/1), 80. 4. Carlos Reutemann (Brabham BT37/2), 80. 5. Clay Regazzoni (Ferrari 312B2 007), 80. 6. Chris Amon (Matra V12 MS120-07), 79.
PP – Revson, 1;13.6; FL – Stewart, 1;15.7, 117.57 mph.
50th GP win for Cosworth DFV engine, 20th for Stewart the driver. Peterson's March led initially, ran second before collision when lapping it on lap 50; Fittipaldi lost time after nose-fin knocked awry when challenging for third place.

8-10-72 UNITED STATES GP,
Watkins Glen, NY – 59 laps, 199.24 miles
1. Jackie Stewart (Tyrrell 005), 59 laps in 1:41;45.354, 117.48 mph.
2. François Cevert (Tyrrell 006), 59 in 1:42;17.622.
3. Denny Hulme (McLaren M19C/1), 59. 4. Ronnie Peterson (March 721G/3), 59. 5. Jacky Ickx (Ferrari 312B2 005), 59. 6. Mario Andretti (Ferrari 312B2 006), 58.
PP – Stewart, 1;40.481; FL – Stewart, 1;41.644, 119.61 mph.
New Tyrrells dominant, Stewart leading throughout while Cevert disposed of Hulme's McLaren for 2nd place.

22-10-72 World Championship Victory Race,
Brands Hatch, GB – 40 laps, 105.96 miles
1. Jean-Pierre Beltoise (BRM V12 P180-02), 40 laps in 59;47.8, 106.36 mph.
2. Carlos Pace (Surtees TS9-006), 40 in 59;54.4.
3. Andrea de Adamich (Surtees TS9-004), 40. 4. Vern Schuppan (BRM V12 P160-05), 39. 5. Peter Gethin (BRM V12 P160-06), 39. 6. John Watson (March 721/4), 39.
PP – Emerson Fittipaldi (Lotus 72 R7), 1;20.8; FL – Fittipaldi, 1;23.8, 113.84 mph.
Wet-dry race gave BRM edge when Beltoise's crew chose dry tyres and track dried out; front-runners Peterson (March), Hailwood (Surtees) and Fittipaldi all started on wets and forced to change tyres.

1973

28-1-73 ARGENTINE GP,
Buenos Aires – 96 laps, 199.56 miles
1. Emerson Fittipaldi (Lotus 72 R7), 96 laps in 1:56;18.22, 104.84 mph.
2. François Cevert (Tyrrell 006), 96 in 1:56;22.91.
3. Jackie Stewart (Tyrrell 005), 96. 4. Jacky Ickx (Ferrari 312B2 005), 96. 5. Denny Hulme (McLaren M19C/1), 95. 6. Wilson Fittipaldi (Brabham BT37/1), 95.
PP – Clay Regazzoni (BRM V12 P160-01), 1;10.54; FL – Fittipaldi, 1;11.22, 104.84 mph.
Regazzoni pole for BRM and led 30 laps before tyres overheated, Cevert took over lead while Stewart, bothered by tyre problems, tried in vain to hold off Lotuses of Fittipaldi and Peterson. The latter retired with engine failure, Fittipaldi made charge and caught Cevert for lead with only 10 laps to run.

11-2-73 BRAZILIAN GP,
Interlagos – 40 laps, 197.84 miles
1. Emerson Fittipaldi (Lotus 72 R7), 40 laps in 1:43;55.6, 114.24 mph.
2. Jackie Stewart (Tyrrell 005), 40 in 1:44;09.1.
3. Denny Hulme (McLaren M19C/1), 40. 4. Arturo Merzario (Ferrari 312B2 008), 39. 5. Jacky Ickx (Ferrari 312B2 005), 39. 6. Clay Regazzoni (BRM V12 P160-01), 39.
PP – Ronnie Peterson (Lotus 72 R8), 2;30.5; FL – Fittipaldi & Hulme, 2;35.0, 114.88 mph.
One of Fittipaldi's easiest victories, led from first corner, never challenged while heat claimed many. Lotus 72 still the car to beat, dominated pace and race though Peterson had rear wheel break when challenging Stewart for 2nd place. Beltoise's BRM 4th until flying stone damaged its electrics.

3-3-73 SOUTH AFRICAN GP,
Kyalami – 79 laps, 201.45 miles
1. Jackie Stewart (Tyrrell 006), 79 laps in 1:43;11.07, 117.14 mph.
2. Peter Revson (McLaren M19C/2), 79 in 1:43;35.62.

14-7-73 BRITISH GP,
Silverstone – 67 laps, 196.11 miles*
Race stopped after two laps, due to multiple accident, restarted over original distance.
1. Peter Revson (McLaren M23/2), 67 laps in 1:29;18.5, 131.75 mph.
2. Ronnie Peterson (Lotus 72 R6), 67 in 1:29;21.3.
3. Denny Hulme (McLaren M23/1), 67. 4. James Hunt (March 731/3), 67. 5. François Cevert (Tyrrell 006), 67. 6. Carlos Reutemann (Brabham BT42/3), 67.
PP – Peterson, 1;16.3; FL – Hunt, 1;18.6, 134.06 mph.
Farcical event, massive pile-up ended first attempt. After restart Peterson led from threatening second place, Revson finally displaced ill-handling Lotus 72 for lead on lap 39.

29-7-73 DUTCH GP,
Zandvoort – 72 laps, 189.06 miles
1. Jackie Stewart (Tyrrell 006/2), 72 laps in 1:39;12.45, 114.35 mph.
2. François Cevert (Tyrrell 006), 72 in 1:39;28.28.
3. James Hunt (March 731/3), 72. 4. Peter Revson (McLaren M23/2), 72. 5. Jean-Pierre Beltoise (BRM V12 P160-07), 72. 6. Gijs van Lennep (Williams FX4/1), 70.
PP – Ronnie Peterson (Lotus 72 R6), 1;19.47; FL – Peterson, 1;20.31, 117.71 mph.
Peterson led from start until lap 64 when gearbox failed, handing Stewart his record-breaking 26th GP win and Tyrrell a fine 1-2; race marred by fatal accident to Roger Williamson in March 731.

5-8-73 GERMAN GP,
Nürburgring – 14 laps, 198.64 miles
1. Jackie Stewart (Tyrrell 006/2), 14 laps in 1:42;03.0, 116.82 mph.
2. François Cevert (Tyrrell 006), 14 in 1:42;04.6.
3. Jacky Ickx (McLaren M23/4), 14. 4. Carlos Pace (Surtees TS14-05), 14. 5. Wilson Fittipaldi (Brabham BT42/2), 14. 6. Emerson Fittipaldi (Lotus 72 R7), 14.
PP – Stewart, 7;07.8; FL – Pace, 7;11.4, 118.43 mph.
Tyrrell race from start to finish, only Ickx's freelance McLaren drive offering any challenge. Pace showed his class in Surtees.

19-8-73 AUSTRIAN GP,
Österreichring – 54 laps, 198.34 miles
1. Ronnie Peterson (Lotus 72 R6), 54 laps in 1:28;48.78, 133.50 mph.
2. Jackie Stewart (Tyrrell 006/2), 54 in 1:28;57.79.
3. Carlos Pace (Surtees TS14-05), 54. 4. Carlos Reutemann (Brabham BT42/3), 54. 5. Jean-Pierre Beltoise (BRM V12 P160-07), 54. 6. Clay Regazzoni (BRM V12 P160-09), 54.
PP – Emerson Fittipaldi (Lotus 72 R7), 1;34.98; FL – Pace, 1;37.29, 135.91 mph.
Lotus 72s back to the fore, Peterson waved Fittipaldi ahead on lap 16 but fuel line failed five laps from end leaving Peterson to win from Stewart. Pace challenged Stewart until fuel pressure fell.

9-9-73 ITALIAN GP,
Monza – 55 laps, 197.34 miles
1. Ronnie Peterson (Lotus 72 R6), 55 laps in 1:29;17.0, 132.63 mph.
2. Emerson Fittipaldi (Lotus 72 R7), 55 in 1:29;17.8.
3. Peter Revson (McLaren M23/4), 55. 4. Jackie Stewart (Tyrrell 006/2), 55. 5. François Cevert (Tyrrell 006), 55. 6. Carlos Reutemann (Brabham BT42/3), 55.
PP – Peterson, 1;34.80; FL – Stewart, 1;35.3, 135.55 mph.
Lotus 72s utterly dominant, but Stewart stopped Tyrrell when 4th in early stages as tyre deflated, rejoined with new tyre in 19th place almost one lap down and soared through field, setting lap record.

23-9-73 CANADIAN GP,
Mosport Pk, Toronto – 80 laps, 196.72 miles
1. Peter Revson (McLaren M23/4), 80 laps in 1:59;04.083, 99.13 mph.
2. Emerson Fittipaldi (Lotus 72 R7), 80 in 1:59;36.817.
3. Jackie Oliver (Shadow DN1/6A), 80. 4. Jean-Pierre Beltoise (BRM V12 P160-07), 80. 5. Jackie Stewart (Tyrrell 006/2), 79. 6. Howden Ganley (Williams FX4/2), 79.
PP – Ronnie Peterson (Lotus 72 R6), 1;13.697; FL – Fittipaldi, 1;15.496, 117.77 mph.
Yet another controversial race won by McLaren, this time rain shower before start put nearly everyone on wet tyres. Lauda's BRM built lead for 20 laps, then track dried and spate of tyre stops commenced. Accident brought out pace car for first time in shepherd field but went ahead of the wrong car – chaos ensued and lap charting went awry; Oliver's Shadow led race at one stage, as did Beltoise's BRM.

7-10-73 UNITED STATES GP,
Watkins Glen, NY – 59 laps, 199.24 miles
1. Ronnie Peterson (Lotus 72 R6), 59 laps in 1:41;15.779, 118.06 mph.
2. James Hunt (March 731/3), 59 in 1:41;16.467.
3. Carlos Reutemann (Brabham BT42/3), 59. 4. Denny Hulme (McLaren M23/1), 59. 5. Peter Revson (McLaren M23/4), 59. 6. Emerson Fittipaldi (Lotus 72 R7), 59.
PP – Peterson, 1;39.657; FL – Hunt, 1;41.652, 119.60 mph.
Cevert killed in practice, Tyrrell team withdrew, end of Stewart's career. Peterson led start to finish staving off fearsome challenge from Hunt's private March. Note winning margin.

1974

13-1-74 ARGENTINE GP,
Buenos Aires – 53 laps, 196.55 miles
1. Denny Hulme (McLaren M23/6), 53 laps in 1:41;02.01, 116.72 mph.
2. Niki Lauda (Ferrari 312B3 012), 53 in 1:41;11.28.

17-3-73 Race of Champions,
Brands Hatch, GB – 40 laps, 105.96 miles
1. Peter Gethin (Chevron-Chevrolet B24 72-05 Formula 5000), 40 laps in 57;22.9, 110.34 mph.
2. Denny Hulme (McLaren M23/1), 40 in 57;26.3.
3. James Hunt (Surtees TS9-006), 40. 4. Tony Trimmer (Williams FX3/1), 40. 5. Tony Dean (Chevron-Chevrolet B24 72-02 Formula 5000), 39. 6. Jean-Pierre Beltoise (BRM V12 P160-03), 39.
PP – Beltoise, 1;21.1; FL – Beltoise, Niki Lauda (BRM V12 P160-01) & Ronnie Peterson (Lotus 72 R6), 1;23.0, 114.94 mph.
Gethin's F5000 beat F1s as they dropped like flies, BRM P160s on front of grid. Peterson led until retirement at 18 laps, Beltoise's BRM punctured, Hailwood's Surtees led and crashed, Hulme first with five laps to go but clutch failed and Gethin passed with one lap to go.

8-4-73 BRDC International Trophy,
Silverstone, GB – 40 laps, 117.08 miles
1. Jackie Stewart (Tyrrell 006/2), 40 laps in 52;53.2, 132.82 mph.
2. Ronnie Peterson (Lotus 72 R8), 40 in 53;03.6.
3. Clay Regazzoni (BRM V12 P160-07), 40. 4. Peter Revson (McLaren M23/2), 40. 5. Jean-Pierre Beltoise (BRM V12 P160-01), 40. 6. George Follmer (Shadow DN1/2A), 39.
PP – Emerson Fittipaldi (Lotus 72 R5), 1;16.4; FL – Peterson, 1;17.5, 135.96 mph.
Victorious debut of new Tyrrell deformable structure car, Stewart spun out of initial lead, Peterson's Lotus took over, Stewart closed again and Swede spun in snow shower!

29-4-73 SPANISH GP,
Montjuich Pk, Barcelona – 75 laps, 176.654 miles
1. Emerson Fittipaldi (Lotus 72 R5), 75 laps in 1:48;18.7, 97.86 mph.
2. François Cevert (Tyrrell 006), 75 in 1:49;01.4.
3. George Follmer (Shadow DN1/2A), 75. 4. Peter Revson (McLaren M23/2), 74. 5. Jean-Pierre Beltoise (BRM V12 P160-03), 74. 6. Denny Hulme (McLaren M23/1), 74.
PP – Ronnie Peterson (Lotus 72 R8), 1;21.8; FL – 1;23.8, 101.19 mph.
Peterson's Lotus led again for 18 laps until gearbox failed, Stewart's Tyrrell had brake problems and Fittipaldi drove steady 25 laps on deflating rear tyre to score Lotus's 50th GP win.

20-5-73 BELGIAN GP,
Zolder – 70 laps, 183.54 miles
1. Jackie Stewart (Tyrrell 006/2), 70 laps in 1:42;13.43, 107.73 mph.
2. François Cevert (Tyrrell 006), 70 in 1:42;45.27.
3. Emerson Fittipaldi (Lotus 72 R7), 70. 4. Andrea de Adamich (Brabham BT37/2), 69. 5. Niki Lauda (BRM V12 P160-08), 69. 6. Chris Amon (Tecno flat-12 PA123/B 006), 67.
PP – Ronnie Peterson (Lotus 72 R6), 1;22.46; FL – Cevert, 1;25.42, 110.51 mph.
Track surface broke up, Cevert led 18 laps, spun and regained ground, Fittipaldi led five laps, Stewart remainder; many accidents on loose surface.

3-6-73 MONACO GP,
Monte Carlo – 78 laps, 158.87 miles
1. Jackie Stewart (Tyrrell 006/2), 78 laps in 1:57;44.3, 80.96 mph.
2. Emerson Fittipaldi (Lotus 72 R7), 78 in 1:57;45.6.
3. Ronnie Peterson (Lotus 72 R6), 77. 4. François Cevert (Tyrrell 006), 77. 5. Peter Revson (McLaren M23/2), 76. 6. Denny Hulme (McLaren M23/1).
PP – Stewart, 1;27.5; FL – Fittipaldi, 1;28.1, 83.23 mph.
Stewart's 25th GP win to equal Clark's record, close and hard-fought battle throughout with Fittipaldi – see winning margin! Cevert and Peterson led early on.

17-6-73 SWEDISH GP,
Anderstorp – 80 laps, 199.61 miles
1. Denny Hulme (McLaren M23/1), 80 laps in 1:56;46.049, 102.65 mph.
2. Ronnie Peterson (Lotus 72 R6), 80 in 1:56;50.088.
3. François Cevert (Tyrrell 006), 80. 4. Carlos Reutemann (Brabham BT42/3), 80. 5. Jackie Stewart (Tyrrell 006/2), 80. 6. Jacky Ickx (Ferrari 312B3 010), 79.
PP – Peterson, 1;23.810; FL – Hulme, 1;26.146, 104.04 mph.
Peterson led 79 of the 80 laps, staving off Fittipaldi and Stewart who slowed with brake problems, Hulme emerged in final 20 laps and won when Lotus rear tyre deflated.

1-7-73 FRENCH GP,
Ricard-Castellet – 54 laps, 194.61 miles
1. Ronnie Peterson (Lotus 72 R6), 54 laps in 1:41;36.52, 115.17 mph.
2. François Cevert (Tyrrell 006), 54 in 1:42;17.44.
3. Carlos Reutemann (Brabham BT42/3), 54. 4. Jackie Stewart (Tyrrell 006/2), 54. 5. Jacky Ickx (Ferrari 312B3 010), 54. 6. James Hunt (March 731/3), 54.
PP – Stewart, 1;48.37; FL – Hulme, 1;51.7, 117.51 mph.
Peterson's long-overdue first GP win, but newcomer Scheckter's McLaren led dominantly up to lap 41 when Fittipaldi tried to go by and their cars collided, Peterson then leading from lap 42 to finish.

3. Clay Regazzoni (Ferrari 312B3 011), 53. **4.** Mike Hailwood (McLaren M23/1), 53. **5.** Jean-Pierre Beltoise (BRM V12 P160-09), 53. **6.** Patrick Depailler (Tyrrell 005), 53.
PP – Ronnie Peterson (Lotus 72 R8), 1;50.78; FL – Regazzoni, 1;52.10, 119.09 mph.

Local hero Carlos Reutemann dominated in Brabham BT44 until engine airbox worked loose then ran out of fuel after 51 of 53 laps; promising debut for Ferrari B3/74s.

27-1-74 BRAZILIAN GP,
Interlagos – 40 laps, 197.84 miles*
Race stopped due to heavy rain after only Fittipaldi and Regazzoni completed 31 laps and were into their 32nd.
1. Emerson Fittipaldi (McLaren M23/5), 32 laps in 1:24;37.06, 112.24 mph.
2. Clay Regazzoni (Ferrari 312B3 011), 32 in 1:24;50.63.
3. Jacky Ickx (Lotus 72 R5), 31. **4.** Carlos Pace (Surtees TS16-02), 31. **5.** Mike Hailwood (McLaren M23/1), 31. **6.** Ronnie Peterson (Lotus 72 R8), 31.
PP – Fittipaldi, 2;32.97; FL – Regazzoni, 2;36.05, 114.11 mph.

Early duel between Fittipaldi and Peterson ended when Lotus's tyre deflated; Reutemann's Brabham led briefly at start until front tyres lost grip.

3-2-74 Grande Prêmio Presidente Medici,
Brasilia, BRA – 40 laps, 136.09 miles
1. Emerson Fittipaldi (McLaren M23/5), 40 laps in 1:15;22.75, 108.27 mph.
2. Jody Scheckter (Tyrrell 006/2), 40 in 1:15;35.15.
3. Arturo Merzario (Williams FX4/1), 40. **4.** Jochen Mass (Surtees TS16-03), 40. **5.** Wilson Fittipaldi (Brabham BT44/2), 39. **6.** Howden Ganley (March 741/2), 39.
PP – Carlos Reutemann (Brabham BT44/1), 1;51.18; FL – E. Fittipaldi, 1;51.62, 109.30 mph.

Reutemann's Brabham form continued, led from pole until piston failed; Scheckter slowed when balance weight fell off wheel, unable to challenge for lead.

17-3-74 Race of Champions,
Brands Hatch, GB – 40 laps, 105.96 miles
1. Jacky Ickx (Lotus 72 R5), 40 laps in 1:03;37.6, 99.96 mph.
2. Niki Lauda (Ferrari 312B3 011), 40 in 1:03;39.1.
3. Emerson Fittipaldi (McLaren M23/4), 40. **4.** Mike Hailwood (McLaren M23/1), 40. **5.** Clay Regazzoni (Ferrari 312B3 012), 40. **6.** Peter Revson (Shadow DN3/1A), 39.
PP – James Hunt (Hesketh 308-1), 1;21.5; FL – Ickx, 1;33.8, 102.80 mph.

Lauda dominated most of race in driving rain, until Ickx passed on outside of difficult Paddock Hill Bend with just five laps to run. Reutemann crashed due to brake trouble after brief initial lead.

30-3-74 SOUTH AFRICAN GP,
Kyalami – 78 laps, 198.80 miles
1. Carlos Reutemann (Brabham BT44/1), 78 laps in 1:42;40.96, 116.24 mph.
2. Jean-Pierre Beltoise (BRM V12 P201-01), 78 in 1:43;14.90.
3. Mike Hailwood (McLaren M23/1), 78. **4.** Patrick Depailler (Tyrrell 005), 78. **5.** Hans Stuck Jr (March 741/1), 78. **6.** Arturo Merzario (Williams FX4/1), 78.
PP – Niki Lauda (Ferrari 312B3 012), 1:16.58; FL – Reutemann, 1;18.16, 117.47 mph.

Brabham luck stayed at last – Reutemann took lead from Lauda end of lap 10, and held off Ferrari until it retired with electrical trouble four laps from end; new BRM finished well when others retired.

7-4-74, BRDC International Trophy,
Silverstone, GB – 40 laps, 117.08 miles
1. James Hunt (Hesketh 308-1), 40 laps in 52;35.4, 133.58 mph.
2. Jochen Mass (Surtees TS16-03), 40 in 53;12.4.
3. Jean-Pierre Jarier (Shadow DN3/2A), 40. **4.** Henri Pescarolo (BRM V12 P160-10), 40. **5.** François Migault (BRM V12 P160-05), 40. **6.** John Nicholson (Lyncar F-1007), 39.
PP – Hunt, 1;16.7; FL – Hunt, 1;17.6, 135.79 mph.

Hunt and Hesketh emerged to take lead from Peterson's Lotus on lap 28.

28-4-74 SPANISH GP,
Jarama, Madrid – 90 laps, 190.15 miles*
Race stopped after two hours under CSI regulation since heavy rain had slowed pace.
1. Niki Lauda (Ferrari 312B3 015), 84 laps in 2:00;29.56, 88.48 mph.
2. Clay Regazzoni (Ferrari 312B3 014), 84 in 2:01;05.17.
3. Emerson Fittipaldi (McLaren M23/5), 83. **4.** Hans Stuck Jr (March 741/1), 82. **5.** Jody Scheckter (Tyrrell 007-1), 82. **6.** Denny Hulme (McLaren M23/4), 82.
PP – Lauda, 1;18.44; FL – Lauda, 1;20.83, 94.20 mph.

Lauda's first GP win, Ferrari's 50th. Peterson's Lotus 76 led first 20 laps before pit stop to change from wet to dry tyres as track dried.

12-5-74 BELGIAN GP,
Nivelles, Brussels – 85 laps, 196.69 miles
1. Emerson Fittipaldi (McLaren M23/5), 85 laps in 1:44;20.57, 114.10 mph.
2. Niki Lauda (Ferrari 312B3 012), 85 in 1:44;20.92.
3. Jody Scheckter (Tyrrell 007-1), 85. **4.** Clay Regazzoni (Ferrari 312B3 014), 85. **5.** Jean-Pierre Beltoise (BRM V12 P201-01), 85. **6.** Denny Hulme (McLaren M23/4), 85.
PP – Regazzoni, 1;09.82; FL – Hulme, 1;11.31, 116.82 mph.

Fittipaldi first driver to win two GPs this season, Scheckter true pole time disallowed, Regazzoni led until lap 39, only lost 3rd as tanks dried on run-in to line; awful new circuit.

26-5-74 MONACO GP,
Monte Carlo – 78 laps, 158.87 miles
1. Ronnie Peterson (Lotus 72 R8), 78 laps in 1:58;03.7, 80.74 mph.

2. Jody Scheckter (Tyrrell 007/1), 78 in 1:58;32.5.
3. Jean-Pierre Jarier (Shadow DN3/2A), 78. **4.** Clay Regazzoni (Ferrari 312B3 016), 78. **5.** Emerson Fittipaldi (McLaren M23/5), 77. **6.** John Watson (Brabham BT42/2), 77.
PP – Niki Lauda (Ferrari 312B3 010), 1;26.3; FL – Peterson, 1;27.9, 83.42 mph.

Lauda led until electrical trouble on lap 33 allowed Peterson to take over in old faithful Lotus 72, replacing failed new model.

9-6-74 SWEDISH GP,
Anderstorp – 80 laps, 199.61 miles
1. Jody Scheckter (Tyrrell 007-1), 80 laps in 1:58;31.391, 101.11 mph.
2. Patrick Depailler (Tyrrell 007-2), 80 in 1:58;31.771.
3. James Hunt (Hesketh 308-2), 80. **4.** Emerson Fittipaldi (McLaren M23/4), 80. **5.** Jean-Pierre Jarier (Shadow DN1/2A), 80. **6.** Graham Hill (Lola T370 HU-2), 79.
PP – Depailler, 1;24.758; FL – Depailler, 1;27.262, 103.01 mph.

Utter Tyrrell domination, 007s shared front row of the grid, Peterson's Lotus split them briefly in second place.

23-6-74 DUTCH GP,
Zandvoort – 75 laps, 196.95 miles
1. Niki Lauda (Ferrari 312B3 015), 75 laps in 1:43;00.35, 114.72 mph.
2. Clay Regazzoni (Ferrari 312B3 014), 75 in 1:43;08.60.
3. Emerson Fittipaldi (McLaren M23/5), 75. **4.** Mike Hailwood (McLaren M23/7), 75. **5.** Jody Scheckter (Tyrrell 007-1), 75. **6.** Patrick Depailler (Tyrrell 007-2), 75.
PP – Lauda, 1;18.31; FL – Ronnie Peterson (Lotus 72 R8), 1;21.44, 116.08 mph.

Ferrari's turn, sharing front row, disposing of Hailwood's McLaren on opening lap but Italian cars dominant thereafter.

7-7-74 FRENCH GP,
Dijon-Prenois – 80 laps, 163.50 miles
1. Ronnie Peterson (Lotus 72 R8), 80 laps in 1:21;55.02, 119.75 mph.
2. Niki Lauda (Ferrari 312B3 012), 80 in 1:22;15.38.
3. Clay Regazzoni (Ferrari 312B3 014), 80. **4.** Jody Scheckter (Tyrrell 007-1), 80. **5.** Jacky Ickx (Lotus 72 R5), 80. **6.** Denny Hulme (McLaren M23/4), 80.
PP – Lauda, 00;58.79 (very short lap distance); FL – Scheckter, 1;00.00, 122.62 mph.

Peterson Lotus tour de force, disposing of Lauda's more powerful Ferrari and keeping ahead on dizzy little circuit.

20-7-74 BRITISH GP,
Brands Hatch – 75 laps, 198.75 miles
1. Jody Scheckter (Tyrrell 007-1), 75 laps in 1:43;02.2, 115.73 mph.
2. Emerson Fittipaldi (McLaren M23/8), 75 in 1:43;17.5.
3. Jacky Ickx (Lotus 72 R5), 74. **4.** Clay Regazzoni (Ferrari 312B3 014), 74. **5.** Niki Lauda (Ferrari 312B3 015), 74. **6.** Carlos Reutemann (Brabham BT44/1), 74.
PP – Lauda, 1;19.7; FL – Lauda, 1;21.1, 117.63 mph.

Lauda led from start but delayed pit stop too late to replace punctured tyre and was trapped in pit lane by organizational failure at finish, allowing Scheckter lucky win; processional race, last-minute farce.

4-8-74 GERMAN GP,
Nürburgring – 14 laps, 198.64 miles
1. Clay Regazzoni (Ferrari 312B3 016), 14 laps in 1:41;35.0, 117.33 mph.
2. Jody Scheckter (Tyrrell 007-1), 14 in 1:42;25.7.
3. Carlos Reutemann (Brabham BT44/1), 14. **4.** Ronnie Peterson (Lotus 76 R10), 14. **5.** Jacky Ickx (Lotus 72 R5), 14. **6.** Tom Pryce (Shadow DN3/5A), 14.
PP – Niki Lauda (Ferrari 312B3 012), 7;00.8; FL – Scheckter, 7;11.1, 118.49 mph.

Young Hunt had said Regazzoni was over the hill, so he was at the Ring, leading start to finish after Lauda immaturity crashed pole Ferrari on second corner – record-breaking Scheckter drive into good second couldn't challenge Ferrari, or Regazzoni.

18-8-74 AUSTRIAN GP,
Österreichring – 54 laps, 198.34 miles
1. Carlos Reutemann (Brabham BT44/1), 54 laps in 1:28;44.72, 134.10 mph.
2. Denny Hulme (McLaren M23/6), 54 in 1:29;27.64.
3. James Hunt (Hesketh 308-3), 54. **4.** John Watson (Brabham BT44/4), 54. **5.** Clay Regazzoni (Ferrari 312B3 014), 54. **6.** Vittorio Brambilla (March 741/2), 54.
PP – Niki Lauda (Ferrari 312B3 015), 1;35.40; FL – Regazzoni, 1;37.22, 136.01 mph.

Brabham start to finish win, Reutemann's team-mate Pace out with fuel leak losing hard-won second place on lap 41, Lauda forced out by engine failure, 3-4-5 all had to change blistered or deflating tyres.

8-9-74 ITALIAN GP,
Monza – 52 laps, 186.76 miles
1. Ronnie Peterson (Lotus 72 R8), 52 laps in 1:22;56.6, 135.41 mph.
2. Emerson Fittipaldi (McLaren M23/8), 52 in 1:22;57.4.
3. Jody Scheckter (Tyrrell 007-1), 52. **4.** Arturo Merzario (Williams FX4/3), 52. **5.** Carlos Pace (Brabham BT44/2), 51. **6.** Denny Hulme (McLaren M23/6), 51.
PP – Niki Lauda (Ferrari 312B3 015), 1;33.16; FL – Pace, 1;34.2, 137.26 mph.

Lauda's 9th pole of season but both Ferraris failed when leading, Peterson inherited lead on lap 39, Fittipaldi headed him for a few yards on one lap, but Lotus held on.

22-9-74 CANADIAN GP,
Mosport Pk, Toronto – 80 laps, 196.72 miles
1. Emerson Fittipaldi (McLaren M23/8), 80 laps in 1:40;26.136, 117.52 mph.
2. Clay Regazzoni (Ferrari 312B3 016), 80 in 1:40;39.170.
3. Ronnie Peterson (Lotus 72 R8), 80. **4.** James Hunt (Hesketh 308-2), 80. **5.** Patrick Depailler (Tyrrell 007-4), 80. **6.** Denny Hulme (McLaren M23/6), 79.
PP – Fittipaldi, 1;13.188; FL – Niki Lauda (Ferrari 312B3 015), 1;13.659, 120.18 mph.

Lauda again led from start but this time hit soil scattered on track by incident and crashed on lap 69, allowing Fittipaldi win to take Championship on into final round, between Fittipaldi, Regazzoni and Scheckter; McLaren, Ferrari, Tyrrell.

6-10-74 UNITED STATES GP,
Watkins Glen, NY – 59 laps, 199.24 miles
1. Carlos Reutemann (Brabham BT44/1), 59 laps in 1:40;21.439, 119.12 mph.
2. Carlos Pace (Brabham BT44/2), 59 in 1:40;32.174.
3. James Hunt (Hesketh 308-2), 59. **4.** Emerson Fittipaldi (McLaren M23/8), 59. **5.** John Watson (Brabham BT44/4), 59. **6.** Patrick Depailler (Tyrrell 007-4), 59.
PP – Reutemann, 1;38.978; FL – Pace, 1;40.608, 120.84 mph.

Brabham all the way for superb 1-2 finish, Hunt shone until Hesketh brakes faded, Ferrari a shambles, Tyrrell failed so McLaren (Fittipaldi) earned titles.

1975

12-1-75 ARGENTINE GP,
Buenos Aires – 53 laps, 196.55 miles
1. Emerson Fittipaldi (McLaren M23/9), 53 laps in 1:39;26.29, 118.60 mph.
2. James Hunt (Hesketh 308-3), 53 in 1:39;32.20.
3. Carlos Reutemann (Brabham BT44B/1), 53. **4.** Clay Regazzoni (Ferrari 312T 014), 53. **5.** Patrick Depailler (Tyrrell 007-4), 53. **6.** Niki Lauda (Ferrari 312T 020), 53.
PP – Jean-Pierre Jarier (Shadow DN5/1A), 1;49.21; FL – Hunt, 1;50.91, 120.37 mph.

Hunt's Hesketh got best of initial battle with Brabhams, but Fittipaldi's new McLaren pressured him into mistake on lap 35 and went on to win, Shadow pole but diff failed on warm-up lap!

26-1-75 BRAZILIAN GP,
Interlagos – 40 laps, 197.84 miles
1. Carlos Pace (Brabham BT44B/2), 40 laps in 1:44;41.17, 113.39 mph.
2. Emerson Fittipaldi (McLaren M23/9), 40 in 1:44;46.96.
3. Jochen Mass (McLaren M23/8), 40. **4.** Clay Regazzoni (Ferrari 312T 014), 40. **5.** Niki Lauda (Ferrari 312T 020), 40. **6.** James Hunt (Hesketh 308-3), 40.
PP – Jean-Pierre Jarier (Shadow DN5/1A), 2;29.88; FL – Jarier, 2;34.16, 115.51 mph.

Reutemann led to lap 5, impressive Jarier Shadow thereafter building big lead until metering unit seized with 8 laps to run, allowing Pace home victory for Brabham.

1-3-75 SOUTH AFRICAN GP,
Kyalami – 78 laps, 198.90 miles
1. Jody Scheckter (Tyrrell 007-2), 78 laps in 1:43;16.90, 115.51 mph.
2. Carlos Reutemann (Brabham BT44B/1), 78 in 1:43;20.64.
3. Patrick Depailler (Tyrrell 007-4), 78. **4.** Carlos Pace (Brabham BT44B/2), 78. **5.** Niki Lauda (Ferrari 312T 018), 78. **6.** Jochen Mass (McLaren M23/8), 78.
PP – Pace, 1;16.41; FL – Pace, 1;17.20, 118.92 mph.

Fine victory in spare Tyrrell with untried spare engine, Scheckter taking home-race lead from lap 3 and holding off Reutemann thereafter.

16-3-75 Race of Champions,
Brands Hatch, GB – 40 laps, 105.96 miles
1. Tom Pryce (Shadow DN5/2A), 40 laps in 55;53.5, 113.79 mph.
2. John Watson (Surtees TS16-04), 40 in 56;24.0.
3. Ronnie Peterson (Lotus 72 R9), 40. **4.** Jacky Ickx (Lotus 72 R5), 39. **5.** Emerson Fittipaldi (McLaren M23/9), 39. **6.** Bob Evans (BRM P201-05), 38.
PP – Pryce, 1;34.9; FL – Pryce, 1;21.1, 117.63 mph.

Scheckter had race in bag for Tyrrell, but Pryce's Shadow then closed rapidly and Tyrrell engine failed on brink of anticipated battle giving Pryce Shadow's first F1 victory.

13-4-75 BRDC International Trophy,
Silverstone, GB – 40 laps, 117.08 miles
1. Niki Lauda (Ferrari 312T 022), 40 laps in 52;17.6, 134.33 mph.
2. Emerson Fittipaldi (McLaren M23/4), 40 in 52;17.7.
3. Mario Andretti (Parnelli VPJ4-002), 40. **4.** John Watson (Surtees TS16-04), 40. **5.** Patrick Depailler (Tyrrell 007-4), 40. **6.** Mark Donohue (Penske PC1-002), 40.
PP – James Hunt (Hesketh 308-2), 1;17.3; FL – Hunt & Fittipaldi, 1;17.7, 135.61 mph.

Hunt's Hesketh led until lap 25 when engine blew, leaving Ferrari/McLaren duel for lead and close finish.

27-4-75 SPANISH GP,
Montjuich Pk, Barcelona – 75 laps, 176.65 miles*
Race stopped after 29 laps due to accident.
1. Jochen Mass (McLaren M23/9), 29 laps in 42;53.7, 95.54 mph.
2. Jacky Ickx (Lotus 72 R5), 29 in 42;54.8.
3. Carlos Reutemann (Brabham BT44B/1), 28. **4.** Jean-Pierre Jarier (Shadow DN5/1A), 29.** **5.** Vittorio Brambilla (March 751/3), 28. **6.** Lella Lombardi (March 751/2), 21.
** One place penalty for overtaking under yellow caution flag.

PP – Niki Lauda (Ferrari 312T 022), 1;23.4; FL – Mario Andretti (Parnelli VPJ4-002), 1;25.1, 99.64 mph.

Circuit safety worries persuaded Fittipaldi to boycott race, the Ferraris rammed each other in first corner, Hunt led briefly but crashed on spilled oil. Andretti took over in new Parnelli until lap 22 crash, then Stommelen's Hill led until rear wing strut failed and car went into bystanders, killing 5, on lap 26 – Pace crashed in avoidance leaving Mass victory as race was stopped.

11-5-75 MONACO GP,
Monte Carlo – 78 laps, 158.87 miles*
Race stopped after 75 laps to comply with two-hour rule.
1. Niki Lauda (Ferrari 312T 023), 75 laps in 2:01;21.31, 75.55 mph.
2. Emerson Fittipaldi (McLaren M23/9), 75 in 2:01;24.09.
3. Carlos Pace (Brabham BT44B/2), 75. **4.** Ronnie Peterson (Lotus 72 R9), 75. **5.** Patrick Depailler (Tyrrell 007-4), 75. **6.** Jochen Mass (McLaren M23/8), 75.
PP – Lauda, 1;26.40; FL – Depailler, 1;28.67, 82.71 mph.

Wet-dry race saw everyone changing to dry tyres after 20 laps or so, Lauda led all but one lap in Ferrari demonstration.

25-5-75 BELGIAN GP,
Zolder – 70 laps, 185.38 miles
1. Niki Lauda (Ferrari 312T 023), 70 laps in 1:43;53.98, 107.06 mph.
2. Jody Scheckter (Tyrrell 007-2), 70 in 1:44;13.20.
3. Carlos Reutemann (Brabham BT44B/1), 70. **4.** Patrick Depailler (Tyrrell 007-4), 70. **5.** Clay Regazzoni (Ferrari 312T 022), 70. **6.** Tom Pryce (Shadow DN5/2A), 70.
PP – Lauda, 1;25.43; FL – Regazzoni, 1;26.76, 109.90 mph.

Lauda won from his 12th pole since joining Ferrari previous year, first five laps saw battle for lead with Pace's Brabham and Brambilla's March.

8-6-75 SWEDISH GP,
Anderstorp – 80 laps, 199.76 miles
1. Niki Lauda (Ferrari 312T 023), 80 laps in 1:59;18.319, 100.41 mph.
2. Carlos Reutemann (Brabham BT44B/1), 80 in 1:59;24.607.
3. Clay Regazzoni (Ferrari 312T 021), 80. **4.** Mario Andretti (Parnelli VPJ4-001), 80. **5.** Mark Donohue (Penske PC1-01), 80. **6.** Tony Brise (Hill GH-1/1), 79.
PP – Vittorio Brambilla (March 751/3), 1;24.360; FL – Lauda, 1;28.267, 101.82 mph.

Brambilla's on-form March led first 15 laps until tyre trouble, Reutemann's Brabham led until front tyres deteriorated, Lauda taking lead with 10 laps to run.

22-6-75 DUTCH GP,
Zandvoort – 75 laps, 196.95 miles
1. James Hunt (Hesketh 308-2), 75 laps in 1:46;57.40, 110.49 mph.
2. Niki Lauda (Ferrari 312T 022), 75 in 1:46;58.46.
3. Clay Regazzoni (Ferrari 312T 021), 75. **4.** Carlos Reutemann (Brabham BT44B/2), 74. **5.** Carlos Pace (Brabham BT44B/2), 74. **6.** Tom Pryce (Shadow DN5/2A), 74.
PP – Lauda, 1;20.29; FL – Lauda, 1;21.54, 115.91 mph.

Another wet-dry tyre race, Hesketh timed Hunt's stop right, and he held off early leader Lauda by might and main.

6-7-75 FRENCH GP,
Ricard-Castellet – 54 laps, 194.61 miles
1. Niki Lauda (Ferrari 312T 022), 54 laps in 1:40;18.84, 116.60 mph.
2. James Hunt (Hesketh 308-2), 54 in 1:40;20.43.
3. Jochen Mass (McLaren M23/8), 54. **4.** Emerson Fittipaldi (McLaren M23/9), 54. **5.** Mario Andretti (Parnelli VPJ4-001), 54. **6.** Patrick Depailler (Tyrrell 007-4), 54.
PP – Lauda, 1;47.82; FL – Mass, 1;50.60, 117.51 mph.

Lauda's race throughout, built large mid-race lead and let it shrink comfortably to final winning margin, Hunt and Mass both very competitive this day.

19-7-75 BRITISH GP,
Silverstone – 67 laps, 196.44 miles*
Race stopped after 56 laps due to multiple crashes in rainstorm.
1. Emerson Fittipaldi (McLaren M23/9), 56 laps in 1:22;05.0, 120.01 mph.
2. Carlos Pace (Brabham BT44B/2), 55.
3. Jody Scheckter (Tyrrell 007-6), 55. **4.** James Hunt (Hesketh 308-2), 55. **5.** Mark Donohue (March 751/5), 55. **6.** Vittorio Brambilla (March 751/3), 55.
PP – Tom Pryce (Shadow DN5/2A), 1;19.36; FL – Clay Regazzoni (Ferrari 312T 024), 1;20.9, 130.47 mph.

Pace led until lap 13 when Regazzoni went by only to spin five laps later in rain shower; Pryce's Shadow led for one lap before crashing, Hunt seven laps until exhaust broke, Fittipaldi inherited lead; 12 laps later storm broke and nine more crashed as another British GP collapsed in farce.

3-8-75 GERMAN GP,
Nürburgring – 14 laps, 198.64 miles
1. Carlos Reutemann (Brabham BT44B/1), 14 laps in 1:41;14.1, 117.73 mph.
2. Jacques Laffite (Williams FX4 IR-03), 14 in 1:42;51.8.
3. Niki Lauda (Ferrari 312T 022), 14. **4.** Tom Pryce (Shadow DN5/2A), 14. **5.** Alan Jones (Hill GH1-3), 14. **6.** Gijs van Lennep (Ensign N175 MN-04), 14.
PP – Lauda, 6;58.6; FL – Clay Regazzoni (Ferrari 312T 021), 7;06.4, 119.79 mph.

Yet another daffy-duck race as flints on track caused spate of punctures; Lauda led first nine laps, Reutemann thereafter, Laffite rising through field as faster runners delayed.

17-8-75 AUSTRIAN GP,
Österreichring – 54 laps, 198.34 miles*
Race stopped after 29 laps due to rains torm.
1. Vittorio Brambilla (March 751/3), 29 laps in 57;56.69, 111.23 mph.
2. James Hunt (Hesketh 308-2), 29 in 5 ;23.72.
3. Tom Pryce (Shadow DN5/2A), 29. **4.** Jochen Mass (McLaren M23/6), 29. **5.** Ronnie Peters on (Lotus 72 R9), 29. **6.** Niki Lauda (Ferrari 312T 022), 29 lap .
PP – Lauda, 1;34.85; FL – Brambilla, 1; 3.90, 116.08 mph.
Hat-trick of strange GPs – Lauda tried Ferrari set-up in hope track would dry, but rain i icreased and Hunt took lead on lap 15 with works Ma rch in contact and taking lead on lap 19 as Hesketh went onto 7 cylinders. Stuck's works March als very fast, Mark Donohue fatally injured in pre-rac March crash.

24-8-75 'Swiss GP,'
Dijon-Prenois, F – 60 laps, 122.63 miles
1. Clay Regazzoni (Ferrari 312T 021), 0 laps in 1:01;25.34, 120.61 mph.
2. Patrick Depailler (Tyrrell 007-4), 60 i 1:01;33.69.
3. Jochen Mass (McLaren M23/6), 60 **4.** Ronnie Peterson (Lotus 72 R9), 60. **5.** John Watson (Sur ees TS16-05), 60. **6.** Carlos Pace (Brabham BT44B/3), 60.
PP – Jean-Pierre Jarier (Shadow DN5/4), 59.25; FL – Jarier, 1;00.44, 121.73 mph.
Jarier's Shadow led handsom ly until gearbox failed, leaving easy if minor vic tory to Regazzoni and Ferrari; only 16 starters, whic would have been a big field in '50s Formula 1!

7-9-75 ITALIAN GP,
Monza – 52 laps, 186.76 miles
1. Clay Regazzoni (Ferrari 312T 024), 52 laps in 1:22;42.6, 135.48 mph.
2. Emerson Fittipaldi (McLaren M23/10 , 52 in 1:22;59.2.
3. Niki Lauda (Ferrari 312T 023), 52. **4.** Carlos Reutemann (Brabham BT44B/1), 52. **5.** James Hu t (Hesketh 308C-1), 52. **6.** Tom Pryce (Shadow DN5/2A), 52
PP – Lauda, 1;32.24; FL – Regazzoni, 1; 3.1, 138.87 mph.
Repeat of Regazzoni's 1970 Ferra i triumph on their home soil, led start to finish, Lau a deposed late on by Fittipaldi for second place.

5-10-75 UNITED STATES GP,
Watkins Glen, NY – 59 laps, 199.2 miles
1. Niki Lauda (Ferrari 312T 023), 59 aps in 1:42;.58.175, 116.10 mph.
2. Emerson Fittipaldi (McLaren M23/10 , 59 in 1:43;03.118.
3. Jochen Mass (McLaren M23/6), 59. **4.** James Hunt (Hesketh 308C-1), 59. **5.** Ronnie Peters on (Lotus 72 R9), 59. **6.** Jody Scheckter (Tyrrell 007-9), 59.
PP – Lauda, 1;42.003; FL – Fittipaldi, 1; 3.374, 117.60 mph.
Lauda all the way, fastest in all four practice sessions and held off Fittipaldi for fi st 20 laps in close duel until lapping delayed Regazz ni and he blocked the McLaren, costing Fittipaldi 1 secs in next five laps, being black-flagged but e ffectively ruining race, Jarier's Shadow strong thir until wheel bearing collapsed after 19 laps.

1976

25-1-76 BRAZILIAN GP,
Interlagos – 40 laps, 197.84 miles
1. Niki Lauda (Ferrari 312T 023), 40 laps in 1:45;16.78, 112.76 mph.
2. Patrick Depailler (Tyrrell 007-4), 40 i 1:45;38.25.
3. Tom Pryce (Shadow DN5/5A), 40. **4.** Hans Stuck Jr (March 761/2), 40. **5.** Jody Scheckter (Tyrrell 07-6), 40. **6.** Jochen Mass (McLaren M23/6), 40.
PP – James Hunt (McLaren M23/8), 2;32.50; FL – Jean-Pierre Jarier (Shadow DN5/6A), 2;35.07 114.83 mph.
Beaten for pole by Hunt's McLare I, Lauda took lead from team-mate Regazzoni after laps, pulled away until Jarier's Shadow closed to w thin 2 secs before sliding off on oil – Pryce's Shado w only lost second place due to brake problems towa ds end.

6-3-76 SOUTH AFRICAN GP,
Kyalami – 78 laps, 198.98 miles
1. Niki Lauda (Ferrari 312T 023), 78 lap s in 1:42;18.4, 116.58 mph.
2. James Hunt (McLaren M23/8), 78 in 1:42;19.7.
3. Jochen Mass (McLaren M23/6), 78. **4.** Jody Scheckter (Tyrrell 007-6), 78. **5.** John Watson (P nske PC3-01), 77. **6.** Mario Andretti (Parnelli VPJ4-002), 77.
PP – Hunt, 1;16.10; FL – Lauda, 1;17.9 , 117.72 mph.
Hunt's McLaren on pole again but Lauda's race throughout, despite deflating tyr e in latter stages; Pryce's Shadow again impress ve, losing fourth place due to puncture.

14-3-76 Race of Champions,
Brands Hatch, GB – 40 laps, 105.96 miles
1. James Hunt (McLaren M23/8), 40 la s in 58;01.23, 107.96 mph.
2. Alan Jones (Surtees TS19-02), 40 in 58;19.65.
3. Jacky Ickx (Hesketh 308C/3), 40. **4.** Vittorio Brambilla (March 761/1), 40. **5.** Chris Amon (Ens gn N174 MN-02), 39. **6.** Tom Pryce (Shadow DN5/5A), 39.
PP – Jody Scheckter (Tyrrell 007-6) 1;20.42; FL – Hunt, 1;23.78, 112.15 mph.
Sensational Surtees debut for l lan Jones, taking lead on first lap, Hunt going by nd pulling away to 18 sec win as Jones baulked by b ck-marker.

28-3-76 UNITED STATES GP W EST,
Long Beach, California – 99 laps, 199.98 miles
1. Clay Regazzoni (Ferrari 312T 024), 0 laps in 1:53;18.471, 85.57 mph.
2. Niki Lauda (Ferrari 312T 023), 80 in ;54;00.885.

3. Patrick Depailler (Tyrrell 007-4), 80. **4.** Jacques Laffite (Ligier-Matra V12 JS5-01), 80. **5.** Jochen Mass (McLaren M23/6), 80. **6.** Emerson Fittipaldi (Fittipaldi FD04-1), 79.
PP – Regazzoni, 1;23.099; FL – Regazzoni, 1;23.076, 87.53 mph.
Utter domination for Regazzoni – pole, led whole distance, fastest lap. Lauda hampered by 'transmission vibration', Depailler pushed Hunt's McLaren out of race on lap 3 . . . Hunt was cross.

11-4-76 BRDC International Trophy,
Silverstone, GB – 40 laps, 117.28 miles
1. James Hunt (McLaren M23/9), 40 laps in 53;04.57, 132.58 mph.
2. Vittorio Brambilla (March 761/3), 40 in 53;15.81.
3. Jody Scheckter (Tyrrell 007-6), 40. **4.** Tom Pryce (Shadow DN5/5A), 40. **5.** Jean-Pierre Jarier (Shadow DN5/4A), 40. **6.** Gunnar Nilsson (Lotus 77 R2), 40.
PP – Hunt, 1;17.91; FL – Hunt, 1;18.81, 133.93 mph.
Dull minor event, Hunt's McLaren led superbly entire distance.

2-5-76 SPANISH GP,
Jarama, Madrid – 75 laps, 158.63 miles
1. James Hunt (McLaren M23/8-2), 75 laps in 1:42;20.43, 92.95 mph.
2. Niki Lauda (Ferrari 312T 026), 75 in 1:42;51.40.
3. Gunnar Nilsson (Lotus 77 R2), 75. **4.** Carlos Reutemann (Brabham-Alfa Romeo f12 BT45/1), 74. **5.** Chris Amon (Ensign N176 MN-05), 74. **6.** Carlos Pace (Brabham-Alfa Romeo f12 BT45/3), 74.
PP – Hunt, 1;18.52; FL – Jochen Mass (McLaren M23/9), 1;20.93, 94.04 mph.
First race for new airbox, wing, cockpit hoop regs. Lauda/Hunt duel resolved when McLaren took lead on lap 32, Lauda handicapped by rib injury but decisive win for McLaren until post-race disqualification for too-wide rear track (decision later reversed by FIA appeal). Lotus 77s impressive, 6-wheel Tyrrell P34 debut.

16-5-76 BELGIAN GP,
Zolder – 70 laps, 185.38 miles
1. Niki Lauda (Ferrari 312T 026), 70 laps in 1:42;53.23, 108.11 mph.
2. Clay Regazzoni (Ferrari 312T 025), 70 in 1:42;56.69.
3. Jacques Laffite (Ligier-Matra V12 JS5-01), 70. **4.** Jody Scheckter (Tyrrell P34/3), 70. **5.** Alan Jones (Surtees TS19-02), 69. **6.** Jochen Mass (McLaren M23/9), 69.
PP – Lauda, 1;26.55; FL – Lauda, 1;25.98, 110.87 mph.
12-cylinders dominant, Ferrari 1-2 from lap 7, Lauda led throughout. Scheckter's first Cosworth car home had broken rear suspension pick-up but gave a length clear of being lapped by winner! Hunt's McLaren fell back from good start, convincing critics its past-Spanish 'legalization' mods had removed its 'cheating' competitiveness . . . they were mistaken.

30-5-76 MONACO GP,
Monte Carlo – 78 laps, 160.52 miles
1. Niki Lauda (Ferrari 312T 026), 78 laps in 1:59;51.47, 80.36 mph.
2. Jody Scheckter (Tyrrell P34/3), 78 in 2:00;02.60.
3. Patrick Depailler (Tyrrell P34/2), 78. **4.** Hans Stuck Jr (March 761/2), 77. **5.** Jochen Mass (McLaren M23/9), 77. **6.** Emerson Fittipaldi (Fittipaldi FD04-1), 77.
PP – Lauda, 1;29.65; FL – Lauda, 1;30.36, 81.99 mph.
Ferrari's fifth win of season for Lauda, leading throughout, Tyrrells impressed though Depailler finished with another broken rear suspension pick-up; Peterson's March started 2nd, ran 2nd and crashed; Regazzoni crashed Ferrari when challenging Scheckter for 2nd place four laps from finish.

13-6-76 SWEDISH GP,
Anderstorp – 72 laps, 179.78 miles
1. Jody Scheckter (Tyrrell P34/3), 72 laps in 1:46;53.729, 100.85 mph.
2. Patrick Depailler (Tyrrell P34/2), 72 in 1:47;13.495.
3. Niki Lauda (Ferrari 312T 026), 72. **4.** Jacques Laffite (Ligier-Matra V12 JS5-01), 72. **5.** James Hunt (McLaren M23/8-2), 72. **6.** Carlos Pace (Brabham-Alfa Romeo f12 BT45/3), 72.
PP – Scheckter, 1;25.659; FL – Mario Andretti (Lotus 77 R1), 1;28.002, 102.13 mph.
Andretti's Lotus 77 started from front row and led 45 laps until engine failed, leaving Tyrrell 6-wheelers triumphant; Amon's Ensign 3rd fastest in practice, ran comfortable 4th until lap 38 crash.

4-7-76 FRENCH GP,
Ricard-Castellet – 54 laps, 194.61 miles
1. James Hunt (McLaren M23/8-2), 54 laps in 1:40;58.60, 115.84 mph.
2. Patrick Depailler (Tyrrell P34/2), 54 in 1:41;11.30.
3. John Watson (Penske PC4-001), 54. **4.** Carlos Pace (Brabham-Alfa Romeo f12 BT45/1), 54. **5.** Mario Andretti (Lotus 77 R1), 54. **6.** Jody Scheckter (Tyrrell P34/3), 54.
PP – Hunt, 1;47.89; FL – Niki Lauda (Ferrari 312T 026), 1;51.0, 117.09 mph.
Both Ferraris retired with engine seizures one-third distance, Hunt's most dominant win thereafter. Peterson 3rd for March until fuel metering unit failure three laps from end, Watson's Penske disqualified for alleged wing height infringement, later reinstated.

18-7-76 BRITISH GP,
Brands Hatch – 76 laps, 201.40 miles*
Race stopped after first-corner multiple collision; restarted over full distance, controversially allowing spare cars to be used.
1. Niki Lauda (Ferrari 312T 028), 76 laps in 1:44;19.66,

114.82 mph.**
2. Jody Scheckter (Tyrrell P34/3), 76 in 1:44;35.84.
3. John Watson (Penske PC4-001), 75. **4.** Tom Pryce (Shadow DN5/5A), 75. **5.** Alan Jones (Surtees TS19-02), 75. **6.** Emerson Fittipaldi (Fittipaldi FD04-3), 74.
PP – Lauda, 1;19.35; FL – James Hunt (McLaren M23/8-2), 1;19.82, 117.71 mph.
First on road was Hunt, but Lauda 2nd in 1:43;27.61, 115.19 mph, later disqualified by FIA appeal hearing.
Yet another silly British GP: Ferraris collided in first corner, involving others, including Hunt's Ferrari – race restarted with Hunt in prime car; he took lead from Lauda after 43 laps, pulled away to dominant win, only 10 cars running at finish. Ferrari protested McLaren's restart car, and won.

1-8-76 GERMAN GP,
Nürburgring – 14 laps, 198.64 miles
1. James Hunt (McLaren M23/6), 14 laps in 1:41;42.7, 117.18 mph.
2. Jody Scheckter (Tyrrell P34/3), 14 in 1:42;10.4.
3. Jochen Mass (McLaren M23/9), 14. **4.** Carlos Pace (Brabham-Alfa Romeo f12 BT45/4), 14. **5.** Gunnar Nilsson (Lotus 77 R2), 14. **6.** Rolf Stommelen (Brabham-Alfa Romeo f12 BT45/1), 14.
PP – Hunt, 7;06.5; FL – Scheckter, 7;10.8, 118.57 mph.
Hunt's third successive on-road GP win, but Lauda crashed and was burned on lap 2; race stopped and restarted, Hunt's task eased when Regazzoni spun off when 2nd.

15-8-76 AUSTRIAN GP,
Österreichring – 54 laps, 198.34 miles
1. John Watson (Penske PC4-001), 54 laps in 1:30;07.86, 132.03 mph.
2. Jacques Laffite (Ligier-Matra V12 JS-02), 54 in 1:30;18.65.
3. Gunnar Nilsson (Lotus 77 R2), 54. **4.** James Hunt (McLaren M23/8-2), 54. **5.** Mario Andretti (Lotus 77 R3), 54. **6.** Ronnie Peterson (March 761/6), 54.
PP – Hunt, 1;35.02; FL – Hunt, 1;35.91, 137.83 mph.
Ferrari cancelled entries, fine race ensued. Peterson (March)/Watson/Scheckter (Tyrrell)/Nilsson (Lotus) battle resolved as Tyrrell broke suspension and crashed and March brakes faded, Nilsson slowed by fluctuating oil pressure at end, allowing Laffite by.

29-8-76 DUTCH GP,
Zandvoort – 75 laps, 196.95 miles
1. James Hunt (McLaren M23/8-2) 75 laps in 1:44;52.09, 112.69 mph.
2. Clay Regazzoni (Ferrari 312T 027), 75 in 1:44;53.01.
3. Mario Andretti (Lotus 77 R1), 75. **4.** Tom Pryce (Shadow DN8/1A), 75. **5.** Jody Scheckter (Tyrrell P34/4), 75. **6.** Vittorio Brambilla (March 761/1), 75.
PP – Ronnie Peterson (March 761/6), 1;21.31; FL – John Watson (Penske PC4-001), 1;23.10, 113.76 mph.
'Drive as you would normally, don't think for one minute the honour of Ferrari and of Italy rests with you' – Mr Ferrari to Regazzoni. Peterson's March and Watson's Penske both led early on, Peterson's engine failed, 30-lap Hunt/Watson battle ended with Penske gearbox failure after 48 laps, Regazzoni started his charge just too late . . . Ferrari disapproved.

12-9-76 ITALIAN GP,
Monza – 52 laps, 187.41 miles
1. Ronnie Peterson (March 761/6), 52 laps in 1:30;35.6, 124.12 mph.
2. Clay Regazzoni (Ferrari 312T 027), 52 in 1:30;37.9.
3. Jacques Laffite (Ligier-Matra V12 JS5-02), 52. **4.** Niki Lauda (Ferrari 312T 026), 52. **5.** Jody Scheckter (Tyrrell P34/4), 52. **6.** Patrick Depailler (Tyrrell P34/2), 52.
PP – Laffite, 1;41.35; FL – Peterson, 1;41.3, 128.08 mph.
McLaren and Penske practice times disallowed after dubious fuel analysis, steamy Hunt went off when brake-tested by Pryce's Shadow in race, Peterson's March passed Scheckter for lead on lap 11 and was never headed thereafter, Lauda's stunning comeback from injury.

3-10-76 CANADIAN GP,
Mosport Pk, Toronto – 80 laps, 196.72 miles
1. James Hunt (McLaren M23/8-2), 80 laps in 1:40;09.626, 117.843 mph.
2. Patrick Depailler (Tyrrell P34/2), 80 in 1:40;15.957.
3. Mario Andretti (Lotus 77 R1), 80. **4.** Jody Scheckter (Tyrrell P34/4), 80. **5.** James Hunt (McLaren M23/9), 80. **6.** Clay Regazzoni (Ferrari 312T 027), 80.
PP – Hunt, 1;12.389; FL – Depailler, 1;13.817, 119.92 mph.
Early bid from Peterson faded leaving Hunt dominant win.

10-10-76 UNITED STATES GP,
Watkins Glen, NY – 59 laps, 199.24 miles
1. James Hunt (McLaren M23/8-2), 59 laps in 1:42;40.741, 116.43 mph.
2. Jody Scheckter (Tyrrell P34/4), 59 in 1:42;48.771.
3. Niki Lauda (Ferrari 312T 026), 59. **4.** Jochen Mass (McLaren M23/9), 59. **5.** Hans Stuck Jr (March 761/2), 59. **6.** John Watson (Penske PC4-02), 59.
PP – Hunt, 1;43.622; FL – Hunt, 1;42.851, 118.20 mph.
Great race between Hunt and Scheckter, McLaren led only 18 of 59 laps, Tyrrell 6-wheeler also second on grid – Hunt now within three points of Lauda's Championship lead.

24-10-76 JAPANESE GP,
Fuji – 73 laps, 197.72 miles
1. Mario Andretti (Lotus 77 R1), 73 laps in 1:43;58.86, 114.09 mph.
2. Patrick Depailler (Tyrrell P34/3), 72.
3. James Hunt (McLaren M23/8-2), 72. **4.** Alan Jones (Surtees TS19-04), 72. **5.** Clay Regazzoni (Ferrari 312T 027), 72. **6.** Gunnar Nilsson (Lotus 77 R2), 72.

PP – Andretti, 1;12.77; FL – Masahiro Hasemi (Kojima KE007/1), 1;18.23, 124.62 mph.
Championship clincher for Hunt, Lauda abandoned race and title in heavy rain. Hunt led to lap 61 when wet tyres failed as track dried, Depailler led two laps before stopping, Andretti ran out winner while Hunt charged back to title-winning third-place finish.

1977

9-1-77 ARGENTINE GP,
Buenos Aires – 53 laps, 196.55 miles
1. Jody Scheckter (Wolf WR1), 53 laps in 1:40;11.19, 117.71 mph.
2. Carlos Pace (Brabham-Alfa Romeo f12 BT45/5), 53 in 1:40;54.43.
3. Carlos Reutemann (Ferrari 312T2 029), 53. **4.** Emerson Fittipaldi (Fittipaldi FD04-3), 53. **5.** Mario Andretti (Lotus 78 R1), 53. **6.** Clay Regazzoni (Ensign N177 MN-06), 51.
PP – James Hunt (McLaren M23/10), 1;48.68; FL – Hunt, 1;51.06, 120.21 mph.
Lucky debut win for Wolf – early leader Watson retired now-competitive Brabham-Alfa when gearbox mounting bolts failed, Hunt's McLaren led comfortably until suspension failure, Pace's Brabham-Alfa led laps 35-47, driver unwell and Scheckter won; Andretti's Lotus should have placed second but rear wheel bearing seized.

23-1-77 BRAZILIAN GP,
Interlagos – 40 laps, 197.84 miles
1. Carlos Reutemann (Ferrari 312T2 029), 40 laps in 1:45;07.72, 112.92 mph.
2. James Hunt (McLaren M23/10), 40 in 1:45;18.43.
3. Niki Lauda (Ferrari 312T2 026), 40. **4.** Emerson Fittipaldi (Fittipaldi FD04-3), 40. **5.** Gunnar Nilsson (Lotus 78 R1), 40. **6.** Renzo Zorzi (Shadow DN5/5A), 39.
PP – Hunt, 2;30.11; FL – Hunt, 2;34.55, 115.21 mph.
Brabham-Alfas potent again, Pace led six laps until collision with Hunt, whose McLaren wore out both front tyres after 24 laps, had to stop to replace them; eight cars crashed on disintegrating track surface.

5-3-77 SOUTH AFRICAN GP,
Kyalami – 78 laps, 198.90 miles
1. Niki Lauda (Ferrari 312T2 030), 78 laps in 1:42;21.6, 116.59 mph.
2. Jody Scheckter (Wolf WR1), 78.
3. Patrick Depailler (Tyrrell P34/2), 78. **4.** James Hunt (McLaren M23/11), 78. **5.** Jochen Mass (McLaren M23/6), 78. **6.** John Watson (Brabham-Alfa Romeo f12 BT45/3), 78.
PP – Hunt, 1;15.96; FL – Watson, 1;17.63, 118.26 mph.
Lauda from lap 7 to finish despite running over debris from tragic Tom Pryce fatal accident, damaging coolers; fine Wolf performance.

20-3-77 Race of Champions,
Brands Hatch, GB – 40 laps, 105.96 miles
1. James Hunt (McLaren M23/10), 40 laps in 53;54.35, 116.36 mph.
2. Jody Scheckter (Wolf WR1), 40 in 54;17.87.
3. John Watson (Brabham-Alfa Romeo f12 BT45/1), 40. **4.** Brian Henton (March 761 Spl), 39. **5.** Jack Oliver (Shadow DN8/1A), 39. **6.** David Purley (LEC Pilbeam R21-01), 39.
PP – Watson, 1;19.05; FL – Hunt, 1;19.48, 118.38 mph.
Andretti's Lotus 78 led for 34 laps until electrical failure, Hunt inheriting win, Watson delayed from pole start by stop to change blistered front tyre.

3-4-77 UNITED STATES GP WEST,
Long Beach, California – 80 laps, 161.60 miles
1. Mario Andretti (Lotus 78 R3), 80 laps in 1:51;35.470, 89.89 mph.
2. Niki Lauda (Ferrari 312T2 030), 80 in 1:51;36.243.
3. Jody Scheckter (Wolf WR1), 80. **4.** Patrick Depailler (Tyrrell P34/2), 80. **5.** Emerson Fittipaldi (Fittipaldi FD04-3), 80. **6.** Jean-Pierre Jarier (ATS Penske PC4-02), 79.
PP – Lauda, 1;21.630; FL – Lauda, 1;21.650, 89.09 mph.
Classic race, first-corner collisions, Scheckter led 77 laps with Lotus and Ferrari in close contact before slow puncture let them by.

8-5-77 SPANISH GP,
Jarama, Madrid – 75 laps, 158.65 miles
1. Mario Andretti (Lotus 78 R3), 75 laps in 1:42;52.22, 91.79 mph.
2. Carlos Reutemann (Ferrari 312T2 029), 75 in 1:43;08.07.
3. Jody Scheckter (Wolf WR1), 75. **4.** Jochen Mass (McLaren M23/12), 75. **5.** Gunnar Nilsson (Lotus 78 R2), 75. **6.** Hans Stuck Jr (Brabham-Alfa Romeo f12 BT45/1), 74.
PP – Andretti, 1;18.70; FL – Jacques Laffite (Ligier-Matra V12 JS7-02), 1;20.81, 94.24 mph.
Lotus 78 dominance begins, though Brabham-Alfas will shine mid-season. Andretti fastest in three practice sessions, led start to finish, only Laffite's Ligier-Matra could keep Lotus in sight but stopped after 12 laps for loose rear wheel to be tightened, miserable McLaren M26 debut for Hunt, Lauda did not start.

22-5-77 MONACO GP,
Monte Carlo – 76 laps, 156.44 miles
1. Jody Scheckter (Wolf WR1), 76 laps in 1:57;52.77, 79.61 mph.
2. Niki Lauda (Ferrari 312T2 030), 76 in 1:57;53.66.
3. Carlos Reutemann (Ferrari 312T2 029), 76. **4.** Jochen Mass (McLaren M23/12), 76. **5.** Mario Andretti (Lotus 78 R3), 76. **6.** Alan Jones (Shadow DN8/3A), 76.
PP – John Watson (Brabham-Alfa Romeo f12 BT45/5), 1;29.86; FL – Scheckter, 1;31.07, 81.35 mph.

Wolf throughout for Cosworth's 100th GP win, Watson's Brabham-Alfa challenged but slowed with brake then terminal gearbox trouble, Scheckter eased off to final winning margin.

5-6-77 BELGIAN GP,
Zolder – 70 laps, 185.38 miles
1. Gunnar Nilsson (Lotus 78 R2), 70 laps in 1:55;05.71, 96.64 mph.
2. Niki Lauda (Ferrari 312T2 030), 70 in 1:55;19.90.
3. Ronnie Peterson (Tyrrell P34/5), 70. 4. Vittorio Brambilla (Surtees TS19-06), 70. 5. Alan Jones (Shadow DN8/3A), 70. 6. Hans Stuck Jr (Brabham-Alfa Romeo f12 BT45/1), 69.
PP – Andretti (Lotus 78 R3), 1;24.64; FL – Nilsson 1;27.54, 108.96 mph.
Very wet race, Andretti/Watson collision on first lap, Nilsson showed Lotus 78 potential by catching Lauda's leading Ferrari after tardy stop to fit dry tyres, took lead with 20 laps to run.

19-6-77 SWEDISH GP,
Anderstorp – 72 laps, 179.78 miles
1. Jacques Laffite (Ligier-Matra V12 JS7-02), 72 laps in 1:46;55.520, 100.85 mph.
2. Jochen Mass (McLaren M23/12), 72 in 1:47;03.969.
3. Carlos Reutemann (Ferrari 312T2 029), 72. 4. Patrick Depailler (Tyrrell P34/5), 72. 5. John Watson (Brabham-Alfa Romeo f12 BT45/6), 72. 6. Mario Andretti (Lotus 78 R3), 72.
PP – Andretti, 1;25.404; FL – Andretti, 1;27.607, 102.61 mph.
Lucky but popular V12 win. Andretti's Lotus 78 took lead from Watson on lap 2 but metering unit flopped onto 'full rich' and forced fuel top-up stop two laps from end, giving Laffite victory; Watson/Wolf collision, Hunt's M26 delayed by stop for tyres.

3-7-77 FRENCH GP,
Dijon-Prenois – 80 laps, 188.89 miles
1. Mario Andretti (Lotus 78 R3), 80 laps in 1:39;40.13, 113.71 mph.
2. John Watson (Brabham-Alfa Romeo f12 BT45/6), 80 in 1:39;41.68.
3. James Hunt (McLaren M26/2), 80. 4. Gunnar Nilsson (Lotus 78 R2), 80. 5. Niki Lauda (Ferrari 312T2 031), 80. 6. Carlos Reutemann (Ferrari 312T2 029), 79.
PP – Andretti, 1;12.21; FL – Andretti, 1;13.75, 115.34 mph.
Watson Brabham-Alfa should have won brilliant victory but fuel dried on final lap, having led from lap 3; Andretti had settled for 2nd place but given very lucky win.

16-7-77 BRITISH GP,
Silverstone – 68 laps, 199.58 miles
1. James Hunt (McLaren M26/2), 68 laps in 1:31;46.06, 130.36 mph.
2. Niki Lauda (Ferrari 312T2 031), 68 in 1:32;04.37.
3. Gunnar Nilsson (Lotus 78 R2), 68. 4. Jochen Mass (McLaren M26/3), 68. 5. Hans Stuck Jr (Brabham-Alfa Romeo f12 BT45/3), 68. 6. Jacques Laffite (Ligier-Matra V12 JS7-01), 67.
PP – Hunt, 1;18.49; FL – Hunt, 1;19.60, 132.60 mph.
Watson and Brabham-Alfa again dominant for 50 laps, first from Lauda, then Hunt, until fuel pick-up then engine problems sidelined it; Andretti engine failure, M26's maiden win. Unimpressive Renault turbo debut.

31-7-77 GERMAN GP,
Hockenheim – 47 laps, 198.25 miles
1. Niki Lauda (Ferrari 312T2 031), 47 laps in 1:31;48.62, 129.48 mph.
2. Jody Scheckter (Wolf WR2), 47 in 1:32;02.95.
3. Hans Stuck Jr (Brabham-Alfa Romeo f12 BT45/3), 47. 4. Carlos Reutemann (Ferrari 312T2 029), 47. 5. Vittorio Brambilla (Surtees TS19-06), 47. 6. Patrick Tambay (Ensign N177 MN-08), 47.
PP – Scheckter, 1;53.07; FL – Lauda, 1;55.99, 130.83 mph.
Wolf led 12 laps before Lauda got by, then handicapped by fuel pick-up problems; Brabham-Alfa again thirsty, Stuck coasting over line with engine dead; Lotus 78 engine failures.

14-8-77 AUSTRIAN GP,
Österreichring – 54 laps, 199.39 miles
1. Alan Jones (Shadow DN8/4A), 54 laps in 1:37;16.49, 122.99 mph.
2. Niki Lauda (Ferrari 312T2 031) 54 in 1:37;36.62.
3. Hans Stuck Jr (Brabham-Alfa Romeo f12 BT45/3), 54. 4. Carlos Reutemann (Ferrari 312T2 029), 54. 5. Ronnie Peterson (Tyrrell P34/6), 54. 6. Jochen Mass (McLaren M26/5), 53.
PP – Lauda, 1;39.32; FL – John Watson (Brabham-Alfa Romeo f12 BT45/5), 1;40.96, 137.83 mph.
Wet start saw Andretti's Lotus 78 lead 10 laps before engine blew; team-mate Nilsson changed onto slicks when 2nd, rocketed back up to third behind Hunt's leading M26 then engine failed; Hunt's leading M26 also blew, leaving maiden victory to Jones and Shadow.

28-8-77 DUTCH GP,
Zandvoort – 75 laps, 196.65 miles
1. Niki Lauda (Ferrari 312T2 030), 75 laps in 1:41;45.93, 116.12 mph.
2. Jacques Laffite (Ligier-Matra V12 JS7-02), 75 in 1:41;47.82.
3. Jody Scheckter (Wolf WR2), 74. 4. Emerson Fittipaldi (Fittipaldi F5/2), 74. 5. Patrick Tambay (Ensign N177 MN-08), 73. 6. Carlos Reutemann (Ferrari 312T2 029), 73.
PP – Mario Andretti (Lotus 78 R3), 1;18.65; FL – Niki Lauda, 1;19.99, 118.18 mph.
Hunt's M26 led five laps until Andretti passed round outside at Tarzan and cars collided, Hunt going out; Andretti's engine broke nine laps later, Lauda consolidated Championship lead.

11-9-77 ITALIAN GP,
Monza – 52 laps, 187.41 miles
1. Mario Andretti (Lotus 78 R3), 52 laps in 1:27;50.30, 128.01 mph.
2. Niki Lauda (Ferrari 312T2 031), 52 in 1:28;07.26.
3. Alan Jones (Shadow DN8/4A), 52. 4. Jochen Mass (McLaren M26/3), 52. 5. Clay Regazzoni (Ensign N177 MN-07), 52. 6. Ronnie Peterson (Tyrrell P34/6), 52.
PP – James Hunt (McLaren M26/2), 1;38.08; FL – Andretti, 1;39.10, 130.92 mph.
Scheckter's Wolf led 10 laps, Andretti went by to dominant victory, Wolf's engine blew in attempt to keep Lotus 78 in sight, Hunt spun when 3rd early on, later retired with brake problems.

2-10-77 UNITED STATES GP,
Watkins Glen, NY – 59 laps, 199.24 miles
1. James Hunt (McLaren M26/2), 59 laps in 1:58;23.267, 100.98 mph.
2. Mario Andretti (Lotus 78 R3), 59 in 1:58;25.293.
3. Jody Scheckter (Wolf WR1), 59. 4. Niki Lauda (Ferrari 312T2 031), 59. 5. Clay Regazzoni (Ensign N177 MN-07), 59. 6. Carlos Reutemann (Ferrari 312T2 030), 58.
PP – Hunt, 1;40.863; FL – Ronnie Peterson (Tyrrell P34/6), 1;51.854, 108.69 mph.
Very wet race dominated by superb Hans Stuck Brabham-Alfa drive until lap 14 crash when clutchless car jumped out of gear; Hunt won from Andretti closing all the time, Lauda's 4th place clinched his title.

9-10-77 CANADIAN GP,
Mosport Pk, Toronto – 80 laps, 196.72 miles
1. Jody Scheckter (Wolf WR1), 80 laps in 1:40;00.00, 118.02 mph.
2. Patrick Depailler (Tyrrell P34/7), 80 in 1:40;06.77.
3. Jochen Mass (McLaren M26/3), 80. 4. Alan Jones (Shadow DN8/5A), 80. 5. Patrick Tambay (Ensign N177 MN-08), 80. 6. Vittorio Brambilla (Surtees TS19-06), 78.
PP – Mario Andretti (Lotus 78 R3), 1;11.385; FL – Andretti, 1;13.299, 120.94 mph.
Andretti's dominant Lotus 78 slowed so much that Scheckter had just unlapped himself in 2nd place when Lotus engine blew. Earlier on, Hunt's narrowly leading McLaren had been inadvertently put out by team-mate Mass while lapping him.

23-10-77 JAPANESE GP,
Fuji – 73 laps, 197.72 miles
1. James Hunt (McLaren M26/3), 73 laps in 1:31;51.68, 129.15 mph.
2. Carlos Reutemann (Ferrari 312T2 029), 73 in 1:32;54.13.
3. Patrick Depailler (Tyrrell P34/7), 73. 4. Alan Jones (Shadow DN8/5A), 73. 5. Jacques Laffite (Ligier-Matra V12 JS7-02), 72. 6. Riccardo Patrese (Shadow DN8/3A), 72.
PP – Mario Andretti (Lotus 78 R3), 1;12.23; FL – Jody Scheckter (Wolf WR3), 1;14.30, 131.04 mph.
Hunt's McLaren all the way; Andretti out in 2nd-lap collision while chasing Hunt, Mass's M26 2nd until lap 28 engine breakage, Regazzoni's Ensign then 2nd until engine failure, Laffite's turn then in Ligier-Matra but out of fuel on last lap, giving Ferrari lucky placing.

1978

15-1-78 ARGENTINE GP,
Buenos Aires – 53 laps, 196.55 miles
1. Mario Andretti (Lotus 78 R3), 52 laps in 1:37;04.47, 119.19 mph.
2. Niki Lauda (Brabham-Alfa Romeo f12 BT45/7), 52 in 1:37;17.68.
3. Patrick Depailler (Tyrrell 008-1), 52. 4. James Hunt (McLaren M26/4), 52. 5. Ronnie Peterson (Lotus 78 R2), 52. 6. Patrick Tambay (McLaren M26/3), 74.
PP – Andretti, 1;47.75; FL – Gilles Villeneuve (Ferrari 312T 027), 1;49.76, 121.63 mph.
Andretti's Lotus from start to finish; brief challenge from Watson's Brabham-Alfa.

29-1-78 BRAZILIAN GP,
Jacarepaguá, Rio de Janeiro – 63 laps, 196.94 miles
1. Carlos Reutemann (Ferrari 312T2 031) 63 laps in 1:49;50.86, 107.43 mph.
2. Emerson Fittipaldi (Fittipaldi F5A/1), 63 in 1:50;48.99.
3. Niki Lauda (Brabham-Alfa Romeo f12 BT45/7), 63. 4. Mario Andretti (Lotus 78 R3), 63. 5. Clay Regazzoni (Shadow DN8/5A), 62. 6. Didier Pironi (Tyrrell 008-2), 62.
PP – Ronnie Peterson (Lotus 78 R2), 1;40.45; FL – Reutemann, 1;43.07, 109.19 mph.
Michelin's first modern GP victory on dominant Ferrari in terrific heat, Fittipaldi's best finish in family F1 car, Andretti lost 2nd place with gearbox trouble.

4-3-78 SOUTH AFRICAN GP,
Kyalami – 78 laps, 198.90 miles
1. Ronnie Peterson (Lotus 78 R2), 78 laps in 1:42;15.76, 116.70 mph.
2. Patrick Depailler (Tyrrell 008-3), 78 in 1:42;16.23.
3. John Watson (Brabham-Alfa Romeo f12 BT46/3), 78. 4. Alan Jones (Williams FW06/1), 78. 5. Jacques Laffite (Ligier-Matra V12 JS7-01), 78. 6. Didier Pironi (Tyrrell 008-2), 77.
PP – Niki Lauda (Brabham-Alfa Romeo f12 BT46/4), 1;14.65; FL – Mario Andretti (Lotus 78 R3), 1;17.09, 119.08 mph.
Classic race with Patrese's new Arrows taking lead on less critical tyre combination when leading Andretti/Scheckter/Lauda group, engine blew 14 laps to go. Depailler led Andretti and Peterson, Mario lost four laps to pit, fuel pick-up hiccup until last lap and Peterson just squeezed by; Watson had spun on oil while leading Peterson towards end.

19-3-78 BRDC International Trophy,
Silverstone, GB – 40 laps, 117.40 miles
1. Keke Rosberg (Theodore TR1/2), 40 laps in 1:12;49.02, 96.64 mph.
2. Emerson Fittipaldi (Fittipaldi F5A/2), 40 in 1:12;50.90.
3. Tony Trimmer (McLaren M23/14), 37. 4. Brett Lunger (McLaren M23/11), 37. UNC '5th'. Rupert Keegan (Surtees TS19-07), 31. UNC '6th'. Hans Stuck Jr (Shadow DN9/1A), 29.
PP – Ronnie Peterson (Lotus 78 R2), 1;16.07; FL – Fittipaldi, 1;38.63, 107.02 mph.
Flooded race, Daly's Hesketh 308E led, new Lotus 79 one of many cars to crash, after dozen laps Rosberg's 'no-hoper' established in winning lead – a day for sheer wet-weather control.

2-4-78 UNITED STATES GP WEST,
Long Beach, California – 80 laps, 162.89 miles
1. Carlos Reutemann (Ferrari 312T3 032), 80 laps in 1:52;01.301, 87.10 mph.
2. Mario Andretti (Lotus 78 R3), 80 in 1:52;12.362.
3. Patrick Depailler (Tyrrell 008-3), 80. 4. Ronnie Peterson (Lotus 78 R2), 80. 5. Jacques Laffite (Ligier-Matra V12 JS7-03), 80. 6. Riccardo Patrese (Arrows FA1/2), 79.
PP – Reutemann, 1;20.636; FL – Alan Jones (Williams FW06/2), 1;22.215, 88.45 mph.
38 laps led by Villeneuve's Ferrari before he ran into back-marker, Reutemann then challenged hard by Jones's Williams until its nose aerofoils collapsed and fuel pick-up faltered.

7-5-78 MONACO GP,
Monte Carlo – 75 laps, 154.35 miles
1. Patrick Depailler (Tyrrell 008-3), 75 laps in 1:55;14.66, 80.36 mph.
2. Niki Lauda (Brabham-Alfa Romeo f12 BT46/4), 75 in 1:55;37.11.
3. Jody Scheckter (Wolf WR1), 75. 4. John Watson (Brabham-Alfa Romeo f12 BT46/3), 75. 5. Didier Pironi (Tyrrell 008-2), 75. 6. Riccardo Patrese (Arrows FA1/2), 75.
PP – Carlos Reutemann (Ferrari 312T3 032), 1;28.34; FL – Lauda, 1;28.65, 83.67 mph.
Depailler's maiden win in six years of F1, beat off Brabhams when Watson's brakes wore and Lauda forced to change deflating tyre. Wolf lost 2nd place only in last three laps when gearbox lost 2nd gear, Ferrari practice promise foiled by collision and crash in race.

21-5-78 BELGIAN GP,
Zolder – 70 laps, 185.38 miles
1. Mario Andretti (Lotus 79 R2), 70 laps in 1:39;52.02, 111.31 mph.
2. Ronnie Peterson (Lotus 78 R2), 70 in 1;40;01.92.
3. Carlos Reutemann (Ferrari 312T3 033), 70. 4. Gilles Villeneuve (Ferrari 312T3 034), 70. 5. Jacques Laffite (Ligier-Matra V12 JS79-01), 69. 6. Didier Pironi (Tyrrell 008-4), 69.
PP – Andretti, 1;20.90; FL – Peterson, 1;23.13, 114.66 mph.
Colin Chapman's 50th birthday Lotus 1-2, Peterson 2nd in 78 after chase through field following stop to change front tyres. Villeneuve delayed when front tyre deflated, drove lap on rim; Reutemann slowed by persistent understeer. Hunt, Lauda, Scheckter hopes end in startline shunt.

4-6-78 SPANISH GP,
Jarama, Madrid – 75 laps, 158.65 miles
1. Mario Andretti (Lotus 79 R3), 75 laps in 1:41;47.06, 93.53 mph.
2. Ronnie Peterson (Lotus 79 R2), 75 in 1:42;06.62.
3. Jacques Laffite (Ligier-Matra V12 JS9-01), 75. 4. Jody Scheckter (Wolf WR5), 75. 5. John Watson (Brabham-Alfa Romeo f12 BT46/4), 75. 6. James Hunt (McLaren M26/3), 74.
PP – Andretti, 1;16.39; FL – Andretti, 1;20.06, 95.10 mph.
Lotus 79s 1-2, Hunt's M26 on sticky tyres led five laps, lay 2nd to 50 before stop for fresh tyres, Peterson recovered from dreadful start.

17-6-78 SWEDISH GP,
Anderstorp – 70 laps, 175.33 miles
1. Niki Lauda (Brabham-Alfa Romeo f12 BT46B/6), 70 laps in 1:41;00.606, 104.14 mph.
2. Riccardo Patrese (Arrows FA1/4), 70 in 1;41;34.625.
3. Ronnie Peterson (Lotus 79 R2), 70 in 1:41;34.711. 4. Patrick Tambay (McLaren M26/5), 69. 5. Clay Regazzoni (Shadow DN9/4A), 69. 6. Emerson Fittipaldi (Fittipaldi F5A/3), 69.
PP – Mario Andretti (Lotus 79 R3), 1;22.058; FL – Lauda, 1;24.836, 106.25 mph.
Ingenious Brabham fan-cars triumphant; Andretti held off Lauda for 40 laps until fan-car exploited advantage on oily surface, Lotus's engine blew on lap 46. Patrese muscled out Peterson's efforts to take 2nd place after early Lotus stop to replace punctured rear tyre, Watson's fan-car spun in 4th place, sand clogging throttle slides causing retirement.

1-7-78 FRENCH GP,
Ricard-Castellet – 54 laps, 194.95 miles
1. Mario Andretti (Lotus 79 R3), 54 laps in 1:38;51.92, 118.31 mph.
2. Ronnie Peterson (Lotus 79 R2), 54 in 1:38;54.85.
3. James Hunt (McLaren M26/3), 54. 4. John Watson (Brabham-Alfa Romeo f12 BT46/4), 54. 5. Alan Jones (Williams FW06/1), 54. 6. Jody Scheckter (Wolf WR5), 54.
PP – Watson, 1;44.41; FL – Carlos Reutemann (Ferrari 312T3 036), 1;48.56, 119.67 mph.
Hunt kept dominant 79s in sight after Watson led first half-lap, in non-fan Brabham – Hunt spun on last lap, physically sick with effort.

16-7-78 BRITISH GP,
Brands Hatch – 76 laps, 198.36 miles
1. Carlos Reutemann (Ferrari 312T3 033), 76 laps in 1:42;12.39, 116.61 mph.
2. Niki Lauda (Brabham-Alfa Romeo f12 BT46/6), 76 in 1:42;13.62.
3. John Watson (Brabham-Alfa Romeo f12 BT46/5), 76. 4. Patrick Depailler (Tyrrell 008-3), 76. 5. Hans Stuck Jr (Shadow DN9/1A), 76. 6. Patrick Tambay (McLaren M26/5), 75.
PP – Ronnie Peterson (Lotus 79 R2), 1;16.80; FL – Lauda, 1;18.60, 119.71 mph.
79s dominated practice, drew away one second per lap in lead before Peterson fuel pump failure and Andretti puncture. New Wolf WR5 wing-car led up to lap 39 when gearbox failed; Lauda inherited lead, caught by when back-marker baulked Brabham-Alfa on lap 60.

30-7-78 GERMAN GP,
Hockenheim – 45 laps, 189.81 miles
1. Mario Andretti (Lotus 79 R3), 45 laps in 1:28;00.90, 129.39 mph.
2. Jody Scheckter (Wolf WR5), 45 in 1:28;16.25.
3. Jacques Laffite (Ligier-Matra V12 JS9-01), 45. 4. Emerson Fittipaldi (Fittipaldi F5A/1), 45. 5. Didier Pironi (Tyrrell 008-2), 45. 6. Hector Rebaque (Lotus 78 R4), 45.
PP – Andretti, 1;51.90; FL – Ronnie Peterson (Lotus 79 R2), 1;55.62, 131.33 mph.
Peterson led five laps, let Andretti by but later stuck in 4th gear before transmission failed; Scheckter last but one due to early fuel vapourization but recovered to take 2nd, Jones's Williams 3rd behind 79s until lap 31 retirement with fuel vapourization.

13-8-78 AUSTRIAN GP,
Österreichring – 54 laps, 199.39 miles*
*Race stopped after seven laps due to torrential rain, restarted over remaining 47 laps.
PART ONE: 1. Peterson; 2. Depailler; 3. Watson; 4. Laffite; 5. Pironi; 6. Lauda.
PART TWO: 1. Peterson; 2. Depailler; 3. Villeneuve; 4. Fittipaldi; 5. Brambilla; 6. Laffite.
AGGREGATE:
1. Ronnie Peterson (Lotus 79 R2), 54 laps in 1:41;21.50, 118.03 mph.
2. Patrick Depailler (Tyrrell 008-3), 54 in 1:42;09.00.
3. Gilles Villeneuve (Ferrari 312T3 034), 54. 4. Emerson Fittipaldi (Fittipaldi F5A/1), 53. 5. Jacques Laffite (Ligier-Matra V12 JS9-02), 53. 6. Vittorio Brambilla (Surtees TS20-02), 53.
Drivers placed in races but not in final aggregate drove following cars; John Watson (Brabham-Alfa Romeo f12 BT46/5); Didier Pironi (Tyrrell 008-2); Niki Lauda (Brabham-Alfa Romeo f12 BT46/6).
PP – Peterson, 1;37.71; FL – Race 2, Peterson, 1;43.12, 128.91 mph.
Peterson spun off on lap 8 only to find race had been stopped ending lap 7. Track dried in Part Two, everyone changed onto slicks, Andretti crashed lap 1 of first race, Peterson easy runaway winner overall.

27-8-78 DUTCH GP,
Zandvoort – 75 laps, 196.65 miles
1. Mario Andretti (Lotus 79 R4), 75 laps in 1:41;04.23, 116.92 mph.
2. Ronnie Peterson (Lotus 79 R2), 75 in 1:41;04.55.
3. Niki Lauda (Brabham-Alfa Romeo f12 BT46/7), 75. 4. John Watson (Brabham-Alfa Romeo f12 BT46/5), 75. 5. Emerson Fittipaldi (Fittipaldi F5A/1), 75. 6. Gilles Villeneuve (Ferrari 312T3 034), 75.
PP – Andretti, 1;16.36; FL – Lauda, 1;19.57, 118.81 mph.
Fourth Lotus 1-2 of year, led Lauda throughout, record eight Lotus GP wins in season.

10-9-78 ITALIAN GP,
Monza – 52 laps, 187.41 miles*
*Race stopped after first-lap multiple collision, restarted over 40 laps, 144.16 miles.
1. Niki Lauda (Brabham-Alfa Romeo f12 BT46/7), 40 laps in 1:07;04.54, 128.95 mph.
2. John Watson (Brabham-Alfa Romeo f12 BT46/5), 40 in 1:07;06.02.
3. Carlos Reutemann (Ferrari 312T3 035), 40. 4. Jacques Laffite (Ligier-Matra V12 JS9-02), 40. 5. Patrick Tambay (McLaren M26/3), 40. 6. Mario Andretti (Lotus 79 R4), 40.**
**Time of 1:07;50.87 includes 60 sec penalty for jumping start; actually first on road with true time of 1:06;50.87, 16 secs ahead of Lauda's Brabham.
PP – Andretti, 1;37.520; FL – Andretti, 1;38.23, 132.08 mph.
Tragic race, fatal Peterson multiple accident. Late afternoon restart saw Villeneuve/Andretti battle resolved five laps from end as Ferrari tyres faded and Andretti easily drove past, both penalized for jumping start leaving cheerless Brabham-Alfa 1-2. Andretti wins World title.

1-10-78 UNITED STATES GP,
Watkins Glen, NY – 59 laps, 199.24 miles
1. Carlos Reutemann (Ferrari 312T3 035), 59 laps in 1:40;48.800, 118.58 mph.
2. Alan Jones (Williams FW06/1), 59 in 1:41;08.539.
3. Jean-Pierre Jabouille (Renault turbo V6 RS01/2), 59. 5. Emerson Fittipaldi (Fittipaldi F5A/2), 59. 6. Patrick Tambay (McLaren M26/7), 59.
PP – Andretti, 1;38.114; FL – Jean-Pierre Jarier (Lotus 79 R1), 1;39.537, 112.11 mph.
Andretti on pole by second, but stub axle sheared on race morning, had to take second 79, held off Ferraris for lap then dropped back until engine blew. Villeneuve 2nd in dominant Ferrari until lap 22 engine failure, good Williams and turbo Renault performances, Jarier in second Lotus out of fuel when 3rd with three laps to run. Renault's first points.

8-10-78 CANADIAN GP,
Ile Notre Dame, Montreal – 70 laps, 195.73 miles
1. Gilles Villeneuve (Ferrari 312T3 034), 70 laps in 1:57;49.196, 99.67 mph.
2. Jody Scheckter (Wolf WR6), 70.
3. Carlos Reutemann (Ferrari 312T3 035), 70. 4. Riccardo Patrese (Arrows A1/3), 70. 5. Patrick Depailler (Tyrrell 008-3), 70. 6. Derek Daly (Ensign N177 MN-06), 70.
PP – Jean-Pierre Jarier (Lotus 79 R3), 1;38.015; FL – Alan Jones (Williams FW06/1), 1;38.077, 10.64 mph.
Jarier confirmed 79's class by leading decisively until major oil leak after 49 laps; Andretti/Watson collision in early stages.

1979

21-1-79 ARGENTINE GP,
Buenos Aires – 53 laps, 196.55 miles*
*Race stopped after first-lap multiple accident, restarted over full distance.
1. Jacques Laffite (Ligier JS11-02), 53 laps in 1:36;03.21, 122.78 mph.
2. Carlos Reutemann (Lotus 79 R2), 53 in 1:36;18.15.
3. John Watson (McLaren M28/2), 53. 4. Patrick Depailler (Ligier JS11-03), 53. 5. Mario Andretti (Lotus 79 R4**), 52. 6. Emerson Fittipaldi (F5A/1), 52.
**Used spare car in restart after damaging 79 R3 in 'first race' accident.
PP – Laffite, 1;44.20; FL – Laffite, 1;28.76, 118.40 mph.
Brilliant Ligier-Cosworth ground effects car debut, 1-2 on grid, restarted race had 20 starters; Depailler led before fuel pressure misfire, Laffite taking over from lap 11.

4-2-79 BRAZILIAN GP,
Interlagos – 40 laps, 197.84 miles
1. Jacques Laffite (Ligier JS11-02), 40 laps in 1:40;09.64, 117.23 mph.
2. Patrick Depailler (Ligier JS11-03), 40 in 1:40;14.92.
3. Carlos Reutemann (Lotus 79 R2), 40. 4. Didier Pironi (Tyrrell 009-2), 40. 5. Gilles Villeneuve (Ferrari 312T3 034), 39. 6. Jody Scheckter (Ferrari 312T3 035), 39.
PP – Laffite, 2;23.07; FL – Laffite, 2;28.76, 118.40 mph.
Ligiers shine again, scoring second successive win; Fittipaldi's F5A challenged Reutemann's position in early stages before stop to fix loose rear wheel.

3-3-79 SOUTH AFRICAN GP,
Kyalami – 78 laps, 198.90 miles
1. Gilles Villeneuve (Ferrari 312T4 037), 79 laps in 1:41;49.96, 117.19 mph.
2. Jody Scheckter (Ferrari 312T4 038), 78 in 1:41;53.38.
3. Jean-Pierre Jarier (Tyrrell 009-3), 78. 4. Mario Andretti (Lotus 79 R5), 78. 5. Carlos Reutemann (Lotus 79 R2), 78. 6. Niki Lauda (Brabham-Alfa Romeo V12 B T48/2), 77.
PP – Jean-Pierre Jabouille (Renault turbo V6 RS01-02), 1;11.80; FL – Villeneuve, 1;14.412, 123.37 mph.
Debut race dominance for Ferrari T4s, race stopped after three laps due to rainstorm when turbo Renaults and Ferraris fighting torrid duel. Race restarted over 76 laps balance, track still wet; Villeneuve on wets, stopped for slicks as track dried at 15 laps; Scheckter led up to lap 52 when he changed slicks, leaving team-mate to win while he recovered 2nd place.

8-4-79 UNITED STATES GP WEST,
Long Beach – 80 laps, 161.52 miles
1. Gilles Villeneuve (Ferrari 312T4 037), 80 laps in 1:50;04.00, 87.81 mph.
2. Jody Scheckter (Ferrari 312T4 038), 80 in 1:50;18.00.
3. Alan Jones (Williams FW06/04), 80. 4. Mario Andretti (Lotus 79 R5), 80. 5. Patrick Depailler (Ligier JS11-03), 80. 6. Jean-Pierre Jarier (Tyrrell 009-3), 77.
PP – Villeneuve, 1;18.825; FL – Villeneuve, 1;21.200, 89.56 mph.
Villeneuve and Ferrari demonstration and fine drive from Jones keeping 'T4s in sight in outdated Williams.

15-4-79 Race of Champions,
Brands Hatch, GB – 40 laps, 104.54 miles
1. Gilles Villeneuve (Ferrari 312T3 034), 40 laps in 53;17.12, 117.72 mph.
2. Nelson Piquet (Brabham-Alfa Romeo V12 BT48/1), 40 in 53;31.19.
3. Mario Andretti (Lotus 79 R4), 40. 4. Jochen Mass (Arrows A1/2A), 40. 5. Niki Lauda (Brabham-Alfa Romeo V12 BT48/2), 39. 6. Elio de Angelis (Shadow DN9/4B), 39.
PP – Andretti, 1;17.52; FL – Piquet, 1;7.46, 121.47 mph.
Lauda led in BT48 ground-effects car until wrong-choice tyres blistered, lap 8; Villeneuve's elderly 'T3 led one lap before Andretti passed but Lotus tyre/gearbox/brake problems allowed Villeneuve through again on lap 28 for third F1 win in a row; promising Piquet 2nd after changing blistered tyres.

29-4-79 SPANISH GP,
Jarama, Madrid – 75 laps, 158.65 miles
1. Patrick Depailler (Ligier JS11-03), 75 laps in 1:39;11.84, 95.97 mph.
2. Carlos Reutemann (Lotus 79 R2), 75 in 1:39;32.78.
3. Mario Andretti (Lotus 80 R1), 75. 4. Jody Scheckter (Ferrari 312T4 039), 75. 5. Jean-Pierre Jarier (Tyrrell 009-3), 75. 6. Didier Pironi (Tyrrell 009-1), 75.
PP – Jacques Laffite (Ligier JS11-04), 1;14.50; FL – Gilles Villeneuve (Ferrari 312T4 037), 1;16.44, 99.61 mph.
Another Ligier 1-2 looked set until Laffite missed gear on lap 16 and blew engine; Depailler led throughout, Andretti impressive in Lotus 80 debut beat Scheckter and Jarier in close battle.

13-5-79 BELGIAN GP,
Zolder – 70 laps 185.38 miles
1. Jody Scheckter (Ferrari 312T4 040), 70 laps in 1:39;59.53, 111.24 mph.
2. Jacques Laffite (Ligier JS11-02), 70 in 1:40;14.89.
3. Didier Pironi (Tyrrell 009-1), 70. 4. Carlos Reutemann (Lotus 79 R2), 70. 5. Riccardo Patrese (Arrows A1/6A), 70. 6. John Watson (McLaren M28/2), 70.
PP – Laffite, 1;21.13; FL – Scheckter, 1;22.39, 115.72 mph.
Scheckter victory through survival rather than pace-making, as team-mate Villeneuve raced back through field after early delay only to run out of fuel on last lap; Jones's superb new Williams FW07 led comfortably before retiring with electrical failure.

27-5-79 MONACO GP,
Monte Carlo – 76 laps, 155.41 miles
1. Jody Scheckter (Ferrari 312T4 040), 76 laps in 1:55;22.48, 81.34 mph.
2. Clay Regazzoni (Williams FW07/2), 76 in 1:55;22.92.
3. Carlos Reutemann (Lotus 79 R4), 76. 4. John Watson (McLaren M28/3), 76. 5. Patrick Depailler (Ligier JS11-03), 74. 6. Jochen Mass (Arrows A1/5A), 69.
PP – Scheckter, 1;26.43; FL – Depailler, 1;28.82, 83.41 mph.
Scheckter's Ferrari all the way from pole but Regazzoni closed to within a half-second at finish after final 15-lap charge; Villeneuve looked stronger challenger for lead, tracking team-mate until transmission failure late in race; Jones's FW07 bent steering arm against barrier when pressing both Ferraris hard.

1-7-79 FRENCH GP,
Dijon-Prenois – 80 laps, 188.90 miles
1. Jean-Pierre Jabouille (Renault turbo V6 RS10-02*), 80 laps in 1:35;20.42, 118.88 mph.
2. Gilles Villeneuve (Ferrari 312T4 041), 80 in 1:35;35.01.
3. René Arnoux (Renault turbo V6 RS10-03*), 80 in 1:35;35.25. 4. Alan Jones (Williams FW07/3), 80. 5. Jean-Pierre Jarier (Tyrrell 009-3), 80. 6. Clay Regazzoni (Williams FW07/2), 80.
*These individual cars are also known as RS11 and RS12, respectively.
PP – Jabouille, 1;07.19; FL – Arnoux, 1;09.16, 122.91 mph.
Renault's great day; both cars on front row but Villeneuve led from start, Jabouille took lead lap 46, Villeneuve's tyres badly worn so fell back into wheel-banging last-lap ruckus with Arnoux – turbo 1.5's maiden win.

14-7-79 BRITISH GP,
Silverstone – 68 laps, 199.38 miles
1. Clay Regazzoni (Williams FW07/2), 68 laps in 1:26;11.17, 138.80 mph.
2. René Arnoux (Renault RS10-03), 68 in 1:26;35.45.
3. Jean-Pierre Jarier (Tyrrell 009-3), 67. 4. John Watson (McLaren M29/1), 67. 5. Jody Scheckter (Ferrari 312T4 039), 67. 6. Jacky Ickx (Ligier JS11-01), 67.
PP – Alan Jones (Williams FW07/1), 1;11.88; FL – Regazzoni, 1;14.40, 141.87 mph.
Great day for Williams – Jones's FW07 set fantastic pace, engine failed after water pump crack leaked coolant away, Regazzoni took over for Williams's maiden GP win, only Jabouille challenged Jones early on before multiple Renault problems.

29-7-79 GERMAN GP,
Hockenheim – 45 laps, 189.81 miles
1. Alan Jones (Williams FW07/4), 45 laps in 1:24;48.83, 134.27 mph.
2. Clay Regazzoni (Williams FW07/2), 45 in 1:24;51.74.
3. Jacques Laffite (Ligier JS11-04), 45. 4. Jody Scheckter (Ferrari 312T4 040), 45. 5. John Watson (McLaren M29/1), 45. 6. Jochen Mass (Arrows A2/2), 44.
PP – Jean-Pierre Jabouille (Renault turbo V6 RS10/02), 1;48.48; FL – Gilles Villeneuve (Ferrari 312T4 041), 1;51.89, 135.71 mph.
Jones beat Jabouille from start but couldn't shake him off until lap 8 driver error spun and stalled Renault. Jones bugged by high-speed misfire and deflating tyre in later stages but scraped home 3 secs clear of team-mate for fine Williams 1-2.

12-8-79 AUSTRIAN GP,
Österreichring – 54 laps, 199.39 miles
1. Alan Jones (Williams FW07/4), 54 laps in 1:27;38.01, 136.52 mph.
2. Gilles Villeneuve (Ferrari 312T4 041), 54 in 1:28;14.06.
3. Jacques Laffite (Ligier JS11-04), 54. 4. Jody Scheckter (Ferrari 312T4 040), 54. 5. Clay Regazzoni (Williams FW07/1), 54. 6. René Arnoux (Renault turbo V6 RS10-03), 53.
PP – Arnoux, 1;34.07; FL – Arnoux, 1;35.77, 138.80 mph.
Williams team hat-trick, Jones's second successive win. Villeneuve led two laps, Renaults both ran 2nd before trouble, Arnoux stopping for fuel only four laps from end, Jabouille stopped by clutch problem.

26-8-79 DUTCH GP,
Zandvoort – 75 laps, 196.94 miles
1. Alan Jones (Williams FW07/1), 75 laps in 1:41;19.775, 116.62 mph.
2. Jody Scheckter (Ferrari 312T4 040), 75 in 1:41;41.558.
3. Jacques Laffite (Ligier JS11-04), 75. 4. Nelson Piquet (Brabham-Alfa Romeo V12 BT48/2), 74. 5. Jacky Ickx (Ligier JS11-01), 74. 6. Jochen Mass (Arrows A2/2), 73.
PP – René Arnoux (Renault turbo V6 RS10), 1;15.461; FL – Gilles Villeneuve (Ferrari 312T4 041), 1;19.438, 119.00 mph.
Four for Williams, hat-trick for Jones – he took early control of race but gearbox problems allowed Villeneuve ahead lap 11, Ferrari 1st until lap 47 spin, two laps later tyre collapsed and off again, driver destroying suspension in brainless but classic high-speed three-wheeled run back to pits . . .

9-9-79 ITALIAN GP,
Monza – 50 laps, 180.20 miles
1. Jody Scheckter (Ferrari 312T4 040), 50 laps in 1:22;00.22, 131.85 mph.
2. Gilles Villeneuve (Ferrari 312T4 038), 50 in 1:22;00.68.
3. Clay Regazzoni (Williams FW07/1), 50. 4. Niki Lauda (Brabham-Alfa Romeo V12 BT48/4), 50. 5. Mario Andretti (Lotus 79 R5), 50. 6. Jean-Pierre Jarier (Tyrrell 009-3), 50.
PP – Jean-Pierre Jabouille (Renault turbo V6 RS10-02), 1;34.580; FL – Regazzoni, 1;35.60, 135.71 mph.
Convincing title-winning drive by Scheckter and fine, very close Ferrari 1-2 finish. Arnoux's Renault led laps 2-12, fell away to retire with misfire, Scheckter untroubled thereafter; Laffite with outside chance of title lost third place with brake/clutch troubles, finally over-revving engine; Jones, delayed by stop to replace dud battery, tore back but only ninth at finish.

16-9-79 Gran Premio Dino Ferrari,
Imola, I – 40 laps, 124.99 miles
1. Niki Lauda (Brabham-Alfa Romeo V12 BT48/4), 40 laps in 1:03;55.89, 117.31 mph.
2. Carlos Reutemann (Lotus 79 R2), 40 in 1:04;02.98.
3. Jody Scheckter (Ferrari 312T4 040), 40. 4. Riccardo Patrese (Arrows A1/5A), 40. 5. Jean-Pierre Jarier (Tyrrell 009-5), 40. 6. Keke Rosberg (Wolf WR8), 40.
PP – Gilles Villeneuve (Ferrari 312T4 038), 1;32.91; FL – Villeneuve, 1;33.61, 120.17 mph.
Brabham-Alfa swansong victory as Cosworth BT49 imminent; duel with Villeneuve's Ferrari ended when 'T4 rammed Lauda's tail under braking, stopping for new nosepiece. This minor race a rehearsal for staging 1980 Italian GP at Imola.

30-9-79 CANADIAN GP,
Ile Notre Dame, Montreal – 72 laps, 201.32 miles
1. Alan Jones (Williams FW07/4), 72 laps in 1:52;06.892, 105.96 mph.
2. Gilles Villeneuve (Ferrari 312T4 041), 72 in 1:52;07.972.
3. Clay Regazzoni (Williams FW07/1), 72. 4. Jody Scheckter (Ferrari 312T4 040), 71. 5. Didier Pironi (Tyrrell 009-6), 71. 6. John Watson (McLaren M29/3), 70.
PP – Jones, 1;29.892; FL – Jones, 1;32.272, 107.95 mph.
Very hard race between Jones and Villeneuve, Ferrari leading 51 laps until ever-present Jones slipped ahead; impressive new Piquet Brabham-Cosworth BT49 chased leaders hard until gearbox failed, leaving place to Regazzoni.

7-10-79 UNITED STATES GP,
Watkins Glen, NY – 59 laps, 199.24 miles
1. Gilles Villeneuve (Ferrari 312T4 041), 59 laps in 1:52;17.734, 106.46 mph.
2. René Arnoux (Renault turbo V6 RS10-03), 59 in 1:53;06.521.
3. Didier Pironi (Tyrrell 009-6), 59. 4. Elio de Angelis (Shadow DN9/1B), 59. 5. Hans Stuck Jr (ATS D3-01), 59. 6. John Watson (McLaren M29/3), 58.
PP – Alan Jones (Williams FW07/4), 1;35.615; FL – Nelson Piquet (Brabham BT49/2), 1;40.054, 121.50 mph.
Villeneuve won as Williams fudged Jones pit stop – 'T4 led in heavy rain on Michelin wets until track dried, lightning Ferrari stop put Villeneuve back out half-minute behind Williams, but Jones lost wheel after his tyre change, leaving Villeneuve comfortable win despite fading oil pressure.

1980

13-1-80 ARGENTINE GP,
Buenos Aires – 53 laps, 196.55 miles
1. Alan Jones (Williams FW07/4), 53 laps in 1:43;24.38, 113.98 mph.
2. Nelson Piquet (Brabham BT49/4), 53 in 1:43;48.97.
3. Keke Rosberg (Fittipaldi F7/2), 53. 4. Derek Daly (Tyrrell 009-6), 53. 5. Bruno Giacomelli (Alfa Romeo 179-004*), 52. 6. Alain Prost (McLaren M29/1B), 52.
*All Alfa Romeo chassis numbers are open to doubt as Autodelta indulged in unparalleled chassis-plate swapping between cars.
PP – Jones, 1;44.17; FL – Jones, 1;50.45, 120.87 mph.
Despite three spins and a stop to remove plastic bag debris blanking Williams's radiator, Jones won 5th GP from last 7. Longer-underwing FW07B version flopped in practice, as did long-underwing Brabhams; floors stripped off for race; BT49 a real threat.

27-1-80 BRAZILIAN GP,
Interlagos – 40 laps, 197.84 miles
1. René Arnoux (Renault turbo V6 RE21), 40 laps in 1:40;01.35, 117.40 mph.
2. Elio de Angelis (Lotus 81 R1), 40 in 1:40;23.19.
3. Alan Jones (Williams FW07/6), 40. 4. Didier Pironi (Ligier JS11-04), 40. 5. Alain Prost (McLaren M29/1B), 40. 6. Riccardo Patrese (Arrows A3/1), 39.
PP – Jean-Pierre Jabouille (Renault RE22), 2;21.40; FL – Arnoux, 2;27.311, 119.57 mph.
Arnoux's maiden win; car ran out of fuel on slowing-down lap. From end of lap 2 Renaults split by Ligiers but the latter had skirt stick (Pironi) and engine cut (Laffite) leaving Renault turbos 1-2 before Jabouille's turbo failed lap 25. De Angelis coped well with ill-handling Lotus.

1-3-80 SOUTH AFRICAN GP,
Kyalami – 78 laps, 198.90 miles
1. René Arnoux (Renault turbo V6 RE21), 78 laps in 1:36;52.54, 123.19 mph.
2. Jacques Laffite (Ligier JS11-03), 78 in 1:37;26.61.
3. Didier Pironi (Ligier JS11-04), 78. 4. Nelson Piquet

(Brabham BT49/4), 78. 5. Carlos Reutemann (Williams FW07/5), 77. 6. Jochen Mass (Arrows A3/4), 77.
PP – Jean-Pierre Jabouille (Renault turbo V6 RE23), 1;10.00; FL – Arnoux, 1;13.15, 125.49 mph.
Turbo advantage at altitude; Jones and Laffite mounted brief challenges but Renaults unmatched, luckless Jabouille tyre deflation 18 laps from end left Arnoux to 2nd consecutive win. French drivers 1-2-3 as Pironi won late-stages dice with Piquet.

30-3-80 UNITED STATES GP WEST,
Long Beach, California – 80.5 laps, 161.52 miles
1. Nelson Piquet (Brabham BT49/6), 80 laps in 1:50;18.550, 88.47 mph.
2. Riccardo Patrese (Arrows A3/3), 80 in 1:51;07.762.
3. Emerson Fittipaldi (Fittipaldi F7/1), 80. 4. John Watson (McLaren M29/2C), 79. 5. Jody Scheckter (Ferrari 312T5 046), 79. 6. Didier Pironi (Ligier JS11-04), 79.
PP – Piquet, 1;17.694; FL – Piquet, 1;19.830, 91.09 mph.
Piquet's maiden win proved class of driver and BT49 car – led throughout. Patrese and Fittipaldi finished well, Ensign crash injuries ended Regazzoni's career.

4-5-80 BELGIAN GP,
Zolder – 72 laps, 190.66 miles
1. Didier Pironi (Ligier JS11-04), 72 laps in 1:38;46.51, 115.82 mph.
2. Alan Jones (Williams FW07B/7), 72 in 1:39;33.88.
3. Carlos Reutemann (Williams FW07B/5), 72. 4. René Arnoux (Renault turbo V6 RE24), 71. 5. Jean-Pierre Jarier (Tyrrell 010/1), 71. 6. Gilles Villeneuve (Ferrari 312T5 045), 71.
PP – Jones, 1;19.12; FL – Jacques Laffite (Ligier JS11-03), 1;20.88, 117.88 mph.
Debut of definitive Williams FW07Bs but Ligier dominated, Pironi's performance superb.

18-5-80 MONACO GP,
Monte Carlo – 76 laps, 156.41 miles
1. Carlos Reutemann (Williams FW07B/5), 76 laps in 1:55;34.365, 81.20 mph.
2. Jacques Laffite (Ligier JS11-03), 76 in 1:56;47.994.
3. Nelson Piquet (Brabham BT49/7), 76. 4. Jochen Mass (Arrows A3/4), 75. 5. Gilles Villeneuve (Ferrari 312T5 045), 75. 6. Emerson Fittipaldi (Fittipaldi F7/1), 74.
PP – Didier Pironi (Ligier JS11-04), 1;24.813; FL – Riccardo Patrese (Arrows A3/5), 1;26.058, 86.09 mph.
Pironi looked set to repeat Zolder win, leading from pole, holding off Jones until Williams transmission failed, then Ligier slid into barrier leaving race to Reutemann's Williams on damp and slippery circuit – first-corner pile-up starred Daly's aviating Tyrrell.

1-6-80 Spanish GP,*
Jarama, Madrid – 80 laps, 164.74 miles
*Race declared non-Championship after being organized as Round 7 of the 1980 series.
1. Alan Jones (Williams FW07B/7), 80 laps in 1:43;14.076, 95.69 mph.
2. Jochen Mass (Arrows A3/4), 80 in 1:44;05.016.
3. Elio de Angelis (Lotus 81 R3), 80. 4. Jean-Pierre Jarier (Tyrrell 010/1), 79. 5. Emerson Fittipaldi (Fittipaldi F7/1), 79. 6. Patrick Gaillard (Ensign N180 MN-14), 75.
PP – Jacques Laffite (Ligier JS11-03), 1;12.647; FL – Jones, 1;15.467, 98.17 mph.
Race declared illegal by FISA after drivers refused to pay summary fines from Zolder dispute; Ferrari, Renault, Alfa boycotted race. Jones started 2nd to Reutemann, missed gearchange and fell to 5th, then car overheated but Reutemann and Laffite collided, Piquet's Brabham broke gearbox, Pironi lost wheel after inheriting lead and Jones couldn't believe his luck . . .

29-6-80 FRENCH GP,
Ricard-Castellet – 54 laps, 194.95 miles
1. Alan Jones (Williams FW07B/7), 54 laps in 1:32;43.42, 126.65 mph.
2. Didier Pironi (Ligier JS11-04), 54 in 1:32;47.94.
3. Jacques Laffite (Ligier JS11-01), 54. 4. Nelson Piquet (Brabham BT49/8), 54. 5. René Arnoux (Renault turbo V6 RE24), 54. 6. Carlos Reutemann (Williams FW07B/5), 54.
PP – Laffite, 1;38.88; FL – Jones, 1;41.45, 128.11 mph.
Brits beat French – after Spanish upset and loss of points, Williams team determined to beat them on their home soil. Ligiers and Renault turbo faster in practice but Jones had fine race set-up in FW07B and battled ahead of Ligiers with 20 laps to go.

13-7-80 BRITISH GP,
Brands Hatch – 76 laps, 198.63 miles
1. Alan Jones (Williams FW07B/7), 76 laps in 1:34;49.228, 125.69 mph.
2. Nelson Piquet (Brabham BT49/8), 76 in 1:35;00.235.
3. Carlos Reutemann (Williams FW07B/5), 76. 4. Derek Daly (Tyrrell 010/4), 75. 5. Jean-Pierre Jarier (Tyrrell 010/4), 75. 6. Alain Prost (McLaren M29/4C), 75.
PP – Didier Pironi (Ligier JS11-04), 1;11.004; FL – Pironi, 1;12.368, 130.02 mph.
Ligiers dominant until rim trouble put Pironi into pits for tyre change, Laffite off road and Jones won 5th GP inherited lead he held thereafter – Pironi rejoined but brilliant recovery drive foiled by another tyre deflation.

10-8-80 GERMAN GP,
Hockenheim – 45 laps, 189.79 miles
1. Jacques Laffite (Ligier JS11-04), 45 laps in 1:22;59.73, 137.26 mph.
2. Carlos Reutemann (Williams FW07B/5), 45 in 1:23;02.32.
3. Alan Jones (Williams FW07B/9), 45. 4. Nelson Piquet (Brabham BT49/8), 45. 5. Bruno Giacomelli (Alfa Romeo 179-03), 45. 6. Gilles Villeneuve (Ferrari 312T5 048), 45.
PP – Jones, 1;45.85; FL – Jones, 1;48.49, 139.96 mph.

Lucky Ligier win; Jabouille and Jones disputed lead, Williams unable to do much about Renaults until both turbos burned valves. Williams pair ran 1-3 sandwiching Laffite until five laps from end when Jones's left-front tyre punctured; Jones just held off Piquet for third after tyre change.

17-8-80 AUSTRIAN GP,
Österreichring – 54 laps, 199.39 miles
1. Jean-Pierre Jabouille (Renault turbo V6 RE23), 54 laps in 1:26;15.73, 138.69 mph.
2. Alan Jones (Williams FW07B/9), 54 in 1:26;16.55.
3. Carlos Reutemann (Williams FW07B/8), 54. 4. Jacques Laffite (Ligier JS11-03), 54. 5. Nelson Piquet (Brabham BT49/7), 54. 6. Elio de Angelis (Lotus 81 R3), 54.
PP – René Arnoux (Renault turbo V6 RE25), 1;30.27; FL – Arnoux,1;32.53, 143.66 mph.

Jones led before Renaults powered past, Arnoux stopped for tyre change while Jabouille paced Jones to finish, fighting real battle only in last few laps; both set their fastest laps on final tour.

31-8-80 DUTCH GP,
Zandvoort – 72 laps, 190.23 miles
1. Nelson Piquet (Brabham BT49/7), 72 laps in 1:38;13.83, 116.19 mph.
2. René Arnoux (Renault turbo V6 RE25), 72 in 1:38;26.76.
3. Jacques Laffite (Ligier JS11-03), 72. 4. Carlos Reutemann (Williams FW07B/8), 72. 5. Jean-Pierre Jarier (Tyrrell 010-5), 72. 6. Alain Prost (McLaren M30/1), 72.
PP – Arnoux, 1;17.44; FL – Arnoux, 1;19.35, 119.87 mph.

Jones built big lead too fast, damaged skirt on kerb and had to stop for it to be changed, allowing Championship rival Piquet to score for Brabham; Laffite robbed of 2nd place right at end when caught napping by Arnoux's late charge.

14-9-80 ITALIAN GP,
Imola – 60 laps, 187.92 miles
1. Nelson Piquet (Brabham BT49/9), 60 laps in 1:38;07.52, 113.98 mph.
2. Alan Jones (Williams FW07B/9), 60 in 1:38;36.45.
3. Carlos Reutemann (Williams FW07B/8), 60. 4. Elio de Angelis (Lotus 81 R3), 59. 5. Keke Rosberg (Fittipaldi F8/1), 59. 6. Didier Pironi (Ligier JS11-04), 59.
PP – René Arnoux (Renault turbo V6 RE25), 1;33.988); FL – Jones, 1;36.089, 116.40 mph.

Piquet disposed of Renaults in first three laps, Jones hampered by indifferent braking had to settle for 2nd, losing Championship lead to Piquet by one point, game drive by Reutemann having lost clutch and 4th gear. Both Ferrari drivers suffered major accidents – Scheckter in practice, Villeneuve a mightier moment in race.

28-9-80 CANADIAN GP,
Ile Notre Dame, Montreal – 70 laps – 191.90 miles
1. Alan Jones (Williams FW07B/9), 70 laps in 1:46;45.53, 110.00 mph.
2. Carlos Reutemann (Williams FW07B/8), 70 in 1:47;01.07.
3. Didier Pironi (Ligier JS11-04), 70. 4. John Watson (McLaren M29/2C), 70. 5. Gilles Villeneuve (Ferrari 312T4 044), 70. 6. Hector Rebaque (Brabham BT49/6), 69.
PP – Nelson Piquet (Brabham BT49/9); FL – Pironi, 1;28.769, 113.40 mph.

Jones/Piquet first-corner collision sparked multiple which stopped race. Piquet restarted in spare car still fitted with practice 'screamer' engine, predictably led until it blew on lap 24; Pironi penalized one minute for jumped start took lead on road and Jones sat back to finish 2nd on road, 1st overall, clinching World title; Watson 4th marked McLaren resurgence.

5-10-80 UNITED STATES GP,
Watkins Glen, NY – 59 laps, 199.24 miles
1. Alan Jones (Williams FW07B/9), 59 laps in 1:34;36.05, 126.37 mph.
2. Carlos Reutemann (Williams FW07B/8), 59 in 1:34;40.26.
3. Didier Pironi (Ligier JS11-02), 59. 4. Elio de Angelis (Lotus 81 R2), 59. 5. Jacques Laffite (Ligier JS11-03), 58. 6. Mario Andretti (Lotus 81 R3), 58.
PP – Bruno Giacomelli (Alfa Romeo 179-06), 1;33.291; FL – Jones, 1;34.068, 129.24 mph.

Fine Williams 1-2 to emphasize Championship success but Giacomelli's Alfa was the star: pole position and led going away until electrics failed at half-distance. Jones left road at first corner, resumed 12th, took 3rd when Piquet spun, overtook team-mate for 2nd then inherited 1st as Alfa failed. Both Lotuses in points for first time in season.

1981

7-2-81 South African GP,
Kyalami – 77 laps, 196.35 miles
1. Carlos Reutemann (Williams FW07B/10), 77 laps in 1:44;54.03, 112.31 mph.
2. Nelson Piquet (Brabham BT49B/10), 77 in 1:45;14.17.
3. Elio de Angelis (Lotus 81 R3), 77. 4. Keke Rosberg (Fittipaldi F8C/3), 76. 5. John Watson (McLaren M29C/4), 76. 6. Riccardo Patrese (Arrows A3/3), 76.
PP – Piquet, 1;12.78; FL – Reutemann, 1;13.61, 124.71 mph.

Another pointless race boycotted by *Grande Costruttori* after FOCA ran skirted rules – excluded from Championship. Great Reutemann drive on slicks from wet weather start while others stopped to change from wets as track dried; Piquet early leader, close Rosberg/Watson battle.

15-3-81 UNITED STATES GP WEST,
Long Beach, California – 80.5 laps, 162.61 miles
1. Alan Jones (Williams FW07C/11), 80 laps in 1:50;41.33,
87.60 mph.
2. Carlos Reutemann (Williams FW07C/12), 80 in 1:50;50.52.
3. Nelson Piquet (Brabham BT49C/11), 80. 4. Mario Andretti (Alfa Romeo 179-02), 80. 5. Eddie Cheever (Tyrrell 010-3), 80. 6. Patrick Tambay (Theodore TR-3), 79.
PP – Riccardo Patrese (Arrows A3/3), 1;19.399; FL – Jones, 1;20.901, 89.89 mph.

Redesigned cars after skirts ban still saw Williams dominant but Patrese's new Arrows A3 dominated practice and early stages until fuel filter blocked one-third distance; new turbo Ferraris promising before retirements, only eight finished. 'Twin-chassis' Lotus 88 excluded in practice controversy. Turbo Ferrari debut.

29-3-81 BRAZILIAN GP,
Jacarepaguà – 62 laps, 193.82 miles*
*Race flagged one lap short of scheduled 63 under two-hour rule due to heavy rain slowing pace.
1. Carlos Reutemann (Williams FW07C/12), 62 laps in 2:00;23.66, 96.59 mph.
2. Alan Jones (Williams FW07C/11), 62 in 2:00;28.10.
3. Riccardo Patrese (Arrows A3/3), 62. 4. Marc Surer (Ensign N180 MN-15) 62. 5. Elio de Angelis (Lotus 81 R3), 62. 6. Jacques Laffite (Ligier-Matra V12 JS17-02), 62.
PP – Nelson Piquet (Brabham BT49C/11), 1;35.079; FL – Surer, 1;54.302, 98.46 mph.

Williams dominant but Reutemann accused of disregarding pit direction to allow Jones by. Fine drives by Patrese and Surer in unfashionable cars, Ferrari's turbos luckless, controversial debut of Brabham lowering suspension.

12-4-81 ARGENTINE GP,
Buenos Aires – 53 laps, 196.55 miles
1. Nelson Piquet (Brabham BT49C/11), 53 laps in 1:34;32.74, 124.67 mph.
2. Carlos Reutemann (Williams FW07C/12), 53 in 1:34;59.35.
3. Alain Prost (Renault turbo V6 RE22B), 53. 4. Alan Jones (Williams FW07C/11), 53. 5. René Arnoux (Renault turbo V6 RE27B), 53. 6. Elio de Angelis (Lotus 81 R3), 52.
PP – Piquet, 1;42.665; FL – Piquet, 1;45.287, 126.80 mph.

Superior Michelin suspension ploy led start-to-finish, number 2 driver Rebaque passing Williams pair for second behind Piquet in mid-race until rotor arm broke; good day for Renault.

3-5-81 'SAN MARINO' GP,
Imola, I – 60 laps, 187.92 miles.
1. Nelson Piquet (Brabham BT49C/11), 60 laps in 1:51;23.97, 101.20 mph.
2. Riccardo Patrese (Arrows A3/5), 60 in 1:51;28.55.
3. Carlos Reutemann (Williams FW07C/12), 60. 4. Hector Rebaque (Brabham BT49C/12), 60. 5. Didier Pironi (Ferrari turbo V6 126C 051), 60. 6. Andrea de Cesaris (McLaren M29F/4), 60.
PP – Gilles Villeneuve (Ferrari turbo V6 126C 052), 1;48.064, 104.33 mph.

Piquet's second successive win but opposed strongly by Reutemann, Arrows and, surprisingly, Ferrari. Villeneuve led first 14 laps in wet before changing to dry tyres, Pironi in command before broken skirt and worn tyres, Piquet took lead with 13 laps to go. Watson's new McLaren 2nd fastest in race but early error; Jones collided with team-mate on first lap.

17-5-81 BELGIAN GP,
Zolder – 70 laps, 185.36 miles
1. Carlos Reutemann (Williams FW07C/12), 54 laps in 1:16;31.61, 112.12 mph.
2. Jacques Laffite (Ligier-Matra V12 JS17-02), 54 in 1:17;07.67.
3. Nigel Mansell (Lotus 81 R1), 54. 4. Gilles Villeneuve (Ferrari turbo V6 126C 050), 54. 5. Elio de Angelis (Lotus 81 R3), 54. 6. Eddie Cheever (Tyrrell 010-3), 54.
PP – Reutemann, 1;22.28; FL – Reutemann, 1;23.30, 114.45 mph.

Race shambles as start accident injured mechanic on grid as lights changed. Restart saw Pironi lead, Piquet and Jones got by, Brabham barged off road, Jones crashed while leading leaving Reutemann to win in 14th consecutive points-scoring finish – including Kyalami – race stopped early as drizzle fell.

31-5-81 MONACO GP,
Monte Carlo – 76 laps, 156.41 miles
1. Gilles Villeneuve (Ferrari turbo V6 126C 052), 76 laps in 1:54;23.38, 82.04 mph.
2. Alan Jones (Williams FW07C/15), 76 in 1:55; 03.29.
3. Jacques Laffite (Ligier-Matra V12 JS17-02), 76. 4. Didier Pironi (Ferrari turbo V6 126C 050), 75. 5. Eddie Cheever (Tyrrell 010-3), 74. 6. Marc Surer (Ensign N190 MN-15), 74.
PP – Nelson Piquet (Brabham BT49C/11), 1;25.710; FL – Jones, 1;27.470, 84.70 mph.

Piquet still rattled by Zolder incident with Jones, pressured into mistake by Williams driver when leading, crashed and gave lead to Jones, who stayed in front until lap 66 when slowed by fuel pick-up problem. Villeneuve inherited win after never-say-die drive in difficult turbo Ferrari.

21-6-81 SPANISH GP,
Jarama, Madrid – 80 laps, 164.64 miles
1. Gilles Villeneuve (Ferrari turbo V6 126C 052), 80 laps in 1:46;35.01, 92.68 mph.
2. Jacques Laffite (Ligier-Matra V12 JS17-04), 80 in 1:46;35.23.
3. John Watson (McLaren MP4/1-2), 80 in 1:46;35.59. 4. Carlos Reutemann (Williams FW07C/12), 80 in 1:46;36.02. 5. Elio de Angelis (Lotus 87 R2), 80 in 1:46;36.25. 6. Nigel Mansell (Lotus 87 R1), 80.
PP – Laffite, 1;13.754; FL – Jones, 1;17.818, 95.21 mph.

Jones threw race away by driver error when well
ahead, leaving Villeneuve to block off pursuers after searing start – superficially looked fabulous race but really a case of speed on straight and blocking 'em all through corners.

5-7-81 FRENCH GP,
Dijon-Prenois – 80 laps, 188.88 miles*
*Race stopped due to torrential rain shower after 58 laps and converted into two-part event with second section covering 22 laps.
PART ONE: 1. Piquet; 2. Prost; 3. Watson; 4. Reutemann; 5. Arnoux; 6. Rebaque.
PART TWO: 1. Prost; 2. Watson; 3. Arnoux; 4. Pironi; 5. Piquet; 6. de Cesaris.
AGGREGATE:
1. Alain Prost (Renault turbo V6 RE30-2), 80 laps in 1:35;48.13, 118.30 mph.
2. John Watson (McLaren MP4/1-2), 80 in 1:35;50.42.
3. Nelson Piquet (Brabham BT49C/11), 80. 4. René Arnoux (Renault turbo V6 RE30-3), 80. 5. Didier Pironi (Ferrari turbo V6 126C 053) 79. 6. Elio de Angelis (Lotus 87 R2), 79.
Drivers placed in 'heats' but not in overall aggregate result drove the following cars. Carlos Reutemann (Williams FW07C/12); Hector Rebaque (Brabham BT49C/12); Andrea de Cesaris (McLaren MP4/1-1).
PP – Part One, Arnoux, 1;05.95; Part Two, result of Part One.
FL – Overall, Prost, 1;09.14, 122.94 mph.

Goodyear servicing Williams and Brabham again for first time since their withdrawal at end of 1980, their race tyres better than result suggests, Michelin qualifiers better – sticky Michelins on Renaults for restart gave them big advantage in unrealistic race.

18-7-81 BRITISH GP,
Silverstone – 68 laps, 199.38 miles
1. John Watson (McLaren MP4/1-2), 68 laps in 1:26;54.80, 137.64 mph.
2. Carlos Reutemann (Williams FW07C/12), 68 in 1:27;35.45.
3. Jacques Laffite (Ligier-Matra V12 JS17-04;, 67. 4. Eddie Cheever (Tyrrell 010-2), 67. 5. Hector Rebaque (Brabham BT49C/12), 67. 6. Slim Borgudd (ATS D5-01), 67.
PP – René Arnoux (Renault turbo V6 RE30-3), 1;11.00; FL – Arnoux, 1;15.067, 140.61 mph.

Villeneuve lost Ferrari lap 4 at Woodcote chicane, taking out Jones, Watson, de Cesaris. Watson rejoined 10th as Renaults extended lead; Piquet crashed 3rd place Brabham when tyre failed, Prost out with burned valves, Arnoux led Watson for 30 laps up to lap 50 when Renault engine began to falter. First win for carbon-fibre McLaren – high retirement rate.

2-8-81 GERMAN GP,
Hockenheim – 45 laps, 189.79 miles
1. Nelson Piquet (Brabham BT49C/14), 45 laps in 1:25;55.60, 132.53 mph.
2. Alain Prost (Renault turbo V6 RE30-2), 45 in 1:26;07.12.
3. Jacques Laffite (Ligier-Matra V12 JS17-04), 45. 4. Hector Rebaque (Brabham BT49C/12), 45. 5. Eddie Cheever (Tyrrell 011-1), 45. 6. John Watson (McLaren MP4/1-2), 44.
PP – Prost, 1;47.50; FL – Alan Jones (Williams FW07C/16), 1;52.42, 135.07 mph.

Early Renault/Williams battle until Jones's Monaco misfire returned; Prost's engine failed and Piquet caught Prost despite damaged Brabham skirt. Good drive by Rebaque; Watson unhappy with spare McLaren's ride.

16-8-81 AUSTRIAN GP,
Österreichring – 53 laps, 195.69 miles
1. Jacques Laffite (Ligier-Matra V12 JS17-04), 53 laps in 1:27;36.47, 134.03 mph.
2. René Arnoux (Renault turbo V6 RE30-3), 53 in 1:27;41.64.
3. Nelson Piquet (Brabham BT49C/14), 53. 4. Alan Jones (Williams FW07D/16), 53. 5. Carlos Reutemann (Williams FW07C/14), 53. 6. John Watson (McLaren MP4/1-3), 53.
PP – Arnoux, 1;32.018; FL – Laffite, 1;37.24, 136.17 mph.

New Ligier team manager Jabouille earmarked Michelin tyre as ideal for Austria during Zandvoort tyre tests – Laffite used it brilliantly to beat Arnoux's Renault in closing stages. Villeneuve led until brake trouble, then Renault monopoly before Prost crashed through suspension failure, and Arnoux fighting understeer was caught by Laffite.

30-8-81 DUTCH GP,
Zandvoort – 72 laps, 190.23 miles
1. Alain Prost (Renault turbo V6 RE30-4), 72 laps in 1:40;22.43, 113.71 mph.
2. Nelson Piquet (Brabham BT49C/14), 72 in 1:40;30.67.
3. Alan Jones (Williams FW07C/16), 72. 4. Hector Rebaque (Brabham BT49C/12), 71. 5. Elio de Angelis (Lotus 87 R3), 71. 6. Eliseo Salazar (Ensign N180 MN-15), 70.
PP – Prost, 1;18.176; FL – Jones, 1;21.83, 116.23 mph.

Fierce Jones/Prost duel decided in Renault's favour when Williams tyres 'went off'; Piquet's Brabham took title lead as Reutemann collided with Laffite's Ligier when disputing 4th place.

13-9-81 ITALIAN GP,
Monza – 52 laps, 187.41 miles
1. Alain Prost (Renault turbo V6 RE30-4), 52 laps in 1:26;33.897, 129.89 mph.
2. Alan Jones (Williams FW07D/16), 52 in 1:26;56.072.
3. Carlos Reutemann (Williams FW07C/17), 52. 4. Elio de Angelis (Lotus 87 R3), 52. 5. Didier Pironi (Ferrari turbo V6 126C 049), 52. 6. Nelson Piquet (Brabham BT49C/14), 51.
PP – René Arnoux (Renault turbo V6 RE30-3), 1;33.467; FL – Reutemann, 1;37.528, 133.03 mph.

Difficult race on damp surface. Prost supreme, Piquet lost 3rd place on last lap when engine blew, Jones overcame handicap of driving with broken finger. Reutemann fast in practice, set car up for dry.

hard drive into 3rd place, led Championship since Brazil.

27-9-81 CANADIAN GP,
Ile Notre Dame, Montreal – 70 laps, 191.90 miles*
*Race affected by rain, stopped after regulation two hours at 63 laps.
1. Jacques Laffite (Ligier-Matra V12 JS17-05), 63 laps in 2:01;25.205, 85.25 mph.
2. John Watson (McLaren MP4/1-4), 63 in 2:01;31.438.
3. Gilles Villeneuve (Ferrari turbo V6 126C 052), 63. 4. Bruno Giacomelli (Alfa Romeo 179-04), 62. 5. Nelson Piquet (Brabham BT49C/15), 62. 6. Elio de Angelis (Lotus 87 R3), 62.
PP – Piquet, 1;29.211; FL – Watson, 1;49.475, 90.11 mph.

Appallingly wet conditions, Michelin rain tyres supreme. Jones spun off when leading, Prost lost lead with locking brakes and Laffite raced home to have an outside chance of winning World Championship in Vegas!

17-10-81 CAESAR'S PALACE GP,
Las Vegas, USA – 75 laps, 169.50 miles
1. Alan Jones (Williams FW07C/D/16), 75 laps in 1:44;09.077, 97.90 mph.
2. Alain Prost (Renault turbo V6 RE30-4), 75 in 1:44;29.125.
3. Bruno Giacomelli (Alfa Romeo 179-04), 75. 4. Nigel Mansell (Lotus 87 R5), 75. 5. Nelson Piquet (Brabham BT49C/15), 75. 6. Jacques Laffite (Ligier-Matra V12 JS17-03), 75.
PP – Carlos Reutemann (Williams FW07C/17), 1;17.821; FL – Didier Pironi (Ferrari turbo V6 126C 049), 1;20.156, 101.86 mph.

Reutemann freaked out of Championship, Jones rubbed in his abilities in farewell race, Laffite rose to 2nd before tyre stop; Watson 7th not enough to deny Piquet title.

1982

23-1-82 SOUTH AFRICAN GP,
Kyalami – 77 laps, 196.35 miles
1. Alain Prost (Renault turbo V6 RE30B-6), 77 laps in 1:32;08.401, 127.86 mph.
2. Carlos Reutemann (Williams FW07D/16), 77 in 1:32;23.347.
3. René Arnoux (Renault turbo V6 RE30B-5), 77. 4. Niki Lauda (McLaren MP4/1-4), 77. 5. Keke Rosberg (Williams FW07C/15), 77. 6. John Watson (McLaren MP4/1-5), 77.
PP – Arnoux, 1;06.351; FL – Prost, 1;08.278, 134.45 mph.

Seven teams on grid – Renaults, Ferraris, Brabham-BMWs and lone Toleman-Hart – filling first three rows. Piquet crashed, Patrese and Villeneuve blew turbos in first quarter, six laps later Pironi in pits. Renaults dominated from Williams pair until Prost had puncture, rejoined 8th, brilliant drive into lead after only 26 laps as Pironi regained 2nd before misfire; Arnoux lost lead to Prost as tyres wore.

21-3-82 BRAZILIAN GP,
Jacarepaguà, Rio de Janeiro – 63 laps, 196.94 miles
1. Alain Prost (Renault turbo V6 RE30B-6), 63 laps in 1:44;33.134, 112.97 mph.*
2. John Watson (McLaren MP4/1-5), 63 in 1:44;36.124.
3. Nigel Mansell (Lotus 91 R7), 63. 4. Michele Alboreto (Tyrrell 011/4), 63. 5. Manfred Winkelhock (ATS D5/3), 63. 6. Didier Pironi (Ferrari turbo V6 126C2 056), 62.
PP – Prost, 1;28.808; FL – Nelson Piquet (Brabham BT49/16), 1;36.582, 116.52 mph.
*Elevated to 1st place after disqualification of:
1. Nelson Piquet (Brabham BT49D/16), 63 laps in 1:43;53.760, 114.08 mph.
2. Keke Rosberg (Williams FW07C/17), 63 in 1:44;05.737.

Like Spain '81, as Villeneuve's turbo power held off lightweight cars of Piquet and Rosberg along straights for 29 laps until Ferrari crashed. Piquet won comfortably as Williams tyres were shot, Prost handicapped by misfire, Reutemann collided with Lauda then later Arnoux, putting them out. 'Brake cooling' ballast ploy judged illegal so first two later disqualified, rest elevated.

4-4-82 UNITED STATES GP WEST,
Long Beach, Calif. – 75.5 laps, 160.91 miles
1. Niki Lauda (McLaren MP4/1-4), 75 laps in 1:58;25.318, 81.40 mph.
2. Keke Rosberg (Williams FW07C/15), 75 in 1:58;39.978.
3. Riccardo Patrese (Brabham BT49C/15), 75. 4. Michele Alboreto (Tyrrell 011-4), 75. 5. Elio de Angelis (Lotus 91 R6), 74. 6. John Watson (McLaren MP4/1-2), 74.
PP – Andrea de Cesaris (Alfa Romeo V12 182/2), 1;27.316; FL – Lauda, 1;30.831, 84.42 mph.

Lauda looked set for pole until last-moment effort by de Cesaris won it for Alfa. Italian led until brush with wall after Lauda got by in clinical charge through field; remade track broke up in places.

25-4-82 'SAN MARINO' GP,
Imola, I – 60 laps, 187.92 miles
1. Didier Pironi (Ferrari turbo V6 126C2 056), 60 in 1:36;38.887, 116.66 mph.
2. Gilles Villeneuve (Ferrari turbo V6 126C2 058), 60 in 1:36;39.253.
3. Michele Alboreto (Tyrrell 011-5), 60. 4. Jean-Pierre Jarier (Osella FA1/003), 59. 5. Eliseo Salazar (ATS D5/3), 57.
UNC '6th'. Teo Fabi (Toleman-Hart 4 hart TG181-07), 52.
PP – René Arnoux (Renault turbo V6 RE30B-7), 1;29.765; FL – Pironi, 1;35.036, 118.63 mph.

Ten FOCA teams boycotted race in ill-judged move marking end of FOCA's dominant power; 14 starters. Ferrari show went wrong as Pironi ignored pit signals and broke lead from aggrieved – if naïve – Villeneuve.

9-5-82 BELGIAN GP,
Zolder – 70 laps, 185.36 miles

1. John Watson (McLaren MP4/1-2). 70 laps in 1:35:41.995, 116.20 mph.
2. Keke Rosberg (Williams FW08/3), 0 in 1:35:49.263.
3. Eddie Cheever (Ligier-Matra V12 , S17-06), 69. 4. Elio de Angelis (Lotus 91 R6), 68. 5. Nelson Piquet (Brabham-turbo 4 BMW BT50/3), 67. 6. Chico Serra (Fittipaldi F8D/3), 67.
PP – Alain Prost (Renault turbo V6 E30B-F) 1:15.701; FL – Watson, 1:20.214, 118.85 mph.

Villeneuve killed in practice crash, Pironi DNS. Rosberg looked set to win from Lauda but tyre trouble for both let Watson win on penultimate lap, running perfect set-up; Lauda 3rd on road, disqualified as car underweight when scrutineered.

23-5-82 MONACO GP,
Monte Carlo – 76 laps, 156.41 miles

1. Riccardo Patrese (Brabham 49D/17), 76 laps in 1:54:11.259, 82.21 mph.
2. Didier Pironi (Ferrari turbo V6 126C2 059), 75 out of fuel.
3. Andrea de Cesaris (Alfa Romeo V12 182/4), 75 out of fuel.
4. Nigel Mansell (Lotus 91 R7), 75. 5. Elio de Angelis (Lotus 91 R6), 75. 6. Derek Daly (Williams FW08/4) 74 crash damage.
PP – René Arnoux (Renault turbo V6 RE30B-8), 1:23.281; FL – Patrese, 1:29.354, 85.79 mph.

Arnoux spun and stalled lap 15, Prost took over with Patrese challenging but tried too hard on damp track and crashed lap 73; lap 75 Patrese spun, Pironi led then ran out of fuel. Daly's Williams potential winner but damaged rear end in spin; de Cesaris's Alfa out of fuel, so Patrese won extraordinary event.

6-6-82 DETROIT GP,
Michigan, USA – 62 laps, 160.58 miles

1. John Watson (McLaren MP4/1-5), 62 laps in 1:58:41.043, 78.20 mph.
2. Eddie Cheever (Ligier-Matra 12 JS17-06), 62 in 1:58;56.769.
3. Didier Pironi (Ferrari turbo V6 126C2 056), 62. 4. Keke Rosberg (Williams FW08/3), 62. 5. Derek Daly (Williams FW08/4), 62. 6. Jacques Laffite (Ligier-Matra V12 JS17-04), 61.
PP – Alain Prost (Renault turbo V6 R30B-6), 1:48.537; FL – Prost, 1:50.438, 81.28 mph.

Race stopped after minor accident lap 7, restarted with McLarens on harder Michelins, Watson tigered through pack to brilliant win. Good drive by Cheever to pass Pironi, Prost/Rosberg led and broke, Lauda crashed when 2nd, spoiling McLaren 1-2.

13-6-82 CANADIAN GP,
Ile Notre Dame, Montreal – 70 laps, 191.90 miles*

*Race stopped on first lap by start line collision, fatal to Ricardo Paletti; restarted with Pironi in spare Ferrari.

1. Nelson Piquet (Brabham-turbo 4 BMW BT50/3), 70 laps in 1:46:39.577, 107.93 mph.
2. Riccardo Patrese (Brabham BT49D/18), 70 in 1:46:53.376.
3. John Watson (McLaren MP4/1-5) 70. 4. Elio de Angelis (Lotus 91 R6), 69. 5. Marc Surer (Arrows A4/1), 69. 6. Andrea de Cesaris (Alfa Romeo V12 182/3), 69.
PP – Didier Pironi (Ferrari turbo V6 126C2 057), 1:27.509; FL – Pironi (Ferrari turbo V6 126C2 059) 1:28.323, 111.68 mph.

Brabham logistical triumph with different types of car 1-2, BMW turbo coming of age. Pironi's new pullrod suspension Ferrari stalled on pole, rammed fatally by Ricardo Paletti's Osella; restart with Pironi in spare car. Another disastrous Renault showing.

3-7-82 DUTCH GP,
Zandvoort – 72 laps, 190.23 miles

1. Didier Pironi (Ferrari turbo V6 126C2 060), 72 laps in 1:38:03.254, 116.40 mph.
2. Nelson Piquet (Brabham-turbo 4 BMW BT50/3), 72 in 1:38:24.903.
3. Keke Rosberg (Williams FW08,5), 72. 4. Niki Lauda (McLaren MP4/1-6), 72. 5. Derek Daly (Williams FW08/4), 71. 6. Mauro Baldi (Arrows A4/2), 71.
PP – Alain Prost (Renault turbo V6 RE30B-7), 1:14.233; FL – Derek Warwick (Toleman-turbo 4 Hart TG181-06), 1:19.780, 119.22 mph.

Renault front row for third successive year, both retired. Pironi dominant for Ferrari on Goodyear race tyres, Arnoux crashed heavily in Renault.

18-7-82 BRITISH GP,
Brands Hatch – 76 laps, 198.63 miles

1. Niki Lauda (McLaren MP4/1-6), 76 laps in 1:35:33.812, 124.70 mph.
2. Didier Pironi (Ferrari turbo V6 126C2 060), 76 in 1:35:59.538.
3. Patrick Tambay (Ferrari 126C2 061), 76. 4. Elio de Angelis (Lotus 91 R8), 76. 5. Derek Daly (Williams FW08/4), 76. 6. Alain Prost (Renault turbo V6 RE30B-6), 76.
PP – Keke Rosberg (Williams FW08/, 1:09.540; FL – Brian Henton (Tyrrell 011-2), 1:13.028, 128 34 mph.

Rosberg failed to start on pole, Patrese startline collision removed Arnoux; Piquet pulled away on light tanks towards scheduled refuelling stop but was out at 9 laps, Lauda taking 19th GP win of career.

25-7-82 FRENCH GP,
Ricard-Castellet – 54 laps, 194.14 miles

1. René Arnoux (Renault turbo V6 RE30B-8), 54 laps in 1:33:33.217, 124.99 mph.
2. Alain Prost (Renault turbo V6 RE30-6), 54 in 1:33:50.525.
3. Didier Pironi (Ferrari turbo V6 126C2 060), 54. 4. Patrick Tambay (Ferrari 126C2 06?), 54. 5. Keke Rosberg (Williams FW08/5), 54. 6. Michele Alboreto (Tyrrell 011/5), 54.
PP – Arnoux, 1:34.406; FL – Riccardo Patrese (Brabham-turbo V6 BM50/4), 1:40.075, 129 37 mph.

Renault intended Prost to win, bolstering outside chance of Championship, but as Arnoux pulled out 20 sec lead he wasn't about to give it up. Brabham-BMWs slaughtered all opposition on half-tanks and soft tyres in early stages, both broke before scheduled stops. Potentially catastrophic lap 11 accident put Mass's March into spectator area, ground-effects safety questions highlighted.

8-8-82 GERMAN GP,
Hockenheim – 45 laps, 189.86 miles

1. Patrick Tambay (Ferrari turbo V6 126C2 061), 45 laps in 1:27:25.178, 130.43 mph.
2. René Arnoux (Renault turbo V6 RE30B-8), 45 in 1:27:41.557.
3. Keke Rosberg (Williams FW08/1), 44. 4. Michele Alboreto (Tyrrell 011-5), 44. 5. Bruno Giacomelli (Alfa Romeo V12 182/3), 44. 6. Marc Surer (Arrows A4/1), 44.
PP – Didier Pironi (Ferrari turbo V6 126C2 061), 1:47.947; FL – Nelson Piquet (Brabham-turbo 4 BMW BT50/3), 1:54.035, 133.33 mph.

Pironi's career ended by ghastly practice accident; Tambay underlined Ferrari potential after Piquet collided with back-marker and took up boxing, Prost slowed with injection trouble, Arnoux unable to respond, Watson crashed when suspension broke. Lauda DNS, injured wrist in practice.

15-8-82 AUSTRIAN GP,
Österreichring – 53 laps, 195.69 miles

1. Elio de Angelis (Lotus 91 R8), 53 laps in 1:25:02.212, 138.07 mph.
2. Keke Rosberg (Williams FW08/1), 53 in 1:25:02.262.
3. Jacques Laffite (Ligier-Matra V12 JS19-03), 52. 4. Patrick Tambay (Ferrari turbo V6 126C2 061), 52. 5. Patrick Tambay (McLaren MP4/1-6), 52. 6. Mauro Baldi (Arrows A4/2), 52.
PP – Nelson Piquet (Brabham-turbo 4 BMW BT50/3), 1:27.612; FL – Piquet, 1:33.699, 141.87 mph.

Brabham pit stops reached for first time, cars still broke; Prost left leading in last turbo until injection failed five laps from end, de Angelis just held off Rosberg who made up 4 secs in those last few laps as Lotus misfired. 150th Cosworth victory, de Angelis was just 9 years old when Clark won first in 1967.

29-8-82 'SWISS GP',
Dijon-Prenois, F – 80 laps, 188.88 miles

1. Keke Rosberg (Williams FW08/5), 80 laps in 1:32:41.087, 122.29 mph.
2. Alain Prost (Renault turbo V6 RE30B-10), 80 in 1:32:45.529.
3. Niki Lauda (McLaren MP4/1-7), 80. 4. Nelson Piquet (Brabham-turbo 4 BMW BT50/5), 79. 5. Riccardo Patrese (Brabham-turbo 4 BMW BT50/4), 79. 6. Elio de Angelis (Lotus 91 R8), 79.
PP – Prost, 1;01.380; FL – Prost, 1:07.477, 125.97 mph.

No Ferraris, Tambay withdrawn due to pinched nerve. Prost dominant first 10 laps until oil went down on track until Prost eased to save car and tyres; Arnoux set to inherit lead when injection trouble intervened, Rosberg fastest on track at end. Organizers almost ended race two laps short with Prost still leading, when Williams management intervened; confusion saw 81 laps run instead of 80! Brabham-BMWs off pace.

12-9-82 ITALIAN GP,
Monza – 52 laps, 187.40 miles

1. René Arnoux (Renault turbo V6 RE30B-5), 52 laps in 1:22:25.734, 136.39 mph.
2. Patrick Tambay (Ferrari turbo V6 126C2 062), 52 in 1:22:39.39.
3. Mario Andretti (Ferrari turbo V6 126C2 061), 52. 4. John Watson (McLaren MP4/1-5), 52. 5. Michele Alboreto (Tyrrell 011-6), 51. 6. Eddie Cheever (Ligier-Matra V12 JS19-01), 51.
PP – Andretti, 1:28.473; FL – Arnoux, 1:33.619, 138.59 mph.

Arnoux took lead from Tambay ending lap 1 and was never headed, Brabham challenge fizzled out, Prost lost 3rd with turbo failure.

25-9-82 CAESAR'S PALACE GP,
Las Vegas, USA – 75 laps, 170.10 miles

1. Michele Alboreto (Tyrrell 011/6), 75 laps in 1:41:56.888, 100.10 mph.
2. John Watson (McLaren MP4/1-5), 75 in 1:42:24.180.
3. Eddie Cheever (Ligier-Matra V12 JS19-01), 75. 4. Alain Prost (Renault turbo V6 RE30B-10), 75. 5. Keke Rosberg (Williams FW08/5), 75. 6. Eddie Cheever (Williams FW08/4), 74.
PP – Prost, 1:16.356; FL – Alboreto, 1:19.639, 102.52 mph.

Rosberg Champion in steady, heady drive, Watson's outside chance taken brilliantly but not lucky enough, Renault again in trouble after leading. Alboreto inherited good lead, cretinous circuit but ideal for Tyrrell and driver – no offence meant.

1983

13-3-83 BRAZILIAN GP,
Jacarepaguà, Rio de Janeiro – 63 laps, 196.945 miles

1. Nelson Piquet (Brabham-turbo 4 BMW BT50/3), 63 laps in 1:48:27.731, 108.926 mph.
2. Keke Rosberg (Williams FW08C/7), 63 in 1:48:48.362.*
3. Niki Lauda (McLaren MP4/1-7), 63 in 1:49:19.614. 4. Jacques Laffite (Williams FW08C/8), 63. 5. Patrick Tambay (Ferrari turbo V6 126C2B 063), 63. 6. Marc Surer (Arrows A6/2), 63.
*Disqualified for alleged push-start, elevating slower finishers including Alain Prost (Renault turbo V6 RE30C-12), 62 laps.
PP – Rosberg, 1:34.526; FL – Piquet, 1:39.829, 112.733 mph.
First 'flat-bottom' race. Rosberg displaced from early lead by Piquet, brief pit fire delayed Williams

in team's first refuelling stop, McLarens strong, Watson out when engine seized while setting up challenge for lead, Prost Renault handicapped by rear tyre vibration.

27-3-83 UNITED STATES GP WEST,
Long Beach, Calif. – 75 laps, 152.625 miles

1. John Watson (McLaren MP4/1-6), 75 laps in 1:53:34.889, 80.6 mph.
2. Niki Lauda (McLaren MP4/1-7), 75 in 1:54:02.882.
3. René Arnoux (Ferrari turbo V6 126C2B 064), 75. 4. Jacques Laffite (Williams FW08C/8), 74. 5. Marc Surer (Arrows A6/3), 74. 6. Johnny Cecotto (Theodore N183-18), 74.
PP – Tambay, (Ferrari turbo V6 126C2B 063), 1:26.117; FL – Lauda, 1:28.33, 82.939 mph.

McLaren classic, 22-23 on grid, ideal race set-up on Michelin tyres. Tambay Ferrari rammed by Rosberg Williams to lose lead, McLarens took lead lap 45, lapped Laffite lap 75.

10-4-83 Race of Champions,
Brands Hatch, GB – 40 laps, 104.544 miles

1. Keke Rosberg (Williams FW08C/6), 40 laps in 53;15.253, 117.886 mph.
2. Danny Sullivan (Tyrrell 011-2), 40 in 53;15.743.
3. Alan Jones (Arrows A6/3), 40. 4. Brian Henton (Theodore N183-18), 40. 5. Raul Boesel (Ligier JS21-03), 40. 6. Jean-Louis Schlesser (March-RAM 01-02), 39.
PP – Rosberg, 1:15.766; FL – René Arnoux (Ferrari turbo V6 126C2B 063), 1:17.826, 120.897 mph.

Sullivan shone in inconsequential minor race, Rosberg slowed by badly blistered tyre.

17-4-83 FRENCH GP,
Ricard-Castellet – 54 laps, 194.95 miles

1. Alain Prost (Renault turbo V6 RE40-01), 54 laps in 1:34:13.913, 124.191 mph.
2. Nelson Piquet (Brabham turbo 4 BMW BT2/3), 54 in 1:34:43.633.
3. Eddie Cheever (Renault turbo V6 RE40-02), 54. 4. Patrick Tambay (Ferrari turbo V6 126C2B 065), 54. 5. Keke Rosberg (Williams FW08C/7), 53. 6. Jacques Laffite (Williams FW08C/8), 53.
PP – Prost, 1;36.672; FL – Prost, 1:42.695, 126.555 mph.

Ferrari and Goodyear problems, Renault dominant on Michelins; Brabham-BMWs matched Renault power but not handling, non-turbo Williams drivers drove their hearts out in hopeless task.

1-5-83 'SAN MARINO' GP,
Imola, I – 60 laps, 187.90 miles

1. Patrick Tambay (Ferrari turbo V6 126C2B 065), 60 laps in 1:37:52.460, 115.251 mph.
2. Alain Prost (Renault turbo V6 RE40-03), 60.
3. René Arnoux (Ferrari 126C2B 064), 59. 4. John Watson (McLaren MP4/1-6), 59. 5. Marc Surer (Arrows A6/2), 59.
PP – René Arnoux (Ferrari 126C2B 064), 1:31.238; FL – Riccardo Patrese (Brabham-turbo 4 BMW BT52/4), 1:34.437, 119.383 mph.

Brabham-BMW dominant, yet Piquet stalled on line, Arnoux lost lead to Patrese lap 6, slow pit stop left Patrese 2nd, he retook lead then crashed, Tambay left to win. Cosworth cars now outclassed even on slower circuits.

15-5-83 MONACO GP,
Monte Carlo – 76 laps, 156.406 miles

1. Keke Rosberg (Williams FW08C/7), 76 laps in 1:56:38.121, 80.521 mph.
2. Nelson Piquet (Brabham-turbo 4 BMW BT52/3), 76 in 1:56;56.596.
3. Alain Prost (Renault turbo V6 RE40-03), 76. 4. Patrick Tambay (Ferrari 126C2B 065), 76. 5. Danny Sullivan (Tyrrell 011-5), 76. 6. Mauro Baldi (Alfa Romeo turbo V8 183T-04), 74.
PP – René Arnoux (Ferrari 126C2B 064), 1:25.182; FL – Piquet, 1:27.283, 84.881 mph.

Wet race won by Rosberg's brilliant natural car control, Laffite's sister Williams lost 2nd place with gearbox trouble.

22-5-83 BELGIAN GP,
Spa-Francorchamps – 40 laps, 173.127 miles

1. Alain Prost (Renault turbo V6 RE40-03), 40 laps in 1:27;11.502, 119.135 mph.
2. Patrick Tambay (Ferrari turbo V6 126C2B 065), 40 in 1:27;34.684.
3. Eddie Cheever (Renault turbo V6 RE40-02), 40. 4. Nelson Piquet (Brabham turbo 4 BMW BT52/3), 40. 5. Keke Rosberg (Williams FW08C/7), 40. 6. Jacques Laffite (Williams FW08C/8), 40.
PP – Prost, 2;04.615; FL – Andrea de Cesaris (Alfa Romeo turbo V8 183T/02), 2;07.493, 121.923 mph.

F1 return to Spa after 13 years, new circuit still put premium on power. Alfa controlled race until pit stop but injection failed 15 laps from end, Prost stroked through, Piquet fell 2nd to 4th when lost 5th gear, Williams consistency paid minor dividends.

5-6-83 DETROIT GP,
Michigan, USA – 60 laps, 150 miles

1. Michele Alboreto (Tyrrell 011-4), 60 laps in 1:50:53.669, 81.158 mph.
2. Keke Rosberg (Williams FW08C/7), 60 in 1:51;01.371.
3. John Watson (McLaren MP4/1C-8), 60. 4. Nelson Piquet (Brabham-turbo 4 BMW BT52/3), 60. 5. Jacques Laffite (Williams FW08C/8), 60. 6. Nigel Mansell (Lotus 92 R10), 59.
PP – René Arnoux (Ferrari turbo V6 126C2B 064), 1:44.734; FL – Arnoux, 1:47.668, 83.590 mph.

Brabham quietly planned to run non-stop but Piquet lost lead with puncture 10 laps from end; Cosworth cars lucky to take five of top six places. Cosworth V8's 155th and last F1 victory.

12-6-83 CANADIAN GP,
Ile Notre Dame, Montreal – 70 laps, 191.82 miles

1. René Arnoux (Ferrari turbo V6 126C2B 064), 70 laps in 1:48;31.838, 106.044 mph.
2. Eddie Cheever (Renault turbo V6 RE40-02), 70 in 1:49;13.867.
3. Patrick Tambay (Ferrari turbo V6 126C2B 065), 70. 4. Keke Rosberg (Williams FW08C/7), 70. 5. Alain Prost (Renault turbo V6 RE40-03), 70. 6. John Watson (McLaren MP4/1C-8), 69.
PP – Arnoux, 1:28.729; FL – Tambay, 1:30.851, 108.583 mph.

Faultless Ferrari win, Arnoux only gave up lead in refuelling stop, Piquet retired when 3rd, Prost's Renault down on power and suffering puncture, Patrese 2nd until gearbox failed.

16-7-83 BRITISH GP,
Silverstone – 67 laps, 196.44 miles

1. Alain Prost (Renault turbo V6 RE40-05), 67 laps in 1:24:39.780, 139.218 mph.
2. Nelson Piquet (Brabham-turbo 4 BMW BT52B/5), 67 in 1:24:58.941.
3. Patrick Tambay (Ferrari turbo V6 126C3 067), 67. 4. Nigel Mansell (Lotus-Renault turbo V6 94T R7), 67. 5. René Arnoux (Ferrari turbo V6 126C3 066), 67. 6. Niki Lauda (McLaren MP4/1C-7) 66.
PP – Arnoux, 1:09.462; FL – Prost, 1:14.212, 142.23 mph.

New Ferraris led 20 laps until tyres lost edge, Prost's Renault took over with Piquet emphasizing Michelin dominance, taking 2nd on lap 31, leading when Prost stopped but later settling for 2nd after his own stop. Much fuss over pace of new Lotuses; Honda returned to F1 with turbo V6 engine in Spirit 201; Lauda's McLaren won 'Cosworth class'.

17-8-83 GERMAN GP,
Hockenheim – 45 laps, 190.055 miles

1. René Arnoux (Ferrari turbo V6 126C3 066), 45 laps in 1:27:10.319, 130.813 mph.
2. Andrea de Cesaris (Alfa Romeo turbo V8 183T/03), 45 in 1:28:20.971.
3. Riccardo Patrese (Brabham-turbo 4 BMW BT52B/6), 45. 4. Alain Prost (Renault turbo V6 RE40-05), 45. 5. Niki Lauda (McLaren MP4/1C-7), 44.* 6. Jacques Laffite (Williams FW08C/8), 44.
*Disqualified for reversing in pit lane after overshooting refuelling marks.
PP – Patrick Tambay (Ferrari turbo V6 126C3 067), 1;49.328; FL – Arnoux, 1;53.938, 133.444 mph.

Tambay led two laps, Arnoux the rest save for refuelling stop; Piquet secure 2nd with three laps to go when fuel filter cracked, fire retired Brabham-BMW, Cheever Renault broke fuel pump drive giving de Cesaris Alfa's best result in modern F1; Prost Renault handicapped by loss of 5th gear.

24-8-83 AUSTRIAN GP,
Österreichring – 53 laps, 195.699 miles

1. Alain Prost (Renault turbo V6 RE40-05), 53 laps in 1:24;32.745, 138.872 mph.
2. René Arnoux (Ferrari turbo V6 126C3 068), 53 in 1:24;39.580.
3. Nelson Piquet (Brabham-turbo 4 BMW BT52B/5), 53. 4. Eddie Cheever (Renault turbo V6 RE40-04), 53. 5. Nigel Mansell (Lotus-Renault turbo V6 94T R2), 52. 6. Niki Lauda (McLaren MP4/1C-7), 51.
PP – Patrick Tambay (Ferrari turbo V6 126C3 067), 1;29.871; FL – Prost, 1:33.961, 141.461 mph.

Ferrari front row, Tambay led until baulked by Jarier's Ligier letting Arnoux and Piquet by; Arnoux gearbox trouble allowed Prost to catch and pass with six laps to run. Cheever, handicapped by wrong tyre choice, almost caught Piquet (losing revs) on line. Lauda McLaren won 'Cosworth class' again.

28-8-83 DUTCH GP,
Zandvoort – 72 laps, 190.228 miles

1. René Arnoux (Ferrari turbo V6 126C3 066), 72 laps in 1:38;41.950, 115.640 mph.
2. Patrick Tambay (Ferrari turbo V6 126C3 067), 72 in 1:39;02.789.
3. John Watson (McLaren MP4/1C-2), 72. 4. Derek Warwick (Toleman-turbo 4 Hart TG183B-04), 72. 5. Mauro Baldi (Alfa Romeo turbo V8 183T/04), 72. 6. Michele Alboreto (Tyrrell 012-1), 71.
PP – Nelson Piquet (Brabham-turbo 4 BMW BT52B/5), 1:15.630; FL – Arnoux, 1:19.863, 119.097 mph.

Tambay, alongside Piquet on grid, muffed start and fell to 21st – Arnoux won from 10th on grid, Tambay fought through to form Ferrari 1-2. Prost/Piquet collision when disputing lead on lap 42, Lauda debut of McLaren MP4/1E TAG-Porsche turbo V6 niggled Watson in old Cosworth car, superb drive to 3rd place, so McLaren won class in their Cosworth swansong.

11-9-83 ITALIAN GP,
Monza – 52 laps, 187.403 miles

1. Nelson Piquet (Brabham-turbo 4 BMW BT52B/5), 52 laps in 1:23;10.880, 135.178 mph.
2. René Arnoux (Ferrari turbo V6 126C3 066), 52 in 1:23;21.092.
3. Eddie Cheever (Renault turbo V6 RE40-04), 52. 4. Patrick Tambay (Ferrari turbo V6 126C3 069), 52. 5. Elio de Angelis (Lotus-Renault turbo V6 94T R1), 52. 6. Derek Warwick (Toleman-turbo 4 Hart TG183B-04), 52.
PP – Riccardo Patrese (Brabham-turbo 4 BMW BT52B/6), 1;29.122; FL – Piquet, 1:34.431, 137.393 mph.

Championship leader Prost's race ended in turbo failure, Patrese blew engine lap 3, Piquet led thereafter. First race to see turbocharged cars filling first six places.

25-9-83 EUROPEAN GP,
Brands Hatch, GB – 76 laps, 198.63 miles
1. Nelson Piquet (Brabham-turbo 4 BT52B/5), 76 laps in 1:36'45.865, 123.165 mph.
2. Alain Prost (Renault turbo V6 RE40-05), 76 in 1:36'52.436.
3. Nigel Mansell (Lotus-Renault turbo V6 94T R2), 76. **4.** Andrea de Cesaris (Alfa Romeo turbo V8 183T/05, 76. **5.** Derek Warwick (Toleman-turbo 4 Hart TG183B-04), 76. **6.** Bruno Giacomelli (Toleman-turbo 4 Hart TG183B-03), 76.
PP – Elio de Angelis (Lotus-Renault turbo V6 94T R1), 1:12.092; FL – Mansell, 1:14.342, 126.563 mph.
Ferrari débâcle – Arnoux 9th, Tambay crashed with brake failure when 4th. De Angelis 1st pole in Lotus but collided with Patrese in early duel for lead, fine Warwick drive delayed by fire extinguisher discharging into cockpit; Piquet unmatchable overall.

15-10-83 SOUTH AFRICAN GP,
Kyalami – 77 laps, 196.35 miles
1. Riccardo Patrese (Brabham-turbo 4 BMW BT52B/6), 77 laps in 1:33'25.708, 126.100 mph.
2. Andrea de Cesaris (Alfa Romeo turbo V8 183T/03), 77 in 1:33'35.027.
3. Nelson Piquet (Brabham-turbo 4 BMW BT52B/5), 77. **4.** Derek Warwick (Toleman-turbo 4 Hart TG183B-02), 76. **5.** Keke Rosberg (Williams-turbo V6 Honda FW09/1), 76. **6.** Eddie Cheever (Renault turbo V6 RE40-04), 76.
PP – Patrick Tambay (Ferrari 126C3 069), 1;06.554; FL – Piquet, 1,09.948, 131.245 mph.
Championship decided as Piquet started very light, tore away from field with team-mate 2nd, stopped early for conservative hard tyres and refuelling then settled back for Champion finish as Prost lost 4th place and title in turbo failure on lap 35. Lauda lost 2nd place after charge from 12th in new McLaren turbo when electrics failed six laps from end.

1984

25-3-84 BRAZILIAN GP,
Jacarepaguà, Rio de Janeiro – 61 laps, 190.692 miles
1. Alain Prost (McLaren-turbo V6 TAG-Porsche MP4/2-2), 61 laps in 1:42'34.492, 111.543 mph.
2. Keke Rosberg (Williams-turbo V6 Honda FW09/4), 61 in 1:43'15.006.
3. Elio de Angelis (Lotus-turbo V6 Renault 95T R3), 61. **4.** Eddie Cheever (Alfa Romeo turbo V8 184T/01), 60. **5.** Martin Brundle (Tyrrell 012-3), 60. **6.** Patrick Tambay (Renault turbo V6 RE50-03), 59.
PP – de Angelis, 1;28.392; FL – Prost, 1,36.499, 116.622 mph.
New 220-litre race fuel restriction serious worry for all but TAG-Porsche. Alboreto's Ferrari spun from lead lap 12, Lauda took over until lap 38 electrical failure, Warwick inherited lead for Renault before front suspension failed following earlier nudge from Lauda, allowing Prost win in largely untested new turbo McLaren.

7-4-84 SOUTH AFRICAN GP,
Kyalami – 75 laps, 191.247 miles
1. Niki Lauda (McLaren-turbo V6 TAG-Porsche MP4/2-1), 75 laps in 1:29;43.430, 126.367 mph.
2. Alain Prost (McLaren-turbo V6 TAG-Porsche MP4/2-3), 75 in 1:30;29.380.
3. Derek Warwick (Renault turbo V6 RE50/04), 74. **4.** Riccardo Patrese (Alfa Romeo turbo V8 184T/02), 73. **5.** Andrea de Cesaris (Ligier-turbo V6 Renault JS23-03), 73. **6.** Ayrton Senna (Toleman-turbo 4 Hart TG183B-05), 72.
PP – Nelson Piquet (Brabham-turbo 4 BMW BT53/5), 1;04.871; FL – Patrick Tambay (Renault turbo V6 RE50/03), 1;08.877, 133.279 mph.
McLarens utterly dominant with brilliant race set-up despite Prost having to race spare car at last moment, not properly adjusted to his needs; superb drive from back of field to team 1-2.

29-4-84 BELGIAN GP,
Zolder – 70 laps, 185.38 miles
1. Michele Alboreto (Ferrari turbo V6 126C4/074), 70 laps in 1:36;32.048, 115.221 mph.
2. Derek Warwick (Renault turbo V6 RE50/04), 70 in 1:37;14.434.
3. René Arnoux (Ferrari turbo V6 126C4/073), 70. **4.** Keke Rosberg (Williams-turbo V6 Honda FW09/4), 69. **5.** Elio de Angelis (Lotus-turbo V6 Renault 95T R3), 69. **6.** Stefan Bellof (Tyrrell 012-2), 69.
PP – Alboreto, 1;14.846; FL – Arnoux, 1;19.294, 120.233 mph.
Alboreto's first Ferrari pole as McLaren and BMW suffered many practice blow-ups, Rosberg bad start followed by meteoric drive into 3rd place at price of running out of fuel last lap, 1st win for Italian Ferrari driver since Monza 1966.

6-5-84 'SAN MARINO' GP,
Imola, I – 60 laps, 187.90 miles
1. Alain Prost (McLaren-turbo V6 TAG-Porsche MP4/2-3), 60 in 1:36'53.679, 116.354 mph.
2. René Arnoux (Ferrari turbo V6 126C4/073), 60 in 1:37'07.095.
3. Elio de Angelis (Lotus-turbo V6 Renault 95T R3), 59. **4.** Derek Warwick (Renault turbo V6 RE50/04), 59. **5.** Stefan Bellof (Tyrrell 012-1), 59. **6.** Thierry Boutsen (Arrows A6/4), 59.
PP – Nelson Piquet (Brabham-turbo 4 BMW BT53/5), 1;28.517; FL – Piquet, 1,33.275, 120.869 mph.
Prost led from start, through spin, through refuelling stop; Lauda delayed by piston failed; worst Williams race since 1978, both retiring; Brabham BMWs burned turbos.

20-5-84 FRENCH GP,
Dijon-Prenois – 79 laps, 186.535 miles
1. Niki Lauda (McLaren-turbo V6 TAG-Porsche MP4/2-1), 79 laps in 1:31;11.951, 125.531 mph.
2. Patrick Tambay (Renault turbo V6 RE50/05), 79 in 1:31;19.105.
3. Nigel Mansell (Lotus-turbo V6 Renault 95T R2), 79. **4.** René Arnoux (Ferrari turbo V6 126C4/073), 79. **5.** Elio de Angelis (Lotus-turbo V6 Renault 95T R3), 79. **6.** Keke Rosberg (Williams-turbo V6 Honda FW09/5, 78.
PP – Lauda, 1;02.200; FL – Alain Prost (McLaren-turbo V6 TAG-Porsche MP4/2-2), 1;05.257, 133.242 mph.
First Renault pole in almost a year, Lauda win after Prost misfortune and major work by Porsche to rush fresh engines from Weissach overnight pre-race after spate of practice problems.

3-6-84 MONACO GP,
Monte Carlo – 31 laps, 63.797 miles*
*Rain shortened race from scheduled 78 laps.
1. Alain Prost (McLaren-turbo V6 TAG-Porsche MP4/2-2), 31 laps in 1:01;07.740, 62.619 mph.
2. Ayrton Senna (Toleman-turbo 4 Hart TG184-02), 31 in 1:01;15.186.
3. Stefan Bellof (Tyrrell 012-4), 31. **4.** René Arnoux (Ferrari turbo V6 126C4/073), 31. **5.** Keke Rosberg (Williams-turbo V6 Honda FW09/5), 31. **6.** Elio de Angelis (Lotus-turbo V6 Renault 95T R3), 31.
PP – Prost, 1;22.661; FL – Senna, 1;54.334, 64.798 mph.
Flooded track; Mansell Lotus led after front-row start before crashing through driver error. Prost lead gobbled up by Senna's Toleman which was bound to take lead when red flag abruptly stopped race, saving very lucky Prost McLaren win. Renault first-corner collision débâcle injured Tambay, Lauda spun out later.

17-6-84 CANADIAN GP,
Ile Notre Dame, Montreal – 70 laps, 191.82 miles
1. Nelson Piquet (Brabham-turbo 4 BMW BT53/5), 70 laps in 1:46;23.748, 108.171 mph.
2. Niki Lauda (McLaren-turbo V6 TAG-Porsche MP4/2-1), 70 in 1:46;26.360.
3. Alain Prost (McLaren-turbo V6 TAG-Porsche MP4/2-2), 70. **4.** Elio de Angelis (Lotus-turbo V6 Renault 95T R3), 69. **5.** René Arnoux (Ferrari turbo V6 126C4/075), 68. **6.** Nigel Mansell (Lotus-turbo V6 Renault 95T R2), 68.
PP – Piquet, 1;25.442; FL – Piquet, 1;28.763, 111.691 mph.
Despite burned foot due to new nose oil cooler, altered weight-distribution Brabham ran superbly for Piquet win; McLarens still 1-2 as usual, only this time Brabham-BMW survived to finish ahead of them!

24-6-84 DETROIT GP,
Michigan, USA – 63 laps, 157.50 miles
1. Nelson Piquet (Brabham-turbo 4 BMW BT53/3), 63 laps in 1:55;41.842, 81.679 mph.
2. Martin Brundle (Tyrrell 012-2), 63 in 1:55;42.679.*
3. Elio de Angelis (Lotus-turbo V6 Renault 95T R3), 63. **4.** Teo Fabi (Brabham-turbo 4 BMW BT53/2), 63. **5.** Alain Prost (McLaren-turbo V6 TAG-Porsche MP4/2-2), 63. **6.** Jacques Laffite (Williams-turbo V6 Honda FW09/3), 62.
*Subsequently disqualified for alleged technical infringement.
PP – Piquet, 1;40.980; FL – Derek Warwick (Renault turbo V6 RE50), 1;46.221, 84.729 mph.
Mansell Lotus sparked first-start collision. Restart with Piquet in spare car still leading start to finish, eased up allowing Brundle to close apparently dramatically near finish in car suiting street circuit.

8-7-84 DALLAS GP,
Fair Park, Texas, USA – 67 laps, 162.408 miles
1. Keke Rosberg (Williams-turbo V6 Honda FW09/5), 67 laps in 2:01;22.617, 80.283 mph.
2. René Arnoux (Ferrari turbo V6 126C4/075), 67 in 2:01;45.081.
3. Elio de Angelis (Lotus-turbo V6 Renault 95T R3), 66. **4.** Jacques Laffite (Williams-turbo V6 Honda FW09/3), 65. **5.** PierCarlo Ghinzani (Osella-turbo V8 Alfa Romeo FA1F-02), 65. **6.** Nigel Mansell (Lotus-turbo V6 Renault 95T R2), 64.
PP – Mansell, 1;37.041; FL – Niki Lauda (McLaren-turbo V6 TAG-Porsche MP4/2-1), 1;45.353, 82.830 mph.
Long hot race on crumbling circuit; 4-5 car battle for lead, Warwick's Renault and McLarens all retired. Mansell led from pole for half race but damaged car, collapsed exhausted in ill-advised and now illegal attempt to push across line at finish; classic drives by Rosberg and Arnoux.

22-7-84 BRITISH GP,
Brands Hatch – 71 laps, 185.566 miles
1. Niki Lauda (McLaren-turbo V6 TAG-Porsche MP4/2-1), 71 laps in 1:29;28.532, 124.406 mph.
2. Derek Warwick (Renault turbo V6 RE50/08), 71 in 1:30;10.655.
3. Ayrton Senna (Toleman-turbo Hart TG184-02), 71. **4.** Elio de Angelis (Lotus-turbo V6 Renault 95T R3), 70. **5.** Michele Alboreto (Ferrari turbo V6 126C4/076), 70. **6.** René Arnoux (Ferrari turbo V6 126C4/075), 70.
PP – Nelson Piquet (Brabham-turbo 4 BMW BT53/4), 1;10.869; FL – Lauda, 1;13.191, 128.523 mph.
Initial Piquet/McLarens battle ended when race stopped after 11 laps by Palmer RAM crash. After restart Piquet lost boost pressure, Prost's gearbox failed; Lauda's day, and Warwick's and Senna's . . .

5-8-84 GERMAN GP,
Hockenheim – 44 laps, 185.83 miles
1. Alain Prost (McLaren-turbo V6 TAG-Porsche MP4/2-2), 44 laps in 1:24;43.210, 131.608 mph.
2. Niki Lauda (McLaren-turbo V6 TAG-Porsche MP4/2-1), 44 in 1:24;46.359.

3. Derek Warwick (Renault turbo V6 RE50/08), 44. **4.** Nigel Mansell (Lotus-turbo V6 Renault 95T R2), 44. **5.** Patrick Tambay (Renault turbo V6 RE50/09), 44. **6.** René Arnoux (Ferrari turbo V6 126C4/075), 43.
PP – Prost, 1;47.012; FL – Prost, 1;53.538, 133.915 mph.
Boring race – de Angelis Lotus led seven laps until Renault engine blew, Piquet led until transmission failed, then McLarens all the way; Senna crashed Toleman when wing fell off after fast start.

19-8-84 AUSTRIAN GP,
Österreichring – 51 laps, 188.313 miles
1. Niki Lauda (McLaren-turbo V6 TAG-Porsche MP4/2-1), 51 laps in 1:21;12.851, 139.11 mph.
2. Nelson Piquet (Brabham-turbo 4 BMW BT53/4), 51 in 1:21;36.376.
3. Michele Alboreto (Ferrari turbo V6 126C4/076), 51. **4.** Teo Fabi (Brabham-turbo 4 BMW BT53/5), 51. **5.** Thierry Boutsen (Arrows-turbo 4 BMW A7/2), 50. **6.** Marc Surer (Arrows-turbo 4 BMW A7/3), 50.
PP – Piquet, 1;26.173; FL – Lauda, 1;32.882, 143.105 mph.
Prost spun off when leading, Piquet lost lead due to worn rear Michelins as Lauda rushed by with 11 laps to go, then 4th gear broke, but McLaren kept running. Lauda nursed it home and Piquet unsuspectingly stroked home to distant 2nd instead of mounting last-laps attack to repass crippled car.

26-8-84 DUTCH GP,
Zandvoort – 71 laps, 187.586 miles
1. Alain Prost (McLaren-turbo V6 TAG-Porsche MP4/2-2), 71 laps in 1:37;21.468, 115.606 mph.
2. Niki Lauda (McLaren-turbo V6 TAG-Porsche MP4/2-1), 71 in 1:37;31.751.
3. Nigel Mansell (Lotus-turbo V6 Renault 95T R2), 71. **4.** Elio de Angelis (Lotus-turbo V6 Renault 95T R3), 70. **5.** Teo Fabi (Brabham-turbo 4 BMW BT53/5), 70. **6.** Patrick Tambay (Renault turbo V6 RE50/09), 70.
PP – Prost, 1;13.567; FL – René Arnoux (Ferrari turbo V6 126C4/077), 1;19.465, 119.693 mph.
Prost pulled away from team-mate, though Piquet led first 10 laps before oil union pulled apart; fine Mansell drive, Rosberg Williams-Honda 3rd at one stage but ran out of fuel near end.

9-9-84 ITALIAN GP,
Monza – 51 laps, 183.801 miles
1. Niki Lauda (McLaren-turbo V6 TAG-Porsche MP4/2-1), 51 laps in 1:20;29.065, 137.021 mph.
2. Michele Alboreto (Ferrari turbo V6 126C4/076), 51 in 1:20;53.314.
3. Riccardo Patrese (Alfa Romeo turbo V8 184T/04), 50. **4.** Stefan Johansson (Toleman-turbo 4 Hart TG184-05), 49. **5.** Jo Gartner (Osella-turbo V8 Alfa Romeo FA1F-04), 49. **6.** Gerhard Berger (ATS-turbo 4 BMW D7/02), 49.
PP – Nelson Piquet (Brabham-turbo 4 BMW BT53/4), 1;26.584; FL – Lauda, 1;31.912, 141.158 mph.
Prost engine broke lap 4, Lauda drove usual fine race despite slipped disc in back. Piquet of course led initially until BMW engine wilted due to coolant loss from split radiator; Brabham led Lauda and Fabi Brabham; at lap 40 Lauda 2nd and on lap 43 took lead from Tambay. Fabi stopped out of oil, Tambay throttle linkage parted, leaving Lauda to cruise away from Alboreto's lucky Ferrari.

7-10-84 EUROPEAN GP,
ersatz Nürburgring, D – 67 laps, 189.091 miles
1. Alain Prost (McLaren-turbo V6 TAG-Porsche MP4/2-2), 67 laps in 1:35;13.284, 119.148 miles.
2. Michele Alboreto (Ferrari turbo V6 126C4/M2-074), 67 in 1:35;37.195.
3. Nelson Piquet (Brabham-turbo 4 BMW BT53/6), 67. **4.** Niki Lauda (McLaren-turbo V6 TAG-Porsche MP4/2-1), 67. **5.** René Arnoux (Ferrari turbo V6 126C4/M2-077), 67. **6.** Riccardo Patrese (Alfa Romeo turbo V8 184T/04), 66.
PP – Piquet, 1;18.871; FL – Piquet & Alboreto, 1;23.146, 122.196 mph.
Prost survived pre-race crash to lead start to finish; Piquet hampered by baulky gearbox, Tambay robbed by misfire, both Piquet and Alboreto cars out of fuel on last lap. Lauda spun mid-race yet could easily have finished 2nd if race was only half a lap longer.

21-10-84 PORTUGUESE GP,
Estoril – 70 laps, 189.207 miles
1. Alain Prost (McLaren-turbo V6 TAG-Porsche MP4/2-2), 70 laps in 1:41;11.753, 112.182 mph.
2. Niki Lauda (McLaren-turbo V6 TAG-Porsche MP4/2-1), 70 in 1:41;25.178.
3. Ayrton Senna (Toleman-turbo 4 Hart TG184-05), 70. **4.** Michele Alboreto (Ferrari turbo V6 126C4/M2-074), 70. **5.** Elio de Angelis (Lotus-turbo V6 Renault 95T R3), 70. **6.** Nelson Piquet (Brabham-turbo 4 BMW BT53/6), 70.
PP – Piquet, 1;21.703; FL – Lauda, 1;22.996, 117.242 mph.
Piquet won second GPs in season yet missed Drivers' title again, Lauda's five wins plus placings taking it. Piquet spun from lead on first lap, Rosberg fought Williams FW09 round eight laps in lead, Senna and Johansson shone, Mansell good 2nd in Lotus with brake failure in lap 52. McLaren 1-2, typifying whole season, for last 18 laps. Lauda's title by half-point was narrowest margin in competition's 35 seasons. McLaren team domination of season unprecedented in modern times . . .

1985

7-4-85 BRAZILIAN GP,
Jacarepaguà – 61 laps, 190.692 miles
1. Alain Prost (McLaren-turbo V6 TAG Turbo-Porsche MP4/2B-5), 61 laps in 1:41;26.115, 112.795 mph.

2. Michele Alboreto (Ferrari turbo V6 156/85 079), 61 in 1:41;29.374.
3. Elio de Angelis (Lotus-turbo V6 Renault 97T-2), 60. **4.** René Arnoux (Ferrari turbo V6 156/85 080), 59. **5.** Patrick Tambay (Ligier-turbo V6 Renault JS25-02), 59. **6.** Jacques Laffite (Ligier-turbo V6 Renault JS25-02), 59.
PP – Alboreto, 1;27.768; FL – Prost, 1;36.702, 116.378 mph.
The rest had closed gap on McLaren, but race lasted only 18 laps between Rosberg's new carbon-tub Williams-Honda and Alboreto, handicapped after first-corner contact with Mansell's Williams. When Rosberg lost a turbo, Alboreto could not resist Prost's charge in updated McLaren.

21-4-85 PORTUGUESE GP,
Estoril – 67 laps, 181.098 miles*
*Wet race scheduled for 69 laps, but shortened in accordance with two-hour rule.
1. Ayrton Senna (Lotus-turbo V6 Renault 97T-2), 67 laps in 2:00;28.006, 90.198 mph.
2. Michele Alboreto (Ferrari turbo V6 156/85 079), 67 in 2:01;30.984.
3. Patrick Tambay (Renault turbo V6 RE60-4), 66. **4.** Elio de Angelis (Lotus-turbo V6 Renault 97T-2), 65. **5.** Nigel Mansell (Williams-turbo V6 Honda FW10-2), 65. **6.** Stefan Bellof (Tyrrell 012-7), 65.
PP – Senna, 1;21.007; FL – Senna, 1;44.121, 93.455 mph.
Senna proved his class with the perfect motor racing performance: pole, led throughout, fastest lap. Prost and Rosberg crashed; Renault picked up early-season points without ever looking competitive.

5-5-85 'SAN MARINO' GP,
Imola, I – 60 laps, 187.90 miles
1.* Elio de Angelis (Lotus-turbo V6 Renault 97T-3), 60 laps in 1:34;35.955, 119.177 mph.
2. Thierry Boutsen (Arrows-turbo 4 BMW A8-4), 59 laps.
3. Patrick Tambay (Renault turbo V6 RE60-4), 59. **4.** Niki Lauda (McLaren-turbo V6 TAG Turbo-Porsche MP42B/4), 59. **5.** Nigel Mansell (Williams-turbo V6 Honda FW10-2), 58. **6.** Stefan Johansson (Ferrari turbo V6 156/85 079), 57.**
*First on road was Alain Prost (McLaren-turbo V6 TAG Turbo-Porsche MP4/2B-5), who completed 60 laps in 1:33;57.118 but car disqualified for being under minimum weight at post-race scrutineering.
**Out of fuel, not running at finish.
PP – Ayrton Senna (Lotus-turbo V6 Renault 97T-2), 1;27.327; FL – Michele Alboreto (Ferrari turbo V6 156/85 081), 1;30.961, 123.945 mph.
Senna dominant again but out of fuel with four laps to run; Johansson inherited lead but ran out of fuel; Prost first but McLaren disqualified; de Angelis's lucky day!

19-5-85 MONACO GP,
Monte Carlo – 78 laps, 160.522 miles
1. Alain Prost (McLaren-turbo V6 TAG Turbo-Porsche MP4/2B-5), 78 laps in 1:51;58.034, 89.654 mph.
2. Michele Alboreto (Ferrari turbo V6 156/85 081), 78 in 1:52;05.575.
3. Elio de Angelis (Lotus-turbo V6 Renault 97T-3), 78 laps. **4.** Andrea de Cesaris (Ligier-turbo V6 Renault JS25-04), 77. **5.** Derek Warwick (Renault turbo V6 RE60-3), 77. **6.** Jacques Laffite (Ligier-turbo V6 Renault JS25-03), 77.
PP – Ayrton Senna (Lotus-turbo V6 Renault 97T-2), 1;20.450; FL – Alboreto, 1;22.637, 89.654 mph.
Senna led until engine broke on lap 13, Prost/Alboreto battle resolved by Ferrari slide on oil spilled in spectacular Piquet/Patrese collision; Italian retook lead, lost it finally with puncture but tigered home second after pit stop. De Angelis led Drivers' Championship.

2-6-85 BELGIAN GP,
Spa-Francorchamps
Race postponed, lifting track surface unsafe.

16-6-85 CANADIAN GP,
Ile Notre Dame, Montreal – 70 laps, 191.82 miles
1. Michele Alboreto (Ferrari turbo V6 156/85 081), 70 laps in 1:46;01.813, 108.544 mph.
2. Stefan Johansson (Ferrari turbo V6 156/85 082), 70 in 1:46;03.770.
3. Alain Prost (McLaren-turbo V6 TAG Turbo-Porsche MP4/2B-5), 70. **4.** Keke Rosberg (Williams-turbo V6 Honda FW10-4), 70. **5.** Elio de Angelis (Lotus-turbo V6 Renault 97T-3), 70. **6.** Nigel Mansell (Williams-turbo V6 Honda FW10-2), 70.
PP – De Angelis (Lotus-turbo V6 Renault 97T-2), 1;24.567; FL – Ayrton Senna (Lotus-turbo V6 Renault 97T-2), 1;27.445, 112.812 mph.
First Ferrari 1-2 since Zandvoort 1983. All-Lotus front row but Senna delayed by early turbo problem, de Angelis led 15 laps but faded. Ferrari fuel economy held off Prost, and his late-charge plans were foiled by de Cesaris's Ligier in his path. New Honda E-Type engine shone in otherwise troubled Williams cars.

23-6-85 DETROIT GP,
Michigan, USA – 63 laps, 157.500 miles
1. Keke Rosberg (Williams-turbo V6 Honda FW10-4), 63 laps in 1:55;39.851, 81.702 mph.
2. Stefan Johansson (Ferrari turbo V6 156/85 082), 63 in 1:56;37.400.
3. Michele Alboreto (Ferrari turbo V6 156/85 081), 63. **4.** Stefan Bellof (Tyrrell 012-7), 63. **5.** Elio de Angelis (Lotus-turbo V6 Renault 97T-3), 63. **6.** Nelson Piquet (Brabham-turbo V6 Renault 97T-2), 62.
PP – Ayrton Senna (Lotus-turbo V6 Renault 97T-2), 1;42.051; FL – Senna, 1;45.612, 85.217 mph.
Senna led seven laps but, like Mansell, Tambay and Prost, crashed. Brundle's Tyrrell-DFY fourth when put out by back-marker. Second US street circuit Rosberg Williams-Honda win after Dallas '84.

7-7-85 FRENCH GP,
Ricard-Castellet – 53 laps, 191. l37 miles
1. Nelson Piquet (Brabham-turbo ` 6 BMW 4 BT54-6), 53 laps in 1:31;46.266, 125.096 mph.
2. Keke Rosberg (Williams-turbo V€ Honda FW10-4), 53 in 1:31;52.926.
3. Alain Prost (McLaren-turbo V 3 TAG Turbo-Porsche MP4/2B-5), 53. **4.** Elio de Angelis (Lotus-turbo V6 Renault 97T-3), 53. **6.** Patrick Tambay (Renault turbo /6 RE60B-6), 53.
PP – Rosberg, 1;32.462; FL – Rosl erg, 1;39.914, 130.077 mph.

Heat-wave suited Brabham's latest Pirellis, and Piquet drove away when heat an d Honda power over-whelmed Williams's Goodyear s after Rosberg had led first 10 laps. Senna crasl ed on own oil after engine blew – Mansell non-star ed after heavy practice crash.

21-7-85 BRITISH GP
Silverstone – 65 laps, 190.580 r iles
1. Alain Prost (McLaren-turbo \ 6 TAG Turbo-Porsche MP4/2B-2), 65 laps in 1:18;10.436, `46.274 mph.
2. Michele Alboreto (Ferrari turbo V6 156/85 081), 64 laps.
3. Jacques Laffite (Ligier-turbo V6 l enault JS25-05), 64. **4.** Nelson Piquet (Brabham-turbo 4 BM V BT54-6), 64. **5.** Derek Warwick (Renault turbo V6 RE60E -7), 64. **6.** Marc Surer (Brabham-turbo 4 BMW BT54-3), 63
PP – Rosberg (Williams-turbo V6 H nda FW10-4), 1;05.591; FL – Prost, 1;09.886, 151.035 mph.
Senna dominant but electronic management failure over-enriched mixture, so f ei ran out after 57 straight laps in lead, with one more after Prost had gone by. Senna recaught, t en Lotus coughed, cleared and finally retired with 5 laps to go. Ferraris not competitive, Hondas failec after blinding qualifying speed. Flag shown a lap € arly otherwise Piquet would have displaced out-of-i uel Laffite. Alboreto two points clear of Prost for Dr ivers' title.

4-8-85 GERMAN GP,
ersatz Nürburgring – 67 laps, 1! 9.091 mph
1. Michele Alboreto (Ferrari turbo V i 156/85 080), 67 laps in 1:35;31.337, 118.773 mph.
2. Alain Prost (McLaren-turbo ` 6 TAG Turbo-Porsche MP4/2B-2), 67 in 1:35;42.998.
3. Jacques Laffite (Ligier-turbo V6 lenault JS25-05), 67. **4.** Thierry Boutsen (Arrows-turbo 4 I MW BMW A8-4), 67. **5.** Niki Lauda (McLaren-turbo V6 TAG Tu bo-Porsche MP4/2B-4), 67. **6.** Nigel Mansell (Williams-turbo V6 Honda FW10-6), 67.
PP – Teo Fabi (Toleman-turbo 4 H art TG185-3*), 1;17.429; FL – Lauda, 1;22.806, 122.698 mph
Pole chassis are numbered as use i in race, not necessarily reflecting that used to set pole time.
Ferraris well matched to co rse in race trim but Alboreto hit Johansson in firs corner, preventing a potential Ferrari 1-2, but Rosl erg led 33 laps, broken for 11 laps by Senna be ore Lotus driveshaft problem; Williams brake troub e then gave Alboreto victory. Fabi's Toleman-Hart fi st-day pole time survived when rain slowed later se ssion.

18-8-85 AUSTRIAN GP,
Österreichring – 52 laps, 191.9 93 mph
1. Alain Prost (McLaren-turbo V6 TAG Turbo-Porsche MP4/2B-3), 52 laps in 1:20;12.583, 143.618 mph.
2. Ayrton Senna (Lotus-turbo V i Renault 97T-4), 52 in 1:20;42.585.
3. Michele Alboreto (Ferrari turbc V6 156/85 080), 52. **4.** Stefan Johansson (Ferrari turbo V6 156/85 079), 52. **5.** Elio de Angelis (Lotus-turbo V6 Renault i7T-3), 52. **6.** Marc Surer (Brabham-turbo 4 BMW BT54-8), 5 .
PP – Prost, 1;25.490; FL – Prost, 1 9.241, 148.943 mph.
Four-car grid pile-up stopped race, spare cars used in restart, utter McLaren do nination once Honda bottom-end troubles hit Willia ms. Prost led first 26 laps, then Lauda's McLaren 3 met engine failure. Prost tied with All oreto for Drivers' Championship lead, Ferrari 72 points to McLaren 55 in Constructors' Cup.

25-8-85 DUTCH GP,
Zandvoort – 70 laps, 184.944 r ph
1. Niki Lauda (McLaren-turbo V6 TAG Turbo-Porsche MP4/2B-4), 70 laps in 1:32;29.263 119.979 mph.
2. Alain Prost (McLaren-turbo V6 TAG Turbo-Porsche MP4/2B-3), 70 in 1:32;29.495.
3. Ayrton Senna (Lotus-turbo V i Renault 97T-4) 70. **4.** Michele Alboreto (Ferrari turbo V6 ` 56/85 080), 70. **5.** Elio de Angelis (Lotus-turbo V6 Renault 97 T-3), 69. **6.** Nigel Mansell (Williams-turbo V6 Honda FW10-6 69.
PP – Nelson Piquet (Brabham-turbo 4 BMW BT54-6), 1;11.074; FL – Prost, 1;16.538, 12 .270 mph.
Abrasive track made tyre c hanges necessary – Lauda's stop-early tactic paid off, just pipped teammate to finish, but Rosberg's Williams-Honda led 32 laps before engine failure. La ada and Prost now had 45 career wins between the n, other 24 drivers in field aggregated only 35 betw en them!

8-9-85 ITALIAN GP,
Monza – 51 laps, 183.801 mil s
1. Alain Prost (McLaren-turbo V6 TAG Turbo-Porsche MP4/2B-5), 51 laps in 1:17;59.451 141.402 mph.
2. Nelson Piquet (Brabham-turb) 4 BMW BT54-6), 51 in 1:18;51.086.
3. Ayrton Senna (Lotus-turbo V6 f enault 97T-4), 51. **4.** Marc Surer (Brabham-turbo 4 BMW BT54-8), 51. **5.** Stefan Johansson (Ferrari turbo V6 15 /85 083), 50. **6.** Elio de Angelis (Lotus-turbo V6 Renault 97 T-3), 50.
PP – Senna, 1;25.084; FL – Nigel Vlansell (Williams-turbo Honda FW10-6), 1;28.283, 146.96 mph.
Ferrari trounced on home g ound; Rosberg's race, lost lead in tyre-change s top, retook it before

engine bottom-end failed again 8 laps from home. Senna underpowered in race, Mansell's Williams-Honda fastest on track after early stop. Prost led 19 of 51 laps, displaced Alboreto, and McLaren displaced Ferrari in respective Championships.

15-9-85 BELGIAN GP,
Spa-Francorchamps – 43 laps, 185.669 miles
1. Ayrton Senna (Lotus-turbo V6 Renault 97T-4), 43 laps in 1:34;19.893, 117.943 mph.
2. Nigel Mansell (Williams-turbo V6 Honda FW10-6), 43 in 1:34;48.315.
3. Alain Prost (McLaren-turbo V6 TAG Turbo-Porsche MP4/2B-5), 43. **4.** Keke Rosberg (Williams-turbo V6 Honda FW10-7), 43. **5.** Nelson Piquet (Brabham-turbo 4 BMW BT54-6), 42. **6.** Derek Warwick (Renault turbo V6 RE60B-3), 42.
PP – Prost, 1;55.306; FL – Prost 2;01.730, 127.531 mph.
Ferraris blew up early, Senna lost lead only in tyre-change stop for pre-heated slicks after part-wet race, thereafter uncatchable. Williams-Hondas and McLaren both strong. Lauda injured wrist in practice crash, non-started.

6-10-85 EUROPEAN GP,
Brands Hatch – 75 laps, 196.050 miles
1. Nigel Mansell (Williams-turbo V6 Honda FW10-6), 75 laps in 1:32;58.109, 126.527 mph.
2. Ayrton Senna (Lotus-turbo V6 Renault 97T-4), 75 in 1:33;19.505.
3. Keke Rosberg (Williams-turbo V6 Honda FW10-7), 75. **4.** Alain Prost (McLaren-turbo V6 TAG Turbo-Porsche MP4/2B-2), 75. **5.** Elio de Angelis (Lotus-turbo V6 Renault 97T-3), 74. **6.** Thierry Boutsen (Arrows-turbo 4 BMW A8-4), 73.
PP – Senna, 1;07.169; FL – Jacques Laffite (Ligier-turbo V6 Renault JS25-05), 1;11.526, 131.566 mph.
Senna Lotus battle with both Williams cars resolved when Rosberg spun and Piquet rammed him, Rosberg rejoined after stop ahead of Senna and gave Mansell chance to pass them both for lead he never lost. Ferrari flopped again, Brabham and Ligier shone on Pirellis, Prost Champion. Watson, deputizing for Lauda, seventh.

19-10-85 SOUTH AFRICAN GP,
Kyalami – 75 laps, 191.247 miles
1. Nigel Mansell (Williams-turbo V6 Honda FW10-6), 75 laps in 1:28;22.866, 129.840 mph.
2. Keke Rosberg (Williams-turbo V6 Honda FW10-7), 75 in 1:28;30.438.
3. Alain Prost (McLaren-turbo V6 TAG Turbo-Porsche MP4/2B-6), 75. **4.** Stefan Johansson (Ferrari turbo V6 156/85 086), 74. **5.** Gerhard Berger (Arrows-turbo 4 BMW A8-2), 74. **6.** Thierry Boutsen (Arrows-turbo 4 BMW A8-4), 74.
PP – Mansell, 1;02.366; FL – Rosberg, 1:08.149, 134.710 mph.
Flawless Mansell drive under pressure from Prost but Rosberg blindingly fast after win into sand trap and two tyre-stops to Mansell's one, Williams-Honda clearly in new class.

3-11-85 AUSTRALIAN GP,
Adelaide – 82 laps, 192.498 miles
1. Keke Rosberg (Williams-turbo V6 Honda FW10-7), 82 laps in 2:00;40.473, 95.71 mph.
2. Jacques Laffite (Ligier-turbo V6 Renault JS25-05), 82 in 2:01;26.603.
3. Philippe Streiff (Ligier-turbo V6 Renault JS25-04), 82. **4.** Ivan Capelli (Tyrrell-turbo V6 Renault 014-2), 81. **5.** Stefan Johansson (Ferrari turbo V6 156/85 086), 81. **6.** Gerhard Berger (Arrows-turbo 4 BMW A8-2), 81.
PP – Ayrton Senna (Lotus-turbo V6 Renault 97T-4), 1;19.843; FL – Rosberg, 1;23.758, 100.899 mph.
Sensational new race, Rosberg/Senna battle included multiple tyre-stops and incidents until Lotus finally blew engine. Lauda led his final GP for two laps before brake failure and crash; Rosberg won despite three stops; Ligier team-mates squabbled near finish, Streiff wrecking his left-front suspension on Lafitte car's rear wheel. McLaren retained Constructors' Cup from Ferrari, Williams displaced Lotus third.

1986

23-3-86 BRAZILIAN GP,
Jacarepaguá, Rio de Janeiro – 61 laps, 190.692 miles
1. Nelson Piquet (Williams-turbo V6 Honda FW11/1), 61 laps in 1:39;32.583, 114.941 mph.
2. Ayrton Senna (Lotus-turbo V6 Renault 98T/3), 61 in 1:40;07.410.
3. Jacques Laffite (Ligier-turbo V6 Renault JS27/01), 61. **4.** René Arnoux (Ligier-turbo V6 Renault JS27/02), 61. **5.** Martin Brundle (Tyrrell-turbo V6 Renault 014/4), 60. **6.** Gerhard Berger (Benetton-turbo 4 BMW B186/2), 59.
PP – Senna, 1;25.501; FL – Piquet, 1;33.546, 120.305 mph.
The latest Williams-Honda proved unbeatable despite Mansell spinning his FW11 on lap 1 trying to take the lead from Senna's Lotus-Renault. Within 2 laps Piquet led, only losing the lead briefly in two planned tyre stops. Prost's McLaren-TAG led 7 laps thanks to a one-stop strategy, but his engine failed at half-distance, as did team-mate Rosberg's. Senna led first 2 laps, Piquet 3-18, Senna 19, Prost 20-26, Piquet 27-40, Senna 41, Piquet 42 to the finish.

13-4-86 SPANISH GP,
Jerez de la Frontera – 72 laps, 188.708 miles
1. Ayrton Senna (Lotus-turbo V6 Renault 98T/3), 72 laps in 1:48;47.735, 104.070 mph.
2. Nigel Mansell (Williams-turbo V6 Honda FW11/2), 72 in 1:48;47.749.
3. Alain Prost (McLaren-turbo V6 TAG Turbo-Porsche

MP4/2C-3), 72. **4.** Keke Rosberg (McLaren-turbo V6 TAG Turbo-Porsche MP4/2C-2), 71. **5.** Teo Fabi (Benetton-turbo 4 BMW B186-1), 71. **6.** Gerhard Berger (Benetton-turbo 4 BMW B186-1), 71.
PP – Senna, 1;21.605; FL – Piquet, 1;27.176, 108.234 mph.
Thrilling finish split Mansell and Senna by 0.01 sec; race began as slow procession with six cars disputing lead, Mansell pitted for tyres with only 8 laps to run, stupendous lunge for the lead all but caught Senna. McLaren drivers slowed by pessimistic cockpit fuel readouts. Senna led laps 1-39, Mansell 40-62, Senna 63 to the end. Johansson survived spectacular head-on crash due to Ferrari brake failure.

27-4-86 'SAN MARINO' GP,
Imola, I – 60 laps, 187.90 miles
1. Alain Prost (McLaren-turbo V6 TAG Turbo-Porsche MP4/2C-3), 60 laps in 1:32;28.408, 121.918 mph.
2. Nelson Piquet (Williams-turbo V6 Honda FW11-4), 60 in 1:32;36.053.
3. Gerhard Berger (Benetton-turbo 4 BMW B186-2), 59. **4.** Stefan Johansson (Ferrari turbo V6 F1/86 '090'), 59. **5.** Keke Rosberg (McLaren-turbo V6 TAG Turbo-Porsche MP4/2C-2), 58.* **6.** Riccardo Patrese (Brabham-turbo 4 BMW BT55/4), 58.*
*Both cars out of fuel.
PP – Ayrton Senna (Lotus-turbo V6 Renault 98T/3), 1;25.050; FL – Piquet, 1;28.667, 127.151 mph.
Prost ran out of fuel before finish but stuttered across the line and still weighed in above minimum limit! Piquet had backed off in mid-race after dire fuel level warnings from onboard computer, but put hammer down in last 10 laps. Rosberg ran out of fuel and lost 2nd place with 2 laps remaining. Piquet led laps 1-28, Rosberg 29-33, Prost 34 to the end.

11-5-86 MONACO GP,
Monte Carlo – 78 laps, 161.298 miles
1. Alain Prost (McLaren-turbo V6 TAG Turbo-Porsche MP4/2C-3), 78 laps in 1:55;41.060, 83.657 mph.
2. Keke Rosberg (McLaren-turbo V6 TAG Turbo-Porsche MP4/2C-2), 78 in 1:56;06.082.
3. Ayrton Senna (Lotus-turbo V6 Renault 98T/3), 78. **4.** Nigel Mansell (Williams-turbo V6 Honda FW11/2), 78. **5.** René Arnoux (Ligier-turbo V6 Renault JS27/02), 77. **6.** Jacques Laffite (Ligier-turbo V6 Renault JS27/03), 77.
PP – Prost, 1;22.627; FL – Prost, 1;26.607, 85.957 mph.
Dull race dominated by Prost's genius. Led throughout except during the pit-stop period, Rosberg charged hard into 2nd place, Senna's Lotus-Renault outclassed in 3rd. Martin Brundle survived violent Tyrrell crash during practice. Prost led laps 1-34, Senna 35-41, Prost 42 to the flag.

25-5-86 BELGIAN GP,
Spa-Francorchamps – 43 laps, 185.429 miles
1. Nigel Mansell (Williams-turbo V6 Honda FW11/2), 43 laps in 1:27;57.925, 126.479 mph.
2. Ayrton Senna (Lotus-turbo V6 Renault 98T/3), 43 in 1:28;17.752.
3. Stefan Johansson (Ferrari turbo V6 F1/86 '090'), 43. **4.** Michele Alboreto (Ferrari turbo V6 F1/86 '089'), 43. **5.** Jacques Laffite (Ligier-turbo V6 Renault JS27/01), 43. **6.** Alain Prost (McLaren-turbo V6 TAG Turbo-Porsche MP4/2C-3), 43.
PP – Nelson Piquet (Williams-turbo V6 Honda FW11/4), 1;54.331; FL – Prost, 1;59.282, 130.148 mph.
Mansell drove intelligent race to balance fuel consumption against pace, defeating Senna – his only threat. Piquet had looked set for an easy win until turbo boost control failure, Prost saw his car's chassis in first-corner collision but set fastest race lap regardless in lonely drive into 6th place, showing what might have been . . . Race overshadowed by death of Elio de Angelis in Brabham testing crash at Ricard few days previously. Piquet led laps 1-16, Senna 17-21, Johansson 22-23, Mansell from lap 25 on.

15-6-86 CANADIAN GP,
Ile Notre Dame, Montreal – 69 laps, 189.07 miles
1. Nigel Mansell (Williams-turbo V6 Honda FW11/2), 69 laps in 1:42;26.415, 110.744 mph.
2. Alain Prost (McLaren-turbo V6 TAG Turbo-Porsche MP4/2C-3), 69 in 1:42;47.074.
3. Nelson Piquet (Williams-turbo V6 Honda FW11/4), 69. **4.** Keke Rosberg (McLaren-turbo V6 TAG Turbo-Porsche MP4/2C-2), 69. **5.** Ayrton Senna (Lotus-turbo V6 Renault 98T/3), 68. **6.** René Arnoux (Ligier-turbo V6 Renault JS27/05), 68.
PP – Mansell, 1;24.118; FL – Piquet, 1;25.443, 115.455 mph.
Mature drive by Mansell to secure fourth GP victory of his career, driver and car in a class of their own, balancing speed and restraint. Lapped all but Piquet, Rosberg. Led laps 1-16, Rosberg 17-21, Mansell 22-30, Prost 31, Mansell 32-40, Piquet 41, then Mansell to the finish.

22-6-86 UNITED STATES (DETROIT) GP,
Detroit, Michigan – 63 laps, 157.50 miles
1. Ayrton Senna (Lotus-turbo V6 Renault 98T/3), 63 laps in 1:51;12.847, 84.971 mph.
2. Jacques Laffite (Ligier-turbo V6 Renault JS27/01), 63 in 1:51;43.864.
3. Alain Prost (McLaren-turbo V6 TAG Turbo-Porsche MP4/2C-3), 63. **4.** Michele Alboreto (Ferrari turbo V6 F1/86 '092'), 63. **5.** Nigel Mansell (Williams-turbo V6 Honda FW11/2), 62. **6.** Riccardo Patrese (Brabham-turbo 4 BMW BT55/4), 62.
PP – Senna, 1;38.301; FL – Nelson Piquet (Williams-turbo V6 Honda FW11/4), 1;41.233, 88.904 mph.
Senna lost early lead with puncture, charged back through field to splendid victory. Mansell developed brake problem as he took the lead, Prost suffered

intermittent engine cut-out, Piquet crashed heavily writing off a Williams-Honda, Arnoux lost 2nd place by colliding with the wreckage some laps later. Senna led first 2 laps, then Mansell laps 3-7, Senna 8-14, Arnoux and the Ligier-Renault laps 15-17, team-mate Laffite 18-30, Piquet 31-39, Senna 40-63.

6-7-86 FRENCH GP,
Ricard-Castellet – 80 laps, 189.543 miles
1. Nigel Mansell (Williams-turbo V6 Honda FW11/2), 80 laps in 1:37;19.272, 116.856 mph.
2. Alain Prost (McLaren-turbo V6 TAG Turbo-Porsche MP4/2C-3), 80 in 1:37;36.400. **3.** Nelson Piquet (Williams-turbo V6 Honda FW11/5), 80. **4.** Keke Rosberg (McLaren-turbo V6 TAG Turbo-Porsche MP4/2C-2), 80. **5.** René Arnoux (Ligier-turbo V6 Renault JS27/04), 79. **6.** Jacques Laffite (Ligier-turbo V6 Renault JS27/01), 79.
PP – Ayrton Senna (Lotus-turbo V6 Renault 98T/3), 1;06.526; FL – Mansell, 1;09.993, 121.861 mph.
Williams planned two tyre changes and fine pit work plus Mansell's newly matured driving flair paid off in the team's fourth win of the year. Mansell beat Prost's McLaren, which made only one tyre-change stop, to head the World Championship pre-Brands Hatch. Mansell led laps 1-25, Prost 26-36, Mansell 37-53, Prost 54-58 then Mansell to the flag.

13-7-86 BRITISH GP,
Brands Hatch – 75 laps, 196.050 miles
1. Nigel Mansell (Williams-turbo V6 Honda FW11/3), 75 laps in 1:30;38.471, 129.775 mph.
2. Nelson Piquet (Williams-turbo V6 Honda FW11/5), 75 in 1:30;44.045.
3. Alain Prost (McLaren-turbo V6 TAG Turbo-Porsche MP4/2C-3), 74. **4.** René Arnoux (Ligier-turbo V6 Renault JS27/02), 73. **5.** Martin Brundle (Tyrrell-turbo V6 Renault 015/1), 72. **6.** Philippe Streiff (Tyrrell-turbo V6 Renault 015/3), 72.
PP – Piquet, 1;06.961; FL – Mansell, 1;09.593, 135.220 mph.
After Mansell broke a half-shaft joint at the start, a first-corner multiple crash saw Jacques Laffite's frontline career ended by severe leg injuries as his Ligier rammed the Armco bank. This race saw him breaking Graham Hill's career record for most number of GPs contested. Race was stopped and restarted with Mansell in spare car set up for Piquet. Mansell on his home ground then beat his team-mate regardless in classic internecine battle. Piquet led laps 1-22, Mansell 23 to victory . . .

27-7-86 GERMAN GP,
Hockenheim – 44 laps, 185.83 miles
1. Nelson Piquet (Williams-turbo V6 Honda FW11/5), 44 laps in 1:22;08.263, 135.746 mph.
2. Ayrton Senna (Lotus-turbo V6 Renault 98T/4), 44 in 1:22;23.700.
3. Nigel Mansell (Williams-turbo V6 Honda FW11/2), 44. **4.** René Arnoux (Ligier-turbo V6 Renault JS27/02), 44. **5.** Keke Rosberg (McLaren-turbo V6 TAG Turbo-Porsche MP4/2C-2), 43. **6.** Alain Prost (McLaren-turbo V6 TAG Turbo-Porsche MP4/2C-3), 43.
PP – Piquet, 1;42.013; FL – Gerhard Berger (Benetton-turbo 4 BMW B186/5), 1;46.604, 142.625 mph.
Commanding victory for Piquet despite two tyre stops which meant he had to battle hard to repass Rosberg's revitalized pole-position McLaren-TAG on Porsche's home ground. Rosberg and Prost both ran out of fuel on last lap – Mansell handicapped throughout by part-detached rear diffuser underbody panel. Leaders: Senna lap 1, Rosberg 2-5, Piquet 6-14, Rosberg 15-19, Prost 20, Piquet 21-27, Rosberg 28-38, Piquet 39-44.

10-8-86 HUNGARIAN GP,
Hungaroring – 76 laps, 189.557 miles*
*Scheduled to run 78 laps, but race stopped after two hours duration as F1 rules require.
1. Nelson Piquet (Williams-turbo V6 Honda FW11/5), 76 laps in 2:00;34.508, 94.326 mph.
2. Ayrton Senna (Lotus-turbo V6 Renault 98T/4), 76 in 2:00;52.181.
3. Nigel Mansell (Williams-turbo Honda V6 FW11/6), 75. **4.** Stefan Johansson (Ferrari turbo V6 F1/86 '090'), 75. **5.** Johnny Dumfries (Lotus-turbo V6 Renault 98T/2), 74. **6.** Martin Brundle (Tyrrell-turbo V6 Renault 015/4), 74.
PP – Senna, 1;29.450; FL – Piquet, 1;31.001, 98.669 mph.
First Communist-bloc World Championship GP saw titanic battle between Piquet and Senna, Williams's Brazilian having found a technical plus pre-race which he kept to himself, overshadowing Mansell (lapped in 3rd place) and dividing the Williams-Honda team against itself. McLaren in eclipse. Laps 1-11, 36-56 led by Senna, Piquet laps 12-35 and 57-76 by Piquet.

17-8-86 AUSTRIAN GP,
Österreichring – 52 laps, 191.993 miles
1. Alain Prost (McLaren-turbo V6 TAG Turbo-Porsche MP4/2C-3), 52 laps in 1:21;22.531, 141.561 mph.
2. Michele Alboreto (Ferrari turbo V6 F1/86 '092'), 51 laps.
3. Stefan Johansson (Ferrari turbo V6 F1/86 '089'), 50. **4.** Alan Jones (Lola-turbo V6 Ford-Cosworth THL-2/004), 50. **5.** Patrick Tambay (Lola-turbo V6 Ford-Cosworth THL-2/005), 50. **6.** Christian Danner (Arrows-turbo 4 BMW A8/05), 49.
PP – Teo Fabi (Benetton-turbo 4 BMW B186/6), 1;23.549; FL – Gerhard Berger (Benetton-turbo 4 BMW B186/5), 1;29.444, 148.604 mph.
Benetton-BMWs stood F1 on its ear in qualifying and led impressively from start until they faltered. Prost profited by others' misfortunes to revive his Championship hopes. McLaren proved reliable for Williams-Hondas, Mansell put out by CV joint failure when 2nd around half-distance. Nobody close enough to take advantage of Prost's dire engine

pick-up problem near finish. Berger led his home race laps 1-25, Mansell led 26-28, Prost 29-52. Berger's hopes sunk by battery fault, Fabi's engine 'buzzed' when he hit a high kerb in opening stages and gearbox jumped out of gear, losing power.

7-9-86 ITALIAN GP,
Monza – 51 laps, 183.801 miles
1. Nelson Piquet (Williams-turbo V6 Honda FW11/5), 51 laps in 1:17:42.889, 141.904 mph.
2. Nigel Mansell (Williams-turbo V6 Honda FW11/6), 51 in 1:17:52.717.
3. Stefan Johansson (Ferrari turbo V6 F1/86 '093), 51. **4.** Keke Rosberg (McLaren-turbo V6 TAG Turbo-Porsche MP4/2C-2), 51. **5.** Gerhard Berger (Benetton-turbo 4 BMW B186/5), 50. **6.** Alan Jones (Lola-turbo V6 Ford-Cosworth THL-2/004), 49.
PP – Teo Fabi (Benetton-turbo 4 BMW B186/6), 1,24.078.*
*Started from back of grid after mechanical trouble on warm-up lap – leaving pole in theory to 2nd fastest qualifier, Alain Prost (McLaren-turbo V6 TAG Turbo-Porsche MP4/2C-3), 1,24.514, but he started from pit lane. Thus pole position at actual race start passed effectively to 3rd fastest qualifier, Mansell, 1,24.882. FL – Fabi, 1,28.099, 147.268 mph.
Berger used more fuel than was prudent in opening charge, Alboreto's Ferrari kept pace with the Williams-Honda pair, Prost allowed to start from pit lane when he should not have been, subsequently black-flagged before engine blew up; race was Mansell v. Piquet, team-mate versus team-mate, and they were on quite friendly terms . . . Piquet's shrewd selection of compromise wing setting perhaps gave his FW11 slight edge which paid off. Berger led laps 1-6, Mansell 7-24, Berger 25-26, Mansell 27-37, Piquet to the flag.

21-9-86 PORTUGUESE GP,
Estoril – 70 laps, 189.207 miles
1. Nigel Mansell (Williams-turbo V6 Honda FW11/6), 70 laps in 1:37:21.900, 116.596 mph.
2. Alain Prost (McLaren-turbo V6 TAG Turbo-Porsche MP4/2C-1), 70 in 1:37:40.672.
3. Nelson Piquet (Williams-turbo V6 Honda FW11/5), 70. **4.** Ayrton Senna (Lotus-turbo V6 Renault 98T/4), 69. **5.** Michele Alboreto (Ferrari turbo V6 F1/86 '092), 69. **6.** Stefan Johansson (Ferrari turbo V6 F1/86 '093), 69.
PP – Senna, 1,16.673; FL – Mansell, 1,20.943, 120.216 mph.
Mansell and Williams-Honda demonstration, leading throughout and trouncing all opposition. Senna's pole-position Lotus lost 2nd place out of fuel on final lap, Piquet gaining a place despite late-stages spin when Williams rear brakes locked.

12-10-86 MEXICAN GP,
Autodromo Hermanos Rodriguez, Mexico City – 68 laps, 186.801 miles
1. Gerhard Berger (Benetton-turbo 4 BMW B186/7), 68 laps in 1:33:18.700, 120.114 mph.
2. Alain Prost (McLaren-turbo V6 TAG Turbo-Porsche MP4/2C-5), 68 in 1:33:44.138.
3. Ayrton Senna (Lotus-turbo V6 Renault 98T/4), 68. **4.** Nelson Piquet (Williams-turbo V6 Honda FW11/5), 67. **5.** Nigel Mansell (Williams-turbo V6 Honda FW11/6), 67. **6.** Philippe Alliot (Ligier-turbo V6 Renault JS27/04), 67.
PP – Senna, 1,16.990; FL – Piquet, 1,19.360, 124.615 mph.
Benetton, BMW and Pirelli tyres had been running stronger for several races, now at altitude they ran non-stop on the one tyre while rival Goodyear runners were beset by repeated stops to replace worn covers. Points leader Mansell failed to select first gear at start, joining at tail of field; Piquet/Prost battle ended by tyre wear problems, Prost inheriting 2nd-place finish. Championship outcome poised three ways between Piquet, Mansell and Prost with one round remaining. Piquet led laps 1-31, Senna 32-35, Berger 36-68.

26-10-86 AUSTRALIAN GP,
Adelaide, South Australia – 82 laps, 192.498 miles
1. Alain Prost (McLaren-turbo V6 TAG Turbo-Porsche MP4/2C-5), 82 laps in 1:54:20.388, 101.040 mph.
2. Nelson Piquet (Williams-turbo V6 Honda FW11/5), 82 in 1:54:24.593.
3. Stefan Johansson (Ferrari turbo V6 F1/86 '094), 81. **4.** Martin Brundle (Tyrrell-turbo V6 Renault 015/5), 81. **5.** Philippe Streiff (Tyrrell-turbo V6 Renault 015/3), 80.* **6.** Johnny Dumfries (Lotus-turbo V6 Renault 98T/2), 80
*Out of fuel but classified as shown.
PP – Nigel Mansell (Williams-turbo V6 Honda FW11/6), 1:18.714; FL – Piquet, 1,20.787, 104.637 mph.
Tyres decided the issue in Australia – Prost pitted lap 32 after puncturing a tired Goodyear against Berger's Benetton, Rosberg had acted as here until a thumping tyre delamination which he misread as engine failure in this, his final GP. Piquet left leading Mansell, with the Englishman set for Championship crown until spectacular 180 mph tyre explosion on lap 63. Concern re tyre wear brought Piquet into pits, delay gave Prost lead he maintained despite fuel readout showing 5 litres short for last 15 laps. Sure he would run out, Prost plugged on, kept Piquet at bay, and won race, and first back-to-back Drivers' Championship title since Jack Brabham of Cooper 1959-1960. Piquet led laps 1-6, Rosberg 7-62, Piquet 63-64, Prost 65 to the title.

1987

12-4-87 BRAZILIAN GP,
Jacarepaguá, Rio de Janeiro – 61 laps, 190.692 miles
1. Alain Prost (McLaren-turbo V6 TAG Turbo-Porsche MP4/3-3), 61 laps in 1:39:45.141, 114.699 mph.

---

2. Nelson Piquet (Williams-turbo V6 Honda FW11B/2), 61 in 1:40:25.688.
3. Stefan Johansson (McLaren-turbo V6 TAG Turbo-Porsche MP4/3-2), 61. **4.** Gerhard Berger (Ferrari turbo V6 Ferrari F1/87 '095), 61. **5.** Thierry Boutsen (Benetton-turbo V6 Ford B187/3), 60. **6.** Nigel Mansell (Williams-turbo V6 Honda FW11B/3), 60.
Top two naturally aspirated 3.5-litre cars and drivers competing in concurrent Colin Chapman and Jim Clark Trophy class placed overall as follows: **10. (1st)** Jonathan Palmer (Tyrrell-Cosworth V8 DG/016-3), 58. **11. (2nd)** Philippe Streiff (Tyrrell-Cosworth V8 DG/016-1), 57.
PP – Mansell, 1;26.128; FL – Piquet, 1,33.861, 119.901 mph.
Cool, tactical tour de force for Prost and McLaren as from 5th fastest in practice he moved relentlessly into 3rd ending lap 8, then before his first scheduled stop on lap 16, then back into the lead which he retained despite a second tyre change. His rivals changed three times, Piquet and Mansell both troubled by overheating. Piquet led laps 1-7, Senna 8-12, Prost 13-16, Piquet again 17-20, then Prost 21 to the flag.

3-5-87 'SAN MARINO' GP,
Imola, I – 59 laps, 185.30 miles
1. Nigel Mansell (Williams-turbo V6 Honda FW11B/3), 59 laps in 1:31;24.076, 121.292 mph.
2. Ayrton Senna (Lotus-turbo V6 Honda 99T/4), 59 in 1:31;51.621.
3. Michele Alboreto (Ferrari turbo V6 F1/87 '096), 59. **4.** Stefan Johansson (McLaren-turbo V6 TAG Turbo-Porsche MP4/3-2), 59. **5.** Martin Brundle (Zakspeed turbo 4 871/1), 57. **6.** Satoru Nakajima (Lotus-turbo V6 Honda 99T/1), 57.
Naturally aspirated class result: **8. (1st)** Philippe Streiff (Tyrrell-Cosworth V8 DG/016-1), 57. **10. (2nd)** Philippe Alliot (Lola-Cosworth V8 LC87/2), 56.
PP – Senna, 1;25.826; FL – Teo Fabi (Benetton-turbo V6 Ford B187/4), 1;29.246, 126.326 mph.
Mansell troubled only by lost wheel balance weights, Piquet non-started after surviving massive practice accident which destroyed his FW11B/2. Senna led the opening lap, then Mansell took over from lap 2-20, Alboreto 22-24, Senna 25-26, Mansell 27 to the close.

17-5-87 BELGIAN GP,
Spa-Francorchamps – 43 laps, 185.429 miles
1. Alain Prost (McLaren-turbo V6 TAG Turbo-Porsche MP4/3-3), 43 laps in 1:27;03.217, 127.803 mph.
2. Stefan Johansson (McLaren-turbo V6 TAG Turbo-Porsche MP4/3-2), 43 in 1:27;27.981.
3. Andrea de Cesaris (Brabham-turbo 4 BMW BT56/2), 42. **4.** Eddie Cheever (Arrows-turbo 4 Megatron-BMW A10/2), 42. **5.** Satoru Nakajima (Lotus-turbo V6 Honda 99T/1), 42. **6.** René Arnoux (Ligier-turbo 4 Megatron-BMW JS29B/2), 41.
Naturally aspirated class result: **8. (1st)** Philippe Alliot (Lola-Cosworth V8 LC87/2), 40. **9. (2nd)** Philippe Streiff (Tyrrell-Cosworth V8 DG/016-3), 39.
PP – Nigel Mansell (Williams-turbo V6 Honda FW11B/3), 1;52.026; FL – Prost, 1;57.153, 132.513 mph.
Race restarted after the Tyrrell team of Streiff and Palmer were involved in high-speed accidents on the climb from Eau Rouge, Mansell then leading by 2 secs. After restart Senna took lead, fought off Mansell's attempted first-lap pass and spun out. Prost left to equal Stewart's career record 27 GP wins, quiet, calm confidence belying the tone of the day. In restarted race Piquet led past the pits for the first 9 laps, Prost for the rest of the way.

31-5-87 MONACO GP,
Monte Carlo – 78 laps, 161.298 miles
1. Ayrton Senna (Lotus-turbo V6 Honda 99T/4), 78 laps in 1:57;54.085, 82.084 mph.
2. Nelson Piquet (Williams-turbo V6 Honda FW11B/4), 78 in 1:58;27.297.
3. Michele Alboreto (Ferrari turbo V6 F1/87 '098), 78. **4.** Gerhard Berger (Ferrari turbo V6 F1/87 '095), 77. **5. (1st)*** Jonathan Palmer (Tyrrell-Cosworth V8 DG/016-2), 76. **6. (2nd)*** Ivan Capelli (March-Cosworth 871/1), 76.
*Bracketed figures indicate naturally aspirated class cars also finishing within top 6 points-scoring positions for World Championship proper.
PP – Nigel Mansell (Williams-turbo V6 Honda FW11B/3), 1;23.039; FL – Senna, 1;27.685, 84.901 mph.
Mansell untouchable during qualifying and for first 30 laps of race until exhaust weld cracked, losing turbo pressure. Easy victory left to Senna, the first for active-suspension Lotus 99T. Piquet still pink after Imola shunt, Prost's engine on 5 cylinders much of the way, blowing up with 2 laps to run when set to 'atmo' 3.5-litre Tyrrell. Palmer's first points of his career in 'atmo' 3.5-litre Tyrrell. Mansell led laps 1-29, Senna 30-78.

21-6-87 UNITED STATES (DETROIT) GP,
Detroit, Michigan – 63 laps, 157.50 miles
1. Ayrton Senna (Lotus-turbo V6 Honda 99T/4), 63 laps in 1:50;16.358, 85.697 mph.
2. Nelson Piquet (Williams-turbo V6 Honda FW11B/4), 63 in 1:50;50.177.
3. Alain Prost (McLaren-turbo V6 TAG Turbo MP4/3-3), 63. **4.** Gerhard Berger (Ferrari turbo V6 '097), 63. **5.** Nigel Mansell (Williams-turbo V6 Honda FW11B/3), 62. **6.** Eddie Cheever (Arrows-turbo 4 Megatron-BMW A10/2), 60.*
*Out of fuel.
Naturally aspirated class result: **11. (1st)** Jonathan Palmer (Tyrrell-Cosworth V8 DG/016-2), 60. **12. (2nd)** Pascal Fabre (AGS-Cosworth V8 JH22/32), 58.
PP – Mansell, 1;39.264; FL – Senna, 1;40.464, 89.584 mph.
Mansell lost race with severe leg cramps, Piquet recovered from early delay caused by puncture which dropped him to 21st. Senna had a comfortable, tactical ride in the active-suspension Lotus,

---

claiming he still felt 'brand new' after the finish. The agonized Mansell led laps 1-33, Senna rest of the way.

5-7-87 FRENCH GP,
Ricard-Castellet – 80 laps, 189.543 miles
1. Nigel Mansell (Williams-turbo V6 Honda FW11B/3), 80 laps in 1:37;03.839, 117.165 mph.
2. Nelson Piquet (Williams-turbo V6 Honda FW11B/4), 80 in 1:37;11.550.
3. Alain Prost (McLaren-turbo V6 TAG Turbo-Porsche MP4/3-3), 80. **4.** Ayrton Senna (Lotus-turbo V6 Honda 99T/4), 79. **5.** Teo Fabi (Benetton-turbo V6 Ford B187/7), 77.* **6. (2nd)** Jonathan Palmer (Tyrrell-Cosworth V8 DG/016-2), 76. **7. (2nd)** Jonathan Palmer (Tyrrell-Cosworth V8 DG/016-2), 76.
*Broken driveshaft.
PP – Mansell, 1,06.454; FL – Piquet, 1,09.548, 122.641 mph.
An internecine Williams-Honda battle, like the previous year's British GP. Mansell very quick on second set of Goodyears, with 17 laps to run Piquet gambled on a second tyre change, and the Brazilian was again out-raced in an even battle. Only Prost's McLaren could challenge the FW11Bs but worsening engine problems dropped him back. Lotus-Honda 99T not in the battle on fast circuit. Mansell led laps 1-35, Piquet 36-45, Mansell to the finish.

12-7-87 BRITISH GP,
Silverstone – 65 laps, 192.985 miles
1. Nigel Mansell (Williams-turbo V6 Honda FW11B/3), 65 laps in 1:19;11.780, 146.208 mph.
2. Nelson Piquet (Williams-turbo V6 Honda FW11B/4), 65 in 1:19;13.698.
3. Ayrton Senna (Lotus-turbo V6 Honda 99T/4), 64. **4.** Satoru Nakajima (Lotus-turbo V6 Honda 99T/5), 63. **5.** Derek Warwick (Arrows-turbo 4 Megatron-BMW A10/4), 63. **6.** Teo Fabi (Benetton-turbo V6 Ford B187/6), 63.
Naturally aspirated class result: **8. (1st)** Jonathan Palmer (Tyrrell-Cosworth V8 DG/016-2), 60. **9. (2nd)** Pascal Fabre (AGS-Cosworth V8 JH22/32), 59.
PP – Piquet, 1;07.110; FL – Mansell, 1;09.832, 153.059 mph.
Classic Piquet v. Mansell battle in the all-conquering Williams-Hondas – Nelson ran non-stop to team advice, Mansell forced to change tyres after losing a balance weight from left-front. Piquet's tyres lost performance, Mansell drove like a man possessed before his home crowd. Three laps to go, Mansell had fuel readout offering no hope – he blitzed regardless past his team-mate at Stowe Corner to win, then ran out of fuel on his cooling-off lap. Williams-Honda's domination was total, Piquet leading laps 1-62, Mansell the crucial final three . . .

26-7-87 GERMAN GP,
Hockenheim – 44 laps, 185.83 miles
1. Nelson Piquet (Williams-turbo V6 Honda FW11B/3), 44 laps in 1:21.25.091, 136.946 mph.
2. Stefan Johansson (McLaren-turbo V6 TAG Turbo-Porsche MP4/3-2), 44 in 1:23;04.682.
3. Ayrton Senna (Lotus-turbo V6 Honda 99T/4), 43. **4. (1st)** Philippe Streiff (Tyrrell-Cosworth V8 DG/016-3), 43. **5. (2nd)** Jonathan Palmer (Tyrrell-Cosworth V8 DG/016-2), 43. **6. (3rd)** Philippe Alliot (Lola-Cosworth V8 LC87/3), 42.
PP – Nigel Mansell (Williams-turbo V6 Honda FW11B/3), 1;42.616; FL – Mansell, 1;45.716, 143.823 mph.
This should have been Prost's 28th record-breaking GP victory, but after seeing off the Williams-Hondas on Porsche's home soil his McLaren's alternator drive parted and he stopped on the Ostkurve with under 4 laps to run. Johansson finished on three wheels with the right-front tyre tattered, Senna's Lotus too was merely wheeling wounded at the flag. Terrific retirement rate included Mansell's Williams. Senna led the opening lap, Mansell laps 2-7, Prost 8-18, Mansell 19-22, Prost 23-39, Piquet the final five.

9-8-87 HUNGARIAN GP,
Hungaroring – 76 laps, 189.557 miles
1. Nelson Piquet (Williams-turbo V6 Honda 99T/4), 76 laps in 1:59;26.793, 95.218 mph.
2. Ayrton Senna (Lotus-turbo V6 Honda 99T/4), 76 in 2:00;04.520.
3. Alain Prost (McLaren-turbo V6 TAG Turbo-Porsche MP4/3-4), 76. **4.** Thierry Boutsen (Benetton-turbo V6 Ford B187/6), 75. **5.** Riccardo Patrese (Brabham-turbo 4 BMW BT56/4), 75. **6.** Derek Warwick (Arrows-turbo 4 Megatron-BMW A10/4), 74.
Naturally aspirated class result: **7. (1st)** Jonathan Palmer (Tyrrell-Cosworth V8 DG/016-6), 74. **8. (2nd)** Philippe Streiff (Tyrrell-Cosworth V8 DG/016-5), 74.
PP – Nigel Mansell (Williams-turbo V6 Honda FW11B/3), 1;28.047; FL – Piquet, 1;30.149, 99.602 mph.
Having been presented with victory in Germany, it happened again for Piquet in Hungary when with 4 laps to go Mansell's right-rear wheel nut worked free and flew off his Williams-Honda. Piquet, troubled for the last 20 laps by severe car vibration, thus inherited his second win in consecutive GPs. McLaren inexplicably off the pace. In an effective reversal of Silverstone fortunes, Mansell led laps 1-70, Piquet 71-76.

16-8-87 AUSTRIAN GP,
Österreichring – 52 laps, 191.993 miles
1. Nigel Mansell (Williams-turbo V6 Honda FW11B/3), 52 laps in 1:18;44.898, 146.283 mph.
2. Nelson Piquet (Williams-turbo V6 Honda FW11B/4), 52 in 1:19;40.602.
3. Teo Fabi (Benetton-turbo V6 Ford B187/7), 51. **4.** Thierry Boutsen (Benetton-turbo V6 Ford B187/6), 51. **5.** Ayrton Senna (Lotus-turbo V6 Honda 99T/6), 50. **6.** Alain Prost (McLaren-turbo V6 TAG Turbo-Porsche MP4/3-4), 50.
Naturally aspirated class result: **11. (1st)** Ivan Capelli

(March-Cosworth V8 871/3), 49. **12. (2nd)** Philippe Alliot (Lola-Cosworth V8 LC87/3), 49.
PP – Piquet, 1;23.357; FL – Mansell, 1;28.318, 150.500 mph.
Two starts, two startline collisions caused the red flag to be shown. Third time lucky Mansell risked his assigned car's clutch rather than opt for the spare FW11B set up for Piquet. It then failed halfway through the ensuing race but his gamble paid off in victory. McLaren lost Johansson's MP4/3 in hideous qualifying collision with a deer crossing the course. The race eventually provided yet another all-Williams leaderboard, Piquet laps 1-20, Mansell 21-52.

9-8-87 ITALIAN GP,
Monza – 50 laps, 180.197 miles
1. Nelson Piquet (Williams-turbo V6 Honda FW11B/5), 50 laps in 1:14;47.707, 144.553 mph.
2. Ayrton Senna (Lotus-turbo V6 Honda 99T/4), 50 in 1:14;49.513.
3. Nigel Mansell (Williams-turbo V6 Honda FW11B/3), 50. **4.** Gerhard Berger (Ferrari turbo V6 F1/87 '098), 50. **5.** Thierry Boutsen (Benetton-turbo V6 Ford B187/6), 50. **6.** Stefan Johansson (McLaren-turbo V6 TAG Turbo-Porsche MP4/3-5), 50.
Naturally aspirated class result: **12. (1st)** Philippe Streiff (Tyrrell-Cosworth V8 DG/016-7), 47. **13. (2nd)** Ivan Capelli (March-Cosworth V8 871/1), 47.
PP – Piquet, 1;23.460; FL – Senna, 1;26.796, 149.479 mph.
Honda announced their decision to sever links with Williams despite one year of their contract still to run, but the Williams cars headed the grid from Ferrari, Lotus-Honda, McLaren-TAG and Benetton-Ford. Using Williams active ride for the first time in anger Piquet inherited victory after Senna's active Lotus slithered off course at the Parabolica with 8 laps to run. Senna had run non-stop but went off line lapping Ghinzani's Ligier and slid wide. Mansell's conventional-suspension FW11B suffered high engine temperatures and power loss. Piquet led the first 23 laps, Senna from 24-42, Piquet the final 8.

21-9-87 PORTUGUESE GP,
Estoril – 70 laps, 189.207 miles
1. Alain Prost (McLaren-turbo V6 TAG Turbo MP4/3-4), 70 laps in 1:37;03.906, 116.957 mph.
2. Gerhard Berger (Ferrari turbo V6 F1/87 '098), 70 in 1:37;24.399.
3. Nelson Piquet (Williams-turbo V6 Honda FW11B/5), 70. **4.** Teo Fabi (Benetton-turbo V6 Ford B187/8), 70.* **5.** Stefan Johansson (McLaren-turbo V6 TAG Turbo-Porsche MP4/3-5), 69. **6.** Eddie Cheever (Arrows-turbo 4 Megatron-BMW A10/3), 68.
*Out of fuel.
Naturally aspirated class result: **9. (1st)** Ivan Capelli (March-Cosworth V8 871/1), 67. **10. (2nd)** Jonathan Palmer (Tyrrell-Cosworth V8 DG/016-6), 67.
PP – Berger, 1;17.620; FL – Berger, 1;19.282, 122.737 mph.
Ferrari clicked in Portugal, the Williams-Hondas were eclipsed and yet Prost shone for McLaren to break Jackie Stewart's long-standing best-career GP wins record. Over the last 20 laps he pressured Berger remorselessly until the Austrian spun with 2 laps to run. Piquet consolidated his Championship lead in the active Williams, Senna delayed to finish 7th, Mansell retired. After Mansell lap 1, Berger tore through to lead 2-33, Alboreto taking over 34-35, then Berger again 36-67, Prost taking the lead for the final 3 only.

27-9-87 SPANISH GP,
Jerez de la Frontera – 72 laps, 188.708 miles
1. Nigel Mansell (Williams-turbo V6 Honda FW11B/8), 72 laps in 1:49;12.692, 103.674 mph.
2. Alain Prost (McLaren-turbo V6 TAG Turbo-Porsche MP4/3-4), 72 in 1:49;34.917.
3. Stefan Johansson (McLaren-turbo V6 TAG Turbo-Porsche MP4/3-5), 72. **4.** Nelson Piquet (Williams-turbo V6 Honda FW11B/5), 72. **5.** Ayrton Senna (Lotus-turbo V6 Honda 99T/4), 72. **6. (1st)** Philippe Alliot (Lola-Cosworth V8 LC87/2), 71. **7. (2nd)** Philippe Streiff (Tyrrell-Cosworth V8 DG/016-2), 71.
PP – Piquet, 1,22.461; FL – Gerhard Berger (Ferrari turbo V6 F1/87), 1;26.986, 108.470 mph.
Mansell led throughout. Piquet drove like a novice, forgetting to keep the brake pedal down during a tyre change, delayed long enough to rejoin race amidst duelling gaggle of cars. Had he beaten them out he could perhaps have exploited his active suspension which Mansell still refused to race. But Mansell was so far ahead his fastest lap was no better than 8th quickest overall! Senna ran non-stop, delaying other front-runners until 62nd lap when he could finally hold out no longer.

18-10-87 MEXICAN GP,
Autodromo Hermanos Rodriguez, Mexico City – 63 laps, 173.065 miles
1. Nigel Mansell (Williams-turbo V6 Honda FW11B/1), 63 laps in 1:26;24.207, 120.179 mph.
2. Nelson Piquet (Williams-turbo V6 Honda FW11B/6), 63 in 1:26;50.383.
3. Riccardo Patrese (Brabham-turbo 4 BMW BT56/4), 63. **4.** Eddie Cheever (Arrows-turbo 4 Megatron-BMW A10/2), 63. **5.** Teo Fabi (Benetton-turbo V6 Ford B187/7), 61. **6. (1st)** Philippe Alliot (Lola-Cosworth V8 LC87/3), 60. **7. (2nd)** Jonathan Palmer (Tyrrell-Cosworth V8 DG/016-5), 60.
PP – Mansell, 1;18.383; FL – Piquet, 1;19.132, 124.974 mph.
Closer competition than ever, with Mansell on pole, Berger's Ferrari alongside, then Boutsen's Benetton-Ford joining Piquet on row two. On lap 1 Piquet and Prost collided, the McLaren retiring, Mansell watched Berger and Boutsen race off for the lead. When they retired Mansell was out on his own,

Piquet 4th, half a minute behind. Then Warwick crashed his Arrows, race was stopped and restarted, Piquet taking the lead, Mansell keeping him in sight to win on aggregate. The Championship now lay purely between the Williams pair, with Honda's home round to follow . . . Bouts en led laps 1-14 for Benetton, Berger 15-20 from second place on the grid, Mansell thereafter.

1-11-87 JAPANESE GP,
Suzuka – 51 laps, 185.670 miles
1. Gerhard Berger (Ferrari turbo V6 F1/87 '098'), 51 laps in 1:32:58.072, 119.829 mph.
2. Ayrton Senna (Lotus-turbo V6 Honda 99T/6), 51 in 1:33:15.456.
3. Stefan Johansson (McLaren-turbo V6 TAG Turbo-Porsche MP4/3-5), 51. **4.** Michele Alboreto (Ferrari turbo V6 F1/87 '101'), 51. **5.** Thierry Boutsen (Benetton-turbo V6 Ford B187/9), 51. **6.** Satoru Nakajima (Lotus-turbo V6 Honda 99T/3), 51.
Naturally aspirated class result: **8.** (**1st**) Jonathan Palmer (Tyrrell-Cosworth V8 DG/016-5), 51. **12.** (**2nd**) Philippe Streiff (Tyrrell-Cosworth V8 DG/016-2), 49.
PP – Senna, 1:40.042; FL – Alain Prost (McLaren-turbo V6 TAG Turbo-Porsche MP4/3-4), 1:43.844, 126.210 mph.
Mansell's hopes of the title evaporated in a practice crash which put him out of the race, deciding the title for Piquet. Berger then spoiled Honda's party by qualifying on pole and leading the first Japanese GP for 10 years on all but lap 25, which was headed by Senna during the Ferrari tyre-change.

15-11-87 AUSTRALIAN GP,
Adelaide, South Australia – 82 laps, 192.454 miles
1. Gerhard Berger (Ferrari turbo V6 F1/87 '098'), 82 laps in 1:52:56.144, 102.299 mph.
2. Michele Alboreto (Ferrari turbo V6 F1/87 '101'), 82 in 1:54:04.028.*
3. Thierry Boutsen (Benetton-turbo V6 Ford B187/9), 81. **4.** (**1st**) Jonathan Palmer (Tyrrell-Cosworth V8 DG/016-5), 80. **5.** (**2nd**) Yannick Dalmas (Lola-Cosworth V8 LC87/2), 79. **6.** (**3rd**) Roberto Moreno (AGS-Cosworth V8 JH22/32), 79.
Second on road was Ayrton Senna Lotus-Honda 99T/6), who completed 82 laps in 1:53:30.989 but was disqualified on a technicality.
PP – Berger, 1:17.267; FL – Berger, 1:20.416, 105.123 mph.
Only real opposition to Ferrari was offered by Senna's Lotus-Honda which finished a strong second on the road but was disqualified for running with greater brake duct cooling intake area than permitted, elevating Alboreto to complete what was officially a Ferrari 1-2. Berger led all 82 laps, starting from pole, and setting fastest race lap, the perfect motor racing performance . . .

1988

3-4-88 BRAZILIAN GP,
Jacarepaguá, Rio de Janeiro – 60 laps, 187.566 miles
1. Alain Prost (McLaren-turbo V6 Honda MP4/4-2), 60 laps in 1:36:06.857, 117.089 mph.
2. Gerhard Berger (Ferrari turbo V6 F1/87/88C '104'), 60 in 1:36:16.730.
3. Nelson Piquet (Lotus-turbo V6 Honda 100T/2), 60. **4.** Derek Warwick (Arrows-turbo 4 Megatron-BMW A10B/2), 60. **5.** Michele Alboreto (Ferrari turbo V6 F1/87/88C '103'), 60. **6.** Satoru Nakajima (Lotus-turbo V6 Honda 100T/1), 59.
1st naturally aspirated car: **9.** Stefan Johansson (Ligier-Judd V8 JS31/3), 57.
PP – Ayrton Senna (McLaren-turbo V6 Honda MP4/4-3), 1:28.096;* FL – Senna, 1:32.943, 121 085 mph.
Started from pit lane leaving effective pole position to Nigel Mansell (Williams-Judd V8 FW12/1), 1:28.632.
Berger's Ferrari had set the pace in pre-season Rio testing but despite setting fastest lap in the GP he could make no impression upon an imperturbable Alain Prost in the lead. His new Steve Nichols-designed MP4/4 with Honda power was untouchable. Ferrari lacked competitive power, and the Ferraris and Lotus 100T needed two tyre changes against Prost's one. Senna had a disappointing McLaren debut, his car's gear linkage being deranged on the warm-up lap, switching cars at the start was delayed and later being black-flagged after a rare chase through the field. Prost led throughout.

1-5-88 'SAN MARINO' GP,
Imola, I – 60 laps, 187.902 miles
1. Ayrton Senna (McLaren-turbo V6 Honda MP4/4-1), 60 laps in 1:32:41.264, 121.635 mph.
2. Alain Prost (McLaren-turbo V6 Honda MP4/4-4), 60 in 1:32:43.598.
3. Nelson Piquet (Lotus-turbo V6 Honda 100T/2), 59. **4.** Thierry Boutsen (Benetton-Ford DFR V8 B188/4), 59. **5.** Gerhard Berger (Ferrari turbo V6 F/87/88C '102'), 59. **6.** Alessandro Nannini (Benetton-Ford DFR V8 B188/3), 59.
PP – Senna, 1:27.148; FL – Prost, 1:29.685, 125.708 mph.
This time, Senna led throughout. There was a terrific duel for third place between Piquet's turbocharged Lotus-Honda, supposedly using an identical engine, and the leading naturally aspirated cars, but this was the race in which the 150-litre-tanked turbos had been expected to be at their most vulnerable. McLaren-Honda were fuel-efficient as well as unbeatably quick.

15-5-88 MONACO GP,
Monte Carlo – 78 laps, 161.298 miles
1. Alain Prost (McLaren-turbo V6 Honda MP4/4-4), 78 laps in 1:57:17.077, 82.516 mph.
2. Gerhard Berger (Ferrari turbo V6 F1/87/88C '104'), 78 in 1:57:37.530.

---

3. Michele Alboreto (Ferrari F1/87/88C '103'), 78. **4.** Derek Warwick (Arrows-turbo 4 Megatron-BMW A10B/2), 77. **5.** Jonathan Palmer (Tyrrell-Cosworth DFZ V8 017/1), 77. **6.** Riccardo Patrese (Williams-Judd V8 FW12/2), 77.
PP – Senna, 1:23.998; FL – Senna, 1:26.321, 86.242 mph.
Senna led until he crashed on lap 67; Prost to the finish. Senna had been fastest in four of the five practice sessions, took pole by 1.5 secs, led from the start, set fastest lap and led Prost by 53 secs, then made a simple error at the *Portier* and hit the barrier. The 'race' was really no contest otherwise, accentuating the fact that amongst first-rate teams McLaren alone had built effective all-new cars for the final year of turbo racing, Ferrari had compromised with old chassis, and Williams were relegated to 'atmo' Judd engines in a bye year.

29-5-88 MEXICAN GP,
Autodromo Hermanos Rodriguez, Mexico City – 67 laps, 184.054 miles
1. Alain Prost (McLaren-turbo V6 Honda MP4/4-4), 67 laps in 1:30:15.737, 122.346 mph.
2. Ayrton Senna (McLaren-turbo V6 Honda MP4/4-1), 67 in 1:30:22.841.
3. Gerhard Berger (Ferrari turbo V6 F1/87/88C '104'), 67. **4.** Michele Alboreto (Ferrari F1/87/88C '103'), 66. **5.** Derek Warwick (Arrows-turbo 4 Megatron-BMW A10B/2), 66. **6.** Eddie Cheever (Arrows-turbo 4 Megatron-BMW A10B/1), 66.
1st naturally aspirated car: **7.** Alessandro Nannini (Benetton-Ford DFR V8 B188/3), 65.
PP – Senna, 1:17.468; FL – Prost, 1:18.608, 125.807 mph.
Prost led from start to finish despite having to deal with an overheating engine and marginal tyre wear in roasting heat. Senna was concerned about tyre wear and unexpectedly high fuel consumption. Berger's Ferrari was the only other runner to complete full distance, and he barely escaped being lapped.

12-6-88 CANADIAN GP,
Ile Notre Dame, Montreal – 69 laps, 188.21 miles
1. Ayrton Senna (McLaren-turbo V6 Honda MP4/4-1), 69 laps in 1:39:46.618, 113.183 mph.
2. Alain Prost (McLaren-turbo V6 Honda MP4/4-4), 69 in 1:39:52.552.
3. Thierry Boutsen (Benetton-Ford DFR V8 B188/5), 69. **4.** Nelson Piquet (Lotus-turbo V6 Honda T100/2), 68. **5.** Ivan Capelli (March-Judd V8 881/3), 68. **6.** Jonathan Palmer (Tyrrell-Cosworth DFZ 017/4), 67.
PP – Senna, 1:21.681; FL – Senna, 1:24.973, 115.567 mph.
Even at reduced-boost 'cruise mode' the McLarens could lap faster than Boutsen's Benetton could manage flat-out. Prost was unable to attack Senna's position due to overheating and brake problems. First 18 laps led by Prost, Senna thereafter.

19-6-88 UNITED STATES (DETROIT) GP,
Detroit, Michigan – 63 laps, 157.50 miles
1. Ayrton Senna (McLaren-turbo V6 Honda MP4/4-2), 63 laps in 1:54:56.035, 82.221 mph.
2. Alain Prost (McLaren-turbo V6 Honda MP4/4-4), 63 in 1:55:34.748.
3. Thierry Boutsen (Benetton-Ford DFR V8 B188/5), 62. **4.** Andrea de Cesaris (Rial-Cosworth DFZ V8 ARC1/2), 62. **5.** Jonathan Palmer (Tyrrell-Cosworth DFZ 017/1), 62. **6.** PierLuigi Martini (Minardi-Cosworth DFZ V8 M188/1), 62.
PP – Senna, 1:40.606; FL – Prost, 1:44.836, 85.848 mph.
Senna led throughout and McLaren-Honda demolished all vain hope of the 'atmo' cars being capable of challenging the reduced boost/reduced fuel tankage turbo cars. Prost hated the Detroit circuit yet still finished a strong second despite a gearchange problem demanding great caution entering the many right-angled walled corners. Again the Benetton proved the best of the rest. De Cesaris shone in minor key – in the Rial, while Palmer climbed from last at the start to finish 5th. Minardi secured their first Championship points after four years' effort.

3-7-88 FRENCH GP,
Ricard-Castellet – 80 laps, 189.543 miles
1. Alain Prost (McLaren-turbo V6 Honda MP4/4-4), 80 laps in 1:37:37.328, 116.495 mph.
2. Ayrton Senna (McLaren-turbo V6 Honda MP4/4-2), 80 in 1:38:09.080.
3. Michele Alboreto (Ferrari turbo V6 F1/87/88C '103'), 80. **4.** Gerhard Berger (Ferrari turbo V6 F1/87/88C '104'), 79. **5.** Nelson Piquet (Lotus-turbo V6 Honda 100T/2), 79. **6.** Alessandro Nannini (Benetton-Ford DFR V8 B188/3), 79.
PP – Prost, 1:07.589; FL – Prost, 1:11.737, 118.898 mph.
Another McLaren-Honda demonstration in this no-contest season. Prost grew horns on his home ground, took his first pole position in two years and carried the race to Senna, who was mildly handicapped by a gearbox problem. Prost led the first 36 laps, Senna laps 37-60, Prost 61-80.

10-7-88 – BRITISH GP,
Silverstone – 65 laps, 192.985 miles
1. Ayrton Senna (McLaren-turbo V6 Honda MP4/4-5), 65 laps in 1:33:16.367, 124.142 mph.
2. Nigel Mansell (Williams-Judd V8 FW12/1), 65 in 1:33:39.711.
3. Alessandro Nannini (Benetton-Ford DFR V8 B188/3), 65. **4.** Mauricio Gugelmin (March-Judd V8 881/2), 65. **5.** Nelson Piquet (Lotus-turbo V6 Honda T100/3), 65. **6.** Derek Warwick (Arrows-turbo 4 Megatron-BMW A10B/3), 64.
PP – Gerhard Berger (Ferrari turbo V6 F1/87/88C '104'), 1:10.133; FL – Mansell, 1:23.308, 128.300 mph.
In pouring rain we saw the first lap of 1988 GP racing not to be led by a McLaren-Honda. Berger led the opening lap of the British GP in heavy rain – a fuel-squandering gesture from the irrepressible Austrian

---

at his peak for Ferrari. Prost opted out in the flooded conditions, Senna won yet again, Mansell put his revised Williams-Judd FW12 into 2nd place in an unusually reliable run while Berger stuttered home 9th, predictably out of fuel. He had led from lap 1-13, Senna 14-65.

24-7-88 GERMAN GP,
Hockenheim – 44 laps, 185.83 miles
1. Ayrton Senna (McLaren-turbo V6 Honda MP4/4-5), 44 laps in 1:32:54.188, 120.016 mph.
2. Alain Prost (McLaren-turbo V6 Honda MP4/4-4), 44 in 1:33:07.797.
3. Gerhard Berger (Ferrari turbo V6 F1/87/88C '104'), 44. **4.** Michele Alboreto (Ferrari turbo V6 F1/87/88C '103'), 44. **5.** Ivan Capelli (March-Judd V8 881/3), 44. **6.** Thierry Boutsen (Benetton-Ford DFR V8 B188/5), 43.
PP – Senna, 1:44.596; FL – Alessandro Nannini (Benetton-Ford DFR V8 B188/6), 2:03.032, 125.581 mph.
Senna's 5th win of the year brought him within 3 points of Prost for the Drivers' title. Senna led from flag to flag. Prost made a poor start, spun later and was beaten by Senna's great expertise in wet-weather racing, narrowing the Championship gap; but in technical terms such continued one-sided racing proved nothing – the McLaren-Hondas were built to one Formula, everything else (in effect) to another.

7-8-88 HUNGARIAN GP,
Hungaroring – 76 laps, 189.557 miles
1. Ayrton Senna (McLaren-turbo V6 Honda MP4/4-5), 76 laps in 1:57:47.081, 96.561 mph.
2. Alain Prost (McLaren-turbo V6 Honda MP4/4-4), 76 in 1:57:47.610.
3. Thierry Boutsen (Benetton-Ford DFR V8 B188/2), 76. **4.** Gerhard Berger (Ferrari turbo V6 F1/87/88C '104'), 76. **5.** Mauricio Gugelmin (March-Judd V8 188/2), 75. **6.** Riccardo Patrese (Williams-Judd V8 FW12/3), 75.
PP – Senna, 1:27.635; FL – Prost, 1:30.639, 99.063 mph.
For the second successive race, Senna led throughout, despite one notable attempt by Prost to pass him, which succeeded for all of 30 yards. Prost was slowed by tyre vibration before coming to terms with it and closing right up on his team-mate at the line.

28-8-88 BELGIAN GP,
Spa-Francorchamps – 43 laps, 185.429 miles
1. Ayrton Senna (McLaren-turbo V6 Honda MP4/4-5), 43 laps in 1:28:00.549, 126.415 mph.
2. Alain Prost (McLaren-turbo V6 Honda MP4/4-4), 43 in 1:28:31.019. **3.** Thierry Boutsen (Benetton-Ford DFR V8 B188/2), 43.* **4.** Alessandro Nannini (Benetton-Ford DFR V8 B188/6), 43.* **5.** Ivan Capelli (March-Judd V8 881/5), 43. **6.** Nelson Piquet (Lotus-turbo V6 Honda 100T/2), 43.
Subsequently disqualified for an alleged fuel irregularity.
PP – Senna, 1:53.718; FL – Gerhard Berger (Ferrari turbo V6 F1/87/88C '104'), 2:00.772, 128.542 mph.
Halfway round the opening lap, Senna displaced Prost for the lead and that's the way it remained. Senna's 4th successive victory made the season score 7-4 to the Brazilian. Capelli shone in his March from 14th on the grid to 5th at the finish, 7 secs behind an equally impressive Nannini. For the third successive race, Senna led every lap.

11-9-88 ITALIAN GP,
Monza – 51 laps, 183.801 miles
1. Gerhard Berger (Ferrari turbo V6 F1/87/88C '102'), 51 laps in 1:17:39.744, 142.000 mph.
2. Michele Alboreto (Ferrari turbo V6 F1/87/88C '103'), 51 in 1:17:40.246.
3. Eddie Cheever (Arrows-turbo 4 Megatron-BMW A10B/4), 51. **4.** Derek Warwick (Arrows-turbo 4 Megatron-BMW A10B/2), 51. **5.** Ivan Capelli (March-Judd V8 881/5), 51. **6.** Thierry Boutsen (Benetton-Ford DFR V8 B188/4), 51.
PP – Senna, 1:25.974; FL – Alboreto, 1:29.070, 145.662 mph.
Glory be, Senna fell over Jean-Louis Schlesser's Williams at the first chicane and crashed out after leading the first 49 laps. For the first time since lap 13 of the British GP at Silverstone, two months previously, somebody else led a GP. If only for two laps they were the vital ones, and Berger's Ferrari won on home soil!

25-9-88 PORTUGUESE GP,
Estoril – 70 laps, 189.207 miles
1. Alain Prost (McLaren-turbo V6 Honda MP4/4-6), 70 laps in 1:37:40.958, 116.217 mph.
2. Ivan Capelli (March-Judd V8 881/5), 70 in 1:37:50.511.
3. Thierry Boutsen (Benetton-Ford DFR V8 B188/2), 70. **4.** Derek Warwick (Arrows-turbo 4 Megatron-BMW A10B/3), 70. **5.** Michele Alboreto (Ferrari turbo V6 F1/87/88C '104'), 70. **6.** Ayrton Senna (McLaren-turbo V6 Honda MP4/4-6), 70.
PP – Prost, 1:17.411; FL – Gerhard Berger (Ferrari turbo V6 F1/87/88C '104'), 1:21.961, 118.722 mph.
The old firm back in business as Senna led lap 1, Prost the rest of the way. Entire meeting depressing for Senna, and Prost was unimpressed by the Brazilian shouldering him tight against the pit wall ending the opening lap. As Senna battled with mechanical problems Prost's main opposition came from Capelli's March-Judd – Alboreto lost 3rd on the final lap as his Ferrari ran out of fuel.

2-10-88 SPANISH GP,
Jerez de la Frontera – 72 laps, 188.708 miles
1. Alain Prost (McLaren-turbo V6 Honda MP4/4-6), 72 laps in 1:48:43.851, 104.133 mph.
2. Nigel Mansell (Williams-Judd V8 FW12/1), 72 in 1:49:10.083.
3. Alessandro Nannini (Benetton-Ford DFR V8 B188/7), 72. **4.** Ayrton Senna (McLaren-turbo V6 Honda MP4/4-5), 72. **5.** Riccardo Patrese (Williams-Judd V8 FW12/3), 72. **6.** Gerhard Berger (Ferrari turbo V6 F1/87/88C '104'), 72.

Prost led Mansell 1-2, McLaren v. Williams, flag to flag. The Frenchman seemed revitalized, while Senna was troubled by fuel consumption readout warnings after starting from pole position. As Nannini beat Senna to the line the Drivers' Championship seemed to open out again – unlike the Constructors' Cup . . .

30-10-88 JAPANESE GP,
Suzuka – 51 laps, 185.670 miles
1. Ayrton Senna (McLaren-turbo V6 Honda MP4/4-2), 51 laps in 1:33:26.173, 119.230 mph.
2. Alain Prost (McLaren-turbo V6 Honda MP4/4-6), 51 in 1:33:39.536.
3. Thierry Boutsen (Benetton-Ford DFR V8 B188/8), 51. **4.** Gerhard Berger (Ferrari turbo V6 F1/87/88C '104'), 51. **5.** Alessandro Nannini (Benetton-Ford DFR V8 B188/7), 51. **6.** Riccardo Patrese (Williams-Judd V8 FW12/3), 51.
PP – Senna, 1:41.853; FL – Senna, 1:46.326, 123.266 mph.
Senna stalled off pole position, bump-started the MP4/4 and lay 14th into the first corner, then 8th ending the lap. Prost quickly disposed of Berger's Ferrari challenge in the March 881 as Prost was slowed by Suzuka's spinning Lola, Capelli led momentarily through the timing beam ending lap 16. Now Senna was 3rd and a March electrical failure left the race a straight fight between the inevitable McLaren-Hondas. De Cesaris delayed Prost exiting the chicane on lap 27, Senna swept by and as he scored his 8th victory of the season the Championship was his. Prost led laps 1-15 and 17-27, Capelli lap 16, Senna laps 28-51.

13-11-88 AUSTRALIAN GP,
Adelaide, South Australia – 82 laps, 192.498 miles
1. Alain Prost (McLaren-turbo V6 Honda MP4/4-6), 82 laps in 1:53:14.676, 102.044 mph.
2. Ayrton Senna (McLaren-turbo V6 Honda MP4/4-2), 82 in 1:53:51.463.
3. Nelson Piquet (Lotus-turbo V6 Honda 100T/2), 82. **4.** Riccardo Patrese (Williams-Judd V8 FW12/3), 82. **5.** Thierry Boutsen (Benetton-Ford DFR V8 B188/8), 81. **6.** Ivan Capelli (March-Judd V8 881/5), 81.
PP – Senna, 1:17.748; FL – Prost, 1:21.216, 104.112 mph.
Prost led laps 1-13 and from 26 to the flag – Berger laps 14-25. But the Frenchman had new worries as Berger had warned him he would run full boost, and hang the consequences . . . a fitting farewell to the era of turbocharged F1 racing. Collision with Arnoux's Ligier ended Berger's doomed run with honour, Senna had gearbox troubles in a final McLaren-turbo Honda 1-2.

1989

26-3-89 BRAZILIAN GP,
Jacarepaguá, Rio de Janeiro – 61 laps, 190.692 miles
1. Nigel Mansell (Ferrari V12 640 '109'), 61 laps in 1:38:58.744, 115.595 mph.
2. Alain Prost (McLaren-Honda V10 MP4/5-3), 61 in 1:39:06.553.
3. Mauricio Gugelmin (March-Judd V8 881/6), 61. **4.** Johnny Herbert (Benetton-Ford DFR V8 B188/8), 61. **5.** Derek Warwick (Arrows-Ford DFR V8 A11/2), 61. **6.** Alessandro Nannini (Benetton-Ford DFR V8 B188/9), 61.
PP – Ayrton Senna (McLaren-Honda V10 MP4/5-2), 1:25.302; FL – Riccardo Patrese (Williams-Renault V10 FW12C/7), 1:32.507, 121.655 mph.
Even during race morning warm-up Nigel Mansell found himself on the end of a tow-rope following yet another failure in his Ferrari's semi-automatic transmission system. Yet with Senna's pole-position McLaren-Honda tangling with Berger's Ferrari at the first corner and Prost's McLaren handicapped by an inoperative clutch Mansell took the lead and held it. His Ferrari proved reliable, largely to his own surprise, and so Maranello's John Barnard creation won its maiden race. Tragically, in a testing accident at Rio 11 days before the race, Philippe Streiff's racing career ended in paralysis following a massive accident in an AGS. On race day, Patrese led laps 1-15 and 21-22, Mansell 16-20, 28-44 and 47 to the finish, Prost laps 23-27 and 45-46.

23-4-89 'SAN MARINO' GP,
Imola, I – 61 laps, 191.033 miles*
Scheduled, but in fact due to Berger's Ferrari accident race run in two parts, of 3 laps and 55 laps – total 58 laps – 181.638 miles.
1. Ayrton Senna (McLaren-Honda V10 MP4/5-1), 58 laps in 1:26:51.245, 125.478 mph.
2. Alain Prost (McLaren-Honda V10 MP4/5-3), 58 in 1:27:31.470.
3. Alessandro Nannini (Benetton-Ford DFR V8 B188/9), 57. **4.** Thierry Boutsen (Williams-Renault V10 FW12C/9), 57.* **5.** Derek Warwick (Arrows-Ford DFR V8 A11/2), 57. **6.** Jonathan Palmer (Tyrrell-Ford DFR V8 018/1), 57.
Disqualified but later reinstated.
PP – Senna, 1:26.010; FL – Prost, 1:26.795, 126.786 mph.
Imola '89 was overshadowed by Berger's massive and fiery shunt on lap 4 when his Ferrari shed a nose wing entering the 170 mph *Tamburello* curve. His escape with minor injuries spoke volumes for the passive safety built into modern F1 monocoques. The race was stopped and restarted, and McLaren-Honda annihilated all opposition, though Senna's victory upset Prost who claimed an agreement had just been broken . . . Senna led throughout.

7-5-89 MONACO GP,
Monte Carlo – 77 laps, 159.229 miles
1. Ayrton Senna (McLaren-Honda V10 MP4/5-1), 77 laps in 1:53;33.251, 84.134 mph.
2. Alain Prost (McLaren-Honda V10 MP4/5-3), 77 in 1:54;25.780.
3. Stefano Modena (Brabham-Judd V8 BT58/2), 76. **4.** Alex Caffi (Dallara-Ford DFR V8 F189/6), 75. **5.** Michele Alboreto (Tyrrell-Ford DFR V8 018/2), 75. **6.** Martin Brundle (Brabham-Judd V8 BT58/3), 75.
PP – Senna, 1:22.308; FL – Prost, 1;25.501, 87.125 mph.
McLarens dominant yet again, lapping all surviving opposition and Senna concealing a major gearbox problem from his pursuing team-mate and increasingly bitter rival, Prost. Brabhams very quick on Pirelli tyres, Brundle looking set for 3rd place until an electrical problem intervened. Mansell's lone Ferrari ran 3rd until gear selection maladies intruded – both Williams-Renaults delayed by rear wing failures. Again, Senna led throughout.

28-5-89 MEXICAN GP,
Autodromo Hermanos Rodriguez, Mexico City – 69 laps, 189.548 miles
1. Ayrton Senna (McLaren-Honda V10 MP4/5-1), 69 laps in 1:35;21.431, 119.266 mph.
2. Riccardo Patrese (Williams-Renault V10 FW12C/7), 69 in 1:35;36.991.
3. Michele Alboreto (Tyrrell-Ford DFR V8 018/2), 69. **4.** Alessandro Nannini (Benetton-Ford V8 B188/9), 69. **5.** Alain Prost (McLaren-Honda V10 MP4/5-3), 69. **6.** Gabriele Tarquini (AGS-Ford DFR V8 JH23B-36), 68.
PP – Senna, 1:17.876; FL – Nigel Mansell (Ferrari V12 640 '109'), 1;20.420, 122.972 mph.
Just for once Prost – master of the art of tyre choice – chose wrong in Mexico and Senna out-smarted him to dominate again. Ferrari came closest to mounting a McLaren challenge but Mansell's transmission suffered an hydraulic pipe failure, and Berger retired from 4th place. Alboreto ran strongly in the Tyrrell. For the third consecutive race, Senna led throughout.

UNITED STATES (PHOENIX) GP,
Phoenix, Arizona – 75 laps, 177.00 miles
1. Ayrton Senna (McLaren-Honda V10 MP4/5-3), 75 laps in 2:01;33.133, 87.370 mph.
2. Riccardo Patrese (Williams-Renault V10 FW12C/7), 75 in 2:02;12.829.
3. Eddie Cheever (Arrows-Ford DFR V8 A11/3), 75. **4.** Christian Danner (Rial-Ford DFR V8 ARC2/1), 74. **5.** Johnny Herbert (Benetton-Ford DFR V8 B188/4), 74. **6.** Thierry Boutsen (Williams-Renault V10 FW12C/9), 74.
PP – Ayrton Senna (McLaren-Honda V10 MP4/5-4), 1;30.108; FL – Senna, 1;33.969, 90.413 mph.
Senna's McLaren season was interrupted by electrical failure in this inaugural Arizonan street race, handing victory to Prost. Senna started from his 34th pole position to break Jim Clark's old record. In practice Prost wrote off a chassis for the first time in 5½ years with McLaren. Patrese and Cheever fought fine battle for 2nd place in race notable for its mechanical carnage. Senna led laps 1-33, Prost 34-75.

18-6-89 CANADIAN GP,
Ile Notre Dame, Montreal – 69 laps, 188.21 miles
1. Thierry Boutsen (Williams-Renault V10 FW12C/9), 69 laps in 2:01;24.073, 93.023 mph.
2. Riccardo Patrese (Williams-Renault V10 FW12C/7), 69 in 2:01;54.080.
3. Andrea de Cesaris (Dallara-Ford DFR V8 F189/7), 69. **4.** Nelson Piquet (Lotus-Judd V8 101/2), 69. **5.** René Arnoux (Ligier-Ford DFR V8 JS33/4), 68. **6.** Alex Caffi (Dallara-Ford DFR V8 F189/5), 67.
PP – Alain Prost (McLaren-Honda V10 MP4/5-3), 1;20.973; FL – Jonathan Palmer (Tyrrell-Ford DFR V8 018/1), 1;31.925, 106.827 mph.
Neither McLaren finished amongst 19 retirements in wet race. Prost had lap 2 suspension failure, Senna's engine blew 3 laps from finish. Williams inherited fortunate 1-2 but Patrese had led for a long way and both cars were still around at the end to benefit. Derek Warwick had looked set to score Arrows' first-ever win until his engine failed, Mansell and Nannini both disqualified after muddled start as they made late decision to change tyres. Prost led opening lap, then Senna laps 2-3, Patrese 4-34, Warwick 35-38, Senna 39-66, Boutsen 67-69.

9-7-89 FRENCH GP,
Ricard-Castellet – 80 laps, 189.543 miles
1. Alain Prost (McLaren-Honda V10 MP4/5-5), 80 laps in 1:38;29.411, 115.469 mph.
2. Nigel Mansell (Ferrari V12 640 '110'), 80 in 1:39;13.428.
3. Riccardo Patrese (Williams-Renault V10 FW12C/10), 80. **4.** Jean Alesi (Tyrrell-Ford DFR V8 018/2), 80. **5.** Stefan Johansson (Onyx-Ford DFR V8 ORE-1/3), 79. **6.** Olivier Grouillard (Ligier-Ford DFR V8 JS33/2), 79.
PP – Prost, 1;07.203; FL – Mauricio Gugelmin (March-Judd V8 CG891/3), 1;12.090, 118.316 mph.
Prost announced he was leaving McLaren and drove a superb race for these to dominate in, in Senna's early absence. He had led into the first corner but Gugelmin rolled his March behind in a multiple collision causing the race to be stopped and restarted. Senna's McLaren then stripped a gear on the restart, leaving Prost to dominate a race enlivened by Mansell's surge into 2nd place driving Berger's Ferrari 640 after his own had been damaged in the first-start collision. Prost led throughout.

7-89 BRITISH GP,
stone – 64 laps, 190.080 miles

1. Alain Prost (McLaren-Honda V10 MP4/5-5), 64 laps in 1:19;22.131, 143.694 mph.
2. Nigel Mansell (Ferrari V12 640 '109'), 64 in 1:19;41.500.
3. Alessandro Nannini (Benetton-Ford V8 B189/4), 64. **4.** Nelson Piquet (Lotus-Judd V8 101/4), 64. **5.** PierLuigi Martini (Minardi-Ford DFR V8 M189/3), 63. **6.** Luis Perez Sala (Minardi-Ford V8 M189/2), 63.
PP – Ayrton Senna (McLaren-Honda V10 MP4/5-6), 1;09.099; FL – Mansell, 1;12.017, 148.465 mph.
Senna spun out of 2nd place leaving it to Mansell's Ferrari and it was delayed by a puncture. Prost made precautionary tyre change extended by baulky wheel nut and rejoined only 12 secs ahead of Mansell who tried hard but could not come to grips with the Honda-powered car. Nannini an encouraging if distant 3rd for Benetton. Senna led laps 1-10 before spinning off when attempting to cope with a gearbox problem on lap 11, Prost the rest of the way.

30-7-89 GERMAN GP,
Hockenheim – 45 laps, 190.055 miles
1. Ayrton Senna (McLaren-Honda V10 MP4/5-3), 45 laps in 1:21;43.302, 139.538 mph.
2. Alain Prost (McLaren-Honda V10 MP4/5-5), 45 in 1:22;01.453.
3. Nigel Mansell (Ferrari V12 640 '109'), 45. **4.** Riccardo Patrese (Williams-Renault V10 FW12C/10), 44. **5.** Nelson Piquet (Lotus-Judd V8 101/4), 44. **6.** Derek Warwick (Arrows-Ford DFR V8 A11/4), 44.
PP – Senna, 1;42.300; FL – Senna, 1;45.884, 143.594 mph.
Usual McLaren domination saw their normal running order reversed by delays during tyre changes. Prost emerged ahead with Senna breathing down his neck until with 2 laps to run the Frenchman's MP4/5 lost 6th gear and Senna ducked by to win. Senna led laps 1-19, Prost 20-42, Senna 43-45.

13-8-89 HUNGARIAN GP,
Hungaroring – 77 laps, 189.850 miles
1. Nigel Mansell (Ferrari V12 640 '109'), 77 laps in 1:49;38.650, 103.821 mph.
2. Ayrton Senna (McLaren-Honda V10 MP4/5-3), 77 in 1:50;04.617.
3. Thierry Boutsen (Williams-Renault V10 FW12C/9), 77. **4.** Alain Prost (McLaren-Honda V10 MP4/5-5), 77. **5.** Eddie Cheever (Arrows-Ford DFR V8 A11/4), 77. **6.** Nelson Piquet (Lotus-Judd V8 101/4), 77.
PP – Riccardo Patrese (Williams-Renault V10 FW12C/10), 1;19.726; FL – Mansell, 1;22.637, 107.411 mph.
Patrese's Williams-Renault appeared ideal for the twisty Hungaroring, he qualified it on pole position and led two-thirds distance until a radiator was punctured. Senna was left leading from Mansell, fully charged-up and the Ferrari 640 fully on song. With 11 laps to run Mansell out-foxed the Brazilian, dashed ahead and held out to the finish. A fine, old-fashioned motor race. Patrese led laps 1-52, Senna 53-57, Mansell 58-77.

27-8-89 BELGIAN GP,
Spa-Francorchamps – 44 laps, 189.741 miles
1. Ayrton Senna (McLaren-Honda V10 MP4/5-7), 44 laps in 1:40;54.196.
2. Alain Prost (McLaren-Honda V10 MP4/5-5), 44 in 1:40;55.500.
3. Nigel Mansell (Ferrari V12 640 '112'), 44. **4.** Thierry Boutsen (Williams-Renault V10 FW12C/9), 44. **5.** Alessandro Nannini (Benetton-Ford V8 B189/4), 44. **6.** Derek Warwick (Arrows-Ford DFR V8 A11/2), 44.
PP – Senna, 1:50.867; FL – Prost, 2;11.571, 117.991 mph.
Wet race on the finest circuit in the calendar dominated by Senna's peerless skills. Prost just fending off Mansell by 0.48 sec for 2nd place. A daunting race in every way, and Senna led throughout.

10-9-89 ITALIAN GP,
Monza – 53 laps, 191.009 miles
1. Alain Prost (McLaren-Honda V10 MP4/5-5), 53 laps in 1:19;27.550, 144.231 mph.
2. Gerhard Berger (Ferrari V12 640 '112BIS'), 53 in 1:19;34.876.
3. Thierry Boutsen (Williams-Renault V10 FW12C/9), 53. **4.** Riccardo Patrese (Williams-Renault V10 FW12C/7), 53. **5.** Jean Alesi (Tyrrell-Ford DFR V8 018/2), 53. **6.** Martin Brundle (Brabham-Judd V8 BT58/5), 52.
PP – Ayrton Senna (McLaren-Honda V10 MP4/5-7), 1;23.720; FL – Prost, 1;28.107, 147.255 mph.
McLaren-Honda clinched the Constructors' Championship as Prost notched his 39th GP win – popular with the Italian crowd because a few days before Prost had signed for Ferrari for 1990. Senna took pole by a staggering 1.79 secs, Prost claiming unfair treatment within the team. Senna led away as he pleased until his engine blew with under 9 laps to run. Prost had disposed of Mansell – soon to retire with transmission trouble – and Berger and inherited untroubled victory. On the victory dais Prost enraged team chief Ron Dennis by tossing his winner's trophy to the crowd below! Senna had led laps 1-44, Prost 45-53.

24-9-89 PORTUGUESE GP,
Estoril – 71 laps, 191.910 miles
1. Gerhard Berger (Ferrari V12 640 '112BIS'), 71 laps in 1:36;48.546, 118.941 mph.
2. Alain Prost (McLaren-Honda V10 MP4/5-5), 71 in 1:37;21.183.
3. Stefan Johansson (Onyx-Ford DFR V8 ORE-1/5), 71. **4.** Alessandro Nannini (Benetton-Ford V8 B189/6), 71. **5.** PierLuigi Martini (Minardi-Ford DFR V8 M189/5), 70. **6.** Jonathan Palmer (Tyrrell-Ford DFR V8 018/4), 70.
PP – Ayrton Senna (McLaren-Honda V10 MP4/5-7), 1;15.468; FL – Berger, 1;18.986, 123.194 mph.

The Barnard Ferraris were dominant at Estoril but trouble began when Mansell overshot his pit stop marks and reversed, breaking the basic rule governing conflicts with the direction of racing. Failing to see, or ignoring, three black flags after rejoining, Mansell then lunged for 2nd place past Senna into the first turn. Senna slammed the door, the cars collided and both spun out. Prost was left to take 2nd place behind Berger's dominant Ferrari but Johansson a staggering 3rd for the tiny Onyx team. Berger led laps 1-23, Mansell 24-39, Martini's Minardi lap 40 (during pit stops), Berger lap 41 to the flag.

1-10-89 SPANISH GP,
Jerez de la Frontera – 73 laps, 191.328 miles
1. Ayrton Senna (McLaren-Honda V10 MP4/5-7), 73 laps in 1:47;48.264, 106.486 mph.
2. Gerhard Berger (Ferrari V12 640 '112BIS'), 73 in 1:48;15.315.
3. Alain Prost (McLaren-Honda V10 MP4/5-5), 73. **4.** Jean Alesi (Tyrrell-Ford DFR V8 018/5), 72. **5.** Riccardo Patrese (Williams-Renault V10 FW12C/9), 72. **6.** Philippe Alliot (Lola-Lamborghini V12 LC89/4), 72.
PP – Senna, 1;20.291; FL – Senna, 1;25.779, 109.996 mph.
Mansell was excluded from taking part as officialdom frowned on perceived Estoril misdemeanours. Senna got away scot-free to dominate at Jerez, Berger could only maintain pressure for first 20 laps, Prost soldiered round 3rd – first three places remaining unchanged throughout.

22-10-89 JAPANESE GP,
Suzuka – 53 laps, 192.952 miles
1. Alessandro Nannini (Benetton-Ford V8 B189/4), 53 laps in 1:35;06.277, 121.730 mph.*
2. Riccardo Patrese (Williams-Renault V10 FW13/1), 53 in 1:35;18.181.
3. Thierry Boutsen (Williams-Renault V10 FW13/3), 53. **4.** Nelson Piquet (Lotus-Judd V8 101/4), 53. **5.** Martin Brundle (Brabham-Judd V8 BT58/1), 52. **6.** Derek Warwick (Arrows-Ford DFR V8 A11/5), 52.
*Awarded 1st place after exclusion of Ayrton Senna (McLaren-Honda V10 MP4/5-7), who won on road after collision with team-mate Alain Prost on lap 47.
PP – Senna, 1;38.041; FL – Prost, 1;43.506, 126.622 mph.
Prost made the better start in his MP4/5 painstakingly set up for greater straightline speed, keeping Senna at bay for 46 laps. On the 47th Senna lunged for the lead, expecting Prost to step aside into the chicane. The Frenchman defended his position, the McLarens collided, Prost retired, Senna rejoined – by-passing the chicane – but lost the lead in a pit stop to replace a tattered nose cone, then regaining it from Nannini's Benetton. He finished 1st on the road but was disqualified. Prost led laps 1-20, Senna 21-23, Prost 24-46, Senna 47-48, Nannini 49-50, Senna 51-53.

5-11-89 AUSTRALIAN GP,
Adelaide, South Australia – 70 laps, 164.290 miles
1. Thierry Boutsen (Williams-Renault V10 FW13/3), 70 laps in 2:00;17.421, 82.00 mph.
2. Alessandro Nannini (Benetton-Ford V8 B189/4), 70 in 2:00;46.079.
3. Riccardo Patrese (Williams-Renault V10 FW13/1), 70. **4.** Satoru Nakajima (Lotus-Judd V8 101/3), 70. **5.** Emanuele Pirro (Benetton-Ford V8 B189/5), 68. **6.** PierLuigi Martini (Minardi-Ford DFR V8 M189/5), 67.
PP – Ayrton Senna (McLaren-Honda V10 MP4/5-7), 1;16.665; FL – Nannini, 1;38.480, 85.860 mph.
Race run in appalling conditions of torrential rain. Senna led at amazing pace considering the conditions until he rammed the tail of Brundle's Brabham hidden in spray cloud. Piquet wrote off a Lotus in similar collision with Ghinzani's Osella. Prost simply declined to take part – the World title was his and he decided that to race in such conditions was an unacceptable lottery. Through all this Boutsen drove exquisitely to win his second wet race for Williams-Renault. Senna's charge led the first 13 laps, Boutsen emerging to lead the final 57.

1990

11-3-90 UNITED STATES (PHOENIX) GP,
Phoenix, Arizona – 72 laps, 169.920 miles
1. Ayrton Senna (McLaren-Honda V10 MP4/5B-4), 72 laps in 1:52;32.829, 90.586 mph.
2. Jean Alesi (Tyrrell-Ford DFR V8 018/5), 72 in 1:52;41.514.
3. Thierry Boutsen (Williams-Renault V10 FW13B/7), 72. **4.** Nelson Piquet (Benetton-Ford HB V8 B189B/5), 72. **5.** Stefano Modena (Brabham-Judd V8 BT58/5), 72. **6.** Satoru Nakajima (Tyrrell-Ford V8 018/2), 71.
PP – Gerhard Berger (McLaren-Honda V10 MP4/5B-2), 1;28.664. FL – Berger, 1;31.050, 93.311 mph.
Jean Alesi emerged as a real find in his Tyrrell, albeit on this relatively low-speed street circuit, leading laps 1-34 before Senna fought his way by, to maintain his winning lead to the finish. Berger's promising pole on his McLaren debut should be regarded against mechanical problems which put Senna back in 5th fastest place. Senna ran 4th in opening stages before mounting a relentless run for the lead. Berger slid off after only 9 laps.

25-3-90 BRAZILIAN GP,
Interlagos – 71 laps, 190.807 miles
1. Alain Prost (Ferrari V12 641 '116BIS'), 71 laps in 1:37;21.258, 117.595 mph.
2. Gerhard Berger (McLaren-Honda V10 MP4/5B-2), 71 in 1:37;34.822.
3. Ayrton Senna (McLaren-Honda V10 MP4/5B-4), 71. **4.** Nigel Mansell (Ferrari V12 641 '116'), 71. **5.** Thierry Boutsen

(Williams-Renault V10 FW13B/7), 70. **6.** Nelson Piquet (Benetton-Ford HB V8 B189B/5), 70.
PP – Senna, 1;17.277; FL – Berger, 1;19.899, 121.086 mph.
Senna led in his home-town race, revived at São Paulo after a 10-year gap. Berger's attack faded early, but on lap 41 Nakajima slid into the McLaren while being lapped, sending Senna into the pits for a replacement nose cone. Senna fell to 3rd and new nose promoted worse handling than original. Prost thus gleefully inherited his 40th GP win, 'and stuffed Senna on his home ground'. Senna led laps 1-40, Prost 41-71.

13-5-90 'SAN MARINO' GP,
Imola, I – 61 laps, 191.033 miles
1. Riccardo Patrese (Williams-Renault V10 FW13B/6), 81 laps in 1:30;55.478, 126.061 mph.
2. Gerhard Berger (McLaren-Honda V10 MP4/5B-5), 61 in 1:31;00.595.
3. Alessandro Nannini (Benetton-Ford V8 B190/2), 61. **4.** Alain Prost (Ferrari V12 641), 81. **5.** Nelson Piquet (Benetton-Ford HB V8 B190/3), 61. **6.** Jean Alesi (Tyrrell-Ford DFR V8 019/3), 60.
PP – Ayrton Senna (McLaren-Honda V10 MP4/5B-4), 1;23.220; FL – Nannini, 1;27.156, 129.355 mph.
Patrese desperately wanted to win at Imola and ended a 7-year F1 drought by defeating Berger's McLaren, aided by a minor Honda engine problem afflicting the Austrian. Senna lost the lead after 4 laps when a stone jammed in a brake caliper, split the wheel rim and deflated a tyre, sending the McLaren slithering off into a sand trap. Mansell proved fastest man on circuit for Ferrari until engine failure after he had been nudged into a spectacular 170 mph spin while attempting to overtake the unsighted Berger. Senna led the first 3 laps, Boutsen laps 4-17, Berger 18-50, Patrese 51-61.

27-5-90 MONACO GP,
Monte Carlo – 78 laps, 161.297 miles
1. Ayrton Senna (McLaren-Honda V10 MP4/5B-4), 78 laps in 1:52;46.982, 85.809 mph.
2. Jean Alesi (Tyrrell-Ford DFR V8 019/3), 78 in 1:52;48.069.
3. Gerhard Berger (McLaren-Honda V10 MP4/5B-3), 78. **4.** Thierry Boutsen (Williams-Renault V10 FW13B/8), 77. **5.** Alex Caffi (Arrows-Ford DFR V8 A11B/1), 76. **6.** Eric Bernard (Lola-Lamborghini V12 L90/3), 76.
PP – Senna, 1;21.314; FL – Senna, 1;24.468, 88.133 mph.
Alesi's Tyrrell overtook Prost's Ferrari on lap 1 entering Mirabeau Supérieur in pursuit of Senna. Berger tried to follow Alesi through, rammed Prost and caused the race to be red-flagged. At the restart Prost shut the door on Alesi and effectively that was the end of racing for the day. Senna simply dominated, and after Prost retired Alesi became the hero in his normally less than top-drawer car. Berger struggled in spare car set up for Senna and lacking bottom gear. Again, Senna led throughout.

10-6-90 CANADIAN GP,
Ile Notre Dame, Montreal – 70 laps, 190.947 miles
1. Ayrton Senna (McLaren-Honda V10 MP4/5B-6), 70 laps in 1:42;56.400, 111.296 mph.
2. Nelson Piquet (Benetton-Ford HB V8 B190/3), 70 in 1:43;06.897.
3. Nigel Mansell (Ferrari V12 641 '118'), 70. **4.** Gerhard Berger (McLaren-Honda V10 MP4/5B-5), 70.* **5.** Alain Prost (Ferrari V12 641 '116BIS'), 70. **6.** Derek Warwick (Lotus-Lamborghini V12 102/4), 68.
*Including 1-minute penalty; won on road in 1:42;11.254.
PP – Senna, 1;20.399; FL – Berger, 1;22.077, 119.645 mph.
Berger jumped the start from the outside of the front row and was penalized one minute. Consequently Senna just trailed him to victory. The Benettons showed great promise, Berger on corrected times placing just ahead of Prost's near-brakeless Ferrari 641 on the final lap. On the road Senna led laps 1-11, Nannini led 12-14, Berger 15-70.

24-6-90 MEXICAN GP,
Autodromo Hermanos Rodriguez, Mexico City – 69 laps, 189.548 miles
1. Alain Prost (Ferrari V12 641 '116BIS'), 69 in 1:32;35.783, 122.822 mph.
2. Nigel Mansell (Ferrari V12 641 '118'), 69 in 1:33;01.134.
3. Gerhard Berger (McLaren-Honda V10 MP4/5B-4), 69. **4.** Alessandro Nannini (Benetton-Ford HB V8 B190/5), 69. **5.** Thierry Boutsen (Williams-Renault V10 FW13B/8), 69. **6.** Nelson Piquet (Benetton-Ford HB V8 B190/3), 69.
PP – Berger, 1;17.227; FL – Prost, 1;17.958, 126.856 mph.
Senna pulled out a 15-sec lead in as many laps before developing a slow puncture which he misinterpreted as excessive tyre wear. Consequently he stayed out too long before changing the wheel, the tyre finally collapsing just before the finish. Prost moved ahead after 60 laps, running non-stop from 13th on the grid. Senna burned out his tyres by pressing too hard too soon, making a pit stop as early as lap 12. He recovered to take 2nd from Mansell but the Briton's response – repassing round the outside of the final Peraltada curve on the penultimate lap – was unanswerable. Senna had led laps 1-60, Prost 61-69.

8-7-90 FRENCH GP,
Ricard-Castellet – 80 laps, 189.543 miles
1. Alain Prost (Ferrari V12 641 '119'), 80 laps in 1:33;29.606, 121.640 mph.
2. Ivan Capelli (Leyton House-Judd V8 CG901/3), 80 in 1:33;38.232.
3. Ayrton Senna (McLaren-Honda V10 MP4/5B-6), 80. **4.** Nelson Piquet (Benetton-Ford HB V8 B190/3), 80. **5.** Gerhard Berger (McLaren-Honda V10 MP4/5B-5), 80. **6.** Riccardo Patrese (Williams-Renault V10 FW13B/6), 80.

PP – Nigel Mansell (Ferrari V12 641 118'), 1;04.402; FL – Mansell, 1;08.012, 125.410 mph.

But for a fuel pick-up problem in the final 3 laps this would have been Capelli's race in the Leyton House. Prost held 6th place for first quarter of race, conserving his tyres in Ricard's customary blistering heat. McLaren lost an early lead in disastrous pit stops, ditto Mansell who led briefly and eventually had his V12 engine break. Prost secured Ferrari's 100th GP victory, Senna was a fortunate 3rd. Berger led laps 1-27, Senna 28-29, Mansell 30-31, Patrese 32, Capelli 33-77, Prost the final – but all-important – 3.

15-7-90 BRITISH GP,
Silverstone – 64 laps, 190.080 miles
1. Alain Prost (Ferrari V12 641 '119'), 64 laps in 1:18;30.999, 145.253 mph.
2. Thierry Boutsen (Williams-Renault V10 FW13B/8), 64 in 1:19;10.091.
3. Ayrton Senna (McLaren-Honda V10 MP4/5B-6), 64.
4. Eric Bernard (Lola-Lamborghini V12 L90/1), 64. **5.** Nelson Piquet (Benetton-Ford HB V8 B190/3), 64. **6.** Aguri Suzuki (Lola-Lamborghini V12 L90/5), 63.
PP – Nigel Mansell (Ferrari V12 641 '118'), 1;07.428; FL – Mansell, 1;11.291, 149.977 mph.
Mansell started from pole on his home course, blasted past Senna to lead from lap 12 but then slowed with gear selection problems to surrender lead to team-mate Prost with 21 laps to run. Nine laps from finish Mansell retired, announcing his imminent retirement from racing come season's end. Prost's 43rd GP win also completed the first hat-trick sequence of his career. Senna led laps 1-11, Mansell 12-21, Berger 22-27, Mansell 28-42, Prost thereafter.

29-7-90 GERMAN GP,
Hockenheim – 45 laps, 190.195 miles
1. Ayrton Senna (McLaren-Honda V10 MP4/5B-6), 45 laps in 1:20;47.164, 141.258 mph.
2. Alessandro Nannini (Benetton-Ford HB V8 B190/4), 45 in 1:20;53.684.
3. Gerhard Berger (McLaren-Honda V10 MP4/5B-5), 45. **4.** Alain Prost (Ferrari V12 641 '116' IS), 45. **5.** Riccardo Patrese (Williams-Renault V10 FW13B/8), 45. **6.** Thierry Boutsen (Williams-Renault V10 FW13B/8), 45.
PP – Senna, 1;40.198; FL – Boutsen, 1;45.602, 144.084 mph.
Mansell retired early after under-steering off course, Senna was complete master of nursing engine and tyres while running considerately, but Nannini and Benetton almost achieved fine tactical victory by running non-stop on hard tyres while Senna stopped. Brazilian led laps 1-17, Nannini 18-33, Senna 34-45.

12-8-90 HUNGARIAN GP,
Hungaroring – 77 laps, 189.850 miles
1. Thierry Boutsen (Williams-Renault V10 FW13B/8), 77 laps in 1:49;30.597, 104.018 mph.
2. Ayrton Senna (McLaren-Honda V10 MP4/5B-4), 77 in 1:49;30.885.
3. Nelson Piquet (Benetton-Ford HB V8 B190/3), 77. **4.** Riccardo Patrese (Williams-Renault V10 FW13B/9), 77. **5.** Derek Warwick (Lotus-Lamborghini V12 102/4), 77. **6.** Eric Bernard (Lola-Lamborghini V12 L90/4), 77.
PP – Boutsen, 1;17.919; FL – Patrese, 1;22.058, 108.169 mph.
Boutsen and Williams-Renault succeeded in controlling a gruelling race from the front while some elbows-out racing behind saw Senna punt Nannini's Benetton high into the air and out of the race. Mansell sidled Berger over against pit wall as the Austrian tried to overtake, and with only 5 laps to run Berger took Mansell out of race in a carbon copy of the Senna/Nannini manoeuvre, and in the self-same ess-bend. But this time Berger retired as well with damaged steering. Boutsen had led throughout, and he just held off Senna at the finish.

25-8-90 BELGIAN GP,
Spa-Francorchamps – 44 laps, 189.741 miles
1. Ayrton Senna (McLaren-Honda V10 MP4/5B-6), 44 laps in 1:26;31.997, 131.562 mph.
2. Alain Prost (Ferrari V12 641 '121'), 44 in 1:26;35.547.
3. Gerhard Berger (McLaren-Honda V10 MP4/5B-5), 44. **4.** Alessandro Nannini (Benetton-Ford HB V8 B190/7), 44. **5.** Nelson Piquet (Benetton-Ford HB V8 B190/8), 44. **6.** Mauricio Gugelmin (Leyton House-Judd V8 CG901/5), 44.
PP – Senna, 1;50.365; FL – Prost, 1;55.087, 134.891 mph.
Prost was Senna's only serious rival in the Ardennes. Three starts were made, early accidents causing two red flags, and again Benetton's non-stop race tactic almost paid off, Senna rejoining just ahead of Nannini after his tyre change and being able to muscle the Italian back with demoralizing vigour, taking the impetus completely out of Nannini's pursuit. Nannini then won a battle with Berger for the minor placings. In the final lap chart, Senna led throughout.

9-9-90 ITALIAN GP,
Monza – 53 laps, 191.009 miles
1. Ayrton Senna (McLaren-Honda V10 MP4/5B-6), 53 laps in 1:17;57.878, 146.996 mph.
2. Alain Prost (Ferrari V12 641 '121') 53 in 1:18;03.932.
3. Gerhard Berger (McLaren-Honda V10 MP4/5B-5), 53. **4.** Nigel Mansell (Ferrari V12 641 '118' 53. **5.** Riccardo Patrese (Williams-Renault V10 FW13B/9), 53. **6.** Satoru Nakajima (Tyrrell-Ford DFR V8 019/4), 52.
PP – Senna, 1;22.533; FL – Senna, 1;26.254, 150.418 mph.
Another perfect performance from Senna and McLaren-Honda, pole position, fastest race lap, led from lights to flag. Yet another crushing demonstration of driver/team dominance as Prost did his best

for Ferrari in their home event but was beaten by 6 seconds to the flag. Derek Warwick fortunate to survive massive first-lap accident exiting the *Parabolica* in his Lotus – race red-flagged and restarted with the rugged Briton competing in his spare car.

23-9-90 PORTUGUESE GP,
Estoril – 61 laps, 164.880 miles*
*Scheduled to run 71 laps but stopped prematurely following collision between Caffi's Arrows and Suzuki's Lola which left Caffi trapped in his car against the barriers.
1. Nigel Mansell (Ferrari V12 641 '120'), 61 laps in 1:22;11.014, 120.374 mph.
2. Ayrton Senna (McLaren-Honda V10 MP4/5B-6), 61 in 1;22;13.822.
3. Alain Prost (Ferrari V12 641 '121'), 61. **4.** Gerhard Berger (McLaren-Honda V10 MP4/5B-5), 61. **5.** Nelson Piquet (Benetton-Ford HB V8 B190/8), 61. **6.** Alessandro Nannini (Benetton-Ford HB V8 B190/7), 61.
PP – Mansell, 1;13.557; FL – Riccardo Patrese (Williams-Renault V10 FW13B/9), 1;18.306, 124.264 mph.
The Ferraris started from the front row, ready to muscle out Senna's Championship charge behind, but as the lights turned green Mansell nearly and almost rammed his team-mate, opening a broad gap through which the Senna and Berger McLarens hurtled. Mansell gave chase but Prost was back in 5th and never recovered. Mansell battled into the lead on lap 50, Prost was troubled by gearbox problems and a slow tyre change, worked his way into 3rd but hopes for further improvement evaporated as Caffi crashed badly and the race was red-flagged 10 laps short.

30-9-90 SPANISH GP,
Jerez de la Frontera – 73 laps, 191.328 miles
1. Alain Prost (Ferrari V12 641 '121'), 73 laps in 1:48;01.461, 106.269 mph.
2. Nigel Mansell (Ferrari V12 641 '120'), 73 in 1:48;23.525.
3. Alessandro Nannini (Benetton-Ford HB V8 B190/7), 73. **4.** Thierry Boutsen (Williams-Renault V10 FW13B/8), 73. **5.** Riccardo Patrese (Williams-Renault V10 FW13B/9), 73. **6.** Aguri Suzuki (Lola-Lamborghini V12 90/5), 73.
PP – Ayrton Senna (McLaren-Honda V10 MP4/5B-6), 1;18.824; FL – Patrese, 1;24.513, 111.644 mph.
Qualifying overshadowed by horrible accident to Martin Donnelly's Lotus following mechanical failure which the Ulster driver was fortunate to survive. Prost tailed Senna until first routine tyre changes, but Frenchman's Ferrari was dominant and Senna settled for 2nd place which would have clinched his World Championship. Dalmas's back-marker AGS then threw up debris which punctured a McLaren radiator and Senna retired starting lap 54, having faded to 6th place. Berger collided foolishly with Boutsen; McLaren's Constructors' Championship lead reduced to 18 points with two races – and a potential 30 points – still available. Senna had led laps 1-26, Piquet 27-28, Prost 29-73.

21-10-90 JAPANESE GP,
Suzuka – 53 laps, 192.952 miles
1. Nelson Piquet (Benetton-Ford HB V8 B190/8), 53 laps in 1:34;36.824, 122.360 mph.
2. Roberto Moreno (Benetton-Ford HB V8 B190/7), 53 in 1:34;44.047.
3. Aguri Suzuki (Lola-Lamborghini V12 L90/5), 53. **4.** Riccardo Patrese (Williams-Renault V10 FW13B/7), 53. **5.** Thierry Boutsen (Williams-Renault V10 FW13B/8), 53. **6.** Satoru Nakajima (Tyrrell-Ford DFR V8 019/7), 53.
PP – Ayrton Senna (McLaren-Honda V10 MP4/5B-7), 1;36.996; FL – Senna, 1;44.233, 125.739 mph.
It took some 15 seconds to decide outcome of the 1990 Championship. Into the first corner Senna and Prost collided and both retired, presenting the Brazilian with the Drivers' title. Senna later admitted his actions to sideline Prost had been deliberate. While the day degenerated into a riot of bitterness and vilification, Berger led 1 lap before needlessly spinning off into a sand trap, Mansell led laps 2-26, his team gave him a fantastic 5.82 sec tyre change and he then snapped a driveshaft joint accelerating away. This left Piquet leading new Benetton team-mate Moreno – replacing poor Nannini, gravely injured in a helicopter crash – to achieve a fine team 1-2.

4-11-90 AUSTRALIAN GP,
Adelaide, South Australia – 81 laps, 190.107 miles
1. Nelson Piquet (Benetton-Ford HB V8 B190/8), 81 laps in 1:49;44.570, 104.016 mph.
2. Nigel Mansell (Ferrari V12 641 '120'), 81 in 1:49;47.699.
3. Alain Prost (Ferrari V12 641 '121'), 81. **4.** Gerhard Berger (McLaren-Honda V10 MP4/5B-5), 81. **5.** Thierry Boutsen (Williams-Renault V10 FW13B/8), 81. **6.** Riccardo Patrese (Williams-Renault V10 FW13B/7), 80.
PP – Ayrton Senna (McLaren-Honda V10 MP4/5B-7), 1;15.671; FL – Mansell, 1;18.203, 108.123 mph.
500th World Championship F1 race fell to Piquet and Benetton using Ford's new HB 75-degree V8 engine after trouble again struck the front-runners. Much of race saw wonderful battle between Senna and Mansell, resolved only when the Ferrari slid down an escape road and made a stop for fresh tyres. Senna emerged with 26 sec lead only to miss 2nd gear in a downchange and slide head-on into a tyre barrier. Piquet again emerged running ahead of the pack, reacting strongly to fend off a closing-stages Mansell Ferrari charge. Prost troubled by fading brakes in final stages; Berger, hampered by cramp and numbness in leg and foot, salvaged distant 4th for Constructors' Champion team. Senna led laps 1-61, Piquet 62-81.

1991

10-3-91 UNITED STATES (PHOENIX) GP,
Phoenix, Arizona – 81 laps, 187.272 miles
1. Ayrton Senna (McLaren-Honda V12 MP4/6-3), 81 laps in 2:00;47.828, 93.018 mph.
2. Alain Prost (Ferrari V12 642 '123'), 81 in 2:01;04.150.
3. Nelson Piquet (Benetton-Ford HB V8 B190/8), 81. **4.** Stefano Modena (Tyrrell-Honda V10 020/3), 81. **5.** Satoru Nakajima (Tyrrell-Honda V10 020/2), 80. **6.** Aguri Suzuki (Lola-Ford DFR V8 L91/1), 79.
PP – Senna, 1;21.434; FL – Jean Alesi (Ferrari V12 642 '124'), 1;26.758, 95.936 mph.
Senna led start to finish, Prost falling away in his Ferrari before a fumbled tyre change dropped him back to 7th, after which the Frenchman recovered in a fighting drive. Senna's 27th GP victory, equalling the old Stewart record. Williams beset by problems with their latest semi-auto gearboxes but showed considerable promise– only 9 runners at the finish on a tough street circuit.

24-3-91 BRAZILIAN GP,
Interlagos – 71 laps, 190.807 miles
1. Ayrton Senna (McLaren-Honda V6 MP4/6-3), 71 laps in 1:38;28.128, 116.264 mph.
2. Riccardo Patrese (Williams-Renault V10 FW14/4), 71 in 1:38;31.119.
3. Gerhard Berger (McLaren-Honda V12 MP4/6-2), 71. **4.** Alain Prost (Ferrari V12 642 '123'), 71. **5.** Nelson Piquet (Benetton-Ford HB V8 B190/8), 71. **6.** Jean Alesi (Ferrari V12 642 '124'), 71.
PP – Senna, 1;16.392; FL – Nigel Mansell (Williams-Renault V10 FW14/2), 1;20.436, 120.278 mph.
Home victory for Senna at his eighth attempt, hounded all the way by resurgent Williams-Renaults, McLaren-Honda's only threat. Mansell pushed Senna hard from the start but suffered more semi-auto gearbox trouble. Senna then encountered transmission troubles of his own, losing 4th gear, then 3rd, 5th and 6th; finally he found 6th on a last lap doused by rain, holding off Patrese's Williams despite the McLaren running on slick tyres.

28-4-91 'SAN MARINO' GP,
Imola, I – 61 laps, 191.033 miles
1. Ayrton Senna (McLaren-Honda V12 MP4/6-5), 61 laps in 1:35;14.750, 120.341 mph.
2. Gerhard Berger (McLaren-Honda V12 MP4/6-6), 61 in 1:35;16.425.
3. J.J. Lehto (Dallara-Judd V10 191/20), 60. **4.** PierLuigi Martini (Minardi-Ferrari V12 M191/5), 59. **5.** Mika Häkkinen (Lotus-Judd V8 102B/3), 58. **6.** Julian Bailey (Lotus-Judd V8 102B/2), 58.
PP – Senna, 1;21.877; FL – Berger, 1;26.531, 130.290 mph.
The dullest Imola in years – the McLaren-Hondas lapped the other 8 finishers at least once. Patrese led 10 laps but his Renault engine faltered. Ferrari lost Prost pre-race on the warm-up lap, Alesi in a sand trap on lap 3. Moreno looked good for 3rd place in the new Benetton before gearbox trouble intruded, Mansell had already gone on lap 1 after a gearchange problem sparked a collision. The teeny points scorers had thus inherited the top teams' rightful places.

12-5-91 MONACO GP,
Monte Carlo – 78 laps, 161.297 miles
1. Ayrton Senna (McLaren-Honda V12 MP4/6-5), 78 laps in 1:53;02.334, 85.611 mph.
2. Nigel Mansell (Williams-Renault V10 FW14/2), 78 in 1:53;20.682.
3. Jean Alesi (Ferrari V12 642 '126'), 78. **4.** Roberto Moreno (Benetton-Ford HB V8 B191/1), 77. **5.** Alain Prost (Ferrari V12 642 '123'), 77. **6.** Emanuele Pirro (Dallara-Judd V10 191/21), 77.
PP – Senna, 1;20.344; FL – Prost, 1;24.368, 88.234 mph.
Senna notched his record-breaking fourth consecutive GP victory to open the 1991 season, dominating both qualifying sessions and leading start to finish. Modena's sprightly Tyrrell-Honda V10 hounded him after qualifying 2nd fastest, only for the engine to disintegrate flat-out through the tunnel, sending Patrese's pursuing Williams into the Armco. Mansell's 2nd place was his first finish of the season. Prost had looked safe in 3rd until a loose front wheel caused him a late-race pit stop in the Ferrari.

2-6-91 CANADIAN GP,
Ile Notre Dame, Montreal – 69 laps, 189.934 miles
1. Nelson Piquet (Benetton-Ford HB V8 B191/2), 69 laps in 1:38;51.490, 115.276 mph.
2. Stefano Modena (Tyrrell-Honda V10 020/5), 69 in 1:39;23.322.
3. Riccardo Patrese (Williams-Renault V10 FW14/3), 69. **4.** Andrea de Cesaris (Jordan-Ford HB V8 191/3), 69. **5.** Bertrand Gachot (Jordan-Ford HB V8 191/4), 69. **6.** Nigel Mansell (Williams-Renault V10 FW14/2), 68.
PP – Patrese, 1;19.837; FL – Mansell, 1;22.385, 120.284 mph.
Mansell's famous 'waving to the crowd' débâcle when the engine of his leading Williams-Renault stalled on the final lap. Mansell had led from the front, lapping ever faster, never under pressure – and then last-mile failure. Piquet, 40 seconds astern, was astonished to find himself the winner. Patrese's Williams-Renault had started from pole but lost 2nd place due to a puncture and pit stop – a sound effort after surviving whiplash in a heavy practice accident. A bad weekend for McLaren – Senna alternator trouble, Berger a short circuit. Both Ferraris failed too.

16-6-91 MEXICAN GP,
Autodromo Hermanos Rodriguez, Mexico City – 67 laps, 184.054 miles*
*Scheduled for 69 laps but reduced after 2 aborted starts.
1. Riccardo Patrese (Williams-Renault V10 FW14/3), 67 laps in 1:29;52.205, 122.880 mph.
2. Nigel Mansell (Williams-Renault V10 FW14/2), 67 in 1:29;53.541.
3. Ayrton Senna (McLaren-Honda V12 MP4/6-5), 67. **4.** Andrea de Cesaris (Jordan-Ford HB V8 191/3), 66. **5.** Roberto Moreno (Benetton-Ford HB V8 B191/4), 66. **6.** Eric Bernard (Lola-Ford DFR V8 L91/2), 66.
PP – Patrese, 1;16.696; FL – Mansell, 1;16.788, 128.789 mph.
Confirmation of Williams-Renault's new dominance – Mansell led for 15 laps, Patrese winged by, subsequent mixture control adjustment brought Mansell's Renault V10 back on full song to take more than a second a lap out of his team-mate's lead towards the end. The first Williams 1-2 since Canada 1989. Senna distant 3rd after rolling his McLaren in practice. Honda V12 clearly outclassed by Renault V10.

7-7-91 FRENCH GP,
Magny-Cours – 72 laps, 191.078 miles
1. Nigel Mansell (Williams-Renault V10 FW14/5), 72 laps in 1:38;00.056, 116.985 mph.
2. Alain Prost (Ferrari V12 643 '128'), 72 in 1:38;05.059.
3. Ayrton Senna (McLaren-Honda V12 MP4/6-5), 72. **4.** Jean Alesi (Ferrari V12 643 '127'), 72. **5.** Riccardo Patrese (Williams-Renault V10 FW14/4), 71. **6.** Andrea de Cesaris (Jordan-Ford HB V8 191/3), 71.
PP – Patrese, 1;14.559; FL – Mansell, 1;19.168, 120.679 mph.
Mansell's luck changed in a superb battling victory, slashing his way past Prost's new raised-nose Ferrari 643, the Frenchman subsequently encountering minor gearchange and handling problems – he said. While Mansell pulled away to an impressive win, Senna, fooled by faulty onboard fuel readout, settled for distant, depressing 3rd. Joint terminal earache afterwards for both McLaren and Honda . . .

14-7-91 BRITISH GP,
Silverstone – 59 laps, 191.573 miles
1. Nigel Mansell (Williams-Renault V10 FW14/5), 59 laps in 1:27;35.479, 131.227 mph.
2. Gerhard Berger (McLaren-Honda V12 MP4/6-7), 59 in 1:28;17.772.
3. Alain Prost (Ferrari V12 643 '128'), 59. **4.** Ayrton Senna (McLaren-Honda V12 MP4/6-5), 58.* **5.** Nelson Piquet (Benetton-Ford HB V8 B191/2), 58. **6.** Bertrand Gachot (Jordan-Ford HB V8 191/5), 58.
*Out of fuel.
PP – Mansell, 1;20.939; FL – Mansell, 1;26.379, 135.325 mph.
Tumultuously popular home victory again for Mansell's Williams – fastest in every session, fastest in morning warm-up, leading virtually all the way and setting fastest race lap. Honda out-powered by Renault on the opening lap, end of story. Patrese out in first-corner collision. Senna lost 2nd place on final lap when misleading fuel read-out left him with tanks dry. Ferrari places inherited, new 643s off the pace.

28-7-91 GERMAN GP,
Hockenheim – 45 laps, 190.180 miles
1. Nigel Mansell (Williams-Renault V10 FW14/5), 45 laps in 1:19;29.661, 143.554 mph.
2. Riccardo Patrese (Williams-Renault V10 FW14/4), 45 in 1:19;43.440.
3. Jean Alesi (Ferrari V12 643 '128'), 45. **4.** Gerhard Berger (McLaren-Honda V12 MP4/6-7), 45. **5.** Andrea de Cesaris (Jordan-Ford HB V8 191/4), 45. **6.** Bertrand Gachot (Jordan-Ford HB V8 191/5), 45.
PP – Mansell, 1;37.087; FL – Patrese, 1;43.569, 146.913 mph.
Williams-Renaults uncatchable at Hockenheim, McLaren-Honda in disarray. Alesi ran non-stop on hard-compound tyres; Senna again ran out of fuel on the final lap after seeming set for 4th. A fierce battle between Senna and Prost had been resolved when the Ferrari was effectively forced up the escape road at the first chicane, the Frenchman bitterly denouncing the Brazilian post-race . . . Against the background of Williams-Renault's continuing dominance it barely seemed significant.

11-8-91 HUNGARIAN GP,
Hungaroring – 77 laps, 189.850 miles
1. Ayrton Senna (McLaren-Honda V12 MP4/6-8), 77 laps in 1:49;12.796, 104.301 mph.
2. Nigel Mansell (Williams-Renault V10 FW14/5), 77 in 1:49;17.395.
3. Riccardo Patrese (Williams-Renault V10 FW14/3), 77. **4.** Gerhard Berger (McLaren-Honda V12 MP4/6-7), 75. **5.** Jean Alesi (Ferrari V12 643 '128'), 77. **6.** Ivan Capelli (Leyton House-Ilmor V10 CG911 x4), 76.
PP – Senna, 1;16.147; FL – Bertrand Gachot (Jordan-Ford HB V8 191/5), 1;21.547, 108.847 mph.
The tight Hungaroring did not suit Williams, and Senna, McLaren and Honda fought back most effectively – pole position by the Brazilian and a good start assuming vital significance on a course where safe overtaking is extremely difficult. By the finish the Williams brakes were cooked and Mansell and Patrese had been forced to ease off.

25-8-91 BELGIAN GP,
Spa-Francorchamps – 44 laps, 189.741 miles
1. Ayrton Senna (McLaren-Honda V12 MP4/6-8), 44 laps in 1:27;17.669, 130.415 mph.
2. Gerhard Berger (McLaren-Honda V12 MP4/6-9), 44 in 1:27;19.570.

3. Nelson Piquet (Benetton-Ford HB V8 B191/4), 44; **4.** Roberto Moreno (Benetton-Ford HB V8 B191/5), 44; **5.** Riccardo Patrese (Williams-Renault V10 FW14/3), 44; **6.** Mark Blundell (Brabham-Yamaha V12 BT60Y/3), 44.
PP – Senna, 1:47.811; FL – Moreno, 1:55.161, 134.806 mph.
Honda's latest engine with 'active' variable-length induction tracts helped Senna qualify on pole. He still had to let Mansell go by and draw away in the race until the Williams-Renault was sidelined by electrical failure. Alesi inherited the lead, only to suffer engine failure in his Ferrari, which returned the lead to Senna despite the Brazilian grappling with gearchange problems. De Cesaris's remarkable Jordan suffered engine failure when set for 2nd with two laps to run, and Patrese's Williams had only 5th gear operable. A lucky McLaren-Honda 1-2 – but crucially they had been 'reliable enough' . . .

8-9-91 ITALIAN GP,
Monza – 53 laps, 191.009 miles
1. Nigel Mansell (Williams-Renault V10 FW14/5), 53 laps in 1:17;54.319, 147.109 mph.
2. Ayrton Senna (McLaren-Honda V12 MP4/6-10), 53 in 1:18;10.581.
3. Alain Prost (Ferrari V12 643 '130'), 53; **4.** Gerhard Berger (McLaren-Honda V12 MP4/6-9), 53; **5.** Michael Schumacher (Benetton-Ford HB V8 B191/5), 53; **6.** Nelson Piquet (Benetton-Ford HB V8 B191/4), 53.
PP – Senna, 1:21.114; FL – Senna, 1:26.061, 150.756 mph.
Mansell had to win to keep the Drivers' Championship open. Senna led, under intense Williams pressure. After 18 laps Mansell let Patrese through to do his best. Lap 26 Patrese led, lap 28 his clutch failed. Mansell mounted another assault on Senna's lead, six laps later he dived through as Senna was fighting front tyre vibration and locking brakes. The McLaren stopped for fresh rubber, Mansell won non-stop – the Championship remained open, Mansell 18 points behind Senna with four races to run.

22-9-91 PORTUGUESE GP,
Estoril – 71 laps, 191.913 miles
1. Riccardo Patrese (Williams-Renault V10 FW14/3), 71 laps in 1:35;42.304, 120.314 mph.
2. Ayrton Senna (McLaren-Honda V12 MP4/6-8), 71 in 1:36;03.245.
3. Jean Alesi (Ferrari V12 643 '129'), 71; **4.** PierLuigi Martini (Minardi-Ferrari V12 M191/6), 71; **5.** Nelson Piquet (Benetton-Ford HB V8 B191/4), 71; **6.** Michael Schumacher (Benetton-Ford HB V8 B191/5), 71.
PP – Patrese, 1:13.001; FL – Nigel Mansell (Williams-Renault V10 FW14/5), 1:18.179, 124.467 mph.*
Disqualified from race, leaving Patrese's best of 1:18.350, 124.196 mph the fastest race lap by a non-disqualified runner.
Mansell led the race in terrific style until a botched scheduled tyre-change stop, being signalled out before the right-rear wheel had been locked tight. The missing wheel was replaced in the pit lane, and Mansell consequently black-flagged. Patrese recovered the situation superbly for the team, but Senna scored strongly in 2nd place. Three races to run, 24 points separating the Drivers' Championship contenders.

29-9-91 SPANISH GP,
Circuit de Catalunya, Barcelona – 65 laps, 191.727 miles
1. Nigel Mansell (Williams-Renault V10 FW14/5), 65 laps in 1:38;41.541, 116.561 mph.
2. Alain Prost (Ferrari V12 643 '130'), 65 in 1:38;52.872.
3. Riccardo Patrese (Williams-Renault V10 FW14/3), 65; **4.** Jean Alesi (Ferrari V12 643 '129'), 65; **5.** Ayrton Senna (McLaren-Honda V12 MP4/6-10), 65; **6.** Michael Schumacher (Benetton-Ford HB V8 B191/2), 65.
PP – Gerhard Berger (McLaren-Honda V12 MP4/6-9), 1:18.751; FL – Patrese, 1:22.837, 128.188 mph.
Race started on a damp track; once the leaders changed onto slick tyres Senna's tactical error became clear, spinning on the wrong tyre choice.

Berger led for McLaren after starting from pole but retired with engine trouble. Now the Drivers' Championship would remain undecided until Japan . . . and the Constructors' title was still wide open between Williams-Renault and McLaren-Honda.

20-10-91 JAPANESE GP,
Suzuka – 53 laps, 193.117 miles
1. Gerhard Berger (McLaren-Honda V12 MP4/6-9), 53 laps in 1:32;10.695, 125.702 mph.
2. Ayrton Senna (McLaren-Honda V12 MP4/6-8), 53 in 1:32;11.039.
3. Riccardo Patrese (Williams-Renault V10 FW14/3), 53; **4.** Alain Prost (Ferrari V12 643 '130'), 53; **5.** Martin Brundle (Brabham-Yamaha V12 BT60Y/4), 52; **6.** Stefano Modena (Tyrrell-Honda V10 020/8), 52.
PP – Berger, 1:34.700; FL – Senna, 1:41.532, 129.195 mph.
All over after 17 minutes' racing as Mansell, caught out under braking, slithered off into a sand trap from 3rd place – Berger leading from a fine pole position, Senna 2nd. With his Drivers' crown assured, Senna cruised past his team-mate to secure the lead, then slowed just before the line to reward Berger with his maiden McLaren-Honda victory. Honda engine development, plus a very Honda-friendly chicane introduced on their own circuit, had combined with driver quality to defeat Williams-Renault.

3-11-91 AUSTRALIAN GP,
Adelaide, South Australia – 14 laps, 32.882 miles*
Scheduled for 81 laps, but stopped due to flooded track and unsafe conditions.
1. Ayrton Senna (McLaren-Honda V12 MP4/6-11), 14 laps in 24;34.899, 80.262 mph.
2. Nigel Mansell (Williams-Renault V10 FW14/5), 14 in 24;36.158.
3. Gerhard Berger (McLaren-Honda V12 MP4/6-9), 14; **4.** Nelson Piquet (Benetton-Ford HB V8 B191/4), 14; **5.** Riccardo Patrese (Williams-Renault V10 FW14/3), 14; **6.** Gianni Morbidelli (Ferrari V12 643 '130'), 14.
PP – Senna, 1:14.041; FL – Berger, 1:41.141, 83.602 mph.
A wet joke, the GP that should never have been started got under way on an already flooded circuit in torrential rain with Mansell just holding on to Senna's leading McLaren in impossible conditions. Race red-flagged after a chapter of accidents, culminating in Mansell spinning hard into a wall. Berger also spun off, but on countback to the end of the previously completed lap the above result was ratified. It was the first 'half-points' race since Monaco 1984 and it provided Senna with his 33rd GP victory and McLaren-Honda with yet another Constructors' Championship. Williams-Renault's final hopes for '91 had just been drowned.

Whatever the technicalities, the name of the game is simply WINNING.